Microeconomics
PRINCIPLES, PROBLEMS, AND POLICIES

THE MCGRAW-HILL SERIES: ECONOMICS

THE FOUR VERSIONS OF MCCONNELL, BRUE, FLYNN

Chapter*	Economics	Microeconomics	Macroeconomics	Essentials of Economics
1. Limits, Alternatives, and Choices	X	X	X	X
2. The Market System and the Circular Flow	X	X	X	X
3. Demand, Supply, and Market Equilibrium	X	X	X	X
4. Market Failures: Public Goods and Externalities	X	X	X	X
5. Government's Role and Government Failure	X	X	X	X
6. Elasticity	X	X		X
7. Utility Maximization	X	X		
8. Behavioral Economics	X	X		
9. Businesses and the Costs of Production	X	X		X
10. Pure Competition in the Short Run	X	X		X
11. Pure Competition in the Long Run	X	X		X
12. Pure Monopoly	X	X		X
13. Monopolistic Competition	X	X		X
14. Oligopoly and Strategic Behavior	X	X		X
15. Technology, R&D, and Efficiency	X	X		
16. The Demand for Resources	X	X		
17. Wage Determination	X	X		X
18. Rent, Interest, and Profit	X	X		
19. Natural Resource and Energy Economics	X	X		
20. Public Finance: Expenditures and Taxes	X	X		
21. Antitrust Policy and Regulation	X	X		
22. Agriculture: Economics and Policy	X	X		
23. Income Inequality, Poverty, and Discrimination	X	X		X
24. Health Care	X	X		
25. Immigration	X	X		
26. An Introduction to Macroeconomics	X		X	
27. Measuring Domestic Output and National Income	X		X	X
28. Economic Growth	X		X	X
29. Business Cycles, Unemployment, and Inflation	X		X	X
30. Basic Macroeconomic Relationships	X		X	
31. The Aggregate Expenditures Model	X		X	
32. Aggregate Demand and Aggregate Supply	X		X	X
33. Fiscal Policy, Deficits, and Debt	X		X	X
34. Money, Banking, and Financial Institutions	X		X	X
35. Money Creation	X		X	
36. Interest Rates and Monetary Policy	X		X	X
37. Financial Economics	X		X	
38. Extending the Analysis of Aggregate Supply	X		X	
39. Current Issues in Macro Theory and Policy	X		X	
40. International Trade	X	X	X	X
41. The Balance of Payments, Exchange Rates, and Trade Deficits	X	X	X	X
42. The Economics of Developing Countries	X	X	X	

*Chapter numbers refer to *Economics: Principles, Problems, and Policies.*
A red "X" indicates chapters that combine or consolidate content from two or more *Economics* chapters.

Twenty-First Edition

Microeconomics

PRINCIPLES, PROBLEMS, AND POLICIES

Campbell R. McConnell
University of Nebraska

Stanley L. Brue
Pacific Lutheran University

Sean M. Flynn
Scripps College

Mc Graw Hill Education

MICROECONOMICS: PRINCIPLES, PROBLEMS, AND POLICIES, TWENTY-FIRST EDITION

Published by McGraw-Hill Education, 2 Penn Plaza, New York, NY 10121. Copyright © 2018 by McGraw-Hill Education. All rights reserved. Printed in the United States of America. Previous editions © 2015, 2012, and 2009. No part of this publication may be reproduced or distributed in any form or by any means, or stored in a database or retrieval system, without the prior written consent of McGraw-Hill Education, including, but not limited to, in any network or other electronic storage or transmission, or broadcast for distance learning.

Some ancillaries, including electronic and print components, may not be available to customers outside the United States.

This book is printed on acid-free paper.

3 4 5 6 7 8 9 LWI 21 20 19 18

ISBN   978-1-259-91572-7 (student edition)
MHID   1-259-91572-7 (student edition)
ISBN   978-1-259-91584-0 (instructor's edition)
MHID   1-259-91584-0 (instructor's edition)

Chief Product Officer, SVP Products & Markets: *G. Scott Virkler*
Vice President, General Manager, Products & Markets: *Marty Lange*
Vice President, Content Design & Delivery: *Betsy Whalen*
Managing Director: *Susan Gouijnstook*
Senior Brand Manager: *Katie Hoenicke*
Director, Product Development: *Rose Koos*
Product Developer: *Adam Huenecke*
Senior Director, Digital Content Development: *Douglas Ruby*
Marketing Manager: *Virgil Lloyd*
Director, Content Design & Delivery: *Linda Avenarius*
Program Manager: *Mark Christianson*
Content Project Managers: *Harvey Yep (Core); Bruce Gin (Assessment)*
Buyer: *Laura Fuller*
Design: *Tara McDermott*
Cover Image: *© Getty Images/Kativ*
Content Licensing Specialists: *Shawntel Schmitt (Image); Beth Thole (Text)*
Typeface: *Stix Mathjax MAIN 10/12*
Compositor: *Aptara®, Inc.*
Printer: *LSC Communications*

All credits appearing on page or at the end of the book are considered to be an extension of the copyright page.

Library of Congress Cataloging-in-Publication Data

Names: McConnell, Campbell R., author. | Brue, Stanley L., 1945- author. |
   Flynn, Sean Masaki, author.
Title: Microeconomics : principles, problems, and policies / Campbell R.
   McConnell, University of Nebraska, Stanley L. Brue, Pacific Lutheran
   University, Sean M. Flynn, Scripps College.
Description: Dubuque : McGraw-Hill Education, [2018] | Revised edition of
   Microeconomics, [2015]
Identifiers: LCCN 2016043809| ISBN 9781259915727 (alk. paper) | ISBN
   1259915727 (alk. paper)
Subjects: LCSH: Microeconomics.
Classification: LCC HB172 .M3925 2018 | DDC 338.5—dc23 LC record available at
https://lccn.loc.gov/2016043809

The Internet addresses listed in the text were accurate at the time of publication. The inclusion of a website does not indicate an endorsement by the authors or McGraw-Hill Education, and McGraw-Hill Education does not guarantee the accuracy of the information presented at these sites.

mheducation.com/highered

To Mem and to Terri and Craig, and to past instructors

CAMPBELL R. MCCONNELL earned his Ph.D. from the University of Iowa after receiving degrees from Cornell College and the University of Illinois. He taught at the University of Nebraska–Lincoln from 1953 until his retirement in 1990. He is also coauthor of *Contemporary Labor Economics,* eleventh edition, and *Essentials of Economics,* third edition, and has edited readers for the principles and labor economics courses. He is a recipient of both the University of Nebraska Distinguished Teaching Award and the James A. Lake Academic Freedom Award and is past president of the Midwest Economics Association. Professor McConnell was awarded an honorary Doctor of Laws degree from Cornell College in 1973 and received its Distinguished Achievement Award in 1994. His primary areas of interest are labor economics and economic education. He has an extensive collection of jazz recordings and enjoys reading jazz history.

STANLEY L. BRUE did his undergraduate work at Augustana College (South Dakota) and received its Distinguished Achievement Award in 1991. He received his Ph.D. from the University of Nebraska–Lincoln. He is retired from a long career at Pacific Lutheran University, where he was honored as a recipient of the Burlington Northern Faculty Achievement Award. Professor Brue has also received the national Leavey Award for excellence in economic education. He has served as national president and chair of the Board of Trustees of Omicron Delta Epsilon International Economics Honorary. He is coauthor of *Economic Scenes,* fifth edition (Prentice-Hall); *Contemporary Labor Economics,* eleventh edition; *Essentials of Economics,* third edition; and *The Evolution of Economic Thought,* eighth edition (Cengage Learning). For relaxation, he enjoys international travel, attending sporting events, and going on fishing trips.

SEAN M. FLYNN did his undergraduate work at the University of Southern California before completing his Ph.D. at U.C. Berkeley, where he served as the Head Graduate Student Instructor for the Department of Economics after receiving the Outstanding Graduate Student Instructor Award. He teaches at Scripps College (of the Claremont Colleges) and is the author of *Economics for Dummies,* second edition (Wiley), and coauthor of *Essentials of Economics,* third edition. His research interests include finance, behavioral economics, and health economics. An accomplished martial artist, he has represented the United States in international aikido tournaments and is the author of *Understanding Shodokan Aikido* (Shodokan Press). Other hobbies include running, traveling, and enjoying ethnic food.

KEY GRAPHS

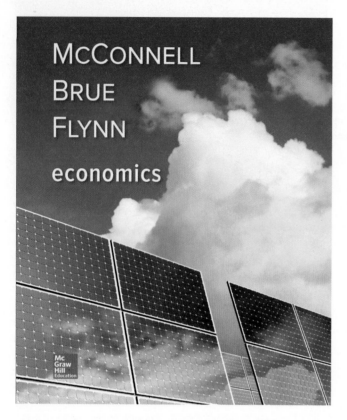

Welcome to the 21st edition of *Economics,* the best-selling economics textbook in the world. An estimated 15 million students have used *Economics* or its companion editions, *Macroeconomics* and *Microeconomics. Economics* has been adapted into Australian and Canadian editions and translated into Italian, Russian, Chinese, French, Spanish, Portuguese, and other languages. We are pleased that *Economics* continues to meet the market test: nearly one out of five U.S. students in principles courses used the 20th edition.

Fundamental Objectives

We have three main goals for *Economics:*

- Help the beginning student master the principles essential for understanding the economizing problem, specific economic issues, and policy alternatives.
- Help the student understand and apply the economic perspective and reason accurately and objectively about economic matters.
- Promote a lasting student interest in economics and the economy.

What's New and Improved?

One of the benefits of writing a successful text is the opportunity to revise—to delete the outdated and install the new, to rewrite misleading or ambiguous statements, to introduce more relevant illustrations, to improve the organizational structure, and to enhance the learning aids.

We trust that you will agree that we have used this opportunity wisely and fully. Some of the more significant changes include the following.

Separate Presentations of Monopolistic Competition and Oligopoly

In response to instructor feedback, we have split the material on monopolistic competition and oligopoly that had together comprised a single chapter in previous editions into two separate chapters. The separated chapters have been made modular so that skipping either or covering both will be equally viable options for instructors. This should be particularly helpful to instructors who want to spend more time on oligopoly.

Onboarding of Web Chapters and COI Material

Economics is everywhere, so the 21st edition continues our commitment to providing instructors with accessible and intuitive coverage of a wide variety of economic subject areas. To that end, we are happy to report that we have been able to pull material that appeared only online in previous editions into the printed book. That includes what were previously two full-length Web Chapters as well as a large fraction of the material that had been posted online as Content Options for Instructors (COIs).

"Technology, R&D, and Efficiency," which had previously been a Web Chapter, is now Chapter 15, while "The Economics of Developing Countries," also previously a Web Chapter, is now Chapter 42. Those chapters as well as the material on "Previous Exchange Rate Systems" that had been posted online as Content Options for Instructors 2 (COI2) are now integrated directly into the printed book, the latter becoming an appendix to Chapter 27 (The Balance of Payments, Exchange Rates, and Trade Deficits). The only online material that was not brought into the book was COI1, "The United States in the Global Economy." That content largely duplicated material that appeared in other chapters and was not much used, so it will no longer be supported either online or in print.

Modernized Presentation of Fixed Exchange Rates and Currency Interventions

For this new edition, we have reorganized and rewritten large parts of Chapter 27 (The Balance of Payments, Exchange Rates, and Trade Deficits). The key revision has to do with our presentation of fixed exchange rates. We now show with greater clarity that under a fixed exchange rate regime, changes in the balance of payments generate automatic changes in both foreign exchange reserves and the domestic money supply that then have to be dealt with by a nation's central bank. Our new presentation uses China as an example of these forces and how they often lead to "sterilization" actions on the part of the central banks that are engaged in currency pegs. Our new presentation also clarifies the relationship between trade deficits and foreign exchange reserves under a currency peg.

We have inserted additional examples into our presentation of flexible exchange rates and have introduced a new Last Word on optimal currency areas to give students insight into some of the European Monetary Union's current problems and how they relate to the fact that a monetary union is equivalent to simultaneous multilateral currency pegs. For instructors who wish to give a larger historical perspective, we have created a brief appendix that covers the gold standard era as well as the Bretton Woods period. This material was previously available in Content Options for Instructors 1 (COI2).

New "Consider This" and "Last Word" Pieces

Our "Consider This" boxes are used to provide analogies, examples, or stories that help drive home central economic ideas in a student-oriented, real-world manner. For instance, a "Consider This" box titled "McHits and McMisses" illustrates consumer sovereignty through a listing of successful and unsuccessful products. How businesses exploit price discrimination is driven home in a "Consider This" box that explains why ballparks charge different admission prices for adults and children but only one set of prices at their concession stands. These brief vignettes, each accompanied by a photo, illustrate key points in a lively, colorful, and easy-to-remember way. We have added 10 new "Consider This" boxes in this edition.

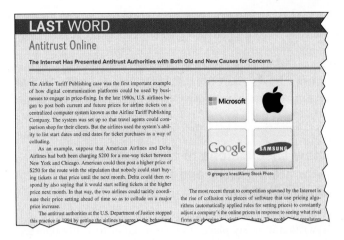

LAST WORD

Antitrust Online

The Internet Has Presented Antitrust Authorities with Both Old and New Causes for Concern.

The Airline Tariff Publishing case was the first important example of how digital communication platforms could be used by businesses to engage in price-fixing. In the late 1980s, U.S. airlines began to post both current and future prices for airline tickets on a centralized computer system known as the Airline Tariff Publishing Company. The system was set up so that travel agents could comparison shop for their clients. But the airlines used the system's ability to list start dates and end dates for ticket purchases as a way of colluding.

As an example, suppose that American Airlines and Delta Airlines had both been charging $200 for a one-way ticket between New York and Chicago. American could then post a higher price of $250 for the route with the stipulation that nobody could start buying tickets at that price until the next month. Delta could then respond by also saying that it would start selling tickets at the higher price next month. In that way, the two airlines could tacitly coordinate their price setting ahead of time so as to collude on a major price increase.

The antitrust authorities at the U.S. Department of Justice stopped this practice in 1994 by getting the airlines to agree to the behavioral

The most recent threat to competition spawned by the Internet is the rise of collusion via pieces of software that use pricing algorithms (automatically applied rules for setting prices) to constantly adjust a company's the online prices in response to seeing what rival firms are charging for similar products. The prob...

Our "Last Word" pieces are lengthier applications or case studies that are placed near the end of each chapter. For example, the "Last Word" section for Chapter 1 (Limits, Alternatives, and Choices) examines pitfalls to sound economic reasoning, while the "Last Word" section for Chapter 4 (Market Failures: Public Goods and Externalities) examines cap-and-trade versus carbon taxes as policy responses to excessive carbon dioxide emissions. There are 7 new "Last Word" sections in this edition.

If you are unfamiliar with *Economics,* we encourage you to thumb through the chapters to take a quick look at these highly visible features.

Enhanced Coverage of Game Theory and Strategic Behavior

The online economy and the tech sector present students with many high-profile examples of oligopolistic firms and industries. A grasp of strategic behavior is consequently more important than ever for principles students. To that end, the 21st edition features extended coverage of game theory and strategic behavior. The new material covers topics related to sequential games, including backward induction, the game-tree (extensive form) representation of strategic games, and subgame perfect Nash equilibrium.

In previous editions, a substantial portion of our game theory coverage appeared in an appendix to a chapter that covered both monopolistic competition and oligopoly. With the material on monopolistic competition now located in a separate chapter, we have been able to eliminate the appendix and fully integrate the game theory material that had appeared there with the treatment of oligopoly that had appeared in the main body of text. The result is our new Chapter 14, which is titled, "Oligopoly and Strategic Behavior."

CONSIDER THIS . . .

A Bright Idea

Source: © Federico Rostagno/Shutterstock.com

In sunny areas, a solar panel can make up for the cost of its installation in just a few years by greatly reducing or even eliminating a household's electricity bill. After those years of payback are finished, there will be almost nothing but benefits because the solar panel will continue to provide free electricity at only modest maintenance costs. Consequently, nearly every household in sunny areas could rationally profit from installing solar panels.

Unfortunately, myopia discourages most people from wanting to reap the net benefits. Because people are myopic, they focus too strongly on the upfront costs of installing solar panels while at the same time discounting the long-run benefits from being able to generate their own electricity. The result is major inefficiency as most homeowners end up foregoing solar panels.

A company called Solar City has figured out a way to work with rather than against people's myopia. It does so by offering leasing and financing options that eliminate the need for consumers to pay for the upfront costs of installing a solar system. Instead, Solar City pays for the upfront costs and then makes its money by splitting the resulting savings on monthly electricity bills with consumers.

This arrangement actually benefits from myopia because consumers get to focus on instant savings rather than initial costs. The same strategy can also be used to promote other investments that would normally be discouraged by myopia, such as installing energy-efficient furnaces, air conditioners, and appliances.

This integrated presentation facilitates student comprehension of both game theory and oligopoly because strategic interactions are always presented in an accessible, intuitive context. Students already understand that Google's actions affect those of rivals like Facebook, and vice versa. So integrating oligopoly with game theory illuminates both sets of material.

New Discussions of Unconventional Monetary Policy and Interest-Rate Normalization

Our macroeconomics chapters on monetary policy have been rewritten in many places to reflect the historically unprecedented monetary policy regimes that have been instituted by central banks since the Financial Crisis. Thus, for instance, we have included material that will allow students to comprehend the negative interest rates that are now common in Europe. Also necessary was a revised treatment of the federal funds rate to reflect the fact that monetary policy has been implemented in recent years in the United States by means of open-market interventions aimed at quantitative easing rather than open-market interventions aimed at lowering the federal funds rate, which has been stuck near the zero lower bound since the Great Recession.

We have also been sure to include intuitive coverage of the monetary policy tools that the Federal Reserve says it will be using in coming years to "normalize" monetary policy and raise short-term interest rates in the context of massive excess bank reserves. To that end, we have truncated our coverage of the federal funds market because the Fed has stated that it intends to normalize via the repo market and the interest rate that it pays banks on excess reserves (IOER). We cover those mechanisms in detail and explain how the Fed intends to use them in coming years.

Tested Content for Peer Instruction

Economics has been at the forefront of pedagogical innovation since our first edition, when we debuted the first separate student study guide and the first explanations next to each figure so that students could understand what was going on without having to hunt around in the main text for an explanation. Successive editions have brought additional firsts, from being the first with prepared overhead slides to being the first with SmartBook and adaptive-learning technology.

While technology has made learning with *Economics* more efficient for the individual student, we wanted to offer new methods to enhance the effectiveness of the classroom experience as well. We are consequently proud that we are now going to be the first textbook to offer Peer Instruction materials that are highly effective, comprehensive, and classroom-tested.

Peer Instruction was pioneered by Eric Mazur of Harvard University's Physics Department. It is a student-focused, interactive teaching method that has been shown to massively increase the depth of student understanding across a wide variety of disciplines. It works by having students, in groups, ponder and discuss questions about challenging scenarios before their instructor steps in to clear up any lingering misconceptions. Along the way, students first answer each question individually before voting as a team after a discussion. Those two answers—individual, then group—provided the evidence for the effectiveness of Peer Instruction.

As explained by Harvard psychologist Stephen Pinker, the group discussions lead to a deeper and more intuitive understanding of concepts and theories than can usually be achieved with lecture-based instruction. That is the case because beginners are often better than experts at explaining challenging ideas to other beginners. The problem with experts—that is, instructors like you and me—is that the process of becoming an expert rewires the brain so that the expert can no longer think like a beginner. Our own expertise makes it difficult to see where students are getting confused and it is consequently very useful to unleash the power of Peer Instruction to help beginners tackle new material.

The effectiveness of Peer Instruction depends, however, on the quality of the questions and scenarios that students are asked to ponder. Developing good questions and effective scenarios is highly time intensive and often a matter of experimentation; you just don't know how well a question or scenario will work until you try it. It is not a surprise, then, that today's busy instructors often shy away from Peer Instruction because of the high start-up costs and the time required to develop truly effective questions and scenarios.

Fortunately for you, we did all the work. Author Sean Flynn and Todd Fitch of the University of San Francisco have field-tested hundreds of questions and scenarios for effectiveness. So with this 21st edition of McConnell, we are ready to offer a fully supported set of Peer Instruction material tied directly to each of the learning objectives in *Economics*. The questions and scenarios, as well as resources to help organize a Peer Instruction classroom can be found in Connect.

If you have ever been in a situation in which more experienced students helped to teach newer students, you have seen the power of Peer Instruction. Our new materials bring us back to that paradigm. So while we are first once again with Peer Instruction in economics, credit belongs to the pioneering work of dedicated teachers like Eric Mazur and Stephen Pinker for making this method available across disciplines.

Full Support for Flipped Classroom Teaching Strategies

We have also designed our new Peer Instruction materials to facilitate flipped-classroom teaching strategies, wherein students learn basic material at home, before lecture, before being challenged in class to reach higher levels of understanding. In K-12 math programs, for example, students study short videos on new content at home before coming to class to work problems. That sequence of learning activities assures that an instructor is present at the stage where students encounter the most difficulties, namely, when they attempt to apply the material. By contrast, the traditional (non-flipped) method for teaching elementary math presents new content in class before sending students home to work problems by themselves. That sequence leaves students without expert help when they are most vulnerable to misunderstandings and errors.

We have designed our new Peer Instruction materials to facilitate the flipped-classroom method by leveraging the adaptive learning materials that are already available in our Connect online learning platform. In particular, students can be assigned new material before lecture via SmartBook, which is an adaptive-learning technology that tutors students through the basic concepts and skills presented in each section of the book. We also recommend that students work before class on end-of-chapter problems and LearnSmart (which also come with adaptive feedback thanks to Connect).

Those pre-class activities will allow students to master the lower levels of Bloom's Taxonomy of learning objectives—things like remembering and understanding—*before* they come to class. They will then be ready to attack the higher levels of Bloom's Taxonomy—things like applying, analyzing, and evaluating. That's where our new Peer Instruction material comes in. Students who have each already worked their way through the lower levels of Bloom's Taxonomy come together in class under the instruction of an expert—their teacher—to work in unison on the higher levels of understanding that are the ultimate goal of economics instruction.

We are consequently happy to be offering students and instructors yet another first, namely, the first high-quality, proven, flipped-classroom package available for principles of economics classes. Not every instructor will choose to use this material, but we are confident that those who do will wish that it had arrived much sooner. For those instructors who are new to either Peer Instruction or the flipped-classroom method, we will be offering extensive complimentary training and support via online seminars and message boards. If you are eager to try these new methods, we will be happy to help you get going and keep going.

Current Discussions and Examples

The 21st edition of *Economics* refers to and discusses many current topics. Examples include surpluses and shortages of tickets at the Olympics; the myriad impacts of ethanol subsidies; creative destruction; applications of behavioral economics; applications of game theory; the most rapidly expanding and disappearing U.S. jobs; oil and gasoline prices; cap-and-trade systems and carbon taxes; occupational licensing; state lotteries; consumption versus income inequality; the impact of electronic medical records on health care costs; the surprising fall in illegal immigration after the 2007–2009 recession; conditional and unconditional cash transfers; the difficulty of targeting fiscal stimulus; the rapid rise in college tuition; the slow recovery from the Great Recession; ballooning federal budget deficits and public debt; the long-run funding shortfalls in Social Security and Medicare; the effect of rising dependency ratios on economic growth; innovative Federal Reserve policies, including quantitative easing, the zero interest rate policy, and explicit inflation targets; the massive excess reserves in the banking system; the jump in the size of the Fed's balance sheet; the effect of the zero interest rate policy on savers; regulation of "too big to fail" banks; trade adjustment assistance; the European Union and the Eurozone; changes in exchange rates; and many other current topics.

Chapter-by-Chapter Changes

Each chapter of *Economics,* 21st edition, contains updated data reflecting the current economy, revised Learning Objectives, and reorganized and expanded end-of-chapter content. Every chapter also contains one or more Quick Review boxes to help students review and solidify content as they are reading along.

Chapter-specific updates include:

Chapter 1: Limits, Alternatives, and Choices features two refreshed Consider This pieces as well as revised new examples and working improvements to clarify the main concepts.

Chapter 2: The Market System and the Circular Flow contains updated examples and a brief new introduction to the concept of residual claimant.

Chapter 3: Demand, Supply, and Market Equilibrium includes a new Last Word on how student lending raises college tuition as well as data updates and updated examples.

Chapter 4: Market Failures: Public Goods and Externalities features updated examples and a new Key Word on Pigovian taxes.

Chapter 5: Government's Role and Government Failure has a new Consider This on government agencies violating government laws, several new examples, and wording revisions for increased clarity.

Chapter 6: Elasticity contains several updated examples.

Chapter 7: Utility Maximization incorporates updated examples and a new Consider This vignette on consumers applying maximizing behavior to the calorie data that are now printed on restaurant menus.

Chapter 8: Behavioral Economics contains a new Consider This piece on the myopia-busting business model employed by Solar City as well as a new Last Word describing the activities of the Behavioral Insights Team.

Chapter 9: Businesses and the Costs of Production incorporates a few wording updates to facilitate rapid comprehension.

Chapter 10: Pure Competition in the Short Run features several wording changes to improve student understanding of the end-of-chapter questions and problems.

Chapter 11: Pure Competition in the Long Run contains several updated examples to keep the content relevant for today's students.

Chapter 12: Pure Monopoly has a new Last Word about individualized online price discrimination as well as updated examples.

Chapter 13: Monopolistic Competition was previously part of a chapter that covered both monopolistic competition and oligopoly. We have split that chapter into two parts for the 21st edition so that instructors who wish to skip either set of material may easily do so.

Chapter 14: Oligopoly and Strategic Behavior was previously part of a chapter that covered both monopolistic competition and oligopoly. The material on oligopoly constitutes the basis for this stand-alone chapter, which also extends the game theory material found in the previous edition. Our extended coverage of game theory and strategic behavior includes extensive-form (game-tree) representations of sequential games and the concept of subgame-perfect Nash equilibrium. As with prior editions, all game theory material is kept concrete by presenting it in the context of strategic behavior among oligopoly firms.

Chapter 15: Technology, R&D, and Efficiency was previously a Web Chapter available only online. It has been brought into the main body of the book and contains extensive data updates as well as several new examples.

Chapter 16: The Demand for Resources incorporates light data updates as well as an entirely new Last Word on capital-labor substitution. This discussion uses ATM machines as its main example, just as the Last Word in the previous edition did. But an update was required because recent research indicates that the main premise of the old Last Word no longer holds true: ATMs did not in fact replace human tellers in the aggregate, at least not after managers adjusted to the new technology. The new Last Word updates the story.

Chapter 17: Wage Determination features extensive data updates, improved wording for clarity, and a new Last Word on how unnecessary occupational licensing requirements are reducing employment opportunities.

Chapter 18: Rent, Interest, and Profit incorporates wording improvements, data updates, and a new Consider This on the subject of profits.

Chapter 19: Natural Resource and Energy Economics has extensive data updates and a new Consider This boxed piece on how the current limitations of electricity-storage technology stymie the wider adoption of renewable energy sources such as solar and wind power.

Chapter 20: Public Finance: Expenditures and Taxes contains extensive data updates and several new examples.

Chapter 21: Antitrust Policy and Regulation has a new Last Word that covers both antitrust prosecutions against human managers who intentionally engage in anticompetitive practices as well as the newly evolving area of price-fixing by artificial intelligence algorithms that unintentionally collude to fix prices when they interact with each other.

Chapter 22: Agriculture: Economics and Policy features extensive data updates as well as a new section on the Agricultural Act of 2014.

Chapter 23: Income Inequality, Poverty, and Discrimination contains a new Consider This about welfare cliffs as well as extensive data updates and several new examples.

Chapter 24: Health Care contains many data updates as well as a completely revised Consider This on the problems that have been encountered during the implementation of the Patient Protection and Affordable Care Act.

Chapter 25: Immigration contains several new examples about the economic contributions of immigrants as well as comprehensive data updates.

Chapter 26: International Trade contains new examples and data updates.

Chapter 27: The Balance of Payments, Exchange Rates, and Trade Deficits is heavily revised for this edition. There is an entirely new presentation of fixed exchange rates and how the balance of payments under a fixed exchange rate determines the direction of change of both foreign exchange reserves as well as the domestic money supply. This presentation is illustrated with a new Consider This on China's currency peg as well as a new Last Word on whether common currencies (which are implicit pegs) are a good idea. This chapter also has a new appendix that includes the material on previous (pre-Bretton Woods) exchange rate systems that was previously presented in Content Options for Instructors 2 (COI2).

Chapter 28: The Economics of Developing Countries has an updated discussion on China's recently terminated one-child policy as well as a new Last Word that reviews the poverty-fighting effectiveness of microcredit, conditional cash transfers, and unconditional cash transfers.

Distinguishing Features

Comprehensive Explanations at an Appropriate Level

Economics is comprehensive, analytical, and challenging yet fully accessible to a wide range of students. The thoroughness and accessibility enable instructors to select topics for special classroom emphasis with confidence that students can read and comprehend other independently assigned material in the book. Where needed, an extra sentence of explanation is provided. Brevity at the expense of clarity is false economy.

Fundamentals of the Market System

Many economies throughout the world are still making difficult transitions from planning to markets while a handful of other countries such as Venezuela seem to be trying to reestablish government-controlled, centrally planned economies. Our detailed description of the institutions and operation of the market system in Chapter 2 (The Market System and the Circular Flow) is therefore even more relevant than before. We pay particular attention to property rights, entrepreneurship, freedom of enterprise and choice, competition, and the role of profits because these concepts are often misunderstood by beginning students worldwide.

Extensive Treatment of International Economics

We give the principles and institutions of the global economy extensive treatment. The appendix to Chapter 3 (Demand, Supply, and Market Equilibrium) has an application on exchange rates. Chapter 26 (International Trade) examines key facts of international trade, specialization and comparative advantage, arguments for protectionism, impacts of tariffs and subsidies, and various trade agreements. Chapter 27 (The Balance of Payments, Exchange Rates, and Trade Deficits) discusses the balance of payments, fixed and floating exchange rates, and U.S. trade deficits.

Chapter 26 (International Trade) is constructed such that instructors who want to cover international trade early in the course can assign it immediately after Chapter 3. Chapter 26 requires only a good understanding of production possibilities analysis and supply and demand analysis to comprehend.

International competition, trade flows, and financial flows are integrated throughout the micro and macro sections. "Global Perspective" boxes add to the international flavor of the book.

Early and Extensive Treatment of Government

The public sector is an integral component of modern capitalism. This book introduces the role of government early. Chapter 4 (Market Failures: Public Goods and Externalities) systematically discusses public goods and government policies toward externalities. Chapter 5 (Government's Role and Government Failure) details the factors that cause government failure. And Chapter 20 (Public Finance: Expenditures and Taxes) examines taxation and government expenditures in detail. Both the micro and the macro sections of the text include issue- and policy-oriented chapters.

Stress on the Theory of the Firm

We have given much attention to microeconomics in general and to the theory of the firm in particular, for two reasons. First, the concepts of microeconomics are difficult for most beginning students; abbreviated expositions usually compound these difficulties by raising more questions than they answer. Second, we wanted to couple analysis of the various market structures with a discussion of the impact of each market arrangement on price, output levels, resource allocation, and the rate of technological advance.

Emphasis on Technological Change and Economic Growth

This edition continues to emphasize economic growth. Chapter 1 (Limits, Alternatives, and Choices) uses the production possibilities curve to show the basic ingredients of growth. Chapter 15 (Technology, R&D, and Efficiency) provides an explicit and cohesive discussion of the microeconomics of technological advance, including topics such as invention, innovation, and diffusion; start-up firms; R&D decision making; market structure and R&D effort; and creative destruction.

Focus on Economic Policy and Issues

For many students, the micro chapters on antitrust, agriculture, income inequality, health care, and immigration, along with the macro chapters on fiscal policy and monetary policy, are where the action is centered. We guide that action along logical lines through the application of appropriate analytical tools. In the micro, we favor inclusiveness; instructors can effectively choose two or three chapters from Part 6.

Organizational Alternatives

Although instructors generally agree on the content of principles of economics courses, they sometimes differ on how to arrange the material. *Economics* includes 11 parts, and thus provides considerable organizational flexibility. We place microeconomics before macroeconomics because this ordering is consistent with how contemporary economists view the direction of linkage between the two components. The introductory material of Parts 1 and 2, however, can be followed immediately by the macro analysis of Parts 7 and 8. Similarly, the two-path macro enables covering the full aggregate expenditures model or advancing directly from the basic macro relationships chapter to the AD-AS model.

Some instructors will prefer to intersperse the microeconomics of Parts 4 and 5 with the issues chapters of Part 6. Chapter 22 on agriculture may follow Chapters 10 and 11 on pure competition; Chapter 21 on antitrust and regulation may follow Chapters 12, 13, 14, and 15 on imperfect competition models and technological advance. Chapter 25 on immigration may follow Chapter 17 on wages; and Chapter 23 on income inequality may follow Chapters 17 and 18 on distributive shares of national income.

Finally, Chapter 26 on international trade can easily be moved up to immediately after Chapter 3 on supply and demand for instructors who want an early discussion of international trade.

Pedagogical Aids

Economics is highly student-oriented. The 21st edition is also accompanied by a variety of high-quality supplements that help students master the subject and help instructors implement customized courses.

Digital Tools

Adaptive Reading Experience. SmartBook contains the same content as the print book, but actively tailors that content to the needs of the individual through adaptive probing. Instructors can assign SmartBook reading assignments for points to create incentives for students to come to class prepared.

Extensive Algorithmic and Graphing Assessment. Robust, auto-gradable question banks for each chapter now include even more questions that make use of the Connect graphing tool. More questions featuring algorithmic variations have also been added.

Interactive Graphs. This new assignable resource within Connect helps students see the relevance of subject matter by providing visual displays of real data for students to manipulate. All graphs are accompanied by assignable assessment questions and feedback to guide students through the experience of learning to read and interpret graphs and data.

Videos New to this edition are videos that provide support for key economics topics. These short, engaging explanations are presented at the moment students may be struggling to help them connect the dots and grasp challenging concepts.

Math Preparedness Tutorials. Our math preparedness assignments have been reworked to help students refresh on important prerequisite topics necessary to be successful in economics.

Digital Image Library Every graph and table in the text is available in the Instructor's Resource section in Connect.

Three Reorganized Test Banks The *Economics* test banks contain around 14,000 multiple-choice and true-false questions, many of which were written by the text authors. While previous editions grouped these questions into two separate test banks,

this edition uses a consolidated test bank with advanced tagging features that will allow instructors to choose familiar questions from Test Banks I and II or create new assignments from the full variety of questions in each chapter. Each test bank question for *Economics* also maps to a specific learning objective. Randy Grant revised Test Bank I for the 21st edition. Felix Kwan of Maryville University updated Test Bank II. All Test Bank questions are organized by learning objective, topic, AACSB Assurance of Learning, and Bloom's Taxonomy guidelines.

Test Bank III, written by William Walstad, contains more than 600 pages of short-answer questions and problems created in the style of the book's end-of-chapter questions. Test Bank III can be used to construct student assignments or design essay and problem exams. Suggested answers to the essay and problem questions are included. In all, nearly 15,000 questions give instructors maximum testing flexibility while ensuring the fullest possible text correlation.

Computerized Test Bank Online TestGen is a complete, state-of-the-art test generator and editing application software that allows instructors to quickly and easily select test items from McGraw-Hill's test bank content. The instructors can then organize, edit and customize questions and answers to rapidly generate tests for paper or online administration. Questions can include stylized text, symbols, graphics, and equations that are inserted directly into questions using built-in mathematical templates. TestGen's random generator provides the option to display different text or calculated number values each time questions are used. With both quick-and-simple test creation and flexible and robust editing tools, TestGen is a complete test generator system for today's educators.

You can use our test bank software, TestGen, or *Connect Economics* to easily query for learning outcomes and objectives that directly relate to the learning objectives for your course. You can then use the reporting features to aggregate student results in a similar fashion, making the collection and presentation of assurance-of-learning data simple and easy.

AACSB Statement The McGraw-Hill Companies is a proud corporate member of the Association to Advance Collegiate Schools of Business (AACSB) International. Understanding the importance and value of AACSB accreditation, *Economics* has sought to recognize the curricula guidelines detailed in the AACSB standards for business accreditation by connecting end-of-chapter questions in *Economics* and the accompanying test banks to the general knowledge and skill guidelines found in the AACSB standards.

This AACSB Statement for *Economics* is provided only as a guide for the users of this text. The AACSB leaves content coverage and assessment within the purview of individual schools, their respective missions, and their respective faculty. While *Economics* and its teaching package make no claim of any specific AACSB qualification or evaluation, we have, within *Economics* labeled selected questions according to the eight general knowledge and skills areas emphasized by AACSB.

Supplements for Students and Instructors

Study Guide One of the world's leading experts on economic education, William Walstad of the University of Nebraska–Lincoln, prepared the *Study Guide*. Many students find either the printed or digital version indispensable. Each chapter contains an introductory statement, a checklist of behavioral objectives, an outline, a list of important terms, fill-in questions, problems and projects, objective questions, and discussion questions.

The *Guide* comprises a superb "portable tutor" for the principles student. Separate *Study Guides* are available for the macro and micro editions of the text.

Instructor's Manual Shawn Knabb of Western Washington University revised and updated the *Instructor's Manual* to accompany the 21st edition of the text. The revised *Instructor's Manual* includes:

- Chapter summaries.
- Listings of "what's new" in each chapter.
- Teaching tips and suggestions.
- Learning objectives.
- Chapter outlines.
- Extra questions and problems.
- Answers to the end-of-chapter questions and problems, plus correlation guides mapping content to learning objectives.

The *Instructor's Manual* is available in the Instructor's Resource section, accessible through the Library tab in Connect.

PowerPoint Presentations A dedicated team of instructors updated the PowerPoint presentations for the 21st edition: Stephanie Campbell of Mineral Area College and Amy Chataginer of Mississippi Gulf Coast Community College. Each chapter is accompanied by a concise yet thorough tour of the key concepts. Instructors can use these presentations in the classroom, and students can use them on their computers.

Digital Solutions
McGraw-Hill *Connect*® Economics

 **Less Managing. More Teaching. Greater Learning.** *Connect Economics* is an online assignment and assessment solution that offers a number of powerful tools and features that make managing assignments easier so faculty can spend more time teaching. With *Connect Economics*, students can engage with their coursework anytime and anywhere, making the learning process more accessible and efficient.

Learning Management System Integration

 McGraw-Hill Campus is a one-stop teaching and learning experience available to use with any learning management system. McGraw-Hill Campus provides single sign-on to faculty and students for all McGraw-Hill material and technology from within a school's website. McGraw-Hill Campus also allows instructors instant access to all supplements and teaching materials for all McGraw-Hill products.

Blackboard and Canvas users also benefit from McGraw-Hill's industry-leading integration, providing single sign-on access to all Connect assignments and automatic feeding of assignment results to the Blackboard grade book.

Tegrity Campus: Lectures 24/7

Tegrity Campus is a service that makes class time available 24/7 by automatically capturing every lecture in a searchable format for students to review when they study and complete assignments. With a simple one-click start-and-stop process, you capture all computer screens and corresponding audio. Students can replay any part of any class with easy-to-use browser-based viewing on a PC or Mac.

Educators know that the more students can see, hear, and experience class resources, the better they learn. In fact, studies prove it. With Tegrity Campus, students quickly recall key moments by using Tegrity Campus's unique search feature. This search function helps students efficiently find what they need, when they need it, across an entire semester of class recordings. Help turn all your students' study time into learning moments immediately supported by your lecture.

To learn more about Tegrity, you can watch a two-minute Flash demo at **tegritycampus.mhhe.com.**

McGraw-Hill Customer Care Contact Information

Getting the most from new technology can be challenging. So McGraw-Hill offers a large suite of complementary support services for faculty using *Economics*. You can contact our Product Specialists 24 hours a day to set up online technology instruction. Or you can contact customer support at any time by either calling **800-331-5094** or by visiting the Customer Experience Group (CXG) Support Center at **www.mhhe.com/support.** They will put you in touch with a Technical Support Analyst familiar with *Economics* and its technology offerings. And, of course, our online knowledge bank of Frequently Asked Questions is always available at the just-mentioned website for instant answers to the most common technology questions.

Acknowledgments

We give special thanks to Ryan Umbeck, Peter Staples, Peggy Dalton, and Matt McMahon for their hard work updating the questions and problems in *Connect,* as well as the material they created for the additional Connect Problems. Thank you Jody Lotz for her dedicated copy editing of the Connect end-of-chapter material. Laura Maghoney's expert revision of the SmartBook content and consultation on many other elements of this project were invaluable. Thanks to the many dedicated instructors who accuracy-checked the end-of-chapter content, test banks, and Instructor's Manuals: Per Norander, Ribhi Daoud, Gretchen Mester, Erwin Erhardt, and Xavier Whitacre. We offer our deepest gratitude to the amazing Laureen Cantwell for her research assistance. Finally, we thank William Walstad and Tom Barbiero (the coauthor of our Canadian edition) for their helpful ideas and insights.

We are greatly indebted to an all-star group of professionals at McGraw-Hill—in particular James Heine, Virgil Lloyd, Trina Maurer, Harvey Yep, Bruce Gin, Tara McDermott, Adam Huenecke, and Katie Hoenicke—for their publishing and marketing expertise.

The 21st edition has benefited from a number of perceptive formal reviews. The reviewers, listed at the end of the preface, were a rich source of suggestions for this revision. To each of you, and others we may have inadvertently overlooked, thank you for your considerable help in improving *Economics.*

Sean M. Flynn
Stanley L. Brue
Campbell R. McConnell

Richard Agesa, *Marshall University*

Carlos Aguilar, *El Paso Community College, Valle Verde*

Yamin Ahmad, *University of Wisconsin–Whitewater*

Eun Ahn, *University of Hawaii, West Oahu*

Miki Anderson, *Pikes Peak Community College*

Giuliana Andreopoulos, *William Paterson University*

Thomas Andrews, *West Chester University of Pennsylvania*

Fatma Antar, *Manchester Community College*

Len Anyanwu, *Union County College*

Emmanuel Asigbee, *Kirkwood Community College*

John Atkins, *Pensacola State College*

Moses Ayiku, *Essex County College*

Wendy Bailey, *Troy University*

Dean Baim, *Pepperdine University*

Herman Baine, *Broward College*

Tyra Barrett, *Pellissippi State Community College*

David Barrus, *Brigham Young University, Idaho*

Jill Beccaris-Pescatore, *Montgomery County Community College*

Kevin Beckwith, *Salem State University*

Christian Beer, *Cape Fear Community College*

Robert Belsterling, *Pennsylvania State University, Altoona*

Laura Jean Bhadra, *Northern Virginia Community College, Manassas*

Priscilla Block, *Broward College*

Augustine Boakye, *Essex County College*

Stephanie Campbell, *Mineral Area College*

Bruce Carpenter, *Mansfield University*

Tom Cate, *Northern Kentucky University*

Semih Emre Çekin, *Texas Tech University*

Suparna Chakraborty, *University of San Francisco*

Claude Chang, *Johnson & Wales University*

Amy Chataginer, *Mississippi Gulf Coast Community College–Gautier*

Shuo Chen, *State University of New York–Geneseo*

Jon Chesbro, *Montana Tech of the University of Montana*

Amod Choudhary, *Lehman College*

Constantinos Christofides, *East Stroudsburg University*

Kathy Clark, *Edison College, Fort Myers*

Wes Clark, *Midlands Technical College*

Jane Clary, *College of Charleston*

Jane Cline, *Forsyth Technical Community College*

Patricia Daigle, *Mount Wachusett Community College*

Anthony Daniele, *St. Petersburg College–Gibbs*

Rosa Lee Danielson, *College of DuPage*

Ribhi Daoud, *Sinclair Community College*

Maria Davis, *Indian River State College, Central*

William L. Davis, *University of Tennessee–Martin*

Richard Dixon, *Thomas Nelson Community College*

Tanya Downing, *Cuesta College*

Scott Dressler, *Villanova University*

Brad Duerson, *Des Moines Area Community College*

Mark J. Eschenfelder, *Robert Morris University*

Maxwell Eseonu, *Virginia State University*

Michael Fenick, *Broward College*

Tyrone Ferdnance, *Hampton University*

Jeffrey Forrest, *St. Louis Community College–Florissant Valley*

Richard Fowles, *University of Utah, Salt Lake City*

Mark Frascatore, *Clarkson University*

Shelby Frost, *Georgia State University*

Sudip Ghosh, *Penn State University–Berks*

Daniel Giedeman, *Grand Valley State University*

Scott Gilbert, *Southern Illinois University*

James Giordano, *Villanova University*

Susan Glanz, *St. John's University*

Lowell Glenn, *Utah Valley University*

Terri Gonzales, *Delgado Community College*

Michael Goode, *Central Piedmont Community College*

Moonsu Han, *North Shore Community College*

Charlie Harrington, *Nova Southeastern University, Main*

Virden Harrison, *Modesto Junior College*

Richard R. Hawkins, *University of West Florida*

Kim Hawtrey, *Hope College*

Glenn Haynes, *Western Illinois University*

Mark Healy, *Harper College*

Dennis Heiner, *College of Southern Idaho*

Michael Heslop, *Northern Virginia Community College, Annandale*

Calvin Hoy, *County College of Morris*

Jesse Hoyt Hill, *Tarrant County College*

Jim Hubert, *Seattle Central Community College*

Greg W. Hunter, *California State Polytechnic University, Pomona*

Christos Ioannou, *University of Minnesota–Minneapolis*

Faridul Islam, *Utah Valley University*

Mahshid Jalilvand, *University of Wisconsin–Stout*

Ricot Jean, *Valencia Community College–Osceola*

Jonatan Jelen, *City College of New York*

Stephen Kaifa, *County College of Morris*

Brad Kamp, *University of South Florida, Sarasota-Manatee*

Gus Karam, *Pace University, Pleasantville*

Kevin Kelley, *Northwest Vista College*

Chris Klein, *Middle Tennessee State University*

Barry Kotlove, *Edmonds Community College*

Richard Kramer, *New England College*

Felix Kwan, *Maryville University*

Ted Labay, *Bishop State Community College*

Tina Lance, *Germanna Community College–Fredericksburg*

Sarah Leahy, *Brookdale Community College*

Yu-Feng Lee, *New Mexico State University–Las Cruces*

Adam Y.C. Lei, *Midwestern State University*

Phillip Letting, *Harrisburg Area Community College*

Brian Lynch, *Lake Land College*

Zagros Madjd-Sadjadi, *Winston-Salem State University*

Laura Maghoney, *Solano Community College*

Vincent Mangum, *Grambling State University*

Benjamin Matta, *New Mexico State University–Las Cruces*

Pete Mavrokordatos, *Tarrant County College–Northeast Campus*

Frederick May, *Trident Technical College*

Katherine McClain, *University of Georgia*

Michael McIntyre, *Copiah-Lincoln Community College*

Robert McKizzie, *Tarrant County College–Southeast Campus*

Kevin McWoodson, *Moraine Valley Community College*

Edwin Mensah, *University of North Carolina at Pembroke*

Randy Methenitis, *Richland College*

Ida Mirzaie, *The Ohio State University*

David Mitch, *University of Maryland–Baltimore County*

Ramesh Mohan, *Bryant University*

Daniel Morvey, *Piedmont Technical College*

Shahriar Mostashari, *Campbell University*

Stefan Mullinax, *College of Lake County*

Ted Muzio, *St. John's University*

Cliff Nowell, *Weber State University*

Alex Obiya, *San Diego City College*

Albert Okunade, *University of Memphis*

Mary Ellen Overbay, *Seton Hall University*

Tammy Parker, *University of Louisiana at Monroe*

Alberto Alexander Perez, *Harford Community College*

David Petersen, *American River College*

Mary Anne Pettit, *Southern Illinois University–Edwardsville*

Jeff Phillips, *Morrisville State College*

Robert Poulton, *Graceland University*

Dezzie Prewitt, *Rio Hondo College*

Joe Prinzinger, *Lynchburg College*

Jaishankar Raman, *Valparaiso University*

Natalie Reaves, *Rowan University*

Virginia Reilly, *Ocean County College*

Tim Reynolds, *Alvin Community College*

Jose Rafael Rodriguez-Solis, *Nova Community College, Annandale*

John Romps, *Saint Anselm College*

Melissa Rueterbusch, *Mott Community College*

Tom Scheiding, *Elizabethtown College*

Amy Schmidt, *Saint Anselm College*

Ron Schuelke, *Santa Rosa Junior College*

Sangheon Shin, *Alabama State University*

Alexandra Shiu, *McLennan Community College*

Dorothy Siden, *Salem State University*

Robert Simonson, *Minnesota State University, Mankato*

Timothy Simpson, *Central New Mexico Community College*

Jonathan Sleeper, *Indian River State College*

Jose Rodriguez Solis, *Northern Virginia Community College*

Camille Soltau-Nelson, *Oregon State University*

Robert Sonora, *Fort Lewis College*

Maritza Sotomayor, *Utah Valley University, Orem*

Nick Spangenberg, *Ozarks Technical Community College*

Dennis Spector, *Naugatuck Valley Community College*

Thomas Stevens, *University of Massachusetts, Amherst*

Tamika Steward, *Tarrant County College, Southeast*

McGraw-Hill Connect®
Learn Without Limits

Connect is a teaching and learning platform that is proven to deliver better results for students and instructors.

Connect empowers students by continually adapting to deliver precisely what they need, when they need it, and how they need it, so your class time is more engaging and effective.

73% of instructors who use **Connect** require it; instructor satisfaction **increases** by 28% when **Connect** is required.

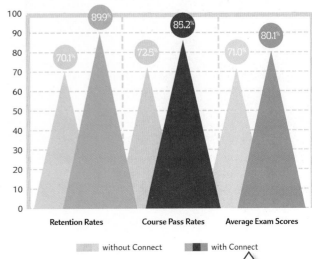

Connect's Impact on Retention Rates, Pass Rates, and Average Exam Scores

without Connect   with Connect

Using **Connect** improves retention rates by **19.8%**, passing rates by **12.7%**, and exam scores by **9.1%**.

Analytics

Connect Insight®

Connect Insight is Connect's new one-of-a-kind visual analytics dashboard that provides at-a-glance information regarding student performance, which is immediately actionable. By presenting assignment, assessment, and topical performance results together with a time metric that is easily visible for aggregate or individual results, Connect Insight gives the user the ability to take a just-in-time approach to teaching and learning, which was never before available. Connect Insight presents data that helps instructors improve class performance in a way that is efficient and effective.

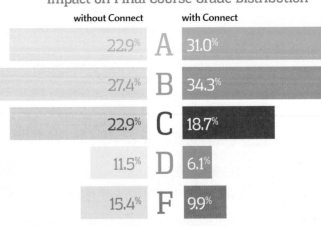

Impact on Final Course Grade Distribution

	without Connect	with Connect
A	22.9%	31.0%
B	27.4%	34.3%
C	22.9%	18.7%
D	11.5%	6.1%
F	15.4%	9.9%

Adaptive

THE **ADAPTIVE READING EXPERIENCE** DESIGNED TO TRANSFORM THE WAY STUDENTS READ

More students earn **A's** and **B's** when they use McGraw-Hill Education **Adaptive** products.

SmartBook®

Proven to help students improve grades and study more efficiently, SmartBook contains the same content within the print book, but actively tailors that content to the needs of the individual. SmartBook's adaptive technology provides precise, personalized instruction on what the student should do next, guiding the student to master and remember key concepts, targeting gaps in knowledge and offering customized feedback, and driving the student toward comprehension and retention of the subject matter. Available on tablets, SmartBook puts learning at the student's fingertips—anywhere, anytime.

Over **8 billion questions** have been answered, making McGraw-Hill Education products more intelligent, reliable, and precise.

www.mheducation.com

STUDENTS WANT

SMARTBOOK®

95% of students reported SmartBook to be a more effective way of reading material.

100% of students want to use the Practice Quiz feature available within SmartBook to help them study.

100% of students reported having reliable access to off-campus wifi.

90% of students say they would purchase SmartBook over print alone.

95% of students reported that SmartBook would impact their study skills in a positive way.

Mc Graw Hill Education

*Findings based on 2015 focus group results administered by McGraw-Hill Education

BRIEF CONTENTS

CONTENTS

	1959	1961	1963	1965	1967	1969	1971	1973	1975	1977
1 Sales by manufacturers (billions of dollars)*	338	356.4	412.7	492.2	575.4	694.6	751.1	1,107.20	1,065.2	1,328.1
2 Profits by manufacturers (billions of dollars)*	29.7	27.5	34.9	46.5	47.8	58.1	52.9	81.4	79.9	115.1
3 After-tax manufacturing profits per dollars of sales (cents)*	4.8	4.3	4.7	5.6	5.0	4.8	4.1	4.7	4.6	5.3
4 Index of business sector productivity (2009 =100)	31.9	33.6	36.5	39.1	41.7	43.3	46.0	48.9	49.8	52.3
5 Annual change in business sector productivity (%)	3.4	3.2	3.0	2.7	2.5	2.3	2.4	2.2	2.2	2.0
6 Nonagricultural employees in goods-producing industries (millions)	19.2	18.6	19.4	20.6	21.9	22.9	21.6	23.5	21.3	23.0
7 Nonagricultural employees in service-providing industries (millions)	34.2	35.5	37.4	40.3	44.0	47.6	49.7	53.5	55.8	59.6
8 Compesation of employees (billions of dollars)	286.3	311.1	351.2	406.3	482.9	586	667	815	950.2	1169
9 Average weekly hours in manufacturing industries**	40.3	39.9	40.6	41.2	37.9	37.5	36.7	36.9	36.0	35.9
10 Average hourly earnings in private nonagrucultural industries (dollars)	–	–	–	2.63	2.85	3.22	3.63	4.14	4.73	5.44
11 Average weekly earnings in private nonagricultural industries (dollars)	–	–	–	101.52	108.07	120.70	133.22	152.59	170.29	195.58
12 Federal minimum wage rate (dollars per hour)	1.00	1.15	1.25	1.25	1.40	1.60	1.60	1.60	2.10	2.30
13 Prime interest rate (%)	4.48	4.50	4.50	4.54	5.63	7.96	5.73	8.03	7.86	6.83
14 Ten-year Treasury bond interest rate (%)	4.33	3.88	4.00	4.28	5.07	6.67	6.16	6.85	7.99	7.42
15 Net farm income (billions of dollars)	62.0	67.5	64.9	68.8	62.2	65.9	62.6	130.2	81.2	56.5
16 Index of prices received by farmers (2011 = 100)	–	–	–	–	–	–	–	–	41	41
17 Index of prices paid by farmers (2011 = 100)	–	–	–	–	–	–	–	–	23	26
18 Persons below poverty level (millions)	39.5	39.6	36.4	33.2	27.8	24.1	25.6	23.0	25.9	24.7
19 Poverty rate (% of population)	22.4	21.9	19.5	17.3	14.2	12.1	12.5	11.1	12.3	11.6
20 U.S. goods exports (billions of dollars)	16.5	20.1	22.3	26.5	30.7	36.4	43.3	71.4	107.1	120.8
21 U.S. goods imports (billions of dollars)	−15.3	−14.5	−17.0	−21.5	−26.9	−35.8	−45.6	−70.5	−98.2	−151.9
22 U.S. population (millions)	177.8	183.7	189.2	194.3	198.7	202.7	207.7	211.9	216.0	220.2
23 Legal immigration (thousands)	260.7	271.3	306.3	296.7	362.0	358.6	370.5	398.5	385.4	458.8
24 Industry R&D expenditures (billions of dollars)	9.2	10.4	12.2	13.8	16.0	17.8	17.8	20.7	23.5	28.9
25 Price of crude oil (U.S. average, dollars per barrel)	2.90	2.89	2.89	2.86	2.92	3.09	3.39	3.89	7.67	8.57

*Revised definition of this series beginning in 1973
**Includes overtime

1979	1981	1983	1985	1986	1987	1988	1989	1990	1991	1992	1993
1,741.8	2,144.7	2,114.3	2,331.4	2,220.9	2,378.2	2,596.2	2,745.1	2,810.7	2,761.1	2,890.2	3,015.1
154.2	158.6	133.1	137.0	129.3	173.0	215.3	187.6	158.1	98.7	31.4	117.9
5.7	4.7	4.1	3.8	3.7	4.9	5.9	4.9	3.9	2.4	.8	2.8
53.0	54.1	55.7	58.5	60.2	60.5	61.4	62.1	63.5	64.6	67.5	67.6
1.9	1.9	1.9	1.8	1.8	1.7	1.7	1.6	1.6	1.6	1.6	1.5
25.0	24.1	22.1	23.6	23.3	23.5	23.9	24.0	23.7	22.6	22.1	22.2
64.9	67.2	68.2	73.9	76.2	78.6	81.4	84.0	85.8	85.8	86.7	88.7
1481	1795.3	2013.9	2389	2543.8	2724.3	2950	3142.6	3342.7	3452	3671.1	3820.7
35.6	35.2	34.9	34.9	34.7	34.7	34.6	34.5	34.3	34.1	34.2	34.3
6.34	7.44	8.20	8.74	8.93	9.14	9.44	9.80	10.20	10.52	10.77	11.05
225.69	261.53	286.43	304.62	309.78	317.39	326.48	338.34	349.72	358.51	368.25	378.94
2.90	3.35	3.35	3.35	3.35	3.35	3.35	3.35	3.80	4.25	4.25	4.25
12.67	18.87	10.79	9.93	8.33	8.21	9.32	10.87	10.01	8.46	6.25	6.00
9.43	13.92	11.10	10.62	7.67	8.39	8.85	8.49	8.55	7.86	7.01	5.87
67.2	55.2	26.6	49.7	53.2	63.4	63.9	72.1	69.2	58.3	71.0	64.6
53	56	55	51	49	50	56	58	58	56	55	57
33	40	42	42	42	43	45	47	49	49	50	51
26.1	31.8	35.3	33.1	32.4	32.2	31.7	31.5	33.6	35.7	38.0	39.3
11.7	14	15.2	14	13.6	13.4	13	12.8	13.5	14.2	14.8	15.1
184.4	237.0	201.8	215.9	223.3	250.2	320.2	359.9	387.4	414.1	439.6	456.9
−212.0	−265.1	−268.9	−338.1	−368.4	−409.8	−447.2	−477.7	−498.4	−491.0	−536.5	−589.4
225.1	229.5	233.8	237.9	240.1	242.3	244.5	246.8	249.5	252.2	255.0	257.8
394.2	595.0	550.1	568.1	600.0	599.9	641.3	1,090.2	1,535.9	1,826.6	973.4	903.9
37.1	50.4	63.7	82.4	85.9	90.2	94.9	99.9	107.4	114.7	116.8	115.4
12.64	31.77	26.19	24.09	12.51	15.40	12.58	15.86	20.03	16.54	15.99	14.25

	1994	1995	1996	1997	1998	1999	2000	2001	2002	2003
1 Sales by manufacturers (billions of dollars)*	3,255.8	3,528.3	3,757.6	3,920.0	3,949.4	4,148.9	4,548.2	4,295.0	4,216.4	4,397.2
2 Profits by manufacturers (billions of dollars)*	243.5	274.5	306.6	331.4	314.7	355.3	381.1	83.2	195.5	305.7
3 After-tax manufacturing profits per dollars of sales (cents)*	5.4	5.6	6.0	6.2	5.9	6.2	6.1	.8	3.2	5.4
4 Index of business sector productivity (2009 = 100)	68.2	68.4	70.5	71.8	74.0	76.7	79.4	81.5	85.0	89.1
5 Annual change in business sector productivity (%)	1.5	1.5	1.5	1.4	1.4	1.4	1.3	1.3	1.3	1.2
6 Nonagricultural employees in goods-producing industries (millions)	22.8	23.2	23.4	23.9	24.4	24.5	24.6	23.9	22.6	21.8
7 Nonagricultural employees in service-providing industries (millions)	91.6	94.2	96.3	99.0	101.7	104.6	107.2	108.0	107.9	108.3
8 Compesation of employees (billions of dollars)	4010.1	4202.6	4422.1	4714.7	5077.8	5410.3	5856.6	6046.5	6141.9	6365.4
9 Average weekly hours in manufacturing industries**	34.5	34.3	34.3	34.5	34.5	34.3	34.3	34.0	33.9	33.7
10 Average hourly earnings in private nonagrucultural industries (dollars)	11.34	11.66	12.05	12.51	13.02	13.49	14.02	14.55	14.97	15.38
11 Average weekly earnings in private nonagricultural industries (dollars)	391.28	400.22	413.47	432.05	448.76	463.35	481.36	494.05	507.03	518.41
12 Federal minimum wage rate (dollars per hour)	4.25	4.25	4.75	4.75	5.15	5.15	5.15	5.15	5.15	5.15
13 Prime interest rate (%)	7.15	8.83	8.27	8.44	8.35	8.00	9.23	6.91	4.67	4.12
14 Ten-year Treasury bond interest rate (%)	7.09	6.57	6.44	6.35	5.26	5.65	6.03	5.02	4.61	4.01
15 Net farm income (billions of dollars)	71.2	52.8	76.8	65.7	59.7	59.6	61.9	60.5	42.5	64.8
16 Index of prices received by farmers (2011 = 100)	56	57	63	60	57	54	54	57	55	60
17 Index of prices paid by farmers (2011 = 100)	52	54	57	58	57	57	59	61	61	63
18 Persons below poverty level (millions)	38.1	36.4	36.5	35.6	34.5	32.8	31.6	32.9	34.6	35.9
19 Poverty rate (% of population)	14.5	13.8	13.7	13.3	12.7	11.9	11.3	11.7	12.1	12.5
20 U.S. goods exports (billions of dollars)	502.9	575.2	612.1	678.4	670.4	698.2	784.8	731.2	697.4	729.8
21 U.S. goods imports (billions of dollars)	−668.7	−749.4	−803.1	−876.8	−918.6	−1,034.4	−1,230.6	−1,152.5	−1,171.9	−1,270.2
22 U.S. population (millions)	260.3	262.8	265.2	267.8	270.2	272.7	282.2	285.0	287.6	290.1
23 Legal immigration (thousands)	804.0	720.2	915.6	797.8	653.2	644.8	841.0	1,058.9	1,059.4	703.5
24 Industry R&D expenditures (billions of dollars)	117.4	129.8	142.4	155.4	167.1	182.1	200.0	202.0	193.9	200.7
25 Price of crude oil (U.S. average, dollars per barrel)	13.19	14.62	18.46	17.23	10.87	15.56	26.72	21.84	22.51	27.56

*Revised definition of this series beginning in 1973
**Includes overtime

2004	2005	2006	2007	2008	2009	2010	2011	2012	2013	2014	2015***
4,934.1	5,411.5	5,782.7	6,060.0	6,374.1	5,109.8	5,756.0	6,485.4	6,681.0	3570.3	6911.8	6428.8
447.5	524.2	604.6	602.8	388.1	360.6	584.3	721.7	507.5	260.1	540.1	511.4
7.1	7.4	8.1	7.3	4.2	5.6	8.3	9.2	7.7	10	9.9	8
92.0	93.9	94.6	95.8	96.8	100.0	103.3	103.6	104.0	104.7	105.4	106.2
1.2	1.1	1.1	1.1	1.1	1.1	1.0	1.0	0.7	0.7	0.6	0.8
21.9	22.2	22.5	22.2	21.3	18.6	17.8	18.0	18.4	18.7	19.2	19.6
109.6	111.6	113.6	115.4	115.5	112.3	112.2	113.5	117.5	119.5	121.9	124.4
6740.5	7087.8	7503.2	7899.1	8079.2	7787.8	7967.3	8278.5	8609.9	8842.4	9253.4	9693.1
33.7	33.8	33.9	33.9	33.6	33.1	33.4	33.6	33.7	33.7	33.7	33.7
15.70	16.13	16.76	17.44	18.08	18.63	19.05	19.44	19.74	20.13	20.61	21.04
529.23	544.44	567.89	590.24	608.11	617.50	636.19	652.89	665.65	677.73	694.91	709.13
5.15	5.15	5.15	5.85	6.55	7.25	7.25	7.25	7.25	7.25	7.25	7.25
4.34	6.19	7.96	8.05	5.09	3.25	3.25	3.25	3.25	3.25	3.25	3.5
4.27	4.29	4.80	4.63	3.66	3.26	3.22	2.78	1.80	2.35	2.54	2.14
90.3	78.8	55.6	65.9	78.4	57.5	76.2	109.9	91.7	115.7	85.2	73.6
66	64	65	76	84	74	79	100	105	107	107	98.8
66	70	74	79	90	88	90	100	104.4	106.3	112	109.9
37.0	37.0	36.5	37.3	39.8	43.6	46.3	46.2	46.5	45.8	46.6	43.1
12.7	12.6	12.3	12.5	13.2	14.3	15.1	15	15	14.7	14.8	13.5
822.0	911.7	1,039.4	1,164.0	1,307.5	1,069.7	1,218.3	1,297.6	1,344.2	1385.7	1447.3	1437.1
−1,485.5	−1,692.4	−1,875.1	−1,982.8	−2,137.6	−1,575.5	−1,826.7	−1,932.1	−1,972.2	−1,995.40	−2,090.80	−2,194.10
292.8	295.5	298.4	301.2	304.1	306.8	309.3	311.6	313.9	316.2	318.6	320.9
957.9	1,122.3	1,266.1	1,052.4	1,107.1	1,130.8	1,042.6	1,062.0	1,031.6	990.5	1,016.50	1,051.00
208.3	226.2	247.7	269.3	290.7	282.4	278.9	294.1	302.3	322.5	340.7	359.4
36.77	50.28	59.69	66.52	94.04	56.35	74.71	95.73	94.52	95.99	87.39	44.39

***Data for 2015 and the immediate prior years are subject to change because of subsequent government data revisions.

Sources: Economic Report of the President; Bureau of Economic Analysis; Bureau of Labor Statistics; National Science Foundation; Federal Reserve Systems; U.S. Census Bureau; U.S. Department of Homeland Security; and U.S. Energy Information Administration

Introduction to Economics and the Economy

Limits, Alternatives, and Choices

Learning Objectives

LO1.1 Define economics and the features of the economic perspective.

LO1.2 Describe the role of economic theory in economics.

LO1.3 Distinguish microeconomics from macroeconomics and positive economics from normative economics.

LO1.4 Explain the individual's economizing problem and how trade-offs, opportunity costs, and attainable combinations can be illustrated with budget lines.

LO1.5 List the categories of scarce resources and delineate the nature of society's economizing problem.

LO1.6 Apply production possibilities analysis, increasing opportunity costs, and economic growth.

LO1.7 Explain how economic growth and international trade increase consumption possibilities.

LO1.8 (Appendix) Understand graphs, curves, and slopes as they relate to economics.

(At the end of this chapter is an appendix is on understanding graphs. If you need a quick review of this mathematical tool, you might benefit by reading the appendix first.) People's wants are numerous and varied. Biologically, people need only air, water, food, clothing, and shelter. But in modern societies people also desire goods and services that provide a more comfortable or affluent standard of living. We want bottled water, soft drinks, and fruit juices, not just water from the creek. We want salads, burgers, and pizzas, not just berries and nuts. We want jeans, suits, and coats, not just woven reeds. We want apartments, condominiums, or houses, not just mud huts. And, as the saying goes, "That is not the half of it." We also want flat-panel TVs, Internet service, education, national defense, cell phones, health care, and much more.

Fortunately, society possesses productive resources, such as labor and managerial talent, tools and machinery, and land and mineral deposits. These resources, employed in the economic system (or simply the economy), help us produce goods and services that satisfy many of our economic wants. But the blunt reality is that our economic wants far exceed the productive capacity of our scarce (limited) resources. We are forced to make choices. This unyielding truth underlies the definition of **economics,** which is the social science concerned with how individuals, institutions, and society make optimal (best) choices under conditions of scarcity.

The Economic Perspective

LO1.1 Define economics and the features of the economic perspective.

Economists view things from a unique perspective. This **economic perspective,** or economic way of thinking, has several critical and closely interrelated features.

Scarcity and Choice

The economic resources needed to make goods and services are in limited supply. This **scarcity** restricts options and demands choices. Because we "can't have it all," we must decide what we will have and what we must forgo.

At the core of economics is the idea that "there is no free lunch." You may be treated to lunch, making it "free" from your perspective, but someone bears a cost. Because all resources are either privately or collectively owned by members of society, ultimately society bears the cost. Scarce inputs of land, equipment, farm labor, the labor of cooks and waiters, and managerial talent are required. Because society could have used these resources to produce other things, it sacrifices those other goods and services in making the lunch available. Economists call such sacrifices **opportunity costs:** To obtain more of one thing, society forgoes the opportunity of getting the next best thing that could have been created with those resources. That sacrifice is the opportunity cost of the choice.

Purposeful Behavior

Economics assumes that human behavior reflects "rational self-interest." Individuals look for and pursue opportunities to increase their **utility**—the pleasure, happiness, or satisfaction obtained from consuming a good or service. They allocate their time, energy, and money to maximize their satisfaction. Because they weigh costs and benefits, their economic decisions are "purposeful" or "rational," not "random" or "chaotic."

Consumers are purposeful in deciding what goods and services to buy. Business firms are purposeful in deciding what products to produce and how to produce them. Government entities are purposeful in deciding what public services to provide and how to finance them.

"Purposeful behavior" does not assume that people and institutions are immune from faulty logic and therefore are perfect decision makers. They sometimes make mistakes. Nor does it mean that people's decisions are unaffected by emotion or the decisions of those around them. Indeed,

economists acknowledge that people are sometimes impulsive or emulative. "Purposeful behavior" simply means that people make decisions with some desired outcome in mind.

Rational self-interest is not the same as selfishness. In the economy, increasing one's own wage, rent, interest, or profit normally requires identifying and satisfying *somebody else's* wants! Also, people make personal sacrifices for others. They contribute time and money to charities because they derive pleasure from doing so. Parents help pay for their children's education for the same reason. These self-interested, but unselfish, acts help maximize the givers' satisfaction as much as any personal purchase of goods or services. Self-interested behavior is simply behavior designed to increase personal satisfaction, however it may be derived.

Marginal Analysis: Comparing Benefits and Costs

The economic perspective focuses largely on **marginal analysis**—comparisons of marginal benefits and marginal costs, usually for decision making. To economists, "marginal"

Fast-Food Lines

Source: © Syracuse Newspapers/The Image Works

The economic perspective is useful in analyzing all sorts of behaviors. Consider an everyday example: the behavior of fast-food customers. When customers enter the restaurant, they go to the shortest line, believing that line will minimize their time cost of obtaining food. They are acting purposefully; time is limited, and people prefer using it in some way other than standing in line.

If one fast-food line is temporarily shorter than other lines, some people will move to that line. These movers apparently view the time saving from the shorter line (marginal benefit) as exceeding the cost of moving from their present line (marginal cost). The line switching tends to equalize line lengths. No further movement of customers between lines occurs once all lines are about equal.

Fast-food customers face another cost-benefit decision when a clerk opens a new station at the counter. Should they move to the new station or stay put? Those who shift to the new line decide that the time saving from the move exceeds the extra cost of physically moving. In so deciding, customers must also consider just how quickly they can get to the new station compared with others who may be contemplating the same move. (Those who hesitate are lost!)

Customers at the fast-food establishment do not have perfect information when they select lines. Thus, not all decisions turn out as expected. For example, you might enter a short line only to find that someone in front of you is ordering hamburgers and fries for 40 people in the Greyhound bus parked out back (and also that the guy taking orders in your new line is a trainee)! Nevertheless, at the time you made your decision, you thought it was optimal.

Finally, customers must decide what food to order when they arrive at the counter. In making their choices, they again compare marginal costs and marginal benefits in attempting to obtain the greatest personal satisfaction for their expenditure.

Economists believe that what is true for the behavior of customers at fast-food restaurants is true for economic behavior in general. Faced with an array of choices, consumers, workers, and businesses rationally compare marginal costs and marginal benefits when making decisions.

means "extra," "additional," or "a change in." Most choices or decisions involve changes in the status quo, meaning the existing state of affairs.

Should you attend school for another year? Should you study an extra hour for an exam? Should you supersize your fries? Similarly, should a business expand or reduce its output? Should government increase or decrease its funding for a missile defense system?

Each option involves marginal benefits and, because of scarce resources, marginal costs. In making choices rationally, the decision maker must compare those two amounts. Example: You and your fiancée are shopping for an engagement ring. Should you buy a $\frac{1}{2}$-carat diamond, a $\frac{3}{4}$-carat diamond, a 1-carat diamond, or something even larger? The marginal cost of a larger-size diamond is the added expense beyond the cost of the smaller-size diamond. The marginal benefit is the perceived lifetime pleasure (utility) from the larger-size stone. If the marginal benefit of the larger diamond exceeds its marginal cost (and you can afford it), buy the larger stone. But if the marginal cost is more than the marginal benefit, you should buy the smaller diamond instead—even if you can afford the larger stone!

In a world of scarcity, the decision to obtain the marginal benefit associated with some specific option always includes the marginal cost of forgoing something else. The money spent on the larger-size diamond means forgoing some other product. An opportunity cost—the value of the next best thing forgone—is always present whenever a choice is made.

Theories, Principles, and Models

LO1.2 Describe the role of economic theory in economics.

Like the physical and life sciences, as well as other social sciences, economics relies on the **scientific method.** That procedure consists of several elements:

- Observing real-world behavior and outcomes.

- Based on those observations, formulating a possible explanation of cause and effect (hypothesis).

- Testing this explanation by comparing the outcomes of specific events to the outcome predicted by the hypothesis.

- Accepting, rejecting, and modifying the hypothesis, based on these comparisons.

- Continuing to test the hypothesis against the facts. If favorable results accumulate, the hypothesis evolves into a theory. A very well-tested and widely accepted theory is referred to as an economic law or an **economic principle**—a statement about economic behavior or the economy that enables prediction of the probable effects of certain actions. Combinations of such laws or principles are incorporated into models, which are simplified representations of how something works, such as a market or segment of the economy.

Economists develop theories of the behavior of individuals (consumers, workers) and institutions (businesses, governments) engaged in the production, exchange, and consumption of goods and services. Theories, principles, and models are "purposeful simplifications." The full scope of economic reality itself is too complex and bewildering to be understood as a whole. In developing theories, principles, and models economists remove the clutter and simplify.

Economic principles and models are highly useful in analyzing economic behavior and understanding how the economy operates. They are the tools for ascertaining cause and effect (or action and outcome) within the economic system. Good theories do a good job of explaining and predicting. They are supported by facts concerning how individuals and institutions actually behave in producing, exchanging, and consuming goods and services.

There are some other things you should know about economic principles.

- *Generalizations* Economic principles are generalizations relating to economic behavior or to the economy itself. Economic principles are expressed as the tendencies of typical or average consumers, workers, or business firms. For example, economists say that consumers buy more of a particular product when its price falls. Economists recognize that some consumers may increase their purchases by a large amount, others by a small amount, and a few not at all. This "price-quantity" principle, however, holds for the typical consumer and for consumers as a group.
- *Other-things-equal assumption* In constructing their theories, economists use the *ceteris paribus* or **other-things-equal assumption**—the assumption that factors other than those being considered do not change. They assume that all variables except those under immediate consideration are held constant for a particular analysis. For example, consider the relationship between the price of Pepsi and the amount of Pepsi that is purchased. Assume that of all the factors that might influence the amount of Pepsi purchased (for example, the price of Pepsi, the price of Coca-Cola, and consumer incomes and preferences), only the price of Pepsi varies. This is helpful because the economist can then focus on the relationship between the price of Pepsi and purchases of Pepsi in isolation without being confused by changes in other variables.
- *Graphical expression* Many economic models are expressed graphically. Be sure to read the special appendix at the end of this chapter as a review of graphs.

Microeconomics and Macroeconomics

LO1.3 Distinguish microeconomics from macroeconomics and positive economics from normative economics.

Economists develop economic principles and models at two levels.

Microeconomics

Microeconomics is the part of economics concerned with decision making by individual customers, workers, households, and business firms. At this level of analysis, we observe the details of their behavior under a figurative microscope. We measure the price of a specific product, the number of workers employed by a single firm, the revenue or income of a particular firm or household, or the expenditures of a specific firm, government entity, or family. In microeconomics, we examine the sand, rocks, and shells, not the beach.

Macroeconomics

Macroeconomics examines the performance and behavior of the economy as a whole. It focuses its attention on economic growth, the business cycle, interest rates, inflation, and the behavior of major economic aggregates such as the government, household, and business sectors. An **aggregate** is a collection of specific economic units treated as if they were one unit. Therefore, we might lump together the millions of consumers in the U.S. economy and treat them as if they were one huge unit called "consumers."

In using aggregates, macroeconomics seeks to obtain an overview, or general outline, of the structure of the economy and the relationships of its major aggregates. Macroeconomics speaks of such economic measures as total output, total employment, total income, aggregate expenditures, and the general level of prices in analyzing various economic problems. Very little attention is given to the specific units making up the various aggregates.

Figuratively, macroeconomics looks at the beach, not the pieces of sand, the rocks, and the shells.

The micro–macro distinction does not mean that economics is so highly compartmentalized that every topic can be readily labeled as either micro or macro; many topics and subdivisions of economics are rooted in both. Example: While the problem of unemployment is usually treated as a macroeconomic topic (because unemployment relates to aggregate production), economists recognize that the decisions made by *individual* workers on how long to search for jobs and the way *specific* labor markets encourage or impede hiring are also critical in determining the unemployment rate.

Positive and Normative Economics

Both microeconomics and macroeconomics contain elements of positive economics and normative economics. **Positive economics** focuses on facts and cause-and-effect relationships. It includes description, theory development, and theory testing. Positive economics avoids value judgments. It tries to establish scientific statements about economic behavior and deals with what the economy is actually like. Such scientific-based analysis is critical to good policy analysis.

Economic policy, on the other hand, involves **normative economics,** which incorporates value judgments about what the economy should be like or what particular policy actions should be recommended to achieve a desirable goal. Normative economics looks at the desirability of certain aspects of the economy. It underlies expressions of support for particular economic policies.

Positive economics concerns *what is,* whereas normative economics embodies subjective feelings about *what ought to be.* Examples: Positive statement: "The unemployment rate in France is higher than that in the United States." Normative statement: "France ought to undertake policies to make its labor market more flexible to reduce unemployment rates." Whenever words such as "ought" or "should" appear in a sentence, you are very likely encountering a normative statement.

Most of the disagreement among economists involves normative, value-based policy questions. Of course, economists sometime disagree about which theories or models best represent the economy and its parts, but they agree on a full range of economic principles. Most economic controversy thus reflects differing opinions or value judgments about what society should be like.

QUICK REVIEW 1.1

✓ Economics examines how individuals, institutions, and society make choices under conditions of scarcity.

✓ The economic perspective stresses (a) resource scarcity and the necessity of making choices, (b) the assumption of purposeful (or rational) behavior, and (c) comparisons of marginal benefit and marginal cost.

✓ In choosing the best option, people incur an opportunity cost—the value of the next-best option.

✓ Economists use the scientific method to establish economic theories—cause-effect generalizations about the economic behavior of individuals and institutions.

✓ Microeconomics focuses on specific decision-making units within the economy. Macroeconomics examines the economy as a whole.

✓ Positive economics deals with factual statements ("what is"); normative economics involves value judgments ("what ought to be").

Individual's Economizing Problem

LO1.4 Explain the individual's economizing problem and how trade-offs, opportunity costs, and attainable combinations can be illustrated with budget lines.

A close examination of the **economizing problem**—the need to make choices because economic wants exceed economic means—will enhance your understanding of economic models and the difference between microeconomic and macroeconomic analysis. Let's first build a microeconomic model of the economizing problem faced by an individual.

Limited Income

We all have a finite amount of income, even the wealthiest among us. Even Bill Gates must decide how to spend his money! And the majority of us have much more limited means. Our income comes to us in the form of wages, interest, rent, and profit, although we may also receive money from government programs or family members. As Global Perspective 1.1 shows, the average income of Americans in 2014 was $55,200. In the poorest nations, it was less than $500.

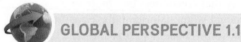

GLOBAL PERSPECTIVE 1.1

Average Income, Selected Nations

Average income (total income/population) and therefore typical individual budget constraints vary greatly among nations.

Country	Country Per Capita Income, 2014 (U.S. dollars, based on exchange rates)
Norway	$103,630
Sweden	61,610
United States	55,200
Singapore	55,150
France	42,960
South Korea	27,090
Mexico	9,870
China	7,400
Iraq	6,500
India	1,570
Madagascar	440
Malawi	250

Source: The World Bank, **www.worldbank.org.**

Unlimited Wants

For better or worse, most people have virtually unlimited wants. We desire various goods and services that provide utility. Our wants extend over a wide range of products, from *necessities* (for example, food, shelter, and clothing) to *luxuries* (for example, perfumes, yachts, and sports cars). Some wants such as basic food, clothing, and shelter have biological roots. Other wants, for example, specific kinds of food, clothing, and shelter, arise from the conventions and customs of society.

Over time, as new and improved products are introduced, economic wants tend to change and multiply. Only recently have people wanted wi-fi connections, tablet computers, or flying drones because those products did not exist a few decades ago. Also, the satisfaction of certain wants may trigger others: the acquisition of a Ford Focus or a Honda Civic has been known to whet the appetite for a Lexus or a Mercedes.

Services, as well as goods, satisfy our wants. Car repair work, the removal of an inflamed appendix, legal and accounting advice, and haircuts all satisfy human wants. Actually, we buy many goods, such as automobiles and washing machines, for the services they render. The differences between goods and services are often smaller than they appear to be.

For most people, the desires for goods and services cannot be fully satisfied. Bill Gates may have all that he wants for himself, but his massive charitable giving suggests that he keenly wants better health care for the world's poor. Our desires for a particular good or service can be satisfied; over a short period of time we can surely get enough toothpaste or pasta. And one appendectomy is plenty. But our broader desire for more goods and services and higher-quality goods and services seems to be another story.

Because we have only limited income (usually through our work) but seemingly insatiable wants, it is in our self-interest to economize: to pick and choose goods and services that maximize our satisfaction given the limitations we face.

A Budget Line

We can clarify the economizing problem facing consumers by visualizing a **budget line** (or, more technically, a *budget constraint*). It is a schedule or curve that shows various combinations of two products a consumer can purchase with a specific money income. Although we assume two products, the analysis generalizes to the full range of products available to consumers.

To understand the idea of a budget line, suppose that you received an Amazon gift card as a birthday present. The $120 card is soon to expire. You go online to Amazon.com and confine your purchase decisions to two alternatives: movies and paperback books. Movies are $20 each and paperback books are $10 each. Your purchase options are shown in the table in Figure 1.1.

At one extreme, you might spend all of your $120 "income" on 6 movies at $20 each and have nothing left to spend on books. Or, by giving up 2 movies and thereby gaining $40, you can have 4 movies at $20 each and 4 books at $10 each. And so on to the other extreme, at which you could buy 12 books at $10 each, spending your entire gift card on books with nothing left to spend on movies.

The graph in Figure 1.1 shows the budget line. Note that the graph is not restricted to whole units of movies and books as is the table. Every point on the graph represents a possible combination of movies and books, including fractional quantities. The slope of the graphed budget line measures the ratio of the price of books (P_b) to the price of movies (P_m); more

FIGURE 1.1 A consumer's budget line. The budget line (or budget constraint) shows all the combinations of any two products that can be purchased, given the prices of the products and the consumer's money income.

The Budget Line: Whole-Unit Combinations of Movies and Paperback Books Attainable with an Income of $120		
Units of Movies (Price = $20)	Units of Books (Price = $10)	Total Expenditure
6	0	$120 (= $120 + $0)
5	2	$120 (= $100 + $20)
4	4	$120 (= $80 + $40)
3	6	$120 (= $60 + $60)
2	8	$120 (= $40 + $80)
1	10	$120 (= $20 + $100)
0	12	$120 (= $0 + $120)

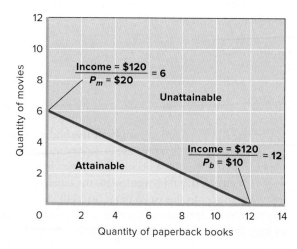

precisely, the slope is $P_b/P_m = \$-10/\$+20 = -\frac{1}{2}$. So you must forgo 1 movie (measured on the vertical axis) to buy 2 books (measured on the horizontal axis). This yields a slope of $-\frac{1}{2}$ or $-.5$.

The budget line illustrates several ideas.

Attainable and Unattainable Combinations All the combinations of movies and books on or inside the budget line are *attainable* from the $120 of money income. You can afford to buy, for example, 3 movies at $20 each and 6 books at $10 each. You also can obviously afford to buy 2 movies and 5 books, thereby using up only $90 of the $120 available on your gift card. But to achieve maximum utility you will want to spend the full $120. The budget line shows all combinations that cost exactly the full $120.

In contrast, all combinations beyond the budget line are *unattainable*. The $120 limit simply does not allow you to purchase, for example, 5 movies at $20 each and 5 books at $10 each. That $150 expenditure would clearly exceed the $120 limit. In Figure 1.1 the attainable combinations are on and within the budget line; the unattainable combinations are beyond the budget line.

Trade-Offs and Opportunity Costs The budget line in Figure 1.1 illustrates the idea of trade-offs arising from limited income. To obtain more movies, you have to give up some books. For example, to obtain the first movie, you trade off 2 books. So the opportunity cost of the first movie is 2 books. To obtain the second movie the opportunity cost is also 2 books. The straight-line budget constraint, with its constant slope, indicates constant opportunity cost. That is, the opportunity cost of 1 extra movie remains the same (= 2 books) as more movies are purchased. And, in reverse, the opportunity cost of 1 extra book does not change ($= \frac{1}{2}$ movie) as more books are bought.

Choice Limited income forces people to choose what to buy and what to forgo to fulfill wants. You will select the combination of movies and paperback books that you think is "best." That is, you will evaluate your marginal benefits and marginal costs (here, product price) to make choices that maximize your satisfaction. Other people, with the same $120 gift card, would undoubtedly make different choices.

Income Changes The location of the budget line varies with money income. An increase in money income shifts the budget line to the right; a decrease in money income shifts it to the left. To verify this, recalculate the table in Figure 1.1, assuming the card value (income) is (a) $240 and (b) $60, and plot the new budget lines in the graph. No wonder people like to have more income: That shifts their budget lines outward

Source: © Helga Esteb/Shutter-stock.com

Did Zuckerberg, Seacrest, and Swift Make Bad Choices?

Opportunity costs come into play in decisions well beyond simple buying decisions. Consider the different choices people make with respect to college. The average salaries earned by college graduates are nearly twice as high as those earned by persons with just high school diplomas. For most capable students, "Go to college, stay in college, and earn a degree" is very sound advice.

Yet Facebook founder Mark Zuckerberg and media personality Ryan Seacrest both dropped out of college, while pop singer Taylor Swift never even bothered to start classes. What were they thinking? Unlike most students, Zuckerberg faced enormous opportunity costs for staying in college. He had a vision for his company, and dropping out helped to ensure Facebook's success. Similarly, Seacrest landed a professional DJ job at his local radio station when he was in high school before moving to Hollywood and eventually becoming America's top radio and TV personality. Finishing his college degree might have interrupted the string of successes that made his career possible. And Swift knew that staying on top in the world of pop takes unceasing work. So after her first album became a massive hit for her at age 16, it made sense for her to skip college in order to relentlessly pursue continuing success.

So Zuckerberg, Seacrest, and Swift understood opportunity costs and made their choices accordingly. The size of opportunity costs matters greatly in making individual decisions.

and enables them to buy more goods and services. But even with more income, people will still face spending trade-offs, choices, and opportunity costs.

QUICK REVIEW 1.2

✓ Because wants exceed incomes, individuals face an economizing problem; they must decide what to buy and what to forgo.

✓ A budget line (budget constraint) shows the various combinations of two goods that a consumer can purchase with a specific money income.

✓ Straight-line budget constraints imply constant opportunity costs for both goods.

Society's Economizing Problem

LO1.5 List the categories of scarce resources and delineate the nature of society's economizing problem.

Society must also make choices under conditions of scarcity. It, too, faces an economizing problem. Should it devote more of its limited resources to the criminal justice system (police, courts, and prisons) or to education (teachers, books, and schools)? If it decides to devote more resources to both, what other goods and services does it forgo? Health care? Energy development?

Scarce Resources

Society has limited or scarce **economic resources,** meaning all natural, human, and manufactured resources that go into the production of goods and services. This includes the entire set of factory and farm buildings and all the equipment, tools, and machinery used to produce manufactured goods and agricultural products; all transportation and communication facilities; all types of labor; and land and mineral resources.

Resource Categories

Economists classify economic resources into four general categories.

Land Land means much more to the economist than it does to most people. To the economist **land** includes all natural resources ("gifts of nature") used in the production process. These include forests, mineral and oil deposits, water resources, wind power, sunlight, and arable land.

Labor The resource **labor** consists of the physical actions and mental activities that people contribute to the production of goods and services. The work-related activities of a logger, retail clerk, machinist, teacher, professional football player, and nuclear physicist all fall under the general heading "labor."

Capital For economists, **capital** (or capital goods) includes all manufactured aids used in producing consumer goods and services. Included are all factory, storage, transportation, and distribution facilities, as well as tools and machinery. Economists use the term **investment** to describe spending that pays for the production and accumulation of capital goods.

Capital goods differ from consumer goods because consumer goods satisfy wants directly, whereas capital goods do so indirectly by aiding the production of consumer goods. For example, large commercial baking ovens (capital goods) help make loaves of bread (consumer goods). Note that the term "capital" as used by economists refers not to money but to tools, machinery, and other productive equipment. Because money produces nothing, economists do not include it as an economic resource. Money (or money capital or financial capital) is simply a means for purchasing goods and services, including capital goods.

Entrepreneurial Ability Finally, there is the special human resource, distinct from labor, called **entrepreneurial ability.** It is supplied by **entrepreneurs,** who perform several critically important economic functions:

- The entrepreneur takes the initiative in combining the resources of land, labor, and capital to produce a good or a service. Both a sparkplug and a catalyst, the entrepreneur is the driving force behind production and the agent who combines the other resources in what is hoped will be a successful business venture.

- The entrepreneur makes the strategic business decisions that set the course of an enterprise.

- The entrepreneur innovates. He or she commercializes new products, new production techniques, or even new forms of business organization.

- The entrepreneur bears risk. Innovation is risky, as nearly all new products and ideas are subject to the possibility of failure as well as success. Progress would cease without entrepreneurs who are willing to take on risk by devoting their time, effort, and ability—as well as their own money and the money of others—to commercializing new products and ideas that may enhance society's standard of living.

Because land, labor, capital, and entrepreneurial ability are combined to produce goods and services, they are called the **factors of production,** or simply "inputs."

Production Possibilities Model

LO1.6 Apply production possibilities analysis, increasing opportunity costs, and economic growth.

Society uses its scarce resources to produce goods and services. The alternatives and choices it faces can best be understood through a macroeconomic model of production possibilities. To keep things simple, let's initially assume:

- *Full employment* The economy is employing all of its available resources.

- *Fixed resources* The quantity and quality of the factors of production are fixed.

- *Fixed technology* The state of technology (the methods used to produce output) is constant.

- *Two goods* The economy is producing only two goods: pizzas and industrial robots. Pizzas symbolize **consumer goods,** products that satisfy our wants directly; industrial robots (for example, the kind used to weld automobile frames) symbolize **capital goods,** products that satisfy our wants indirectly by making possible more efficient production of consumer goods.

TABLE 1.1 Production Possibilities of Pizzas and Industrial Robots

	Production Alternatives				
Type of Product	**A**	**B**	**C**	**D**	**E**
Pizzas (in hundred thousands)	0	1	2	3	4
Robots (in thousands)	10	9	7	4	0

Production Possibilities Table

A production possibilities table lists the different combinations of two products that can be produced with a specific set of resources, assuming full employment. Table 1.1 presents a simple, hypothetical economy that is producing pizzas and industrial robots; the data are, of course, hypothetical, too. At alternative A, this economy would be devoting all its available resources to the production of industrial robots (capital goods); at alternative E, all resources would go to pizza production (consumer goods). Those alternatives are unrealistic extremes; an economy typically produces both capital goods and consumer goods, as in B, C, and D. As we move from alternative A to E, we increase the production of pizzas at the expense of the production of industrial robots.

Because consumer goods satisfy our wants directly, any movement toward E looks tempting. In producing more pizzas, society increases the satisfaction of its current wants. But there is a cost: More pizzas mean fewer industrial robots. This shift of resources to consumer goods catches up with society over time because the stock of capital goods expands more slowly, thereby reducing potential future production. By moving toward alternative E, society chooses "more now" at the expense of "much more later."

By moving toward A, society chooses to forgo current consumption, thereby freeing up resources that can be used to increase the production of capital goods. By building up its stock of capital this way, society will have greater future production and, therefore, greater future consumption. By moving toward A, society is choosing "more later" at the cost of "less now."

Generalization: At any point in time, a fully employed economy must sacrifice some of one good to obtain more of another good. Scarce resources prohibit a fully employed economy from having more of both goods. Society must choose among alternatives. There is no such thing as a free pizza, or a free industrial robot. Having more of one thing means having less of something else.

Production Possibilities Curve

The data presented in a production possibilities table are shown graphically as a **production possibilities curve.** Such a curve displays the different combinations of goods and services that society can produce in a fully employed economy, assuming a fixed availability of supplies of resources and fixed technology. We arbitrarily represent the economy's

output of capital goods (here, industrial robots) on the vertical axis and the output of consumer goods (here, pizzas) on the horizontal axis, as shown in **Figure 1.2 (Key Graph).**

Each point on the production possibilities curve represents some maximum output of the two products. The curve is a "constraint" because it shows the limit of attainable outputs. Points on the curve are attainable as long as the economy uses all its available resources. Points lying inside the curve are also attainable, but they reflect less total output and therefore are not as desirable as points on the curve. Points inside the curve imply that the economy could have more of both industrial robots and pizzas if it achieved full employment of its resources. Points lying beyond the production possibilities curve, like W, would represent a greater output than the output at any point on the curve. Such points, however, are unattainable with the current availability of resources and technology.

Law of Increasing Opportunity Costs

Figure 1.2 clearly shows that more pizzas mean fewer industrial robots. The number of units of industrial robots that must be given up to obtain another unit of pizzas, of course, is the opportunity cost of that unit of pizzas.

In moving from alternative A to alternative B in Table 1.1, the cost of 1 additional unit of pizzas is 1 fewer unit of industrial robots. But when additional units are considered—B to C, C to D, and D to E—an important economic principle is revealed: For society, the opportunity cost of each additional unit of pizzas is greater than the opportunity cost of the preceding one. When we move from A to B, just 1 unit of industrial robots is sacrificed for 1 more unit of pizzas; but in going from B to C we sacrifice 2 additional units of industrial robots for 1 more unit of pizzas; then 3 more of industrial robots for 1 more of pizzas; and finally 4 for 1. Conversely, confirm that as we move from E to A, the cost of an additional unit of industrial robots (on average) is $\frac{1}{4}, \frac{1}{3}, \frac{1}{2}$, and 1 unit of pizzas, respectively, for the four successive moves.

Our example illustrates the **law of increasing opportunity costs.** As the production of a particular good increases, the opportunity cost of producing an additional unit rises.

Shape of the Curve The law of increasing opportunity costs is reflected in the shape of the production possibilities curve: The curve is bowed out from the origin of the graph. Figure 1.2 shows that when the economy moves from A to E, it must give up successively larger amounts of industrial robots (1, 2, 3, and 4) to acquire equal increments of pizzas (1, 1, 1, and 1). This is shown in the slope of the production possibilities curve, which becomes steeper as we move from A to E.

Economic Rationale The law of increasing opportunity costs is driven by the fact that economic resources are not

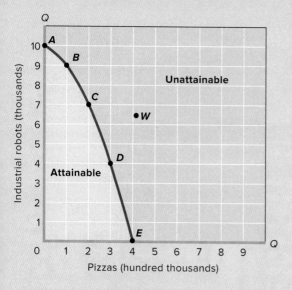

FIGURE 1.2 The production possibilities curve. Each point on the production possibilities curve represents some maximum combination of two products that can be produced if resources are fully employed. When an economy is operating on the curve, more industrial robots means fewer pizzas, and vice versa. Limited resources and a fixed technology make any combination of industrial robots and pizzas lying outside the curve (such as at *W*) unattainable. Points inside the curve are attainable, but they indicate that full employment is not being realized.

QUICK QUIZ FOR FIGURE 1.2

1. Production possibilities curve *ABCDE* is bowed out from the origin because:
   a. the marginal benefit of pizzas declines as more pizzas are consumed.
   b. the curve gets steeper as we move from *E* to *A*.
   c. it reflects the law of increasing opportunity costs.
   d. resources are scarce.

2. The marginal opportunity cost of the second unit of pizza is:
   a. 2 units of robots.
   b. 3 units of robots.
   c. 7 units of robots.
   d. 9 units of robots.

3. The total opportunity cost of 7 units of robots is:
   a. 1 unit of pizza.
   b. 2 units of pizza.
   c. 3 units of pizza.
   d. 4 units of pizza.

4. All points on this production possibilities curve necessarily represent:
   a. society's optimal choice.
   b. less than full use of resources.
   c. unattainable levels of output.
   d. full employment.

Answers: 1. c; 2. a; 3. b; 4. d

completely adaptable to alternative uses. Many resources are better at producing one type of good than at producing others. Consider land. Some land is highly suited to growing the ingredients necessary for pizza production. But as pizza production expands, society has to start using land that is less bountiful for farming. Other land is rich in mineral deposits and therefore well-suited to producing the materials needed to make industrial robots. That land will be the first land devoted to the production of industrial robots. But as society steps up the production of robots, it must use land that is less and less suited to making their components.

If we start at *A* and move to *B* in Figure 1.2, we can shift resources whose productivity is relatively high in pizza production and low in industrial robots. But as we move from *B* to *C*, *C* to *D*, and so on, resources highly productive in pizzas become increasingly scarce. To get more pizzas, resources whose productivity in industrial robots is relatively great will be needed. Increasingly more of such resources, and hence greater sacrifices of industrial robots, will be needed to achieve each 1-unit increase in pizzas. This lack of perfect flexibility, or interchangeability, on the part of resources is the cause of increasing opportunity costs for society.

Optimal Allocation

Of all the attainable combinations of pizzas and industrial robots on the curve in Figure 1.2, which is optimal (best)? That is, what specific quantities of resources should be allocated to pizzas and what specific quantities should be allocated to industrial robots in order to maximize satisfaction?

Recall that economic decisions center on comparisons of marginal benefit (MB) and marginal cost (MC). Any economic activity should be expanded as long as marginal

FIGURE 1.3 Optimal output: MB = MC. Achieving the optimal output requires the expansion of a good's output until its marginal benefit (MB) and marginal cost (MC) are equal. No resources beyond that point should be allocated to the product. Here, optimal output occurs at point *e*, where 200,000 units of pizzas are produced.

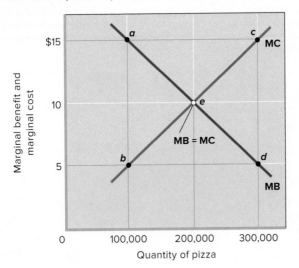

benefit exceeds marginal cost and should be reduced if marginal cost exceeds marginal benefit. The optimal amount of the activity occurs where MB = MC. Society needs to make a similar assessment about its production decision.

Consider pizzas. We already know from the law of increasing opportunity costs that the marginal cost of additional units of pizza will rise as more units are produced. At the same time, we need to recognize that the extra or marginal benefits that come from producing and consuming pizza decline with each successive unit of pizza. Consequently, each successive unit of pizza brings with it both increasing marginal costs and decreasing marginal benefits.

The optimal quantity of pizza production is indicated in Figure 1.3 by point *e* at the intersection of the MB and MC curves: 200,000 units. Why is this amount the optimal quantity? If only 100,000 units of pizzas were produced, the marginal benefit of an extra unit of pizza (point *a*) would exceed its marginal cost (point *b*). In money terms, MB is $15, while MC is only $5. When society gains something worth $15 at a marginal cost of only $5, it is better off. In Figure 1.3, net gains can continue to be realized until pizza-product production has been increased to 200,000.

In contrast, the production of 300,000 units of pizzas is excessive. There the MC of an added unit is $15 (point *c*) and its MB is only $5 (point *d*). This means that 1 unit of pizza is worth only $5 to society but costs it $15 to obtain. This is a losing proposition for society!

So resources are being efficiently allocated to any product when the marginal benefit and marginal cost of its output are equal (MB = MC). Suppose that by applying the same analysis

CONSIDER THIS . . .

Source: © Royalty-Free/Corbis RF

The Economics of War

Production possibilities analysis is helpful in assessing the costs and benefits of waging the post-9/11 war on terrorism, including the wars in Afghanistan and Iraq. At the end of 2015, the estimated cumulative cost of these efforts exceeded $1.7 trillion.

If we categorize all U.S. production as either "defense goods" or "civilian goods," we can measure them on the axes of a production possibilities diagram such as that shown in Figure 1.2. The opportunity cost of using more resources for defense goods is the civilian goods sacrificed. In a fully employed economy, more defense goods are achieved at the opportunity cost of fewer civilian goods—health care, education, pollution control, personal computers, houses, and so on. The cost of war and defense is the other goods forgone. The benefits of these activities are numerous and diverse but clearly include the gains from protecting against future loss of American lives, assets, income, and well-being.

Society must assess the marginal benefit (MB) and marginal cost (MC) of additional defense goods to determine their optimal amounts—where to locate on the defense goods–civilian goods production possibilities curve. Although estimating marginal benefits and marginal costs is an imprecise art, the MB-MC framework is a useful way of approaching choices. An optimal allocation of resources requires that society expand production of defense goods until MB = MC.

The events of September 11, 2001, and the future threats they foreshadowed increased the marginal benefits of defense goods, as perceived by Americans. If we label the horizontal axis in Figure 1.3 "defense goods" and draw in a rightward shift of the MB curve, you will see that the optimal quantity of defense goods rises. In view of the concerns relating to September 11, the United States allocated more of its resources to defense. But the MB-MC analysis also reminds us we can spend too much on defense, as well as too little. The United States should not expand defense goods beyond the point where MB = MC. If it does, it will be sacrificing civilian goods of greater value than the defense goods obtained.

to industrial robots, we find that the optimal (MB = MC) quantity of robots is 7,000. This would mean that alternative *C* (200,000 units of pizzas and 7,000 units of industrial robots) on the production possibilities curve in Figure 1.2 would be optimal for this economy.

Unemployment, Growth, and the Future

LO1.7 Explain how economic growth and international trade increase consumption possibilities.

In the depths of the Great Depression of the 1930s, one-quarter of U.S. workers were unemployed and one-third of U.S. production capacity was idle. Subsequent downturns have been much less severe. During the deep 2007–2009 recession, for instance, production fell by a comparably smaller 3.7 percent and 1-in-10 workers was without a job.

Almost all nations have experienced widespread unemployment and unused production capacity from business downturns at one time or another. Since 2010, for example, many nations—including Argentina, Italy, Russia, Japan, and France—have had economic downturns and elevated unemployment.

How do these realities relate to the production possibilities model? Our analysis and conclusions change if we relax the assumption that all available resources are fully employed. The five alternatives in Table 1.1 represent maximum outputs; they illustrate the combinations of pizzas and industrial robots that can be produced when the economy is operating at full employment. With unemployment, this economy would produce less than each alternative shown in the table.

Graphically, we represent situations of unemployment by points inside the original production possibilities curve (reproduced here in Figure 1.4). Point *U* is one such point. Here the economy is falling short of the various maximum combinations of pizzas and industrial robots represented by the points on the production possibilities curve. The arrows in Figure 1.4 indicate three possible paths back to full employment. A move toward full employment would yield a greater output of one or both products.

FIGURE 1.4 Unemployment and the production possibilities curve. Any point inside the production possibilities curve, such as *U*, represents unemployment or a failure to achieve full employment. The arrows indicate that by realizing full employment, the economy could operate on the curve. This means it could produce more of one or both products than it is producing at point *U*.

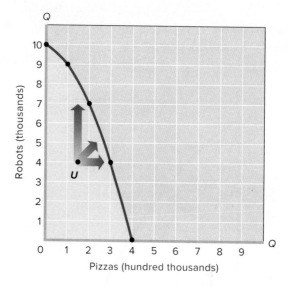

A Growing Economy

When we drop the assumptions that the quantity and quality of resources and technology are fixed, the production possibilities curve shifts positions and the potential maximum output of the economy changes.

Increases in Resource Supplies Although resource supplies are fixed at any specific moment, they change over time. For example, a nation's growing population brings about increases in the supplies of labor and entrepreneurial ability. Also, labor quality usually improves over time via more education and training. Historically, the economy's stock of capital has increased at a significant, though unsteady, rate. And although some of our energy and mineral resources are being depleted, new sources are also being discovered. The development of irrigation systems, for example, adds to the supply of arable land.

The net result of these increased supplies of the factors of production is the ability to produce more of both consumer goods and capital goods. Thus, 20 years from now, the production possibilities may supersede those shown in Table 1.1. The new production possibilities might look like those in the table in Figure 1.5. The greater abundance of resources will result in a greater potential output of one or both products at each alternative. The economy will have achieved economic growth in the form of expanded potential output. Thus, when an increase in the quantity or quality of resources occurs, the production possibilities curve shifts outward and to the right,

FIGURE 1.5 Economic growth and the production possibilities curve. The increase in supplies of resources, improvements in resource quality, and technological advances that occur in a dynamic economy move the production possibilities curve outward and to the right, allowing the economy to have larger quantities of both types of goods.

Type of Product	Production Alternatives				
	A'	B'	C'	D'	E'
Pizzas (in hundred thousands)	0	2	4	6	8
Robots (in thousands)	14	12	9	5	0

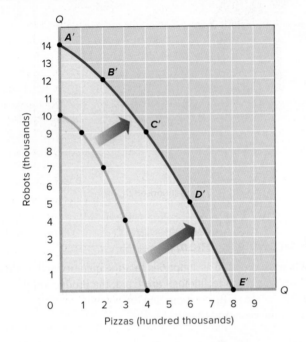

as illustrated by the move from the inner curve to curve A'B'C'D'E' in Figure 1.5. This sort of shift represents growth of economic capacity, which, when used, means **economic growth:** a larger total output.

Advances in Technology An advancing technology brings both new and better goods and improved ways of producing them. For now, let's think of technological advance as being only improvements in the methods of production, for example, the introduction of computerized systems to manage inventories and schedule production. These advances alter our previous discussion of the economizing problem by allowing society to produce more goods with available resources. As with increases in resource supplies, technological advances make possible the production of more industrial robots *and* more pizzas.

A real-world example of improved technology is the recent surge of new technologies relating to computers, communications, and biotechnology. Technological advances have dropped the prices of computers and greatly increased their

speed. Improved software has greatly increased the everyday usefulness of computers. Cellular phones and the Internet have increased communications capacity, enhancing production and improving the efficiency of markets. Advances in biotechnology have resulted in important agricultural and medical discoveries. These and other new and improved technologies have contributed to U.S. economic growth (outward shifts of the nation's production possibilities curve).

Conclusion: Economic growth is the result of (1) increases in supplies of resources, (2) improvements in resource quality, and (3) technological advances. The consequence of growth is that a full-employment economy can enjoy a greater output of both consumption goods and capital goods. Whereas static, no-growth economies must sacrifice some of one good to obtain more of another, dynamic, growing economies can have larger quantities of both goods.

Present Choices and Future Possibilities

An economy's current choice of positions on its production possibilities curve helps determine the future location of that curve. Let's designate the two axes of the production possibilities curve as "goods for the future" and "goods for the present," as in Figure 1.6. Goods for the future are such things as capital goods, research and education, and preventive medicine. They increase the quantity and quality of property resources, enlarge the stock of technological information, and improve the quality of human resources. As we have already seen, goods for the future such as capital goods are the ingredients of economic growth. Goods for the present are consumer goods such as food, clothing, and entertainment.

Now suppose there are two hypothetical economies, Presentville and Futureville, that are initially identical in every respect except one: Presentville's current choice of positions on its production possibilities curve strongly favors present goods over future goods. Point *P* in Figure 1.6a indicates that choice. It is located quite far down the curve to the right, indicating a high priority for goods for the present, at the expense of less goods for the future. Futureville, in contrast, makes a current choice that stresses larger amounts of future goods and smaller amounts of present goods, as shown by point *F* in Figure 1.6b.

Now, other things equal, we can expect Futureville's future production possibilities curve to be farther to the right than Presentville's future production possibilities curve. By currently choosing an output more favorable to technological advances and to increases in the quantity and quality of resources, Futureville will achieve greater economic growth than Presentville. In terms of capital goods, Futureville is choosing to make larger current additions to its "national factory" by devoting more of its current output to capital than

FIGURE 1.6 Present choices and future locations of production possibilities curves. (a) Presentville's current choice to produce more "present goods" and fewer "future goods," as represented by point *P,* will result in a modest outward shift of the production possibilities curve in the future. (b) Futureville's current choice of producing fewer "present goods" and more "future goods," as depicted by point *F,* will lead to a greater outward shift of the production possibilities curve in the future.

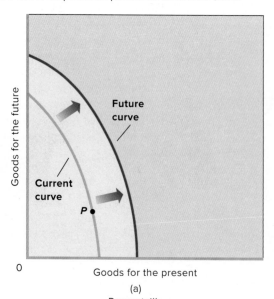

(a)
Presentville

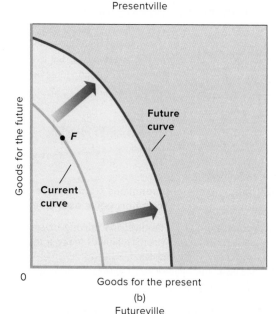

(b)
Futureville

does Presentville. The payoff from this choice for Futureville is greater future production capacity and economic growth. The opportunity cost is fewer consumer goods in the present for Futureville to enjoy.

Is Futureville's choice thus necessarily "better" than Presentville's? That, we cannot say. The different outcomes sim-

ply reflect different preferences and priorities in the two countries. But each country will have to live with the economic consequences of its choice.

A Qualification: International Trade

Production possibilities analysis implies that an individual nation is limited to the combinations of output indicated by its production possibilities curve. But we must modify this principle when international specialization and trade exist.

You will see in later chapters that an economy can circumvent, through international specialization and trade, the output limits imposed by its domestic production possibilities curve. Under international specialization and trade, each nation first specializes in the production of those items for which it has the lowest opportunity costs (due to an abundance of the necessary resources). Countries then engage in international trade, with each country exchanging the items that it can produce at the lowest opportunity costs for the items that other countries can produce at the lowest opportunity costs.

International specialization and trade allow a nation to get more of a desired good at less sacrifice of some other good. Rather than sacrifice three units of domestically produced robots to get a third unit of domestically produced pizza, as in Table 1.1, a nation that engages in international specialization and trade might be able to do much better. If it specializes in robots while another country specializes in pizza, then it may be able to obtain the third unit of pizza by trading only two units of domestically produced robots for one unit of foreign-produced pizza. Specialization and trade have the same effect as having more and better resources or discovering improved production techniques; both increase the quantities of capital and consumer goods available to society. Expansion of domestic production possibilities and international trade are two separate routes for obtaining greater output.

QUICK REVIEW 1.4

✓ Unemployment causes an economy to operate at a point inside its production possibilities curve.

✓ Increases in resource supplies, improvements in resource quality, and technological advance cause economic growth, which is depicted as an outward shift of the production possibilities curve.

✓ An economy's present choice of capital and consumer goods helps determine the future location of its production possibilities curve.

✓ International specialization and trade enable a nation to obtain more goods than its production possibilities curve indicates.

Pitfalls to Sound Economic Reasoning

Because They Affect Us So Personally, We Often Have Difficulty Thinking Accurately and Objectively about Economic Issues.

Here are some common pitfalls to avoid in successfully applying the economic perspective.

Biases Most people bring a bundle of biases and preconceptions to the field of economics. For example, some may think that corporate profits are excessive or that lending money is always superior to borrowing money. Others may believe that government is necessarily less efficient than businesses or that more government regulation is always better than less. Biases cloud thinking and interfere with objective analysis. All of us must be willing to shed biases and preconceptions that are not supported by facts.

Loaded Terminology The economic terminology used in newspapers and broadcast media is sometimes emotionally biased, or loaded. The writer or spokesperson may have a cause to promote or an ax to grind and may slant comments accordingly. High profits may be labeled "obscene," low wages may be called "exploitative," or self-interested behavior may be "greed." Government workers may be referred to as "mindless bureaucrats" and those favoring stronger government regulations may be called "socialists." To objectively analyze economic issues, you must be prepared to reject or discount such terminology.

Source: © James Leynse/Corbis RF

Fallacy of Composition Another pitfall in economic thinking is the assumption that what is true for one individual or part of a whole is necessarily true for a group of individuals or the whole. This is a logical fallacy called the *fallacy of composition;* the assumption is not correct. A statement that is valid for an individual or part is not

SUMMARY

LO1.1 Define economics and the features of the economic perspective.

Economics is the social science that examines how individuals, institutions, and society make optimal choices under conditions of scarcity. Central to economics is the idea of opportunity cost: the value of the next-best good or service forgone to obtain something.

The economic perspective includes three elements: scarcity and choice, purposeful behavior, and marginal analysis. It sees individuals and institutions as making rational decisions based on comparisons of marginal costs and marginal benefits.

LO1.2 Describe the role of economic theory in economics.

Economists employ the scientific method, in which they form and test hypotheses of cause-and-effect relationships to generate theories, laws, and principles. Economists often combine theories into representations called models.

LO1.3 Distinguish microeconomics from macroeconomics and positive economics from normative economics.

Microeconomics examines the decision making of specific economic units or institutions. Macroeconomics looks at the economy as a whole or its major aggregates.

Positive economic analysis deals with facts; normative economics reflects value judgments.

LO1.4 Explain the individual's economizing problem and how trade-offs, opportunity costs, and attainable combinations can be illustrated with budget lines.

Individuals face an economizing problem. Because their wants exceed their incomes, they must decide what to purchase and what to forgo. Society also faces an economizing problem. Societal wants exceed the available resources necessary to fulfill them. Society therefore must decide what to produce and what to forgo.

Graphically, a budget line (or budget constraint) illustrates the economizing problem for individuals. The line shows the various necessarily valid for the larger group or whole. Noneconomic example: You may see the action better if you leap to your feet to see an outstanding play at a football game. But if all the spectators leap to their feet at the same time, nobody—including you—will have a better view than when all remained seated.

Here are two economic examples: An individual stockholder can sell shares of, say, Google stock without affecting the price of the stock. The individual's sale will not noticeably reduce the share price because the sale is a negligible fraction of the total shares of Google being bought and sold. But if all the Google shareholders decide to sell their shares the same day, the market will be flooded with shares and the stock price will fall precipitously. Similarly, a single cattle ranch can increase its revenue by expanding the size of its livestock herd. The extra cattle will not affect the price of cattle when they are brought to market. But if all ranchers as a group expand their herds, the total output of cattle will increase so much that the price of cattle will decline when the cattle are sold. If the price reduction is relatively large, ranchers as a group might find that their income has fallen despite their having sold a greater number of cattle because the fall in price overwhelms the increase in quantity.

Post Hoc Fallacy You must think very carefully before concluding that because event A precedes event B, A is the cause of B. This kind of faulty reasoning is known as the *post hoc, ergo propter hoc,* or "after this, therefore because of this," fallacy. Noneconomic example: A professional football team hires a new coach and the team's record improves. Is the new coach the cause? Maybe. Perhaps the presence of more experienced and talented players or an easier

schedule is the true cause. The rooster crows before dawn but does not cause the sunrise.

Economic example: Many people blamed the Great Depression of the 1930s on the stock market crash of 1929. But the crash did not cause the Great Depression. The same severe weaknesses in the economy that caused the crash caused the Great Depression. The depression would have occurred even without the preceding stock market crash.

Correlation but Not Causation Do not confuse correlation, or connection, with causation. Correlation between two events or two sets of data indicates only that they are associated in some systematic and dependable way. For example, we may find that when variable X increases, Y also increases. But this correlation does not necessarily mean that there is causation—that increases in X cause increases in Y. The relationship could be purely coincidental or dependent on some other factor, Z, not included in the analysis.

Here is an example: Economists have found a positive correlation between education and income. In general, people with more education earn higher incomes than those with less education. Common sense suggests education is the cause and higher incomes are the effect; more education implies a more knowledgeable and productive worker, and such workers receive larger salaries.

But might the relationship be explainable in other ways? Are education and income correlated because the characteristics required for succeeding in education—ability and motivation—are the same ones required to be a productive and highly paid worker? If so, then people with those traits will probably both obtain more education and earn higher incomes. Greater education will not be the sole cause of the higher income.

combinations of two products that a consumer can purchase with a specific money income, given the prices of the two products.

LO1.5 List the categories of scarce resources and delineate the nature of society's economizing problem.

Economic resources are inputs into the production process and can be classified as land, labor, capital, or entrepreneurial ability. Economic resources are also known as factors of production or inputs.

Economists illustrate society's economizing problem through production possibilities analysis. Production possibilities tables and curves show the different combinations of goods and services that can be produced in a fully employed economy, assuming that resource quantity, resource quality, and technology are fixed.

LO1.6 Apply production possibilities analysis, increasing opportunity costs, and economic growth.

An economy that is fully employed and thus operating on its production possibilities curve must sacrifice the output of some types of goods and services to increase the production of others. The gain of one type of good or service is always accompanied by an opportunity cost in the form of the loss of some of the other type of good or service.

Because resources are not equally productive in all possible uses, shifting resources from one use to another creates increasing opportunity costs. The production of additional units of one product requires the sacrifice of increasing amounts of the other product.

The optimal (best) point on the production possibilities curve represents the most desirable mix of goods and is determined by expanding the production of each good until its marginal benefit (MB) equals its marginal cost (MC).

LO1.7 Explain how economic growth and international trade increase consumption possibilities.

Over time, technological advances and increases in the quantity and quality of resources enable the economy to produce more of all goods and services, that is, to experience economic growth. Society's choice as to the mix of consumer goods and capital goods in current output is a major determinant of the future location of the production possibilities curve and thus of the extent of economic growth.

International trade enables a nation to obtain more goods from its limited resources than its production possibilities curve indicates.

TERMS AND CONCEPTS

economics

economic perspective

scarcity

opportunity cost

utility

marginal analysis

scientific method

economic principle

other-things-equal assumption

microeconomics

macroeconomics

aggregate

positive economics

normative economics

economizing problem

budget line

economic resources

land

labor

capital

investment

entrepreneurial ability

entrepreneurs

factors of production

consumer goods

capital goods

production possibilities curve

law of increasing opportunity costs

economic growth

The following and additional problems can be found in ■ connect

DISCUSSION QUESTIONS

1. What is an opportunity cost? How does the idea relate to the definition of economics? Which of the following decisions would entail the greater opportunity cost: allocating a square block in the heart of New York City for a surface parking lot or allocating a square block at the edge of a typical suburb for such a lot? Explain. **LO1.1**

2. Cite three examples of recent decisions that you made in which you, at least implicitly, weighed marginal cost and marginal benefit. **LO1.1**

3. What is meant by the term "utility" and how does the idea relate to purposeful behavior? **LO1.1**

4. What are the key elements of the scientific method and how does this method relate to economic principles and laws? **LO1.2**

5. State (a) a positive economic statement of your choice, and then (b) a normative economic statement relating to your first statement. **LO1.3**

6. How does the slope of a budget line illustrate opportunity costs and trade-offs? How does a budget line illustrate scarcity and the effect of limited incomes? **LO1.4**

7. What are economic resources? What categories do economists use to classify them? Why are resources also called factors of production? Why are they called inputs? **LO1.5**

8. Why is money not considered to be a capital resource in economics? Why is entrepreneurial ability considered a category of economic resource, distinct from labor? What are the major functions of the entrepreneur? **LO1.5**

9. Specify and explain the typical shapes of marginal-benefit and marginal-cost curves. How are these curves used to determine the optimal allocation of resources to a particular product? If current output is such that marginal cost exceeds marginal benefit, should more or fewer resources be allocated to this product? Explain. **LO1.6**

10. Suppose that, on the basis of a nation's production possibilities curve, an economy must sacrifice 10,000 pizzas domestically to get the 1 additional industrial robot it desires but that it can get the robot from another country in exchange for 9,000 pizzas. Relate this information to the following statement: "Through international specialization and trade, a nation can reduce its opportunity cost of obtaining goods and thus 'move outside its production possibilities curve.'" **LO1.7**

11. **LAST WORD** Studies indicate that married men on average earn more income than unmarried men of the same age and education level. Why must we be cautious in concluding that marriage is the cause and higher income is the effect?

REVIEW QUESTIONS

1. Match each term with the correct definition. **LO1.1**
   economics
   opportunity cost
   marginal analysis
   utility
   a. The next-best thing that must be forgone in order to produce one more unit of a given product.
   b. The pleasure, happiness, or satisfaction obtained from consuming a good or service.

   c. The social science concerned with how individuals, institutions, and society make optimal (best) choices under conditions of scarcity.
   d. Making choices based on comparing marginal benefits with marginal costs.

2. Indicate whether each of the following statements applies to microeconomics or macroeconomics: **LO1.3**
   a. The unemployment rate in the United States was 5.1 percent in September 2015.

b. A U.S. software firm discharged 15 workers last month and transferred the work to India.

c. An unexpected freeze in central Florida reduced the citrus crop and caused the price of oranges to rise.

d. U.S. output, adjusted for inflation, increased by 2.4 percent in 2014.

e. Last week Wells Fargo Bank lowered its interest rate on business loans by one-half of 1 percentage point.

f. The consumer price index rose by 0.2 percent from August 2014 to August 2015.

3. Suppose that you initially have $100 to spend on books or movie tickets. The books start off costing $25 each and the movie tickets start off costing $10 each. For each of the following situations, would the attainable set of combinations that you can afford increase or decrease? LO1.4

a. Your budget increases from $100 to $150 while the prices stay the same.

b. Your budget remains $100, the price of books remains $25, but the price of movie tickets rises to $20.

c. Your budget remains $100, the price of movie tickets remains $10, but the price of a book falls to $15.

4. Suppose that you are given a $100 budget at work that can be spent only on two items: staplers and pens. If staplers cost $10 each and pens cost $2.50 each, then the opportunity cost of purchasing one stapler is: LO1.4

a. 10 pens.

b. 5 pens.

c. zero pens.

d. 4 pens.

5. For each of the following situations involving marginal cost (MC) and marginal benefit (MB), indicate whether it would be best to produce more, fewer, or the current number of units. LO1.4

a. 3,000 units at which MC = $10 and MB = $13.

b. 11 units at which MC = $4 and MB = $3.

c. 43,277 units at which MC = $99 and MB = $99.

d. 82 units at which MC < MB.

e. 5 units at which MB < MC.

6. Explain how (if at all) each of the following events affects the location of a country's production possibilities curve: LO1.6

a. The quality of education increases.

b. The number of unemployed workers increases.

c. A new technique improves the efficiency of extracting copper from ore.

d. A devastating earthquake destroys numerous production facilities.

7. What are the two major ways in which an economy can grow and push out its production possibilities curve? LO1.7

a. Better weather and nicer cars.

b. Higher taxes and lower spending.

c. Increases in resource supplies and advances in technology.

d. Decreases in scarcity and advances in auditing.

PROBLEMS

1. Potatoes cost Janice $1 per pound, and she has $5.00 that she could possibly spend on potatoes or other items. If she feels that the first pound of potatoes is worth $1.50, the second pound is worth $1.14, the third pound is worth $1.05, and all subsequent pounds are worth $0.30, how many pounds of potatoes will she purchase? What if she only had $2 to spend? LO1.1

2. Pham can work as many or as few hours as she wants at the college bookstore for $9 per hour. But due to her hectic schedule, she has just 15 hours per week that she can spend working at either the bookstore or other potential jobs. One potential job, at a café, will pay her $12 per hour for up to 6 hours per week. She has another job offer at a garage that will pay her $10 an hour for up to 5 hours per week. And she has a potential job at a daycare center that will pay her $8.50 per hour for as many hours as she can work. If her goal is to maximize the amount of money she can make each week, how many hours will she work at the bookstore? LO1.1

3. Suppose you won $15 on a lotto ticket at the local 7-Eleven and decided to spend all the winnings on candy bars and bags of peanuts. Candy bars cost $0.75 each while bags of peanuts cost $1.50 each. LO1.5

a. Construct a table showing the alternative combinations of the two products that are available.

b. Plot the data in your table as a budget line in a graph. What is the slope of the budget line? What is the opportunity cost

of one more candy bar? Of one more bag of peanuts? Do these opportunity costs rise, fall, or remain constant as additional units are purchased?

c. Does the budget line tell you which of the available combinations of candy bars and bags of peanuts to buy?

d. Suppose that you had won $30 on your ticket, not $15. Show the $30 budget line in your diagram. Has the number of available combinations increased or decreased?

4. Suppose that you are on a desert island and possess exactly 20 coconuts. Your neighbor, Friday, is a fisherman, and he is willing to trade 2 fish for every 1 coconut that you are willing to give him. Another neighbor, Kwame, is also a fisherman, and he is willing to trade 3 fish for every 1 coconut. LO1.5

a. On a single figure, draw budget lines for trading with Friday and for trading with Kwame. (Put coconuts on the vertical axis.)

b. What is the slope of the budget line from trading with Friday?

c. What is the slope of the budget line from trading with Kwame?

d. Which budget line features a larger set of attainable combinations of coconuts and fish?

e. If you are going to trade coconuts for fish, would you rather trade with Friday or Kwame?

5. Refer to the following production possibilities table for consumer goods (automobiles) and capital goods (forklifts): **LO1.6**
   a. Show these data graphically. Upon what specific assumptions is this production possibilities curve based?
   b. If the economy is at point C, what is the cost of one more automobile? Of one more forklift? Which characteristic of the production possibilities curve reflects the law of increasing opportunity costs: its shape or its length?
   c. If the economy characterized by this production possibilities table and curve were producing 3 automobiles and 20 forklifts, what could you conclude about its use of its available resources?
   d. Is production at a point outside the production possibilities curve currently possible? Could a future advance in technology allow production beyond the current production possibilities curve? Could international trade allow a country to consume beyond its current production possibilities curve?

Type of Production	Production Alternatives				
	A	B	C	D	E
Automobiles	0	2	4	6	8
Forklifts	30	27	21	12	0

6. Look at Figure 1.3. Suppose that the cost of cheese falls, so that the marginal cost of producing pizza decreases. Will the MC curve shift up or down? Will the optimal amount of pizza increase or decrease? **LO1.6**

7. Referring to the table in problem 5, suppose improvement occurs in the technology of producing forklifts but not in the technology of producing automobiles. Draw the new production possibilities curve. Now assume that a technological advance occurs in producing automobiles but not in producing forklifts. Draw the new production possibilities curve. Now draw a production possibilities curve that reflects technological improvement in the production of both goods. **LO1.7**

8. Because investment and capital goods are paid for with savings, higher savings rates reflect a decision to consume fewer goods for the present in order to be able to invest in more goods for the future. Households in China save 40 percent of their annual incomes each year, whereas U.S. households save less than 5 percent. At the same time, production possibilities are growing at roughly 9 percent per year in China but only about 3.5 percent per year in the United States. Use graphical analysis of "present goods" versus "future goods" to explain the difference between China's growth rate and the U.S. growth rate. **LO1.7**

Graphs and Their Meaning

LO1.8 Understand graphs, curves, and slopes as they relate to economics.

If you glance quickly through this text, you will find many graphs. Some seem simple, while others seem more formidable. All are included to help you visualize and understand economic relationships. Physicists and chemists sometimes illustrate their theories by building arrangements of multicolored wooden balls, representing protons, neutrons, and electrons, that are held in proper relation to one another by wires or sticks. Economists most often use graphs to illustrate their models. By understanding these "pictures," you can more readily comprehend economic relationships.

Construction of a Graph

A *graph* is a visual representation of the relationship between two economic quantities, or variables. The table in Figure 1 is a hypothetical illustration showing the relationship between income and consumption for the economy as a whole. Without even studying economics, we would logically expect that people would buy more goods and services when their incomes go up. Thus, it is not surprising to find in the table that total consumption in the economy increases as total income increases.

The information in the table is expressed graphically in Figure 1. Here is how it is done: We want to show visually how consumption changes as income changes. We therefore represent income on the **horizontal axis** of the graph and consumption on the **vertical axis.**

Now we arrange the vertical and horizontal scales of the graph to reflect the ranges of values of consumption and income and mark the scales in convenient increments. As you can see, the values marked on the scales cover all the values in the table. The increments on both scales are $100.

Because the graph has two dimensions, each point within it represents an income value and its associated consumption value. To find a point that represents one of the five income-consumption combinations in the table in Figure 1, we draw straight lines from the appropriate values on the vertical and horizontal axes. For example, to plot point *c* (the $200 income–$150 consumption point), we draw straight lines up from the horizontal (income) axis at $200 and across from the vertical (consumption) axis at $150. These lines intersect at point *c,* which represents this particular income-consumption combination. You should verify that the other income-consumption combinations shown in the table are properly located in the graph in Figure 1. Finally, by assuming that the same general relationship between income and consumption prevails for all other incomes, we draw a line or smooth curve to connect these points. That line or curve represents the income-consumption relationship.

If the curve is a straight line, as in Figure 1, we say the relationship is *linear.* (It is permissible, and even customary, to refer to straight lines in graphs as "curves.")

Direct and Inverse Relationships

The line in Figure 1 slopes upward to the right, so it depicts a direct relationship between income and consumption. By a **direct relationship** (or positive relationship) we mean that two variables—in this case, consumption and income—change in the *same* direction. An increase in consumption is

FIGURE 1 **Graphing the direct relationship between consumption and income.** Two sets of data that are positively or directly related, such as consumption and income, graph as an upsloping line.

Income per Week	Consumption per Week	Point
$ 0	$ 50	a
100	100	b
200	150	c
300	200	d
400	250	e

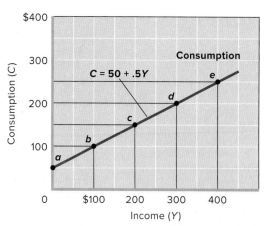

associated with an increase in income; a decrease in consumption accompanies a decrease in income. When two sets of data are positively or directly related, they always graph as an *upsloping* line, as in Figure 1.

In contrast, two sets of data may be inversely related. Consider the table in Figure 2, which shows the relationship between the price of basketball tickets and game attendance at Gigantic State University (GSU). Here we have an **inverse relationship** (or negative relationship) because the two variables change in *opposite* directions. When ticket prices decrease, attendance increases. When ticket prices increase, attendance decreases. The six data points in the table in Figure 2 are plotted in the graph. Observe that an inverse relationship always graphs as a *downsloping* line.

Dependent and Independent Variables

Although it is not always easy, economists seek to determine which variable is the "cause" and which is the "effect." Or, more formally, they seek the independent variable and the dependent variable. The **independent variable** is the cause or source; it is the variable that changes first. The **dependent variable** is the effect or outcome; it is the variable that changes because of the change in the independent variable. As in our income-consumption example, income generally is the independent variable and consumption the dependent variable. Income causes consumption to be what it is rather than the other way around. Similarly, ticket prices (set in advance of the season and printed on the ticket) determine attendance at GSU basketball games; attendance at games does not determine the printed ticket prices for those games. Ticket price is the independent variable and the quantity of tickets purchased is the dependent variable.

You may recall from your high school courses that mathematicians put the independent variable (cause) on the horizontal axis and the dependent variable (effect) on the vertical axis. Economists are less tidy; their graphing of independent and dependent variables is more arbitrary. Their conventional graphing of the income-consumption relationship is consistent with mathematical convention, but economists put price and cost data on the vertical axis. Hence, economists' graphing of GSU's ticket price–attendance data differs from normal mathematical procedure. This does not present a problem, but we want you to be aware of this fact to avoid any possible confusion.

Other Things Equal

Our simple two-variable graphs purposely ignore many other factors that might affect the amount of consumption occurring at each income level or the number of people who attend GSU basketball games at each possible ticket price. When economists plot the relationship between any two variables, they employ the *ceteris paribus* (other-things-equal) assumption. Thus, in Figure 1 all factors other than income that might affect the amount of consumption are presumed to be constant or unchanged. Similarly, in Figure 2 all factors other than ticket price that might influence attendance at GSU basketball games are assumed constant. In reality, "other things" are not equal; they often change, and when they do, the relationship represented in our two tables and graphs will change. Specifically, the lines we have plotted would *shift* to new locations.

Consider a stock market "crash." The dramatic drop in the value of stocks might cause people to feel less wealthy and therefore less willing to consume at each level of income. The result might be a downward shift of the consumption line. To see this,

FIGURE 2 **Graphing the inverse relationship between ticket prices and game attendance.** Two sets of data that are negatively or inversely related, such as ticket price and the attendance at basketball games, graph as a downsloping line.

Ticket Price	Attendance, Thousands	Point
$50	0	a
40	4	b
30	8	c
20	12	d
10	16	e
0	20	f

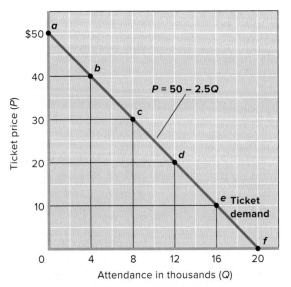

you should plot a new consumption line in Figure 1, assuming that consumption is, say, $20 less at each income level. Note that the relationship remains direct; the line merely shifts downward to reflect less consumption spending at each income level.

Similarly, factors other than ticket prices might affect GSU game attendance. If GSU loses most of its games, attendance at GSU games might be less at each ticket price. To see this, redraw Figure 2 assuming that 2,000 fewer fans attend GSU games at each ticket price.

Slope of a Line

Lines can be described in terms of their slopes. The **slope of a straight line** is the ratio of the vertical change (the rise or drop) to the horizontal change (the run) between any two points of the line.

Positive Slope Between point b and point c in Figure 1, the rise or vertical change (the change in consumption) is +$50 and the run or horizontal change (the change in income) is +$100. Therefore:

$$\text{slope} = \frac{\text{vertical change}}{\text{horizontal change}} = \frac{+50}{+100} = \frac{1}{2} = .5$$

Note that our slope of or .5 is positive because consumption and income change in the same direction; that is, consumption and income are directly or positively related.

The slope of .5 tells us there will be a $0.50 increase in consumption for every $1 increase in income. Similarly, there will be a $0.50 decrease in consumption for every $1 decrease in income.

Negative Slope Between any two of the identified points in Figure 2, say, point c and point d, the vertical change is −10 (the drop) and the horizontal change is +4 (the run). Therefore:

$$\text{Slope} = \frac{\text{vertical change}}{\text{horizontal change}} = \frac{-10}{+4}$$
$$= -2\frac{1}{2} = -2.5$$

This slope is negative because ticket price and attendance have an inverse relationship.

Note that on the horizontal axis attendance is stated in thousands of people. So the slope of −10/+4 or −2.5 means that lowering the price by $10 will increase attendance by 4,000 people. That ratio also implies that a $2.50 price reduction will increase attendance by 1,000 persons.

Slopes and Measurement Units The slope of a line will be affected by the choice of units for either variable. If, in our ticket price illustration, we had chosen to measure attendance in individual people, our horizontal change would have been 4,000 and the slope would have been

$$\text{slope} = \frac{-10}{+4,000} = \frac{-1}{+400} = -.0025$$

The slope depends on the way the relevant variables are measured.

Slopes and Marginal Analysis Recall that economics is largely concerned with changes from the status quo. The concept of slope is important in economics because it reflects marginal changes—those involving 1 more (or 1 fewer) unit. For example, in Figure 1 the .5 slope shows that $0.50 of extra or marginal consumption is associated with each $1 change in income. In this example, people collectively will consume $0.50 of any $1 increase in their incomes and reduce their consumption by $0.50 for each $1 decline in income.

Infinite and Zero Slopes Many variables are unrelated or independent of one another. For example, the quantity of wristwatches purchased is not related to the price of bananas. In Figure 3a we represent the price of bananas on the vertical axis and the quantity of watches demanded on the horizontal axis. The graph of their relationship is the line parallel to the vertical axis. The line's vertical slope indicates that the same quantity of watches is purchased no matter what the price of bananas. The slope of vertical lines is *infinite*.

Similarly, aggregate consumption is completely unrelated to the nation's divorce rate. In Figure 3b we put consumption

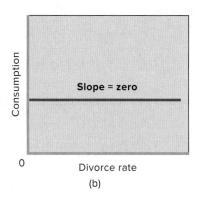

FIGURE 3 Infinite and zero slopes. (a) A line parallel to the vertical axis has an infinite slope. Here, purchases of watches remain the same no matter what happens to the price of bananas. (b) A line parallel to the horizontal axis has a slope of zero. In this case, consumption remains the same no matter what happens to the divorce rate. In both (a) and (b), the two variables are totally unrelated to one another.

on the vertical axis and the divorce rate on the horizontal axis. The line parallel to the horizontal axis represents this lack of relatedness because the amount of consumption remains the same no matter what happens to the divorce rate. The slope of horizontal lines is *zero*.

Vertical Intercept

A line can be positioned on a graph (without plotting points) if we know just two things: its slope and its vertical intercept. We have already discussed slope. The **vertical intercept** of a line is the point where the line meets the vertical axis. In Figure 1 the intercept is $50. This intercept means that if current income were zero, consumers would still spend $50. They might do this through borrowing or by selling some of their assets. Similarly, the $50 vertical intercept in Figure 2 shows that at a $50 ticket price, GSU's basketball team would be playing in an empty arena.

Equation of a Linear Relationship

If we know the vertical intercept and slope, we can describe a line succinctly in equation form. In its general form, the equation of a straight line is

$$y = a + bx$$

where y = dependent variable
a = vertical intercept
b = slope of line
x = independent variable

For our income-consumption example, if C represents consumption (the dependent variable) and Y represents income (the independent variable), we can write $C = a + bY$. By substituting the known values of the intercept and the slope, we get

$$C = 50 + .5Y$$

This equation also allows us to determine the amount of consumption C at any specific level of income. You should use it to confirm that at the $250 income level, consumption is $175.

When economists reverse mathematical convention by putting the independent variable on the vertical axis and the dependent variable on the horizontal axis, then y stands for the independent variable, rather than the dependent variable in the general form. We noted previously that this case is relevant for our GSU ticket price–attendance data. If P represents the ticket price (independent variable) and Q represents attendance (dependent variable), their relationship is given by

$$P = 50 - 2.5Q$$

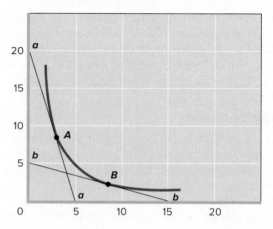

FIGURE 4 **Determining the slopes of curves.** The slope of a nonlinear curve changes from point to point on the curve. The slope at any point (say, *B*) can be determined by drawing a straight line that is tangent to that point (line *bb*) and calculating the slope of that line.

where the vertical intercept is 50 and the negative slope is $-2\frac{1}{2}$, or -2.5. Knowing the value of P lets us solve for Q, our dependent variable. You should use this equation to predict GSU ticket sales when the ticket price is $15.

Slope of a Nonlinear Curve

We now move from the simple world of linear relationships (straight lines) to the more complex world of nonlinear relationships (curvy lines). The slope of a straight line is the same at all its points. The slope of a line representing a nonlinear relationship changes from one point to another. Such lines are always referred to as *curves*.

Consider the downsloping curve in Figure 4. Its slope is negative throughout, but the curve flattens as we move down along it. Thus, its slope constantly changes; the curve has a different slope at each point.

To measure the slope at a specific point, we draw a straight line tangent to the curve at that point. A straight line is *tangent* at a point if it touches, but does not intersect, the curve at that point. Thus line *aa* is tangent to the curve in Figure 4 at point A. The slope of the curve at that point is equal to the slope of the tangent line. Specifically, the total vertical change (drop) in the tangent line *aa* is -20 and the total horizontal change (run) is $+5$. Because the slope of the tangent line *aa* is $-20/+5$, or -4, the slope of the curve at point A is also -4.

Line *bb* in Figure 4 is tangent to the curve at point B. Following the same procedure, we find the slope at B to be $-5/+15$, or $-\frac{1}{3}$. Thus, in this flatter part of the curve, the slope is less negative.

APPENDIX SUMMARY

LO1.8 Understand graphs, curves, and slopes as they relate to economics.

Graphs are a convenient and revealing way to represent economic relationships.

Two variables are positively or directly related when their values change in the same direction. The line (curve) representing two directly related variables slopes upward.

Two variables are negatively or inversely related when their values change in opposite directions. The line (curve) representing two inversely related variables slopes downward.

The value of the dependent variable (the "effect") is determined by the value of the independent variable (the "cause").

When the "other factors" that might affect a two-variable relationship are allowed to change, the graph of the relationship will likely shift to a new location.

The slope of a straight line is the ratio of the vertical change to the horizontal change between any two points. The slope of an upsloping line is positive; the slope of a downsloping line is negative.

The slope of a line or curve depends on the units used in measuring the variables. The slope is especially relevant for economics because it measures marginal changes.

The slope of a horizontal line is zero; the slope of a vertical line is infinite.

Together, the vertical intercept and slope of a line determine its location; they are used in expressing the line—and the relationship between the two variables—as an equation.

The slope of a curve at any point is determined by calculating the slope of a straight line tangent to the curve at that point.

APPENDIX TERMS AND CONCEPTS

horizontal axis

vertical axis

direct relationship

inverse relationship

independent variable

dependent variable

slope of a straight line

vertical intercept

The following and additional problems can be found in ■ connect

APPENDIX DISCUSSION QUESTIONS

1. Briefly explain the use of graphs as a way to represent economic relationships. What is an inverse relationship? How does it graph? What is a direct relationship? How does it graph? **LO1.8**
2. Describe the graphical relationship between ticket prices and the number of people choosing to visit amusement parks. Is that relationship consistent with the fact that, historically, park attendance and ticket prices have both risen? Explain. **LO1.8**
3. Look back at Figure 2, which shows the inverse relationship between ticket prices and game attendance at Gigantic State University. (a) Interpret the meaning of both the slope and the intercept. (b) If the slope of the line were steeper, what would that say about the amount by which ticket sales respond to increases in ticket prices? (c) If the slope of the line stayed the same but the intercept increased, what can you say about the amount by which ticket sales respond to increases in ticket prices? **LO1.8**

APPENDIX REVIEW QUESTIONS

1. Indicate whether each of the following relationships is usually a direct relationship or an inverse relationship. **LO1.8**
   a. A sports team's winning percentage and attendance at its home games.
   b. Higher temperatures and sweater sales.
   c. A person's income and how often he or she shops at discount stores.
   d. Higher gasoline prices and miles driven in automobiles.
2. Erin grows pecans. The number of bushels (B) that she can produce depends on the number of inches of rainfall (R) that her orchards get. The relationship is given algebraically as follows: $B = 3,000 + 800R$. Match each part of this equation with the correct term. **LO1.8**

B	slope
3,000	dependent variable
800	vertical intercept
R	independent variable

APPENDIX PROBLEMS

1. Graph and label as either direct or indirect the relationships you would expect to find between (a) the number of inches of rainfall per month and the sale of umbrellas, (b) the amount of tuition and the level of enrollment at a university, and (c) the popularity of an entertainer and the price of her concert tickets. **LO1.8**
2. Indicate how each of the following might affect the data shown in the table and graph in Figure 2 of this appendix: **LO1.8**
   a. GSU's athletic director schedules higher-quality opponents.
   b. An NBA team locates in the city where GSU plays.
   c. GSU contracts to have all its home games televised.

3. The following table contains data on the relationship between saving and income. Rearrange these data into a meaningful order and graph them on the accompanying grid. What is the slope of the line? The vertical intercept? Write the equation that represents this line. What would you predict saving to be at the $12,500 level of income? **LO1.8**

Income per Year	Saving per Year
$15,000	$1,000
0	−500
10,000	500
5,000	0
20,000	1,500

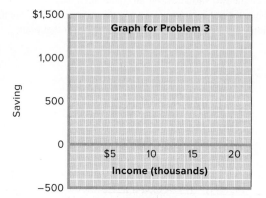

4. Construct a table from the data shown in the accompanying graph. Which is the dependent variable and which is the independent variable? Summarize the data in equation form. **LO1.8**

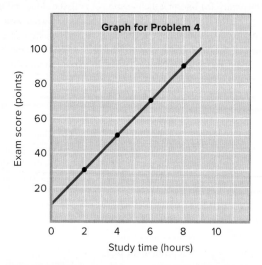

5. Suppose that when the interest rate on loans is 16 percent, businesses find it unprofitable to invest in machinery and equipment. However, when the interest rate is 14 percent, $5 billion worth of investment is profitable. At 12 percent interest, a total of $10 billion of investment is profitable. Similarly, total investment increases by $5 billion for each successive 2-percentage-point decline in the interest rate. Describe the relevant

relationship between the interest rate and investment in a table, on a graph, and as an equation. Put the interest rate on the vertical axis and investment on the horizontal axis. In your equation use the form $i = a + bI$, where i is the interest rate, a is the vertical intercept, b is the slope of the line (which is negative), and I is the level of investment. **LO1.8**

6. Suppose that $C = a + bY$, where C = consumption, a = consumption at zero income, b = slope, and Y = income. **LO1.8**
   a. Are C and Y positively related or are they negatively related?
   b. If graphed, would the curve for this equation slope upward or slope downward?
   c. Are the variables C and Y inversely related or directly related?
   d. What is the value of C if $a = 10$, $b = 0.50$, and $Y = 200$?
   e. What is the value of Y if $C = 100$, $a = 10$, and $b = 0.25$?

7. The accompanying graph shows curve XX' and tangents at points A, B, and C. Calculate the slope of the curve at these three points. **LO1.8**

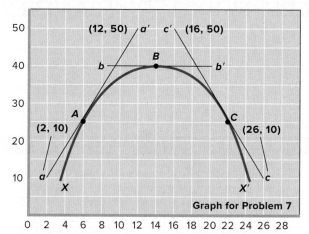

8. In the accompanying graph, is the slope of curve AA' positive or negative? Does the slope increase or decrease as we move along the curve from A to A'? Answer the same two questions for curve BB'. **LO1.8**

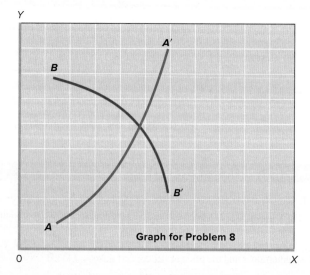

The Market System and the Circular Flow

Learning Objectives

LO2.1 Differentiate between laissez-faire capitalism, the command system, and the market system.

LO2.2 List the main characteristics of the market system.

LO2.3 Explain how the market system answers the five fundamental questions of what to produce, how to produce, who obtains the output, how to adjust to change, and how to promote progress.

LO2.4 Explain the operation of the "invisible hand" and why market economies usually do a better job than command economies at efficiently transforming economic resources into desirable output.

LO2.5 Describe the mechanics of the circular flow model.

LO2.6 Explain how the market system deals with risk.

You are at the mall. Suppose you were assigned to compile a list of all the individual goods and services there, including the different brands and variations of each type of product.

That task would be daunting and the list would be long! And even though a single shopping mall contains a remarkable quantity and variety of goods, it is only a tiny part of the national economy.

Who decided that the particular goods and services available at the mall and in the broader economy should be produced? How did the producers determine which technology and types of resources to use in producing these particular goods? Who will obtain these products? What accounts for the new and improved products among these goods? This chapter will answer these and related questions.

Economic Systems

LO2.1 Differentiate between laissez-faire capitalism, the command system, and the market system.

Every society needs to develop an **economic system**—a particular set of institutional arrangements and a coordinating mechanism—to respond to the economizing problem. The economic system has to determine what goods are produced, how they are produced, who gets them, how to accommodate change, and how to promote technological progress.

Economic systems differ as to (1) who owns the factors of production and (2) the method used to motivate, coordinate, and direct economic activity.

Economics systems can be classified by the degree to which they rely upon decentralized decision making based upon markets and prices or centralized government control based upon orders and mandates. At one extreme lies *laissez-faire capitalism,* in which government intervention is at a very minimum and markets and prices are allowed to direct nearly all economic activity. At the other extreme lie *command systems,* in which governments have total control over all economic activity. The vast majority of national economies lie somewhere in the middle, utilizing some mixture of centralized government regulation and decentralized markets and prices. These economies are said to have *market systems* or *mixed economies.*

Laissez-Faire Capitalism

In **laissez-faire capitalism**—or "pure capitalism"—the government's role would be limited to protecting private property from theft and aggression and establishing a legal environment in which contracts would be enforced and people could interact in markets to buy and sell goods, services, and resources.

The term "laissez-faire" is the French for "let it be," that is, keep the government from interfering with the economy. Proponents of laissez-faire believe that such interference reduces human welfare. They maintain that any government that intervenes widely in the economy will end up being corrupted by special interests that will use the government's economic influence to benefit themselves rather than society at large.

To prevent that from happening, the proponents of laissez-faire argue that government should restrict itself to preventing individuals and firms from coercing each other. By doing so, it will ensure that only mutually beneficial economic transactions get negotiated and completed. That should lead to the highest possible level of human satisfaction because, after all, who knows better what people want than the people themselves?

It is important to note, however, that no society has ever employed a laissez-faire system. In fact, no government has *ever* limited its economic actions to the short list of functions that would be allowed under laissez-faire. Instead, every government known to history has undertaken a wider range of economic activities, many of which are widely popular and which include industrial safety regulations, various taxes and subsidies, occupational licensing requirements, and income redistribution.

Thus, you should think of laissez-faire capitalism as a hypothetical system that is viewed by proponents as the ideal to which all economic systems should strive—but which is opposed by those who welcome greater government intervention in the economy.

The Command System

The polar opposite of laissez-faire capitalism is the **command system,** in which government owns most property resources and economic decision making is set by a central economic plan created and enforced by the government. The command system is also known as *socialism* or *communism.*

Under the command system, a central planning board appointed by the government makes all the major decisions concerning the use of resources, the composition and distribution of output, and the organization of production. The government owns most of the business firms, which produce according to government directives. The central planning board determines production goals for each enterprise and specifies the amount of resources to be allocated to each enterprise so that it can reach its production goals. The division of output between capital and consumer goods is centrally decided, and capital goods are allocated among industries on the basis of the central planning board's long-term priorities.

A pure command economy would rely exclusively on a central plan to allocate the government-owned property resources. But, in reality, even the preeminent command economy—the Soviet Union—tolerated some private ownership and incorporated some markets before its collapse in 1992. Subsequent reforms in Russia and most of the eastern European nations have, to one degree or another, transformed their command economies to capitalistic, market-oriented systems. China's reforms have not gone as far, but they have greatly reduced China's reliance on central planning. Although government ownership of resources and capital in China is still extensive, the nation has increasingly relied on free markets to organize and coordinate its economy. North Korea and Cuba are the last prominent remaining examples of largely centrally planned economies. Other countries using mainly the command system include Turkmenistan, Laos, Belarus, Myanmar, Venezuela, and Iran. Later in this chapter, we will explore the main reasons for the general demise of command systems.

The Market System

The vast majority of the world's economies utilize the **market system,** which is also known as *capitalism* or the *mixed economy.*

The market system is characterized by a mixture of centralized government economic initiatives and decentralized actions taken by individuals and firms. The precise mixture varies from country to country, but in each case the system features the private ownership of resources and the use of markets and prices to coordinate and direct economic activity.

In the market system, individuals and businesses seek to achieve their economic goals through their own decisions regarding work, consumption, or production. The system allows for the private ownership of capital, communicates through prices, and coordinates economic activity through markets—places where buyers and sellers come together to buy and sell goods, services, and resources.

Participants act in their own self-interest, and goods and services are produced and resources are supplied by whoever is willing and able to do so. The result is competition among independently acting buyers and sellers of each product and resource and an economic system in which decision making is widely dispersed.

The market system also offers high potential monetary rewards that create powerful incentives for existing firms to innovate and for entrepreneurs to pioneer new products and processes despite the financial risks involved and despite most innovations failing to catch on with consumers.

It is the case, however, that in the capitalism practiced in the United States and most other countries, the government plays a substantial role in the economy. It not only provides the rules for economic activity but also promotes economic stability and growth, provides certain goods and services that would otherwise be underproduced or not produced at all, and modifies the distribution of income. The government, however, is not the dominant economic force in deciding what to produce, how to produce it, and who will get it. That force is the market.

Characteristics of the Market System

LO2.2 List the main characteristics of the market system.

An examination of some of the key features of the market system in detail will be very instructive.

Private Property

In a market system, private individuals and firms, not the government, own most of the property resources (land and capital). It is this extensive private ownership of capital that gives capitalism its name. This right of **private property,** coupled with the freedom to negotiate binding legal contracts, enables individuals and businesses to obtain, use, and dispose of property resources as they see fit. The right of property owners to designate who will receive their property when they die helps sustain the institution of private property.

The most important consequence of property rights is that they encourage people to cooperate by helping to ensure that only *mutually agreeable* economic transactions take place. To consider why this is true, imagine a world without legally enforceable property rights. In such a world, the strong could simply take whatever they wanted from the weak without giving them any compensation. But in a world of legally enforceable property rights, any person wanting something from you has to get you to agree to give it to them. And you can say no. The result is that if they really want what you have, they must offer you something that you value more highly in return. That is, they must offer you a mutually agreeable economic transaction—one that benefits you as well as them.

Property rights also encourage investment, innovation, exchange, maintenance of property, and economic growth.

Nobody would stock a store, build a factory, or clear land for farming if someone else, or the government itself, could take that property for his or her own benefit.

Property rights also extend to intellectual property through patents, copyrights, and trademarks. Such long-term protection encourages people to write books, music, and computer programs and to invent new products and production processes without fear that others will steal them and the rewards they may bring.

Moreover, property rights facilitate exchange. The title to an automobile or the deed to a cattle ranch assures the buyer that the seller is the legitimate owner. Also, property rights encourage owners to maintain or improve their property so as to preserve or increase its value. Finally, property rights enable people to use their time and resources to produce more goods and services, rather than using them to protect and retain the property they have already produced or acquired.

Freedom of Enterprise and Choice

Closely related to private ownership of property is freedom of enterprise and choice. The market system requires that various economic units make certain choices, which are expressed and implemented in the economy's markets:

- **Freedom of enterprise** ensures that entrepreneurs and private businesses are free to obtain and use economic resources to produce their choice of goods and services and to sell them in their chosen markets.

- **Freedom of choice** enables owners to employ or dispose of their property and money as they see fit. It also allows workers to try to enter any line of work for which they are qualified. Finally, it ensures that consumers are free to buy the goods and services that best satisfy their wants and that their budgets allow.

These choices are free only within broad legal limitations, of course. Illegal choices such as selling human organs or buying illicit drugs are punished through fines and imprisonment. (Global Perspective 2.1 reveals that the degree of economic freedom varies greatly from economy to economy.)

Self-Interest

In the market system, **self-interest** is the motivating force of the various economic units as they express their free choices. Self-interest simply means that each economic unit tries to achieve its own particular goal, which usually requires delivering something of value to others. Entrepreneurs try to maximize profit or minimize loss. Property owners try to get the highest price for the sale or rent of their resources. Workers try to maximize their utility (satisfaction) by finding jobs that offer the best combination of wages, hours, fringe benefits, and working conditions. Consumers try to obtain the products they want at the lowest possible price and apportion their

GLOBAL PERSPECTIVE 2.1

Index of Economic Freedom, Selected Economies

The Index of Economic Freedom measures economic freedom using 10 major groupings such as trade policy, property rights, and government intervention, with each category containing more than 50 specific criteria. The index then ranks 179 economies according to their degree of economic freedom. A few selected rankings for 2015 are listed below.

FREE
| 1 Hong Kong |
| 3 New Zeland |
| 5 Switzerland |

MOSTLY FREE
| 12 United States |
| 20 Japan |
| 28 Colombia |

MOSTLY UNFREE
| 117 Brazil |
| 128 India |
| 143 Russia |

REPRESSED
| 169 Argentina |
| 171 Iran |
| 178 North Korea |

Source: The Heritage Foundation, **www.heritage.org**.

expenditures to maximize their utility. The motive of self-interest gives direction and consistency to what might otherwise be a chaotic economy.

Competition

The market system depends on **competition** among economic units. The basis of this competition is freedom of choice exercised in pursuit of a monetary return. Very broadly defined, competition requires

- Two or more buyers and two or more sellers acting independently in a particular product or resource market. (Usually there are many more than two buyers and two sellers.)
- Freedom of sellers and buyers to enter or leave markets, on the basis of their economic self-interest.

Competition among buyers and sellers diffuses economic power within the businesses and households that make up the economy. When there are many buyers and sellers acting independently in a market, no single buyer or seller can dictate the price of the product or resource because others can undercut that price.

Competition also implies that producers can enter or leave an industry; no insurmountable barriers prevent an industry's expanding or contracting. This freedom of an industry to expand or contract provides the economy with the flexibility needed to remain efficient over time. Freedom of entry and exit enables the economy to adjust to changes in consumer tastes, technology, and resource availability.

The diffusion of economic power inherent in competition limits the potential abuse of that power. A producer that charges more than the competitive market price will lose sales to other producers. An employer who pays less than the competitive market wage rate will lose workers to other employers. A firm that fails to exploit new technology will lose profits to firms that do. A firm that produces shoddy products will be punished as customers switch to higher-quality items made by rival firms. Competition is the basic regulatory force in the market system.

Markets and Prices

We may wonder why an economy based on self-interest does not collapse in chaos. If consumers want breakfast cereal, but businesses choose to produce running shoes and resource suppliers decide to make computer software, production would seem to be deadlocked by the apparent inconsistencies of free choices.

In reality, the millions of decisions made by households and businesses are highly coordinated with one another by markets and prices, which are key components of the market system. They give the system its ability to coordinate millions of daily economic decisions. A **market** is an institution or mechanism that brings buyers ("demanders") and sellers ("suppliers") into contact. A market system conveys the decisions made by buyers and sellers of products and resources. The decisions made on each side of the market determine a set of product and resource prices that guide resource owners, entrepreneurs, and consumers as they make and revise their choices and pursue their self-interest.

Just as competition is the regulatory mechanism of the market system, the market system itself is the organizing and coordinating mechanism. It is an elaborate communication network through which innumerable individual free choices are recorded, summarized, and balanced. Those who respond to market signals and heed market dictates are rewarded with greater profit and income; those who do not respond to those signals and choose to ignore market dictates are penalized. Through this mechanism society decides what the economy should produce, how production can be organized efficiently, and how the fruits of production are to be distributed among the various units that make up the economy.

QUICK REVIEW 2.1

✓ The market system rests on the private ownership of property and on freedom of enterprise and freedom of choice.

✓ Property rights encourage people to cooperate and make mutually agreeable economic transactions.

✓ The market system permits consumers, resource suppliers, and businesses to pursue and further their self-interest.

✓ Competition diffuses economic power and limits the actions of any single seller or buyer.

✓ The coordinating mechanism of capitalism is a system of markets and prices.

Technology and Capital Goods

In the market system, competition, freedom of choice, self-interest, and personal reward provide the opportunity and motivation for technological advance. The monetary rewards for new products or production techniques accrue directly to the innovator. The market system therefore encourages extensive use and rapid development of complex capital goods: tools, machinery, large-scale factories, and facilities for storage, communication, transportation, and marketing.

Advanced technology and capital goods are important because the most direct methods of production are often the least efficient. The only way to avoid that inefficiency is to rely on capital goods. It would be ridiculous for a farmer to go at production with bare hands. There are huge benefits to be derived from creating and using such capital equipment as plows, tractors, and storage bins. More efficient production means much more abundant output.

Specialization

The extent to which market economies rely on **specialization** is extraordinary. Specialization means using the resources of an individual, firm, region, or nation to produce one or a few goods or services rather than the entire range of goods and services. Those goods and services are then exchanged for a full range of desired products. The majority of consumers produce virtually none of the goods and services they consume, and they consume little or nothing of the items they produce. The person working nine to five installing windows in commercial aircraft may rarely fly. Many farmers sell their milk to the local dairy and then buy margarine at the local grocery store. Society learned long ago that self-sufficiency breeds inefficiency. The jack-of-all-trades may be a very colorful individual but is certainly not an efficient producer.

Division of Labor Human specialization—called the **division of labor**—contributes to a society's output in several ways:

- *Specialization makes use of differences in ability.* Specialization enables individuals to take advantage of existing differences in their abilities and skills. If LeBron is strong, athletic, and good at shooting a basketball and Beyoncé is beautiful, agile, and can sing, their distribution of talents can be most efficiently used if LeBron plays professional basketball while Beyoncé records songs and gives concerts.

- *Specialization fosters learning by doing.* Even if the abilities of two people are identical, specialization may still be advantageous. By devoting time to a single task, a person is more likely to develop the skills required and to improve techniques than by working at a number of different tasks. You learn to be a good lawyer by studying and practicing law.

- *Specialization saves time.* By devoting time to a single task, a person avoids the loss of time incurred in shifting from one job to another. Also, time is saved by not "fumbling around" with tasks that one is not trained to do.

For all these reasons, specialization increases the total output society derives from limited resources.

Geographic Specialization Specialization also works on a regional and international basis. It is conceivable that oranges could be grown in Nebraska, but because of the unsuitability of the land, rainfall, and temperature, the costs would be very high. And it is conceivable that wheat could be grown in Florida, but such production would be costly for similar geographical reasons. So Nebraskans produce products—wheat in particular—for which their resources are best suited, and Floridians do the same, producing oranges and other citrus fruits. By specializing, both economies produce more than is needed locally. Then, very sensibly, Nebraskans and Floridians swap some of their surpluses—wheat for oranges, oranges for wheat.

Similarly, on an international scale, the United States specializes in producing such items as commercial aircraft and software, which it sells abroad in exchange for mobile phones from China, bananas from Honduras, and woven baskets from Thailand. Both human specialization and geographic specialization are needed to achieve efficiency in the use of limited resources.

Use of Money

A rather obvious characteristic of any economic system is the extensive use of money. Money performs several functions, but first and foremost it is a **medium of exchange.** It makes trade easier.

Specialization requires exchange. Exchange can, and sometimes does, occur through **barter**—swapping goods for

FIGURE 2.1 Money facilitates trade when wants do not coincide. The use of money as a medium of exchange permits trade to be accomplished despite a noncoincidence of wants. (1) Nebraska trades the wheat that Florida wants for money from Floridians; (2) Nebraska trades the money it receives from Florida for the potatoes it wants from Idaho; (3) Idaho trades the money it receives from Nebraska for the oranges it wants from Florida.

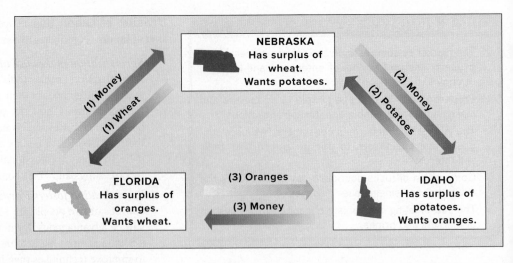

goods, say, wheat for oranges. But barter poses serious problems because it requires a *coincidence of wants* between the buyer and the seller. In our example, we assumed that Nebraskans had excess wheat to trade and wanted oranges. And we assumed that Floridians had excess oranges to trade and wanted wheat. So an exchange occurred. But if such a coincidence of wants is missing, trade is stymied.

Suppose that Nebraska has no interest in Florida's oranges but wants potatoes from Idaho. And suppose that Idaho wants Florida's oranges but not Nebraska's wheat. And, to complicate matters, suppose that Florida wants some of Nebraska's wheat but none of Idaho's potatoes. We summarize the situation in Figure 2.1.

In none of the cases shown in the figure is there a coincidence of wants. Trade by barter clearly would be difficult. Instead, people in each state use **money,** which is simply a convenient social invention to facilitate exchanges of goods and services. Historically, people have used cattle, cigarettes, shells, stones, pieces of metal, and many other commodities, with varying degrees of success, as money. To serve as money, an item needs to pass only one test: It must be generally acceptable to sellers in exchange for their goods and services. Money is socially defined; whatever society accepts as a medium of exchange *is* money.

Today, most economies use pieces of paper as money. The use of paper dollars (currency) as a medium of exchange is what enables Nebraska, Florida, and Idaho to overcome their trade stalemate, as demonstrated in Figure 2.1.

On a global basis, specialization and exchange are complicated by the fact that different nations have different currencies. But markets in which currencies are bought and sold make it possible for people living in different countries to exchange goods and services without resorting to barter.

Active, but Limited, Government

An active, but limited, government is the final characteristic of market systems in modern advanced industrial economies.

Although a market system promotes a high degree of efficiency in the use of its resources, it has certain inherent shortcomings, called "market failures." We will discover in subsequent chapters that governments can often increase the overall effectiveness of a market system in several ways. That being said, governments have their own set of shortcomings that can themselves cause substantial misallocations of resources. Consequently, we will also investigate several types of "government failure."

QUICK REVIEW 2.2

✓ The market systems of modern industrial economies are characterized by extensive use of technologically advanced capital goods. Such goods help these economies achieve greater efficiency in production.

✓ Specialization is extensive in market systems; it enhances efficiency and output by enabling individuals, regions, and nations to produce the goods and services for which their resources are best suited.

✓ The use of money in market systems facilitates the exchange of goods and services that specialization requires.

Five Fundamental Questions

LO2.3 Explain how the market system answers the five fundamental questions of what to produce, how to produce, who obtains the output, how to adjust to change, and how to promote progress.

The key features of the market system help explain how market economies respond to five fundamental questions:

- What goods and services will be produced?
- How will the goods and services be produced?
- Who will get the goods and services?
- How will the system accommodate change?
- How will the system promote progress?

These five questions highlight the economic choices underlying the production possibilities curve discussed in Chapter 1. They reflect the reality of scarce resources in a world of unlimited wants. All economies, whether market or command, must address these five questions.

What Will Be Produced?

How will a market system decide on the specific types and quantities of goods to be produced? The simple answer is this: The goods and services that can be produced at a continuing profit will be produced, while those whose production generates a continuing loss will be discontinued. Profits and losses are the difference between the total revenue (TR) a firm receives from the sale of its products and the total cost (TC) of producing those products. (For economists, total costs include not only wage and salary payments to labor, and interest and rental payments for capital and land, but also payments to the entrepreneur for organizing and combining the other resources to produce a product.)

Continuing economic profit (TR > TC) in an industry results in expanded production and the movement of resources toward that industry. Existing firms grow and new firms enter. The industry expands. Continuing losses (TC > TR) in an industry lead to reduced production and the exit of resources from that industry. Some existing firms shrink in size; others go out of business. The industry contracts. In the market system, consumers are sovereign (in command). **Consumer sovereignty** is crucial in determining the types and quantities of goods produced. Consumers spend their income on the goods they are most willing and able to buy. Through these **"dollar votes"** they register their wants in the market. If the dollar votes for a certain product are great enough to create a profit, businesses will produce that product and offer it for sale. In contrast, if the dollar votes do not create sufficient revenues to cover costs, businesses will not produce the product. So the consumers are sovereign. They collectively direct resources to industries that are meeting consumer wants and away from industries that are not meeting consumer wants.

The dollar votes of consumers determine not only which industries will continue to exist but also which products will survive or fail. Only profitable industries, firms, and products survive. So firms are not as free to produce whatever products they wish as one might otherwise think. Consumers' buying decisions make the production of some products profitable and the production of other products unprofitable, thus restricting the choice of businesses in deciding what to produce. Businesses must match their production choices with consumer choices or else face losses and eventual bankruptcy.

The same holds true for resource suppliers. The employment of resources derives from the sale of the goods and services that the resources help produce. Autoworkers are employed because automobiles are sold. There are few remaining professors of early Latin because there are few

people desiring to learn the Latin language. Resource suppliers, desiring to earn income, are not truly free to allocate their resources to the production of goods that consumers do not value highly. Consumers register their preferences in the market; producers and resource suppliers, prompted by their own self-interest, respond appropriately.

How Will the Goods and Services Be Produced?

What combinations of resources and technologies will be used to produce goods and services? How will the production be organized? The answer: In combinations and ways that minimize the cost per unit of output. This is true because inefficiency drives up costs and lowers profits. As a result, any firm wishing to maximize its profits will make great efforts to minimize production costs. These efforts will include using the right mix of labor and capital, given the prices and productivity of those resources. They also mean locating production facilities optimally to hold down production and transportation expenses.

Those efforts will be intensified if the firm faces competition, as consumers strongly prefer low prices and will shift their purchases over to the firms that can produce a quality product at the lowest possible price. Any firm foolish enough to use higher-cost production methods will go bankrupt as it is undersold by its more efficient competitors who can still make a profit when selling at a lower price. Simply stated: Competition eliminates high-cost producers.

Least-cost production means that firms must employ the most economically efficient technique of production in producing their output. The most efficient production technique depends on

- The available technology, that is, the available body of knowledge and techniques that can be used to combine economic resources to produce the desired results.
- The prices of the needed resources.

A technique that requires just a few inputs of resources to produce a specific output may be highly inefficient economically if those resources are valued very highly in the market. Economic efficiency requires obtaining a particular output of product with the least input of scarce resources, when both output and resource inputs are measured in dollars and cents. The combination of resources that will produce, say, $15 worth of bathroom soap at the lowest possible cost is the most efficient.

Suppose there are three possible techniques for producing the desired $15 worth of bars of soap. Suppose also that the quantity of each resource required by each production technique and the prices of the required resources are as shown in Table 2.1. By multiplying the required quantities of each resource by its price in each of the three techniques, we can determine the total cost of producing $15 worth of soap by means of each technique.

Technique 2 is economically the most efficient because it is the least costly. It enables society to obtain $15 worth of output by using a smaller amount of resources—$13 worth— than the $15 worth required by the two other techniques. Competition will dictate that producers use technique 2. Thus, the question of how goods will be produced is answered. They will be produced in a least-cost way.

A change in either technology or resource prices, however, may cause a firm to shift from the technology it is using. If the price of labor falls to $0.50, technique 1 becomes more desirable than technique 2. Firms will find they can lower their costs by shifting to a technology that uses more of the resource whose price has fallen. Exercise: Would a new technique involving 1 unit of labor, 4 of land, 1 of capital, and 1 of entrepreneurial ability be preferable to the techniques listed in Table 2.1, assuming the resource prices shown there?

Who Will Get the Output?

The market system enters the picture in two ways when determining the distribution of total output. Generally, any product will be distributed to consumers on the basis of their ability and willingness to pay its existing market price. If the price of some product, say, a small sailboat, is $3,000, then buyers who are willing and able to pay that price will "sail, sail away." Consumers who are unwilling or unable to pay the price will be "sitting on the dock of the bay."

The ability to pay the prices for sailboats and other products depends on the amount of income that consumers have, along with the prices of, and preferences for, various goods. If consumers have sufficient income and want to spend their money on a particular good, they can have it. The amount of income they have depends on (1) the quantities of the property and human resources they supply and (2) the prices those resources command in the resource market. Resource prices (wages, interest, rent, profit) are crucial in determining the size of each person's income and therefore each person's ability to buy part of the economy's output. If a lawyer earning $130 an hour and a janitor earning $13 an hour both work the same number of hours each year, then each year the lawyer will be able to purchase 10 times more of society's output than the janitor.

How Will the System Accommodate Change?

Market systems are dynamic: Consumer preferences, technologies, and resource supplies all change. This means that the particular allocation of resources that is now the most efficient for a specific pattern of consumer tastes, range of

TABLE 2.1 Three Techniques for Producing $15 Worth of Bar Soap

Resource	Price per Unit of Resource	Technique 1 Units	Technique 1 Cost	Technique 2 Units	Technique 2 Cost	Technique 3 Units	Technique 3 Cost
Labor	$2	4	$ 8	2	$ 4	1	$ 2
Land	1	1	1	3	3	4	4
Capital	3	1	3	1	3	2	6
Entrepreneurial ability	3	1	3	1	3	1	3
Total cost of $15 worth of bar soap			$15		$13		$15

technological alternatives, and amount of available resources will become obsolete and inefficient as consumer preferences change, new techniques of production are discovered, and resource supplies change over time. Can the market economy adjust to such changes?

Suppose consumer tastes change. For instance, assume that consumers decide they want more fruit juice and less milk than the economy currently provides. Those changes in consumer tastes will be communicated to producers through an increase in spending on fruit and a decline in spending on milk. Other things equal, prices and profits in the fruit juice industry will rise and those in the milk industry will fall. Self-interest will induce existing competitors to expand output and entice new competitors to enter the prosperous fruit industry and will in time force firms to scale down—or even exit—the depressed milk industry.

The higher prices and greater economic profit in the fruit-juice industry will not only induce that industry to expand but also give it the revenue needed to obtain the resources essential to its growth. Higher prices and profits will permit fruit producers to attract more resources from less urgent alternative uses. The reverse occurs in the milk industry, where fewer workers and other resources are employed. These adjustments in the economy are appropriate responses to the changes in consumer tastes. This is consumer sovereignty at work.

The market system is a gigantic communications system. Through changes in prices and profits, it communicates changes in such basic matters as consumer tastes and elicits appropriate responses from businesses and resource suppliers. By affecting price and profits, changes in consumer tastes direct the expansion of some industries and the contraction of others. Those adjustments are conveyed to the resource market. As expanding industries employ more resources and contracting industries employ fewer, the resulting changes in resource prices (wages and salaries, for example) and income flows guide resources from the contracting industries to the expanding industries.

This directing or guiding function of prices and profits is a core element of the market system. Without such a system, a government planning board or some other administrative agency would have to direct businesses and resources into the appropriate industries. A similar analysis shows that the system can and does adjust to other fundamental changes—for example, to changes in technology and in the prices of various resources.

How Will the System Promote Progress?

Society desires economic growth (greater output) and higher standards of living (greater output *per person*). How does the market system promote technological improvements and capital accumulation, both of which contribute to a higher standard of living for society?

Technological Advance The market system provides a strong incentive for technological advance and enables better products and processes to supplant inferior ones. An entrepreneur or firm that introduces a popular new product will gain revenue and economic profit at the expense of rivals. Firms that are highly profitable one year may find they are in financial trouble just a few years later. Technological advance also includes new and improved methods that reduce production or distribution costs. By passing part of its cost reduction on to the consumer through a lower product price, a firm can increase sales and obtain economic profit at the expense of rival firms.

Moreover, the market system promotes the *rapid spread* of technological advance throughout an industry. Rival firms must follow the lead of the most innovative firm or else suffer immediate losses and eventual failure. In some cases, the result is **creative destruction:** The creation of new products and production methods completely destroys the market positions of firms that are wedded to existing products and older ways of doing business. Example: Compact discs largely demolished vinyl records before MP3 players and then online streaming subsequently supplanted compact discs.

Capital Accumulation Most technological advances require additional capital goods. The market system provides the resources necessary to produce additional capital goods through increased dollar votes for those goods. That is, the market system acknowledges dollar voting for capital goods as well as for consumer goods.

But who counts the dollar votes for capital goods? Answer: Entrepreneurs and business owners. As receivers of profit income, they often use part of that income to purchase capital goods. Doing so yields even greater profit income in the future if the technological innovation that required the additional capital goods is successful. Also, by paying interest or selling ownership shares, the entrepreneur and firm can attract some of the income of households as saving to increase their dollar votes for the production of more capital goods.

QUICK REVIEW 2.3

✓ The output mix of the market system is determined by profits, which in turn depend heavily on consumer preferences. Economic profits cause industries to expand; losses cause industries to contract.

✓ Competition forces industries to use the least costly production methods.

✓ Competitive markets reallocate resources in response to changes in consumer tastes, technological advances, and changes in availability of resources.

✓ In a market economy, consumer income and product prices determine how output will be distributed.

✓ Competitive markets create incentives for technological advance and capital accumulation, both of which contribute to increases in standards of living.

The "Invisible Hand"

LO2.4 Explain the operation of the "invisible hand" and why market economies usually do a better job than command economies at efficiently transforming economic resources into desirable output.

In his 1776 book *The Wealth of Nations,* Adam Smith first noted that the operation of a market system creates a curious unity between private interests and social interests. Firms and resource suppliers, seeking to further their own self-interest and operating within the framework of a highly competitive market system, will simultaneously, as though guided by an **"invisible hand,"** promote the public or social interest. For example, we have seen that in a competitive environment, businesses seek to build new and improved products to increase profits. Those enhanced products increase society's well-being. Businesses also use the least costly combination of resources to produce a specific output because doing so is in their self-interest. To act otherwise would be to forgo profit or even to risk business failure. But, at the same time, to use scarce resources in the least costly way is clearly in the social interest as well. It "frees up" resources to produce other things that society desires.

Self-interest, awakened and guided by the competitive market system, is what induces responses appropriate to the changes in society's wants. Businesses seeking to make higher profits and to avoid losses, and resource suppliers pursuing greater monetary rewards, negotiate changes in the allocation of resources and end up with the output that society wants. Competition controls or guides self-interest such that self-interest automatically and quite unintentionally furthers the best interest of society. The invisible hand ensures that when firms maximize their profits and resource suppliers maximize their incomes, these groups also help maximize society's output and income.

Of the various virtues of the market system, three merit reemphasis:

- *Efficiency* The market system promotes the efficient use of resources by guiding them into the production of the goods and services most wanted by society. It forces the use of the most efficient techniques in organizing resources for production, and it encourages the development and adoption of new and more efficient production techniques.
- *Incentives* The market system encourages skill acquisition, hard work, and innovation. Greater work skills and effort mean greater production and higher incomes, which usually translate into a higher standard of living. Similarly, the assuming of risks by entrepreneurs can result in substantial profit incomes. Successful innovations generate economic rewards.
- *Freedom* The major noneconomic argument for the market system is its emphasis on personal freedom. In

contrast to central planning, the market system coordinates economic activity without coercion. The market system permits—indeed, it thrives on—freedom of enterprise and choice. Entrepreneurs and workers are free to further their own self-interest, subject to the rewards and penalties imposed by the market system itself.

Of course, no economic system, including the market system, is flawless. In Chapter 4 we will explain two well-known shortcomings of the market system and examine the government policies that try to remedy them.

The Demise of the Command Systems

Our discussion of how a market system answers the five fundamental questions provides insights on why the command systems of the Soviet Union, eastern Europe, and China (prior to its market reforms) failed. Those systems encountered two insurmountable problems.

The Coordination Problem The first difficulty was the coordination problem. The central planners had to coordinate the millions of individual decisions by consumers, resource suppliers, and businesses. Consider the setting up of a factory to produce tractors. The central planners had to establish a realistic annual production target, for example, 1,000 tractors. They then had to make available all the necessary inputs—labor, machinery, electric power, steel, tires, glass, paint, transportation—for the production and delivery of those 1,000 tractors.

Because the outputs of many industries serve as inputs to other industries, the failure of any single industry to achieve its output target caused a chain reaction of repercussions. For example, if iron mines, for want of machinery or labor or transportation, did not supply the steel industry with the required inputs of iron ore, the steel mills were unable to fulfill the input needs of the many industries that depended on steel. Those steel-using industries (such as tractor, automobile, and transportation) were unable to fulfill their planned production goals. Eventually the chain reaction spread to all firms that used steel as an input and from there to other input buyers or final consumers.

The coordination problem became more difficult as the economies expanded. Products and production processes grew more sophisticated and the number of industries requiring planning increased. Planning techniques that worked for the simpler economy proved highly inadequate and inefficient for the larger economy. Bottlenecks and production stoppages became the norm, not the exception. In trying to cope, planners further suppressed product variety, focusing on one or two products in each product category.

A lack of a reliable success indicator added to the coordination problem in the Soviet Union and China prior to its market reforms. We have seen that market economies rely on profit as a success indicator. Profit depends on consumer demand, production efficiency, and product quality. In contrast, the major success indicator for the command economies usually was a quantitative production target that the central planners assigned. Production costs, product quality, and product mix were secondary considerations. Managers and workers often sacrificed product quality and variety because they were being awarded bonuses for meeting quantitative, not qualitative, targets. If meeting production goals meant sloppy assembly work and little product variety, so be it.

It was difficult at best for planners to assign quantitative production targets without unintentionally producing distortions in output. If the plan specified a production target for producing nails in terms of *weight* (tons of nails), the enterprise made only large nails. But if it specified the target as a *quantity* (thousands of nails), the firm made all small nails, and lots of them! That is precisely what happened in the centrally planned economies.

The Incentive Problem

The command economies also faced an incentive problem. Central planners determined the output mix. When they misjudged how many automobiles, shoes, shirts, and chickens were wanted at the government-determined prices, persistent shortages and surpluses of those products arose. But as long as the managers who oversaw the production of those goods were rewarded for meeting their assigned production goals, they had no incentive to adjust production in response to the shortages and surpluses. And there were no fluctuations in prices and profitability to signal that more or less of certain products was desired. Thus, many products were unavailable or in short supply, while other products were overproduced and sat for months or years in warehouses.

The command systems of the former Soviet Union and China before its market reforms also lacked entrepreneurship. Central planning did not trigger the profit motive, nor did it reward innovation and enterprise. The route for getting ahead was through participation in the political hierarchy of the Communist Party. Moving up the hierarchy meant better housing, better access to health care, and the right to shop in special stores. Meeting production targets and maneuvering through the minefields of party politics were measures of success in "business." But a definition of business success based solely on political savvy was not conducive to technological advance, which is often disruptive to existing products, production methods, and organizational structures.

The Circular Flow Model

LO2.5 Describe the mechanics of the circular flow model.

The dynamic market economy creates continuous, repetitive flows of goods and services, resources, and money. The **circular flow diagram,** shown in **Figure 2.2 (Key Graph),** illustrates those flows for a simplified economy in which there is no government. Observe that in the diagram we group this economy's decision makers into *businesses* and *households.* Additionally, we divide this economy's markets into the *resource market* and the *product market.*

Households

The blue rectangle on the right side of the circular flow diagram in Figure 2.2 represents **households,** which are defined as one or more persons occupying a housing unit. There are currently about 118 million households in the U.S. economy. Households buy the goods and services that businesses make available in the product market. Households obtain the income needed to buy those products by selling resources in the resource market.

All the resources in our no-government economy are ultimately owned or provided by households. For instance, the members of one household or another directly provide all of the labor and entrepreneurial ability in the economy. Households also own all of the land and all of the capital in the economy either directly, as personal property, or indirectly, as a consequence of owning all of the businesses in the economy

CONSIDER THIS . . .

Source: © Stocktrek Images/Getty Images RF

The Two Koreas

North Korea is one of the few command economies still standing. After the Second World War, the Korean peninsula was divided into North Korea and South Korea. North Korea, under the influence of the Soviet Union, established a command economy that emphasized government ownership and central government planning. South Korea, protected by the United States, established a market economy based upon private ownership and the profit motive. Today, the differences in the economic outcomes of the two systems are striking:

	North Korea	South Korea
GDP	$40 billion*	$1.8 trillion*
GDP per capita	$1,800*	$34,200*
Exports	$2.2 billion	$911 billion
Imports	$4.4 billion	$815 billion
Agriculture as % of GDP	23 percent	2.3 percent

*Based on purchasing power equivalencies to the U.S. dollar.

Source: CIA World Fact Book, 2014, **www.cia.gov.**

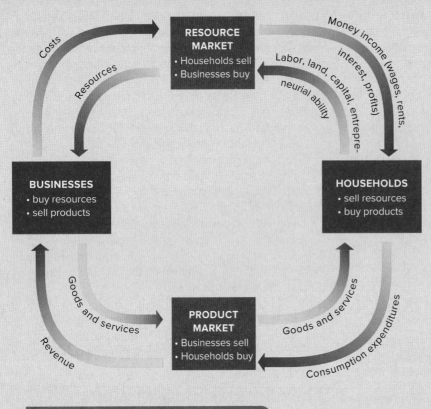

FIGURE 2.2 **The circular flow diagram.**
Resources flow from households to businesses through the resource market, and products flow from businesses to households through the product market. Opposite these real flows are monetary flows. Households receive income from businesses (their costs) through the resource market, and businesses receive revenue from households (their expenditures) through the product market.

QUICK QUIZ FOR FIGURE 2.2

1. The resource market is the place where:
   a. households sell products and businesses buy products.
   b. businesses sell resources and households sell products.
   c. households sell resources and businesses buy resources (or the services of resources).
   d. businesses sell resources and households buy resources (or the services of resources).

2. Which of the following would be determined in the product market?
   a. a manager's salary.
   b. the price of equipment used in a bottling plant.
   c. the price of 80 acres of farmland.
   d. the price of a new pair of athletic shoes.

3. In this circular flow diagram:
   a. money flows counterclockwise.
   b. resources flow counterclockwise.
   c. goods and services flow clockwise.
   d. households are on the selling side of the product market.

4. In this circular flow diagram:
   a. households spend income in the product market.
   b. firms sell resources to households.
   c. households receive income through the product market.
   d. households produce goods.

Answers: 1. c; 2. d; 3. b; 4. a

(and thereby controlling all of the land and capital owned by businesses). Thus, all of the income in the economy—all wages, rents, interest, and profits—flows to households because they provide the economy's labor, land, capital, and entrepreneurial ability.

Businesses

The blue rectangle on the left side of the circular flow diagram represents **businesses,** which are commercial establishments that attempt to earn profits for their owners by offering goods and services for sale. Businesses fall into three main categories.

- A **sole proprietorship** is a business owned and managed by a single person. The proprietor (the owner) may work alone or have employees. Examples include a woman who runs her own tree-cutting business and an independent accountant who, with two assistants, helps his clients with their taxes.

- The **partnership** form of business organization is a natural outgrowth of the sole proprietorship. In a partnership, two or more individuals (the partners) agree to own and operate a business together. They pool their financial resources and business skills to operate the business, and they share any profits or losses that the business may generate. Many law firms and dental practices are organized as partnerships, as are a wide variety of firms in many other industries.

- A **corporation** is an independent legal entity that can—on its own behalf—acquire resources, own assets, produce and sell products, incur debts, extend credit, sue and be sued, and otherwise engage in any legal business activity.

The fact that a corporation is an independent legal entity means that its owners bear no personal financial responsibility for the fulfillment of the corporation's debts and obligations. For instance, if a corporation has failed to repay a loan to a bank, the bank can sue the corporation but not its owners. Professional managers run most corporations. They are hired and supervised by a board of directors that is elected annually by the corporation's owners. Google, Ford, and American Airlines are examples of large corporations, but corporations come in all sizes and operate in every type of industry.

There currently are about 30 million businesses in the United States, ranging from enormous corporations like Walmart, with 2012 sales of $444 billion and 2.2 million employees, to single-person sole proprietorships with sales of less than $100 per day.

Businesses sell goods and services in the product market in order to obtain revenue, and they incur costs in the resource market when they purchase the labor, land, capital, and entrepreneurial ability that they need to produce their respective goods and services.

Product Market

The red rectangle at the bottom of the diagram represents the **product market,** the place where the goods and services produced by businesses are bought and sold. Households use the income they receive from the sale of resources to buy goods and services. The money that they spend on goods and services flows to businesses as revenue.

Resource Market

Finally, the red rectangle at the top of the circular flow diagram represents the **resource market** in which households sell resources to businesses. The households sell resources to generate income, and the businesses buy resources to produce goods and services. Productive resources flow from households to businesses, while money flows from businesses to households in the form of wages, rents, interest, and profits.

To summarize, the circular flow model depicts a complex web of economic activity in which businesses and households are both buyers and sellers. Businesses buy resources and sell products. Households buy products and sell resources. The counterclockwise flow of economic resources and finished products that is illustrated by the red arrows in Figure 2.2 is paid for by the clockwise flow of money income and consumption expenditures illustrated by the blue arrows.

> ### QUICK REVIEW 2.4
>
> ✓ Competition directs individuals and firms to unwittingly promote the social interest, as if guided by a benevolent "invisible hand."
> ✓ The command systems of the Soviet Union and pre-reform China failed as a result of the coordination problem and the incentive problem.
> ✓ The circular flow model illustrates how resources flow from households to businesses and how payments for those resources flow from businesses to households.

How the Market System Deals with Risk

LO2.6 Explain how the market system deals with risk.

Producing goods and services is risky. Input shortages can suddenly arise. Consumer preferences can quickly change. Natural disasters can destroy factories and cripple supply chains.

For an economic system to maximize its potential, it must develop methods for assessing and managing risk. The market system does so by confronting business owners with the financial consequences of their decisions. If they manage risks well, they may prosper. If they manage risks poorly, they may lose everything.

The Profit System

As explained in Chapter 1, entrepreneurial ability is the economic resource that organizes and directs the other three resources of land, labor, and capital toward productive uses. The owners of a firm may attempt to supply the entrepreneurial ability themselves. Or they can hire professional managers to supply the necessary leadership and decision making. Either way, it falls to those acting as the firm's entrepreneurs to deal with risk.

They are guided toward sensible decisions by the so-called *profit system*. This system is actually a *profit and loss* system because the entrepreneurs who must deal with risk and uncertainty gain profits if they choose wisely but suffer losses if they choose poorly. That provides them with a large financial incentive to avoid unnecessary risks and make prudent decisions.

By contrast, risk management tends to be done very poorly in command economies because the central planners who must allocate resources and deal with risk do not themselves face the possibility of losing money if they make bad decisions. As government employees, they tend to receive the same salaries whether things go well or poorly.

Shielding Employees and Suppliers from Business Risk

Under the market system, only a firm's owners are subject to business risk and the possibility of losing money. By contrast, the firm's employees and suppliers are shielded from business risk because they are legally entitled to receive their contracted wages and payments on time and in full regardless of whether the firm is earning a profit or generating a loss.

To see how this works, consider a pizza parlor that is being started in a small town. Its investors put up $50,000 to get it going. They rent a storefront, lease ovens, purchase computers, and leave some money set aside as a reserve.

The firm then has to attract employees. To do so, it will offer wage contracts that promise to pay employees every two weeks without regard to whether the firm is making a profit or generating a loss. This guarantee shields the firm's employees from the risks of owning and operating the business. They will get paid even if the pizza parlor is losing money.

In the same way, the contracts that the firm signs with its suppliers and with anyone who loans the firm money (for instance, the local bank) will also specify that they will be paid on time and in full no matter how the firm is doing in terms of profitability.

Because everyone else is legally entitled to get paid before the firm's owners, the firm's owners are referred to as **residual claimants** in business law. The owners are obligated to receive (claim) whatever profit or loss remains (is residual) after all other parties have been paid.

Dealing with Losses   So what happens if the firm starts losing money? In that case, the owners will take the financial hit. To be concrete, suppose that the pizza parlor loses $1,500 during the month of October because it runs up $11,500 in costs but generates only $10,000 in revenue. In that situation, the investors' wealth will shrink by $1,500 as the firm is forced to dip into its reserve to cover the loss. If the firm continues to lose money in subsequent months and exhausts the reserve, the owners will then have to decide whether they want to close the shop or put in additional money in the hope that things will turn around.

But throughout all those months of losses, the suppliers and employees are safeguarded. Because they are paid on time and in full, they are shielded from the firm's business risks and whether it is generating a profit or a loss.

As a result, however, they are not legally entitled to share in the profits if the firm does end up being profitable. That privilege is reserved under the market system for the firm's owners as their reward for bearing business risk. In exchange for making sure that everyone else is shielded if things go badly, the owners are legally entitled to take all of the profits if things go well.

Benefits of Restricting Business Risk to Owners

There are two major benefits that arise from the market system's restriction of business risk to owners and investors.

Shuffling the Deck

Economist Donald Boudreaux Marvels at the Way the Market System Systematically and Purposefully Arranges the World's Tens of Billions of Individual Resources.

In *The Future and Its Enemies,* Virginia Postrel notes the astonishing fact that if you thoroughly shuffle an ordinary deck of 52 playing cards, chances are practically 100 percent that the resulting arrangement of cards has never before existed. *Never.* Every time you shuffle a deck, you produce an arrangement of cards that exists for the first time in history.

The arithmetic works out that way. For a very small number of items, the number of possible arrangements is small. Three items, for example, can be arranged only six different ways. But the number of possible arrangements grows very large very quickly. The number of different ways to arrange five items is 120 . . . for ten items it's 3,628,800 . . . for fifteen items it's 1,307,674,368,000.

The number of different ways to arrange 52 items is 8.066×10^{67}. This is a *big* number. No human can comprehend its enormousness. By way of comparison, the number of possible ways to arrange a mere 20 items is 2,432,902,008,176,640,000—a number larger than the total number of seconds that have elapsed since the beginning of time ten billion years ago—and this number is Lilliputian compared to 8.066×10^{67}.

What's the significance of these facts about numbers? Consider the number of different resources available in the world—my labor, your labor, your land, oil, tungsten, cedar, coffee beans, chickens, rivers, the Empire State Building, [Microsoft] Windows, the wharves at Houston, the classrooms at Oxford, the airport at Miami, and on and on and on. No one can possibly count all of the different productive resources available for our use. But we can be sure that this number is at least in the tens of billions.

When you reflect on how incomprehensibly large is the number of ways to arrange a deck containing a mere 52 cards, the mind boggles at the number of different ways to arrange all the world's resources.

If our world were random—if resources combined together haphazardly, as if a giant took them all into his hands and tossed them down like so many [cards]—it's a virtual certainty that the resulting combination of resources would be useless. Unless this chance arrangement were quickly rearranged according to some productive logic, nothing worthwhile would be produced. We would all starve to death. Because only a tiny fraction of possible arrangements serves

Source: © Royalty-Free/Corbis RF

human ends, any arrangement will be useless if it is chosen randomly or with inadequate knowledge of how each and every resource might be productively combined with each other.

And yet, we witness all around us an arrangement of resources that's productive and serves human goals. Today's arrangement of resources might not be perfect, but it is vastly superior to most of the trillions upon trillions of other possible arrangements.

How have we managed to get one of the minuscule number of arrangements that works? The answer is private property—a social institution that encourages mutual accommodation.

Private property eliminates the possibility that resource arrangements will be random, for each resource owner chooses a course of action only if it promises rewards to the owner that exceed the rewards promised by all other available courses.

[The result] is a breathtakingly complex and productive arrangement of countless resources. This arrangement emerged over time (and is still emerging) as the result of billions upon billions of individual, daily, small decisions made by people seeking to better employ their resources and labor in ways that other people find helpful.

Source: Abridged from Donald J. Boudreaux, "Mutual Accommodation," *Ideas on Liberty,* May 2000, pp. 4–5. Used by permission of *The Freeman.*

Attracting Inputs Many people deeply dislike risk and would not be willing to participate in a business venture if they were exposed to the possibility of losing money. That is the case with many workers, who just want to do their jobs and get paid twice a month without having to worry about whether their employer is doing well or not. The same is true for most suppliers, who just want to get paid on time and in full for the inputs they supply to the firm.

For both groups, the concentration of business risk on owners and investors is very welcome because they can supply their resources to a firm without having to worry about the firm's profitability. That sense of security makes it much easier for firms to attract labor and other inputs, which in turn helps the economy innovate and grow.

Focusing Attention The profit system helps to achieve prudent risk management by focusing both the responsibility and the rewards for successfully managing risk onto a firm's owners. They can provide the risk-managing input of entrepreneurial ability themselves or hire it by paying a skilled manager. But either way, some individual's full-time job includes the specialized task of managing risk and making prudent decisions about the allocation of resources. By contrast, in a command system, the responsibility for managing risk tends to be spread out over several layers of government and many different committees so that nobody is personally responsible for bad outcomes.

QUICK REVIEW 2.5

✓ The market system incentivizes the prudent management of business risk by concentrating any profit or loss upon a firm's owners and investors.

✓ The market system shields employees, suppliers, and lenders from business risks, but in exchange for that protection, they are excluded from any profit that may be earned.

✓ By focusing risk on owners and investors, the market system (a) creates an incentive for owners and investors to hire managerial and entrepreneurial specialists to prudently manage business risks and (b) encourages the participation of workers, suppliers, and lenders who dislike risk.

SUMMARY

LO2.1 Differentiate between laissez-faire capitalism, the command system, and the market system.

Laissez-faire capitalism is a hypothetical economic system in which government's role would be restricted to protecting private property and enforcing contracts. All real-world economic systems have featured a more extensive role for government. Governments in command systems own nearly all property and resources and make nearly all decisions about what to produce, how to produce it, and who gets the output. Most countries today, including the United States, have market systems in which the government does play a large role, but in which most property and resources are privately owned and markets are the major force in determining what to produce, how to produce it, and who gets it.

LO2.2 List the main characteristics of the market system.

The market system is characterized by the private ownership of resources, including capital, and the freedom of individuals to engage in economic activities of their choice to advance their material well-being. Self-interest is the driving force of such an economy and competition functions as a regulatory or control mechanism.

In the market system, markets, prices, and profits organize and make effective the many millions of individual economic decisions that occur daily.

Specialization, use of advanced technology, and the extensive use of capital goods are common features of market systems. Functioning as a medium of exchange, money eliminates the problems of bartering and permits easy trade and greater specialization, both domestically and internationally.

LO2.3 Explain how the market system answers the five fundamental questions of what to produce, how to produce, who obtains the output, how to adjust to change, and how to promote progress.

Every economy faces five fundamental questions: (a) What goods and services will be produced? (b) How will the goods and services be produced? (c) Who will get the goods and services? (d) How will the system accommodate change? (e) How will the system promote progress?

The market system produces products whose production and sale yield total revenue sufficient to cover total cost. It does not produce products for which total revenue continuously falls short of total cost. Competition forces firms to use the lowest-cost production techniques.

Economic profit (total revenue minus total cost) indicates that an industry is prosperous and promotes its expansion. Losses signify that an industry is not prosperous and hasten its contraction.

Consumer sovereignty means that both businesses and resource suppliers are subject to the wants of consumers. Through their dollar votes, consumers decide on the composition of output.

The prices that a household receives for the resources it supplies to the economy determine that household's income. This income determines the household's claim on the economy's output. Those who have income to spend get the products produced in the market system.

By communicating changes in consumer tastes to entrepreneurs and resource suppliers, the market system prompts appropriate adjustments in the allocation of the economy's resources. The market system also encourages technological advance and capital accumulation, both of which raise a nation's standard of living.

LO2.4 Explain the operation of the "invisible hand" and why market economies usually do a better job than command economies at efficiently transforming economic resources into desirable output.

Competition, the primary mechanism of control in the market economy, promotes a unity of self-interest and social interests. As if directed by an invisible hand, competition harnesses the self-interested motives of businesses and resource suppliers to further the social interest.

The command systems of the Soviet Union and pre-reform China met their demise because of coordination difficulties caused by central planning and the lack of a profit incentive. The coordination problem resulted in bottlenecks, inefficiencies, and a focus on a limited number of products. The incentive problem discouraged product improvement, new product development, and entrepreneurship.

LO2.5 Describe the mechanics of the circular flow model.

The circular flow model illustrates the flows of resources and products from households to businesses and from businesses to households, along with the corresponding monetary flows. Businesses are on the buying side of the resource market and the selling side of the product market. Households are on the selling side of the resource market and the buying side of the product market.

LO2.6 Explain how the market system deals with risk.

By focusing business risks onto owners, the market system encourages the participation of workers and suppliers who dislike risk while at the same time creating a strong incentive for owners to manage business risks prudently.

TERMS AND CONCEPTS

economic system	specialization	households
laissez-faire capitalism	division of labor	businesses
command system	medium of exchange	sole proprietorship
market system	barter	partnership
private property	money	corporation
freedom of enterprise	consumer sovereignty	product market
freedom of choice	dollar votes	resource market
self-interest	creative destruction	residual claimant
competition	invisible hand	
market	circular flow diagram	

The following and additional problems can be found in ▣ **connect**

DISCUSSION QUESTIONS

1. Contrast how a market system and a command economy try to cope with economic scarcity. **LO2.1**
2. How does self-interest help achieve society's economic goals? Why is there such a wide variety of desired goods and services in a market system? In what way are entrepreneurs and businesses at the helm of the economy but commanded by consumers? **LO2.2**
3. Why is private property, and the protection of property rights, so critical to the success of the market system? How do property rights encourage cooperation? **LO2.2**
4. What are the advantages of using capital in the production process? What is meant by the term "division of labor"? What are the advantages of specialization in the use of human and material resources? Explain why exchange is the necessary consequence of specialization. **LO2.2**
5. What problem does barter entail? Indicate the economic significance of money as a medium of exchange. What is meant by the statement "We want money only to part with it"? **LO2.2**
6. Evaluate and explain the following statements: **LO2.2**
   a. The market system is a profit-and-loss system.
   b. Competition is the disciplinarian of the market economy.
7. Some large hardware stores, such as Home Depot, boast of carrying as many as 20,000 different products in each store. What motivated the producers of those individual products to make them and offer them for sale? How did the producers decide on the best combinations of resources to use? Who made those resources available, and why? Who decides whether these particular hardware products should continue to be produced and offered for sale? **LO2.3**

8. What is meant by the term "creative destruction"? How does the emergence of MP3 (or iPod) technology relate to this idea? **LO2.3**

9. In a sentence, describe the meaning of the phrase "invisible hand." **LO2.4**

10. In market economies, firms rarely worry about the availability of inputs to produce their products, whereas in command economies input availability is a constant concern. Why the difference? **LO2.4**

11. Distinguish between the resource market and the product market in the circular flow model. In what way are businesses and households both sellers and buyers in this model? What are the flows in the circular flow model? **LO2.5**

12. How does shielding employees and suppliers from business risk help to improve economic outcomes? Who is responsible for managing business risks in the market system? **LO2.6**

13. **LAST WORD** What explains why millions of economic resources tend to get arranged logically and productively rather than haphazardly and unproductively?

REVIEW QUESTIONS

1. Decide whether each of the following descriptions most closely corresponds to being part of a command system, a market system, or a laissez-faire system. **LO2.1**
   a. A woman who wants to start a flower shop finds she cannot do so unless the central government has already decided to allow a flower shop in her area.
   b. Shops stock and sell the goods their customers want but the government levies a sales tax on each transaction in order to fund elementary schools, public libraries, and welfare programs for the poor.
   c. The only taxes levied by the government are to pay for national defense, law enforcement, and a legal system designed to enforce contracts between private citizens.

2. Match each term with the correct definition. **LO2.2**
   private property
   freedom of enterprise
   mutually agreeable
   freedom of choice
   self-interest
   competition
   market
   a. An institution that brings buyers and sellers together.
   b. The right of private persons and firms to obtain, control, employ, dispose of, and bequeath land, capital, and other property.
   c. The presence in a market of independent buyers and sellers who compete with one another and who are free to enter and exit the market as they each see fit.
   d. The freedom of firms to obtain economic resources, decide what products to produce with those resources, and sell those products in markets of their choice.
   e. What each individual or firm believes is best for itself and seeks to obtain.
   f. Economic transactions willingly undertaken by both the buyer and the seller because each feels that the transaction will make him or her better off.
   g. The freedom of resource owners to dispose of their resources as they think best; of workers to enter any line of work for which they are qualified; and of consumers to spend their incomes in whatever way they feel is most appropriate.

3. True or False: Money must be issued by a government for people to accept it. **LO2.2**

4. Assume that a business firm finds that its profit is greatest when it produces $40 worth of product A. Suppose also that each of the three techniques shown in the following table will produce the desired output. **LO2.3**
   a. With the resource prices shown, which technique will the firm choose? Why? Will production using that technique entail profit or loss? What will be the amount of that profit or loss? Will the industry expand or contract? When will that expansion or contraction end?
   b. Assume now that a new technique, technique 4, is developed. It combines 2 units of labor, 2 of land, 6 of capital, and 3 of entrepreneurial ability. In view of the resource prices in the table, will the firm adopt the new technique? Explain your answer.
   c. Suppose that an increase in the labor supply causes the price of labor to fall to $1.50 per unit, all other resource prices remaining unchanged. Which technique will the producer now choose? Explain.
   d. "The market system causes the economy to conserve most in the use of resources that are particularly scarce in supply. Resources that are scarcest relative to the demand for them have the highest prices. As a result, producers use these resources as sparingly as is possible." Evaluate this statement. Does your answer to part c, above, bear out this contention? Explain.

Resource	Price per Unit of Resource	Resource Units Required		
		Technique 1	Technique 2	Technique 3
Labor	$3	5	2	3
Land	4	2	4	2
Capital	2	2	4	5
Entrepreneurial ability	2	4	2	4

5. Identify each of the following quotes as being an example of either: the coordination problem, the invisible hand, creative destruction, or the incentive problem. **LO2.4**
   a. "If you compare a list of today's most powerful and profitable companies with a similar list from 30 years ago, you will see lots of new entries."

b. "Managers in the old Soviet Union often sacrificed product quality and variety because they were being awarded bonuses for quantitative, not qualitative, targets."

c. "Each day, central planners in the old Soviet Union were tasked with setting 27 million prices—correctly."

d. "It is not from the benevolence of the butcher, the brewer, or the baker that we expect our dinner, but from their regard to their own interest."

6. True or False: Households sell finished products to businesses. LO2.6

7. Franklin, John, Henry, and Harry have decided to pool their financial resources and business skills in order to open up and run a coffee shop. They will share any profits or losses that the business generates and will be personally responsible for making good on any debt that their business undertakes. Their business should be classified as a: LO2.6
   a. corporation.
   b. sole proprietorship.
   c. partnership.
   d. none of the above.

8. Ted and Fred are the owners of a gas station. They invested $150,000 each and pay an employee named Lawrence $35,000 per year. This year revenues are $900,000, while costs are $940,000. Who is legally responsible for bearing the $40,000 loss? LO2.6
   a. Lawrence.
   b. Ted.
   c. Fred.
   d. Ted and Fred.
   e. Lawrence, Ted, and Fred.

PROBLEMS

1. Table 2.1 contains information on three techniques for producing $15 worth of bar soap. Assume that we said "$15 worth of bar soap" because soap costs $3 per bar and all three techniques produce 5 bars of soap ($15 = $3 per bar × 5 bars). So you know each technique produces 5 bars of soap. LO2.3
   a. What technique will you want to use if the price of a bar of soap falls to $2.75? What if the price of a bar of soap rises to $4? To $5?
   b. How many bars of soap will you want to produce if the price of a bar of soap falls to $2.00?
   c. Suppose that the price of soap is again $3 per bar but that the prices of all four resources are now $1 per unit. Which is now the least-profitable technique?
   d. If the resource prices return to their original levels (the ones shown in the table), but a new technique is invented that can produce 3 bars of soap (yes, 3 bars, not 5 bars!), using 1 unit of each of the four resources, will firms prefer the new technique?

2. Suppose Natasha currently makes $50,000 per year working as a manager at a cable TV company. She then develops two possible entrepreneurial business opportunities. In one, she will quit her job to start an organic soap company. In the other, she will try to develop an Internet-based competitor to the local cable company. For the soap-making opportunity, she anticipates annual revenue of $465,000 and costs for the necessary land, labor, and capital of $395,000 per year. For the Internet opportunity, she anticipates costs for land, labor, and capital of $3,250,000 per year as compared to revenues of $3,275,000 per year. (a) Should she quit her current job to become an entrepreneur? (b) If she does quit her current job, which opportunity would she pursue? LO2.3

3. With current technology, suppose a firm is producing 400 loaves of banana bread daily. Also assume that the least-cost combination of resources in producing those loaves is 5 units of labor, 7 units of land, 2 units of capital, and 1 unit of entrepreneurial ability, selling at prices of $40, $60, $60, and $20, respectively. If the firm can sell these 400 loaves at $2 per unit, what is its total revenue? Its total cost? Its profit or loss? Will it continue to produce banana bread? If this firm's situation is typical for the other makers of banana bread, will resources flow toward or away from this bakery good? LO2.3

4. Let's put dollar amounts on the flows in the circular flow diagram of Figure 2.2. LO2.5
   a. Suppose that businesses buy a total of $100 billion of the four resources (labor, land, capital, and entrepreneurial ability) from households. If households receive $60 billion in wages, $10 billion in rent, and $20 billion in interest, how much are households paid for providing entrepreneurial ability?
   b. If households spend $55 billion on goods and $45 billion on services, how much in revenues do businesses receive in the product market?

Price, Quantity, and Efficiency

Demand, Supply, and Market Equilibrium

Learning Objectives

LO3.1 Characterize and give examples of markets.

LO3.2 Describe *demand* and explain how it can change.

LO3.3 Describe *supply* and explain how it can change.

LO3.4 Relate how supply and demand interact to determine market equilibrium.

LO3.5 Explain how changes in supply and demand affect equilibrium prices and quantities.

LO3.6 Identify what government-set prices are and how they can cause product surpluses and shortages.

LO3.7 (Appendix) Illustrate how supply and demand analysis can provide insights on actual-economy situations.

The model of supply and demand is the economics profession's greatest contribution to human understanding because it explains the operation of the markets on which we depend for nearly everything that we eat, drink, or consume. The model is so powerful and so widely used that to many people it *is* economics.

This chapter explains how the model works and how it can explain both the *quantities* that are bought and sold in markets as well as the *prices* at which they trade.

Markets

LO3.1 Characterize and give examples of markets.

Markets bring together buyers ("demanders") and sellers ("suppliers"). The corner gas station, an e-commerce site, the local bakery shop, a farmer's roadside stand—all are familiar markets. The New York Stock Exchange and the Chicago Board of Trade are markets in which buyers and sellers from all over the world communicate with one another to buy and sell bonds, stocks, and commodities. Auctioneers bring together potential buyers and sellers of art, livestock, used farm equipment, and, sometimes, real estate. In labor markets, new college graduates "sell" and employers "buy" specific labor services.

Some markets are local; others are national or international. Some are highly personal, involving face-to-face contact between demander and supplier; others are faceless, with buyer and seller never seeing or knowing each other.

To keep things simple, we will focus in this chapter on markets in which large numbers of independently acting buyers and sellers come together to buy and sell standardized products. Markets with these characteristics are the economy's most highly competitive. They include the wheat market, the stock market, and the market for foreign currencies. All such markets involve demand, supply, price, and quantity. As you will soon see, the price is "discovered" through the interacting decisions of buyers and sellers.

Demand

LO3.2 Describe *demand* and explain how it can change.

Demand is a schedule or a curve that shows the various amounts of a product that consumers are willing and able to purchase at each of a series of possible prices during a specified period of time.[1] Demand shows the quantities of a product that will be purchased at various possible prices, *other things equal*. Demand can easily be shown in table form. The table in Figure 3.1 is a hypothetical **demand schedule** for a *single consumer* purchasing bushels of corn.

The table reveals the relationship between the various prices of corn and the quantity of corn a particular consumer would be willing and able to purchase at each of these prices. We say "willing and able" because willingness alone is not effective in the market. You may be willing to buy a plasma television set, but if that willingness is not backed by the necessary dollars, it will not be effective and, therefore, will not be reflected in the market. In the table in Figure 3.1, if the price of corn were $5 per bushel, our consumer would be willing and able to buy 10 bushels per week; if it were $4, the consumer would be willing and able to buy 20 bushels per week; and so forth.

---

[1]This definition obviously is worded to apply to product markets. To adjust it to apply to resource markets, substitute the word "resource" for "product" and the word "businesses" for "consumers."

FIGURE 3.1 An individual buyer's demand for corn. Because price and quantity demanded are inversely related, an individual's demand schedule graphs as a downsloping curve such as *D*. Other things equal, consumers will buy more of a product as its price declines and less of the product as its price rises. (Here and in later figures, *P* stands for price and *Q* stands for quantity demanded or supplied.)

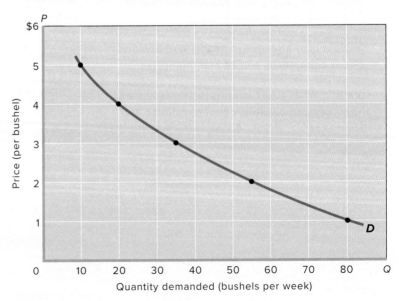

Demand for Corn	
Price per Bushel	Quantity Demanded per Week
$5	10
4	20
3	35
2	55
1	80

The table does not tell us which of the five possible prices will actually exist in the corn market. That depends on the interaction between demand and supply. Demand is simply a statement of a buyer's plans, or intentions, with respect to the purchase of a product.

To be meaningful, the quantities demanded at each price must relate to a specific period—a day, a week, a month. Saying "A consumer will buy 10 bushels of corn at $5 per bushel" is meaningless. Saying "A consumer will buy 10 bushels of corn *per week* at $5 per bushel" is meaningful. Unless a specific time period is stated, we do not know whether the demand for a product is large or small.

Law of Demand

A fundamental characteristic of demand is this: Other things equal, as price falls, the quantity demanded rises, and as price rises, the quantity demanded falls. In short, there is a negative or *inverse* relationship between price and quantity demanded. Economists call this inverse relationship the **law of demand.**

The other-things-equal assumption is critical here. Many factors other than the price of the product being considered affect the amount purchased. For example, the quantity of Nikes purchased will depend not only on the price of Nikes but also on the prices of such substitutes as Reeboks, Adidas, and New Balances. The law of demand in this case says that fewer Nikes will be purchased if the price of Nikes rises and if the prices of Reeboks, Adidas, and New Balances all remain constant. In short, if the *relative price* of Nikes rises, fewer Nikes will be bought. However, if the price of Nikes and the prices of all other competing shoes increase by some amount—say, $5—consumers might buy more, fewer, or the same number of Nikes.

Why the inverse relationship between price and quantity demanded? Let's look at three explanations, beginning with the simplest one:

- The law of demand is consistent with common sense. People ordinarily *do* buy more of a product at a low price than at a high price. Price is an obstacle that deters consumers from buying. The higher that obstacle, the less of a product they will buy; the lower the price obstacle, the more they will buy. The fact that businesses have "sales" to clear out unsold items is evidence of their belief in the law of demand.

- In any specific time period, each buyer of a product will derive less satisfaction (or benefit, or utility) from each successive unit of the product consumed. The second Big Mac will yield less satisfaction to the consumer than the first, and the third still less than the second. That is, consumption is subject to **diminishing marginal utility.** And because successive units of a particular product yield less and less marginal utility,

consumers will buy additional units only if the price of those units is progressively reduced.

- We can also explain the law of demand in terms of income and substitution effects. The **income effect** indicates that a lower price increases the purchasing power of a buyer's money income, enabling the buyer to purchase more of the product than before. A higher price has the opposite effect. The **substitution effect** suggests that at a lower price buyers have the incentive to substitute what is now a less expensive product for other products that are now *relatively* more expensive. The product whose price has fallen is now "a better deal" relative to the other products.

For example, a decline in the price of chicken will increase the purchasing power of consumer incomes, enabling people to buy more chicken (the income effect). At a lower price, chicken is relatively more attractive and consumers tend to substitute it for pork, lamb, beef, and fish (the substitution effect). The income and substitution effects combine to make consumers able and willing to buy more of a product at a low price than at a high price.

The Demand Curve

The inverse relationship between price and quantity demanded for any product can be represented on a simple graph, in which, by convention, we measure *quantity demanded* on the horizontal axis and *price* on the vertical axis. In the graph in Figure 3.1 we have plotted the five price-quantity data points listed in the accompanying table and connected the points with a smooth curve, labeled *D*. Such a curve is called a **demand curve.** Its downward slope reflects the law of demand—people buy more of a product, service, or resource as its price falls. The relationship between price and quantity demanded is inverse (or negative).

The table and graph in Figure 3.1 contain exactly the same data and reflect the same relationship between price and quantity demanded. But the graph shows that relationship much more simply and clearly than a table or a description in words.

Market Demand

So far, we have concentrated on just one consumer. But competition requires that more than one buyer be present in each market. By adding the quantities demanded by all consumers at each of the various possible prices, we can get from *individual* demand to *market* demand. If there are just three buyers in the market, as represented in the table in Figure 3.2, it is relatively easy to determine the total quantity demanded at each price. Figure 3.2 shows the graphical summing procedure: At each price we sum horizontally the quantities demanded by Joe, Jen,

FIGURE 3.2 **Market demand for corn, three buyers.** The market demand curve *D* is the horizontal summation of the individual demand curves (D_1, D_2, and D_3) of all the consumers in the market. At the price of $3, for example, the three individual curves yield a total quantity demanded of 100 bushels (= 35 + 39 + 26).

Market Demand for Corn, Three Buyers						
Price per Bushel	Quantity Demanded					Total Quantity Demanded per Week
	Joe		Jen		Jay	
$5	10	+	12	+	8	= 30
4	20	+	23	+	17	= 60
3	35	+	39	+	26	= 100
2	55	+	60	+	39	= 154
1	80	+	87	+	54	= 221

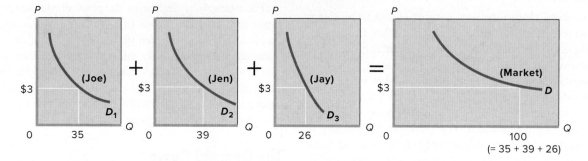

and Jay to obtain the total quantity demanded at that price; we then plot the price and the total quantity demanded as one point on the market demand curve. At the price of $3, for example, the three individual curves yield a total quantity demanded of 100 bushels (= 35 + 39 + 26).

Competition, of course, ordinarily entails many more than three buyers of a product. To avoid hundreds or thousands or millions of additions, we suppose that all the buyers in a market are willing and able to buy the same amounts at each of the possible prices. Then we just multiply those amounts by the number of buyers to obtain the market demand. That is how we arrived at the demand schedule and demand curve D_1 in Figure 3.3 for a market of 200 corn buyers, each with a demand as shown in the table in Figure 3.1.

In constructing a demand curve such as D_1 in Figure 3.3, economists assume that price is the most important influence on the amount of any product purchased. But economists know that other factors can and do affect purchases. These factors, called **determinants of demand,** are assumed to be constant when a demand curve like D_1 is drawn. They are the "other things equal" in the relationship between price and quantity demanded. When any of these determinants changes, the demand curve will shift to the right or left. For this reason, determinants of demand are sometimes referred to as *demand shifters.*

The basic determinants of demand are (1) consumers' tastes (preferences), (2) the number of buyers in the market, (3) consumers' incomes, (4) the prices of related goods, and (5) consumer expectations.

Changes in Demand

A change in one or more of the determinants of demand will change the demand data (the demand schedule) in the table accompanying Figure 3.3 and therefore the location of the demand curve there. A change in the demand schedule or, graphically, a shift in the demand curve is called a *change in demand.*

If consumers desire to buy more corn at each possible price than is reflected in column 2 in the table in Figure 3.3, that *increase in demand* is shown as a shift of the demand curve to the right, say, from D_1 to D_2. Conversely, a *decrease in demand* occurs when consumers buy less corn at each possible price than is indicated in column 2. The leftward shift of the demand curve from D_1 to D_3 in Figure 3.3 shows that situation.

Now let's see how changes in each determinant affect demand.

Tastes A favorable change in consumer tastes (preferences) for a product—a change that makes the product more desirable—means that more of it will be demanded at each price. Demand will increase; the demand curve will shift rightward. An unfavorable change in consumer preferences will decrease demand, shifting the demand curve to the left.

New products may affect consumer tastes; for example, the introduction of digital cameras greatly decreased the demand for film cameras. Consumers' concern over the health hazards of cholesterol and obesity have increased the demand

FIGURE 3.3 Changes in the demand for corn. A change in one or more of the determinants of demand causes a change in demand. An increase in demand is shown as a shift of the demand curve to the right, as from D_1 to D_2. A decrease in demand is shown as a shift of the demand curve to the left, as from D_1 to D_3. These changes in demand are to be distinguished from a change in quantity demanded, which is caused by a change in the price of the product, as shown by a movement from, say, point a to point b on fixed demand curve D_1.

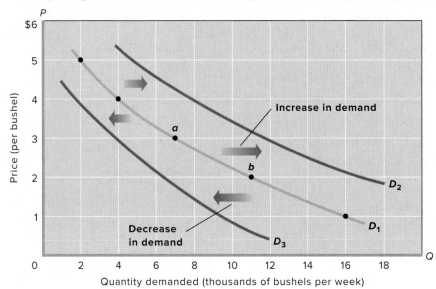

Market Demand for Corn, 200 Buyers, (D_1)	
(1) Price per Bushel	(2) Total Quantity Demanded per Week
$5	2,000
4	4,000
3	7,000
2	11,000
1	16,000

for broccoli, low-calorie beverages, and fresh fruit while decreasing the demand for beef, veal, eggs, and whole milk. Over the past twenty years, the demand for coffee drinks and table wine has greatly increased, driven by a change in tastes. So, too, has the demand for touch-screen mobile phones and fuel-efficient hybrid vehicles.

Number of Buyers An increase in the number of buyers in a market is likely to increase demand; a decrease in the number of buyers will probably decrease demand. For example, the rising number of older persons in the United States in recent years has increased the demand for motor homes, medical care, and retirement communities. Large-scale immigration from Mexico has greatly increased the demand for a range of goods and services in the Southwest, including Mexican food products in local grocery stores. Improvements in communications have given financial markets international range and have thus increased the demand for stocks and bonds. International trade agreements have reduced foreign trade barriers to American farm commodities, increasing the number of buyers and therefore the demand for those products.

In contrast, emigration (out-migration) from many small rural communities has reduced the population and thus the demand for housing, home appliances, and auto repair in those towns.

Income How changes in income affect demand is a more complex matter. For most products, a rise in income causes an increase in demand. Consumers typically buy more steaks, furniture, and electronic equipment as their incomes increase.

Conversely, the demand for such products declines as their incomes fall. Products whose demand varies *directly* with money income are called *superior goods,* or **normal goods.**

Although most products are normal goods, there are some exceptions. As incomes increase beyond some point, the demand for used clothing, retread tires, and third-hand automobiles may decrease because the higher incomes enable consumers to buy new versions of those products. Rising incomes may also decrease the demand for soy-enhanced hamburger. Similarly, rising incomes may cause the demand for charcoal grills to decline as wealthier consumers switch to gas grills. Goods whose demand varies *inversely* with money income are called **inferior goods.**

Prices of Related Goods A change in the price of a related good may either increase or decrease the demand for a product, depending on whether the related good is a substitute or a complement:

- A **substitute good** is one that can be used in place of another good.

- A **complementary good** is one that is used together with another good.

Substitutes Häagen-Dazs ice cream and Ben & Jerry's ice cream are substitute goods or, simply, *substitutes.* When two products are substitutes, an increase in the price of one will increase the demand for the other. Conversely, a decrease in the price of one will decrease the demand for the other. For example, when the price of Häagen-Dazs ice cream rises, consumers will buy less of it and increase their demand for Ben & Jerry's ice cream. When the price of Colgate toothpaste declines, the demand for Crest decreases. So it is with other product pairs such as Nikes and Reeboks, Budweiser and Miller beer, or Chevrolets and Fords. They are *substitutes in consumption*.

Complements Because complementary goods (or, simply, *complements*) are used together, they are typically demanded jointly. Examples include computers and software, cell phones and cellular service, and snowboards and lift tickets. If the price of a complement (for example, lettuce) goes up, the demand for the related good (salad dressing) will decline. Conversely, if the price of a complement (for example, tuition) falls, the demand for a related good (textbooks) will increase.

Unrelated Goods The vast majority of goods are not related to one another and are called *independent goods*. Examples are butter and golf balls, potatoes and automobiles, and bananas and wristwatches. A change in the price of one has little or no effect on the demand for the other.

Consumer Expectations Changes in consumer expectations may shift demand. A newly formed expectation of higher future prices may cause consumers to buy now in order to "beat" the anticipated price rises, thus increasing current demand. That is often what happens in so-called hot real estate markets. Buyers rush in because they think the price of new homes will continue to escalate rapidly. Some buyers fear being "priced out of the market" and therefore not obtaining the home they desire. Other buyers—speculators—believe they will be able to sell the houses later at a higher price. Whichever their motivation, these buyers increase the current demand for houses.

Similarly, a change in expectations concerning future income may prompt consumers to change their current spending. For example, first-round NFL draft choices may splurge on new luxury cars in anticipation of lucrative professional football contracts. Or workers who become fearful of losing their jobs may reduce their demand for, say, vacation travel.

In summary, an *increase* in demand—the decision by consumers to buy larger quantities of a product at each possible price—may be caused by:

- A favorable change in consumer tastes.
- An increase in the number of buyers.
- Rising incomes if the product is a normal good.
- Falling incomes if the product is an inferior good.
- An increase in the price of a substitute good.
- A decrease in the price of a complementary good.
- A new consumer expectation that either prices or income will be higher in the future.

TABLE 3.1 Determinants of Demand: Factors That Shift the Demand Curve

Determinant	Examples
Change in buyer tastes	Physical fitness rises in popularity, increasing the demand for jogging shoes and bicycles; cell phone popularity rises, reducing the demand for landline phones.
Change in number of buyers	A decline in the birthrate reduces the demand for children's toys.
Change in income	A rise in incomes increases the demand for normal goods such as restaurant meals, sports tickets, and necklaces while reducing the demand for inferior goods such as cabbage, turnips, and inexpensive wine.
Change in the prices of related goods	A reduction in airfares reduces the demand for bus transportation (substitute goods); a decline in the price of DVD players increases the demand for DVD movies (complementary goods).
Change in consumer expectations	Inclement weather in South America creates an expectation of higher future coffee bean prices, thereby increasing today's demand for coffee beans.

You should "reverse" these generalizations to explain a *decrease* in demand. Table 3.1 provides additional illustrations of the determinants of demand.

Changes in Quantity Demanded

A *change in demand* must not be confused with a *change in quantity demanded*. A **change in demand** is a shift of the demand curve to the right (an increase in demand) or to the left (a decrease in demand). It occurs because the consumer's state of mind about purchasing the product has been altered in response to a change in one or more of the determinants of demand. Recall that "demand" is a schedule or a curve; therefore, a "change in demand" means a change in the schedule and a shift of the curve.

In contrast, a **change in quantity demanded** is a movement from one point to another point—from one price-quantity combination to another—on a fixed demand curve. The cause of such a change is an increase or decrease in the price of the product under consideration. In the table in Figure 3.3, for example, a decline in the price of corn from $5 to $4 will increase the quantity demanded of corn from 2,000 to 4,000 bushels.

In Figure 3.3 the shift of the demand curve D_1 to either D_2 or D_3 is a change in demand. But the movement from point *a* to point *b* on curve D_1 represents a change in quantity demanded: Demand has not changed; it is the entire curve, and it remains fixed in place.

Supply

LO3.3 Describe *supply* and explain how it can change.

Supply is a schedule or curve showing the various amounts of a product that producers are willing and able to make available for sale at each of a series of possible prices during a specific period.[2] The table in Figure 3.4 is a hypothetical **supply schedule** for a single producer of corn. It shows the quantities of corn that will be supplied at various prices, other things equal.

---

[2]This definition is worded to apply to product markets. To adjust it to apply to resource markets, substitute "resource" for "product" and "owners" for "producers.

Law of Supply

The table in Figure 3.4 shows that a positive or direct relationship prevails between price and quantity supplied. As price rises, the quantity supplied rises; as price falls, the quantity supplied falls. This relationship is called the **law of supply.** A supply schedule tells us that, other things equal, firms will produce and offer for sale more of their product at a high price than at a low price. This, again, is basically common sense.

Price is an obstacle from the standpoint of the consumer, who is on the paying end. The higher the price, the less the consumer will buy. But the supplier is on the receiving end of the product's price. To a supplier, price represents *revenue,* which serves as an incentive to produce and sell a product. The higher the price, the greater this incentive and the greater the quantity supplied.

Consider a farmer who is deciding on how much corn to plant. As corn prices rise, as shown in the table in Figure 3.4, the farmer finds it profitable to plant more corn. And the higher corn prices enable the farmer to cover the increased costs associated with more intensive cultivation and the use of more seed, fertilizer, and pesticides. The overall result is more corn.

Now consider a manufacturer. Beyond some quantity of production, manufacturers usually encounter increases in *marginal cost*—the added cost of producing one more unit of output. Certain productive resources—in particular, the firm's plant and machinery—cannot be expanded quickly, so the firm uses more of other resources such as labor to produce more output. But as labor becomes more abundant relative to the fixed plant and equipment, the additional workers have relatively less space and access to equipment. For example, the added workers may have to wait to gain access to machines. As a result, each added worker produces less added output, and the marginal cost

---

FIGURE 3.4 An individual producer's supply of corn. Because price and quantity supplied are directly related, the supply curve for an individual producer graphs as an upsloping curve. Other things equal, producers will offer more of a product for sale as its price rises and less of the product for sale as its price falls.

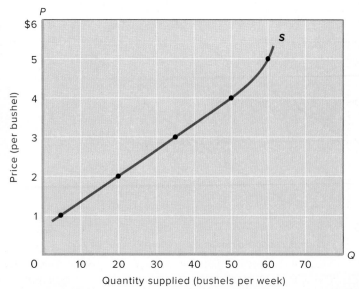

Supply of Corn	
Price per Bushel	Quantity Supplied per Week
$5	60
4	50
3	35
2	20
1	5

of successive units of output rises accordingly. The firm will not produce the more costly units unless it receives a higher price for them. Again, price and quantity supplied are directly related.

The Supply Curve

As with demand, it is convenient to represent individual supply graphically. In Figure 3.4, curve S is the **supply curve** that corresponds with the price–quantity supplied data in the accompanying table. The upward slope of the curve reflects the law of supply—producers offer more of a good, service, or resource for sale as its price rises. The relationship between price and quantity supplied is positive, or direct.

Market Supply

Market supply is derived from individual supply in exactly the same way that market demand is derived from individual demand. We sum the quantities supplied by each producer at each price. That is, we obtain the market supply curve by "horizontally adding" the supply curves of the individual producers. The price–quantity supplied data in the table accompanying Figure 3.5 are for an assumed 200 identical producers in the market, each willing to supply corn according to the supply schedule shown in Figure 3.4. Curve S_1 in Figure 3.5 is a graph of the market supply data. Note that the values of the axes in Figure 3.5 are the same as those used in our graph of market demand (Figure 3.3). The only difference is that we change the label on the horizontal axis from "quantity demanded" to "quantity supplied."

Determinants of Supply

In constructing a supply curve, we assume that price is the most significant influence on the quantity supplied of any product. But other factors (the "other things equal") can and do affect supply. The supply curve is drawn on the assumption that these other things are fixed and do not change. If one of them does change, a *change in supply* will occur, meaning that the entire supply curve will shift.

The basic **determinants of supply** are (1) resource prices, (2) technology, (3) taxes and subsidies, (4) prices of other goods, (5) producer expectations, and (6) the number of sellers in the market. A change in any one or more of these determinants of supply, or *supply shifters,* will move the supply curve for a product either right or left. A shift to the *right,* as from S_1 to S_2 in Figure 3.5, signifies an *increase* in supply: Producers supply larger quantities of the product at each possible price. A shift to the *left,* as from S_1 to S_3, indicates a *decrease* in supply: Producers offer less output at each price.

Changes in Supply

Let's consider how changes in each of the determinants affect supply. The key idea is that costs are a major factor underlying supply curves; anything that affects costs (other than changes in output itself) usually shifts the supply curve.

Resource Prices   The prices of the resources used in the production process help determine the costs of production incurred by firms. Higher *resource* prices raise production costs and, assuming a particular *product* price, squeeze profits. That reduction in profits reduces the incentive for firms to supply output at each product price. For example, an increase in the price of sand, crushed rock, or Portland cement will increase the cost of producing concrete and reduce its supply.

In contrast, lower *resource* prices reduce production costs and increase profits. So when resource prices fall, firms

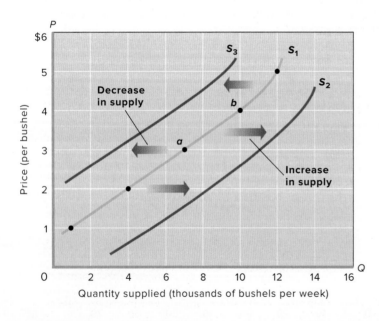

FIGURE 3.5 Changes in the supply of corn. A change in one or more of the determinants of supply causes a change in supply. An increase in supply is shown as a rightward shift of the supply curve, as from S_1 to S_2. A decrease in supply is depicted as a leftward shift of the curve, as from S_1 to S_3. In contrast, a change in the *quantity supplied* is caused by a change in the product's price and is shown by a movement from one point to another, as from *b* to *a* on fixed supply curve S_1.

Market Supply of Corn, 200 Producers, (S_1)	
(1) **Price per Bushel**	**(2)** **Total Quantity Supplied per Week**
$5	12,000
4	10,000
3	7,000
2	4,000
1	1,000

supply greater output at each product price. For example, a decrease in the price of iron ore will decrease the price of steel.

Technology Improvements in technology (techniques of production) enable firms to produce units of output with fewer resources. Because resources are costly, using fewer of them lowers production costs and increases supply. Example: Technological advances in producing flat-panel computer monitors have greatly reduced their cost. Thus, manufacturers will now offer more such monitors than previously at the various prices; the supply of flat-panel monitors has increased.

Taxes and Subsidies Businesses treat most taxes as costs. An increase in sales or property taxes will increase production costs and reduce supply. In contrast, subsidies are "taxes in reverse." If the government subsidizes the production of a good, it in effect lowers the producers' costs and increases supply.

Prices of Other Goods Firms that produce a particular product, say, soccer balls, can sometimes use their plant and equipment to produce alternative goods, say, basketballs and volleyballs. The higher prices of these "other goods" may entice soccer ball producers to switch production to those other goods in order to increase profits. This *substitution in production* results in a decline in the supply of soccer balls. Alternatively, when the prices of basketballs and volleyballs decline relative to the price of soccer balls, producers of those goods may decide to produce more soccer balls instead, increasing their supply.

Producer Expectations Changes in expectations about the future price of a product may affect the producer's current willingness to supply that product. It is difficult, however, to generalize about how a new expectation of higher prices affects the present supply of a product. Farmers anticipating a higher wheat price in the future might withhold some of their current wheat harvest from the market, thereby causing a decrease in the current supply of wheat. In contrast, in many types of manufacturing industries, newly formed expectations that price will increase may induce firms to add another shift of workers or to expand their production facilities, causing current supply to increase.

Number of Sellers Other things equal, the larger the number of suppliers, the greater the market supply. As more firms enter an industry, the supply curve shifts to the right. Conversely, the smaller the number of firms in the industry, the less the market supply. This means that as firms leave an industry, the supply curve shifts to the left. Example: The United States and Canada have imposed restrictions on haddock fishing to replenish dwindling stocks. As part of that

TABLE 3.2 Determinants of Supply: Factors That Shift the Supply Curve

Determinant	Examples
Change in resource prices	A decrease in the price of microchips increases the supply of computers; an increase in the price of crude oil reduces the supply of gasoline.
Change in technology	The development of more effective wireless technology increases the supply of cell phones.
Changes in taxes and subsidies	An increase in the excise tax on cigarettes reduces the supply of cigarettes; a decline in subsidies to state universities reduces the supply of higher education.
Change in prices of other goods	An increase in the price of cucumbers decreases the supply of watermelons.
Change in producer expectations	An expectation of a substantial rise in future log prices decreases the supply of logs today.
Change in number of suppliers	An increase in the number of tattoo parlors increases the supply of tattoos; the formation of women's professional basketball leagues increases the supply of women's professional basketball games.

policy, the federal government has bought the boats of some of the haddock fishers as a way of putting them out of business and decreasing the catch. The result has been a decline in the market supply of haddock.

Table 3.2 is a checklist of the determinants of supply, along with further illustrations.

Changes in Quantity Supplied

The distinction between a *change in supply* and a *change in quantity supplied* parallels the distinction between a change in demand and a change in quantity demanded. Because supply is a schedule or curve, a **change in supply** means a change in the schedule and a shift of the curve. An increase in supply shifts the curve to the right; a decrease in supply shifts it to the left. The cause of a change in supply is a change in one or more of the determinants of supply.

In contrast, a **change in quantity supplied** is a movement from one point to another on a fixed supply curve. The cause of such a movement is a change in the price of the specific product being considered.

Consider supply curve S_1 in Figure 3.5. A decline in the price of corn from $4 to $3 decreases the quantity of corn supplied per week from 10,000 to 7,000 bushels. This movement from point *b* to point *a* along S_1 is a change in quantity supplied, not a change in supply. Supply is the full schedule of prices and quantities shown, and this schedule does not change when the price of corn changes.

Market Equilibrium

LO3.4 Relate how supply and demand interact to determine market equilibrium.

With our understanding of demand and supply, we can now show how the decisions of buyers of corn and sellers of corn interact to determine the equilibrium price and quantity of corn. In the table in Figure 3.6, columns 1 and 2 repeat the market supply of corn (from the table in Figure 3.5), and columns 2 and 3 repeat the market demand for corn (from the table in Figure 3.3). We assume this is a competitive market so that neither buyers nor sellers can set the price.

Equilibrium Price and Quantity

We are looking for the equilibrium price and equilibrium quantity. The **equilibrium price** (or *market-clearing price*) is the price where the intentions of buyers and sellers match. It is the price where quantity demanded equals quantity supplied. The table in Figure 3.6 reveals that at $3, *and only at that price,* the number of bushels of corn that sellers wish to sell (7,000) is identical to the number consumers want to buy (also 7,000). At $3 and 7,000 bushels of corn, there is neither a shortage nor a surplus of corn. So 7,000 bushels of corn is the **equilibrium quantity:** the quantity at which the intentions of buyers and sellers match, so that the quantity demanded and the quantity supplied are equal.

Graphically, the equilibrium price is indicated by the intersection of the supply curve and the demand curve in **Figure 3.6 (Key Graph).** (The horizontal axis now measures both quantity demanded and quantity supplied.) With neither a shortage nor a surplus at $3, the market is *in equilibrium,* meaning "in balance" or "at rest."

Competition among buyers and among sellers drives the price to the equilibrium price; once there, it will remain there unless it is subsequently disturbed by changes in demand or supply (shifts of the curves). To better understand the uniqueness of the equilibrium price, let's consider other prices. At

any above-equilibrium price, quantity supplied exceeds quantity demanded. For example, at the $4 price, sellers will offer 10,000 bushels of corn, but buyers will purchase only 4,000. The $4 price encourages sellers to offer lots of corn but discourages many consumers from buying it. The result is a **surplus** (or *excess supply*) of 6,000 bushels. If corn sellers produced them all, they would find themselves with 6,000 unsold bushels of corn.

Surpluses drive prices down. Even if the $4 price existed temporarily, it could not persist. The large surplus would prompt competing sellers to lower the price to encourage buyers to take the surplus off their hands. As the price fell, the incentive to produce corn would decline and the incentive for consumers to buy corn would increase. As shown in Figure 3.6, the market would move to its equilibrium at $3.

Any price below the $3 equilibrium price would create a shortage; quantity demanded would exceed quantity supplied. Consider a $2 price, for example. We see both from column 2 of the table and from the demand curve in Figure 3.6 that quantity demanded exceeds quantity supplied at that price. The result is a **shortage** (or *excess demand*) of 7,000 bushels of corn. The $2 price discourages sellers from devoting resources to corn and encourages consumers to desire more bushels than are available. The $2 price cannot persist as the equilibrium price. Many consumers who want to buy corn at this price will not obtain it. They will express a willingness to pay more than $2 to get corn. Competition among these buyers will drive up the price, eventually to the $3 equilibrium level. Unless disrupted by changes of supply or demand, this $3 price of corn will continue to prevail.

Rationing Function of Prices

The ability of the competitive forces of supply and demand to establish a price at which selling and buying decisions are consistent is called the rationing function of prices. In our case, the equilibrium price of $3 clears the market, leaving no burdensome surplus for sellers and no inconvenient shortage for potential buyers. And it is the combination of freely made individual decisions that sets this market-clearing price. In effect, the market outcome says that all buyers who are willing and able to pay $3 for a bushel of corn will obtain it; all buyers who cannot or will not pay $3 will go without corn. Similarly, all producers who are willing and able to offer corn for sale at $3 a bushel will sell it; all producers who cannot or will not sell for $3 per bushel will not sell their product.

Efficient Allocation

A competitive market such as that we have described not only rations goods to consumers but also allocates society's

FIGURE 3.6 Equilibrium price and quantity. The intersection of the downsloping demand curve *D* and the upsloping supply curve *S* indicates the equilibrium price and quantity, here $3 and 7,000 bushels of corn. The shortages of corn at below-equilibrium prices (for example, 7,000 bushels at $2) drive up price. The higher prices increase the quantity supplied and reduce the quantity demanded until equilibrium is achieved. The surpluses caused by above-equilibrium prices (for example, 6,000 bushels at $4) push price down. As price drops, the quantity demanded rises and the quantity supplied falls until equilibrium is established. At the equilibrium price and quantity, there are neither shortages nor surpluses of corn.

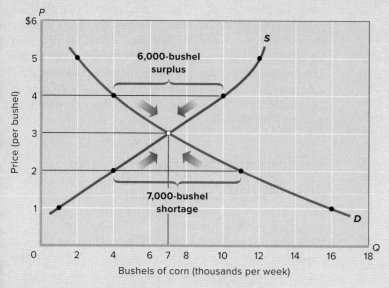

Market Supply of and Demand for Corn			
(1) Total Quantity Supplied per Week	(2) Price per Bushel	(3) Total Quantity Demanded per Week	(4) Surplus (+) or Shortage (−)*
12,000	$5	2,000	+10,000 ↓
10,000	4	4,000	+6,000 ↓
7,000	3	7,000	0
4,000	2	11,000	−7,000 ↑
1,000	1	16,000	−15,000 ↑

*Arrows indicate the effect on price.

QUICK QUIZ FOR FIGURE 3.6

1. Demand curve *D* is downsloping because:
   a. producers offer less of a product for sale as the price of the product falls.
   b. lower prices of a product create income and substitution effects that lead consumers to purchase more of it.
   c. the larger the number of buyers in a market, the lower the product price.
   d. price and quantity demanded are directly (positively) related.

2. Supply curve *S*:
   a. reflects an inverse (negative) relationship between price and quantity supplied.
   b. reflects a direct (positive) relationship between price and quantity supplied.
   c. depicts the collective behavior of buyers in this market.

   d. shows that producers will offer more of a product for sale at a low product price than at a high product price.

3. At the $3 price:
   a. quantity supplied exceeds quantity demanded.
   b. quantity demanded exceeds quantity supplied.
   c. the product is abundant and a surplus exists.
   d. there is no pressure on price to rise or fall.

4. At price $5 in this market:
   a. there will be a shortage of 10,000 units.
   b. there will be a surplus of 10,000 units.
   c. quantity demanded will be 12,000 units.
   d. quantity demanded will equal quantity supplied.

Answers: 1. b; 2. b; 3. d; 4. b

resources efficiently to the particular product. Competition among corn producers forces them to use the best technology and right mix of productive resources. If they didn't, their costs would be too high relative to the market price, and they would be unprofitable. The result is **productive efficiency:** the production of any particular good in the least costly way. When society produces corn at the lowest achievable per-unit cost, it is expending the least-valued combination of resources to produce that product and therefore is making available more-valued resources to produce other desired goods. Suppose society has only $100 worth of resources available. If it can produce a bushel of corn using $3 of those resources, then it will have available $97 of resources remaining to produce other goods. This is clearly better than producing the corn for $5 and having only $95 of resources available for the alternative uses.

Competitive markets also produce **allocative efficiency:** the *particular mix* of goods and services most

CONSIDER THIS . . .

Source: Uber Manila Tips, http://ubermanilatips.com/wp-content/uploads/2015/02/surge-price-icon.jpg

Uber and Dynamic Pricing

The ride-sharing service known as Uber rose to prominence in 2013 by offering consumers an alternative to government-regulated taxi companies. Uber works via the Internet, matching people who need a ride with people who are willing to use their own vehicles to provide rides. Both parties can find each other easily and instantly via a mobile phone app and Uber makes its money by taking a percentage of the fare.

Uber is innovative in many ways, including empowering anybody to become a paid driver, breaking up local taxi monopolies, and making it effortless to arrange a quick pickup. But Uber's most interesting feature is dynamic pricing, under which Uber sets equilibrium prices in real time, constantly adjusting fares so as to equalize quantity demanded and quality supplied. The result is extremely short waiting times for both riders and drivers as Uber will, for instance, set a substantially higher "surge price" in a given location if demand suddenly increases due to, say, a bunch of people leaving a concert all at once and wanting rides. The higher fare encourages more Uber drivers to converge on the area, thereby minimizing wait times for both drivers and passengers.

The short wait times created by Uber's use of dynamic pricing stand in sharp contrast to taxi fares, which are fixed by law and therefore unable to adjust to ongoing changes in supply and demand. On days when demand is high relative to supply, taxi shortages arise. On days when demand is low relative to supply, drivers sit idle for long stretches of time. All of that inefficiency and inconvenience is eliminated by Uber's use of market equilibrium prices to equalize the demand and supply of rides.

highly valued by society (minimum-cost production assumed). For example, society wants land suitable for growing corn used for that purpose, not to grow dandelions. It wants diamonds to be used for jewelry, not crushed up and used as an additive to give concrete more sparkle. It wants streaming online music, not cassette players and tapes. Moreover, society does not want to devote all its resources to corn, diamonds, and streaming music. It wants to assign some resources to wheat, gasoline, and cell

phones. Competitive markets make those allocatively efficient assignments.

The equilibrium price and quantity in competitive markets usually produce an assignment of resources that is "right" from an economic perspective. Demand essentially reflects the marginal benefit (MB) of the good, based on the utility received. Supply reflects the marginal cost (MC) of producing the good. The market ensures that firms produce all units of goods for which MB exceeds MC and no units for which MC exceeds MB. At the intersection of the demand and supply curves, MB equals MC and allocative efficiency results. As economists say, there is neither an "underallocaton of resources" nor an "overallocation of resources" to the product.

Changes in Supply, Demand, and Equilibrium

LO3.5 Explain how changes in supply and demand affect equilibrium prices and quantities.

We know that demand might change because of fluctuations in consumer tastes or incomes, changes in consumer expectations, or variations in the prices of related goods. Supply might change in response to changes in resource prices, technology, or taxes. What effects will such changes in supply and demand have on equilibrium price and quantity?

Changes in Demand

Suppose that the supply of some good (for example, health care) is constant and demand increases, as shown in Figure 3.7a. As a result, the new intersection of the supply and demand curves is at higher values on both the price and the quantity axes. Clearly, an increase in demand raises both equilibrium price and equilibrium quantity. Conversely, a decrease in demand such as that shown in Figure 3.7b reduces both equilibrium price and equilibrium quantity. (The value of graphical analysis is now apparent: We need not fumble with columns of figures to determine the outcomes; we need only compare the new and the old points of intersection on the graph.)

Changes in Supply

What happens if the demand for some good (for example, automobiles) is constant but supply increases, as in Figure 3.7c? The new intersection of supply and demand is located at a lower equilibrium price but at a higher equilibrium quantity. An increase in supply reduces equilibrium price but increases equilibrium quantity. In contrast, if supply decreases, as in Figure 3.7d, equilibrium price rises while equilibrium quantity declines.

FIGURE 3.7 **Changes in demand and supply and the effects on price and quantity.** The increase in demand from D_1 to D_2 in (a) increases both equilibrium price and equilibrium quantity. The decrease in demand from D_3 to D_4 in (b) decreases both equilibrium price and equilibrium quantity. The increase in supply from S_1 to S_2 in (c) decreases equilibrium price and increases equilibrium quantity. The decline in supply from S_3 to S_4 in (d) increases equilibrium price and decreases equilibrium quantity. The boxes in the top right corners summarize the respective changes and outcomes. The upward arrows in the boxes signify increases in equilibrium price (P) and equilibrium quantity (Q); the downward arrows signify decreases in these items.

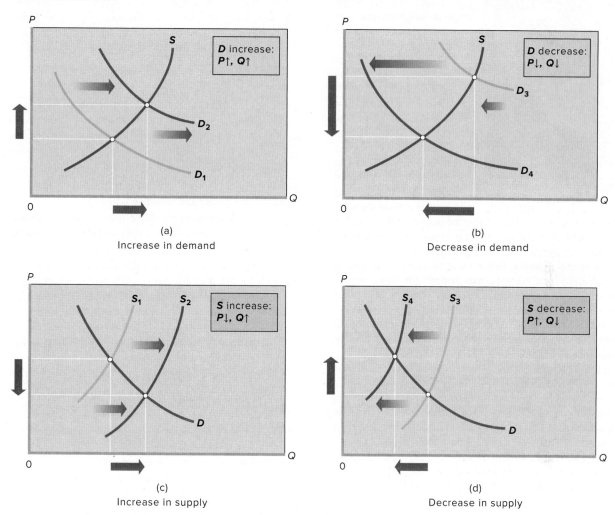

Complex Cases

When both supply and demand change, the effect is a combination of the individual effects.

Supply Increase; Demand Decrease What effect will a supply increase and a demand decrease for some good (for example, apples) have on equilibrium price? Both changes decrease price, so the net result is a price drop greater than that resulting from either change alone.

What about equilibrium quantity? Here the effects of the changes in supply and demand are opposed: the increase in supply increases equilibrium quantity, but the decrease in demand reduces it. The direction of the change in equilibrium

quantity depends on the relative sizes of the changes in supply and demand. If the increase in supply is larger than the decrease in demand, the equilibrium quantity will increase. But if the decrease in demand is greater than the increase in supply, the equilibrium quantity will decrease.

Supply Decrease; Demand Increase A decrease in supply and an increase in demand for some good (for example, gasoline) both increase price. Their combined effect is an increase in equilibrium price greater than that caused by either change separately. But their effect on the equilibrium quantity is again indeterminate, depending on the relative sizes of the changes in supply and demand. If the decrease in

CONSIDER THIS . . .

© Nancy R. Cohen/Getty Images RF

Salsa and Coffee Beans

If you forget the other-things-equal assumption, you can encounter situations that *seem* to be in conflict with the laws of demand and supply. For example, suppose salsa manufacturers sell 1 million bottles of salsa at $4 a bottle in one year; 2 million bottles at $5 in the next year; and 3 million at $6 in the year thereafter. Price and quantity purchased vary directly, and these data seem to be at odds with the law of demand.

But there is no conflict here; the data do not refute the law of demand. The catch is that the law of demand's other-things-equal assumption has been violated over the three years in the example. Specifically, because of changing tastes and rising incomes, the demand for salsa has increased sharply, as in Figure 3.7a. The result is higher prices *and* larger quantities purchased.

Another example: The price of coffee beans occasionally shoots upward at the same time that the quantity of coffee beans harvested declines. These events seemingly contradict the direct relationship between price and quantity denoted by supply. The catch again is that the other-things-equal assumption underlying the upsloping supply curve is violated. Poor coffee harvests decrease supply, as in Figure 3.7d, increasing the equilibrium price of coffee and reducing the equilibrium quantity.

The laws of demand and supply are not refuted by observations of price and quantity made over periods of time in which either demand or supply curves shift.

supply is larger than the increase in demand, the equilibrium quantity will decrease. In contrast, if the increase in demand is greater than the decrease in supply, the equilibrium quantity will increase.

Supply Increase; Demand Increase

What if supply and demand both increase for some good (for example, cell phones)? A supply increase drops equilibrium price, while a demand increase boosts it. If the increase in supply is greater than the increase in demand, the equilibrium price will fall. If the opposite holds, the equilibrium price will rise.

The effect on equilibrium quantity is certain: The increases in supply and demand both raise the equilibrium quantity. Therefore, the equilibrium quantity will increase by an amount greater than that caused by either change alone.

TABLE 3.3 Effects of Changes in Both Supply and Demand

Change in Supply	Change in Demand	Effect on Equilibrium Price	Effect on Equilibrium Quantity
1. Increase	Decrease	Decrease	Indeterminate
2. Decrease	Increase	Increase	Indeterminate
3. Increase	Increase	Indeterminate	Increase
4. Decrease	Decrease	Indeterminate	Decrease

Supply Decrease; Demand Decrease   What about decreases in both supply and demand for some good (for example, new homes)? If the decrease in supply is greater than the decrease in demand, equilibrium price will rise. If the reverse is true, equilibrium price will fall. Because the decreases in supply and demand each reduce equilibrium quantity, we can be sure that equilibrium quantity will fall.

Table 3.3 summarizes these four cases. To understand them fully, you should draw supply and demand diagrams for each case to confirm the effects listed in this table.

Special cases arise when a decrease in demand and a decrease in supply, or an increase in demand and an increase in supply, exactly cancel out. In both cases, the net effect on equilibrium price will be zero; price will not change.

The optional appendix accompanying this chapter provides additional examples of situations in which both supply and demand change at the same time.

Application: Government-Set Prices

LO3.6 Identify what government-set prices are and how they can cause product surpluses and shortages.

Prices in most markets are free to rise or fall to their equilibrium levels, no matter how high or low those levels might be. However, government sometimes concludes that supply and demand will produce prices that are unfairly high for buyers or unfairly low for sellers. So government may place legal limits on how high or low a price or prices may go. Is that a good idea?

Price Ceilings on Gasoline

A **price ceiling** sets the maximum legal price a seller may charge for a product or service. A price at or below the ceiling is legal; a price above it is not. The rationale for establishing price ceilings (or ceiling prices) on specific products is that they purportedly enable consumers to obtain some "essential" good or service that they could not afford at the equilibrium price. Examples are rent controls and usury laws, which specify maximum "prices" in the forms of rent and interest that can be charged to borrowers.

FIGURE 3.8 A price ceiling. A price ceiling is a maximum legal price such as P_c. When the ceiling price is below the equilibrium price, a persistent product shortage results. Here that shortage is shown by the horizontal distance between Q_d and Q_s.

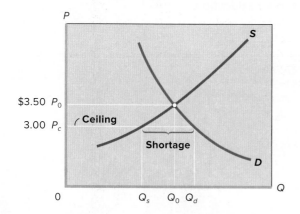

Graphical Analysis

We can easily show the effects of price ceilings graphically. Suppose that rapidly rising world income boosts the purchase of automobiles and shifts the demand for gasoline to the right so that the market equilibrium price reaches $3.50 per gallon, shown as P_0 in Figure 3.8. The rapidly rising price of gasoline greatly burdens low- and moderate-income households, which pressure government to "do something." To keep gasoline prices down, the government imposes a ceiling price P_c of $3 per gallon. To impact the market, a price ceiling must be below the equilibrium price. A ceiling price of $4, for example, would have had no effect on the price of gasoline in the current situation.

What are the effects of this $3 ceiling price? The rationing ability of the free market is rendered ineffective. Because the ceiling price P_c is below the market-clearing price P_0, there is a lasting shortage of gasoline. The quantity of gasoline demanded at P_c is Q_d and the quantity supplied is only Q_s; a persistent excess demand or shortage of amount $Q_d - Q_s$ occurs.

The price ceiling P_c prevents the usual market adjustment in which competition among buyers bids up price, inducing more production and rationing some buyers out of the market. That process would normally continue until the shortage disappeared at the equilibrium price and quantity, P_0 and Q_0.

By preventing these market adjustments from occurring, the price ceiling poses two related problems.

Rationing Problem

How will the available supply Q_s be apportioned among buyers who want the greater amount Q_d? Should gasoline be distributed on a first-come, first-served basis, that is, to those willing and able to get in line the soonest or stay in line the longest? Or should gas stations distrib-

ute it on the basis of favoritism? Since an unregulated shortage does not lead to an equitable distribution of gasoline, the government must establish some formal system for rationing it to consumers. One option is to issue ration coupons, which authorize bearers to purchase a fixed amount of gasoline per month. The rationing system might entail first the printing of coupons for Q_s gallons of gasoline and then the equal distribution of the coupons among consumers so that the wealthy family of four and the poor family of four both receive the same number of coupons.

Black Markets But ration coupons would not prevent a second problem from arising. The demand curve in Figure 3.8 reveals that many buyers are willing to pay more than the ceiling price P_c. And, of course, it is more profitable for gasoline stations to sell at prices above the ceiling. Thus, despite a sizable enforcement bureaucracy that would have to accompany the price controls, *black markets* in which gasoline is illegally bought and sold at prices above the legal limits will flourish. Counterfeiting of ration coupons will also be a problem. And since the price of gasoline is now "set by government," government might face political pressure to set the price even lower.

Rent Controls

About 200 cities in the United States, including New York City, Boston, and San Francisco, have at one time or another enacted rent controls: maximum rents established by law (or, more recently, maximum rent increases for existing tenants). Such laws are well intended. Their goals are to protect low-income families from escalating rents caused by perceived housing shortages and to make housing more affordable to the poor.

What have been the actual economic effects? On the demand side, the below-equilibrium rents attract a larger number of renters. Some are locals seeking to move into their own places after sharing housing with friends or family. Others are outsiders attracted into the area by the artificially lower rents. But a large problem occurs on the supply side. Price controls make it less attractive for landlords to offer housing on the rental market. In the short run, owners may sell their rental units or convert them to condominiums. In the long run, low rents make it unprofitable for owners to repair or renovate their rental units. (Rent controls are one cause of the many abandoned apartment buildings found in larger cities.) Also, insurance companies, pension funds, and other potential new investors in housing will find it more profitable to invest in office buildings, shopping malls, or motels, where rents are not controlled.

In brief, rent controls distort market signals and thus resources are misallocated: Too few resources are allocated to rental housing and too many to alternative uses. Ironically, although rent controls are often legislated to lessen the effects

Student Loans and Tuition Costs

By Increasing Demand, Student Loans Increase the Price of Higher Education.

Since 1958, the federal government has attempted to make college more affordable by subsidizing student loans. The subsidies come in the form of lower interest rates and fewer credit checks than if students tried to borrow privately.

At first glance, that assistance appears to be entirely helpful. After all, college tuition costs are now very high after having risen steadily for decades. Between 1971-1972 school year and the 2014-2015 school year, the average cost of tuition, fees, room, and board increased from $2,929 to $42,419 at private four-year colleges and universities. Over the same period, they increased from $1,405 to $18,943 at public institutions.

It may seem obvious that student loans have helped students keep up with rising college costs. Under this commonly held hypothesis, college costs have risen over time due to outside factors like having to pay higher salaries to faculty and administrators, having to install the equipment necessary for digital classrooms and Internet connectivity, and having to hire larger staffs as colleges and universities added a wider variety of student services, including career centers and tutoring programs. From this point of view, outside factors increased costs and one of the only ways for students to keep up was by taking out loans.

But as far back as 1987, William Bennett, who was then the U.S. Secretary of Education, proposed that the commonly held hypothesis

© baona/Getty Images RF

had things backward. Instead of loans helping students to keep up with rising tuition costs, loans were a major *cause* of rising tuition costs. As he wrote in the *New York Times*, ". . . increases in financial aid in recent years have enabled colleges and universities to blithely raise their tuitions, confident that Federal loan subsidies would help cushion the increase."

of perceived housing shortages, controls in fact are a primary cause of such shortages. For that reason, most American cities either have abandoned or are in the process of dismantling rent controls.

Price Floors on Wheat

A **price floor** is a minimum price fixed by the government. A price at or above the price floor is legal; a price below it is not. Price floors above equilibrium prices are usually invoked when society feels that the free functioning of the market system has not provided a sufficient income for certain groups of resource suppliers or producers. Supported prices for agricultural products and current minimum wages are two examples of price (or wage) floors. Let's look at the former.

Suppose that many farmers have extremely low incomes when the price of wheat is at its equilibrium value of $2 per bushel. The government decides to help out by establishing a legal price floor or price support of $3 per bushel.

What will be the effects? At any price above the equilibrium price, quantity supplied will exceed quantity demanded—that is, there will be a persistent excess supply or surplus of the product. Farmers will be willing to produce and offer for sale more than private buyers are willing to purchase at the price floor. As we saw with a price ceiling, an imposed legal price disrupts the rationing ability of the free market.

Graphical Analysis Figure 3.9 illustrates the effect of a price floor graphically. Suppose that S and D are the supply and demand curves for wheat. Equilibrium price and quantity are P_0 and Q_0, respectively. If the government imposes a price floor of P_f, farmers will produce Q_s but private buyers will purchase only Q_d. The surplus is the excess of Q_s over Q_d.

The government may cope with the surplus resulting from a price floor in two ways:

- It can restrict supply (for example, by instituting acreage allotments by which farmers agree to take a

Recent research by the New York Federal Reserve Bank confirms Bennett's view.[1] Each $1 increase in the average amount of student loans received per full-time student increases tuition costs by an average of 70 cents. In addition, researchers were able to demonstrate the order of causation because the federal government increased the borrowing limits on student loans in the mid-2000s. When the limits were raised, students borrowed more. And when they did, tuition increased. So the order of causation was clear: more loans lead to higher tuition (rather than higher tuition causing students to take out more loans).

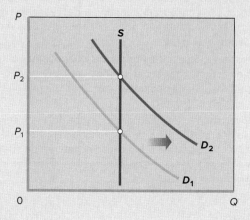

[1]David O. Lucca, Taylor Nauld, and Karen Shen, "Credit Supply and the Rise in College Tuition: Evidence from the Expansion in Federal Student Aid Programs," Staff Report No. 733, Federal Reserve Bank of New York, July 2015.

The model of demand and supply can explain why taking out more loans raises tuition. Take a look at the accompanying figure. At any given time, the quantity supplied of higher education is essentially fixed because it is not easy for colleges and universities to expand enrollments without constructing new classrooms. But the demand curve for higher education is not fixed. It shifts rightward whenever any factor increases either the willingness or ability of students to pay for higher education.

That is important because student loans increase the ability to pay. Student loans consequently shift the demand curve for higher education to the right from D_1 to D_2. That rightward shift in demand coupled with the fixed supply results in the equilibrium price of higher education rising from P_1 to P_2. More loans mean higher tuition costs.

This suggests that student loans are the wrong approach for the government to be taking in its attempt to increase access to higher education. With each $1 increase in the average amount of student loans received per full-time student causing a 70 cent increase in tuition, the student lending program is largely self-defeating as it ends up dramatically raising the price of the thing that it is striving to make more affordable.

One alternative would be for the government to redirect its efforts toward subsidizing supply rather than demand. If the government set up programs to increase the supply of higher education, the equilibrium price of higher education would naturally fall as the supply curve for higher education S shifted rightward. This was the approach taken after World War II, when the heavily subsidized state university systems expanded rapidly.

certain amount of land out of production) or increase demand (for example, by researching new uses for the product involved). These actions may reduce the difference between the equilibrium price and the price floor and that way reduce the size of the resulting surplus.

- If these efforts are not wholly successful, then the government must purchase the surplus output at the $3 price (thereby subsidizing farmers) and store or otherwise dispose of it.

Additional Consequences
Price floors such as P_f in Figure 3.9 not only disrupt the rationing ability of prices but distort resource allocation. Without the price floor, the $2 equilibrium price of wheat would cause financial losses and force high-cost wheat producers to plant other crops or abandon farming altogether. But the $3 price floor allows them to continue to grow wheat and remain farmers. So society devotes too many of its scarce resources to wheat production and too few to

FIGURE 3.9 A price floor. A price floor is a minimum legal price such as P_f. When the price floor is above the equilibrium price, a persistent product surplus results. Here that surplus is shown by the horizontal distance between Q_s and Q_d.

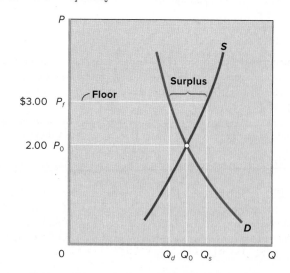

producing other, more valuable, goods and services. It fails to achieve allocative efficiency.

That's not all. Consumers of wheat-based products pay higher prices because of the price floor. Taxpayers pay higher taxes to finance the government's purchase of the surplus. Also, the price floor causes potential environmental damage by encouraging wheat farmers to bring hilly, erosion-prone "marginal land" into production. The higher price also prompts imports of wheat. But, since such imports would increase the quantity of wheat supplied and thus undermine the price floor, the government needs to erect tariffs (taxes on imports) to keep the foreign wheat out. Such tariffs usually prompt other countries to retaliate with their own tariffs against U.S. agricultural or manufacturing exports.

So it is easy to see why economists "sound the alarm" when politicians advocate imposing price ceilings or price floors such as price controls, rent controls, interest-rate lids, or agricultural price supports. In all these cases, good intentions lead to bad economic outcomes. Government-controlled prices cause shortages or surpluses, distort resource allocation, and produce negative side effects.

> ## QUICK REVIEW 3.3
>
> ✓ In competitive markets, prices adjust to the equilibrium level at which quantity demanded equals quantity supplied.
> ✓ The equilibrium price and quantity are those indicated by the intersection of the supply and demand curves for any product or resource.
> ✓ An increase in demand increases equilibrium price and quantity; a decrease in demand decreases equilibrium price and quantity.
> ✓ An increase in supply reduces equilibrium price but increases equilibrium quantity; a decrease in supply increases equilibrium price but reduces equilibrium quantity.
> ✓ Over time, equilibrium price and quantity may change in directions that seem at odds with the laws of demand and supply because the other-things-equal assumption is violated.
> ✓ Government-controlled prices in the form of ceilings and floors stifle the rationing function of prices, distort resource allocations, and cause negative side effects.

SUMMARY

LO3.1 Characterize and give examples of markets.

Markets bring buyers and sellers together. Some markets are local, others international. Some have physical locations while others are online. For simplicity, this chapter focuses on highly competitive markets in which large numbers of buyers and sellers come together to buy and sell standardized products. All such markets involve demand, supply, price, and quantity, with price being "discovered" through the interacting decisions of buyers and sellers.

LO3.2 Describe *demand* and explain how it can change.

Demand is a schedule or curve representing the willingness of buyers in a specific period to purchase a particular product at each of various prices. The law of demand implies that consumers will buy more of a product at a low price than at a high price. So, other things equal, the relationship between price and quantity demanded is negative or inverse and is graphed as a downsloping curve.

Market demand curves are found by adding horizontally the demand curves of the many individual consumers in the market.

Changes in one or more of the determinants of demand (consumer tastes, the number of buyers in the market, the money incomes of consumers, the prices of related goods, and consumer expectations) shift the market demand curve. A shift to the right is an increase in demand; a shift to the left is a decrease in demand. A change in demand is different from a change in the quantity demanded, the latter being a movement from one point to another point on a fixed demand curve because of a change in the product's price.

LO3.3 Describe *supply* and explain how it can change.

Supply is a schedule or curve showing the amounts of a product that producers are willing to offer in the market at each possible price during a specific period. The law of supply states that, other things equal, producers will offer more of a product at a high price than at a low price. Thus, the relationship between price and quantity supplied is positive or direct, and supply is graphed as an upsloping curve.

The market supply curve is the horizontal summation of the supply curves of the individual producers of the product.

Changes in one or more of the determinants of supply (resource prices, production techniques, taxes or subsidies, the prices of other goods, producer expectations, or the number of sellers in the market) shift the supply curve of a product. A shift to the right is an increase in supply; a shift to the left is a decrease in supply. In contrast, a change in the price of the product being considered causes a change in the quantity supplied, which is shown as a movement from one point to another point on a fixed supply curve.

LO3.4 Relate how supply and demand interact to determine market equilibrium.

The equilibrium price and quantity are established at the intersection of the supply and demand curves. The interaction of market demand and market supply adjusts the price to the point at which the quantities demanded and supplied are equal. This is the equilibrium price. The corresponding quantity is the equilibrium quantity.

The ability of market forces to synchronize selling and buying decisions to eliminate potential surpluses and shortages is known as the rationing function of prices. The equilibrium quantity in competitive markets reflects both productive efficiency (least-cost production) and allocative efficiency (producing the right amount of the product relative to other products).

LO3.5 Explain how changes in supply and demand affect equilibrium prices and quantities.

A change in either demand or supply changes the equilibrium price and quantity. Increases in demand raise both equilibrium price and equilibrium quantity; decreases in demand lower both equilibrium price and equilibrium quantity. Increases in supply lower equilibrium price and raise equilibrium quantity; decreases in supply raise equilibrium price and lower equilibrium quantity.

Simultaneous changes in demand and supply affect equilibrium price and quantity in various ways, depending on their direction and relative magnitudes (see Table 3.3).

LO3.6 Identify what government-set prices are and how they can cause product surpluses and shortages.

A price ceiling is a maximum price set by government and is designed to help consumers. Effective price ceilings produce persistent product shortages, and if an equitable distribution of the product is sought, government must ration the product to consumers.

A price floor is a minimum price set by government and is designed to aid producers. Effective price floors lead to persistent product surpluses; the government must either purchase the product or eliminate the surplus by imposing restrictions on production or increasing private demand.

Legally fixed prices stifle the rationing function of prices and distort the allocation of resources.

TERMS AND CONCEPTS

demand	substitute good	change in quantity supplied
demand schedule	complementary good	equilibrium price
law of demand	change in demand	equilibrium quantity
diminishing marginal utility	change in quantity demanded	surplus
income effect	supply	shortage
substitution effect	supply schedule	productive efficiency
demand curve	law of supply	allocative efficiency
determinants of demand	supply curve	price ceiling
normal goods	determinants of supply	price floor
inferior goods	change in supply	

The following and additional problems can be found in **connect**

DISCUSSION QUESTIONS

1. Explain the law of demand. Why does a demand curve slope downward? How is a market demand curve derived from individual demand curves? **LO3.2**

2. What are the determinants of demand? What happens to the demand curve when any of these determinants change? Distinguish between a change in demand and a movement along a fixed demand curve, noting the cause(s) of each. **LO3.2**

3. Explain the law of supply. Why does the supply curve slope upward? How is the market supply curve derived from the supply curves of individual producers? **LO3.3**

4. What are the determinants of supply? What happens to the supply curve when any of these determinants change? Distinguish between a change in supply and a change in the quantity supplied, noting the cause(s) of each. **LO3.3**

5. In 2001 an outbreak of hoof-and-mouth disease in Europe led to the burning of millions of cattle carcasses. What impact do you think this had on the supply of cattle hides, hide prices, the supply of leather goods, and the price of leather goods? **LO3.5**

6. For each stock in the stock market, the number of shares sold daily equals the number of shares purchased. That is, the quantity of each firm's shares demanded equals the quantity supplied. So, if this equality always occurs, why do the prices of stock shares ever change? **LO3.5**

7. What do economists mean when they say "price floors and ceilings stifle the rationing function of prices and distort resource allocation"? **LO3.6**

8. **LAST WORD** Real (inflation-adjusted) tuition costs were nearly constant during the 1960s despite a huge increase in the number of college students as the very large Baby Boom generation came of age. What does this suggest about the supply of higher education during that period? When the much smaller Baby Bust generation followed in the 1970s, real tuition costs fell. What does that suggest about demand relative to supply during the 1970s?

REVIEW QUESTIONS

1. What effect will each of the following have on the demand for small automobiles such as the Mini-Cooper and Fiat 500? **LO3.2**
   a. Small automobiles become more fashionable.
   b. The price of large automobiles rises (with the price of small autos remaining the same).
   c. Income declines and small autos are an inferior good.
   d. Consumers anticipate that the price of small autos will greatly come down in the near future.
   e. The price of gasoline substantially drops.

2. True or False: A "change in quantity demanded" is a shift of the entire demand curve to the right or to the left. **LO3.2**

3. What effect will each of the following have on the supply of auto tires? **LO3.3**
   a. A technological advance in the methods of producing tires.
   b. A decline in the number of firms in the tire industry.
   c. An increase in the prices of rubber used in the production of tires.
   d. The expectation that the equilibrium price of auto tires will be lower in the future than currently.
   e. A decline in the price of the large tires used for semi trucks and earth-hauling rigs (with no change in the price of auto tires).
   f. The levying of a per-unit tax on each auto tire sold.
   g. The granting of a 50-cent-per-unit subsidy for each auto tire produced.

4. "In the corn market, demand often exceeds supply and supply sometimes exceeds demand." "The price of corn rises and falls in response to changes in supply and demand." In which of these two statements are the terms "supply" and "demand" used correctly? Explain. **LO3.3**

5. Suppose that in the market for computer memory chips, the equilibrium price is $50 per chip. If the current price is $55 per chip, then there will be _____ of memory chips. **LO3.4**
   a. A shortage.
   b. A surplus.
   c. An equilibrium quantity.
   d. None of the above.

6. Critically evaluate: "In comparing the two equilibrium positions in Figure 3.7b, I note that a smaller amount is actually demanded at a lower price. This refutes the law of demand." **LO3.5**

7. Label each of the following scenarios with the set of symbols that best indicates the price change and quantity change that occur in the scenario. In some scenarios, it may not be possible from the information given to determine the direction of a particular price change or a particular quantity change. We will symbolize those cases as, respectively, "P?" and "Q?". The four possible combinations of price and quantity changes are: **LO3.5**

P↓ Q?	P? Q↓
P↑ Q?	P? Q↑

   a. On a hot day, both the demand for lemonade and the supply of lemonade increase.
   b. On a cold day, both the demand for ice cream and the supply of ice cream decrease.
   c. When Hawaii's Mt. Kilauea erupts violently, the demand on the part of tourists for sightseeing flights increases but the supply of pilots willing to provide these dangerous flights decreases.
   d. In a hot area of Arizona where they generate a lot of their electricity with wind turbines, the demand for electricity falls on windy days as people switch off their air conditioners and enjoy the breeze. But at the same time, the amount of electricity supplied increases as the wind turbines spin faster.

8. Suppose the total demand for wheat and the total supply of wheat per month in the Kansas City grain market are as shown in the following table. Suppose that the government establishes a price ceiling of $3.70 for wheat. What might prompt the government to establish this price ceiling? Explain carefully the main effects. Demonstrate your answer graphically. Next, suppose that the government establishes a price floor of $4.60 for wheat. What will be the main effects of this price floor? Demonstrate your answer graphically. **LO3.6**

Thousands of Bushels Demanded	Price per Bushel	Thousands of Bushels Supplied
85	$3.40	72
80	3.70	73
75	4.00	75
70	4.30	77
65	4.60	79
60	4.90	81

9. A price ceiling will result in a shortage only if the ceiling price is _____ the equilibrium price. **LO3.6**
   a. Less than.
   b. Equal to.
   c. Greater than.
   d. Louder than.

PROBLEMS

1. Suppose there are three buyers of candy in a market: Tex, Dex, and Rex. The market demand and the individual demands of Tex, Dex, and Rex are shown in the following table. **LO3.2**
   a. Fill in the table for the missing values.
   b. Which buyer demands the least at a price of $5? The most at a price of $7?
   c. Which buyer's quantity demanded increases the most when the price is lowered from $7 to $6?
   d. Which direction would the market demand curve shift if Tex withdrew from the market? What if Dex doubled his purchases at each possible price?
   e. Suppose that at a price of $6, the total quantity demanded increases from 19 to 38. Is this a "change in the quantity demanded" or a "change in demand"?

Price per Candy	Individual Quantities Demanded			Total Quantity Demanded
	Tex	Dex	Rex	
$8	3 +	1 +	0 =	___
7	8 +	2 +	___ =	12
6	___ +	3 +	4 =	19
5	17 +	___ +	6 =	27
4	23 +	5 +	8 =	___

2. The figure below shows the supply curve for tennis balls, S_1, for Drop Volley Tennis, a producer of tennis equipment. Use the figure and the table below to give your answers to the following questions. **LO3.3**

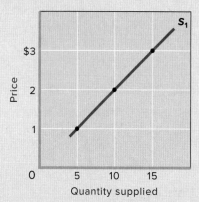

a. Use the figure to fill in the quantity supplied on supply curve S_1 for each price in the following table.

Price	S_1 Quantity Supplied	S_2 Quantity Supplied	Change in Quantity Supplied
$3	___	4	___
2	___	2	___
1	___	0	___

b. If production costs were to increase, the quantities supplied at each price would be as shown by the third column of the table ("S_2 Quantity Supplied"). Use those data to draw supply curve S_2 on the same graph as supply curve S_1.
c. In the fourth column of the table, enter the amount by which the quantity supplied at each price changes due to the increase in product costs. (Use positive numbers for increases and negative numbers for decreases.)
d. Did the increase in production costs cause a "decrease in supply" or a "decrease in quantity supplied"?

3. Refer to the following expanded table from review question 8. **LO3.4**
   a. What is the equilibrium price? At what price is there neither a shortage nor a surplus? Fill in the surplus-shortage column and use it to confirm your answers.
   b. Graph the demand for wheat and the supply of wheat. Be sure to label the axes of your graph correctly. Label equilibrium price P and equilibrium quantity Q.
   c. How big is the surplus or shortage at $3.40? At $4.90? How big a surplus or shortage results if the price is 60 cents higher than the equilibrium price? 30 cents lower than the equilibrium price?

Thousands of Bushels Demanded	Price per Bushel	Thousands of Bushels Supplied	Surplus (+) or Shortage (−)
85	$3.40	72	___
80	3.70	73	___
75	4.00	75	___
70	4.30	77	___
65	4.60	79	___
60	4.90	81	___

4. How will each of the following changes in demand and/or supply affect equilibrium price and equilibrium quantity in a competitive market; that is, do price and quantity rise, fall, or remain unchanged, or are the answers indeterminate because they depend on the magnitudes of the shifts? Use supply and demand to verify your answers. **LO3.5**
   a. Supply decreases and demand is constant.
   b. Demand decreases and supply is constant.
   c. Supply increases and demand is constant.
   d. Demand increases and supply increases.
   e. Demand increases and supply is constant.
   f. Supply increases and demand decreases.
   g. Demand increases and supply decreases.
   h. Demand decreases and supply decreases.

5. Use two market diagrams to explain how an increase in state subsidies to public colleges might affect tuition and enrollments in both public and private colleges. **LO3.5**

6. **ADVANCED ANALYSIS** Assume that demand for a commodity is represented by the equation $P = 10 - .2Q_d$ and supply by the equation $P = 2 + .2Q_s$, where Q_d and Q_s are quantity demanded and quantity supplied, respectively, and P is price. Using the equilibrium condition $Q_s = Q_d$, solve the equations to determine equilibrium price. Now determine equilibrium quantity. **LO3.5**

7. Suppose that the demand and supply schedules for rental apartments in the city of Gotham are as given in the following table. **LO3.6**

Monthly Rent	Apartments Demanded	Apartments Supplied
$2,500	10,000	15,000
2,000	12,500	12,500
1,500	15,000	10,000
1,000	17,500	7,500
500	20,000	5,000

a. What is the market equilibrium rental price per month and the market equilibrium number of apartments demanded and supplied?

b. If the local government can enforce a rent-control law that sets the maximum monthly rent at $1,500, will there be a surplus or a shortage? Of how many units? And how many units will actually be rented each month?

c. Suppose that a new government is elected that wants to keep out the poor. It declares that the minimum rent that can be charged is $2,500 per month. If the government can enforce that price floor, will there be a surplus or a shortage? Of how many units? And how many units will actually be rented each month?

d. Suppose that the government wishes to decrease the market equilibrium monthly rent by increasing the supply of housing. Assuming that demand remains unchanged, by how many units of housing would the government have to increase the supply of housing in order to get the market equilibrium rental price to fall to $1,500 per month? To $1,000 per month? To $500 per month?

Additional Examples of Supply and Demand

LO3.7 Illustrate how supply and demand analysis can provide insights on actual-economy situations.

Our discussion has clearly demonstrated that supply and demand analysis is a powerful tool for understanding equilibrium prices and quantities. The information provided in the main body of this chapter is fully sufficient for moving forward in the book, but you may find that additional examples of supply and demand are helpful. This optional appendix provides several concrete illustrations of changes in supply and demand.

Your instructor may assign all, some, or none of this appendix, depending on time availability and personal preference.

Changes in Supply and Demand

As Figure 3.7 of this chapter demonstrates, changes in supply and demand cause changes in price, quantity, or both. The following applications illustrate this fact in several real-world markets. The simplest situations are those in which either supply changes while demand remains constant or demand changes while supply remains constant. Let's consider two such simple cases first, before looking at more complex applications.

Lettuce

Every now and then we hear on the news that extreme weather has severely reduced the size of some crop. Suppose, for example, that a severe freeze destroys a sizable portion of the lettuce crop. This unfortunate situation implies a significant decline in supply, which we represent as a leftward shift of the supply curve from S_1 to S_2 in Figure 1. At each price, consumers desire as much lettuce as before, so the freeze does not affect the demand for lettuce. That is, demand curve D_1 does not shift.

What are the consequences of the reduced supply of lettuce for equilibrium price and quantity? As shown in Figure 1, the leftward shift of the supply curve disrupts the previous equilibrium in the market for lettuce and drives the equilibrium price upward from P_1 to P_2. Consumers respond to that price hike by reducing the quantity of lettuce demanded from Q_1 to Q_2. Equilibrium is restored at P_2 and Q_2.

Consumers who are willing and able to pay price P_2 obtain lettuce; consumers unwilling or unable to pay that price do not. Some consumers continue to buy as much lettuce as before, even at the higher price. Others buy some lettuce but not as much as before, and still others opt out of the market completely. The latter two groups use the money they would

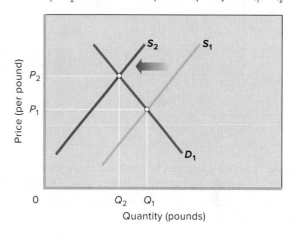

FIGURE 1 The market for lettuce. The decrease in the supply of lettuce, shown here by the shift from S_1 to S_2, increases the equilibrium price of lettuce from P_1 to P_2 and reduces the equilibrium quantity from Q_1 to Q_2.

have spent on lettuce to obtain other products, say, carrots. (Because of our other-things-equal assumption, the prices of other products have not changed.)

Exchange Rates

Exchange rates are the prices at which one currency can be traded (exchanged) for another. Exchange rates are normally determined in foreign exchange markets. One of the largest foreign exchange markets is the euro-dollar market in which the currency used in most of Europe, the *euro,* is exchanged for U.S. dollars. In the United States, this market is set up so that euros are priced in dollars—that is, the "product" being traded is euros and the "price" to buy that product is quoted in dollars. Thus, the market equilibrium price one day might be $1.25 to buy 1 euro, while on another day it might be $1.50 to buy 1 euro.

Foreign exchange markets are used by individuals and companies that need to make purchases or payments in a different currency. U.S. companies exporting goods to Germany, for instance, wish to be paid in U.S. dollars. Thus, their German customers will need to convert euros into dollars. The euros that they bring to the euro-dollar market will become part of the overall market supply of euros. Conversely, an American mutual fund may wish to purchase some French real estate outside of Paris. But to purchase that real estate, it will need to pay in euros because the current French owners will only accept payment in euros. Thus, the American

FIGURE 2 The market for euros. The increase in the demand for euros, shown here by the shift from D_1 to D_2, increases the equilibrium price of one euro from $1.25 to $1.50 and increases the equilibrium quantity of euros that are exchanged from Q_1 to Q_2. The dollar has depreciated.

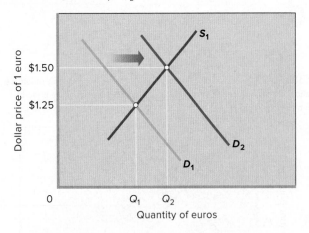

FIGURE 3 The market for pink salmon. In the last several decades, the supply of pink salmon has increased and the demand for pink salmon has decreased. As a result, the price of pink salmon has declined, as from P_1 to P_2. Because supply has increased by more than demand has decreased, the equilibrium quantity of pink salmon has increased, as from Q_1 to Q_2.

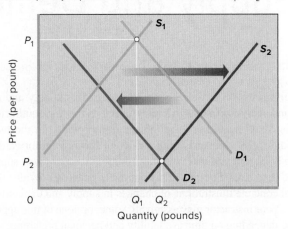

mutual fund has a demand to purchase euros that will form part of the overall market demand for euros. The fund will bring dollars to the euro-dollar foreign exchange market in order to purchase the euros it desires.

Sometimes, the demand for euros increases. This might be because a European product surges in popularity in foreign countries. For example, if a new German-made automobile is a big hit in the United States, American car dealers will demand more euros with which to pay for more units of that new model. This will shift the demand curve for euros to the right, as from D_1 to D_2 in Figure 2. Given the fixed euro supply curve S_1, the increase in demand raises the equilibrium exchange rate (the equilibrium number of dollars needed to purchase 1 euro) from $1.25 to $1.50. The equilibrium quantity of euros purchased increases from Q_1 to Q_2. Because a higher dollar amount is now needed to purchase one euro, economists say that the dollar has *depreciated*— gone down in value—relative to the euro. Alternatively, the euro has *appreciated*—gone up in value—relative to the dollar, because one euro now buys $1.50 rather than $1.25.

Pink Salmon

Now let's see what happens when both supply and demand change at the same time. Several decades ago, people who caught salmon earned as much as $1 for each pound of pink salmon—the type of salmon most commonly used for canning. In Figure 3 that price is represented as P_1, at the intersection of supply curve S_1 and demand curve D_1. The corresponding quantity of pink salmon is shown as Q_1 pounds.

As time passed, supply and demand changed in the market for pink salmon. On the supply side, improved technology in the form of larger, more efficient fishing boats greatly increased the catch and lowered the cost of obtaining it. Also,

high profits at price P_1 encouraged many new fishers to enter the industry. As a result of these changes, the supply of pink salmon greatly increased and the supply curve shifted to the right, as from S_1 to S_2 in Figure 3.

Over the same years, the demand for pink salmon declined, as represented by the leftward shift from D_1 to D_2 in Figure 3. That decrease was caused by increases in consumer income and reductions of the price of substitute products. As buyers' incomes rose, consumers shifted demand away from canned fish and toward higher-quality fresh or frozen fish, including more-valued Atlantic, chinook, sockeye, and coho salmon. Moreover, the emergence of fish farming, in which salmon are raised in ocean net pens, lowered the prices of these substitute species. That, too, reduced the demand for pink salmon.

The altered supply and demand reduced the price of pink salmon to as low as $0.10 per pound, as represented by the drop in price from P_1 to P_2 in Figure 3. Both the supply increase and the demand decrease helped reduce the equilibrium price. However, in this particular case the equilibrium quantity of pink salmon increased, as represented by the move from Q_1 to Q_2. Both shifts reduced the equilibrium price, but equilibrium quantity increased because the increase in supply exceeded the decrease in demand.

Gasoline

The price of gasoline in the United States has increased rapidly several times during the past several years. For example, the average price of a gallon of gasoline rose from around $2.60 in October 2010 to about $3.90 in May 2011. What caused this 50 percent rise in the price of gasoline? How would we diagram this increase?

We begin in Figure 4 with the price of a gallon of gasoline at P_1, representing the $2.60 price. Simultaneous

FIGURE 4 **The market for gasoline.** An increase in the demand for gasoline, as shown by the shift from D_1 to D_2, coupled with a decrease in supply, as shown by the shift from S_1 to S_2, boosts equilibrium price (here from P_1 to P_2). In this case, equilibrium quantity increases from Q_1 to Q_2 because the increase in demand outweighs the decrease in supply.

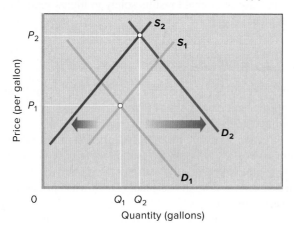

FIGURE 5 **The market for sushi.** Equal increases in the demand for sushi, as from D_1 to D_2, and in the supply of sushi, as from S_1 to S_2, expand the equilibrium quantity of sushi (here from Q_1 to Q_2) while leaving the price of sushi unchanged at P_1.

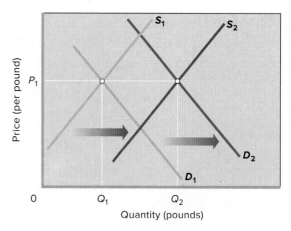

supply and demand factors disturbed this equilibrium. Supply uncertainties relating to Middle East politics and warfare and expanded demand for oil by fast-growing countries such as China pushed up the price of a barrel of oil from under $80 per barrel in October 2010 to well over $100 per barrel in May 2011. Oil is the main input for producing gasoline, so any sustained rise in its price boosts the per-unit cost of producing gasoline. Such cost rises decrease the supply of gasoline, as represented by the leftward shift of the supply curve from S_1 to S_2 in Figure 4. At times refinery breakdowns in the United States also contributed to this reduced supply.

While the supply of gasoline declined between October 2010 and May 2011, the demand for gasoline increased, as depicted by the rightward shift of the demand curve from D_1 to D_2. Incomes in general were rising over this period because the U.S. economy was expanding. Rising incomes raise demand for all normal goods, including gasoline. An increased number of low-gas-mileage SUVs and light trucks on the road also contributed to growing gas demand.

The combined decline in gasoline supply and increase in gasoline demand boosted the price of gasoline from $2.60 to $3.90, as represented by the rise from P_1 to P_2 in Figure 4. Because the demand increase outweighed the supply decrease, the equilibrium quantity expanded, here from Q_1 to Q_2.

In other periods the price of gasoline has *declined* as the demand for gasoline has increased. Test your understanding of the analysis by explaining how such a price decrease could occur.

Sushi

Sushi bars are springing up like Starbucks in American cities (well, maybe not that fast!). Consumption of sushi, the raw-fish delicacy from Japan, has soared in the United States in

recent years. Nevertheless, the price of sushi has remained relatively constant.

Supply and demand analysis helps explain this circumstance of increased quantity and constant price. A change in tastes has increased the U.S. demand for sushi. Many consumers of sushi find it highly tasty when they try it. And, as implied by the growing number of sushi bars in the United States, the supply of sushi has also expanded.

We represent these supply and demand changes in Figure 5 as the rightward shift of the demand curve from D_1 to D_2 and the rightward shift of the supply curve from S_1 to S_2. Observe that the equilibrium quantity of sushi increases from Q_1 to Q_2 and equilibrium price remains constant at P_1. The increase in supply, which taken alone would reduce price, has perfectly offset the increase in demand, which taken alone would raise price. The price of sushi does not change, but the equilibrium quantity greatly increases because both the increase in demand and the increase in supply expand purchases and sales.

Simultaneous increases in demand and supply can cause price to either rise, fall, or remain constant, depending on the relative magnitudes of the supply and demand increases. In this case, price remained constant.

Upsloping versus Vertical Supply Curves

As you already know, the typical good or service possesses an upsloping supply curve because a higher market price will cause producers to increase the quantity supplied. There are, however, some goods and services whose quantities supplied are fixed and totally unresponsive to changes in price. Examples include the amount of land in a given area, the number of seats in a stadium, and the limited part of the electromagnetic spectrum that is reserved for cellular telephone transmissions. These sorts of goods and services have vertical supply curves because the same fixed amount is available no matter what price is offered to suppliers.

Reactions to Demand Shifts

Markets react very differently to a shift in demand depending upon whether they have upsloping or vertical supply curves.

Upsloping Supply Curves When a market has an upsloping supply curve, any shift in demand will cause both the equilibrium price *and* the equilibrium quantity to adjust. Consider Figure 2. When the demand for euros increases, the movement from the initial equilibrium to the final equilibrium involves the equilibrium price rising from $1.25 to $1.50 while the equilibrium quantity increases from Q_1 to Q_2. Price and quantity *both* change.

Vertical Supply Curves When a market has a vertical supply curve, any shift in demand will cause only the equilibrium price to change; the equilibrium quantity remains the same because the quantity supplied is fixed and cannot adjust.

Consider Figure 6, in which the supply of land in San Francisco is fixed at quantity Q_0. If demand increases from D_1 to D_2, the movement from the initial equilibrium at point *a* to the final equilibrium at point *b* is accomplished solely by a rise in the equilibrium price from P_1 to P_2. Because the quantity of land is fixed, the increase in demand cannot cause any change in the equilibrium quantity supplied. The entire adjustment from the initial equilibrium to the final equilibrium has to come in the form of a higher equilibrium price.

FIGURE 6 **The market for land in San Francisco.** Because the quantity of land in San Francisco is fixed at Q_0, the supply curve is vertical above Q_0 in order to indicate that the same quantity of land will be supplied no matter what the price is. As demand increases from D_1 to D_2, the equilibrium price rises from P_1 to P_2. Because the quantity of land is fixed at Q_0, the movement from equilibrium *a* to equilibrium *b* involves only a change in the equilibrium price; the equilibrium quantity remains at Q_0 due to land being in fixed supply.

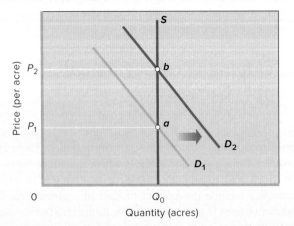

This fact explains why real estate prices are so high in San Francisco and other major cities. Any increase in demand cannot be met by a combination of increases in price and increases in quantity. With the quantity of land in fixed supply, any increase in demand results solely in higher equilibrium land prices.

Preset Prices

In the body of this chapter, we saw that an effective government-imposed price ceiling (legal maximum price) causes quantity demanded to exceed quantity supplied—a shortage. An effective government-imposed price floor (legal minimum price) causes quantity supplied to exceed quantity demanded—a surplus. Put simply: Shortages result when prices are set below, and surpluses result when prices are set above, equilibrium prices.

We now want to establish that shortages and surpluses can occur in markets other than those in which government imposes price floors and ceilings. Such market imbalances happen when the seller or sellers set prices in advance of sales and the prices selected turn out to be below or above equilibrium prices. Consider the following two examples.

Olympic Figure Skating Finals

Tickets for the women's figure skating championship at the Olympics are among the world's "hottest tickets." The popularity of this event and the high incomes of buyers translate into tremendous ticket demand. The Olympic officials set the price for the tickets in advance. Invariably, the price, although high, is considerably below the equilibrium price that would equate quantity demanded and quantity supplied. A severe shortage of tickets therefore occurs in this *primary market*—the market involving the official ticket office.

The shortage, in turn, creates a *secondary market* in which buyers bid for tickets held by initial purchasers rather than the original seller. Scalping tickets—selling them above the original ticket price—may be legal or illegal, depending on local laws.

Figure 7 shows how the shortage in the primary ticket market looks in terms of supply and demand analysis. Demand curve D represents the strong demand for tickets and supply curve S represents the supply of tickets. The supply curve is vertical because a fixed number of tickets are printed to match the capacity of the arena. At the printed ticket price of P_1, the quantity of tickets demanded, Q_2, exceeds the quantity supplied, Q_1. The result is a shortage of *ab*—the horizontal distance between Q_2 and Q_1 in the primary market.

If the printed ticket price had been the higher equilibrium price P_2, no shortage of tickets would have occurred. But at the lower price P_1, a shortage and secondary ticket market will emerge among those buyers willing to pay more than the printed ticket price and those sellers willing to sell their

FIGURE 7 The market for tickets to the Olympic women's figure skating finals. The demand curve D and supply curve S for the Olympic women's figure skating finals produce an equilibrium price that is above the P_1 price printed on the ticket. At price P_1 the quantity of tickets demanded, Q_2, greatly exceeds the quantity of tickets available, Q_1. The resulting shortage of ab $(= Q_2 - Q_1)$ gives rise to a legal or illegal secondary market.

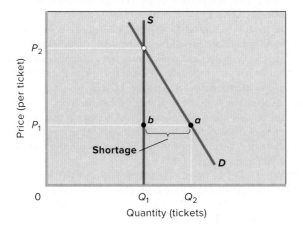

FIGURE 8 The market for tickets to the Olympic curling preliminaries. The demand curve D and supply curve S for the Olympic curling preliminaries produce an equilibrium price below the P_1 price printed on the ticket. At price P_1 the quantity of tickets demanded is less than the quantity of tickets available. The resulting surplus of ba $(= Q_1 - Q_2)$ means the event is not sold out.

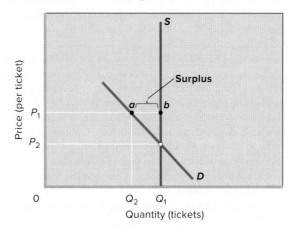

purchased tickets for more than the original price. Wherever there are shortages and secondary markets, it is safe to assume the original price was set below the equilibrium price.

Olympic Curling Preliminaries

Contrast the shortage of tickets for the women's figure skating finals at the Olympics to the surplus of tickets for one of the preliminary curling matches. For the uninitiated, curling is a sport in which participants slide a heavy round object called a "stone" down the ice toward a target while teammates called "sweepers" use brooms to alter the course of the stone when desired.

Curling is a popular spectator sport in a few nations such as Canada, but it does not draw many fans in most countries. So the demand for tickets to most of the preliminary curling

events is not very strong. We demonstrate this weak demand as D in Figure 8. As in our previous example, the supply of tickets is fixed by the size of the arena and is shown as vertical line S.

We represent the printed ticket price as P_1 in Figure 8. In this case the printed price is much higher than the equilibrium price of P_2. At the printed ticket price, quantity supplied is Q_1 and quantity demanded is Q_2. So a surplus of tickets of ba $(= Q_1 - Q_2)$ occurs. No ticket scalping occurs and there are numerous empty seats. Only if the Olympic officials had priced the tickets at the lower price P_2 would the event have been a sellout. (Actually, the Olympic officials try to adjust to demand realities for curling contests by holding them in smaller arenas and by charging less for tickets. Nevertheless, the stands are rarely full for the preliminary contests, which compete against final events in other winter Olympic sports.)

APPENDIX SUMMARY

LO3.7 Illustrate how supply and demand analysis can provide insights on actual-economy situations.

A decrease in the supply of a product increases its equilibrium price and reduces its equilibrium quantity. In contrast, an increase in the demand for a product boosts both its equilibrium price and its equilibrium quantity.

Simultaneous changes in supply and demand affect equilibrium price and quantity in various ways, depending on the relative magnitudes of the changes in supply and demand. Equal increases in supply and demand, for example, leave equilibrium price unchanged.

Products (such as land) whose quantities supplied do not vary with price have vertical supply curves. For these products, any shift in demand will lead to a change in the equilibrium price but no change in the equilibrium quantity.

Sellers set prices of some items such as tickets in advance of the event. These items are sold in the primary market that involves the original sellers and buyers. If preset prices turn out to be below the equilibrium prices, shortages occur and scalping in legal or illegal secondary markets arises. The prices in the secondary market then rise above the preset prices. In contrast, surpluses occur when the preset prices happen to exceed the equilibrium prices.

The following and additional problems can be found in ▉ connect

APPENDIX DISCUSSION QUESTIONS

1. Why are shortages or surpluses more likely with preset prices, such as those on tickets, than flexible prices, such as those on gasoline? **LO3.7**

2. Most scalping laws make it illegal to sell—but not to buy—tickets at prices above those printed on the tickets. Assuming that is the case, use supply and demand analysis to explain why the equilibrium ticket price in an illegal secondary market tends to be higher than in a legal secondary market. **LO3.7**

3. Go to the website of the Energy Information Administration, **www.eia.doe.gov,** and follow the links to find the current retail price of gasoline. How does the current price of regular gasoline compare with the price a year ago? What must have happened to either supply, demand, or both to explain the observed price change? **LO3.7**

4. Suppose the supply of apples sharply increases because of perfect weather conditions throughout the growing season. Assuming no change in demand, explain the effect on the equilibrium price and quantity of apples. Explain why quantity demanded increases even though demand does not change. **LO3.7**

5. Assume the demand for lumber suddenly rises because of a rapid growth of demand for new housing. Assume no change in supply. Why does the equilibrium price of lumber rise? What would happen if the price did not rise under the demand and supply circumstances described? **LO3.7**

6. Assume that both the supply of bottled water and the demand for bottled water rise during the summer but that supply increases more rapidly than demand. What can you conclude about the directions of the impacts on equilibrium price and equilibrium quantity? **LO3.7**

7. When asked for investment advice, humorist Will Rogers joked that people should "[b]uy land. They ain't making any more of the stuff." Explain his advice in terms of the supply and demand model. **LO3.7**

APPENDIX REVIEW QUESTIONS

1. Will the equilibrium price of orange juice increase or decrease in each of the following situations? **LO3.7**
   a. A medical study reporting that orange juice reduces cancer is released at the same time that a freak storm destroys half of the orange crop in Florida.
   b. The prices of all beverages except orange juice fall by half while unexpectedly perfect weather in Florida results in an orange crop that is 20 percent larger than normal.

2. Consider the market for coffee beans. Suppose that the prices of all other caffeinated beverages go up 30 percent while at the same time a new fertilizer boosts production at coffee plantations dramatically. Which of the following best describes what is likely to happen to the equilibrium price and quantity of coffee beans? **LO3.7**
   a. Both the equilibrium price and the quantity will rise.
   b. The equilibrium price will rise but the equilibrium quantity will fall.
   c. The equilibrium price may rise or fall but the equilibrium quantity will rise for certain.
   d. Neither the price change nor the quantity change can be determined for certain.
   e. None of the above.

3. A price ceiling will result in a shortage only if the ceiling price is _____ the equilibrium price. **LO3.7**
   a. Less than.
   b. Equal to.
   c. Greater than.
   d. Faster than.

4. Suppose that you are the economic advisor to a local government that has to deal with a politically embarrassing surplus that was caused by a price floor that the government recently imposed. Your first suggestion is to get rid of the price floor, but the politicians don't want to do that. Instead, they present you with the following list of options that they hope will get rid of the surplus while keeping the price floor. Identify each one as either *could work* or *can't work*. **LO3.7**
   a. Restricting supply.
   b. Decreasing demand.
   c. Purchasing the surplus at the floor price.

5. Suppose both the demand for olives and the supply of olives decline by equal amounts over some time period. Use graphical analysis to show the effect on equilibrium price and quantity. **LO3.7**

6. Governments can use subsidies to increase demand. For instance, a government can pay farmers to use organic fertilizers rather than traditional fertilizers. That subsidy increases the demand for organic fertilizer. Consider two industries, one in which supply is nearly vertical and the other in which supply is nearly horizontal. Assume that firms in both industries would prefer a higher market equilibrium price because a higher market equilibrium price would mean higher profits. Which industry would probably spend more resources lobbying the government to increase the demand for its output? (Assume that both industries have similarly sloped demand curves.) **LO3.7**
   a. The industry with a nearly flat supply curve.
   b. The industry with a nearly vertical supply curve.

APPENDIX PROBLEMS

1. Demand and supply often shift in the retail market for gasoline. Below are two demand curves and two supply curves for gallons of gasoline in the month of May in a small town in Maine. Some of the data are missing. **LO3.7**

Price	Quantities Demanded D_1	D_2	Quantities Supplied S_1	S_2
$4.00	5,000	7,500	9,000	9,500
____	6,000	8,000	8,000	9,000
2.00	____	8,500	____	8,500
____	____	9,000	5,000	____

a. Use the following facts to fill in the missing data in the table. If demand is D_1 and supply is S_1, the equilibrium quantity is 7,000 gallons per month. When demand is D_2 and supply is S_1, the equilibrium price is $3.00 per gallon. When demand is D_2 and supply is S_1, there is an excess demand of 4,000 gallons per month at a price of $1.00 per gallon. If demand is D_1 and supply is S_2, the equilibrium quantity is 8,000 gallons per month.

b. Compare two equilibriums. In the first, demand is D_1 and supply is S_1. In the second, demand is D_1 and supply is S_2. By how much does the equilibrium quantity change? By how much does the equilibrium price change?

c. If supply falls from S_2 to S_1 while demand declines from D_2 to D_1, does the equilibrium price rise, fall, or stay the same? What if only supply falls? What if only demand falls?

d. Suppose that supply is fixed at S_1 and that demand starts at D_1. By how many gallons per month would demand have to increase at each price level such that the equilibrium price per gallon would be $3.00? $4.00?

2. The following table shows two demand schedules for a given style of men's shoe—that is, how many pairs per month will be demanded at various prices at a men's clothing store in Seattle called Stromnord.

Price	D_1 Quantity Demanded	D_2 Quantity Demanded
$75	53	13
70	60	15
65	68	18
60	77	22
55	87	27

Suppose that Stromnord has exactly 65 pairs of this style of shoe in inventory at the start of the month of July and will not receive any more pairs of this style until at least August 1. **LO3.7**

a. If demand is D_1, what is the lowest price that Stromnord can charge so that it will not run out of this model of shoe in the month of July? What if demand is D_2?

b. If the price of shoes is set at $75 for both July and August and demand will be D_2 in July and D_1 in August, how many pairs of shoes should Stromnord order if it wants to end the month of August with exactly zero pairs of shoes in its inventory? What if the price is set at $55 for both months?

3. Use the following table to answer the questions that follow: **LO3.7**

a. If this table reflects the supply of and demand for tickets to a particular World Cup soccer game, what is the stadium capacity?

b. If the preset ticket price is $45, would we expect to see a secondary market for tickets? Would the price of a ticket in the secondary market be higher than, the same as, or lower than the price in the primary (original) market?

c. Suppose for some other World Cup game the quantity of tickets demanded is 20,000 lower at each ticket price than shown in the table. If the ticket price remains $45, would the event be a sellout?

Quantity Demanded, Thousands	Price	Quantity Supplied, Thousands
80	$25	60
75	35	60
70	45	60
65	55	60
60	65	60
55	75	60
50	85	60

4

Market Failures: Public Goods and Externalities

Learning Objectives

LO4.1 Differentiate between demand-side market failures and supply-side market failures.

LO4.2 Explain the origin of both consumer surplus and producer surplus and explain how properly functioning markets maximize their sum, total surplus, while optimally allocating resources.

LO4.3 Describe free riding and public goods and illustrate why private firms cannot normally produce public goods.

LO4.4 Explain how positive and negative externalities cause under- and overallocations of resources.

LO4.5 Show why we normally won't want to pay what it would cost to eliminate every last bit of a negative externality such as air pollution.

LO4.6 (Appendix) Describe how information failures may justify government intervention in some markets.

Competitive markets usually do a remarkably effective job of allocating society's scarce resources to their most highly valued uses. Thus, we begin this chapter by demonstrating how properly functioning markets efficiently allocate resources. We then explore what happens when markets don't function properly. In some circumstances, economically desirable goods are not produced at all. In other situations, they are either overproduced or underproduced. This chapter focuses on these situations, which economists refer to as **market failures.**

In such situations, an economic role for government may arise. We will examine that role as it relates to public goods and so-called externalities—situations where market failures lead to suboptimal outcomes that the government may be able to improve upon by using its powers to tax, spend, and regulate. The government may, for instance, pay for the production of goods that the private sector fails to produce. It may also act to reduce the production of those goods and services that the private sector overproduces. Implementing such policies can, however, be both costly and complicated. Thus, we conclude the chapter by noting the government inefficiencies that can hinder government efforts to improve economic outcomes.

Market Failures in Competitive Markets[1]

LO4.1 Differentiate between demand-side market failures and supply-side market failures.

In Chapter 3 we asserted that "competitive markets usually produce an assignment of resources that is 'right' from an economic perspective." We now want to focus on the word "usually" and discuss exceptions. We must do this because it is unfortunately the case that the presence of robust competition involving many buyers and many sellers may not, by itself, be enough to guarantee that a market will allocate resources correctly. Market failures sometimes happen in competitive markets. The focus of this chapter is to explain how and why such market failures can arise.

Fortunately, the broad picture is simple. Market failures in competitive markets fall into just two categories:

- **Demand-side market failures** happen when demand curves do not reflect consumers' full willingness to pay for a good or service.

- **Supply-side market failures** occur when supply curves do not reflect the full cost of producing a good or service.

Demand-Side Market Failures

Demand-side market failures arise because it is impossible in certain cases to charge consumers what they are willing to pay for a product. Consider outdoor fireworks displays. People enjoy fireworks and would therefore be *willing* to pay to see a fireworks display if the only way to see it was to have to pay for the right to do so. But because such displays are outdoors and in public, people don't actually *have* to pay to see the display because there is no way to exclude those who haven't paid from also enjoying the show. Private firms will therefore be unwilling to produce outdoor fireworks displays, as it will be nearly impossible for them to raise enough revenue to cover production costs.

Supply-Side Market Failures

Supply-side market failures arise in situations in which a firm does not have to pay the full cost of producing its output. Consider a coal-burning power plant. The firm running the plant will have to pay for all of the land, labor, capital, and entrepreneurship that it uses to generate electricity by burning coal. But if the firm is not charged for the smoke that it releases into the atmosphere, it will fail to pay another set of costs—the costs that its pollution imposes on other people. These include future harm from global warming, toxins that affect wildlife, and possible damage to agricultural crops downwind.

A market failure arises because it is not possible for the market to correctly weigh costs and benefits in a situation in which some of the costs are completely unaccounted for. The coal-burning power plant produces more electricity and generates more pollution than it would if it had to pay for each ton of smoke that it released into the atmosphere. The extra units that are produced are units of output for which the costs are *greater than* the benefits. Obviously, these units should not be produced.

Efficiently Functioning Markets

LO4.2 Explain the origin of both consumer surplus and producer surplus and explain how properly functioning markets maximize their sum, total surplus, while optimally allocating resources.

The best way to understand market failure is to first understand how properly functioning competitive markets achieve economic efficiency. We touched on this subject in Chapter 3, but we now want to expand and deepen that analysis, both for its own sake and to set up our discussion of public goods and externalities. Two conditions must hold if a competitive market is to produce efficient outcomes: The demand curve in the market must reflect consumers' full willingness to pay, and the supply curve in the market must reflect all the costs of production. If these conditions hold, then the market will produce only units for which benefits are at least equal to costs. It will also maximize the amount of "benefit surpluses" that are shared between consumers and producers.

Consumer Surplus

The benefit surplus received by a consumer or consumers in a market is called **consumer surplus.** It is defined as the difference between the maximum price a consumer is (or consumers are) willing to pay for a product and the actual price that they do pay.

The maximum price that a person is willing to pay for a unit of a product depends on the opportunity cost of that person's consumption alternatives. Suppose that Ted is offered the chance to purchase an apple. He would of course like to have it for free, but the maximum amount he would be willing to pay depends on the alternative uses to which he can put his money. If his maximum willingness to pay for that particular apple is $1.25, then we know that he is willing to forgo up to—but not more than—$1.25 of other goods and services. Paying even one cent more would entail having to give up too much of other goods and services.

It also means that if Ted is charged any market price less than $1.25, he will receive a consumer surplus equal to the

---

[1]Other market failures arise when there are not enough buyers or sellers to ensure competition. In those situations, the lack of competition allows either buyers or sellers to restrict purchases or sales below optimal levels for their own benefit. As an example, a monopoly—a firm that is the only producer in its industry—can restrict the amount of output that it supplies in order to drive up the market price and thereby increase its own profit.

TABLE 4.1 Consumer Surplus

(1) Person	(2) Maximum Price Willing to Pay	(3) Actual Price (Equilibrium Price)	(4) Consumer Surplus
Bob	$13	$8	$5 (= $13 − $8)
Barb	12	8	4 (= $12 − $8)
Bill	11	8	3 (= $11 − $8)
Bart	10	8	2 (= $10 − $8)
Brent	9	8	1 (= $ 9 − $8)
Betty	8	8	0 (= $ 8 − $8)

difference between the $1.25 maximum price that he would have been willing to pay and the lower market price. For instance, if the market price is $0.50 per apple, Ted will receive a consumer surplus of $0.75 per apple (= $1.25 − $0.50). In nearly all markets, consumers individually and collectively gain greater total utility or satisfaction in dollar terms from their purchases than the amount of their expenditures (= product price × quantity). This utility surplus arises because each consumer who buys the product only has to pay the market equilibrium price even though many of them would have been willing to pay more than the equilibrium price to obtain the product.

The concept of maximum willingness to pay also gives us another way to understand demand curves. Consider Table 4.1, where the first two columns show the maximum amounts that six consumers would each be willing to pay for a bag of oranges. Bob, for instance, would be willing to pay a maximum of $13 for a bag of oranges. Betty, by contrast, would only be willing to pay a maximum of $8 for a bag of oranges.

Notice that the maximum prices that these individuals are willing to pay represent points on a demand curve because the lower the market price, the more bags of oranges will be demanded. At a price of $12.50, for instance, Bob will be the only person listed in the table who will purchase a bag. But at a price of $11.50, both Bob and Barb will want to purchase a bag. And at a price of $10.50, Bob, Barb, and Bill will each want to purchase a bag. The lower the price, the greater the total quantity demanded as the market price falls below the maximum prices of more and more consumers.

Lower prices also imply larger consumer surpluses. When the price is $12.50, Bob only gets $0.50 in consumer surplus because his maximum willingness to pay of $13 is only $0.50 higher than the market price of $12.50. But if the market price were to fall to $8, then his consumer surplus would be $5 (= $13 − $8). The third and fourth columns of Table 4.1 show how much consumer surplus each of our six consumers will receive if the market price of a bag of oranges is $8. Only Betty receives no consumer surplus because her maximum willingness to pay exactly matches the $8 equilibrium price.

FIGURE 4.1 Consumer surplus. Consumer surplus—shown as the green triangle—is the difference between the maximum prices consumers are willing to pay for a product and the lower equilibrium price, here assumed to be $8. For quantity Q_1, consumers are willing to pay the sum of the amounts represented by the green triangle and the yellow rectangle. Because they need to pay only the amount shown as the yellow rectangle, the green triangle shows consumer surplus.

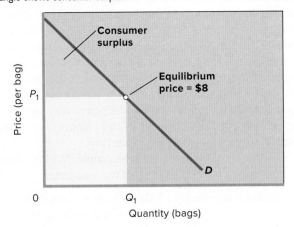

It is easy to show on a graph both the individual consumer surplus received by each particular buyer in a market as well as the collective consumer surplus received by all buyers. Consider Figure 4.1, which shows the market equilibrium price P_1 = $8 as well as the downsloping demand curve D for bags of oranges. Demand curve D includes not only the six consumers named in Table 4.1 but also every other consumer of oranges in the market. The individual consumer surplus of each particular person who is willing to buy at the $8 market price is simply the vertical distance from the horizontal line that marks the $8 market price up to that particular buyer's maximum willingness to pay. The collective consumer surplus obtained by all of our named and unnamed buyers is found by adding together each of their individual consumer surpluses. To obtain the Q_1 bags of oranges represented, consumers collectively are willing to pay the total amount shown by the sum of the green triangle and yellow rectangle under the demand curve and to the left of Q_1. But consumers need pay only the amount represented by the yellow rectangle (= $P_1 \times Q_1$). So the green triangle is the consumer surplus in this market. It is the sum of the vertical distances between the demand curve and the $8 equilibrium price at each quantity up to Q_1. Alternatively, it is the sum of the gaps between maximum willingness to pay and actual price, such as those we calculated in Table 4.1. Thus, consumer surplus can also be defined as the area that lies below the demand curve and above the price line that extends horizontally from P_1.

Consumer surplus and price are inversely (negatively) related. Given the demand curve, higher prices reduce consumer surplus; lower prices increase it. To test this generalization, draw in an equilibrium price above $8 in Figure 4.1

and observe the reduced size of the triangle representing consumer surplus. When price goes up, the gap narrows between the maximum willingness to pay and the actual price. Next, draw in an equilibrium price below $8 and see that consumer surplus increases. When price declines, the gap widens between maximum willingness to pay and actual price.

Producer Surplus

Like consumers, producers also receive a benefit surplus in markets. This **producer surplus** is the difference between the actual price a producer receives (or producers receive) and the minimum acceptable price that a consumer would have to pay the producer to make a particular unit of output available.

A producer's minimum acceptable price for a particular unit will equal the producer's marginal cost of producing that particular unit. That marginal cost will be the sum of the rent, wages, interest, and profit that the producer will need to pay in order to obtain the land, labor, capital, and entrepreneurship required to produce that particular unit. In this section, we are assuming that the marginal cost of producing a unit will include *all* of the costs of production. Unlike the coal-burning power plant mentioned previously, the producer must pay for all of its costs, including the cost of pollution. In later sections, we will explore the market failures that arise in situations where firms do not have to pay all their costs.

In addition to equaling marginal cost, a producer's minimum acceptable price can also be interpreted as the opportunity cost of bidding resources away from the production of other products. To see why this is true, suppose that Leah is an apple grower. The resources necessary for her to produce one apple could be used to produce other things. To get them directed toward producing an apple, it is necessary to pay Leah what it will cost her to bid the necessary resources away from other entrepreneurs who would like to use them to produce other products. Leah would, naturally, like to get paid as much as possible to produce the apple for you. But her minimum acceptable price is the lowest price you could pay her such that she can just break even after bidding away from other uses the land, labor, capital, and entrepreneurship necessary to produce the apple.

The size of the producer surplus earned on any particular unit will be the difference between the market price that the producer actually receives and the producer's minimum acceptable price. Consider Table 4.2, which shows the minimum acceptable prices of six different orange growers. With a market price of $8, Carlos, for instance, has a producer surplus of $5, which is equal to the market price of $8 minus his minimum acceptable price of $3. Chad, by contrast, receives no producer surplus because his minimum acceptable price of $8 just equals the market equilibrium price of $8.

Carlos's minimum acceptable price is lower than Chad's minimum acceptable price because Carlos is a more efficient

TABLE 4.2 Producer Surplus

(1) Person	(2) Minimum Acceptable Price	(3) Actual Price (Equilibrium Price)	(4) Consumer Surplus
Carlos	$3	$8	$5 (= $8 − $3)
Courtney	4	8	4 (= $8 − $4)
Chuck	5	8	3 (= $8 − $5)
Cindy	6	8	2 (= $8 − $6)
Craig	7	8	1 (= $8 − $7)
Chad	8	8	0 (= $8 − $8)

producer than Chad, by which we mean that Carlos produces oranges using a less-costly combination of resources than Chad uses. The differences in efficiency between Carlos and Chad are likely due to differences in the type and quality of resources available to them. Carlos, for instance, may own land perfectly suited to growing oranges, while Chad has land in the desert that requires costly irrigation if it is to be used to grow oranges. Thus, Chad has a higher marginal cost of producing oranges.

The minimum acceptable prices that producers are willing to accept form points on a supply curve because the higher the price, the more bags of oranges will be supplied. At a price of $3.50, for instance, only Carlos would be willing to supply a bag of oranges. But at a price of $5.50, Carlos, Courtney, and Chuck would all be willing to supply a bag of oranges. The higher the market price, the more oranges will be supplied, as the market price surpasses the marginal costs and minimum acceptable prices of more and more producers. Thus, supply curves shown in this competitive market are both marginal-cost curves and minimum-acceptable-price curves.

The supply curve in Figure 4.2 includes not only the six producers named in Table 4.2 but also every other producer of oranges in the market. At the market price of $8 per bag, Q_1 bags are produced because only those producers whose minimum acceptable prices are less than $8 per bag will choose to produce oranges with their resources. Those lower acceptable prices for each of the units up to Q_1 are shown by the portion of the supply curve lying to the left of and below the assumed $8 market price.

The individual producer surplus of each of these sellers is thus the vertical distance from each seller's respective minimum acceptable price on the supply curve up to the $8 market price. Their collective producer surplus is shown by the blue triangle in Figure 4.2. In that figure, producers collect revenues of $P_1 \times Q_1$, which is the sum of the blue triangle and the yellow area. As shown by the supply curve, however, revenues of only those illustrated by the yellow area would be required to entice producers to offer Q_1 bags of oranges for sale. The sellers therefore receive a producer surplus shown by the blue triangle. That surplus is the sum of the vertical

FIGURE 4.2 Producer surplus. Producer surplus—shown as the blue triangle—is the difference between the actual price producers receive for a product (here $8) and the lower minimum payments they are willing to accept. For quantity Q_1, producers receive the sum of the amounts represented by the blue triangle plus the yellow area. Because they need to receive only the amount shown by the yellow area to produce Q_1, the blue triangle represents producer surplus.

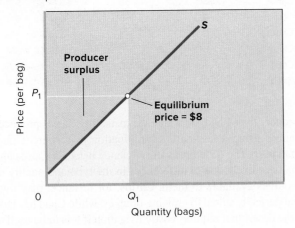

FIGURE 4.3 Efficiency: maximum combined consumer and producer surplus. At quantity Q_1 the combined amount of consumer surplus, shown as the green triangle, and producer surplus, shown as the blue triangle, is maximized. Efficiency occurs because, at Q_1, maximum willingness to pay, indicated by the points on the demand curve, equals minimum acceptable price, shown by the points on the supply curve.

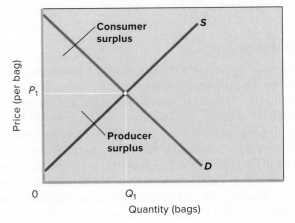

distances between the supply curve and the $8 equilibrium price at each of the quantities to the left of Q_1.

There is a direct (positive) relationship between equilibrium price and the amount of producer surplus. Given the supply curve, lower prices reduce producer surplus; higher prices increase it. If you pencil in a lower equilibrium price than $8, you will see that the producer surplus triangle gets smaller. The gaps between the minimum acceptable payments and the actual prices narrow when the price falls. If you pencil in an equilibrium price above $8, the size of the producer surplus triangle increases. The gaps between minimum acceptable payments and actual prices widen when the price increases.

Efficiency Revisited

In Figure 4.3 we bring together the demand and supply curves of Figures 4.1 and 4.2 to show the equilibrium price and quantity and the previously described regions of consumer and producer surplus. All markets that have downsloping demand curves and upsloping supply curves yield consumer and producer surplus.

Because we are assuming in Figure 4.3 that the demand curve reflects buyers' full willingness to pay and the supply curve reflects all of the costs facing sellers, the equilibrium quantity in Figure 4.3 reflects economic efficiency, which consists of productive efficiency and allocative efficiency.

- *Productive efficiency* is achieved because competition forces orange growers to use the best technologies and combinations of resources available. Doing so minimizes the per-unit cost of the output produced.
- *Allocative efficiency* is achieved because the correct quantity of oranges—Q_1—is produced relative to other goods and services.

There are two ways to understand why Q_1 is the correct quantity of oranges. Both involve realizing that any resources directed toward the production of oranges are resources that could have been used to produce other products. Thus, the only way to justify taking any amount of any resource (land, labor, capital, entrepreneurship) away from the production of other products is if it brings more utility or satisfaction when devoted to the production of oranges than it would if it were used to produce other products.

The first way to see why Q_1 is the allocatively efficient quantity of oranges is to note that demand and supply curves can be interpreted as measuring marginal benefit (MB) and marginal cost (MC). Recall from the discussion relating to Figure 1.3 that optimal allocation is achieved at the output level where MB = MC. We have already seen that supply curves are marginal cost curves. As it turns out, demand curves are marginal benefit curves. This is true because the maximum price that a consumer would be willing to pay for any particular unit is equal to the benefit that she would get if she were to consume that unit. Thus, each point on a demand curve represents both some consumer's maximum willingness to pay as well as the marginal benefit that he or she would get from consuming the particular unit in question.

Combining the fact that supply curves are MC curves with the fact that demand curves are MB curves, we see that points on the demand curve in Figure 4.3 measure the marginal benefit of oranges at each level of output, while points on the supply curve measure the marginal cost of oranges at each level of output. As a result, MB = MC where the demand and supply curves intersect—which means that the equilibrium quantity Q_1 must be allocatively efficient.

To gain a deeper understanding of why Q_1 is allocatively efficient, notice that for every unit up to Q_1 marginal benefit exceeds marginal cost (MB > MC). And because marginal cost includes the opportunity cost of not making other things with the resources needed to make these units, we know that people are made better off when the resources necessary to make these units are allocated to producing oranges rather than to producing anything else.

The second way to see why Q_1 is the correct quantity of oranges is based on our analysis of consumer and producer surplus and the fact that we can interpret demand and supply curves in terms of maximum willingness to pay and minimum acceptable price. In Figure 4.3, the maximum willingness to pay on the demand curve for each bag of oranges up to Q_1 exceeds the corresponding minimum acceptable price on the supply curve. Thus, each of these bags adds a positive amount (= maximum willingness to pay *minus* minimum acceptable price) to the *total* of consumer and producer surplus.

The fact that maximum willingness to pay exceeds minimum acceptable price for every unit up to Q_1 means that people gain more utility from producing and consuming those units than they would if they produced and consumed anything else that could be made with the resources that went into making those units. This is true because both the maximum willingness to pay and the minimum acceptable price take opportunity costs into account. As long as the maximum willingness to pay exceeds the minimum acceptable price, people are willing to pay more to consume a unit of the good in question (here, bags of oranges) than they would pay to consume anything else that could be made with the same resources. Only at the equilibrium quantity Q_1—where the maximum willingness to pay exactly equals the minimum acceptable price—does society exhaust all opportunities to produce units for which benefits exceed costs (including opportunity costs). Producing Q_1 units therefore achieves allocative efficiency because the market is producing and distributing only those units that make people happier with bags of oranges than they would be with anything else that could be produced with the same resources.

Geometrically, producing Q_1 units maximizes the combined area of consumer and producer surplus in Figure 4.3. In this context, the combined area is referred to as *total surplus*. Thus, when Q_1 units are produced, total surplus is equal to the large triangle formed by the green consumer-surplus triangle and the blue producer-surplus triangle.

When demand curves reflect buyers' full willingness to pay and when supply curves reflect all the costs facing sellers, competitive markets produce equilibrium quantities that maximize the sum of consumer and producer surplus. Allocative efficiency occurs at the market equilibrium quantity where three conditions exist simultaneously:

- MB = MC (Figure 1.3).

- Maximum willingness to pay = minimum acceptable price.

- Total surplus (= sum of consumer and producer surplus) is at a maximum.

Economists are enamored of markets because properly functioning markets automatically achieve allocative efficiency. Other methods of allocating resources—such as government central planning—do exist. But because other methods cannot do any better than properly functioning markets—and may, in many cases, do much worse—economists usually prefer that resources be allocated through markets whenever properly functioning markets are available.

Efficiency Losses (or Deadweight Losses)

Figures 4.4a and 4.4b demonstrate that **efficiency losses**—reductions of combined consumer and producer surplus—result from both underproduction and overproduction. First, consider Figure 4.4a, which analyzes the case of underproduction by considering what happens if output falls from the efficient level Q_1 to the smaller amount Q_2. When that happens, the sum of consumer and producer surplus, previously *abc*, falls to *adec*. So the combined consumer and producer surplus declines by the amount of the gray triangle to the left

FIGURE 4.4 Efficiency losses (or deadweight losses). Quantity levels either less than or greater than the efficient quantity Q_1 create efficiency losses. (a) Triangle *dbe* shows the efficiency loss associated with underproduction at output Q_2. (b) Triangle *bfg* illustrates the efficiency loss associated with overproduction at output level Q_3.

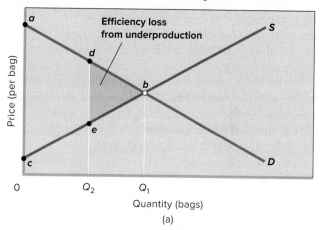

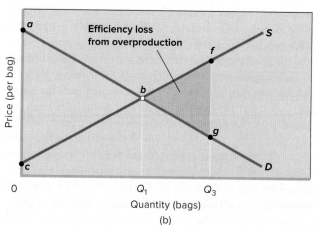

of Q_1. That triangle represents an efficiency loss to buyers and sellers. And because buyers and sellers are members of society, it represents an efficiency loss (or a so-called **deadweight loss**) to society.

For output levels from Q_2 to Q_1, consumers' maximum willingness to pay (as reflected by points on the demand curve) exceeds producers' minimum acceptable price (as reflected by points on the supply curve). By failing to produce units of this product for which a consumer is willing to pay more than a producer is willing to accept, society suffers a loss of net benefits. As a concrete example, consider a particular unit for which a consumer is willing to pay $10 and a producer is willing to accept $6. The $4 difference between those values is a net benefit that will not be realized if this unit is not produced. In addition, the resources that should have gone to producing this unit will go instead to producing other products that will not generate as much utility as if those resources had been used here to produce this unit of this product. The triangle *dbe* in Figure 4.4a shows the total loss of net benefits that results from failing to produce the units from Q_2 to Q_1.

In contrast, consider the case of overproduction shown in Figure 4.4b, in which the number of oranges produced is Q_3 rather than the efficient level Q_1. In Figure 4.4b the combined consumer and producer surplus therefore declines by *bfg*—the gray triangle to the right of Q_1. This triangle subtracts from the total consumer and producer surplus of *abc* that would occur if the quantity had been Q_1. That is, for all units from 0 to Q_1, benefits exceed costs, so that those units generate the economic surplus shown by triangle *abc*. But the units from Q_1 to Q_3 are such that costs exceed benefits. Thus, they generate an economic loss shown by triangle *bfg*. The total economic surplus for all units from 0 to Q_3 is therefore the economic surplus given by *abc* for the units from 0 to Q_1 *minus* the economic loss given by *bfg* for the units from Q_1 to Q_3.

Producing any unit beyond Q_1 generates an economic loss because the willingness to pay for such units on the part of consumers is less than the minimum acceptable price to produce such units on the part of producers. As a concrete example, note that producing an item for which the maximum willingness to pay is, say, $7 and the minimum acceptable price is, say, $10 subtracts $3 from society's net benefits. Such production is uneconomical and creates an efficiency loss (or deadweight loss) for society. Because the net benefit of each bag of oranges from Q_1 to Q_3 is negative, we know that the benefits from these units are smaller than the opportunity costs of the other products that could have been produced with the resources that were used to produce these bags of oranges. The resources used to produce the bags from Q_1 to Q_3 could have generated net benefits instead of net losses if they had been directed toward producing other products. The gray triangle *bfg* to the right of Q_1 in Figure 4.4b shows the total efficiency loss from overproduction at Q_3.

The magic of markets is that when demand reflects consumers' full willingness to pay and when supply reflects all costs, the market equilibrium quantity will automatically equal the allocatively efficient output level. Under these conditions, the market equilibrium quantity will ensure that there are neither efficiency losses from underproduction nor efficiency losses from overproduction. As we are about to see, however, such losses do happen when either demand does not reflect consumers' full willingness to pay or supply does not reflect all costs.

Public Goods

LO4.3 Describe free riding and public goods and illustrate why private firms cannot normally produce public goods.

Demand-side market failures arise in competitive markets when demand curves fail to reflect consumers' full willingness to pay for a good or service. In such situations, markets fail to produce all of the units for which there are net benefits because demand curves underreport how much consumers are willing and able to pay. This underreporting problem reaches its most extreme form in the case of a public good: Markets may fail to produce *any* of the public good because its demand curve may reflect *none* of its consumers' willingness to pay.

To understand public goods, we first need to understand the characteristics that define private goods.

Private Goods Characteristics

We have seen that the market system produces a wide range of **private goods**. These are the goods offered for sale in stores, in shops, and on the Internet. Examples include automobiles, clothing, personal computers, household appliances, and sporting goods. Private goods are distinguished by rivalry and excludability.

- **Rivalry** (in consumption) means that when one person buys and consumes a product, it is not available for another person to buy and consume. When Adams purchases and drinks a bottle of mineral water, it is not available for Benson to purchase and consume.

- **Excludability** means that sellers can keep people who do not pay for a product from obtaining its benefits. Only people who are willing and able to pay the market price for bottles of water can obtain these drinks and the benefits they confer.

Consumers fully express their personal demands for private goods in the market. If Adams likes bottled mineral water, that fact will be known by her desire to purchase the product. Other things equal, the higher the price of bottled water, the fewer bottles she will buy. So Adams's demand for bottled water will reflect an inverse relationship between the price of bottled water and the quantity of it demanded. This is simply *individual* demand, as described in Chapter 3.

The *market* demand for a private good is the horizontal summation of the individual demand schedules (review Figure 3.2). Suppose just two consumers comprise the market for bottled water and the price is $1 per bottle. If Adams will purchase 3 bottles and Benson will buy 2, the market demand will reflect consumers' demand for 5 bottles at the $1 price. Similar summations of quantities demanded at other prices will generate the market demand schedule and curve.

Suppose the equilibrium price of bottled water is $1. Adams and Benson will buy a total of 5 bottles, and the sellers will obtain total revenue of $5 (= $1 × 5). If the sellers' cost per bottle is $0.80, their total cost will be $4 (= $0.80 × 5). So sellers charging $1 per bottle will obtain $5 of total revenue, incur $4 of total cost, and earn $1 of profit on the 5 bottles sold.

Because firms can profitably "tap market demand" for private goods, they will produce and offer them for sale. Consumers demand private goods, and profit-seeking suppliers produce goods that satisfy the demand. Consumers willing to pay the market price obtain the goods; nonpayers go without. A competitive market not only makes private goods available to consumers but also allocates society's resources efficiently to the particular product. There is neither underproduction nor overproduction of the product.

Public Goods Characteristics

Public goods have the opposite characteristics of private goods. Public goods are distinguished by nonrivalry and nonexcludability.

- **Nonrivalry** (in consumption) means that one person's consumption of a good does not preclude consumption of the good by others. Everyone can simultaneously obtain the benefit from a public good such as national defense, street lighting, a global positioning system, or environmental protection.

- **Nonexcludability** means there is no effective way of excluding individuals from the benefit of the good once it comes into existence. Once in place, you cannot exclude someone from benefiting from national defense, street lighting, a global positioning system, or environmental protection.

These two characteristics create a **free-rider problem.** Once a producer has provided a public good, everyone, including nonpayers, can obtain the benefit.

Because most people do not voluntarily pay for something that they can obtain for free, most people become free riders. These free riders like the public good and would be willing to pay for it if producers could somehow force them to pay—but nonexcludability means that there is no way for producers to withhold the good from the free riders without also denying it to the few who do pay. As a result, free riding means that the willingness to pay of the free riders is not expressed in the market. From the viewpoint of producers, free riding reduces demand. The more free riding, the less demand. And if all consumers free ride, demand will collapse all the way to zero.

The low or even zero demand caused by free riding makes it virtually impossible for private firms to profitably provide public goods. With little or no demand, firms cannot effectively "tap market demand" for revenues and profits. As a result, they will not produce public goods. Society will therefore suffer efficiency losses because goods for which marginal benefits exceed marginal costs are not produced. Thus, if society wants a public good to be produced, it will have to direct government to provide it. Because the public good will still feature nonexcludability, the government won't have any better luck preventing free riding or charging people for it. But because the government can finance the provision of the public good through the taxation of other things, the government does not have to worry about profitability. It can therefore provide the public good even when private firms can't.

Examples of public goods include national defense, outdoor fireworks displays, the light beams thrown out by lighthouses, public art displays, public music concerts, MP3 music files posted to file-sharing websites, and ideas and inventions that are not protected by patents or copyrights. Each of these goods or services shows both nonrivalry and nonexcludability.

In a few special cases, private firms can provide public goods because the production costs of these public goods can be covered by the profits generated by closely related private

CONSIDER THIS . . .

Street Entertainers

Street entertainers are often found in tourist areas of major cities. These entertainers illuminate the concepts of free riders and public goods.

Source: © Colin Young-Wolff/PhotoEdit

Most street entertainers have a hard time earning a living from their activities (unless event organizers pay them) because they have no way of excluding nonpayers from the benefits of their entertainment. They essentially are providing public, not private, goods and must rely on voluntary payments.

The result is a significant free-rider problem. Only a few in the audience put money in the container or instrument case, and many who do so contribute only token amounts. The rest are free riders who obtain the benefits of the street entertainment and retain their money for purchases that they initiate.

Street entertainers are acutely aware of the free-rider problem, and some have found creative ways to lessen it. For example, some entertainers involve the audience directly in the act. This usually creates a greater sense of audience willingness (or obligation) to contribute money at the end of the performance.

"Pay for performance" is another creative approach to lessening the free-rider problem. A good example is the street entertainer painted up to look like a statue. When people drop coins into the container, the "statue" makes a slight movement. The greater the contributions, the greater the movement. But these human "statues" still face a free-rider problem: Nonpayers also get to enjoy the acts.

goods. For instance, private companies can make a profit providing broadcast TV—which is a nonrival, nonexcludable public good—because they control who gets to air TV commercials, which are rival and excludable private goods. The money that broadcasters make from selling airtime for ads allows them to turn a profit despite having to give their main product, broadcast TV, away for free.

Unfortunately, only a few public goods can be subsidized in this way by closely related private goods. For the large majority of public goods, private provision is unprofitable. As a result, there are only two remaining ways for a public good to be provided: private philanthropy or government provision. For many less expensive or less important public goods like fireworks displays or public art, society may feel comfortable relying on private philanthropy. But when it comes to public goods like national defense, people normally look to the government.

This leads to an important question: Once a government decides to produce a particular public good, how can it determine the optimal amount that it should produce? How can it avoid either underallocating or overallocating society's scarce resources to the production of the public good?

Optimal Quantity of a Public Good

If consumers need not reveal their true demand for a public good in the marketplace, how can society determine the optimal amount of that good? The answer is that the government has to try to estimate the demand for a public good through surveys or public votes. It can then compare the marginal benefit (MB) of an added unit of the good against the government's marginal cost (MC) of providing it. Adhering to the MB = MC rule, government can provide the "right," meaning "efficient," amount of the public good.

Demand for Public Goods

The demand for a public good is somewhat unusual. Suppose Adams and Benson are the only two people in the society, and their marginal willingness to pay for a public good, national defense, is as shown in columns 1 and 2 and columns 1 and 3 in Table 4.3. Economists might have discovered these schedules through a survey asking hypothetical questions about how much each citizen was willing to pay for various types and amounts of public goods rather than go without them.

Notice that the schedules in Table 4.3 are price-quantity schedules, implying that they are demand schedules. Rather than depicting demand in the usual way—the quantity of a product someone is willing to buy at each possible price—these schedules show the price someone is willing to pay for an extra unit at each possible quantity. That is, Adams is willing to pay $4 for the first unit of the public good, $3 for the second, $2 for the third, and so on.

Suppose the government produces 1 unit of this public good. Because of nonrivalry, Adams's consumption of the good does not preclude Benson from also consuming it, and vice versa. So both consume the good, and neither volunteers to pay for it. But from Table 4.3 we can find the amount these

TABLE 4.3   Demand for a Public Good, Two Individuals

(1) Quantity of Public Good	(2) Adams's Willingness to Pay (Price)		(3) Benson's Willingness to Pay (Price)		(4) Collective Willingness to Pay (Price)
1	$4	+	$5	=	$9
2	3	+	4	=	7
3	2	+	3	=	5
4	1	+	2	=	3
5	0	+	1	=	1

Source: © Robert Kohlhuber/Getty Images RF

Responding to Digital Free Riding

Four teenage friends start a rock band. They practice hard, master their instruments, write their own songs, and do gig after gig for nearly nothing at local bars to gain experience and perfect their music.

After nearly five years of effort, they get signed to a major record label. But the year is 2005 and record sales are collapsing due to digital piracy. The rise of Internet file sharing has turned music into a public good and sales of recorded music have collapsed as hundreds of millions of music lovers have become digital free riders.

At first, the band struggles with the new reality. If they can't make a living selling music, they might have to quit music and get regular jobs. But then they realize that while recorded music is now free for anyone who wants it to be free, live music isn't. And neither are T-shirts or memorabilia.

So the band promotes itself online and allows free downloads to help propel its popularity. But then it charges steep prices at live concerts and makes sure that its T-shirts and memorabilia also generate substantial revenues. By doing so, the band adjusts to the new reality in which music has become a public good, but live concerts and T-shirts have not. They charge for the items that are still private goods.

Benson's willingness-to-pay curves *vertically* to derive the collective willingness-to-pay curve (demand curve). The summing procedure is downward from the top graph to the middle graph to the bottom (total) graph. For example, the height of the collective demand curve D_c at 2 units of

FIGURE 4.5 The optimal amount of a public good. Two people—Adams and Benson—are the only members of a hypothetical economy. (a) D_1 shows Adams's willingness to pay for various quantities of a particular public good. (b) D_2 shows Benson's willingness to pay pay for these same quantities of this public good. (c) The collective demand for this public good is shown by D_c and is found by summing vertically Adams's and Benson's individual willingness-to-pay curves. The supply (S) of the public good is upsloping, reflecting rising marginal costs. The optimal amount of the public good is 3 units, determined by the intersection of D_c and S. At that output, marginal benefit (reflected in the collective demand curve D_c) equals marginal cost (reflected in the supply curve S).

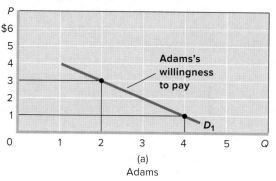

(a)
Adams

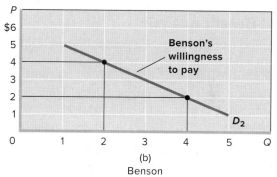

(b)
Benson

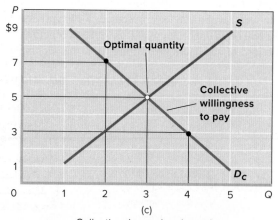

(c)
Collective demand and supply

two people would be willing to pay, together, rather than do without this 1 unit of the good. Columns 1 and 2 show that Adams would be willing to pay $4 for the first unit of the public good; columns 1 and 3 show that Benson would be willing to pay $5 for it. So the two people are jointly willing to pay $9 (= $4 + $5) for this first unit.

For the second unit of the public good, the collective price they are willing to pay is $7 (= $3 from Adams + $4 from Benson); for the third unit they would pay $5 (= $2 + $3); and so on. By finding the collective willingness to pay for each additional unit (column 4), we can construct a collective demand schedule (a willingness-to-pay schedule) for the public good. Here we are *not* adding the quantities demanded at each possible price, as we do when we determine the market demand for a private good. Instead, we are adding the prices that people are willing to pay for the last unit of the public good at each possible quantity demanded.

Figure 4.5 shows the same adding procedure graphically, using the data from Table 4.3. Note that we sum Adams's and output in the bottom graph is $7, the sum of the amounts that Adams and Benson are each willing to pay for the second unit (= $3 + $4). Likewise, the height of the collective demand curve at 4 units of the public good is $3 (= $1 + $2).

What does it mean in Figure 4.5a that, for example, Adams is willing to pay $3 for the second unit of the public good? It means that Adams expects to receive $3 of extra benefit or utility from that unit. And we know from our discussion of diminishing marginal utility in Chapter 3 that successive units of any good yield less and less added benefit. This is also true for public goods, explaining the downward slope of the willingness-to-pay curves of Adams, Benson, and society. These curves, in essence, are marginal-benefit (MB) curves.

Comparing MB and MC

We can now determine the optimal quantity of the public good. The collective demand curve D_c in Figure 4.5c measures society's marginal benefit of each unit of this particular good. The supply curve S in that figure measures society's marginal cost of each unit. The optimal quantity of this public good occurs where marginal benefit equals marginal cost, or where the two curves intersect. In Figure 4.5c that point is 3 units of the public good, where the collective willingness to pay for the last (third) unit—the marginal benefit—just matches that unit's marginal cost ($5 = $5). As we saw in Chapter 1, equating marginal benefit and marginal cost efficiently allocates society's scarce resources.

Cost-Benefit Analysis

The above example suggests a practical means, called **cost-benefit analysis,** for deciding whether to provide a particular public good and how much of it to provide. Like our example, cost-benefit analysis (or marginal-benefit–marginal-cost analysis) involves a comparison of marginal costs and marginal benefits.

Concept Suppose the federal government is contemplating a highway construction plan. Because the economy's resources are limited, any decision to use more resources in the public sector will mean fewer resources for the private sector. There will be an opportunity cost, as well as a benefit. The cost is the loss of satisfaction resulting from the accompanying

decline in the production of private goods; the benefit is the extra satisfaction resulting from the output of more public goods. Should the needed resources be shifted from the private to the public sector? The answer is yes if the benefit from the extra public goods exceeds the cost that results from having fewer private goods. The answer is no if the cost of the forgone private goods is greater than the benefit associated with the extra public goods.

Cost-benefit analysis, however, can indicate more than whether a public program is worth doing. It can also help the government decide on the *extent* to which a project should be pursued. Real economic questions cannot usually be answered simply by "yes" or "no" but, rather, involve questions such as "how much" or "how little."

Illustration Roads and highways can be run privately, as excludability is possible with toll gates. However, the federal highway system is almost entirely nonexclusive because anyone with a car can get on and off most federal highways without restriction any time they want. Federal highways therefore satisfy one characteristic of a public good, nonexcludability. The other characteristic, nonrivalry, is also satisfied by the fact that unless a highway is already extremely crowded, one person's driving on the highway does not preclude another person's driving on the highway. Thus, the federal highway system is effectively a public good. This leads us to ask: Should the federal government expand the federal highway system? If so, what is the proper size or scope for the overall project?

Table 4.4 lists a series of increasingly ambitious and increasingly costly highway projects: widening existing two-lane highways; building new two-lane highways; building new four-lane highways; building new six-lane highways. The extent to which government should undertake highway construction depends on the costs and benefits. The costs are largely the costs of constructing and maintaining the highways; the benefits are improved flows of people and goods throughout the country.[2]

---

[2]Because the costs of public goods typically are immediate while the benefits often accrue over longer time periods, economists convert both costs and benefits to present values for comparison. Doing so properly accounts for the time-value of money, discussed at length in later chapters.

TABLE 4.4 **Cost-Benefit Analysis for a National Highway Construction Project (in Billions)**

(1) Plan	(2) Total Cost of Project	(3) Marginal Cost	(4) Total Benefit	(5) Marginal Benefit	(6) Net Benefit (4) − (2)
No new construction	$ 0		$ 0		$ 0
		$ 4		$ 5	
A: Widen existing highways	4		5		1
		6		8	
B: New 2-lane highways	10		13		3
		8		10	
C: New 4-lane highways	18		23		5
		10		3	
D: New 6-lane highways	28		26		−2

The table shows that total annual benefit (column 4) exceeds total annual cost (column 2) for plans A, B, and C, indicating that some highway construction is economically justifiable. We see this directly in column 6, where total costs (column 2) are subtracted from total annual benefits (column 4). Net benefits are positive for plans A, B, and C. Plan D is not economically justifiable because net benefits are negative.

But the question of optimal size or scope for this project remains. Comparing the marginal cost (the change in total cost) and the marginal benefit (the change in total benefit) relating to each plan determines the answer. The guideline is well known to you from previous discussions: Increase an activity, project, or output as long as the marginal benefit (column 5) exceeds the marginal cost (column 3). Stop the activity at, or as close as possible to, the point at which the marginal benefit equals the marginal cost. Do not undertake a project for which marginal cost exceeds marginal benefit.

In this case plan C (building new four-lane highways) is the best plan. Plans A and B are too modest; the marginal benefits exceed the marginal costs, and there is a better option. Plan D's marginal cost ($10 billion) exceeds the marginal benefit ($3 billion) and therefore cannot be justified; it overallocates resources to the project. Plan C is closest to the theoretical optimum because its marginal benefit ($10 billion) still exceeds marginal cost ($8 billion) but approaches the MB = MC (or MC = MB) ideal.

This **marginal-cost–marginal-benefit rule** actually tells us which plan provides the maximum excess of total benefits over total costs or, in other words, the plan that provides society with the maximum net benefit. You can confirm directly in column 6 that the maximum net benefit (= $5 billion) is associated with plan C.

Cost-benefit analysis shatters the myth that "economy in government" and "reduced government spending" are synonymous. "Economy" is concerned with using scarce resources efficiently. If the marginal cost of a proposed government program exceeds its marginal benefit, then the proposed public program should not be undertaken. But if the marginal benefit exceeds the marginal cost, then it would be uneconomical or "wasteful" not to spend on that government program. Economy in government does not mean minimization of public spending. It means allocating resources between the private and public sectors and among public goods to achieve maximum net benefit.

Quasi-Public Goods

Government provides many goods that fit the economist's definition of a public good. However, it also provides other goods and services that could be produced and delivered in such a way that exclusion would be possible. Such goods, called **quasi-public goods**, include education, streets and highways, police and fire protection, libraries and museums,

preventive medicine, and sewage disposal. They could all be priced and provided by private firms through the market system. But, because the benefits of these goods flow well beyond the benefit to individual buyers, these goods would be underproduced by the market system. Therefore, government often provides them to avoid the underallocation of resources that would otherwise occur.

The Reallocation Process

How are resources reallocated from the production of private goods to the production of public and quasi-public goods? If the resources of the economy are fully employed, government must free up resources from the production of private goods and make them available for producing public and quasi-public goods. It does so by reducing private demand for them. And it does that by levying taxes on households and businesses, taking some of their income out of the circular flow. With lower incomes and hence less purchasing power, households and businesses must curtail their consumption and investment spending. As a result, the private demand for goods and services declines, as does the private demand for resources. So by diverting purchasing power from private spenders to government, taxes remove resources from private use.

Government then spends the tax proceeds to provide public and quasi-public goods and services. Taxation releases resources from the production of private consumer goods (food, clothing, television sets) and private investment goods (wi-fi networks, boxcars, warehouses). Government shifts those resources to the production of public and quasi-public goods (post offices, submarines, parks), changing the composition of the economy's total output.

QUICK REVIEW 4.2

✓ Public goods are characterized by nonrivalry and nonexcludability.

✓ The demand (marginal-benefit) curve for a public good is found by vertically adding the prices that all the members of society are willing to pay for the last unit of output at various output levels.

✓ The socially optimal amount of a public good is the amount at which the marginal cost and marginal benefit of the good are equal.

✓ Cost-benefit analysis is the method of evaluating alternative projects or sizes of projects by comparing the marginal cost and marginal benefit and applying the MC = MB rule.

✓ The government uses taxes to reallocate resources from the production of private goods to the production of public and quasi-public goods.

Externalities

LO4.4 Explain how positive and negative externalities cause under- and overallocations of resources.

In addition to providing public goods, governments can also improve the allocation of resources in the economy by correcting for market failures caused by externalities. An **externality** occurs when some of the costs or the benefits of a good or service are passed onto or "spill over to" someone other than the immediate buyer or seller. Such spillovers are called externalities because they are benefits or costs that accrue to some third party that is external to the market transaction.

There are both positive and negative externalities. An example of a negative externality is the cost of breathing polluted air; an example of a positive externality is the benefit of having everyone else inoculated against some disease. When there are negative externalities, an overproduction of the related product occurs and there is an overallocation of resources to this product. Conversely, underproduction and underallocation of resources result when positive externalities are present.

Negative Externalities

Negative externalities cause supply-side market failures. These failures happen because producers do not take into account the costs that their negative externalities impose on others. This failure to account for all production costs causes firms' supply curves to shift to the right of (or below) where they would be if firms properly accounted for all costs. Consider the costs of breathing polluted air that are imposed on third parties living downwind of smoke-spewing factories. Because polluting firms do not take account of such costs, they oversupply the products they make, producing units for which total costs (including those that fall on third parties) exceed total benefits. The same is true when airlines fail to account for the costs that noisy jet engines impose on people living near airports and when biodiesel factories that convert dead animal parts into fuel release foul smelling gases that disgust those living nearby.

Figure 4.6a illustrates how negative externalities affect the allocation of resources. When producers shift some of their costs onto the community as external costs, producers' marginal costs are lower than they would be if they had to pay for those costs. So their supply curves do not include or "capture" all the costs legitimately associated with the production of their goods. A polluting producer's supply curve such as S in Figure 4.6a therefore understates the total cost of production. The firm's supply curve lies to the right of (or below) the total-cost supply curve S_t, which would include the spillover cost. Through polluting and thus transferring costs to society, the firm enjoys lower production costs and has the supply curve S.

The outcome is shown in Figure 4.6a, where equilibrium output Q_e is larger than the optimal output Q_o. This means that resources are overallocated to the production of this commodity; too many units of it are produced. In fact, there is a net loss to society for every unit from Q_o to Q_e because, for those units, the supply curve that accounts for all costs, S_t, lies above the demand curve. Therefore, MC exceeds MB for those units. The resources that went into producing those units should have been used elsewhere in the economy to produce other things.

In terms of our previous analysis, the negative externality results in an efficiency loss represented by triangle abc.

Positive Externalities

Positive externalities cause demand-side market failures. These failures happen because market demand curves in such cases fail to include the willingness to pay of the third parties who receive the external benefits caused by the positive externality. This failure to account for all benefits shifts market demand curves to the left of (or below) where they would be if they included all benefits and the willingness to pay of both the third parties as well as the primary beneficiaries. Because demand curves fail to take into account all benefits when there are positive externalities, markets in such cases fail to produce all units for which benefits (including those that are received by third parties) exceed costs. As a result, products featuring positive externalities are underproduced.

Vaccinations are a good example of how positive externalities reduce demand and shift demand curves down and to the left. When John gets vaccinated against a disease, he benefits not only himself (because he can no longer contract the

FIGURE 4.6 Negative externalities and positive externalities. (a) With negative externalities borne by society, the producers' supply curve S is to the right of (below) the total-cost supply curve S_t. Consequently, the equilibrium output Q_e is greater than the optimal output Q_o, and the efficiency loss is abc. (b) When positive externalities accrue to society, the market demand curve D is to the left of (below) the total-benefit demand curve D_t. As a result, the equilibrium output Q_e is less than the optimal output Q_o, and the efficiency loss is xyz.

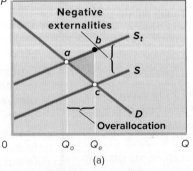

(a)
Negative externalities

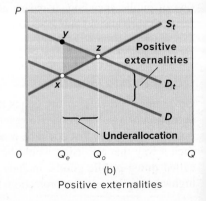

(b)
Positive externalities

disease) but also everyone else around him (because they know that in the future he will never be able to infect them). These other people would presumably be willing to pay some positive amount of money for the benefits they receive when John is vaccinated. But because his vaccination is a public good, there is no way to make them pay.

To see why his vaccination is a public good, note that the vaccination benefits that John provides to others feature non-rivalry and nonexcludability. There is nonrivalry because the protection his vaccination provides to one person does not lessen the protection that it provides to other people. There is nonexcludability because once he is vaccinated, there is no way to exclude anyone in particular from benefiting from his vaccination. Thus, the market demand for vaccinations will only include John's personal willingness to pay for the benefits that he personally receives from the vaccination. The market demand will fail to include the benefits that others receive. As a result, demand will be too low and vaccinations will be underproduced.

Figure 4.6b shows the impact of positive externalities on resource allocation. When external benefits occur, the market demand curve D lies to the left of (or below) the total-benefits demand curve, D_t. That is, D does not include the external benefits of the product, whereas D_t does.

The outcome is that the equilibrium output Q_e is less than the optimal output Q_o. The market fails to produce enough vaccinations, and resources are underallocated to this product. The underproduction implies that society is missing out on a significant amount of potential net benefits. For every unit from Q_e to Q_o, the demand curve that accounts for all benefits, D_t, lies above the supply curve that accounts for all costs—including the opportunity cost of producing other items with the resources that would be needed to produce these units. Therefore, MB exceeds MC for each of these units, and we know that society should redeploy some of its resources away from the production of other things in order to produce these units that generate net benefits.

In terms of our previous analysis, the positive externality results in an efficiency loss represented by triangle xyz.

Government Intervention

Government intervention may be called upon to achieve economic efficiency when externalities affect large numbers of people or when community interests are at stake. Government can use direct controls and taxes to counter negative externalities; it may provide subsidies or public goods to deal with positive externalities.

Direct Controls The direct way to reduce negative externalities from a certain activity is to pass legislation limiting that activity. Such direct controls force the offending firms to incur the actual costs of the offending activity. Historically, direct controls in the form of uniform emission standards—limits on allowable pollution—have dominated American air pollution policy. For example, the Clean Air Act of 1990 (1) forced factories and businesses to install "maximum achievable control technology" to reduce emissions of 189 toxic chemicals by 90 percent between 1990 and 2000; (2) required a 30 to 60 percent reduction in tailpipe emissions from automobiles by 2000; (3) mandated a 50 percent reduction in the use of chlorofluorocarbons (CFCs), which deplete the ozone layer (CFCs were used widely as a coolant in refrigeration, a blowing agent for foam, and a solvent in the electronics industry); and (4) forced coal-burning utilities to cut their emissions of sulfur dioxide by about 50 percent to reduce the acid-rain destruction of lakes and forests. Clean-water legislation limits the amount of heavy metals, detergents, and other pollutants firms can discharge into rivers and bays. Toxic-waste laws dictate special procedures and dump sites for disposing of contaminated soil and solvents. Violating these laws means fines and, in some cases, imprisonment.

Direct controls raise the marginal cost of production because the firms must operate and maintain pollution-control equipment. The supply curve S in Figure 4.7b, which does not

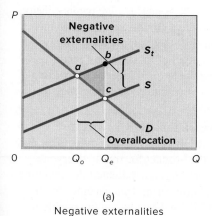

(a)
Negative externalities

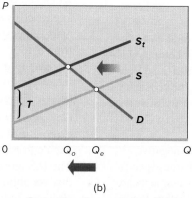

(b)
Correcting the overallocation
of resources via direct controls
or via a tax

FIGURE 4.7 Correcting for negative externalities.
(a) Negative externalities result in an overallocation of resources. (b) Government can correct this overallocation in two ways: (1) using direct controls, which would shift the supply curve from S to S_t and reduce output from Q_e to Q_o, or (2) imposing a specific tax T, which would also shift the supply curve from S to S_t, eliminating the overallocation of resources and thus the efficiency loss.

CONSIDER THIS . . .

Source: © Digital Vision/Getty Images RF

The Fable of the Bees

Economist Ronald Coase received the Nobel Prize for his so-called **Coase theorem**, which pointed out that under the right conditions, private individuals could often negotiate their own mutually agreeable solutions to externality problems through *private bargaining* without the need for government interventions like pollution taxes.

This is a very important insight because it means that we shouldn't automatically call for government intervention every time we see a potential externality problem. Consider the positive externalities that bees provide by pollinating farmers' crops. Should we assume that beekeeping will be underprovided unless the government intervenes with, for instance, subsidies to encourage more hives and hence more pollination?

As it turns out, no. Research has shown that farmers and beekeepers long ago used private bargaining to develop customs and payment systems that avoid free riding by farmers and encourage beekeepers to keep the optimal number of hives. Free riding is avoided by the custom that all farmers in an area simultaneously hire beekeepers to provide bees to pollinate their crops. And farmers always pay the beekeepers for their pollination services because if they didn't, then no beekeeper would ever work with them in the future—a situation that would lead to massively reduced crop yields due to a lack of pollination.

The "Fable of the Bees" is a good reminder that it is a fallacy to assume that the government must always get involved to remedy externalities. In many cases, the private sector can solve both positive and negative externality problems on its own.

reflect the external costs, shifts leftward to the total-cost supply curve, S_t. Product price increases, equilibrium output falls from Q_e to Q_o, and the initial overallocation of resources shown in Figure 4.7a is corrected. Observe that the efficiency loss shown by triangle *abc* in Figure 4.7a disappears after the overallocation is corrected in Figure 4.7b.

Pigovian Taxes A second policy approach to negative externalities is for government to levy taxes or charges specifically on the related good. These targeted tax assessments are often referred to as **Pigovian taxes** in honor of Arthur Pigou, the first economist to study externalities. Example: The government has placed a manufacturing excise tax on CFCs,

which deplete the stratospheric ozone layer protecting the earth from excessive solar ultraviolet radiation. Facing such an excise tax, manufacturers must decide whether to pay the tax or expend additional funds to purchase or develop substitute products. In either case, the tax raises the marginal cost of producing CFCs, shifting the private supply curve for this product leftward (or upward).

In Figure 4.7b, a tax equal to T per unit increases the firm's marginal cost, shifting the supply curve from S to S_t. The equilibrium price rises, and the equilibrium output declines from Q_e to the economically efficient level Q_o. The tax thus eliminates the initial overallocation of resources and therefore the efficiency loss.

Subsidies and Government Provision Where spillover benefits are large and diffuse, as in our earlier example of inoculations, government has three options for correcting the underallocation of resources:

- *Subsidies to buyers* Figure 4.8a again shows the supply-demand situation for positive externalities. Government could correct the underallocation of resources, for example, to inoculations, by subsidizing consumers of the product. It could give each new mother in the United States a discount coupon to be used to obtain a series of inoculations for her child. The coupon would reduce the "price" to the mother by, say, 50 percent. As shown in Figure 4.8b, this program would shift the demand curve for inoculations from too-low D to the appropriate D_t. The number of inoculations would rise from Q_e to the economically optimal Q_o, eliminating the underallocation of resources and efficiency loss shown in Figure 4.8a.

- *Subsidies to producers* A subsidy to producers is a tax in reverse. Taxes are payments *to* the government that increase producers' costs. Subsidies are payments *from* the government that decrease producers' costs. As shown in Figure 4.8c, a subsidy of U per inoculation to physicians and medical clinics would reduce their marginal costs and shift their supply curve rightward from S_t to S_t'. The output of inoculations would increase from Q_e to the optimal level Q_o, correcting the underallocation of resources and efficiency loss shown in Figure 4.8a.

- *Government provision* Finally, where positive externalities are extremely large, the government may decide to provide the product for free to everyone. The U.S. government largely eradicated the crippling disease polio by administering free vaccines to all children. India ended smallpox by paying people in rural areas to come to public clinics to have their children vaccinated.

FIGURE 4.8 Correcting for positive externalities. (a) Positive externalities result in an underallocation of resources. (b) This underallocation can be corrected through a subsidy to consumers, which shifts market demand from D to D_t and increases output from Q_e to Q_o. (c) Alternatively, the underallocation can be eliminated by providing producers with a subsidy of U, which shifts their supply curve from S_t to S_t', increasing output from Q_e to Q_o and eliminating the underallocation, and thus the efficiency loss, shown in graph a.

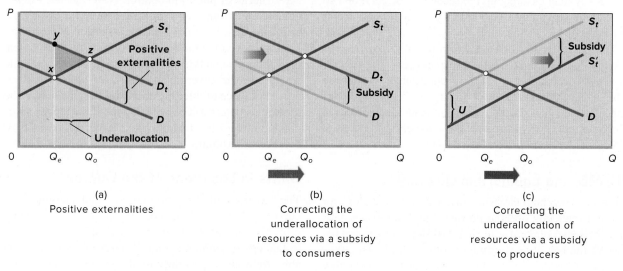

(a)	(b)	(c)
Positive externalities	Correcting the underallocation of resources via a subsidy to consumers	Correcting the underallocation of resources via a subsidy to producers

TABLE 4.5 Methods for Dealing with Externalities

Problem	Resource Allocation Outcome	Ways to Correct
Negative externalities (spillover costs)	Overproduction of output and therefore overallocation of resources	1. Private bargaining 2. Liability rules and lawsuits 3. Tax on producers 4. Direct controls 5. Market for externality rights
Positive externalities (spillover benefits)	Underproduction of output and therefore underallocation of resources	1. Private bargaining 2. Subsidy to consumers 3. Subsidy to producers 4. Government provision

Table 4.5 lists several methods for correcting externalities, including those we have discussed thus far.

Society's Optimal Amount of Externality Reduction

LO4.5 Show why we normally won't want to pay what it would cost to eliminate every last bit of a negative externality such as air pollution.

Negative externalities such as pollution reduce the utility of those affected, rather than increase it. These spillovers are not economic goods but economic "bads." If something is bad, shouldn't society eliminate it? Why should society allow firms or municipalities to discharge *any* impure waste into public waterways or to emit *any* pollution into the air?

Economists answer these questions by pointing out that reducing pollution and negative externalities is not free. There are costs as well as benefits to reducing pollution. As a result, the correct question to ask when it comes to cleaning up negative externalities is not, "Do we pollute a lot or pollute zero?" That is an all-or-nothing question that ignores marginal costs and marginal benefits. Instead, the correct question is, "What is the optimal amount to clean up—the amount that equalizes the marginal cost of cleaning up with the marginal benefit of a cleaner environment?"

If we ask that question, we see that reducing a negative externality has a "price." Society must decide how much of a reduction it wants to "buy." High costs may mean that totally eliminating pollution might not be desirable, even if it is technologically feasible. Because of the law of diminishing returns, cleaning up the second 10 percent of pollutants from an industrial smokestack normally is more costly than cleaning up the first 10 percent. Eliminating the third 10 percent is more costly than cleaning up the second 10 percent, and so on. Therefore, cleaning up the last 10 percent of pollutants is the most costly reduction of all.

The marginal cost (MC) to the firm and hence to society—the opportunity cost of the extra resources used—rises as pollution is reduced more and more. At some point MC may rise so high that it exceeds society's marginal benefit (MB) of further pollution abatement (reduction). Additional actions to reduce pollution will therefore lower society's well-being; total cost will rise more than total benefit.

MC, MB, and Equilibrium Quantity

Figure 4.9 shows both the rising marginal-cost curve, MC, for pollution reduction and the downsloping marginal-benefit curve, MB, for pollution reduction. MB slopes downward because of the law of diminishing marginal utility: The more pollution reduction society accomplishes, the lower the utility (and benefit) of the next unit of pollution reduction.

The **optimal reduction of an externality** occurs when society's marginal cost and marginal benefit of reducing that externality are equal (MC = MB). In Figure 4.9 this optimal amount of pollution abatement is Q_1 units. When MB exceeds MC, additional abatement moves society toward economic efficiency; the added benefit of cleaner air or water exceeds the benefit of any alternative use of the required resources. When MC exceeds MB, additional abatement reduces economic

efficiency; there would be greater benefits from using resources in some other way than to further reduce pollution.

In reality, it is difficult to measure the marginal costs and benefits of pollution control. Nevertheless, Figure 4.9 demonstrates that some pollution may be economically efficient. This is so not because pollution is desirable but because beyond some level of control, further abatement may reduce society's net well-being. As an example, it would cost the government billions of dollars to clean up every last piece of litter in America. Thus, it would be better to tolerate some trash blowing around if the money saved by picking up less trash would yield larger net benefits when spent on other things.

Shifts in Locations of the Curves

The locations of the marginal-cost and marginal-benefit curves in Figure 4.9 are not forever fixed. They can, and probably do, shift over time. For example, suppose that the technology of pollution-control equipment improved noticeably. We would expect the cost of pollution abatement to fall, society's MC curve to shift rightward, and the optimal level of abatement to rise. Or suppose that society were to decide that it wanted cleaner air and water because of new information about the adverse health effects of pollution. The MB curve in Figure 4.9 would shift rightward, and the optimal level of pollution control would increase beyond Q_1. Test your understanding of these statements by drawing the new MC and MB curves in Figure 4.9.

Government's Role in the Economy

Market failures can be used to justify government interventions in the economy. The inability of private-sector firms to break even when attempting to provide public goods and the over- and underproduction problems caused by positive and negative externalities mean that government can have an important role to play if society's resources are to be efficiently allocated to the goods and services that people most highly desire.

Correcting for market failures is not, however, an easy task. To begin with, government officials must correctly identify the existence and the cause of any given market failure. That by itself may be difficult, time-consuming, and costly. But even if a market failure is correctly identified and diagnosed, government may still fail to take appropriate corrective action due to the fact that government undertakes its economic role in the context of politics.

To serve the public, politicians need to get elected. To stay elected, officials (presidents, senators, representatives, mayors, council members, school board members) need to satisfy their particular constituencies. At best, the political realities complicate government's role in the economy; at worst, they produce undesirable economic outcomes.

FIGURE 4.9 Society's optimal amount of pollution abatement. The optimal amount of externality reduction—in this case, pollution abatement—occurs at Q_1, where society's marginal cost MC and marginal benefit MB of reducing the spillover are equal.

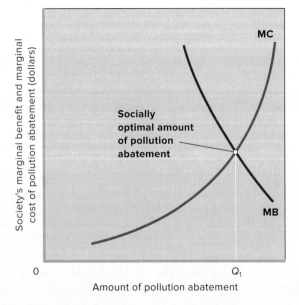

Carbon Dioxide Emissions, Cap and Trade, and Carbon Taxes

Cap-and-Trade Systems and Carbon Taxes Are Two Approaches to Reducing Carbon Dioxide (CO_2) Emissions.

Externality problems are property rights problems. Consider a landfill. Because the owner of the landfill has full rights to his land, people wishing to dump their trash into the landfill have to pay him. This payment implies that there is no externality: He happily accepts their trash in exchange for a dumping fee. By contrast, because nobody owns the atmosphere, all air pollution is an externality, since there is no way for those doing the polluting to work out a payment to compensate those affected by the pollution or for those threatened with pollution to simply refuse to be polluted on.

Conventional property rights therefore cannot fix the externalities associated with air pollution. But that does not mean property rights can't help fight pollution. The trick to making them work is to assign property rights not to the atmosphere itself, but to *polluting* the atmosphere. This is done in "cap-and-trade" systems, under which the government sets an annual limit, or cap, to the number of tons of a pollutant that firms can emit into the atmosphere.

Consider carbon dioxide, or CO_2. It is a colorless, odorless gas that many scientists consider to be a contributing cause of climate change, specifically global warming. To reduce CO_2 emissions, the U.S. government might set a cap of 5 billion tons of CO_2 emissions per year in the United States (which would be about 25 percent below 2010 emissions levels for that molecule). The government then prints out emissions permits that sum to the limit set in the cap and distributes them to polluting firms. Once they are distributed, the only way a firm can legally emit a ton of CO_2 is if it owns a permit to do so.

Under this policy, the government can obviously adjust the total amount of air pollution by adjusting the cap. This by itself improves efficiency because the cap imposes scarcity. Because each firm has only a limited number of permits, each firm has a strong incentive to maximize the net benefit that it produces from every ton of pollution that it emits. But the *cap-and-trade* scheme leads to even greater improvements in efficiency because firms are free to trade (sell) them to each other in what are referred to as *markets for externality rights*.

For instance, suppose Smokestack Toys owns permits for 100 tons of CO_2 emissions and that it could use them to produce toy cars that would generate profits of $100,000. There is a power plant, however, that could make up to $1 million of profits by using those 100 tons of emissions permits to generate electricity. Because firms can trade their permits, Smokestack Toys will sell its permits to the power plant for more than the $100,000 in profits that it could make if it kept them and produced toy cars. And the power plant will gladly pay more than $100,000 for those permits because it can turn around and use them to make up $1 million of profits by using them to generate electricity.

Society will benefit hugely from this transaction because while 100 tons of CO_2 will be emitted no matter which firm uses the permits, society will receive much greater net benefits when they are

Source: © Larry Lee Photography/Corbis RF

used by the power plant, as indicated by the fact that the power plant can produce much larger profits than the toy company when using the same amount of this scarce resource.

Several words of caution, however! Cap-and-trade systems have proven very difficult to implement in cases where it is difficult for regulators to effectively check whether firms are obeying the system. This has been a major problem with the European Union's cap-and-trade system for CO_2 emissions. Because nearly every type of industrial activity releases CO_2 into the atmosphere, enforcement involves monitoring many thousands of factories of all sizes. That is very difficult and cheating has resulted. In addition, politically connected industries got politicians to give them exemptions or free permits.

By contrast, a cap-and-trade system on sulfur dioxide emissions from coal-burning public utilities has worked well in the United States since the 1980s. But in that case, there were only a few hundred polluting utilities, and they were already being monitored for emissions. So there was little ability to cheat. In addition, all of the firms were treated equally, with no firms allowed exemptions or free permits.

Due to the mixed results, many economists have concluded that a cap-and-trade system would not be the best way to curb CO_2 emissions in the United States. They believe that there are simply too many sources of pollution to make monitoring either possible or cost-effective. And it seems likely that politically connected industries will be granted exemptions. So, instead, many economists favor a carbon tax, which would involve taxing each ton of coal, each gallon of gasoline, and each barrel of oil on the basis of how much carbon it contains (and thus how much CO_2 will eventually be released into the atmosphere when it is used). By raising the cost of polluting, the tax would reduce consumption and lessen the externalities associated with CO_2 emissions. It would also be nearly impossible to evade, so that we would not have to worry about cheating.

In the political context, overregulation can occur in some cases; underregulation, in others. Some public goods and quasi-public goods can be produced not because their benefits exceed their costs but because their benefits accrue to firms located in states served by powerful elected officials. Inefficiency can easily creep into government activities because of the lack of a profit incentive to hold down costs. Policies to correct negative externalities can be politically blocked by the very parties that are producing the spillovers. In short, the economic role of government, although critical to a well-functioning economy, is not always perfectly carried out.

Economists use the term "government failure" to describe economically inefficient outcomes caused by shortcomings in the public sector.

QUICK REVIEW 4.3

✓ Policies for coping with the overallocation of resources, and therefore efficiency losses, caused by negative externalities are (a) private bargaining, (b) liability rules and lawsuits, (c) direct controls, (d) specific taxes, and (e) markets for externality rights (Last Word).

✓ Policies for correcting the underallocation of resources, and therefore efficiency losses, associated with positive externalities are (a) private bargaining, (b) subsidies to producers, (c) subsidies to consumers, and (d) government provision.

✓ The optimal amount of negative-externality reduction occurs where society's marginal cost and marginal benefit of reducing the externality are equal.

✓ Political pressures often lead government to respond inefficiently when attempting to correct for market failures.

SUMMARY

LO4.1 Differentiate between demand-side market failures and supply-side market failures.

A market failure happens in a particular market when the market produces an equilibrium level of output that either overallocates or underallocates resources to the product being traded in the market. In competitive markets that feature many buyers and many sellers, market failures can be divided into two types: Demand-side market failures occur when demand curves do not reflect consumers' full willingness to pay; supply-side market failures occur when supply curves do not reflect all production costs, including those that may be borne by third parties.

LO4.2 Explain the origin of both consumer surplus and producer surplus and explain how properly functioning markets maximize their sum, total surplus, while optimally allocating resources.

Consumer surplus is the difference between the maximum price that a consumer is willing to pay for a product and the lower price actually paid; producer surplus is the difference between the minimum price that a producer is willing to accept for a product and the higher price actually received. Collectively, consumer surplus is represented by the triangle under the demand curve and above the actual price, whereas producer surplus is shown by the triangle above the supply curve and below the actual price.

Graphically, the combined amount of producer and consumer surplus is represented by the triangle to the left of the intersection of the supply and demand curves that is below the demand curve and above the supply curve. At the equilibrium price and quantity in competitive markets, marginal benefit equals marginal cost, maximum willingness to pay equals minimum acceptable price, and the combined amount of consumer surplus and producer surplus is maximized.

Output levels that are either less than or greater than the equilibrium output create efficiency losses, also called deadweight losses. These losses are reductions in the combined amount of consumer surplus and producer surplus. Underproduction creates efficiency losses because output is not being produced for which maximum willingness to pay exceeds minimum acceptable price. Overproduction creates efficiency losses because output is being produced for which minimum acceptable price exceeds maximum willingness to pay.

LO4.3 Describe free riding and public goods and illustrate why private firms cannot normally produce public goods.

Public goods are distinguished from private goods. Private goods are characterized by rivalry (in consumption) and excludability. One person's purchase and consumption of a private good precludes others from also buying and consuming it. Producers can exclude nonpayers (free riders) from receiving the benefits. In contrast, public goods are characterized by nonrivalry (in consumption) and nonexcludability. Public goods are not profitable to private firms because nonpayers (free riders) can obtain and consume those goods without paying. Government can, however, provide desirable public goods, financing them through taxation.

The collective demand schedule for a particular public good is found by summing the prices that each individual is willing to pay for an additional unit. Graphically, that demand curve is found by summing vertically the individual demand curves for that good. The resulting total demand curve indicates the collective willingness to pay for (or marginal benefit of) any given amount of the public good.

The optimal quantity of a public good occurs where the society's willingness to pay for the last unit—the marginal benefit of the good—equals the marginal cost of the good.

LO4.4 Explain how positive and negative externalities cause under- and overallocations of resources.

Externalities, or spillovers, are costs or benefits that accrue to someone other than the immediate buyer or seller. Such costs or benefits are not captured in market demand or supply curves and therefore cause the output of certain goods to vary from society's optimal output. Negative externalities (or spillover costs or external costs) result in an overallocation of resources to a particular product. Positive externalities (or spillover benefits or external benefits) are accompanied by an underallocaton of resources to a particular product.

Direct controls and specifically targeted Pigovian taxes can improve resource allocation in situations where negative externalities affect many people and community resources. Both direct controls (for example, smokestack emission standards) and Pigovian taxes (for example, taxes on firms producing toxic chemicals) increase production costs and hence product price. As product price rises, the externality, overallocation of resources, and efficiency loss are reduced since less of the output is produced.

Government can correct the underallocation of resources and therefore the efficiency losses that result from positive externalities in a particular market either by subsidizing consumers (which increases market demand) or by subsidizing producers (which increases market supply). Such subsidies increase the equilibrium output, reducing or eliminating the positive externality and consequent underallocation of resources and efficiency loss.

The Coase theorem suggests that under the right circumstances private bargaining can solve externality problems. Thus, government intervention is not always needed to deal with externality problems.

LO4.5 Show why we normally won't want to pay what it would cost to eliminate every last bit of a negative externality such as air pollution.

The socially optimal amount of externality abatement occurs where society's marginal cost and marginal benefit of reducing the externality are equal. With pollution, for example, this optimal amount of pollution abatement is likely to be less than a 100 percent reduction. Changes in technology or changes in society's attitudes toward pollution can affect the optimal amount of pollution abatement.

Market failures present government with opportunities to improve the allocation of society's resources and thereby enhance society's total well-being. But even when government correctly identifies the existence and cause of a market failure, political pressures may make it difficult or impossible for government officials to implement a proper solution.

TERMS AND CONCEPTS

market failures	rivalry	marginal-cost–marginal-benefit rule
demand-side market failures	excludability	quasi-public goods
supply-side market failures	public goods	externality
consumer surplus	nonrivalry	Coase theorem
producer surplus	nonexcludability	Pigovian tax
efficiency losses (or deadweight losses)	free-rider problem	optimal reduction of an externality
private goods	cost-benefit analysis	

The following and additional problems can be found in ▇ connect

DISCUSSION QUESTIONS

1. Explain the two causes of market failures. Given their definitions, could a market be affected by both types of market failures simultaneously? **LO4.1**

2. Use the ideas of consumer surplus and producer surplus to explain why economists say competitive markets are efficient. Why are below- or above-equilibrium levels of output inefficient, according to these two sets of ideas? **LO4.2**

3. What are the two characteristics of public goods? Explain the significance of each for public provision as opposed to private provision. What is the free-rider problem as it relates to public goods? Is U.S. border patrol a public good or a private good? Why? How about satellite TV? Explain. **LO4.3**

4. What divergences arise between equilibrium output and efficient output when (a) negative externalities and (b) positive externalities are present? How might government correct these divergences? Cite an example (other than the text examples) of an external cost and an external benefit. **LO4.4**

5. Why are spillover costs and spillover benefits also called negative and positive externalities? Show graphically how a tax can correct for a negative externality and how a subsidy to producers can correct for a positive externality. How does a subsidy to consumers differ from a subsidy to producers in correcting for a positive externality? **LO4.4**

6. An apple grower's orchard provides nectar to a neighbor's bees, while the beekeeper's bees help the apple grower by pollinating his apple blossoms. Use Figure 4.6b to explain why this situation of dual positive externalities might lead to an underallocation of resources to both apple growing and beekeeping. How might this underallocation get resolved via the means suggested by the Coase theorem? **LO4.4**

7. The LoJack car recovery system allows the police to track stolen cars. As a result, they not only recover 90 percent of LoJack-equipped cars that are stolen but also arrest many auto thieves and shut down many "chop shops" that take apart stolen

vehicles to get at their used parts. Thus, LoJack provides both private benefits and positive externalities. Should the government consider subsidizing LoJack purchases? **LO4.4**

8. Explain why zoning laws, which allow certain land uses only in specific locations, might be justified in dealing with a problem of negative externalities. Explain why in areas where buildings sit close together tax breaks to property owners for installing extra fire prevention equipment might be justified in view of positive externalities. Explain why excise taxes on beer might be justified in dealing with a problem of external costs. **LO4.5**

9. **LAST WORD** Distinguish between a carbon-tax and a cap-and-trade strategy for reducing carbon dioxide and other so-called greenhouse gases (that are believed by many scientists to be causing global warming). Which of the two strategies do you think would have the most political support in an election in your home state? Explain your thinking.

REVIEW QUESTIONS

1. Draw a supply and demand graph and identify the areas of consumer surplus and producer surplus. Given the demand curve, what impact will an increase in supply have on the amount of consumer surplus shown in your diagram? Explain why. **LO4.2**

2. Assume that candle wax is traded in a perfectly competitive market in which the demand curve captures buyers' full willingness to pay while the supply curve reflects all production costs. For each of the following situations, indicate whether the total output should be increased, decreased, or kept the same in order to achieve allocative and productive efficiency. **LO4.2**
   a. Maximum willingness to pay exceeds minimum acceptable price.
   b. MC > MB.
   c. Total surplus is at a maximum.
   d. The current quantity produced exceeds the market equilibrium quantity.

3. Efficiency losses _____. **LO4.2**
   a. Are not possible if suppliers are willing to produce and sell a product.
   b. Can only result from underproduction.
   c. Can only result from overproduction.
   d. None of the above.

4. Draw a production possibilities curve with public goods on the vertical axis and private goods on the horizontal axis. Assuming the economy is initially operating on the curve, indicate how the production of public goods might be increased. How might the output of public goods be increased if the economy is initially operating at a point inside the curve? **LO4.3**

5. Use the distinction between the characteristics of private and public goods to determine whether the following should be produced through the market system or provided by government: (a) French fries, (b) airport screening, (c) court systems, (d) mail delivery, and (e) medical care. State why you answered as you did in each case. **LO4.3**

6. Match each of the following characteristics or scenarios with either the term *negative externality* or the term *positive externality*. **LO4.4**
   a. Overallocation of resources.
   b. Tammy installs a very nice front garden, raising the property values of all the other houses on her block.
   c. Market demand curves are too far to the left (too low).
   d. Underallocation of resources.
   e. Water pollution from a factory forces neighbors to buy water purifiers.

7. Use marginal cost/marginal benefit analysis to determine if the following statement is true or false: "The optimal amount of pollution abatement for some substances, say, dirty water from storm drains, is very low; the optimal amount of abatement for other substances, say, cyanide poison, is close to 100 percent." **LO4.5**

PROBLEMS

1. Refer to Table 4.1. If the six people listed in the table are the only consumers in the market and the equilibrium price is $11 (not the $8 shown), how much consumer surplus will the market generate? **LO4.2**

2. Refer to Table 4.2. If the six people listed in the table are the only producers in the market and the equilibrium price is $6 (not the $8 shown), how much producer surplus will the market generate? **LO4.2**

3. Look at Tables 4.1 and 4.2 together. What is the total surplus if Bob buys a unit from Carlos? If Barb buys a unit from Courtney? If Bob buys a unit from Chad? If you match up pairs of buyers and sellers so as to maximize the total surplus of all transactions, what is the largest total surplus that can be achieved? **LO4.2**

4. **ADVANCED ANALYSIS** Assume the following values for Figures 4.4a and 4.4b: $Q_1 = 20$ bags. $Q_2 = 15$ bags. $Q_3 = 27$ bags. The market equilibrium price is $45 per bag. The price at a is $85 per bag. The price at c is $5 per bag. The price at f is $59 per bag. The price at g is $31 per bag. Apply the formula for the area of a triangle (Area = ½ × Base × Height) to answer the following questions. **LO4.2**
   a. What is the dollar value of the total surplus (producer surplus plus consumer surplus) when the allocatively efficient output level is being produced? How large is the dollar value of the consumer surplus at that output level?
   b. What is the dollar value of the deadweight loss when output level Q_2 is being produced? What is the total surplus when output level Q_2 is being produced?
   c. What is the dollar value of the deadweight loss when output level Q_3 is produced? What is the dollar value of the total surplus when output level Q_3 is produced?

5. On the basis of the three individual demand schedules in the following table, and assuming these three people are the only ones in the society, determine (a) the market demand schedule on the assumption that the good is a private good and (b) the

collective demand schedule on the assumption that the good is a public good. **LO4.3**

P	Q_d (D_1)	Q_d (D_2)	Q_d (D_3)
$8	0	1	0
7	0	2	0
6	0	3	1
5	1	4	2
4	2	5	3
3	3	6	4
2	4	7	5
1	5	8	6

6. Use your demand schedule for a public good, determined in problem 5, and the following supply schedule to ascertain the optimal quantity of this public good. **LO4.3**

P	Q_s
$19	10
16	8
13	6
10	4
7	2
4	1

7. Look at Tables 4.1 and 4.2, which show, respectively, the willingness to pay and willingness to accept of buyers and sellers of bags of oranges. For the following questions, assume that the equilibrium price and quantity will depend on the indicated changes in supply and demand. Assume that the only market participants are those listed by name in the two tables. **LO4.4**

   a. What are the equilibrium price and quantity for the data displayed in the two tables?

   b. What if, instead of bags of oranges, the data in the two tables dealt with a public good like fireworks displays? If all the buyers free ride, what will be the quantity supplied by private sellers?

   c. Assume that we are back to talking about bags of oranges (a private good), but that the government has decided that tossed orange peels impose a negative externality on the public that must be rectified by imposing a $2-per-bag tax on sellers. What is the new equilibrium price and quantity? If the new equilibrium quantity is the optimal quantity, by how many bags were oranges being overproduced before?

McGraw Hill Education **connect**

Information Failures

LO4.6 Describe how information failures may justify government intervention in some markets.

This chapter discussed the two most common types of market failure, public goods and externalities. But there is also another, subtler, type of market failure. This one results when either buyers or sellers have incomplete or inaccurate information and their cost of obtaining better information is prohibitive. Technically stated, this market failure occurs because of **asymmetric information**—unequal knowledge possessed by the parties to a market transaction. Buyers and sellers do not have identical information about price, quality, or some other aspect of the good or service.

Sufficient market information is normally available to ensure that goods and services are produced and purchased efficiently. But in some cases inadequate information makes it difficult to distinguish trustworthy from untrustworthy sellers or trustworthy from untrustworthy buyers. In these markets, society's scarce resources may not be used efficiently, thus implying that the government should intervene by increasing the information available to the market participants. Under rare circumstances the government may itself supply a good for which information problems have prohibited efficient production.

Inadequate Buyer Information about Sellers

Inadequate information among buyers about sellers and their products can cause market failure in the form of underallocation of resources. Two examples will help you understand this point.

Example: Gasoline Market

Assume an absurd situation: Suppose there is no system of weights and measures established by law, no government inspection of gasoline pumps, and no law against false advertising. Each gas station can use whatever measure it chooses; it can define a gallon of gas as it pleases. A station can advertise that its gas is 87 octane when in fact it is only 75. It can rig its pumps to indicate that it is providing more gas than the amount being delivered.

Obviously, the consumer's cost of obtaining reliable information under such chaotic conditions is exceptionally high, if not prohibitive. Customers or their representatives would have to buy samples of gas from various gas stations, have them tested for octane level, and test the accuracy of calibrations at the pump. And these activities would have to be repeated regularly, since a station owner could alter the product quality and the accuracy of the pump at will.

Because of the high cost of obtaining information about the seller, many consumers would opt out of this chaotic market. One tankful of a 50 percent mixture of gasoline and water would be enough to discourage most motorists from further driving. More realistically, the conditions in this market would encourage consumers to vote for political candidates who promise to provide a government solution. The oil companies and honest gasoline stations would most likely welcome government intervention. They would realize that accurate information, by enabling this market to work, would expand their total sales and profits.

The government has in fact intervened in the market for gasoline and other markets with similar potential information difficulties. It has established a system of weights and measures, employed inspectors to check the accuracy of gasoline pumps, and passed laws against fraudulent claims and misleading advertising. Clearly, these government activities have produced net benefits for society.

Example: Licensing of Surgeons

Suppose now that anyone could hang out a shingle and claim to be a surgeon, much as anyone can become a house painter. The market would eventually sort out the true surgeons from those who are "learning by doing" or are fly-by-night operators who move into and out of an area. As people died from unsuccessful surgeries, lawsuits for malpractice eventually would identify and eliminate most of the medical impostors. People needing surgery for themselves or their loved ones could obtain information from newspaper reports, Internet sites, or people who have undergone similar operations.

But this process of obtaining information for those needing surgery would take considerable time and would impose unacceptably high human and economic costs. There is a fundamental difference between getting an amateurish paint job on one's house and being on the receiving end of heart surgery by a bogus physician. The marginal cost of obtaining information about sellers in the surgery market would be excessively high. The risk of proceeding without good information would result in much less surgery than desirable—an underallocation of resources to surgery.

The government has remedied this market failure through a system of qualifying tests and licensing. The licensing provides consumers with inexpensive information about a service they only infrequently buy. The government has taken a similar role in several other areas of the economy. For example, it approves new medicines, regulates the securities industry, and requires warnings on containers of potentially hazardous substances.

It also requires warning labels on cigarette packages and disseminates information about communicable diseases. And it issues warnings about unsafe toys and inspects restaurants for health-related violations.

Inadequate Seller Information about Buyers

Just as inadequate information about sellers can keep markets from achieving economic efficiency, so can inadequate information about buyers. The buyers may be consumers who buy products or firms that buy resources.

Moral Hazard Problem

Private markets may underallocate resources to a particular good or service for which there is a severe **moral hazard problem.** The moral hazard problem is the tendency of one party to a contract or agreement to alter her or his behavior, after the contract is signed, in ways that could be costly to the other party.

Suppose a firm offers an insurance policy that pays a set amount of money per month to people who suffer divorces. The attractiveness of such insurance is that it would pool the economic risk of divorce among thousands of people and, in particular, would protect spouses and children from the economic hardship that divorce often brings. Unfortunately, the moral hazard problem reduces the likelihood that insurance companies can profitably provide this type of insurance.

After taking out such insurance, some people would alter their behavior in ways that impose heavy costs on the insurer. For example, married couples would have less of an incentive to get along and to iron out marital difficulties. At the extreme, some people might be motivated to obtain a divorce, collect the insurance, and then continue to live together. Such insurance could even promote divorce, the very outcome that it is intended to protect against. The moral hazard problem would force the insurer to charge such high premiums for this insurance that few policies would be bought. If the insurer could identify in advance those people most prone to alter their behavior, the firm could exclude them from buying the insurance. But the firm's marginal cost of getting such information is too high compared with the marginal benefit. Thus, this market would fail.

Although divorce insurance is not available in the marketplace, society recognizes the benefits of insuring against the hardships of divorce. It has corrected for this underallocation of "hardship insurance" through child-support laws that dictate payments to the spouse who retains the children, when the economic circumstances warrant them. Alimony laws also play a role.

The government also supplies "divorce insurance" of a sort through the Temporary Assistance for Needy Families (TANF) program. Though aimed at helping poor children in general rather than children of divorce specifically, parents with children can receive TANF payments if they are left destitute by divorce. Because government does not have to earn a profit when supplying services, it can offer this type of "divorce insurance" despite the fact that it, too, may be susceptible to the moral hazard problem.

The moral hazard problem is also illustrated in the following statements:

- Drivers may be less cautious because they have car insurance.
- Medical malpractice insurance may increase the amount of malpractice.
- Guaranteed contracts for professional athletes may reduce the quality of their performance.
- Unemployment compensation insurance may lead some workers to shirk.
- Government insurance on bank deposits may encourage banks to make risky loans.

Adverse Selection Problem

Another information problem resulting from inadequate information about buyers is the **adverse selection problem.** This problem arises when information known by the first party to a contract or agreement is not known by the second and, as a result, the second party incurs major costs. Unlike the moral hazard problem, which arises after a person signs a contract, the adverse selection problem arises at the time a person signs a contract.

In insurance, the adverse selection problem is that people who are most likely to need insurance payouts are those who buy insurance. For example, those in poorest health will seek to buy the most generous health insurance policies. Or, at the extreme, a person planning to hire an arsonist to "torch" his failing business has an incentive to buy fire insurance.

Our hypothetical divorce insurance sheds further light on the adverse selection problem. If the insurance firm sets the premiums on the basis of the average divorce rate, many married couples who are about to obtain a divorce will buy insurance. An insurance premium based on average probabilities will make a great buy for those about to get divorced. Meanwhile, those in highly stable marriages will not buy it.

The adverse selection problem thus tends to eliminate the pooling of low and high risks, which is the basis of profitable insurance. Insurance rates then must be so high that few people would want to (or be able to) buy such insurance.

Where private firms underprovide insurance because of information problems, the government often establishes some type of social insurance. It can require that everyone in a particular group take the insurance and thereby can overcome the adverse selection problem. Example: Although the Social

Security system in the United States is partly insurance and partly an income transfer program, in its broadest sense it is insurance against poverty during old age. The Social Security program requires nearly universal participation: People who are most likely to need the minimum benefits that Social Security provides are automatically participants in the program. So, too, are those not likely to need the benefits. Consequently, no adverse selection problem emerges.

Qualification

Households and businesses have found many ingenious ways to overcome information difficulties without government intervention. For example, many firms offer product warranties to overcome the lack of information about themselves and their products. Franchising also helps overcome this problem.

When you visit a Wendy's or a Marriott, you know what you are going to get, as opposed to stopping at Slim's Hamburger Shop or the Triple Six Motel.

Also, some private firms and organizations specialize in providing information to buyers and sellers. *Consumer Reports, Mobil Travel Guide,* and numerous Internet sites provide product information; labor unions collect and disseminate information about job safety; and credit bureaus provide information about credit histories and past bankruptcies to lending institutions and insurance companies. Brokers, bonding agencies, and intermediaries also provide information to clients.

Economists agree, however, that the private sector cannot remedy all information problems. In some situations, government intervention is desirable to promote an efficient allocation of society's scarce resources.

APPENDIX SUMMARY

LO4.6 Describe how information failures may justify government intervention in some markets.

Asymmetric information occurs when buyers and sellers do not have the same information about a product. It is a source of potential market failure, causing society's scarce resources to be allocated inefficiently.

Asymmetric information can cause a market to fail if the party that has less information decides to withdraw from the market because it fears that its lack of knowledge may be exploited by the party that has more information.

If the party that has less information reduces its participation in a market, the reduction in the size of the market may cause an underallocation of resources to the product produced for the market.

The moral hazard problem is the tendency of one party to a contract or agreement to alter its behavior in ways that are costly to the other party; for example, a person who buys insurance may willingly incur added risk.

The adverse selection problem arises when one party to a contract or agreement has less information than the other party and incurs a cost because of that asymmetrical information. For example, an insurance company offering "no medical-exam-required" life insurance policies may attract customers who have life-threatening diseases.

APPENDIX TERMS AND CONCEPTS

asymmetric information

moral hazard problem

adverse selection problem

The following and additional problems can be found in ▓ **connect**

APPENDIX DISCUSSION QUESTIONS

1. Because medical records are private, an individual applying for health insurance will know more about his own health conditions than will the insurance companies to which he is applying for coverage. Is this likely to increase or decrease the insurance premium that he will be offered? Why? **LO4.6**
2. Why is it in the interest of new homebuyers and builders of new homes to have government building codes and building inspectors? **LO4.6**
3. Place an "M" beside the items in the following list that describe a moral hazard problem and an "A" beside those that describe an adverse selection problem. **LO4.6**

   a. A person with a terminal illness buys several life insurance policies through the mail.
   b. A person drives carelessly because she has automobile insurance.
   c. A person who intends to torch his warehouse takes out a large fire insurance policy.
   d. A professional athlete who has a guaranteed contract fails to stay in shape during the off season.
   e. A woman who anticipates having a large family takes a job with a firm that offers exceptional child care benefits.

APPENDIX REVIEW QUESTIONS

1. People drive faster when they have auto insurance. This is an example of: **LO4.6**
   a. Adverse selection.
   b. Asymmetric information.
   c. Moral hazard.
2. Government inspectors who check on the quality of services provided by retailers as well as government requirements for licensing in various professions are both attempts to resolve: **LO4.6**
   a. The moral hazard problem.
   b. The asymmetric information problem.
3. True or False: A market may collapse and have relatively few transactions between buyers and sellers if buyers have more information than sellers. **LO4.6**

APPENDIX PROBLEMS

1. Consider a used car market with asymmetric information. The owners of used cars know what their vehicles are worth but have no way of credibly demonstrating those values to potential buyers. Thus, potential buyers must always worry that the used car they are being offered may be a low quality "lemon." **LO4.6**
   a. Suppose that there are equal numbers of good and bad used cars in the market and that good used cars are worth $13,000 while bad used cars are worth $5,000. What is the average value of a used car?
   b. By how much does the average value exceed the value of a bad used car? By how much does the value of a good used car exceed the average value?
   c. Would a potential seller of a good used car be willing to accept the average value as payment for her vehicle?
   d. If a buyer negotiates with a seller to purchase the seller's used car for a price equal to the average value, is the car more likely to be good or bad?
   e. Will the used-car market come to feature mostly—if not exclusively—lemons? How much will used cars end up costing if all the good cars are withdrawn?

5 Chapter

Government's Role and Government Failure

Learning Objectives

LO5.1 Describe how government's power to coerce can be economically beneficial and list some of the difficulties associated with managing and directing the government.

LO5.2 Discuss "government failure" and explain why it happens.

LO5.3 (Appendix) Explain the difficulties of conveying economic preferences through majority voting.

Governments perform a variety of economic tasks in market economies. As discussed in various places in the book, these include promoting production and trade by defining property rights, enforcing contracts, and settling disputes; enforcing laws designed to maintain competition; redistributing income via taxes and transfers; reallocating resources by producing public goods and intervening to correct negative and positive externalities; and promoting economic growth and full employment.

In this chapter, we deepen our understanding of government's role in the market economy by examining some

of the difficulties that democratic governments face when making specific laws related to the economy. We will find that governments sometimes pursue policies for which costs outweigh benefits. These inefficient outcomes happen often enough that we need to be just as vigilant in looking for instances of *government failure* as we are in looking for instances of *market failure*.

Government's Economic Role

LO5.1 Describe how government's power to coerce can be economically beneficial and list some of the difficulties associated with managing and directing the government.

As discussed in Chapter 2, the U.S. economy is a *market system* that uses mostly markets and prices to coordinate and direct economic activity. But the government also has a prominent role in how the economy functions. Among other things, the government sets the laws governing economic activity, provides goods and services that would otherwise be underproduced by private firms, and modifies the distribution of income. The government also promotes both economic stability and economic growth.

Government's Right to Coerce

One key difference between the economic activities of government and those of private firms and individuals is that government possesses the legal right to force people to do things. Whereas private-sector economic activities consist primarily of voluntary transactions, government has the legal right to enforce involuntary transactions. Among other things, the government can put you in jail if you do not pay your taxes, fine you if you violate pollution laws, jail you if you commit fraud, and remove your business license if you violate health and safety regulations.

Force and Economic Efficiency From an economic perspective, the government's ability to force people to do things can be quite beneficial because it can be used to increase economic efficiency.

Correcting for Market Failures Consider public goods and externalities. As discussed in Chapter 4, these market failures cause resource misallocations. When it comes to both public goods and products offering positive externalities, private producers fail to produce enough output because it is impossible to charge many of the beneficiaries for the benefits that they receive from the producers' products. In such cases, the government can improve economic efficiency by using involuntarily collected tax money to subsidize production.

By contrast, products that generate negative externalities are overproduced by the private sector because many of their costs are borne by third parties rather than by their producers. The government can reduce that overproduction and improve economic efficiency by using involuntary policies such as direct controls, pollution taxes, and cap-and-trade schemes to force producers to bear higher costs.

Reducing Private-Sector Economic Risks Government's ability to force people to do things is also crucial in reducing private-sector economic risks. To begin with, the government helps to ensure that only mutually agreeable transactions take place by making blackmail, extortion, and other forms of private coercion illegal. The government also uses its legal powers to outlaw various forms of theft, deception, and discrimination as well as restraints on trade, price-fixing, and refusal to honor a contract.

These limitations encourage economic activity by giving greater security to both individuals and firms. Because they know that the government will use its massive resources to arrest and punish those who break the law, they know that other individuals and firms are less likely to try to take advantage of them. That reduction in risk encourages higher levels of investment, the formation of more new businesses, and the introduction of more new goods and services. In economic terminology, both allocative and productive efficiency increase.

The Problem of Directing and Managing Government

As just discussed, the government can substantially improve allocative and productive efficiency if it directs its awesome

CONSIDER THIS . . .

Source: © Antenna/Getty Images RF

Does Big Government Equal Bad Government?

You will sometimes hear politicians (and maybe your grumpy uncle) complaining about Big Government. Their implication is that large government initiatives are inherently inefficient or incompetent.

Since economics is focused on efficiency, you might wonder where economists stand on the subject.

The answer is that economists focus not on bigness or smallness *per se*, but on marginal benefit (MB) and marginal cost (MC). Spending should be increased up to the point where MB = MC. For some programs, that will be a small dollar amount. For other programs, that will be a large dollar amount.

Thus, economists don't see much point in having an abstract debate over "big government" versus "small government." What matters is allocative and productive efficiency and directing government's limited resources toward the programs that generate the largest net benefits for society.

From that vantage point, we should not condemn large government programs just for being large. We must first compare MB with MC. Only if MB < MC should large programs be reduced or eliminated.

coercive powers toward rectifying market failures and providing a low-risk economic environment for the private sector. However, it has only been in recent centuries that democratic political institutions have been able to tame government and direct it toward those goals. Until that happened, most governments were tyrannical, with their powers almost always directed toward enriching the small minority that controlled each government.

Because modern democratic governments serve much broader constituencies, they are much more likely to pursue economic policies with widespread social benefits. Their ability to deliver economically optimal outcomes is hindered, however, by the wide variety of government failures that this chapter will discuss in detail.

But before discussing them, it will be useful to first point out that governing a nation is not easy. In particular, governments face the daunting challenge of organizing millions of employees to carry out thousands of tasks—everything from cleaning sewers to researching cures for cancer to delivering the mail. An understanding of those challenges and complexities will give you a better sense of how well most governments manage to do *despite* all of the problems associated with government failure.

No Invisible Hand Government economic polices are not self-correcting. Unlike the private sector—where competitive forces and Adam Smith's "invisible hand" help to automatically direct resources to their best uses—poorly designed government policies can misallocate resources indefinitely unless active steps are taken by legislators or administrators.

Massive Size and Scope Identifying and correcting inefficient government policies is hampered by government's massive size and scope. Consider the U.S. federal government. In 2014, it had 4.2 million employees spread over 500 agencies that were collectively charged with enforcing hundreds of thousands of pages of laws and regulations while attempting to wisely spend $3.5 trillion.

The Need for Bureaucracy By law, those 4.2 million federal employees are ultimately supervised and directed by just 536 elected officials: one president, 435 representatives, and 100 senators. Because 536 elected officials could never hope to directly supervise 4.2 million people, governments rely on many layers of supervisors and supervisors-of-supervisors to manage the government's affairs. They collectively form a massive, hierarchical, many-layered bureaucracy.

The Need for Paperwork and Inflexibility To make sure that laws are uniformly enforced and do not vary at the whim of individual bureaucrats, the bureaucracy is regulated by detailed rules and regulations governing nearly every possible action that any individual bureaucrat might be called upon to make. These rules and regulations ensure that laws and regulations are uniformly applied. But they do so at the cost of massive amounts of paperwork and an inability to expeditiously process nonroutine situations and requests.

The Information Aggregation Problem Because of their massive size and scope, bureaucracies have difficulty with effectively aggregating and conveying information from their bottom layers to their top layers. As a result, top officials will tend to make many inefficient choices because they do not have enough information to sensibly compare the marginal benefits and marginal costs of individual programs and because they are unable to comprehensively assess opportunity costs and where to best spend funds across the wide variety of programs run by the government.

Lack of Accountability Governments also struggle with accountability. Democratic elections do take place for the elected officials at the top, but because the government undertakes so many activities simultaneously, it is difficult for the electorate to know the details of even a small fraction of what the government is up to at any particular time. As a result, hundreds or even thousands of individual programs may be poorly run without affecting the reelection chances of the

incumbent politicians who are supposed to be supervising everything.

Within the bureaucracy itself, individual accountability is also hard to enforce because most bureaucrats have civil service protections that effectively guarantee them a job for life. Those protections reduce corruption by shielding bureaucrats from political pressures. But they also severely constrain the ability of elected officials to hold individual bureaucrats personally responsible for bad decisions.

> **QUICK REVIEW 5.1**
>
> ✓ Government's ability to enforce nonvoluntary transactions can improve economic outcomes by compensating for resource misallocations and by providing a low-risk economic environment for individuals and firms.
> ✓ Government economic actions are not automatically self-correcting (as with the "invisible hand" in competitive markets).
> ✓ Democratic governments face several challenges in directing and supervising government's actions, including inflexibility, information aggregation, comparing marginal costs with marginal benefits, assessment of opportunity costs, and accountability.

Government Failure

LO5.2 Discuss "government failure" and explain why it happens.

The term **government failure** refers to economically inefficient outcomes caused by shortcomings in the public sector. One cause of government failure is the voting problems that we discuss at length in this chapter's appendix. But government failures caused by voting problems are somewhat unique in that they are driven by a lack of information about voter preferences. By contrast, most instances of government failure happen *despite* government officials knowing what voters prefer.

In these situations, government failures occur because the incentive structures facing government officials lead them to either put their own interests ahead of voter interests or to put the interests of a minority of voters ahead of those of the majority of voters. Let's examine what economic theory has to say about these situations.

Representative Democracy and the Principal-Agent Problem

Our system of representative democracy has the advantage of allowing us to elect full-time representatives who can specialize in understanding the pros and cons of different potential laws and who have more time to digest their details than the average citizen. But the system also suffers from principal-agent problems.

Principal-agent problems are conflicts that arise when tasks are delegated by one group of people (principals) to another group of people (agents). The conflicts arise because the interests of the agents may not be the same as the interests of the principals, so that the agents may end up taking actions that are opposed by the principals whom they are supposed to be representing.

In the business world, principal-agent problems often arise when the company's managers (the agents) take actions that are not in the best interests of the company's shareholders (the principals). Examples include the managers spending huge amounts of company money on executive jets and lavish offices or holding meetings at expensive resorts. These luxuries are obviously enjoyable to managers but are, of course, not in the best interest of shareholders because the money spent on them could either be reinvested back into the firm to increase future profits or paid out to shareholders immediately as dividends. But to the extent that managers are free to follow their own interests rather than those of their shareholders, they may indeed take these and other actions that are not in the better interests of their shareholders. Hence the conflicts.

In a representative democracy, principal-agent problems often arise because politicians have goals such as reelection that may be inconsistent with pursuing the best interests of their constituents. Indeed, casual reflection suggests that "sound economics" and "good politics" often differ. Sound economics calls for the public sector to pursue various programs as long as marginal benefits exceed marginal costs. Good politics, however, suggests that politicians support programs and policies that will maximize their chances of getting reelected. The result may be that the government will promote the goals of groups of voters that have special interests to the detriment of the larger public. Economic inefficiency is the likely outcome.

Special-Interest Effect   Efficient public decision making is often impaired by the **special-interest effect.** This is any outcome of the political process whereby a small number of people obtain a government program or policy that gives them large gains at the expense of a much greater number of persons who individually suffer small losses.

The small group of potential beneficiaries is well informed and highly vocal on the issue in question, and they press politicians for approval by making campaign contributions and by hiring well-connected professional advocates known as "lobbyists" to aggressively make their case. By contrast, the large number of people facing the very small individual losses are generally unaware of the issue. So politicians feel they will lose the campaign contributions and votes of the small special-interest group that backs the issue if

CONSIDER THIS . . .

Source: © Hein von Horsten/Getty Images

Mohair and the Collective-Action Problem

Smaller groups can sometimes achieve political victories against larger groups by taking advantage of the **collective-action problem**—the fact that larger groups are more difficult to organize and motivate than smaller groups.

Larger groups are harder to organize and motivate for two main reasons. First, the larger the group, the smaller each member's share of the benefits if the group gets its way. Second, the larger the group, the higher its organizing costs, as it will have to contact and recruit large numbers of strangers via e-mails, telephone calls, and mass mailings.

Smaller groups can take advantage of these difficulties and generally get their way against larger groups as long as they are pressing for policies that only cause small amounts of harm to the members of the larger groups.

Consider the infamous subsidy for mohair, the wool produced by Angora goats. Each year the federal government provides millions of dollars in subsidized loans to Angora goat farmers in Texas, Arizona, and New Mexico. The federal government began the subsidy in the late 1940s to ensure a large supply of insulation for the jackets needed to keep pilots and other crew members warm in the unheated airplanes used during that period.

The mohair subsidy should have ended in the 1950s when heated cabins were developed, but it survives because it costs taxpayers only a few cents each. This means that it would cost them more to organize and defeat the mohair subsidy than they would save by having the subsidy terminated.

More generally, the collective-action problem explains why nearly every example of the special-interest effect is characterized by "concentrated benefits and diffuse costs." Concentrated benefits make proponents easy to organize, while diffuse costs make opponents difficult to organize.

they legislate against it but will lose very little support from the large group of uninformed voters, who are likely to evaluate the politicians on other issues of greater importance to them.

The special-interest effect is also evident in so-called *pork-barrel politics*, a means of securing a government project that yields benefits mainly to a single political district and its political representative. In this case, the special-interest group comprises local constituents, while the larger group consists of relatively uninformed taxpayers scattered across a much larger geographic area. Politicians clearly have a strong incentive to secure government projects ("pork") for their local constituents. Such projects win political favor because they are highly valued by constituents and the costs are borne mainly by taxpayers located elsewhere.

At the federal level, pork-barrel politics often consist of congressional members inserting specific provisions that authorize spending for local projects (that will benefit only local constituents) into comprehensive legislation (that is supposed to be about making laws for the entire country). Such narrow, specifically designated authorizations of expenditure are called **earmarks.** In 2015, legislation contained 105 such earmarks, totaling $4.2 billion. These earmarks enable senators and representatives to provide benefits to in-state firms and organizations without subjecting the proposals to the usual evaluation and competitive bidding. Although some of the earmarked projects deliver benefits that exceed costs, many others are questionable, at best. These latter expenditures very likely reallocate some of society's scarce resources from higher-valued uses to lower-valued uses. Moreover, logrolling, discussed in the chapter appendix, typically enters the picture. "Vote for my special local project and I will vote for yours" becomes part of the overall strategy for securing "pork" and remaining elected.

Finally, a politician's inclination to support the smaller group of special beneficiaries is enhanced because special-interest groups are often quite willing to help finance the campaigns of "right-minded" politicians and politicians who "bring home the pork." The result is that politicians may support special-interest programs and projects that cannot be justified on economic grounds.

Rent-Seeking Behavior The appeal to government for special benefits at taxpayers' or someone else's expense is called **rent seeking.** The term "rent" in "rent seeking" is used loosely to refer to any payment in excess of the minimum amount that would be needed to keep a resource employed in its current use. Those engaged in "rent seeking" are attempting to use government influence to get themselves into a situation in which they will get paid more for providing a good or service than the minimum amount you would actually have to pay them to provide that good or service. (These excess, or surplus, payments are akin to *land rent,* which is also a surplus payment.)

Rent seeking goes beyond the usual profit seeking through which firms try to increase their profits by adjusting their output levels, improving their products, and incorporating cost-saving technologies. Rent seeking looks to obtain extra profit or income by influencing government policies. Corporations, trade associations, labor unions, and professional organizations employ vast resources to secure favorable government policies that result in rent—higher profit or income than would otherwise occur. The government is able to dispense such rent directly or indirectly through laws, rules, hiring, and purchases. Elected officials are willing to provide such rent because they want to be responsive to the key constituents who can help them remain in office.

Here are some examples of "rent-providing" legislation or policies: tariffs on foreign products that limit competition and raise prices to consumers, tax breaks that benefit specific corporations, government construction projects that create union jobs but cost more than the benefits they yield, occupational licensing that goes beyond what is needed to protect consumers, and large subsidies to farmers by taxpayers. None of these is justified by economic efficiency.

Clear Benefits, Hidden Costs

Some critics say that vote-seeking politicians will ignore economic rationality by failing to objectively weigh costs and benefits when deciding which programs to support. Because political officeholders must seek voter support every few years, they favor programs that have immediate and clear-cut benefits and vague or deferred costs. Conversely, politicians will reject programs with immediate and easily identifiable costs but with less measurable but very high long-term benefits.

Such biases may lead politicians to reject economically justifiable programs and to accept programs that are economically irrational. Example: A proposal to construct or expand mass-transit systems in large metropolitan areas may be economically rational on the basis of cost-benefit analysis. But if (1) the program is to be financed by immediate increases in highly visible income or sales taxes and (2) benefits will occur only years from now when the project is completed, then the vote-seeking politician may oppose the program.

Assume, on the other hand, that a program of federal aid to municipal police forces is not justifiable on the basis of cost-benefit analysis. But if the cost is paid for from budget surpluses, the program's modest benefits may seem so large that it will gain approval.

Unfunded Liabilities

The political tendency to favor spending priorities that have immediate payouts but deferred costs also leads to many government programs having unfunded liabilities. A government creates an **unfunded liability** when it commits to making a series of future expenditures without simultaneously committing to collect enough tax revenues to pay for those expenditures.

The most famous example of an unfunded liability belongs to the Social Security program, under which the U.S. federal government supplements the incomes of the elderly and the disabled. The government does collect Social Security taxes to help defray the expected future costs of the program, but the current tax rates will not generate nearly enough revenue to pay for all of the expected outlays. In fact, it is estimated that Social Security has an unfunded liability

(= total value of spending commitments minus expected value of tax revenues) of $20.5 trillion.

Social Security is not the only major unfunded government liability. Medicare, which provides health care to the elderly and disabled in the United States, has an unfunded liability of $4.8 trillion, while state and local governments are estimated to have $4.6 trillion in unfunded retirement and health care commitments.

Chronic Budget Deficits

A government runs an annual **budget deficit** whenever its tax revenues are less than its spending during a particular year. To make up for the shortfall, the government must borrow money, usually by issuing bonds. Whatever it borrows in a given year gets added to its overall pile of debt, which is the accumulation of all past budget deficits and budget surpluses.

Many governments run budget deficits year after year. These chronic deficits can be attributed to a pair of conflicting incentives that confront politicians. On the one hand, many government programs are highly popular with voters, so that there is almost always political pressure to either maintain or increase spending. On the other hand, hardly anyone likes paying taxes, so there is almost always political pressure to reduce taxes. Faced with those two conflicting pressures, politicians tend to opt for spending levels that exceed tax revenues.

That may be problematic because chronic deficits can pose several economic challenges, including

- *Economic inefficiency* Deficits may allow the government to control and direct an inefficiently large fraction of the economy's resources. To the extent that deficit spending facilitates an underallocation of resources to the private sector and an overallocation of resources to the government sector, there will be a tendency to underproduce private goods and overproduce public goods. If that occurs, the economy will experience a decrease in both allocative and productive efficiency.

- *Debt crises* A government's accumulated debt level may rise so high that investors lose faith in the government's ability or willingness to repay its debts. If that happens, the government will find itself in the middle of a **debt crisis,** unable to borrow any more money. Cut off from borrowing, the government will be forced to undertake some combination of drastic spending cuts or massive tax increases. Either of those actions will tend to plunge the economy into a recessionary period in which unemployment rises and output falls.

To prevent politicians from succumbing to voter preferences for deficits, many state and local governments have balanced-budget laws that make deficits illegal. No such law exists at the national level, however. As a result, federal politicians were able to run budget deficits in 51 of the 56 years between 1960 and 2015.

Misdirection of Stabilization Policy

Economies go through alternating periods of expansion and recession. Multiyear periods during which output expands, employment increases, and living standards rise alternate with periods during which output contracts, employment decreases, and living standards fall.

Governments often attempt to smooth out these so-called *business cycles* by using two types of macroeconomic stabilization policy:

- **Fiscal policy** attempts to use changes in tax rates and spending levels to offset the business cycle. For example, if the economy is going into a recessionary period with falling output and rising unemployment, the government may attempt to stimulate the economy by lowering tax rates or increasing government spending. Either action should increase spending on goods and services and consequently induce business to produce more output and hire more workers.

- **Monetary policy** attempts to use changes in interest rates to regulate the economy. In particular, the government can use its control over the money supply to lower interest rates during a recession. The lower interest rates stimulate spending by making it cheaper for individuals and businesses to borrow money to pay for capital goods such as houses, cars, and machinery. As spending on those items increases, firms are induced to produce more output and hire more workers.

Politicization of Fiscal and Monetary Policy Fiscal and monetary policy are both subject to politicization. In the case of fiscal policy, if the economy goes into recession and there are calls to stimulate the economy through lower taxes or increased spending, politicians often spend more time attempting to target any tax cuts or spending increases toward special interests than they do making sure that their fiscal policy actions will actually stimulate the overall economy. The recession also provides political cover for increasing the size of the deficit.

Monetary policy can be similarly politicized, with the biggest problem being that incumbent politicians will want to cut interest rates to boost the economy right before they are up for reelection. That is problematic because monetary stimulus is only helpful if the economy is in recession. If the economy is doing well, monetary stimulus can actually make things worse because it can raise the rate of inflation and drive up prices all over the economy.

To prevent that, most countries have put politically independent central banks in charge of monetary policy. In the

United States, the Federal Reserve serves this function. Other top central banks include the Bank of Japan, the Bank of England, and the European Central Bank. Each is run by professional economists who are insulated from political pressures so that they may use their independent expertise and judgment to decide if and when monetary stimulus should be used.

QUICK REVIEW 5.2

✓ Principal-agent problems are conflicts that occur when the agents who are supposed to be acting in the best interests of their principals instead take actions that help themselves but hurt their principals.

✓ Because larger groups are more difficult to organize and motivate than smaller groups, special interests can often obtain what they want politically even when what they want is opposed by a majority of voters.

✓ Rent seeking involves influencing government policies so that one can get paid more for providing a good or service than it costs to produce.

✓ Political pressures cause politicians to favor policies such as unfunded liabilities and budget deficits that have immediate benefits and delayed costs.

Limited and Bundled Choice

Economic theory points out that the political process forces citizens and their elected representatives to be less selective in choosing public goods and services than they are in choosing private goods and services.

In the marketplace, the citizen as a consumer can exactly satisfy personal preferences by buying certain goods and not buying others. However, in the public sector the citizen as a voter is confronted with, say, only two or three candidates for an office, each representing a different "bundle" of programs (public goods and services). None of these bundles of public goods is likely to fit exactly the preferences of any particular voter. Yet the voter must choose one of them. The candidate who comes closest to voter Smith's preference may endorse national health insurance, increases in Social Security benefits, subsidies to tobacco farmers, and tariffs on imported goods. Smith is likely to vote for that candidate even though Smith strongly opposes tobacco subsidies.

In other words, the voter must take the bad with the good. In the public sector, people are forced to "buy" goods and services they do not want. It is as if, in going to a sporting-goods store, you were forced to buy an unwanted pool cue to get a wanted pair of running shoes. This is a situation where resources are not being used efficiently to satisfy consumer wants. In this sense, the provision of public goods and services is inherently inefficient.

Congress is confronted with a similar limited-choice, bundled-goods problem. Appropriations legislation combines hundreds, even thousands, of spending items into a single bill. Many of these spending items may be completely unrelated to the main purpose of the legislation. Yet congressional representatives must vote on the entire package—yea or nay. Unlike consumers in the marketplace, they cannot be selective.

Bureaucracy and Inefficiency

Some economists contend that public agencies are generally less efficient than private businesses. The reason is not that lazy and incompetent workers somehow end up in the public sector while ambitious and capable people gravitate to the private sector. Rather, it is that the market system creates incentives for internal efficiency that are absent from the public sector. Private enterprises have a clear goal—profit. Whether a private firm is in a competitive or monopolistic market, efficient management means lower costs and higher profit. The higher profit not only benefits the firm's owners but enhances the promotion prospects of the firm's managers. Moreover, part of the managers' pay may be tied to profit via profit-sharing plans, bonuses, and stock options. There is no similar

---

CONSIDER THIS . . .

Source: © Jerry McBride/The Durango Herald/Polaris/Newscom

Government, Scofflaw
An interesting example of government failure occurs when public companies that are completely owned and operated by the government violate the law at higher rates than private companies.

A 2015 study of 1,000 hospitals, 3,000 power plants, and 4,200 water utilities found that public providers were substantially more likely than private companies to violate health and safety laws. Public hospitals and public power plants had 20 percent more high-priority violations of the Clean Air Act, while public water companies had 14 percent more health violations of the Safe Drinking Water Act as well as 29 percent more monitoring violations.

One explanation is that public companies may have difficulty getting taxpayers and politicians to approve the funding that would be needed to improve their facilities by enough to comply with the law. But the law also appears to be applied much more leniently against public companies because public power plants and public hospitals are 20 percent less likely to be fined when found to be in violation of the Clean Air Act. In addition, there is evidence that public violators are allowed to delay or avoid paying fines even when they are assessed. So they are under substantially less pressure than private firms to comply with the law.

gain to government agencies and their managers—no counterpart to profit—to create a strong incentive to achieve efficiency.

The market system imposes a very obvious test of performance on private firms: the test of profit and loss. An efficient firm is profitable and therefore successful; it survives, prospers, and grows. An inefficient firm is unprofitable and unsuccessful; it declines and in time goes out of business. But there is no similar, clear-cut test with which to assess the efficiency or inefficiency of public agencies. How can anyone determine whether a public hydroelectricity provider, a state university, a local fire department, the Department of Agriculture, or the Bureau of Indian Affairs is operating efficiently?

Cynics even argue that a public agency that inefficiently uses its resources is likely to survive and grow! In the private sector, inefficiency and monetary loss lead to the abandonment of certain activities or products or even firms. But the government, they say, does not like to abandon activities in which it has failed. Some suggest that the typical response of the government to a program's failure is to increase its budget and staff. This means that public sector inefficiency just continues on a larger scale.

Furthermore, economists assert that government employees, together with the special-interest groups they serve, often gain sufficient political clout to block attempts to pare down or eliminate their agencies. Politicians who attempt to reduce the size of huge federal bureaucracies such as those relating to agriculture, education, health and welfare, and national defense incur sizable political risk because bureaucrats and special-interest groups will team up to defeat them.

Finally, critics point out that government bureaucrats tend to justify their continued employment by looking for and eventually finding new problems to solve. It is not surprising that social "problems," as defined by government, persist or even expand.

The Last Word at the end of this chapter highlights several recent media-reported examples of the special-interest effect (including earmarks), the problem of limited and bundled choices, and problems of government bureaucracy.

Inefficient Regulation and Intervention

Governments regulate many aspects of the market economy. Examples include health and safety regulations, environmental laws, banking supervision, restrictions on monopoly power, and the imposition of wage and price controls.

These interventions are designed to improve economic outcomes, but several forms of regulation and intervention have been known to generate outcomes that are less beneficial than intended.

Regulatory Capture A government agency that is supposed to supervise a particular industry is said to have suffered from **regulatory capture** if its regulations and enforcement activities come to be heavily influenced by the industry that it is supposed to be regulating.

Regulatory capture is often facilitated by the fact that nearly everyone who knows anything about the details of a regulated industry works in the industry. So when it comes time for the regulatory agency to find qualified people to help write intelligent regulations, it ends up hiring a lot of people from regulated firms. Those individuals bring their old opinions and sympathies with them when they become bureaucrats. As a result, many regulations end up favoring the interests of the regulated firms.

Regulatory Capture in the Railroad Industry The classic example of regulatory capture is that of railroad regulation during the nineteenth and twentieth centuries. In response to public complaints that the nation's railroads were often charging exorbitant rates, the federal government established the Interstate Commerce Commission (ICC) in 1887 as the government agency charged with regulating competition and prices within the railroad industry.

Within a generation, railroad executives had achieved regulatory capture by manipulating the ICC into a policy that simultaneously fixed rates at profitable levels while also eliminating competition between different railroad companies. The public justification for these policies was that competition had to be restricted in order to prevent larger railroads from bankrupting smaller railroads and thereby becoming monopolies that could easily exploit the public. But the railroad industry's true motive was to establish a regulatory regime in which both larger and small railroads were guaranteed steady, competition-free profits.

These days, activists often complain that various government bureaucracies are subject to regulatory capture. At the federal level, complaints are voiced about the Food and Drug Administration's supervision of the pharmaceutical industry, the Securities and Exchange Commission's supervision of Wall Street financial firms, and the Bureau of Land Management's policies with respect to leasing federal lands for oil drilling, mining, and forestry.

Deregulation as an Alternative Economists are divided about the intensity and inefficiency of regulatory capture as well as what to do about it. One potential solution is for the government to engage in **deregulation** and intentionally remove most or even all of the regulations governing an industry.

Deregulation solves the problem of regulatory capture because there is no regulatory agency left to capture. But it only works well in terms of economic efficiency if the deregulated industry becomes competitive and is automatically guided toward allocative and productive efficiency by competitive forces and the invisible hand. If the deregulated industry instead tends toward monopoly or ends up generating substantial negative externalities, continued regulation might be the better option.

Proponents of deregulation often cite the deregulation of interstate trucking, railroads, and airlines in the 1970s and 1980s as examples of competition successfully replacing regulation. They do so because after regulation was removed, robust competition led to lower prices, increased output, and higher levels of productivity and efficiency.

But for government agencies tasked with environmental protection, human safety, and financial regulation, there is less confidence as to whether competitive pressures might be able to replace regulation. For those industries, regulation may always be necessary. If so, then some amount of regulatory capture may always be likely due to the fact that regulated firms will always want to capture their regulators.

Government's Poor Investment Track Record

Governments are often asked to use taxpayer money to directly invest in private businesses that have been unable to secure funding from private sources such as banks. Unfortunately, researchers have found that low and negative rates of return are the norm for government investments. In addition, government funding often allows inefficient firms to persist in operation long after competitive forces would have put them out of operation and freed up their resources for higher-valued projects elsewhere in the economy.

Critics also note that many government investments look like prime examples of rent seeking and the special-interest effect, especially when the firms receiving government investments are found to have made substantial financial contributions to influential politicians. In too many cases, the government's investment decisions appear to be based on political connections rather than on whether specific investments can produce substantial net benefits for society.

Loan Guarantees   The government also tends to earn low or negative returns when it subsidizes private-sector investments with **loan guarantees.** The start-up company named Solyndra provides a good example of what can go wrong.

The Solyndra Subsidy   In 2009, Solyndra was unable to convince private investors to lend it enough money to start producing solar panels with its new technology. The private investors sensibly feared that the company's new technology was too expensive and that its solar panels would not be able to compete with those made by the industry's more established firms.

At that point, Solyndra turned to a federal loan-guarantee program under which the Department of Energy told potential investors that it would cosign any loan taken out by Solyndra and thereby guarantee that if Solyndra went bankrupt, the federal government would use taxpayer money to repay the loan.

With that loan guarantee in place, the otherwise-reluctant private investors were willing to put in $535 million. After all, they had nothing to lose and everything to gain. If Solyndra went bankrupt, they would get their money back from the government. But if Solyndra somehow did well, they would collect substantial returns.

Unfortunately, the investors' original doubts proved to be well founded. Solyndra was unable to compete effectively with incumbent firms and went bankrupt in 2011, leaving taxpayers on the hook for the full $535 million.

Socializing Losses, Privatizing Gains   Government loan guarantees can be socially beneficial if they help to increase the production of beneficial products that are being underproduced by the private sector—as would be the case for products that generated positive externalities. But the loan guarantees also provide an inducement toward reckless investing because they remove from private investors any consideration of losses. Indeed, loan guarantees are often criticized for "socializing losses and privatizing gains" because if things go wrong, any losses go to the taxpayer, while if things go well, any profits go to private investors.

In addition, the process by which loan guarantees are awarded is often criticized for being highly politicized and likely to award loan guarantees not to the firms whose projects are the most likely to increase economic efficiency but to those with the best political connections.

On the other hand, there may be legitimate cases where a new technology that would generate net benefits cannot be developed without government loan guarantees, so proponents of loan-guarantee programs argue that the programs should remain in place, but with tight controls against rent seeking and the special-interest effect.

Corruption

Political corruption is the unlawful misdirection of governmental resources or actions that occurs when government officials abuse their entrusted powers for personal gain. For instance, a police supervisor engages in political corruption if she accepts a bribe in exchange for illegally freeing a thief who had been lawfully arrested by another officer. Similarly, a government bureaucrat engages in political corruption if he refuses to issue a building permit to a homebuilder who is in full compliance with the law unless the homebuilder makes a "voluntary contribution" to the bureaucrat's favorite charity.

While relatively uncommon in the United States, political corruption is a daily reality in many parts of the world, as can be seen in Global Perspective 5.1, which gives the percentages of survey respondents in 10 countries who reported that they or someone else in their respective households paid a bribe during the previous 12 months.

Political corruption comes in two basic forms. In the first, a government official must be bribed to do what he should be doing as part of his job—as with the bureaucrat in our earlier example who demands a bribe to issue a

GLOBAL PERSPECTIVE 5.1

Percentage of Households Paying a Bribe in the Past Year

The Global Corruption Barometer is an international survey that asks individuals about their personal experiences with government corruption. The 2013 survey of over 114,000 people in 107 countries included a question that asked participants whether they or anyone in their respective households had paid a bribe in any form during the previous 12 months. Here are the results for 10 selected countries.

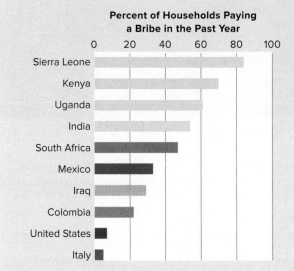

Percent of Households Paying a Bribe in the Past Year

Source: Data from Transparency International, *Global Corruption Barometer*, 2013, visit **transparency.org.**

permit to a homebuilder who is in full compliance with the law. In the second, a government official demands a bribe to do something that she is not legally entitled to do—as with the police supervisor in our earlier example who illegally freed a thief.

If a candidate accepts campaign contributions from a special-interest group and then shows subsequent support for that group's legislative goals, has a subtle form of political corruption taken place? While there are strong opinions on both sides of the issue, it is often hard to tell in any particular case whether a special interest's campaign contribution amounts to a bribe. On the one hand, the special interest may indeed be trying to influence the politician's vote. On the other hand, the special interest may simply be trying to support and get elected a person who already sees things their way and who would vote the way they wanted no matter what.

That being said, the impression of impropriety lingers, and so laws have been passed in the United States limiting the amount of money that individuals can donate to specific candidates and making it illegal for certain groups such as companies to donate money directly to individual politicians

(as distinct from directing funds toward supporting specific issues or advocacy groups—which is both legal and unrestricted). Proponents of these laws hope that the limitations strike a good balance—allowing contributions to be large enough that individuals and groups can meaningfully support candidates they agree with but keeping contributions small enough that no one individual or group can singlehandedly donate enough money to sway a politician's vote.

Imperfect Institutions

It is possible to argue that the wide variety of criticisms of public sector inefficiency that we have discussed in this chapter are exaggerated and cynical. Perhaps they are. Nevertheless, they do tend to shatter the concept of a benevolent government that responds with precision and efficiency to the wants of its citizens. The market system of the private sector is far from perfectly efficient, and government's economic function is mainly to correct that system's shortcomings. But the public sector is also subject to deficiencies in fulfilling its economic function. "The relevant comparison is not between perfect markets and imperfect governments, nor between faulty markets and all-knowing, rational, benevolent governments, but between inevitably imperfect institutions."[1]

Because markets and governments are both imperfect, it is sometimes difficult to determine whether a particular activity can be performed with greater success in the private sector or in the public sector. It is easy to reach agreement on opposite extremes: National defense must lie with the public sector, while automobile production can best be accomplished by the private sector. But what about health insurance? Parks and recreation areas? Fire protection? Garbage collection? Housing? Education? It is hard to assess every good or service and to say absolutely that it should be assigned to either the public sector or the private sector. Evidence: All the goods and services just mentioned are provided in part by *both* private enterprises and public agencies.

QUICK REVIEW 5.3

✓ Unlike the private sector—where the profit motive helps to ensure efficiency and variety—government lacks a strong incentive to be efficient and typically offers only limited and bundled choices.

✓ Regulatory capture occurs when a regulated industry can control its government regulator and get it to implement policies that favor the industry.

✓ Political corruption occurs when government officials abuse their powers for personal gain.

[1]Otto Eckstein, *Public Finance*, 3d ed. (Englewood Cliffs, NJ: Prentice-Hall, 1973), P. 17.

"Government Failure" in the News

The Media Continually Report Government Actions That Illustrate Pork-Barrel Politics, Limited and Bundled Choices, or Bureaucratic Inefficiency.

Examples:

- The corporate tax relief bill of 2004 contained 633 pages, with 276 special provisions. Included were provisions that benefited "restaurant owners and Hollywood producers; makers of bows, arrows, tackle boxes, and sonar fish finders; NASCAR track owners; native Alaska whalers; and even importers of Chinese fans." (*The Washington Post*)

- The $878 billion American Recovery and Reinvestment Act of 2009 was laden with many dubious spending projects, including $10 million to renovate a train station in Elizabethtown, Pennsylvania, that hadn't been used in 30 years; $1.15 million to build a guardrail for an artificial lake in Woodward, Oklahoma, that had never been filled with water; and an unrequested $587,661 grant that was given to the upscale town of Union, New York, to fight a homeless problem that it didn't have. (*Lancaster Newspapers*, **newson6.com**, *Binghamton Press & Sun Union*)

- Congress funded a sanctuary for white squirrels, an antique bicycle museum, and a giant roadside coffee pot as part of 2011 federal highway spending. It also spent $765,828 to subsidize the construction of an IHOP restaurant and $113,277 to aid in the historical preservation of video games. (*Human Events, Washington Examiner, Gamasutra*)

- A 2011 audit revealed that the federal government had paid $600 million in retirement benefits to deceased federal retirees over the previous five years. Checks had been illegally cashed by living relatives. One son received cumulative payments of $515,000 over the 37 years after his father died in 1971. The fraud was only discovered after the son died in 2008. (*Associated Press*)

Source: © Royalty-Free/Corbis RF

- Despite Disney making a profit of over $2 billion per year running nine of the world's 10 largest amusement parks, two Disney contractors asked for and received $1.4 million of federal loan guarantees in 2014 to help expand the Polynesian Resort at Disney World. (*Daily Mail*)

- Between 2009 and 2014, the U.S. Department of Agriculture spent $34 million on a program to encourage Afghanis to cultivate and consume soybeans—despite soybeans growing poorly in Afghanistan and locals having no desire to eat soybeans. (*NBC News*)

- In 2014, Congress earmarked $194 million and ordered the U.S. Army to retrofit its entire fleet of M1 Abrams tanks— despite the Army stating that the tanks are obsolete for likely future conflicts. (*Fiscal Times*)

SUMMARY

LO5.1 Describe how government's power to coerce can be economically beneficial and list some of the difficulties associated with managing and directing the government.

Government's legal right to use coercion and force can help to improve economic efficiency by correcting for market failures and by enforcing laws and regulations that reduce the risk that individuals and firms will be taken advantage of.

LO5.2 Discuss "government failure" and explain why it happens.

Special interests can succeed in perpetuating policies that are opposed by the majority of voters because the costs of organizing and

motivating groups to take political action increase with group size. This collective-action problem implies that special interests can perpetuate unpopular policies as long as the costs of organizing an opposition exceed the costs that the general public is currently suffering as a result of those policies.

There are powerful incentives for politicians to accommodate rent seeking and support special-interest legislation.

Because voters like receiving the benefits of government programs but do not like having to pay the taxes necessary to finance them, politicians tend to favor programs that offer easily identified immediate benefits but vague or deferred costs. This tendency helps to explain the unfunded liabilities of programs including Social Security as well as the federal government's tendency to run budget deficits.

When the economy goes into recession, politicians often use the need for fiscal policy stimulus as political cover to direct lower taxes or increased spending toward politically powerful special-interest groups. To prevent politicians from using lower interest rates and monetary stimulus as a way of increasing their reelection chances, most governments have put politically independent central banks in charge of monetary policy.

Economic theorists cite several reasons why government might be inefficient in providing public goods. (a) Citizens as voters and congressional representatives face limited and bundled choices as to public goods, whereas consumers in the private sector can be highly selective in their choices. (b) Government bureaucracies have less incentive to operate efficiently than do private businesses. (c) Regulated industries may sometimes capture their government regulatory agencies and mold government polices toward their own best interests.

Government's track record as an investor in private-sector firms is very poor, with most government investments into private sector businesses generating low or negative returns for taxpayers.

Government attempts to increase private investment by offering loan guarantees often cause resources to be misdirected toward high-risk projects that have an extremely low likelihood of success. These arrangements "socialize losses and privatize gains" because if the businesses go bankrupt, the government bears the losses, but if they do well, private individuals receive the profits.

Political corruption may cause governmental resources or actions to be misdirected.

Neither governments nor markets are perfect economic institutions. Each has its own set of shortcomings and citizens should be aware of where each is likely to fail and where each is likely to succeed.

TERMS AND CONCEPTS

government failure	rent seeking	monetary policy
principal-agent problems	unfunded liability	regulatory capture
special-interest effect	budget deficit	deregulation
collective-action problem	debt crisis	loan guarantees
earmarks	fiscal policy	political corruption

The following and additional problems can be found in **connect**

DISCUSSION QUESTIONS

1. Why might citizens interested in maximizing economic efficiency be happy to invest their government with the right to coerce them in at least some situations? **LO5.1**
2. Jean-Baptiste Colbert was the Minister of Finance under King Louis XIV of France. He famously observed, "The art of taxation consists in so plucking the goose as to obtain the largest possible amount of feathers with the smallest possible amount of hissing." How does his comment relate to special interests and the collective-action problem? **LO5.2**
3. What is rent seeking and how does it differ from the kinds of profit maximization and profit seeking that we discussed in previous chapters? Provide an actual or hypothetical example of rent seeking by firms in an industry. By a union. By a professional association (for example, physicians, school teachers, or lawyers). Why do elected officials often accommodate rent-seeking behavior, particularly by firms, unions, and professional groups located in their home states? **LO5.2**

4. How does the problem of limited and bundled choice in the public sector relate to economic efficiency? Why are public bureaucracies possibly less efficient than business firms? **LO5.2**
5. Discuss the political incentives that helped motivate federal politicians to approve budget deficits in all but five years between 1960 and 2015. **LO5.2**
6. Explain: "Politicians would make more rational economic decisions if they weren't running for reelection every few years." **LO5.2**
7. Critique: "Thank goodness we have so many government regulatory agencies. They keep Big Business in check." **LO5.2**
8. **LAST WORD** How do the concepts of pork-barrel politics and the special-interest effect relate to the items listed in the Last Word?

REVIEW QUESTIONS

1. Select all of the following that are true. To an economist, a coercive government can be useful in order to: **LO5.1**
   a. Reallocate resources in order to improve efficiency.
   b. Fight negative externalities.
   c. Ensure low gasoline prices.
   d. Provide a low-risk economic environment for individuals and firms.

2. To an economist, a government program is too big if an analysis of that program finds that MB _____ MC. **LO5.1**
   a. Is greater than.
   b. Is less than.
   c. Is equal to.
   d. Is less than twice as large as.
   e. Is more than twice as large as.

3. Tammy Hall is the mayor of a large U.S. city. She has just established the Office of Window Safety. Because windows sometimes break and spray glass shards, every window in the city will now have to pass an annual safety inspection. Property owners must pay the $5-per-window cost—and by the way, Tammy has made her nephew the new head of the Office of Window Safety. This new policy is an example of: **LO5.2**
   a. Political corruption.
   b. Earmarks.
   c. Rent seeking.
   d. Adverse selection.

4. A few hundred U.S. sugar makers lobby the U.S. government each year to make sure that the government taxes imported sugar at a high rate. They do so because the policy drives up the domestic price of sugar and increases their profits. It is estimated that the policy benefits U.S. sugar producers by about $1 billion per year while costing U.S. consumers upwards of $2 billion per year. Which of the following concepts apply to the U.S. sugar tax? **LO5.2**
   a. Political corruption.
   b. Rent-seeking behavior.
   c. The collective-action problem.
   d. The special-interest effect.

5. _____ occur when politicians commit to making a series of future expenditures without simultaneously committing to collect enough tax revenues to pay for those expenditures. **LO5.2**
   a. Budget deficits
   b. Debt crises
   c. Loan guarantees
   d. Unfunded liabilities

PROBLEMS

1. Suppose that there are 1 million federal workers at the lowest level of the federal bureaucracy and that above them there are multiple layers of supervisors and supervisors-of-supervisors. Assume that each higher level is one-tenth the size of the one below it because the government is using a 10:1 ratio of supervisees to supervisors. That is, for every 10 workers at the bottom, there is 1 supervisor; for every 10 of those supervisors, there is 1 supervisor-of-supervisors; for every one of those supervisors-of-supervisors, there is a supervisor-of-supervisors-of-supervisors; and so on, all the way up the bureaucratic pyramid to the president. **LO5.1**
   a. How many supervisors will there be in each supervisory layer of the federal bureaucracy? Start with the layer of supervisors directly above the 1 million workers at the bottom.
   b. How many supervisors are there in total at all levels of the federal bureaucratic pyramid, including the president?
   c. If you count the 1 million workers at the bottom as the first layer of the federal bureaucracy, how many total layers are there, including the president?
   d. How many federal employees are there in total at all layers, including the president?
   e. What fraction of all federal employees are supervisory, including the president?

2. Consider a specific example of the special-interest effect and the collective-action problem. In 2012, it was estimated that the total value of all corn production subsidies in the United States was about $3 billion. The population of the United States was approximately 300 million people that year. **LO5.2**
   a. On average, how much did corn subsidies cost per person in the United States in 2012? (Hint: A billion is a 1 followed by nine zeros. A million is a 1 followed by six zeros.)
   b. If each person in the United States is only willing to spend $0.50 to support efforts to overturn the corn subsidy, and if antisubsidy advocates can only raise funds from 10 percent of the population, how much money will they be able to raise for their lobbying efforts?
   c. If the recipients of corn subsidies donate just 1 percent of the total amount that they receive in subsidies, how much could they raise to support lobbying efforts to continue the corn subsidy?
   d. By how many dollars does the amount raised by the recipients of the corn subsidy exceed the amount raised by the opponents of the corn subsidy?

3. Consider a corrupt provincial government in which each housing inspector examines two newly built structures each week. All the builders in the province are unethical and want to increase their profits by using substandard construction materials, but they can't do that unless they can bribe a housing inspector into approving a substandard building. **LO5.2**
   a. If bribes cost $1,000 each, how much will a housing inspector make each year in bribes? (Assume that each inspector works 52 weeks a year and gets bribed for every house he inspects.)
   b. There is a provincial construction supervisor who gets to hire all of the housing inspectors. He himself is corrupt and expects his housing inspectors to share their bribes with him. Suppose that 20 inspectors work for him and that each passes along half the bribes collected from builders. How much will the construction supervisor collect each year?
   c. Corrupt officials may have an incentive to reduce the provision of government services to help line their own pockets. Suppose that the provincial construction supervisor decides to cut the total number of housing inspectors from 20 to 10 in order to decrease the supply of new housing permits. This decrease in the supply of permits raises the equilibrium bribe from $1,000 to $2,500. How much per year will the construction supervisor now receive if he is still getting half of all the bribes collected by the 10 inspectors? How much more is the construction supervisor getting now than when he had 20 inspectors working in part *b*? Will he personally be happy with the reduction in government services?
   d. What if reducing the number of inspectors from 20 to 10 only increased the equilibrium bribe from $1,000 to $1,500? In this case, how much per year would the construction supervisor collect from his 10 inspectors? How much *less* is the construction supervisor getting than when he had 20 inspectors working in part *b*? In this case, will the construction supervisor be happy with the reduction in government services? Will he want to go back to using 20 inspectors?

Public Choice Theory and Voting Paradoxes

LO5.3 Explain the difficulties of conveying economic preferences through majority voting.

Public Choice Theory

Market failures, such as public goods and externalities, impede economic efficiency and justify government intervention in the economy.

But the government's response to market failures is not without its own problems and pitfalls. In fact, government can sometimes fail as badly or even worse than markets in terms of delivering economic efficiency and directing resources to the uses where they will bring the largest net benefits.

That is why it is important to study **public choice theory**—the economic analysis of government decision making, politics, and elections. Just as the study of *market failure* helps us to understand how regulating markets may help to improve the allocation of resources, the study of *government failure* can help us to understand how changes in the way government functions might help it to operate more efficiently.

As we will discuss shortly, many instances of government failure can be traced to incentive structures that lead political representatives to pursue policies that go against the preferences of the people that they are representing. But an even more fundamental problem exists. The majority voting systems that we rely upon may make it difficult or even impossible to correctly discern voter preferences. In such cases, it is not surprising that government fails to deliver what the voters actually want.

Revealing Preferences through Majority Voting

Through some process, society must decide which public goods it wants and in what amounts. It also must determine the extent to which it wants government to intervene in private markets to correct externalities. Decisions need to be made about the extent and type of regulation of business that is necessary, the amount of income redistribution that is desirable, what policies the government might enact to mitigate asymmetric information problems, and other such choices. Furthermore, society must determine the set of taxes it thinks is best for financing government. How should government apportion (divide) the total tax burden among the public?

Decisions such as these are made collectively in the United States through a democratic process that relies heavily on majority voting. Candidates for office offer alternative policy packages, and citizens elect people who they think will make the best decisions on their collective behalf. Voters "retire" officials who do not adequately represent their collective wishes and elect persons they think do. Also, citizens periodically have opportunities at the state and local levels to vote directly on public expenditures or new legislation.

Although the democratic process does a reasonably good job of revealing society's preferences, it is imperfect. Public choice theory demonstrates that majority voting can produce inefficiencies and inconsistencies.

Inefficient Voting Outcomes Society's well-being is enhanced when government provides a public good whose total benefit exceeds its total cost. Unfortunately, majority voting does not always deliver that outcome.

Illustration: Inefficient "No" Vote Assume that the government can provide a public good, say, national defense, at a total expense of $900. Also assume that there are only three individuals—Adams, Benson, and Conrad—in the society and that they will share the $900 tax expense equally, each being taxed $300 if the proposed public good is provided. And assume, as Figure 1a illustrates, that Adams would receive $700 worth of benefits from having this public good; Benson, $250; and Conrad, $200.

What will be the result if a majority vote determines whether or not this public good is provided? Although people do not always vote strictly according to their own economic interest, it is likely Benson and Conrad will vote "no" because they will incur tax costs of $300 each while gaining benefits of only $250 and $200, respectively. Adams will vote "yes." So the majority vote will defeat the proposal even though the total benefit of $1,150 (= $700 for Adams + $250 for Benson + $200 for Conrad) exceeds the total cost of $900. Resources should be devoted to this good, but they will not be. Too little of this public good will be produced.

Illustration: Inefficient "Yes" Vote Now consider a situation in which the majority favors a public good even though its total cost exceeds its total benefit. Figure 1b shows the details. Again, Adams, Benson, and Conrad will equally share the $900 cost of the public good; each will be taxed $300. But since Adams' benefit now is only $100 from the public good, she will vote against it. Meanwhile, Benson and Conrad will

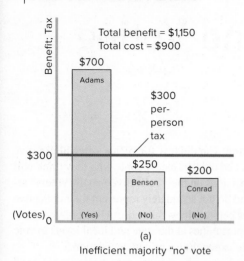

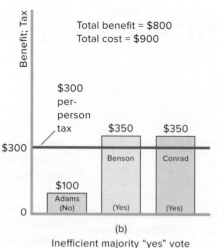

FIGURE 1 Inefficient voting outcomes. Majority voting can produce inefficient decisions. (a) Majority voting leads to rejection of a public good that would entail a greater total benefit than total cost. (b) Majority voting results in acceptance of a public good that has a higher total cost than total benefit.

(a) Inefficient majority "no" vote

(b) Inefficient majority "yes" vote

benefit by $350 each. They will vote for the public good because that benefit ($350) exceeds their tax payments ($300). The majority vote will provide a public good costing $900 that produces total benefits of only $800 (= $100 for Adams + $350 for Benson + $350 for Conrad). Society's resources will be inefficiently allocated to this public good. Too much of it will be produced.

Implications The point is that an inefficient outcome may occur as either an overproduction or an underproduction of a specific public good, and therefore as an overallocation or underallocation of resources for that particular use. In Chapter 4 we saw that government can improve economic efficiency by providing public goods that the market system will not make available. Now we have extended that analysis to reveal that government may not provide some of those public goods or may provide them in the wrong amounts. In other cases, it may provide public goods that are not economically warranted.

In our examples, each person has only a single vote, no matter how much he or she might gain or lose from a public good. In the first example (inefficient "no" vote), Adams would be willing to purchase a vote from either Benson or Conrad if buying votes were legal. That way Adams could be assured of obtaining the national defense she so highly values. But since buying votes is illegal, many people with strong preferences for certain public goods may have to go without them.

When individual consumers have a strong preference for a specific *private good*, they usually can find that good in the marketplace even though it may be unpopular with the majority of consumers. A consumer can buy beef tongue, liver, and squid in some supermarkets, although it is doubtful that any of these products would be available if majority voting stocked the shelves. But a person cannot easily "buy" a *public good* such as national defense once the majority has decided against it.

Conversely, a consumer in the marketplace can decide against buying a particular product, even a popular one. But although you may not want national defense, you must "buy" it through your tax payments when the majority have decided they want it.

Conclusion: Because majority voting fails to incorporate the *strength* of the preferences of the individual voter, it may produce economically inefficient outcomes.

Interest Groups and Logrolling Some, but not all, of the inefficiencies of majority voting get resolved through the political process. Two examples follow.

Interest Groups People who share strong preferences for a public good may band together into interest groups and use advertisements, mailings, and direct persuasion to convince others of the merits of that public good. Adams might try to persuade Benson and Conrad that it is in their best interest to vote for national defense—that national defense is much more valuable to them than their $250 and $200 valuations. Such appeals are common in democratic politics. Sometimes they are successful; sometimes they are not.

Political Logrolling Perhaps surprisingly, **logrolling**—the trading of votes to secure desired outcomes—can also turn an inefficient outcome into an efficient one. In our first example (Figure 1a), suppose that Benson has a strong preference for a different public good, for example, a new road, which Adams and Conrad do not think is worth the tax expense. That would provide an opportunity for Adams and Benson to trade votes to ensure provision of both national defense and the new road. That is, Adams and Benson would each vote "yes" on both measures. Adams would get the national defense and Benson would get the road. Without the logrolling, both public goods would have been rejected. This logrolling will add to society's well-being if, as was true for national defense, the road creates a greater overall benefit than cost.

But logrolling need not increase economic efficiency. Even if national defense and the road each cost more than the total benefit each produces, both might still be provided if there is vote trading. Adams and Benson might still engage in logrolling if each expects to secure a sufficient net gain from her or his favored public good, even though the gains would come at the clear expense of Conrad.

Logrolling is very common in state legislatures and Congress. It can either increase or diminish economic efficiency, depending on the circumstances.

Paradox of Voting

Another difficulty with majority voting is the **paradox of voting,** a situation in which society may not be able to rank its preferences consistently through paired-choice majority voting.

Preferences Consider Table 1, in which we again assume a community of three voters: Adams, Benson, and Conrad. Suppose the community has three alternative public goods from which to choose: national defense, a road, and a weather warning system. We expect that each member of the community prefers the three alternatives in a certain order. For example, one person might prefer national defense to a road and a road to a weather warning system. We can attempt to determine the preferences of the community through paired-choice majority voting. Specifically, a vote can be held between any two of the public goods, and the winner of that vote can then be matched against the third public good in another vote.

The three goods and the assumed individual preferences of the three voters are listed in the top part of Table 1. The data indicate that Adams prefers national defense to the road and the road to the weather warning system. This implies also that Adams prefers national defense to the weather warning system. Benson values the road more than the weather warning system and the warning system more than national defense. Conrad's order of preference is weather warning system, national defense, and road.

TABLE 1 Paradox of Voting

Public Good	Preferences		
	Adams	Benson	Conrad
National defense	1st choice	3d choice	2d choice
Road	2d choice	1st choice	3d choice
Weather warning system	3d choice	2d choice	1st choice

Election	Voting Outcomes: Winner
1. National defense vs. road	National defense (preferred by Adams and Conrad)
2. Road vs. weather warning system	Road (preferred by Adams and Benson)
3. National defense vs. weather warning system	Weather warning system (preferred by Benson and Conrad)

Voting Outcomes The lower part of Table 1 shows the outcomes of three hypothetical elections decided through majority vote. In the first, national defense wins against the road because a majority of voters (Adams and Conrad) prefer national defense to the road. In the second election, to see whether this community wants a road or a weather warning system, a majority of voters (Adams and Benson) prefer the road.

We have determined that the majority of people in this community prefer national defense to a road and prefer a road to a weather warning system. It seems logical to conclude that the community prefers national defense to a weather warning system. But it does not!

To demonstrate this conclusion, we hold a direct election between national defense and the weather warning system. Row 3 shows that a majority of voters (Benson and Conrad) prefer the weather warning system to national defense. As listed in Table 1, then, the three paired-choice majority votes imply that this community is irrational: It seems to prefer national defense to a road and a road to a weather warning system, but would rather have a weather warning system than national defense.

The problem is not irrational community preferences but rather a flawed procedure for determining those preferences. We see that the outcome from paired-choice majority voting may depend on the order in which the votes are taken. Different sequences of majority votes can lead to different outcomes, many of which may fail to reflect the electorate's underlying preferences. As a consequence, government may find it difficult to provide the "correct" public goods by acting in accordance with majority voting. Important note: This critique is not meant to suggest that some better procedure exists. Majority voting is much more likely to reflect community preferences than decisions by, say, a dictator or a group of self-appointed leaders.

Median-Voter Model One other aspect of majority voting reveals further insights into real-world phenomena. The **median-voter model** suggests that, under majority rule and consistent voting preferences, the median voter will in a sense determine the outcomes of elections. The median voter is the person holding the middle position on an issue: Half the other voters have stronger preferences for a public good, amount of taxation, or degree of government regulation, while half have weaker or negative preferences. The extreme voters on each side of an issue prefer the median choice rather than the other extreme position, so the median voter's choice predominates.

Example Suppose a society composed of Adams, Benson, and Conrad has reached agreement that as a society it needs a weather warning system. Each person independently is to submit a total dollar amount he or she thinks should be spent on the warning system, assuming each will be taxed one-third of that amount. An election will determine the size of the

CONSIDER THIS . . .

Source: © Blend Images/Superstock RF

Voter Failure

Inefficient voting outcomes and the paradox of voting imply that governments may sometimes fail to deliver the best combination of public goods because it may be very difficult for politicians to discern what voters actually want. In other cases, though, economists worry that governments may end up failing to deliver allocative and productive efficiency not because politicians can't tell what people want—but because they *can*.

The problem is that voters sometimes support policies that reduce rather than enhance allocative and productive efficiency. Examples include several types of wage and price controls, punitive tariffs on foreign products, and various industrial and agricultural subsidies.

These policies almost always reduce economic efficiency, but they are also extremely popular with voters in many countries. Faced with that reality, a politician may well end up supporting such policies even if he personally understands that they will create more economic harm than benefit.

That behavior makes some observers wish for braver politicians who might be willing to oppose these instances of "voter failure." But others argue that it is too much to hope for braver politicians. Instead, efforts should be directed toward educating the public and convincing them to support government policies that are economically efficient.

system. Because each person can be expected to vote for his or her own proposal, no majority will occur if all the proposals are placed on the ballot at the same time. Thus, the group decides on a paired-choice vote: They will first vote between two of the proposals and then match the winner of that vote against the remaining proposal.

The three proposals are as follows: Adams desires a $400 system; Benson wants an $800 system; Conrad opts for a $300 system. Which proposal will win? The median-voter model suggests it will be the $400 proposal submitted by the median voter, Adams. Half the other voters favor a more costly system; half favor a less costly system. To understand why the $400 system will be the outcome, let's conduct the two elections.

First, suppose that the $400 proposal is matched against the $800 proposal. Adams naturally votes for her $400 proposal, and Benson votes for his own $800 proposal. Conrad, who proposed the $300 expenditure for the warning system,

votes for the $400 proposal because it is closer to his own. So Adams's $400 proposal is selected by a 2-to-1 majority vote.

Next, we match the $400 proposal against the $300 proposal. Again the $400 proposal wins. It gets a vote from Adams and one from Benson, who proposed the $800 expenditure and for that reason prefers a $400 expenditure to a $300 one. Adams, the median voter in this case, is in a sense the person who has decided the level of expenditure on a weather warning system for this society.

Real-World Applicability Although our illustration is simple, it explains a great deal. We do note a tendency for public choices to match most closely the median view. Political candidates, for example, take one set of positions to win the nomination of their political parties; in so doing, they tend to appeal to the median voter within the party to get the nomination. They then shift their views more closely to the political center when they square off against opponents from the opposite political party. In effect, they redirect their appeal toward the median voter within the total population. They also try to label their opponents as being too liberal, or too conservative, and out of touch with "mainstream America." And they conduct polls and adjust their positions on issues accordingly.

Implications The median-voter model has two important implications:

- At any point in time, many people will be dissatisfied by the extent of government involvement in the economy. The size of government will largely be determined by the median preference, leaving many people desiring a much larger, or a much smaller, public sector. In the marketplace you can buy no zucchinis, 2 zucchinis, or 200 zucchinis, depending on how much you enjoy them. In the public sector you will tend to get the number of Stealth bombers and new highway projects that the median voter prefers.

- Some people may "vote with their feet" by moving into political jurisdictions where the median voter's preferences are closer to their own. They may move from the city to a suburb where the level of government services, and therefore taxes, is lower. Or they may move into an area known for its excellent, but expensive, school system. Some may move to other states; a few may even move to other countries.

For these reasons, and because our personal preferences for publicly provided goods and services are not static, the median preference shifts over time. Moreover, information about people's preferences is imperfect, leaving much room for politicians to misjudge the true median position. When they do, they may have a difficult time getting elected or reelected.

APPENDIX SUMMARY

LO5.3 Explain the difficulties of conveying economic preferences through majority voting.

Public choice theory suggests that governments may sometimes suffer from government failures because majority voting fails to correctly indicate voter preferences.

Majority voting creates the possibility of (a) underallocations or overallocations of resources to particular public goods and (b) inconsistent voting outcomes that make it impossible for a democratic political system to definitively determine the will of the people.

The median-voter model predicts that, under majority rule, the person holding the middle position on an issue will determine the outcome of an election involving that issue.

APPENDIX TERMS AND CONCEPTS

public choice theory

logrolling

paradox of voting

median-voter model

The following and additional problems can be found in ▩ **connect**

APPENDIX DISCUSSION QUESTIONS

1. Explain how affirmative and negative majority votes can sometimes lead to inefficient allocations of resources to public goods. Is this problem likely to be greater under a benefits-received or an ability-to-pay tax system? Use the information in Figures 1a and 1b to show how society might be better off if Adams were allowed to buy votes. **LO5.3**

2. "Majority voting ensures that government will produce only those public goods for which benefits exceed costs." Discuss. **LO5.3**

3. "The problem with our democratic institutions is that they don't correctly reflect the will of the people! If the people—rather than self-interested politicians or lobbyists—had control, we wouldn't have to worry about government taking actions that don't maximize allocative and productive efficiency." Critique. **LO5.3**

APPENDIX REVIEW QUESTIONS

1. Explain the paradox of voting through reference to the accompanying table, which shows the ranking of three public goods by voters Jay, Dave, and Conan: **LO5.3**

Public Good	Rankings		
	Jay	**Dave**	**Conan**
Courthouse	2nd choice	1st choice	3d choice
School	3d choice	2d choice	1st choice
Park	1st choice	3d choice	2d choice

2. We can apply voting paradoxes to the highway construction example of Chapter 4. Suppose there are only five people in a society and each favors one of the five highway construction options listed in Table 4.4 ("No new construction" is one of the five options). Explain which of these highway options will be selected using a majority paired-choice vote. Will this option be the optimal size of the project from an economic perspective? **LO5.3**

3. True or False: The median-voter model explains why politicians so often stake out fringe positions that appeal only to a small segment of the electorate. **LO5.3**

APPENDIX PROBLEMS

1. Look back at Figures 1a and 1b, which show the costs and benefits to voters Adams, Benson, and Conrad of two different public goods that the government will produce if a majority of Adams, Benson, and Conrad support them. Suppose that Adams, Benson, and Conrad have decided to have one single vote at which the funding for both of those public goods will be decided simultaneously. **LO5.3**

   a. Given the $300 cost per person of each public good, what are Adams's net benefits for each public good individually and for the two combined? Will he want to vote yes or no on the proposal to fund both projects simultaneously?

   b. What are Conrad's net benefits for each public good individually and for the two combined? Will he want to vote yes or no on the proposal to fund both projects simultaneously?

   c. What are Benson's net benefits for each public good individually and for the two combined? Will he want to vote yes or no on the proposal to fund both projects simultaneously—or will he be indifferent?

    d. Who is the median voter here? Who will the two other voters be attempting to persuade?

2. Political advertising is often directed at winning over so-called swing voters, whose votes might go either way. Suppose that two political parties—the Freedom Party and the Liberty Party—disagree on whether to build a new road. Polling shows that of 1,000 total voters, 450 are firmly for the new road and 450 are firmly against the new road. Thus, each party will try to win over a majority of the 100 remaining swing voters. **LO5.3**

    a. Suppose that each party spends $5,000 on untargeted TV, radio, and newspaper ads that are equally likely to reach any and all voters. How much per voter will be spent by both parties combined?

    b. Suppose that, instead, each party could direct all of its spending toward just the swing voters by using targeted ads that exploit Internet social media. If all of the two parties' combined spending was targeted at just swing voters, how much would be spent per swing voter?

    c. Suppose that only the Freedom Party knows how to target voters using social media. How much per swing voter will it be spending? If at the same time the Liberty Party is still using only untargeted TV, radio, and newspaper ads, what portion of its total spending is likely to be reaching the 100 swing voters? How much per swing voter does that portion amount to?

    d. Looking at your answers to part *c*, how much more per swing voter will the Freedom Party be spending than the Liberty Party? If spending per swing voter influences elections, which party is more likely to win?

Consumer Behavior

3

Elasticity

Learning Objectives

LO6.1 Discuss price elasticity of demand and how it is calculated.

LO6.2 Explain the usefulness of the total-revenue test for price elasticity of demand.

LO6.3 List the factors that affect price elasticity of demand and describe some applications of price elasticity of demand.

LO6.4 Describe price elasticity of supply and how it can be applied.

LO6.5 Apply cross elasticity of demand and income elasticity of demand.

In this chapter we extend Chapter 3's discussion of demand and supply by explaining *elasticity,* an extremely important concept that helps us answer such questions as: Why do buyers of some products (for example, ocean cruises) respond to price increases by substantially reducing their purchases while buyers of other products (say, gasoline) respond by only slightly cutting back their purchases? Why do higher market prices for some products (for example, chicken) cause producers to greatly increase

their output while price rises for other products (say, gold) cause only limited increases in output? Why does the demand for some products (for example, books) rise a great deal when household income increases while the demand for other products (say, milk) rises just a little?

Elasticity extends our understanding of markets by letting us know the degree to which changes in prices and incomes affect supply and demand. Sometimes the responses are substantial, other times minimal or even nonexistent. But by knowing what to expect, businesses and the government can do a better job in deciding what to produce, how much to charge, and, surprisingly, what items to tax.

Price Elasticity of Demand

LO6.1 Discuss price elasticity of demand and how it is calculated.
The law of demand tells us that, other things equal, consumers will buy more of a product when its price declines and less when its price increases. But how much more or less will they buy? The amount varies from product to product and over different price ranges for the same product. It also may vary over time. And such variations matter. For example, a firm contemplating a price hike will want to know how consumers will respond. If they remain highly loyal and continue to buy, the firm's revenue will rise. But if consumers defect en masse to other sellers or other products, the firm's revenue will tumble.

The responsiveness (or sensitivity) of consumers to a price change is measured by a product's **price elasticity of demand.** For some products—for example, restaurant meals—consumers are highly responsive to price changes. Modest price changes cause very large changes in the quantity purchased. Economists say that the demand for such products is *relatively elastic* or simply *elastic.*

For other products—for example, toothpaste—consumers pay much less attention to price changes. Substantial price changes cause only small changes in the amount purchased. The demand for such products is *relatively inelastic* or simply *inelastic.*

The Price-Elasticity Coefficient and Formula

Economists measure the degree to which demand is price elastic or inelastic with the coefficient E_d, defined as

$$E_d = \frac{\text{percentage change in quantity demanded of product X}}{\text{percentage change in price of product X}}$$

The percentage changes in the equation are calculated by dividing the *change* in quantity demanded by the original quantity demanded and by dividing the *change* in price by the original price. So we can restate the formula as

$$E_d = \frac{\dfrac{\text{change in quantity demanded of X}}{\text{original quantity demanded of X}}}{\div \dfrac{\text{change in price of X}}{\text{original price of X}}}$$

Using Averages Unfortunately, an annoying problem arises in computing the price-elasticity coefficient. A price change from, say, $4 to $5 along a demand curve is a 25 percent (= $1/$4) increase, but the opposite price change from $5 to $4 along the same curve is a 20 percent (= $1/$5) decrease. Which percentage change in price should we use in the denominator to compute the price-elasticity coefficient? And when quantity changes, for example, from 10 to 20, it is a 100 percent (= 10/10) increase. But when quantity falls from 20 to 10 along the identical demand curve, it is a 50 percent (= 10/20) decrease. Should we use 100 percent or 50 percent in the numerator of the elasticity formula? Elasticity should be the same whether price rises or falls!

The simplest solution to the problem is to use the **midpoint formula** for calculating elasticity. This formula simply averages the two prices and the two quantities as the reference points for computing the percentages. That is,

$$E_d = \frac{\text{change in quantity}}{\text{sum of quantities/2}} \div \frac{\text{change in price}}{\text{sum of prices/2}}$$

For the same $5–$4 price range, the price reference is $4.50 [= ($5 + $4)/2], and for the same 10–20 quantity range, the quantity reference is 15 units [= (10 + 20)/2]. The percentage change in price is now $1/$4.50, or about 22 percent, and the percentage change in quantity is $\frac{10}{15}$, or about 67 percent. So E_d is about 3. This solution eliminates the "up versus down" problem. All the price-elasticity coefficients that follow are calculated using this midpoint formula.

Using Percentages Why use percentages rather than absolute amounts in measuring consumer responsiveness? There are two reasons.

First, if we use absolute changes, the choice of units will arbitrarily affect our impression of buyer responsiveness. To illustrate: If the price of a bag of popcorn at the local softball game is reduced from $3 to $2 and consumers increase their purchases from 60 to 100 bags, it will seem that consumers are quite sensitive to price changes and therefore that demand is elastic. After all, a price change of 1 unit has caused a change in the amount demanded of 40 units. But by changing the monetary unit from dollars to pennies (why not?), we find that a price change of 100 units (pennies) causes a quantity change of 40 units. This may falsely lead us to believe that demand is inelastic. We avoid this problem by using percentage changes. This particular price decline is the same whether we measure it in dollars or pennies.

Second, by using percentages, we can correctly compare consumer responsiveness to changes in the prices of different products. It makes little sense to compare the effects on quantity demanded of (1) a $1 increase in the price of a $10,000 used car with (2) a $1 increase in the price of a $1 soft drink. Here the price of the used car has increased by 0.01 percent while the price of the soft drink is up by 100 percent. We can more sensibly compare the consumer responsiveness to price increases by using some common percentage increase in price for both.

Elimination of Minus Sign We know from the downsloping demand curve that price and quantity demanded are inversely related. Thus, the price-elasticity coefficient of demand E_d will always be a negative number. As an example, if price declines, then quantity demanded will increase. This means that the numerator in our formula will be positive and the denominator negative, yielding a negative E_d. For an increase in price, the numerator will be negative but the denominator positive, again yielding a negative E_d.

Economists usually ignore the minus sign and simply present the absolute value of the elasticity coefficient to avoid an ambiguity that might otherwise arise. It can be confusing to say that an E_d of −4 is greater than one of −2. This possible confusion is avoided when we say an E_d of 4 reveals greater elasticity than one of 2. So, in what follows, we ignore the minus sign in the coefficient of price elasticity of demand

and show only the absolute value. Incidentally, the ambiguity does not arise with supply because price and quantity supplied are positively related. All elasticity of supply coefficients therefore are positive numbers.

Interpretations of E_d

We can interpret the coefficient of price elasticity of demand as follows.

Elastic Demand Demand is **elastic** if a specific percentage change in price results in a larger percentage change in quantity demanded. In such cases, E_d will be greater than 1. Example: Suppose that a 2 percent decline in the price of cut flowers results in a 4 percent increase in quantity demanded. Then demand for cut flowers is elastic and

$$E_d = \frac{.04}{.02} = 2$$

Inelastic Demand If a specific percentage change in price produces a smaller percentage change in quantity demanded, demand is **inelastic.** In such cases, E_d will be less than 1. Example: Suppose that a 2 percent decline in the price of coffee leads to only a 1 percent increase in quantity demanded. Then demand is inelastic and

$$E_d = \frac{.01}{.02} = .5$$

Unit Elasticity The case separating elastic and inelastic demands occurs where a percentage change in price and the resulting percentage change in quantity demanded are the same. Example: Suppose that a 2 percent drop in the price of chocolate causes a 2 percent increase in quantity demanded. This special case is termed **unit elasticity** because E_d is exactly 1, or unity. In this example,

$$E_d = \frac{.02}{.02} = 1$$

Extreme Cases When we say demand is "inelastic," we do not mean that consumers are completely unresponsive to a price change. In that extreme situation, where a price change results in no change whatsoever in the quantity demanded, economists say that demand is **perfectly inelastic.** The price-elasticity coefficient is zero because there is no response to a change in price. Approximate examples include an acute diabetic's demand for insulin or an addict's demand for heroin. A line parallel to the vertical axis, such as D_1 in Figure 6.1a, shows perfectly inelastic demand graphically.

Conversely, when we say demand is "elastic," we do not mean that consumers are completely responsive to a price change. In that extreme situation, where a small price reduction

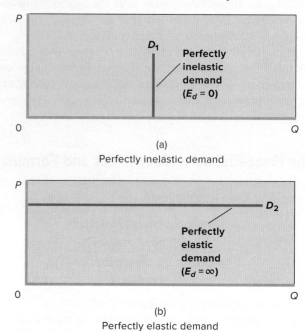

FIGURE 6.1 Perfectly inelastic and elastic demands. Demand curve D_1 in (a) represents perfectly inelastic demand ($E_d = 0$). A price increase will result in no change in quantity demanded. Demand curve D_2 in (b) represents perfectly elastic demand. A price increase will cause quantity demanded to decline from an infinite amount to zero ($E_d = \infty$).

(a)
Perfectly inelastic demand

(b)
Perfectly elastic demand

causes buyers to increase their purchases from zero to all they can obtain, the elasticity coefficient is infinite ($= \infty$) and economists say demand is **perfectly elastic.** A line parallel to the horizontal axis, such as D_2 in Figure 6.1b, shows perfectly elastic demand. You will see in Chapter 10 that such a demand applies to a firm—say, a mining firm—that is selling its output in a purely competitive market.

The Total-Revenue Test

LO6.2 Explain the usefulness of the total-revenue test for price elasticity of demand.

The importance of elasticity for firms relates to the effect of price changes on total revenue and thus on profits (= total revenue minus total costs).

Total revenue (TR) is the total amount the seller receives from the sale of a product in a particular time period; it is calculated by multiplying the product price (P) by the quantity sold (Q). In equation form:

$$TR = P \times Q$$

Graphically, total revenue is represented by the $P \times Q$ rectangle lying below a point on a demand curve. At point a in Figure 6.2a, for example, price is $2 and quantity demanded is 10 units. So total revenue is $20 (= $2 × 10), shown by the rectangle composed of the yellow and green areas under the demand curve. We know from basic geometry that the area of

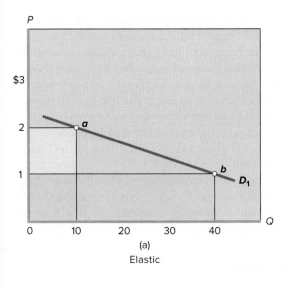

(a)
Elastic

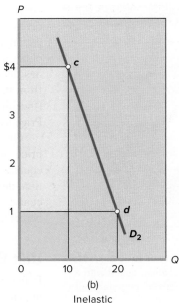

(b)
Inelastic

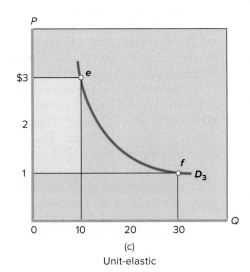

(c)
Unit-elastic

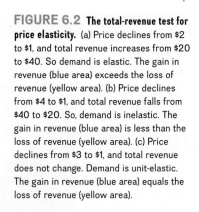

FIGURE 6.2 The total-revenue test for price elasticity. (a) Price declines from $2 to $1, and total revenue increases from $20 to $40. So demand is elastic. The gain in revenue (blue area) exceeds the loss of revenue (yellow area). (b) Price declines from $4 to $1, and total revenue falls from $40 to $20. So, demand is inelastic. The gain in revenue (blue area) is less than the loss of revenue (yellow area). (c) Price declines from $3 to $1, and total revenue does not change. Demand is unit-elastic. The gain in revenue (blue area) equals the loss of revenue (yellow area).

a rectangle is found by multiplying one side by the other. Here, one side is "price" ($2) and the other is "quantity demanded" (10 units).

Total revenue and the price elasticity of demand are related. In fact, the easiest way to infer whether demand is elastic or inelastic is to employ the **total-revenue test.** Here is the test: Note what happens to total revenue when price changes. If total revenue changes in the opposite direction from price, demand is elastic. If total revenue changes in the same direction as price, demand is inelastic. If total revenue does not change when price changes, demand is unit-elastic.

Elastic Demand

If demand is elastic, a decrease in price will increase total revenue. Even though a lesser price is received per unit,

enough additional units are sold to more than make up for the lower price. For an example, look at demand curve D_1 in Figure 6.2a. We have already established that at point a, total revenue is $20 (= $2 × 10), shown as the yellow plus green area. If the price declines from $2 to $1 (point b), the quantity demanded becomes 40 units and total revenue is $40 (= $1 × 40). As a result of the price decline, total revenue has increased from $20 to $40. Total revenue has increased in this case because the $1 decline in price applies to 10 units, with a consequent revenue loss of $10 (the yellow area). But 30 more units are sold at $1 each, resulting in a revenue gain of $30 (the blue area). Visually, the gain of the blue area clearly exceeds the loss of the yellow area. As indicated, the overall result is a net increase in total revenue of $20 (= $30 − $10).

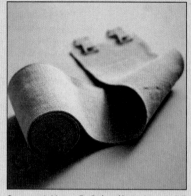
The analysis is reversible: If demand is elastic, a price increase will reduce total revenue. The revenue gained on the higher-priced units will be more than offset by the revenue lost from the lower quantity sold. Bottom line: Other things equal, when price and total revenue move in opposite directions, demand is elastic. E_d is greater than 1, meaning the percentage change in quantity demanded is greater than the percentage change in price.

Inelastic Demand

If demand is inelastic, a price decrease will reduce total revenue. The increase in sales will not fully offset the decline in revenue per unit, and total revenue will decline. To see this, look at demand curve D_2 in Figure 6.2b. At point c on the curve, price is $4 and quantity demanded is 10. Thus total revenue is $40, shown by the combined yellow and green rectangle. If the price drops to $1 (point d), total revenue declines to $20, which obviously is less than $40. Total revenue has declined because the loss of revenue (the yellow area) from the lower unit price is larger than the gain in revenue (the blue area) from the accompanying increase in sales. Price has fallen, and total revenue has also declined.

Our analysis is again reversible: If demand is inelastic, a price increase will increase total revenue. So, other things equal, when price and total revenue move in the same direction, demand is inelastic. E_d is less than 1, meaning the percentage change in quantity demanded is less than the percentage change in price.

Unit Elasticity

In the special case of unit elasticity, an increase or a decrease in price leaves total revenue unchanged. The loss in revenue from a lower unit price is exactly offset by the gain in revenue from the accompanying increase in sales. Conversely, the gain in revenue from a higher unit price is exactly offset by the revenue loss associated with the accompanying decline in the amount demanded.

In Figure 6.2c (demand curve D_3) we find that at the price of $3, 10 units will be sold, yielding total revenue of $30. At the lower $1 price, a total of 30 units will be sold, again resulting in $30 of total revenue. The $2 price reduction causes the loss of revenue shown by the yellow area, but this is exactly offset by the revenue gain shown by the blue area. Total revenue does not change. In fact, that would be true for all price changes along this particular curve.

Other things equal, when price changes and total revenue remains constant, demand is unit-elastic (or unitary). E_d is 1, meaning the percentage change in quantity equals the percentage change in price.

Price Elasticity along a Linear Demand Curve

Now a major confession! Although the demand curves depicted in Figure 6.2 nicely illustrate the total-revenue test for elasticity, two of the graphs involve specific movements along linear (straight-line) demand curves. That presents no problem for explaining the total-revenue test. However, you need to know that elasticity typically varies over different price ranges of the same demand curve. (The exception is the curve in Figure 6.2c. Elasticity is 1 along the entire curve.)

Table 6.1 and Figure 6.3 demonstrate that elasticity typically varies over different price ranges of the same demand schedule or curve. Plotting the hypothetical data for movie tickets shown in columns 1 and 2 of Table 6.1 yields demand curve D in Figure 6.3. Observe that the demand curve is

TABLE 6.1 Price Elasticity of Demand for Movie Tickets as Measured by the Elasticity Coefficient and the Total-Revenue Test

(1) Total Quantity of Tickets Demanded per Week, Thousands	(2) Price per Ticket	(3) Elasticity Coefficient (E_d)	(4) Total Revenue, (1) × (2)	(5) Total-Revenue Test
1	$8		$ 8,000	
2	7	5.00	14,000	Elastic
3	6	2.60	18,000	Elastic
4	5	1.57	20,000	Elastic
5	4	1.00	20,000	Unit-elastic
6	3	0.64	18,000	Inelastic
7	2	0.38	14,000	Inelastic
8	1	0.20	8,000	Inelastic

linear. But we see from column 3 of the table that the price elasticity coefficient for this demand curve declines as we move from higher to lower prices. For all downsloping straight-line and most other demand curves, demand is more price-elastic toward the upper left (here, the $5–$8 price range of D) than toward the lower right (here, the $4–$1 price range of D).

This is the consequence of the arithmetic properties of the elasticity measure. Specifically, in the upper-left segment of the demand curve, the percentage change in quantity is large because the original reference quantity is small. Similarly, the percentage change in price is small in that segment because the original reference price is large. The relatively large percentage change in quantity divided by the relatively small change in price yields a large E_d—an elastic demand.

The reverse holds true for the lower-right segment of the demand curve. Here the percentage change in quantity is small because the original reference quantity is large; similarly, the percentage change in price is large because the original reference price is small. The relatively small percentage

FIGURE 6.3 The relation between price elasticity of demand for movie tickets and total revenue. (a) Demand curve D is based on Table 6.1 and is marked to show that the hypothetical weekly demand for movie tickets is elastic at higher price ranges and inelastic at lower price ranges. (b) The total-revenue curve TR is derived from demand curve D. When price falls and TR increases, demand is elastic; when price falls and TR is unchanged, demand is unit-elastic; and when price falls and TR declines, demand is inelastic.

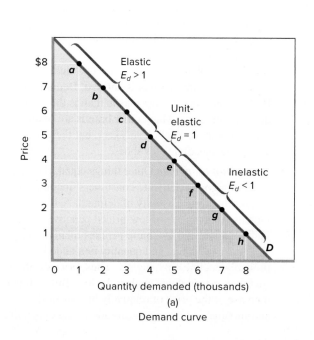

(a)
Demand curve

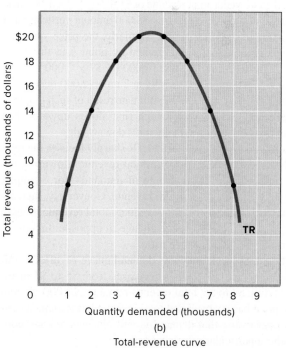

(b)
Total-revenue curve

TABLE 6.2 Price Elasticity of Demand: A Summary

Absolute Value of Elasticity Coefficient	Demand Is:	Description	Impact on Total Revenue of a:	
			Price Increase	**Price Decrease**
Greater than 1 ($E_d > 1$)	Elastic or relatively elastic	Quantity demanded changes by a larger percentage than does price	Total revenue decreases	Total revenue increases
Equal to 1 ($E_d = 1$)	Unit- or unitary elastic	Quantity demanded changes by the same percentage as does price	Total revenue is unchanged	Total revenue is unchanged
Less than 1 ($E_d < 1$)	Inelastic or relatively inelastic	Quantity demanded changes by a smaller percentage than does price	Total revenue increases	Total revenue decreases

change in quantity divided by the relatively large percentage change in price results in a small E_d—an inelastic demand.

The demand curve in Figure 6.3a also illustrates that the slope of a demand curve—its flatness or steepness—is not a sound basis for judging elasticity. The catch is that the slope of the curve is computed from *absolute* changes in price and quantity, while elasticity involves *relative* or *percentage* changes in price and quantity. The demand curve in Figure 6.3a is linear, which by definition means that the slope is constant throughout. But we have demonstrated that such a curve is elastic in its high-price ($8–$5) range and inelastic in its low-price ($4–$1) range.

Price Elasticity and the Total-Revenue Curve

In Figure 6.3b we plot the total revenue per week to the theater owner that corresponds to each price-quantity combination indicated along demand curve *D* in Figure 6.3a. The price–quantity-demanded combination represented by point *a* on the demand curve yields total revenue of $8,000 (= $8 × 1,000 tickets). In Figure 6.3b, we plot this $8,000 amount vertically at 1 unit (1,000 tickets) demanded. Similarly, the price–quantity-demanded combination represented by point *b* in the upper panel yields total revenue of $14,000 (= $7 × 2,000 tickets). This amount is graphed vertically at 2 units (2,000 tickets) demanded in the lower panel. The ultimate result of such graphing is total-revenue curve TR, which first slopes upward, then reaches a maximum, and finally turns downward.

Comparison of curves *D* and TR sharply focuses the relationship between elasticity and total revenue. Lowering the ticket price in the elastic range of demand—for example, from $8 to $5—increases total revenue. Conversely, increasing the ticket price in that range reduces total revenue. In both cases, price and total revenue change in opposite directions, confirming that demand is elastic.

The $5–$4 price range of demand curve *D* reflects unit elasticity. When price either decreases from $5 to $4 or increases from $4 to $5, total revenue remains $20,000. In both cases, price has changed and total revenue has remained constant, confirming that demand is unit-elastic when we consider these particular price changes.

In the inelastic range of demand curve *D*, lowering the price—for example, from $4 to $1—decreases total revenue, as shown in Figure 6.3b. Raising the price boosts total revenue. In both cases, price and total revenue move in the same direction, confirming that demand is inelastic.

Table 6.2 summarizes the characteristics of price elasticity of demand. You should review it carefully.

Determinants of Price Elasticity of Demand

LO6.3 List the factors that affect price elasticity of demand and describe some applications of price elasticity of demand.

We cannot say just what will determine the price elasticity of demand in each individual situation. However, the following generalizations are often helpful.

- *Substitutability* Generally, the larger the number of substitute goods that are available, the greater the price elasticity of demand. Various brands of candy bars are generally substitutable for one another, making the demand for one brand of candy bar, say Snickers, highly elastic. Toward the other extreme, the demand for tooth repair (or tooth pulling) is quite inelastic because there simply are no close substitutes when those procedures are required.

  The elasticity of demand for a product depends on how narrowly the product is defined. Demand for Reebok sneakers is more elastic than is the overall demand for shoes. Many other brands are readily substitutable for Reebok sneakers, but there are few, if any, good substitutes for shoes.

- *Proportion of income* Other things equal, the higher the price of a good relative to consumers' incomes, the greater the price elasticity of demand. A 10 percent increase in the price of low-priced pencils or chewing gum amounts to a few more pennies relative to a consumer's income, and quantity demanded will probably decline only slightly. Thus, price elasticity for such low-priced items tends to be low. But a 10 percent increase in the price of relatively high-priced automobiles or housing means additional expenditures

TABLE 6.3 **Selected Price Elasticities of Demand**

Product or Service	Coefficient of Price Elasticity of Demand (E_d)	Product or Service	Coefficient of Price Elasticity of Demand (E_d)
Newspapers	.10	Milk	.63
Electricity (household)	.13	Household appliances	.63
Bread	.15	Liquor	.70
Major League Baseball tickets	.23	Movies	.87
Cigarettes	.25	Beer	.90
Telephone service	.26	Shoes	.91
Sugar	.30	Motor vehicles	1.14
Medical care	.31	Beef	1.27
Eggs	.32	China, glassware, tableware	1.54
Legal services	.37	Residential land	1.60
Automobile repair	.40	Restaurant meals	2.27
Clothing	.49	Lamb and mutton	2.65
Gasoline	.60	Fresh peas	2.83

Source: Compiled from numerous studies and sources reporting price elasticity of demand.

of perhaps $3,000 or $20,000, respectively. These price increases are significant fractions of the annual incomes and budgets of most families, and quantities demanded will likely diminish significantly. The price elasticities for such items tend to be high.

- ***Luxuries versus necessities*** In general, the more that a good is considered to be a "luxury" rather than a "necessity," the greater is the price elasticity of demand. Electricity is generally regarded as a necessity; it is difficult to get along without it. A price increase will not significantly reduce the amount of lighting and power used in a household. (Note the very low price-elasticity coefficient of this good in Table 6.3.) An extreme case: A person does not decline an operation for acute appendicitis because the physician's fee has just gone up.

  On the other hand, vacation travel and jewelry are luxuries, which, by definition, can easily be forgone. If the prices of vacation travel and jewelry rise, a consumer need not buy them and will suffer no great hardship without them.

  What about the demand for a common product like salt? It is highly inelastic on three counts: Few good substitutes are available; salt is a negligible item in the family budget; and it is a "necessity" rather than a luxury.

- ***Time*** Generally, product demand is more elastic the longer the time period under consideration. Consumers often need time to adjust to changes in prices. For example, when the price of a product rises, time is needed to find and experiment with other products to see if they are acceptable. Consumers may not

immediately reduce their purchases very much when the price of beef rises by 10 percent, but in time they may shift to chicken, pork, or fish.

Another consideration is product durability. Studies show that "short-run" demand for gasoline is more inelastic ($E_d = 0.2$) than is "long-run" demand ($E_d = 0.7$). In the short run, people are "stuck" with their present cars and trucks, but with rising gasoline prices they eventually replace them with smaller, more fuel-efficient vehicles. They also switch to mass transit where it is available.

Table 6.3 shows estimated price-elasticity coefficients for a number of products. Each reflects some combination of the elasticity determinants just discussed.

Applications of Price Elasticity of Demand

The concept of price elasticity of demand has great practical significance, as the following examples suggest.

Large Crop Yields The demand for most farm products is highly inelastic; E_d is perhaps 0.20 or 0.25. As a result, increases in the supply of farm products arising from a good growing season or from increased productivity tend to depress both the prices of farm products and the total revenues (incomes) of farmers. For farmers as a group, the inelastic demand for their products means that large crop yields may be undesirable. For policymakers it means that achieving the goal of higher total farm income requires that farm output be restricted.

Excise Taxes The government pays attention to elasticity of demand when it selects goods and services on which to levy excise taxes. If a $1 tax is levied on a product and 10,000 units are sold, tax revenue will be $10,000 (= $1 × 10,000 units sold). If the government raises the tax to $1.50, but the higher price that results reduces sales to 4,000 because of elastic demand, tax revenue will decline to $6,000 (= $1.50 × 4,000 units sold). Because a higher tax on a product with elastic demand will bring in less tax revenue, legislatures tend to seek out products that have inelastic demand—such as liquor, gasoline, and cigarettes—when levying excises.

Decriminalization of Illegal Drugs In recent years proposals to legalize drugs have been widely debated. Proponents contend that drugs should be treated like alcohol; they should be made legal for adults and regulated for purity and potency. The current war on drugs, it is argued, has been unsuccessful, and the associated costs—including enlarged police forces, the construction of more prisons, an overburdened court system, and untold human costs—have increased markedly. Legalization would allegedly reduce drug trafficking significantly by taking the profit out of it. Crack cocaine and heroin, for example, are cheap to produce and could be sold at low prices in legal markets. Because the demand of addicts is highly inelastic, the amounts consumed at the lower prices would increase only modestly. Addicts' total expenditures for cocaine and heroin would decline, and so would the street crime that finances those expenditures.

Opponents of legalization say that the overall demand for cocaine and heroin is far more elastic than proponents think. In addition to the inelastic demand of addicts, there is another market segment whose demand is relatively elastic. This segment consists of the occasional users or "dabblers," who use hard drugs when their prices are low but who abstain or substitute, say, alcohol when their prices are high. Thus, the lower prices associated with the legalization of hard drugs would increase consumption by dabblers. Also, removal of the legal prohibitions against using drugs might make drug use more socially acceptable, increasing the demand for cocaine and heroin.

Many economists predict that the legalization of cocaine and heroin would reduce street prices by up to 60 percent, depending on if and how much they were taxed. According to an important study, price declines of that size would increase the number of occasional users of heroin by 54 percent and the number of occasional users of cocaine by 33 percent. The total quantity of heroin demanded would rise by an estimated 100 percent, and the quantity of cocaine demanded would rise by 50 percent.[1] Moreover, many existing and first-time dabblers might in time become addicts. The overall result, say the opponents of legalization, would be higher social costs, possibly including an increase in street crime.

[1] Henry Saffer and Frank Chaloupka, "The Demand for Illegal Drugs," *Economic Inquiry,* July 1999, pp. 401–411.

QUICK REVIEW 6.1

✓ The price elasticity of demand coefficient E_d is the ratio of the percentage change in quantity demanded to the percentage change in price. The *averages* of the two prices and two quantities are used as the base references in calculating the percentage changes.

✓ When E_d is greater than 1, demand is elastic; when E_d is less than 1, demand is inelastic; when E_d is equal to 1, demand is of unit elasticity.

✓ When price changes, total revenue will change in the opposite direction if demand is price-elastic, in the same direction if demand is price-inelastic, and not at all if demand is unit-elastic.

✓ Demand is typically elastic in the high-price (low-quantity) range of the demand curve and inelastic in the low-price (high-quantity) range of the demand curve.

✓ Price elasticity of demand is greater (a) the larger the number of substitutes available; (b) the higher the price of a product relative to one's budget; (c) the greater the extent to which the product is a luxury; and (d) the longer the time period involved.

Price Elasticity of Supply

LO6.4 Describe price elasticity of supply and how it can be applied.

The concept of price elasticity also applies to supply. If the quantity supplied by producers is relatively responsive to price changes, supply is elastic. If it is relatively insensitive to price changes, supply is inelastic.

We measure the degree of price elasticity or inelasticity of supply with the coefficient E_s, defined almost like E_d except that we substitute "percentage change in quantity supplied" for "percentage change in quantity demanded":

$$E_s = \frac{\text{Percentage change in quantity supplied of product X}}{\text{Percentage change in price of product X}}$$

For reasons explained earlier, the averages, or midpoints, of the before and after quantities supplied and the before and after prices are used as reference points for the percentage changes. Suppose an increase in the price of a good from $4 to $6 increases the quantity supplied from 10 units to 14 units. The percentage change in price would be $\frac{2}{5}$, or 40 percent, and the percentage change in quantity would be $\frac{4}{12}$, or 33 percent. Consequently,

$$E_s = \frac{.33}{.40} = .83$$

In this case, supply is inelastic because the price-elasticity coefficient is less than 1. If E_s is greater than 1, supply is elastic. If it is equal to 1, supply is unit-elastic. Also, E_s is never negative, since price and quantity supplied are directly related. Thus, there are no minus signs to drop, as was necessary with elasticity of demand.

The degree of **price elasticity of supply** depends on how easily—and therefore quickly—producers can shift resources between alternative uses. The easier and more rapidly producers can shift resources between alternative uses, the greater the price elasticity of supply. Take the case of Christmas trees. A firm's response to, say, an increase in the price of trees depends on its ability to shift resources from the production of other products (whose prices we assume remain constant) to

the production of trees. And shifting resource takes time: The longer the time, the greater the "shiftability." So we can expect a greater response, and therefore greater elasticity of supply, the longer a firm has to adjust to a price change.

In analyzing the impact of time on elasticity, economists distinguish among the immediate market period, the short run, and the long run.

Price Elasticity of Supply: The Immediate Market Period

The **immediate market period** is the length of time over which producers are unable to respond to a change in price with a change in quantity supplied. Suppose the owner of a small farm brings to market one truckload of tomatoes that is the entire season's output. The supply curve for the tomatoes is perfectly inelastic (vertical); the farmer will sell the truckload whether the price is high or low. Why? Because the farmer can offer only one truckload of tomatoes even if the price of tomatoes is much higher than anticipated. The farmer might like to offer more tomatoes, but tomatoes cannot be produced overnight. Another full growing season is needed to respond to a higher-than-expected price by producing more than one truckload. Similarly, because the product is perishable, the farmer cannot withhold it from the market. If the price is lower than anticipated, the farmer will still sell the entire truckload.

The farmer's costs of production, incidentally, will not enter into this decision to sell. Though the price of tomatoes may fall far short of production costs, the farmer will nevertheless sell everything he brought to market to avoid a total loss through spoilage. In the immediate market period, both the supply of tomatoes and the quantity of tomatoes supplied are fixed. The farmer offers only one truckload no matter how high or low the price.

Figure 6.4a shows the farmer's vertical supply curve during the immediate market period. Supply is perfectly inelastic because the farmer does not have time to respond to a change in demand, say, from D_1 to D_2. The resulting price increase from P_0 to P_m simply determines which buyers get the fixed quantity supplied; it elicits no increase in output.

However, not all supply curves are perfectly inelastic immediately after a price change. If the product is not perishable and the price rises, producers may choose to increase quantity supplied by drawing down their inventories of unsold, stored goods. This will cause the market supply curve to attain some positive slope. For our tomato farmer, the immediate market period may be a full growing season; for producers of goods that can be inexpensively stored, there may be no immediate market period at all.

Price Elasticity of Supply: The Short Run

The **short run** in microeconomics is a period of time too short to change plant capacity but long enough to use the

CONSIDER THIS . . .

Source: © Punchstock RF

Elasticity and College Costs

Why does college cost so much? Elasticity offers some clues.

From the end of World War II through the 1970s, the supply of higher education increased massively as state and local governments spent billions of dollars expanding their higher education systems. This massive increase in supply helped to offset the huge increase in demand that took place as the large Baby Boom generation flooded the higher education system starting in the early 1960s. With supply increasing nearly as fast as demand, the equilibrium price of higher education only increased modestly.

Things changed dramatically beginning in the early 1980s. With respect to supply, state and local governments slowed the growth of higher education spending, so that many college and university systems saw only modest subsequent increases in capacity. At the same time, the federal government dramatically increased both subsidized student lending and the volume of federal student grant money. Those policy innovations were of great benefit to poor and middle-class students, but they also meant that the demand curve for higher education continued to shift to the right.

That turned out to be problematic because, with the supply of seats largely fixed by the changing priorities of state and local governments, the supply of higher education was highly inelastic even in the long run. As a result, the increases in demand caused by student loans and grant money resulted in substantially higher equilibrium prices for higher education.

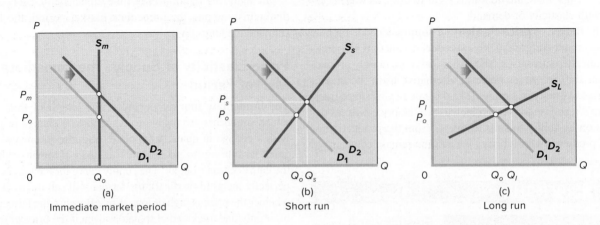

FIGURE 6.4 Time and the elasticity of supply. The greater the amount of time producers have to adjust to a change in demand, here from D_1 to D_2, the greater will be their output response. (a) In the immediate market period, there is insufficient time to change output, and so supply is perfectly inelastic. (b) In the short run, plant capacity is fixed, but changing the intensity of its use can alter output; supply is therefore more elastic. (c) In the long run, all desired adjustments, including changes in plant capacity, can be made, and supply becomes still more elastic.

fixed-sized plant more or less intensively. In the short run, our farmer's plant (land and farm machinery) is fixed. But he does have time in the short run to cultivate tomatoes more intensively by applying more labor and more fertilizer and pesticides to the crop. The result is a somewhat greater output in response to a presumed increase in demand; this greater output is reflected in a more elastic supply of tomatoes, as shown by S_s in Figure 6.4b. Note now that the increase in demand from D_1 to D_2 is met by an increase in quantity (from Q_0 to Q_s), so there is a smaller price adjustment (from P_0 to P_s) than would be the case in the immediate market period. The equilibrium price is therefore lower in the short run than in the immediate market period.

Price Elasticity of Supply: The Long Run

The **long run** in microeconomics is a time period long enough for firms to adjust their plant sizes and for new firms to enter (or existing firms to leave) the industry. In the "tomato industry," for example, our farmer has time to acquire additional land and buy more machinery and equipment. Furthermore, other farmers may, over time, be attracted to tomato farming by the increased demand and higher price. Such adjustments create a larger supply response, as represented by the more elastic supply curve S_L in Figure 6.4c. The outcome is a smaller price rise (P_0 to P_l) and a larger output increase (Q_0 to Q_l) in response to the increase in demand from D_1 to D_2.

There is no total-revenue test for elasticity of supply. Supply shows a positive or direct relationship between price and amount supplied; the supply curve is upsloping. Regardless of the degree of elasticity or inelasticity, price and total revenue always move together.

Applications of Price Elasticity of Supply

The idea of price elasticity of supply has widespread applicability, as suggested by the following examples.

Antiques and Reproductions *Antiques Roadshow* is a popular PBS television program in which people bring antiques to a central location for appraisal by experts. Some people are pleased to learn that their old piece of furniture or funky folk art is worth a large amount, say, $30,000 or more.

The high price of an antique results from strong demand and limited, highly inelastic supply. Because a genuine antique can no longer be reproduced, its quantity supplied either does not rise or rises only slightly as price goes up. The higher price might prompt the discovery of a few more of the remaining originals and thus add to the quantity available for sale, but this quantity response is usually quite small. So the supply of antiques and other collectibles tends to be inelastic. For one-of-a-kind antiques, the supply is perfectly inelastic.

Factors such as increased population, higher income, and greater enthusiasm for collecting antiques have increased the demand for antiques over time. Because the supply of antiques is limited and inelastic, those increases in demand have greatly boosted the prices of antiques.

Contrast the inelastic supply of original antiques with the elastic supply of modern "made-to-look-old" reproductions. Such faux antiques are quite popular and widely available at furniture stores and knickknack shops. When the demand for reproductions increases, the firms making them simply boost production. Because the supply of reproductions is highly elastic, increased demand raises their prices only slightly.

Volatile Gold Prices The price of gold is quite volatile, sometimes shooting upward one period and plummeting downward the next. The main sources of these fluctuations are shifts in demand interacting with highly inelastic supply. Gold production is a costly and time-consuming process of exploration, mining, and refining. Moreover, the physical availability of gold is highly limited. For both reasons, increases in gold prices do not elicit substantial increases in quantity supplied. Conversely, gold mining is costly to shut down and existing gold bars are expensive to store. Price decreases therefore do not produce large drops in the quantity of gold supplied. In short, the supply of gold is inelastic.

The demand for gold is partly derived from the demand for its uses, such as for jewelry, dental fillings, and coins. But people also demand gold as a speculative financial investment. They increase their demand for gold when they fear general inflation or domestic or international turmoil that might undermine the value of currency and more traditional investments. They reduce their demand when events settle down. Because of the inelastic supply of gold, even relatively small changes in demand produce relatively large changes in price.

Cross Elasticity and Income Elasticity of Demand

LO6.5 Apply cross elasticity of demand and income elasticity of demand.

Price elasticities measure the responsiveness of the quantity of a product demanded or supplied when its price changes. The consumption of a good also is affected by a change in the price of a related product or by a change in income.

Cross Elasticity of Demand

The **cross elasticity of demand** measures how sensitive consumer purchases of one product (say, X) are to a change in the price of some other product (say, Y). We calculate the coefficient of cross elasticity of demand E_{xy} just as we do the coefficient of simple price elasticity, except that we relate the percentage change in the consumption of X to the percentage change in the price of Y:

$$E_{xy} = \frac{\text{percentage change in quantity demanded of product X}}{\text{percentage change in price of product Y}}$$

This cross-elasticity (or cross-price-elasticity) concept allows us to quantify and more fully understand substitute and complementary goods, introduced in Chapter 3's. Unlike price elasticity, we allow the coefficient of cross elasticity of demand to be either positive or negative.

Substitute Goods If cross elasticity of demand is positive, meaning that sales of X move in the same direction as a change in the price of Y, then X and Y are substitute goods. An example is Evian water (X) and Dasani water (Y). An increase in the price of Evian causes consumers to buy more Dasani, resulting in a positive cross elasticity. The larger the positive cross-elasticity coefficient, the greater is the substitutability between the two products.

Complementary Goods When cross elasticity is negative, we know that X and Y "go together"; an increase in the price of one decreases the demand for the other. So the two are complementary goods. For example, a decrease in the price of digital cameras will increase the number of memory sticks purchased. The larger the negative cross-elasticity coefficient, the greater is the complementarity between the two goods.

Independent Goods A zero or near-zero cross elasticity suggests that the two products being considered are unrelated or independent goods. An example is walnuts and plums: We would not expect a change in the price of walnuts to have any effect on purchases of plums, and vice versa.

Application The degree of substitutability of products, measured by the cross-elasticity coefficient, is important to businesses and government. For example, suppose that Coca-Cola is considering whether or not to lower the price of its Sprite brand. Not only will it want to know something about the price elasticity of demand for Sprite (will the price cut increase or decrease total revenue?), but it will also be interested in knowing if the increased sales of Sprite will come at the expense of its Coke brand. How sensitive are the sales of one of its products (Coke) to a change in the price of another of its products (Sprite)? By how much will the increased sales of Sprite "cannibalize" the sales of Coke? A low cross elasticity would indicate that Coke and Sprite are weak substitutes for each other and that a lower price for Sprite would have little effect on Coke sales.

Government also implicitly uses the idea of cross elasticity of demand in assessing whether a proposed merger between two large firms will substantially reduce competition and therefore violate the antitrust laws. For example, the cross elasticity between Coke and Pepsi is high, making them strong substitutes for each other. In addition, Coke and Pepsi together sell about 70 percent of all carbonated cola drinks consumed in the United States. Taken together, the high cross elasticities and the large market shares suggest that the government would likely block a merger between Coke and Pepsi because the merger would substantially lessen competition. In contrast, the cross elasticity between cola and gasoline is low or zero. A merger between Coke and Shell oil company would have a minimal effect on competition. So government would let that merger happen.

Elasticity and Pricing Power: Why Different Consumers Pay Different Prices

Firms and Nonprofit Institutions Often Recognize and Exploit Differences in Price Elasticity of Demand.

All the buyers of a product traded in a highly competitive market pay the same market price for the product, regardless of their individual price elasticities of demand. If the price rises, Jones may have an elastic demand and greatly reduce her purchases. Green may have a unit-elastic demand and reduce his purchases less than Jones. Lopez may have an inelastic demand and hardly curtail his purchases at all. But all three consumers will pay the single higher price regardless of their respective demand elasticities.

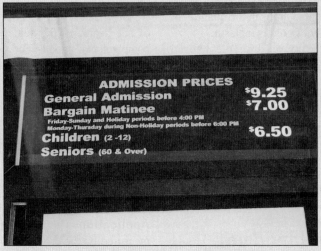

Source: © Tom Prettyman/PhotoEdit

In later chapters we will find that not all sellers must passively accept a "one-for-all" price. Some firms have "market power" or "pricing power" that allows them to set their product prices in their best interests. For some goods and services, firms may find it advantageous to determine differences in price elasticity of demand and then charge different prices to different buyers.

It is extremely difficult to tailor prices for each customer on the basis of price elasticity of demand, but it is relatively easy to

Income Elasticity of Demand

Income elasticity of demand measures the degree to which consumers respond to a change in their incomes by buying more or less of a particular good. The coefficient of income elasticity of demand E_i is determined with the formula

$$E_i = \frac{\text{percentage change in quantity demanded}}{\text{percentage change in income}}$$

Normal Goods For most goods, the income-elasticity coefficient E_i is positive, meaning that more of them are demanded as incomes rise. Such goods are called normal or superior goods (and were first described in Chapter 3's). But the value of E_i varies greatly among normal goods. For example, income elasticity of demand for automobiles is about +3, while income elasticity for most farm products is only about +0.20.

Inferior Goods A negative income-elasticity coefficient designates an inferior good. Retread tires, cabbage, long-distance bus tickets, used clothing, and muscatel wine are likely candidates. Consumers decrease their purchases of inferior goods as incomes rise.

TABLE 6.4 Cross and Income Elasticities of Demand

Value of Coefficient	Description	Type of Good(s)
Cross elasticity: Positive ($E_{wz} > 0$)	Quantity demanded of W changes in same direction as change in price of Z	Substitutes
Negative ($E_{xy} < 0$)	Quantity demanded of X changes in opposite direction from change in price of Y	Complements
Income elasticity: Positive ($E_i > 0$)	Quantity demanded of the product changes in same direction as change in income	Normal or superior
Negative ($E_i < 0$)	Quantity demanded of the product changes in opposite direction from change in income	Inferior

observe differences in group elasticities. Consider airline tickets. Business travelers generally have inelastic demand for air travel. Because their time is highly valuable, they do not see slower modes of transportation as realistic substitutes. Also, their employers pay for their tickets as part of their business expenses. In contrast, leisure travelers tend to have elastic demand. They have the option to drive rather than fly or to simply not travel at all. They also pay for their tickets out of their own pockets and thus are more sensitive to price.

Airlines recognize the difference between the groups in terms of price elasticity of demand and charge business travelers more than leisure travelers. To accomplish that, they have to dissuade business travelers from buying the less expensive round-trip tickets aimed at leisure travelers. One way to do this is by placing restrictions on the lower-priced tickets. For instance, airlines have at times made such tickets nonrefundable, required at least a 2-week advance purchase, and required Saturday-night stays. These restrictions chase off most business travelers who engage in last-minute travel and want to be home for the weekend. As a result, a business traveler often pays hundreds of dollars more for a ticket than a leisure traveler on the same plane.

Discounts for children are another example of pricing based on group differences in price elasticity of demand. For many products, children have more elastic demands than adults because children have low budgets, often financed by their parents. Sellers recognize the elasticity difference and price accordingly. The barber spends as much time cutting a child's hair as an adult's but charges the child much less. A child takes up a full seat at the baseball game but pays a lower price than an adult. A child snowboarder occupies the same space on a chairlift as an adult snowboarder but qualifies for a discounted lift ticket.

Finally, consider pricing by colleges and universities. Price elasticity of demand for higher education is greater for prospective students from low-income families than similar students from high-income families. This makes sense because tuition is a much larger proportion of household income for a low-income student or family than for his or her high-income counterpart. Desiring a diverse student body, colleges charge different *net* prices (= tuition *minus* financial aid) to the two groups on the basis of price elasticity of demand. High-income students pay full tuition, unless they receive merit-based scholarships. Low-income students receive considerable financial aid in addition to merit-based scholarships and, in effect, pay a lower *net* price.

It is common for colleges to announce a large tuition increase and immediately cushion the news by emphasizing that they also are increasing financial aid. In effect, the college is increasing the tuition for students who have inelastic demand by the full amount and raising the *net* tuition of those with elastic demand by some lesser amount or not at all. Through this strategy, colleges boost revenue to cover rising costs while maintaining affordability for a wide range of students.

There are a number of other examples of dual or multiple pricing. All relate directly to price elasticity of demand. We will revisit this topic again in Chapter 12 when we analyze *price discrimination*—charging different prices to different customers for the same product.

Insights Coefficients of income elasticity of demand provide insights into the economy. For example, when recessions (business downturns) occur and incomes fall, income elasticity of demand helps predict which products will decline in demand more rapidly than others.

Products with relatively high income-elasticity coefficients, such as automobiles ($E_i = +3$), housing ($E_i = +1.5$), and restaurant meals ($E_i = +1.4$), are generally hit hardest by recessions. Those with low or negative income-elasticity coefficients are much less affected. For example, food products prepared at home ($E_i = +0.20$) respond relatively little to income fluctuations. When incomes drop, purchases of food (and toothpaste and toilet paper) drop little compared to purchases of movie tickets, luxury vacations, and plasma screen TVs. Products we view as essential tend to have lower income-elasticity coefficients than products we view as luxuries. When our incomes fall, we cannot easily eliminate or postpone the purchase of essential products.

In Table 6.4 we provide a convenient synopsis of the cross-elasticity and income-elasticity concepts.

SUMMARY

LO6.1 Discuss price elasticity of demand and how it is calculated.

Price elasticity of demand measures consumer response to price changes. If consumers are relatively sensitive to price changes, demand is elastic. If they are relatively unresponsive to price changes, demand is inelastic.

The price-elasticity coefficient E_d measures the degree of elasticity or inelasticity of demand. The coefficient is found by the formula

$$E_d = \frac{\text{percentage change in quantity demanded of X}}{\text{percentage change in price of X}}$$

Economists use the averages of prices and quantities under consideration as reference points in determining percentage changes in price and quantity. If E_d is greater than 1, demand is elastic. If E_d is less than 1, demand is inelastic. Unit elasticity is the special case in which E_d equals 1.

Perfectly inelastic demand is graphed as a line parallel to the vertical axis; perfectly elastic demand is shown by a line above and parallel to the horizontal axis.

Elasticity varies at different price ranges on a demand curve, tending to be elastic in the upper-left segment and inelastic in the lower-right segment. Elasticity cannot be judged by the steepness or flatness of a demand curve.

LO6.2 Explain the usefulness of the total-revenue test for price elasticity of demand.

If total revenue changes in the opposite direction from prices, demand is elastic. If price and total revenue change in the same direction, demand is inelastic. Where demand is of unit elasticity, a change in price leaves total revenue unchanged.

LO6.3 List the factors that affect price elasticity of demand and describe some applications of price elasticity of demand.

The number of available substitutes, the size of an item's price relative to one's budget, whether the product is a luxury or a necessity, and length of time to adjust are all determinants of elasticity of demand.

LO6.4 Describe price elasticity of supply and how it can be applied.

The elasticity concept also applies to supply. The coefficient of price elasticity of supply is found by the formula

$$E_s = \frac{\text{percentage change in quantity supplied of X}}{\text{percentage change in price of X}}$$

The averages of the prices and quantities under consideration are used as reference points for computing percentage changes. Elasticity of supply depends on the ease of shifting resources between alternative uses, which varies directly with the time producers have to adjust to a price change.

LO6.5 Apply cross elasticity of demand and income elasticity of demand.

Cross elasticity of demand indicates how sensitive the purchase of one product is to changes in the price of another product. The coefficient of cross elasticity of demand is found by the formula

$$E_{xy} = \frac{\text{percentage change in quantity demanded of X}}{\text{percentage change in price of Y}}$$

Positive cross elasticity of demand identifies substitute goods; negative cross elasticity identifies complementary goods.

Income elasticity of demand indicates the responsiveness of consumer purchases to a change in income. The coefficient of income elasticity of demand is found by the formula

$$E_i = \frac{\text{percentage change in quantity demanded of X}}{\text{percentage change in income}}$$

The coefficient is positive for normal goods and negative for inferior goods.

Industries that sell products that have high income-elasticity-of-demand coefficients are particularly hard hit by recessions. Those with products that have low or negative income-elasticity-of-demand coefficients fare much better.

TERMS AND CONCEPTS

price elasticity of demand	perfectly inelastic demand	immediate market period
midpoint formula	perfectly elastic demand	short run
elastic demand	total revenue (TR)	long run
inelastic demand	total-revenue test	cross elasticity of demand
unit elasticity	price elasticity of supply	income elasticity of demand

The following and additional problems can be found in ▨ connect

DISCUSSION QUESTIONS

1. Explain why the choice between 1, 2, 3, 4, 5, 6, 7, and 8 "units," or 1,000, 2,000, 3,000, 4,000, 5,000, 6,000, 7,000, and 8,000 movie tickets, makes no difference in determining elasticity in Table 6.1. **LO6.1**

2. What effect would a rule stating that university students must live in university dormitories have on the price elasticity of demand for dormitory space? What impact might this in turn have on room rates? **LO6.1**

3. The income elasticities of demand for movies, dental services, and clothing have been estimated to be +3.4, +1, and +0.5, respectively. Interpret these coefficients. What does it mean if an income-elasticity coefficient is negative? **LO6.5**

4. Research has found that an increase in the price of beer would reduce the amount of marijuana consumed. Is cross elasticity of demand between the two products positive or negative? Are these products substitutes or complements? What might be the logic behind this relationship? **LO6.5**

5. **LAST WORD** What is the purpose of charging different groups of customers different prices? Supplement the three broad examples in the Last Word with two additional examples of your own. Hint: Think of price discounts based on group characteristics or time of purchase.

REVIEW QUESTIONS

1. Suppose that the total revenue received by a company selling basketballs is $600 when the price is set at $30 per basketball and $600 when the price is set at $20 per basketball. Without using the midpoint formula, can you tell whether demand is elastic, inelastic, or unit-elastic over this price range? **LO6.2**

2. What are the major determinants of price elasticity of demand? Use those determinants and your own reasoning in judging whether demand for each of the following products is probably elastic or inelastic: (*a*) bottled water; (*b*) toothpaste, (*c*) Crest toothpaste, (*d*) ketchup, (*e*) diamond bracelets, (*f*) Microsoft's Windows operating system. **LO6.3**

3. Calculate total-revenue data from the demand schedule in review question 1. Graph total revenue below your demand curve. Generalize about the relationship between price elasticity and total revenue. **LO6.2**

4. How would the following changes in price affect total revenue? That is, would total revenue increase, decrease, or remain unchanged? **LO6.2**

a. Price falls and demand is inelastic.
b. Price rises and demand is elastic.
c. Price rises and supply is elastic.
d. Price rises and supply is inelastic.
e. Price rises and demand is inelastic.
f. Price falls and demand is elastic.
g. Price falls and demand is of unit-elasticity.

5. In 2015, Paul Gauguin's painting *When Will You Marry* sold for $300 million. Portray this sale in a demand and supply diagram and comment on the elasticity of supply. Comedian George Carlin once mused, "If a painting can be forged well enough to fool some experts, why is the original so valuable?" Provide an answer. **LO6.4**

6. Suppose the cross elasticity of demand for products A and B is +3.6 and for products C and D is −5.4. What can you conclude about how products A and B are related? Products C and D? **LO6.5**

PROBLEMS

1. Look at the demand curve in Figure 6.2a. Use the midpoint formula and points *a* and *b* to calculate the elasticity of demand for that range of the demand curve. Do the same for the demand curves in Figures 6.2b and 6.2c using, respectively, points *c* and *d* for Figure 6.2b and points *e* and *f* for Figure 6.2c. **LO6.1**

2. Investigate how demand elasticities are affected by increases in demand. Shift each of the demand curves in Figures 6.2a, 6.2b, and 6.2c to the right by 10 units. For example, point *a* in Figure 6.2a would shift rightward from location (10 units, $2) to (20 units, $2), while point *b* would shift rightward from location (40 units, $1) to (50 units, $1). After making these shifts, apply the midpoint formula to calculate the demand elasticities for the shifted points. Are they larger or smaller than the elasticities you calculated in problem 1 for the original points? In terms of the midpoint formula, what explains the change in elasticities? **LO6.1**

3. Graph the accompanying demand data, and then use the midpoint formula for *Ed* to determine price elasticity of demand for each of the four possible $1 price changes. What can you conclude about the relationship between the slope of a curve and its elasticity? Explain in a nontechnical way why demand is elastic in the northwest segment of the demand curve and inelastic in the southeast segment. **LO6.1**

Product Price	Quantity Demanded
$5	1
4	2
3	3
2	4
1	5

4. Danny "Dimes" Donahue is a neighborhood's 9-year-old entrepreneur. His most recent venture is selling homemade brownies that he bakes himself. At a price of $1.50 each, he sells 100. At a price of $1 each, he sells 300. Is demand elastic or inelastic over this price range? If demand had the same elasticity for a price decline from $1.00 to $0.50 as it does for the decline from $1.50 to $1, would cutting the price from $1.00 to $0.50 increase or decrease Danny's total revenue? **LO6.2**

5. What is the formula for measuring the price elasticity of supply? Suppose the price of apples goes up from $20 to $22 a box. In direct response, Goldsboro Farms supplies 1,200 boxes of apples instead of 1,000 boxes. Compute the coefficient of price elasticity (midpoint approach) for Goldsboro's supply. Is its supply elastic, or is it inelastic? **LO6.4**

6. **ADVANCED ANALYSIS** Currently, at a price of $1 each, 100 popsicles are sold per day in the perpetually hot town of Rostin. Consider the elasticity of supply. In the short run, a price increase from $1 to $2 is unit-elastic ($E_s = 1.0$). So how many popsicles will be sold each day in the short run if the price rises to $2 each? In the long run, a price increase from $1 to $2 has an elasticity of supply of 1.50. So how many popsicles will be sold per day in the long run if the price rises to $2 each? (Hint: Apply the midpoint approach to the elasticity of supply.) **LO6.4**

7. Lorena likes to play golf. The number of times per year that she plays depends on both the price of playing a round of golf as well as Lorena's income and the cost of other types of entertainment—in particular, how much it costs to go see a movie instead of playing golf. The three demand schedules in the following table show how many rounds of golf per year Lorena will demand at each price under three different scenarios. In scenario D_1, Lorena's income is $50,000 per year and movies cost $9 each. In scenario D_2, Lorena's income is also $50,000 per year, but the price of seeing a movie rises to $11. And in scenario D_3, Lorena's income goes up to $70,000 per year, while movies cost $11. **LO6.5**

	Quantity Demanded		
Price	D_1	D_2	D_3
$50	15	10	15
35	25	15	30
20	40	20	50

a. Using the data under D_1 and D_2, calculate the cross elasticity of Lorena's demand for golf at all three prices. (To do this, apply the midpoints approach to the cross elasticity of demand.) Is the cross elasticity the same at all three prices? Are movies and golf substitute goods, complementary goods, or independent goods?

b. Using the data under D_2 and D_3, calculate the income elasticity of Lorena's demand for golf at all three prices. (To do this, apply the midpoint approach to the income elasticity of demand.) Is the income elasticity the same at all three prices? Is golf an inferior good?

Utility Maximization

Learning Objectives

LO7.1 Define and explain the relationship between total utility, marginal utility, and the law of diminishing marginal utility.

LO7.2 Describe how rational consumers maximize utility by comparing the marginal utility-to-price ratios of all the products they could possibly purchase.

LO7.3 Explain how a demand curve can be derived by observing the outcomes of price changes in the utility-maximization model.

LO7.4 Discuss how the utility-maximization model helps highlight the income and substitution effects of a price change.

LO7.5 Give examples of several real-world phenomena that can be explained by applying the theory of consumer behavior.

LO7.6 (Appendix) Relate how the indifference curve model of consumer behavior derives demand curves from budget lines, indifference curves, and utility maximization.

If you were to compare the shopping carts of almost any two consumers, you would observe striking differences. Why does Paula have potatoes, peaches, and Pepsi in her cart, while Sam has sugar, saltines, and 7-Up in his? Why didn't Paula also buy pasta and plums? Why didn't Sam have soup and spaghetti on his grocery list?

In this chapter, you will see how individual consumers allocate their incomes among the various goods and services available to them. Given a certain budget, how does a consumer decide which goods and services to buy? This chapter will develop a model to answer this question.

Law of Diminishing Marginal Utility

LO7.1 Define and explain the relationship between total utility, marginal utility, and the law of diminishing marginal utility.

The simplest theory of consumer behavior rests squarely on the **law of diminishing marginal utility.** This principle, first discussed in Chapter 3, is that added satisfaction declines as a consumer acquires additional units of a given product. Although consumer wants in general may be insatiable, wants for particular items can be satisfied. In a specific span of time over which consumers' tastes remain unchanged, consumers can obtain as much of a particular good or service as they can afford. But the more of that product they obtain, the less they want still more of it.

Consider durable goods, for example. A consumer's desire for an automobile, when he or she has none, may be very strong. But the desire for a second car is less intense; and for a third or fourth, weaker and weaker. Unless they are collectors, even the wealthiest families rarely have more than a half-dozen cars, although their incomes would allow them to purchase a whole fleet of vehicles.

Terminology

Evidence indicates that consumers can fulfill specific wants with succeeding units of a product but that each added unit provides less utility than the last unit purchased. Recall that a consumer derives utility from a product if it can satisfy a want: **Utility** is want-satisfying power. The utility of a good or service is the satisfaction or pleasure one gets from consuming it. Keep in mind three characteristics of this concept:

- "Utility" and "usefulness" are not synonymous. Paintings by Picasso may offer great utility to art connoisseurs but are useless functionally (other than for hiding a crack on a wall).

- Utility is subjective. The utility of a specific product may vary widely from person to person. A lifted pickup truck may have great utility to someone who drives off-road but little utility to someone unable or unwilling to climb into the rig. Eyeglasses have tremendous utility to someone who has poor eyesight but no utility to a person with 20-20 vision.

- Utility is difficult to quantify. But for purposes of illustration we assume that people can measure satisfaction with units called *utils* (units of utility). For example, a particular consumer may get 100 utils of satisfaction from a smoothie, 10 utils of satisfaction from a candy bar, and 1 util of satisfaction from a stick of gum. These imaginary units of satisfaction are convenient for quantifying consumer behavior for explanatory purposes.

Total Utility and Marginal Utility

Total utility and marginal utility are related, but different, ideas. **Total utility** is the total amount of satisfaction or pleasure a person derives from consuming some specific quantity—for example, 10 units—of a good or service. **Marginal utility** is the *extra* satisfaction a consumer realizes from an additional unit of that product—for example, from the eleventh unit. Alternatively, marginal utility is the change in total utility that results from the consumption of 1 more unit of a product.

Figure 7.1 (Key Graph) and the accompanying table demonstrate the relation between total utility and marginal utility. The curves reflect the data in the table. Column 2 shows the total utility associated with each level of consumption of tacos. Column 3 shows the marginal utility—the change in total utility—that results from the consumption of each successive taco. Starting at the origin in Figure 7.1a, observe that each of the first five units increases total utility (TU), but by a diminishing amount. Total utility reaches a maximum with the addition of the sixth unit and then declines.

So in Figure 7.1b marginal utility (MU) remains positive but diminishes through the first five units (because total utility increases at a declining rate). Marginal utility is zero for the sixth unit (because that unit doesn't change total utility). Marginal utility then becomes negative with the seventh unit and beyond (because total utility is falling). Figure 7.1b and table column 3 reveal that each successive taco yields less extra utility, meaning fewer utils, than the preceding taco.[1] That is, the table and graph illustrate the law of diminishing marginal utility.

Marginal Utility and Demand

The law of diminishing marginal utility explains why the demand curve for a given product slopes downward. If successive units of a good yield smaller and smaller amounts of marginal, or extra, utility, then the consumer will buy additional units of a product only if its price falls. The consumer for whom Figure 7.1 is relevant may buy two tacos at a price of $1 each. But because he or she obtains less marginal utility from additional tacos, the consumer will choose not to buy more at that price. The consumer would rather spend additional dollars on products that provide more utility, not less utility. Therefore, additional tacos with less utility are not worth buying unless the price declines. (When marginal utility becomes negative, Taco Bell would have to pay you to consume another taco!) Thus, diminishing marginal utility supports the idea that price must decrease in order for quantity demanded to increase. In other words, consumers behave in ways that make demand curves downsloping.

> ### QUICK REVIEW 7.1
>
> ✓ Utility is the benefit or satisfaction a person receives from consuming a good or a service.
> ✓ The law of diminishing marginal utility indicates that gains in satisfaction become smaller as successive units of a specific product are consumed.
> ✓ Diminishing marginal utility provides a simple rationale for the law of demand.

---

[1]Technical footnote: In Figure 7.1b we graphed marginal utility at half-units. For example, we graphed the marginal utility of 4 utils at 3 1/2 units because "4 utils" refers neither to the third nor the fourth unit per se but to the *addition* or *subtraction* of the fourth unit.

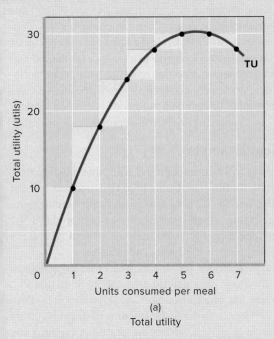

(a)
Total utility

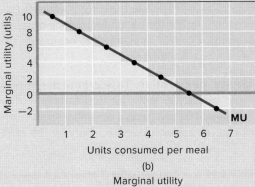

(b)
Marginal utility

FIGURE 7.1 Total and marginal utility. Curves TU and MU are graphed from the data in the table. (a) As more of a product is consumed, total utility increases at a diminishing rate, reaches a maximum, and then declines. (b) Marginal utility, by definition, reflects the changes in total utility. Thus marginal utility diminishes with increased consumption, becomes zero when total utility is at a maximum, and is negative when total utility declines. As shown by the shaded rectangles in (a) and (b), marginal utility is the change in total utility associated with each additional taco. Or, alternatively, each new level of total utility is found by adding marginal utility to the preceding level of total utility.

(1) Tacos Consumed per Meal	(2) Total Utility, Utils	(3) Marginal Utility, Utils
0	0	
1	10	10
2	18	8
3	24	6
4	28	4
5	30	2
6	30	0
7	28	−2

QUICK QUIZ FOR FIGURE 7.1

1. Marginal utility:
   a. is the extra output a firm obtains when it adds another unit of labor.
   b. explains why product supply curves slope upward.
   c. typically rises as successive units of a good are consumed.
   d. is the extra satisfaction from the consumption of 1 more unit of some good or service.

2. Marginal utility in Figure 7.1b is positive, but declining, when total utility in Figure 7.1a is positive and:
   a. rising at an increasing rate.
   b. falling at an increasing rate.
   c. rising at a decreasing rate.
   d. falling at a decreasing rate.

3. When marginal utility is zero in graph (b), total utility in graph (a) is:
   a. also zero.
   b. neither rising nor falling.
   c. negative.
   d. rising, but at a declining rate.

4. Suppose the person represented by these graphs experienced a diminished taste for tacos. As a result the:
   a. TU curve would get steeper.
   b. MU curve would get flatter.
   c. TU and MU curves would shift downward.
   d. MU curve, but not the TU curve, would collapse to the horizontal axis.

Answers: 1. d; 2. c; 3. b; 4. c

Theory of Consumer Behavior

LO7.2 Describe how rational consumers maximize utility by comparing the marginal utility-to-price ratios of all the products they could possibly purchase.

In addition to explaining the law of demand, the idea of diminishing marginal utility explains how consumers allocate their money incomes among the many goods and services available for purchase.

Consumer Choice and the Budget Constraint

For simplicity, we will assume that the situation for the typical consumer has the following dimensions.

- *Rational behavior* The consumer is a rational person, who tries to use his or her money income to derive the greatest amount of satisfaction, or utility, from it. Consumers want to get "the most for their money" or, technically, to maximize their total utility. They engage in **rational behavior.**
- *Preferences* Each consumer has clear-cut preferences for certain of the goods and services that are available in the market. Buyers also have a good idea of how much marginal utility they will get from successive units of the various products they might purchase.
- *Budget constraint* At any point in time the consumer has a fixed, limited amount of money income. Since each consumer supplies a finite amount of human and property resources to society, he or she earns only limited income. Thus, as noted in Chapter 1, every consumer faces a **budget constraint,** even consumers who earn millions of dollars a year. Of course, this budget limitation is more severe for a consumer with an average income than for a consumer with an extraordinarily high income.
- *Prices* Goods are scarce relative to the demand for them, so every good carries a price tag. We assume that the price of each good is unaffected by the amount of it that is bought by any particular person. After all, each person's purchase is a tiny part of total demand. Also, because the consumer has a limited number of dollars, he or she cannot buy everything wanted. This point drives home the reality of scarcity to each consumer.

So the consumer must compromise; he or she must choose the most personally satisfying mix of goods and services. Different individuals will choose different mixes.

Utility-Maximizing Rule

Of all the different combinations of goods and services a consumer can obtain within his or her budget, which specific combination will yield the maximum utility or satisfaction? *To maximize satisfaction, the consumer should allocate his or her money income so that the last dollar spent on each product yields the same amount of extra (marginal) utility.* We call this the **utility-maximizing rule.** When the consumer has "balanced his margins" using this rule, he has achieved **consumer equilibrium** and has no incentive to alter his expenditure pattern. In fact, any person who has achieved consumer equilibrium would be worse off—total utility would decline—if there were any alteration in the bundle of goods purchased, providing there is no change in taste, income, products, or prices.

Numerical Example

An illustration will help explain the utility-maximizing rule. For simplicity we limit our example to two products, but the analysis also applies if there are more. Suppose consumer Holly is analyzing which combination of two products she should purchase with her fixed daily income of $10. Let's suppose these products are apples and oranges.

Holly's preferences for apples and oranges and their prices are the basic data determining the combination that will maximize her satisfaction. Table 7.1 summarizes those data, with column 2a showing the amounts of marginal utility she will derive from each successive unit of A (apples) and with column 3a showing the same thing for product B (oranges). Both columns reflect the law of diminishing marginal utility, which, in this example, is assumed to begin with the second unit of each product purchased.

Marginal Utility per Dollar To see how the utility-maximizing rule works, we must put the marginal-utility information in columns 2a and 3a on a per-dollar-spent basis. A consumer's choices are influenced not only by the extra

TABLE 7.1 The Utility-Maximizing Combination of Apples and Oranges Obtainable with an Income of $10*

(1) Unit of Product	(2) Apple (Product A): Price = $1		(3) Orange (Product B): Price 5 = $2	
	(a) Marginal Utility, Utils	(b) Marginal Utility per Dollar (MU/Price)	(a) Marginal Utility, Utils	(b) Marginal Utility per Dollar (MU/Price)
First	10	10	24	12
Second	8	**8**	20	10
Third	7	7	18	9
Fourth	6	6	16	**8**
Fifth	5	5	12	6
Sixth	4	4	6	3
Seventh	3	3	4	2

*It is assumed in this table that the amount of marginal utility received from additional units of each of the two products is independent of the quantity of the other product. For example, the marginal-utility schedule for apples is independent of the number of oranges obtained by the consumer.

utility that successive apples will yield but also by how many dollars (and therefore how many oranges) she must give up to obtain additional apples.

The rational consumer must compare the extra utility from each product with its added cost (that is, its price). Switching examples for a moment, suppose that you prefer a pizza whose marginal utility is, say, 36 utils to a movie whose marginal utility is 24 utils. But if the pizza's price is $12 and the movie costs only $6, you would choose the movie rather than the pizza! Why? Because the marginal utility per dollar spent would be 4 utils for the movie (= 24 utils/$6) compared to only 3 utils for the pizza (= 36 utils/$12). You could see two movies for $12 and, assuming that the marginal utility of the second movie is, say, 16 utils, your total utility would be 40 utils. Clearly, 40 units of satisfaction (= 24 utils + 16 utils) from two movies are superior to 36 utils from the same $12 expenditure on one pizza.

To make the amounts of extra utility derived from differently priced goods comparable, marginal utilities must be put on a per-dollar-spent basis. We do this in columns 2b and 3b by dividing the marginal-utility data of columns 2a and 3a by the prices of apples and oranges—$1 and $2, respectively.

Decision-Making Process Table 7.1 shows Holly's preferences on a unit basis and a per-dollar basis as well as the price tags of apples and oranges. With $10 to spend, in what order should Holly allocate her dollars on units of apples and oranges to achieve the highest amount of utility within the $10 limit imposed by her income? And what specific combination of the two products will she have obtained at the time she uses up her $10?

Concentrating on columns 2b and 3b in Table 7.1, we find that Holly should first spend $2 on the first orange because its marginal utility per dollar of 12 utils is higher than the first apple's 10 utils. But now Holly finds herself indifferent about whether to buy a second orange or the first apple because the marginal utility per dollar of both is 10 utils per dollar. So she buys both of them. Holly now has 1 apple and 2 oranges. Also, the last dollar she spent on each good yielded the same marginal utility per dollar (10). But this combination of apples and oranges does not represent the maximum amount of

utility that Holly can obtain. It cost her only $5 [= (1 × $1) + (2 × $2)], so she has $5 remaining, which she can spend to achieve a still higher level of total utility.

Examining columns 2b and 3b again, we find that Holly should spend the next $2 on a third orange because marginal utility per dollar for the third orange is 9 compared with 8 for the second apple. But now, with 1 apple and 3 oranges, she is again indifferent between a second apple and a fourth orange because both provide 8 utils per dollar. So Holly purchases 1 more of each. Now the last dollar spent on each product provides the same marginal utility per dollar (8), and Holly's money income of $10 is exhausted.

The utility-maximizing combination of goods attainable by Holly is 2 apples and 4 oranges. By summing marginal-utility information from columns 2a and 3a, we find that Holly is obtaining 18 (= 10 + 8) utils of satisfaction from the 2 apples and 78 (= 24 + 20 + 18 + 16) utils of satisfaction from the 4 oranges. Her $10, optimally spent, yields 96 (= 18 + 78) utils of satisfaction.

Table 7.2 summarizes our step-by-step process for maximizing Holly's utility. Note that we have implicitly assumed that Holly spends her entire income. She neither borrows nor saves. However, saving can be regarded as a "commodity" that yields utility and can be incorporated into our analysis. In fact, we treat it that way in problem 4 at the end of this chapter.

Inferior Options Holly can obtain other combinations of apples and oranges with $10, but none will yield as great a total utility as do 2 apples and 4 oranges. As an example, she can obtain 4 apples and 3 oranges for $10. But this combination yields only 93 utils, clearly inferior to the 96 utils provided by 2 apples and 4 oranges. True, there are other combinations of apples and oranges (such as 4 apples and 5 oranges or 1 apple and 2 oranges) in which the marginal utility of the last dollar spent is the same for both goods. But all such combinations either are unobtainable with Holly's limited money income (as 4 apples and 5 oranges) or do not exhaust her money income (as 1 apple and 2 oranges) and therefore do not yield the maximum utility attainable.

TABLE 7.2 Sequence of Purchases to Achieve Consumer Equilibrium, Given the Data in Table 7.1

Choice Number	Potential Choices	Marginal Utility per Dollar	Purchase Decision	Income Remaining
1	First apple	10	First orange for $2	$8 = $10 − $2
	First orange	12		
2	First apple	10	First apple for $1	$5 = $8 − $3
	Second orange	10	and second orange for $2	
3	Second apple	8	Third orange for $2	$3 = $5 − $2
	Third orange	9		
4	Second apple	8	Second apple for $1	$0 = $3 − $3
	Fourth orange	8	and fourth orange for $2	

Algebraic Generalization

Economists generalize the utility-maximizing rule by saying that a consumer will maximize her satisfaction when she allocates her money income so that the last dollar spent on product A, the last on product B, and so forth, yield equal amounts of additional, or marginal, utility. The marginal utility per dollar spent on A is indicated by the MU of product A divided by the price of A (column 2b in Table 7.1), and the marginal utility per dollar spent on B by the MU of product B divided by the price of B (column 3b in Table 7.1). Our utility-maximizing rule merely requires that these ratios be equal for the last dollar spent on A and the last dollar spent on B. Algebraically,

$$\frac{\text{MU of product A}}{\text{Price of A}} = \frac{\text{MU of product B}}{\text{Price of B}}$$

And, of course, the consumer must exhaust her available income. Table 7.1 shows us that the combination of 2 units of A (apples) and 4 of B (oranges) fulfills these conditions in that

$$\frac{8 \text{ utils}}{\$1} = \frac{16 \text{ utils}}{\$2}$$

and the consumer's $10 income is all spent.

If the equation is not fulfilled, then some reallocation of the consumer's expenditures between A and B (from the low to the high marginal-utility-per-dollar product) will increase the consumer's total utility. For example, if the consumer spent $10 on 4 of A (apples) and 3 of B (oranges), we would find that

$$\frac{\text{MU of A of 6 utils}}{\text{Price of A of }\$1} < \frac{\text{MU of B of 18 utils}}{\text{Price of B of }\$2}$$

Here the last dollar spent on A provides only 6 utils of satisfaction, while the last dollar spent on B provides 9 (= 18/$2). So the consumer can increase total satisfaction by purchasing more of B and less of A. As dollars are reallocated from A to B, the marginal utility per dollar of A will increase while the marginal utility per dollar of B will decrease. At some new combination of A and B the two will be equal and consumer equilibrium will be achieved. Here that combination is 2 of A (apples) and 4 of B (oranges).

Utility Maximization and the Demand Curve

LO7.3 Explain how a demand curve can be derived by observing the outcomes of price changes in the utility-maximization model.

Once you understand the utility-maximizing rule, you can easily see why product price and quantity demanded are inversely related. Recall that the basic determinants of an individual's demand for a specific product are (1) preferences or tastes, (2) money income, and (3) the prices of other goods. The utility data in Table 7.1 reflect our consumer's preferences. We continue to suppose that her money income is $10. And, concentrating on the construction of an individual demand curve for oranges, we assume that the price of apples, now representing all "other goods," is still $1.

Deriving the Demand Schedule and Curve

We can derive a single consumer's demand schedule for oranges by considering alternative prices at which oranges might be sold and then determining the quantity the consumer will purchase. We already know one such price-quantity combination in the utility-maximizing example: Given tastes, income, and the prices of other goods, Holly will purchase 4 oranges at $2.

Now let's assume the price of oranges falls to $1. The marginal-utility-per-dollar data of column 3b in Table 7.1 will double because the price of oranges has been halved; the new data for column 3b are (by coincidence) identical to the data in column 3a. The doubling of the MU per dollar for each successive orange means that the purchase of 2 apples and 4 oranges is no longer an equilibrium combination. By applying the same reasoning we used previously, we now find that Holly's utility-maximizing combination is 4 apples and 6 oranges. As summarized in the table in Figure 7.2, Holly will purchase

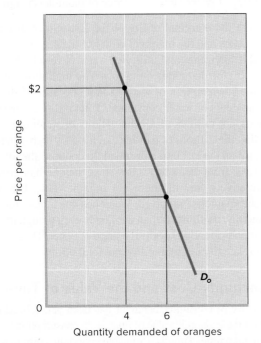

FIGURE 7.2 Deriving an individual demand curve. The consumer represented by the data in the table maximizes utility by purchasing 4 oranges at a price of $2. The decline in the price of oranges to $1 disrupts the consumer's initial utility-maximizing equilibrium. The consumer restores equilibrium by purchasing 6 rather than 4 oranges. Thus, a simple price-quantity schedule emerges, which locates two points on a downsloping demand curve.

Price per Orange	Quantity Demanded
$2	4
1	6

6 oranges when the price of oranges is $1. Using the data in this table, we can sketch the downward-sloping demand curve for oranges, D_o, shown in Figure 7.2. This exercise, then, clearly links the utility-maximizing behavior of a consumer and that person's downsloping demand curve for a particular product.

Income and Substitution Effects

LO7.4 Discuss how the utility-maximization model helps highlight the income and substitution effects of a price change.

Recall from Chapter 3 that the **income effect** is the impact that a change in the price of a product has on a consumer's real income and consequently on the quantity demanded of that good. In contrast, the **substitution effect** is the impact that a change in a product's price has on its relative expensiveness and consequently on the quantity demanded. Both effects help explain why a demand curve such as that in Figure 7.2 is downsloping.

Let's first look at the substitution effect. Recall that before the price of oranges declined, Holly was in equilibrium

when purchasing 2 apples and 4 oranges because

$$\frac{\text{MU of apples of 8}}{\text{Price of apples of \$1}} = \frac{\text{MU of oranges of 16}}{\text{Price of oranges of \$2}}$$

But after the price of oranges declines from $2 to $1,

$$\frac{\text{MU of apples of 8}}{\text{Price of apples of \$1}} < \frac{\text{MU of oranges of 16}}{\text{Price of oranges of \$1}}$$

Clearly, the last dollar spent on oranges now yields greater utility (16 utils) than does the last dollar spent on apples (8 utils). This will lead Holly to switch, or substitute, purchases away from apples and toward oranges so as to restore consumer equilibrium. This substitution effect contributes to the inverse relationship between price and quantity that is found along her demand curve for oranges: When the price of oranges declines, the substitution effect causes Holly to buy more oranges.

What about the income effect? The decline in the price of oranges from $2 to $1 increases Holly's real income. Before the price decline, she maximized her utility and achieved consumer equilibrium by selecting 2 apples and 4 oranges. But at the lower $1 price for oranges, Holly would have to spend only $6 rather than $10 to buy that particular combination of goods. That means that the lower price of oranges has freed up $4 that can be spent on buying more apples, more oranges, or more of both. How many more of each fruit she ends up buying will be determined by applying the utility-maximizing rule to the new situation. But it is quite likely that the increase in real income caused by the reduction in the price of oranges will cause Holly to end up buying more oranges than before the price reduction. Any such increase in orange purchases is referred to as the income effect of the reduction in the price of oranges and it, too, helps to explain why demand curves are downward sloping: When the price of oranges falls, the income effect causes Holly to buy more oranges.

> ## QUICK REVIEW 7.2
>
> ✓ The theory of consumer behavior assumes that, with limited income and a set of product prices, consumers make rational choices on the basis of well-defined preferences.
>
> ✓ A consumer maximizes utility by allocating income so that the marginal utility per dollar spent is the same for every good purchased.
>
> ✓ A downsloping demand curve can be derived by changing the price of one product in the consumer-behavior model and noting the change in the utility-maximizing quantity of that product demanded.
>
> ✓ By providing insights on the income effect and substitution effect of a price decline, the utility-maximization model helps explain why demand curves are downsloping.

Applications and Extensions

LO7.5 Give examples of several real-world phenomena that can be explained by applying the theory of consumer behavior.

Many real-world phenomena can be explained by applying the theory of consumer behavior.

iPads

Every so often a new product totally captures consumers' imaginations. One such product is Apple's iPad, which debuted in April 2010. Less than three years later, Apple sold its 100-millionth unit.

The swift ascendancy of the iPad resulted mainly from a leapfrog in technology. It was the first touchscreen tablet computer and became a hit because it was much better for the consumption of digital media—music, pictures, videos, and many games—than existing laptop or desktop computers. Those larger machines still held the advantage if a consumer wanted to create content or edit documents, but for consuming digital content the iPad was far superior in the eyes of millions of consumers.

In the language of our analysis, Apple's introduction of the iPad severely disrupted consumer equilibrium. Consumers en masse concluded that iPads had a higher marginal-utility-to-price ratio (= MU/P) than the ratios for alternative products. They therefore shifted spending away from those other products and toward iPads as a way to increase total utility. Of course, for most people the marginal utility of a second or third iPad relative to price is quite low, so most consumers purchased only a single iPad. But Apple continued to enhance the iPad, enticing some of the buyers of older models to buy new models.

This example demonstrates a simple but important point: New products succeed by enhancing consumers' total utility. This "delivery of value" generates a revenue stream. If revenues exceed production costs, substantial profits can result—as they have for Apple.

The Diamond-Water Paradox

Early economists such as Adam Smith were puzzled by the fact that some "essential" goods had much lower prices than some "unimportant" goods. Why would water, essential to life, be priced below diamonds, which have much less usefulness? The paradox is resolved when we acknowledge that water is in great supply relative to demand and thus has a very low price per gallon. Diamonds, in contrast, are rare. Their supply is small relative to demand and, as a result, they have a very high price per carat.

Moreover, the marginal utility of the last unit of water consumed is very low. The reason follows from our utility-maximizing rule. Consumers (and producers) respond to the very low price of water by using a great deal of it—for generating electricity, irrigating crops, heating buildings, watering lawns, quenching thirst, and so on. Consumption is expanded until marginal utility, which declines as more water is consumed,

equals its low price. On the other hand, relatively few diamonds are purchased because of their prohibitively high price, meaning that their marginal utility remains high. In equilibrium:

$$\frac{\text{MU of water (low)}}{\text{Price of water (low)}} = \frac{\text{MU of diamonds (high)}}{\text{Price of diamonds (high)}}$$

Although the marginal utility of the last unit of water consumed is low and the marginal utility of the last diamond purchased is high, the total utility of water is very high and the total utility of diamonds quite low. The total utility derived from the consumption of water is large because of the enormous amounts of water consumed. Total utility is the sum of the marginal utilities of all the gallons of water consumed, including the trillions of gallons that have far higher marginal utilities than the last unit consumed. In contrast, the total utility derived from diamonds is low since their high price means that relatively few of them are bought. Thus the water-diamond "paradox" is solved: Water has much more total utility (roughly, usefulness) than diamonds even though the price of diamonds greatly exceeds the price of water. These relative prices relate to marginal utility, not total utility.

Opportunity Cost and the Value of Time

The theory of consumer behavior has been generalized to account for the economic value of *time*. Both consumption and production take time. Time is a valuable economic commodity; by using an hour in productive work a person can earn $6, $10, $50, or more, depending on her or his education and skills. By using that hour for leisure or in consumption activities, the individual incurs the opportunity cost of forgone income; she or he sacrifices the $6, $10, or $50 that could have been earned by working.

Imagine a self-employed consumer named Linden who is considering buying a round of golf, on the one hand, and a concert, on the other. The market price of the golf game is $30 and that of the concert is $40. But the golf game takes more time than the concert. Suppose Linden spends 4 hours on the golf course but only 2 hours at the concert. If her time is worth $10 per hour, as evidenced by the $10 wage she can obtain by working, then the "full price" of the golf game is $70 (the $30 market price plus $40 worth of time). Similarly, the full price of the concert is $60 (the $40 market price plus $20 worth of time). We find that, contrary to what market prices alone indicate, the full price of the concert is really less than the full price of the golf game.

If we now assume that the marginal utilities derived from successive golf games and concerts are identical, traditional theory would indicate that Linden should consume more golf games than concerts because the market price of the former ($30) is lower than that of the latter ($40). But when time is taken into account, the situation is reversed and golf games ($70) are more expensive than concerts ($60). So it is rational for Linden to consume more concerts than golf games.

Criminal Behavior

Although Economic Analysis Is Not Particularly Relevant in Explaining Some Crimes of Passion and Violence, It Does Provide Interesting Insights on Such Property Crimes as Robbery, Burglary, and Auto Theft.

The theory of rational consumer behavior can be extended to provide some useful insights on criminal behavior. Both the lawful consumer and the criminal try to maximize their total utility (or net benefit). For example, you can remove a textbook from the campus bookstore by either purchasing it or stealing it. If you *buy* the book, your action is legal; you have fully compensated the bookstore for the product. (The bookstore would rather have your money than the book.) If you *steal* the book, you have broken the law. Theft is outlawed because it imposes uncompensated costs on others. In this case, your action reduces the bookstore's revenue and profit and also may impose costs on other buyers who now must pay higher prices for their textbooks.

Why might someone engage in a criminal activity such as stealing? Just like the consumer who compares the marginal utility of a good with its price, the potential criminal compares the marginal benefit from his or her action with the "price" or cost. If the marginal benefit (to the criminal) exceeds the price or marginal cost (also to the criminal), the individual undertakes the criminal activity.

Most people, however, do not engage in theft, burglary, or fraud. Why not? The answer is that they perceive the personal price of engaging in these illegal activities to be too high relative to the marginal benefit. The price or marginal cost to the potential criminal has several facets. First, there are the "guilt costs," which for many people are substantial. Such individuals would not steal from others even if there were no penalties for doing so. Their moral sense of right and wrong would entail too great a guilt cost relative to the benefit from the stolen good. Other types of costs include the direct cost of the criminal activity (supplies and tools) and the forgone income from legitimate activities (the opportunity cost to the criminal).

Unfortunately, guilt costs, direct costs, and forgone income are not sufficient to deter some people from stealing. So society imposes other costs, mainly fines and imprisonment, on lawbreakers. The potential of being fined increases the marginal cost to the criminal. The potential of being imprisoned boosts marginal cost still further. Most people highly value their personal freedom and lose considerable legitimate earnings while incarcerated.

Given these types of costs, the potential criminal estimates the marginal cost and benefit of committing the crime. As a simple example, suppose that the direct cost and the opportunity cost of stealing an $80 textbook are both zero. The probability of getting caught

Source: © Digital Vision/Getty Images RF

is 10 percent and, if apprehended, there will be a $500 fine. The potential criminal will estimate the marginal cost of stealing the book as $50 (= $500 fine × .10 chance of apprehension). Someone who has a guilt cost of zero will choose to steal the book because the marginal benefit of $80 would exceed the marginal cost of $50. In contrast, someone having a guilt cost of, say, $40 will not steal the book. The marginal benefit of $80 will not be as great as the marginal cost of $90 (= $50 of penalty cost + $40 of guilt cost).

This perspective on illegal behavior has some interesting implications. For example, other things equal, crime will rise (more of it will be "bought") when its price falls. This explains, for instance, why some people who do not steal from stores under normal circumstances participate in looting stores during riots, when the marginal cost of being apprehended has substantially declined.

Another implication is that society can reduce unlawful behavior by increasing the "price of crime." It can nourish and increase guilt costs through family, educational, and religious efforts. It can increase the direct cost of crime by using more sophisticated security systems (locks, alarms, video surveillance) so that criminals will have to buy and use more sophisticated tools. It can undertake education and training initiatives to enhance the legitimate earnings of people who might otherwise engage in illegal activity. It can increase policing to raise the probability of being apprehended for crime. And it can impose greater penalties for those who are caught and convicted.

By accounting for the opportunity cost of a consumer's time, we can explain certain phenomena that are otherwise quite puzzling. It may be rational for the unskilled worker or retiree whose time has little market value to ride a bus from Chicago to Pittsburgh. But the corporate executive, whose time is very valuable, will find it cheaper to fly, even though bus fare is only a fraction of plane fare. It is sensible for the retiree, living on a modest company pension and a Social Security check, to spend many hours shopping for bargains at the mall or taking long trips in a motor home. It is equally intelligent for the highly paid physician, working 55 hours per week, to buy a new personal computer over the Internet and take short vacations at expensive resorts.

People in other nations often feel affluent Americans are "wasteful" of food and other material goods but "overly economical" in their use of time. Americans who visit developing countries find that time is used casually or "squandered," while material goods are very highly prized and carefully used. These differences are not a paradox or a case of radically different temperaments. The differences are primarily a rational reflection of the fact that the high productivity of labor in an industrially advanced society gives time a high market value, whereas the opposite is true in a low-income, developing country.

Medical Care Purchases

The method of payment for certain goods and services affects their prices at the time we buy them and significantly changes the amount purchased. Let's go back to Table 7.1. Suppose the $1 price for apples is its "true" value or opportunity cost. But now, for some reason, its price is only, say, $0.20. A rational consumer clearly would buy more apples at the $0.20 price than at the $1 price.

That is what happens with medical care. People in the United States who have health insurance pay a fixed premium once a month that covers, say, 80 percent of all incurred health care costs. This means that when they actually need health care, its price to them will be only 20 percent of the actual market price. How would you act in such a situation? When you are ill, you would likely purchase a great deal more medical care than you would if you were confronted with the full price. As a result, financing health care through insurance is an important factor in explaining today's high expenditures on health care and the historical growth of such spending as a percentage of domestic output.

Similar reasoning applies to purchases of buffet meals. If you buy a meal at an all-you-can-eat buffet, you will tend to eat more than if you purchased it item by item. Why not eat that second dessert? Its marginal utility is positive and its "price" is zero!

Cash and Noncash Gifts

Marginal-utility analysis also helps us understand why people generally prefer cash gifts to noncash gifts costing the same amount. The reason is simply that the noncash gifts may not match the recipient's preferences and thus may not add as much as cash to total utility. Thought of differently, consumers know their own preferences better than the gift giver does, and the $100 cash gift provides more choices.

Look back at Table 7.1. Suppose Holly has zero earned income but is given the choice of a $2 cash gift or a noncash gift of 2 apples. Because 2 apples can be bought with $2, these two gifts are of equal monetary value. But by spending the $2 cash gift on the first orange, Holly could obtain 24 utils. The noncash gift of the first 2 apples would yield only 18 (= 10 + 8) units of utility. Conclusion: The noncash gift yields less utility to the beneficiary than does the cash gift.

Since giving noncash gifts is common, a considerable value of those gifts is potentially lost because they do not match their recipients' tastes. For example, Uncle Fred may have paid $30 for the ski goggles he gave you for the holidays, but you would pay only $15 for them. Thus, a $15, or 50 percent, value loss is involved. Multiplied by billions of gifts a year, the total potential loss of value is huge.

But some of that loss is avoided by the creative ways individuals handle the problem. For example, newlyweds set up gift registries for their weddings to help match up their wants to the noncash gifts received. Also, people obtain cash refunds or exchanges for gifts so they can buy goods that provide more utility. And people have even been known to "recycle gifts" by giving them to someone else at a later time. All three actions support the proposition that individuals take actions to maximize their total utility.

SUMMARY

LO7.1 Define and explain the relationship between total utility, marginal utility, and the law of diminishing marginal utility.

The law of diminishing marginal utility states that beyond a certain quantity, additional units of a specific good will yield declining amounts of extra satisfaction to a consumer.

LO7.2 Describe how rational consumers maximize utility by comparing the marginal utility-to-price ratios of all the products they could possibly purchase.

The utility-maximization model assumes that the typical consumer is rational and acts on the basis of well-defined preferences. Because income is limited and goods have prices, the consumer cannot purchase all the goods and services he or she might want. The consumer therefore selects the attainable combination of goods that maximizes his or her utility or satisfaction.

A consumer's utility is maximized when income is allocated so that the last dollar spent on each product purchased yields the same amount of extra satisfaction. Algebraically, the utility-maximizing rule is fulfilled when

$$\frac{\text{MU of product A}}{\text{Price of A}} = \frac{\text{MU of product B}}{\text{Price of B}}$$

and the consumer's total income is spent.

LO7.3 Explain how a demand curve can be derived by observing the outcomes of price changes in the utility-maximization model.

The utility-maximizing rule and the demand curve are logically consistent. Because marginal utility declines, a lower price is needed to induce the consumer to buy more of a particular product.

LO7.4 Discuss how the utility-maximization model helps highlight the income and substitution effects of a price change.

The utility-maximization model illuminates the income and substitution effects of a price change. The income effect implies that a decline in the price of a product increases the consumer's real income and enables the consumer to buy more of that product with a fixed money income. The substitution effect implies that a lower price makes a product relatively more attractive and therefore increases the consumer's willingness to substitute it for other products.

LO7.5 Give examples of several real-world phenomena that can be explained by applying the theory of consumer behavior.

The theory of consumer behavior can explain many real world phenomena, including the rapid adoption of popular consumer goods like the iPad that feature disruptive technologies, the overconsumption of products like health care that have artificially low prices, and people's preference for gifts of cash over gifts of particular items or objects of the same monetary value.

TERMS AND CONCEPTS

law of diminishing marginal utility

utility

total utility

marginal utility

rational behavior

budget constraint

utility-maximizing rule

consumer equilibrium

income effect

substitution effect

The following and additional problems can be found in ▇ connect

DISCUSSION QUESTIONS

1. Complete the following table and answer the questions below: **LO7.1**

Units Consumed	Total Utility	Marginal Utility
0	0	
1	10	10
2	—	8
3	25	—
4	30	—
5	—	3
6	34	—

   a. At which rate is total utility increasing: a constant rate, a decreasing rate, or an increasing rate? How do you know?
   b. "A rational consumer will purchase only 1 unit of the product represented by these data, since that amount maximizes marginal utility." Do you agree? Explain why or why not.
   c. "It is possible that a rational consumer will not purchase any units of the product represented by these data." Do you agree? Explain why or why not.

2. Mrs. Simpson buys loaves of bread and quarts of milk each week at prices of $1 and 80 cents, respectively. At present she is buying these products in amounts such that the marginal utilities from the last units purchased of the two products are 80 and 70 utils, respectively. Is she buying the utility-maximizing combination of bread and milk? If not, how should she reallocate her expenditures between the two goods? **LO7.2**

3. How can time be incorporated into the theory of consumer behavior? Explain the following comment: "Want to make millions of dollars? Devise a product that saves Americans lots of time." **LO7.2**

4. Explain: **LO7.2**
   a. Before economic growth, there were too few goods; after growth, there is too little time.
   b. It is irrational for an individual to take the time to be completely rational in economic decision making.
   c. Telling your spouse where you would like to go out to eat for your birthday makes sense in terms of utility maximization.

5. In the last decade or so, there has been a dramatic expansion of small retail convenience stores (such as 7-Eleven, Kwik Shop, and Circle K), although their prices are generally much higher than prices in large supermarkets. What explains the success of the convenience stores? **LO7.2**

6. Many apartment-complex owners are installing water meters for each apartment and billing the occupants according to the amount of water they use. This is in contrast to the former procedure of having a central meter for the entire complex and dividing up the collective water expense as part of the rent. Where individual meters have been installed, water usage has declined 10 to 40 percent. Explain that drop, referring to price and marginal utility. **LO7.3**

7. Using the utility-maximization rule as your point of reference, explain the income and substitution effects of an increase in the price of product B, with no change in the price of product A. **LO7.4**

8. **ADVANCED ANALYSIS** A "mathematically fair bet" is one in which the amount won will on average equal the amount bet, for example, when a gambler bets, say, $100 for a 10 percent chance to win $1,000 ($100 = 0.10 × $1,000). Assuming diminishing marginal utility of dollars, explain why this is not a fair bet in terms of utility. Why is it even a less fair bet when the "house" takes a cut of each dollar bet? So is gambling irrational? **LO7.4**

9. Rank each of the following three gift possibilities in terms of how much utility they are likely to bring and explain your reasoning. A store-specific gift card worth $15, a $15 item from that specific store, and $15 of cash that can be spent anywhere. **LO7.5**

10. **LAST WORD** In what way is criminal behavior similar to consumer behavior? Why do most people obtain goods via legal behavior as opposed to illegal behavior? What are society's main options for reducing illegal behavior?

REVIEW QUESTIONS

1. True or false. The law of diminishing marginal utility predicts the consumption behavior of addicts quite well. **LO7.1**

2. Frank spends $75 on 10 magazines and 25 newspapers. The magazines cost $5 each and the newspapers cost $2.50 each. Suppose that his MU from the final magazine is 10 utils while his MU from the final newspaper is also 10 utils. According to the utility-maximizing rule, Frank should: **LO7.2**
   a. Reallocate spending from magazines to newspapers.
   b. Reallocate spending from newspapers to magazines.
   c. Be satisfied because he is already maximizing his total utility.
   d. None of the above.

3. Demand curves slope downward because, other things held equal, **LO7.3**
   a. An increase in a product's price lowers MU.
   b. A decrease in a product's price lowers MU.
   c. A decrease in a product's price raises MU per dollar and makes consumers wish to purchase more units.
   d. An increase in a product's price raises MU per dollar and makes consumers wish to purchase more units.

4. Jermaine spends his money on cucumbers and lettuce. If the price of cucumbers falls, the MU per dollar of cucumbers will _____ and Jermaine will _____ cucumbers for lettuce. **LO7.4**
   a. Fall; substitute
   b. Rise; substitute
   c. Fall; supply
   d. Rise; demand

5. Tammy spends her money on lemonade and iced tea. If the price of lemonade falls, it is as though her income _____. **LO7.4**
   a. Increases.
   b. Decreases.
   c. Stays the same.

PROBLEMS

1. Mylie's total utility from singing the same song over and over is 50 utils after one repetition, 90 utils after two repetitions, 70 utils after three repetitions, 20 utils after four repetitions, −50 utils after five repetitions, and −200 utils after six repetitions. Write down her marginal utility for each repetition. Once Mylie's total utility begins to decrease, does each additional singing of the song hurt more than the previous one or less than the previous one? **LO7.1**

2. John likes Coca-Cola. After consuming one Coke, John has a total utility of 10 utils. After two Cokes, he has a total utility of 25 utils. After three Cokes, he has a total utility of 50 utils. Does John show diminishing marginal utility for Coke, or does he show increasing marginal utility for Coke? Suppose that John has $3 in his pocket. If Cokes cost $1 each and John is willing to spend one of his dollars on purchasing a first can of Coke, would he spend his second dollar on a Coke, too? What about the third dollar? If John's marginal utility for Coke keeps on increasing no matter how many Cokes he drinks, would it be fair to say that he is addicted to Coke? **LO7.1**

3. Suppose that Omar's marginal utility for cups of coffee is constant at 1.5 utils per cup no matter how many cups he drinks. On the other hand, his marginal utility per doughnut is 10 for the first doughnut he eats, 9 for the second he eats, 8 for the third he eats, and so on (that is, declining by 1 util per additional doughnut). In addition, suppose that coffee costs $1 per cup, doughnuts cost $1 each, and Omar has a budget that he can spend only on doughnuts, coffee, or both. How big would that budget have to be before he would spend a dollar buying a first cup of coffee? **LO7.2**

4. Columns 1 through 4 in the following table show the marginal utility, measured in utils, that Ricardo would get by purchasing various amounts of products A, B, C, and D. Column 5 shows the marginal utility Ricardo gets from saving. Assume that the prices of A, B, C, and D are, respectively, $18, $6, $4, and $24 and that Ricardo has an income of $106. **LO7.2**
   a. What quantities of A, B, C, and D will Ricardo purchase in maximizing his utility?
   b. How many dollars will Ricardo choose to save?
   c. Check your answers by substituting them into the algebraic statement of the utility-maximizing rule.

Column 1		Column 2		Column 3		Column 4		Column 5	
Units of A	MU	Units of B	MU	Units of C	MU	Units of D	MU	Number of Dollars Saved	MU
1	72	1	24	1	15	1	36	1	5
2	54	2	15	2	12	2	30	2	4
3	45	3	12	3	8	3	24	3	3
4	36	4	9	4	7	4	18	4	2
5	27	5	7	5	5	5	13	5	1
6	18	6	5	6	4	6	7	6	$\frac{1}{2}$
7	15	7	2	7	$3\frac{1}{2}$	7	4	7	$\frac{1}{4}$
8	12	8	1	8	3	8	2	8	$\frac{1}{8}$

5. You are choosing between two goods, X and Y, and your marginal utility from each is as shown in the following table. If your income is $9 and the prices of X and Y are $2 and $1, respectively, what quantities of each will you purchase to maximize utility? What total utility will you realize? Assume that, other things remaining unchanged, the price of X falls to $1. What quantities of X and Y will you now purchase? Using the two prices and quantities for X, derive a demand schedule (a table showing prices and quantities demanded) for X. **LO7.3**

Units of X	MU_x	Units of Y	MU_y
1	10	1	8
2	8	2	7
3	6	3	6
4	4	4	5
5	3	5	4
6	2	6	3

6. **ADVANCED ANALYSIS** Let $MU_A = z = 10 - x$ and $MU_B = z = 21 - 2y$, where z is marginal utility per dollar measured in utils, x is the amount spent on product A, and y is the amount spent on product B. Assume that the consumer has $10 to spend on A and B—that is, $x + y = 10$. How is the $10 best allocated between A and B? How much utility will the marginal dollar yield? **LO7.3**

7. Suppose that with a budget of $100, Deborah spends $60 on sushi and $40 on bagels when sushi costs $2 per piece and bagels cost $2 per bagel. But then, after the price of bagels falls to $1 per bagel, she spends $50 on sushi and $50 on bagels. How many pieces of sushi and how many bagels did Deborah consume before the price change? At the new prices, how much money would it have cost Deborah to buy those same quantities (the ones that she consumed before the price change)? Given that it used to take Deborah's entire $100 to buy those quantities, how big is the income effect caused by the reduction in the price of bagels? **LO7.4**

Indifference Curve Analysis

LO7.6 Relate how the indifference curve model of consumer behavior derives demand curves from budget lines, indifference curves, and utility maximization.

The utility-maximization rule previously discussed requires individuals to measure and compare utility, much as a business would measure and compare costs or revenues. Such *cardinal utility* is measured in units such as 1, 2, 3, and 4 and can be added, subtracted, multiplied, and divided, just like the cardinal numbers in mathematics. More importantly, cardinal utility allows precise quantification of the marginal utilities upon which the utility-maximizing rule depends. In fact, the marginal-utility theory of consumer demand that we explained in the body of this chapter rests squarely on the assumption that economists be able to measure cardinal utility. The reality, however, is that measuring cardinal utility is highly difficult, at best. (Can you, for instance, state exactly how many utils you are getting from reading this book right now or how many utils you would get from watching a sunset?)

To avoid this measurement problem, economists have developed an alternative explanation of consumer behavior and equilibrium in which cardinal measurement is not required. In this more-advanced analysis, the consumer must simply *rank* various combinations of goods in terms of preference. For instance, Sally can simply report that she *prefers* 4 units of A to 6 units of B without having to put number values on how much she likes either option. The model of consumer behavior that is based upon such *ordinal utility* rankings is called indifference curve analysis. It has two main elements: budget lines and indifference curves.

The Budget Line: What Is Attainable

We know from Chapter 1 that a **budget line** (or, more technically, a *budget constraint*) is a schedule or curve showing various combinations of two products a consumer can purchase with a specific money income. If the price of product A is $1.50 and the price of product B is $1, a consumer could purchase all the combinations of A and B shown in the table in Figure 1 with $12 of money income. At one extreme, the consumer might spend all of his or her income on 8 units of A and have nothing left to spend on B. Or, by giving up 2 units of A and thereby "freeing" $3, the consumer could have 6 units of A and 3 of B. And so on to the other extreme, at which the consumer could buy 12 units of B at $1 each, spending his or her entire money income on B with nothing left to spend on A.

Figure 1 also shows the budget line graphically. Note that the graph is not restricted to whole units of A and B as is the table. Every point on the graph represents a possible combination of A and B, including fractional quantities. The slope of the graphed budget line measures the ratio of the price of B to the price of A; more precisely, the absolute value of the slope is $P_B/P_A = \$1.00/\$1.50 = \frac{2}{3}$. This is the mathematical way of saying that the consumer must forgo 2 units of A (measured on the vertical axis) to buy 3 units of B (measured on the horizontal axis). In moving down the budget or price line, 2 units of A (at $1.50 each) must be given up to obtain 3 more units of B (at $1 each). This yields a slope of $\frac{2}{3}$.

Note that all combinations of A and B that lie on or inside the budget line are attainable from the consumer's $12 of

FIGURE 1 A consumer's budget line. The budget line shows all the combinations of any two products that someone can purchase, given the prices of the products and the person's money income.

Units of A (Price = $1.50)	Units of B (Price = $1)	Total Expenditure
8	0	$12 (= $12 + $0)
6	3	$12 (= $9 + $3)
4	6	$12 (= $6 + $6)
2	9	$12 (= $3 + $9)
0	12	$12 (= $0 + $12)

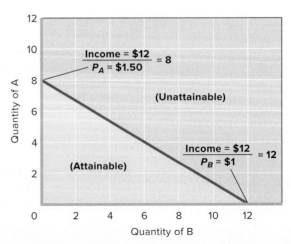

money income. He can afford to buy not only the combinations of A and B that lie along the budget line itself but also those that lie below it. He could, for instance, afford to buy 2 units of A and 4 units of B, thereby using up only $7 (= $3 spent on 2 units of A at a price of $1.50 each + $4 spent on 4 units of B at a price of $1 each). That combination is clearly attainable because it would use up only half of the consumer's $12 budget. But to achieve maximum utility, the consumer will want to spend the full $12. The budget line shows all combinations that cost exactly the full $12.

The budget line has two other significant characteristics:

- **Income changes** The location of the budget line varies with money income. An increase in money income shifts the budget line to the right; a decrease in money income shifts it to the left. To verify this, recalculate the table in Figure 1, assuming that money income is (a) $24 and (b) $6, and plot the new budget lines in Figure 1.

- **Price changes** A change in product prices also shifts the budget line. A decline in the prices of both products— the equivalent of an increase in real income—shifts the curve to the right. (You can verify this by recalculating the table in Figure 1 and replotting Figure 1 assuming that $P_A = \$0.75$ and $P_B = \$0.50$.) Conversely, an increase in the prices of A and B shifts the curve to the left. (Assume $P_A = \$3$ and $P_B = \$2$, and rework the table and Figure 1 to substantiate this statement.)

Note what happens if P_B changes while P_A and money income remain constant. In particular, if P_B drops, say, from $1 to $0.50, the lower end of the budget line fans outward to the right. Conversely, if P_B increases, say, from $1 to $1.50, the lower end of the line fans inward to the left. In both instances the line remains "anchored" at 8 units on the vertical axis because P_A has not changed.

Indifference Curves: What Is Preferred

Budget lines reflect "objective" market data, specifically income and prices. They reveal combinations of products A and B that can be purchased, given current money income and prices.

Indifference curves, on the other hand, reflect "subjective" information about consumer preferences for A and B. An **indifference curve** shows all the combinations of two products A and B that will yield the same total satisfaction or total utility to a consumer. The table and graph in Figure 2 present a hypothetical indifference curve for products A and B. The consumer's subjective preferences are such that he or she will realize the same total utility from each combination of A and B shown in the table or on the curve. So the consumer will be indifferent (will not care) as to which combination is actually obtained.

Indifference curves have several important characteristics.

Indifference Curves Are Downsloping
An indifference curve slopes downward because more of one product means less of the other if total utility is to remain unchanged. Suppose the consumer moves from one combination of A and B to another, say, from j to k in Figure 2. In so doing, the consumer obtains more of product B, increasing his or her total utility. But because total utility is the same everywhere on the curve, the consumer must give up some of the other product, A, to reduce total utility by a precisely offsetting amount. Thus "more of B" necessitates "less of A," and the quantities of A and B are inversely related. A curve that reflects inversely related variables is downsloping.

Indifference Curves Are Convex to the Origin
Recall from the appendix to Chapter 1 that the slope of a curve at a particular point is measured by drawing a straight line that is tangent to that point and then measuring the "rise over run"

FIGURE 2 A consumer's indifference curve. Every point on indifference curve *I* represents some combination of products A and B, and all those combinations are equally satisfactory to the consumer. That is, each combination of A and B on the curve yields the same total utility.

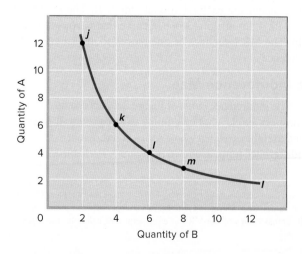

Combination	Units of A	Units of B
j	12	2
k	6	4
l	4	6
m	3	8

of the straight line. If you drew such straight lines for several points on the curve in Figure 2, you would find that their slopes decline (in absolute terms) as you move down the curve. An indifference curve is therefore convex (bowed inward) to the origin of the graph. Its slope diminishes or becomes flatter as we move down the curve from j to k to l, and so on. Technically, the slope of an indifference curve at each point measures the **marginal rate of substitution (MRS)** of the combination of two goods represented by that point. The slope or MRS shows the rate at which the consumer who possesses the combination must substitute one good for the other (say, B for A) to remain equally satisfied. The diminishing slope of the indifference curve means that the willingness to substitute B for A diminishes as more of B is obtained.

The rationale for this convexity—that is, for a diminishing MRS—is that a consumer's subjective willingness to substitute B for A (or A for B) will depend on the amounts of B and A he or she has to begin with. Consider the table and graph in Figure 2 again, beginning at point j. Here, in relative terms, the consumer has a substantial amount of A and very little of B. Within this combination, a unit of B is very valuable (that is, its marginal utility is high), while a unit of A is less valuable (its marginal utility is low). The consumer will then be willing to give up a substantial amount of A to get, say, 2 more units of B. In this case, the consumer is willing to forgo 6 units of A to get 2 more units of B; the MRS is $\frac{6}{2}$, or 3, for the jk segment of the curve.

But at point k the consumer has less A and more B. Here A is somewhat more valuable, and B less valuable, "at the margin." In a move from point k to point l, the consumer is willing to give up only 2 units of A to get 2 more units of B, so the MRS is only $\frac{2}{2}$, or 1. Having still less of A and more of B at point l, the consumer is willing to give up only 1 unit of A in return for 2 more units of B and the MRS falls to $\frac{1}{2}$ between l and m.[1]

In general, as the amount of B *increases,* the marginal utility of additional units of B *decreases.* Similarly, as the quantity of A *decreases,* its marginal utility *increases.* In Figure 2 we see that in moving down the curve, the consumer will be willing to give up smaller and smaller amounts of A to offset acquiring each additional unit of B. The result is a curve with a diminishing slope, a curve that is convex to the origin. The MRS declines as one moves southeast along the indifference curve.

The Indifference Map

The single indifference curve of Figure 2 reflects some constant (but unspecified) level of total utility or satisfaction. It is possible and useful to sketch a whole series of indifference curves or an **indifference map,** as shown in Figure 3. Each curve reflects

---

[1]MRS declines continuously between j and k, k and l, and l and m. Our numerical values for MRS relate to the curve segments between points and are not the actual values of the MRS at each point. For example, the MRS at point l is $\frac{2}{3}$.

FIGURE 3 An indifference map. An indifference map is a set of indifference curves. Curves farther from the origin indicate higher levels of total utility. Thus any combination of products A and B represented by a point on I_4 has greater total utility than any combination of A and B represented by a point on I_3, I_2, or I_1.

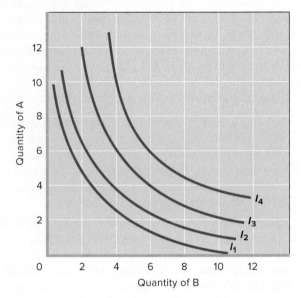

a different level of total utility and therefore never crosses another indifference curve. Specifically, each curve to the right of our original curve (labeled I_3 in Figure 3) reflects combinations of A and B that yield more utility than I_3. Each curve to the left of I_3 reflects less total utility than I_3. As we move out from the origin, each successive indifference curve represents a higher level of utility. To demonstrate this fact, draw a line in a northeasterly direction from the origin; note that its points of intersection with successive curves entail larger amounts of both A and B and therefore higher levels of total utility.

Equilibrium at Tangency

Since the axes in Figures 1 and 3 are identical, we can superimpose a budget line on the consumer's indifference map, as shown in Figure 4. By definition, the budget line indicates all the combinations of A and B that the consumer can attain with his or her money income, given the prices of A and B. Of these attainable combinations, the consumer will prefer the combination that yields the greatest satisfaction or utility. Specifically, the utility-maximizing combination will be the combination lying on the highest attainable indifference curve. It is called the consumer's **equilibrium position.**

In Figure 4 the consumer's equilibrium position is at point X, where the budget line is *tangent* to I_3. Why not point Y? Because Y is on a lower indifference curve, I_2. By moving "down" the budget line—by shifting dollars from purchases of A to purchases of B—the consumer can attain an indifference curve farther from the origin and thereby increase the

FIGURE 4 **The consumer's equilibrium position.** The consumer's equilibrium position is represented by point X, where the black budget line is tangent to indifference curve I_3. The consumer buys 4 units of A at $1.50 per unit and 6 of B at $1 per unit with a $12 money income. Points Z and Y represent attainable combinations of A and B but yield less total utility, as is evidenced by the fact that they are on lower indifference curves. Point W would entail more utility than X, but it requires a greater income than the $12 represented by the budget line.

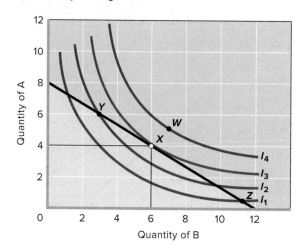

total utility derived from the same income. Why not point Z? For the same reason: Point Z is on a lower indifference curve, I_1. By moving "up" the budget line—by reallocating dollars from B to A—the consumer can get on higher indifference curve I_3 and increase total utility.

How about point W on indifference curve I_4? While it is true that W would yield a greater total utility than X, point W is beyond (outside) the budget line and hence is *not* attainable by the consumer. Point X represents the optimal *attainable* combination of products A and B. Note that at the equilibrium position, X, the definition of tangency implies that the slope of the highest attainable indifference curve equals the slope of the budget line. Because the slope of the indifference curve reflects the MRS (marginal rate of substitution) and the slope of the budget line is P_B/P_A, the consumer's optimal or equilibrium position is the point where

$$MRS = \frac{P_B}{P_A}$$

(You may benefit by trying Appendix Discussion Question 3 at this time.)

Equivalency at Equilibrium

As indicated at the beginning of this appendix, an important difference exists between the marginal-utility theory of consumer demand and the indifference curve theory. The marginal-utility theory assumes that utility is *numerically* measurable, that is, that the consumer can say how much extra utility he or she derives from each extra

unit of A or B. The consumer needs that information to determine the utility-maximizing (equilibrium) position, which is defined by

$$\frac{\text{Marginal utility of A}}{\text{Price of A}} = \frac{\text{Marginal utility of B}}{\text{Price of B}}$$

The indifference curve approach imposes a less stringent requirement on the consumer. He or she need only specify whether a particular combination of A and B will yield more than, less than, or the same amount of utility as some other combination of A and B will yield. The consumer need only say, for example, that 6 of A and 7 of B will yield more (or less) satisfaction than will 4 of A and 9 of B. Indifference curve theory does not require that the consumer specify *how much* more (or less) satisfaction will be realized.

That being said, it is a remarkable mathematical fact that both models of consumer behavior will, in any given situation, point to exactly the same consumer equilibrium and, consequently, exactly the same demand behavior. This fact allows us to combine the separate pieces of information that each theory gives us about equilibrium in order to deduce an interesting property about marginal utilities that must also hold true in equilibrium. To see this, note that when we compare the equilibrium situations in the two theories, we find that in the indifference curve analysis the MRS equals P_B/P_A at equilibrium; however, in the marginal-utility approach the ratio of marginal utilities equals P_B/P_A. We therefore deduce that at equilibrium the MRS is equivalent in the marginal-utility approach to the ratio of the marginal utilities of the last purchased units of the two products.[2]

The Derivation of the Demand Curve

We noted earlier that with a fixed price for A, an increase in the price of B will cause the bottom of the budget line to fan inward to the left. We can use that fact to derive a demand curve for product B. In Figure 5a we reproduce the part of Figure 4 that shows our initial consumer equilibrium at point X. The budget line determining this equilibrium position assumes that money income is $12 and that P_A = $1.50 and P_B = $1. Let's see what happens to the equilibrium position when we increase P_B to $1.50 and hold both money income and the price of A constant. The result is shown in Figure 5a. The budget line fans to the left, yielding a new equilibrium point X' where it is tangent to lower indifference curve I_2. At X' the consumer buys 3 units of B and 5 of A, compared with 4 of A and 6 of B at X. Our interest is in B, and we now have

---

[2]Technical footnote: If we begin with the utility-maximizing rule, $MU_A/P_A = MU_B/P_B$, and then multiply through by P_B and divide through by MU_A, we obtain $P_B/P_A = MU_B/MU_A$. In indifference curve analysis we know that at the equilibrium position $MRS = P_B/P_A$. Hence, at equilibrium, MRS also equals MU_B/MU_A.

CONSIDER THIS . . .

© Ryan McVay/Getty Images RF

Indifference Maps and Topographical Maps

The familiar topographical map may help you understand the idea of indifference curves and indifference maps. Each line on a topographical map represents a particular elevation above sea level, such as 500 feet. Similarly, an indifference curve represents a particular level of total utility. When you move from one point on a specific elevation line to another, the elevation remains the same. So it is with an indifference curve. A move from one position to another on the curve leaves total utility unchanged. Neither elevation lines nor indifference curves can intersect. If they did, the meaning of each line or curve would be violated. An elevation line is "an equal-elevation line"; an indifference curve is "an equal-total-utility curve."

Like the topographical map, an indifference map contains not just one line but a series of lines. That is, the topographical map may have elevation lines representing successively higher elevations of 100, 200, 300, 400, and 500 feet. Similarly, the indifference curves on the indifference map represent successively higher levels of total utility. The climber whose goal is to maximize elevation wants to get to the highest attainable elevation line; the consumer desiring to maximize total utility wants to get to the highest attainable indifference curve.

Finally, both topographical maps and indifference maps show only a few of the many such lines that could be drawn. The topographical map, for example, leaves out the elevation lines for 501 feet, 502, 503, and so on. The indifference map leaves out all the indifference curves that could be drawn between those that are displayed.

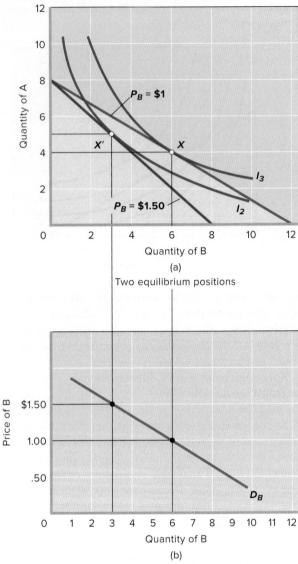

FIGURE 5 **Deriving the demand curve.** (a) When the price of product B is increased from $1 to $1.50, the equilibrium position moves from X to X', decreasing the quantity demanded of product B from 6 to 3 units. (b) The demand curve for product B is determined by plotting the $1–6-unit and the $1.50–3-unit price-quantity combinations for product B.

(a)
Two equilibrium positions

(b)
The demand curve for product B

sufficient information to locate two points on the demand curve for product B. We know that at equilibrium point X the price of B is $1 and 6 units are purchased; at equilibrium point X' the price of B is $1.50 and 3 units are purchased.

These data are shown graphically in Figure 5b as points on the consumer's demand curve for B. Note that the horizontal axes of Figures 5a and 5b are identical; both measure the quantity demanded of B. We can therefore drop vertical reference lines from Figure 5a down to the horizontal axis of Figure 5b. On the vertical axis of Figure 5b we locate the two chosen prices of B. Knowing that these prices yield the relevant quantities demanded, we locate two points on the demand curve for B. By simple manipulation of the price of B in an

indifference curve–budget line context, we have obtained a downward-sloping demand curve for B. We have thus again derived the law of demand assuming "other things equal," since only the price of B was changed (the price of A and the consumer's money income and tastes remained constant). But, in this case, we have derived the demand curve without resorting to the questionable assumption that consumers can measure utility in units called "utils." In this indifference curve approach, consumers simply compare combinations of products A and B and determine which combination they prefer, given their incomes and the prices of the two products.

APPENDIX SUMMARY

LO7.6 **Relate how the indifference curve model of consumer behavior derives demand curves from budget lines, indifference curves, and utility maximization.**

The indifference curve approach to consumer behavior is based on the consumer's budget line and indifference curves.

The budget line shows all combinations of two products that the consumer can purchase, given product prices and his or her money income. A change in either product prices or money income moves the budget line.

An indifference curve shows all combinations of two products that will yield the same total utility to a consumer. Indifference curves are downsloping and convex to the origin.

An indifference map consists of a number of indifference curves; the farther from the origin, the higher the total utility associated with a curve.

The consumer is in equilibrium (utility is maximized) at the point on the budget line that lies on the highest attainable indifference curve. At that point the budget line and indifference curve are tangent.

Changing the price of one product shifts the budget line and determines a new equilibrium point. A downsloping demand curve can be determined by plotting the price-quantity combinations associated with two or more equilibrium points.

APPENDIX TERMS AND CONCEPTS

budget line

indifference curve

marginal rate of substitution (MRS)

indifference map

equilibrium position

The following and additional problems can be found in ▪ **connect**

APPENDIX DISCUSSION QUESTIONS

1. What information is embodied in a budget line? What shifts occur in the budget line when money income (*a*) increases and (*b*) decreases? What shifts occur in the budget line when the price of the product shown on the vertical axis (*c*) increases and (*d*) decreases? **LO7.6**

2. What information is contained in an indifference curve? Why are such curves (*a*) downsloping and (*b*) convex to the origin? Why does total utility increase as the consumer moves to indifference curves farther from the origin? Why can't indifference curves intersect? **LO7.6**

3. Using Figure 4, explain why the point of tangency of the budget line with an indifference curve is the consumer's equilibrium position. Explain why any point where the budget line intersects an indifference curve is not equilibrium. Explain: "The consumer is in equilibrium where $MRS = P_B/P_A$." **LO7.6**

APPENDIX REVIEW QUESTIONS

1. Consider two bundles of coffee and chocolate and how Ted feels about them. The first bundle consists of two cups of coffee and two chocolate bars. The second bundle consists of one cup of coffee and three chocolate bars. If the first bundle gives Ted a total utility of 18 utils while the second bundle gives Ted a total utility of 19 bundles, could the two bundles be on the same indifference curve? Answer yes or no. **LO7.6**

2. Bill spends his money on flowers and cookies so as to maximize his total utility. Both flowers and cookies start off costing $2 each. At that price, Bill buys three flowers and two cookies.

When the price of flowers is lowered to $1, Bill buys eight flowers and one cookie. Which of the following statements about Bill's reaction to the price change is **not** true? **LO7.6**
   a. Bill's budget line shifted outward when the price of flowers fell.
   b. Bill moved to a higher indifference curve after the price of flowers fell.
   c. Bill's demand curve for flowers shifted to the right.
   d. Bill's attainable set was smaller before the price of flowers fell.

APPENDIX PROBLEMS

1. Assume that the data in the following table give an indifference curve for Mr. Chen. Graph this curve, putting A on the vertical axis and B on the horizontal axis. Assuming that the prices of A and B are $1.50 and $1, respectively, and that Mr. Chen has $24 to spend, add his budget line to your graph. What combination of A and B will Mr. Chen purchase? Does your answer meet the MRS $= P_B/P_A$ rule for equilibrium? **LO7.6**

Units of A	Units of B
16	6
12	8
8	12
4	24

2. Explain graphically how indifference analysis can be used to derive a demand curve. **LO7.6**

3. **ADVANCED ANALYSIS** First, graphically illustrate a doubling of income without price changes in the indifference curve model. Next, on the same graph, show a situation in which the person whose indifference curves you are drawing buys considerably more of good B than good A after the income increase. What can you conclude about the relative coefficients of the income elasticity of demand for goods A and B (Chapter 6)? **LO7.6**

Behavioral Economics

Learning Objectives

LO8.1 Define behavioral economics and explain how it contrasts with neoclassical economics.

LO8.2 Discuss the evidence for the brain being modular, computationally restricted, reliant on heuristics, and prone to various forms of cognitive error.

LO8.3 Relate how prospect theory helps to explain many consumer behaviors, including framing effects, mental accounting, anchoring, loss aversion, and the endowment effect.

LO8.4 Describe how time inconsistency and myopia cause people to make suboptimal long-run decisions.

LO8.5 Define fairness and give examples of how it affects behavior in the economy and in the dictator and ultimatum games.

Scientific theories are judged by the accuracy of their predictions. As an example, nobody would take physics seriously if it weren't possible to use the equations taught in college physics classes to predict the best trajectory for putting a satellite into orbit or the best radio frequency to penetrate buildings and provide good indoor cellular service.

Conventional **neoclassical economics** makes many accurate predictions about human choice behavior, especially when it comes to financial incentives and how consumers and businesses respond to changing prices. On the other hand, a number of neoclassical predictions fail quite dramatically. These include predictions about how people deal with risk and uncertainty; choices that require willpower or commitment; and decisions that involve fairness, reciprocity, or trust.

Behavioral economics attempts to make better predictions about human choice behavior by combining insights from economics, psychology, and biology. This chapter introduces you to behavioral economics and the areas in which it has most dramatically increased our understanding of economic behavior. Among the highlights is prospect theory, which was such a large advance on our understanding of how people deal with risk and uncertainty that its inventor, Daniel Kahneman, received the Nobel Prize in economics.

Systematic Errors and the Origin of Behavioral Economics

LO8.1 Define behavioral economics and explain how it contrasts with neoclassical economics.

We tend to think of ourselves as being very good at making decisions. While we may make a few mistakes here and there, we generally proceed through life with confidence, believing firmly that we will react sensibly and make good choices whenever decisions have to be made. In terms of economic terminology, we feel that our decisions are **rational,** meaning that they maximize our chances of achieving what we want.

Unfortunately, scientists have amassed overwhelming evidence to the contrary. People constantly make decision errors that reduce—rather than enhance—the likelihood of getting what they want. In addition, many errors are **systematic errors,** meaning that people tend to repeat them over and over, no matter how many times they encounter a similar situation.

Behavioral economics developed as a separate field of study because neoclassical economics could not explain why people make so many systematic errors. The underlying problem for neoclassical economics is that it assumes that people are fundamentally rational. Under that worldview, people might make some initial mistakes when encountering a new situation. But as they gain experience, they should learn and adapt to the situation. As a result, decision errors should be rare—and definitely not systematic or regularly repeated.

When evidence began to pile up in the late twentieth century that even highly experienced people made systematic errors, neoclassical economists assumed that people were just ignorant of what was in their best interests. They assumed that a little education would fix everything. But people often persisted in making the same error even after they were informed that they were behaving against their own interests.

As a result, several researchers realized that it would be necessary to drop the neoclassical assumption that people are fundamentally rational. With that assumption relaxed, economists could develop alternative theories that could make more accurate predictions about human behavior—including the tendency people have toward making systematic errors in certain situations. The result of those efforts is what we today refer to as behavioral economics. Its distinguishing feature is that it is based upon people's actual behavior—which is in many cases substantially irrational, prone to systematic errors, and difficult to modify.

Comparing Behavioral Economics with Neoclassical Economics

While rationality is the most fundamental point of disagreement between behavioral economics and neoclassical economics, it is not the only one. Behavioral economics also contends that neoclassical economics makes a number of highly unrealistic assumptions about human capabilities and motivations, including

- People have stable preferences that aren't affected by context.
- People are eager and accurate calculating machines.
- People are good planners who possess plenty of willpower.
- People are almost entirely selfish and self-interested.

Neoclassical economics made these "simplifying assumptions" for two main reasons. First, they render neoclassical models of human behavior both mathematically elegant and easy enough to solve. Second, they enable neoclassical models to generate very precise predictions about human behavior.

Unfortunately, precision is not the same thing as accuracy. As noted behavioral economist Richard Thaler has written, "Would you rather be elegant and precisely wrong—or messy and vaguely right?"

Behavioral economists err on the side of being messy and vaguely right. As a result, behavioral economics replaces the simplifying assumptions made by neoclassical economics with much more realistic and complex models of human capabilities, motivations, and mental processes.

Table 8.1 summarizes how the two approaches differ in several areas.

Focusing on the Mental Processes behind Decisions

Another major difference between behavioral economics and neoclassical economics is in the amount of weight and importance that they attach to predicting decisions on the one hand and in understanding the mental processes used to reach those decisions on the other. While neoclassical economics focuses almost entirely on predicting behavior, behavioral economics puts significant emphasis on the mental processes driving behavior.

Neoclassical economics focuses its attention on prediction because its assumption that people are rational allows it to fully separate what people do from how they do it. In particular, perfectly rational people will always choose the course of action that will maximize the likelihood of getting what they want. How they actually come to those optimal decisions might be interesting—but you don't need to know anything about that process to predict a perfectly rational person's behavior. He will simply end up doing whatever it is that will best advance his interests. Consequently, neoclassical economists have felt free to ignore the underlying mental processes by which people make decisions.

Behavioral economists disagree sharply with the neoclassical neglect of mental processes. To them, the fact that people are not perfectly rational implies two important reasons

TABLE 8.1 **Major Differences between Behavioral Economics and Conventional Neoclassical Economics**

Topic	Neoclassical Economics	Behavioral Economics
Rationality	People are fundamentally rational and will adjust their choices and behaviors to best achieve their goals. Consequently, they will not make systematic errors.	People are irrational and make many errors that reduce their chances of achieving their goals. Some errors are regularly repeated systematic errors.
Stability of preferences	People's preferences are completely stable and unaffected by context.	People's preferences are unstable and often inconsistent because they depend on context (framing effects).
Capability for making mental calculations	People are eager and accurate calculators.	People are bad at math and avoid difficult computations if possible.
Ability to assess future options and possibilities	People are just as good at assessing future options as current options.	People place insufficient weight on future events and outcomes.
Strength of willpower	People have no trouble resisting temptation.	People lack sufficient willpower and often fall prey to temptation.
Degree of selfishness	People are almost entirely self-interested and self-centered.	People are often selfless and generous.
Fairness	People do not care about fairness and only treat others well if doing so will get them something they want.	Many people care deeply about fairness and will often give to others even when doing so will yield no personal benefits.

for understanding the underlying mental processes that determine decisions:

- It should allow us to make better predictions about behavior.

- It should provide guidance about how to get people to make better decisions.

Improving Outcomes by Improving Decision Making

Neoclassical economics and behavioral economics differ on how to improve human welfare. Neoclassical economics focuses its attention on providing people with more options. That's because a fully rational person can be trusted to select from any set of options the one that will make him best off. As a result, the only way to make him even happier would be to provide an additional option that is even better.

By contrast, the existence of irrationality leads behavioral economists to conclude that it may be possible to make people better off without providing additional options. In particular, improvements in utility and happiness may be possible simply by getting people to make better selections from the set of options that is already available to them.

This focus on improving outcomes by improving decisions is one of the distinguishing characteristics of behavioral economics. This chapter's Last Word reviews several instances where substantial benefits arise from helping people to make better choices from among the options that they already have.

Viewing Behavioral Economics and Neoclassical Economics as Complements

It would be hasty to view behavioral economics and neoclassical economics as fundamentally opposed or mutually exclusive. Instead, many economists prefer to think of them as complementary approaches

that can be used in conjunction to help improve our understanding of human behavior.

As an example of their complementary nature, consider how using the two approaches in tandem can help us achieve a better understanding of how customers behave at a local supermarket.

Neoclassical Economics at the Supermarket The major neoclassical contribution to our understanding of the customers' shopping behavior can be summarized by the phrase "incentives matter." In particular, the customers will care a great deal about prices. When prices go up, they buy less. When prices go down, they buy more.

That insight goes a long way toward explaining how customers behave. But there are other shopping behaviors that neoclassical economics cannot explain with its emphasis on people reacting rationally to incentives and prices. In those cases, behavioral economics may be able to help us figure out what people are up to.

Behavioral Economics at the Supermarket A good example of a shopping behavior that neoclassical economics can't explain very well is that people tend to buy what they happen to see. This behavior is called *impulse buying* and it contradicts the neoclassical assumption that consumers carefully calculate marginal utilities and compare prices before making their purchases. On the other hand, it is a very common behavior that is regularly exploited by retailers.

For instance, nearly all supermarkets attempt to take advantage of impulse buying by placing staple products like milk and eggs against the back walls of their stores. Placing those products at the rear increases impulse buying by forcing customers to walk past hundreds of other items on the way to

CONSIDER THIS . . .

Source: Library of Congress, Prints & Photographs Division, Reproduction number LC-DIG-ggbain-04978 (digital file from original neg.)

Wannamaker's Lament

Marketing experts try to increase sales or launch new products by applying what they think they know about consumer behavior. Many people find those efforts spooky and wonder if they are being constantly manipulated into purchasing products that they don't want. But how much do the marketing experts really know?

Judging by their success rate, not so much. Most advertising campaigns show little effect on sales. Eighty percent of newly launched consumer products fail within just three months. And the vast majority of Hollywood films end up as flops despite studios spending billions of dollars each year on market research and advertising.

The difficulties facing marketers were best described in the late nineteenth century by John Wannamaker, the marketing genius and department store entrepreneur who, among other things, invented the price tag and the money-back guarantee. He famously complained, "Half the money I spend on advertising is wasted—the trouble is, I don't know which half!"

A recent response to Wannamaker's lament has been to run lots of simple experiments to see if anything at all can increase sales. Amazon.com runs hundreds of experiments per month, systematically showing different groups of customers different versions of its website in order to see if any of those different versions can increase sales. Las Vegas casinos also run experiments, systematically varying the scents injected into their air-conditioning systems to see which ones cause the largest increases in gambling. Vanilla apparently works very well and some scents are said to increase revenues by up to 20 percent.

the milk and eggs. A few of those items will catch their eyes and thereby increase sales as customers end up purchasing products that they had no intention of buying when they first entered the store.

Marketers also know that impulse purchases are highest for items that are stacked on shelves at eye level. So, believe it or not, food manufacturers actively bid against each other and pay supermarkets for the privilege of having their brands stacked at eye level. In cereal aisles, the most expensive shelf space isn't at eye level for an adult, but a foot or two lower—at the eye level of a toddler sitting in a shopping cart or of a child walking with a parent. Because kids are even more prone to impulse buying than adults, cereal makers are more

than happy to pay to have their products stacked at kid-friendly eye levels.

Complementary Explanations at the Supermarket Behavioral economics explains impulse buying and other irrational behaviors as the result of a wide variety of underlying factors, including cognitive biases, heuristics, and ongoing battles between different areas of the brain.

You will learn about these underlying factors in the remainder of this chapter. But for now, take to heart the idea that we typically need both neoclassical *and* behavioral methods to figure out what people are doing. Some behaviors—including the fact that shoppers respond strongly to incentives and prices—can be explained very well by neoclassical models that assume people are perfectly rational. But other behaviors—including impulse buying—are very much inconsistent with rationality and are therefore better explained by using the methods of behavioral economics.

Our Efficient, Error-Prone Brains

LO8.2 Discuss the evidence for the brain being modular, computationally restricted, reliant on heuristics, and prone to various forms of cognitive error.

The human brain is the most complex object in the universe. One hundred billion neurons share 10,000 times as many connections. Working together, they allow you to observe your environment, think creatively, and interact with people and objects.

The brain, however, is rather error-prone. Its many weaknesses are most dramatically illustrated by visual illusions, such as the one shown in Figure 8.1. If you follow the

FIGURE 8.1 A visual illusion. The human brain uses a large number of heuristics (shortcuts) to process both visual and other types of information. Many of them utilize context to interpret specific bits of information. When that context changes (as it does here when you put your finger horizontally across the middle of the image), so does the brain's heuristic-filtered interpretation.

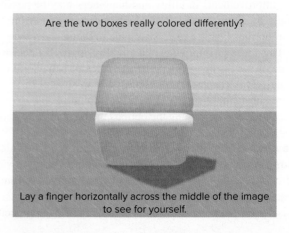

Are the two boxes really colored differently?

Lay a finger horizontally across the middle of the image to see for yourself.

instructions printed in that figure, you will quickly discover that your brain can't consistently tell what color an object is.

This inability to properly process visual information is especially informative about the brain's limitations because the brain devotes more neurons toward processing and interpreting visual information than it does anything else. So, if the brain makes errors with visual processing, we should expect to find errors in everything else it does, too.

Heuristics Are Energy Savers

The brain's information-processing limitations are the result of evolutionary pressures. In particular, it was normally very difficult for our ancestors to get enough food to eat. That matters because our brains are extremely energy intensive. In fact, while your brain accounts for just 5 percent of your body weight, it burns 20 percent of all the energy you consume each day. So back when our ancestors had to hunt and gather and scavenge to survive, getting enough energy was a constant challenge.

In response, the brain evolved many low-energy mental shortcuts, or **heuristics.** Because they are shortcuts, heuristics are not the most accurate mental-processing options. But in a world where calories were hard to come by, a low-energy "good enough" heuristic was superior to a "perfect but costly" alternative.

Your brain's susceptibility to the visual-processing failure demonstrated in Figure 8.1 is the result of your brain using a host of error-prone heuristics to process visual information. But think about what a good trade-off you are getting. In everyday life, the visual-processing failure demonstrated in Figure 8.1 hardly ever comes up. So, it would be a waste of resources to devote more brainpower to fixing the issue. Put in economic terms, there are diminishing returns to employing additional units of brainpower. Heuristics are used because the opportunity cost of perfection is too high.

Some Common Heuristics The following examples will give you a sense of how the brain employs heuristics for nearly every type of action and decision we make.

Catching a Baseball with the Gaze Heuristic Consider the problem faced by a centerfielder in a baseball game when a ball is hit in his general direction. The mentally expensive way to catch the ball would be for the player to use the laws of physics to determine where the ball is heading so that he could run to that spot before the ball arrives.

What baseball players actually do is lock their eyes on the ball and then adjust their position on the field as necessary to keep the ball in front of them and at the same angle as when they first locked their eyes on it. Just as long as they can run fast enough, this *gaze heuristic* always gets them to the correct place to make the catch. You don't need to learn physics to catch a baseball!

Riding a Bicycle with the Steering Heuristic There is a simple heuristic for staying upright as you ride a bicycle: if you begin to fall, steer in the direction you are falling. This *steering heuristic* works because turning in the direction of a fall generates a centrifugal force that can be used to hold you up long enough for you to steady the bike. This heuristic is almost never articulated, but it is precisely what little kids subconsciously learn to do when they are using training wheels.

Guesstimating Ranks with the Recognition Heuristic Which German city has the larger population, Munich or Stuttgart?

Even people who know nothing about Germany tend to get the right answer to this question. They correctly guess "Munich" by employing the *recognition heuristic,* which says to assume that if one option is more easily recognized, it is probably more important or more highly ranked.

The recognition heuristic isn't foolproof, but it tends to work because relatively important people and places are much more likely to be mentioned in the media. Thus, whichever option is easier to recognize will probably be larger or more important.

Much of advertising is based on exploiting the recognition heuristic. Indeed, companies spend billions to ensure that consumers are familiar with their products because when it comes time to buy, consumers will be biased toward the products that seem the most familiar.

Interpreting Depth with the Shadow Heuristic The world is three-dimensional, but the light-sensing surfaces at the back of our eyes are two-dimensional. As a result, our brains are forced to use a cluster of heuristics to estimate depth when interpreting the two-dimensional images registered by our eyes.

Figure 8.2 shows how the *shadow heuristic* causes you to interpret shaded, two-dimensional circles as either humps or holes depending upon whether each circle is shaded on the top or on the bottom. Look at Figure 8.2 and count how many of the six shaded circles look like humps rather than holes. Now turn the picture upside down and count again. If your vision is typical, you will find that all the humps have become holes, and vice versa.

Here's what's happening. The shadow heuristic evolved back when sunlight was the only important source of light. As a result, it presumes that light always falls from above. Under that assumption, anything that sticks out from a surface will cast a shadow below it while anything indented will have a shadow on top due to the top of the recessed area casting a shadow on whatever lies below. Because your brain applies the shadow heuristic no matter what, you are tricked into believing that the shaded circles in Figure 8.2 are three-dimensional and either humps or holes depending upon whether they are shaded on the top or on the bottom.

FIGURE 8.2 **The shadow heuristic.** The brain processes light with a heuristic that assumes that light always comes from above. Under that assumption, anything that sticks out will have a shadow on the bottom while anything that is recessed will have a shadow on top. As a result, your brain interprets five of the six shaded circles as humps that stick out while the bottom middle circle is interpreted as a recess. See what happens when you turn the picture upside down. Surprised?

The Implications of Hardwired Heuristics

As you study the rest of the chapter, keep in mind that most heuristics appear to be hardwired into the brain, and, consequently, impossible to unlearn or avoid. That possibility has three important implications:

1. It may be very difficult for people to alter detrimental behaviors or routines even after you point out what they're doing wrong.

2. People may be easy prey for those who understand their hardwired tendencies.

3. If you want people to make a positive behavioral change, it might be helpful to see if you can put them in a situation where a heuristic will kick in and subconsciously lead them toward the desired outcome.

Brain Modularity

The modern human brain is modular, so that specific areas deal with specific sensations, activities, and emotions—such as vision, breathing, and anger.

This modular structure is the result of millions of years of evolution, with the modern human brain evolving in stages from the much less complex brains of our hominid ancestors. The oldest parts of the brain are located in the back of the head, where the spine enters the skull. The newest parts are up front, near the forehead.

The older parts control subconscious activities like breathing and sweating as well as automatic emotional reactions such as fear and joy. The newer parts allow you to think creatively, imagine the future, and keep track of everyone in your social network. They are largely under conscious control.

System 1 and System 2

It is useful to think of the brain's decision-making systems as falling into two categories, which are informally referred to as System 1 and System 2. System 1 uses a lot of heuristics in the older parts of your brain to produce quick, unconscious reactions. If you ever get a "gut instinct," System 1 is responsible. By contrast, System 2 uses the newer parts of your brain to undertake slow, deliberate, and conscious calculations of costs and benefits. If you ever find yourself "thinking things over," you are using System 2.

Conflicts may sometimes arise between our unconscious System 1 intuitions and our conscious System 2 deliberations. For example, System 1 may urge you to eat an entire pile of cookies as fast as possible, while System 2 admonishes you to stick to your diet and have only one. That being said, a large body of evidence suggests that most decisions are probably either fully or mostly the result of System 1 intuitions and heuristics. That matters because those unconscious mental processes suffer from a variety of cognitive biases.

Cognitive Biases

Cognitive biases are the misperceptions or misunderstandings that cause systematic errors.

There are a wide variety of cognitive biases, but they can be placed into two general categories. The first are mental-processing errors that result from faulty heuristics. As previously discussed, faulty heuristics are the result of evolution trading off accuracy for speed and efficiency.

The second category of cognitive biases consists of mental-processing errors that result from our brains not having any evolved capacities for dealing with modern problems and challenges, such as solving calculus problems or programming computers. Because our ancestors never encountered things like math, engineering, or statistics, our brains have a total absence of System 1 heuristics for dealing with those sorts of problems. In addition, our slower and more deliberative System 2 mental processes are also of only limited assistance because they were evolved to deal with other types of problems, such as keeping track of everyone in a social network or attempting to think through whether it would be better to go hunting in the morning or in the evening.

As a result, most people find recently developed mental challenges like math and physics to be very tiresome. In addition, cognitive biases often result because the System 2 processes that we are recruiting to solve modern problems were in fact designed for other purposes and don't work particularly well when directed at modern problems.

Psychologists have identified scores of cognitive biases. Here are a few that are relevant to economics and decision making.

Confirmation Bias

The term *confirmation bias* refers to the human tendency to pay attention only to information that agrees with one's preconceptions. Information that contradicts those preconceptions is either ignored completely or rationalized away. Confirmation bias is problematic because it allows bad decisions to continue long after an impartial weighing of the evidence would have put a stop to them. When you see someone persisting with a failed policy or incorrect opinion despite overwhelming evidence that he or she should try something else, confirmation bias is probably at work.

Self-Serving Bias The term *self-serving bias* refers to people's tendency to attribute their successes to personal effort or personal character traits while at the same time attributing any failures to factors that were out of their control. While helping to preserve people's self-esteem, this bias makes it difficult for people to learn from their mistakes because they incorrectly assume that anything that went wrong was beyond their control.

Overconfidence Effect The *overconfidence effect* refers to people's tendency to be overly confident about how likely their judgments and opinions are to be correct. As an example, people who rated their answers to a particular quiz as being "99 percent likely to be right" were in fact wrong more than 40 percent of the time. Such overconfidence can lead to bad decisions because people will tend to take actions without pausing to verify if their initial hunches are actually true.

Hindsight Bias People engage in *hindsight bias* when they retroactively believe that they were able to predict past events. As an example, consider an election between candidates named Terence and Philip. Before the election happens, many people will predict that Terence will lose. But after Terence ends up winning, many of those same people will convince themselves that they "knew all along" that Terence was going to win. This faulty "I-knew-it-all-along" perspective causes people to massively overestimate their predictive abilities.

Availability Heuristic The *availability heuristic* causes people to base their estimates about the likelihood of an event not on objective facts but on whether or not similar events come to mind quickly and are readily available in their memories. Because vivid, emotionally charged images come to mind more easily, people tend to think that events like homicides, shark attacks, and lightning strikes are much more common than they actually are. At the same time, they underestimate the likelihood of unmemorable events.

As an example, you are five times more likely to die of stomach cancer than be murdered, but most people rate the likelihood of being murdered as much higher. They do this because they have many vivid memories of both real and fictional murders but almost no recollections whatsoever of anyone dying of stomach cancer.

The availability heuristic causes people to spend too much of their time and effort attempting to protect themselves against charismatic dangers of low actual probability while neglecting to protect themselves against dull threats of substantially higher probability.

Planning Fallacy The *planning fallacy* is the tendency people have to massively underestimate the time needed to complete a task. A good example is when last-minute test cramming gets really frantic. The student doing the cramming probably underestimated by many hours how much time he needed to prepare for the exam. The planning fallacy also helps to explain why construction projects, business initiatives, and government reform efforts all tend to come in substantially behind schedule.

Framing Effects **Framing effects** occur when a change in context (frame) causes people to react differently to a particular piece of information or to an otherwise identical situation.

Figure 8.3 gives an example of a framing effect. The middle symbol is identical in both rows, but it is interpreted differently depending upon whether it is surrounded by letters or numbers. When surrounded by letters in the top row, the brain tends to interpret the symbol as the letter B. When surrounded by numbers in the bottom row, the brain tends to interpret the symbol as the number 13.

Changes in context can also cause extraordinary changes in behavior. Experiments have shown that ordinary people are twice as likely to litter, steal, or trespass if experimenters tag an area with graffiti and scatter lots of trash around. By changing the area's appearance from neat and orderly to run-down and chaotic, experimenters got ordinary people to subconsciously choose to engage in more crime.

Framing effects can also cause consumers to change their purchases. At the local supermarket, apples command a higher price if each one comes with a pretty sticker and meat

FIGURE 8.3 The letter illusion is the result of a framing effect. In each row, the middle symbol is the same. When that symbol is surrounded by the letters A and C in the top row, our brains tend to register the symbol as the letter B. But when it is surrounded by the numbers 12 and 14 in the bottom row, our brains tend to register it as the number 13. What our brain "sees" is largely a matter of context (frame).

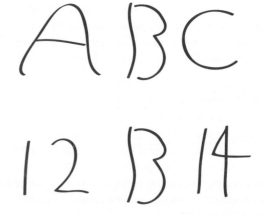

sells faster if it is packaged in shiny plastic containers. At a high-end retailer, expensive packaging increases the perceived value of the shop's merchandise. So does having a nice physical space in which to shop. Thus, high-end retailers spend a lot on architecture and displays.

Prospect Theory

LO8.3 Relate how prospect theory helps to explain many consumer behaviors, including framing effects, mental accounting, anchoring, loss aversion, and the endowment effect.
Neoclassical economics focuses much of its attention on consumer-choice situations in which people only have to deal with "goods" as opposed to "bads." When deciding on how to spend a budget, a consumer considers only items that would bring her positive marginal utility—that is, "good" things. She then uses the utility-maximizing rule to select how much of each of those good things she should consume to get as much utility as possible from her limited budget.

Unfortunately, life often forces us to deal with bad things, too. Our houses may burn down. A potential investment may go bad. The money we lend out may not be repaid.

How people cope with negative possibilities is a central focus of behavioral economics. Many thousands of observations have been cataloged as to how people actually deal with the prospect of bad things as well as good things. Three very interesting facts summarize how people deal with goods and bads:

- People judge good things and bad things in relative terms, as gains and losses relative to their current situation, or **status quo.**
- People experience both diminishing marginal utility for gains (meaning that each successive unit of gain feels good, but not as good as the previous unit) as well as diminishing marginal disutility for losses (meaning that each successive unit of loss hurts, but less painfully than the previous unit).

- People experience **loss aversion,** meaning that for losses and gains near the status quo, losses are felt *much* more intensely than gains—in fact, about 2.5 times more intensely. Thus, for instance, the pain experienced by an investor who loses one dollar from his status quo level of wealth will be about 2.5 times more intense than the pleasure he would have felt if he had gained one dollar relative to his status quo level of wealth.

These three facts about how people deal with goods and bads form the basis of **prospect theory,** which sheds important light on how consumers plan for and deal with life's ups and downs as well as why they often appear narrow-minded and

---

CONSIDER THIS . . .

Source: © Stewart Cohen/Stockbyte/Getty Images RF

Rising Consumption and the Hedonic Treadmill

For many sensations, people's brains are wired to notice changes rather than states. For example, your brain can sense acceleration—your change in speed—but not speed itself. As a result, standing still feels the same as moving at a constant 50 miles per hour. And if you accelerate from one constant speed to another—say, from 50 miles per hour to 70 miles per hour—you will feel the acceleration only while it's happening. Once you settle down at the new higher speed, it will feel like you are standing still again.

Consumption appears to work in much the same way. If you are used to a given level of consumption—say, $50,000 per year—then you will get a lot of enjoyment for a while if your consumption accelerates to $100,000 per year. But, as time passes, you will get used to that higher level of consumption, so that $100,000 per year seems ordinary and doesn't bring you any more pleasure than $50,000 per year used to bring you when it was your status quo.

Economist Richard Easterlin coined the term *hedonic treadmill* (pleasure treadmill) to describe this phenomenon. Just as a person walking on a real treadmill gets nowhere, people trying to make themselves permanently happier by consuming more also get nowhere because they end up getting used to any higher level of consumption. Indeed, except for the extremely poor, people across the income spectrum report similar levels of happiness and satisfaction with their lives. This has led several economists, including Robert Frank, to argue that we should all stop trying to consume more because doing so doesn't make us any happier in the long run. What do you think? Should we all step off of the hedonic treadmill?

fail to "see the big picture." To give you an idea of how powerful prospect theory is—and why its pioneer, Daniel Kahneman, was awarded the Nobel Prize in Economics—let's go through some examples of consumer behavior that would be hard to explain without the insights provided by prospect theory.

Losses and Shrinking Packages

Because people see the world in terms of gains and losses relative to the status quo situations that they are used to, businesses have to be very careful about increasing the prices they charge for their products. This is because once consumers become used to a given price, they will view any increase in the price as a loss relative to the status quo price they had been accustomed to.

The fact that consumers may view a price increase as a loss explains the otherwise curious fact that many food producers react to rising input costs by shrinking the sizes of their products. The company most famous for doing this is Hershey's chocolates. During its first decades of operation about 100 years ago, it would always charge exactly 5 cents for one of its Hershey's chocolate bars. But the size of the bars would increase or decrease depending on the cost of the company's inputs. When the cost of raw materials rose, the company would keep the price fixed at 5 cents but decrease the size of the bar. When the cost of raw materials fell, it would again keep the price fixed at 5 cents but increase the size of the bar.

This seems rather bizarre when you consider that consumers were not in any way *actually* being shielded from the changes in input prices. That is because what should rationally matter to consumers is the price per ounce that they are paying for Hershey's Bars. And that *does* go up and down when the price remains fixed but the size of the bars changes.

But people aren't being fully rational here. They mentally fixate on the product's price because that is the characteristic that they are used to focusing on when making their purchasing decisions. And because the 5-cent price had become the status quo that they were used to, Hershey's understood that any price increase would be mentally categorized as a loss. Thus, Hershey's wisely chose to keep the price of its product fixed at 5 cents even when input prices were rising.

Other companies employ the same strategy today. In the years following the 2007–2008 recession, the prices of many raw materials, including sugar, soybeans, and corn, rose substantially. Many major manufacturers reacted by reducing product sizes while keeping prices fixed. Häagen-Dazs reduced the size of its supermarket ice cream tubs from 16 to 14 ounces. Kraft reduced the number of slices of cheese in a package of Kraft Singles from 24 to 22 slices. A bottle of Tropicana orange juice shrank from 64 ounces (the traditional half-gallon size) to just 59 ounces. And Procter & Gamble reduced the size of Bounty paper towel rolls from 60 to 52 sheets.

Framing Effects and Advertising

Because people evaluate situations in terms of gains and losses, their decision making can be very sensitive to the mental frame that they use to evaluate whether a possible outcome should be viewed as a gain or a loss. Here are a couple of examples in which differences in the context or "frame" change the perception of whether a situation should be treated as a gain or loss. See how you react to them.

- Would you be happy with a salary of $100,000 per year? You might say yes. But what if your salary last year had been $140,000? Are you still going to say yes? Now that you know you are taking a $40,000 pay cut, does that $100,000 salary seem as good as it did before?

- Similarly, suppose you have a part-time job. One day, your boss Joe walks in and says that he is going to give you a 10 percent raise. Would that please you? Now, what if he also mentioned that *everyone else* at your firm would be getting a 15 percent raise. Are you still going to be just as pleased? Or does your raise now seem like a loss compared to what everyone else will be getting?

Prospect theory takes into account the fact that people's preferences can change drastically depending on whether contextual information causes them to define a situation as a gain or a loss. These framing effects are important to recognize because they can be manipulated by advertisers, lawyers, and politicians to try to alter people's decisions. For instance, would an advertising company be better off marketing a particular brand of hamburger as "20% fat" or as "80% lean"? Both phrases describe the same meat, but one frames the situation as a loss (20 percent fat) while the other frames it as a gain (80 percent lean).

And would you be more willing to take a particular medicine if you were told that 99.9 percent of the people who take it live or if you were told that 0.1 percent of the people who take it die? Continuing to live is a gain, whereas dying is clearly a loss. Which frame sounds better to you?

Framing effects have major consequences for consumer behavior because any frame that alters whether consumers consider a situation to be a gain or a loss *will* affect their consumption decisions!

Anchoring and Credit Card Bills

Before people can calculate their gains and losses, they must first define the status quo from which to measure those changes. But it turns out that irrelevant information can unconsciously influence people's feelings about the status quo. Here's a striking example. Find a group of people and ask each person to write down the last two digits of his or her Social Security number. Then ask each person to write down his or her best estimate of the value of some object that you display to them—say, a nice wireless keyboard. What you will find is that the people whose Social Security numbers end in higher numbers—say, 67 or 89—will give higher estimates for the value of the keyboard than people whose Social Security numbers end in smaller numbers like 18 or 37. The effect can be huge. Among students in one MBA class at MIT, those with Social Security numbers ending between 80 and 99 gave an average estimate of $56 for a wireless keyboard, while their classmates whose Social Security numbers ended between 00 and 20 gave an average estimate of just $16.

Psychologists and behavioral economists refer to this phenomenon as **anchoring** because people's estimates about the value of the keyboard are influenced, or "anchored," by the recently considered information about the last two digits of their Social Security numbers. Why irrelevant information can anchor subsequent valuations is not fully understood. But the anchoring effect is real and can lead people to unconsciously alter how they evaluate different options.

Unfortunately, credit card companies have figured this out. They use anchoring to increase their profits by showing very small minimum-payment amounts on borrowers' monthly credit card statements. The companies could require larger minimum payments, but the minimum-payment numbers that they present are only typically about 2 percent of what a customer owes. Why such a small amount? Because it acts as an anchor that causes people to unconsciously make smaller payments each month. This can make a huge difference in how long it takes to pay off their bill and how much in total interest they will end up paying. For a customer who owes $1,000 on a credit card that charges the typical interest rate of 19 percent per year, it will take 22 years and $3,398.12 in total payments (including accumulated interest) to pay off the debt if he only makes 2 percent monthly payments. By showing such small minimum-payment amounts, credit card companies anchor many customers into the expensive habit of paying off their debts slowly rather than quickly.

Mental Accounting and Overpriced Warranties

The utility-maximizing rule (Chapter 7) assumes that people will look at all of their potential consumption options simultaneously when trying to maximize the total utility that they can get from spending their limited incomes. But economist Richard Thaler famously noted that people sometimes look at consumption options in isolation, thereby irrationally failing to look at all their options simultaneously. Thaler coined the term **mental accounting** to describe this behavior because it was as if people arbitrarily put certain options into totally separate "mental accounts" that they dealt with without any thought to options outside of those accounts.

As an example of where this suboptimal tendency leads, consider the extended warranties offered by big electronic stores whenever customers purchase expensive products like plasma TVs. These warranties are very much overpriced given that the products they insure hardly ever break down. Personal financial experts universally tell people not to buy them. Yet many people do buy them because they engage in mental accounting.

They do this by mentally labeling their purchase of the TV as an isolated, individual transaction, sticking it into a separate mental account in their brain that might have a title like "Purchase of New TV." Viewing the purchase in isolation exaggerates the size of the potential loss that would come from a broken TV. Customers who view the transaction in isolation see the possibility of a $1,000 loss on their $1,000 purchase as a potential total loss—"Holy cow! I could lose $1,000 on a $1,000 TV!" By contrast, people who can see the big picture are able to compare the potential $1,000 loss with the much larger value of their entire future income stream. That allows them to realize that the potential loss is relatively minor—and thus not a good enough reason to purchase an expensive warranty.

The Endowment Effect and Market Transactions

Prospect theory also offers an explanation for the **endowment effect,** which is the tendency that people have to put a higher valuation on anything that they currently possess (are endowed with) than on identical items that they do not own but might purchase. For instance, if we show a person a new coffee mug and ask him what the maximum amount is that he would pay to buy it, he might say $10. But if we then give the mug to him so that he now owns it, and we then ask how much we would have to pay him to buy it back, he will very likely report a much higher value—say, $15.

The interesting thing is that he is not just bluffing or driving a hard bargain. Rather, the human brain appears wired to put a higher value on things we own than on things we don't. Economist John List has shown that this tendency can moderate if people are used to buying things for resale—that is, buying them with the intention of getting rid of them. But without such experience, the endowment effect can be quite strong. If it is, it can make market transactions between buyers and sellers harder because sellers will be demanding higher prices for the items they are selling ("Hey, *my* mug is worth $15 to me!") than the values put on those items by potential buyers ("Dude, *your* mug is only worth $10 to me").

Several researchers have suggested that loss aversion may be responsible for the endowment effect and the higher values demanded by sellers. They argue that once a person possesses something, the thought of parting with it seems like a potential loss. As a result, the person will demand a lot of money as compensation if he or she is asked to sell the item. On the other hand, potential purchasers do not feel any potential sense of loss, so they end up assigning lower values to the same items.

GLOBAL PERSPECTIVE 8.1

Percent of Population Consenting to Be Organ Donors

People tend to stick with whatever option is presented as the default option. Thus, the seven countries with high percentages consenting to be organ donors have organ-donation programs in which the default option is participation. By contrast, the four countries with low percentages consenting to be organ donors have organ-donation programs where the default option is *not* participating.

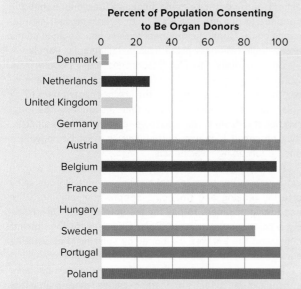

Percent of Population Consenting to Be Organ Donors

Source: Eric Johnson and Daniel Goldstein, "Defaults and Donation Decisions," *Transplantation* 78, no. 12, December 27, 2004. Used by permission of Wolters Kluwer Health via Copyright Clearance Center.

Status Quo Bias

Prospect theory also explains **status quo bias,** which is the tendency that people have to favor any option that is presented to them as being the default (status quo) option. As an example, consider Global Perspective 8.1. It shows, for a selection of European countries, the percentages of their respective populations that have indicated their willingness to participate in organ-donation programs.

As you can see, seven of the 11 countries have very high participation rates while the other four have low participation rates. You might suspect that cultural differences are at play, but that doesn't make sense when you note that countries like Germany and Austria that are culturally very similar still have massively different participation rates.

What is actually going on is a difference in the default option that people are presented with when they are asked whether they wish to participate. In the seven countries with high participation rates, the default option is participation, so

that those who don't want to participate must explicitly check off a box indicating that they don't want to participate. By contrast, in the four countries with low participation rates, the default option is *not* participating, so that those wishing to participate must explicitly check off a box indicating that they want to participate.

What we see in all countries is that nearly everyone chooses to do nothing. They almost never check off the box that would indicate doing the opposite of the default option. Consequently, they end up agreeing to whatever the default option happens to be. Thus, the huge differences in participation rates among the 11 countries are driven almost entirely by what the default option happens to be.

Prospect theory explains this and other examples of status quo bias as a combination of the endowment effect and loss aversion. When people are put into a novel situation, they have no preexisting preferences for any of the options. As a result, the way the options are framed becomes very important because if any of them is presented as the default option, people will tend to treat it as an endowment that they wish to hold on to. At the same time, they will treat any other option as a prospect that could potentially cause a loss. Loss aversion then kicks in and causes most people to stick with the default option in order to avoid the possibility of incurring a loss. The result is a bias toward the status quo.

Status quo bias can be used to explain several consumer behaviors. Consider brand loyalty. If you have gotten used to eating Heinz ketchup, then status quo bias will make you reluctant to purchase any other brand of ketchup. Overcoming that feeling of potential loss is a difficult challenge for competing brands, as attested to by the fact that rivals seeking to challenge an established brand are often forced to resort to deep discounts or free samples to get consumers to even try their products.

Myopia and Time Inconsistency

LO8.4 Describe how time inconsistency and myopia cause people to make suboptimal long-run decisions.

Our ancient ancestors had little cause to spend much time worrying about anything that would happen in the distant future. Infectious diseases, predatory animals, and the constant threat of starvation made life extremely precarious. Consequently, they had to be almost entirely focused on the present moment and how to get through the next few weeks or the next few months.

Today, however, people living in industrialized countries only rarely die from infectious diseases, mostly see predatory animals in zoos, and are under no threat at all of starvation. Living past 80 is now routine and most of us will die of old age. As a result, long-run challenges like planning for retirement and saving for college are now common tasks that nearly everyone faces.

Unfortunately, our brains were designed for our ancestors' more immediate concerns. Thus, we often have difficulty with long-run planning and decisions that involve trade-offs between the present and the future. Two of the major stumbling blocks are myopia and time inconsistency.

Myopia

In biology, myopia, or nearsightedness, refers to a defect of the eye that makes distant objects appear fuzzy, out of focus, and hard to see. By analogy, economists use the word **myopia** to describe the fact that our brains have a hard time conceptualizing the future. Compared with the present, the future seems fuzzy, out of focus, and hard to see.

As an example, our brains are very good at weighing current benefits against current costs in order to make immediate decisions. But our brains almost seem "future blind" when it comes to conceptualizing either future costs or future benefits. As a result, we have difficulty evaluating possibilities that will occur more than a few weeks or months into the future.

The primary consequence of myopia is that when people are forced to choose between something that will generate benefits quickly and something that won't yield benefits for a long time, they will have a very strong tendency to favor the more immediate option. As an example, imagine that Terence has $1,000 that he can either spend on a vacation next month or save for his retirement in 30 years.

Myopia will cause him to have great difficulty imagining the additional spending power that he will be able to enjoy in 30 years if he saves the money. On the other hand, it is very easy for him to imagine all the fun he could have next month if he were to go on vacation. As a result, he will be strongly biased toward spending the money next month. With myopia obscuring the benefits of the long-term option, the short-term option will seem much more attractive.

Myopia also makes it hard to stick with a diet or follow an exercise plan. Compared with the immediate and clearly visible pleasures of eating doughnuts or hanging out, the future benefits from eating better or exercising consistently are just too hazy in most people's minds to be very attractive.

Time Inconsistency

Time inconsistency is the tendency to systematically misjudge at the present time what you will want to do at some future time. This misperception causes a disconnect between what you currently think you will want to do at some particular point in the future and what you actually end up wanting to do when that moment arrives. It is as though your present self does not understand what your future self will want.

Waking up early is a good example. At 8 p.m. on a Tuesday, you may really like the idea of waking up early the next morning so that you can exercise before starting the rest of your day. So you set your alarm 90 minutes earlier than you

CONSIDER THIS . . .

Source: © Federico Rostagno/ Shutterstock.com

A Bright Idea

In sunny areas, a solar panel can make up for the cost of its installation in just a few years by greatly reducing or even eliminating a household's electricity bill. After those years of payback are finished, there will be almost nothing but benefits because the solar panel will continue to provide free electricity at only modest maintenance costs. Consequently, nearly every household in sunny areas could rationally profit from installing solar panels.

Unfortunately, myopia discourages most people from wanting to reap the net benefits. Because people are myopic, they focus too strongly on the upfront costs of installing solar panels while at the same time discounting the long-run benefits from being able to generate their own electricity. The result is major inefficiency as most homeowners end up foregoing solar panels.

A company called Solar City has figured out a way to work with rather than against people's myopia. It does so by offering leasing and financing options that eliminate the need for consumers to pay for the upfront costs of installing a solar system. Instead, Solar City pays for the upfront costs and then makes its money by splitting the resulting savings on monthly electricity bills with consumers.

This arrangement actually benefits from myopia because consumers get to focus on instant savings rather than initial costs. The same strategy can also be used to promote other investments that would normally be discouraged by myopia, such as installing energy-efficient furnaces, air conditioners, and appliances.

normally do. But when your alarm goes off the next morning at that earlier time, you loath the concept, throw the alarm across the room, and go back to sleep. That switch in your preferences from the night before is the essence of time inconsistency. Your future self ends up disagreeing with your current self.

Self-Control Problems Time inconsistency is important because it is a major cause of **self-control problems.** To see why, imagine that before heading out to a restaurant with friends, you think that you will be happy sticking to your diet and only ordering a salad. After all, that particular restaurant has very tasty salads. But then, after you get there, you find the dessert menu overwhelmingly attractive and end up ordering two servings of cheesecake.

Because you were time inconsistent and didn't understand what your future self would want, you placed yourself into a situation in which it was very difficult for you to stick to your diet. If you had, instead, been able to correctly predict what your future self would want, you might have decided to stay home for the evening rather than putting yourself in temptation's way. Alternatively, you could have gone, but not before making your friends promise to prevent you from ordering dessert.

Time inconsistency also makes it hard for many workers to save money. Before their paychecks arrive, they mistakenly assume that their future selves will want to save money as much as their current selves do. But once the money becomes available, their future selves end up wanting to spend everything and save nothing.

Fighting Self-Control Problems with Precommitments

The key to fighting time inconsistency and self-control problems is to have a good understanding of what your future self is likely to want. You can then make **precommitments** and take actions ahead of time to prevent your future self from doing much damage.

Hiding the Alarm Clock Consider again the problem of wanting to wake up 90 minutes early on Wednesday morning so that you can work out before starting the rest of your day. If you understand that your future self is not going to want to cooperate, you can take steps to prevent that future self from flaking out. Some people set multiple alarms. Others put their alarms on the other side of the room, underneath a pile of stuff that will have to be moved if the future self wants to turn the damned thing off. But the point is that each of these methods ensures that it will be nearly impossible for the future self to easily get back to sleep. They set things up so that the future self will be forced to do what the present self desires.

Automatic Payroll Deductions Precommitment strategies have also been used to help future selves save more. Consider automatic payroll deductions. If a worker named Blaire signs up for such a program, a fixed percentage will be automatically deducted from each of her paychecks and deposited directly into her retirement savings account. Because that money never gets to her checking account, there is no way for Blaire's future self to fall prey to temptation and spend it. As the old saying goes, "Out of sight, out of mind."

Salary Smoothing School teachers and college professors often have the choice of having their annual salaries paid out over 9 larger monthly installments (to match the length of the school year) or 12 smaller monthly installments (to match the length of the calendar year). If we observe which option they actually choose, we find that the vast majority opt to have their salaries spread out over 12 months rather than 9 months.

They do so because they fear self-control problems. In particular, they are afraid that if they opt to be paid over 9 months, they won't have the self-control to save enough

money during the 9-month period when they will be getting paid to last them through the three months of summer vacation when they won't be getting paid. To avoid that situation, they opt to have their salaries spread out evenly over the entire calendar year. That precommitment ensures that their future selves are never given the chance to blow through all the money too quickly.

Early Withdrawal Penalties Sometimes, one cognitive bias can be used to offset another. Retirement accounts that have early-withdrawal penalties are a good example. They use loss aversion to offset time inconsistency and self-control problems.

In some cases, the penalties on these sorts of accounts are as high as 25 percent, meaning that if a saver wanted to withdraw $1,000 before reaching retirement, he would have to give up an additional $250 (= 25 percent of $1,000) as a penalty. While that amount is substantial in itself, loss aversion makes it even more painful to contemplate. As a result, most people can't bring themselves to make an early withdrawal.

Weight-Loss Competitions Loss aversion also drives the effectiveness of weight-loss competitions. For a person who has agreed to participate, the prospect of losing the competition can be a great motivator because loss aversion applies just as much to future selves as to present selves. Even after the future rolls around and the future self is in charge, the future self won't like the prospect of losing either. Thus, the present self can be confident that the future self will also be motivated to stick to the weight-loss goals that the present self wants to achieve.

QUICK REVIEW 8.2

✓ Prospect theory models decision making by accounting for the fact that people's choices are affected by whether a possible outcome is perceived as a prospective gain or a prospective loss relative to the current status quo situation.

✓ Because our ancestors were focused on short-term survival, our brains suffer from myopia and are not good at dealing with decisions that involve the future.

✓ Precommitments can be used to compensate for time inconsistency and the self-control problems that arise when the future self doesn't want to do what the present self prefers.

Fairness and Self-Interest

LO8.5 Define fairness and give examples of how it affects behavior in the economy and in the dictator and ultimatum games.
Neoclassical models assume that people are purely self-interested. They do so because "pure self-interest" seems like a good basis for predicting many economic behaviors, especially those happening in market situations where people are

dealing mostly with strangers and are, consequently, unlikely to be particularly sentimental or charity-minded.

Adam Smith, the founder of modern economics, put this line of thinking into words. The most-quoted passage from *The Wealth of Nations* reads,

> It is not from the benevolence of the butcher, the brewer, or the baker that we expect our dinner, but from their regard to their own interest. We address ourselves not to their humanity but to their self-love, and never talk to them of our own necessities but of *their* advantages.

Smith, however, did not believe that people are *exclusively* focused on self-love and their own interests. He believed that we are also strongly motivated by emotions such as charity, selflessness, and the desire to work for the common good. He expressed this view at length in his other influential book, *The Theory of Moral Sentiments*. The book's opening sentence reads:

> How selfish soever man may be supposed, there are evidently some principles in his nature which interest him in the fortune of others and render their happiness necessary to him though he derives nothing from it except the pleasure of seeing it.

What behavioral economists have discovered is that this human propensity to care about others extends into every type of economic behavior. While self-interest is always present, most people care deeply about others and how they are interacting with others. As a result, economic transactions are heavily influenced by moral and ethical factors.

Field Evidence for Fairness

Many real-world behaviors support the contention that economic transactions are heavily influenced by beliefs and values. This "field evidence" has helped behavioral economists identify the ethical and moral factors that appear to have the largest influence on economic behavior. Fairness is among the most important.

Fairness is a person's opinion as to whether a price, wage, or allocation is considered morally or ethically acceptable. Standards of fairness vary from person to person and economists generally take no stand on what people consider to be right or wrong. But fairness has been studied extensively because many everyday economic behaviors indicate that people care substantially about fairness and not just about maximizing what they can get for themselves.

Consider the following examples—none of which would be undertaken by a purely self-interested person.

- *Giving to Charity* Each year, U.S. charities receive over $300 billion of cash donations and 8 billion hours of free labor. These donations of time and money are inconsistent with the idea that people are only interested in themselves. What is more, many of the cash donations are anonymous. That suggests that many donors have extremely pure motives and are not donating just to make themselves look good.

- *Obeying the Law* In many countries, the large majority of citizens are law-abiding despite having many opportunities to break the law without getting caught. In the same way, the large majority of taxpayers complete their tax returns honestly despite having many opportunities to cut corners and hide income.

- *Fixing Prices* During hurricanes and other natural disasters, shortages of crucial products such as gasoline and electric generators often develop. The shortages imply that retailers could raise prices, but they mostly keep prices fixed because they do not want to be thought of as taking advantage of the situation.

- *Purchasing "Fair-Trade" Products* Many consumers are willing to pay premium prices to purchase products that have been certified by the Fair Trade organization as having been produced by companies that meet high standards with respect to workers' rights and environmental sustainability. These customers clearly care about more than just getting the lowest price.

Experimental Evidence for Fairness

Our understanding of fairness and how it affects economic transactions has been reinforced and refined in recent decades by examining experimental games that were specifically designed to test people's feelings about fairness.

The most important feature of these games is that they are played for real money. That matters because if people were only motivated by self-interest, you would expect everyone playing the games to utilize only those strategies that are most likely to maximize their own winnings.

As it turns out, however, only a few people behave that way. The majority actually play fairly and generously, often going out of their way to share with less-fortunate players even when they are under no compulsion to do so. That being said, their kindness only goes so far. If other players are acting selfishly, the average person will withhold cooperation and may even retaliate.

The Dictator Game The strongest experimental evidence against the idea that people are only interested in what they can get for themselves comes from the **dictator game.**

The Rules In the game, two people interact anonymously. One of them is randomly designated as the "dictator." It is his job to split an amount of money that is put up for that purpose by the researcher running the game. A typical amount is $10.

The defining feature of the game is that the dictator can dictate whatever split he prefers. It could be to keep all the money for himself. It could be to give all the money to the other player. It could be to split it in any other possible way, such as $8.67 for himself and $1.33 for the other person.

Because the game is fully anonymous, the dictator doesn't have to worry about retaliation by the other person. He can get away with being as selfish as he wants.

How Players Behave So what actually happens when people play the dictator game? After running the experiment many thousands of times in many different countries, experimenters have found that only one-third of dictators keep all of the money for themselves. The other two-thirds show substantial generosity, allocating an average of 42 percent of the money to the other player. In addition, 17 percent of all dictators split the money perfectly evenly and a little over 5 percent of all dictators give the other player everything.

Implications for Fairness The way dictators behave suggests two important things about fairness.

First, the majority of people appear to be genuinely concerned about being fair to other people. They are willing to take less for themselves in order to ensure that the other player receives something, too. And they are willing to give substantially to the other player even though the game's guarantee of anonymity would allow them to take everything for themselves without fear of retaliation.

Second, generosity varies quite widely. Between the third of dictators who keep everything for themselves and the 5 percent who give everything to the other person lie the large majority who allocate some but not all of the money to the other person. Within that group, every possible split of the money can be found. As a result, behavioral economists believe that individuals vary widely in their beliefs about fairness. Some are incredibly selfish. Others are incredibly generous. And most of us lie somewhere in between.

To help get a better handle on how those widely divergent beliefs affect behavior in more realistic situations, economists designed a slightly more complex game.

The Ultimatum Game Like the dictator game, the **ultimatum game** involves two players anonymously splitting an amount of money. But there is no longer a dictator who can arbitrarily decide how the money is split. Instead, both players need to agree on any proposed split if it is to take place.

That difference in the rules ensures that the ultimatum game mirrors the many real-world situations in which a project or proposal must obtain the consent and support of all parties if it is to be undertaken. As an example, consider a business transaction between a potential seller and a potential buyer. Even if there are substantial net benefits available to both parties, no transaction will take place unless the buyer and the seller can come to an agreement on the selling price.

The Rules As with the dictator game, the researcher puts up an amount of money to be split. This pot of money is similar in spirit to the net benefits that a buyer and a seller can split if they can agree on a price. It also represents the net benefits that will be forgone if the two parties cannot reach an agreement.

At the start of the experiment, one of the players is randomly assigned to be "the proposer" while the other player is randomly assigned to be "the responder." The game begins with the proposer proposing a split. As in the dictator game, the proposed split can range anywhere from suggesting that all the money go to the proposer to suggesting that all the money go to the responder.

The responder examines the proposed split and decides whether to accept it or reject it. If she accepts it, the split is made and both players are immediately paid their shares by the researcher. But if the responder rejects the proposed split, neither player gets anything. The game simply ends and both players go home without receiving any money at all—a situation similar to when a business negotiation fails and all the potential benefits are forgone.

How Players Behave When the ultimatum game is played, two behaviors stand out.

The more important is that the splits proposed by proposers in the ultimatum game are much more equal on average than the splits imposed by dictators in the dictator game. This is best seen by noting that whereas one-third of dictators keep all the money for themselves in the dictator game, almost no proposers suggest allocating all the money to themselves in the ultimatum game.

This extremely large difference in behavior arises because the people acting as proposers in the ultimatum game realize that suggesting a highly unequal split is almost certain to greatly offend a responder's sense of fairness and lead to a rejection. In addition, most proposers also seem to understand that even moderately unfair offers might also offend responders. As a result, the large majority of proposers suggest either perfectly equal splits or splits that are only slightly biased in the proposer's favor (such as 55 percent going to the proposer).

The second behavior that stands out is the decisiveness and emotional intensity with which responders reject offers that they consider unfair. Of particular interest is the fact that rejection decisions are not made in a cool and calculating fashion. Responders do *not* calmly weigh the costs and benefits of accepting an unfair offer. They actually become extremely angry and reject as a way of retaliating against the proposer. Their rejections are not just negative responses; they are acts of vengeance designed to hurt the proposer by denying him money.

The full extent to which unfair offers make responders angry can be gauged by looking at high-stakes versions of the ultimatum game in which proposers and responders attempt to split hundreds or even thousands of dollars. You might

The Behavioral Insights Team

A Crack Team of Researchers Uses People's Behavioral Biases to "Nudge" them Toward Making Better Decisions.*

In 2010, the government of the United Kingdom established the Behavioral Insights Team. It was tasked with finding low-cost ways to gently nudge people toward making better choices for themselves and others.

A key feature of "nudges" is that they are subtle. This subtlety means that nudges can cause large changes in behavior without making people feel bullied or coerced—and also without imposing stringent new rules or having to offer people big monetary incentives or disincentives to get them to do something.

Consider tax collections. The Behavioral Insights Team (BIT) found that it could substantially increase the total amount of income tax collected each year in the United Kingdom by simply mailing letters to those who had not yet paid stating that most of their neighbors had already paid. That little bit of peer pressure was all it took to get many people to pay up. A similar experiment in Guatemala tripled tax collections.

Little personalized reminders are often all that is needed to make big changes in people's behavior. The BIT found that it could increase the attendance rates at adult literacy classes by over one-third just by sending students a text message each Sunday night that read, "I hope you had a good break, we look forward to seeing you next week. Remember to plan how you will get to your class."

The BIT uses randomized controlled trials to discover what works. Whenever it comes up with a potential nudge, it tests that potential nudge on a randomly selected group of people. At the same time, it also recruits a control (comparison) group who do not get the nudge. After waiting to see how both groups behave, the potential nudge is only deemed a success if the people receiving it make better choices than the people in the control group.

That was the case when it came to savings behavior in a poor rural area of the Philippines. The BIT worked with local researchers

Source: © Manoj Shah/Getty Images

to see whether local people would save more at their local banks if they were offered a new type of "commitment" savings account. These commitment accounts restricted people from withdrawing money until they reached either a specific date or a specific savings target (that participants chose for themselves). By contrast, the people in the control group received ordinary savings accounts that had no such restrictions—meaning that people could withdraw money at any time they wanted and there were no savings targets.

The results of the experiment were startling. Over the course of one year, the people with ordinary accounts increased their stockpile of savings by only 12 percent. By contrast, the people randomized into having to use commitment accounts increased their savings by 82 percent—or nearly seven times more.

That large increase in savings is important because one of the surest ways out of poverty is for poorer people to pile up wealth that can be used for education, starting small businesses, and surviving periods of severe financial distress.

The introduction of commitment accounts made higher savings rates possible by providing locals with a simple way to overcome self-control problems. But please note that successful nudges can be viewed as a form of manipulation. That interpretation can be even more disturbing when you consider that the changes in behavior generated by successful nudges are most likely unconscious on the part of those being nudged. Keep this in mind as you consider for yourself whether is it morally or ethically acceptable to use nudges to guide people's behavior.

---

*The term "nudge" was popularized by Richard Thaler and Cass Sunstein in their book *Nudge: Improving Decisions about Health, Wealth, and Happiness,* Yale University Press, 2008.

think that when such large amounts of money are on the line, responders would be willing to accept unfair splits. But what we actually see is responders continuing to reject splits that they consider to be unfair. Their preference for fair treatment is so strong that they will reject unfair offers even when doing so means giving up a *lot* of money.

Why the Threat of Rejection Increases Cooperation Some people won't offer anything to other people unless they are coerced into doing so. This is best understood by comparing

the behavior of dictators in the dictator game with the behavior of proposers in the ultimatum game. In the dictator game, a full third of dictators award themselves all the money and leave nothing for the other player. In the ultimatum game, by contrast, nearly every proposer offers a substantial split to the responder.

That dramatic increase in generosity and fairness is, of course, related to the different rules used in the two games. When one person has total control over the split, selfish tendencies are given free reign. But when rejections become possible, the player in charge of proposing the split has to take the other player's feelings into account. That causes even selfish proposers to make generous offers because they quickly realize that the only way they can get any money for themselves is by making proposals that will not be rejected.

Implications for Market Efficiency   The willingness of proposers to make more generous offers when faced with the threat of rejection can be thought of as the simplest expression of the invisible hand.

As we discussed in Chapter 2, the invisible hand is a metaphor that summarizes the tendency of the market system to align private interests with social interests and get people behaving in ways that benefit not only themselves but other people, too.

In the case of the ultimatum game, the threat of rejection helps to align private interests with social interests. It does so by motivating selfish people to make substantially more generous offers. The result is a higher level of cooperation and utility as offers get accepted and players split the money.

A similar process can be seen in the real world with respect to consumer sovereignty. As discussed in Chapter 2, consumer sovereignty is the right of consumers to spend their incomes on the goods and services that they are most willing and able to buy. Crucially, that right includes the ability to reject any product that does not meet the consumer's expectations.

That right of rejection leads to substantial social benefits because it motivates producers to work hard at producing products that will be acceptable to consumers. Over time, those efforts lead to increased allocative and productive efficiency as better products get produced at lower prices.

SUMMARY

LO8.1 Define behavioral economics and explain how it contrasts with neoclassical economics.

Neoclassical economics bases its predictions about human behavior on the assumption that people are fully rational decision makers who have no trouble making mental calculations and no problems dealing with temptation. While some of its predictions are accurate, many are not.

The key difficulty facing neoclassical economics is that people make systematic errors, meaning that they regularly and repeatedly engage in behaviors that reduce their likelihood of achieving what they want.

Behavioral economics attempts to explain systematic errors by combining insights from economics, psychology, and biology. Its goal is to make more accurate predictions about human choice behavior by taking into account the mental mistakes that lead to systematic errors.

LO8.2 Discuss the evidence for the brain being modular, computationally restricted, reliant on heuristics, and prone to various forms of cognitive error.

Our brains make systematic errors for two reasons. First, our brains were not prepared by evolution for dealing with many modern problems, especially those having to do with math, physics, and statistics. Second, our brains also make mistakes when dealing with long-standing challenges (like interpreting visual information) because caloric limitations forced our brains to adopt low-energy heuristics (shortcuts) for completing mental tasks.

Heuristics sacrifice accuracy for speed and low energy usage. In most cases, the lack of accuracy is not important because the errors that result are relatively minor. However, in some cases, those errors can generate cognitive biases that substantially impede rational decision making. Examples include confirmation bias, the overconfidence effect, the availability heuristic, and framing effects.

LO8.3 Relate how prospect theory helps to explain many consumer behaviors, including framing effects, mental accounting, anchoring, loss aversion, and the endowment effect.

Prospect theory is the behavioral economics theory that attempts to accurately describe how people deal with risk and uncertainty. Its key feature is that it models a person's preferences about uncertain outcomes as being based on whether those outcomes will cause gains or losses relative to the current status quo situation to which the person has become accustomed.

Prospect theory also accounts for loss aversion and the fact that most people perceive the pain of losing a given amount of money as being about 2.5 times more intense than the pleasure they would receive from an equal-sized gain.

LO8.4 Describe how time inconsistency and myopia cause people to make suboptimal long-run decisions.

Myopia refers to the difficulty that most people have in conceptualizing the future. It causes people to put insufficient weight on future outcomes when making decisions.

Time inconsistency refers to the difficulty that most people have in correctly predicting what their future selves will want. It causes self-control problems because people are not able to correctly anticipate the degree to which their future selves may fall prey to various sorts of temptation.

People sometimes utilize precommitments to help them overcome self-control problems. Precommitments are courses of action that would be very difficult for the future self to alter. They consequently force the future self to do what the present self desires.

LO8.5 Define fairness and give examples of how it affects behavior in the economy and in the dictator and ultimatum games.

Behavioral economists have found extensive evidence that people are *not* purely self-interested. Rather, they care substantially about fairness and are often willing to give up money and other possessions in order to benefit other people.

The field evidence for fairness includes donations to charity, law-abiding behavior, the reluctance of retailers to raise prices during natural disasters, and the willingness of many consumers to pay premium prices for Fair Trade products.

The dictator and ultimatum games provide experimental evidence on fairness by showing how pairs of people interact to split a pot of money that is provided by the researcher. In the dictator game, one person has total control over the split. In the ultimatum game, both players must agree to the split.

The dictator game shows that many people will share with others even when anonymity would allow them to be perfectly selfish and keep all the money for themselves. The ultimatum game shows that people put a very high value on being treated fairly. They would rather reject an unfair offer and get nothing than accept it and get something.

TERMS AND CONCEPTS

neoclassical economics	status quo	myopia
behavioral economics	loss aversion	time inconsistency
rational	prospect theory	self-control problems
systematic errors	anchoring	precommitments
heuristics	mental accounting	fairness
cognitive biases	endowment effect	dictator game
framing effects	status quo bias	ultimatum game

The following and additional problems can be found in ▥ **connect**

DISCUSSION QUESTIONS

1. Suppose that Joe enjoys and repeatedly does stupid things like getting heavily into debt and insulting police officers. Do these actions constitute systematic errors? If he gets what he wants each time, are his stupid actions even considered to be errors by economists? Explain. **LO8.1**

2. Why do behavioral economists consider it helpful to base a theory of economic behavior on the actual mental processes that people use to make decisions? Why do neoclassical economists not care about whether a theory incorporates those actual mental processes? **LO8.1**

3. Economist Gerd Gigerenzer characterizes heuristics as "fast and frugal" ways of reaching decisions. Are there any costs to heuristics being "fast and frugal"? Explain and give an example of how a fast and frugal method for doing something in everyday life comes at some costs in terms of other attributes forgone. **LO8.2**

4. "There's no such thing as bad publicity." Evaluate this statement in terms of the recognition heuristic. **LO8.2**

5. For each of the following cognitive biases, come up with at least one example from your own life. **LO8.2**
   a. Confirmation bias.
   b. Self-serving bias.
   c. The overconfidence effect.
   d. Hindsight bias.
   e. The availability heuristic.
   f. The planning fallacy.
   g. Framing effects.

6. Suppose that Ike is loss averse. In the morning, Ike's stockbroker calls to tell him that he has gained $1,000 on his stock portfolio. In the evening, his accountant calls to tell him that he owes an extra $1,000 in taxes. At the end of the day, does Ike feel emotionally neutral since the dollar value of the gain in his stock portfolio exactly offsets the amount of extra taxes he has to pay? Explain. **LO8.3**

7. You just accepted a campus job helping to raise money for your school's athletic program. You are told to draft a fund-raising letter. The bottom of the letter asks recipients to write down a donation amount. If you want to raise as much money as possible, would it be better if the text of that section mentioned that your school is ranked third in the nation in sports or that you are better than 99 percent of other schools at sports? Explain. **LO8.3**

8. In the early 1990s, New Jersey and Pennsylvania both reformed their automobile insurance systems so that citizens could opt for either a less-expensive policy that did not allow people to sue if they got into accidents or a more-expensive policy that did allow people to sue if they got into accidents. In New Jersey, the default option was the less-expensive policy that did not allow suing. In Pennsylvania, the default option was the more-expensive policy that did allow suing. Given those options, which policy do you think most people in New Jersey ended up with? What about in Pennsylvania? Explain. **LO8.3**

9. Give an example from your own life of a situation where you or someone you know uses a precommitment to overcome a

self-control problem. Describe why the precommitment is useful and what it compensates for. Avoid any precommitment that was mentioned in the book. **LO8.4**

10. What does behavioral economics have to say about each of the following statements? **LO8.5**
    a. "Nobody is truly charitable—they just give money to show off."
    b. "America has a ruthless capitalist system. Considerations of fairness are totally ignored."
    c. "Selfish people always get ahead. It's like nobody even notices!"

11. Do people playing the dictator game show only self-interested behavior? How much divergence is there in the splits given by dictators to the other player? **LO8.5**

12. Evaluate the following statement. "We shouldn't generalize from what people do in the ultimatum game because $10 is a trivial amount of money. When larger amounts of money are on the line, people will act differently." **LO8.5**

13. **LAST WORD** What do you think of the ethics of using unconscious nudges to alter people's behavior? Before you answer, consider the following argument made by economists Richard Thaler and Cass Sunstein, who favor the use of nudges. They argue that in most situations, we couldn't avoid nudging even if we wanted to because whatever policy we choose will contain some set of unconscious nudges and incentives that will influence people. Thus, they say, we might as well choose the wisest set of nudges.

REVIEW QUESTIONS

1. Which of the following are systematic errors? **LO8.1**
    a. A colorblind person who repeatedly runs red lights.
    b. An accountant whose occasional math errors are sometimes on the high side and sometimes on the low side.
    c. The tendency many people have to see faces in clouds.
    d. Miranda paying good money for a nice-looking apple that turns out to be rotten inside.
    e. Elvis always wanting to save more but then spending his whole paycheck, month after month.

2. Identify each statement as being associated with neoclassical economics or behavioral economics. **LO8.1**
    a. People are eager and accurate calculators.
    b. People are often selfless and generous.
    c. People have no trouble resisting temptation.
    d. People place insufficient weight on future events and outcomes.
    e. People treat others well only if doing so will get them something they want.

3. Label each of the following behaviors with the correct bias or heuristic. **LO8.3**
    a. Your uncle says that he knew all along that the stock market was going to crash in 2008.
    b. When Fred does well at work, he credits his intelligence. When anything goes wrong, he blames his secretary.

    c. Ellen thinks that being struck dead by lightning is much more likely than dying from an accidental fall at home.
    d. The sales of a TV that is priced at $999 rise after another very similar TV priced at $1,300 is placed next to it at the store.
    e. The sales of a brand of toothpaste rise after new TV commercials announce that the brand "is preferred by 4 out of 5 dentists."

4. Erik wants to save more, but whenever a paycheck arrives, he ends up spending everything. One way to help him overcome this tendency would be to: **LO8.4**
    a. Teach him about time inconsistency.
    b. Tell him that self-control problems are common.
    c. Have him engage in precommitments that will make it difficult for his future self to overspend.

5. Many proposers in the ultimatum game offer half to the responder with whom they are paired. This behavior could be motivated by (select as many as might apply): **LO8.5**
    a. Fear that an unequal split might be rejected by a fair-minded responder.
    b. A desire to induce the responder to reject the offer.
    c. A strong sense of fairness on the part of the proposers.
    d. Unrestrained greed on the part of the proposers.

PROBLEMS

1. One type of systematic error arises because people tend to think of benefits in percentage terms rather than in absolute dollar amounts. As an example, Samir is willing to drive 20 minutes out of his way to save $4 on a grocery item that costs $10 at a local market. But he is unwilling to drive 20 minutes out of his way to save $10 on a laptop that costs $400 at a local store. In percentage terms, how big is the savings on the grocery item? On the laptop? In absolute terms, how big is the savings on the grocery item? On the laptop? If Samir is willing to sacrifice 20 minutes of his time to save $4 in one case, shouldn't he also be willing to sacrifice 20 minutes of his time to save $10? **LO8.2**

2. Anne is a bargain-minded shopper. Normally, her favorite toothpaste costs the same at both of her local supermarkets, but the stores are having competing sales this week. At one store, there is a bonus offer: buy 2, get 1 free. At the other store, toothpaste is being sold at 40 percent off. Anne instantly opts for the first offer. Was that really the less-expensive choice? (Hint: Is "buy 2, get 1 free" the same as 50 percent off?) **LO8.2**

3. The coffee shop near the local college normally sells 10 ounces of roasted coffee beans for $10. But the shop sometimes puts the beans on sale. During some sales, it offers "33 percent more for free." Other weeks, it takes "33 percent off" the normal

price. After reviewing the shop's sales data, the shop's manager finds that "33 percent more for free" sells a lot more coffee than "33 percent off." Are the store's customers making a systematic error? Which is actually the better deal? **LO8.2**

4. Angela owes $500 on a credit card and $2,000 on a student loan. The credit card has a 15 percent annual interest rate and the student loan has a 7 percent annual interest rate. Her sense of loss aversion makes her more anxious about the larger loan. As a result, she plans to pay it off first—despite the fact that professional financial advisors always tell people to pay off their highest-interest-rate loans first. Suppose Angela has only $500 at the present time to help pay down her loans and that this $500 will be the only money she will have for making debt payments for at least the next year. If she uses the $500 to pay off the credit card, how much interest will accrue on the other loan over the coming year? On the other hand, if she uses the $500 to pay off part of the student loan, how much in combined interest will she owe over the next year on the remaining balances on the two loans? By how many dollars will she be better off if she uses the $500 to completely pay off the credit card rather than partly paying down the student loan? (Hint: If you owe X dollars at an annual interest rate of Y percent, your annual interest payment will be $X \times Y$, where the interest rate Y is expressed as a decimal.) **LO8.3**

5. **ADVANCED ANALYSIS** In the algebraic version of prospect theory, the variable x represents gains and losses. A positive value for x is a gain, a negative value for x is a loss, and a zero value for x represents remaining at the status quo. The so-called value function, $v(x)$, has separate equations for translating gains and losses into, respectively, positive values (utility) and negative values (disutility). The gain or loss is typically measured in dollars while the resulting value (utility or disutility) is measured in utils. A typical person values gains ($x > 0$) using the function $v(x) = x^{0.88}$ and losses ($x < 0$) using the function $v(x) = -2.5*(-x)^{0.88}$. In addition, if she stays at the status quo ($x = 0$), then $v(x) = 0$. First use a scientific calculator (or a spreadsheet program) and the typical person's value functions for gains and losses to fill out the missing spaces in the following table. Then answer the questions that follow. **LO8.3**

a. What is the total value of gaining $1? Of gaining $2?

b. What is the marginal value of going from $0 to gaining $1? Of going from gaining $1 to gaining $2? Does the typical person experience diminishing marginal utility from gains?

c. What is the marginal value of going from $0 to losing $1? Of going from losing $1 to losing $2? Does the typical person experience diminishing marginal disutility from losses?

d. Suppose that a person simultaneously gains $1 from one source and loses $1 from another source. What is the person's total utility after summing the values from these two events? Can a *combination* of events that leaves a person with the same wealth as they started with be perceived negatively? Does this shed light on status quo bias?

e. Suppose that an investor has one investment that gains $2 while another investment simultaneously loses $1. What is the person's total utility after summing the values from these two events? Will an investor need to have gains that are bigger than her losses just to feel as good as she would if she did not invest at all and simply remained at the status quo?

6. Ted has always had difficulty saving money, so on June 1, Ted enrolls in a Christmas savings program at his local bank and deposits $750. That money is totally locked away until December 1 so that Ted can be certain that he will still have it once the holiday shopping season begins. Suppose that the annual rate of interest is 10 percent on ordinary savings accounts (that allow depositors to withdraw their money at any time). How much interest is Ted giving up by precommitting his money into the Christmas savings account for six months instead of depositing it into an ordinary savings account? (Hint: If you invest X dollars at an annual interest rate of Y percent, you will receive interest equal to $X \times Y$, where the interest rate Y is expressed as a decimal.) **LO8.4**

Gain or Loss	Total Value of Gain or Loss	Marginal Value of Gain or Loss
−3	−6.57	___
−2	___	−2.10
−1	−2.50	−2.50
0	0.00	___
1	___	1.00
2	1.84	___
3	___	0.79

Microeconomics of Product Markets

Businesses and the Costs of Production

Learning Objectives

LO9.1 Explain why economic costs include both explicit (revealed and expressed) costs and implicit (present but not obvious) costs.

LO9.2 Relate the law of diminishing returns to a firm's short-run production costs.

LO9.3 Describe the distinctions between fixed and variable costs and among total, average, and marginal costs.

LO9.4 Use economies of scale to link a firm's size and its average costs in the long run.

LO9.5 Give business examples of short-run costs, economies of scale, and minimum efficient scale (MES).

Our attention now turns from the behavior of consumers to the behavior of producers. In market economies, a wide variety of businesses produce an even wider variety of goods and services. Each of those businesses requires economic resources in order to produce its products. In obtaining and using resources, a firm makes monetary payments to resource owners (for example, workers) and incurs opportunity costs when using resources it already owns (for example, entrepreneurial talent). Those payments and opportunity costs together make up the firm's *costs of production,* which we discuss in this chapter.

Then, in the next several chapters, we bring product demand, product prices, and revenue back into the analysis and explain how firms compare revenues and costs in determining how much to produce. Our ultimate purpose is to show how those comparisons relate to economic efficiency.

Economic Costs

LO9.1 Explain why economic costs include both explicit (revealed and expressed) costs and implicit (present but not obvious) costs.

Firms face costs because the resources they need to produce their products are scarce and have alternative uses. Because of scarcity, firms wanting a particular resource have to bid it away from other firms. That process is costly for firms because it requires a payment to the resource owner. This reality causes economists to define an **economic cost** as the payment that must be made to obtain and retain the services of a resource. It is the income the firm must provide to resource suppliers to attract resources away from alternative uses.

This section explains how firms incorporate opportunity costs to calculate economic costs. If you need a refresher on opportunity costs, a brief review of the section on opportunity costs in Chapter 1 might be useful before continuing on with the rest of this section.

Explicit and Implicit Costs

To properly calculate a firm's economic costs, you must remember that each of the resources used by the firm has an opportunity cost. This is true both for the resources that a firm purchases from outsiders as well as for the resources that it already owns.

As an example, consider a table-making firm that starts this month with $5,000 in cash as well as ownership of a small oak forest from which it gets the oak that it turns into tables.

Suppose that during the month the firm uses the entire $5,000 of cash to pay its workers. Clearly, the $5,000 it spends purchasing their labor comes at the opportunity cost of forgoing the best alternatives that could have been bought with that money.

Less obvious, however, is the opportunity cost of the oak that the firm grows itself and which it uses to make tables. Suppose that the oak has a market value of $1,500, meaning that our table-making firm could sell it to outsiders for $1,500. This implies that using the oak to make tables has an opportunity cost of $1,500. Choosing to convert the oak into tables means giving up the best alternatives that the firm could have purchased with the $1,500.

As a result, keep in mind that *all* of the resources that a firm uses—whether purchased from outside or already owned—have opportunity costs and thus economic costs. Economists refer to these two types of economic costs as *explicit costs* and *implicit costs*:

- A firm's **explicit costs** are the monetary payments it makes to those from whom it must purchase resources that it does not own. Because these costs involve an obvious cash transaction, they are referred to as explicit costs. Be sure to remember that explicit costs are opportunity costs because every monetary payment used to purchase outside resources necessarily involves forgoing the best alternatives that could have been purchased with the money.

- A firm's **implicit costs** are the opportunity costs of using the resources that it already owns to make the firm's own product rather than selling those resources to outsiders for cash. Because these costs are present but not obvious, they are referred to as implicit costs.

A firm's economic costs are the sum of its explicit costs and its implicit costs:

Economic costs = Explicit costs + Implicit costs

The following example makes clear how both explicit costs and implicit costs affect firm profits and firm behavior.

Accounting Profit and Normal Profit

Suppose that after many years working as a sales representative for a large T-shirt manufacturer, you decide to strike out on your own. After considering many potential business ventures, you settle on opening a retail T-shirt shop. As we explain in Chapter 2, you will be providing two different economic resources to your new enterprise: labor and entrepreneurial ability. The part of your job that involves providing labor includes any of the routine tasks that are needed to help run the business—things like answering customer e-mails, taking inventory, and sweeping the floor. The part of your job that involves providing entrepreneurial ability includes any of the nonroutine tasks involved with organizing the business and directing its strategy—things like deciding on whether to use Internet ads or in-person events to promote your business, whether to include children's clothing in your product mix, and how to decorate your store to maximize its appeal to potential customers.

You begin providing entrepreneurial ability to your new firm by making some initial organizational decisions. You decide to work full time at your new business, so you quit your old job that paid you $22,000 per year. You invest $20,000 of savings that has been earning $1,000 per year. You decide that your new firm will occupy a small retail space that you own and had been previously renting out for $5,000 per year. Finally, you decide to hire one clerk to help you in the store. She agrees to work for you for $18,000 per year.

After a year in business, you total up your accounts and find the following:

Total sales revenue		$120,000
Cost of T-shirts	$40,000	
Clerk's salary	18,000	
Utilities	5,000	
Total (explicit) costs		63,000
Accounting profit		57,000

These numbers look very good. In particular, you are happy with your $57,000 **accounting profit,** the profit number that accountants calculate by subtracting total explicit costs from total sales revenue. This is the profit (or "net income") that would appear on your accounting statement and that you would report to the government for tax purposes.

But don't celebrate yet! Your $57,000 accounting profit overstates the economic success of your business because it ignores your implicit costs. Success is not defined as "having a total sales revenue that exceeds total explicit costs." Rather, the true measure of success is doing as well as you possibly can—that is, making more money in your new venture selling T-shirts than you could pursuing any other business venture.

To figure out whether you are achieving that goal, you must take into account all of your opportunity costs—both your implicit costs as well as your explicit costs. Doing so will indicate whether your new business venture is earning more money than what you could have earned in any other business venture.

To see how these calculations are made, let's continue with our example.

By providing your own financial capital, retail space, and labor, you incurred three different implicit costs during the year: $1,000 of forgone interest, $5,000 of forgone rent, and $22,000 of forgone wages. But don't forget that there is another implicit cost that you must also take account of—how much income you chose to forgo by applying your entrepreneurial abilities to your current retail T-shirt venture rather than applying them to other potential business ventures.

But what dollar value should we place on the size of the profits that you might have made if you had provided your entrepreneurial ability to one of those other ventures?

The answer is given by estimating a **normal profit,** the typical (or "normal") amount of accounting profit that you would most likely have earned in one of these other ventures. For the sake of argument, let us assume that with your particular set of skills and talents your entrepreneurial abilities would have on average yielded a normal profit of $5,000 in one of the other potential ventures. Knowing that value, we can take all of your implicit costs properly into account by subtracting them from your accounting profit:

Accounting profit		$57,000
Forgone interest	$ 1,000	
Forgone rent	5,000	
Forgone wages	22,000	
Forgone entrepreneurial income	5,000	
Total implicit costs		33,000
Economic profit		24,000

Economic Profit

After subtracting your $33,000 of implicit costs from your accounting profit of $57,000, we are left with an *economic profit* of $24,000.

Please distinguish clearly between accounting profit and economic profit. Accounting profit is the result of subtracting only explicit costs from revenue: *Accounting Profit = Revenue − Explicit Costs*. By contrast, **economic profit** is the result of subtracting all of your economic costs—both explicit costs and implicit costs—from revenue: *Economic Profit = Revenue − Explicit Costs − Implicit Costs*.

By subtracting *all* of your economic costs from your revenue, you determine how your current business venture compares with your best alternative business venture. In our

example, the fact that you are generating an economic profit of $24,000 means that you are making $24,000 more than you could expect to make in your best alternative business venture.

By contrast, suppose that you had instead done poorly in business, so that this year your firm generated an economic loss (a negative economic profit) of $8,000. This would mean that you were doing worse in your current venture than you could have done in your best alternative venture. You would, as a result, wish to switch to that alternative.

Generalizing this point, we see that there is an important behavioral threshold at $0 of economic profit. If a firm is breaking even (that is, earning exactly $0 of economic profit), then its entrepreneurs know that they are doing exactly as well as they could expect to do in their best alternative business venture. They are earning enough to cover all their explicit and implicit costs, including the normal profit that they could expect to earn in other business ventures. Thus, they have no incentive to change. By contrast, anyone running a positive economic profit knows they are doing better than they could in alternative ventures and will want to continue doing what they are doing or maybe even expand their business. And anyone running an economic loss (a negative economic profit) knows that they could do better by switching to something else.

It is for this reason that economists focus on economic profits rather than accounting profits. Simply put, economic profits direct how resources are allocated in the economy. Entrepreneurs running economic losses close their current businesses, thereby liberating the land, labor, capital, and entrepreneurial ability that they had been using. These resources are freed up to be used by firms that are generating positive economic profits or that are at least breaking even. Resources thus flow from producing goods and services with lower net benefits toward producing goods and services with higher net benefits. Allocative efficiency increases as firms are led by their profit signals to produce more of what consumers want the most.

Figure 9.1 shows the relationship among the various cost and profit concepts that we have just discussed. To test

FIGURE 9.1 Economic profit versus accounting profit. Economic profit is equal to total revenue less economic costs. Economic costs are the sum of explicit and implicit costs and include a normal profit to the entrepreneur. Accounting profit is equal to total revenue less accounting (explicit) costs.

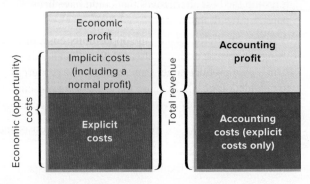

yourself, you might want to enter the cost numbers used in our example in the appropriate blocks.

Short Run and Long Run

When the demand for a firm's product changes, the firm's profitability may depend on how quickly it can adjust the amounts of the various resources it employs. It can easily and quickly adjust the quantities employed of many resources such as hourly labor, raw materials, fuel, and power. It needs much more time, however, to adjust its *plant capacity*—the size of the factory building, the amount of machinery and equipment, and other capital resources. In some heavy industries such as aircraft manufacturing, a firm may need several years to alter plant capacity. Because of these differences in adjustment time, economists find it useful to distinguish between two conceptual periods: the short run and the long run. We will discover that costs differ in these two time periods.

Short Run: Fixed Plant In microeconomics, the **short run** is a period too brief for a firm to alter its plant capacity, yet long enough to permit a change in the degree to which the plant's current capacity is used. The firm's plant capacity is fixed in the short run. However, the firm can vary its output by applying larger or smaller amounts of labor, materials, and other resources to that plant. It can use its existing plant capacity more or less intensively in the short run.

Long Run: Variable Plant In microeconomics, the **long run** is a period long enough for a firm to adjust the quantities of all the resources that it employs, including plant capacity. From the industry's viewpoint, the long run also includes enough time for existing firms to dissolve and leave the industry or for new firms to be created and enter the industry. While the short run is a "fixed-plant" period, the long run is a "variable-plant" period.

Illustrations If Boeing hires 100 extra workers for one of its commercial airline plants or adds an entire shift of workers, we are speaking of the short run. If it adds a new production facility and installs more equipment, we are referring to the long run. The first situation is a *short-run adjustment;* the second is a *long-run adjustment.*

    The short run and the long run are conceptual periods rather than calendar time periods. In light-manufacturing industries, changes in plant capacity may be accomplished almost overnight. A small T-shirt manufacturer can increase its plant capacity in a matter of days by ordering and installing two or three new cutting tables and several extra sewing machines. But for heavy industry the long run is a different matter. Shell Oil may need several years to construct a new gasoline refinery.

> ### QUICK REVIEW 9.1
> ✓ Explicit costs are money payments a firm makes to outside suppliers of resources; implicit costs are the opportunity costs associated with a firm's use of resources it owns.
> ✓ Normal profit is the implicit cost of entrepreneurship. Economic profit is total revenue less all explicit and implicit costs, including a normal profit.
> ✓ In the short run, a firm's plant capacity is fixed; in the long run, a firm can vary its plant size and firms can enter or leave the industry.

Short-Run Production Relationships

LO9.2 Relate the law of diminishing returns to a firm's short-run production costs.

A firm's costs of producing a specific output depend on both the prices and the quantities of the resources (inputs) needed to produce that output. Resource supply and demand determine resource prices. The technological aspects of production, specifically the relationships between inputs and output, determine the quantities of resources needed. Our focus will be on the *labor*-output relationship, given a fixed plant capacity. But before examining that relationship, we need to define three terms:

- **Total product (TP)** is the total quantity, or total output, of a particular good or service produced.
- **Marginal product (MP)** is the extra output or added product associated with adding a unit of a variable resource, in this case labor, to the production process. Thus,

$$\text{Marginal product} = \frac{\text{change in total product}}{\text{change in labor input}}$$

- **Average product (AP),** also called labor productivity, is output per unit of labor input:

$$\text{Average product} = \frac{\text{total product}}{\text{units of labor}}$$

In the short run, a firm can for a time increase its output by adding units of labor to its fixed plant. But by how much will output rise when it adds more labor? And why do we say "for a time"?

Law of Diminishing Returns

The answers are provided in general terms by the **law of diminishing returns.** This law assumes that technology is fixed and thus the techniques of production do not change. It states that as successive units of a variable resource (say, labor) are added to a fixed resource (say, capital or land), beyond some point the extra, or marginal, product that can be attributed to each additional unit of the variable resource will decline. For example, if additional workers are hired to work with a constant amount of capital equipment, output will eventually rise by smaller and smaller amounts as more workers are hired.

Rationale   Suppose a farmer has a fixed resource—80 acres of land—planted in corn. If the farmer does not cultivate the cornfields (clear the weeds) at all, the yield will be 40 bushels per acre. If he cultivates the land once, output may rise to 50 bushels per acre. A second cultivation may increase output to 57 bushels per acre, a third to 61, and a fourth to 63. Succeeding cultivations will add less and less to the land's yield. If this were not so, the world's needs for corn could be fulfilled by extremely intense cultivation of this single 80-acre plot of land. Indeed, if diminishing returns did not occur, the world could be fed out of a flowerpot. Why not? Just keep adding more seed, fertilizer, and harvesters!

The law of diminishing returns also holds true in nonagricultural industries. Assume a wood shop is manufacturing furniture frames. It has a specific amount of equipment such as lathes, planes, saws, and sanders. If this shop hired just one or two workers, total output and productivity (output per worker) would be very low. The workers would have to perform many different jobs, and the advantages of specialization would not be realized. Time would be lost in switching from one job to another, and machines would stand idle much of the time. In short, the plant would be understaffed, and production would be inefficient because there would be too much capital relative to the amount of labor.

The shop could eliminate those difficulties by hiring more workers. Then the equipment would be more fully used, and workers could specialize on doing a single job. Time would no longer be lost switching from job to job. As more workers were added, production would become more efficient and the marginal product of each succeeding worker would rise.

But the rise could not go on indefinitely. Beyond a certain point, adding more workers would cause overcrowding. Since workers would then have to wait in line to use the machinery, they would be underused. Total output would increase at a diminishing rate because, given the fixed size of the plant, each worker would have less capital equipment to work with as more and more labor was hired. The marginal product of additional workers would decline because there would be more labor in proportion to the fixed amount of capital. Eventually, adding still more workers would cause so much congestion that marginal product would become negative and total product would decline. At the extreme, the addition of more and more labor would exhaust all the standing room, and total product would fall to zero.

Note that the law of diminishing returns assumes that all units of labor are of equal quality. Each successive worker is presumed to have the same innate ability, motor coordination, education, training, and work experience. Marginal product ultimately diminishes, but not because successive workers are less skilled or less energetic. It declines because the firm is using more workers relative to the amount of plant and equipment available.

TABLE 9.1 **Total, Marginal, and Average Product: The Law of Diminishing Returns**

(1) Units of the Variable Resource (Labor)	(2) Total Product (TP)	(3) Marginal Product (MP), Change in (2)/ Change in (1)	(4) Average Product (AP), (2)/(1)
0	0		—
1	10	10 ⎤ Increasing	10.00
2	25	15 ⎬ marginal	12.50
3	45	20 ⎦ returns	15.00
4	60	15 ⎤ Diminishing	15.00
5	70	10 ⎬ marginal	14.00
6	75	5 ⎦ returns	12.50
7	75	0 ⎤ Negative	10.71
8	70	−5 ⎬ marginal ⎦ returns	8.75

Tabular Example

Table 9.1 is a numerical illustration of the law of diminishing returns. Column 2 shows the total product, or total output, resulting from combining each level of a variable input (labor) in column 1 with a fixed amount of capital.

Column 3 shows the marginal product (MP), the change in total product associated with each additional unit of labor. Note that with no labor input, total product is zero; a plant with no workers will produce no output. The first three units of labor generate increasing marginal returns, with marginal products of 10, 15, and 20 units, respectively. But beginning with the fourth unit of labor, marginal product diminishes continuously, becoming zero with the seventh unit of labor and negative with the eighth.

Average product, or output per labor unit, is shown in column 4. It is calculated by dividing total product (column 2) by the number of labor units needed to produce it (column 1). At 5 units of labor, for example, AP is 14 (= 70/5).

Graphical Portrayal

Figure 9.2 (**Key Graph**) shows the diminishing-returns data in Table 9.1 graphically and further clarifies the relationships between total, marginal, and average products. (Marginal product in Figure 9.2b is plotted halfway between the units of labor since it applies to the addition of each labor unit.)

Note first in Figure 9.2a that total product, TP, goes through three phases: It rises initially at an increasing rate; then it increases, but at a diminishing rate; finally, after reaching a maximum, it declines.

Geometrically, marginal product—shown by the MP curve in Figure 9.2b—is the slope of the total-product curve. Marginal product measures the change in total product associated with each succeeding unit of labor. Thus, the three phases of total product are also reflected in marginal product. Where total product is increasing at an increasing rate, marginal product is rising. Here, extra units of labor are adding

larger and larger amounts to total product. Similarly, where total product is increasing but at a decreasing rate, marginal product is positive but falling. Each additional unit of labor adds less to total product than did the previous unit. When total product is at a maximum, marginal product is zero. When total product declines, marginal product becomes negative.

Average product, AP (Figure 9.2b), displays the same tendencies as marginal product. It increases, reaches a maximum, and then decreases as more and more units of labor are added to the fixed plant. But note the relationship between marginal product and average product: Where marginal product exceeds average product, average product rises. And where marginal product is less than average product, average product declines. It follows that marginal product intersects average product where average product is at a maximum.

This relationship is a mathematical necessity. If you add a larger number to a total than the current average of that total, the average must rise. And if you add a smaller number to a total than the current average of that total, the average must fall. You raise your average examination grade only when your score on an additional (marginal) examination is greater than the average of all your past scores. You lower your average when your grade on an additional exam is below your current average. In our production example, when the amount an extra worker adds to total product exceeds the average product of all workers currently employed, average product will rise. Conversely, when the amount an extra worker adds to total product is less than the current average product, average product will decrease.

The law of diminishing returns is embodied in the shapes of all three curves. But, as our definition of the law of diminishing returns indicates, economists are most concerned with its effects on marginal product. The regions of increasing, diminishing, and negative marginal product (returns) are shown in Figure 9.2b.

KEY GRAPH

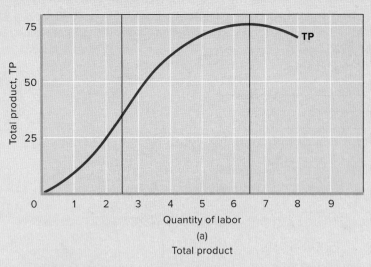

(a)
Total product

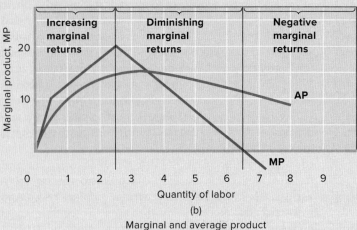

(b)
Marginal and average product

FIGURE 9.2 **The law of diminishing returns.** (a) As a variable resource (labor) is added to fixed amounts of other resources (land or capital), the total product that results will eventually increase by diminishing amounts, reach a maximum, and then decline. (b) Marginal product is the change in total product associated with each new unit of labor. Average product is simply output per labor unit. Note that marginal product intersects average product at the maximum average product.

QUICK QUIZ FOR FIGURE 9.2

1. Which of the following is an assumption underlying these figures?
   a. Firms first hire "better" workers and then hire "poorer" workers.
   b. Capital and labor are both variable, but labor increases more rapidly than capital.
   c. Consumers will buy all the output (total product) produced.
   d. Workers are of equal quality.

2. Marginal product is:
   a. the change in total product divided by the change in the quantity of labor.
   b. total product divided by the quantity of labor.
   c. always positive.
   d. unrelated to total product.

3. Marginal product in graph (b) is zero when:
   a. average product in graph (b) stops rising.
   b. the slope of the marginal-product curve in graph (b) is zero.
   c. total product in graph (a) begins to rise at a diminishing rate.
   d. the slope of the total-product curve in graph (a) is zero.

4. Average product in graph (b):
   a. rises when it is less than marginal product.
   b. is the change in total product divided by the change in the quantity of labor.
   c. can never exceed marginal product.
   d. falls whenever total product in graph (a) rises at a diminishing rate.

Answers: 1. d; 2. a; 3. d; 4. a

Short-Run Production Costs

LO9.3 Describe the distinctions between fixed and variable costs and among total, average, and marginal costs.

Production information such as that provided in Table 9.1 and Figures 9.2a and 9.2b must be coupled with resource prices to determine the total and per-unit costs of producing various levels of output. We know that in the short run, resources associated with the firm's plant are fixed. Other resources, however, are variable in the short run. As a result, short-run costs can be either fixed or variable.

Fixed, Variable, and Total Costs

Let's see what distinguishes fixed costs, variable costs, and total costs from one another.

Fixed Costs **Fixed costs** are those costs that do not vary with changes in output. Fixed costs are associated with the very existence of a firm's plant and therefore must be paid even if its output is zero. Such costs as rental payments, interest on a firm's debts, a portion of depreciation on equipment and buildings, and insurance premiums are generally fixed costs; they are fixed and do not change even if a firm produces more. In column 2 of Table 9.2 we assume that the firm's total fixed cost is $100. By definition, this fixed cost is incurred at all levels of output, including zero. The firm cannot avoid paying fixed costs in the short run.

Variable Costs **Variable costs** are those costs that change with the level of output. They include payments for materials, fuel, power, transportation services, most labor, and similar

variable resources. In column 3 of Table 9.2 we find that the total of variable costs changes directly with output. But note that the increases in variable cost associated with succeeding one-unit increases in output are not equal. As production begins, variable cost will for a time increase by a decreasing amount; this is true through the fourth unit of output in Table 9.2. Beyond the fourth unit, however, variable cost rises by increasing amounts for succeeding units of output.

The reason lies in the shape of the marginal-product curve. At first, as in Figure 9.2b, marginal product is increasing, so smaller and smaller increases in the amounts of variable resources are needed to produce successive units of output. Hence the variable cost of successive units of output decreases. But when, as diminishing returns are encountered, marginal product begins to decline, larger and larger additional amounts of variable resources are needed to produce successive units of output. Total variable cost therefore increases by increasing amounts.

Total Cost **Total cost** is the sum of fixed cost and variable cost at each level of output:

$$TC = TFC + TVC$$

TC is shown in column 4 of Table 9.2. At zero units of output, total cost is equal to the firm's fixed cost. Then for each unit of the 10 units of production, total cost increases by the same amount as variable cost.

Figure 9.3 shows graphically the fixed-, variable-, and total-cost data given in Table 9.2. Observe that total variable cost, TVC, is measured vertically from the horizontal axis at each level of output. The amount of fixed cost, shown as

TABLE 9.2 Total-, Average-, and Marginal-Cost Schedules for an Individual Firm in the Short Run

	Total-Cost Data			Average-Cost Data			Marginal Cost
(1) Total Product (Q)	(2) Total Fixed Cost (TFC)	(3) Total Variable Cost (TVC)	(4) Total Cost (TC) TC = TFC + TVC	(5) Average Fixed Cost (AFC) $AFC = \frac{TFC}{Q}$	(6) Average Variable Cost (AVC) $AVC = \frac{TVC}{Q}$	(7) Average Total Cost (ATC) $ATC = \frac{TC}{Q}$	(8) Marginal Cost (MC) $MC = \frac{\text{change in TC}}{\text{change in Q}}$
0	$100	$ 0	$ 100				$ 90
1	100	90	190	$100.00	$90.00	$190.00	80
2	100	170	270	50.00	85.00	135.00	70
3	100	240	340	33.33	80.00	113.33	60
4	100	300	400	25.00	75.00	100.00	70
5	100	370	470	20.00	74.00	94.00	80
6	100	450	550	16.67	75.00	91.67	90
7	100	540	640	14.29	77.14	91.43	110
8	100	650	750	12.50	81.25	93.75	130
9	100	780	880	11.11	86.67	97.78	150
10	100	930	1,030	10.00	93.00	103.00	

FIGURE 9.3 **Total cost is the sum of fixed cost and variable cost.** Total variable cost (TVC) changes with output. Total fixed cost (TFC) is independent of the level of output. The total cost (TC) at any output is the vertical sum of the fixed cost and variable cost at that output.

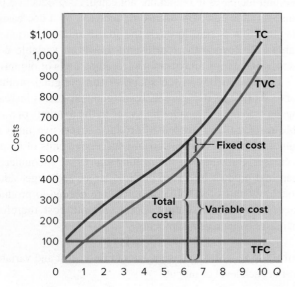

TFC, is added vertically to the total-variable-cost curve to obtain the points on the total-cost curve TC.

The distinction between fixed and variable costs is significant to the business manager. Variable costs can be controlled or altered in the short run by changing production levels. Fixed costs are beyond the business manager's current control; they are incurred in the short run and must be paid regardless of output level.

Per-Unit, or Average, Costs

Producers are certainly interested in their total costs, but they are equally concerned with per-unit, or average, costs. In particular, average-cost data are more meaningful for making comparisons with product price, which is always stated on a per-unit basis. Average fixed cost, average variable cost, and average total cost are shown in columns 5 to 7, Table 9.2.

AFC **Average fixed cost (AFC)** for any output level is found by dividing total fixed cost (TFC) by that amount of output (Q). That is,

$$AFC = \frac{TFC}{Q}$$

Because the total fixed cost is, by definition, the same regardless of output, AFC must decline as output increases. As output rises, the total fixed cost is spread over a larger and larger output. When output is just 1 unit in Table 9.2, TFC and AFC are the same at $100. But at 2 units of output, the total fixed cost of $100 becomes $50 of AFC or fixed cost per unit; then it becomes $33.33 per unit as $100 is spread over 3 units,

and $25 per unit when spread over 4 units. This process is sometimes referred to as "spreading the overhead." Figure 9.4 shows that AFC graphs as a continuously declining curve as total output is increased.

AVC **Average variable cost (AVC)** for any output level is calculated by dividing total variable cost (TVC) by that amount of output (Q):

$$AVC = \frac{TVC}{Q}$$

Due to increasing and then diminishing returns, AVC declines initially, reaches a minimum, and then increases again. A graph of AVC is a U-shaped or saucer-shaped curve, as shown in Figure 9.4.

Because total variable cost reflects the law of diminishing returns, so must AVC, which is derived from total variable cost. Because marginal returns increase initially, fewer and fewer additional variable resources are needed to produce each of the first four units of output. As a result, variable cost per unit declines. AVC hits a minimum with the fifth unit of output, and beyond that point AVC rises as diminishing returns require more and more variable resources to produce each additional unit of output.

Rephrased, production is relatively inefficient—and therefore costly—at low levels of output. Because the firm's fixed plant is understaffed, average variable cost is relatively high. As output expands, however, greater specialization and better use of the firm's capital equipment yield more efficiency, and variable cost per unit of output declines. As still more variable resources are added, a point is reached where crowding causes diminishing returns to set in. Once diminishing returns start, each additional unit of input does not

FIGURE 9.4 **The average-cost curves.** AFC falls as a given amount of fixed costs is apportioned over a larger and larger output. AVC initially falls because of increasing marginal returns but then rises because of diminishing marginal returns. Average total cost (ATC) is the vertical sum of average variable cost (AVC) and average fixed cost (AFC).

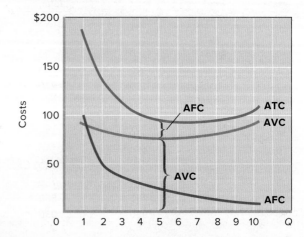

increase output by as much as preceding units did. This means that AVC eventually increases.

You can verify the U or saucer shape of the AVC curve by returning to Table 9.1. Assume the price of labor is $10 per unit. Labor cost per unit of output is then $10 (the price per labor unit in this example) divided by average product (output per labor unit). Because we have assumed labor to be the only variable input, the labor cost per unit of output is the variable cost per unit of output, or AVC. When average product is initially low, AVC is high. As workers are added, average product rises and AVC falls. When average product is at its maximum, AVC is at its minimum. Then, as still more workers are added and average product declines, AVC rises. The "hump" of the average-product curve is reflected in the saucer or U shape of the AVC curve. As you will soon see, the two are mirror images of each other.

ATC Average total cost (ATC) for any output level is found by dividing total cost (TC) by that output (Q) or by adding AFC and AVC at that output:

$$ATC = \frac{TC}{Q} = \frac{TFC}{Q} + \frac{TVC}{Q} = AFC + AVC$$

Graphically, ATC can be found by adding vertically the AFC and AVC curves, as in Figure 9.4. Thus the vertical distance between the ATC and AVC curves measures AFC at any level of output.

Marginal Cost

One final and very crucial cost concept remains: **Marginal cost (MC)** is the extra, or additional, cost of producing one more unit of output. MC can be determined for each added unit of output by noting the change in total cost entailed by that unit's production:

$$MC = \frac{\text{change in TC}}{\text{change in } Q}$$

Calculations In column 4 of Table 9.2, production of the first unit of output increases total cost from $100 to $190. Therefore, the additional, or marginal, cost of that first unit is $90 (column 8). The marginal cost of the second unit is $80 (= $270 − $190); the MC of the third is $70 (= $340 − $270); and so forth. The MC for each of the 10 units of output is shown in column 8.

MC can also be calculated from the total-variable-cost column because the only difference between total cost and total variable cost is the constant amount of fixed costs ($100). Thus, the change in total cost and the change in total variable cost associated with each additional unit of output are always the same.

Marginal Decisions Marginal costs are costs the firm can control directly and immediately. Specifically, MC designates all the cost incurred in producing the last unit of output. Thus, it also designates the cost that can be "saved" by not producing that last unit. Average-cost figures do not provide this information. For example, suppose the firm is undecided whether to produce 3 or 4 units of output. At 4 units Table 9.2 indicates that ATC is $100. But the firm does not increase its total costs by $100 by producing the fourth unit, nor does it save $100 by not producing that unit. Rather, the change in costs involved here is only $60, as the MC column in Table 9.2 reveals.

A firm's decisions as to what output level to produce are typically marginal decisions, that is, decisions to produce a few more or a few less units. Marginal cost is the change in costs when one more or one less unit of output is produced.

CONSIDER THIS . . .

Ignoring Sunk Costs

It is a deep-seated human tendency to drag past costs—so-called sunk costs—into marginal-benefit versus marginal-cost calculations. Doing so is known as the *sunk cost fallacy*.

Source: © Don Farrall/Getty Images RF

As an example of this error, suppose a family that's on vacation stops at a roadside stand to buy some apples. After driving a bit, the family discovers that the apples are mushy and gross. Would it be logical for the father to insist that everyone eat the apples "because we paid a premium price for them"?

Absolutely not. In making a new decision, you should ignore all costs that are not affected by that new decision. The prior bad decision (in retrospect) to buy the apples should not dictate a subsequent decision for which marginal benefit is less than marginal cost.

Consider a business example. Suppose that a firm spends $1 million on R&D to bring out a new product, only to discover that the product sells very poorly. Should the firm continue to produce the product at a loss even when there is no realistic hope for future success? Obviously, it should not. In making this decision, the firm should realize that the amount it spent developing the product is irrelevant; it should stop production and cut its losses.

The emotional tendency that drives the sunk cost fallacy is the desire to "get one's money's worth" out of a past expenditure. But giving in to that emotion can lead to "throwing good money after bad." Instead, you should ignore all past costs and focus solely on those that depend on the decision at hand.

KEY GRAPH

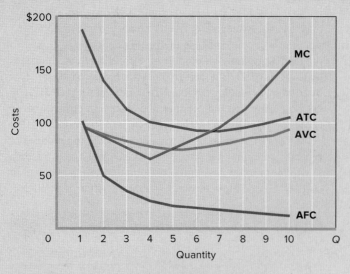

QUICK QUIZ FOR FIGURE 9.5

1. The marginal-cost curve first declines and then increases because of:
   a. increasing, then diminishing, marginal utility.
   b. the decline in the gap between ATC and AVC as output expands.
   c. increasing, then diminishing, marginal returns.
   d. constant marginal revenue.
2. The vertical distance between ATC and AVC measures:
   a. marginal cost.
   b. total fixed cost.
   c. average fixed cost.
   d. economic profit per unit.

3. ATC is:
   a. AVC − AFC.
   b. MC + AVC.
   c. AFC + AVC.
   d. (AFC + AVC) + Q.
4. When the marginal-cost curve lies:
   a. above the ATC curve, ATC rises.
   b. above the AVC curve, ATC rises.
   c. below the AVC curve, total fixed cost increases.
   d. below the ATC curve, total fixed cost falls.

Answers: 1. c; 2. c; 3. c; 4. a

When coupled with marginal revenue (which, as you will see in Chapter 10, indicates the change in revenue from one more or one less unit of output), marginal cost allows a firm to determine if it is profitable to expand or contract its production. The analysis in the next four chapters focuses on those marginal calculations.

Graphical Portrayal Marginal cost is shown graphically in **Figure 9.5 (Key Graph)**. Marginal cost at first declines sharply, reaches a minimum, and then rises rather abruptly. This reflects the fact that variable cost, and therefore total cost, increase at first by decreasing amounts and then by increasing amounts (see columns 3 and 4, Table 9.2).

MC and Marginal Product The marginal-cost curve's shape is a consequence of the law of diminishing returns. Looking back at Table 9.1, we can see the relationship between marginal product and marginal cost. If all units of a variable resource (here labor) are hired at the same price, the

marginal cost of each extra unit of output will fall as long as the marginal product of each additional worker is rising. This is true because marginal cost is the (constant) cost of an extra worker divided by his or her marginal product. Therefore, in Table 9.1, suppose that each worker can be hired for $10. Because the first worker's marginal product is 10 units of output, and hiring this worker increases the firm's costs by $10, the marginal cost of each of these 10 extra units of output is $1 (= $10/10 units). The second worker also increases costs by $10, but the marginal product is 15, so the marginal cost of each of these 15 extra units of output is $0.67 (= $10/15 units). Similarly, the MC of each of the 20 extra units of output contributed by the third worker is $.50 (= $10/20 units). To generalize, as long as marginal product is rising, marginal cost will fall.

But with the fourth worker diminishing returns set in and marginal cost begins to rise. For the fourth worker, marginal cost is $0.67 (= $10/15 units); for the fifth worker, MC is $1 ($10/10 units); for the sixth, MC is $2 (= $10/5 units); and so

FIGURE 9.6 The relationship between productivity curves and cost curves. The marginal-cost (MC) curve and the average-variable-cost (AVC) curve in (b) are mirror images of the marginal-product (MP) and average-product (AP) curves in (a). Assuming that labor is the only variable input and that its price (the wage rate) is constant, then when MP is rising, MC is falling, and when MP is falling, MC is rising. Under the same assumptions, when AP is rising, AVC is falling, and when AP is falling, AVC is rising.

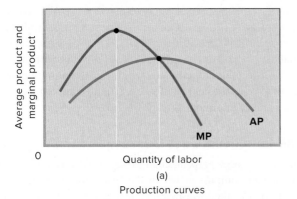

(a)
Production curves

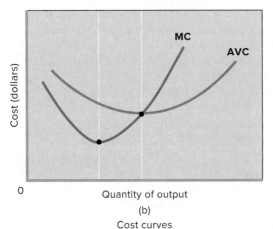

(b)
Cost curves

on. If the price (cost) of the variable resource remains constant, increasing marginal returns will be reflected in a declining marginal cost, and diminishing marginal returns in a rising marginal cost. The MC curve is a mirror reflection of the marginal-product curve. As you can see in Figure 9.6, when marginal product is rising, marginal cost is necessarily falling. When marginal product is at its maximum, marginal cost is at its minimum. And when marginal product is falling, marginal cost is rising.

Relation of MC to AVC and ATC Figure 9.5 shows that the marginal-cost curve MC intersects both the AVC and the ATC curves at their respective minimum points. As noted earlier, this marginal-average relationship is a mathematical necessity, which a simple illustration will reveal. Suppose an NBA basketball player has scored an average of 20 points a game over the first three games of the season. Now, whether his average rises or falls as a result of playing a fourth (marginal) game will depend on whether the additional points he

scores in that game are fewer or more than his current 20-point average. If in the fourth game he scores fewer than 20 points, his average will fall. For example, if he scores 16 points in the fourth game, his total points will rise from 60 to 76 and his average will fall from 20 to 19 (= 76/4). Conversely, if in the fourth (marginal) game he scores more than 20 points, say, 24, his total will increase from 60 to 84 and his average will rise from 20 to 21 (= 84/4).

So it is with costs. When the amount (the marginal cost) added to total cost is less than the current average total cost, ATC will fall. Conversely, when the marginal cost exceeds ATC, ATC will rise. This means in Figure 9.5 that as long as MC lies below ATC, ATC will fall, and whenever MC lies above ATC, ATC will rise. Therefore, at the point of intersection where MC equals ATC, ATC has just ceased to fall but has not yet begun to rise. This, by definition, is the minimum point on the ATC curve. The marginal-cost curve intersects the average-total-cost curve at the ATC curve's minimum point.

Marginal cost can be defined as the addition either to total cost or to total variable cost resulting from one more unit of output; thus this same rationale explains why the MC curve also crosses the AVC curve at the AVC curve's minimum point. No such relationship exists between the MC curve and the average-fixed-cost curve because the two are not related; marginal cost includes only those costs that change with output, and fixed costs by definition are those that are independent of output.

Shifts of the Cost Curves

Changes in either resource prices or technology will cause costs to change and cost curves to shift. If fixed costs double from $100 to $200, the AFC curve in Figure 9.5 would be shifted upward. At each level of output, fixed costs are higher. The ATC curve would also move upward because AFC is a component of ATC. But the positions of the AVC and MC curves would be unaltered because their locations are based on the prices of variable rather than fixed resources. However, if the price (wage) of labor or some other variable input rose, AVC, ATC, and MC would rise and those cost curves would all shift upward. The AFC curve would remain in place because fixed costs have not changed. And, of course, reductions in the prices of fixed or variable resources would reduce costs and produce shifts of the cost curves exactly opposite to those just described.

The discovery of a more efficient technology would increase the productivity of all inputs. The cost figures in Table 9.2 would all be lower. To illustrate, if labor is the only variable input, if wages are $10 per hour, and if average product is 10 units, then AVC would be $1. But if a technological improvement increases the average product of labor to 20 units, then AVC will decline to $0.50. More generally, an upward shift in the productivity curves shown in Figure 9.6a means a downward shift in the cost curves portrayed in Figure 9.6b.

QUICK REVIEW 9.2

✓ The law of diminishing returns indicates that, beyond some point, output will increase by diminishing amounts as more units of a variable resource (labor) are added to a fixed resource (capital).

✓ In the short run, the total cost of any level of output is the sum of fixed and variable costs (TC = TFC + TVC).

✓ Average fixed, average variable, and average total costs are fixed, variable, and total costs per unit of output; marginal cost is the extra cost of producing one more unit of output.

✓ Average fixed cost declines continuously as output increases; the average-variable-cost and average-total-cost curves are U-shaped, reflecting increasing and then diminishing returns; the marginal-cost curve falls but then rises, intersecting both the average-variable-cost curve and the average-total-cost curve at their minimum points.

Long-Run Production Costs

LO9.4 Use economies of scale to link a firm's size and its average costs in the long run.

In the long run an industry and its individual firms can undertake all desired resource adjustments. That is, they can change the amount of all inputs used. The firm can alter its plant capacity; it can build a larger plant or revert to a smaller plant than that assumed in Table 9.2. The industry also can change its overall capacity; the long run allows sufficient time for new firms to enter or for existing firms to leave an industry. We will discuss the impact of the entry and exit of firms to and from an industry in the next chapter; here we are concerned only with changes in plant capacity made by a single firm. Let's couch our analysis in terms of average total cost (ATC), making no distinction between fixed and variable costs because all resources, and therefore all costs, are variable in the long run.

Firm Size and Costs

Suppose a manufacturer with a single plant begins on a small scale and, as the result of successful operations, expands to successively larger plant sizes with larger output capacities. What happens to average total cost as this occurs? For a time, successively larger plants will reduce average total cost. However, eventually the building of a still larger plant will cause ATC to rise.

Figure 9.7 illustrates this situation for five possible plant sizes. ATC-1 is the short-run average-total-cost curve for the smallest of the five plants, and ATC-5, the curve for the largest. Constructing larger plants will lower the minimum average total costs through plant size 3. But then larger plants will mean higher minimum average total costs.

The Long-Run Cost Curve

The vertical lines perpendicular to the output axis in Figure 9.7 indicate the outputs at which the firm should change plant size to realize the lowest attainable average total costs of production. These are the outputs at which the per-unit costs for a larger plant drop below those for the current, smaller plant. For all outputs up to 20 units, the lowest average total costs are attainable with plant size 1. However, if the firm's volume of sales expands beyond 20 units but less than 30, it can achieve lower per-unit costs by constructing a larger plant, size 2. Although total cost will be higher at the expanded levels of production, the cost per unit of output will be less. For any output between 30 and 50 units, plant size 3 will yield the lowest average total costs. From 50 to 60 units of output, the firm must build the size-4 plant to achieve the lowest unit costs. Lowest average total costs for any output over 60 units require construction of the still larger plant, size 5.

Tracing these adjustments, we find that the long-run ATC curve for the enterprise is made up of segments of the short-run ATC curves for the various plant sizes that can be constructed. The long-run ATC curve shows the lowest average total cost at which *any output level* can be produced after the firm has had

FIGURE 9.7 The long-run average-total-cost curve: five possible plant sizes. The long-run average-total-cost curve is made up of segments of the short-run cost curves (ATC-1, ATC-2, etc.) of the various-size plants from which the firm might choose. Each point on the bumpy planning curve shows the lowest unit cost attainable for any output when the firm has had time to make all desired changes in its plant size.

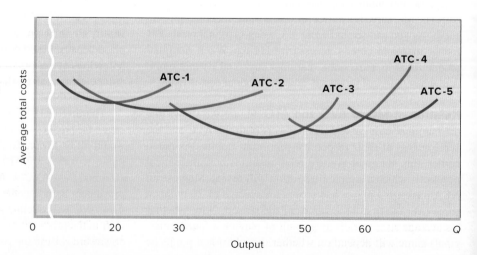

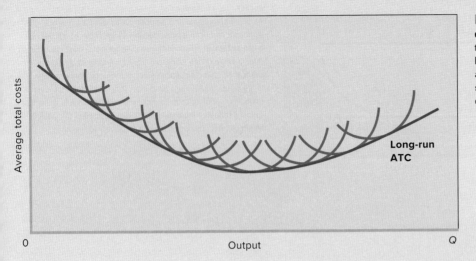

QUICK QUIZ FOR FIGURE 9.8

1. The unlabeled red curves in this figure illustrate the:
   a. long-run average-total-cost curves of various firms constituting the industry.
   b. short-run average-total-cost curves of various firms constituting the industry.
   c. short-run average-total-cost curves of various plant sizes available to a particular firm.
   d. short-run marginal-cost curves of various plant sizes available to a particular firm.

2. The unlabeled red curves in this figure derive their shapes from:
   a. decreasing, then increasing, short-run returns.
   b. increasing, then decreasing, short-run returns.
   c. economies, then diseconomies, of scale.
   d. diseconomies, then economies, of scale.

3. The long-run ATC curve in this figure derives its shape from:
   a. decreasing, then increasing, short-run returns.
   b. increasing, then decreasing, short-run returns.
   c. economies, then diseconomies, of scale.
   d. diseconomies, then economies, of scale.

4. The long-run ATC curve is often called the firm's:
   a. planning curve.
   b. capital-expansion path.
   c. total-product curve.
   d. production possibilities curve.

Answers: 1. c; 2. b; 3. c; 4. a

---

time to make all appropriate adjustments in its plant size. In Figure 9.7 the blue, bumpy curve is the firm's long-run ATC curve or, as it is often called, the firm's *planning curve.*

In most lines of production the choice of plant size is much wider than in our illustration. In many industries the number of possible plant sizes is virtually unlimited, and in time quite small changes in the volume of output will lead to changes in plant size. Graphically, this implies an unlimited number of short-run ATC curves, one for each output level, as suggested by **Figure 9.8 (Key Graph).** Then, rather than being made up of segments of short-run ATC curves as in Figure 9.7, the long-run ATC curve is made up of all the points of tangency of the unlimited number of short-run ATC curves from which the long-run ATC curve is derived. Therefore, the planning curve is smooth rather than bumpy. Each point on it tells us the minimum ATC of producing the corresponding level of output.

Economies and Diseconomies of Scale

We have assumed that, for a time, larger and larger plant sizes will lead to lower unit costs but that, beyond some point, successively larger plants will mean higher average total costs. That is, we have assumed the long-run ATC curve is U-shaped. But why should this be? It turns out that the U shape is caused by economies and diseconomies of large-scale production, as we explain in a moment. But before we do, please understand that the U shape of the long-run average-total-cost curve *cannot* be the result of rising resource prices or the law of diminishing returns. First, our discussion assumes that resource prices are constant. Second, the law of diminishing returns does not apply to production in the long run. This is true because the law of diminishing returns only deals with situations in which a productive resource or input is held constant. Under our definition of "long run," all resources and inputs are variable.

193

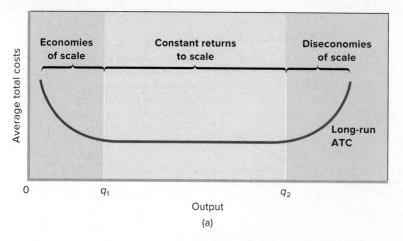

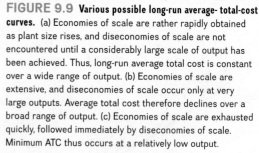

FIGURE 9.9 **Various possible long-run average- total-cost curves.** (a) Economies of scale are rather rapidly obtained as plant size rises, and diseconomies of scale are not encountered until a considerably large scale of output has been achieved. Thus, long-run average total cost is constant over a wide range of output. (b) Economies of scale are extensive, and diseconomies of scale occur only at very large outputs. Average total cost therefore declines over a broad range of output. (c) Economies of scale are exhausted quickly, followed immediately by diseconomies of scale. Minimum ATC thus occurs at a relatively low output.

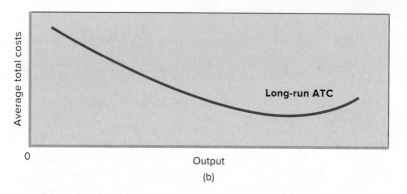

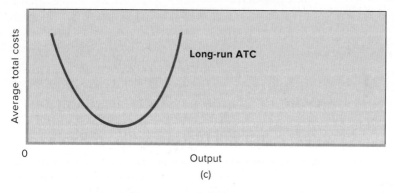

Economies of Scale

Economies of scale, or economies of mass production, explain the downsloping part of the long-run ATC curve, as indicated in Figure 9.9, graphs (a), (b), and (c). As plant size increases, a number of factors will for a time lead to lower average costs of production.

Labor Specialization Increased specialization in the use of labor becomes more achievable as a plant increases in size. Hiring more workers means jobs can be divided and subdivided. Each worker may now have just one task to perform instead of five or six. Workers can work full-time on the tasks for which they have special skills. By contrast, skilled machinists in a small plant may spend half their time performing unskilled tasks, leading to higher production costs.

Further, by working at fewer tasks, workers become even more proficient at those tasks. The jack-of-all-trades doing five or six jobs is not likely to be efficient in any of them. Concentrating on one task, the same worker may become highly efficient.

Finally, greater labor specialization eliminates the loss of time that occurs whenever a worker shifts from one task to another.

Managerial Specialization Large-scale production also means better use of, and greater specialization in, management. A supervisor who can handle 20 workers is underused in a small plant that employs only 10 people. The production staff could be doubled with no increase in supervisory costs.

CHAPTER 9   Businesses and the Costs of Production | 195

Small firms cannot use management specialists to best advantage. For example, a marketing specialist working in a small plant may have to spend some of her time on functions outside of her area of expertise—for example, accounting, personnel, and finance. A larger scale of operations would allow her to supervise marketing full time, while other specialists perform other managerial functions. Greater productivity and efficiency, along with lower unit costs, would be the net result.

Efficient Capital Small firms often cannot afford the most efficient equipment. In many lines of production such machinery is available only in very large and extremely expensive units. Furthermore, effective use of the equipment demands a high volume of production, and that again requires large-scale producers.

In the automobile industry the most efficient fabrication method employs robotics and elaborate assembly-line equipment. Effective use of this equipment demands an annual output of several hundred thousand automobiles. Only very large-scale producers can afford to purchase and use this equipment efficiently. The small-scale producer is faced with a dilemma. To fabricate automobiles using other equipment is inefficient and therefore more costly per unit. But so, too, is buying and underutilizing the equipment used by the large manufacturers. Because it cannot spread the high equipment cost over very many units of output, the small-scale producer will be stuck with high costs per unit of output.

Other Factors Many products entail design and development costs, as well as other "start-up" costs, which must be incurred regardless of projected sales. These costs decline per unit as output is increased. Similarly, advertising costs decline per auto, per computer, per stereo system, and per box of detergent as more units are produced and sold. Also, the firm's production and marketing expertise usually rises as it produces and sells more output. This *learning by doing* is a further source of economies of scale.

All these factors contribute to lower average total costs for the firm that is able to expand its scale of operations. Where economies of scale are possible, an increase in all resources of, say, 10 percent will cause a more-than-proportionate increase in output of, say, 20 percent. The result will be a decline in ATC.

In many U.S. manufacturing industries, economies of scale have been of great significance. Firms that have expanded their scale of operations to obtain economies of mass production have survived and flourished. Those unable to expand have become relatively high-cost producers, doomed to struggle to survive.

Diseconomies of Scale In time the expansion of a firm may lead to diseconomies and therefore higher average total costs.

The main factor causing **diseconomies of scale** is the difficulty of efficiently controlling and coordinating a firm's operations as it becomes a large-scale producer. In a small plant a single key executive may make all the basic decisions for the plant's operation. Because of the firm's small size, the executive is close to the production line, understands the firm's operations, and can make efficient decisions because the small plant size requires only a relatively small amount of information to be examined and understood in order to optimize production.

This neat picture changes as a firm grows. One person cannot assemble, digest, and understand all the information essential to decision making on a large scale. Authority must be delegated to many vice presidents, second vice presidents, and so forth. This expansion of the management hierarchy leads to problems of communication and cooperation, bureaucratic red tape, and the possibility that decisions will not be coordinated. At the same time, each new manager must be paid a salary. Thus, declining efficiency in making and executing decisions goes hand-in-hand with rising average total costs as bureaucracy expands beyond a certain point.

Also, in massive production facilities workers may feel alienated from their employers and care little about working efficiently. Opportunities to shirk, by avoiding work in favor of on-the-job leisure, may be greater in large plants than in small ones. Countering worker alienation and shirking may require additional worker supervision, which increases costs.

Where diseconomies of scale are operative, an increase in all inputs of, say, 10 percent will cause a less-than-proportionate increase in output of, say, 5 percent. As a consequence, ATC will increase. The rising portion of the long-run cost curves in Figure 9.9 illustrates diseconomies of scale.

Constant Returns to Scale In some industries a rather wide range of output may exist between the output at which economies of scale end and the output at which diseconomies of scale begin. That is, there may be a range of **constant returns to scale** over which long-run average cost does not change. The q_1q_2 output range of Figure 9.9a is an example. Here a given percentage increase in all inputs of, say, 10 percent will cause a proportionate 10 percent increase in output. Thus, in this range ATC is constant.

Minimum Efficient Scale and Industry Structure

Economies and diseconomies of scale are an important determinant of an industry's structure. Here we introduce the concept of **minimum efficient scale (MES),** which is the lowest level of output at which a firm can minimize long-run average costs. In Figure 9.9a that level occurs at q_1 units of output. Because of the extended range of constant returns to scale, firms producing substantially greater outputs could also realize the minimum attainable long-run average costs. Specifically, firms within the q_1 to q_2 range would be equally efficient. So we would not be surprised to find an industry with such cost conditions to be populated by firms of quite

3-D Printers

3-D Printers Are Poised to Replace Mass Production with Mass Customization.

Both a billionaire and your Average Joe can buy a pocketknife for $10. They can also both buy an iPhone for $199. And they can both purchase a new compact car for under $15,000.

The fact that all of these items are affordable to both a billionaire and your Average Joe is due to mass production and economies of scale. The iPhone, for instance, is one of the most complicated devices ever made. It contains cutting-edge technologies for graphics, voice recognition, battery length, screen durability, and many other features. Most of those technologies took hundreds of millions—if not billions—of dollars to develop and the factories that manufacture the iPhone and its components themselves cost many billions of dollars to set up. Yet, the iPhone is so inexpensive that Average Joes can afford to buy one.

That mass affordability is the result of mass production coupled with mass sales. Marginal costs are typically quite low with mass production. So if manufacturers can tap mass markets and sell their products in large numbers, they can achieve low per-unit costs by spreading the massive fixed costs (for developing the new technologies and setting up the factories) over many units. Doing so results in economies of scale, low average total costs per unit, and low prices that even average folks can afford.

Mass production and mass sales first became possible during the Industrial Revolution, which began in England during the late 1700s and then spread through most of the rest of the world

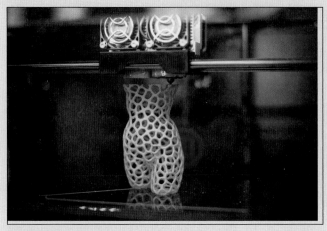

Source: © Timur Emek/Getty Images

during the next two centuries. The Industrial Revolution occurred when steam-powered engines became powerful enough to drive factory equipment, propel ships, and pull trains. Engineers and inventors used steam power to automate factories and initiate the low-cost mass production of consumer goods. That process only accelerated when, in the late nineteenth century, the so-called Second Industrial Revolution saw electricity harnessed to drive factories and provide lighting.

different sizes. The apparel, food processing, furniture, wood products, snowboard, banking, and small-appliance industries are examples. With an extended range of constant returns to scale, relatively large and relatively small firms can coexist in an industry and be equally successful.

Compare this with Figure 9.9b, where economies of scale continue over a wide range of outputs and diseconomies of scale appear only at very high levels of output. This pattern of declining long-run average total cost occurs in the automobile, aluminum, steel, and other heavy industries. The same pattern holds in several of the new industries related to information technology, for example, computer microchips, operating system software, and Internet service provision.

Given consumer demand, efficient production will be achieved with a few large-scale producers. Small firms cannot realize the minimum efficient scale and will not be able to compete. In the extreme, economies of scale might extend beyond the market's size, resulting in what is termed **natural monopoly,** a relatively rare market situation in which average

total cost is minimized when only one firm produces the particular good or service.

Where economies of scale are few and diseconomies come into play quickly, the minimum efficient size occurs at a low level of output, as shown in Figure 9.9c. In such industries a particular level of consumer demand will support a large number of relatively small producers. Many retail trades and some types of farming fall into this category. So do certain kinds of light manufacturing such as the baking, clothing, and shoe industries. Fairly small firms are more efficient than larger-scale producers in such industries.

Our point here is that the shape of the long-run average-total-cost curve is determined by technology and the economies and diseconomies of scale that result. The shape of the long-run ATC curve, in turn, can be significant in determining whether an industry is populated by a relatively large number of small firms or is dominated by a few large producers, or lies somewhere in between.

But we must be cautious in our assessment because industry structure does not depend on cost conditions alone.

Mass sales, however, are not easy. They require large distribution networks, massive advertising budgets, and, perhaps most important, cheap ways of shipping products from factories to consumers. Thus, it was crucially important that transportation was also vastly improved during the First and Second Industrial Revolutions. If not for better ships, smoother roads, and cheap transportation by railroad, transportation costs would have been so high that consumers would not have been able to afford mass-produced products shipped from distant factories.

Now, a new technology promises to deliver a Third Industrial Revolution that will feature not only low production costs but also zero transportation costs. Even better, both of those highly attractive features will be possible *even if you make only a single unit of a product*. In addition, each unit can be fully customized to a consumer's wants and needs. As a result, our world of affordable mass production may soon be replaced by a world of affordable mass customization.

The new technology is called additive manufacturing and it creates objects using computer-controlled devices known as "3-D printers." The 3-D (three-dimensional) printers contain a fine powder of metal or plastic particles that sit in a bin. A laser moves rapidly over the powder, the heat of its beam fusing small clumps of the powder together. Guided by a computerized blueprint, the rapidly moving laser can fuse a single layer of a complicated object together in just a few seconds.

The bin is then lowered a bit, another layer of powder is placed on top, and the laser again begins to shoot, this time fusing together both the previous layer as well as the current layer. Doing this over and over, one layer atop another, results in a solid object whose shape is limited only by the complexity of the blueprint. Any of the powder that is not struck by the laser and incorporated into the object is simply recycled for later use.

Because 3-D printers are inexpensive, they could potentially be located anywhere. Thus, there is no need to worry about transportation costs since objects could be manufactured by consumers in their own homes or in local workshops located only a short drive away. And because the powders are cheap and the machines only require a modest amount of electricity, anything that could be made using a 3-D printer would be inexpensive even if you were only making a single unit.

The First Industrial Revolution delivered low prices by spreading massive fixed costs over many units. The Third Industrial Revolution is set to deliver even lower prices by eliminating two types of costs—the massive fixed costs necessary to set up large factories and the transportation costs needed to ship resources to factories and then finished goods to consumers.

One major cost might still remain, however. That is the cost of paying people to make the blueprints that drive the 3-D printers. But just as digital file sharing has pushed the price of recorded music toward zero, many analysts suspect that digital file sharing will also drive the price of blueprints very low. If so, the cost of manufactured goods may soon plunge to levels even lower than what has been achieved through mass production.

So far, only relatively simple objects can be made with 3-D printers. But some engineers see a day in the not-so-distant future when it may be possible to create even complicated devices like an iPhone using additive manufacturing. If so, people will simply download inexpensive blueprints, make a few changes to customize the product, and then "print" what they want.

Government policies, the geographic size of markets, managerial strategy and skill, and other factors must be considered in explaining the structure of a particular industry.

QUICK REVIEW 9.3

✓ Most firms have U-shaped long-run average-total-cost curves, reflecting economies and then diseconomies of scale.

✓ Economies of scale are the consequence of greater specialization of labor and management, more efficient capital equipment, and the spreading of start-up costs over more units of output.

✓ Diseconomies of scale are caused by the problems of coordination and communication that arise in large firms.

✓ Minimum efficient scale (MES) is the lowest level of output at which a firm's long-run average total cost is at a minimum.

Applications and Illustrations

LO9.5 Give business examples of short-run costs, economies of scale, and minimum efficient scale (MES).

The business world offers many examples relating to short-run costs, economies of scale, and minimum efficient scale (MES). Here are just a few.

Rising Gasoline Prices

As we discuss in the appendix to Chapter 3, changes in supply and demand often lead to rapid increases in the price of gasoline. Because gasoline is used to power the vast majority of all motor vehicles, including those used by businesses, increases in the price of gasoline lead to increases in firms' short-run variable costs, marginal costs, and average total costs. In terms of our analysis, their AVC, MC, and ATC curves all shift upward when an increase in the price of gasoline increases production costs.

The extent of these upward shifts depends upon the relative importance of gasoline as a variable input in the various firms' individual production processes. Package-delivery companies like FedEx that use a lot of gasoline-powered vehicles will see substantial upward shifts while software companies like Symantec (Norton) that mainly deliver their products through Internet downloads may see only small upward shifts.

Successful Start-Up Firms

The U.S. economy has greatly benefited over the past several decades from the explosive growth of scores of highly successful start-up firms. These firms typically reduce their costs by moving from higher to lower points on their short-run cost curves and by downward and to-the-right shifts of their short-run cost curves via economies of scale. That has certainly been the case for such former start-up firms as Intel (microchips), Starbucks (coffee), Microsoft (software), Dell (personal computers), Google (Internet searches), and Cisco Systems (Internet switching).

A major source of lower average total cost for rapidly growing firms is the ability to spread huge product development and advertising costs over a larger number of units of output. These firms also achieve economies of scale from learning by doing and through increased specialization of labor, management, and equipment. After starting up, such firms experience declining average total costs over the years or even decades it takes them to eventually reach their respective MESs.

The Verson Stamping Machine

In 1996 Verson (a U.S. firm located in Chicago) introduced a 49-foot-tall metal-stamping machine that is the size of a house and weighs as much as 12 locomotives. This $30 million machine, which cuts and sculpts raw sheets of steel into automobile hoods and fenders, enables automakers to make new parts in just 5 minutes, compared with 8 hours for older stamping presses. A single machine is designed to make 5 million auto parts per year. So, to achieve the cost saving from the machine, an auto manufacturer must have sufficient auto production to use all these parts. By allowing the use of this cost-saving piece of equipment, large firm size achieves economies of scale.

The Daily Newspaper

Daily newspapers have been going bankrupt in rapid succession over the past several years as both advertising dollars and news readership have shifted to the Internet. The falling circulation numbers have caused average fixed costs to rise significantly as newspapers are forced to spread their substantial fixed costs over fewer and fewer papers. The spike in average fixed costs has, in turn, forced newspapers to sharply increase their prices. Between July 2007 and July 2009, for instance, the *New York Times* had to raise its cover price three times as advertising revenues plunged and fixed costs had to be spread over fewer and fewer papers. Starting at $1 per copy, the cover price had to be raised to $1.25, then $1.50, and then $2.00.

With readership continuing to fall, newspapers face an average-fixed-cost death spiral. The more they raise their prices, the less they will sell. But the less their sales, the higher their average fixed costs and thus the more they must raise their prices. As a result, printed newspapers could ultimately be a thing of the past, with both advertising and news delivery shifting mainly to the Internet.

Aircraft and Concrete Plants

Why are there only two plants in the United States (both operated by Boeing) that produce large commercial aircraft and thousands of plants (owned by hundreds of firms) that produce ready-mixed concrete? The simple answer is that MES is radically different in the two industries. Why is that? First, while economies of scale are extensive in assembling large commercial aircraft, they are only very modest in mixing concrete. Manufacturing airplanes is a complex process that requires huge facilities, thousands of workers, and very expensive, specialized machinery. Economies of scale extend to huge plant sizes. But mixing portland cement, sand, gravel, and water to produce concrete requires only a handful of workers and relatively inexpensive equipment. Economies of scale are exhausted at relatively small size.

The differing MESs also derive from the vastly different sizes of the geographic markets. The market for commercial airplanes is global, and aircraft manufacturers can deliver new airplanes anywhere in the world by flying them there. In contrast, the geographic market for a concrete plant is roughly the 50-mile radius within which the concrete can be delivered before it "sets up." So thousands of small concrete plants locate close to their customers in hundreds of small and large cities in the United States.

SUMMARY

LO9.1 Explain why economic costs include both explicit (revealed and expressed) costs and implicit (present but not obvious) costs.

The economic cost of using a resource to produce a good or service is the value or worth that the resource would have had in its best alternative use. Economic costs include explicit costs, which flow to resources owned and supplied by others, and implicit costs, which are payments for the use of self-owned and self-employed resources. One implicit cost is a normal profit to the entrepreneur. Economic profit occurs when total revenue exceeds total cost (= explicit costs + implicit costs, including a normal profit).

In the short run a firm's plant capacity is fixed. The firm can use its plant more or less intensively by adding or subtracting units of variable resources, but it does not have sufficient time in the short run to alter plant size.

LO9.2 Relate the law of diminishing returns to a firm's short-run production costs.

The law of diminishing returns describes what happens to output as a fixed plant is used more intensively. As successive units of a variable resource such as labor are added to a fixed plant, beyond some point the marginal product associated with each additional unit of a resource declines.

LO9.3 Describe the distinctions between fixed and variable costs and among total, average, and marginal costs.

Because some resources are variable and others are fixed, costs can be classified as variable or fixed in the short run. Fixed costs are independent of the level of output; variable costs vary with output. The total cost of any output is the sum of fixed and variable costs at that output.

Average fixed, average variable, and average total costs are fixed, variable, and total costs per unit of output. Average fixed cost declines continuously as output increases because a fixed sum is being spread over a larger and larger number of units of production. A graph of average variable cost is U-shaped, reflecting increasing returns followed by diminishing returns. Average total cost is the sum of average fixed and average variable costs; its graph is also U-shaped.

Marginal cost is the extra, or additional, cost of producing one more unit of output. It is the amount by which total cost and total variable cost change when one more or one less unit of output is produced. Graphically, the marginal-cost curve intersects the ATC and AVC curves at their minimum points.

Lower resource prices shift cost curves downward, as does technological progress. Higher input prices shift cost curves upward.

LO9.4 Use economies of scale to link a firm's size and its average costs in the long run.

The long run is a period of time sufficiently long for a firm to vary the amounts of all resources used, including plant size. In the long run all costs are variable. The long-run ATC, or planning, curve is composed of segments of short-run ATC curves, and it represents the various plant sizes a firm can construct in the long run.

The long-run ATC curve is generally U-shaped. Economies of scale are first encountered as a small firm expands. Greater specialization in the use of labor and management, the ability to use the most efficient equipment, and the spreading of start-up costs among more units of output all contribute to economies of scale. As the firm continues to grow, it will encounter diseconomies of scale stemming from the managerial complexities that accompany large-scale production. The output ranges over which economies and diseconomies of scale occur in an industry are often an important determinant of the structure of that industry.

A firm's minimum efficient scale (MES) is the lowest level of output at which it can minimize its long-run average cost. In some industries, MES occurs at such low levels of output that numerous firms can populate the industry. In other industries, MES occurs at such high output levels that only a few firms can exist in the long run.

LO9.5 Give business examples of short-run costs, economies of scale, and minimum efficient scale (MES).

Rising gasoline prices increase (shift upward) the AVC, ATC, and MC cost curves of firms like FedEx that use gasoline as an input in their production processes.

Starbucks, Facebook, and many other successful start-up firms that experienced rapid growth reduced costs and shifted their cost curves down and to the right by spreading product-development and advertising costs over larger numbers of units and by exploiting the economies of scale that can be generated through learning by doing and increased specialization of labor, management, and equipment.

Because minimum efficient scale (MES) is extremely large for commercial aircraft, Boeing only has two production facilities in the United States. By contrast, MES is very small in concrete manufacturing. So there are thousands of concrete makers in the United States.

TERMS AND CONCEPTS

economic cost	marginal product (MP)	marginal cost (MC)
explicit costs	average product (AP)	economies of scale
implicit costs	law of diminishing returns	diseconomies of scale
accounting profit	fixed costs	constant returns to scale
normal profit	variable costs	minimum efficient scale (MES)
economic profit	total cost	natural monopoly
short run	average fixed cost (AFC)	
long run	average variable cost (AVC)	
total product (TP)	average total cost (ATC)	

The following and additional problems can be found in ▣ **connect**

DISCUSSION QUESTIONS

1. Distinguish between explicit and implicit costs, giving examples of each. What are some explicit and implicit costs of attending college? **LO9.1**

2. Distinguish among accounting profit, economic profit, and normal profit. Does accounting profit or economic profit determine how entrepreneurs allocate resources between different business ventures? Explain. **LO9.1**

3. Complete the following table by calculating marginal product and average product.

Inputs of Labor	Total Product	Marginal Product	Average Product
0	0	_____	
1	15	_____	_____
2	34	_____	_____
3	51	_____	_____
4	65	_____	_____
5	74	_____	_____
6	80	_____	_____
7	83	_____	_____
8	82	_____	_____

Plot the total, marginal, and average products and explain in detail the relationship between each pair of curves. Explain why marginal product first rises, then declines, and ultimately becomes negative. What bearing does the law of diminishing returns have on short-run costs? Be specific. "When marginal product is rising, marginal cost is falling. And when marginal product is diminishing, marginal cost is rising." Illustrate and explain graphically. **LO9.2**

4. Why can the distinction between fixed costs and variable costs be made in the short run? Classify the following as fixed or variable costs: advertising expenditures, fuel, interest on company-issued bonds, shipping charges, payments for raw materials, real estate taxes, executive salaries, insurance premiums, wage payments, depreciation and obsolescence charges, sales taxes, and rental payments on leased office machinery. "There are no fixed costs in the long run; all costs are variable." Explain. **LO9.3**

5. List several fixed and variable costs associated with owning and operating an automobile. Suppose you are considering whether to drive your car or fly 1,000 miles to Florida for spring break. Which costs—fixed, variable, or both—would you take into account in making your decision? Would any implicit costs be relevant? Explain. **LO9.3**

6. Use the concepts of economies and diseconomies of scale to explain the shape of a firm's long-run ATC curve. What is the concept of minimum efficient scale? What bearing can the shape of the long-run ATC curve have on the structure of an industry? **LO9.4**

7. **LAST WORD** Does additive manufacturing rely on economies of scale to deliver low costs? What are two ways in which additive manufacturing lowers costs? Besides what's written in the book, might there be another reason to expect 3-D blueprints to be inexpensive? (Hint: Think in terms of supply and demand.)

REVIEW QUESTIONS

1. Linda sells 100 bottles of homemade ketchup for $10 each. The cost of the ingredients, the bottles, and the labels was $700. In addition, it took her 20 hours to make the ketchup and to do so she took time off from a job that paid her $20 per hour. Linda's accounting profit is _____ while her economic profit is _____ . **LO9.1**
   a. $700; $400
   b. $300; $100
   c. $300; negative $100
   d. $1,000; negative $1,100

2. Which of the following are short-run and which are long-run adjustments? **LO9.1**
   a. Wendy's builds a new restaurant.
   b. Harley-Davidson Corporation hires 200 more production workers.
   c. A farmer increases the amount of fertilizer used on his corn crop.
   d. An Alcoa aluminum plant adds a third shift of workers.

3. A firm has fixed costs of $60 and variable costs as indicated in the table at the top of the next page. Complete the table and check your calculations by referring to problem 4 at the end of Chapter 10. **LO9.3**
   a. Graph total fixed cost, total variable cost, and total cost. Explain how the law of diminishing returns influences the shapes of the variable-cost and total-cost curves.
   b. Graph AFC, AVC, ATC, and MC. Explain the derivation and shape of each of these four curves and their relationships to one another. Specifically, explain in nontechnical terms why the MC curve intersects both the AVC and the ATC curves at their minimum points.
   c. Explain how the location of each curve graphed in question 3b would be altered if (1) total fixed cost had been $100 rather than $60 and (2) total variable cost had been $10 less at each level of output.

4. Indicate how each of the following would shift the (1) marginal-cost curve, (2) average-variable-cost curve, (3) average-fixed-cost

Total Product	Total Fixed Cost	Total Variable Cost	Total Cost	Average Fixed Cost	Average Variable Cost	Average Total Cost	Marginal Cost
0	$ ____	$ 0	$ ____			$ ____	
1	____	45	____	$ ____	$ ____	____	$ ____
2	____	85	____	____	____	____	____
3	____	120	____	____	____	____	____
4	____	150	____	____	____	____	____
5	____	185	____	____	____	____	____
6	____	225	____	____	____	____	____
7	____	270	____	____	____	____	____
8	____	325	____	____	____	____	____
9	____	390	____	____	____	____	____
10	____	465	____	____	____	____	____

curve, and (4) average-total-cost curve of a manufacturing firm. In each case specify the direction of the shift. LO9.3
   a. A reduction in business property taxes.
   b. An increase in the nominal wages of production workers.
   c. A decrease in the price of electricity.
   d. An increase in insurance rates on plant and equipment.
   e. An increase in transportation costs.
5. True or false. The U shape of the long-run ATC curve is the result of diminishing returns. LO9.4
6. Suppose a firm has only three possible plant-size options, represented by the ATC curves shown in the figure to the right. What plant size will the firm choose in producing (a) 50, (b) 130, (c) 160, and (d) 250 units of output? Draw the

firm's long-run average-cost curve on the diagram and describe this curve. LO9.4

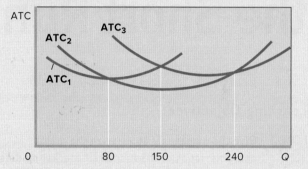

PROBLEMS

1. Gomez runs a small pottery firm. He hires one helper at $12,000 per year, pays annual rent of $5,000 for his shop, and spends $20,000 per year on materials. He has $40,000 of his own funds invested in equipment (pottery wheels, kilns, and so forth) that could earn him $4,000 per year if alternatively invested. He has been offered $15,000 per year to work as a potter for a competitor. He estimates his entrepreneurial talents are worth $3,000 per year. Total annual revenue from pottery sales is $72,000. Calculate the accounting profit and the economic profit for Gomez's pottery firm. LO9.1

2. Imagine you have some workers and some handheld computers that you can use to take inventory at a warehouse. There are diminishing returns to taking inventory. If one worker uses one computer, he can inventory 100 items per hour. Two workers sharing a computer can together inventory 150 items per hour. Three workers sharing a computer can together inventory 160 items per hour. And four or more workers sharing a computer can together inventory fewer than 160 items per hour. Computers cost $100 each and you must pay each worker $25 per hour. If you assign one worker per computer, what is the cost of inventorying a single item? What if you assign two workers per computer? Three? How many workers per computer should you assign if you wish to minimize the cost of inventorying a single item? LO9.2

3. You are a newspaper publisher. You are in the middle of a one-year rental contract for your factory that requires you to pay $500,000 per month, and you have contractual labor obligations of $1 million per month that you can't get out of. You also have a marginal printing cost of $0.25 per paper as well as a marginal delivery cost of $0.10 per paper. If sales fall by 20 percent from 1 million papers per month to 800,000 papers per month, what happens to the AFC per paper, the MC per paper, and the minimum amount that you must charge to break even on these costs? LO9.3

4. There are economies of scale in ranching, especially with regard to fencing land. Suppose that barbed-wire fencing costs $10,000 per mile to set up. How much would it cost to fence a single property whose area is one square mile if that property also happens to be perfectly square, with sides that are each one mile long? How much would it cost to fence exactly four such properties, which together would contain four square miles of area? Now, consider how much it would cost to fence in four square miles of ranch land if, instead, it comes as a single large square that is two miles long on each side. Which is more costly—fencing in the four, one-square-mile properties or the single four-square-mile property? LO9.4

Pure Competition in the Short Run

Learning Objectives

LO10.1 Give the names and summarize the main characteristics of the four basic market models.

LO10.2 List the conditions required for purely competitive markets.

LO10.3 Explain how demand is seen by a purely competitive seller.

LO10.4 Convey how purely competitive firms can use the total-revenue–total-cost approach to maximize profits or minimize losses in the short run.

LO10.5 Explain how purely competitive firms can use the marginal-revenue–marginal-cost approach to maximize profits or minimize losses in the short run.

LO10.6 Explain why a competitive firm's marginal cost curve is the same as its supply curve.

In Chapter 6 we examined the relationship between product demand and total revenue, and in Chapter 9 we discussed production costs. Now we want to connect revenues and costs to see how a business decides what price to charge and how much output to produce. A firm's decisions concerning price and production depend greatly on the character of the industry in which it is operating. There is no "average" or "typical" industry. At one extreme is an industry in which a single producer dominates the market; at the other extreme are industries in which there are thousands of firms that each produce a tiny fraction of market supply. Between these extremes are many other types of industries.

Since we cannot examine each industry individually, we will focus on four basic *models* of **market structure.** Together, these models will help you understand how price and output are determined in the many product markets in the economy. They also will help you evaluate the efficiency or inefficiency of those markets. Finally, these four models will provide a crucial background for assessing public policies (such as antitrust policy) relating to certain firms and industries.

Four Market Models

LO10.1 Give the names and summarize the main characteristics of the four basic market models.

Economists group industries into four distinct market structures: pure competition, pure monopoly, monopolistic competition, and oligopoly. These four market models differ in several respects: the number of firms in the industry, whether those firms produce a standardized product or try to differentiate their products from those of other firms, and how easy or how difficult it is for firms to enter the industry.

Very briefly the four models are as follows:

- **Pure competition** involves a very large number of firms producing a standardized product (that is, a product like cotton, for which each producer's output is virtually identical to that of every other producer.) New firms can enter or exit the industry very easily.

- **Pure monopoly** is a market structure in which one firm is the sole seller of a product or service (for example, a local electric utility). Since the entry of additional firms is blocked, one firm constitutes the entire industry. The pure monopolist produces a single unique product, so product differentiation is not an issue.

- **Monopolistic competition** is characterized by a relatively large number of sellers producing differentiated products (clothing, furniture, books). Present in this model is widespread *nonprice competition,* a selling strategy in which a firm does not try to distinguish its product on the basis of price but instead on attributes like design and workmanship (an approach called *product differentiation*). Either entry to or exit from monopolistically competitive industries is quite easy.

- **Oligopoly** involves only a few sellers of a standardized or differentiated product, so each firm is affected by the decisions of its rivals and must take those decisions into account in determining its own price and output.

Table 10.1 summarizes the characteristics of the four models for easy comparison and later reference. In discussing these market models, we will occasionally distinguish the characteristics of *pure competition* from those of the three other basic market structures, which together we will designate as **imperfect competition.**

Pure Competition: Characteristics and Occurrence

LO10.2 List the conditions required for purely competitive markets.

Although pure competition is relatively rare in the real world, this market model is highly relevant to several industries. In particular, we can learn much about markets for agricultural goods, fish products, foreign exchange, basic metals, and stock shares by studying the pure-competition model. Also, pure competition is a meaningful starting point for any discussion of price and output determination. Moreover, the operation of a purely competitive economy provides a standard, or norm, for evaluating the efficiency of the real-world economy.

Let's take a fuller look at pure competition, the focus of the remainder of this chapter:

- ***Very large numbers*** A basic feature of a purely competitive market is the presence of a large number of independently acting sellers, often offering their products in large national or international markets. Examples: markets for farm commodities, the stock market, and the foreign exchange market.

- ***Standardized product*** Purely competitive firms produce a standardized (identical or homogeneous) product. As long as the price is the same, consumers will be indifferent about which seller to buy the product from. Buyers view the products of firms B, C, D, and E as perfect substitutes for the product of firm A. Because purely competitive firms sell standardized products,

TABLE 10.1 Characteristics of the Four Basic Market Models

Characteristic	Market Model			
	Pure Competition	**Monopolistic Competition**	**Oligopoly**	**Pure Monopoly**
Number of firms	A very large number	Many	Few	One
Type of product	Standardized	Differentiated	Standardized or differentiated	Unique; no close substitutes
Control over price	None	Some, but within rather narrow limits	Limited by mutual interdependence; considerable with collusion	Considerable
Conditions of entry	Very easy, no obstacles	Relatively easy	Significant obstacles	Blocked
Nonprice competition	None	Considerable emphasis on advertising, brand names, trademarks	Typically a great deal, particularly with product differentiation	Mostly public relations advertising
Examples	Agriculture	Retail trade, dresses, shoes	Steel, automobiles, farm implements, many household appliances	Local utilities

they make no attempt to differentiate their products and do not engage in other forms of nonprice competition.

- *"Price takers"* In a purely competitive market, individual firms do not exert control over product price. Each firm produces such a small fraction of total output that increasing or decreasing its output will not perceptibly influence total supply or, therefore, product price. In short, the competitive firm is a **price taker:** It cannot change market price; it can only adjust to it. That means that the individual competitive producer is at the mercy of the market. Asking a price higher than the market price would be futile. Consumers will not buy from firm A at $2.05 when its 9,999 competitors are selling an identical product, and therefore a perfect substitute, at $2 per unit. Conversely, because firm A can sell as much as it chooses at $2 per unit, it has no reason to charge a lower price, say, $1.95. Doing that would shrink its profit.

- *Free entry and exit* New firms can freely enter and existing firms can freely leave purely competitive industries. No significant legal, technological, financial, or other obstacles prohibit new firms from selling their output in any competitive market.

Demand as Seen by a Purely Competitive Seller

LO10.3 Explain how demand is seen by a purely competitive seller.
We begin by examining demand from a purely competitive seller's viewpoint to see how it affects revenue. This seller might be a wheat farmer, a strawberry grower, a sheep rancher, a foreign-currency broker, or some other pure competitor. Because each purely competitive firm offers only a negligible fraction of total market supply, it must accept the price determined by the market; it is a price taker, not a price maker.

Perfectly Elastic Demand

The demand schedule faced by the *individual firm* in a purely competitive industry is perfectly elastic at the market price, as demonstrated in Figure 10.1. As shown in column 1 of the table in Figure 10.1, the market price is $131. The firm represented cannot obtain a higher price by restricting its output, nor does it need to lower its price to increase its sales volume. Columns 1 and 2 show that the firm can produce and sell as many or as few units as it likes at the market price of $131.

We are *not* saying that *market* demand is perfectly elastic in a competitive market. Rather, market demand graphs as a downsloping curve. An entire industry (all firms producing a particular product) can affect price by changing industry output. For example, all firms, acting independently but simultaneously, can increase price by reducing output. But the individual competitive firm cannot do that because its output represents such a small fraction of its industry's total output.

For the individual competitive firm, the market price is therefore a fixed value at which it can sell as many or as few units as it cares to. Graphically, this implies that the individual competitive firm's demand curve will plot as a straight, horizontal line such as *D* in Figure 10.1.

Average, Total, and Marginal Revenue

The firm's demand schedule is also its average-revenue schedule. Price per unit to the purchaser is also revenue per unit, or average revenue, to the seller. To say that all buyers must pay $131 per unit is to say that the revenue per unit, or **average revenue** received by the seller, is $131. Price and average revenue are the same thing.

The **total revenue** for each sales level is found by multiplying price by the corresponding quantity the firm can sell. (Column 1 multiplied by column 2 in the table in Figure 10.1 yields column 3.) In this case, total revenue increases by a constant amount, $131, for each additional unit of sales. Each unit sold adds exactly its constant price—no more or no less—to total revenue.

When a firm is pondering a change in its output, it will consider how its total revenue will change as a result. **Marginal revenue** is the change in total revenue (or the extra revenue) that results from selling one more unit of output. In column 3 of the table in Figure 10.1, total revenue is zero when zero units are sold. The first unit of output sold increases total revenue from zero to $131, so marginal revenue for that unit is $131. The second unit sold increases total revenue from $131 to $262, and marginal revenue is again $131. Note in column 4 that marginal revenue is a constant $131, as is price. *In pure competition, marginal revenue and price are equal.*

Figure 10.1 shows the purely competitive firm's total-revenue, demand, marginal-revenue, and average-revenue curves. Total revenue (TR) is a straight line that slopes upward to the right. Its slope is constant because each extra unit of sales increases TR by $131. The demand curve (*D*) is horizontal, indicating perfect price elasticity. The marginal-revenue (MR) curve coincides with the demand curve because the product price (and hence MR) is constant. The average revenue (AR) curve equals price and therefore also coincides with the demand curve.

> ## QUICK REVIEW 10.1
>
> ✓ In a purely competitive industry a large number of firms produce a standardized product and there are no significant barriers to entry.
>
> ✓ The demand seen by a purely competitive firm is perfectly elastic—horizontal on a graph—at the market price.
>
> ✓ Marginal revenue and average revenue for a purely competitive firm coincide with the firm's demand curve; total revenue rises by the product price for each additional unit sold.

FIGURE 10.1 A purely competitive firm's demand and revenue curves. The demand curve (D) of a purely competitive firm is a horizontal line (perfectly elastic) because the firm can sell as much output as it wants at the market price (here, $131). Because each additional unit sold increases total revenue by the amount of the price, the firm's total-revenue (TR) curve is a straight upsloping line and its marginal-revenue (MR) curve coincides with the firm's demand curve. The average-revenue (AR) curve also coincides with the demand curve.

Firm's Demand Schedule		Firm's Revenue Data	
(1) Product Price (P) (Average Revenue)	(2) Quantity Demanded (Q)	(3) Total Revenue (TR), (1) × (2)	(4) Marginal Revenue (MR)
$131	0	$ 0	
131	1	131	$131
131	2	262	131
131	3	393	131
131	4	524	131
131	5	655	131
131	6	786	131
131	7	917	131
131	8	1048	131
131	9	1179	131
131	10	1310	131

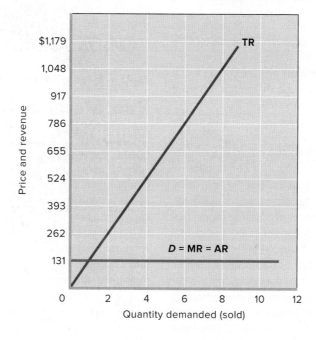

Profit Maximization in the Short Run: Total-Revenue–Total-Cost Approach

LO10.4 Convey how purely competitive firms can use the total-revenue–total-cost approach to maximize profits or minimize losses in the short run.

Because the purely competitive firm is a price taker, it cannot attempt to maximize its profit by raising or lowering the price it charges. With its price set by supply and demand in the overall market, the only variable that the firm can control is its output. As a result, the purely competitive firm attempts to maximize its economic profit (or minimize its economic loss) by adjusting its *output*. And, in the short run, the firm has a fixed plant. Thus it can adjust its output only through changes in the amount of variable resources (materials, labor) it uses. It adjusts its variable resources to achieve the output level that maximizes its profit or minimizes its loss.

There are two ways to determine the level of output at which a competitive firm will realize maximum profit or minimum loss. One method is to compare total revenue and total cost; the other is to compare marginal revenue and marginal cost. Both approaches apply to all firms, whether they are pure competitors, pure monopolists, monopolistic competitors, or oligopolists.[1]

We begin by examining profit maximization using the total-revenue–total-cost approach. Confronted with the market price of its product, the competitive producer will ask three questions: (1) Should we produce this product? (2) If so, in what amount? (3) What economic profit (or loss) will we realize?

Let's demonstrate how a pure competitor answers these questions, given a particular set of cost data and a specific market price. Our cost data are already familiar because they are the fixed-cost, variable-cost, and total-cost data in Table 9.2, repeated in columns 1 to 4 of the table in Figure 10.2. (Recall that these data reflect explicit and implicit costs, including a normal profit.) Assuming that the market price is $131, the total revenue for each output level is found by multiplying output (total product) by price. Total-revenue data are in column 5. Then in column 6 we find the profit or loss at each output level by subtracting total cost, TC (column 4), from total revenue, TR (column 5).

Should the firm produce? Definitely. It can obtain a profit by doing so. How much should it produce? Nine units. Column 6 tells us that this is the output at which total economic profit is at a maximum. What economic profit (or loss) will it realize? A $299 economic profit—the difference between total revenue ($1,179) and total cost ($880).

Figure 10.2a compares total revenue and total cost graphically for this profit-maximizing case. Observe again that the total-revenue curve for a purely competitive firm is a straight line (Figure 10.1). Total cost increases with output because more production requires more resources. But the *rate* of increase in total cost varies with the efficiency of the firm, which in turn varies with the amount of variable inputs that are being combined with the firm's current amount of capital (which is fixed in the short run). Stated slightly differently, the cost data reflect Chapter 9's law of diminishing returns. From zero to four units of output, total cost increases at a decreasing rate as the firm temporarily experiences increasing returns. At higher levels of output, however, efficiency falls as crowding causes diminishing returns to set in. Once that happens, the firm's total cost increases at an increasing rate because each additional unit of input yields less output than the previous unit.

Total revenue and total cost are equal where the two curves in Figure 10.2a intersect (at roughly 2 units of output). Total

revenue covers all costs (including a normal profit, which is included in the cost curve), but there is no economic profit. For this reason economists call this output a **break-even point:** an output at which a firm makes a *normal profit* but not an economic profit. If we extended the data beyond 10 units of output, another break-even point would occur where total cost catches up with total revenue, somewhere between 13 and 14 units of output in Figure 10.2a. Any output within the two break-even points identified in the figure will yield an economic profit. The firm achieves maximum profit, however, where the vertical distance between the total-revenue and total-cost curves is greatest. For our particular data, this is at 9 units of output, where maximum profit is $299.

The profit-maximizing output is easier to see in Figure 10.2b, where total profit is graphed for each level of output. Where the total-revenue and total-cost curves intersect in Figure 10.2a, economic profit is zero, as shown by the total-profit line in Figure 10.2b. Where the vertical distance between TR and TC is greatest in the upper graph, economic profit is at its peak ($299), as shown in the lower graph. This firm will choose to produce 9 units since that output maximizes its profit.

Profit Maximization in the Short Run: Marginal-Revenue–Marginal-Cost Approach

LO10.5 Explain how purely competitive firms can use the marginal-revenue–marginal-cost approach to maximize profits or minimize losses in the short run.

In the second approach, the firm compares the amounts that each *additional* unit of output would add to total revenue and to total cost. In other words, the firm compares the *marginal revenue* (MR) and the *marginal cost* (MC) of each successive unit of output. Assuming that producing is preferable to shutting down, the firm should produce any unit of output whose marginal revenue exceeds its marginal cost because the firm would gain more in revenue from selling that unit than it would add to its costs by producing it. Conversely, if the marginal cost of a unit of output exceeds its marginal revenue, the firm should not produce that unit. Producing it would add more to costs than to revenue, and profit would decline or loss would increase.

In the initial stages of production, where output is relatively low, marginal revenue will usually (but not always) exceed marginal cost. So it is profitable to produce through this range of output. But at later stages of production, where output is relatively high, rising marginal costs will exceed marginal revenue. Obviously, a profit-maximizing firm will want to avoid output levels in that range. Separating these two production ranges is a unique point at which marginal revenue

---

[1]To make sure you understand these two approaches, we will apply both of them to output determination under pure competition. But since we want to emphasize the marginal approach, we will limit our graphical application of the total-revenue approach to a situation where the firm maximizes profits. We will then use the marginal approach to examine three cases: profit maximization, loss minimization, and shutdown.

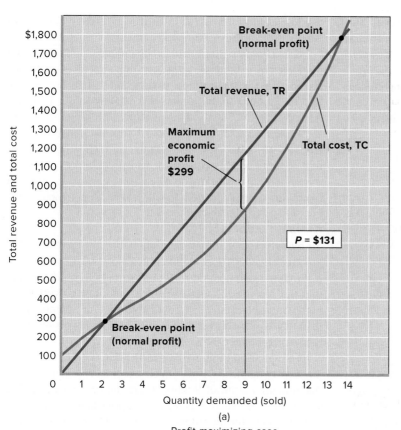

FIGURE 10.2 **Total-revenue–total-cost approach to profit maximization for a purely competitive firm.** (a) The firm's profit is maximized at that output (9 units) where total revenue, TR, exceeds total cost, TC, by the maximum amount. (b) The vertical distance between TR and TC in (a) is plotted as a total-economic-profit curve. Maximum economic profit is $299 at 9 units of output.

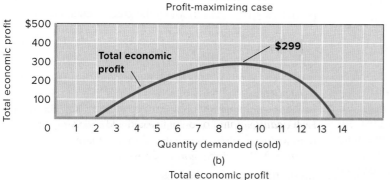

(1) Total Product (Output) (Q)	(2) Total Fixed Cost (TFC)	(3) Total Variable Cost (TVC)	(4) Total Cost (TC)	PRICE: $131	
				(5) Total Revenue (TR)	(6) Profit (+) or Loss (−)
0	$100	$ 0	$ 100	$ 0	$−100
1	100	90	190	131	−59
2	100	170	270	262	−8
3	100	240	340	393	+53
4	100	300	400	524	+124
5	100	370	470	655	+185
6	100	450	550	786	+236
7	100	540	640	917	+277
8	100	650	750	1,048	+298
9	100	780	**880**	**1,179**	**+299**
10	100	930	1,030	1,310	+280

equals marginal cost. This point is the key to the output-determining rule: *In the short run, the firm will maximize profit or minimize loss by producing the output at which marginal revenue equals marginal cost (as long as producing is preferable to shutting down).* This profit-maximizing guide is known as the **MR = MC rule.**

Keep in mind these features of the MR = MC rule:

- For most sets of MR and MC data, MR and MC will be precisely equal at a fractional level of output. In such instances the firm should produce the last complete unit of output for which MR exceeds MC.

- As noted, the rule applies only if producing is preferable to shutting down. We will show shortly that if marginal revenue does not equal or exceed average variable cost, the firm will shut down rather than produce the amount of output at which MR = MC.

- The rule is an accurate guide to profit maximization for all firms whether they are purely competitive, monopolistic, monopolistically competitive, or oligopolistic.

- The rule can be restated as $P = MC$ when applied to a purely competitive firm. Because the demand schedule faced by a competitive seller is perfectly elastic at the going market price, product price and marginal revenue are equal. So under pure competition (and only under pure competition) we may substitute P for MR in the rule: When producing is preferable to shutting down, the competitive firm that wants to maximize its profit or minimize its loss should produce at that point where price equals marginal cost ($P = MC$).

Now let's apply the MR = MC rule or, because we are considering pure competition, the $P = MC$ rule, first using the same price as used in our total-revenue–total-cost approach to profit maximization. Then, by considering other prices, we will demonstrate two additional cases: loss minimization and shutdown. It is crucial that you understand the MR = MC analysis that follows since it reappears in Chapters 12 through 16.

Profit-Maximizing Case

The first five columns of the table in **Figure 10.3 (Key Graph)** reproduce the AFC, AVC, ATC, and MC data derived for our product in Table 9.2. It is the marginal-cost data of column 5 that we will compare with price (equals marginal revenue) for each unit of output. Suppose first that the market price, and therefore marginal revenue, is $131, as shown in column 6.

What is the profit-maximizing output? Every unit of output up to and including the ninth unit represents greater marginal revenue than marginal cost of output. Each of the first 9 units therefore adds to the firm's profit and should be produced. The tenth unit, however, should not be produced. It

would add more to cost ($150) than to revenue ($131). So 9 units is the profit-maximizing output.

The economic profit realized by producing 9 units can be calculated by subtracting total cost from total revenue. Multiplying price ($131) by output (9), we find that total revenue is $1,179. From the average-total-cost data in column 4, we see that ATC is $97.78 at 9 units of output. Multiplying $97.78 by 9 gives us total cost of $880.[2] The difference of $299 (= $1,179 − $880) is the economic profit. Clearly, this firm will prefer to operate rather than shut down.

Perhaps an easier way to calculate the economic profit is to use this simple equation, in which A is average total cost:

$$\text{Profit} = (P - A) \times Q$$

So by subtracting the average total cost ($97.78) from the product price ($131), we obtain a per-unit profit of $33.22. Multiplying that amount by 9 units of output, we determine that the profit is $299. Take some time now to verify the numbers in column 7. You will find that any output other than that which adheres to the MR = MC rule will mean either profits below $299 or losses.

The graph in Figure 10.3 shows price (= MR) and marginal cost graphically. Price equals marginal cost at the profit-maximizing output of 9 units. There the per-unit economic profit is $P - A$, where P is the market price and A is the average total cost for an output of 9 units. The total economic profit is $9 \times (P - A)$, shown by the green rectangular area.

Note that the firm wants to maximize its total profit, not its per-unit profit. Per-unit profit is greatest at 7 units of output, where price exceeds average total cost by $39.57 (= $131 − $91.43). But by producing only 7 units, the firm would be forgoing the production of 2 additional units of output that would clearly contribute to total profit. The firm is happy to accept lower per-unit profits for additional units of output because they nonetheless add to total profit.

Loss-Minimizing Case

Now let's assume that the market price is $81 rather than $131. Should the firm still produce? If so, how much? And what will be the resulting profit or loss? The answers, respectively, are "Yes," "Six units," and "A loss of $64."

The first five columns of the table in Figure 10.4 are the same as the first five columns of the table in Figure 10.3. But column 6 of the table in Figure 10.4 shows the new price (equal to MR), $81. Comparing columns 5 and 6, we find that the first unit of output adds $90 to total cost but only $81 to total revenue. One might conclude: "Don't produce—close down!" But

---

[2]Most of the unit-cost data are rounded figures. Therefore, economic profits calculated from them will typically vary by a few cents from the profits determined in the total-revenue–total-cost approach. Here we simply ignore the few-cents differentials to make our answers consistent with the results of the total-revenue–total-cost approach.

FIGURE 10.3 Short-run profit maximization for a purely competitive firm. The MR = MC output enables the purely competitive firm to maximize profits or to minimize losses. In this case MR (= P in pure competition) and MC are equal at an output Q of 9 units. There, P exceeds the average total cost A = $97.78, so the firm realizes an economic profit of P − A per unit. The total economic profit is represented by the green rectangle and is 9 × (P − A).

(1) Total Product (Output)	(2) Average Fixed Cost (AFC)	(3) Average Variable Cost (AVC)	(4) Average Total Cost (ATC)	(5) Marginal Cost (MC)	(6) Price = Marginal Revenue (MR)	(7) Total Economic Profit (+) or Loss (−)
0						$−100
				$ 90	$131	
1	$100.00	$90.00	$190.00			−59
				80	131	
2	50.00	85.00	135.00			−8
				70	131	
3	33.33	80.00	113.33			+53
				60	131	
4	25.00	75.00	100.00			+124
				70	131	
5	20.00	74.00	94.00			+185
				80	131	
6	16.67	75.00	91.67			+236
				90	131	
7	14.29	77.14	91.43			+277
				110	131	
8	12.50	81.25	93.75			+298
				130	131	
9	11.11	86.67	97.78			+299
				150	131	
10	10.00	93.00	103.00			+280

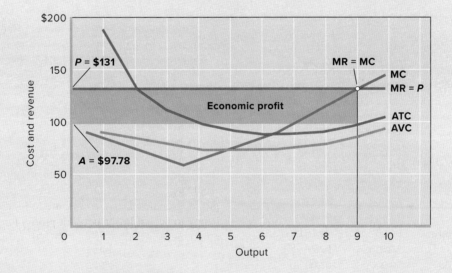

QUICK QUIZ FOR FIGURE 10.3

1. Curve MR is horizontal because:
   a. product price falls as output increases.
   b. the law of diminishing marginal utility is at work.
   c. the market demand for this product is perfectly elastic.
   d. the firm is a price taker.

2. At a price of $131 and 7 units of output:
   a. MR exceeds MC, and the firm should expand its output.
   b. total revenue is less than total cost.
   c. AVC exceeds ATC.
   d. the firm would earn only a normal profit.

3. In maximizing profits at 9 units of output, this firm is adhering to which of the following decision rules?

   a. Produce where MR exceeds MC by the greatest amount.
   b. Produce where P exceeds ATC by the greatest amount.
   c. Produce where total revenue exceeds total cost by the greatest amount.
   d. Produce where average fixed costs are zero.

4. Suppose price declined from $131 to $100. This firm's:
   a. marginal-cost curve would shift downward.
   b. economic profit would fall to zero.
   c. profit-maximizing output would decline.
   d. total cost would fall by more than its total revenue.

Answers: 1. d; 2. a; 3. c; 4. c

FIGURE 10.4 Short-run loss minimization for a purely competitive firm. If price *P* exceeds the minimum AVC (here, $74 at *Q* = 5) but is less than ATC, the MR = MC output (here, 6 units) will permit the firm to minimize its losses. In this instance the loss is *A* − *P* per unit, where *A* is the average total cost at 6 units of output. The total loss is shown by the red area and is equal to 6 × (*A* − *P*).

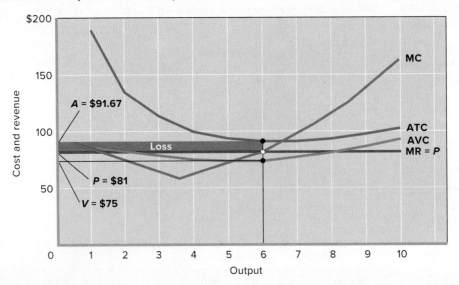

(1) Total Product (Output)	(2) Average Fixed Cost (AFC)	(3) Average Variable Cost (AVC)	(4) Average Total Cost (ATC)	(5) Marginal Cost (MC)	Loss-Minimizing Case		Shutdown Case	
					(6) $81 Price = Marginal Revenue (MR)	(7) Profit (+) or Loss (−), $81 Price	(8) $71 Price = Marginal Revenue (MR)	(9) Profit (+) or Loss (−), $71 Price
0				$ 90	$81	$−100	$71	$−100
1	$100.00	$90.00	$190.00	80	81	−109	71	−119
2	50.00	85.00	135.00	70	81	−108	71	−128
3	33.33	80.00	113.33	60	81	−97	71	−127
4	25.00	75.00	100.00	70	81	−76	71	−116
5	20.00	74.00	94.00	80	81	−65	71	−115
6	16.67	75.00	91.67	90	81	−64	71	−124
7	14.29	77.14	91.43	110	81	−73	71	−143
8	12.50	81.25	93.75	130	81	−102	71	−182
9	11.11	86.67	97.78	150	81	−151	71	−241
10	10.00	93.00	103.00			−220		−320

that would be hasty. Remember that in the very early stages of production, marginal product is low, making marginal cost unusually high. The price–marginal cost relationship improves with increased production. For units 2 through 6, price exceeds marginal cost. Each of these 5 units adds more to revenue than to cost, and as shown in column 7, they decrease the total loss. Together they more than compensate for the "loss" taken on the first unit. Beyond 6 units, however, MC exceeds MR (= *P*). The firm should therefore produce 6 units. In general, the profit-seeking producer should always compare marginal revenue (or price under pure competition) with the rising portion of the marginal-cost schedule or curve.

Will production be profitable? No, because at 6 units of output the average total cost of $91.67 exceeds the price of

$81 by $10.67 per unit. If we multiply that by the 6 units of output, we find the firm's total loss is $64. Alternatively, comparing the total revenue of $486 (= 6 × $81) with the total cost of $550 (= 6 × $91.67), we see again that the firm's loss is $64.

Then why produce? Because this loss is less than the firm's $100 of fixed costs, which is the $100 loss the firm would incur in the short run by closing down. The firm receives enough revenue per unit ($81) to cover its average variable costs of $75 and also provide $6 per unit, or a total of $36, to apply against fixed costs. Therefore, the firm's loss is only $64 (= $100 − $36), not $100.

This loss-minimizing case is illustrated in the graph in Figure 10.4. Wherever price *P* exceeds average variable cost

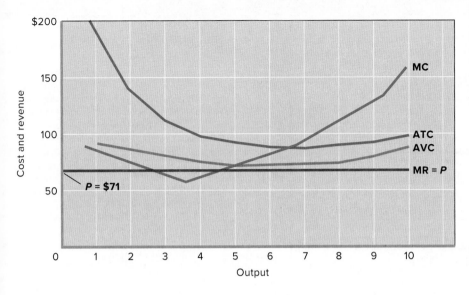

FIGURE 10.5 The short-run shutdown case for a purely competitive firm. If price P falls below the minimum AVC (here, $74 at $Q = 5$), the competitive firm will minimize its losses in the short run by shutting down. There is no level of output at which the firm can produce and incur a loss smaller than its total fixed cost.

AVC but is less than ATC, the firm can pay part, but not all, of its fixed costs by producing. The loss is minimized by producing the output at which MC = MR (here, 6 units). At that output, each unit contributes $P - V$ to covering fixed cost, where V is the AVC at 6 units of output. The per-unit loss is $A - P = \$10.67$, and the total loss is $6 \times (A - P)$, or $64, as shown by the red area.

Shutdown Case

Suppose now that the market yields a price of only $71. Should the firm produce? No, because at every output level the firm's average variable cost is greater than the price (compare columns 3 and 8 of the table in Figure 10.4). The smallest loss it can incur by producing is greater than the $100 fixed cost it will lose by shutting down (as shown by column 9). The best action is to shut down.

You can see this shutdown situation in Figure 10.5. Price comes closest to covering average variable costs at the MR ($= P$) = MC output of 5 units. But even here, price or revenue per unit would fall short of average variable cost by $3 ($= \$74 - \$71$). By producing at the MR ($= P$) = MC output, the firm would lose its $100 worth of fixed cost plus $15 ($3 of variable cost on each of the 5 units), for a total loss of $115. This compares unfavorably with the $100 fixed-cost loss the firm would incur by shutting down and producing no output. So it will make sense for the firm to shut down rather than produce at a $71 price—or at any price less than the minimum average variable cost of $74.

The shutdown case reminds us of the qualifier to our MR ($= P$) = MC rule. A competitive firm will maximize profit or minimize loss in the short run by producing that output at which MR ($= P$) = MC, *provided that market price exceeds minimum average variable cost.*

> **QUICK REVIEW 10.2**
>
> ✓ A firm will choose to produce if it can at least break even and generate a normal profit.
> ✓ Profit is maximized, or loss minimized, at the output at which marginal revenue (or price in pure competition) equals marginal cost, provided that price exceeds variable cost.
> ✓ If the market price is below the minimum average variable cost, the firm will minimize its losses by shutting down.

Marginal Cost and Short-Run Supply

LO10.6 Explain why a competitive firm's marginal cost curve is the same as its supply curve.

In the preceding section we simply selected three different prices and asked what quantity the profit-seeking competitive firm, faced with certain costs, would choose to offer in the market at each price. This set of product prices and corresponding quantities supplied constitutes part of the supply schedule for the competitive firm.

Table 10.2 summarizes the supply schedule data for those three prices ($131, $81, and $71) and four others. This table confirms the direct relationship between product price and quantity supplied that we identified in Chapter 3. Note first that the firm will not produce at price $61 or $71 because both are less than the $74 minimum AVC. Then note that quantity supplied increases as price increases. Observe finally that economic profit is higher at higher prices.

KEY GRAPH

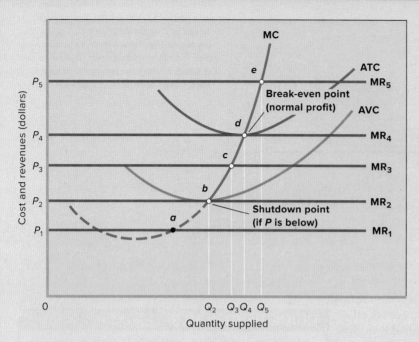

FIGURE 10.6 The $P = MC$ rule and the competitive firm's short-run supply curve. Application of the $P = MC$ rule, as modified by the shutdown case, reveals that the (solid) segment of the firm's MC curve that lies above AVC is the firm's short-run supply curve. More specifically, at price P_1, $P = MC$ at point a, but the firm will produce no output because P_1 is less than minimum AVC. At price P_2 the firm will operate at point b, where it produces Q_2 units and incurs a loss equal to its total fixed cost. At P_3 it operates at point c, where output is Q_3 and the loss is less than total fixed cost. With the price of P_4, the firm operates at point d; in this case the firm earns a normal profit because at output Q_4 price equals ATC. At price P_5 the firm operates at point e and maximizes its economic profit by producing Q_5 units.

Generalized Depiction

Figure 10.6 (Key Graph) generalizes the MR $=$ MC rule and the relationship between short-run production costs and the firm's supply behavior. The ATC, AVC, and MC curves are shown, along with several marginal-revenue lines drawn at possible market prices. Let's observe quantity supplied at each of these prices:

- Price P_1 is below the firm's minimum average variable cost, so at this price the firm won't operate at all. Quantity supplied will be zero, as it will be at all other prices below P_2.

TABLE 10.2 The Supply Schedule of a Competitive Firm Confronted with the Cost Data in the Table in Figure 10.3

Price	Quantity Supplied	Maximum Profit (+) or Minimum Loss (−)
$151	10	$+480
131	9	+299
111	8	+138
91	7	−3
81	6	−64
71	0	−100
61	0	−100

CONSIDER THIS . . .

Source: © LWA/Getty RF

The "Still There" Motel

Have you ever driven by a poorly maintained business facility and wondered why the owner does not either fix up the property or go out of business? The somewhat surprising reason is that it may be unprofitable to improve the facility yet profitable to continue to operate the business as it deteriorates. Seeing why will aid your understanding of the "stay open or shut down" decision facing firms experiencing declining demand.

Consider the story of the Still There Motel on Old Highway North, Anytown, USA. The owner built the motel on the basis of traffic patterns and competition existing several decades ago. But as interstate highways were built, the motel found itself located on a relatively untraveled stretch of road. Also, it faced severe competition from "chain" motels located much closer to the interstate highway.

As demand and revenue fell, Still There moved from profitability to loss ($P <$ ATC). But at first its room rates and annual revenue were sufficient to cover its total variable costs and contribute some to the payment of fixed costs such as insurance and property taxes ($P >$ AVC). By staying open, Still There lost less than it would have if it shut down. But since its total revenue did not cover its total costs (or $P <$ ATC), the owner realized that something must be done in the long run. The owner decided to lower total costs by reducing annual maintenance. In effect, the owner opted to allow the motel to deteriorate as a way of temporarily regaining profitability.

This renewed profitability of Still There cannot last because in time no further reduction of maintenance costs will be possible. The deterioration of the motel structure will produce even lower room rates, and therefore even less total revenue. The owner of Still There knows that sooner or later total revenue will again fall below total cost (or P will again fall below ATC), even with an annual maintenance expense of zero. When that occurs, the owner will close down the business, tear down the structure, and sell the vacant property. But, in the meantime, the motel is still there—open, deteriorating, and profitable.

- Price P_2 is just equal to the minimum average variable cost. The firm will supply Q_2 units of output (where $MR_2 =$ MC) and just cover its total variable cost. Its loss will equal its total fixed cost. (Actually, the firm would be indifferent as to shutting down or supplying Q_2 units of output, but we assume it produces.)

- At price P_3 the firm will supply Q_3 units of output to minimize its short-run losses. At any of the other prices between P_2 and P_4 the firm will also minimize its losses by producing and supplying the quantity at which MR $(= P) =$ MC.

- The firm will just break even at price P_4. There it will supply Q_4 units of output (where $MR_4 =$ MC), earning a normal profit but not an economic profit. Total revenue will just cover total cost, including a normal profit, because the revenue per unit $(MR_4 = P_4)$ and the total cost per unit (ATC) are the same.

- At price P_5 the firm will realize an economic profit by producing and supplying Q_5 units of output. In fact, at any price above P_4 the firm will obtain economic profit by producing to the point where MR $(= P) =$ MC.

Note that each of the MR $(= P) =$ MC intersection points labeled *b, c, d,* and *e* in Figure 10.6 indicates a possible product price (on the vertical axis) and the corresponding quantity that the firm would supply at that price (on the horizontal axis). Thus, points such as these are on the upsloping supply curve of the competitive firm. Note, too, that quantity supplied would be zero at any price below the minimum average variable cost (AVC). *We can conclude that the portion of the firm's marginal-cost curve lying above its average-variable-cost curve is its short-run supply curve.* In Figure 10.6, the solid segment of the marginal-cost curve MC is this firm's **short-run supply curve.** It tells us the amount of output the firm will supply at each price in a series of prices.

Table 10.3 summarizes the MR = MC approach to determining the competitive firm's profit-maximizing output level. It also shows the equivalent analysis in terms of total revenue and total cost.

TABLE 10.3 Output Determination in Pure Competition in the Short Run

Question	Answer
Should this firm produce?	Yes, if price is equal to, or greater than, minimum average variable cost. This means that the firm is profitable or that its losses are less than its fixed cost.
What quantity should this firm produce?	Produce where MR $(= P) =$ MC; there, profit is maximized (TR exceeds TC by a maximum amount) or loss is minimized.
Will production result in economic profit?	Yes, if price exceeds average total cost (so that TR exceeds TC). No, if average total cost exceeds price (so that TC exceeds TR).

Fixed Costs: Digging Yourself Out of a Hole

For Firms Facing Losses Due to Fixed Costs, Shutting Down in the Short Run Does Not Mean Shutting Down Forever.

A firm with fixed costs starts each month standing at the bottom of a deep financial hole. The depth of that "money pit" is equal to the dollar value of all the payments that the firm is legally obligated to make even if it is producing nothing. These fixed costs include contractually guaranteed salaries, interest payments on loans, and equipment rental fees that are locked in by long-term contracts. As the firm stands at the bottom of this fixed-cost financial hole and stares upward looking for a way out, it has to ask itself the following question: Will producing output make the hole even deeper?

Naturally, the firm hopes that producing output will generate positive cash flows that will offset its fixed costs and start filling in the hole. If those positive flows are large enough, they may completely offset the firm's fixed costs and fill up the hole, thereby allowing the firm to break even. And if they are just a bit larger, they will not only fill up the hole but also accumulate a nice little pile of profits above ground.

But those are just the firm's hopes. The firm's reality may be quite unpleasant. In particular, the firm may be facing a situation in which producing output would make its financial situation

Source: © pixhook/Getty RF

worse rather than better. As explained in this chapter, if the price of the firm's output falls too low, then producing output will yield cash flows that are negative rather than positive because revenues will be less than variable costs. If that happens,

Diminishing Returns, Production Costs, and Product Supply

We have now identified the links between the law of diminishing returns (Chapter 9), production costs, and product supply in the short run. Because of the law of diminishing returns, marginal costs eventually rise as more units of output are produced. And because marginal costs rise with output, a purely competitive firm must get successively higher prices to motivate it to produce additional units of output.

Viewed alternatively, higher product prices and marginal revenue encourage a purely competitive firm to expand output. As its output increases, the firm's marginal costs rise as a result of the law of diminishing returns. At some now greater output, the higher MC equals the new product price and MR. Profit once again is maximized, but at a greater total amount. Quantity supplied has increased in direct response to an increase in product price and the desire to maximize profit.

Changes in Supply

In Chapter 9 we saw that changes in such factors as the prices of variable inputs or in technology will alter costs and shift the marginal-cost or short-run supply curve to a new location. All else equal, for example, a wage increase would increase marginal cost and shift the supply curve in Figure 10.6 upward as viewed from the horizontal axis (leftward as viewed from the vertical axis). That is, supply would decrease. Similarly, technological progress that increases the productivity of labor would reduce marginal cost and shift the marginal-cost or supply curve downward as viewed from the horizontal axis (rightward as viewed from the vertical axis). This represents an increase in supply.

Firm and Industry: Equilibrium Price

In the preceding section we established the competitive firm's short-run supply curve by applying the MR (= P) = MC rule. But which of the various possible prices will actually be the market equilibrium price?

producing output will lose money for the firm so that the firm would be better off shutting down production rather than producing output. By shutting down, it will lose only its fixed costs. By shutting down, its financial hole won't get even deeper.

A crucial thing to understand, however, is that the low prices that cause firms to shut down production are often temporary—so that shutdowns are also often temporary. Just because a firm shuts down at a given moment to prevent its financial hole from getting any deeper does not mean that the firm will go out of business forever. To the contrary, many industries are characterized by firms that regularly switch production on and off depending upon the market price they can get for their output and, consequently, whether producing output will generate positive or negative cash flows.

Oil production is a good example. Different wells have different variable production costs. If the price of oil drops below a given well's variable costs, then it would be better to halt production on that well and just lose the value of its fixed costs rather than pumping oil whose variable cost exceeds the revenue that it generates when sold.

Seasonal resorts are another good example of turning production on and off depending on the price. The demand for hotel rooms near ski resorts in New Hampshire, for instance, is much higher during the winter ski season than it is during the summer. As a result, the market price of hotel rooms falls so low during the summer that many inns and resorts close during the warmer months. They have all sorts of fixed costs, but it makes more sense for them to shut down rather than remain open because operating in the summer would cost more in variable costs than it would generate in revenues. Better to lose only their fixed costs.

Numerous other examples of temporary shutdowns occur during recessions, the occasional economy-wide economic slowdowns during which demand declines for nearly all goods and services. The 2007–2009 recession in the United States, for instance, saw many manufacturing companies temporarily shut down and mothball their production facilities. The recession witnessed the mothballing of electric generating plants, factories that make fiber optic cable, automobile factories, chemical plants, textile mills, and even the plant in McIntosh, Alabama, that makes the artificial sweetener Splenda. Many other firms also shut down production to wait out the recession—so many, in fact, that there was a mini-boom for consulting firms that specialized in helping firms mothball their factories (the main problem being how to properly store idle machinery so that it will work again when it is eventually brought back into service).

Firms that mothball factories or equipment during a recession do so expecting to eventually turn them back on. But the lengths of recessions vary, as do the specific circumstances of individual firms. So while many firms shut down in the short run with the expectation of reopening as soon as their particular business conditions improve, sometimes their business conditions do not improve. Sometimes the only way to terminate fixed costs is to terminate the firm.

From Chapter 3 we know that the market equilibrium price will be the price at which the total quantity supplied of the product equals the total quantity demanded. So to determine the equilibrium price, we first need to obtain a total supply schedule and a total demand schedule. We find the total supply schedule by assuming a particular number of firms in the industry and supposing that each firm has the same individual supply schedule as the firm represented in Figure 10.6. Then we sum the quantities supplied at each price level to obtain the total (or market) supply schedule. Columns 1 and 3 in Table 10.4 repeat the supply schedule for the individual competitive firm, as derived in Table 10.2. Suppose 1,000 firms compete in this industry, all having the same total and unit costs as the single firm we discussed. This lets us calculate the market supply schedule (columns 2 and 3) by multiplying the quantity-supplied figures of the single firm (column 1) by 1,000.

Market Price and Profits To determine the equilibrium price and output, these total-supply data must be compared

TABLE 10.4 **Firm and Market Supply and Market Demand**

(1) Quantity Supplied, Single Firm	(2) Total Quantity Supplied, 1,000 Firms	(3) Product Price	(4) Total Quantity Demanded
10	10,000	$151	4,000
9	9,000	131	6,000
8	**8,000**	**111**	**8,000**
7	7,000	91	9,000
6	6,000	81	11,000
0	0	71	13,000
0	0	61	16,000

with total-demand data. Let's assume that total demand is as shown in columns 3 and 4 in Table 10.4. By comparing the total quantity supplied and the total quantity demanded at the seven possible prices, we determine that the equilibrium price

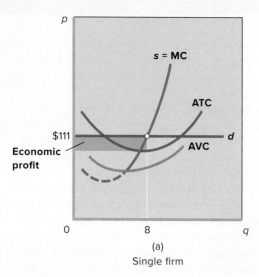

(a)
Single firm

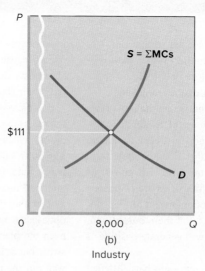

(b)
Industry

FIGURE 10.7 Short-run competitive equilibrium for (a) a firm and (b) the industry. The horizontal sum of the 1,000 firms' individual supply curves (*s*) determines the industry supply curve (*S*). Given industry demand (*D*), the short-run equilibrium price and output for the industry are $111 and 8,000 units. Taking the equilibrium price as given, the individual firm establishes its profit-maximizing output at 8 units and, in this case, realizes the economic profit represented by the green area.

is $111 and the equilibrium quantity is 8,000 units for the industry—8 units for each of the 1,000 identical firms.

Will these conditions of market supply and demand make this a profitable or unprofitable industry? Multiplying product price ($111) by output (8 units), we find that the total revenue of each firm is $888. The total cost is $750, found by looking at column 4 of the table in Figure 10.2. The $138 difference is the economic profit of each firm. For the industry, total economic profit is $138,000. This, then, is a profitable industry.

Another way of calculating economic profit is to determine per-unit profit by subtracting average total cost ($93.75) from product price ($111) and multiplying the difference (per-unit profit of $17.25) by the firm's equilibrium level of output (8). Again we obtain an economic profit of $138 per firm and $138,000 for the industry.

Figure 10.7 shows this analysis graphically. The individual supply curves of each of the 1,000 identical firms—one of which is shown as *s* = MC in Figure 10.7a—are summed horizontally to get the total-supply curve *S* = SMC of Figure 10.7b. With total-demand curve *D*, it yields the equilibrium price $111 and equilibrium quantity (for the industry) 8,000 units. This equilibrium price is given and unalterable to the individual firm; that is, each firm's demand curve is perfectly elastic at the equilibrium price, as indicated by *d* in Figure 10.7a. Because the individual firm is a price taker, the marginal-revenue curve coincides with the firm's demand curve *d*. This $111 price exceeds the average total cost at the firm's equilibrium MR = MC output of 8 units, so the firm earns an economic profit represented by the green area in Figure 10.7a.

Assuming no changes in costs or market demand, these diagrams reveal a genuine equilibrium in the short run. No shortages or surpluses occur in the market to cause price or

total quantity to change. Nor can any firm in the industry increase its profit by altering its output. Note, too, that higher unit and marginal costs, on the one hand, or weaker market demand, on the other, could change the situation so that Figure 10.7a resembles Figure 10.4 or Figure 10.5.

Firm versus Industry Figure 10.7 underscores a point made earlier: Product price is a given fact to the *individual* competitive firm, but the supply plans of all competitive producers *as a group* are a basic determinant of product price. If we recall the fallacy of composition (Last Word, Chapter 1), we find there is no inconsistency here. Although one firm, supplying a negligible fraction of total supply, cannot affect price, the sum of the supply curves of all the firms in the industry constitutes the industry supply curve, and that curve does have an important bearing on price.

> ### QUICK REVIEW 10.3
>
> ✓ A competitive firm's short-run supply curve is the portion of its marginal cost (MC) curve that lies above its average variable cost (AVC) curve.
>
> ✓ If price *P* is greater than minimum average variable cost, the firm will produce the amount of output where MR (= *P*) = MC in order to either maximize its profit (if price exceeds minimum ATC) or minimize its loss (if price lies between minimum AVC and minimum ATC).
>
> ✓ Market supply in a competitive industry is the horizontal sum of the individual supply curves of all of the firms in the industry. The market equilibrium price is determined by where the industry's market supply curve intersects the industry's market demand curve.

SUMMARY

LO10.1 Give the names and summarize the main characteristics of the four basic market models.

Economists group industries into four models based on their market structures: (*a*) pure competition, (*b*) pure monopoly, (*c*) monopolistic competition, and (*d*) oligopoly.

LO10.2 List the conditions required for purely competitive markets.

A purely competitive industry consists of a large number of independent firms producing a standardized product. Pure competition assumes that firms and resources are mobile among different industries.

LO10.3 Explain how demand is seen by a purely competitive seller.

In a competitive industry, no single firm can influence market price. This means that the firm's demand curve is perfectly elastic and price equals marginal revenue.

LO10.4 Convey how purely competitive firms can use the total-revenue–total-cost approach to maximize profits or minimize losses in the short run.

We can analyze short-run profit maximization by a competitive firm by comparing total revenue and total cost or by applying marginal analysis. A firm maximizes its short-run profit by producing the output at which total revenue exceeds total cost by the greatest amount.

LO10.5 Explain how purely competitive firms can use the marginal-revenue–marginal-cost approach to maximize profits or minimize losses in the short run.

Provided price exceeds minimum average variable cost, a competitive firm maximizes profit or minimizes loss in the short run by producing the output at which price or marginal revenue equals marginal cost.

If price is less than minimum average variable cost, a competitive firm minimizes its loss by shutting down. If price is greater than average variable cost but is less than average total cost, a competitive firm minimizes its loss by producing the $P = MC$ amount of output. If price also exceeds average total cost, the firm maximizes its economic profit at the $P = MC$ amount of output.

LO10.6 Explain why a competitive firm's marginal cost curve is the same as its supply curve.

Applying the MR ($= P$) = MC rule at various possible market prices leads to the conclusion that the segment of the firm's short-run marginal-cost curve that lies above the firm's average-variable-cost curve is its short-run supply curve.

A competitive firm shuts down production at least temporarily if price is less than minimum average variable cost because, in those situations, producing any amount of output will always result in variable costs exceeding revenues. Shutting down therefore results in a smaller loss because the firm will lose only its fixed cost, whereas, if it operated, it would lose its fixed cost plus whatever money is lost due to variable costs exceeding revenues.

Competitive firms choose to operate rather than shut down whenever price is greater than average variable cost but less than average total cost because, in those situations, revenues will always exceed variable costs. The amount by which revenues exceed variable costs can be used to help pay down some of the firm's fixed costs. Thus, the firm loses less money by operating (and paying down some of its fixed costs) than it would if it shut down (in which case it would suffer a loss equal to the full amount of its fixed costs).

TERMS AND CONCEPTS

market structure	imperfect competition	marginal revenue
pure competition	price taker	break-even point
pure monopoly	average revenue	MR = MC rule
monopolistic competition	total revenue	short-run supply curve
oligopoly		

The following and additional problems can be found in ▪ connect

DISCUSSION QUESTIONS

1. Briefly state the basic characteristics of pure competition, pure monopoly, monopolistic competition, and oligopoly. Under which of these market classifications does each of the following most accurately fit? (*a*) a supermarket in your hometown; (*b*) the steel industry; (*c*) a Kansas wheat farm; (*d*) the commercial bank in which you or your family has an account; (*e*) the automobile industry. In each case, justify your classification. **LO10.1**

2. Strictly speaking, pure competition is relatively rare. Then why study it? **LO10.2**

3. "Even if a firm is losing money, it may be better to stay in business in the short run." Is this statement ever true? Under what condition(s)? **LO10.5**

4. Consider a firm that has no fixed costs and that is currently losing money. Are there any situations in which it would want to stay open for business in the short run? If a firm has no fixed costs, is it sensible to speak of the firm distinguishing between the short run and the long run? **LO10.5**

5. Why is the equality of marginal revenue and marginal cost essential for profit maximization in all market structures? Explain why price can be substituted for marginal revenue in the MR = MC rule when an industry is purely competitive. **LO10.5**

6. "That segment of a competitive firm's marginal-cost curve that lies above its average-variable-cost curve constitutes the short-run supply curve for the firm." Explain using a graph and words. **LO10.5**

7. **LAST WORD** If a firm's current revenues are less than its current variable costs, when should it shut down? If the firm decides to shut down, should we expect that decision to be final? Explain using an example that is not in the book.

REVIEW QUESTIONS

1. Suppose that the paper clip industry is perfectly competitive. Also assume that the market price for paper clips is 2 cents per paper clip. The demand curve faced by each firm in the industry is: **LO10.3**
   a. A horizontal line at 2 cents per paper clip.
   b. A vertical line at 2 cents per paper clip.
   c. The same as the market demand curve for paper clips.
   d. Always higher than the firm's MC curve.

2. Use the following demand schedule to determine total revenue and marginal revenue for each possible level of sales: **LO10.3**
   a. What can you conclude about the structure of the industry in which this firm is operating? Explain.

Product Price	Quantity Demanded	Total Revenue	Marginal Revenue
$2	0	$_____	
2	1	_____	$_____
2	2	_____	_____
2	3	_____	_____
2	4	_____	_____
2	5	_____	_____

   b. Graph the demand, total-revenue, and marginal-revenue curves for this firm.
   c. Why do the demand and marginal-revenue curves coincide?
   d. "Marginal revenue is the change in total revenue associated with additional units of output." Explain verbally and graphically, using the data in the table.

3. A purely competitive firm whose goal is to maximize profit will choose to produce the amount of output at which: **LO10.4**
   a. TR and TC are equal.
   b. TR exceeds TC by as much as possible.
   c. TC exceeds TR by as much as possible.
   d. none of the above.

4. If it is possible for a perfectly competitive firm to do better financially by producing rather than shutting down, then it should produce the amount of output at which: **LO10.5**
   a. MR < MC.
   b. MR = MC.
   c. MR > MC.
   d. none of the above.

5. A perfectly competitive firm that makes car batteries has a fixed cost of $10,000 per month. The market price at which it can sell its output is $100 per battery. The firm's minimum AVC is $105 per battery. The firm is currently producing 500 batteries a month (the output level at which MR = MC). This firm is making a _____ and should _____ production **LO10.5**
   a. profit; increase
   b. profit; shut down
   c. loss; increase
   d. loss; shut down

6. Consider a profit-maximizing firm in a competitive industry. For each of the following situations, indicate whether the firm should shut down production or produce where MR = MC. **LO10.5**
   a. P < minimum AVC.
   b. P > minimum ATC.
   c. Minimum AVC < P < minimum ATC.

PROBLEMS

1. A purely competitive firm finds that the market price for its product is $20. It has a fixed cost of $100 and a variable cost of $10 per unit for the first 50 units and then $25 per unit for all successive units. Does price exceed average variable cost for the first 50 units? What about for the first 100 units? What is the marginal cost per unit for the first 50 units? What about for units 51 and higher? For each of the first 50 units, does MR exceed MC? What about for units 51 and higher? What output level will yield the largest possible profit for this purely competitive firm? (Hint: Draw a graph similar to Figure 10.2 using data for this firm.) **LO10.5**

2. A purely competitive wheat farmer can sell any wheat he grows for $10 per bushel. His five acres of land show diminishing returns because some are better suited for wheat production than others. The first acre can produce 1,000 bushels of wheat, the second acre 900, the third 800, and so on. Draw a table with multiple columns to help you answer the following questions. How many bushels will each of the farmer's five acres produce? How much revenue will each acre generate? What are the TR and MR for each acre? If the marginal cost of planting and harvesting an acre is $7,000 per acre for each of the five acres, how many acres should the farmer plant and harvest? LO10.5

3. Karen runs a print shop that makes posters for large companies. It is a very competitive business. The market price is currently $1 per poster. She has fixed costs of $250. Her variable costs are $1,000 for the first thousand posters, $800 for the second thousand, and then $750 for each additional thousand posters. What is her AFC per poster (not per thousand!) if she prints 1,000 posters? 2,000? 10,000? What is her ATC per poster if she prints 1,000? 2,000? 10,000? If the market price fell to 70 cents per poster, would there be any output level at which Karen would not shut down production immediately? LO10.5

4. Assume that the cost data in the following table are for a purely competitive producer: LO10.5

Total Product	Average Fixed Cost	Average Variable Cost	Average Total Cost	Marginal Cost
0				
1	$60.00	$45.00	$105.00	$45
2	30.00	42.50	72.50	40
3	20.00	40.00	60.00	35
4	15.00	37.50	52.50	30
5	12.00	37.00	49.00	35
6	10.00	37.50	47.50	40
7	8.57	38.57	47.14	45
8	7.50	40.63	48.13	55
9	6.67	43.33	50.00	65
10	6.00	46.50	52.50	75

a. At a product price of $56, will this firm produce in the short run? If it is preferable to produce, what will be the profit-maximizing or loss-minimizing output? What economic profit or loss will the firm realize per unit of output?

b. Answer the questions of 4a assuming product price is $41.

c. Answer the questions of 4a assuming product price is $32.

d. In the following table, complete the short-run supply schedule for the firm (columns 1 and 2) and indicate the profit or loss incurred at each output (column 3).

(1) Price	(2) Quantity Supplied, Single Firm	(3) Profit (+) or Loss (−)	(4) Quantity Supplied 1,500 Firms
$26	_____	$_____	_____
32	_____	_____	_____
38	_____	_____	_____
41	_____	_____	_____
46	_____	_____	_____
56	_____	_____	_____
66	_____	_____	_____

e. Now assume that there are 1,500 identical firms in this competitive industry; that is, there are 1,500 firms, each of which has the cost data shown in the table. Complete the industry supply schedule (column 4).

f. Suppose the market demand data for the product are as follows:

Price	Total Quantity Demanded
$26	17,000
32	15,000
38	13,500
41	12,000
46	10,500
56	9,500
66	8,000

What will be the equilibrium price? What will be the equilibrium output for the industry? For each firm? What will profit or loss be per unit? Per firm? Will this industry expand or contract in the long run?

Pure Competition in the Long Run

Learning Objectives

LO11.1 Explain how the long run differs from the short run in pure competition.

LO11.2 Describe how profits and losses drive the long-run adjustment process of pure competition.

LO11.3 Explain the differences between constant-cost, increasing-cost, and decreasing-cost industries.

LO11.4 Show how long-run equilibrium in pure competition produces an efficient allocation of resources.

LO11.5 Discuss creative destruction and the profit incentives for innovation.

The previous chapter discussed how pure competition operates in the short run, the time period during which the individual firms in an industry are stuck with their current plant sizes and fixed-cost commitments. As you know, pure competitors shut down production if prices are too low or, if prices are high enough, produce where MR = MC to minimize their losses or maximize their profits. Whether they make a profit or a loss depends on how high the market price is relative to their costs.

That being said, profits and losses cannot be the end of the pure competition story because one of the key characteristics of pure competition is the freedom of firms to enter or exit the industry. We know from Chapter 2 that profits attract entry and losses prompt exit.

In this chapter, we are keenly interested in how entry and exit relate to allocative and productive efficiency. We are also interested in how continuing competition leads to new products and new business methods replacing older products and older business methods through a process aptly referred to as *creative destruction*.

The Long Run in Pure Competition

LO11.1 Explain how the long run differs from the short run in pure competition.

The entry and exit of firms in our market models can only take place in the long run. In the short run, the industry is composed of a specific number of firms, each with a plant size that is fixed and unalterable in the short run. Firms may shut down in the sense that they can produce zero units of output in the short run, but they do not have sufficient time to liquidate their assets and go out of business.

In the long run, by contrast, the firms already in an industry have sufficient time to either expand or contract their capacities. More important, the number of firms in the industry may either increase or decrease as new firms enter or existing firms leave.

The length of time constituting the long run varies substantially by industry, however, so that you should not fix in your mind any specific number of years, months, or days. Instead, focus your attention on the incentives provided by profits and losses for the entry and exit of firms into any purely competitive industry and, later in the chapter, on how those incentives lead to productive and allocative efficiency. The time horizons are far less important than the process by which profits and losses guide business managers toward the efficient use of society's resources.

Profit Maximization in the Long Run

The first part of the pure competition story (Chapter 10) was about profit, loss, and shutdown in the short run. The rest of the story (this chapter) is about entry and exit and their effects on industry size and allocative and productive efficiency in the long run.

To tell the rest of story well, we need to return to our graphical analysis and examine profit maximization by pure competitors in the long run. Several assumptions, none of which affect our conclusions, will keep things simple:

- **Entry and exit only** The only long-run adjustment in our graphical analysis is caused by the entry or exit of firms. Moreover, we ignore all short-run adjustments in order to concentrate on the effects of the long-run adjustments.
- **Identical costs** All firms in the industry have identical cost curves. This assumption lets us discuss an "average," or "representative," firm, knowing that all other firms in the industry are similarly affected by any long-run adjustments that occur.

- **Constant-cost industry** The industry is a constant-cost industry. This means that the entry and exit of firms does not affect resource prices or, consequently, the locations of the average-total-cost curves of individual firms.

The Long-Run Adjustment Process in Pure Competition

LO11.2 Describe how profits and losses drive the long-run adjustment process of pure competition.

The basic conclusion we seek to explain is this: After all long-run adjustments are completed in a purely competitive industry, product price will be exactly equal to, and production will occur at, each firm's minimum average total cost.

This conclusion follows from two basic facts: (1) Firms seek profits and shun losses, and (2) under pure competition, firms are free to enter and leave an industry. If market price initially exceeds minimum average total cost, the resulting economic profit will attract new firms to the industry. But this industry expansion will increase supply until price is brought back down to equality with minimum average total cost. Conversely, if price is initially less than minimum average total cost, the resulting loss will cause firms to leave the industry. As they leave, total supply will decline, bringing the price back up to equality with minimum average total cost.

Long-Run Equilibrium

Consider the average firm in a purely competitive industry that is initially in long-run equilibrium. This firm is represented in Figure 11.1a, where MR = MC and price and minimum average total cost are equal at $50. Economic profit here is zero; the industry is in equilibrium or "at rest" because there is no tendency for firms to enter or to leave. The existing firms are earning normal profits, which means that their accounting profits are equal to those that the owners of these

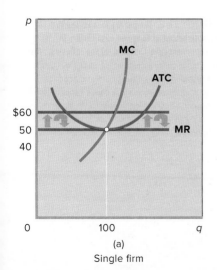

(a)
Single firm

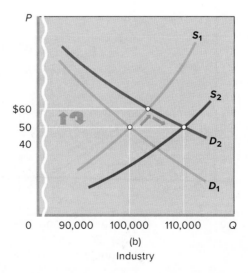

(b)
Industry

FIGURE 11.1 Temporary profits and the reestablishment of long-run equilibrium in (a) a representative firm and (b) the industry. A favorable shift in demand (D_1 to D_2) will upset the original industry equilibrium and produce economic profits. But those profits will entice new firms to enter the industry, increasing supply (S_1 to S_2) and lowering product price until economic profits are once again zero.

firms could expect to receive on average in other industries. It is because their current profits are the same as they could expect to earn elsewhere that there is no tendency for firms to enter or leave the industry. The $50 market price is determined in Figure 11.1b by market or industry demand D_1 and supply S_1. (S_1 is a short-run supply curve; we will develop the long-run industry supply curve in our discussion.) And remember that normal profits earned by these firms are considered an opportunity cost and, therefore, are included in the firms' cost curves.

As shown on the quantity axes of the two graphs, equilibrium output in the industry is 100,000 while equilibrium output for the single firm is 100. If all firms in the industry are identical, there must be 1,000 firms (= 100,000/100).

Entry Eliminates Economic Profits Let's upset the long-run equilibrium in Figure 11.1 and see what happens. Suppose a change in consumer tastes increases product demand from D_1 to D_2. Price will rise to $60, as determined at the intersection of D_2 and S_1, and the firm's marginal-revenue curve will shift upward to $60. This $60 price exceeds the firm's average total cost of $50 at output 100, creating an economic profit of $10 per unit. This economic profit will lure new firms into the industry. Some entrants will be newly created firms; others will shift from less prosperous industries.

As firms enter, the market supply of the product increases, pushing the product price below $60. Economic profits persist, and entry continues until short-run supply increases to S_2. Market price falls to $50, as does marginal revenue for the firm. Price and minimum average total cost are again equal at $50. The economic profits caused by the boost in demand have been eliminated, and, as a result, the previous incentive for more firms to enter the industry has disappeared because the firms that remain are earning only a normal profit (zero economic profit). Entry ceases and a new long-run equilibrium is reached.

Observe in Figure 11.1a and 11.1b that total quantity supplied is now 110,000 units and each firm is producing 100 units. Now 1,100 firms rather than the original 1,000 populate the industry. Economic profits have attracted 100 more firms.

Exit Eliminates Losses Now let's consider a shift in the opposite direction. We begin in Figure 11.2b with curves S_1 and D_1 setting the same initial long-run equilibrium situation as in our previous analysis, including the $50 price.

Suppose consumer demand declines from D_1 to D_3. This forces the market price and marginal revenue down to $40, making production unprofitable at the minimum ATC of $50. In time the resulting economic losses will induce firms to leave the industry. Their owners will seek a normal profit elsewhere rather than accept the below-normal profits (losses) now confronting them. As this exodus of firms proceeds, however, industry supply decreases, pushing the price up from $40 toward $50. Losses continue and more firms leave the industry until the supply curve shifts to S_3. Once this happens, price is again $50, just equal to the minimum average total cost. Losses have been eliminated so that the firms that remain are earning only a normal profit (zero economic profit). Since this is no better or worse than entrepreneurs could expect to earn in other business ventures, there is no longer any incentive to exit the industry. Long-run equilibrium is restored.

In Figure 11.2a and 11.2b, total quantity supplied is now 90,000 units and each firm is producing 100 units. Only 900 firms, not the original 1,000, populate the industry. Losses have forced 100 firms out.

You may have noted that we have sidestepped the question of which firms will leave the industry when losses occur by assuming that all firms have identical cost curves. In the real world, of course, managerial talents differ. Even if resource prices and technology are the same for all firms, less skillfully managed firms tend to incur higher

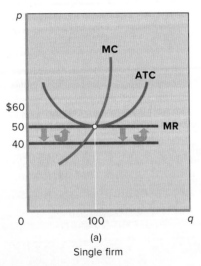

(a)
Single firm

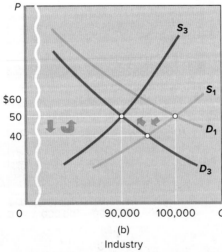

(b)
Industry

FIGURE 11.2 Temporary losses and the reestablishment of long-run equilibrium in (a) a representative firm and (b) the industry. An unfavorable shift in demand (D_1 to D_3) will upset the original industry equilibrium and produce losses. But those losses will cause firms to leave the industry, decreasing supply (S_1 to S_3) and increasing product price until all losses have disappeared.

costs and therefore are the first to leave an industry when demand declines. Similarly, firms with less productive labor forces or higher transportation costs will be higher-cost producers and likely candidates to quit an industry when demand decreases.

We have now reached an intermediate goal: Our analysis verifies that competition, reflected in the entry and exit of firms, eliminates economic profits or losses by adjusting price to equal minimum long-run average total cost. In addition, this competition forces firms to select output levels at which average total cost is minimized.

Long-Run Supply Curves

LO11.3 Explain the differences between constant-cost, increasing-cost, and decreasing-cost industries.

Although our analysis has dealt with the long run, we have noted that the market supply curves in Figures 11.1b and 11.2b are short-run curves. What then is the character of the **long-run supply curve** of a competitive industry? Our analysis points us toward an answer. The crucial factor here is the effect, if any, that changes in the number of firms in the industry will have on costs of the individual firms in the industry.

Long-Run Supply for a Constant-Cost Industry

In our analysis of long-run competitive equilibrium we assumed that the industry under discussion was a **constant-cost industry.** This means that industry expansion or contraction will not affect resource prices and therefore production costs. Graphically, it means that the entry or exit of firms does not shift the long-run ATC curves of individual firms. This is the case when the industry's demand for resources is small in relation to the total demand for those resources. Then the industry can expand or contract without significantly affecting resource prices and costs.

What does the long-run supply curve of a constant-cost industry look like? The answer is contained in our previous analysis. There we saw that the entry and exit of firms changes industry output but always brings the product price back to its original level, where it is just equal to the constant minimum ATC. Specifically, we discovered that the industry would supply 90,000, 100,000, or 110,000 units of output, all at a price of $50 per unit. In other words, the long-run supply curve of a constant-cost industry is perfectly elastic.

This is demonstrated graphically in Figure 11.3, which uses data from Figures 11.1 and 11.2. Suppose industry demand is originally D_1, industry output is Q_1 (100,000 units), and product price is P_1 ($50). This situation, from Figure 11.1, is one of long-run equilibrium. We saw that when

FIGURE 11.3 **The long-run supply curve for a constant-cost industry.**
In a constant-cost industry, the entry and exit of firms do not affect resource prices, or, therefore, unit costs. So an increase in demand (D_1 to D_2) raises industry output (Q_1 to Q_2) but not price ($50). Similarly, a decrease in demand (D_1 to D_3) reduces output (Q_1 to Q_3) but not price. Thus, the long-run industry supply curve (S) is horizontal through points Z_1, Z_2, and Z_3.

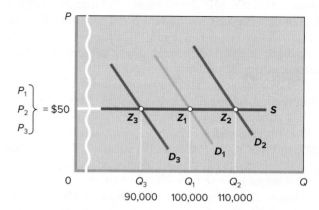

demand increases to D_2, upsetting this equilibrium, the resulting economic profits attract new firms. Because this is a constant-cost industry, entry continues and industry output expands until the price is driven back down to the level of the unchanged minimum ATC. This is at price P_2 ($50) and output Q_2 (110,000).

From Figure 11.2, we saw that a decline in market demand from D_1 to D_3 causes an exit of firms and ultimately restores equilibrium at price P_3 ($50) and output Q_3 (90,000 units). The points Z_1, Z_2, and Z_3 in Figure 11.3 represent these three price-quantity combinations. A line or curve connecting all such points shows the various price-quantity combinations that firms would produce if they had enough time to make all desired adjustments to changes in demand. This line or curve is the industry's long-run supply curve. In a constant-cost industry this curve (straight line) is horizontal, as in Figure 11.3, thus representing perfectly elastic supply.

Long-Run Supply for an Increasing-Cost Industry

Constant-cost industries are a special case. Most industries are **increasing-cost industries,** in which firms' ATC curves shift upward as the industry expands and downward as the industry contracts. Usually, the entry of new firms will increase resource prices, particularly in industries using specialized resources whose long-run supplies do not readily increase in response to increases in resource demand. Higher resource prices result in higher long-run average total costs for all firms in the industry. These higher costs cause upward shifts in each firm's long-run ATC curve.

Thus, when an increase in product demand results in economic profits and attracts new firms to an increasing-cost industry, a two-way squeeze works to eliminate those profits. As before, the entry of new firms increases market supply and lowers the market price. But now each firm's entire ATC curve also shifts upward. The overall result is a higher-than-original equilibrium price. The industry produces a larger output at a higher product price because the industry expansion has increased resource prices and the minimum average total cost.

Since greater output will be supplied at a higher price, the long-run industry supply curve is upsloping. Instead of supplying 90,000, 100,000, or 110,000 units at the same price of $50, an increasing-cost industry might supply 90,000 units at $45, 100,000 units at $50, and 110,000 units at $55. A higher price is required to induce more production because costs per unit of output increase as production rises.

Figure 11.4 nicely illustrates the situation. Original market demand is D_1 and industry price and output are P_1 ($50) and Q_1 (100,000 units), respectively, at equilibrium point Y_1. An increase in demand to D_2 upsets this equilibrium and leads to economic profits. New firms enter the industry, increasing both market supply and the production costs of individual firms. A new price is established at point Y_2, where P_2 is $55 and Q_2 is 110,000 units.

Conversely, a decline in demand from D_1 to D_3 makes production unprofitable and causes firms to leave the industry. The resulting decline in resource prices reduces the minimum average total cost of production for firms that stay. A new equilibrium price is established at some level below the original price, say, at point Y_3, where P_3 is $45 and Q_3 is 90,000 units. Connecting these three equilibrium positions, we derive the upsloping long-run supply curve S in Figure 11.4.

Long-Run Supply for a Decreasing-Cost Industry

In **decreasing-cost industries,** firms experience lower costs as their industry expands. The personal computer industry is an example. As demand for personal computers increased, new manufacturers of computers entered the industry and greatly increased the resource demand for the components used to build them (for example, memory chips, hard drives, monitors, and operating software). The expanded production of the components enabled the producers of those items to achieve substantial economies of scale. The decreased production costs of the components reduced their prices, which greatly lowered the computer manufacturers' average costs of production. The supply of personal computers increased by more than demand, and the price of personal computers declined.

Unfortunately, however, the industries that show decreasing costs when output expands also show increasing costs if output contracts. A good example is the American shoe-manufacturing industry as it contracted due to foreign competition. Back when the industry was doing well and there were many shoemaking firms, the cost of specialized technicians who repair shoemaking machinery could be spread across many firms. This was because the repairmen worked as independent contractors going from one firm's factory to another firm's factory on a daily basis as various pieces of equipment at different factories needed repairs. But as the demand for American footwear fell over time, there were fewer and fewer factories, so the cost of a repair technician had to be spread over fewer and fewer firms. Thus, costs per firm and per unit of output increased.

Figure 11.5 illustrates the situation. The original market demand is D_1 and industry price and output are P_1 ($50) and Q_1 (100,000 units), respectively, at equilibrium point X_1. An increase in demand to D_2 upsets this equilibrium and leads to

FIGURE 11.4 The long-run supply curve for an increasing-cost industry. In an increasing-cost industry, the entry of new firms in response to an increase in demand (D_3 to D_1 to D_2) will bid up resource prices and thereby increase unit costs. As a result, an increased industry output (Q_3 to Q_1 to Q_2) will be forthcoming only at higher prices ($45 < $50 < $55). The long-run industry supply curve (S) therefore slopes upward through points Y_3, Y_1, and Y_2.

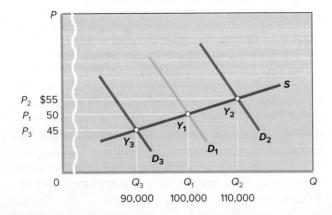

FIGURE 11.5 The long-run supply curve for a decreasing-cost industry. In a decreasing-cost industry, the entry of new firms in response to an increase in demand (D_3 to D_1 to D_2) will lead to decreased input prices and, consequently, decreased unit costs. As a result, an increase in industry output (Q_3 to Q_1 to Q_2) will be accompanied by lower prices ($55 > $50 > $45). The long-run industry supply curve (S) therefore slopes downward through points X_3, X_1, and X_2.

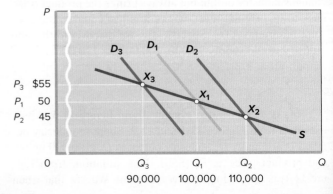

economic profits. New firms enter the industry, increasing market supply but decreasing the production costs of individual firms. A new price is established at point X_2, where P_2 is \$45 and Q_2 is 110,000 units.

Conversely, a decline in demand from D_1 to D_3 makes production unprofitable and causes firms to leave the industry. The resulting increase in input prices increases the minimum average total cost of production for the firms that remain. A new equilibrium price is established at some level above the original price, say at point X_3, where P_3 is \$55 and Q_3 is 90,000 units. Connecting these three equilibrium positions in Figure 11.5, we derive the downsloping long-run supply curve S for this decreasing-cost industry.

QUICK REVIEW 11.1

✓ In pure competition, entrepreneurs remove resources from industries and firms that are generating economic losses in order to transfer them to industries and firms that are generating economic profits.

✓ In the long run, the entry of firms into an industry will compete away any economic profits, and the exit of firms will eliminate economic losses, so price and minimum average total cost are equal. Entry and exit cease when the firms in the industry return to making a normal profit (zero economic profit).

✓ The long-run supply curves of constant-, increasing-, and decreasing-cost industries are horizontal, upsloping, and downsloping, respectively.

Pure Competition and Efficiency

LO11.4 Show how long-run equilibrium in pure competition produces an efficient allocation of resources.

Figure 11.6 (Key Graph) demonstrates the efficiency characteristics of the individual firms (Figure 11.6a) and the market (Figure 11.6b) after long-run adjustments in pure competition. Assuming a constant- or increasing-cost industry, the final long-run equilibrium positions of all firms have the same basic efficiency characteristics. As shown in Figure 11.6a, price (and marginal revenue) will settle where it is equal to minimum average total cost: P (and MR) = minimum ATC. Moreover, since the marginal-cost curve intersects the average-total-cost curve at its minimum point, marginal cost and average total cost are equal: MC = minimum ATC. So in long-run equilibrium a triple equality occurs: P (and MR) = MC = minimum ATC. Thus, in long-run equilibrium, each firm produces at the output level Q_f that is associated with this triple equality.[1]

The triple equality tells us two very important things about long-run equilibrium. First, it tells us that although a competitive firm may realize economic profit or loss in the short run, it will earn only a normal profit by producing in accordance with the MR (= P) = MC rule in the long run. Second, the triple equality tells us that in long-run equilibrium, the profit-maximizing decision rule that leads each firm to produce the quantity at which P = MR also implies that each firm will produce at the output level Q_f that is associated with the minimum point on each identical firm's ATC curve.

This is very important because it suggests that pure competition leads to the most efficient possible use of society's resources. Indeed, subject only to Chapter 4's qualifications relating to public goods and externalities, an idealized purely competitive market economy composed of constant- or increasing-cost industries will generate both productive efficiency and allocative efficiency.

Productive Efficiency: P = Minimum ATC

Productive efficiency requires that goods be produced in the least costly way. In the long run, pure competition forces firms to produce at the minimum average total cost of production and to charge a price that is just consistent with that cost. This is true because firms that do not use the best available (least-cost) production methods and combinations of inputs will not survive.

To see why that is true, let's suppose that Figure 11.6 has to do with pure competition in the cucumber industry. In the final equilibrium position shown in Figure 11.6a, suppose each firm in the cucumber industry is producing 100 units (say, truckloads) of cucumbers by using \$5,000 (equal to average total cost of \$50 × 100 units) worth of resources. If any firm produced that same amount of output at any higher total cost, say \$7,000, it would be wasting resources because all of the other firms in the industry are able to produce that same amount of output using only \$5,000 of resources. Society would be faced with a net loss of \$2,000 worth of alternative products. But this cannot happen in pure competition; this firm would incur a loss of \$2,000, requiring it to either reduce its costs or go out of business.

Note, too, that consumers benefit from productive efficiency by paying the lowest product price possible under the prevailing technology and cost conditions. And the firm receives only a normal profit, which is part of its economic costs and thus incorporated in its ATC curve.

Allocative Efficiency: P = MC

Long-run equilibrium in pure competition guarantees productive efficiency, such that output will be produced in the least-cost way. But productive efficiency by itself does not guarantee that anyone will want to buy the items that are being produced in the least-cost manner. For all

---

[1]This triple equality does not always hold for decreasing-cost industries in which individual firms produce a large fraction of the total market output. In such cases, MC may remain below ATC if average costs are decreasing. We will discuss this situation of "natural monopoly" in Chapter 12.

KEY GRAPH

FIGURE 11.6 Long-run equilibrium: a competitive firm and market. (a) The equality of price (*P*), marginal cost (MC), and minimum average total cost (ATC) at output Q_f indicates that the firm is achieving productive efficiency and allocative efficiency. It is using the most efficient technology, charging the lowest price, and producing the greatest output consistent with its costs. It is receiving only a normal profit, which is incorporated into the ATC curve. The equality of price and marginal cost indicates that society allocated its scarce resources in accordance with consumer preferences. (b) In the purely competitive market, allocative efficiency occurs at the market equilibrium output Q_e. The sum of consumer surplus (green area) and producer surplus (blue area) is maximized.

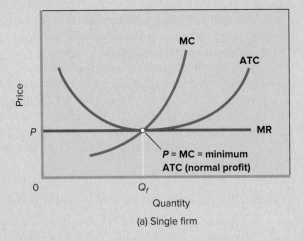

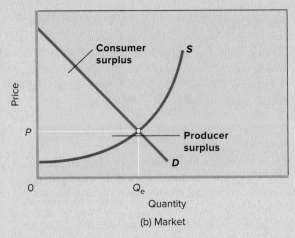

(a) Single firm

(b) Market

QUICK QUIZ FOR FIGURE 11.6

1. We know the firm is a price taker because:
   a. its MC curve slopes upward.
   b. its ATC curve is U-shaped.
   c. its MR curve is horizontal.
   d. MC and ATC are equal at the profit-maximizing output.

2. At this firm's profit-maximizing output:
   a. total revenue equals total cost.
   b. it is earning an economic profit.
   c. allocative, but not necessarily productive, efficiency is achieved.
   d. productive, but not necessarily allocative, efficiency is achieved.

3. The equality of *P*, MC, and minimum ATC:
   a. occurs only in constant-cost industries.
   b. encourages entry of new firms.
   c. means that the "right goods" are being produced in the "right ways."
   d. results in a zero accounting profit.

4. When *P* = MC = lowest ATC for individual firms, in the market:
   a. consumer surplus necessarily exceeds producer surplus.
   b. consumer surplus plus producer surplus is at a maximum.
   c. producer surplus necessarily exceeds consumer surplus.
   d. supply and demand are identical.

Answers: 1. c; 2. a; 3. c; 4. b

---

we know, consumers might prefer that the resources used to produce those items be redirected toward producing other products instead.

Fortunately, long-run equilibrium in pure competition also guarantees **allocative efficiency,** so we can be certain that society's scarce resources are directed toward producing the goods and services that people most want to consume. Stated formally, allocative efficiency occurs when it is impossible to produce any net gains for society by altering the combination of goods and services that are produced from society's limited supply of resources.

To understand how pure competition leads to allocative efficiency, recall the concept of opportunity cost while looking at Figure 11.6b, where Q_e total units are being produced in equilibrium by the firms in a purely competitive industry. For every unit up to Q_e, market demand curve *D* lies above

market supply curve *S*. Recall from Chapter 4 what this means in terms of marginal benefits and marginal costs.

- For each unit of output on the horizontal axis, the point directly above it on demand curve *D* shows how many dollars' worth of other goods and services consumers are willing to give up to obtain that unit of output. Consequently, the demand curve shows the dollar value of the marginal benefit that consumers place on each unit.

- For each unit of output on the horizontal axis, the point directly above it on supply curve *S* shows how many dollars' worth of other products have to be sacrificed in order to direct the underlying resources toward producing each unit of this product. Consequently, supply curve *S* shows the dollar value of the marginal opportunity cost of each unit.

Keeping these definitions in mind, the fact that the demand curve lies above the supply curve for every unit up to Q_e means that marginal benefit exceeds marginal cost for every one of these units. Stated slightly differently, producing and consuming these units brings net benefits because consumers are willing to give up more of other goods to obtain these units than must actually be forgone to produce them. Furthermore, because the supply curve includes the opportunity cost of the other goods that must be given up when resources are directed to producing these units, we can be certain that consumers prefer to have the necessary resources directed toward producing these units rather than anything else. In other words, allocative efficiency has been achieved because redirecting the necessary resources toward producing anything else would make people less happy.

The fact that pure competition yields allocative efficiency can also be understood by looking at the situation facing each individual firm in long-run equilibrium. To see this, take the market equilibrium price P that is determined in Figure 11.6b and see how it affects the behavior of the individual firm shown in Figure 11.6a. This profit-maximizing firm takes P as fixed and produces Q_f units, the output level at which $P = MC$.

By comparing the horizontal line at P with the upsloping MC curve, it is clear that for every unit up to Q_f, the price at which each unit can be sold exceeds the marginal cost of producing it. That is equivalent to saying that these units are worth more to consumers than they cost to make. Why? Because consumers are willing to forgo P dollars' worth of other goods and services when they pay P dollars for these units, but at the same time the firm only has to use less than P dollars' worth of resources to produce them. Thus, if these units are produced and consumed, there are net benefits and society comes out ahead. And, as with our previous analysis, allocative efficiency also obtains because by spending their P dollars per unit on these units rather than anything else, consumers are indicating that they would rather have the necessary resources directed toward producing these units rather than anything else.

Maximum Consumer and Producer Surplus

We confirm the existence of allocative efficiency in Figure 11.6b, where we see that pure competition maximizes the sum of the "benefit surpluses" to consumers and producers. Recall from Chapter 4 that **consumer surplus** is the difference between the maximum prices that consumers are willing to pay for a product (as shown by the demand curve) and the market price of the product. In Figure 11.6b, consumer surplus is the green triangle, which is the sum of the vertical distances between the demand curve and equilibrium price. In contrast, **producer surplus** is the difference between the minimum prices that producers are willing to accept for a

product (as shown by the supply curve) and the market price of the product. Producer surplus is the sum of the vertical distances between the equilibrium price and the supply curve. Here producer surplus is the blue area.

At the equilibrium quantity Q_e, the combined amount of consumer surplus and producer surplus is maximized. Allocative efficiency occurs because, at Q_e, marginal benefit, reflected by points on the demand curve, equals marginal cost, reflected by points on the supply curve. Alternatively, the maximum willingness of consumers to pay for unit Q_e equals the minimum acceptable price of that unit to producers. At any output less than Q_e, the sum of consumer and producer surplus—the combined size of the green and blue area—would be less than that shown. At any output greater than Q_e, an efficiency loss (deadweight loss) would subtract from the combined consumer and producer surplus shown by the green and blue area.

After long-run adjustments, pure competition produces both productive and allocative efficiency. It yields a level of output at which $P = MC = $ lowest ATC, marginal benefit = marginal cost, maximum willingness to pay for the last unit = minimum acceptable price for that unit, and combined consumer and producer surplus are maximized.

Dynamic Adjustments

A further attribute of purely competitive markets is their ability to restore the efficiency just described when disrupted by changes in the economy. A change in consumer tastes, resource supplies, or technology will automatically set in motion the appropriate realignments of resources. For example, suppose that cucumbers and pickles become dramatically more popular. First, the demand for cucumbers will increase in the market, increasing the price of cucumbers. So, at current output, the price of cucumbers will exceed their marginal cost. At this point efficiency will be lost, but the higher price will create economic profits in the cucumber industry and stimulate its expansion. The profitability of cucumbers will permit the industry to bid resources away from now-less-pressing uses, say, watermelons. Expansion of the industry will end only when the supply of cucumbers has expanded such that the price of cucumbers and their marginal cost are equal—that is, when allocative efficiency has been restored.

Similarly, a change in the supply of a particular resource—for example, the field laborers who pick cucumbers—or in a production technique will upset an existing price–marginal-cost equality by either raising or lowering marginal cost. The resulting inequality of MC and P will cause producers, in either pursuing profit or avoiding loss, to reallocate resources until product supply is such that price once again equals marginal cost. In so doing, they will correct any inefficiency in the allocation of resources

A Patent Failure?

Patents May Hinder Creative Destruction. If So, Should We Consider Abolishing Patents?

Patents give inventors the sole legal right to market and sell their new ideas for a period of 20 years. So when considering the plusses and minuses of the patent system, it is important to begin with the fact that the possibility of obtaining a patent gives inventors a strong financial incentive to bear the research and development (R&D) costs necessary to come up with innovative solutions to old problems.

At the same time, however, the patent system also gives patent holders the ability to stifle the creative energies of other inventors by suing or threating to sue any individual or firm that they believe is "infringing" on their patent by producing or utilizing their invention without permission.

The problem is most acute for products like cell phones that incorporate thousands of different technologies into a single product. That's because each of those technologies might possibly infringe on one or more patents. If so, a single lawsuit filed over just one of those patents could halt the production and sale of the entire product. The alleged infringement may be totally unintentional or a matter of honest dispute. But if a patent holder believes that some part of the phone is infringing on his patent, he can threaten to sue the manufacturer and demand the shutdown of all production unless he receives royalty payments in compensation.

Consider Microsoft, which 30 years ago was a successful innovator thanks to its Windows operating system. Over the last 10 years, however, its Windows-based cell phones have been a failure. Yet Microsoft CEO Steve Balmer threatened to shut down the production

of all Android phones because the Android software used to run those extremely popular phones happens to incorporate the ability to schedule a meeting. That is a feature that most Android users don't even know about. But it is a functionality over which Microsoft holds a patent for mobile devices. So to avoid a lawsuit that could have shut down the production of all Android phones, Android's parent company, Google, is now paying Microsoft a licensing fee on each and every Android phone.

That situation is very problematic for creative destruction because the patent system is being used to help an old company that hasn't had a successful product in many years to effectively tax and benefit from the successful innovations of a young rival. That ability to tax is a form of life support that allows stodgy old firms to survive longer than they should against innovative rivals and the pressures of creative destruction.

Even worse, companies known as "patent trolls" have been created to buy up patents simply for the chance to sue other companies and collect royalties. The patent trolls invent nothing and produce nothing. But they are free under the current system to make billions of dollars every year by suing innovative companies.

In response, some economists have begun to argue that the net benefits of the patent system have been overstated and that innovation might proceed faster in certain industries if patents were abolished. Their key insight is that the net benefits of patents depend upon how easy it is for rivals to successfully copy and market an innovative product.

---

that the original change may have temporarily imposed on the economy.

"Invisible Hand" Revisited

The highly efficient allocation of resources that a purely competitive economy promotes comes about because businesses and resource suppliers seek to further their self-interest. For private goods with no externalities (Chapter 4), the "invisible hand" (Chapter 2) is at work. The competitive system not only maximizes profits for individual producers but also, at the same time, creates a pattern of resource allocation that maximizes consumer satisfaction. The invisible hand thus organizes the private interests of producers in a way that is fully in sync with society's interest in using scarce resources efficiently. Striving to obtain a profit produces highly desirable economic outcomes.

Technological Advance and Competition

LO11.5 Discuss creative destruction and the profit incentives for innovation.

In explaining the model of pure competition, we assumed for simplicity that all the firms in an industry had the same cost curves. Competition, as a result, only involved entrepreneurs entering and exiting industries in response to changes in profits caused by changes in the market price. This form of competition is important, but it is just a game of copycat because firms entering an industry simply duplicate the production methods and cost curves of existing firms in order to duplicate their above-normal profits. In this type of competition, there is no dynamism and no innovation, just more of the same.

Consider pharmaceuticals. Once the chemical formula for a new drug becomes known, it is very easy for rivals to make chemically identical versions that will be easy to market because they will be just as effective as the version sold by the firm that invented the drug. At the same time, competition is so fierce in the pharmaceutical industry that without patent protection the price of the new drug would be driven down almost immediately to its marginal production cost. That is highly problematic because the market price would be too low to ever recoup the large R&D costs necessary to identify and develop effective new medications. Thus, without patent protection, R&D would cease and no new drugs would be developed.

So for industries like pharmaceuticals that have easy-to-copy products, patents should continue to exist as they are the only way to provide the financial incentive necessary to get firms to invest the R&D monies that must be spent if you want innovation and creative destruction.

Things are very different, however, for complicated consumer products that are made up of thousands of separate technologies that are each difficult to copy and market. As an example, even if Apple's rivals obtained the blueprints for the iPhone, it would still be extremely costly for them to build the factories necessary to make copies. And even if they did that, they would still have to convince consumers that their copycat iPhones were as good as the original. Thus, unlike pharmaceuticals, patents are not necessary to provide the firms that produce complicated consumer goods with an incentive to develop new products and invest in R&D.

On the other hand, society would likely see great benefits if patents were eliminated for complicated consumer goods like cell phones and automobiles because creative destruction would likely increase as innovative companies would no longer fear

patent-infringement lawsuits and old rivals could no longer delay their own demise by taxing innovators.

As a result, some economists now argue that patents should only be available for industries with simple products that are easy to copy and market. For industries with complicated products that are hard to copy and market, patents should be eliminated.

By contrast, the most dynamic and interesting parts of competition are the fights between firms over the creation of new production technologies and new products. As we explain in detail in Chapter 15, firms have a strong profit incentive to develop both improved ways of making existing products as well as totally new products. To put that incentive in context, recall one fact that you just learned about long-run equilibrium in perfect competition. When each firm in a purely competitive industry has the same productive technology and therefore the same cost structure for producing output, entry and exit assure that in the long run every firm will make the exact same normal profit.

Entrepreneurs, of course, would like to earn more than a normal profit. As a result, they are constantly attempting two different strategies for increasing their profits. The first involves attempting to lower the production costs of existing products through better technology or improved business organization. Because pure competition implies that individual firms cannot affect the market price, anything that lowers an innovating firm's production costs will result in higher profits, since the innovating firm's revenues per unit (which are equal to the market price per unit) will stay the same while its costs per unit fall due to its improved production technology.

The second strategy for earning a rate of return greater than a normal profit is to try to develop a totally new product that is popular with consumers. If a firm is first-to-market with a popular new product, it will face no competition, as it is the only producer. As long as the product remains popular and the firm remains the only producer, it will be able to charge prices that are higher than production costs, thereby allowing it to earn above-normal profits. (We say much more about this in the next chapter, which covers pure monopoly.)

CONSIDER THIS . . .

Source: © Katrin Thomas/Getty Images RF

Running a Company Is Hard Business

The life expectancy of a U.S. business is just 10.2 years. About 9.5 percent of U.S. firms go out of business each year. In addition, 22 percent of new start-up firms go bankrupt within 2 years, 53 percent within 5 years, and nearly 65 percent within 10 years.

These numbers testify to the ability of competition to quickly dispose of firms that have high production costs or unpopular products. In a competitive environment, such firms quickly prove unprofitable and are shut down by their owners.

Balancing out the dying firms are start-ups that hope to use the resources freed up by the closed firms to deliver better products or lower costs. In a typical year, more than 650,000 new businesses are started in the United States. Most of these new firms will themselves eventually fall victim to creative destruction and the pressures of competition, but one of them may just be the next Google, Starbucks, or Walmart.

Notably, however, any advantages that innovative firms gain either by lowering the production costs of existing products or by introducing entirely new products will not normally persist. An innovative entrepreneur may put some of her current rivals out of business, but there are always other entrepreneurs with new ideas so that soon it may be *her* firm that is going out of business due to innovations made by others. The nearby Consider This box shows just how rapidly new firms are created and destroyed.

Creative Destruction

The innovations that firms achieve thanks to competition are considered by many economists to be the driving force behind economic growth and rising living standards. The transformative effects of competition are often referred to as **creative destruction** to capture the idea that the creation of new products and new production methods destroys the market positions of firms committed to existing products and old ways of doing business. In addition, just the *threat* that a rival may soon come out with a new technology or product can cause other firms to innovate and thereby replace or rectify their old ways of doing business. As argued decades ago by

Harvard economist Joseph Schumpeter, the most important type of competition is

> competition from the new commodity, the new technology, the new source of supply, the new type of business organization—competition which commands a decisive cost or quality advantage and which strikes not at the margins of profits of the existing firms but at their foundation and their very lives. This kind of competition is . . . so . . . important that it becomes a matter of comparative indifference whether competition in the ordinary [short-run or long-run] sense functions more or less promptly. . . .
>
> . . . Competition of the kind we now have in mind acts not only when in being but also when it is merely an ever-present threat. It disciplines before it attacks. The businessman feels himself to be in a competitive situation even if he is alone in his field.[2]

There are many examples of creative destruction. In the 1800s wagons, ships, and barges were the only means of transporting freight until the railroads broke up their monopoly; the dominant market position of the railroads was, in turn, undermined by trucks and, later, by airplanes. Movies brought new competition to live theater, at one time the "only show in town." But movies were later challenged by broadcast television, which was then challenged by cable TV. Both are now challenged by Netflix, Amazon Instant Video, and other online video-on-demand services. Cassettes replaced records before being supplanted in turn by compact discs. Then compact discs were done in by iPods and MP3 players, which in turn were done in by the availability of smartphones to play music—including music streamed (instead of purchased) via services like Spotify and Pandora. Electronic communications—including faxes and e-mails—have pushed the U.S. Postal Service toward bankruptcy, including a $5.1 billion loss in 2015. And online retailers like Amazon.com have stolen substantial business away from brick-and-mortar retailers.

The "creative" part of "creative destruction" leads to new products and lower-cost production methods that are of great benefit to society because they allow for a more efficient use of society's scarce resources. Keep in mind, however, that the "destruction" part of "creative destruction" can be hard on workers in the industries being displaced by new technologies. A worker at a CD-making factory may see her job eliminated as consumers switch to online music downloads. The U.S. Postal Service cut 213,000 jobs (30 percent of its workforce) between 2005 and 2015 partly because of the impact that e-mail has had on the demand for postal services. And many jobs in retail have been eliminated due to competition with Amazon.com and other online retailers.

Normally, the process of creative destruction goes slowly enough that workers at firms being downsized can transition smoothly to jobs in firms that are expanding. But sometimes

---

[2]Joseph A. Schumpeter, *Capitalism, Socialism, and Democracy,* 3d ed. (New York: Harper & Row, 1950), pp. 84–85.

the change is too swift for all of them to find new jobs easily. And in other instances, such as a town with only one major employer—like a rural coal-mining town or a small town with a large auto factory—the loss of that one major employer can be devastating because there are not enough other firms in the local area to employ the workers laid off by the major employer.

While the net effects of creative destruction are indisputably positive—including ongoing economic growth and rising living standards—creative destruction involves costs as well as benefits. And while the benefits are widespread, the costs tend to be borne almost entirely by the relatively few workers in declining industries who are not positioned to make easy transitions to new jobs.

SUMMARY

LO11.1 Explain how the long run differs from the short run in pure competition.

In the short run, when plant and equipment are fixed, the firms in a purely competitive industry may earn profits or suffer losses. In the long run, when plant and equipment are adjustable, profits will attract new entrants, while losses will cause existing firms to leave the industry.

LO11.2 Describe how profits and losses drive the long-run adjustment process of pure competition.

The entry or exit of firms will change industry supply. Entry or exit will continue until the market price determined by industry supply interacting with market demand generates a normal profit for firms in the industry. With firms earning a normal profit, there will be no incentive to either enter or exit the industry. This situation constitutes long-run equilibrium in a purely competitive industry.

Entry and exit help to improve resource allocation. Firms that exit an industry due to low profits release their resources to be used more profitably in other industries. Firms that enter an industry chasing higher profits bring with them resources that were less profitably used in other industries. Both processes increase allocative efficiency.

In the long run, the market price of a product will equal the minimum average total cost of production. At a higher price, economic profits will cause firms to enter the industry until those profits have been competed away. At a lower price, losses will force the exit of firms from the industry until the product price rises to equal average total cost.

LO11.3 Explain the differences between constant-cost, increasing-cost, and decreasing-cost industries.

The long-run supply curve is horizontal for a constant-cost industry, upsloping for an increasing-cost industry, and downsloping for a decreasing-cost industry.

LO11.4 Show how long-run equilibrium in pure competition produces an efficient allocation of resources.

The long-run equality of price and minimum average total cost means that competitive firms will use the most efficient known technology and charge the lowest price consistent with their production costs. That is, the purely competitive firms will achieve productive efficiency.

The long-run equality of price and marginal cost implies that resources will be allocated in accordance with consumer tastes. Allocative efficiency will occur. In the market, the combined amount of consumer surplus and producer surplus will be at a maximum.

The competitive price system will reallocate resources in response to a change in consumer tastes, in technology, or in resource supplies and will thereby maintain allocative efficiency over time.

LO11.5 Discuss creative destruction and the profit incentives for innovation.

Competition involves never-ending attempts by entrepreneurs and managers to earn above-normal profits by either creating new products or developing lower-cost production methods for existing products. These efforts cause creative destruction, the financial undoing of the market positions of firms committed to existing products and old ways of doing business by new firms with new products and innovative ways of doing business.

TERMS AND CONCEPTS

long-run supply curve	decreasing-cost industry	consumer surplus
constant-cost industry	productive efficiency	producer surplus
increasing-cost industry	allocative efficiency	creative destruction

The following and additional problems can be found in ▓ connect

DISCUSSION QUESTIONS

1. Explain how the long run differs from the short run in pure competition. **LO11.1**
2. Relate opportunity costs to why profits encourage entry into purely competitive industries and how losses encourage exit from purely competitive industries. **LO11.2**
3. How do the entry and exit of firms in a purely competitive industry affect resource flows and long-run profits and losses? **LO11.2**
4. In long-run equilibrium, P = minimum ATC = MC. Of what significance for economic efficiency is the equality of P and minimum ATC? The equality of P and MC? Distinguish between productive efficiency and allocative efficiency in your answer. **LO11.4**
5. The basic model of pure competition reviewed in this chapter finds that in the long run all firms in a purely competitive industry will earn normal profits. If all firms will only earn a normal profit in the long run, why would any firms bother to develop new products or lower-cost production methods? Explain. **LO11.5**
6. "Ninety percent of new products fail within two years—so you shouldn't be so eager to innovate." Do you agree? Explain why or why not. **LO11.5**
7. **LAST WORD** How can patents speed up the process of creative destruction? How can patents slow down the process of creative destruction? How do differences in manufacturing costs affect which industries would be most likely to be affected by the removal of patents?

REVIEW QUESTIONS

1. When discussing pure competition, the term *long run* refers to a period of time long enough to allow: **LO11.1**
   a. Firms already in an industry to either expand or contract their capacities.
   b. New firms to enter or existing firms to leave.
   c. Both *a* and *b*.
   d. None of the above.
2. Suppose that the pen-making industry is perfectly competitive. Also suppose that each current firm and any potential firms that might enter the industry all have identical cost curves, with minimum ATC = $1.25 per pen. If the market equilibrium price of pens is currently $1.50, what would you expect it to be in the long run? **LO11.2**
   a. $0.25.
   b. $1.00.
   c. $1.25.
   d. $1.50.
3. Suppose that as the output of mobile phones increases, the cost of touch screens and other component parts decreases. If the mobile phone industry features pure competition, we would expect the long-run supply curve for mobile phones to be: **LO11.3**
   a. Upward sloping.
   b. Downward sloping.
   c. Horizontal.
   d. U-shaped.
4. Using diagrams for both the industry and a representative firm, illustrate competitive long-run equilibrium. Assuming constant costs, employ these diagrams to show how (*a*) an increase and (*b*) a decrease in market demand will upset that long-run equilibrium. Trace graphically and describe verbally the adjustment processes by which long-run equilibrium is restored. Now rework your analysis for increasing- and decreasing-cost industries and compare the three long-run supply curves. **LO11.3**
5. Suppose that purely competitive firms producing cashews discover that P exceeds MC. Is their combined output of cashews too little, too much, or just right to achieve allocative efficiency? In the long run, what will happen to the supply of cashews and the price of cashews? Use a supply and demand diagram to show how that response will change the combined amount of consumer surplus and producer surplus in the market for cashews. **LO11.4**

PROBLEMS

1. A firm in a purely competitive industry has a typical cost structure. The normal rate of profit in the economy is 5 percent. This firm is earning $5.50 on every $50 invested by its founders. What is its percentage rate of return? Is the firm earning an economic profit? If so, how large? Will this industry see entry or exit? What will be the rate of return earned by firms in this industry once the industry reaches long-run equilibrium? **LO11.2**
2. A firm in a purely competitive industry is currently producing 1,000 units per day at a total cost of $450. If the firm produced 800 units per day, its total cost would be $300, and if it produced 500 units per day, its total cost would be $275.

What are the firm's ATC per unit at these three levels of production? If every firm in this industry has the same cost structure, is the industry in long-run competitive equilibrium? From what you know about these firms' cost structures, what is the highest possible price per unit that could exist as the market price in long-run equilibrium? If that price ends up being the market price and if the normal rate of profit is 10 percent, then how big will each firm's accounting profit per unit be? **LO11.4**

3. There are 300 purely competitive farms in the local dairy market. Of the 300 dairy farms, 298 have a cost structure that generates profits of $24 for every $300 invested. What is their percentage rate of return? The other two dairies have a cost structure that generates profits of $22 for every $200 invested. What is their percentage rate of return? Assuming that the normal rate of profit in the economy is 10 percent, will there be entry or exit? Will the change in the number of firms affect the two that earn $22 for every $200 invested? What will be the rate of return earned by most firms in the industry in long-run equilibrium? If firms can copy each other's technology, what will be the rate of return eventually earned by all firms? **LO11.4**

Pure Monopoly

Learning Objectives

LO12.1 List the characteristics of pure monopoly.

LO12.2 List and explain the barriers to entry that shield pure monopolies from competition.

LO12.3 Explain how demand is seen by a pure monopoly.

LO12.4 Explain how a pure monopoly sets its profit-maximizing output and price.

LO12.5 Discuss the economic effects of monopoly.

LO12.6 Describe why a monopolist might prefer to charge different prices in different markets.

LO12.7 Distinguish among the monopoly price, the socially optimal price, and the fair-return price of a government-regulated monopoly.

We turn now from pure competition to pure monopoly, which is at the opposite end of the spectrum of industry structures listed in Table 10.1. You deal with monopolies more often than you might think. If you see the logo for Microsoft's Windows on your computer, you are dealing

with a monopoly (or, at least, a near-monopoly). When you purchase certain prescription drugs, you are buying monopolized products. When you make a local telephone call, turn on your lights, or subscribe to cable TV, you may be patronizing a monopoly, depending on your location.

What precisely do we mean by pure monopoly, and what conditions enable it to arise and survive? How does a pure monopolist determine its profit-maximizing price and output? Does a pure monopolist achieve the efficiency associated with pure competition? If not, what, if anything, should the government do about it? A simplified model of pure monopoly will help us answer these questions. It will be the first of three models of imperfect competition.

An Introduction to Pure Monopoly

LO12.1 List the characteristics of pure monopoly.

Pure monopoly exists when a single firm is the sole producer of a product for which there are no close substitutes. Here are the main characteristics of pure monopoly:

- *Single seller* A pure, or absolute, monopoly is an industry in which a single firm is the sole producer of a specific good or the sole supplier of a service; the firm and the industry are synonymous.

- *No close substitutes* A pure monopoly's product is unique in that there are no close substitutes. The consumer who chooses not to buy the monopolized product must do without it.

- *Price maker* The pure monopolist controls the total quantity supplied and thus has considerable control over price; it is a *price maker* (unlike a pure competitor, which has no such control and therefore is a *price taker*). The pure monopolist confronts the usual downsloping product demand curve. It can change its product price by changing the quantity of the product it produces. The monopolist will use this power whenever it is advantageous to do so.

- *Blocked entry* A pure monopolist has no immediate competitors because certain barriers keep potential competitors from entering the industry. Those barriers may be economic, technological, legal, or of some other type. But entry is totally blocked in pure monopoly.

- *Nonprice competition* The product produced by a pure monopolist may be either standardized (as with natural gas and electricity) or differentiated (as with Windows or Frisbees). Monopolists that have standardized products engage mainly in public relations advertising, whereas those with differentiated products sometimes advertise their products' attributes.

Examples of Monopoly

Examples of *pure* monopoly are relatively rare, but there are many examples of less pure forms. In most cities, government-owned or government-regulated public utilities—natural gas and electric companies, the water company, the cable TV company, and the local telephone company—are all monopolies or virtually so.

There are also many "near-monopolies" in which a single firm has the bulk of sales in a specific market. Intel, for example, produces 80 percent of the central microprocessors used in personal computers. First Data Corporation, via its Western Union subsidiary, accounts for 80 percent of the market for money order transfers. Brannock Device Company has an 80 percent market share of the shoe sizing devices found in shoe stores. Wham-O, through its Frisbee brand, sells 90 percent of plastic throwing disks. Google executes nearly 70 percent of all U.S. Internet searches and consequently controls nearly 75 percent of all the revenue generated by search ads in the United States.

Professional sports teams are, in a sense, monopolies because they are the sole suppliers of specific services in large geographic areas. With a few exceptions, a single major-league team in each sport serves each large American city. If you want to see a live Major League Baseball game in St. Louis or Seattle, you must patronize the Cardinals or the Mariners, respectively. Other geographic monopolies exist. For example, a small town may be served by only one airline or railroad. In a small, isolated community, the local barber shop, dry cleaner, or grocery store may approximate a monopoly. And in the skies above, airlines control the only Internet access that is available to the passengers flying on their planes.

Of course, there is almost always some competition. Satellite television is a substitute for cable, and amateur softball is a substitute for professional baseball. The Linux operating system can substitute for Windows, and so on. But such substitutes are typically either more costly or in some way less appealing.

Dual Objectives of the Study of Monopoly

Monopoly is worth studying both for its own sake and because it provides insights about the more common market structures of monopolistic competition and oligopoly (Chapters 13 and 14). These two market structures combine, in differing degrees, characteristics of pure competition and pure monopoly.

Barriers to Entry

LO12.2 List and explain the barriers to entry that shield pure monopolies from competition.

The factors that prohibit firms from entering an industry are called **barriers to entry.** In pure monopoly, strong barriers to entry effectively block all potential competition. Somewhat weaker barriers may permit oligopoly, a market structure dominated by a few firms. Still weaker barriers may permit the entry of a fairly large number of competing firms giving rise to monopolistic competition. And the absence of any effective entry barriers permits the entry of a very large number of firms, which provide the basis of pure competition. So barriers to entry are pertinent not only to the extreme case of pure monopoly but also to other market structures in which there are monopoly-like characteristics or monopoly-like behaviors.

We now discuss the four most prominent barriers to entry.

Economies of Scale

Modern technology in some industries is such that economies of scale—declining average total cost with added firm size—are extensive. In such cases, a firm's long-run average-cost schedule will decline over a wide range of output. Given market demand, only a few large firms or, in the extreme, only a single large firm can achieve low average total costs.

Figure 12.1 indicates economies of scale over a wide range of outputs. If total consumer demand is within that output range, then only a single producer can satisfy demand at least cost. Note, for example, that a monopolist can produce

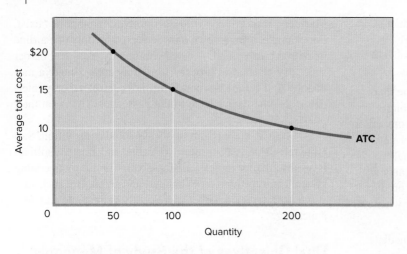

FIGURE 12.1 **Economies of scale: the natural monopoly case.** A declining long-run average-total-cost curve over a wide range of output quantities indicates extensive economies of scale. A single monopoly firm can produce, say, 200 units of output at lower cost ($10 each) than could two or more firms that had a combined output of 200 units.

200 units at a per-unit cost of $10 and a total cost of $2,000. If the industry has two firms and each produces 100 units, the unit cost is $15 and total cost rises to $3,000 (= 200 units × $15). A still more competitive situation with four firms each producing 50 units would boost unit and total cost to $20 and $4,000, respectively. Conclusion: When long-run ATC is declining, only a single producer, a monopolist, can produce any particular amount of output at minimum total cost.

If a pure monopoly exists in such an industry, economies of scale will serve as an entry barrier and will protect the monopolist from competition. New firms that try to enter the industry as small-scale producers cannot realize the cost economies of the monopolist. They therefore will be undercut and forced out of business by the monopolist, which can sell at a much lower price and still make a profit because of its lower per-unit cost associated with its economies of scale. A new firm might try to start out big, that is, to enter the industry as a large-scale producer so as to achieve the necessary economies of scale. But the massive expense of the plant facilities along with customer loyalty to the existing product would make the entry highly risky. Therefore, the new and untried enterprise would find it difficult to secure financing for its venture. In most cases the risks and financial obstacles to "starting big" are prohibitive. This explains why efforts to enter such industries as computer operating software, commercial aircraft, and household laundry equipment are so rare.

A monopoly firm is referred to as a *natural monopoly* if the market demand curve intersects the long-run ATC curve at any point where average total costs are declining. If a natural monopoly were to set its price where market demand intersects long-run ATC, its price would be lower than if the industry were more competitive. But it will probably set a higher price. As with any monopolist, a natural monopolist may, instead, set its price far above ATC and obtain substantial economic profit. In that event, the lowest-unit-cost advantage of a natural monopolist would accrue to the monopolist as profit and not as lower prices to consumers. That is why the government regulates some natural monopolies, specifying the price they may charge. We will say more about that later.

Legal Barriers to Entry: Patents and Licenses

Government also creates legal barriers to entry by awarding patents and licenses.

Patents   A *patent* is the exclusive right of an inventor to use, or to allow another to use, her or his invention. Patents and patent laws aim to protect the inventor from rivals who would use the invention without having shared in the effort and expense of developing it. At the same time, patents provide the inventor with a monopoly position for the life of the patent. The world's nations have agreed on a uniform patent length of 20 years from the time of application. Patents have figured prominently in the growth of modern-day giants such as IBM, Pfizer, Intel, Xerox, General Electric, and DuPont.

Research and development (R&D) is what leads to most patentable inventions and products. Firms that gain monopoly power through their own research or by purchasing the patents of others can use patents to strengthen their market position. The profit from one patent can finance the research required to develop new patentable products. In the pharmaceutical industry, patents on prescription drugs have produced large monopoly profits that have helped finance the discovery of new patentable medicines. So monopoly power achieved through patents may well be self-sustaining, even though patents eventually expire and generic drugs then compete with the original brand. (Chapter 11's Last Word has more on the costs and benefits of patents.)

Licenses Government may also limit entry into an industry or occupation through *licensing*. At the national level, the Federal Communications Commission licenses only so many radio and television stations in each geographic area. In many large cities one of a limited number of municipal licenses is required to drive a taxicab. The consequent restriction of the supply of cabs creates economic profit for cab owners and drivers. New cabs cannot enter the industry to drive down prices and profits. In a few instances the government might "license" itself to provide some product and thereby create a public monopoly. For example, in some states only state-owned retail outlets can sell liquor. Similarly, many states have "licensed" themselves to run lotteries.

Ownership or Control of Essential Resources

A monopolist can use private property as an obstacle to potential rivals. For example, a firm that owns or controls a resource essential to the production process can prohibit the entry of rival firms. At one time the International Nickel Company of Canada (now called Vale Canada Limited) controlled 90 percent of the world's known nickel reserves. A local firm may own all the nearby deposits of sand and gravel. And it is very difficult for new sports leagues to be created because existing professional sports leagues have contracts with the best players and have long-term leases on the major stadiums and arenas.

Pricing and Other Strategic Barriers to Entry

Even if a firm is not protected from entry by, say, extensive economies of scale or ownership of essential resources, entry may effectively be blocked by the way the monopolist responds to attempts by rivals to enter the industry. Confronted with a new entrant, the monopolist may "create an entry barrier" by slashing its price, stepping up its advertising, or taking other strategic actions to make it difficult for the entrant to succeed.

Some examples of entry deterrence: In 2005 Dentsply, the dominant American maker of false teeth (80 percent market share) was found to have unlawfully precluded independent distributors of false teeth from carrying competing brands. The lack of access to the distributors deterred potential foreign competitors from entering the U.S. market. As another example, in 2015 American Express was found guilty of an unlawful restraint of trade because it prohibited any merchant who had signed up to accept American Express credit cards from promoting rival credit cards—such as Visa or MasterCard—to their customers.

Monopoly Demand

LO12.3 Explain how demand is seen by a pure monopoly.

Now that we have explained the sources of monopoly, we want to build a model of pure monopoly so that we can analyze its price and output decisions. Let's start by making three assumptions:

- Patents, economies of scale, or resource ownership secures the firm's monopoly.
- No unit of government regulates the firm.
- The firm is a single-price monopolist; it charges the same price for all units of output.

The crucial difference between a pure monopolist and a purely competitive seller lies on the demand side of the market. The purely competitive seller faces a perfectly elastic demand at the price determined by market supply and demand. It is a price taker that can sell as much or as little as it wants at the going market price. Each additional unit sold will add the amount of the constant product price to the firm's total revenue. That means that marginal revenue for the competitive seller is constant and equal to product price. (Refer to the table and graph in Figure 10.1 for price, marginal-revenue, and total-revenue relationships for the purely competitive firm.)

The demand curve for the monopolist (and for any imperfectly competitive seller) is quite different from that of the pure competitor. Because the pure monopolist *is* the industry, its demand curve *is* the market demand curve. And because market demand is not perfectly elastic, the monopolist's demand curve is downsloping. Columns 1 and 2 in Table 12.1 illustrate this concept. Note that quantity demanded increases as price decreases.

In Figure 10.7 we drew separate demand curves for the purely competitive industry and for a single firm in such an industry. But only a single demand curve is needed in pure monopoly because the firm and the industry are one and the same. We have graphed part of the demand data in Table 12.1 as demand curve *D* in Figure 12.2. This is the monopolist's demand curve *and* the market demand curve. The downsloping demand curve has three implications that are essential to understanding the monopoly model.

Marginal Revenue Is Less Than Price

With a fixed downsloping demand curve, the pure monopolist can increase sales only by charging a lower price. Consequently, marginal revenue—the change in total revenue associated with a one-unit change in output—is less than price (average revenue) for every unit of output except the first. Why so? The reason is that the lower price of the extra unit of output also applies to all prior units of output. The

TABLE 12.1 Revenue and Cost Data of a Pure Monopolist

	Revenue Data				Cost Data			
(1) Quantity of Output	(2) Price (Average Revenue)	(3) Total Revenue, (1) × (2)	(4) Marginal Revenue		(5) Average Total Cost	(6) Total Cost, (1) × (5)	(7) Marginal Cost	(8) Profit [+] or Loss [−]
0	$172	$ 0				$ 100		$−100
			$162				$ 90	
1	162	162			$190.00	190		−28
			142				80	
2	152	304			135.00	270		+34
			122				70	
3	142	426			113.33	340		+86
			102				60	
4	132	528			100.00	400		+128
			82				70	
5	122	610			94.00	470		+140
			62				80	
6	112	672			91.67	550		+122
			42				90	
7	102	714			91.43	640		+74
			22				110	
8	92	736			93.75	750		−14
			2				130	
9	82	738			97.78	880		−142
			−18				150	
10	72	720			103.00	1030		−310

monopolist could have sold these prior units at a higher price if it had not produced and sold the extra output. Each additional unit of output sold increases total revenue by an amount equal to its own price less the sum of the price cuts that apply to all prior units of output.

Figure 12.2 confirms this point. There, we have highlighted two price-quantity combinations from the monopolist's demand curve. The monopolist can sell 1 more unit at $132 than it can at $142 and that way obtain $132 (the blue

FIGURE 12.2 Price and marginal revenue in pure monopoly. A pure monopolist, or any other imperfect competitor with a downsloping demand curve such as *D*, must set a lower price in order to sell more output. Here, by charging $132 rather than $142, the monopolist sells an extra unit (the fourth unit) and gains $132 from that sale. But from this gain must be subtracted $30, which reflects the $10 less the monopolist charged for each of the first 3 units. Thus, the marginal revenue of the fourth unit is $102 (= $132 − $30), considerably less than its $132 price.

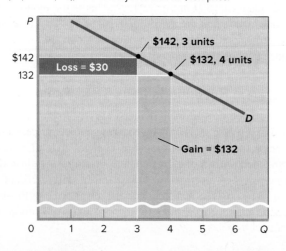

area) of extra revenue. But to sell that fourth unit for $132, the monopolist must also sell the first 3 units at $132 rather than $142. The $10 reduction in revenue on 3 units results in a $30 revenue loss (the red area). Thus, the net difference in total revenue from selling a fourth unit is $102: the $132 gain from the fourth unit minus the $30 forgone on the first 3 units. This net gain (marginal revenue) of $102 from the fourth unit is clearly less than the $132 price of the fourth unit.

Column 4 in Table 12.1 shows that marginal revenue is always less than the corresponding product price in column 2, except for the first unit of output. Because marginal revenue is the change in total revenue associated with each additional unit of output, the declining amounts of marginal revenue in column 4 mean that total revenue increases at a diminishing rate (as shown in column 3).

We show the relationship between the monopolist's marginal-revenue curve and total-revenue curve in Figure 12.3. For this figure, we extended the demand and revenue data of columns 1 through 4 in Table 12.1, assuming that each successive $10 price cut elicits 1 additional unit of sales. That is, the monopolist can sell 11 units at $62, 12 units at $52, and so on.

Note that the monopolist's MR curve lies below the demand curve, indicating that marginal revenue is less than price at every output quantity but the very first unit. Observe also the special relationship between total revenue (shown in the lower graph) and marginal revenue (shown in the top graph). Because marginal revenue is the change in total revenue, marginal revenue is positive while total revenue is increasing. When total revenue reaches its maximum, marginal revenue is zero. When total revenue is diminishing, marginal revenue is negative.

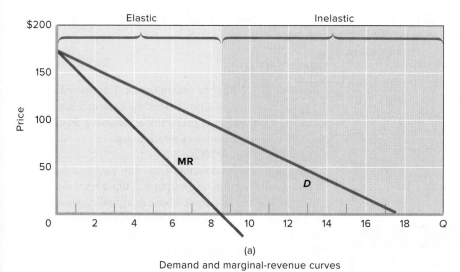

(a)
Demand and marginal-revenue curves

FIGURE 12.3 **Demand, marginal revenue, and total revenue for a pure monopolist.**
(a) Because it must lower price on all units sold in order to increase its sales, an imperfectly competitive firm's marginal-revenue curve (MR) lies below its downsloping demand curve (D). The elastic and inelastic regions of demand are highlighted. (b) Total revenue (TR) increases at a decreasing rate, reaches a maximum, and then declines. Note that in the elastic region, TR is increasing and hence MR is positive. When TR reaches its maximum, MR is zero. In the inelastic region of demand, TR is declining, so MR is negative.

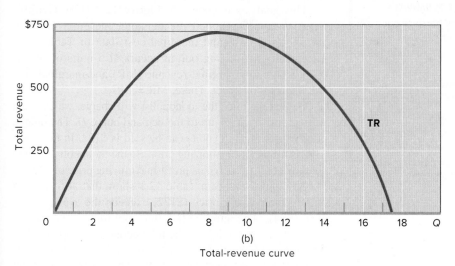

(b)
Total-revenue curve

The Monopolist Is a Price Maker

All imperfect competitors, whether pure monopolists, oligopolists, or monopolistic competitors, face downsloping demand curves. As a result, any change in quantity produced causes a movement along their respective demand curves and a change in the price they can charge for their respective products. Economists summarize this fact by saying that firms with downsloping demand curves are *price makers*.

This is most evident in pure monopoly, where an industry consists of a single monopoly firm so that total industry output is exactly equal to whatever the single monopoly firm chooses to produce. As we just mentioned, the monopolist faces a downsloping demand curve in which each amount of output is associated with some unique price. Thus, in deciding on the quantity of output to produce, the monopolist is also determining the price it will charge. Through control of output, it can "make the price." From columns 1 and 2 in Table 12.1 we find that the monopolist

can charge a price of $72 if it produces and offers for sale 10 units, a price of $82 if it produces and offers for sale 9 units, and so forth.

The Monopolist Sets Prices in the Elastic Region of Demand

The total-revenue test for price elasticity of demand is the basis for our third implication. Recall from Chapter 6 that the total-revenue test reveals that when demand is elastic, a decline in price will increase total revenue. Similarly, when demand is inelastic, a decline in price will reduce total revenue. Beginning at the top of demand curve D in Figure 12.3a, observe that as the price declines from $172 to approximately $82, total revenue increases (and marginal revenue therefore is positive). This means that demand is elastic in this price range. Conversely, for price declines below $82, total revenue decreases (marginal revenue is negative), indicating that demand is inelastic there.

The implication is that a monopolist will never choose a price-quantity combination where price reductions cause total revenue to decrease (marginal revenue to be negative). The profit-maximizing monopolist will always want to avoid the inelastic segment of its demand curve in favor of some price-quantity combination in the elastic region. Here's why: To get into the inelastic region, the monopolist must lower price and increase output. In the inelastic region a lower price means less total revenue. And increased output always means increased total cost. Less total revenue and higher total cost yield lower profit.

QUICK REVIEW 12.1

✓ A pure monopolist is the sole supplier of a product or service for which there are no close substitutes.

✓ A monopoly survives because of entry barriers such as economies of scale, patents and licenses, the ownership of essential resources, and strategic actions to exclude rivals.

✓ The monopolist's demand curve is downsloping and its marginal-revenue curve lies below its demand curve.

✓ The downsloping demand curve means that the monopolist is a price maker.

✓ The monopolist will operate in the elastic region of demand since in the inelastic region it can increase total revenue and reduce total cost by reducing output.

Output and Price Determination

LO12.4 Explain how a pure monopoly sets its profit-maximizing output and price.

At what specific price-quantity combination will a profit-maximizing monopolist choose to operate? To answer this question, we must add production costs to our analysis.

Cost Data

On the cost side, we will assume that although the firm is a monopolist in the product market, it hires resources competitively and employs the same technology and, therefore, has the same cost structure as the purely competitive firm that we studied in Chapters 10 and 11. By using the same cost data that we developed in Chapter 9 and applied to the competitive firm in Chapters 10 and 11, we will be able to directly compare the price and output decisions of a pure monopoly with those of a pure competitor. This will help us demonstrate that the price and output differences between a pure monopolist and a pure competitor are not the result of two different sets of costs. Columns 5 through 7 in Table 12.1 restate the pertinent cost data from Table 9.2.

MR = MC Rule

A monopolist seeking to maximize total profit will employ the same rationale as a profit-seeking firm in a competitive industry. If producing is preferable to shutting down, it will produce up to the output at which marginal revenue equals marginal cost (MR = MC).

A comparison of columns 4 and 7 in Table 12.1 indicates that the profit-maximizing output is 5 units because the fifth unit is the last unit of output whose marginal revenue exceeds its marginal cost. What price will the monopolist charge? The demand schedule shown as columns 1 and 2 in Table 12.1 indicates there is only one price at which 5 units can be sold: $122.

This analysis is shown in **Figure 12.4 (Key Graph)**, where we have graphed the demand, marginal-revenue, average-total-cost, and marginal-cost data of Table 12.1. The profit-maximizing output occurs at 5 units of output (Q_m), where the marginal-revenue (MR) and marginal-cost (MC) curves intersect. There, MR = MC.

To find the price the monopolist will charge, we extend a vertical line from Q_m up to the demand curve D. The unique price P_m at which Q_m units can be sold is $122. In this case, $122 is the profit-maximizing price. So the monopolist sets the quantity at Q_m to charge its profit-maximizing price of $122.

Columns 2 and 5 in Table 12.1 show that at 5 units of output, the product price ($122) exceeds the average total cost ($94). The monopolist thus obtains an economic profit of $28 per unit, and the total economic profit is $140 (= 5 units × $28). In Figure 12.4, per-unit profit is $P_m - A$, where A is the average total cost of producing Q_m units. Total economic profit—the green rectangle—is found by multiplying this per-unit profit by the profit-maximizing output Q_m.

Another way to determine the profit-maximizing output is by comparing total revenue and total cost at each possible level of production and choosing the output with the greatest positive difference. Use columns 3 and 6 in Table 12.1 to verify that 5 units is the profit-maximizing output. An accurate graphing of total revenue and total cost against output would also show the greatest difference (the maximum profit) at 5 units of output. Table 12.2 summarizes the process for determining the profit-maximizing output, profit-maximizing price, and economic profit in pure monopoly.

No Monopoly Supply Curve

Recall that MR equals P in pure competition and that the supply curve of a purely competitive firm is determined by applying the MR (= P) = MC profit-maximizing rule. At any specific market-determined price, the purely competitive seller

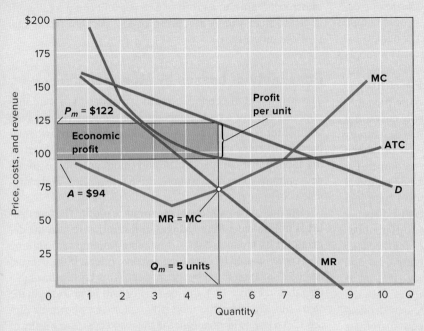

FIGURE 12.4 **Profit maximization by a pure monopolist.** The pure monopolist maximizes profit by producing at the MR = MC output, here Q_m = 5 units. Then, as seen from the demand curve, it will charge price P_m = $122. Average total cost will be A = $94, meaning that per-unit profit is $P_m - A$ and total profit is $5 \times (P_m - A)$. Total economic profit is thus represented by the green rectangle.

QUICK QUIZ FOR FIGURE 12.4

1. The MR curve lies below the demand curve in this figure because the:
   a. demand curve is linear (a straight line).
   b. demand curve is highly inelastic throughout its full length.
   c. demand curve is highly elastic throughout its full length.
   d. gain in revenue from an extra unit of output is less than the price charged for that unit of output.

2. The area labeled "Economic profit" can be found by multiplying the difference between P and ATC by quantity. It also can be found by:
   a. dividing profit per unit by quantity.
   b. subtracting total cost from total revenue.
   c. multiplying the coefficient of demand elasticity by quantity.
   d. multiplying the difference between P and MC by quantity.

3. This pure monopolist:
   a. charges the highest price that it could achieve.
   b. earns only a normal profit in the long run.
   c. restricts output to create an insurmountable entry barrier.
   d. restricts output to increase its price and total economic profit.

4. At this monopolist's profit-maximizing output:
   a. price equals marginal revenue.
   b. price equals marginal cost.
   c. price exceeds marginal cost.
   d. profit per unit is maximized.

Answers: 1. d; 2. b; 3. d; 4. c

TABLE 12.2 **Steps for Graphically Determining the Profit-Maximizing Output, Profit-Maximizing Price, and Economic Profit (if Any) in Pure Monopoly**

Step 1. Determine the profit-maximizing output by finding where MR = MC.

Step 2. Determine the profit-maximizing price by extending a vertical line upward from the output determined in step 1 to the pure monopolist's demand curve

Step 3. Determine the pure monopolist's economic profit using one of two methods:

Method 1. Find profit per unit by subtracting the average total cost of the profit-maximizing output from the profit-maximizing price. Then multiply the difference by the profit-maximizing output to determine economic profit (if any).

Method 2. Find total cost by multiplying the average total cost of the profit-maximizing output by that output. Find total revenue by multiplying the profit-maximizing output by the profit-maximizing price. Then subtract total cost from total revenue to determine economic profit (if any).

will maximize profit by supplying the quantity at which MC is equal to that price. When the market price increases or decreases, the competitive firm produces more or less output. Each market price is thus associated with a specific output, and all such price-output pairs define the supply curve. This supply curve turns out to be the portion of the firm's MC curve that lies above the average-variable-cost curve (see Figure 10.6).

At first glance we would suspect that the pure monopolist's marginal-cost curve would also be its supply curve. But that is *not* the case. *The pure monopolist has no supply curve.* There is no unique relationship between price and quantity supplied for a monopolist. Like the competitive firm, the monopolist equates marginal revenue and marginal cost to determine output, but for the monopolist marginal revenue is less than price. Because the monopolist does not equate marginal cost to price, it is possible for different demand conditions to bring about different prices for the same output. To understand this point, refer to Figure 12.4 and pencil in a new, steeper marginal-revenue curve that intersects the marginal-cost curve at the same point as does the present marginal-revenue curve. Then draw in a new demand curve that is roughly consistent with your new marginal-revenue curve. With the new curves, the same MR = MC output of 5 units now means a higher profit-maximizing price. Conclusion: There is no single, unique price associated with each output level Q_m, and so there is no supply curve for the pure monopolist.

Misconceptions Concerning Monopoly Pricing

Our analysis exposes two fallacies concerning monopoly behavior.

Not Highest Price Because a monopolist can manipulate output and price, people often believe it "will charge the highest price possible." That is incorrect. There are many prices above P_m in Figure 12.4, but the monopolist shuns them because they yield a smaller-than-maximum total profit. The monopolist seeks maximum total profit, not maximum price. Some high prices that could be charged would reduce sales and total revenue too severely to offset any decrease in total cost.

Total, Not Unit, Profit The monopolist seeks maximum *total* profit, not maximum *unit* profit. In Figure 12.4 a careful comparison of the vertical distance between average total cost and price at various possible outputs indicates that per-unit profit is greater at a point slightly to the left of the profit-maximizing output Q_m. This is seen in Table 12.1, where the per-unit profit at 4 units of output is $32 (= $132 − $100) compared with $28 (= $122 − $94) at the profit-maximizing output of 5 units. Here the monopolist accepts a lower-than-maximum per-unit profit because additional sales more than compensate for the lower unit profit. A monopolist would rather sell 5 units at a profit of $28 per unit (for a total profit of $140) than 4 units at a profit of $32 per unit (for a total profit of only $128).

Possibility of Losses by Monopolist

The likelihood of economic profit is greater for a pure monopolist than for a pure competitor. In the long run the pure competitor is destined to have only a normal profit, whereas barriers to entry mean that any economic profit realized by the monopolist can persist. In pure monopoly there are no new entrants to increase supply, drive down price, and eliminate economic profit.

But pure monopoly does not guarantee profit. The monopolist is not immune from changes in tastes that reduce the demand for its product. Nor is it immune from upward-shifting cost curves caused by escalating resource prices. If the demand and cost situation faced by the monopolist is far less favorable than that in Figure 12.4, the monopolist will incur losses in the short run. Consider the monopoly enterprise shown in Figure 12.5. Despite its dominance in the market (as, say, a seller of home sewing machines), it suffers a loss, as shown, because of weak demand and relatively high costs. Yet it continues to operate for the time being because its total loss is less than its fixed cost. More precisely, at output Q_m the monopolist's price P_m exceeds its average variable cost V. Its loss per unit is $A − P_m$, and the total loss is shown by the red rectangle.

Like the pure competitor, the monopolist will not persist in operating at a loss. Faced with continuing losses, in the long run the firm's owners will move their resources to alternative industries that offer better profit opportunities. A

FIGURE 12.5 The loss-minimizing position of a pure monopolist. If demand *D* is weak and costs are high, the pure monopolist may be unable to make a profit. Because P_m exceeds *V*, the average variable cost at the MR = MC output Q_m, the monopolist will minimize losses in the short run by producing at that output. The loss per unit is $A − P_m$, and the total loss is indicated by the red rectangle.

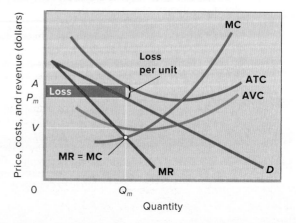

monopolist such as the one depicted in Figure 12.5 must obtain a minimum of a normal profit in the long run or it will go out of business.

Economic Effects of Monopoly

LO12.5 Discuss the economic effects of monopoly.

Let's now evaluate pure monopoly from the standpoint of society as a whole. Our reference for this evaluation will be the outcome of long-run efficiency in a purely competitive market, identified by the triple equality $P = MC = $ minimum ATC.

Price, Output, and Efficiency

Figure 12.6 graphically contrasts the price, output, and efficiency outcomes of pure monopoly and a purely competitive *industry*. The $S = MC$ curve in Figure 12.6a reminds us that the market supply curve S for a purely competitive industry is the horizontal sum of the marginal-cost curves of all the firms in the industry. Suppose there are 1,000 such firms. Comparing their combined supply curves S with market demand D, we see that the purely competitive price and output are P_c and Q_c.

Recall that this price-output combination results in both productive efficiency and allocative efficiency. *Productive efficiency* is achieved because free entry and exit force firms to operate where average total cost is at a minimum. The sum of the minimum-ATC outputs of the 1,000 pure competitors is the industry output, here, Q_c. Product price is at the lowest

level consistent with minimum average total cost. The *allocative efficiency* of pure competition results because production occurs up to that output at which price (the measure of a product's value or marginal benefit to society) equals marginal cost (the worth of the alternative products forgone by society in producing any given commodity). In short: $P = MC = $ minimum ATC.

Now let's suppose that this industry becomes a pure monopoly (Figure 12.6b) as a result of one firm acquiring all its competitors. We also assume that no changes in costs or market demand result from this dramatic change in the industry structure. What formerly were 1,000 competing firms is now a single pure monopolist consisting of 1,000 noncompeting branches.

The competitive market supply curve S has become the marginal-cost curve (MC) of the monopolist, the summation of the individual marginal-cost curves of its many branch plants. (Since the monopolist does not have a supply curve, as such, we have removed the S label.) The important change, however, is on the demand side. From the viewpoint of each of the 1,000 individual competitive firms, demand was perfectly elastic, and marginal revenue was therefore equal to the market equilibrium price P_c. So each firm equated its marginal revenue of P_c dollars per unit with its individual marginal cost curve to maximize profits. But market demand and individual demand are the same to the pure monopolist. The firm *is* the industry, and thus the monopolist sees the downsloping demand curve D shown in Figure 12.6b.

FIGURE 12.6 Inefficiency of pure monopoly relative to a purely competitive industry. (a) In a purely competitive industry, entry and exit of firms ensure that price (P_c) equals marginal cost (MC) and that the minimum average-total-cost output (Q_c) is produced. Both productive efficiency ($P = $ minimum ATC) and allocative efficiency ($P = MC$) are obtained. (b) In pure monopoly, the MR curve lies below the demand curve. The monopolist maximizes profit at output Q_m, where MR = MC, and charges price P_m. Thus, output is lower (Q_m rather than Q_c) and price is higher (P_m rather than P_c) than they would be in a purely competitive industry. Monopoly is inefficient, since output is less than that required for achieving minimum ATC (here, at Q_c) and because the monopolist's price exceeds MC. Monopoly creates an efficiency loss (here, of triangle *abc*). There is also a transfer of income from consumers to the monopoly (here, of rectangle $P_cP_m bd$).

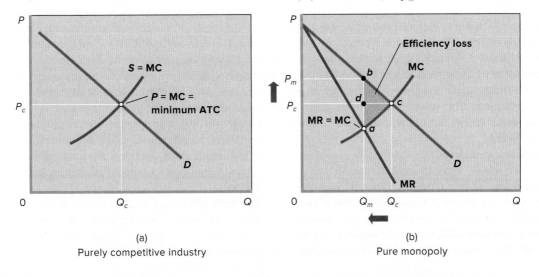

(a)
Purely competitive industry

(b)
Pure monopoly

This means that marginal revenue is less than price, that graphically the MR curve lies below demand curve D. In using the MR = MC rule, the monopolist selects output Q_m and price P_m. A comparison of both graphs in Figure 12.6 reveals that the monopolist finds it profitable to sell a smaller output at a higher price than do the competitive producers.

Monopoly yields neither productive nor allocative efficiency. The lack of productive efficiency can be understood most directly by noting that the monopolist's output Q_m is less than Q_c, the output at which average total cost is lowest. In addition, the monopoly price P_m is higher than the competitive price P_c that we know in long-run equilibrium in pure competition equals minimum average total cost. Thus, the monopoly price exceeds minimum average total cost, thereby demonstrating in another way that the monopoly will not be productively efficient.

The monopolist's underproduction also implies allocative inefficiency. One way to see this is to note that at the monopoly output level Q_m, the monopoly price P_m that consumers are willing to pay exceeds the marginal cost of production. This means that consumers value additional units of this product more highly than they do the alternative products that could be produced from the resources that would be necessary to make more units of the monopolist's product.

The monopolist's allocative inefficiency can also be understood by noting that for every unit between Q_m and Q_c, marginal benefit exceeds marginal cost because the demand curve lies above the supply curve. By choosing not to produce these units, the monopolist reduces allocative efficiency because the resources that should have been used to make these units will be redirected instead toward producing items that bring lower net benefits to society. The total dollar value of this efficiency loss (or *deadweight loss*) is equal to the area of the gray triangle labeled *abc* in Figure 12.6b.

Income Transfer

In general, a monopoly transfers income from consumers to the owners of the monopoly. The income is received by the owners as revenue. Because a monopoly has market power, it can charge a higher price than would a purely competitive firm with the same costs. So the monopoly in effect levies a "private tax" on consumers. This private tax can often generate substantial economic profits that can persist because entry to the industry is blocked.

The transfer from consumers to the monopolist is evident in Figure 12.6b. For the Q_m units of output demanded, consumers pay price P_m rather than the price P_c that they would pay to a pure competitor. The total amount of income transferred from consumers to the monopolist is $P_m - P_c$ multiplied by the number of units sold, Q_m. So the total transfer is the dollar amount of rectangle P_cP_mbd. What the consumer

loses, the monopolist gains. In contrast, the efficiency loss *abc* is a *deadweight* loss—society totally loses the net benefits of the Q_c minus Q_m units that are not produced.

Cost Complications

Our evaluation of pure monopoly has led us to conclude that, given identical costs, a purely monopolistic industry will charge a higher price, produce a smaller output, and allocate economic resources less efficiently than a purely competitive industry. These inferior results are rooted in the entry barriers characterizing monopoly.

Now we must recognize that costs may not be the same for purely competitive and monopolistic producers. The unit cost incurred by a monopolist may be either larger or smaller than that incurred by a purely competitive firm. There are four reasons costs may differ: (1) economies of scale, (2) a factor called "X-inefficiency," (3) the need for monopoly-preserving expenditures, and (4) the "very long run" perspective, which allows for technological advance.

Economies of Scale Once Again Where economies of scale are extensive, market demand may not be sufficient to support a large number of competing firms, each producing at minimum efficient scale. In such cases, an industry of one or two firms would have a lower average total cost than would the same industry made up of numerous competitive firms. At the extreme, only a single firm—a natural monopoly—might be able to achieve the lowest long-run average total cost.

Some firms relating to new information technologies—for example, computer software, Internet service, and wireless communications—have displayed extensive economies of scale. As these firms have grown, their long-run average total costs have declined because of greater use of specialized inputs, the spreading of product development costs, and learning by doing. Also, *simultaneous consumption* and *network effects* have reduced costs.

A product's ability to satisfy a large number of consumers at the same time is called **simultaneous consumption** (or *nonrivalrous consumption*). Dell Computers needs to produce a personal computer for each customer, but Microsoft needs to produce its Windows program only once. Then, at very low marginal cost, Microsoft delivers its program by disk or Internet to millions of consumers. A similarly low cost of delivering product to additional customers is true for Internet service providers, music producers, and wireless communication firms. Because marginal costs are so low, the average total cost of output declines as more customers are added.

Network effects are present if the value of a product to each user, including existing users, increases as the total number of users rises. Good examples are computer software, cell phones, and website like Facebook where the content is provided by users. When other people have Internet service and devices to access it, a person can conveniently send e-mail messages to them. And when they have similar software, various documents, spreadsheets, and photos can be attached to the e-mail messages. The greater the number of persons connected to the system, the more the benefits of the product to each person are magnified.

Such network effects may drive a market toward monopoly because consumers tend to choose standard products that everyone else is using. The focused demand for these products permits their producers to grow rapidly and thus achieve economies of scale. Smaller firms, which either have higher-cost "right" products or "wrong" products, get acquired or go out of business.

Economists generally agree that some new information firms have not yet exhausted their economies of scale. But most economists question whether such firms are truly natural monopolies. Most firms eventually achieve their minimum efficient scale at less than the full size of the market. That means competition among firms is possible.

But even if natural monopoly develops, the monopolist is unlikely to pass cost reductions along to consumers as price reductions. So, with perhaps a handful of exceptions, economies of scale do not change the general conclusion that monopoly industries are inefficient relative to competitive industries.

X-Inefficiency

In constructing all the average-total-cost curves used in this book, we have assumed that the firm uses the most efficient existing technology. This assumption is only natural because firms cannot maximize profits unless they are minimizing costs. **X-inefficiency** occurs when a firm produces output at a higher cost than is necessary to produce it. In Figure 12.7 X-inefficiency is represented by operation at points X and X' above the lowest-cost ATC curve. At these points, per-unit costs are ATC_X (as opposed to ATC_1) for output Q_1

and $ATC_{X'}$ (as opposed to ATC_2) for output Q_2. Producing at any point above the average-total-cost curve in Figure 12.7 reflects inefficiency or "bad management" by the firm.

Why is X-inefficiency allowed to occur if it reduces profits? The answer is that managers may have goals, such as expanding power, an easier work life, avoiding business risk, or giving jobs to incompetent relatives, that conflict with cost minimization. Or X-inefficiency may arise because a firm's workers are poorly motivated or ineffectively supervised. Or a firm may simply become lethargic and inert, relying on rules of thumb in decision making as opposed to careful calculations of costs and revenues.

For our purposes the relevant question is whether monopolistic firms tend more toward X-inefficiency than competitive producers do. Presumably they do. Firms in competitive industries are continually under pressure from rivals, forcing them to be internally efficient to survive. But monopolists are sheltered from such competitive forces by entry barriers. That lack of pressure may lead to X-inefficiency.

Rent-Seeking Expenditures

Rent-seeking behavior is any activity designed to transfer income or wealth to a particular firm or resource supplier at someone else's, or even society's, expense. We have seen that a monopolist can obtain an economic profit even in the long run. Therefore, it is no surprise that a firm may go to great expense to acquire or maintain a monopoly granted by government through legislation or an exclusive license. Such rent-seeking expenditures add nothing to the firm's output, but they clearly increase its costs. Taken alone, rent seeking implies that monopoly involves even higher costs and even less efficiency than suggested in Figure 12.6b.

Technological Advance

In the very long run, firms can reduce their costs through the discovery and implementation of new technology. If monopolists are more likely than

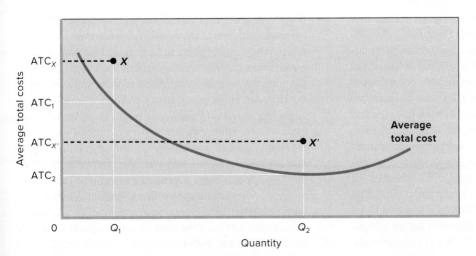

FIGURE 12.7 X-inefficiency. The average-total-cost curve (ATC) is assumed to reflect the minimum cost of producing each particular level of output. Any point above this "lowest-cost" ATC curve, such as X or X', implies X-inefficiency: operation at greater than lowest cost for a particular level of output.

competitive producers to develop more efficient production techniques over time, then the inefficiency of monopoly might be overstated. Because research and development (R&D) is the topic of Chapter 15, we will provide only a brief assessment here.

The general view of economists is that a pure monopolist will not be technologically progressive. Although its economic profit provides ample means to finance research and development, it has little incentive to implement new techniques (or products). The absence of competitors means that there is no external pressure for technological advance in a monopolized market. Because of its sheltered market position, the pure monopolist can afford to be complacent and lethargic. There simply is no major penalty for not being innovative.

One caveat: Research and technological advance may be one of the monopolist's barriers to entry. Thus, the monopolist may continue to seek technological advance to avoid falling prey to new rivals. In this case technological advance is essential to the maintenance of monopoly. But then it is *potential* competition, not the monopoly market structure, that is driving the technological advance. By assumption, no such competition exists in the pure monopoly model; entry is completely blocked.

Assessment and Policy Options

Monopoly is a legitimate concern. Monopolists can charge higher-than-competitive prices that result in an underallocation of resources to the monopolized product. They can stifle innovation, engage in rent-seeking behavior, and foster X-inefficiency. Even when their costs are low because of economies of scale, there is no guarantee that the price they charge will reflect those low costs. The cost savings may simply accrue to the monopoly as greater economic profit.

Fortunately, however, monopoly is not widespread in the United States. Barriers to entry are seldom completely successful. Although research and technological advance may strengthen the market position of a monopoly, technology may also undermine monopoly power. Over time, the creation of new technologies may work to destroy monopoly positions. For example, the development of courier delivery, fax machines, and e-mail has eroded the monopoly power of the U.S. Postal Service. Similarly, cable television monopolies are now challenged by satellite TV and by technologies that permit the transmission of audio and video over the Internet.

Patents eventually expire; and even before they do, the development of new and distinct substitutable products often circumvents existing patent advantages. New sources of monopolized resources sometimes are found and competition from foreign firms may emerge. (See Global Perspective 12.1.) Finally, if a monopoly is sufficiently fearful of future competition from new products, it may keep its prices relatively low

GLOBAL PERSPECTIVE 12.1

Competition from Foreign Multinational Corporations

Competition from foreign multinational corporations diminishes the market power of firms in the United States. Here are just a few of the hundreds of foreign multinational corporations that compete strongly with U.S. firms in certain American markets.

Company (Country)	Main Products
Bayer (Germany)	chemicals
Daimler (Germany)	automobiles
Michelin (France)	tires
Lenovo (China)	electronics
Nestlé (Switzerland)	food products
Nokia (Finland)	wireless phones
Panasonic (Japan)	electronics
Petrobras (Brazil)	gasoline
Royal Dutch Shell (Netherlands)	gasoline
Samsung (South Korea)	electronics
Toyota (Japan)	automobiles

Source: Compiled from the Fortune 500 listing of the world's largest firms, "FORTUNE Global 500," 2016, **www.fortune.com.**

so as to discourage rivals from developing such products. If so, consumers may pay nearly competitive prices even though competition is currently lacking.

So what should government do about monopoly when it arises in the real world? Economists agree that government needs to look carefully at monopoly on a case-by-case basis. Three general policy options are available:

- If the monopoly is achieved and sustained through anticompetitive actions, creates substantial economic inefficiency, and appears to be long-lasting, the government can file charges against the monopoly under the antitrust laws. If found guilty of monopoly abuse, the firm can either be expressly prohibited from engaging in certain business activities or be broken into two or more competing firms. An example of the breakup approach was the dissolution of Standard Oil into several competing firms in 1911. In contrast, in 2001 an appeals court overruled a lower-court decision to divide Microsoft into two firms. Instead, Microsoft was prohibited from engaging in a number of specific anticompetitive business activities. (We discuss the antitrust laws and the Microsoft case in Chapter 21.)

- If the monopoly is a natural monopoly, society can allow it to continue to expand. If no competition emerges from new products, government may then decide to regulate its prices and operations. (We discuss this option later in this chapter and also in Chapter 21.)

- If the monopoly appears to be unsustainable because of emerging new technology, society can simply choose to ignore it. In such cases, society simply lets the process of creative destruction (discussed in Chapter 11) do its work. In Chapter 15, we discuss in detail the likelihood that real-world monopolies will collapse due to creative destruction and competition brought on by new technologies.

QUICK REVIEW 12.2

✓ The monopolist maximizes profit (or minimizes loss) at the output where MR = MC and charges the price that corresponds to that output on its demand curve.

✓ The monopolist has no supply curve, since any of several prices can be associated with a specific quantity of output supplied.

✓ Assuming identical costs, a monopolist will be less efficient than a purely competitive industry because it will fail to produce units of output for which marginal benefits exceed marginal costs.

✓ The inefficiencies of monopoly may be offset or lessened by economies of scale and, less likely, by technological progress, but they may be intensified by the presence of X-inefficiency and rent-seeking expenditures.

Price Discrimination

LO12.6 Describe why a monopolist might prefer to charge different prices in different markets.

We have assumed in this chapter that the monopolist charges a single price to all buyers. But under certain conditions the monopolist can increase its profit by charging different prices to different buyers. In so doing, the monopolist is engaging in **price discrimination,** the practice of selling a specific product at more than one price when the price differences are not justified by cost differences. Price discrimination can take three forms:

- Charging each customer in a single market the maximum price she or he is willing to pay.

- Charging each customer one price for the first set of units purchased and a lower price for subsequent units purchased.

- Charging some customers one price and other customers another price.

Conditions

The opportunity to engage in price discrimination is not readily available to all sellers. Price discrimination is possible when the following conditions are met:

- *Monopoly power* The seller must be a monopolist or, at least, must possess some degree of monopoly power, that is, some ability to control output and price.

- *Market segregation* At relatively low cost to itself, the seller must be able to segregate buyers into distinct classes, each of which has a different willingness or ability to pay for the product. This separation of buyers is usually based on different price elasticities of demand, as the examples below will make clear.

- *No resale* The original purchaser cannot resell the product or service. If buyers in the low-price segment of the market could easily resell in the high-price segment, the monopolist's price-discrimination strategy would create competition in the high-price segment. This competition would reduce the price in the high-price segment and undermine the monopolist's price-discrimination policy. This condition suggests that service industries such as the transportation industry or legal and medical services, where resale is impossible, are good candidates for price discrimination.

Examples of Price Discrimination

Price discrimination is widely practiced in the U.S. economy. For example, we noted in Chapter 6's Last Word that airlines charge high fares to business travelers, whose demand for travel is inelastic, and offer lower, highly restricted, non-refundable fares to attract vacationers and others whose demands are more elastic.

Electric utilities frequently segment their markets by end uses, such as lighting and heating. The absence of reasonable lighting substitutes means that the demand for electricity for illumination is inelastic and that the price per kilowatt-hour for such use is high. But the availability of natural gas and petroleum for heating makes the demand for electricity for this purpose less inelastic and the price lower.

Movie theaters and golf courses vary their charges on the basis of time (for example, higher evening and weekend rates) and age (for example, lower rates for children, senior discounts). Railroads vary the rate charged per ton-mile of freight according to the market value of the product being shipped. The shipper of 10 tons of television sets or refrigerators is charged more than the shipper of 10 tons of gravel or coal.

The issuance of discount coupons, redeemable at purchase, is a form of price discrimination. It enables firms to

CONSIDER THIS . . .

Source: © Stephen Dunn/Getty Images

Some Price Differences at the Ballpark

Take me out to the ball game...

Buy me some peanuts and Cracker Jack...

Professional baseball teams earn substantial revenues through ticket sales. To maximize profit, they offer significantly lower ticket prices for children (whose demand is elastic) than for adults (whose demand is inelastic). This discount may be as much as 50 percent.

If this type of price discrimination increases revenue and profit, why don't teams also price discriminate at the concession stands? Why don't they offer half-price hot dogs, soft drinks, peanuts, and Cracker Jack to children?

The answer involves the three requirements for successful price discrimination. All three requirements are met for game tickets: (1) The team has monopoly power; (2) it can segregate ticket buyers by age group, each group having a different elasticity of demand; and (3) children cannot resell their discounted tickets to adults.

It's a different situation at the concession stands. Specifically, the third condition is *not* met. If the team had dual prices, it could not prevent the exchange or "resale" of the concession goods from children to adults. Many adults would send children to buy food and soft drinks for them: "Here's some money, Billy. Go buy *six* hot dogs." In this case, price discrimination would reduce, not increase, team profit. Thus, children and adults are charged the same high prices at the concession stands. (These prices are high relative to those for the same goods at the local convenience store because the stadium sellers have a captive audience and thus considerable monopoly power.)

give price discounts to their most price-sensitive customers who have elastic demand. Less price-sensitive consumers who have less elastic demand are not as likely to take the time to clip and redeem coupons. The firm thus makes a larger profit than if it had used a single-price, no-coupon strategy.

Finally, price discrimination often occurs in international trade. A Russian aluminum producer, for example, might sell aluminum for less in the United States than in Russia. In the United States, this seller faces an elastic demand because several substitute suppliers are available. But in Russia, where the manufacturer dominates the market and trade barriers impede imports, consumers have fewer choices and thus demand is less elastic.

Graphical Analysis

Figure 12.8 demonstrates graphically the most frequently seen form of price discrimination—charging different prices to different classes of buyers. The two side-to-side graphs are for a single pure monopolist selling its product, say, software, in two segregated parts of the market. Figure 12.8a illustrates demand for software by small-business customers; Figure 12.8b, the demand for software by students. Student versions of the software are identical to the versions sold to businesses but are available (1 per person) only to customers with a student ID. Presumably, students have lower ability to pay for the software and are charged a discounted price.

The demand curve D_b in the graph to the left indicates a relatively inelastic demand for the product on the part of business customers. The demand curve D_s in the right-hand graph reflects the more elastic demand of students. The marginal revenue curves (MR_b and MR_s) lie below their respective demand curves, reflecting the demand–marginal revenue relationship previously described.

For visual clarity we have assumed that average total cost (ATC) is constant. Therefore marginal cost (MC) equals average total cost (ATC) at all quantities of output. These costs are the same for both versions of the software and therefore appear as the identical straight lines labeled "MC = ATC."

What price will the pure monopolist charge to each set of customers? Using the MR = MC rule for profit maximization, the firm will offer Q_b units of the software for sale to small businesses. It can sell that profit-maximizing output by charging price P_b. Again using the MR = MC rule, the monopolist will offer Q_s units of software to students. To sell those Q_s units, the firm will charge students the lower price P_s.

Firms engage in price discrimination because it enhances their profit. The numbers (not shown) behind the curves in Figure 12.8 would clearly reveal that the sum of the two profit rectangles shown in green exceeds the single profit rectangle the firm would obtain from a single monopoly price. How do consumers fare? In this case, students clearly benefit by paying a lower price than they would if the firm charged a single monopoly price; in contrast, the price discrimination results in a higher price for business customers. Therefore, compared to the single-price situation, students buy more of the software and small businesses buy less.

Such price discrimination is widespread in the economy and is illegal only when it is part of a firm's strategy to lessen or eliminate competition. We will discuss illegal price discrimination in Chapter 21, which covers antitrust policy.

FIGURE 12.8 Price discrimination to different groups of buyers. The price-discriminating monopolist represented here maximizes its total profit by dividing the market into two segments based on differences in elasticity of demand. It then produces and sells the MR = MC output in each market segment. (For visual clarity, average total cost, ATC, is assumed to be constant. Therefore, MC equals ATC at all output levels.) (a) The price-discriminating monopolist charges a high price (here P_b) to small-business customers because they have a relatively inelastic demand curve for the product. (b) The firm charges a low price (here P_s) to students because their demand curve is relatively elastic. The firm's total profit from using price discrimination (here, the sum of the two green rectangles) exceeds the profit (not shown) that would have occurred if the monopolist had charged the same price to all customers.

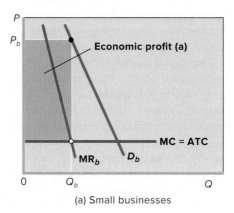

(a) Small businesses

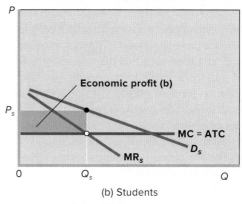

(b) Students

Regulated Monopoly

LO12.7 Distinguish among the monopoly price, the socially optimal price, and the fair-return price of a government-regulated monopoly.

Natural monopolies traditionally have been subject to *rate regulation* (price regulation), although the recent trend has been to deregulate wherever competition seems possible. For example, long-distance telephone calls, natural gas distribution, wireless communications, cable television, and long-distance electricity transmission have been, to one degree or another, deregulated over the past several decades. And regulators in some states are beginning to allow new entrants to compete with existing local telephone and electricity providers. Nevertheless, state and local regulatory commissions still regulate the prices that most local natural gas distributors, regional telephone companies, and local electricity suppliers can charge. These locally regulated monopolies are commonly called "public utilities."

Let's consider the regulation of a local natural monopoly. Our example will be a single firm that is the only seller of natural gas in the town of Springfield. Figure 12.9 shows the demand and the long-run cost curves facing our firm. Because of extensive economies of scale, the demand curve cuts the natural monopolist's long-run average-total-cost curve at a point where that curve is still falling. It would be inefficient to have several firms in this industry because each would produce a much smaller output, operating well to the left on the long-run average-total-cost curve. In short, each firm's lowest average total cost would be substantially higher than that of a single firm. So efficient, lowest-cost production requires a single seller.

We know by application of the MR = MC rule that Q_m and P_m are the profit-maximizing output and price that an unregulated monopolist would choose. Because price exceeds average total cost at output Q_m, the monopolist enjoys a substantial economic profit. Furthermore, price exceeds marginal cost, indicating an underallocation of resources to this product or service. Can government regulation bring about better results from society's point of view?

FIGURE 12.9 Regulated monopoly. The socially optimal price P_r, found where D and MC intersect, will result in an efficient allocation of resources but may entail losses to the monopoly. The fair-return price P_f will allow the monopolist to break even but will not fully correct the underallocation of resources.

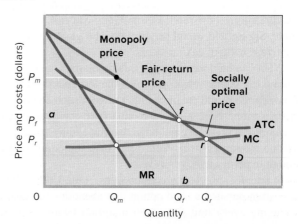

Socially Optimal Price: $P = MC$

One sensible goal for regulators would be to get the monopoly to produce the allocatively efficient output level. For our monopolist in Figure 12.9, this is output level Q_r, determined by where the demand curve D intersects the MC curve. Q_r is the allocatively efficient output level because for each unit of output up to Q_r, the demand curve lies above the MC curve, indicating that for all of these units marginal benefits exceed marginal costs.

But how can the regulatory commission actually motivate the monopoly to produce this output level? The trick is to set the regulated price P_r at a level such that the monopoly will be led by its profit-maximizing rule to voluntarily produce the allocatively efficient level of output. To see how this works, note that because the monopoly will receive the regulated price P_r for all units that it sells, P_r becomes the monopoly's marginal revenue per unit. Thus, the monopoly's MR curve becomes the horizontal white line moving rightward from price P_r on the vertical axis.

The monopoly will at this point follow its usual rule for maximizing profits or minimizing losses: It will produce where marginal revenue equals marginal cost. As a result, the monopoly will produce where the horizontal white MR ($= P_r$) line intersects the MC curve at point r. That is, the monopoly will end up producing the socially optimal output Q_r not because it is socially minded but because Q_r happens to be the output that either maximizes profits or minimizes losses when the firm is forced by the regulators to sell all units at the regulated price P_r.

The regulated price P_r that achieves allocative efficiency is called the **socially optimal price.** Because it is determined by where the MC curve intersects the demand curve, this type of regulation is often summarized by the equation $P = MC$.

Fair-Return Price: $P = ATC$

The socially optimal price suffers from a potentially fatal problem. P_r may be so low that average total costs are not covered, as is the case in Figure 12.9. In such situations, forcing the socially optimal price on the regulated monopoly would result in short-run losses and long-run exit. In our example, Springfield would be left without a gas company and its citizens without gas.

What can be done to rectify this problem? One option is to provide a public subsidy to cover the loss that the socially optimal price would entail. Another possibility is to condone price discrimination, allow the monopoly to charge some customers prices above P_r, and hope that the additional revenue that the monopoly gains from price discrimination will be enough to permit it to break even.

In practice, regulatory commissions in the United States have often pursued a third option that abandons the goal of producing every unit for which marginal benefits exceed marginal costs but that guarantees that regulated monopolies will be able to break even and continue in operation. Under this third option, regulators set a regulated price that is high enough for monopolists to break even and continue in operation. This price has come to be referred to as a **fair-return price** because of a ruling in which the Supreme Court held that regulatory agencies must permit regulated utility owners to enjoy a "fair return" on their investments.

In practice, a fair return is equal to a normal profit. That is, a fair return is an accounting profit equal in size to what the owners of the monopoly would on average receive if they entered another type of business.

The regulator determines the fair-return price P_f by where the average total cost curve intersects the demand curve at point f. As we will explain, setting the regulated price at this level will cause the monopoly to produce Q_f units while guaranteeing that it will break even and not wish to exit the industry. To see why the monopoly will voluntarily produce Q_f units, note that because the monopoly will receive P_f dollars for each unit it sells, its marginal revenue per unit becomes P_f dollars so that the horizontal line moving rightward from P_f on the vertical axis becomes the regulated monopoly's MR curve. Because this horizontal MR curve is always higher than the monopoly's MC curve, it is obvious that marginal revenues will exceed marginal costs for every possible level of output shown in Figure 12.9. Thus, the monopoly should be willing to supply whatever quantity of output is demanded by consumers at the regulated price P_f. That quantity is, of course, given by the demand curve. At price P_f consumers will demand exactly Q_f units. Thus, by setting the regulated price at P_f, the regulator gets the monopoly to voluntarily supply exactly Q_f units.

Even better, the regulator also guarantees that the monopoly firm will earn exactly a normal profit. This can be seen in Figure 12.9 by noting that the rectangle $0afb$ is equal to both the monopoly's total cost and its total revenue. Its economic profit is therefore equal to zero, implying that it must be earning a normal accounting profit for its owners.

One final point about allocative efficiency: By choosing the fair-return price P_f, the regulator leads the monopoly to produce Q_f units. This is less than the socially optimal quantity Q_r, but still more than the Q_m units that the monopolist would produce if left unregulated. So while fair-return pricing does not lead to full allocative efficiency, it is still an improvement on what the monopoly would do if left to its own devices.

Dilemma of Regulation

Comparing results of the socially optimal price ($P = MC$) and the fair-return price ($P = ATC$) suggests a policy dilemma, sometimes termed the *dilemma of regulation*. When its price is set to achieve the most efficient allocation of resources ($P = MC$), the regulated monopoly is likely to suffer losses. Survival of the firm would presumably depend on permanent public

Personalized Pricing

The Potential Perils of Online Price Discrimination

Internet retailers collect vast amounts of data about their customers. They know what you buy, who your friends are, what posts you like on Facebook, what websites you visit, and—by connecting that information with other data—how old you are, where you live, your credit history, and so on.

This huge collection of "Big Data" can be used by retailers with monopoly power to engage in an individually tailored form of price discrimination known as personalized pricing. As discussed in this chapter, price discrimination involves selling the same product to different buyers at different prices when the price differences are not justified by cost differences.

Traditionally, price discrimination has operated at the group level with, for example, senior citizens getting discounts at restaurants and children under 12 getting discounts on movie tickets. Groups with relatively inelastic demand get charged higher prices while groups with relatively elastic demand get charged lower prices.

The trick behind personalized pricing is that online retailers now have the ability to set individualized prices for most patrons. When that is possible, a firm with monopoly power can set the very lowest price for the person with the most elastic demand, a slightly higher price for the person with the next-most elastic demand, and so on all the way up to the highest price being presented to the person with the most *in*elastic demand.

By proceeding in this manner, the monopoly seller can attempt to set a price for each individual that is just below his or her reservation price. Doing so allows the monopoly seller to squeeze out as much revenue as possible from each customer while still leaving him or her with a bit of consumer surplus (and thus with a motive to still buy the product).

For an offline example of how personalized pricing works, think about car dealerships, where the final price paid by a buyer is usually the result of a negotiation. In particular, keep in mind that a car salesman will negotiate much more aggressively if you drive up in a fancy BMW rather than an average Hyundai. The salesman will try to tailor the final price to your perceived ability to pay. Big Data allows the same tactic to be used online. The more online retailers know about your buying habits, background, and preferences, the more they can attempt to set a price tailored to maximize how much they think they can get from you.

But personalized pricing has its limits. Most importantly, very few firms actually have any substantial monopoly power. As just one example, car dealers have to compete with each other. So a dealership

Source: © Miss Ty/Shutterstock.com

that is driving too hard a bargain will drive customers toward rival dealers. That competitive pressure is probably even stronger online, where search engines and vast digital retail sites like eBay and Amazon often list multiple competing sellers for every item.

But even if a seller were to have monopoly power online, it would still confront another problem. Even with Big Data, it is hard for sellers to figure out what each potential buyer's reservation price is. So even if a firm with monopoly power wished to attempt personalized pricing, it probably wouldn't ever be able to figure out how to set a customized price for each individual.

On the other hand, online shoppers give up all their advantages if they fail to comparison shop. If they treat the first seller that they deal with as the only seller, they are implicitly giving that seller monopoly power over them. In those situations, online merchants can run wild with personalized pricing. In 2014, for example, Allstate Insurance admitted to Wisconsin insurance regulators that its personalized pricing computer algorithms had presented essentially identical online customers with insurance prices that varied massively, in some cased by more than 800 percent. In many instances, the differences were driven by factors as trivial as one customer having a birthdate of January 12, 1968, and another having a birthdate of April 9, 1968.

Allstate customers who failed to shop around left themselves open to paying much more than they had to. Online shopping is speedy and convenient—but it still pays to shop around.

subsidies out of tax revenues. On the other hand, although a fair-return price (P = ATC) allows the monopolist to cover costs, it only partially resolves the underallocation of resources that the unregulated monopoly price would foster. Despite this dilemma, regulation can improve on the results of monopoly from the social point of view. Price regulation (even at the fair-return price) can simultaneously reduce price, increase output, and reduce the economic profit of monopolies.

That said, we need to provide an important caution: "Fair-price" regulation of monopoly looks rather simple in theory but is amazingly complex in practice. In the actual economy, rate regulation is accompanied by large, expensive rate-setting bureaucracies and maze-like sets of procedures. Also, rate decisions require extensive public input via letters and through public hearings. Rate decisions are subject to lengthy legal challenges. Further, because regulatory commissions must set prices sufficiently above costs to create fair returns, regulated monopolists have little incentive to minimize average total costs. When these costs creep up, the regulatory commissions must set higher prices.

Regulated firms therefore are noted for higher-than-competitive wages, more managers and staff than necessary, nicer-than-typical office buildings, and other forms of X-inefficiency. These inefficiencies help explain the

trend of federal, state, and local governments abandoning price regulation where the possibility of competition looks promising.

> ## QUICK REVIEW 12.3
>
> ✓ Price discrimination occurs when a firm sells a product at different prices that are not based on cost differences.
>
> ✓ The conditions necessary for price discrimination are (a) monopoly power, (b) the ability to segregate buyers on the basis of demand elasticities, and (c) the inability of buyers to resell the product.
>
> ✓ Compared with single pricing by a monopolist, perfect price discrimination results in greater profit and greater output. Many consumers pay higher prices, but other buyers pay prices below the single price.
>
> ✓ Monopoly price can be reduced and output increased through government regulation.
>
> ✓ The socially optimal price (P = MC) achieves allocative efficiency but may result in losses; the fair-return price (P = ATC) yields a normal profit but fails to achieve allocative efficiency.

SUMMARY

LO12.1 List the characteristics of pure monopoly.

A pure monopolist is the sole producer of a commodity for which there are no close substitutes.

LO12.2 List and explain the barriers to entry that shield pure monopolies from competition.

The existence of pure monopoly and other imperfectly competitive market structures is explained by barriers to entry in the form of (a) economies of scale, (b) patent ownership and research, (c) ownership or control of essential resources, and (d) pricing and other strategic behavior.

LO12.3 Explain how demand is seen by a pure monopoly.

The pure monopolist's market situation differs from that of a competitive firm in that the monopolist's demand curve is downsloping, causing the marginal-revenue curve to lie below the demand curve. Like the competitive seller, the pure monopolist will maximize profit by equating marginal revenue and marginal cost. Barriers to entry may permit a monopolist to acquire economic profit even in the long run. However, (a) the monopolist does not charge "the highest price possible," (b) the price that yields maximum total

profit to the monopolist rarely coincides with the price that yields maximum unit profit, (c) high costs and a weak demand may prevent the monopolist from realizing any profit at all, and (d) the monopolist avoids the inelastic region of its demand curve.

LO12.4 Explain how a pure monopoly sets its profit-maximizing output and price.

With the same costs, the pure monopolist will find it profitable to restrict output and charge a higher price than would sellers in a purely competitive industry. This restriction of output causes resources to be misallocated, as is evidenced by the fact that price exceeds marginal cost in monopolized markets. Monopoly creates an efficiency loss (or deadweight loss) for society.

Monopoly transfers income from consumers to monopolists because a monopolist can charge a higher price than would a purely competitive firm with the same costs. So monopolists in effect levy a "private tax" on consumers and, if demand is strong enough, obtain substantial economic profits.

LO12.5 Discuss the economic effects of monopoly.

The costs monopolists and competitive producers face may not be the same. On the one hand, economies of scale may make lower unit costs available to monopolists but not to competitors. Also, pure monopoly may be more likely than pure competition to reduce costs via technological advance because of the monopolist's ability to realize economic profit, which can be used to finance research. On the other hand, X-inefficiency—the failure to produce with the least costly combination of inputs—is more common among monopolists than among competitive firms. Also, monopolists may make costly expenditures to maintain monopoly privileges that are conferred by government. Finally, the blocked entry of rival firms weakens the monopolist's incentive to be technologically progressive.

LO12.6 Describe why a monopolist might prefer to charge different prices in different markets.

A monopolist can increase its profit by practicing price discrimination, provided (*a*) it can segregate buyers on the basis of elasticities of demand and (*b*) its product or service cannot be readily transferred between the segregated markets.

LO12.7 Distinguish among the monopoly price, the socially optimal price, and the fair-return price of a government-regulated monopoly.

Price regulation can be invoked to eliminate wholly or partially the tendency of monopolists to underallocate resources and to earn economic profits. The socially optimal price is determined where the demand and marginal-cost curves intersect; the fair-return price is determined where the demand and average-total-cost curves intersect.

TERMS AND CONCEPTS

pure monopoly	network effects	price discrimination
barriers to entry	X-inefficiency	socially optimal price
simultaneous consumption	rent-seeking behavior	fair-return price

The following and additional problems can be found in ▪ **connect**

DISCUSSION QUESTIONS

1. "No firm is completely sheltered from rivals; all firms compete for consumer dollars. If that is so, then pure monopoly does not exist." Do you agree? Explain. How might you use Chapter 6's concept of cross elasticity of demand to judge whether monopoly exists? **LO12.1**

2. Discuss the major barriers to entry into an industry. Explain how each barrier can foster either monopoly or oligopoly. Which barriers, if any, do you feel give rise to monopoly that is socially justifiable? **LO12.2**

3. How does the demand curve faced by a purely monopolistic seller differ from that confronting a purely competitive firm? Why does it differ? Of what significance is the difference? Why is the pure monopolist's demand curve not perfectly inelastic? **LO12.3**

4. Assume that a pure monopolist and a purely competitive firm have the same unit costs. Contrast the two with respect to (*a*) price, (*b*) output, (*c*) profits, (*d*) allocation of resources, and (*e*) impact on income transfers. Since both monopolists and competitive firms follow the MC = MR rule in maximizing profits, how do you account for the different results? Why might the costs of a purely competitive firm and those of a monopolist be different? What are the implications of such a cost difference? **LO12.5**

5. Critically evaluate and explain each statement: **LO12.5**
   a. Because they can control product price, monopolists are always assured of profitable production by simply charging the highest price consumers will pay.
   b. The pure monopolist seeks the output that will yield the greatest per-unit profit.
   c. An excess of price over marginal cost is the market's way of signaling the need for more production of a good.
   d. The more profitable a firm, the greater its monopoly power.
   e. The monopolist has a pricing policy; the competitive producer does not.
   f. With respect to resource allocation, the interests of the seller and of society coincide in a purely competitive market but conflict in a monopolized market.

6. Assume a monopolistic publisher has agreed to pay an author 10 percent of the total revenue from the sales of a text. Will the author and the publisher want to charge the same price for the text? Explain. **LO12.5**

7. U.S. pharmaceutical companies charge different prices for prescription drugs to buyers in different nations, depending on elasticity of demand and government-imposed price ceilings. Explain why these companies, for profit reasons, oppose laws allowing re-importation of drugs to the United States. **LO12.6**

8. Explain verbally and graphically how price (rate) regulation may improve the performance of monopolies. In your answer distinguish between (*a*) socially optimal (marginal-cost) pricing and (*b*) fair-return (average-total-cost) pricing. What is the "dilemma of regulation"? **LO12.7**

9. It has been proposed that natural monopolists should be allowed to determine their profit-maximizing outputs and prices and then government should tax their profits away and distribute them to consumers in proportion to their purchases from the monopoly. Is this proposal as socially desirable as requiring monopolists to equate price with marginal cost or average total cost? **LO12.7**

10. **LAST WORD** Using Big Data to set personalized prices cannot be done with 100 percent precision. What would happen if personalized prices were set higher than customers' reservation prices? Would this possibility reduce the incentive to set the highest possible personalized prices? How can consumers protect themselves from personalized prices?

REVIEW QUESTIONS

1. Which of the following could explain why a firm is a monopoly? Select one or more answers from the choices shown. **LO12.2**
   - **a.** Patents.
   - **b.** Economies of scale.
   - **c.** Inelastic demand.
   - **d.** Government licenses.
   - **e.** Downsloping market demand.

2. The MR curve of a perfectly competitive firm is horizontal. The MR curve of a monopoly firm is: **LO12.3**
   - **a.** Horizontal, too.
   - **b.** Upsloping.
   - **c.** Downsloping.
   - **d.** It depends.

3. Use the following demand schedule to calculate total revenue and marginal revenue at each quantity. Plot the demand, total-revenue, and marginal-revenue curves, and explain the relationships between them. Explain why the marginal revenue of the fourth unit of output is $3.50, even though its price is $5. Use Chapter 6's total-revenue test for price elasticity to designate the elastic and inelastic segments of your graphed demand curve. What generalization can you make as to the relationship between marginal revenue and elasticity of demand? Suppose the marginal cost of successive units of output was zero. What output would the profit-seeking firm produce? Finally, use your analysis to explain why a monopolist would never produce in the inelastic region of demand. **LO12.3**

Price (*P*)	Quantity Demanded (*Q*)	Price (*P*)	Quantity Demanded (*Q*)
$7.00	0	$4.50	5
6.50	1	4.00	6
6.00	2	3.50	7
5.50	3	3.00	8
5.00	4	2.50	9

4. How often do *perfectly competitive* firms engage in price discrimination? **LO12.6**
   - **a.** Never.
   - **b.** Rarely.
   - **c.** Often.
   - **d.** Always.

5. Suppose that a monopolist can segregate his buyers into two different groups to which he can charge two different prices. In order to maximize profit, the monopolist should charge a higher price to the group that has: **LO12.6**
   - **a.** The higher elasticity of demand.
   - **b.** The lower elasticity of demand.
   - **c.** Richer members.

6. The socially optimal price (*P* = MC) is socially optimal because: **LO12.7**
   - **a.** It reduces the monopolist's profit.
   - **b.** It yields a normal profit.
   - **c.** It minimizes ATC.
   - **d.** It achieves allocative efficiency.

7. The main problem with imposing the socially optimal price (*P* = MC) on a monopoly is that the socially optimal price: **LO12.7**
   - **a.** May be so low that the regulated monopoly can't break even.
   - **b.** May cause the regulated monopoly to engage in price discrimination.
   - **c.** May be higher than the monopoly price.

PROBLEMS

1. Suppose a pure monopolist is faced with the following demand schedule and the same cost data as the competitive producer discussed in problem 4 at the end of Chapter 10. Calculate the missing total-revenue and marginal-revenue amounts, and determine the profit-maximizing price and profit-maximizing output for this monopolist. What is the monopolist's profit? Verify your answer graphically and by comparing total revenue and total cost. **LO12.4**

Price	Quantity Demanded	Total Revenue	Marginal Revenue
$115	0	$_____	
100	1	_____	$_____
83	2	_____	_____
71	3	_____	_____
63	4	_____	_____
55	5	_____	_____
48	6	_____	_____
42	7	_____	_____
37	8	_____	_____
33	9	_____	_____
29	10	_____	_____

2. Suppose that a price-discriminating monopolist has segregated its market into two groups of buyers. The first group is described by the demand and revenue data that you developed for problem 1. The demand and revenue data for the second group of buyers is shown in the following table. Assume that MC is $13 in both markets and MC = ATC at all output levels. What price will the firm charge in each market? Based solely on these two prices, which market has the higher price elasticity of demand? What will be this monopolist's total economic profit? LO12.6

Price	Quantity Demanded	Total Revenue	Marginal Revenue
$71	0	$ 0	
63	1	63	$63
55	2	110	47
48	3	144	34
42	4	168	24
37	5	185	17
33	6	198	13
29	7	203	5

3. Assume that the most efficient production technology available for making vitamin pills has the cost structure given in the following table. Note that output is measured as the number of bottles of vitamins produced per day and that costs include a normal profit. LO12.6

Output	TC	MC
25,000	$100,000	$0.50
50,000	150,000	1.00
75,000	187,500	2.50
100,000	275,500	3.00

a. What is ATC per unit for each level of output listed in the table?
b. Is this a decreasing-cost industry? (Answer yes or no.)
c. Suppose that the market price for a bottle of vitamins is $2.50 and that at that price the total market quantity demanded is 75,000,000 bottles. How many firms will there be in this industry?

d. Suppose that, instead, the market quantity demanded at a price of $2.50 is only 75,000. How many firms do you expect there to be in this industry?
e. Review your answers to parts b, c, and d. Does the level of demand determine this industry's market structure?

4. A new production technology for making vitamins is invented by a college professor who decides not to patent it. Thus, it is available for anybody to copy and put into use. The TC per bottle for production up to 100,000 bottles per day is given in the following table. LO12.6

Output	TC
25,000	$50,000
50,000	70,000
75,000	75,000
100,000	80,000

a. What is ATC for each level of output listed in the table?
b. Suppose that for each 25,000-bottle-per-day increase in production above 100,000 bottles per day, TC increases by $5,000 (so that, for instance, 125,000 bottles per day would generate total costs of $85,000 and 150,000 bottles per day would generate total costs of $90,000). Is this a decreasing-cost industry?
c. Suppose that the price of a bottle of vitamins is $1.33 and that at that price the total quantity demanded by consumers is 75,000,000 bottles. How many firms will there be in this industry?
d. Suppose that, instead, the market quantity demanded at a price of $1.33 is only 75,000. How many firms do you expect there to be in this industry?
e. Review your answers to parts b, c, and d. Does the level of demand determine this industry's market structure?
f. Compare your answer to part d of this problem with your answer to part d of problem 3. Do both production technologies show constant returns to scale?

5. Suppose you have been tasked with regulating a single monopoly firm that sells 50-pound bags of concrete. The firm has fixed costs of $10 million per year and a variable cost of $1 per bag no matter how many bags are produced. LO12.7

a. If this firm kept on increasing its output level, would ATC per bag ever increase? Is this a decreasing-cost industry?
b. If you wished to regulate this monopoly by charging the socially optimal price, what price would you charge? At that price, what would be the size of the firm's profit or loss? Would the firm want to exit the industry?
c. You find out that if you set the price at $2 per bag, consumers will demand 10 million bags. How big will the firm's profit or loss be at that price?
d. If consumers instead demanded 20 million bags at a price of $2 per bag, how big would the firm's profit or loss be?
e. Suppose that demand is perfectly inelastic at 20 million bags, so that consumers demand 20 million bags no matter what the price is. What price should you charge if you want the firm to earn only a fair rate of return? Assume as always that TC includes a normal profit.

13 Chapter

Monopolistic Competition

Learning Objectives

LO13.1 List the characteristics of monopolistic competition.

LO13.2 Explain why monopolistic competitors earn only a normal profit in the long run.

LO13.3 Explain why monopolistic competition delivers neither productive nor allocative efficiency.

LO13.4 Relate how the ability of monopolistic competition to deliver product differentiation helps to compensate for its failure to deliver economic efficiency.

In the United States, most industries have a market structure that falls somewhere between the two poles of pure competition and pure monopoly. To begin with, most real-world industries have fewer than the large number of producers required for pure competition but more than the single producer that defines pure monopoly. In addition, most firms in most industries have both distinguishable rather than standardized products as well as some discretion over the prices they charge. As a result, competition often occurs on the basis of price, quality, location, service, and advertising. Finally, entry to most real-world industries ranges from easy to very difficult but is rarely completely blocked.

This chapter examines the first of two models that more closely approximate these widespread industry structures. In this chapter, you will discover that *monopolistic competition* mixes a small amount of monopoly power with a large amount of competition. In the next chapter, you will see how *oligopoly* blends a large amount of monopoly power with both considerable rivalry among existing firms and the threat of increased future competition due to foreign firms and new technologies. (You should quickly review Table 10.1, at this point.)

Monopolistic Competition

LO13.1 List the characteristics of monopolistic competition.

Let's begin by examining **monopolistic competition,** which is characterized by (1) a relatively large number of sellers; (2) differentiated products (often promoted by heavy advertising); and (3) easy entry to, and exit from, the industry. The first and third characteristics provide the "competitive" aspect of monopolistic competition; the second characteristic provides the "monopolistic" aspect. In general, however, monopolistically competitive industries are much more competitive than they are monopolistic.

Relatively Large Number of Sellers

Monopolistic competition is characterized by a fairly large number of firms, say, 25, 35, 60, or 70, not by the hundreds or thousands of firms in pure competition. Consequently, monopolistic competition involves:

- *Small market shares* Each firm has a comparatively small percentage of the total market and consequently has limited control over market price.

- *No collusion* The presence of a relatively large number of firms ensures that collusion by a group of firms to restrict output and set prices is unlikely.

- *Independent action* With numerous firms in an industry, there is no feeling of interdependence among them; each firm can determine its own pricing policy without considering the possible reactions of rival firms. A single firm may realize a modest increase in sales by cutting its price, but the effect of that action on competitors' sales will be nearly imperceptible and will probably trigger no response.

Differentiated Products

In contrast to pure competition, in which there is a standardized product, monopolistic competition is distinguished by **product differentiation.** Monopolistically competitive firms turn out variations of a particular product. They produce products with slightly different physical characteristics, offer varying degrees of customer service, provide varying amounts of locational convenience, or proclaim special qualities, real or imagined, for their products.

Let's examine these aspects of product differentiation in more detail.

Product Attributes Product differentiation may entail physical or qualitative differences in the products themselves. Real differences in functional features, materials, design, and workmanship are vital aspects of product differentiation. Personal computers, for example, differ in terms of storage capacity, speed, graphic displays, and included software. There are dozens of competing principles of economics textbooks that differ in content, organization, presentation and readability, pedagogical aids, and graphics and design. Most cities have a variety of retail stores selling men's and women's clothes that differ greatly in styling, materials, and quality of work. Similarly, one pizza place may feature thin-crust Neapolitan style pizza, while another may tout its thick-crust Chicago-style pizza.

Service Service and the conditions surrounding the sale of a product are forms of product differentiation too. One shoe store may stress the fashion knowledge and helpfulness of its clerks. A competitor may leave trying on shoes and carrying

them to the register to its customers but feature lower prices. Customers may prefer one-day over three-day dry cleaning of equal quality. The prestige appeal of a store, the courteousness and helpfulness of clerks, the firm's reputation for servicing or exchanging its products, and the credit it makes available are all service aspects of product differentiation.

Location Products may also be differentiated through the location and accessibility of the stores that sell them. Small convenience stores manage to compete with large supermarkets, even though these minimarts have a more limited range of products and charge higher prices. They compete mainly on the basis of location—being close to customers and situated on busy streets. A motel's proximity to an interstate highway gives it a locational advantage that may enable it to charge a higher room rate than nearby motels in less convenient locations.

Brand Names and Packaging Product differentiation may also be created through the use of brand names and trademarks, packaging, and celebrity connections. Most aspirin tablets are very much alike, but many headache sufferers believe that one brand—for example, Bayer, Anacin, or Bufferin—is superior and worth a higher price than a generic substitute. A celebrity's name associated with watches, perfume, or athletic shoes may enhance the appeal of those products for some buyers. Many customers prefer one style of ballpoint pen to another. Packaging that touts "natural spring" bottled water may attract additional customers.

Some Control over Price Despite the relatively large number of firms, monopolistic competitors do have some control over their product prices because of product differentiation. If consumers prefer the products of specific sellers, then within limits they will pay more to satisfy their preferences. Sellers and buyers are not linked randomly, as in a purely competitive market. But the monopolistic competitor's control over price is quite limited since there are numerous potential substitutes for its product.

Easy Entry and Exit

Entry into monopolistically competitive industries is relatively easy compared to oligopoly or pure monopoly. Because monopolistic competitors are typically small firms, both absolutely and relatively, economies of scale are few and capital requirements are low. On the other hand, compared with pure competition, financial barriers may result from the need to develop and advertise a product that differs from rivals' products. Some firms have trade secrets relating to their products or hold trademarks on their brand names, making it difficult and costly for other firms to imitate them.

Exit from monopolistically competitive industries is relatively easy. Nothing prevents an unprofitable monopolistic competitor from holding a going-out-of-business sale and shutting down.

Advertising

The expense and effort involved in product differentiation would be wasted if consumers were not made aware of product differences. Thus, monopolistic competitors advertise their products, often heavily. The goal of product differentiation and advertising—so-called **nonprice competition**—is to make price less of a factor in consumer purchases and make product differences a greater factor. If successful, the firm's demand curve will shift to the right and will become less elastic.

Monopolistically Competitive Industries

Table 13.1 lists several manufacturing industries that approximate monopolistic competition. Economists measure the degree of industry concentration—the extent to which the largest firms account for the bulk of the industry's output—to identify monopolistically competitive (versus oligopolistic) industries. Two such measures are the four-firm concentration ratio and the Herfindahl index. They are listed in columns 2 and 3 of the table.

A **four-firm concentration ratio,** expressed as a percentage, is the ratio of the output (sales) of the four largest firms in an industry relative to total industry sales.

$$\text{Four-firm concentration ratio} = \frac{\text{Output of four largest firms}}{\text{Total output in the industry}}$$

Four-firm concentration ratios are very low in purely competitive industries in which there are hundreds or even thousands of firms, each with a tiny market share. In contrast, four-firm ratios are high in oligopoly and pure monopoly. Industries in which the largest four firms account for 40 percent or more of the market are generally considered to be oligopolies. If the largest four firms account for less than 40 percent, they are likely to be monopolistically competitive. Observe that the four-firm concentration ratios in Table 13.1 range from 5 percent to 32 percent.

Published concentration ratios such as those in Table 13.1 are helpful in categorizing industries but must be used cautiously because the market shares (percentage of total sales) that they list are national in scope, whereas competition in many industries is often local in scope. As a result, some industries with low national concentration ratios are in fact substantially concentrated if one focuses on local markets.

As an example, the national four-firm concentration ratio for ready-mix concrete shown in Table 13.1 is only 14 percent. This suggests that ready-mix concrete is a monopolistically competitive industry. But the sheer bulk of ready-mix concrete and the fact that it "sets up" as it dries limits the relevant market to a specific town, city, or metropolitan area. In most of these local markets, only a few firms compete, not the numerous firms needed for monopolistic competition.

Column 3 of Table 13.1 lists a second measure of concentration: the **Herfindahl index.** This index is the sum of the squared percentage market shares of all firms in the industry. In equation form:

$$\text{Herfindahl index} = (\%S_1)^2 + (\%S_2)^2 + (\%S_3)^2 + \cdots + (\%S_n)^2$$

TABLE 13.1 Percentage of Output Produced by Firms in Selected Low-Concentration U.S. Manufacturing Industries

(1) Industry	(2) Percentage of Industry Output* Produced by the Four Largest Firms	(3) Herfindahl Index for the Top 50 Firms	(1) Industry	(2) Percentage of Industry Output* Produced by the Four Largest Firms	(3) Herfindahl Index for the Top 50 Firms
Jewelry	32	550	Ready-mix concrete	14	89
Plastic pipe	31	303	Sawmills	14	93
Plastic bags	28	320	Textile bags	13	93
Asphalt paving	25	230	Wood pallets	12	55
Bolts, nuts, and rivets	23	198	Stone products	12	56
Women's dresses	22	236	Textile machinery	10	58
Wood trusses	21	158	Metal stamping	10	52
Curtains and draperies	20	172	Signs	9	36
Metal windows and doors	17	143	Sheet metal work	8	29
Quick printing	17	108	Retail bakeries	5	12

*As measured by value of shipments. Data are for 2012. See **www.census.gov/econ/manufacturing.html.**

Source: Bureau of Census, *Census of Manufacturers,* 2012.

where $\%S_1$ is the percentage market share of firm 1, $\%S_2$ is the percentage market share of firm 2, and so on for each of the n total firms in the industry. By squaring the percentage market shares of all firms in the industry, the Herfindahl index purposely gives much greater weight to larger, and thus more powerful, firms than to smaller ones. For a purely competitive industry, the index would approach zero since each firm's market share—$\%S$ in the equation—is extremely small. In the case of a single-firm industry, the index would be at its maximum of 10,000 ($= 100^2$), indicating an industry with complete monopoly power.

We will discover later in this chapter that the Herfindahl index is important for assessing oligopolistic industries. But for now, the relevant generalization is that the lower the Herfindahl index, the greater is the likelihood that an industry is monopolistically competitive rather than oligopolistic. Column 3 of Table 13.1 lists the Herfindahl index (computed for the top 50 firms, not all the industry firms) for several industries. Note that the index values are decidedly closer to the bottom limit of the Herfindahl index—0—than to its top limit—10,000.

The numbers in Table 13.1 are for manufacturing industries. In addition, many retail establishments in metropolitan areas are monopolistically competitive, including grocery stores, gasoline stations, hair salons, dry cleaners, clothing stores, and restaurants. Also, many providers of professional services such as medical care, legal assistance, real estate sales, and basic bookkeeping are monopolistic competitors.

Price and Output in Monopolistic Competition

LO13.2 Explain why monopolistic competitors earn only a normal profit in the long run.

How does a monopolistic competitor decide on its price and output? To explain, we initially assume that each firm in the industry is producing a specific differentiated product and engaging in a particular amount of advertising. Later we will see how changes in the product and in the amount of advertising modify our conclusions.

The Firm's Demand Curve

Our explanation is based on **Figure 13.1 (Key Graph)**, which shows that the demand curve faced by a monopolistically competitive seller is highly, but not perfectly, elastic. It is precisely this feature that distinguishes monopolistic competition from both pure monopoly and pure competition. The monopolistic competitor's demand is more elastic than the demand faced by a pure monopolist because the monopolistically competitive seller has many competitors producing closely substitutable goods. The pure monopolist has no rivals at all. Yet, for two reasons, the monopolistic competitor's demand is not perfectly elastic like that of the pure competitor. First, the monopolistic competitor has fewer rivals; second, its products are differentiated, so they are not perfect substitutes.

The price elasticity of demand faced by the monopolistically competitive firm depends on the number of rivals and the degree of product differentiation. The larger the number of rivals and the weaker the product differentiation, the greater the price elasticity of each seller's demand, that is, the closer monopolistic competition will be to pure competition.

The Short Run: Profit or Loss

In the short run, monopolistically competitive firms maximize profit or minimize loss using exactly the same strategy as pure competitors and monopolists: They produce the level of output at which marginal revenue equals marginal cost (MR = MC). Thus, the monopolistically competitive firm in Figure 13.1a produces output Q_1, where MR = MC. As shown by demand curve D_1, it then can charge price P_1. It realizes an economic profit, shown by the green area $[= (P_1 - A_1) \times Q_1]$.

But with less favorable demand or costs, the firm may incur a loss in the short run. We show this possibility in Figure 13.1b, where the firm's best strategy is to minimize its loss. It does so by producing output Q_2 (where MR = MC) and, as determined by demand curve D_2, by charging price P_2. Because price P_2 is less than average total cost A_2, the firm incurs a per-unit loss of $A_2 - P_2$ and a total loss represented as the red area $[= (A_2 - P_2) \times Q_2]$.

The Long Run: Only a Normal Profit

In the long run, firms will enter a profitable monopolistically competitive industry and leave an unprofitable one. So a monopolistic competitor will earn only a normal profit in the long run or, in other words, will only break even. (Remember that the cost curves include both explicit and implicit costs, including a normal profit.)

Profits: Firms Enter In the case of short-run profit (Figure 13.1a), economic profits attract new rivals because entry to the industry is relatively easy. As new firms enter, the demand curve faced by the typical firm shifts to the left (falls). Why? Because each firm has a smaller share of total demand and now faces a larger number of close-substitute products. This decline in the firm's demand reduces its economic profit. When entry of new firms has reduced demand to the extent that the demand curve is tangent to the average-total-cost curve at the profit-maximizing output, the firm is just making a normal profit. This situation is shown in Figure 13.1c, where demand is D_3 and the firm's

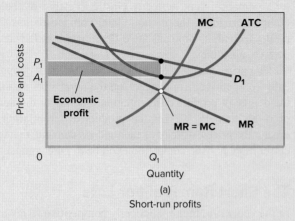

(a)
Short-run profits

FIGURE 13.1 A monopolistically competitive firm: short run and long run. The monopolistic competitor maximizes profit or minimizes loss by producing the output at which MR = MC. The economic profit shown in (a) will induce new firms to enter, eventually eliminating economic profit. The loss shown in (b) will cause an exit of firms until normal profit is restored. After such entry and exit, the price will settle in (c) to where it just equals average total cost at the MR = MC output. At this price P_3 and output Q_3, the monopolistic competitor earns only a normal profit, and the industry is in long-run equilibrium.

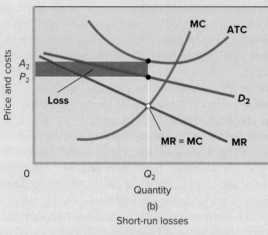

(b)
Short-run losses

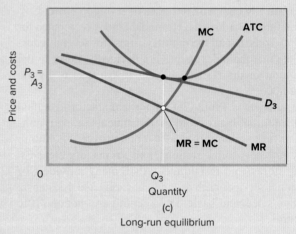

(c)
Long-run equilibrium

QUICK QUIZ FOR FIGURE 13.1

1. Price exceeds MC in:
   a. graph (a) only.
   b. graph (b) only.
   c. graphs (a) and (b) only.
   d. graphs (a), (b), and (c).

2. Price exceeds ATC in:
   a. graph (a) only.
   b. graph (b) only.
   c. graphs (a) and (b) only.
   d. graphs (a), (b), and (c).

3. The firm represented by Figure 13.1c is:
   a. making a normal profit.
   b. incurring a loss.

c. producing at the same level of output as a purely competitive firm.
   d. producing a standardized product.

4. Which of the following pairs are both "competition-like elements" in monopolistic competition?
   a. Price exceeds MR; standardized product.
   b. Entry is relatively easy; only a normal profit in the long run.
   c. Price equals MC at the profit-maximizing output; economic profits are likely in the long run.
   d. A firm's demand curve is downsloping; differentiated products.

Answers: 1. d; 2. a; 3. a; 4. b

long-run equilibrium output is Q_3. As Figure 13.1c indicates, any greater or lesser output will entail an average total cost that exceeds product price P_3, meaning a loss for the firm. At the tangency point between the demand curve and ATC, total revenue equals total costs. With the economic

profit gone, there is no further incentive for additional firms to enter.

Losses: Firms Leave When the industry suffers short-run losses, as in Figure 13.1b, some firms will exit in the long run. Faced with fewer substitute products and blessed with an expanded share of total demand, the surviving firms will see their demand curves shift to the right (rise), as to D_3. Their losses will disappear and give way to normal profits (Figure 13.1c). (For simplicity we have assumed constant costs; shifts in the cost curves as firms enter or leave would complicate our discussion slightly but would not alter our conclusions.)

Complications The representative firm in the monopolistic competition model earns only a normal profit in the long run. That outcome may not always occur, however, in the real world of small firms as opposed to the theoretical model.

- Some firms may achieve sufficient product differentiation such that other firms cannot duplicate them, even over time. One hotel in a major city may have the best location relative to business and tourist activities. Or a firm may have developed a well-known brand name that gives it a slight but very long-lasting advantage over imitators. Such firms may have sufficient monopoly power to realize modest economic profits even in the long run.

- Entry to some industries populated by small firms is not as free in reality as it is in theory. Because of product differentiation, financial barriers to entry are likely to be greater than they would be if the product were standardized. This suggests some monopoly power, with small economic profits continuing even in the long run.

With all things considered, however, the outcome that yields only a normal profit—the long-run equilibrium shown in Figure 13.1c—is a reasonable approximation of reality.

QUICK REVIEW 13.1

✓ Monopolistic competition involves a relatively large number of firms operating in a noncollusive way and producing differentiated products with easy industry entry and exit.

✓ In the short run, a monopolistic competitor will maximize profit or minimize loss by producing the level of output at which marginal revenue equals marginal cost.

✓ In the long run, easy entry and exit of firms causes monopolistic competitors to earn only a normal profit.

Monopolistic Competition and Efficiency

LO13.3 Explain why monopolistic competition delivers neither productive nor allocative efficiency.

We know from Chapter 11 that economic efficiency requires each firm to produce the amount of output at which

$P = \text{MC} = \text{minimum ATC}$. The equality of price and minimum average total cost yields *productive efficiency*. The good is being produced in the least costly way, and the price is just sufficient to cover average total cost, including a normal profit. The equality of price and marginal cost yields *allocative efficiency*. The right amount of output is being produced, and thus the right amount of society's scarce resources is being devoted to this specific use.

How efficient is monopolistic competition, as measured against this triple equality? In particular, do monopolistically competitive firms produce the efficient output level associated with $P = \text{MC} = \text{minimum ATC}$?

Neither Productive nor Allocative Efficiency

In monopolistic competition, neither productive nor allocative efficiency occurs in long-run equilibrium. Figure 13.2 includes an enlargement of part of Figure 13.1c and clearly shows this. First note that the profit-maximizing price P_3 slightly exceeds the lowest average total cost, A_4. In producing the profit-maximizing output Q_3, the firm's average total cost therefore is slightly higher than optimal from society's perspective—productive efficiency is not achieved. Also note that the profit-maximizing price P_3 exceeds marginal cost (here M_3), meaning that monopolistic competition causes an underallocation of resources. To measure the size of this inefficiency, note that the allocatively optimal amount of output is determined by point c, where demand curve D intersects the MC curve. So for all units between Q_3 and the level of output associated with point c, marginal benefits exceed marginal costs. Consequently, by producing only Q_3 units, this monopolistic competitor creates an efficiency loss (deadweight loss) equal in size to area acd. The total efficiency loss for the industry as a whole will be the sum of the individual efficiency losses generated by each of the firms in the industry.

Excess Capacity

In monopolistic competition, the gap between the minimum-ATC output and the profit-maximizing output identifies **excess capacity**: plant and equipment that are underused because firms are producing less than the minimum-ATC output. This gap is shown as the distance between Q_4 and Q_3 in Figure 13.2. Note in the figure that the minimum ATC is at point b. If each monopolistic competitor could profitably produce at this point on its ATC curve, the lower average total cost would enable a lower price than P_3. More importantly, if each firm produced at b rather than at a, fewer firms would be needed to produce the industry output. But because monopolistically competitive firms produce at a in long-run equilibrium, monopolistically competitive industries are overpopulated with firms, each operating below its optimal

FIGURE 13.2 The inefficiency of monopolistic competition. In long-run equilibrium a monopolistic competitor achieves neither productive nor allocative efficiency. Productive efficiency is not realized because production occurs where the average total cost A_3 exceeds the minimum average total cost A_4. Allocative efficiency is not achieved because the product price P_3 exceeds the marginal cost M_3. The results are an underallocation of resources as well as an efficiency loss and excess production capacity at every firm in the industry. This firm's efficiency loss is area acd and its excess production capacity is $Q_4 - Q_3$.

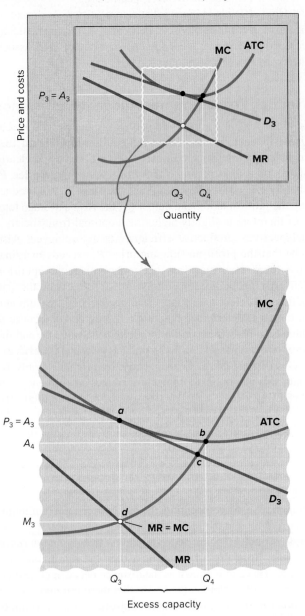

Excess capacity

capacity. This situation is typified by many kinds of retail establishments. For example, in most cities there is an abundance of small motels and restaurants that operate well below half capacity.

Product Variety

LO13.4 Relate how the ability of monopolistic competition to deliver product differentiation helps to compensate for its failure to deliver economic efficiency.

The situation portrayed in Figures 13.1c and 13.2 is not very satisfying to monopolistic competitors, since it foretells only a normal profit. But the profit-realizing firm of Figure 13.1a need not stand by and watch new competitors eliminate its profit by imitating its product, matching its customer service, and copying its advertising. Each firm has a product that is distinguishable in some way from those of the other producers. So the firm can attempt to stay ahead of competitors and sustain its profit through further product differentiation and better advertising. By developing or improving its product, it may be able to postpone, at least for a while, the outcome of Figure 13.1c.

Although product differentiation and advertising will add to the firm's costs, they can also increase the demand for its product. If demand increases by more than enough to compensate for the added costs, the firm will have improved its profit position. As Figure 13.2 suggests, the firm has little or no prospect of increasing profit by price cutting. So why not engage in nonprice competition?

Benefits of Product Variety

The product variety and product improvement that accompany the drive to maintain economic profit in monopolistic competition are a benefit for society—one that may offset the cost of the inefficiency associated with monopolistic competition. Consumers have a wide diversity of tastes: Some like regular fries, others like curly fries; some like contemporary furniture, others like traditional furniture. If a product is differentiated, then at any time the consumer will be offered a wide range of types, styles, brands, and quality gradations of that product. Compared with pure competition, this provides an advantage to the consumer. The range of choice is widened, and producers more fully meet the wide variation in consumer tastes.

The product improvement promoted by monopolistic competition further differentiates products and expands choices. And a successful product improvement by one firm obligates rivals to imitate or improve on that firm's temporary market advantage or else lose business. So society benefits from better products.

In fact, product differentiation creates a trade-off between consumer choice and productive efficiency. The stronger the product differentiation, the greater is the excess capacity and, therefore, the greater is the productive inefficiency. But the greater the product differentiation, the more likely it is that the firms will satisfy the great diversity of consumer tastes. The greater the excess-capacity problem, the wider the range of consumer choice.

Higher Wages, More McRestaurants

In the Monopolistically Competitive Restaurant Market, Higher Wages Favor Big Chain Restaurants over Small "Mom and Pop" Operations.

Restaurants are monopolistic competitors. Because each one has a unique location, it has some monopoly power. Additional bits of monopoly power are generated by product differentiation. Restaurants can differ on menu items, decor, speed of service, price, drive-through convenience, and a wide variety of additional characteristics.

Restaurants also differ in their production methods. Compare a McDonald's hamburger restaurant with a small "mom and pop" hamburger stand. The McDonald's will have a huge amount of specialized equipment. There will be special machines for frying, microwaving, making milkshakes, dispensing beverages into cups automatically, and of course cooking the hamburgers.

There will also in most cases be digital touchscreen computers for taking walk-up orders; wireless headsets for taking drive-through orders, and a fully computerized register system for keeping track of cash, credit; and debit transactions. And there will be a dining area that is often tastefully decorated in modern styles at substantial expense. All these things imply that a McDonald's restaurant is capital intensive. It uses a large amount of capital equipment to produce and serve a hamburger.

By contrast, a small mom and pop hamburger stand will typically have only the bare minimum in terms of cooking equipment—a grill, a fryer, an unautomated beverage dispenser, and a refrigerator. Seating will be plain. The decor will be inexpensive and probably out of style. The mom and pop hamburger stand will use relatively little capital to produce and serve a hamburger.

In a monopolistically competitive restaurant market, equilibrium can often include both highly capitalized chain stores like McDonald's as well as lightly capitalized mom and pop operations. As long as both types of hamburger restaurant can make zero economic profits, each type will have representatives in the local restaurant market.

Economists have recently discovered, however, that wage increases can tilt the local restaurant market in favor of highly capitalized chain stores. In particular, increases in the minimum wage tend to reduce the proportion of mom and pop restaurants.

This happens because increases in the minimum wage have a relatively small impact on the cost curves of highly capitalized chain restaurants. While it is true that a highly capitalized McDonald's *does* hire minimum wage workers, the fact that it uses so much capital to produce hamburgers means that a large fraction

Source: © Sorbis/Shutterstock.com

of its costs derive from machinery and equipment. So when the minimum wage goes up, only a relatively minor part of its production costs go up.

By contrast, mom and pop restaurants use relatively little capital combined with lots of labor. After all, if you don't have much in the way of machinery and specialized equipment, you need to have lots of labor to make up for the lack of capital. So when the minimum wage is increased, the cost curves of mom and pop stores shift upward by more than the cost curves of highly capitalized chain restaurants. In both cases, economic profits will turn negative—but they will become much more negative at the mom and pop restaurants, which are heavily reliant on labor.

The result is a greater tendency on the part of mom and pop restaurants to exit the industry. Both types of restaurant will see exits. But when a new equilibrium is eventually reestablished, there will be a higher proportion of highly capitalized chain restaurants and a lower proportion of labor-intensive mom and pop restaurants.

Higher minimum wages are often promoted as a way to help low-wage workers. But they generate an unintended consequence in the restaurant market, where they favor big chain stores over small local operations. Voters and politicians need to be aware that this happens when they consider raising the minimum wage.

CONSIDER THIS . . .

Source: © Chuck Nacke/Alamy Stock Photo

The Spice of Life

The Wendy's hamburger chain debuted a hilarious TV commercial in 1987. The commercial depicts a Soviet communist fashion show. A woman walks down the runway in a drab grey factory uniform. The emcee shouts out, "Day wear!" Then she marches down the runway again in the same uniform but holding a flashlight. The emcee shouts out, "Evening wear!" She then marches out in the same uniform again but holding an inflatable beach ball. "Swimwear!"

Communist central planners didn't care about product differentiation. They typically made one design of a given product to be able to mass produce it at the lowest possible cost. The result was a society of painful sameness.

The Wendy's TV commercial hammered home a single idea—that we should embrace the fact that the food produced by Wendy's was different from that produced by its main rivals, McDonald's and Burger King. Unlike the communist central planning of the old Soviet Union, the free market system of the United States allows for huge amounts of product differentiation. If "variety is the spice of life," American capitalism is extremely well seasoned.

Source: Wendy's, "Soviet Fashion Show," 1987.

Further Complexity

Finally, the ability to engage in nonprice competition makes the market situation of a monopolistic competitor more complex than Figure 13.1 indicates. That figure assumes a given (unchanging) product and a given level of advertising expenditures. But we know that, in practice, product attributes and advertising are not fixed. The monopolistically competitive firm juggles three factors—price, product, and advertising—in seeking maximum profit. It must determine what variety of product, selling at what price, and supplemented by what level of advertising will result in the greatest profit. This complex situation is not easily expressed in a simple, meaningful economic model. At best, we can say that each possible combination of price, product, and advertising poses a different demand and cost (production cost plus advertising cost) situation for the firm and that one combination yields the maximum profit. In practice, this optimal combination cannot be readily forecast but must be found by trial and error.

> ### QUICK REVIEW 13.2
>
> ✓ A monopolistic competitor's long-run equilibrium output is such that price exceeds the minimum average total cost (implying that consumers do not get the product at the lowest price attainable) and price exceeds marginal cost (indicating that resources are underallocated to the product).
> ✓ The efficiency loss (or deadweight loss) associated with monopolistic competition is greatly muted by the benefits consumers receive from product variety.

SUMMARY

LO13.1 List the characteristics of monopolistic competition.

The distinguishing features of monopolistic competition are (*a*) there are enough firms in the industry to ensure that each firm has only limited control over price, mutual interdependence is absent, and collusion is nearly impossible; (*b*) products are characterized by real or perceived differences so that economic rivalry entails both price and nonprice competition; and (*c*) entry to the industry is relatively easy. Many aspects of retailing, and some manufacturing industries in which economies of scale are few, approximate monopolistic competition.

The four-firm concentration ratio measures the percentage of total industry output accounted for by the largest four firms. The

Herfindahl index sums the squares of the percentage market shares of all firms in the industry.

LO13.2 Explain why monopolistic competitors earn only a normal profit in the long run.

Monopolistically competitive firms may earn economic profits or incur losses in the short run. The easy entry and exit of firms results in only normal profits in the long run.

LO13.3 Explain why monopolistic competition delivers neither productive nor allocative efficiency.

The long-run equilibrium position of the monopolistically competitive producer is less efficient than that of the pure competitor. Under monopolistic competition, price exceeds marginal cost, indicating an underallocation of resources to the product, and price exceeds minimum average total cost, indicating that consumers do not get the product at the lowest price that cost conditions might allow.

LO13.4 Relate how the ability of monopolistic competition to deliver product differentiation helps to compensate for its failure to deliver economic efficiency.

Nonprice competition provides a way that monopolistically competitive firms can offset the long-run tendency for economic profit to fall to zero. Through product differentiation, product development, and advertising, a firm may strive to increase the demand for its product more than enough to cover the added cost of such nonprice competition. Consumers benefit from the wide diversity of product choice that monopolistic competition provides.

In practice, the monopolistic competitor seeks the specific combination of price, product, and advertising that will maximize profit.

TERMS AND CONCEPTS

monopolistic competition	nonprice competition	Herfindahl index
product differentiation	four-firm concentration ratio	excess capacity

The following and additional problems can be found in ▪**connect**

DISCUSSION QUESTIONS

1. How does monopolistic competition differ from pure competition in its basic characteristics? From pure monopoly? Explain fully what product differentiation may involve. Explain how the entry of firms into its industry affects the demand curve facing a monopolistic competitor and how that, in turn, affects its economic profit. **LO13.1**

2. Compare the elasticity of a monopolistic competitor's demand with that of a pure competitor and a pure monopolist. Assuming identical long-run costs, compare graphically the prices and outputs that would result in the long run under pure competition and under monopolistic competition. Contrast the two market structures in terms of productive and allocative efficiency. Explain: "Monopolistically competitive industries are populated by too many firms, each of which produces too little." **LO13.2**

3. "Monopolistic competition is monopolistic up to the point at which consumers become willing to buy close substitute products and competitive beyond that point." Explain. **LO13.2**

4. "Competition in quality and service may be just as effective as price competition in giving buyers more for their money." Do you agree? Why? Explain why monopolistically competitive firms frequently prefer nonprice competition to price competition. **LO13.2**

5. Critically evaluate and explain: **LO13.2**
   a. In monopolistically competitive industries, economic profits are competed away in the long run; hence, there is no valid reason to criticize the performance and efficiency of such industries.
   b. In the long run, monopolistic competition leads to a monopolistic price but not to monopolistic profits.

6. **LAST WORD** What would you expect to happen to the proportion of big chain restaurants relative to mom and pop restaurants in a town that lowered its minimum wage? Will the proportion change due to exits or entrances? Which type of restaurant will see more in the way of exits or entrances? Why?

REVIEW QUESTIONS

1. There are 10 firms in an industry, and each firm has a market share of 10 percent. The industry's Herfindahl index is: **LO13.1**
   a. 10.
   b. 100.
   c. 1,000.
   d. 10,000.

2. In the small town of Geneva, there are five firms that make watches. The firms' respective output levels are 30 watches per year, 20 watches per year, 20 watches per year, 20 watches per year, and 10 watches per year. The four-firm concentration ratio for the town's watch-making industry is: **LO13.1**
   a. 5.   c. 90.
   b. 70.   d. 100.

3. Which of the following best describes the efficiency of monopolistically competitive firms? **LO13.3**
   a. Allocatively efficient but productively inefficient.
   b. Allocatively inefficient but productively efficient.
   c. Both allocatively efficient and productively efficient.
   d. Neither allocatively efficient nor productively efficient.

PROBLEMS

1. Suppose that a small town has seven burger shops whose respective shares of the local hamburger market are (as percentages of all hamburgers sold): 23 percent, 22 percent, 18 percent, 12 percent, 11 percent, 8 percent, and 6 percent. What is the four-firm concentration ratio of the hamburger industry in this town? What is the Herfindahl index for the hamburger industry in this town? If the top three sellers combined to form a single firm, what would happen to the four-firm concentration ratio and to the Herfindahl index? **LO13.1**

2. Suppose that the most popular car dealer in your area sells 10 percent of all vehicles. If all other car dealers sell either the same number of vehicles or fewer, what is the largest value that the Herfindahl index could possibly take for car dealers in your area? In that same situation, what would the four-firm concentration ratio be? **LO13.1**

3. Suppose that a monopolistically competitive restaurant is currently serving 230 meals per day (the output where MR = MC). At that output level, ATC per meal is $10 and consumers are willing to pay $12 per meal. What is the size of this firm's profit or loss? Will there be entry or exit? Will this restaurant's demand curve shift left or right? In long-run equilibrium, suppose that this restaurant charges $11 per meal for 180 meals and that the marginal cost of the 180th meal is $8. What is the size of the firm's profit? Suppose that the allocatively efficient output level in long-run equilibrium is 200 meals. Is the deadweight loss for this firm greater than or less than $60? **LO13.1**

Chapter 14

Oligopoly and Strategic Behavior

Learning Objectives

LO14.1 Describe the characteristics of oligopoly.

LO14.2 Discuss how game theory relates to oligopoly.

LO14.3 Explain the three main models of oligopoly pricing and output: kinked-demand theory, collusive pricing, and price leadership.

LO14.4 Contrast the potential positive and negative effects of advertising.

LO14.5 Discuss the efficiency of oligopoly from society's standpoint and whether it is more or less efficient than monopoly.

LO14.6 Utilize additional game-theory terminology and demonstrate how to find Nash equilibriums in both simultaneous and sequential games.

In the United States, most industries have a market structure that falls somewhere between the two poles of pure competition and pure monopoly. To begin with, most real-world industries have fewer than the large number of producers required for pure competition but more than the single producer that defines pure monopoly. In addition, most firms in most industries have both distinguishable rather than standardized products as well as some discretion over the prices they charge. As a result, competition often occurs on the basis of price, quality, location, service, and advertising. Finally, entry to most real-world industries ranges from easy to very difficult but is rarely completely blocked.

This chapter examines the second of two models that more closely approximate these widespread industry structures. While the *monopolistic competition* model of the previous chapter mixes a small amount of monopoly power with a large amount of competition, the *oligopoly* model covered in this chapter blends a large amount of monopoly power with both considerable rivalry among existing firms and the threat of increased future competition due to foreign firms and new technologies. (You should quickly review Table 10.1 at this point.)

Oligopoly

LO14.1 Describe the characteristics of oligopoly.

In terms of competitiveness, the spectrum of market structures reaches from pure competition, to monopolistic competition, to oligopoly, to pure monopoly (review Table 10.1). We now direct our attention to **oligopoly,** a market dominated by a few large producers of a homogeneous or differentiated product. Because of their "fewness," oligopolists have considerable control over their prices, but each must consider the possible reaction of rivals to its own pricing, output, and advertising decisions.

A Few Large Producers

The phrase "a few large producers" is necessarily vague because the market model of oligopoly covers much ground, ranging between pure monopoly, on the one hand, and monopolistic competition, on the other. Oligopoly encompasses the U.S. aluminum industry, in which three huge firms dominate an entire national market, and the situation in which four or five much smaller auto-parts stores enjoy roughly equal shares of the market in a medium-size town. Generally, however, when you hear a term such as "Big Three," "Big Four," or "Big Six," you can be sure it refers to an oligopolistic industry.

Homogeneous or Differentiated Products

An oligopoly may be either a **homogeneous oligopoly** or a **differentiated oligopoly,** depending on whether the firms in the oligopoly produce standardized (homogeneous) or differentiated products. Many industrial products (steel, zinc, copper, aluminum, lead, cement, industrial alcohol) are virtually standardized products that are produced in oligopolies. Alternatively, many consumer goods industries (automobiles, tires, household appliances, electronics equipment, breakfast cereals, cigarettes, and many sporting goods) are differentiated oligopolies. These differentiated oligopolies typically engage in considerable nonprice competition supported by heavy advertising.

Control over Price, but Mutual Interdependence

Because firms are few in oligopolistic industries, each firm is a "price maker"; like the monopolist, it can set its price and output levels to maximize its profit. But unlike the monopolist, which has no rivals, the oligopolist must consider how its rivals will react to any change in its price, output, product characteristics, or advertising. Oligopoly is thus characterized by *strategic behavior* and *mutual interdependence*. By **strategic behavior,** we simply mean self-interested behavior that takes into account the reactions of others. Firms develop and implement price, quality, location, service, and advertising strategies

to "grow their business" and expand their profits. But because rivals are few, there is **mutual interdependence:** a situation in which each firm's profit depends not just on its own price and sales strategies but also on those of the other firms in its highly concentrated industry. So oligopolistic firms base their decisions on how they think their rivals will react. Example: In deciding whether to increase the price of its cosmetics, L'Oréal will try to predict the response of the other major producers, such as Clinique. Second example: In deciding on its advertising strategy, Burger King will take into consideration how McDonald's might react.

Entry Barriers

The same barriers to entry that create pure monopoly also contribute to the creation of oligopoly. Economies of scale are important entry barriers in a number of oligopolistic industries, such as the aircraft, rubber, and copper industries. In those industries, three or four firms might each have sufficient sales to achieve economies of scale, but new firms would have such a small market share that they could not do so. They would then be high-cost producers, and as such they could not survive. A closely related barrier is the large expenditure for capital—the cost of obtaining necessary plant and equipment—required for entering certain industries. The jet engine, automobile, commercial aircraft, and petroleum-refining industries, for example, are all characterized by very high capital requirements.

The ownership and control of raw materials help explain why oligopoly exists in many mining industries, including gold, silver, and copper. In the computer, chemicals, consumer electronics, and pharmaceutical industries, patents have served as entry barriers. Moreover, oligopolists can preclude the entry of new competitors through preemptive and retaliatory pricing and advertising strategies.

Mergers

Some oligopolies have emerged mainly through the growth of the dominant firms in a given industry (examples: breakfast cereals, chewing gum, candy bars). But for other industries the route to oligopoly has been through mergers (examples: steel, in its early history, and, more recently, airlines, banking, and entertainment). The merging, or combining, of two or more competing firms may substantially increase their market share, and this in turn may allow the new firm to achieve greater economies of scale.

Another motive underlying the "urge to merge" is the desire for monopoly power. The larger firm that results from a merger has greater control over market supply and thus the price of its product. Also, since it is a larger buyer of inputs, it may be able to demand and obtain lower prices (costs) on its production inputs.

CONSIDER THIS . . .

Creative Strategic Behavior

Source: © Richard Cummins/Corbis

The following story, offered with tongue in cheek, illustrates a localized market that exhibits some characteristics of oligopoly, including strategic behavior.

Tracy Martinez's Native American Arts and Crafts store is located in the center of a small tourist town that borders on a national park. In its early days, Tracy had a mini-monopoly. Business was brisk, and prices and profits were high.

To Tracy's annoyance, two "copycat" shops opened adjacent to her store, one on either side of her shop. Worse yet, the competitors named their shops to take advantage of Tracy's advertising. One was "Native Arts and Crafts"; the other, "Indian Arts and Crafts." These new sellers drew business away from Tracy's store, forcing her to lower her prices. The three side-by-side stores in the small, isolated town constituted a localized oligopoly for Native American arts and crafts.

Tracy began to think strategically about ways to boost profit. She decided to distinguish her shop from those on either side by offering a greater mix of high-quality, expensive products and a lesser mix of inexpensive souvenir items. The tactic worked for a while, but the other stores eventually imitated her product mix.

Then, one of the competitors next door escalated the rivalry by hanging up a large sign proclaiming: "We Sell for Less!" Shortly thereafter, the other shop put up a large sign stating: "We Won't Be Undersold!"

Not to be outdone, Tracy painted a colorful sign of her own and hung it above her door. It read: "Main Entrance."

Oligopolistic Industries

In the previous chapter, we listed the four-firm concentration ratio—the percentage of total industry sales accounted for by the four largest firms—for a number of monopolistically competitive industries (see Table 13.1). Column 2 of Table 14.1 shows the four-firm concentration ratios for 22 oligopolistic industries. For example, the four largest U.S. producers of aircraft make 80 percent of all aircraft produced in the United States.

When the largest four firms in an industry control 40 percent or more of the market (as in Table 14.1), that industry is considered oligopolistic. Using this benchmark, about one-half of all U.S. manufacturing industries are oligopolies.

Although concentration ratios help identify oligopoly, they have four shortcomings.

Localized Markets We have already noted that concentration ratios apply to the nation as a whole, whereas the markets for some products are highly localized because of high transportation costs. Local oligopolies can exist even though national concentration ratios are low.

Interindustry Competition Concentration ratios are based on somewhat arbitrary definitions of industries. In some cases, they disguise significant **interindustry competition**—competition between two products associated with different industries. The high concentration ratio for the primary aluminum industry shown in Table 14.1 understates the competition in that industry because aluminum competes with copper in many applications (for example, in the market for long-distance power lines).

World Trade The data in Table 14.1 only take account of output produced in the United States and may overstate concentration because they do not account for the **import competition** of foreign suppliers. The truck and auto tire industry is a good example. Although Table 14.1 shows that four U.S. firms produce 73 percent of the domestic output of tires, it ignores the fact that a very large portion of the truck and auto tires bought in the United States are imports. Many of the world's largest corporations are foreign, and many of them do business in the United States.

Dominant Firms The four-firm concentration ratio does not reveal the extent to which one or two firms dominate an industry. Suppose that in industry X one firm produces the entire industry output. In a second industry, Y, four firms compete, each with 25 percent of the market. The concentration ratio is 100 percent for both these industries. But industry X is a pure monopoly, while industry Y is an oligopoly that may be experiencing significant economic rivalry. Most economists would agree that monopoly power (or market power) is substantially greater in industry X than in industry Y, a fact disguised by their identical 100 percent concentration ratios.

The Herfindahl index addresses this problem. Recall that this index is the sum of the squared percentage market shares of all firms in the industry. In equation form:

$$\text{Herfindahl index} = (\%S_1)^2 + (\%S_2)^2 + (\%S_3)^2 + \cdots + (\%S_n)^2$$

where $\%S_1$ is the percentage market share of firm 1, $\%S_2$ is the percentage market share of firm 2, and so on for each firm

TABLE 14.1 Percentage of Output Produced by Firms in Selected High-Concentration U.S. Manufacturing Industries

(1) Industry	(2) Percentage of Industry Output* Produced by the Four Largest Firms	(3) Herfindahl Index for the Top 50 Firms	(1) Industry	(2) Percentage of Industry Output* Produced by the Four Largest Firms	(3) Herfindahl Index for the Top 50 Firms
Household laundry equipment	100	ND†	Primary aluminum	74	2,089
Household refrigerators and freezers	93	ND	Tires	73	1,531
			Bottled water	71	1,564
Cigarettes	88	2,897	Gasoline pumps	70	1,611
Beer	88	3,561	Bar soaps	70	2,250
Glass containers	86	ND	Burial caskets	69	1,699
Phosphate fertilizers	85	3,152	Printer toner cartridges	67	1,449
Small-arms ammunition	84	2,848	Alcohol distilleries	65	1,394
Electric light bulbs	84	3,395	Turbines and generators	61	1,263
Aircraft	80	3,287	Motor vehicles	60	1,178
Breakfast cereals	79	2,333	Primary copper	50	879
Aerosol cans	75	1,667			

*As measured by value of shipments. Data are for 2012. See **www.census.gov/econ/manufacturing.html**.

†ND = not disclosed.

Source: Bureau of Census, *Census of Manufacturers, 2012.*

in the industry. Also remember that by squaring the percentage market shares of all firms in the industry, the Herfindahl index gives much greater weight to larger, and thus more powerful, firms than to smaller ones. In the case of the single-firm industry X, the index would be at its maximum of 100^2, or 10,000, indicating an industry with complete monopoly power. For our supposed four-firm industry Y, the index would be $25^2 + 25^2 + 25^2 + 25^2$, or 2,500, indicating much less market power.

The larger the Herfindahl index, the greater the market power within an industry. Note in Table 14.1 that the four-firm concentration ratios for the gasoline pumps industry and the bar soaps industry are identical at 70 percent. But the Herfindahl index of 2,250 for the bar soaps industry suggests greater market power than the 1,611 index for the gasoline pumps industry. Also, contrast the much larger Herfindahl indexes in Table 14.1 with those for the low-concentration industries in Table 13.1.

Oligopoly Behavior: A Game-Theory Overview

LO14.2 Discuss how game theory relates to oligopoly.

Oligopoly pricing behavior has the characteristics of certain games of strategy such as poker, chess, and bridge. The best way to play such a game depends on the way one's opponent plays. Players (and oligopolists) must pattern their actions according to the actions and expected reactions of rivals. The study of how people behave in strategic situations is called **game theory.** A classic example of game theory is called the prisoner's dilemma, in which each of two prisoners confesses to a crime even though they might go free if neither confesses. The logic of this outcome is explained in the nearby Consider This box, which you should read now.

The "confess-confess" outcome of the prisoner's dilemma is conceptually identical to the "low price–low price" outcome in the game shown in Figure 14.1. In Figure 14.1 we assume that a duopoly, or two-firm oligopoly, is producing athletic shoes. Each of the two firms—let's call them RareAir and Uptown—has a choice of two pricing strategies: price high or price low. The profit each firm earns will depend on the strategy it chooses *and* the strategy its rival chooses.

There are four possible combinations of strategies for the two firms, and a lettered cell in Figure 14.1 represents each combination. For example, cell C represents a low-price strategy for Uptown along with a high-price strategy for RareAir. Figure 14.1 is called a *payoff matrix* because each cell shows the payoff (profit) to each firm that would result from each combination of strategies. Cell C shows that if Uptown adopts a low-price strategy and RareAir a high-price strategy, then Uptown will earn $15 million (yellow portion) and RareAir will earn $6 million (blue portion).

FIGURE 14.1 Profit payoff (in millions) for a two-firm oligopoly. Each firm has two possible pricing strategies. RareAir's strategies are shown in the top margin, and Uptown's in the left margin. Each lettered cell of this four-cell payoff matrix represents one combination of a RareAir strategy and an Uptown strategy and shows the profit that combination would earn for each. Assuming no collusion, the outcome of this game is Cell D, with both parties using low-price strategies and earning $8 million of profits.

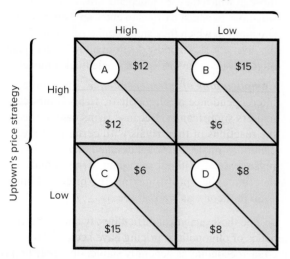

RareAir's price strategy

CONSIDER THIS . . .

The Prisoner's Dilemma

One of the classic illustrations of game theory is the prisoner's dilemma game in which two people—let's call them Betty and Al—have committed a diamond heist and are being detained by the police as prime suspects. Unbeknownst to the two, the evidence against them is weak, so the best hope the police have for getting a conviction is if one or both of the thieves confess to the crime. The police place Betty and Al in separate holding cells and offer each the same deal: Confess to the crime and receive a lighter prison sentence.

Each detainee therefore faces a dilemma. If Betty remains silent and Al confesses, Betty will end up with a long prison sentence. If Betty confesses and Al says nothing, Al will receive a long prison sentence. What happens? Fearful that the other person will confess, both confess, even though they each would be better off saying nothing.

Mutual Interdependence Revisited

The data in Figure 14.1 are hypothetical, but their relationships are typical of real situations. Recall that oligopolistic firms can increase their profits, and influence their rivals' profits, by changing their pricing strategies. Each firm's profit depends on its own pricing strategy and that of its rivals. This mutual interdependence of oligopolists is the most obvious point demonstrated by Figure 14.1. If Uptown adopts a high-price strategy, its profit will be $12 million provided that RareAir also employs a high-price strategy (cell A). But if RareAir uses a low-price strategy against Uptown's high-price strategy (cell B), RareAir will increase its market share and boost its profit from $12 to $15 million. RareAir's higher profit will come at the expense of Uptown, whose profit will fall from $12 million to $6 million. Uptown's high-price strategy is a good strategy only if RareAir also employs a high-price strategy.

Collusion

Figure 14.1 also suggests that oligopolists often can benefit from **collusion**—that is, cooperation with rivals. To see the benefits of collusion, first suppose that both firms in Figure 14.1 are acting independently and following high-price strategies. Each realizes a $12 million profit (cell A).

Note that either RareAir or Uptown could increase its profit by switching to a low-price strategy (cell B or C). The low-price firm would increase its profit to $15 million and

the high-price firm's profit would fall to $6 million. The high-price firm would be better off if it, too, adopted a low-price policy. Doing so would increase its profit from $6 million to $8 million (cell D). The effect of all this independent strategy shifting would be the reduction of both firms' profits from $12 million (cell A) to $8 million (cell D).

In real situations, too, independent action by oligopolists may lead to mutually "competitive" low-price strategies: Independent oligopolists compete with respect to price, and this leads to lower prices and lower profits. This outcome is clearly beneficial to consumers but not to the oligopolists, whose profits decrease.

How could oligopolists avoid the low-profit outcome of cell D? The answer is that they could collude, rather than establish prices competitively or independently. In our example, the two firms could agree to establish and maintain a high-price policy. So each firm will increase its profit from $8 million (cell D) to $12 million (cell A).

Incentive to Cheat

The payoff matrix also explains why an oligopolist might be strongly tempted to cheat on a collusive agreement. Suppose Uptown and RareAir agree to maintain high-price policies, with each earning $12 million in profit (cell A). Both are tempted to cheat on this collusive pricing agreement because either firm can increase its profit to $15 million by lowering its price.

For instance, if Uptown secretly cheats and sells at the low price while RareAir keeps on charging the high price, the payoff would move from cell A to cell C so that Uptown's profit would rise to $15 million while RareAir's profit would fall to $6 million. On the other hand, if RareAir cheats and sets a low price while Uptown keeps the agreement and charges the high price, the payoff matrix would move from cell A to cell B so that RareAir would get $15 million while Uptown would get only $6 million.

As you can see, cheating is both very lucrative to the cheater as well as very costly to the firm that gets cheated on. As a result, both firms will probably cheat so that the game will settle back to cell D, with each firm using its low-price strategy. (The Consider This box on the prisoner's dilemma is highly relevant, and we urge you to read it over again right now. Also, the final section in this chapter provides several additional applications of game theory.)

QUICK REVIEW 14.1

✓ An oligopoly is made up of relatively few firms producing either homogeneous or differentiated products; these firms are mutually interdependent.

✓ Barriers to entry such as scale economies, control of patents or strategic resources, or the ability to engage in retaliatory pricing characterize oligopolies. Oligopolies may result from internal growth of firms, mergers, or both.

✓ The four-firm concentration ratio shows the percentage of an industry's sales accounted for by its four largest firms; the Herfindahl index measures the degree of market power in an industry by summing the squares of the percentage market shares held by the individual firms in the industry.

✓ Game theory reveals that (a) oligopolies are mutually interdependent in their pricing policies, (b) collusion enhances oligopoly profits, and (c) there is a temptation for oligopolists to cheat on a collusive agreement.

Three Oligopoly Models

LO14.3 Explain the three main models of oligopoly pricing and output: kinked-demand theory, collusive pricing, and price leadership.

To gain further insight into oligopolistic pricing and output behavior, we will examine three distinct pricing models: (1) the kinked-demand curve, (2) collusive pricing, and (3) price leadership.

Why not a single model, as in our discussions of the other market structures? There are two reasons:

- **Diversity of oligopolies** Oligopoly encompasses a greater range and diversity of market situations than

do other market structures. It includes the *tight* oligopoly, in which two or three firms dominate an entire market, and the *loose* oligopoly, in which six or seven firms share, say, 70 or 80 percent of a market while a "competitive fringe" of firms shares the remainder. It includes both differentiated and standardized products. It includes cases in which firms act in collusion and those in which they act independently. It embodies situations in which barriers to entry are very strong and situations in which they are not quite so strong. In short, the diversity of oligopoly does not allow us to explain all oligopolistic behaviors with a single market model.

- **Complications of interdependence** The mutual interdependence of oligopolistic firms complicates matters significantly. Because firms cannot predict the reactions of their rivals with certainty, they cannot estimate their own demand and marginal-revenue data. Without such data, firms cannot determine their profit-maximizing price and output, even in theory, as we will see.

Despite these analytical difficulties, two interrelated characteristics of oligopolistic pricing have been observed. First, if the macroeconomy is generally stable, oligopolistic prices are typically inflexible (or "rigid" or "sticky"). Prices change less frequently under oligopoly than under pure competition, monopolistic competition, and, in some instances, pure monopoly. Second, when oligopolistic prices do change, firms are likely to change their prices together, suggesting that there is a tendency to act in concert, or collusively, in setting and changing prices (as we mentioned in the preceding section). The diversity of oligopolies and the presence of mutual interdependence are reflected in the models that follow.

Kinked-Demand Theory: Noncollusive Oligopoly

Imagine an oligopolistic industry made up of three hypothetical firms (Arch, King, and Dave's), each having about one-third of the total market for a differentiated product. Assume that the firms are "independent," meaning that they do not engage in collusive price practices. Assume, too, that the going price for Arch's product is P_0 and its current sales are Q_0, as shown in **Figure 14.2a (Key Graph)**.

Now the question is, "What does the firm's demand curve look like?" Mutual interdependence and the uncertainty about rivals' reactions make this question hard to answer. The location and shape of an oligopolist's demand curve depend on how the firm's rivals will react to a price change introduced by Arch. There are two plausible assumptions about the reactions of Arch's rivals:

- **Match price changes** One possibility is that King and Dave's will exactly match any price change initiated by

FIGURE 14.2 The kinked-demand curve. (a) The slope of a noncollusive oligopolist's demand and marginal-revenue curves depends on whether its rivals match (straight lines D_1 and MR_1) or ignore (straight lines D_2 and MR_2) any price changes that it may initiate from the current price P_0. (b) In all likelihood an oligopolist's rivals will ignore a price increase but follow a price cut. This causes the oligopolist's demand curve to be kinked (D_2eD_1) and the marginal-revenue curve to have a vertical break, or gap (fg). Because any shift in marginal costs between MC_1 and MC_2 will cut the vertical (dashed) segment of the marginal-revenue curve, no change in either price P_0 or output Q_0 will result from such a shift.

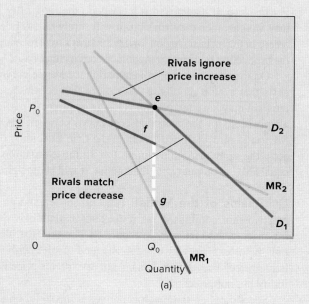

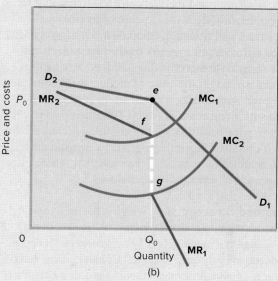

QUICK QUIZ FOR FIGURE 14.2

1. Suppose Q_0 in this figure represents annual sales of 5 million units for this firm. The other two firms in this three-firm industry sell 3 million and 2 million units, respectively. The Herfindahl index for this industry is:
   a. 100 percent.
   b. 400.
   c. 10.
   d. 3,800.

2. The D_2e segment of the demand curve D_2eD_1 in graph (b) implies that:
   a. this firm's total revenue will fall if it increases its price above P_0.
   b. other firms will match a price increase above P_0.
   c. the firm's relevant marginal-revenue curve will be MR_1 for price increases above P_0.
   d. the product in this industry is necessarily standardized.

3. By matching a price cut, this firm's rivals can:
   a. increase their market shares.
   b. increase their marginal revenues.
   c. maintain their market shares.
   d. lower their total costs.

4. A shift of the marginal-cost curve from MC_2 to MC_1 in graph (b) would:
   a. increase the "going price" above P_0.
   b. leave price at P_0 but reduce this firm's total profit.
   c. leave price at P_0 but reduce this firm's total revenue.
   d. make this firm's demand curve more elastic.

Answers: 1. d; 2. a; 3. c; 4. b

Arch. In this case, Arch's demand and marginal-revenue curves will look like the straight lines labeled D_1 and MR_1 in Figure 14.2a. Why are they so steep? Reason: If Arch cuts its price, its sales will increase only modestly because its two rivals will also cut their prices to prevent Arch from gaining an advantage over them. The small increase in sales that Arch (and its two rivals) will realize is at the expense of other industries; Arch will gain no sales from King and Dave's. In a similar fashion, if Arch raises its price, its sales will fall only modestly because King and Dave's will match its price increase. The industry will lose sales to other industries, but Arch will lose no customers to King and Dave's.

- *Ignore price changes* The other possibility is that King and Dave's will ignore any price change by Arch. In this case, the demand and marginal-revenue curves faced by Arch will resemble the straight lines D_2 and MR_2 in Figure 14.2a. Demand in this case is considerably more elastic than it was under the previous assumption. The reasons are clear: If Arch lowers its price and its rivals do not, Arch will gain sales significantly at the expense of its two rivals because it will be underselling them. Conversely, if Arch raises its price and its rivals do not, Arch will lose many customers to King and Dave's, which will be underselling it. Because of product differentiation, however, Arch's sales will not fall to zero when it raises its price; some of Arch's customers will pay the higher price because they have a strong preference for Arch's product. Nevertheless, Arch's demand curve will be much more elastic when its rivals ignore price changes than when they match them.

A Combined Strategy Now, which is the most logical assumption for Arch to make about how its rivals will react to any price change it might initiate? The answer is, "It depends on the direction of the price change." Common sense and observation of oligopolistic industries suggest that a firm's rivals will match price declines below P_0 as they act to prevent the price cutter from taking their customers. But they will ignore price increases above P_0 because the rivals of the price-increasing firm stand to gain the business lost by the price booster. In other words, the dark-green left-hand segment of the "rivals ignore" demand curve D_2 in Figure 14.2a seems relevant for price increases, and the dark-green right-hand segment of the "rivals match" demand curve D_1 seems relevant for price cuts. It is therefore reasonable to assume that the noncollusive oligopolist faces the **kinked-demand curve** D_2eD_1, as shown in Figure 14.2b. Demand is highly elastic above the going price P_0 but much less elastic or even inelastic below that price.

Note also that if rivals match a price cut but ignore an increase, the marginal-revenue curve of the oligopolist will also have an odd shape. It, too, will be made up of two segments: the dark gray left-hand part of marginal-revenue curve MR_2 in Figure 14.2a and the dark gray right-hand part of marginal-revenue curve MR_1. Because of the sharp difference in elasticity of demand above and below the going price, there is a gap, or what we can simply treat as a vertical segment, in the marginal-revenue curve. We show this gap as the dashed segment in the combined marginal-revenue curve MR_2fgMR_1 in Figure 14.2b.

Price Inflexibility This analysis helps explain why prices are generally stable in noncollusive oligopolistic industries. There are both demand and cost reasons.

On the demand side, the kinked-demand curve gives each oligopolist reason to believe that any change in price will be for the worse. If it raises its price, many of its customers will desert it. If it lowers its price, its sales at best will increase very modestly since rivals will match the lower price. Even if a price cut increases the oligopolist's total revenue somewhat, its costs may increase by a greater amount, depending on demand elasticity. For instance, if its demand is inelastic to the right of Q_0, as it may well be, then the firm's profit will surely fall. A price decrease in the inelastic region lowers the firm's total revenue, and the production of a larger output increases its total costs.

On the cost side, the broken marginal-revenue curve suggests that even if an oligopolist's costs change substantially, the firm may have no reason to change its price. In particular, all positions of the marginal-cost curve between MC_1 and MC_2 in Figure 14.2b will result in the firm's deciding on exactly the same price and output. For all those positions, MR equals MC at output Q_0; at that output, it will charge price P_0.

Criticisms of the Model The kinked-demand analysis has two shortcomings. First, it does not explain how the going price gets to be at P_0 in Figure 14.2 in the first place. It only helps explain why oligopolists tend to stick with an existing price. The kinked-demand curve explains price inflexibility but not price itself.

Second, when the macroeconomy is unstable, oligopoly prices are not as rigid as the kinked-demand theory implies. During inflationary periods, many oligopolists have raised their prices often and substantially. And during downturns (recessions), some oligopolists have cut prices. In some instances these price reductions have set off a **price war:** successive and continuous rounds of price cuts by rivals as they attempt to maintain their market shares.

Cartels and Other Collusion

Our game-theory model demonstrated that oligopolists might benefit from collusion. We can say that collusion occurs whenever firms in an industry reach an agreement to fix prices, divide up the market, or otherwise restrict competition among themselves. The disadvantages and uncertainties of noncollusive, kinked-demand oligopolies are obvious. There is always the danger of a price war breaking out, especially during a general business recession. Then each firm finds that, because of unsold goods and excess capacity, it can reduce per-unit costs by increasing market share. Then, too, a new firm may surmount entry barriers and initiate aggressive price cutting to gain a foothold in the market. In addition, the kinked-demand curve's tendency toward rigid prices may adversely affect profits if general inflationary pressures increase costs. However, by controlling price through collusion, oligopolists may be able to reduce uncertainty, increase profits, and perhaps even prohibit the entry of new rivals.

Price and Output Assume once again that there are three hypothetical oligopolistic firms (Gypsum, Sheetrock, and GSR) producing, in this instance, gypsum drywall panels for finishing interior walls. All three firms produce a homogeneous product and have identical cost curves. Each firm's demand curve is indeterminate unless we know how its rivals will react to any price change. Therefore, we suppose each firm assumes that its two rivals will match either a price cut or a price increase. In other words, each firm has a demand curve like the straight line D_1 in Figure 14.2a. And since they have identical cost data, and the same demand and thus marginal-revenue data, we can say that Figure 14.3 represents the position of each of our three oligopolistic firms.

What price and output combination should, say, Gypsum select? If Gypsum were a pure monopolist, the answer would be clear: Establish output at Q_0, where marginal revenue equals marginal cost, charge the corresponding price P_0, and enjoy the maximum profit attainable. However, Gypsum does have two rivals selling identical products, and if Gypsum's assumption that its rivals will match its price of P_0 proves to be incorrect, the consequences could be disastrous for Gypsum. Specifically, if Sheetrock and GSR actually charge prices below P_0, then Gypsum's demand curve D will shift sharply to the left as its potential customers turn to its rivals, which are now selling the same product at a lower price. Of course, Gypsum can retaliate by cutting its price too, but this will move all three firms down their demand curves, lowering their profits. It may even drive them to a point where average total cost exceeds price and losses are incurred.

FIGURE 14.3 Collusion and the tendency toward joint-profit maximization. If oligopolistic firms face identical or highly similar demand and cost conditions, they may collude to limit their joint output and to set a single, common price. Thus each firm acts as if it were a pure monopolist, setting output at Q_0 and charging price P_0. This price and output combination maximizes each oligopolist's profit (green area) and thus the combined or joint profit of the colluding firms.

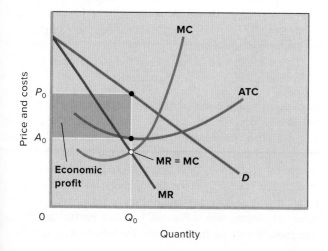

So the question becomes, "Will Sheetrock and GSR want to charge a price below P_0?" Under our assumptions, and recognizing that Gypsum has little choice except to match any price they may set below P_0, the answer is no. Faced with the same demand and cost circumstances, Sheetrock and GSR will find it in their interest to produce Q_0 and charge P_0. This is a curious situation; each firm finds it most profitable to charge the same price, P_0, but only if its rivals actually do so! How can the three firms ensure the price P_0 and quantity Q_0 solution in which each is keenly interested? How can they avoid the less profitable outcomes associated with either higher or lower prices?

The answer is evident: They can collude. They can get together, talk it over, and agree to charge the same price, P_0, and thereby enjoy the maximum profit available $[= (P_0 - A_0) \times Q_0$ units]. In addition to reducing the possibility of price wars, this will give each firm the maximum profit. (But it will also subject them to antitrust prosecution if they are caught!) For society, the result will be the same as would occur if the industry were a pure monopoly composed of three identical plants.

Overt Collusion: The OPEC Cartel Collusion may assume a variety of forms. The most comprehensive form of collusion is the **cartel,** a group of producers that typically creates a formal written agreement specifying how much each member will produce and charge. Output must be controlled—the market must be divided up—in order to maintain the agreed-upon price. The collusion is overt, or open to view.

Undoubtedly the most significant international cartel is the Organization of Petroleum Exporting Countries (OPEC), comprising 14 oil-producing nations (see Global Perspective 14.1). OPEC produces 34 percent of the world's oil and supplies 34 percent of all oil traded internationally.

OPEC has in some cases been able to drastically alter oil prices by increasing or decreasing supply. In 1973, for instance, it caused the price of oil to more than triple by getting its members to restrict output. And again, in the late 1990s it caused oil prices to rise from $11 per barrel to $34 per barrel over a 15-month period.

That being said, it should be kept in mind that most increases in the price of oil are not caused by OPEC. Between 2005 and 2008, for example, oil prices went from $40 per barrel to $140 per barrel due to rapidly rising demand from China and supply uncertainties related to armed conflict in the Middle East. But as the recession that began in December 2007 took hold, demand slumped and oil prices collapsed back down to about $40 per barrel. OPEC was largely a nonfactor in this rise and fall in the price of oil. But in those cases where OPEC can effectively enforce its production agreements, there is little doubt that it can hold the price of oil substantially above the marginal cost of production.

Covert Collusion: Examples Cartels are illegal in the United States, and hence any collusion that exists is covert or

GLOBAL PERSPECTIVE 14.1

The 14 OPEC Nations, Daily Oil Production, December 2015

The OPEC nations produce about 34 percent of the world's oil and about 34 percent of the oil sold in world markets.

OPEC Country	Barrels of Oil
Saudi Arabia	10,088,000
Iraq	4,309,000
UAE	2,895,000
Iran	2,882,000
Kuwait	2,708,000
Venezuela	2,348,000
Nigeria	1,789,000
Angola	1,751,000
Algeria	1,103,000
Indonesia	693,000
Qatar	674,000
Ecuador	551,000
Libya	394,000
Gabon	219,000

Source: OPEC, OPEC Monthly Oil Market Report, January 2016.

secret. Yet there are numerous examples, as shown by evidence from antitrust (antimonopoly) cases. In 2011, U.S.-based Whirlpool, Japan-headquartered Panasonic, the Danish firm Danfoss, and the Italian company Appliance Components were fined over $200 million for attempting to run an international cartel that could rig the worldwide prices of refrigerator compressors. In 2012, several Japanese autoparts makers pleaded guilty to rigging the bids that they submitted to a major carmaker. The conspirators employed measures to keep their conduct secret, including using code names and instructing participants to destroy evidence of collusion.

In many other instances collusion is much subtler. Unwritten, informal understandings (historically called "gentlemen's agreements") are frequently made at cocktail parties, on golf courses, through phone calls, or at trade association meetings. In such agreements, executives reach verbal or even tacit (unspoken) understandings on product price, leaving market shares to be decided by nonprice competition. Although these agreements, too, violate antitrust laws—and can result in severe personal and corporate penalties—the elusive character of informal understandings makes them more difficult to detect.

Obstacles to Collusion Normally, cartels and similar collusive arrangements are difficult to establish and maintain. Here are several barriers to collusion:

Demand and Cost Differences When oligopolists face different costs and demand curves, it is difficult for them to agree on a price. This is particularly the case in industries where products are differentiated and change frequently. Even with highly standardized products, firms usually have somewhat different market shares and operate with differing degrees of productive efficiency. Thus it is unlikely that even homogeneous oligopolists would have the same demand and cost curves.

In either case, differences in costs and demand mean that the profit-maximizing price will differ among firms; no single price will be readily acceptable to all, as we assumed was true in Figure 14.3. So price collusion depends on compromises and concessions that are not always easy to obtain and hence act as an obstacle to collusion.

Number of Firms Other things equal, the larger the number of firms, the more difficult it is to create a cartel or some other form of price collusion. Agreement on price by three or four producers that control an entire market may be relatively easy to accomplish. But such agreement is more difficult to achieve where there are, say, 10 firms, each with roughly 10 percent of the market, or where the Big Three have 70 percent of the market while a competitive fringe of 8 or 10 smaller firms battles for the remainder.

Cheating As the game-theory model makes clear, collusive oligopolists are tempted to engage in secret price cutting to increase sales and profit. The difficulty with such cheating is that buyers who are paying a high price for a product may become aware of the lower-priced sales and demand similar treatment. Or buyers receiving a price concession from one producer may use the concession as a wedge to get even larger price concessions from a rival producer. Buyers' attempts to play producers against one another may precipitate price wars among the producers. Although secret price concessions are potentially profitable, they threaten collusive oligopolies over time. Collusion is more likely to succeed when cheating is easy to detect and punish. Then the conspirators are less likely to cheat on the price agreement.

Recession Long-lasting recession usually serves as an enemy of collusion because slumping markets increase average total cost. In technical terms, as the oligopolists' demand and marginal-revenue curves shift to the left in Figure 14.3 in response to a recession, each firm moves leftward and upward to a higher operating point on its average-total-cost curve. Firms find they have substantial excess production capacity, sales are down, unit costs are up, and profits are being squeezed. Under such conditions, businesses may feel they can avoid serious profit reductions (or even losses) by cutting price and thus gaining sales at the expense of rivals.

Potential Entry The greater prices and profits that result from collusion may attract new entrants, including foreign firms. Since that would increase market supply and reduce prices and profits, successful collusion requires that colluding oligopolists block the entry of new producers.

Legal Obstacles: Antitrust Law U.S. antitrust laws prohibit cartels and price-fixing collusion. So less obvious means of price control have evolved in the United States.

Price Leadership Model

Price leadership entails a type of implicit understanding by which oligopolists can coordinate prices without engaging in outright collusion based on formal agreements and secret meetings. Rather, a practice evolves whereby the "dominant firm"—usually the largest or most efficient in the industry—initiates price changes and all other firms more or less automatically follow the leader. Many industries, including farm machinery, cement, copper, newsprint, glass containers, steel, beer, fertilizer, cigarettes, and tin, are practicing, or have in the recent past practiced, price leadership.

Leadership Tactics An examination of price leadership in a variety of industries suggests that the price leader is likely to observe the following tactics.

Infrequent Price Changes Because price changes always carry the risk that rivals will not follow the lead, price adjustments are made only infrequently. The price leader does not respond to minuscule day-to-day changes in costs and demand. Price is changed only when cost and demand conditions have been altered significantly and on an industrywide basis as the result of, for example, industrywide wage increases, an increase in excise taxes, or an increase in the price of some basic input such as energy. In the automobile industry, price adjustments traditionally have been made when new models are introduced each fall.

Communications The price leader often communicates impending price adjustments to the industry through speeches by major executives, trade publication interviews, or press releases. By publicizing "the need to raise prices," the price leader seeks agreement among its competitors regarding the actual increase.

Limit Pricing The price leader does not always choose the price that maximizes short-run profits for the industry because the industry may want to discourage new firms from entering. If the cost advantages (economies of scale) of existing firms are a major barrier to entry, new entrants could surmount that barrier if the price leader and the other firms set product price high enough. New firms that are relatively inefficient because of their small size might survive and grow if the industry sets price very high. So, in order to discourage new competitors and to maintain the current oligopolistic structure of the industry, the price leader may keep price below the short-run profit-maximizing level. The strategy of establishing a price that blocks the entry of new firms is called *limit pricing*.

Breakdowns in Price Leadership: Price Wars Price leadership in oligopoly occasionally breaks down, at least temporarily, and sometimes results in a price war. An example of price leadership temporarily breaking down occurred in the breakfast cereal industry, in which Kellogg traditionally had been the price leader. General Mills countered Kellogg's leadership in 1995 by reducing the prices of its cereals by 11 percent. In 1996 Post responded with a 20 percent price cut, which Kellogg then followed. Not to be outdone, Post reduced its prices by another 11 percent.

As another example, in October 2009 with the Christmas shopping season just getting under way, Walmart cut its price on 10 highly anticipated new books to just $10 each. Within hours, Amazon.com matched the price cut. Walmart then retaliated by cutting its price for the books to just $9 each. Amazon.com matched that reduction—at which point Walmart went to $8.99! Then, out of nowhere, Target jumped in at $8.98, a price that Amazon.com and Walmart immediately matched. And that is where the price finally came to rest—at a level so low that each company was losing money on each book it sold.

Most price wars eventually run their course. After a period of low or negative profits, they again yield price leadership to one of the industry's leading firms. That firm then begins to raise prices, and the other firms willingly follow suit.

> ## QUICK REVIEW 14.2
>
> ✓ In the kinked-demand theory of oligopoly, price is relatively inflexible because a firm contemplating a price change assumes that its rivals will follow a price cut and ignore a price increase.
>
> ✓ Cartels agree on production limits and set a common price to maximize the joint profit of their members as if each were a subsidiary of a single pure monopoly.
>
> ✓ Collusion among oligopolists is difficult because of (a) demand and cost differences among sellers, (b) the complexity of output coordination among producers, (c) the potential for cheating, (d) a tendency for agreements to break down during recessions, (e) the potential entry of new firms, and (f) antitrust laws.
>
> ✓ Price leadership involves an informal understanding among oligopolists to match any price change initiated by a designated firm (often the industry's dominant firm).

Oligopoly and Advertising

LO14.4 Contrast the potential positive and negative effects of advertising.

We have noted that oligopolists would rather not compete on the basis of price and may become involved in price collusion. Nonetheless, each firm's share of the total market is typically determined through product development and advertising, for two reasons:

- Product development and advertising campaigns are less easily duplicated than price cuts. Price cuts can be quickly and easily matched by a firm's rivals to cancel any potential gain in sales derived from that strategy. Product improvements and successful advertising, however, can produce more permanent gains in market share because they cannot be duplicated as quickly and completely as price reductions.

- Oligopolists have sufficient financial resources to engage in product development and advertising. For most oligopolists, the economic profits earned in the past can help finance current advertising and product development.

Product development (or, more broadly, "research and development") is the subject of Chapter 15, so we will confine our present discussion to advertising. In 2014, firms spent an estimated $141 billion on advertising in the United States and $539 billion worldwide. Advertising is prevalent in both monopolistic competition and oligopoly. Table 14.2 lists the 10 leading U.S. advertisers in 2014.

Advertising may affect prices, competition, and efficiency both positively and negatively, depending on the circumstances. While our focus here is on advertising by oligopolists, the analysis is equally applicable to advertising by monopolistic competitors.

TABLE 14.2 The Largest U.S. Advertisers, 2014

Company	Advertising Spending Millions of $
Procter & Gamble	$4,607
AT&T	3,272
General Motors	3,120
Comcast	3,029
Verizon	2,526
Ford Motor	2,467
American Express	2,364
Fiat Chrysler	2,250
L'Oréal	2,158
Walt Disney	2,109

Source: Advertising Age, **www.adage.com.**

Positive Effects of Advertising

In order to make rational (efficient) decisions, consumers need information about product characteristics and prices. Media advertising may be a low-cost means for consumers to obtain that information. Suppose you are in the market for a high-quality camera that is not advertised or promoted in newspapers, in magazines, or on the Internet. To make a rational choice, you may have to spend several days visiting stores to determine the availability, prices, and features of various brands. This search entails both direct costs (gasoline, parking fees) and indirect costs (the value of your time). By providing information about the available options, advertising and Internet promotion reduce your search time and minimize these direct and indirect costs.

By providing information about the various competing goods that are available, advertising diminishes monopoly power. In fact, advertising is frequently associated with the introduction of new products designed to compete with existing brands. Could Toyota and Honda have so strongly challenged U.S. auto producers without advertising? Could FedEx have sliced market share away from UPS and the U.S. Postal Service without advertising?

Viewed this way, advertising is an efficiency-enhancing activity. It is a relatively inexpensive means of providing useful information to consumers and thus lowering their search costs. By enhancing competition, advertising results in greater economic efficiency. By facilitating the introduction of new products, advertising speeds up technological progress. By increasing sales and output, advertising can reduce long-run average total cost by enabling firms to obtain economies of scale.

Potential Negative Effects of Advertising

Not all the effects of advertising are positive, of course. Much advertising is designed simply to manipulate or persuade consumers—that is, to alter their preferences in favor of the advertiser's product. A television commercial that indicates that a popular personality drinks a particular brand of soft drink—and therefore that you should too—conveys little or no information to consumers about price or quality. In addition, advertising is sometimes based on misleading and extravagant claims that confuse consumers rather than enlighten them. Indeed, in some cases advertising may well persuade consumers to pay high prices for much-acclaimed but inferior products, forgoing better but unadvertised products selling at lower prices. Example: *Consumer Reports* has found that heavily advertised premium motor oils provide no better engine performance and longevity than do cheaper brands.

Firms often establish substantial brand-name loyalty and thus achieve monopoly power via their advertising (see Global Perspective 14.2). As a consequence, they are able to increase their sales, expand their market shares, and enjoy greater profits. Larger profits permit still more advertising and further enlargement of the firm's market share and profit. In time, consumers may lose the advantages of competitive markets and face the disadvantages of monopolized markets. Moreover, new entrants to the industry need to incur large advertising costs in order to establish their products in the marketplace; thus, advertising costs may be a barrier to entry.

Advertising can also be self-canceling. The advertising campaign of one fast-food hamburger chain may be offset by equally costly campaigns waged by rivals, so each firm's demand actually remains unchanged. Few, if any, extra burgers will be purchased and each firm's market share will stay the same. But because of the advertising, all firms will experience higher costs and either their profits will fall or, through successful price leadership, their product prices will rise.

When advertising either leads to increased monopoly power or is self-canceling, economic inefficiency results.

Oligopoly and Efficiency

LO14.5 Discuss the efficiency of oligopoly from society's standpoint and whether it is more or less efficient than monopoly.

Is oligopoly, then, an efficient market structure from society's standpoint? How do the price and output decisions of the oligopolist measure up to the triple equality $P = MC = $ minimum ATC that occurs in pure competition?

Productive and Allocative Efficiency

Many economists believe that the outcome of some oligopolistic markets is approximately as shown in Figure 14.3. This view is bolstered by evidence that many oligopolists sustain sizable economic profits year after year. In that case, the oligopolist's production occurs where price exceeds marginal cost and average total cost. Moreover, production is below the output at which average total cost is minimized. In this view, neither productive efficiency ($P = $ minimum ATC) nor allocative efficiency ($P = MC$) is likely to occur under oligopoly.

A few observers assert that oligopoly is actually less desirable than pure monopoly because government usually regulates pure monopoly in the United States to guard against abuses of monopoly power. Informal collusion among oligopolists may yield price and output results similar to those under pure monopoly yet give the outward appearance of competition involving independent firms.

Qualifications

We should note, however, three qualifications to this view:

- ***Increased foreign competition*** In recent decades foreign competition has increased rivalry in a number of oligopolistic industries—steel, automobiles, video games, electric shavers, outboard motors, and copy machines, for example. This has helped to break down such cozy arrangements as price leadership and to stimulate much more competitive pricing.

- ***Limit pricing*** Recall that some oligopolists may purposely keep prices below the short-run profit-maximizing level in order to bolster entry barriers. In essence, consumers and society may get some of the benefits of competition—prices closer to marginal cost and minimum average total cost—even without the competition that free entry would provide.

- ***Technological advance*** Over time, oligopolistic industries may foster more rapid product development and greater improvement of production techniques than would be possible if they were purely competitive. Oligopolists have large economic profits from which they can fund expensive research and development (R&D). Moreover, the existence of barriers to entry may give the oligopolist some assurance that it will reap the rewards of successful R&D. Thus, the short-run economic inefficiencies of oligopolists may be partly or wholly offset by the oligopolists' contributions to better products, lower prices, and lower costs over time. We say more about these dynamic aspects of rivalry in Chapter 15.

Game Theory and Strategic Behavior

LO14.6 Utilize additional game-theory terminology and demonstrate how to find Nash equilibriums in both simultaneous and sequential games.

We have seen that game theory is helpful in explaining mutual interdependence and strategic behavior by oligopolists. This section provides additional oligopoly-based applications of game theory.

A One-Time Game: Strategies and Equilibrium

Consider Figure 14.4, which lists strategies and outcomes for two fictitious producers of the computer memory chips referred to as DRAMs (Dynamic Random Access Memory circuits). Chipco is the single producer of these chips in the United States and Dramco is the only producer in China. Each firm has two alternative strategies: an international strategy, in which it competes directly against the other firm in both countries; and a national strategy, in which it sells only in its home country.

The game and payoff matrix shown in Figure 14.4 is a **one-time game** because the firms select their optimal strategies in a single time period without regard to possible interactions in subsequent time periods. The game is also a **simultaneous game** because the firms choose their strategies at the same time; and a **positive-sum game,** a game in which the sum of the two firms' outcomes (here, profits) is positive. In contrast, the net gain in a **zero-sum game** is zero because one firm's gain must equal the other firm's loss, and the net gain in a **negative-sum game** is negative. In some positive-sum games, both firms may have positive outcomes. That is the case in Figure 14.4.

To determine optimal strategies, Chipco looks across the two rows in the payoff matrix (yellow portion of cells in millions of dollars) and Dramco looks down the two columns (blue portion of cells). These payoffs indicate that both firms

FIGURE 14.4 A one-time game. In this single-period, positive-sum game, Chipco's international strategy is its dominant strategy—the alternative that is superior to any other strategy regardless of whatever Dramco does. Similarly, Dramco's international strategy is also its dominant strategy. With both firms choosing international strategies, the outcome of the game is cell A, where each firm receives an $11 million profit. Cell A is a Nash equilibrium because neither firm will independently want to move away from it given the other firm's strategy.

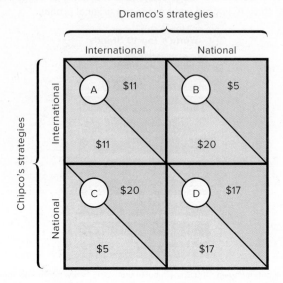

have a **dominant strategy**—an option that is better than any alternative option *regardless of what the other firm does.* To see this, notice that Chipco's international strategy will give it a higher profit than its national strategy—regardless of whether Dramco chooses to utilize an international or a national strategy. An international strategy will produce an $11 million profit for Chipco (yellow portion of cell A) if Dramco also uses an international strategy while a national strategy will result in a $20 million profit for Chipco (yellow portion of cell B) if Dramco uses a national strategy. Chipco's possible $11 million and $20 million outcomes are clearly better than the $5 million (cell C) and $17 million (cell D) outcomes it could receive if it chose to pursue a national strategy. Chipco's international strategy is, consequently, its dominant strategy. Using similar logic, Dramco also concludes that its international strategy is its dominant strategy.

In this particular case, the outcome (cell A) of the two dominant strategies is the game's **Nash equilibrium**—an outcome from which neither rival wants to deviate.[1] At the Nash equilibrium, both rivals see their current strategy as optimal *given the other firm's strategic choice.* The Nash equilibrium is the only outcome in the payoff matrix in Figure 14.4 that, once achieved, is stable and therefore will persist.[2]

---

[1]The Nash equilibrium is named for its discoverer, John F. Nash. Nash's life and Nobel Prize are the subject of the motion picture *A Beautiful Mind,* directed by Ron Howard and starring Russell Crowe.

[2]Nash equilibriums can exist even in games that lack dominant strategies.

Credible and Empty Threats

In looking for optimal strategies, Chipco and Dramco both note that they could increase their profit from $11 million to $17 million if they could agree to jointly pursue national strategies (cell D) instead of independently pursuing international strategies (cell A). Presumably the national strategies would leave the firms as pure monopolists in their domestic economies, with each able to set higher prices and obtain greater profits as a result. But if this territorial agreement were put in place, both firms would have an incentive to cheat on the agreement by secretly selling DRAMs in the other's country. That would temporarily move the game to either cell B or cell C. Once discovered, however, such cheating would undermine the territorial agreement and return the game to the Nash equilibrium (cell A).

Now let's add a new twist—a credible threat—to the game shown in Figure 14.4. A **credible threat** is a statement of coercion (a threat!) that is believable by the other firm. Suppose that Chipco is the lower-cost producer of DRAMs because of its superior technology. Also, suppose that Chipco approaches Dramco saying that Chipco intends to use its national strategy and expects Dramco to do the same. If Dramco decides against the national strategy or agrees to the strategy and then later cheats on the agreement, Chipco will immediately drop its price to an ultra-low level equal to its average total cost (ATC). Both firms know that Chipco's ATC price is below Dramco's ATC. Although Chipco will see its economic profit fall to zero, Dramco will suffer an economic loss and possibly go out of business.

If Chipco's threat is credible, the two firms represented in Figure 14.4 will abandon the Nash equilibrium (cell A) to deploy their national strategies and achieve highly profitable cell D. In game theory, credible threats such as this can help establish and maintain collusive agreements. A strong "enforcer" can help prevent cheating and maintain the group discipline needed for cartels, price-fixing conspiracies, and territorial understandings to successfully generate high profits.

But credible threats are difficult to achieve in the actual economy. For example, Dramco might rightly wonder why Chipco had not previously driven it out of business through an ultra-low price strategy. Is Chipco fearful of the U.S. antitrust authorities?

If Dramco does not wish to participate in the proposed scheme, it might counter Chipco's threat with its own: Forget that you ever talked to us and we will not take this illegal "offer" to the U.S. Justice Department. Dramco can make this threat because strict laws are in place against attempts to restrain trade through price-fixing and territorial agreements.

So Dramco may view Chipco's threat as simply an **empty threat**—a statement of coercion that is not believable by the threatened firm. If so, the Nash equilibrium will prevail, with both firms pursuing an international strategy.

Repeated Games and Reciprocity Strategies

The Chipco-Dramco game was a one-time game, but many strategic situations are repeated by the same oligopolists over and over again. For example, Coca-Cola and Pepsi are mutually interdependent on pricing, advertising, and product development year after year, decade after decade. The same is true for Boeing and Airbus, Walmart and Target, Toyota and General Motors, Budweiser and Miller, Nike and Adidas, and numerous other dominant pairs.

In a **repeated game**—a game that recurs more than once—the optimal strategy may be to cooperate and restrain oneself from competing as hard as possible so long as the other firm reciprocates by also not competing as hard as possible.[3] To see how this works, consider two hypothetical producers of soft drinks: 2Cool and ThirstQ. If ThirstQ competes hard with 2Cool in today's situation in which 2Cool would like ThirstQ to take things easy, 2Cool will most likely retaliate against ThirstQ in any subsequent situation where the circumstances are reversed. In contrast, if ThirstQ cooperates with 2Cool in game 1, ThirstQ can expect 2Cool to reciprocate in game 2 of their repeated interaction. Both firms know full well the negative long-run consequences of ever refusing to cooperate. So the cooperation continues, not only in game 2, but in games 3, 4, 5, and beyond.

Figure 14.5 shows two side-by-side payoff matrixes for the two games. In Figure 14.5a, 2Cool and ThirstQ face a situation in which 2Cool is introducing a new cola called Cool Cola and has two advertising options: a high promotional budget to introduce the new product and a normal advertising budget. ThirstQ has the same two options: a high promotional budget to try to counter 2Cool's product introduction and a normal advertising budget.

The analysis is now familiar to you. The dominant strategies for both firms in game 1 (Figure 14.5a) are their large promotional advertising budgets and the Nash equilibrium is cell A. Both firms could do better at cell D if each agreed to use normal advertising budgets. But 2Cool could do better still. It could achieve the $16 million of profit in cell B, but only if ThirstQ holds its advertising budget to its normal level during the introduction of Cool Cola.

ThirstQ might voluntarily do just that! It knows that game 2 (Figure 14.5b) is forthcoming in which it will be introducing its new product, Quench It. By leaving its advertising budget at its normal level during 2Cool's introduction of Cool Cola, and thereby sacrificing profit of $2 million (= $10 million in cell A − $8 million in cell B), ThirstQ can expect 2Cool to reciprocate in the subsequent game in which ThirstQ introduces Quench It.

Without formally colluding—and risking antitrust penalties—game 1 ends at cell B and repeated game 2 ends at

---

[3]We are assuming either an infinitely repeated game or a game of unknown time horizon. Games with a known ending date undermine reciprocity strategies.

FIGURE 14.5 A repeated game with reciprocity. (a) In the first payoff matrix, 2Cool introduces its new Cool Cola with a large promotional advertising budget, but its rival ThirstQ maintains its normal advertising budget even though it could counter 2Cool with a large advertising budget of its own and drive the outcome from cell B to cell A. ThirstQ forgoes this $2 million of extra profit because it knows that it will soon be introducing its own new product (Quench It). (b) In the second payoff matrix, ThirstQ introduces Quench It with a large promotional advertising budget. Cool2 reciprocates ThirstQ's earlier accommodation by not matching ThirstQ's promotional advertising budget and instead allowing the outcome of the repeated game to be cell C. The profit of both 2Cool and ThirstQ therefore is larger over the two periods than if each firm had aggressively countered each other's single-period strategy.

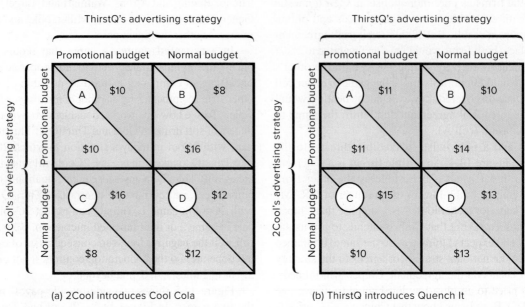

(a) 2Cool introduces Cool Cola

(b) ThirstQ introduces Quench It

cell C. With reciprocity, 2Cool's total profit of $26 million (= $16 million in game 1 + $10 million in game 2) exceeds the $21 million (= $10 million + $11 million) it would have earned without the reciprocity. ThirstQ similarly benefits. To check your understanding, confirm this fact using the numbers in the two matrixes.

First-Mover Advantages and Preemption of Entry

The games we have highlighted thus far have been games in which the two firms simultaneously select their optimal strategies. But in some actual economic circumstances, firms apply strategies sequentially: One firm moves first and commits to a strategy to which a rival firm must subsequently respond. In such a **sequential game,** the final outcome may depend critically upon which firm moves first since the first mover may have the opportunity to establish a Nash equilibrium that works in its favor.

Consider Figure 14.6, which identifies a game in which two large retailers—let's call them Big Box and Huge Box—are each considering building a large retail store in a small rural city. As indicated in the figure, each firm has two strategies: Build or Don't Build. The payoff matrix reflects the fact that the city is not large enough to support two big box retailers profitably. If

FIGURE 14.6 A first-mover advantage and the preemption of entry. In this game in which strategies are pursued sequentially, the firm that moves first can take advantage of the particular situation represented in which only a single firm can exist profitably in some geographical market. Here, we suppose that Big Box moves first with its "Build" strategy to achieve the $12 million profit outcome in cell C. Huge Box then will find that it will lose money if it also builds because that will result in a $5 million loss, as shown in cell A.

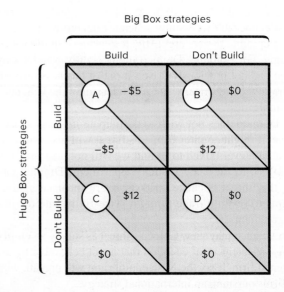

both retailers simultaneously build, the outcome will be cell A and each firm will lose $5 million. If neither firm builds, the outcome will be cell D with both firms securing zero profit. If only Big Box builds, the outcome will be cell C and Big Box will profit handsomely at $12 million. If Huge Box builds, but Big Box stays out, the outcome will be cell B and Huge Box will secure the $12 million profit. Either cell B or cell C is the possible Nash equilibrium. At either cell, both firms will have selected their best option in view of the strategy taken by the other firm.

The payoff matrix in Figure 14.6 clearly reveals that whoever builds first will preempt the other retailer from entering the market. An extremely large **first-mover advantage** exists in this particular game. Suppose that a well-thought-out strategy and adequate financing leave Big Box better prepared than Huge Box to move quickly to build a large retail store in this city. By exploiting its first-mover advantage, Big Box drives the outcome to Cell C and preempts Huge Box's entry into this market.

Many firms in the actual economy have used variations of this first-mover strategy to a greater or lesser extent to preempt major rivals, or at least greatly slow their entry. Examples are Walmart, Home Depot, Costco, Walgreens, Starbucks, and many more. The strategy, however, is highly risky because it requires the commitment of huge amounts of investment funds to saturate the market and preclude entry by other firms. Also, to be the first mover in places that are being transformed from rural land into urban areas, firms may need to build their stores many months prior to the time when the area in question becomes developed enough to provide the store with significant business. That may mean losses until the market grows sufficiently for profitability. Some firms such as Walmart have become huge, profitable international enterprises by using a first-mover strategy. Other firms, such as Krispy Kreme Donuts, have lost millions of dollars because their extremely rapid expansion turned out to be unprofitable in many of their outlets because the expected customers never materialized.

QUICK REVIEW 14.4

✓ Positive-sum, zero-sum, and negative-sum games have combined payoffs across all players that sum to, respectively, something positive, zero, and something negative. Positive-sum games correspond to "win-win" situations; zero-sum games to "I win-you lose" situations; and negative-sum games to "we both lose" situations.

✓ A dominant strategy for a firm in a two-firm game is a strategy that leads to better outcomes for the firm no matter what the other firm does.

✓ A Nash equilibrium occurs when both firms are simultaneously playing dominant strategies, so that neither firm has any incentive to alter its behavior.

✓ Reciprocity can improve outcomes in repeated games.

Extensive Form Representation of Sequential Games

Summarizing a game using a payoff matrix is referred to as displaying the game in strategic form because the rows and columns of the matrix represent each firm's strategy choices (such as Build or Don't Build in Figure 14.6). But sequential games can also be displayed in an alternative format called extensive form in which an extensive (spread out) "game tree" is used to display not only which strategy choices are available but the order in which decisions are made, starting with the first mover.

Figure 14.7 presents the extensive form representation of the first-mover game that was displayed in strategic form in Figure 14.6. As you will recall, Big Box (BB) gets to move first and then Huge Box (HB) gets to move second. There are three circular **decision nodes** labeled BB, HB_1, and HB_2. Decision node BB represents the two choices that Big Box must choose between as first mover. It can either choose Build or Don't Build. If it chooses Build, we follow the upsloping path from decision node BB. But if Big Box chooses Don't Build, we take the downsloping path from decision note BB.

The upsloping path leads to decision node HB_1 while the downsloping path leads to decision node HB_2. HB_1 represents the decision that Huge Box will have to face as second mover if Big Box has chosen Build in the first stage. HB_2 represents the choice that Huge Box will have to face as second mover if Big Box has chosen Don't Build in the first stage. In either case, Huge Box must choose either Build or Don't Build. Those choices lead to the **terminal nodes** A, C, B, and D, which correspond to the identically labeled cells in the strategic form representation shown in Figure 14.6.

Associated with each terminal node is a pair of numbers representing the profits that will be earned by each firm if the sequential decisions made by Big Box and Huge Box lead to that particular terminal node. The profits are presented as a pair of numbers in the format: (Big Box profit, Huge Box profit). As an example, the profits of the two firms at terminal node C are $12 million for Big Box and $0 for Huge Box.

In Figure 14.7, two segments of the game tree have been drawn bolder to make them stand out: the upsloping segment that begins at BB and the downsloping segment that begins at HB_1. The lines are bolded because they represent the Nash equilibrium of the game. The way you determine the Nash Equilibrium when a game is displayed in extensive form is by using a two-stage process called **backward induction** that first divides the overall game tree into nested "subgames" before working backwards from right to left—from the profits shown at each terminal node on the right to the preceding decisions that are necessary to end up at any particular terminal node.

To see how this works, notice that the upsloping and downsloping choices that emanate from decision node HB_1 form a **subgame** (or mini-game) within the overall game. Starting from HB_1, Huge Box can choose either Build or

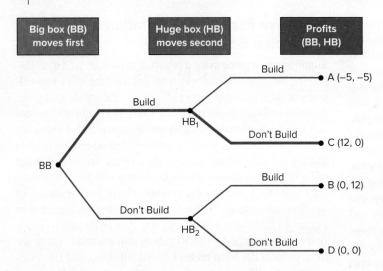

Here we display the game shown in Figure 14.6 in extensive form (game-tree format) rather than in strategic form (payoff-matrix format). The extensive form allows us to study the sequence in which decisions are made, moving from left to right. Big Box (BB) moves first at decision node BB. Its decision about Build or Don't Build will lead, respectively, to either decision node HB_1 or HB_2. Huge Box moves second from either HB_1 or HB_2 (depending upon what Big Box did at decision node BB). Huge Box's decision at HB_1 or HB_2 will lead to one of the four terminal nodes: A, C, B, and D (which correspond to the identically labeled cells in Figure 14.6). The bold line segments indicate the subgame perfect Nash equilibrium path that shows how the game will be played out if each company always does what is most profitable for itself given what it knows about the profit incentives facing its rival.

Don't Build. If we look at the payouts from those two choices, we see that Huge Box would prefer Don't Build so that it will receive a profit of $0 at terminal node C rather than a loss of −$5 million at terminal node A. So in the subgame that starts at decision node HB_1, Huge Box would prefer Don't Build. By contrast, in the subgame that starts at decision node HB_2, Huge box would prefer Build over Don't Build because choosing Build would lead to a profit of $12 million while choosing Don't Build would lead to a profit of $0.

We now know that if Huge Box ends up at decision node HB_1 it will choose Don't Build, so that the overall game will end at terminal node C. We also know that if Huge Box ends up at decision node HB_2 it will choose Build, thus forcing the overall game to end up at terminal node B. Those facts will be known perfectly well not only to us but to the managers of Big Box, too. So when Big Box makes its choice as the first mover at decision node BB, it will know that choosing Build will definitely lead to terminal node C because Huge Box will definitely choose Don't Build if it finds itself at decision node HB_1. Big Box will also understand that if it chooses Don't Build at decision node BB, the game will end up at terminal node B because Huge Box will definitely choose Build if it finds itself at decision node HB_2.

Thus, from Big Box's perspective, choosing Build will lead to the profits associated with C while choosing Don't Build will lead to the profits associated with B. Thus, Big Box's optimal decision at decision node BB comes down to seeing whether it will profit more highly at C than at B. If we compare Big Box's profits at C and B, we find that Big Box would prefer to end up at C rather than B because its profit at C would be $12 million while its profit at B would be $0. As a result, Big Box will choose Build at decision node BB. That choice leads upward to decision node HB_1, where Huge Box will definitely choose Don't Build. And that decision, in turn, will lead to both firms receiving the profits associated with terminal node C.

The two bold segments of the game tree show the path that results from those sequential decisions. It is a Nash

equilibrium from which neither party has an incentive to deviate because by working backward from right to left through each of the subgames we have made sure that both firms will be making rational (profit-maximizing) choices at every decision node. Thus, when the game is played out in proper sequence from left to right, neither firm will want to deviate from the decisions indicated by the bold path. Economists sometimes refer to the bold path as the **subgame perfect Nash equilibrium** because the process of backward induction used to find the bold path relies on both firms having perfect information about (i.e., a complete understanding of) the decisions that will be made in each subgame.

Note that the subgame perfect Nash equilibrium path shown in Figure 14.7 implies the same outcome with regard to preemption of entry as we discovered when we studied the same game in strategic form in Figure 14.6. Along the bold equilibrium path, Big Box will choose Build as first mover and Huge Box will chose Don't Build as second mover. As a result, Big Box will be able to preempt Huge Box from entering the local market.

A Leader-Follower (Stackelberg Duopoly) Game

Extensive form representation and backward induction can also be used to solve for situations in which a leader (first mover) firm cannot preempt a follower firm from entering its industry. The subgame perfect Nash equilibrium involves both firms entering the industry and producing positive levels of output.

As an example, let us consider a duopoloy (two-firm) automobile manufacturing industry in which both firms have to make sequential decisions about factory size and output levels. In other duopoly models, both firms move simultaneously. But in this section we are assuming a Stackelberg duopoly model in which the two competitors move sequentially.

In this sequential model, an established truck maker that has political connections will get to move first and decide how big a factory it will build. Its rival will then move second and determine how big its factory will be. Both firms are aware that the more the two firms produce and supply in total, the lower will be the market price of trucks. So there is a trade-off between building higher-capacity factories on the one hand and getting less revenue per truck on the other hand.

In this strategic situation, the leader firm's choice of factory size must attempt to rationally anticipate what the follower firm's factory-size choice will be. As an example, if the leader firm anticipates that the follower firm will end up building a huge factory, the leader firm may want to build a small factory to keep total output low enough that the market price of trucks does not collapse.

In Figure 14.8, the leader firm chooses first, at decision node L. Its choices are to either set up a smaller factory that can produce 5,000 trucks per year or a larger factory that can produce 10,000 trucks per year. If the leader firm chooses the smaller factory, the upward sloping option will lead to decision node F_1, where the follower firm can either choose to set up a factory that will produce 7,000 trucks per year or a factory that can produce 12,000 trucks per year. Note that when starting at decision node F_1, both of the follower firm's factory-size options will produce more vehicles per year than the 5,000 trucks per year that the leader firm would have had to have chosen at decision node L to have moved the game to decision node F_1. This reflects the fact that the follower firm would take the leader firm's decision to produce only 5,000 cars per year as an opportunity to become the larger player in the two-firm industry. The only question for the follower firm at decision node F_1 is to decide on how much larger it will want its output of trucks to be.

By contrast, if the leader firm chooses to build the larger factory at decision node L, the game will follow the downsloping path to decision node F_2, where the follower firm can either choose to set up a factory that will produce 5,000 cars per year or a factory that will produce 7,000 cars

per year. In this case, the follower firm is resigned to being the smaller firm in the industry, since both options will produce fewer cars per year than the 10,000 that the leader would have had to have chosen for the game to have ended up at decision node F_2.

We can now use subgames and backward induction to solve for the subgame perfect Nash equilibrium, which is indicated in Figure 14.8 by the bold segments of the game tree. As before, we solve the game tree backward, from right to left. Consider first the subgame that begins at decision node F_1. There, the follower firm will want to choose to produce 7,000 cars per year because the $210 million profit it would obtain from doing so will be nearly double the $120 million profit it would obtain if it chose to produce 12,000 cars per year. Next, consider the subgame that begins at decision node F_2. There, the follower firm will want to produce 7,000 cars per year rather than 5,000 cars per year because the former will generate a profit of $140 million per year while the latter would generate a profit of only $50 million per year.

The leader firm can now take into account at decision node L how the follower firm will behave if the game ends up at either decision node F_1 or decision node F_2. If the leader firm chooses to produce 5,000 cars per year at decision node L, the follower firm will choose to produce 7,000 cars at decision node F_1, thereby leading to terminal node A and a payoff of $150 million for the leader firm. By contrast, if the leader firm chooses to produce 10,000 cars per year at decision node L, the follower firm will choose to produce 7,000 cars per year at decision node F_2, thereby leading to terminal node D and a payoff of $200 million for the leader firm.

The leader firm can see that it would be better off ending up at terminal node D rather than at terminal node A. It will consequently choose to build a factory that can produce 10,000 cars per year. The subgame perfect Nash equilibrium therefore consists of the line segment that leads downward from decision node L followed by the line segment that leads

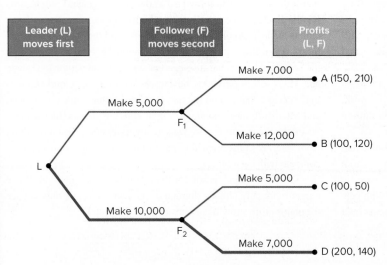

FIGURE 14.8 **Extensive form representation of leader-follower (Stackelberg duopoly) game.** There is a Leader firm and a Follower firm that sequentially must decide on their respective factory sizes. The Leader firm moves first at decision node L. The Follower firm moves second, starting from either decision node F_1 or decision node F_2 (depending on the Leader firm's decision at decision node L). Each firm wishes to make as much money as possible, but knows that there is a trade-off between producing more cars and reducing the market price per vehicle. Moving from right to left, backward induction indicates that the subgame perfect Nash equilibrium corresponds to the path indicated by the bold line segments.

LAST WORD

Internet Oligopolies

A Few Big Companies Dominate the Internet—and Act as Highly Competitive Oligopolists.

The Internet only became accessible to the average person in the mid-1990s. Over the past 10 years, it has evolved into a medium dominated by a few major firms. Chief among them are Google, Facebook, and Amazon. Other major players include Microsoft and Apple.

A key characteristic of each of these firms is that it holds a near-monopoly in a particular part of the tech business. Google dominates search. Facebook holds sway in social networking. Amazon rules the roost in online shopping. Microsoft holds a near-monopoly on PC operating systems and business-productivity software. And Apple became the world's most valuable company in 2012 by way of being the planet's most profitable manufacturer of computers, mobile phones, and tablets—all of which run on Apple's own operating software.

But instead of just trying to maintain dominance in its own sector, each of these Internet titans has used the profits generated by its own near-monopoly to try to steal business from one or more of the other titans. The result has been intense oligopolistic competition between a few well-funded rivals.

Source: © Anatolii Babii/Alamy Stock Photo

Consider search. Google's 64 percent share of the search market creates massive amounts of advertising revenue for Google. In fact, Google's 2015 ad revenues of $16 billion exceeded the ad revenues received by all U.S. magazines and newspapers combined. So it may not be surprising that Microsoft created its Bing search engine to compete with Google. As of late 2015, Bing held 21 percent of the search market. Along with Yahoo, which held 13 percent, Bing maintains competitive pressure on Google, forcing ad rates lower.

Facebook is by far the largest social networking website, with more than 1.8 billion regular users. But in 2011, Google succeeded in creating a large enough social network to challenge Facebook. Google did so by encouraging the users of its various free services—such as Gmail and YouTube—to join the Google+ social network. By late 2012, Google+ had 500 million total users and 235 million regular users—enough to compete credibly with Facebook.

Google+ was important for Google because Facebook had been encouraging advertisers to switch from using Google search ads to using Facebook banner ads that could be targeted at specific types of Facebook users (such as, "25–30-year-old males with pets living in Pittsburgh"). Google can now counter by offering its own social network on which advertisers can place those sorts of targeted ads.

Google has also challenged Apple by releasing its very popular Android operating system for mobile devices to compete with the iOS operating system that Apple uses on both its iPhone cell phones and its iPad tablet computers. By doing so, Google reduced the threat that Apple could at some point in the future substantially reduce Google's search revenues by directing searches done on Apple devices to a proprietary search engine of Apple's own design.

Apple's dominance in smartphones and tablets has also been challenged by some of the other Internet titans. In addition to licensing the Android operating system to any manufacturer who wants to use it on their own cell phones or tablets, Google launched its own line of Nexus mobile devices to compete with Apple's iPhone and iPad. Also seeking to challenge Apple in mobile devices, Microsoft updated its Windows operating system to handle phones and tablets, launched its Surface line of tablets to compete with the iPad, and attempted to compete with the iPhone by marketing its own Windows Phone as well as by purchasing long-time cell-phone maker Nokia.

Microsoft's fundamental problem is that smartphone and tablet sales are rising rapidly while PC sales are falling quickly. So unless Microsoft can generate revenues from smartphones, tablets, or search, it will suffer an inexorable decline as the PC sector continues to shrink.

Amazon has also made forays outside of the online retail sector that it dominates. The foray best known to the general public is its Kindle line of tablet computers, which compete directly with the tablets made by Apple, Google, Microsoft, and the various manufacturers that utilize Google's Android operating system. But behind the scenes, Amazon has also become a major competitor to Google and Microsoft in providing businesses with online "cloud computing" services that run on the massive servers that Amazon, Google, and Microsoft must maintain for their core businesses (like search). So in cloud computing, too, we see oligopoly competition resulting from Internet titans branching out of their own dominant sectors to compete with each other.

There's a simple reason for their aggressive competition. When a near-monopoly already dominates its own sector, its only chance for major profit growth is to invade a rival's sector.

downward from decision node F_2. Along that path, neither firm has any reason to change its behavior given the perfect (complete) knowledge it possesses about both its own incentives and those of the other firm.

Note that there is no preemption of entry in this game. Both firms produce, but at different levels of output. The leader firm produces more and the follower firm produces less. This intuition can be generalized from duopoly industries with just two firms to oligopoly industries with several firms. The leader goes first but the profit possibilities at the various terminal nodes imply a subgame perfect Nash equilibrium in which additional firms enter the industry as followers. The followers produce less than the leader but are still able to survive and carry on. Examples include microchips, where Intel was the leader and several other firms such as AMD became followers, and smartphones, where Apple was the leader and several other firms such as Samsung, LG, and Google became followers.

Please note, however, that once entry has occurred and competition is possible, it may be the case that one or more of the follower firms may come to dominate the industry, pushing aside the leader firm that once held sway. This happened with televisions. Early leaders such as Sylvania got pushed aside in the 1980s by Japanese brands such as Sony before Korean brands such as Samsung came to dominate in the 2000s.

SUMMARY

LO14.1 Describe the characteristics of oligopoly.

Oligopolistic industries are characterized by the presence of few firms, each having a significant fraction of the market. Firms thus situated engage in strategic behavior and are mutually interdependent: The behavior of any one firm directly affects, and is affected by, the actions of rivals. Products may be either virtually uniform or significantly differentiated. Various barriers to entry, including economies of scale, underlie and maintain oligopoly.

High concentration ratios are an indication of oligopoly (monopoly) power. By giving more weight to larger firms, the Herfindahl index is designed to measure market dominance in an industry.

LO14.2 Discuss how game theory relates to oligopoly.

Game theory (a) shows the interdependence of oligopolists' pricing policies, (b) reveals the tendency of oligopolists to collude, and (c) explains the temptation of oligopolists to cheat on collusive arrangements.

LO14.3 Explain the three main models of oligopoly pricing and output: kinked-demand theory, collusive pricing, and price leadership.

Noncollusive oligopolists may face a kinked-demand curve. This curve and the accompanying marginal-revenue curve help explain the price rigidity that often characterizes oligopolies; they do not, however, explain how the actual prices of products were first established.

The uncertainties inherent in oligopoly promote collusion. Collusive oligopolists such as cartels maximize joint profits—that is, they behave like pure monopolists. Demand and cost differences, a "large" number of firms, cheating through secret price concessions, recessions, and the antitrust laws are all obstacles to collusive oligopoly.

Price leadership is an informal means of collusion whereby one firm, usually the largest or most efficient, initiates price changes and the other firms in the industry follow the leader.

LO14.4 Contrast the potential positive and negative effects of advertising.

Market shares in oligopolistic industries are usually determined on the basis of product development and advertising. Oligopolists emphasize nonprice competition because (a) advertising and product variations are less easy for rivals to match and (b) oligopolists frequently have ample resources to finance nonprice competition.

Advertising may affect prices, competition, and efficiency either positively or negatively. Positive: It can provide consumers with low-cost information about competing products, help introduce new competing products into concentrated industries, and generally reduce monopoly power and its attendant inefficiencies. Negative: It can promote monopoly power via persuasion and the creation of entry barriers. Moreover, it can be self-canceling when engaged in by rivals; then it boosts costs and creates inefficiency while accomplishing little else.

LO14.5 Discuss the efficiency of oligopoly from society's standpoint and whether it is more or less efficient than monopoly.

Neither productive nor allocative efficiency is realized in oligopolistic markets, but oligopoly may be superior to pure competition in promoting research and development and technological progress.

Table 10.1 provides a concise review of the characteristics of monopolistic competition and oligopoly as they compare to those of pure competition and pure monopoly.

LO14.6 Utilize additional game-theory terminology and demonstrate how to find Nash equilibriums in both simultaneous and sequential games.

Positive-sum games are games in which the payoffs to the firms sum to a positive number; zero-sum games are games in which the payoffs sum to zero; and negative-sum games are games in which the payoffs sum to less than zero. Positive-sum games allow for "win-win" opportunities, whereas zero-sum games always feature "I win–you lose" outcomes. Games can be either one-time games or repeated games. Decisions in games may be made either simultaneously or sequentially.

When two firms are playing a strategic game, a firm is said to have a dominant strategy if there is an option that leads to better outcomes for the firm no matter what the other firm does. Not all games have dominant strategies. The Nash equilibrium is an outcome from which neither firm wants to deviate because both firms see their current strategy as optimal given the other firm's chosen strategy. The Nash equilibrium is stable and persistent. Attempts by the firms to rig games to achieve some other outcome are difficult to accomplish and maintain, although credible threats can sometimes work. In contrast, empty threats accomplish nothing and leave the outcome at the Nash equilibrium.

Reciprocity can improve outcomes for firms participating in repeated games. In such games, one firm avoids taking advantage of the other firm because it knows that the other firm can take

advantage of it in subsequent games. This reciprocity increases firm profits relative to what they would have been without reciprocity.

Two possible Nash equilibriums can exist in sequential games with first-mover advantages. Which one occurs depends on which firm moves first since that firm can preempt the other firm, making it unprofitable for the other firm to match the choice made by the firm that moves first. Several real-world firms, including Walmart, have successfully used first-mover advantages to saturate markets and preempt entry by rivals.

Sequential games can be represented as game trees in extensive form. In extensive form, the order of decisions made by players is displayed in sequence from left to right. The game can be solved for a subgame perfect Nash equilibrium by using backward induction to examine each of the overall game's nested subgames from right to left.

TERMS AND CONCEPTS

oligopoly	price war	credible threat
homogeneous oligopoly	cartel	empty threat
differentiated oligopoly	price leadership	repeated game
strategic behavior	one-time game	sequential game
mutual interdependence	simultaneous game	first-mover advantage
interindustry competition	positive-sum game	decision node
import competition	zero-sum game	terminal node
game theory	negative-sum game	backward induction
collusion	dominant strategy	subgame
kinked-demand curve	Nash equilibrium	subgame perfect Nash equilibrium

The following and additional problems can be found in **connect**

DISCUSSION QUESTIONS

1. Why do oligopolies exist? List five or six oligopolists whose products you own or regularly purchase. What distinguishes oligopoly from monopolistic competition? **LO14.1**
2. Answer the following questions, which relate to measures of concentration: **LO14.1**
   a. What is the meaning of a four-firm concentration ratio of 60 percent? 90 percent? What are the shortcomings of concentration ratios as measures of monopoly power?
   b. Suppose that the five firms in industry A have annual sales of 30, 30, 20, 10, and 10 percent of total industry sales. For

the five firms in industry B, the figures are 60, 25, 5, 5, and 5 percent. Calculate the Herfindahl index for each industry and compare their likely competitiveness.

3. Explain the general meaning of the profit payoff matrix below for oligopolists X and Y. All profit figures are in thousands. **LO14.2**
   a. Use the payoff matrix to explain the mutual interdependence that characterizes oligopolistic industries.
   b. Assuming no collusion between X and Y, what is the likely pricing outcome?

c. In view of your answer to 3b, explain why price collusion is mutually profitable. Why might there be a temptation to cheat on the collusive agreement?

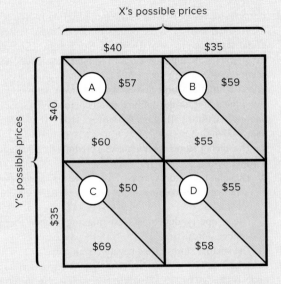

X's possible prices

Y's possible prices

4. What assumptions about a rival's response to price changes underlie the kinked-demand curve for oligopolists? Why is there a gap in the oligopolist's marginal-revenue curve? How does the kinked-demand curve explain price rigidity in oligopoly? What are the shortcomings of the kinked-demand model? **LO14.3**

5. Why might price collusion occur in oligopolistic industries? Assess the economic desirability of collusive pricing. What are the main obstacles to collusion? Speculate as to why price leadership is legal in the United States, whereas price-fixing is not. **LO14.3**

6. Why is there so much advertising in monopolistic competition and oligopoly? How does such advertising help consumers and promote efficiency? Why might it be excessive at times? **LO14.4**

7. **ADVANCED ANALYSIS** Construct a strategic form payoff matrix involving two firms and their decisions on high versus low advertising budgets and the effects of each on profits. Show a circumstance in which both firms select high advertising budgets even though both would be more profitable with low advertising budgets. Why won't they unilaterally cut their advertising budgets? **LO14.4**

8. Is the game shown by Figure 14.1 a zero-sum game or is it a positive-sum game? How can you tell? Are there dominant strategies in this game? If so, what are they? What cell represents a Nash equilibrium and why? Explain why it is so difficult for Uptown and RareAir to achieve and maintain a more favorable cell than the Nash equilibrium in this single-period pricing game. **LO14.6**

9. Refer to the payoff matrix in discussion question 3. First, assume this is a one-time game. Explain how the $60/$57 outcome might be achieved through a credible threat.

Next, assume this is a repeated game (rather than a one-time game) and that the interaction between the two firms occurs indefinitely. Why might collusion with a credible threat not be necessary to achieve the $60/$57 outcome? **LO14.6**

10. Refer to the following payoff matrix. **LO14.6**

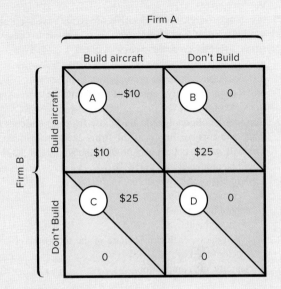

Firm A

Firm B

Assuming this is a sequential game with no collusion, what is the outcome if Firm A moves first to build a new type of commercial aircraft? Explain why first-mover strategies in the real world are only as good as the profit projections on which they are based. How could a supposed "win" from moving first turn out to be a big loss, whereas the "loss" of being preempted turn out to be a blessing in disguise?

11. **ADVANCED ANALYSIS** Suppose you are playing a game in which you and one other person each picks a number between 1 and 100, with the person closest to some randomly selected number between 1 and 100 winning the jackpot. (Ask your instructor to fund the jackpot.) Your opponent picks first. What number do you expect her to choose? Why? What number would you then pick? Why are the two numbers so close? How might this example relate to why Home Depot and Lowes, Walgreens and Rite-Aid, McDonald's and Burger King, and other major pairs of rivals locate so close to each other in many well-defined geographical markets that are large enough for both firms to be profitable? **LO14.6**

12. Are the subgames of a sequential game visible when the entire game is presented in strategic form? Explain. **LO14.6**

13. Can backward induction be readily applied when a sequential game is presented as a payoff matrix? Discuss. **LO14.6**

14. **LAST WORD** Why have tech firms with near monopolies in their own sectors sought to compete with tech firms that have extremely strong, near-monopoly positions in other sectors?

REVIEW QUESTIONS

1. Which of the following apply to oligopoly industries? Select one or more answers from the choices shown. **LO14.1**
   a. A few large producers.
   b. Many small producers.
   c. Strategic behavior.
   d. Price taking.

2. Faceblock, Gargle+, and SnapHat are rival firms in an oligopoly industry. If kinked-demand theory applies to these three firms, Faceblock's demand curve will be: **LO14.3**
   a. More elastic above the current price than below it.
   b. Less elastic above the current price than below it.
   c. Of equal elasticity both above and below the current price.
   d. None of the above.

3. Consider an oligopoly industry whose firms have identical demand and cost conditions. If the firms decide to collude, then they will want to collectively produce the amount of output that would be produced by: **LO14.3**
   a. A monopolistic competitor.
   b. A pure competitor.
   c. A pure monopolist.
   d. None of the above.

4. In an oligopoly, each firm's share of the total market is typically determined by: **LO14.4**
   a. Scarcity and competition.
   b. Kinked-demand curves and payoff matrices.
   c. Homogeneous products and import competition.
   d. Product development and advertising.

5. Some analysts consider oligopolies to be potentially less efficient than monopoly firms because at least monopoly firms tend to be regulated. Arguments in favor of a more benign view of oligopolies include: **LO14.5**
   a. Oligopolies are self-regulating.
   b. Oligopolies can be kept in line by foreign competition.
   c. Oligopolistic industries may promote technological progress.
   d. Oligopolies may engage in limit pricing to keep out potential entrants.

6. Collusive agreements can be established and maintained by: **LO14.6**
   a. Credible threats.   c. Empty threats.
   b. One-time games.   d. First-mover advantage.

7. True or false. Potential rivals may be more likely to collude if they view themselves as playing a repeated game rather than a one-time game. **LO14.6**

8. Property developers who build shopping malls like to have them "anchored" with the outlets of one or more famous national retail chains, like Target or Nordstrom. Having such "anchors" is obviously good for the mall developers because anchor stores bring a lot of foot traffic that can help generate sales for smaller stores that lack well-known national brands. But what's in it for the national retail chains? Why become an anchor? Choose the best answer from the following list. **LO14.6**
   a. The anchor stores want to make a credible threat against the developer.
   b. The anchor stores may feel there is a first-mover advantage to becoming one of only a few anchor stores at a new mall.
   c. The property developers are making empty threats to smaller stores.
   d. The smaller stores face a negative-sum game.

9. Look back at Figure 14.7. Suppose that the payouts at terminal node B change to (13,12) while everything else in the game stays the same. The new subgame perfect Nash equilibrium will consist of the two line segments: **LO14.6**
   a. Build at BB followed by Build at HB_1.
   b. Build at BB followed by Don't Build at HB_1.
   c. Don't Build at BB followed by Build at HB_2.
   d. Don't Build at BB followed by Don't Build at HB_2.

10. Look back at Figure 14.8. Suppose that the two firms switch places—the firm that was the follower now gets to go first while the firm that was the leader now has to go second. The new subgame perfect Nash equilibrium will lead to terminal node: **LO14.6**
    a. A.
    b. B.
    c. C.
    d. D.

PROBLEMS

1. Consider a "punishment" variation of the two-firm oligopoly situation shown in Figure 14.1. Suppose that if one firm sets a low price while the other sets a high price, then the firm setting the high price can fine the firm setting the low price. Suppose that whenever a fine is imposed, X dollars is taken from the low-price firm and given to the high-price firm. What is the smallest amount that the fine X can be such that both firms will want to always set the high price? **LO14.6**

2. Consider whether the promises and threats made toward each other by duopolists and oligopolists are always credible (believable). Look back at Figure 14.1. Imagine that the two

firms will play this game twice in sequence and that each firm claims the following policy. Each says that if both it and the other firm choose the high price in the first game, then it will also choose the high price in the second game (as a reward to the other firm for cooperating in the first game). **LO14.6**
   a. As a first step toward thinking about whether this policy is credible, consider the situation facing both firms in the second game. If each firm bases its decision on what to do in the second game entirely on the payoffs facing the firms in the second game, which strategy will each firm choose in the second game?

b. Now move backward in time one step. Imagine that it is the start of the first game and each firm must decide what to do during the first game. Given your answer to 2a, is the publicly stated policy credible? (Hint: No matter what happens in the first game, what will both firms do in the second game?)

c. Given your answers to 2a and 2b, what strategy will each firm choose in the first game?

3. Examine the following game tree. Fred and Sally are planning on running competing restaurants. Each must decide whether to rent space or buy space. Fred goes first at decision node F. Sally goes second at either decision node S_1 or decision node S_2 (depending on what Fred chose to do at decision node F). Note that the payoff to Sally at terminal node A is X. **LO14.6**

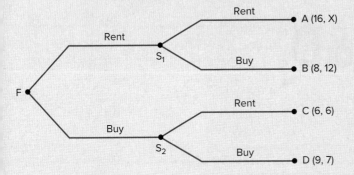

a. If X < 12, what terminal node will the subgame perfect Nash equilibrium path lead to?

b. If X > 12, what terminal node will the subgame perfect Nash Equilibrium path lead to?

c. Suppose that X = 11 and that it is now possible for Fred to make a side payment of value V to Sally that will boost her payout at terminal node A from X = 11 to X = 11 + V. What is the minimum amount that V can be such that the subgame perfect Nash equilibrium path will lead to terminal node A? Assume that V can take on only discrete units (0, 1, 2, 3,...).

Technology, R&D, and Efficiency

Learning Objectives

LO15.1 Differentiate among invention, innovation, and technological diffusion.

LO15.2 Explain how entrepreneurs and other innovators further technological advance.

LO15.3 Summarize how a firm determines its optimal amount of research and development (R&D).

LO15.4 Discuss how technological change can increase profits by raising revenues or lowering costs.

LO15.5 Relate why firms can benefit from their innovation even though rivals have an incentive to imitate it.

LO15.6 Discuss the role of market structure in promoting technological advance.

LO15.7 Show how technological advance enhances productive efficiency and allocative efficiency.

- "Just Do It." In 1968 two entrepreneurs from Oregon developed a lightweight sport shoe and formed a new company called Nike, incorporating a "swoosh" logo (designed by a graduate student for $35). Today, Nike sells $24 billion worth of goods annually.

- "Leap Ahead." In 1967 neither Intel nor its product existed. Today it is the world's largest producer of microprocessors for personal computers, with about $54 billion of annual sales.

- "Save money, live better." Expanding from a single store in 1962 to about 7,000 stores worldwide today, Walmart's annual revenue ($444 billion) exceeds that of General Motors or IBM.

Nike, Intel, and Walmart owe much of their success to **technological advance,** broadly defined as new and better goods and services or new and better ways of producing or distributing them. Nike and Intel pioneered innovative new products, and Walmart developed creative ways to manage inventories and distribute goods.

Multiply these examples—perhaps on a smaller scale—by thousands in the economy! The pursuit of technological advance is a major competitive activity among firms. In this chapter, we examine some of the microeconomics of that activity.

Invention, Innovation, and Diffusion

LO15.1 Differentiate among invention, innovation, and technological diffusion.

For economists, technological advance occurs over a theoretical time period called the *very long run,* which can be as short as a few months or as long as many years. Compare the concept of the very long run with the two shorter-duration time concepts that we developed while discussing our four market models (pure competition, monopolistic competition, oligopoly, and pure monopoly). In the short run, technology and plant and equipment are fixed. In the long run, technology is constant but firms can change their plant sizes and are free to enter or exit industries. In contrast, the **very long run** is a period in which technology can change and in which firms can develop and offer entirely new products.

In Chapter 1 we saw that technological advance shifts an economy's production possibilities curve outward, enabling the economy to obtain more goods and services. Technological advance is a three-step process of invention, innovation, and diffusion.

Invention

The basis of technological advance is **invention:** the conception of a new product or process combined with the first proof that it will work. Invention is a process of imagination, ingenious thinking, and experimentation. The result of the process is called *an* invention. The prototypes (basic working models) of the telephone, the automobile, and the microchip were inventions.

Invention usually is based on scientific knowledge and is the product of individuals, working either on their own or as members of corporate research and development (R&D) teams. Later on you will see how governments encourage invention by providing the inventor with a **patent,** an exclusive right to sell any new and useful process, machine, or product for a set period of time. In 2015, the top 10 firms in terms of securing the most U.S. patents were IBM (7,355), Samsung (5,072), Canon (4,134), Qualcomm (2,900), Google (2,835), Toshiba (2,627), Sony (2,455), LG (2,242), Intel (2,048), and Microsoft (1,956). Numbers like these, of course, do not reveal the quality of the patents received; some patents are much more significant than other patents. Patents have a worldwide duration of 20 years from the time of application for the patent.

Innovation

Innovation draws directly on invention. While invention is the discovery and first proof of workability, **innovation** is the first successful commercial introduction of a new product, the first use of a new method, or the creation of a new form of business enterprise. Innovation is of two types: **product innovation,** which refers to new and improved products or services; and **process innovation,** which refers to new and improved methods of production or distribution.

Unlike inventions, innovations cannot be patented. Nevertheless, innovation is a major factor in competition, since it sometimes enables a firm to leapfrog competitors by rendering their products or processes obsolete. For example, personal computers coupled with software for word processing pushed some major typewriter manufacturers into obscurity. More recently, innovations in hardware retailing (by large warehouse stores such as Home Depot and Lowe's) have threatened the existence of smaller, more traditional hardware stores.

But innovation need not weaken or destroy existing firms. Aware that new products and processes may threaten their survival, existing firms have a powerful incentive to engage continuously in R&D of their own. Innovative products and processes often enable such firms to maintain or increase their profits. The introduction of disposable contact lenses by Johnson & Johnson, scientific calculators by Hewlett-Packard, and iPhones by Apple are good examples. Thus, innovation can either diminish or strengthen market power.

Diffusion

Diffusion is the spread of an innovation to other products or processes through imitation or copying. To take advantage of new profit opportunities or to slow the erosion of profit, both new and existing firms emulate the successful innovations of others. Alamo greatly increased its auto rentals by offering customers unlimited mileage, and Hertz, Avis, Budget, and others eventually followed. Chrysler profitably introduced a luxury version of its Jeep Grand Cherokee; other manufacturers, including Acura, Mercedes, and Lexus, countered with luxury sport-utility vehicles of their own. In 2007 Apple introduced the iPhone, a palm-sized telephone that was also a music player, camera, Internet browser, and mini personal computer. BlackBerry, Nokia, Samsung, and Palm soon brought out similar products.

Other recent examples: Early successful cholesterol-reducing drugs (statins) such as Bristol-Myers Squibb's Pravachol were soon followed by chemically distinct but similar statins such as Merck's Zocor and Pfizer's Lipitor. Early video game consoles such as those by Atari eventually gave rise to more popular consoles by Nintendo (Wii), Sony (PlayStation), and Microsoft (Xbox). Facebook, LinkedIn, Pinterest, and Instagram mimicked the social networking innovation pioneered by Classmates.com.

In each of these cases, other firms incorporated the new innovation into their own businesses and products through imitation, modification, and extension. The original innovation thus became commonplace and mainly of historical interest.

Although not as dramatic as invention and innovation, diffusion is a critical element of technological change.

R&D Expenditures

As related to *businesses,* the term "research and development" is used loosely to include direct efforts toward invention, innovation, and diffusion. However, *government* also engages in R&D, particularly R&D having to do with national defense. In 2012 *total* U.S. R&D expenditures (business *plus* government) were $400 billion. Relative to GDP that amount was about 2.8 percent, which is a reasonable measure of the emphasis the U.S. economy puts on technological advance. As shown in Global Perspective 15.1, this is a high percentage of GDP compared to several other nations.

American businesses spent $277 billion on R&D in 2012. Figure 15.1 shows how these R&D expenditures were allocated. Observe that U.S. firms collectively channeled 79 percent of their R&D expenditures to "development" (innovation and imitation, the route to diffusion). They spent another 16 percent on applied research, or on pursuing invention. For reasons we will mention later, only 5 percent of business R&D expenditures went for basic research, the search for general scientific principles. Of course, industries, and firms within industries, vary greatly in the amount of emphasis they place on these three processes.

GLOBAL PERSPECTIVE 15.1

Total R&D Expenditures as a Percentage of GDP, Selected Nations

Relative R&D spending varies among leading industrial nations. From a microeconomic perspective, R&D helps promote economic efficiency; from a macroeconomic perspective, R&D helps promote economic growth.

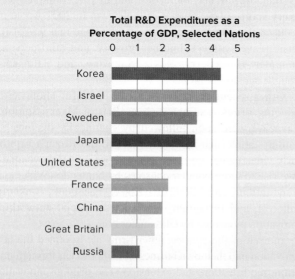

Source: National Science Foundation, **www.nsf.gov**, and *OECD Factbook 2014: Economic, Environmental and Social Statistics,* **www.oecd.org**. Latest available data.

FIGURE 15.1 The composition of business R&D outlays in the United States, 2012. Firms channel the bulk of their R&D spending to innovation and imitation because both have direct commercial value; less to applied research, that is, invention; and a relatively small amount to basic scientific research.

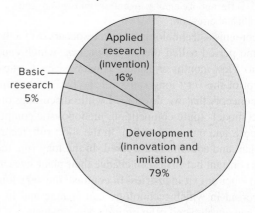

Source: Science Resource Statistics, National Science Foundation, **www.nsf.gov**.

Modern View of Technological Advance

For decades most economists regarded technological advance as being a random *external* force to which the economy adjusted. In their opinion, advances in scientific and technological knowledge were unforeseeable lucky events unrelated to anything going on in the economy. But when they occurred from time to time, they paved the way for major new products (automobiles, airplanes) and major new production processes (assembly lines). Firms and industries incorporated a new technology into their products or processes to enhance or maintain their profits. After integrating the new technology, they settled back into new long-run equilibrium positions. Although they agreed with modern economists that technological advance was vitally important to the economy, economists of that era believed that the development of new technologies was rooted in the independent advance of science, which is largely external to the market system.

Most contemporary economists have a different view. They see capitalism itself as the driving force behind technological advance. Invention, innovation, and diffusion occur in response to incentives within the economy, meaning that technological advance is *internal* to capitalism. Specifically, technological advance arises from intense rivalry among individuals and firms that motivates them to seek and exploit new profit opportunities or to expand existing opportunities. That rivalry occurs both among existing firms and between existing firms and newly created firms. Moreover, many advances in "pure" scientific knowledge are motivated, at least in part, by the prospect of commercial applicability and eventual profit. In the modern view, entrepreneurs and other innovators are at the heart of technological advance.

Role of Entrepreneurs and Other Innovators

LO15.2 Explain how entrepreneurs and other innovators further technological advance.

It will be helpful to distinguish between "entrepreneurs" and "other innovators":

- **Entrepreneurs** Recall that the entrepreneur is an initiator, innovator, and risk bearer. His or her entrepreneurial ability is the productive resource that combines the other productive resources of land, labor, and capital in new and unique ways to produce new goods and services. In the past a single individual, for example, Andrew Carnegie in steel, Henry Ford in automobiles, or Levi Strauss in blue jeans, carried out the entrepreneurial role. Such advances as air conditioning, the ballpoint pen, cellophane, the jet engine, insulin, xerography, and the helicopter all have an individualistic heritage. But in today's more technologically complex economy, entrepreneurship is just as likely to be carried out by entrepreneurial teams. Such teams may include only two or three people working "as their own bosses" on some new product idea or it may consist of larger groups of entrepreneurs who have pooled their financial resources to pursue a business idea.

- **Other innovators** This designation includes other key people involved in the pursuit of innovation who do not bear personal financial risk. Among them are key executives, scientists, and other salaried employees engaged in commercial R&D activities. (They are sometimes referred to as *intrapreneurs* since they provide the spirit of entrepreneurship within existing firms.)

Forming Start-Ups

Entrepreneurs often form small new companies called **start-ups** that focus on creating and introducing a new product or employing a new production or distribution technique. Two twenty-somethings named Steve Jobs and Steve Wozniak formed such a start-up in the mid-1970s after months of tinkering on a prototype personal computer that they had built in a garage during their free time. When neither of their employers—Hewlett-Packard and Atari, the developer of Pong (the first video game)—was interested in funding the development of their new computer, they founded their own computer company: Apple. Other examples of successful start-ups are Amgen, a biotechnology firm specializing in new medical treatments; Starbucks, a seller of gourmet coffee; Amazon, an Internet retailer; and Google, an Internet search provider.

Innovating within Existing Firms

Innovators are also at work within existing corporations, large and small. Such innovators are salaried workers, although many firms have pay systems that provide them with substantial bonuses or profit shares. Examples of firms known for their skillful internal innovators are 3M Corporation, the U.S. developer of Scotch tape, Post-it notes, and Thinsulate insulation; and General Electric, the developer of innovative major kitchen appliances, medical imaging machines, and jet aircraft engines. R&D work in major corporations has produced significant technological improvements in such products as television sets, telephones, home appliances, automobiles, automobile tires, and sporting equipment.

Some large firms, aware that excessive bureaucracy can stifle creative thinking and technological advance, have separated part of their R&D and manufacturing divisions to form new, more flexible, innovative firms. Three significant examples of such "spin-off firms" are Lucent Technologies (now Alcatel-Lucent), a telephone equipment and R&D firm created by AT&T; Imation, a high-technology firm spun off by the 3M Corporation; and Yum! Brands, which operates restaurant chains Taco Bell, KFC, and Pizza Hut. It was spun off by Pepsi.

Anticipating the Future

In 1949 a writer for *Popular Mechanics* magazine boldly predicted, "Computers in the future may weigh no more than 1.5 tons." Today's notebook computers weigh less than 3 pounds, while an iPhone weighs under 4 ounces.

Anticipating the future is difficult, but that is what innovators try to do. Those with strong anticipatory ability and determination have a knack for introducing new and improved products or services at just the right time.

The rewards for success are both monetary and nonmonetary. Product innovation and development are creative endeavors, with such intangible rewards as personal satisfaction. Also, many people simply enjoy participating in the competitive "contest." Of course, the "winners" can reap huge monetary rewards in the form of economic profits, stock appreciation, or large bonuses. Extreme examples are Bill Gates and Paul Allen, who founded Microsoft in 1975, and had net worths in 2016 of $75.4 billion and $18.1 billion, respectively, mainly in the form of Microsoft stock.

Past successes often give entrepreneurs and innovative firms access to resources for further innovations that anticipate consumer wants. Although they may not succeed a second time, the market tends to entrust the production of goods and services to businesses that have consistently succeeded in filling consumer wants. And the market does not care whether these "winning" entrepreneurs and innovative firms are American, Brazilian, Japanese, German, or Swiss. Entrepreneurship and innovation are global in scope.

Exploiting University and Government Scientific Research

In Figure 15.1 we saw that only 5 percent of business R&D spending in the United States goes to basic scientific research. The reason the percentage is so small is that scientific principles, as such, cannot be patented, nor do they usually have immediate commercial uses. Yet new scientific knowledge is highly important to technological advance. For that reason, entrepreneurs study the scientific output of university and government laboratories to identify discoveries with commercial applicability.

Government and university labs have been the scene of many technological breakthroughs, including hybrid seeds, nuclear energy, satellite communications, the computer mouse, genetic engineering, and the Internet. Entire high-tech industries such as computers and biotechnology have their roots in major research universities and government laboratories. And nations with strong scientific communities tend to have the most technologically progressive firms and industries.

Also, firms increasingly help fund university research that relates to their products. Business funding of R&D at universities has grown rapidly, rising to more than $3.5 billion in 2013. Today, the separation between university scientists and innovators is narrowing; scientists and universities increasingly realize that their work may have commercial value and are teaming up with innovators to share in the potential profit.

A few firms, of course, find it profitable to conduct basic scientific research on their own. New scientific knowledge can give them a head start in creating an invention or a new product. This is particularly true in the pharmaceutical industry, where it is not uncommon for firms to parlay new scientific knowledge generated in their corporate labs into new, patentable drugs.

QUICK REVIEW 15.1

✓ Broadly defined, technological advance means new or improved products and services as well as new or improved production and distribution processes.

✓ Invention is the *discovery* of a new product or method; innovation is the *successful commercial application* of some invention; and diffusion is the *widespread adoption* of the innovation.

✓ Many economists view technological advance as mainly a response to profit opportunities arising within a capitalist economy.

✓ Technological advance is fostered by entrepreneurs and other innovators and is supported by the scientific research of universities and government-sponsored laboratories.

A Firm's Optimal Amount of R&D

LO15.3 Summarize how a firm determines its optimal amount of research and development (R&D).

How does a firm decide on its optimal amount of research and development? That amount depends on the firm's perception of the marginal benefit and marginal cost of R&D activity. The decision rule here flows from basic economics: To earn the greatest profit, expand a particular activity until its marginal benefit (MB) equals its marginal cost (MC). A firm that sees the marginal benefit of a particular R&D activity, say, innovation, as exceeding the marginal cost should expand that activity. In contrast, an activity whose marginal benefit promises to be less than its marginal cost should be cut back. But the R&D spending decision is complex since it involves a present sacrifice for a future expected gain. While the cost of R&D is immediate, the expected benefits occur at some future time and are highly uncertain. So estimating those benefits is often more art than science. Nevertheless, the MB = MC way of thinking remains relevant for analyzing R&D decisions.

Interest-Rate Cost of Funds

Firms have several ways of obtaining the funds they need to finance R&D activities:

- **Bank loans** Some firms are able to obtain a loan from a bank or other financial institution. The cost of using the funds is the interest paid to the lender. The marginal cost is the cost per extra dollar borrowed, which is simply the market interest rate for borrowed funds.

- **Bonds** Bonds are financial contracts through which a borrower (typically a firm or a government) is obligated to pay the owner of a bond both the principal and interest due on a loan on dates specified in the bond contract. Established, profitable firms may be able to borrow funds for R&D by issuing bonds and selling them in the bond market. In this case, the cost is the interest paid to the lenders—the bondholders. Again the marginal cost of using the funds is the interest rate.

- **Retained earnings** A large, well-established firm may be able to draw on its own corporate savings to finance R&D. Typically, such a firm retains part of its profit rather than paying it all out as dividends to the firm's shareholders (owners). Some of the undistributed profit, called *retained earnings,* can be used to finance R&D activity. The marginal cost of using retained earnings for R&D is an opportunity cost—the rate of interest that those funds could have earned as deposits in a financial institution.

- **Venture capital** A small start-up firm may be able to attract venture capital to finance its R&D projects. Venture capital is financial capital, or simply money, not real capital. **Venture capital** consists of that part of household saving used to finance high-risk business ventures in exchange for shares of the profit if the ventures succeed. The marginal cost of venture capital is the share of expected profit that the firm will have to pay to those who provided the money. This can be stated as a percentage of the venture capital, so it is essentially an interest rate.

- *Personal savings* Finally, individual entrepreneurs might draw on their own savings to finance the R&D for a new venture. The marginal cost of the financing is again the forgone interest rate.

Thus, whatever the source of the R&D funds, we can state the marginal cost of these funds as an interest rate *i*. For simplicity, let's assume that this interest rate is the same no matter how much financing is required. Further, we assume that a certain firm called MedTech must pay an interest rate of 8 percent for the least expensive funding available to it. Then a graph of the marginal cost of each funding amount for this firm is a horizontal line at the 8 percent interest rate, as shown in Figure 15.2. Such a graph is called an **interest-rate cost-of-funds curve.** This one tells us that MedTech can borrow any amount of money at the 8 percent interest rate. The table accompanying the graph contains the data used to construct the graph and tells us much the same thing.

With these data in hand, MedTech wants to determine how much R&D it should finance in the coming year.

Expected Rate of Return

A firm's marginal benefit from R&D is its expected profit (or return) from the last (marginal) dollar spent on R&D. That is, the R&D is expected to result in a new product or production method that will increase revenue, reduce production costs, or both (in ways we will soon explain). This return is expected, not certain—there is risk in R&D decisions. Let's suppose that after considering such risks, MedTech anticipates that an R&D expenditure of $1 million will result in a new product that will yield a one-time added profit of $1.2 million a year later. As a result, the expected rate of return *r* on the $1 million R&D expenditure (after the $1 million has been repaid) is 20 percent (= $200,000/$1,000,000). This is the marginal benefit of the first $1 million of R&D. (Stretching the return over several years complicates the computation of *r*, but it does not alter the basic analysis. We discuss this "present-value complication" in Chapter 19.)

MedTech can use this same method to estimate the expected rates of return for R&D expenditures of $2 million, $3 million, $4 million, and so on. Suppose those marginal rates of return are the ones indicated in the table in Figure 15.3, where they are also graphed as the **expected-rate-of-return curve.** This curve shows the expected rate of return, which is the marginal benefit of each dollar of expenditure on

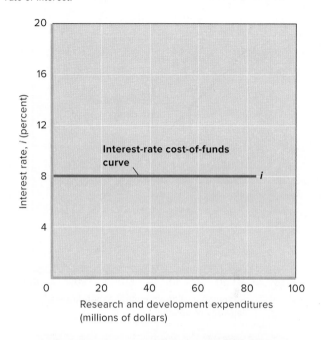

FIGURE 15.2 The interest-rate cost-of-funds schedule and curve. As it relates to R&D, a firm's interest-rate cost-of-funds schedule (the table) and curve (the graph) show the interest rate the firm must pay to obtain any particular amount of funds to finance R&D. Curve *i* indicates the firm can finance as little or as much R&D as it wants at a constant 8 percent rate of interest.

R&D, Millions	Interest-Rate Cost of Funds, %
$10	8
20	8
30	8
40	8
50	8
60	8
70	8
80	8

R&D. The curve slopes downward because of diminishing returns to R&D expenditures. A firm will direct its initial R&D expenditures to the highest expected-rate-of-return activities and then use additional funding for activities with successively lower expected rates of return. That is, the firm will experience lower and lower expected rates of return as it expands its R&D spending.

Optimal R&D Expenditures

Figure 15.4 combines the interest-rate cost-of-funds curve (Figure 15.2) and the expected-rate-of-return curve (Figure 15.3). The curves intersect at MedTech's **optimal amount of R&D,** which is $60 million. This amount can also be

FIGURE 15.3 The expected-rate-of-return schedule and curve. As they relate to R&D, a firm's expected-rate-of-return schedule (the table) and curve (the graph) show the firm's expected gain in profit, as a percentage of R&D spending, for each level of R&D spending. Curve *r* slopes downward because the firm assesses its potential R&D projects in descending order of expected rates of return.

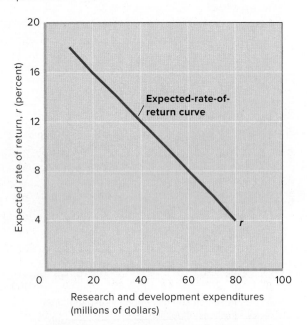

R&D, Millions	Expected Rate of Return, %
$10	18
20	16
30	14
40	12
50	10
60	8
70	6
80	4

FIGURE 15.4 A firm's optimal level of R&D expenditures. The firm's optimal level of R&D expenditures ($60 million) occurs where its expected rate of return equals the interest-rate cost of funds, as shown in both the table and the graph. At $60 million of R&D spending, the firm has taken advantage of all R&D opportunities for which the expected rate of return, *r*, exceeds or equals the 8 percent interest cost of borrowing, *i*.

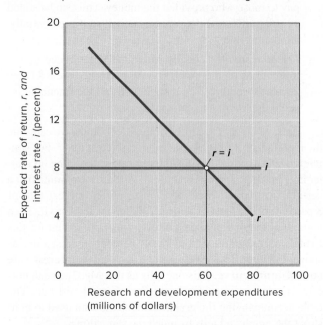

Expected Rate of Return, %	R&D, Millions	Interest-Rate Cost-of-Funds, %
18	$10	8
16	20	8
14	30	8
12	40	8
10	50	8
8	**60**	**8**
6	70	8
4	80	8

determined from the table as the amount of funding for which the expected rate of return and the interest cost of borrowing are equal (here, 8 percent).

Both the curve and the table in Figure 15.4 tell us that at $60 million of R&D expenditures, the marginal benefit and marginal cost of the last dollar spent on R&D are equal. MedTech should undertake all R&D expenditures up to $60 million since those outlays yield a higher marginal benefit or expected rate of return, *r*, than the 8 percent marginal cost or interest-rate cost of borrowing, *i*. But it should not undertake R&D expenditures beyond $60 million; for these outlays, *r* (marginal benefit) is less than *i* (marginal cost). Only at $60 million do we have *r = i*, telling us that MedTech will spend $60 million on R&D.

Our analysis reinforces three important points:

- *Optimal versus affordable R&D* From earlier discussions we know there can be too much, as well as too little, of a "good thing." So it is with R&D and technological advance. Figure 15.4 shows that R&D expenditures make sense to a firm only as long as the expected return from the outlay equals or exceeds the cost of obtaining the funds needed to finance it. Many R&D expenditures may be affordable but not worthwhile because their marginal benefit is likely to be less than their marginal cost.

- *Expected, not guaranteed, returns* The outcomes from R&D are expected, not guaranteed. With 20-20 hindsight, a firm can always look back and decide whether a particular expenditure for R&D was worthwhile. But that assessment is irrelevant to the original decision. At the time of the decision, the expenditure was thought to be worthwhile on the basis of existing information and expectations. Some R&D decisions may be more like an informed gamble than the typical business decision. Invention and innovation, in particular, carry with them a great deal of risk. For every successful outcome, there are scores of costly disappointments.

- *Adjustments* Firms adjust their R&D expenditures when expected rates of return on various projects change (when curves such as *r* in Figure 15.4 shift). The U.S. war on terrorism, for example, increased the expected rate of return on R&D for improved security devices used at airports, train stations, harbors, and other public places. It also increased the expected return on new methods of detecting and responding to potential bioterrorism. The revised realities prompted many firms to increase their R&D expenditures for these purposes.

Increased Profit via Innovation

LO15.4 Discuss how technological change can increase profits by raising revenues or lowering costs.

In discussing how a firm determines its optimal amount of R&D spending, we sidestepped the question of how technological change can increase a firm's profit. Although the answer may seem obvious—by increasing revenue or reducing production costs—insights can be gained by exploring these two possibilities in some detail.

Increased Revenue via Product Innovation

Firms here and abroad have profitably introduced hundreds of new products in the past two or three decades. Examples include roller blades, microwave popcorn, cordless drills, digital cameras, camcorders, and high-definition TVs. Other new products are snowboards, cellular phones, tablet computers, and automobile air bags. All these items reflect technological advance in the form of product innovation.

How do such new products gain consumer acceptance? As you know from Chapter 7, to maximize their satisfaction, consumers purchase products that have the highest marginal utility per dollar. They determine which products to buy in view of their limited money incomes by comparing the ratios of MU/price for the various goods. They first select the unit of the good with the highest MU/price ratio, then the one with the next highest, and so on, until their incomes are used up.

The first five columns of Table 15.1 repeat some of the information in Table 7.1. Before the introduction of new product C, the consumer maximized the total utility she could get from $10 of income by buying 2 units of A at $1 per unit and 4 units of B at $2 per unit. Her total budget of $10 was thus fully expended, with $2 spent on A and $8 on B. As shown in columns 2b and 3b, the marginal utility per dollar spent on the last unit of each product was 8 (= 8/$1 = 16/$2). The total utility, derived from columns 2a and 3a, was 96 utils (= 10 + 8 from the first 2 units of A plus 24 + 20 + 18 + 16 from the first 4 units of B). (If you are uncertain about this outcome, please review the discussion of Table 7.1.)

Now suppose an innovative firm offers new product C (columns 4a and 4b in Table 15.1), priced at $4 per unit. Note that the first unit of C has a higher marginal utility per dollar (13) than any unit of A or B and that the second unit of C and the first unit of B have equal MU/price ratios of 12. To maximize satisfaction, the consumer now buys 2 units of C at $4 per unit, 1 unit of B at $2 per unit, and zero units of A. Our consumer has spent all of her $10 income ($8 on C and $2 on B), and the MU/price ratios of the last units of B and C are equal at 12. But as determined via columns 3a and 4a, the consumer's total utility is now 124 utils (= 24 from the first unit of B plus 52 + 48 from the first 2 units of C).

TABLE 15.1 Utility Maximization with the Introduction of a New Product (Income = $10)*

(1) Unit of Product	(2) Product A: Price = $1		(3) Product B: Price = $2		(4) New Product C: Price = $4	
	(a) Marginal Utility, Utils	(b) Marginal Utility per Dollar (MU/Price)	(a) Marginal Utility, Utils	(b) Marginal Utility per Dollar (MU/Price)	(a) Marginal Utility, Utils	(b) Marginal Utility per Dollar (MU/Price)
First	10	10	24	12	52	13
Second	8	8	20	10	48	12
Third	7	7	18	9	44	11
Fourth	6	6	16	8	36	9
Fifth	5	5	12	6	32	8

*It is assumed in this table that the amount of marginal utility received from additional units of each of the three products is independent of the quantity purchased of the other products. For example, the marginal-utility schedule for product C is independent of the amount of A and B purchased by the consumer.

Total utility has increased by 28 utils (= 124 utils − 96 utils), and that is why product C was purchased. Consumers will buy a new product only if it increases the total utility they obtain from their limited incomes.

From the innovating firm's perspective, these "dollar votes" represent new product demand that yields increased revenue. When per-unit revenue exceeds per-unit cost, the product innovation creates per-unit profit. Total profit rises by the per-unit profit multiplied by the number of units sold. As a percentage of the original R&D expenditure, the rise in total profit is the return on that R&D expenditure. It was the basis for the expected-rate-of-return curve *r* in Figure 15.4.

Other related points:

- **Importance of price** Consumer acceptance of a new product depends on both its marginal utility and its price. (Confirm that the consumer represented in Table 15.1 would buy zero units of new product C if its price were $8 rather than $4.) To be successful, a new product must not only deliver utility to consumers but do so at an acceptable price.

- **Unsuccessful new products** For every successful new product, hundreds do not succeed; the expected return that motivates product innovation is not always realized. Examples of colossal product flops are Ford's Edsel automobile, quadraphonic stereo, New Coke by Coca-Cola, Kodak disc cameras, and XFL football. Less dramatic failures include the hundreds of dot-com firms that have gone out of business since the late 1990s. In each case, millions of dollars of R&D and promotion expense ultimately resulted in loss, not profit.

- **Product improvements** Most product innovation consists of incremental improvements to existing products rather than radical inventions. Examples: more fuel-efficient automobile engines, new varieties of pizza, lighter-weight shafts for golf clubs, more flavorful bubble gum, "rock shocks" for mountain bikes, and clothing made of wrinkle-free fabrics.

Reduced Cost via Process Innovation

The introduction of better methods of producing products—process innovation—is also a path toward enhanced profit and a positive return on R&D expenditures. Suppose a firm introduces a new and better production process, say, assembling its product by teams rather than by a standard assembly line. Alternatively, suppose this firm replaces old equipment with more productive equipment embodying a technological advance. In either case, the innovation yields an upward shift in the firm's total-product curve from TP_1 to TP_2 in Figure 15.5a. As a result, more units of output can now be produced at each level of resource usage. Note from the figure, for example, that this firm can now produce 2,500 units of output, rather than 2,000 units, when using 1,000 units of

FIGURE 15.5 Process innovation, total product, and average total cost. (a) Process innovation shifts a firm's total-product curve upward from TP_1 to TP_2, meaning that with a given amount of capital the firm can produce more output at each level of labor input. As shown, with 1,000 units of labor it can produce 2,500 rather than 2,000 units of output. (b) The upward shift in the total-product curve results in a downward shift in the firm's average-total-cost curve, from ATC_1 to ATC_2. This means the firm can produce any particular unit of output at a lower average total cost than it could previously. For example, the original 2,000 units can be produced at less than $4 per unit, versus $5 per unit originally. Or 2,500 units can now be produced at $4 per unit.

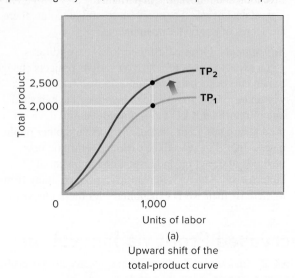

(a)
Upward shift of the
total-product curve

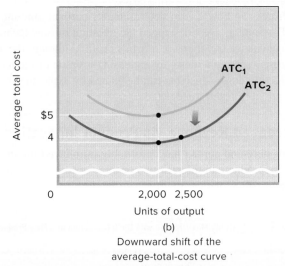

(b)
Downward shift of the
average-total-cost curve

labor. So its average product has increased from 2 (= 2,000 units of output/1,000 units of labor) to 2.5 (= 2,500 units of output/1,000 units of labor).

The result is a downward shift in the firm's average-total-cost curve, from ATC_1 to ATC_2 in Figure 15.5b. To understand why, let's assume this firm pays $1,000 for the use of its capital and $9 for each unit of labor. Since it uses 1,000 units of labor, its labor cost is $9,000 (= $9 × 1,000); its capital cost is $1,000; and thus its total cost is $10,000. When its output increases from 2,000 to 2,500 units as a result of the process innovation, its total cost remains $10,000. So its average total cost declines from $5 (= $10,000/2,000) to $4 (= $10,000/2,500). Alternatively, the firm could produce the original 2,000 units of output with fewer units of labor at an even lower average total cost.

This reduction in average total cost enhances the firm's profit. As a percentage of the R&D expenditure that fostered it, this extra profit is the expected return *r* that was the basis for the rate-of-return curve in Figure 15.3. In this case, the expected increase in profit arose from the prospect of lower production costs through process innovation.

Example: Computer-based inventory control systems, such as those pioneered by Walmart, enabled innovators to reduce the number of people needed to keep track of inventories. The new systems also enabled firms to keep goods arriving "just in time," reducing the cost of storing inventories. The consequence? Significant increases in sales per worker, declines in average total cost, and increased profit.

Imitation and R&D Incentives

LO15.5 Relate why firms can benefit from their innovation even though rivals have an incentive to imitate it.

Our analysis of product and process innovation explains how technological advance enhances a firm's profit. But it also hints at a potential **imitation problem:** A firm's rivals may be able to imitate its new product or process, greatly reducing the originator's profit from its R&D effort. As just one example, in the 1980s U.S. auto firms took apart Japanese Honda Accords, piece by piece, to discover the secrets of their high quality. This reverse engineering—which ironically was perfected earlier by the Japanese—helped the U.S. firms incorporate innovative features into their own cars. This type of imitation is perfectly legitimate and fully anticipated; it is often the main path to widespread diffusion of an innovation.

In fact, a dominant firm that is making large profits from its existing products may let smaller firms in the industry incur the high costs of product innovation while it closely monitors their successes and failures. The dominant firm then moves quickly to imitate any successful new product; its goal is to become the second firm to embrace the innovation. In using this so-called **fast-second strategy,** the dominant firm counts on its own product-improvement abilities, marketing prowess, or economies of scale to prevail.

Examples abound: Royal Crown introduced the first diet cola, but Diet Coke and Diet Pepsi dominate diet-cola sales today. Meister Brau introduced the first low-calorie beer, but Miller popularized the product with its Miller Lite. Gillette moved quickly with its own stainless-steel razor blade only after a smaller firm, Wilkinson, introduced this product innovation. Creative Technology (the maker of Sound Blaster audio cards for personal computers) introduced the first miniature MP3 player, but Apple popularized the product with its iPod before incorporating a music player into its iPhone smartphone.

Benefits of Being First

Imitation and the fast-second strategy raise an important question: What incentive is there for any firm to bear the expenses and risks of innovation if competitors can imitate its new or improved product? Why not let others bear the costs and risks of product development and then just imitate the successful innovations? Although we have seen that this may be a plausible strategy in some situations, there are several protections for, and potential advantages to, taking the lead.

Patents   Some technological breakthroughs, specifically inventions, can be patented. Once patented, they cannot be legally imitated for two decades from time of patent application. The purpose of patents is, in fact, to reduce imitation and its negative effect on the incentive for engaging in R&D. Example: Polaroid's patent of its instant camera enabled it to earn high economic profits for many years. When Kodak "cloned" the camera, Polaroid won a patent-infringement lawsuit against its rival. Kodak not only had to stop producing its version of the camera but had to buy back the Kodak instant cameras it had sold and pay millions of dollars in damages to Polaroid.

There are hundreds of other examples of long-run profits based on U.S. patents; they involve products from prescription drugs to pop-top cans to weed trimmers. As shown in Global Perspective 15.2, foreign citizens and firms hold U.S. patents along with American citizens and firms.

GLOBAL PERSPECTIVE 15.2

Distribution of U.S. Patents, by Foreign Nation

Foreign citizens, corporations, and governments hold 42 percent of U.S. patents. The top 10 foreign countries in terms of U.S. patent holdings since 1963 are listed below, with the number of U.S. patents (through 2014) in parentheses.

Top 10 Foreign Countries

Japan (1,014,977)

Germany (347,875)

Taiwan (150,121)

South Korea (146,153)

United Kingdom (133,063)

France (132,840)

Canada (116,413)

Italy (59,058)

Switzerland (54,294)

Netherlands (47,556)

Source: U.S. Patent and Trademark Office, **www.uspto.gov.**

Copyrights and Trademarks *Copyrights* protect publishers of books, computer software, movies, videos, and musical compositions from having their works copied. *Trademarks* give the original innovators of products the exclusive right to use a particular product name ("M&Ms," "Barbie" dolls, "Wheaties"). By reducing the problem of direct copying, these legal protections increase the incentive for product innovation. They have been strengthened worldwide through recent international trade agreements.

Brand-Name Recognition Along with trademark protection, brand-name recognition may give the original innovator a major marketing advantage for years or even decades. Consumers often identify a new product with the firm that first introduced and popularized it in the mass market. Examples: Levi's blue jeans, Kleenex soft tissues, Johnson & Johnson's Band-Aids, Gatorade sports drink, and Kellogg's Corn Flakes.

Trade Secrets and Learning by Doing Some innovations involve trade secrets, without which competitors cannot imitate the product or process. Example: Coca-Cola has successfully kept its formula for Coke a secret from potential rivals. Many other firms have perfected special production techniques known only to them. In a related advantage, a firm's head start with a new product often allows it to achieve substantial cost reductions through learning by doing. The innovator's lower cost may enable it to continue to profit even after imitators have entered the market.

Time Lags Time lags between innovation and diffusion often enable innovating firms to realize a substantial economic profit. It takes time for an imitator to gain knowledge of the properties of a new innovation. And once it has that knowledge, the imitator must design a substitute product, gear up a factory for its production, and conduct a marketing campaign. Various entry barriers, such as large financial requirements, economies of scale, and price-cutting, may extend the time lag between innovation and imitation. In practice, it may take years or even decades before rival firms can successfully imitate a profitable new product and cut into the market share of the innovator. In the meantime, the innovator continues to profit.

Profitable Buyouts

A final advantage of being first arises from the possibility of a buyout (outright purchase) of the innovating firm by a larger firm. Here, the innovative entrepreneurs take their rewards immediately, as cash or as shares in the purchasing firm, rather than waiting for perhaps uncertain long-run profits from their own production and marketing efforts.

Examples: Once the popularity of cellular communications became evident, AT&T bought out McCaw Communications,

an early leader in this new technology. When Minnetonka's Softsoap became a huge success, it sold its product to Colgate-Palmolive. More recently, Swiss conglomerate Nestlé bought out Chef America, the highly successful maker of Hot Pockets frozen meat-and-cheese sandwiches. Such buyouts are legal under current antitrust laws as long as they do not substantially lessen competition in the affected industry. For this to be the case, there must be other strong competitors in the market. That was not true, for example, when Microsoft tried to buy out Intuit (maker of Quicken, the best-selling financial software). That buyout was disallowed because Intuit and Microsoft were the two main suppliers of financial software for personal computers.

In short, despite the imitation problem, significant protections and advantages enable most innovating firms to profit from their R&D efforts, as implied by the continuing high levels of R&D spending by firms year after year. As shown in Figure 15.6, business R&D spending in the United States not only remains substantial but has grown over the past quarter-century. The high levels of spending simply would not continue if imitation consistently and severely depressed rates of return on R&D expenditures.

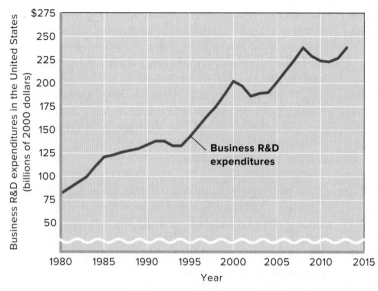

FIGURE 15.6 The growth of business R&D expenditures in the United States, 1980–2013. Inflation-adjusted R&D expenditures by firms are substantial and growing, suggesting that R&D continues to be profitable for firms, even in the face of possible imitation.

Source: Science and Engineering Indicators, National Science Foundation, **www.nsf.gov**.

QUICK REVIEW 15.2

✓ A firm's optimal R&D expenditure is the amount at which the expected rate of return (marginal benefit) from the R&D expenditure just equals the interest-rate cost of borrowing (marginal cost) required to finance it.

✓ Product innovation can entice consumers to substitute a new product for existing products to increase their total utility, thereby increasing the innovating firm's revenue and profit.

✓ Process innovation can lower a firm's production costs and increase its profit by increasing total product and decreasing average total cost.

✓ A firm faces reduced profitability from R&D if competitors can successfully imitate its new product or process. Nevertheless, there are significant potential protections and benefits to being first, including patents, copyrights, and trademarks; brand-name recognition; trade secrets; cost reductions from learning by doing; and major time lags between innovation and imitation.

Role of Market Structure

LO15.6 Discuss the role of market structure in promoting technological advance.

In view of our discussion of market structures in the previous four chapters, asking whether some particular market structure or firm size is best suited to technological progress is logical. Is a highly competitive industry consisting of thousands of relatively small firms likely to produce faster technological progress than a monopoly? Or is perhaps an intermediate market structure like oligopoly the most likely to produce rapid technological progress?

Market Structure and Technological Advance

As a first step toward answering these questions, we survey the strengths and shortcomings of our four market models as related to technological advance.

Pure Competition Does a pure competitor have a strong incentive and strong ability to undertake R&D? On the positive side, strong competition provides a reason for such firms to innovate; competitive firms tend to be less complacent than monopolists. If a pure competitor does not seize the initiative, one or more rivals may introduce a new product or cost-reducing production technique that could drive it from the market. As a matter of short-term profit and long-term survival, the pure competitor is under continual pressure to improve products and lower costs through innovation. Also, where there are many competing firms, there is less chance that an idea for improving a product or process will be overlooked by a single firm.

On the negative side, the expected rate of return on R&D may be low or even negative for a pure competitor. Because of easy entry, its profit rewards from innovation may quickly be competed away by existing or entering firms that also produce the new product or adopt the new technology. Also, the small size of competitive firms and the fact that they earn only a normal profit in the long run lead to serious questions as to whether they can finance substantial R&D programs. Observers have noted that the high rate of technological advance in the purely competitive agricultural industry, for example, has come not from the R&D of individual farmers but from government-sponsored research and from the development of fertilizers, hybrid seed, and farm implements by oligopolistic firms.

Monopolistic Competition Like pure competitors, monopolistic competitors cannot afford to be complacent. But unlike pure competitors, which sell standardized products, monopolistic competitors have a strong profit incentive to engage in product innovation. This incentive to differentiate products from those of competitors stems from the fact that sufficiently novel products may create monopoly power and thus economic profit. There are many examples of innovative firms (McDonald's, Starbucks, Redbox video rentals) that started out as monopolistic competitors in localized markets but soon gained considerable national market power, with the attendant economic profit.

For the typical firm, however, the shortcomings of monopolistic competition in relation to technological advance are the same as those of pure competition. Most monopolistic competitors remain small, which limits their ability to secure inexpensive financing for R&D. In addition, monopolistic competitors find it difficult to extract large profits from technological advances. Any economic profits from innovation are usually temporary because entry to monopolistically competitive industries is relatively easy. In the long run, new entrants with similar goods reduce the demand for the innovator's product, leaving the innovator with only a normal profit. Monopolistic competitors therefore usually have relatively low expected rates of return on R&D expenditures.

Oligopoly Many of the characteristics of oligopoly are conducive to technological advance. First, the large size of oligopolists enables them to finance the often large R&D costs associated with major product or process innovation. In particular, the typical oligopolist realizes an ongoing economic profit, a part of which is retained. This undistributed profit serves as a major source of readily available, relatively low-cost funding for R&D. Moreover, the existence of barriers to entry gives the oligopolist some assurance that it can maintain any economic profit it gains from innovation. Then, too, the large sales volume of the oligopolist enables it to spread the cost of specialized R&D equipment and teams of specialized researchers over a great many units of output. Finally, the broad scope of R&D activity within oligopolistic firms helps them offset the inevitable R&D "misses" with more-than-compensating R&D "hits." Thus, oligopolists clearly have the means and incentive to innovate.

But there is also a negative side to R&D in oligopoly. In many instances, the oligopolist's incentive to innovate may be far less than we have just implied because oligopoly tends to breed complacency. An oligopolist may reason that introducing costly new technology and producing new products

makes little sense when it currently is earning a sizable economic profit without them. The oligopolist wants to maximize its profit by exploiting fully all its capital assets. Why rush to develop a new product (say, batteries for electric automobiles) when that product's success will render obsolete much of the firm's current equipment designed to produce its existing product (say, gasoline engines)? It is not difficult to cite oligopolistic industries in which the largest firms' interest in R&D has been quite modest. Examples: the steel, cigarette, and aluminum industries.

Pure Monopoly In general, the pure monopolist has little incentive to engage in R&D; it maintains its high profit through entry barriers that, in theory, are complete. The only incentive for the pure monopolist to engage in R&D is defensive: to reduce the risk of being blindsided by some new product or production process that destroys its monopoly. If such a product is out there to be discovered, the monopolist may have an incentive to find it. By so doing, it can either exploit the new product or process for continued monopoly profit or suppress the product until the monopolist has extracted the maximum profit from its current capital assets. But, in general, economists agree that pure monopoly is the market structure least conducive to innovation.

Inverted-U Theory of R&D

Analysis like this has led some experts on technological progress to postulate a so-called **inverted-U theory of R&D,** which deals with the relationship between market structure and technological advance. This theory is illustrated in Figure 15.7, which relates R&D spending as a percentage of a firm's sales (vertical axis) to the industry's four-firm concentration ratio (horizontal axis). The "inverted-U" shape of the curve suggests that R&D effort is at best weak in both very-low-concentration industries (pure competition) and very-high-concentration industries (pure monopoly). Starting from the lowest concentrations, R&D spending as a percentage of sales rises with concentration until a concentration ratio of 50 percent or so is reached, meaning that the four largest firms account for about one-half the total industry output. Beyond that, relative R&D spending decreases as concentration rises.

The logic of the inverted-U theory follows from our discussion. Firms in industries with very low concentration ratios are mainly competitive firms. They are small, and this makes it difficult for them to finance R&D. Moreover, entry to these industries is easy, making it difficult to sustain economic profit from innovations that are not supported by patents. As a result, firms in these industries spend little on R&D relative to their sales. At the other end (far right) of the curve, where concentration is exceptionally high, monopoly profit is already high and innovation will not add much more profit. Furthermore, innovation typically requires costly

FIGURE 15.7 The inverted-U theory of R&D expenditures. The inverted-U theory suggests that R&D expenditures as a percentage of sales rise with industry concentration until the four-firm concentration ratio reaches about 50 percent. Further increases in industry concentration are associated with lower relative R&D expenditures.

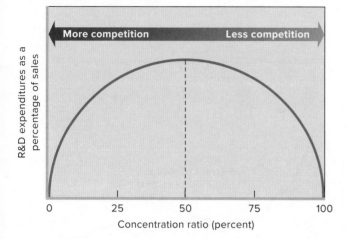

retooling of very large factories, which will cut into whatever additional profit is realized. As a result, the expected rate of return from R&D is quite low, as are expenditures for R&D relative to sales. Finally, the lack of rivals makes the monopolist quite complacent about R&D.

The optimal industry structure for R&D is one in which expected returns on R&D spending are high and funds to finance it are readily available and inexpensive. From our discussion, those factors seem to occur in industries where a few firms are absolutely and relatively large but where the concentration ratio is not so high as to prohibit vigorous competition by smaller rivals. Rivalry among the larger oligopolistic firms and competition between the larger and the smaller firms then provide a strong incentive for R&D. The inverted-U theory of R&D, as represented by Figure 15.7, also points toward this "loose" oligopoly as the optimal structure for R&D spending.

Market Structure and Technological Advance: The Evidence

Various industry studies and cross-industry studies collectively support the inverted-U theory of R&D.[1] Other things equal, the optimal market structure for technological advance seems to be an industry in which there is a mix of large oligopolistic firms (a 40 to 60 percent concentration ratio), with several highly innovative smaller firms.

But our "other-things-equal" qualification is quite important here. Whether or not a particular industry is highly technical may well be a more important determinant of

R&D than its structure. While some concentrated industries (electronics, aircraft, and petroleum) devote large quantities of resources to R&D and are very innovative, others (cigarettes, aluminum, gypsum products) are not. The level of R&D spending within an industry seems to depend as much on its technical character and "technological opportunities" as on its market structure. There simply may be more opportunities to innovate in the computer and pharmaceutical industries, for example, than in the brick-making and coal-mining industries.

Conclusion: The inverted-U curve shown in Figure 15.7 is a useful depiction of the general relationship between R&D spending and market structure, other things equal.

Technological Advance and Efficiency

LO15.7 Show how technological advance enhances productive efficiency and allocative efficiency.

Technological advance contributes significantly to economic efficiency. New and better processes and products enable society to produce more output, as well as a higher-valued mix of output.

Productive Efficiency

Technological advance as embodied in process innovation improves *productive efficiency* by increasing the productivity of inputs (as indicated in Figure 15.5a) and by reducing average total costs (as in Figure 15.5b). In other words, it enables society to produce the same amount of a particular good or service while using fewer scarce resources, thereby freeing the unused resources to produce other goods and services. Or if society desires more of the now less expensive good, process innovation enables it to have that greater quantity without sacrificing other goods. Viewed either way, process innovation enhances productive efficiency: It reduces society's per-unit cost of whatever mix of goods and services it chooses. It is thus an important means of shifting an economy's production possibilities curve rightward.

Allocative Efficiency

Technological advance as embodied in *product* (or service) innovation enhances allocative efficiency by giving society a more preferred mix of goods and services. Recall from our earlier discussion that consumers buy a new product rather than an old product only when buying the new one increases the total utility obtained from their limited incomes. Obviously, then, a popular new product—and the new mix of products it implies—creates a higher level of total utility for society.

In terms of markets, the demand for the new product rises and the demand for the old product declines. The high economic profit engendered by the new product attracts resources

---

[1]One such study is that by Philippe Aghion et al., "Competition and Innovation: An Inverted-U Relationship," *Quarterly Journal of Economics,* May 2005, pp. 701–728.

The Relative Decline of Federal R&D Spending

Should the Federal Government Go Back to Spending a Larger Portion of Its Budget on Basic Scientific Research?

Figure 15.6 shows that R&D spending by U.S. businesses has risen tremendously in recent decades. Measured in constant year-2000 dollars to adjust for inflation, private R&D spending increased from $80 billion in 1980 to $238 billion in 2013. At the same time, the federal government's inflation-adjusted spending on R&D also went up significantly, from $30 billion in 1980 to $90 billion in 2013.

That large increase in federal research spending is good news for long-term economic growth because most of it flows to basic scientific research, which produces fundamental discoveries that in turn generate widespread applications. Some examples of federal research dollars leading to important products include the packet-switching technology that guides data through the Internet, the photovoltaic technology used in many types of solar panels, and several major classes of therapeutic drugs.

It should be noted, however, that basic scientific research typically generates ideas that are years—if not decades—away from commercialization. It was over 25 years, for instance, between the development of packet-switching in the late 1960s and when the Internet became commercially viable in the early 1990s.

As a result, private firms concentrate their R&D efforts on more developed technologies that are closer to commercialization. That strategy minimizes the risk that their R&D spending will fail to yield profitable products. But it also means that only about 5 percent

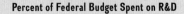

Percent of Federal Budget Spent on R&D

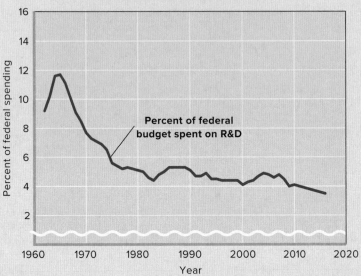

Percent of federal budget spent on R&D

of private R&D spending goes toward basic scientific research. As a result, businesses only spent an inflation-adjusted $12 billon on basic scientific research in 2013.

Comparing that $12 billion of private funding for basic scientific research with the federal government's $90 billion of R&D spending the same year, we see that the economy is overwhelmingly

away from less valued uses and to the production of the new product. In theory, such shifting of resources continues until the price of the new product equals its marginal cost.

There is a caveat here, however. Innovation (either product or process) can create monopoly power through patents or through the many advantages of being first. When new monopoly power results from an innovation, society may lose part of the improved efficiency it otherwise would have gained from that innovation. The reason is that the profit-maximizing monopolist restricts output to keep its product price above marginal cost. For example, Microsoft's innovative Windows product has resulted in dominance in the market for operating systems for personal computers. Microsoft's substantial monopoly power permits it to charge prices that are well above marginal cost and minimum average total cost.

Creative Destruction

Although innovation can create monopoly power, it also can reduce or eliminate it. By increasing competition where it previously was weak, innovation can push prices down toward marginal cost. For example, Intel's microprocessor enabled the use of personal computers, and their ease of production eventually diminished IBM's monopoly power in the sale of computer hardware. More recently, Google's Android operating system has provided some promising competition for Microsoft Windows.

At the extreme, innovation may cause *creative destruction,* the phenomenon discussed in Chapter 11 whereby the market positions of firms committed to existing products and old ways of doing business are destroyed by the creation and spread of new products and new production methods.

dependent on government spending when it comes to basic scientific research. As a result, the first figure displayed in this Last Word troubles many economists.

It shows that the percentage of the federal budget devoted to basic scientific research has fallen drastically over the past 50 years—from a high of 11.7 percent in 1965 to just 3.5 percent in 2015.

Many economists consider that decline as indicating a misallocation of resources. They argue that the federal government is spending too much on programs that fund current consumption and not enough on the productivity-enhancing research activities that could raise future consumption.

The second figure can be used to support their case. It shows how much more the federal government spent in 2015 on several programs that fund the current consumption of goods and services as opposed to all of the programs that fund basic scientific research.

The consumption spending includes the $888 billion paid out by the Social Security system to retirees and the disabled, the $546 billion spent by Medicare to provide health care to the elderly, the $525 billion of non-R&D spending undertaken by the Defense Department, and the $350 billion spent by Medicaid to provide health care to the poor. By contrast, the two most famous federal R&D funding agencies—the National Science Foundation and the National Institutes of Health—received only $7 billion and $29 billion, respectively, while all other federal R&D spending (most of it military) amounted to just $135 billion.

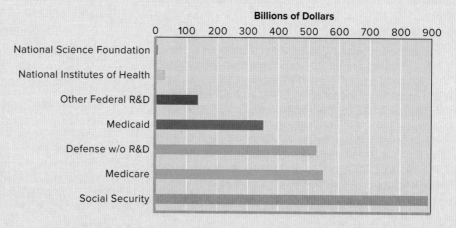

Federal Spending on Various Programs, 2015

The economists who argue for more R&D spending note that the $3,766 billion of non-R&D federal expenditures in 2015 were nearly 28 times more than the $135 billion that the federal government spent on R&D that year. They argue that because scientific knowledge is a public good with huge positive externalities, government should heavily subsidize its production. And they point out that for anyone wishing for more money in the future for programs like Social Security, Medicare, or defense, their best bet would be to spend more now on R&D so as to increase productivity, income, and tax revenues in the future. That way, we could give up a small amount of current consumption in exchange for a substantial boost in future consumption.

Sources: Federal R&D funding data for 2015 and previous years from *Federal Funds for Research and Development: Fiscal Years 2013–15*, National Science Foundation, www.nsf.gov. 2015 federal spending and historical GDP data from Bureau of Economic Analysis, **www.bea.gov.**

According to early proponents like MIT economist Joseph Schumpeter, creative destruction is such a powerful force that it will automatically displace any monopolist that no longer delivers superior performance. But many contemporary economists think this notion reflects more wishful thinking than fact. In this view, the idea that creative destruction is automatic

> ... neglects the ability of powerful established firms to erect private storm shelters—or lobby government to build public storm shelters for them—in order to shield themselves from the Schumpeterian gales of creative destruction. It ignores the difference between the legal freedom of entry and the economic reality deterring the entry of potential newcomers into concentrated industries.[2]

That is, some dominant firms may be able to use strategies such as selective price cutting, buyouts, and massive advertising to block entry and competition from even the most innovative new firms and existing rivals. Moreover, politically active dominant firms have been known to persuade government to give them tax breaks, subsidies, and tariff protection that strengthen their market power.

In short, while innovation in general enhances economic efficiency, in some cases it may lead to entrenched monopoly power. Further innovation may eventually destroy that monopoly power, but the process of creative destruction is neither automatic nor inevitable. On the other hand, the possession of monopoly power does not necessarily preclude rapid technological advance, innovation, or efficiency.

[2]Walter Adams and James Brock, *The Structure of American Industry,* 10th ed. (Upper Saddle River, NJ: Prentice Hall, 2001), pp. 363–64.

SUMMARY

LO15.1 Differentiate among invention, innovation, and technological diffusion.

Technological advance is evidenced by new and improved goods and services and new and improved production or distribution processes. In economists' models, technological advance occurs only in the *very long run*.

Invention is the discovery of a product or process through the use of imagination, ingenuity, and experimentation. Innovation is the first successful commercial introduction of a new product, the first use of a new method, or the creation of a new form of business enterprise. Diffusion is the spread of an earlier innovation among competing firms. Firms channel a majority of their R&D expenditures to innovation and imitation, rather than to basic scientific research and invention.

LO15.2 Explain how entrepreneurs and other innovators further technological advance.

Historically, most economists viewed technological advance as a random, external force to which the economy adjusted. Many contemporary economists see technological advance as occurring in response to profit incentives within the economy and thus as an integral part of capitalism.

Entrepreneurs and other innovators try to anticipate the future. They play a central role in technological advance by initiating changes in products and processes. Entrepreneurs often form start-up firms that focus on creating and introducing new products. Sometimes, innovators work in the R&D labs of major corporations. Entrepreneurs and innovative firms often rely heavily on the basic research done by university and government scientists.

LO15.3 Summarize how a firm determines its optimal amount of research and development (R&D).

A firm's optimal amount of R&D spending occurs where its expected return (marginal benefit) from R&D equals its interest-rate cost of funds (marginal cost) to finance R&D. Entrepreneurs and firms use several sources to finance R&D, including (a) bank loans, (b) bonds, (c) venture capital (funds given in return for a share of the profits if the business succeeds), (d) undistributed corporate profits (retained earnings), and (e) personal savings.

LO15.4 Discuss how technological change can increase profits by raising revenues or lowering costs.

Process innovation can lower a firm's production costs by improving its internal production techniques. Such improvement increases the

firm's total product, thereby lowering its average total cost and increasing its profit. The added profit provides a positive rate of return on the R&D spending that produced the process innovation.

LO15.5 Relate why firms can benefit from their innovation even though rivals have an incentive to imitate it.

Product innovation, the introduction of new products, succeeds when it provides consumers with a higher marginal utility per dollar spent than do existing products. The new product enables consumers to obtain greater total utility from a given income. From the firm's perspective, product innovation increases net revenue sufficiently to yield a positive rate of return on the R&D spending that produced the innovation.

Imitation poses a potential problem for innovators since it threatens their returns on R&D expenditures. Some dominant firms use a fast-second strategy, letting smaller firms initiate new products and then quickly imitating the successes. Nevertheless, there are significant protections and potential benefits for firms that take the lead with R&D and innovation, including (a) patent protection, (b) copyrights and trademarks, (c) lasting brand-name recognition, (d) benefits from trade secrets and learning by doing, (e) high economic profits during the time lag between a product's introduction and its imitation, and (f) the possibility of lucrative buyout offers from larger firms.

LO15.6 Discuss the role of market structure in promoting technological advance.

Each of the four basic market structures has potential strengths and weaknesses regarding the likelihood of R&D and innovation. The inverted-U theory of R&D holds that a firm's R&D spending as a percentage of its sales rises with its industry four-firm concentration ratio, reaches a peak at a 50 percent concentration ratio, and then declines as concentration increases further. Empirical evidence is not clear-cut but lends general support to this theory. For any specific industry, however, the technological opportunities that are available may count more than market structure in determining R&D spending and innovation.

LO15.7 Show how technological advance enhances productive efficiency and allocative efficiency.

In general, technological advance enhances both productive and allocative efficiency. But in some situations patents and the advantages of being first with an innovation can increase monopoly power. While in some cases creative destruction eventually destroys monopolies, most economists doubt that this process is either automatic or inevitable.

TERMS AND CONCEPTS

technological advance	process innovation	optimal amount of R&D
very long run	diffusion	imitation problem
invention	start-ups	fast-second strategy
patent	venture capital	inverted-U theory of R&D
innovation	interest-rate cost-of-funds curve	
product innovation	expected-rate-of-return curve	

The following and additional problems can be found in ▪connect

DISCUSSION QUESTIONS

1. What is meant by technological advance, as broadly defined? How does technological advance enter into the definition of the very long run? Which of the following are examples of technological advance, and which are not: an improved production process; entry of a firm into a profitable purely competitive industry; the imitation of a new production process by another firm; an increase in a firm's advertising expenditures? **LO15.1**

2. Contrast the older and the modern views of technological advance as they relate to the economy. What is the role of entrepreneurs and other innovators in technological advance? How does research by universities and government affect innovators and technological advance? Why do you think some university researchers are becoming more like entrepreneurs and less like "pure scientists"? **LO15.2**

3. Consider the effect that corporate profit taxes have on investing. Look back at Figure 15.4. Suppose that the *r* line is the rate of return a firm earns before taxes. If corporate profit taxes are imposed, the firm's after-tax returns will be lower (and the higher the tax rate, the lower the after-tax returns). If the firm's decisions about R&D spending are based on comparing after-tax returns with the interest-rate cost of funds, how will increased corporate profit taxes affect R&D spending? Does this effect modify your views on corporate profit taxes? Discuss. **LO15.3**

4. Answer the following lettered questions on the basis of the information in this table: **LO15.3**

Amount of R&D, Millions	Expected Rate of Return on R&D, %
$10	16
20	14
30	12
40	10
50	8
60	6

a. If the interest-rate cost of funds is 8 percent, what will be the optimal amount of R&D spending for this firm?

b. Explain why $20 million of R&D spending will not be optimal.

c. Why won't $60 million be optimal either?

5. Explain: "The success of a new product depends not only on its marginal utility but also on its price." **LO15.4**

6. Learning how to use software takes time. So once customers have learned to use a particular software package, it is easier to sell them software upgrades than to convince them to switch to new software. What implications does this have for expected rates of return on R&D spending for software firms developing upgrades versus firms developing imitative products? **LO15.5**

7. Why might a firm making a large economic profit from its existing product employ a fast-second strategy in relationship to new or improved products? What risks does it run in pursuing this strategy? What incentive does a firm have to engage in R&D when rivals can imitate its new product? **LO15.5**

8. Do you think the overall level of R&D would increase or decrease over the next 20 to 30 years if the lengths of new patents were extended from 20 years to, say, "forever"? What if the duration were reduced from 20 years to, say, 3 years? **LO15.5**

9. Make a case that neither pure competition nor pure monopoly is conducive to a great deal of R&D spending and innovation. Why might oligopoly be more favorable to R&D spending and innovation than either pure competition or pure monopoly? What is the inverted-U theory of R&D, and how does it relate to your answers to these questions? **LO15.6**

10. Evaluate: "Society does not need laws outlawing monopolization and monopoly. Inevitably, monopoly causes its own self-destruction, since its high profit is the lure for other firms or entrepreneurs to develop substitute products." **LO15.7**

11. **LAST WORD** How could spending less on Social Security now lead to an ability to increase Social Security funding in the future? Why don't businesses devote more of their R&D spending toward basic scientific research?

REVIEW QUESTIONS

1. Listed below are several possible actions by firms. Write "INV" beside those that reflect invention, "INN" beside those that reflect innovation, and "DIF" beside those that reflect diffusion. **LO15.1**

   a. An auto manufacturer adds "heated seats" as a standard feature in its luxury cars to keep pace with a rival firm whose luxury cars already have this feature.

   b. A television production company pioneers the first music video channel.

   c. A firm develops and patents a working model of a self-erasing whiteboard for classrooms.

   d. A light bulb firm is the first to produce and market lighting fixtures with LEDs (light-emitting diodes).

   e. A rival toy maker introduces a new Jezebel doll to compete with Mattel's Barbie doll.

2. A firm is considering three possible one-year investments, which we will name X, Y, and Z.
   - Investment X would cost $10 million now and would return $11 million next year, for a net gain of $1 million.
   - Investment Y would cost $100 million now and would return $105 million next year, for a net gain of $5 million.
   - Investment Z would cost $1 million now and would return $1.2 million next year, for a net gain of $200,000.

   The firm currently has $150 million of cash on hand that it can loan out at 15 percent interest. Which of the three possible investments should it undertake? **LO15.3**

   a. X only.

   b. Y only.

   c. Z only.

d. X and Y.

e. X and Z.

f. X, Y, and Z.

3. An additional unit of Old Product X will bring Cindy an MU of 15 utils, an additional unit of New Product Y will bring Cindy an MU of 30 utils, and an additional unit of New Product Z will bring Cindy an MU of 40 utils. If a unit of Old Product X costs $10, a unit of New Product Y costs $30, and a unit of New Product Z costs $20, which product will Cindy prefer to spend her money on? **LO15.4**

a. Old Product X.

b. New Product Y.

c. New Product Z.

d. More information is required.

4. The inverted-U theory suggests that R&D expenditures as a percentage of sales _____ with industry concentration after the four-firm concentration ratio exceeds about 50 percent. **LO15.6**

a. Rise.

b. Fall.

c. Fluctuate.

d. Flat-line.

5. Which statement about market structure and innovation is true? **LO15.7**

a. Innovation helps only dominant firms.

b. Innovation keeps new firms from ever catching up with leading firms.

c. Innovation often leads to creative destruction and the replacement of established firms by new firms.

d. Innovation always leads to entrenched monopoly power.

PROBLEMS

1. Suppose a firm expects that a $20 million expenditure on R&D in the current year will result in a new product that can be sold next year. Selling that product next year would increase the firm's revenue next year by $30 million and its costs next year by $29 million. **LO15.3**

   a. What is the expected rate of return on this R&D expenditure?

   b. Suppose the firm can get a bank loan at 6 percent interest to finance its $20 million R&D project. Will the firm undertake the project?

   c. Now suppose the interest-rate cost of borrowing, in effect, falls to 4 percent because the firm decides to use its own retained earnings to finance the R&D. Will this lower interest rate change the firm's R&D decision?

   d. Now suppose that the firm has savings of $20 million— enough money to fund the R&D expenditure without borrowing. If the firm has the chance to invest this money either in the R&D project or in government bonds that pay 3.5 percent per year, which should it do?

   e. What if the government bonds were paying 6.5 percent per year?

2. A firm faces the following costs: total cost of capital = $1,000; price paid for labor = $12 per labor unit; and price paid for raw materials = $4 per raw-material unit. **LO15.4**

   a. Suppose the firm can produce 5,000 units of output this year by combining its fixed capital with 100 units of labor and 450 units of raw materials. What are the total cost and average total cost of producing the 5,000 units of output?

   b. Now assume the firm improves its production process so that it can produce 6,000 units of output this year by combining its fixed capital with 100 units of labor and 450 units of raw materials. What are the total cost and average total cost of producing the 6,000 units of output?

   c. If units of output can always be sold for $1 each, then by how much does the firm's profit increase after it improves its production process?

   d. Suppose that implementing the improved production process would require a one-time-only cost of $1,100. If the firm only considers this year's profit, would the firm implement the improved production process? What if the firm considers its profit not just this year but in future years as well?

Part FIVE

Microeconomics of Resource Markets and Government

The Demand for Resources

Learning Objectives

LO16.1 Explain the significance of resource pricing.

LO16.2 Convey how the marginal revenue productivity of a resource relates to a firm's demand for that resource.

LO16.3 List the factors that increase or decrease resource demand.

LO16.4 Discuss the determinants of elasticity of resource demand.

LO16.5 Determine how a competitive firm selects its optimal combination of resources.

LO16.6 Explain the marginal productivity theory of income distribution.

When you finish your education, you probably will look for a new job. Employers have a demand for educated, productive workers like you. To learn more about the demand for labor and other resources, we now turn from the pricing and production of *goods and services* to the pricing and employment of *resources*. Although firms come in various sizes and operate under different market conditions, each has a demand for productive resources. Firms obtain needed resources from households—the direct or indirect owners of land, labor, capital, and entrepreneurial resources. We shift our attention from the bottom loop of the circular flow model (Figure 2.2), where businesses supply products that households demand, to the top loop, where businesses demand resources that households supply.

This chapter looks at the *demand* for economic resources. Although the discussion is couched in terms of labor, the principles developed also apply to land, capital, and entrepreneurial ability. In Chapter 17 we will combine resource (labor) demand with labor *supply* to analyze wage rates. In Chapter 18 we will use resource demand and resource supply to examine the prices of, and returns to, other productive resources. Issues relating to the use of natural resources are the subject of Chapter 19.

Significance of Resource Pricing

LO16.1 Explain the significance of resource pricing.

Studying resource pricing is important for several reasons:

- *Money-income determination* Resource prices are a major factor in determining the income of households. The expenditures that firms make in acquiring economic resources flow as wage, rent, interest, and profit incomes to the households that supply those resources.

- *Cost minimization* To the firm, resource prices are costs. And to obtain the greatest profit, the firm must produce the profit-maximizing output with the most efficient (least costly) combination of resources. Resource prices play the main role in determining the quantities of land, labor, capital, and entrepreneurial ability that will be combined in producing each good or service (see Table 2.1).

- *Resource allocation* Just as product prices allocate finished goods and services to consumers, resource prices allocate resources among industries and firms. In a dynamic economy, where technology and product demand often change, the efficient allocation of resources over time calls for the continuing shift of resources from one use to another. Resource pricing is a major factor in producing those shifts.

- *Policy issues* Many policy issues surround the resource market. Examples: To what extent should government redistribute income through taxes and transfers? Should government do anything to discourage "excess" pay to corporate executives? Should it increase the legal minimum wage? Is the provision of subsidies to farmers efficient? Should government encourage or restrict labor unions? The facts and debates relating to these policy questions are grounded on resource pricing.

Marginal Productivity Theory of Resource Demand

LO16.2 Convey how the marginal revenue productivity of a resource relates to a firm's demand for that resource.

In discussing resource demand, we will first assume that a firm sells its output in a purely competitive product market and hires a certain resource in a purely competitive resource market. This assumption keeps things simple and is consistent with the model of a competitive labor market that we will develop in Chapter 17. In a competitive *product market,* the firm is a "price taker" and can dispose of as little or as much output as it chooses at the market price. The firm is selling such a negligible fraction of total output that its output decisions exert no influence on product price. Similarly, the firm also is a "price taker" (or "wage taker") in the com-petitive *resource market*. It purchases such a negligible fraction of the total supply of the resource that its buying (or hiring) decisions do not influence the resource price.

Resource Demand as a Derived Demand

Resource demand is the starting point for any discussion of resource prices. Resource demand is a schedule or a curve showing the amounts of a resource that buyers are willing and able to purchase at various prices over some period of time. Crucially, resource demand is a **derived demand,** meaning that the demand for a resource is derived from the demand for the products that the resource helps to produce. This is true because resources usually do not directly satisfy customer wants but do so indirectly through their use in producing goods and services. Almost nobody wants to consume an acre of land, a John Deere tractor, or the labor services of a farmer, but millions of households do want to consume the food and fiber products that these resources help produce. Similarly, the demand for airplanes generates a demand for assemblers, and the demands for such services as income-tax preparation, haircuts, and child care create derived demands for accountants, barbers, and child care workers.

Marginal Revenue Product

Because resource demand is derived from product demand, the strength of the demand for any resource will depend on:

- The productivity of the resource in helping to create a good or service.

- The market value or price of the good or service it helps produce.

Other things equal, a resource that is highly productive in turning out a highly valued commodity will be in great demand. On the other hand, a relatively unproductive resource that is capable of producing only a minimally valued commodity will be in little demand. And no demand whatsoever will exist for a resource that is phenomenally efficient in producing something that no one wants to buy.

Productivity Table 16.1 shows the roles of resource productivity and product price in determining resource demand. Here we assume that a firm adds a single variable resource, labor, to its fixed plant. Columns 1 and 2 give the number of units of the resource applied to production and the resulting total product (output). Column 3 provides the **marginal product (MP),** or additional output, resulting from using each additional unit of labor. Columns 1 through 3 remind us that the law of diminishing returns applies here, causing the marginal product of labor to fall beyond some point. For simplicity, we assume that these diminishing marginal returns—these declines in marginal product—begin with the first worker hired.

TABLE 16.1 **The Demand for Labor: Pure Competition in the Sale of the Product**

(1) Units of Resource	(2) Total Product (Output)	(3) Marginal Product (MP)	(4) Product Price	(5) Total Revenue, (2) × (4)	(6) Marginal Revenue Product (MRP)
0	0		$2	$ 0	
		7			$14
1	7		2	14	
		6			12
2	13		2	26	
		5			10
3	18		2	36	
		4			8
4	22		2	44	
		3			6
5	25		2	50	
		2			4
6	27		2	54	
		1			2
7	28		2	56	

Product Price But the derived demand for a resource depends also on the price of the product it produces. Column 4 in Table 16.1 adds this price information. Product price is constant, in this case at $2, because the product market is competitive. The firm is a price taker and can sell units of output only at this market price.

Multiplying column 2 by column 4 provides the total-revenue data of column 5. These are the amounts of revenue the firm realizes from the various levels of resource usage. From these total-revenue data we can compute **marginal revenue product (MRP)**—the change in total revenue resulting from the use of each additional unit of a resource (labor, in this case). In equation form,

$$\text{Marginal revenue product} = \frac{\text{Change in total revenue}}{\text{Unit change in resource quantity}}$$

The MRPs are listed in column 6 in Table 16.1.

Rule for Employing Resources: MRP = MRC

The MRP schedule, shown as columns 1 and 6, is the firm's demand schedule for labor. To understand why, you must first know the rule that guides a profit-seeking firm in hiring any resource: To maximize profit, a firm should hire additional units of a specific resource as long as each successive unit adds more to the firm's total revenue than it adds to the firm's total cost.

Economists use special terms to designate what each additional unit of labor or other variable resource adds to total cost and what it adds to total revenue. We have seen that MRP measures how much each successive unit of a resource adds to total revenue. The amount that each additional unit of a resource adds to the firm's total (resource) cost is called its **marginal resource cost (MRC).** In equation form,

$$\text{Marginal resource cost} = \frac{\text{change in total (resource) cost}}{\text{unit change in resource quantity}}$$

So we can restate our rule for hiring resources as follows: It will be profitable for a firm to hire additional units of a resource up to the point at which that resource's MRP is equal to its MRC. For example, as the rule applies to labor, if the number of workers a firm is currently hiring is such that the MRP of the last worker exceeds his or her MRC, the firm can profit by hiring more workers. But if the number being hired is such that the MRC of the last worker exceeds his or her MRP, the firm is hiring workers who are not "paying their way" and it can increase its profit by discharging some workers. You may have recognized that this **MRP = MRC rule** is similar to the MR = MC profit-maximizing rule employed throughout our discussion of price and output determination. The rationale of the two rules is the same, but the point of reference is now *inputs* of a resource, not *outputs* of a product.

MRP as Resource Demand Schedule

Let's continue with our focus on labor, knowing that the analysis also applies to other resources. In a purely competitive labor market, market supply and market demand establish the wage rate. Because each firm hires such a small fraction of market supply, it cannot influence the market wage rate; it is a wage taker, not a wage maker. This means that for each additional unit of labor hired, each firm's total resource cost increases by exactly the amount of the constant market wage rate. More specifically, the MRC of labor exactly equals the market wage rate. Thus, resource "price" (the market wage rate) and resource "cost" (marginal resource cost) are equal for a firm that hires a resource in a competitive labor market. As a result, the MRP = MRC rule tells us that, in pure competition, the firm will hire workers up to the point at which the market *wage rate* (its MRC) is equal to its MRP.

In terms of the data in columns 1 and 6 of Table 16.1, if the market wage rate is, say, $13.95, the firm will hire only one worker. This is so because only the hiring of the first worker results in an increase in profits. To see this, note that for the first worker MRP (= $14) exceeds MRC (= $13.95). Thus, hiring the first worker is profitable. For each successive worker, however, MRC (= $13.95) exceeds MRP (= $12 or less), indicating that it will not be profitable to hire any of

FIGURE 16.1 The purely competitive seller's demand for a resource.
The MRP curve is the resource demand curve; each of its points relates
a particular resource price (= MRP when profit is maximized) with a
corresponding quantity of the resource demanded. Under pure competition,
product price is constant; therefore, the downward slope of the $D = MRP$
curve is due solely to the decline in the resource's marginal product (law of
diminishing marginal returns).

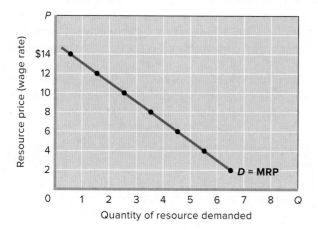

those workers. If the wage rate is $11.95, by the same reason-
ing we discover that it will pay the firm to hire both the first
and second workers. Similarly, if the wage rate is $9.95, three
workers will be hired. If it is $7.95, four. If it is $5.95, five.
And so forth. So here is the key generalization: The MRP
schedule constitutes the firm's demand for labor because
each point on this schedule (or curve) indicates the number of
workers the firm would hire at each possible wage rate.

In Figure 16.1, we show the $D = MRP$ curve based on
the data in Table 16.1.[1] The competitive firm's resource

---

[1]Note that we plot the points in Figure 16.1 halfway between succeeding
numbers of resource units because MRP is associated with the addition of 1
more unit. Thus in Figure 16.1, for example, we plot the MRP of the second
unit ($12) not at 1 or 2 but at 1½. This "smoothing" enables us to sketch a
continuously downsloping curve rather than one that moves downward in
discrete steps (like a staircase) as each new unit of labor is hired.

demand curve identifies an inverse relationship between the
wage rate and the quantity of labor demanded, other things
equal. The curve slopes downward because of diminishing
marginal returns.

Resource Demand under Imperfect Product Market Competition

Resource demand (here, labor demand) is more complex
when the firm is selling its product in an imperfectly competitive market, one in which the firm is a price maker. That
is because imperfect competitors (pure monopolists, oligopolists, and monopolistic competitors) face downsloping product demand curves. As a result, whenever an imperfect
competitor's product demand curve is fixed in place, the only
way to increase sales is by setting a lower price (and thereby
moving down along the fixed demand curve).

The productivity data in Table 16.1 are retained in columns
1 to 3 in Table 16.2. But here in Table 16.2 we show in column 4
that product price must be lowered to sell the marginal product
of each successive worker. The MRP of the purely competitive
seller of Table 16.1 falls for only one reason: Marginal product
diminishes. But the MRP of the imperfectly competitive seller
of Table 16.2 falls for two reasons: Marginal product diminishes *and* product price falls as output increases.

We emphasize that the lower price accompanying each
increase in output (total product) applies not only to the
marginal product of each successive worker but also to all
prior output units that otherwise could have been sold at a
higher price. Observe that the marginal product of the second worker is 6 units of output. These 6 units can be sold
for $2.40 each, or, as a group, for $14.40. But $14.40 is not
the MRP of the second worker. To sell these 6 units, the
firm must take a 20-cent price cut on the 7 units produced
by the first worker—units that otherwise could have been
sold for $2.60 each. Thus, the MRP of the second worker is
only $13 [= $14.40 − (7 × 20 cents)], as shown.

Similarly, the third worker adds 5 units to total product,
and these units are worth $2.20 each, or $11 total. But to sell

---

TABLE 16.2 The Demand for Labor: Imperfect Competition in the Sale of the Product

(1) Units of Resource	(2) Total Product (Output)	(3) Marginal Product (MP)	(4) Product Price	(5) Total Revenue, (2) × (4)	(6) Marginal Revenue Product (MRP)
0	0		$2.80	$ 0	
1	7	7	2.60	18.20	$18.20
2	13	6	2.40	31.20	13.00
3	18	5	2.20	39.60	8.40
4	22	4	2.00	44.00	4.40
5	25	3	1.85	46.25	2.25
6	27	2	1.75	47.25	1.00
7	28	1	1.65	46.20	−1.05

these 5 units, the firm must take a 20-cent price cut on the 13 units produced by the first two workers. So the third worker's MRP is only $8.40 [= $11 − (13 × 20 cents)]. The numbers in column 6 reflect such calculations.

In Figure 16.2 we graph the MRP data from Table 16.2 and label it "D = MRP (imperfect competition)." The broken-line resource demand curve, in contrast, is that of the purely competitive seller represented in Figure 16.1. A comparison of the two curves demonstrates that, other things equal, the resource demand curve of an imperfectly competitive seller is less elastic than that of a purely competitive seller. Consider the effects of an identical percentage decline in the wage rate (resource price) from $11 to $6 in Figure 16.2. Comparison of the two curves reveals that the imperfectly competitive seller (solid curve) does not expand the quantity of labor it employs by as large a percentage as does the purely competitive seller (broken curve).

It is not surprising that the imperfectly competitive producer is less responsive to resource price cuts than the purely competitive producer. When resource prices fall, MC per unit declines for both imperfectly competitive firms as well as purely competitive firms. Because both types of firms maximize profits by producing where MR = MC, the decline in MC will cause both types of firms to produce more. But the effect will be muted for imperfectly competitive firms because their downsloping demand curves cause them to also face downsloping MR curves—so that for each additional unit sold, MR declines. By contrast, MR is constant (and equal to the market equilibrium price P) for competitive firms, so that they do not have to worry about MR per unit falling as they produce more units. As a result, competitive

firms increase production by a larger amount than imperfectly competitive firms whenever resource prices fall.

Market Demand for a Resource

The total, or market, demand curve for a specific resource shows the various total amounts of the resource that firms will purchase or hire at various resource prices, other things equal. Recall that the total, or market, demand curve for a *product* is found by summing horizontally the demand curves of all individual buyers in the market. The market demand curve for a particular *resource* is derived in essentially the same way—by summing horizontally the individual demand or MRP curves for all firms hiring that resource.

Determinants of Resource Demand

LO16.3 List the factors that increase or decrease resource demand.

What will alter the demand for a resource—that is, shift the resource demand curve? The fact that resource demand is derived from *product demand* and depends on *resource productivity* suggests two "resource demand shifters." Also, our analysis of how changes in the prices of other products can shift a product's demand curve (Chapter 3) suggests another factor: changes in the *prices of other resources*.

Changes in Product Demand

Other things equal, an increase in the demand for a product will increase the demand for a resource used in its production, whereas a decrease in product demand will decrease the demand for that resource.

Let's see how this works. The first thing to recall is that a change in the demand for a product will change its price. In

FIGURE 16.2 The imperfectly competitive seller's demand curve for a resource. An imperfectly competitive seller's resource demand curve D (solid) slopes downward because both marginal product and product price fall as resource employment and output rise. This downward slope is greater than that for a purely competitive seller (dashed resource demand curve) because the pure competitor can sell the added output at a constant price.

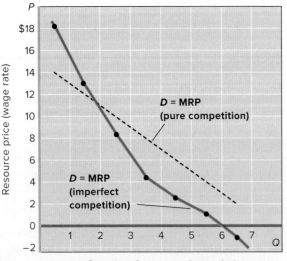

Quantity of resource demanded

Superstars

In what economist Robert Frank calls "winner-take-all markets," a few highly talented performers have huge earnings relative to the average performers in the market. Because consumers and firms seek out "top" performers, small differences in talent or popularity get magnified into huge differences in pay.

Source: © PRNewsFoto/Diamond Information Center/AP Images

In these markets, consumer spending gets channeled toward a few performers. The media then "hypes" these individuals, which further increases the public's awareness of their talents. Many more consumers then buy the stars' products. Although it is not easy to stay on top, several superstars emerge.

The high earnings of superstars result from the high revenues they generate from their work. Consider Beyoncé Knowles. If she sold only a few thousand songs and attracted only a few hundred fans to each concert, the revenue she would produce—her marginal revenue product—would be quite modest. So, too, would be her earnings.

But consumers have anointed Beyoncé as queen of the R&B and hip-hop portion of pop culture. The demand for her music and concerts is extraordinarily high. She sells *millions* of songs, not thousands, and draws *thousands* to her concerts, not hundreds. Her extraordinarily high net earnings derive from her extraordinarily high MRP.

So it is for the other superstars in the "winner-take-all markets." Influenced by the media, but coerced by no one, consumers direct their spending toward a select few. The resulting strong demand for these stars' services reflects their high MRP. And because top talent (by definition) is very limited, superstars receive amazingly high earnings.

Table 16.1, let's assume that an increase in product demand boosts product price from $2 to $3. You should calculate the new resource demand schedule (columns 1 and 6) that would result and plot it in Figure 16.1 to verify that the new resource demand curve lies to the right of the old demand curve. Similarly, a decline in the product demand (and price) will shift the resource demand curve to the left. This effect—resource demand changing along with product demand—demonstrates that resource demand is derived from product demand.

Example: Assuming no offsetting change in supply, a decrease in the demand for new houses will drive down house prices. Those lower prices will decrease the MRP of construction workers, and therefore the demand for construction

workers will fall. The resource demand curve such as in Figure 16.1 or Figure 16.2 will shift to the left.

Changes in Productivity

Other things equal, an increase in the productivity of a resource will increase the demand for the resource and a decrease in productivity will reduce the demand for the resource. If we doubled the MP data of column 3 in Table 16.1, the MRP data of column 6 would also double, indicating a rightward shift of the resource demand curve.

The productivity of any resource may be altered over the long run in several ways:

- *Quantities of other resources* The marginal productivity of any resource will vary with the quantities of the other resources used with it. The greater the amount of capital and land resources used with, say, labor, the greater will be labor's marginal productivity and, thus, labor demand.

- *Technological advance* Technological improvements that increase the quality of other resources, such as capital, have the same effect. The better the *quality* of capital, the greater the productivity of labor used with it. Dockworkers employed with a specific amount of real capital in the form of unloading cranes are more productive than dockworkers with the same amount of real capital embodied in older conveyor-belt systems.

- *Quality of the variable resource* Improvements in the quality of the variable resource, such as labor, will increase its marginal productivity and therefore its demand. In effect, there will be a new demand curve for a different, more skilled, kind of labor.

All these considerations help explain why the average level of (real) wages is higher in industrially advanced nations (for example, the United States, Germany, Japan, and France) than in developing nations (for example, Nicaragua, Ethiopia, Angola, and Cambodia). Workers in industrially advanced nations are generally healthier, better educated, and better trained than are workers in developing countries. Also, in most industries they work with a larger and more efficient stock of capital goods and more abundant natural resources. This increases productivity and creates a strong demand for labor. On the supply side of the market, labor is scarcer relative to capital in industrially advanced than in most developing nations. A strong demand and a relatively scarce supply of labor result in high wage rates in the industrially advanced nations.

Changes in the Prices of Other Resources

Changes in the prices of other resources may change the demand for a specific resource. For example, a change in the price of capital may change the demand for labor. The direction of the change in labor demand will depend on whether labor and capital are substitutes or complements in production.

Substitute Resources

Substitute Resources Suppose the technology in a certain production process is such that labor and capital are substitutable. A firm can produce some specific amount of output using a relatively small amount of labor and a relatively large amount of capital, or vice versa. Now assume that the price of machinery (capital) falls. The effect on the demand for labor will be the net result of two opposed effects: the substitution effect and the output effect.

- *Substitution effect* The decline in the price of machinery prompts the firm to substitute machinery for labor. This allows the firm to produce its output at lower cost. So at the fixed wage rate, smaller quantities of labor are now employed. This **substitution effect** decreases the demand for labor. More generally, the substitution effect indicates that a firm will purchase more of an input whose relative price has declined and, conversely, use less of an input whose relative price has increased.

- *Output effect* Because the price of machinery has fallen, the costs of producing various outputs must also decline. With lower costs, the firm finds it profitable to produce and sell a greater output. The greater output increases the demand for all resources, including labor. So this **output effect** increases the demand for labor. More generally, the output effect means that the firm will purchase more of one particular input when the price of the other input falls and less of that particular input when the price of the other input rises.

- *Net effect* The substitution and output effects are both present when the price of an input changes, but they work in opposite directions. For a decline in the price of capital, the substitution effect decreases the demand for labor and the output effect increases it. The net change in labor demand depends on the relative sizes of the two effects: If the substitution effect outweighs the output effect, a decrease in the price of capital decreases the demand for labor. If the output effect exceeds the substitution effect, a decrease in the price of capital increases the demand for labor.

Complementary Resources Recall from Chapter 3 that certain products, such as computers and software, are complementary goods; they "go together" and are jointly demanded. Resources may also be complementary; an increase in the quantity of one of them used in the production process requires an increase in the amount used of the other as well, and vice versa. Suppose a small design firm does computer-assisted design (CAD) with relatively expensive personal computers as its basic piece of capital equipment. Each computer requires exactly one design engineer to operate it; the machine is not automated—it will not run itself—and a second engineer would have nothing to do.

Now assume that a technological advance in the production of these computers substantially reduces their price. There can be no substitution effect because labor and capital must be used in *fixed proportions,* one person for one machine. Capital cannot be substituted for labor. But there *is* an output effect. Other things equal, the reduction in the price of capital goods means lower production costs. Producing a larger output will therefore be profitable. In doing so, the firm will use both more capital and more labor. When labor and capital are complementary, a decline in the price of capital increases the demand for labor through the output effect.

We have cast our analysis of substitute resources and complementary resources mainly in terms of a decline in the price of capital. Table 16.3 summarizes the effects of an *increase* in the price of capital on the demand for labor. Please study it carefully.

Now that we have discussed the full list of the determinants of labor demand, let's again review their effects. Stated in terms of the labor resource, the demand for labor will increase (the labor demand curve will shift rightward) when:

- The demand for (and therefore the price of) the product produced by that labor *increases.*

- The productivity (MP) of labor *increases.*

- The price of a substitute input *decreases,* provided the output effect exceeds the substitution effect.

- The price of a substitute input *increases,* provided the substitution effect exceeds the output effect.

- The price of a complementary input *decreases.*

TABLE 16.3 The Effect of an Increase in the Price of Capital on the Demand for Labor, D_L

(1) Relationship of Inputs	(2) Increase in the Price of Capital		
	(a) Substitution Effect	(b) Output Effect	(c) Combined Effect
Substitutes in production	Labor substituted for capital	Production costs up, output down, and less of both capital and labor used	D_L increases if the substitution effect exceeds the output effect; D_L decreases if the output effect exceeds the substitution effect
Complements in production	No substitution of labor for capital	Production costs up, output down, and less of both capital and labor used	D_L decreases (because only the output effect applies)

TABLE 16.4 Determinants of Labor Demand: Factors That Shift the Labor Demand Curve

Determinant	Examples
Change in product demand	Gambling increases in popularity, increasing the demand for workers at casinos.
	Consumers decrease their demand for leather coats, decreasing the demand for tanners.
	The federal government increases spending on homeland security, increasing the demand for security personnel.
Change in productivity	An increase in the skill levels of physicians increases the demand for their services.
	Computer-assisted graphic design increases the productivity of, and demand for, graphic artists.
Change in the price of another resource	An increase in the price of electricity increases the cost of producing aluminum and reduces the demand for aluminum workers.
	The price of security equipment used by businesses to protect against illegal entry falls, decreasing the demand for night guards.
	The price of cell phone equipment decreases, reducing the cost of cell phone service; this in turn increases the demand for cell phone assemblers.
	Health-insurance premiums rise, and firms substitute part-time workers who are not covered by insurance for full-time workers who are.

Be sure that you can "reverse" these effects to explain a *decrease* in labor demand.

Table 16.4 provides several illustrations of the determinants of labor demand, listed by the categories of determinants we have discussed. You will benefit by giving them a close look.

Occupational Employment Trends

Changes in labor demand have considerable significance since they affect wage rates and employment in specific occupations. Increases in labor demand for certain occupational groups result in increases in their employment; decreases in labor demand result in decreases in their employment. For illustration, let's first look at occupations for which labor demand is growing and then examine occupations for which it is declining. (Wage rates are the subject of the next chapter.)

The Fastest-Growing Occupations Table 16.5 lists the 10 fastest-growing U.S. occupations for 2010 to 2020, as measured by percentage changes and projected by the Bureau of Labor Statistics. It is no coincidence that the service occupations dominate the list. In general, the demand for service workers in the United States is rapidly outpacing the demand for manufacturing, construction, and mining workers.

Of the 10 fastest-growing occupations in percentage terms, seven—occupational therapy assistants, physical therapist assistants, physical therapy aids, home health aides, nurse practitioners, physical therapists, and ambulance drivers—are related to the health field. The rising demand for these types of labor is derived from the growing demand for health services, caused by several factors. The aging of the U.S. population has brought with it more medical problems; the rising standard of income has led to greater expenditures on health care; and the continued presence of private and public insurance has allowed people to purchase more health care than most could afford individually.

TABLE 16.5 The 10 Fastest-Growing U.S. Occupations in Percentage Terms, 2014–2024

Occupation	Employment, Thousands of Jobs		Percentage Increase*
	2014	**2024**	
Wind turbine service technicians	4	9	108
Occupational therapy assistants	33	47	43
Physical therapist assistants	79	111	41
Physical therapist aides	50	70	39
Home health aides	914	1,262	38
Commercial drivers	4	6	37
Nurse practitioners	127	172	35
Physical therapists	211	283	34
Statisticians	30	40	34
Ambulance drivers and attendants, except EMTs	20	26	33

*Percentages and employment numbers may not reconcile due to rounding.

Source: Bureau of Labor Statistics, "Employment Projections," **www.bls.gov**.

The Most Rapidly Declining Occupations In contrast, Table 16.6 lists the 10 U.S. occupations with the greatest projected job loss (in percentage terms) between 2014 and 2024. Several of the occupations owe their declines mainly to "labor-saving" technological change. For example, automated or computerized equipment has greatly reduced the need for postal employees, sewing machine operators, and photographic process workers.

Two of the occupations in the declining employment list are related to textiles and apparel. The U.S. demand for these

TABLE 16.6 The 10 Most Rapidly Declining U.S. Occupations in Percentage Terms, 2014–2024

Occupation	Employment, Thousands of Jobs		Percentage Decrease*
	2014	2024	
Locomotive firers	2	0.5	70
Electronic equipment technicians, motor vehicles	12	6	50
Telephone operators	13	8	42
Postal service mail sorters and processors	118	78	34
Switchboard operators and answering service operators	112	75	33
Photographic process workers	29	19	31
Shoe machine operators	4	3	30
Manufactured building and mobile home installers	4	3	28
Foundry mold and coremakers	12	9	27
Sewing machine operators	154	112	27

*Percentages and employment numbers may not reconcile due to rounding.
Source: Bureau of Labor Statistics, "Employment Projections," **www.bls.gov**.

goods is increasingly being filled through imports. Those jobs are therefore rapidly disappearing in the United States.

As we indicated, the "top-10" lists shown in Tables 16.5 and 16.6 are based on percentage changes. In terms of absolute job growth and loss, the greatest projected employment growth between 2014 and 2024 is for home health aides (348,000 jobs) and physical therapists (72,000 jobs). The greatest projected absolute decline in employment is for sewing machine operators (−42,000).

Elasticity of Resource Demand

LO16.4 Discuss the determinants of elasticity of resource demand.

The employment changes we have just discussed have resulted from shifts in the locations of resource demand curves. Such changes in demand must be distinguished from changes in the quantity of a resource demanded caused by a change in the price of the specific resource under consideration. Such a change is caused not by a shift of the demand curve but,

rather, by a movement from one point to another on a fixed resource demand curve. Example: In Figure 16.1 we note that an increase in the wage rate from $5 to $7 will reduce the quantity of labor demanded from 5 to 4 units. This is a change in the *quantity of labor demanded* as distinct from a *change in the demand for labor*.

The sensitivity of resource quantity to changes in resource prices along a fixed resource demand curve is measured by the **elasticity of resource demand.** In coefficient form,

$$E_{rd} = \frac{\text{percentage change in resource quantity demanded}}{\text{percentage change in resource price}}$$

When E_{rd} is greater than 1, resource demand is elastic; when E_{rd} is less than 1, resource demand is inelastic; and when E_{rd} equals 1, resource demand is unit-elastic. What determines the elasticity of resource demand? Several factors are at work.

Ease of Resource Substitutability   The degree to which resources are substitutable is a fundamental determinant of elasticity. More specifically, the greater the substitutability of other resources, the more elastic is the demand for a particular resource. As an example, the high degree to which computerized voice recognition systems are substitutable for human beings implies that the demand for human beings answering phone calls at call centers is quite elastic. In contrast, good substitutes for physicians are rare, so demand for them is less elastic or even inelastic. If a furniture manufacturer finds that several types of wood are equally satisfactory in making coffee tables, a rise in the price of any one type of wood may cause a sharp drop in the amount demanded as the producer substitutes some other type of wood for the type of wood whose price has gone up. At the other extreme, there may be no reasonable substitutes; bauxite is absolutely essential in the production of aluminum ingots. Thus, the demand for bauxite by aluminum producers is inelastic.

Time can play a role in the ease of input substitution. For example, a firm's truck drivers may obtain a substantial wage increase with little or no immediate decline in employment. But over time, as the firm's trucks wear out and are replaced, that wage increase may motivate the company to purchase larger trucks and in that way deliver the same total output with fewer drivers.

Elasticity of Product Demand   Because the demand for labor is a derived demand, the elasticity of the demand for the output that the labor is producing will influence the elasticity of the demand for labor. Other things equal, the greater the price elasticity of product demand, the greater the elasticity of resource demand. For example, suppose that the wage rate falls. This means a decline in the cost of producing the product and a drop in the product's price. If the elasticity of product demand is great, the resulting increase in the quantity of the product demanded will be large and thus necessitate a large increase in the quantity of labor to produce the additional output. This implies an elastic demand for labor. But if the demand for the product is inelastic, the increase in the amount of the product demanded will be small, as will be the increases in the quantity of labor demanded. This suggests an inelastic demand for labor.

Remember that the resource demand curve in Figure 16.1 is more elastic than the resource demand curve shown in Figure 16.2. The difference arises because in Figure 16.1 we assume a perfectly elastic product demand curve, whereas Figure 16.2 is based on a downsloping or less than perfectly elastic product demand curve.

Ratio of Resource Cost to Total Cost The larger the proportion of total production costs accounted for by a resource, the greater the elasticity of demand for that resource. In the extreme, if labor cost is the only production cost, then a 20 percent increase in wage rates will shift all the firm's cost curves upward by 20 percent. If product demand is elastic, this substantial increase in costs will cause a relatively large decline in sales and a sharp decline in the amount of labor demanded. So labor demand is highly elastic. But if labor cost is only 50 percent of production cost, then a 20 percent increase in wage rates will increase costs by only 10 percent. With the same elasticity of product demand, this will cause a relatively small decline in sales and therefore in the amount of labor demanded. In this case the demand for labor is much less elastic.

QUICK REVIEW 16.2

✓ A resource demand curve will shift because of changes in product demand, changes in the productivity of the resource, and changes in the prices of other inputs.

✓ If resources A and B are substitutable, a decline in the price of A will decrease the demand for B provided the substitution effect exceeds the output effect. But if the output effect exceeds the substitution effect, the demand for B will increase.

✓ If resources C and D are complements, a decline in the price of C will increase the demand for D.

✓ Elasticity of resource demand measures the extent to which producers change the quantity of a resource they hire when its price changes.

✓ For any particular resource, the elasticity of resource demand will be less the greater the difficulty of substituting other resources for the resource, the smaller the elasticity of product demand, and the smaller the proportion of total cost accounted for by the resource.

Optimal Combination of Resources*

LO16.5 Determine how a competitive firm selects its optimal combination of resources.

So far, our main focus has been on one variable input, labor. But in the long run firms can vary the amounts of all the resources they use. That's why we need to consider what combination of resources a firm will choose when *all* its inputs are variable. While our analysis is based on two resources, it can be extended to any number of inputs.

We will consider two interrelated questions:

- What combination of resources will minimize costs at a specific level of output?
- What combination of resources will maximize profit?

The Least-Cost Rule

A firm is producing a specific output with the **least-cost combination of resources** when the last dollar spent on each resource yields the same marginal product. That is, the cost of any output is minimized when the ratios of marginal product to price of the last units of resources used are the same for each resource. To see how this rule maximizes profits in a more concrete setting, consider firms that are competitive buyers in resource markets. Because each firm is too small to affect resource prices, each firm's marginal resource costs will equal market resource prices and each firm will be able to hire as many or as few units as it would like of any and all resources at their respective market prices. Thus, if there are just two resources, labor and capital, a competitive firm will minimize its total cost of a specific output when

$$\frac{\text{Marginal product of labor (MP}_L)}{\text{Price of labor (}P_L)} = \frac{\text{Marginal product of capital (MP}_C)}{\text{Price of capital (}P_C)} \quad (1)$$

Throughout, we will refer to the marginal products of labor and capital as MP_L and MP_C, respectively, and symbolize the price of labor by P_L and the price of capital by P_C.

A concrete example will show why fulfilling the condition in equation 1 leads to least-cost production. Assume that the price of both capital and labor is $1 per unit but that Siam Soups currently employs them in such amounts that the marginal product of labor is 10 and the marginal product of capital is 5. Our equation immediately tells us that this is not the least costly combination of resources:

$$\frac{MP_L = 10}{P_L = \$1} > \frac{MP_C = 5}{P_C = \$1}$$

---

*Note to Instructors: We consider this section to be optional. If desired, it can be skipped without loss of continuity. It can also be deferred until after the discussion of wage determination in the next chapter.

Suppose Siam spends $1 less on capital and shifts that dollar to labor. It loses 5 units of output produced by the last dollar's worth of capital, but it gains 10 units of output from the extra dollar's worth of labor. Net output increases by 5 (= 10 − 5) units for the same total cost. More such shifting of dollars from capital to labor will push the firm *down* along its MP curve for labor and *up* along its MP curve for capital, increasing output and moving the firm toward a position of equilibrium where equation 1 is fulfilled. At that equilibrium position, the MP per dollar for the last unit of both labor and capital might be, for example, 7. And Siam will be producing a greater output for the same (original) cost.

Whenever the same total-resource cost can result in a greater total output, the cost per unit—and therefore the total cost of any specific level of output—can be reduced. Being able to produce a *larger* output with a *specific* total cost is the same as being able to produce a *specific* output with a *smaller* total cost. If Siam buys $1 less of capital, its output will fall by 5 units. If it spends only $.50 of that dollar on labor, the firm will increase its output by a compensating 5 units (= $\frac{1}{2}$ of the MP per dollar). Then the firm will realize the same total output at a $0.50 lower total cost.

The cost of producing any specific output can be reduced as long as equation 1 does not hold. But when dollars have been shifted between capital and labor to the point where equation 1 holds, no additional changes in the use of capital and labor will reduce costs further. Siam will be producing that output using the least-cost combination of capital and labor.

All the long-run cost curves developed in Chapter 9 and used thereafter assume that the least-cost combination of inputs has been realized at each level of output. Any firm that combines resources in violation of the least-cost rule would have a higher-than-necessary average total cost at each level of output. That is, it would incur *X-inefficiency,* as discussed in Figure 12.7.

The producer's least-cost rule is analogous to the consumer's utility-maximizing rule described in Chapter 7. In achieving the utility-maximizing combination of goods, the consumer considers both his or her preferences as reflected in diminishing-marginal-utility data and the prices of the various products. Similarly, in achieving the cost-minimizing combination of resources, the producer considers both the marginal-product data and the prices (costs) of the various resources.

The Profit-Maximizing Rule

Minimizing cost is not sufficient for maximizing profit. A firm can produce any level of output in the least costly way by applying equation 1. But only one unique level of output maximizes profit. Our earlier analysis of product markets showed that this profit-maximizing output occurs where marginal revenue equals marginal cost (MR = MC). Near the beginning of this chapter we determined that we could write this profit-maximizing condition as MRP = MRC as it relates to resource inputs.

In a purely competitive resource market the marginal resource cost (MRC) is equal to the resource price P. Thus, for any competitive resource market, we have as our profit-maximizing equation

$$\text{MRP (resource)} = P \text{ (resource)}$$

This condition must hold for every variable resource, and in the long run all resources are variable. In competitive markets, a firm will therefore achieve its **profit-maximizing combination of resources** when each resource is employed to the point at which its marginal revenue product equals its resource price. For two resources, labor and capital, we need both

$$P_L = \text{MRP}_L \quad \text{and} \quad P_C = \text{MRP}_C$$

We can combine these conditions by dividing both sides of each equation by their respective prices and equating the results to get

$$\frac{\text{MRP}_L}{P_L} = \frac{\text{MRP}_C}{P_C} = 1 \tag{2}$$

Note in equation 2 that it is not sufficient that the MRPs of the two resources be *proportionate* to their prices; the MRPs must be *equal* to their prices and the ratios therefore equal to 1. For example, if $\text{MRP}_L = \$15$, $P_L = \$5$, $\text{MRP}_C = \$9$, and $P_C = \$3$, Siam is underemploying both capital and labor even though the ratios of MRP to resource price are identical for both resources. The firm can expand its profit by hiring additional amounts of both capital and labor until it moves down its downsloping MRP curves to the points at which $\text{MRP}_L = \$5$ and $\text{MRP}_C = \$3$. The ratios will then be 5/5 and 3/3 and equal to 1.

The profit-maximizing position in equation 2 includes the cost-minimizing condition of equation 1. That is, if a firm is maximizing profit according to equation 2, then it must be using the least-cost combination of inputs to do so. However, the converse is not true: A firm operating at least cost according to equation 1 may not be operating at the output that maximizes its profit.

Numerical Illustration

A numerical illustration will help you understand the least-cost and profit-maximizing rules. In columns 2, 3, 2′, and 3′ in Table 16.7 we show the total products and marginal products for various amounts of labor and capital that are assumed to be the only inputs Siam needs in producing its soup. Both inputs are subject to diminishing returns.

We also assume that labor and capital are supplied in competitive resource markets at $8 and $12, respectively, and that Siam's soup sells competitively at $2 per unit. For both labor and capital we can determine the total revenue associated with each input level by multiplying total product by the

TABLE 16.7 Data for Finding the Least-Cost and Profit-Maximizing Combination of Labor and Capital, Siam's Soups*

	Labor (Price = $8)					Capital (Price = $12)			
(1) Quantity	(2) Total Product (Output)	(3) Marginal Product	(4) Total Revenue	(5) Marginal Revenue Product	(1') Quantity	(2') Total Product (Output)	(3') Marginal Product	(4') Total Revenue	(5') Marginal Revenue Product
0	0		$ 0		0	0		$ 0	
		12		$24			13		$26
1	12		24		1	13		26	
		10		20			9		18
2	22		44		2	22		44	
		6		12			6		12
3	28		56		3	28		56	
		5		10			4		8
4	33		66		4	32		64	
		4		8			3		6
5	37		74		5	35		70	
		3		6			2		4
6	40		80		6	37		74	
		2		4			1		2
7	42		84		7	38		76	

*To simplify, it is assumed in this table that the productivity of each resource is independent of the quantity of the other. For example, the total and marginal products of labor are assumed not to vary with the quantity of capital employed.

$2 product price. These data are shown in columns 4 and 4'. They enable us to calculate the marginal revenue product of each successive input of labor and capital as shown in columns 5 and 5', respectively.

Producing at Least Cost What is the least-cost combination of labor and capital for Siam to use in producing, say, 50 units of output? The answer, which we can obtain by trial and error, is 3 units of labor and 2 units of capital. Columns 2 and 2' indicate that this combination of labor and capital does, indeed, result in the required 50 (= 28 + 22) units of output. Now, note from columns 3 and 3' that hiring 3 units of labor gives us $MP_L/P_L = \frac{6}{8} = \frac{3}{4}$ and hiring 2 units of capital gives us $MP_C/P_C = \frac{9}{12} = \frac{3}{4}$. So equation 1 is fulfilled. How can we verify that costs are actually minimized? First, we see that the total cost of employing 3 units of labor and 2 of capital is $48 [= (3 × $8) + (2 × $12)].

Other combinations of labor and capital will also yield 50 units of output, but at a higher cost than $48. For example, 5 units of labor and 1 unit of capital will produce 50 (= 37 + 13) units, but total cost is higher, at $52 [= (5 × $8) + (1 × $12)]. This comes as no surprise because 5 units of labor and 1 unit of capital violate the least-cost rule—$MP_L/P_L = \frac{4}{8}$, $MP_C/P_C = \frac{13}{12}$. Only the combination (3 units of labor and 2 units of capital) that minimizes total cost will satisfy equation 1. All other combinations capable of producing 50 units of output violate the cost-minimizing rule, and therefore cost more than $48.

Maximizing Profit Will 50 units of output maximize Siam's profit? No, because the profit-maximizing terms of equation 2 are not satisfied when the firm employs 3 units of labor and 2 of capital. To maximize profit, each input should be employed until its price equals its marginal revenue

product. But for 3 units of labor, labor's MRP in column 5 is $12 while its price is only $8. This means the firm could increase its profit by hiring more labor. Similarly, for 2 units of capital, we see in column 5' that capital's MRP is $18 and its price is only $12. This indicates that more capital should also be employed. By producing only 50 units of output (even though they are produced at least cost), labor and capital are being used in less-than-profit-maximizing amounts. The firm needs to expand its employment of labor and capital, thereby increasing its output.

Table 16.7 shows that the MRPs of labor and capital are equal to their prices, so equation 2 is fulfilled when Siam is employing 5 units of labor and 3 units of capital. So this is the profit-maximizing combination of inputs.[2] The firm's total cost will be $76, made up of $40 (= 5 × $8) of labor and $36 (= 3 × $12) of capital. Total revenue will be $130, found either by multiplying the total output of 65 (= 37 + 28) by the $2 product price or by summing the total revenues attributable to labor ($74) and to capital ($56). The difference between total revenue and total cost in this instance is $54 (= $130 − $76). Experiment with other combinations of labor and capital to demonstrate that they yield an economic profit of less than $54.

Note that the profit-maximizing combination of 5 units of labor and 3 units of capital is also a least-cost combination for this particular level of output. Using these resource amounts satisfies the least-cost requirement of equation 1 in that $MP_L/P_L = \frac{4}{8} = \frac{1}{2}$ and $MP_C/P_C = \frac{6}{12} = \frac{1}{2}$.

---

[2]Because we are dealing with discrete (nonfractional) units of the two outputs here, the use of 4 units of labor and 2 units of capital is equally profitable. The fifth unit of labor's MRP and its price (cost) are equal at $8, so that the fifth labor unit neither adds to nor subtracts from the firm's profit; similarly, the third unit of capital has no effect on profit.

Labor and Capital: Substitutes or Complements?

Automatic Teller Machines (ATMs) Have Complemented Some Types of Labor While Substituting for Other Types of Labor.

As you have learned from this chapter, a firm achieves its least-cost combination of inputs when the last dollar it spends on each input makes the same contribution to total output. This raises an interesting real-world question: What happens when technological advance makes available a new, highly productive capital good for which MP/P is greater than it is for other inputs, say, a particular type of labor?

The answer is that the least-cost mix of resources abruptly changes, and the firm responds accordingly. If the new capital is a substitute for a particular type of labor, the firm will replace that particular type of labor with the new capital. But if the new capital is a complement for a particular type of labor, the firm will add additional amounts of that type of labor.

Consider bank tellers. One of their core functions, before ATMs became common in the 1980s, was to handle deposits and withdrawals of cash. Bank tellers had several other tasks that they needed to handle, but one particular type of labor they supplied was handling cash transactions. The task of handling cash trans-

Source: © Picturenet/Getty Images RF

actions can, however, be equally well-managed by ATMs—but at one-quarter the cost. Naturally, banks responded to that cost advantage by installing more ATMs.

That might make you think that ATMs displaced tellers because it would seem natural in this scenario that ATMs were a substitute for bank tellers. But the data tells a different story! The number of human bank tellers actually *increased* over time as the number of ATMs soared. In 1985, there were 60,000 ATMs and 485,000 bank tellers. In 2015, there were 425,000 ATMs and 526,000 bank tellers. This means that over that entire time period, ATM machines must have been a complement to the labor provided by bank tellers.

To understand what happened, you have to keep in mind that bank tellers can be put to work doing many different tasks. Only one of those many possible tasks is handling cash. So while it is true that ATMs were indeed a substitute for bank tellers in terms of cash handling, ATMs did not offer a cheaper alternative for the other tasks

that bank tellers could engage in. Thus, while there was a strong tendency for ATMs to substitute for the labor involved in handling cash, ATMs could not substitute for other bank teller activities. In fact, ATMs ended up becoming a complement for those other activities.

The process was not instantaneous. Eighty thousand bank teller jobs were indeed lost during the 1990s because bank managers at first *did* think of ATMs and bank tellers as substitutes. But by the early 2000s, bank managers realized that the cost savings offered by ATMs had given them the chance to operate in new ways that would actually require more tellers rather than fewer tellers.

Before ATMs, the average branch employed 20 employees. After ATMs, the average branch employed 13 employees. That ma-

Source: © Keith Brofsky/Getty Images RF

jor increase in efficiency gave banks the chance to compete against one another by opening more branches—and more branches meant having to hire more human tellers. Thus, the efficiencies generated by having ATMs handle cash transactions at one-fourth the cost caused the demand for bank tellers to increase.

In addition, the banks also realized that bank tellers could be trained in more complex tasks like selling financial products and helping to issue home mortgages. Once banks figured out these new ways to employ tellers, ATMs turned from a substitute for bank teller labor into a complement for bank teller labor. By freeing human beings from having to handle cash transactions, ATMs acted as a complement for other types of human labor, such as selling financial products.

We can generalize from the history of ATMs. Capital is, overall, a complement for human labor, not a substitute for human labor. Certain types of human labor are substituted away as new technologies arrive, but humans end up being complemented by capital as they perform other tasks. Some types of work will disappear and the government may need to help displaced workers train for new jobs. But the newly deployed capital will end up increasing wages because it will increase the overall demand for human labor.

Marginal Productivity Theory of Income Distribution

LO16.6 Explain the marginal productivity theory of income distribution.

Our discussion of resource pricing is the cornerstone of the controversial view that fairness and economic justice are one of the outcomes of a competitive capitalist economy. Table 16.7 demonstrates, in effect, that workers receive income payments (wages) equal to the marginal contributions they make to their employers' outputs and revenues. In other words, workers are paid according to the value of the labor services that they contribute to production. Similarly, owners of the other resources receive income based on the value of the resources they supply in the production process.

In this **marginal productivity theory of income distribution,** income is distributed according to contribution to society's output. So, if you are willing to accept the proposition "To each according to the value of what he or she creates," income payments based on marginal revenue product provide a fair and equitable distribution of society's income.

This sounds reasonable, but you need to be aware of serious criticisms of this theory of income distribution:

- *Inequality* Critics argue that the distribution of income resulting from payment according to marginal productivity may be highly unequal because productive resources are very unequally distributed in the first place. Aside from their differences in mental and physical attributes, individuals encounter substantially different opportunities to enhance their productivity through education and training and the use of more and better equipment. Some people may not be able to participate in production at all because of mental or physical disabilities, and they would obtain no income under a system of distribution based solely on marginal productivity. Ownership of property resources is also highly unequal. Many owners of land and capital resources obtain their property by inheritance rather than through their own productive effort. Hence, income from inherited property

resources conflicts with the "To each according to the value of what he or she creates" idea. Critics say that these inequalities call for progressive taxation and government spending programs aimed at creating an income distribution that will be more equitable than that which would occur if the income distribution were made strictly according to marginal productivity.

- *Market imperfections* The marginal productivity theory of income distribution rests on the assumptions of competitive markets. But, as we will see in Chapter 17, not all labor markets are highly competitive. In some labor markets employers exert their wage-setting power to pay less-than-competitive wages. And some workers, through labor unions, professional associations, and occupational licensing laws, wield wage-setting power in selling their services. Even the process of collective bargaining over wages suggests a power struggle over the division of income. In wage setting through negotiations, market forces—and income shares based on marginal productivity—may get partially pushed into the background. In addition, discrimination in the labor market can distort earnings patterns. In short, because of real-world market imperfections, wage rates and other resource prices are not always based solely on contributions to output.

> ## QUICK REVIEW 16.3
>
> ✓ Any specific level of output will be produced with the least-costly combination of variable resources when the marginal product per dollar's worth of each input is the same.
>
> ✓ A firm is employing the profit-maximizing combination of resources when each resource is used to the point where its marginal revenue product equals its price.
>
> ✓ The marginal productivity theory of income distribution holds that all resources are paid according to their marginal contributions to output.

SUMMARY

LO16.1 Explain the significance of resource pricing.

Resource prices help determine money incomes, and they simultaneously ration resources to various industries and firms.

LO16.2 Convey how the marginal revenue productivity of a resource relates to a firm's demand for that resource.

The demand for any resource is derived from the product it helps produce. That means the demand for a resource will depend on its

productivity and on the market value (price) of the good it is used to produce.

Marginal revenue product is the extra revenue a firm obtains when it employs 1 more unit of a resource. The marginal revenue product curve for any resource is the demand curve for that resource because the firm equates resource price and MRP in determining its profit-maximizing level of resource employment. Thus each point on the MRP curve indicates how many resource units the firm will hire at a specific resource price.

The firm's demand curve for a resource slopes downward because the marginal product of additional units declines in accordance with the law of diminishing returns. When a firm is selling in an imperfectly competitive market, the resource demand curve falls for a second reason: Product price must be reduced for the firm to sell a larger output. The market demand curve for a resource is derived by summing horizontally the demand curves of all the firms hiring that resource.

LO16.3 List the factors that increase or decrease resource demand.

The demand curve for a resource will shift as the result of (*a*) a change in the demand for, and therefore the price of, the product the resource is producing; (*b*) changes in the productivity of the resource; and (*c*) changes in the prices of other resources.

If resources A and B are substitutable for each other, a decline in the price of A will decrease the demand for B provided the substitution effect is greater than the output effect. But if the output effect *exceeds* the substitution effect, a decline in the price of A will increase the demand for B.

If resources C and D are complementary or jointly demanded, there is only an output effect; a change in the price of C will change the demand for D in the opposite direction.

The majority of the 10 fastest-growing occupations in the United States—by percentage increase—relate to health care and computers (review Table 16.5); the 10 most rapidly declining occupations by percentage decrease, however, are more mixed (review Table 16.6).

LO16.4 Discuss the determinants of elasticity of resource demand.

The elasticity of demand for a resource measures the responsiveness of producers to a change in the resource's price. The coefficient of the elasticity of resource demand is

$$E_{rd} = \frac{\text{percentage change in resource quantity demanded}}{\text{percentage change in resource price}}$$

When E_{rd} is greater than 1, resource demand is elastic; when E_{rd} is less than 1, resource demand is inelastic; and when E_{rd} equals 1, resource demand is unit-elastic.

The elasticity of demand for a resource will be greater (*a*) the greater the ease of substituting other resources for labor, (*b*) the greater the elasticity of demand for the product, and (*c*) the larger the proportion of total production costs attributable to the resource.

LO16.5 Determine how a competitive firm selects its optimal combination of resources.

Any specific level of output will be produced with the least costly combination of variable resources when the marginal product per dollar's worth of each input is the same—that is, when

$$\frac{\text{MP of labor}}{\text{Price of labor}} = \frac{\text{MP of capital}}{\text{Price of capital}}$$

A firm is employing the profit-maximizing combination of resources when each resource is used to the point where its marginal revenue product equals its price. In terms of labor and capital, that occurs when the MRP of labor equals the price of labor and the MRP of capital equals the price of capital—that is, when

$$\frac{\text{MP of labor}}{\text{Price of labor}} = \frac{\text{MP of capital}}{\text{Price of capital}} = 1$$

LO16.6 Explain the marginal productivity theory of income distribution.

The marginal productivity theory of income distribution holds that resources are paid according to their marginal contribution to output. Critics say that such an income distribution is too unequal and that real-world market imperfections result in pay above and below marginal contributions to output.

TERMS AND CONCEPTS

derived demand	MRP = MRC rule	least-cost combination of resources
marginal product (MP)	substitution effect	profit-maximizing combination of resources
marginal revenue product (MRP)	output effect	marginal productivity theory of income distribution
marginal resource cost (MRC)	elasticity of resource demand	

The following and additional problems can be found in ▪ **connect**

DISCUSSION QUESTIONS

1. What is the significance of resource pricing? Explain how the factors determining resource demand differ from those determining product demand. Explain the meaning and significance of the fact that the demand for a resource is a derived demand. Why do resource demand curves slope downward? **LO16.1**

2. In 2009 General Motors (GM) announced that it would reduce employment by 21,000 workers. What does this decision reveal about how GM viewed its marginal revenue product (MRP) and marginal resource cost (MRC)? Why didn't GM reduce employment by more than 21,000 workers? By fewer than 21,000 workers? **LO16.3**

3. What factors determine the elasticity of resource demand? What effect will each of the following have on the elasticity or the location of the demand for resource C, which is being used to produce commodity X? Where there is any uncertainty as to the outcome, specify the causes of that uncertainty. **LO16.4**
   a. An increase in the demand for product X.
   b. An increase in the price of substitute resource D.
   c. An increase in the number of resources substitutable for C in producing X.
   d. A technological improvement in the capital equipment with which resource C is combined.
   e. A fall in the price of complementary resource E.
   f. A decline in the elasticity of demand for product X due to a decline in the competitiveness of product market X.

4. In each of the following four cases, MRP_L and MRP_C refer to the marginal revenue products of labor and capital, respectively, and P_L and P_C refer to their prices. Indicate in each case whether the conditions are consistent with maximum profits for the firm. If not, state which resource(s) should be used in larger amounts and which resource(s) should be used in smaller amounts. **LO16.5**
   a. $MRP_L = \$8$; $P_L = \$4$; $MRP_C = \$8$; $P_C = \$4$.
   b. $MRP_L = \$10$; $P_L = \$12$; $MRP_C = \$14$; $P_C = \$9$.
   c. $MRP_L = \$6$; $P_L = \$6$; $MRP_C = \$12$; $P_C = \$12$.
   d. $MRP_L = \$22$; $P_L = \$26$; $MRP_C = \$16$; $P_C = \$19$.

5. Florida citrus growers say that the recent crackdown on illegal immigration is increasing the market wage rates necessary to get their oranges picked. Some are turning to $100,000 to $300,000 mechanical harvesters known as "trunk, shake, and catch" pickers, which vigorously shake oranges from the trees. If widely adopted, what will be the effect on the demand for human orange pickers? What does that imply about the relative strengths of the substitution and output effects? **LO16.5**

6. **LAST WORD** To save money, some fast food chains are now having their customers place their orders at computer kiosks. Will the kiosks necessarily reduce the total number of workers employed in the fast food industry?

REVIEW QUESTIONS

1. Cindy is a baker and runs a large cupcake shop. She has already hired 11 employees and is thinking of hiring a 12th. Cindy estimates that a 12th worker would cost her $100 per day in wages and benefits while increasing her total revenue from $2,600 per day to $2,750 per day. Should Cindy hire a 12th worker? **LO16.2**
   a. Yes.
   b. No.
   c. You need more information to figure this out.

2. Complete the following labor demand table for a firm that is hiring labor competitively and selling its product in a competitive market. **LO16.2**

Units of Labor	Total Product	Marginal Product	Product Price	Total Revenue	Marginal Revenue Product
0	0	_____	$2	$_____	$_____
1	17	_____	2	_____	_____
2	31	_____	2	_____	_____
3	43	_____	2	_____	_____
4	53	_____	2	_____	_____
5	60	_____	2	_____	_____
6	65	_____	2	_____	

   a. How many workers will the firm hire if the market wage rate is $27.95? $19.95? Explain why the firm will not hire a larger or smaller number of units of labor at each of these wage rates.
   b. Show in schedule form and graphically the labor demand curve of this firm.
   c. Now again determine the firm's demand curve for labor, assuming that it is selling in an imperfectly competitive market and that, although it can sell 17 units at $2.20 per unit, it must lower product price by 5 cents in order to sell the marginal product of each successive labor unit. Compare this demand curve with that derived in part b. Which curve is more elastic? Explain.

3. Alice runs a shoemaking factory that utilizes both labor and capital to make shoes. Which of the following would shift the factory's demand for capital? You can select one or more answers from the choices shown. **LO16.3**
   a. Many consumers decide to walk barefoot all the time.
   b. New shoemaking machines are twice as efficient as older machines.
   c. The wages that the factory has to pay its workers rise due to an economy-wide labor shortage.

4. FreshLeaf is a commercial salad maker that produces "salad in a bag" that is sold at many local supermarkets. Its customers like lettuce but don't care so much what type of lettuce is included in each bag of salad, so you would expect FreshLeaf's demand for iceberg lettuce to be: **LO16.4**
   a. Elastic.
   b. Inelastic.
   c. Unit elastic.
   d. All of the above.

5. Suppose the productivity of capital and labor are as shown in the table below. The output of these resources sells in a purely competitive market for $1 per unit. Both capital and labor are hired under purely competitive conditions at $3 and $1, respectively. **LO16.5**
   a. What is the least-cost combination of labor and capital the firm should employ in producing 80 units of output? Explain.
   b. What is the profit-maximizing combination of labor and capital the firm should use? Explain. What is the resulting

level of output? What is the economic profit? Is this the least costly way of producing the profit-maximizing output?

Units of Capital	MP of Capital	Units of Labor	MP of Labor
0		0	
	24		11
1		1	
	21		9
2		2	
	18		8
3		3	
	15		7
4		4	
	9		6
5		5	
	6		4
6		6	
	3		1
7		7	
	1		$\frac{1}{2}$
8		8	

6. A software company in Silicon Valley uses programmers (labor) and computers (capital) to produce apps for mobile devices. The firm estimates that when it comes to labor, $MP_L = 5$ apps per month while $P_L = \$1,000$ per month. And when it comes to capital, $MP_C = 8$ apps per month while $P_C = \$1,000$ per month. If the company wants to maximize its profits, it should: **LO16.5**
   a. Increase labor while decreasing capital.
   b. Decrease labor while increasing capital.
   c. Keep the current amounts of capital and labor just as they are.
   d. None of the above.

PROBLEMS

1. A delivery company is considering adding another vehicle to its delivery fleet; each vehicle is rented for $100 per day. Assume that the additional vehicle would be capable of delivering 1,500 packages per day and that each package that is delivered brings in 10 cents in revenue. Also assume that adding the delivery vehicle would not affect any other costs. **LO16.2**
   a. What is the MRP? What is the MRC? Should the firm add this delivery vehicle?
   b. Now suppose that the cost of renting a vehicle doubles to $200 per day. What are the MRP and MRC? Should the firm add a delivery vehicle under these circumstances?
   c. Next suppose that the cost of renting a vehicle falls back down to $100 per day but, due to extremely congested freeways, an additional vehicle would only be able to deliver 750 packages per day. What are the MRP and MRC in this situation? Would adding a vehicle under these circumstances increase the firm's profits?

2. Suppose that marginal product tripled while product price fell by one-half in Table 16.1. What would be the new MRP values in Table 16.1? What would be the net impact on the location of the resource demand curve in Figure 16.1? **LO16.2**

3. Suppose that a monopoly firm finds that its MR is $50 for the first unit sold each day, $49 for the second unit sold each day, $48 for the third unit sold each day, and so on. Further suppose that the first worker hired produces 5 units per day, the second 4 units per day, the third 3 units per day, and so on. **LO16.3**
   a. What is the firm's MRP for each of the first five workers?
   b. Suppose that the monopolist is subjected to rate regulation and the regulator stipulates that it must charge exactly $40 per unit for all units sold. At that price, what is the firm's MRP for each of the first five workers?

   c. If the daily wage paid to workers is $170 per day, how many workers will the unregulated monopoly demand? How many will the regulated monopoly demand? Looking at those figures, will the regulated or the unregulated monopoly demand more workers at that wage?
   d. If the daily wage paid to workers falls to $77 per day, how many workers will the unregulated monopoly demand? How many will the regulated monopoly demand? Looking at those figures, will the regulated or the unregulated monopoly demand more workers at that wage?
   e. Comparing your answers to parts c and d, does regulating a monopoly's output price *always* increase its demand for resources?

4. Consider a small landscaping company run by Mr. Viemeister. He is considering increasing his firm's capacity. If he adds one more worker, the firm's total monthly revenue will increase from $50,000 to $58,000. If he adds one more tractor, monthly revenue will increase from $50,000 to $62,000. Each additional worker costs $4,000 per month, while an additional tractor would also cost $4,000 per month. **LO16.5**
   a. What is the marginal product of labor? The marginal product of capital?
   b. What is the ratio of the marginal product of labor to the price of labor (MP_L/P_L)? What is the ratio of the marginal product of capital to the price of capital (MP_K/P_K)?
   c. Is the firm using the least-costly combination of inputs?
   d. Does adding an additional worker or adding an additional tractor yield a larger increase in total revenue for each dollar spent?

Wage Determination

Learning Objectives

LO17.1 Explain why labor productivity and real hourly compensation track so closely over time.

LO17.2 Show how wage rates and employment levels are determined in competitive labor markets.

LO17.3 Demonstrate how monopsony (a market with a single employer) can reduce wages below competitive levels.

LO17.4 Discuss how unions increase wage rates by pursuing the demand-enhancement model, the craft union model, or the industrial union model.

LO17.5 Explain why wages and employment are determined by collective bargaining in a situation of bilateral monopoly.

LO17.6 Discuss how minimum wage laws affect labor markets.

LO17.7 List the major causes of wage differentials.

LO17.8 Identify the types, benefits, and costs of "pay-for-performance" plans.

LO17.9 (Appendix) Relate who belongs to U.S. unions, the basics of collective bargaining, and the economic effects of unions.

Roughly 150 million Americans go to work each day. We work at an amazing variety of jobs for thousands of different firms and receive considerable differences in pay. What determines our hourly wage or annual salary? Why is the salary for, say, a topflight major-league baseball player $15 million or more a year, whereas the pay for a first-rate schoolteacher is $50,000? Why are starting salaries for college graduates who major in engineering and accounting so much higher than those for graduates majoring in journalism and sociology?

Having explored the major factors that underlie labor demand, we now bring *labor supply* into our analysis to help answer these questions. Generally speaking, labor supply and labor demand interact to determine the level of hourly wage rates or annual salaries in each occupation. Collectively, those wages and salaries make up about 70 percent of all income paid to American resource suppliers.

Labor, Wages, and Earnings

LO17.1 Explain why labor productivity and real hourly compensation track so closely over time.

Economists use the term "labor" broadly to apply to (1) blue- and white-collar workers of all varieties; (2) professional people such as lawyers, physicians, dentists, and teachers; and (3) owners of small businesses, including barbers, plumbers, and a host of retailers who provide labor as they operate their own businesses.

Wages are the price that employers pay for labor. Wages take the form of not only direct money payments such as hourly pay, annual salaries, bonuses, commissions, and royalties, but also fringe benefits such as paid vacations, health insurance, and pensions. Unless stated otherwise, we will use the term "wages" to mean all such payments and benefits converted to an hourly basis. That will remind us that the **wage rate** is the price paid per unit of labor services, in this case an hour of work. It will also let us distinguish between the wage rate and labor earnings, the latter determined by multiplying the number of hours worked by the hourly wage rate.

We must also distinguish between nominal wages and real wages. A **nominal wage** is the amount of money received per hour, day, or year. A **real wage** is the quantity of goods and services a worker can obtain with nominal wages; real wages reveal the "purchasing power" of nominal wages.

Your real wage depends on your nominal wage and the prices of the goods and services you purchase. Suppose you receive a 5 percent increase in your nominal wage during a certain year but in that same year the price level increases by 3 percent. Then your real wage has increased by 2 percent (= 5 percent − 3 percent). Unless otherwise indicated, we will assume that the overall level of prices remains constant. In other words, we will discuss only *real* wages.

General Level of Wages

Wages differ among nations, regions, occupations, and individuals. Wage rates are much higher in the United States than in China or India. They are slightly higher in the north and east of the United States than in the south. Plumbers are paid less than NFL punters. And one physician may earn twice as much as another physician for the same number of hours of work. The average wages earned by workers also differ by gender, race, and ethnic background.

The general, or average, level of wages, like the general level of prices, includes a wide range of different wage rates. It includes the wages of bakers, barbers, brick masons, and brain surgeons. By averaging such wages, we can more easily compare wages among regions and among nations.

GLOBAL PERSPECTIVE 17.1

Hourly Wages of Production Workers, Selected Nations

Wage differences are pronounced worldwide. The data shown here indicate that hourly compensation in the United States is not as high as in some European nations. It is important to note, however, that the prices of goods and services vary greatly among nations, and the process of converting foreign wages into dollars may not accurately reflect such variations.

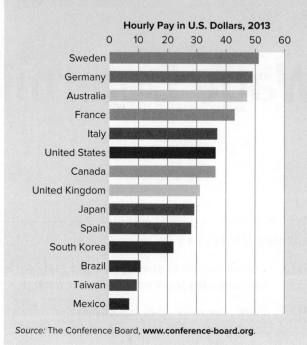

Source: The Conference Board, **www.conference-board.org**.

As Global Perspective 17.1 suggests, the general level of real wages in the United States is relatively high—although clearly not the highest in the world.

The simplest explanation for the high real wages in the United States and other industrially advanced economies (referred to hereafter as advanced economies) is that the demand for labor in those nations is relatively large compared to the supply of labor.

Role of Productivity

We know from the previous chapter that the demand for labor, or for any other resource, depends on its productivity. In general, the greater the productivity of labor, the greater is the demand for it. And if the total supply of labor is fixed, then the stronger the demand for labor, the higher is the average level of real wages. The demand for labor in the United States and the other major advanced economies is large because labor in those countries is highly productive. There are several reasons for that high productivity:

- *Plentiful capital* Workers in the advanced economies have access to large amounts of physical capital equipment (machinery and buildings). In the United States in 2015, $180,076 of physical capital was available, on average, for each worker.

- *Access to abundant natural resources* In advanced economies, natural resources tend to be abundant in relation to the size of the labor force. Some of those resources are available domestically and others are imported from abroad. The United States, for example, is richly endowed with arable land, mineral resources, and sources of energy for industry.

- *Advanced technology* The level of production technology is generally high in advanced economies. Not only do workers in these economies have more capital equipment to work with, but that equipment is technologically superior to the equipment available to the vast majority of workers worldwide. Moreover, work methods in the advanced economies are steadily being improved through scientific study and research.

- *Labor quality* The health, vigor, education, and training of workers in advanced economies are generally superior to those in developing nations. This means that, even with the same quantity and quality of natural and capital resources, workers in advanced economies tend to be more efficient than many of their foreign counterparts.

- *Other factors* Less obvious factors also may underlie the high productivity in some of the advanced economies. In the United States, for example, such factors include (a) the efficiency and flexibility of management; (b) a business, social, and political environment that emphasizes production and productivity; (c) the vast size of the domestic market, which enables firms to engage in mass production; and (d) the increased specialization of production enabled by free-trade agreements with other nations.

Real Wages and Productivity

Figure 17.1 shows the close long-run relationship in the United States between output per hour of work and real hourly compensation (= wages and salaries + employers' contributions to social insurance and private benefit plans). Because real income and real output are two ways of viewing the same thing, real income (compensation) per worker can increase only at about the same rate as output per worker. When workers produce more real output per hour, more real income is available to distribute to them for each hour worked.

In the actual economy, however, suppliers of land, capital, and entrepreneurial talent also share in the income from production. Real wages therefore do not always rise in lockstep with gains in productivity over short spans of time. But over long periods, productivity and real wages tend to rise together.

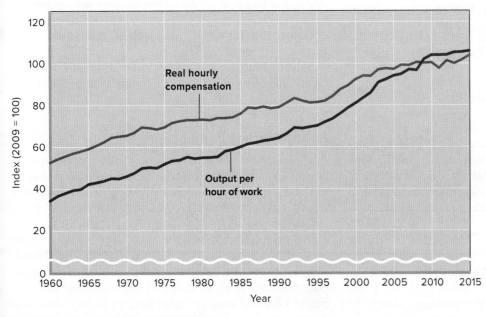

FIGURE 17.1 Output per hour and real hourly compensation in the United States, 1960–2015. Over long time periods, output per hour of work and real hourly compensation are closely related.

Source: Bureau of Labor Statistics, **www.bls.gov.**

FIGURE 17.2 The long-run trend of real wages in the United States. The productivity of U.S. labor has increased substantially over the long run, causing the demand for labor *D* to shift rightward (that is, to increase) more rapidly than increases in the supply of labor *S*. The result has been increases in real wages.

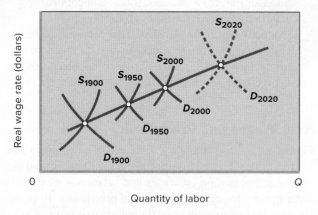

Long-Run Trend of Real Wages

Basic supply and demand analysis helps explain the long-term trend of real-wage growth in the United States. The nation's labor force has grown significantly over the decades. But as a result of the productivity-increasing factors we have mentioned, increases in labor demand have outstripped increases in labor supply. Figure 17.2 shows several such increases in labor supply and labor demand. The result has been a long-run, or secular, increase in wage rates and employment. For example, real hourly compensation in the United States has roughly doubled since 1960. Over that same period, employment has increased by about 80 million workers.

A Purely Competitive Labor Market

LO17.2 Show how wage rates and employment levels are determined in competitive labor markets.

Average levels of wages, however, disguise the great variation of wage rates among occupations and within occupations. What determines the wage rate paid for a specific type of labor? Demand and supply analysis again is revealing. Let's begin by examining labor demand and labor supply in a **purely competitive labor market.** In this type of market:

- Numerous firms compete with one another in hiring a specific type of labor.

- Each of many qualified workers with identical skills supplies that type of labor.

- Individual firms and individual workers are "wage takers" since neither can exert any control over the market wage rate.

Market Demand for Labor

Suppose 200 firms demand a particular type of labor, say, carpenters. These firms need not be in the same industry; industries are defined according to the products they produce and not the resources they employ. Thus, firms producing wood-framed furniture, wood windows and doors, houses and apartment buildings, and wood cabinets will demand carpenters. To find the total, or market, labor demand curve for a particular labor service, we sum horizontally the labor demand curves (the marginal revenue product curves) of the individual firms, as indicated in **Figure 17.3 (Key Graph).** The horizontal summing of the 200 labor demand curves like *d* in Figure 17.3b yields the market labor demand curve *D* in Figure 17.3a.

Market Supply of Labor

On the supply side of a purely competitive labor market, we assume that no union is present and that workers individually compete for available jobs. The supply curve for each type of labor slopes upward, indicating that employers as a group must pay higher wage rates to obtain more workers. They must do this to bid workers away from other industries, occupations, and localities. Within limits, workers have alternative job opportunities. For example, they may work in other industries in the same locality, or they may work in their present occupations in different cities or states, or they may work in other occupations.

Firms that want to hire these workers (here, carpenters) must pay higher wage rates to attract them away from the alternative job opportunities available to them. They must also pay higher wages to induce people who are not currently in the labor force—who are perhaps doing household activities or enjoying leisure—to seek employment. In short, assuming that wages are constant in other labor markets, higher wages in a particular labor market entice more workers to offer their labor services in that market—a fact expressed graphically by the upsloping market supply-of-labor curve *S* in Figure 17.3a.

Labor Market Equilibrium

The intersection of the market labor demand curve and the market labor supply curve determines the equilibrium wage rate and level of employment in a purely competitive labor market. In Figure 17.3a the equilibrium wage rate is W_c ($10) and the number of workers hired is Q_c (1,000). To the individual firm the market wage rate W_c is given. Each of the many firms employs such a small fraction of the total available supply of this type of labor that no single firm can influence the wage rate. As shown by the horizontal line *s* in Figure 17.3b, the supply of labor faced by an individual firm is perfectly elastic. It can hire as many or as few workers as it wants to at the market wage rate.

FIGURE 17.3 **Labor supply and labor demand in (a) a purely competitive labor market and (b) a single competitive firm.** In a purely competitive labor market (a), market labor supply *S* and market labor demand *D* determine the equilibrium wage rate W_c and the equilibrium number of workers Q_c. Each individual competitive firm (b) takes this competitive wage W_c as given. Thus, the individual firm's labor supply curve *s* = MRC is perfectly elastic at the going wage W_c. Its labor demand curve, *d*, is its MRP curve (here labeled *mrp*). The firm maximizes its profit by hiring workers up to where MRP = MRC. Area 0*abc* represents both the firm's total revenue and its total cost. The green area is its total wage cost; the blue area is its nonlabor costs, including a normal profit—that is, the firm's payments to the suppliers of land, capital, and entrepreneurship.

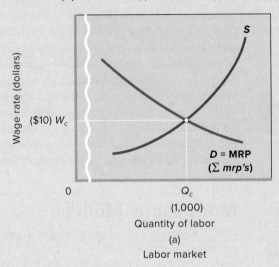

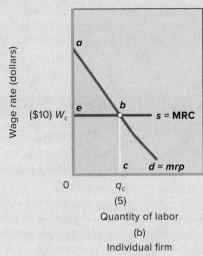

(a)
Labor market

(b)
Individual firm

QUICK QUIZ FOR FIGURE 17.3

1. The supply-of-labor curve *S* slopes upward in graph (a) because:
   a. the law of diminishing marginal utility applies.
   b. the law of diminishing returns applies.
   c. workers can afford to "buy" more leisure when the wage rate increases.
   d. higher wages are needed to attract workers away from other labor markets, household activities, and leisure.

2. This firm's labor demand curve *d* in graph (b) slopes downward because:
   a. the law of diminishing marginal utility applies.
   b. the law of diminishing returns applies.
   c. the firm must lower its price to sell additional units of its product.
   d. the firm is a competitive employer, not a monopsonist.

3. In employing five workers, the firm represented in graph (b):
   a. has a total wage cost of $6,000.
   b. is adhering to the general principle of undertaking all actions for which the marginal benefit exceeds the marginal cost.
   c. uses less labor than would be ideal from society's perspective.
   d. experiences increasing marginal returns.

4. A rightward shift of the labor supply curve in graph (a) would shift curve:
   a. *d* = *mrp* leftward in graph (b).
   b. *d* = *mrp* rightward in graph (b).
   c. *s* = MRC upward in graph (b).
   d. *s* = MRC downward in graph (b).

Answers: 1. d; 2. b; 3. b; 4. d

Each individual firm will maximize its profit (or minimize its loss) by hiring this type of labor up to the point at which marginal revenue product is equal to marginal resource cost. This is merely an application of the MRP = MRC rule we developed in Chapter 16.

As Table 17.1 indicates, when an individual competitive firm faces the market price for a resource, the marginal cost of that resource (MRC) is constant and is equal to the market price for each and every unit that the competitive firm may choose to purchase. Note that MRC is constant at

$10 and matches the $10 wage rate. Each additional worker hired adds precisely his or her own wage rate ($10 in this case) to the firm's total resource cost. So the firm in a purely competitive labor market maximizes its profit by hiring workers up to the point at which its wage rate equals MRP. In Figure 17.3b this firm will hire q_c (5) workers, paying each worker the market wage rate W_c ($10). The other 199 firms (not shown) that are hiring workers in this labor market will also each employ 5 workers and pay $10 per hour.

TABLE 17.1 The Supply of Labor: Pure Competition in the Hire of Labor

(1) Units of Labor	(2) Wage Rate	(3) Total Labor Cost	(4) Marginal Resource (Labor) Cost
0	$10	$ 0	$10
1	10	10	10
2	10	20	10
3	10	30	10
4	10	40	10
5	10	50	10
6	10	60	

CONSIDER THIS . . .

Source: © numbeos/E-plus /Getty Images RF

Fringe Benefits vs. Take-Home Pay

Figure 17.2 shows that total compensation has risen significantly over the past several decades. Not shown in that figure, however, is the fact that the amount of take-home pay received by middle-class American workers has increased by much less. One contributing factor has been the rise of fringe benefits.

To see why fringe benefits matter, recall that throughout this chapter we have defined the wage as the total price that employers pay to obtain labor and compensate workers for providing it. Under our definition, wages are the sum of take-home pay (such as hourly pay and annual salaries) and fringe benefits (such as paid vacations, health insurance, and pensions).

So now consider an equilibrium wage, such as W_c in Figure 17.3. If workers want higher fringe benefits, they can have them—but only if take-home pay falls by an equal amount. With the equilibrium wage fixed by supply and demand, the only way workers can get more fringe benefits is by accepting lower take-home pay.

This is an important point to understand because in recent decades, workers have received an increasing fraction of their total compensation in the form of fringe benefits—especially health insurance. Those fringe benefits are costly and in a competitive labor market, each $1 increase in fringe benefits means $1 less for paychecks.

That trade-off helps to explain why take-home pay has increased by less than total compensation in recent decades. With a rising fraction of total compensation flowing toward fringe benefits, the increase in take-home pay was much less than the overall increase in total compensation.

To determine a firm's total revenue from employing a particular number of labor units, we sum the MRPs of those units. For example, if a firm employs 3 labor units with marginal revenue products of $14, $13, and $12, respectively, then the firm's total revenue is $39 (= $14 + $13 + $12). In Figure 17.3b, where we are not restricted to whole units of labor, total revenue is represented by area 0*abc* under the MRP curve to the left of q_c. And what area represents the firm's total cost, including a normal profit? Answer: For q_c units, the same area—0*abc*. The green rectangle represents the firm's total wage cost (0q_c × 0W_c). The blue triangle (total revenue minus total wage cost) represents the firm's nonlabor costs—its explicit and implicit payments to land, capital, and entrepreneurship. Thus, in this case, total cost (wages plus other income payments) equals total revenue. This firm and others like it are earning only a normal profit. So Figure 17.3b represents a long-run equilibrium for a firm that is selling its product in a purely competitive product market and hiring its labor in a purely competitive labor market.

Monopsony Model

LO17.3 Demonstrate how monopsony (a market with a single employer) can reduce wages below competitive levels.

In the purely competitive labor market described in the preceding section, each employer hires too small an amount of labor to influence the wage rate. Each firm can hire as little or as much labor as it needs, but only at the market wage rate, as reflected in its horizontal labor supply curve. The situation is quite different when the labor market is a **monopsony,** a market structure in which there is only a single buyer. A labor market monopsony has the following characteristics:

- There is only a single buyer of a particular type of labor.

- The workers providing this type of labor have few employment options other than working for the monopsony because they are either geographically immobile or because finding alternative employment would mean having to acquire new skills.

- The firm is a "wage maker" because the wage rate it must pay varies directly with the number of workers it employs.

As is true of monopoly power, there are various degrees of monopsony power. In *pure* monopsony such power is at its maximum because only a single employer hires labor in the labor market. The best real-world examples are probably the labor markets in some towns that depend almost entirely on one major firm. For example, a silver-mining company may be almost the only source of employment in a remote Idaho town. A Colorado ski resort, a Wisconsin paper mill, or an Alaskan fish processor may provide most of the employment in its geographically isolated locale.

In other cases three or four firms may each hire a large portion of the supply of labor in a certain market and therefore have some monopsony power. Moreover, if they tacitly or openly act in concert in hiring labor, they greatly enhance their monopsony power.

Upsloping Labor Supply to Firm

When a firm hires most of the available supply of a certain type of labor, its decision to employ more or fewer workers affects the wage rate it pays to those workers. Specifically, if a firm is large in relation to the size of the labor market, it will have to pay a higher wage rate to attract labor away from other employment or from leisure. Suppose that there is only one employer of a particular type of labor in a certain geographic area. In this pure monopsony situation, the labor supply curve for the *firm* and the total labor supply curve for the *labor market* are identical. The monopsonist's supply curve—represented by curve *S* in Figure 17.4—is upsloping because the firm must pay higher wage rates if it wants to attract and hire additional workers. This same curve is also the monopsonist's average-cost-of-labor curve. Each point on curve *S* indicates the wage rate (cost) per worker that must be paid to attract the corresponding number of workers.

MRC Higher Than the Wage Rate

When a monopsonist pays a higher wage to attract an additional worker, it must pay that higher wage not only to the additional worker, but to all the workers it is currently employing at a lower wage. If not, labor morale will deteriorate, and the employer will be plagued with labor unrest because of wage-rate differences existing for the same job. Paying a uniform wage to all workers means that the cost of an extra worker—the marginal resource (labor) cost (MRC)—is the sum of that

TABLE 17.2 The Supply of Labor: Monopsony in the Hiring of Labor

(1) Units of Labor	(2) Wage Rate	(3) Total Labor Cost	(4) Marginal Resource (Labor) Cost
0	$ 5	$ 0	
1	6	6	$ 6
2	7	14	8
3	8	24	10
4	9	36	12
5	10	50	14
6	11	66	16

worker's wage rate and the amount necessary to bring the wage rate of all current workers up to the new wage level.

Table 17.2 illustrates this point. One worker can be hired at a wage rate of $6. But hiring a second worker forces the firm to pay a higher wage rate of $7. The marginal resource (labor) cost of the second worker is $8—the $7 paid to the second worker plus a $1 raise for the first worker. From another viewpoint, total labor cost is now $14 (= 2 × $7), up from $6 (= 1 × $6). So the MRC of the second worker is $8 (= $14 − $6), not just the $7 wage rate paid to that worker. Similarly, the marginal labor cost of the third worker is $10—the $8 that must be paid to attract this worker from alternative employment plus $1 raises, from $7 to $8, for the first two workers.

Here is the key point: Because the monopsonist is the only employer in the labor market, its marginal resource (labor) cost exceeds the wage rate. Graphically, the monopsonist's MRC curve lies above the average-cost-of-labor curve, or labor supply curve *S*, as is clearly shown in Figure 17.4.

Equilibrium Wage and Employment

How many units of labor will the monopsonist hire, and what wage rate will it pay? To maximize profit, the monopsonist will employ the quantity of labor Q_m in Figure 17.4, because at that quantity MRC and MRP are equal (point *b*).[1] The

FIGURE 17.4 **The wage rate and level of employment in a monopsonistic labor market.** In a monopsonistic labor market the employer's marginal resource (labor) cost curve (MRC) lies above the labor supply curve *S*. Equating MRC with MRP at point *b*, the monopsonist hires Q_m workers (compared with Q_c under competition). As indicated by point *c* on *S*, it pays only wage rate W_m (compared with the competitive wage W_c).

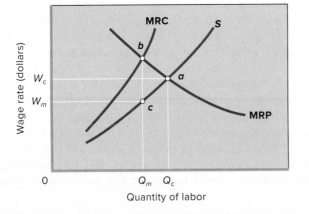

[1] The fact that MRC exceeds resource price when resources are hired or purchased under imperfectly competitive (monopsonistic) conditions calls for adjustments in Chapter 16's least-cost and profit-maximizing rules for hiring resources. (See equations 1 and 2 in the "Optimal Combination of Resources" section of Chapter 16.) Specifically, we must substitute MRC for resource price in the denominators of our two equations. That is, with imperfect competition in the hiring of both labor and capital, equation 1 becomes

$$\frac{MP_L}{MRC_L} = \frac{MP_C}{MRC_C} \tag{1'}$$

and equation 2 is restated as

$$\frac{MRP_L}{MRC_L} = \frac{MRP_C}{MRC_C} = 1 \tag{2'}$$

In fact, equations 1 and 2 can be regarded as special cases of 1' and 2' in which firms happen to be hiring under purely competitive conditions and resource price is therefore equal to, and can be substituted for, marginal resource cost.

monopsonist next determines how much it must pay to attract these Q_m workers. From the supply curve S, specifically point c, it sees that it must pay wage rate W_m. Clearly, it need not pay a wage equal to MRP; it can attract and hire exactly the number of workers it wants (Q_m) with wage rate W_m. And that is the wage that it will pay.

Contrast these results with those that would prevail in a competitive labor market. With competition in the hiring of labor, the level of employment would be greater (at Q_c) and the wage rate would be higher (at W_c). Other things equal, the monopsonist maximizes its profit by hiring a smaller number of workers and thereby paying a less-than-competitive wage rate. Society obtains a smaller output, and workers receive a wage rate that is less by bc than their marginal revenue product. Just as a monopolistic seller finds it profitable to restrict product output to realize an above-competitive price for its goods, the monopsonistic employer of resources finds it profitable to restrict employment in order to reduce wage rates below those that would occur under competitive conditions.

Examples of Monopsony Power

Fortunately, monopsonistic labor markets are uncommon in the United States. In most labor markets, several potential employers compete for most workers, particularly for workers who are occupationally and geographically mobile. Also, where monopsony labor market outcomes might have otherwise occurred, unions have often sprung up to counteract that power by forcing firms to negotiate wages. Nevertheless, economists have found some evidence of monopsony power in such diverse labor markets as the markets for nurses, professional athletes, public school teachers, newspaper employees, and some building-trade workers.

In the case of nurses, the major employers in most locales are a relatively small number of hospitals. Further, the highly specialized skills of nurses are not readily transferable to other occupations. It has been found, in accordance with the monopsony model, that, other things equal, the smaller the number of hospitals in a town or city (that is, the greater the degree of monopsony), the lower the beginning salaries of nurses.

Professional sports leagues also provide a good example of monopsony, particularly as it relates to the pay of first-year players. The National Football League, the National Basketball Association, and Major League Baseball assign first-year players to teams through "player drafts." That device prohibits other teams from competing for a player's services, at least for several years, until the player becomes a "free agent." In this way each league exercises monopsony power, which results in lower salaries than would occur under competitive conditions.

> ## QUICK REVIEW 17.1
>
> ✓ Real wages have increased over time in the United States because labor demand has increased relative to labor supply.
>
> ✓ Over the long term, real wages per worker have increased at approximately the same rate as worker productivity.
>
> ✓ The competitive employer is a wage taker and employs workers at the point where the wage rate (= MRC) equals MRP.
>
> ✓ The labor supply curve to a monopsonist is upsloping, causing MRC to exceed the wage rate for each worker. Other things equal, the monopsonist, hiring where MRC = MRP, will employ fewer workers and pay a lower wage rate than would a purely competitive employer.

Three Union Models

LO17.4 Discuss how unions increase wage rates by pursuing the demand-enhancement model, the craft union model, or the industrial union model.

Our assumption thus far has been that workers compete with one another in selling their labor services. But in some labor markets workers unionize and sell their labor services collectively. (We examine union membership, collective bargaining, and union impacts in detail in an appendix to this chapter. Here our focus is on three union wage models.)

When a union is formed in an otherwise competitive labor market, it usually bargains with a relatively large number of employers. It has many goals, the most important of which is to raise wage rates. It can pursue that objective in several ways.

Demand-Enhancement Model

Unions recognize that their ability to influence the demand for labor is limited. But from the union's viewpoint, increasing the demand for union labor is highly desirable. As Figure 17.5 shows, an increase in the demand for union labor will create a higher union wage along with more jobs.

Unions can increase the demand for their labor by increasing the demand for the goods or services they help produce. Political lobbying is the main tool for increasing the demand for union-produced goods or services. For example, construction unions have lobbied for new highways, mass-transit systems, and stadium projects. Teachers' unions and associations have pushed for increased public spending on education. Unions in the aerospace industry have lobbied to increase spending on the military and on space exploration. U.S. steel unions and forest-product workers have lobbied for tariffs and quotas on foreign

FIGURE 17.5 Unions and demand enhancement. When unions can increase the demand for union labor (say, from D_1 to D_2), they can realize higher wage rates (W_c to W_u) and more jobs (Q_c to Q_u).

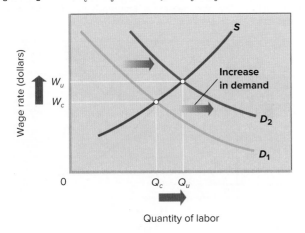

imports of steel and lumber, respectively. Such trade restrictions shift the demand for labor away from foreign countries and toward unionized U.S. labor.

Unions can also increase the demand for union labor by altering the price of other inputs. For example, although union members are generally paid significantly more than the minimum wage, unions have strongly supported increases in the minimum wage. The purpose may be to raise the price of low-wage, nonunion labor, which in some cases is substitutable for union labor. A higher minimum wage for nonunion workers will discourage employers from substituting such workers for union workers and will thereby bolster the demand for union members.

Similarly, unions have sometimes sought to increase the demand for their labor by supporting policies that will reduce or hold down the price of a complementary resource. For example, unions in industries that represent workers who transport fruits and vegetables may support legislation that allows low-wage foreign agricultural workers to temporarily work in the United States. Where union labor and another resource are complementary, a price decrease for the other resource will increase the demand for union labor through Chapter 16's output effect.

Exclusive or Craft Union Model

Unions can also boost wage rates by reducing the supply of labor, and over the years organized labor has favored policies to do just that. For example, labor unions have supported legislation that has (1) restricted permanent immigration, (2) reduced child labor, (3) encouraged compulsory retirement, and (4) enforced a shorter workweek.

Moreover, certain types of workers have adopted techniques designed to restrict the number of workers who can join their union. This is especially true of *craft unions*, whose members possess a particular skill, such as carpenters, brick masons, or plumbers. Craft unions have frequently forced employers to agree to hire only union members, thereby gaining virtually complete control of the labor supply. Then, by following restrictive membership policies—for example, long apprenticeships, very high initiation fees, and limits on the number of new members admitted—they have artificially restricted labor supply. As indicated in Figure 17.6, such practices result in higher wage rates and constitute what is called **exclusive unionism.** By excluding workers from unions and therefore from the labor supply, craft unions succeed in elevating wage rates.

This craft union model is also applicable to many professional organizations, such as the American Medical Association, the National Education Association, the American Bar Association, and hundreds of others. Such groups seek to prohibit competition for their services from less qualified labor suppliers by leveraging the special interest effect under which a small group of insiders is able to obtain favorable political treatment despite imposing substantial costs on outsiders. One way to accomplish that is through **occupational licensing.** Here a group of workers in a given occupation pressure federal, state, or municipal government to pass a law that says that some occupational group (for example, barbers, physicians, lawyers, plumbers, cosmetologists, egg graders, pest controllers) can practice their trade only if they meet certain requirements. Those requirements might include level of education, amount of work experience, the passing of an examination, and personal characteristics ("the practitioner must be of good moral character"). Members of the licensed occupation typically dominate the licensing board that administers such laws. The result is self-regulation, which often leads to policies that serve only to restrict entry to the occupation and reduce labor supply.

FIGURE 17.6 Exclusive or craft unionism. By reducing the supply of labor (say, from S_1 to S_2) through the use of restrictive membership policies, exclusive unions achieve higher wage rates (W_c to W_u). However, restriction of the labor supply also reduces the number of workers employed (Q_c to Q_u).

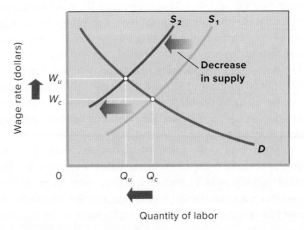

The expressed purpose of licensing is to protect consumers from incompetent practitioners—surely a worthy goal. But such licensing, if abused, results in above-competitive wages and earnings for those in the licensed occupation (Figure 17.6). Moreover, licensing requirements often include a residency requirement, which inhibits the interstate movement of qualified workers. Some 1,100 occupations are now licensed in the United States. This chapter's Last Word gives examples of excessive licensing requirements that hurt the employment prospects of lower-income workers.

Inclusive or Industrial Union Model

Instead of trying to limit their membership, however, most unions seek to organize all available workers. This is especially true of the *industrial unions,* such as those of the automobile workers and steelworkers. Such unions seek as members all available unskilled, semiskilled, and skilled workers in an industry. It makes sense for a union to be exclusive when its members are skilled craft workers for whom the employer has few substitutes. But it does not make sense for a union to be exclusive when trying to organize unskilled and semiskilled workers. To break a strike, employers could then easily substitute unskilled or semiskilled nonunion workers for the unskilled or semiskilled union workers.

By contrast, an industrial union that includes virtually all available workers in its membership can put firms under great pressure to agree to its wage demands. Because of its legal right to strike, such a union can threaten to deprive firms of their entire labor supply. And an actual strike can do just that. Further, with virtually all available workers in the union, it will be difficult in the short run for new nonunion firms to emerge and thereby undermine what the union is demanding from existing firms.

We illustrate such **inclusive unionism** in Figure 17.7. Initially, the competitive equilibrium wage rate is W_c and the level of employment is Q_c. Now suppose an industrial union is formed that demands a higher, above-equilibrium wage rate of, say, W_u. That wage rate W_u would create a perfectly elastic labor supply over the range ae in Figure 17.7. If firms wanted to hire any workers in this range, they would have to pay the union-imposed wage rate. If they decide against meeting this wage demand, the union will supply no labor at all, and the firms will be faced with a strike. If firms decide it is better to pay the higher wage rate than to suffer a strike, they will cut back on employment from Q_c to Q_u.

By agreeing to the union's wage demand, individual employers become wage takers at the union wage rate W_u. Because labor supply is perfectly elastic over range ae, the marginal resource (labor) cost is equal to the wage rate W_u over this range. The Q_u level of employment is the result of

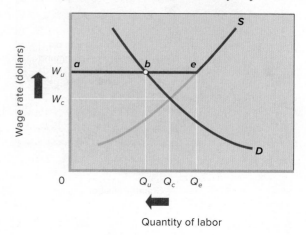

FIGURE 17.7 Inclusive or industrial unionism. By organizing virtually all available workers in order to control the supply of labor, inclusive industrial unions may impose a wage rate, such as W_u, which is above the competitive wage rate W_c. In effect, this changes the labor supply curve from S to aeS. At wage rate W_u, employers will cut employment from Q_c to Q_u.

employers' equating this MRC (now equal to the union wage rate) with MRP, according to our profit-maximizing rule.

Note from point e on labor supply curve S that Q_e workers desire employment at wage W_u. But as indicated by point b on labor demand curve D, only Q_u workers are employed. The result is a surplus of labor of $Q_e - Q_u$ (also shown by distance eb). In a purely competitive labor market without the union, the effect of a surplus of unemployed workers would be lower wages. Specifically, the wage rate would fall to the equilibrium level W_c where the quantity of labor supplied equals the quantity of labor demanded (each Q_c). But this drop in wages does not happen because workers are acting collectively through their union. Individual workers cannot offer to work for less than W_u nor can employers pay less than that.

Wage Increases and Job Loss

Have U.S. unions been successful in raising the wages of their members? Evidence suggests that union members on average achieve a 15 percent wage advantage over nonunion workers. But when unions are successful in raising wages, their efforts also have another major effect.

As Figures 17.6 and 17.7 suggest, the wage-raising actions achieved by both exclusive and inclusive unionism reduce employment in unionized firms. Simply put, a union's success in achieving above-equilibrium wage rates tends to be accompanied by a decline in the number of workers employed. That result acts as a restraining influence on union wage demands. A union cannot expect to maintain solidarity within its ranks if it seeks a wage rate so high that 20 to 30 percent of its members lose their jobs.

Bilateral Monopoly Model

LO17.5 Explain why wages and employment are determined by collective bargaining in a situation of bilateral monopoly.

Suppose a strong industrial union is formed in a monopsonist labor market rather that a competitive labor market, thereby creating a combination of the monopsony model and the inclusive unionism model. Economists call the result **bilateral monopoly** because in its pure form there is a single seller and a single buyer. The union is a monopolistic "seller" of labor that controls labor supply and can influence wage rates, but it faces a monopsonistic "buyer" of labor that can also affect wages by altering the amount of labor that it employs. This is not an uncommon case, particularly in less pure forms in which a single union confronts two, three, or four large employers. Examples: steel, automobiles, construction equipment, professional sports, and commercial aircraft.

Indeterminate Outcome of Bilateral Monopoly

We show this situation in Figure 17.8, where Figure 17.7 is superimposed onto Figure 17.4. The monopsonistic employer will seek the below-competitive-equilibrium wage rate W_m, and the union will press for some above-competitive-equilibrium wage rate such as W_u. Which will be the outcome? We cannot say with certainty. The outcome is "logically indeterminate" because the bilateral monopoly model does not explain what will happen at the bargaining table. We can expect the wage outcome to lie somewhere between W_m and W_u. Beyond that, about all we can say is that the party with the greater bargaining power and the more effective bargaining strategy will probably get a wage closer to the one it seeks.

FIGURE 17.8 Bilateral monopoly in the labor market. A monopsonist seeks to hire Q_m workers (where MRC = MRP) and pay wage rate W_m corresponding to quantity Q_m on labor supply curve S. The inclusive union it faces seeks the above-equilibrium wage rate W_u. The actual outcome cannot be predicted by economic theory. It will result from bargaining between the two parties.

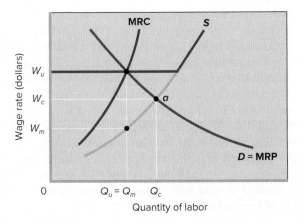

Desirability of Bilateral Monopoly

The wage and employment outcomes in this situation might be more economically desirable than the term "bilateral monopoly" implies. The monopoly on one side of the market might in effect cancel out the monopoly on the other side, yielding competitive or near-competitive results. If either the union or management prevailed in this market—that is, if the actual wage rate were either W_u or W_m—employment would be restricted to Q_m (where MRP = MRC), which is below the competitive level.

But now suppose the monopoly power of the union roughly offsets the monopsony power of management, and the union and management agree on wage rate W_c, which is the competitive wage. Once management accepts this wage rate, its incentive to restrict employment disappears; no longer can it depress wage rates by restricting employment. Instead, management hires at the most profitable resource quantity, where the bargained wage rate W_c (which is now the firm's MRC) is equal to the MRP. It hires Q_c workers. Thus, with monopoly on both sides of the labor market, the resulting wage rate and level of employment may be closer to competitive levels than would be the case if monopoly existed on only one side of the market.

QUICK REVIEW 17.2

✓ In the demand-enhancement union model, a union increases the wage rate by increasing labor demand through actions that increase product demand or alter the prices of related inputs.

✓ In the exclusive (craft) union model, a union increases wage rates by artificially restricting labor supply, through, say, long apprenticeships or occupational licensing.

✓ In the inclusive (industrial) union model, a union raises the wage rate by gaining control over a firm's labor supply and threatening to withhold labor via a strike unless a negotiated wage is obtained.

✓ Bilateral monopoly occurs in a labor market where a monopsonist bargains with an inclusive, or industrial, union. Wage and employment outcomes are determined by collective bargaining in this situation.

The Minimum-Wage Controversy

LO17.6 Discuss how minimum wage laws affect labor markets.

Since the passage of the Fair Labor Standards Act in 1938, the United States has had a federal **minimum wage.** That wage has ranged between 30 and 50 percent of the average wage paid to manufacturing workers and was most recently raised to $7.25 in July 2009. Numerous states, however, have minimum wages that are higher than the federal minimum wage. Some of these state minimum wages are considerably higher. For example, in 2016 the minimum wage in the state of Washington was $9.47 an hour. The purpose of the minimum wage is to provide a "wage floor" that will help less-skilled workers earn enough income to escape poverty.

Case against the Minimum Wage

Critics, reasoning in terms of Figure 17.7, contend that an above-equilibrium minimum wage (say, W_u) will simply cause employers to hire fewer workers. Downsloping labor demand curves are a reality. The higher labor costs may even force some firms out of business. Then some of the poor, low-wage workers whom the minimum wage was designed to help will find themselves out of work. Critics point out that a worker who is *unemployed* and desperate to find a job at a minimum wage of $7.25 per hour is clearly worse off than he or she would be if *employed* at a market wage rate of, say, $6.50 per hour.

A second criticism of the minimum wage is that it is "poorly targeted" to reduce household poverty. Critics point out that much of the benefit of the minimum wage accrues to workers, including many teenagers, who do not live in impoverished households.

Case for the Minimum Wage

Advocates of the minimum wage say that critics analyze its impact in an unrealistic context. Figure 17.7, advocates claim, assumes a competitive labor market. But in a less competitive, low-pay labor market where employers possess some monopsony power (Figure 17.8), the minimum wage can increase wage rates without causing significant unemployment. Indeed, a higher minimum wage may even produce more jobs by eliminating the motive that monopsonistic firms have for restricting employment. For example, a minimum-wage floor of W_c in Figure 17.8 would change the firm's labor supply curve to $W_c aS$ and prompt the firm to increase its employment from Q_m workers to Q_c workers.

Moreover, even if the labor market is competitive, the higher wage rate might prompt firms to find more productive tasks for low-paid workers, thereby raising their productivity. Alternatively, the minimum wage may reduce *labor turnover* (the rate at which workers voluntarily quit). With fewer low-productive trainees, the *average* productivity of the firm's workers would rise. In either case, the alleged negative employment effects of the minimum wage might not occur.

Evidence and Conclusions

Which view is correct? Unfortunately, there is no clear answer. All economists agree that firms will not hire workers who cost more per hour than the value of their hourly output.

So there is some minimum wage sufficiently high that it would severely reduce employment. Consider $30 an hour, as an absurd example. Because the majority of U.S. workers earned barely over $20 per hour in 2015, a minimum wage of $30 per hour would render the majority of American workers unemployable because the minimum wage that they would have to be paid by potential employers would far exceed their marginal revenue products.

It has to be remembered, though, that a minimum wage will only cause unemployment in labor markets where the minimum wage is higher than the equilibrium wage. Because the current minimum wage of $7.25 per hour is much lower than the average hourly wage of about $21.04 that was earned by American workers in 2015, any unemployment caused by the $7.25 per hour minimum wage is most likely to fall on low-skilled workers who earn low wages due to their low productivity. These workers are mostly teenagers, adults who did not complete high school, and immigrants with low levels of education and poor English proficiency. For members of such groups, recent research suggests that a 10 percent increase in the minimum wage will cause a 1 to 3 percent decline in employment. However, estimates of the employment effect of minimum wage laws vary from study to study so that significant controversy remains.

The overall effect of the minimum wage is thus uncertain. On the one hand, the employment and unemployment effects of the minimum wage do not appear to be as great as many critics fear. On the other hand, because a large part of its effect is dissipated on nonpoverty families, the minimum wage is not as strong an antipoverty tool as many supporters contend.

Voting patterns and surveys make it clear, however, that the minimum wage has strong political support. Perhaps this stems from two realities: (1) More workers are believed to be helped than hurt by the minimum wage, and (2) the minimum wage gives society some assurance that employers are not "taking undue advantage" of vulnerable, low-skilled workers.

Wage Differentials

LO17.7 List the major causes of wage differentials.

Hourly wage rates and annual salaries differ greatly among occupations. In Table 17.3 we list average annual salaries for a number of occupations to illustrate such occupational **wage differentials.** For example, observe that surgeons on average earn nine times as much as retail salespersons. Not shown, there are also large wage differentials within some of the occupations listed. For example, some highly experienced surgeons earn several times as much income as surgeons just starting their careers. And although average wages for retail salespersons are relatively low, some top salespersons selling on commission make several times the average wages listed for their occupation.

TABLE 17.3 Average Annual Wages in Selected Occupations, 2014

Occupation	Average Annual Wages
1. Surgeons	$240,440
2. Petroleum engineers	147,520
3. Financial managers	130,320
4. Law professors	126,270
5. Pharmacists	118,470
6. Civil engineers	87,130
7. Dental hygienists	71,970
8. Registered nurses	69,790
9. Police officers	59,530
10. Electricians	54,520
11. Carpenters	45,490
12. Travel agents	37,370
13. Barbers	28,430
14. Retail salespersons	25,760
15. Janitors	25,460
16. Child care workers	21,710
17. Fast food cooks	19,030

Source: Bureau of Labor Statistics, **www.bls.gov**.

What explains wage differentials such as these? Once again, the forces of demand and supply are revealing. As we demonstrate in Figure 17.9, wage differentials can arise on either the supply or the demand side of labor markets. Figure 17.9a and Figure 17.9b represent labor markets for two occupational groups that have identical *labor supply curves*. Labor market (a) has a relatively high equilibrium wage (W_a) because labor demand is very strong. In labor market (b) the equilibrium wage is relatively low (W_b) because labor demand is weak. Clearly, the wage differential between occupations (a) and (b) results solely from differences in the magnitude of labor demand.

Contrast that situation with Figure 17.9c and 17.9d, where the *labor demand curves* are identical. In labor market (c) the equilibrium wage is relatively high (W_c) because labor supply is low. In labor market (d) labor supply is highly abundant, so the equilibrium wage (W_d) is relatively low. The wage differential between (c) and (d) results solely from the differences in the magnitude of labor supply.

Although Figure 17.9 provides a good starting point for understanding wage differentials, we need to know *why* demand and supply conditions differ in various labor markets. There are several reasons.

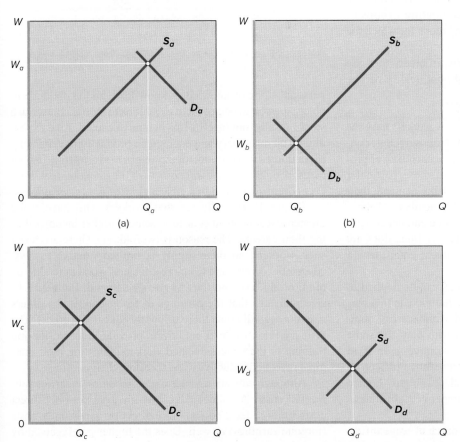

FIGURE 17.9 Labor demand, labor supply, and wage differentials. Wage differentials in labor markets are caused by varying supply and demand conditions (a) and (b). Because the labor supply curves S_a and S_b are identical in the labor markets depicted in the two top graphs, differences in demand are the sole cause of the $W_a - W_b$ wage differential (c) and (d). Because the labor demand curves D_c and D_d are identical in the bottom two graphs, the $W_c - W_d$ wage differential results solely from differences in labor supply.

Marginal Revenue Productivity

The strength of labor demand—how far rightward the labor demand curve is located—differs greatly among occupations due to differences in how much various occupational groups contribute to the revenue of their respective employers. This revenue contribution, in turn, depends on the workers' productivity and the strength of the demand for the products they are helping to produce. Where labor is highly productive and product demand is strong, labor demand also is strong and, other things equal, pay is high. Top professional athletes, for example, are highly productive at producing sports entertainment, for which millions of people are willing to pay billions of dollars over the course of a season. Because the **marginal revenue productivity** of these players is so high, they are in very high demand by sports teams. This high demand leads to their extremely high salaries (as in Figure 17.9a). In contrast, most workers generate much more modest revenue for their employers. This results in much lower demand for their labor and, consequently, much lower wages (as in Figure 17.9b).

Noncompeting Groups

On the supply side of the labor market, workers are not homogeneous; they differ in their mental and physical capacities and in their education and training. At any given time the labor force is made up of many **noncompeting groups** of workers, each representing several occupations for which the members of a particular group qualify. In some groups qualified workers are relatively few, whereas in others they are plentiful. And workers in one group do not qualify for the occupations of other groups.

Ability At any moment in time, only a few workers have the skills or physical attributes to be hired as brain surgeons, concert violinists, top fashion models, research chemists, or professional athletes. Because the supply of these particular types of labor is very small in relation to labor demand, their wages are high (as in Figure 17.9c). The members of these and similar groups do not compete with one another or with other skilled or semiskilled workers. The violinist does not compete with the surgeon, nor does the surgeon compete with the violinist or the fashion model.

The concept of noncompeting groups can be applied to various subgroups and even to specific individuals in a particular group. Some especially skilled violinists can command higher salaries than colleagues who play the same instrument. A handful of top corporate executives earn 10 to 20 times as much as the average chief executive officer. In each of these cases, the supply of top talent is highly limited since less-talented colleagues are only imperfect substitutes.

Education and Training Another source of wage differentials is differing amounts of **human capital**, which is the

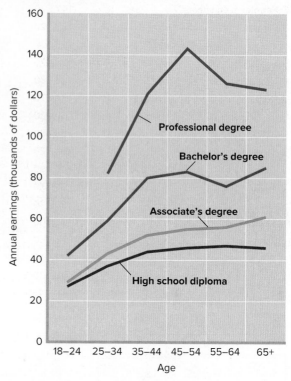

FIGURE 17.10 Education levels and individual annual earnings. Annual income by age is higher for workers with more education than less. Investment in education yields a return in the form of earnings differences enjoyed over one's work life.

Source: U.S. Bureau of the Census. Data are for both sexes in 2014.

personal stock of knowledge, know-how, and skills that enables a person to be productive and thus to earn income. Such stocks result from investments in human capital. Like expenditures on machinery and equipment, productivity-enhancing expenditures on education or training are investments. In both cases, people incur *present costs* with the intention that those expenditures will lead to a greater flow of *future earnings*.

Figure 17.10 indicates that workers who have made greater investments in education achieve higher incomes during their careers. The reason is twofold: (1) There are fewer such workers, so their supply is limited relative to less-educated workers, and (2) more-educated workers tend to be more productive and thus in greater demand. Figure 17.10 also indicates that the earnings of better-educated workers rise more rapidly than those of poorly educated workers. The primary reason is that employers provide more on-the-job training to the better-educated workers, boosting their marginal revenue productivity and therefore their earnings.

Although education yields higher incomes, it carries substantial costs. A college education involves not only direct costs (tuition, fees, books) but indirect or opportunity costs (forgone earnings) as well. Does the higher pay received by better-educated workers compensate for these costs? The answer is yes. Rates of return are estimated to be 10 to 13 percent for investments in secondary education and 8 to 12 percent for investments in college education. One generally accepted estimate is that each year of schooling raises a worker's wage by about 8 percent.

Compensating Differences

If the workers in a particular noncompeting group are equally capable of performing several different jobs, you might expect the wage rates to be identical for all these jobs. Not so. A group of high school graduates may be equally capable of becoming salesclerks or general construction workers. But these jobs pay different wages. In virtually all locales, construction laborers receive much higher wages than salesclerks. These wage differentials are called **compensating differences** because they must be paid to compensate for nonmonetary differences in various jobs.

The construction job involves dirty hands, a sore back, the hazard of accidents, and irregular employment, both seasonally and during recessions (the economywide economic slowdowns that periodically affect the economy). The retail sales job means clean clothing, pleasant air-conditioned surroundings, and little fear of injury or layoff. Other things equal, it is easy to see why workers would rather pick up a credit card than a shovel. So the amount of labor that is supplied to construction firms (as in Figure 17.9c) is smaller than that which is supplied to retail shops (as in Figure 17.9d). Construction firms must pay higher wages than retailers to compensate for the unattractive nonmonetary aspects of construction jobs.

Such compensating differences spring up throughout the economy. Other things equal, jobs having high risk of injury or death pay more than comparable, safer jobs. Jobs lacking employer-paid health insurance, pensions, and vacation time pay more than comparable jobs that provide these "fringe benefits." Jobs with more flexible hours pay less than jobs with rigid work-hour requirements. Jobs with greater risk of unemployment pay more than comparable jobs with little unemployment risk. Entry-level jobs in occupations that provide very poor prospects for pay advancement pay more than entry-level jobs that have clearly defined "job ladders."

These and other compensating differences play an important role in allocating society's scarce labor resources. If very few workers want to be garbage collectors, then society must pay high wages to garbage collectors to get the garbage collected. If many more people want to be salesclerks, then society need not pay them as much as it pays garbage collectors to get those services performed.

Market Imperfections

Differences in marginal revenue productivity, amounts of human capital, and nonmonetary aspects of jobs explain most of the wage differentials in the economy. But some persistent

CONSIDER THIS . . .

Source: © Grand Palais/Art Resource, NY

My Entire Life

Human capital is the accumulation of outcomes of prior investments in education, training, and other factors that increase productivity and earnings. It is the stock of knowledge, know-how, and skills that enables individuals to be productive and thus earn income. A valuable stock of human capital, together with a strong demand for one's services, can add up to a large capacity to earn income. For some people, high earnings have little to do with actual hours of work and much to do with their tremendous skill, which reflects their accumulated stock of human capital.

The point is demonstrated in the following story: It is said that a tourist once spotted the famous Spanish artist Pablo Picasso (1881–1973) in a Paris café. The tourist asked Picasso if he would do a sketch of his wife for pay. Picasso sketched the wife in a matter of minutes and said, "That will be 10,000 francs [roughly $2,000]." Hearing the high price, the tourist became irritated, saying, "But that took you only a few minutes."

"No," replied Picasso, "it took me my entire life!"

differentials result from various market imperfections that impede workers from moving from lower-paying jobs to higher-paying jobs.

Lack of Job Information Workers may simply be unaware of job opportunities and wage rates in other geographic areas and in other jobs for which they qualify. Consequently, the flow of qualified labor from lower-paying to higher-paying jobs—and thus the adjustments in labor supply—may not be sufficient to equalize wages within occupations.

Geographic Immobility Workers take root geographically. Many are reluctant to move to new places. Doing so would involve leaving friends, relatives, and associates. It would mean forcing their children to change schools, having to sell their homes, and incurring the costs and inconveniences of adjusting to a new job and a new community. As Adam Smith noted over two centuries ago, "A [person] is of all sorts of luggage the most difficult to be transported." The reluctance or inability of workers to move enables geographic wage differentials within the same occupation to persist.

Unions and Government Restraints Wage differentials may be reinforced by artificial restrictions on mobility imposed by unions and government. We have noted that craft unions find it to their advantage to restrict membership. After all, if carpenters and bricklayers become too plentiful, the wages they can command will decline. Thus the low-paid nonunion carpenter of Brush, Colorado, may be willing to move to Chicago in the pursuit of higher wages. But her chances for succeeding are slim. She may be unable to get a union card, and no card means no job. Similarly, an optometrist or lawyer qualified to practice in one state may not meet the licensing requirements of other states, so his or her ability to move is limited. Other artificial barriers involve pension plans, health insurance benefits, and seniority rights that might be jeopardized by moving from one job to another.

Discrimination Despite legislation to the contrary, discrimination sometimes results in lower wages being paid to women and minority workers than to white males doing very similar or even identical work. Also, women and minorities may be crowded into certain low-paying occupations, driving down wages there and raising them elsewhere. If this *occupational segregation* keeps qualified women and minorities from taking higher-paying jobs, then differences in pay will persist. (We discuss discrimination in Chapter 23.)

All four considerations—differences in marginal revenue productivity, noncompeting groups, nonmonetary differences, and market imperfections—come into play in explaining actual wage differentials. For example, the differential between the wages of a physician and those of a construction worker can be explained on the basis of marginal revenue productivity and noncompeting groups. Physicians generate considerable revenue because of their high productivity and the strong willingness of consumers (via insurance) to pay for health care. Physicians also fall into a noncompeting group where, because of stringent training requirements, only relatively few persons qualify. So the supply of labor is small in relation to demand.

In construction work, where training requirements are much less significant, the supply of labor is great relative to demand. So wages are much lower for construction workers than for physicians. However, if not for the unpleasantness of the construction worker's job and the fact that his or her craft union observes restrictive membership policies, the differential would be even greater than it is.

Pay for Performance

LO17.8 Identify the types, benefits, and costs of "pay-for-performance" plans.

The models of wage determination we have described in this chapter assume that worker pay is always a standard amount for each hour's work, for example, $15 per hour. But pay schemes are often more complex than that both in composition and in purpose. For instance, many workers receive annual salaries rather than hourly pay. And workers receive differing proportions of fringe benefits (health insurance, life insurance, paid vacations, paid sick-leave days, pension contributions, and so on) as part of their pay. Finally, some pay plans are designed to elicit a desired level of performance from workers. This last aspect of pay plans requires further elaboration.

The Principal-Agent Problem

The **principal-agent problem** is usually associated with the possible differences in the interests of corporate stockholders (principals) and the executives (agents) they hire. But this problem extends to all paid employees. Firms hire workers because they are needed to help produce the goods and services the firms sell in their attempts to turn a profit. Workers are the firms' agents; they are hired to advance the interest (profit) of the firms. The principals are the firms; they hire agents to advance their goals. Firms and workers have one interest in common: They both want the firm to survive and thrive. That will ensure profit for the firm and continued employment and wages for the workers.

But the interests of firms and workers are not identical. As a result, a principal-agent problem arises. Workers may seek to increase their utility by shirking on the job, that is, by providing less than the agreed-upon effort or by taking unauthorized breaks. They may improve their well-being by increasing their leisure during paid work hours, without forfeiting income. The night security guard in a warehouse may leave work early or spend time reading a novel rather than making the assigned rounds. A salaried manager may spend time away from the office visiting with friends rather than attending to company business.

Firms (principals) have a profit incentive to reduce or eliminate shirking. One option is to monitor workers, but monitoring is difficult and costly. Hiring another worker to supervise or monitor the security guard might double the cost of maintaining a secure warehouse. Another way of resolving a principal-agent problem is through some sort of **incentive pay plan** that ties worker compensation more closely to worker output or performance. Such incentive pay schemes include piece rates; commissions and royalties; bonuses, stock options, and profit sharing; and efficiency wages.

Piece Rates Piece rates consist of compensation paid according to the number of units of output a worker produces. If a principal pays fruit pickers by the bushel or typists by the page, it need not be concerned with shirking or with monitoring costs.

Commissions or Royalties Unlike piece rates, commissions and royalties tie compensation to the value of sales.

Employees who sell products or services—including real estate agents, insurance agents, stockbrokers, and retail salespersons—commonly receive *commissions* that are computed as a percentage of the monetary value of their sales. Recording artists and authors are paid *royalties,* computed as a certain percentage of sales revenues from their works. Such types of compensation link the financial interests of the salespeople, artists, and authors to the profit interest of the firms.

Bonuses, Stock Options, and Profit Sharing *Bonuses* are payments in addition to one's annual salary that are based on some factor such as the performance of the individual worker, or of a group of workers, or of the firm itself. A professional baseball player may receive a bonus based on a high batting average, the number of home runs hit, or the number of runs batted in. A business manager may receive a bonus based on the profitability of her or his unit. *Stock options* allow workers to buy shares of their employer's stock at a fixed, lower price when the stock price rises. Such options are part of the compensation packages of top corporate officials, as well as many workers in relatively high-technology firms. *Profit-sharing plans* allocate a percentage of a firm's profit to its employees.

Efficiency Wages The rationale behind *efficiency wages* is that employers will enjoy greater effort from their workers by paying them above-equilibrium wage rates. Glance back at Figure 17.3, which shows a competitive labor market in which the equilibrium wage rate is $10. What if an employer decides to pay an above-equilibrium wage of $12 per hour? Rather than putting the firm at a cost disadvantage compared with rival firms paying only $10, the higher wage might improve worker effort and productivity so that unit labor costs actually fall. For example, if each worker produces 10 units of output per hour at the $12 wage rate compared with only 6 units at the $10 wage rate, unit labor costs for the high-wage firm will be only $1.20 (= $12/10) compared to $1.67 (= $10/6) for firms paying the equilibrium wage.

An above-equilibrium wage may enhance worker efficiency in several ways. It enables the firm to attract higher-quality workers. It lifts worker morale. And it lowers turnover, resulting in a more experienced workforce, greater worker productivity, and lower recruitment and training costs. Because the opportunity cost of losing a higher-wage job is greater, workers are more likely to put forth their best efforts with less supervision and monitoring. In fact, efficiency wage payments have proved effective for many employers.

Addenda: Negative Side Effects of Pay for Performance

Although pay for performance may help overcome the principal-agent problem and enhance worker productivity, such plans may have negative side effects and require careful design. Here are a few examples:

- The rapid production pace that piece rates encourage may result in poor product quality and may compromise the safety of workers. Such outcomes can be costly to the firm over the long run.

- Commissions may cause some salespeople to engage in questionable or even fraudulent sales practices, such as making exaggerated claims about products or recommending unneeded repairs. Such practices may lead to private lawsuits or government legal action.

- Bonuses based on personal performance may disrupt the close cooperation needed for maximum team production. A professional basketball player who receives a bonus for points scored may be reluctant to pass the ball to teammates.

- Since profit sharing is usually tied to the performance of the entire firm, less energetic workers can "free ride" by obtaining their profit share on the basis of the hard work by others.

- Stock options may prompt some unscrupulous executives to manipulate the cost and revenue streams of their firms to create a false appearance of rapidly rising profit. When the firm's stock value rises, the executives exercise their stock options at inflated share prices and reap a personal fortune.

- There may be a downside to the reduced turnover resulting from above-market wages: Firms that pay efficiency wages have fewer opportunities to hire new workers and suffer the loss of the creative energy that they often bring to the workplace.

> **QUICK REVIEW 17.3**
>
> ✓ Proponents of the minimum wage argue that it is needed to assist the working poor and to counter monopsony where it might exist; critics say that it is poorly targeted to reduce poverty and that it reduces employment.
>
> ✓ Wage differentials are attributable in general to the forces of supply and demand, influenced by differences in workers' marginal revenue productivity, education, and skills and by nonmonetary differences in jobs. But several labor market imperfections also play a role.
>
> ✓ As it applies to labor, the principal-agent problem is one of workers pursuing their own interests to the detriment of the employer's profit objective.
>
> ✓ Pay-for-performance plans (piece rates, commissions, royalties, bonuses, stock options, profit sharing, and efficiency wages) are designed to improve worker productivity by overcoming the principal-agent problem.

Occupational Licensing

Many Industries Impose Unnecessary Licensing Requirements as a Way of Restricting Competition.

Occupational licensing laws operate at the state and local level. They were originally created to protect the public from harm by ensuring that the members of licensed professions met high standards for training and expertise. This makes perfect sense for physicians and emergency medical technicians (EMTs), who are literally responsible for people's lives. But various business groups whose activities pose little or no threat to anyone have managed to get their industries covered by unnecessary licensing requirements as a way of limiting competition and driving up prices.

The most egregious example is interior design. You have probably put up a poster, painted a wall, or rearranged your furniture at least a few times in your life. These acts of interior design probably didn't strike you as requiring any particular training or being in any way a threat to the public. But the National Association of Interior Designers disagrees. They have spent decades lobbying state governments to impose occupational licensing requirements on interior designers. And they have succeeded in Florida, Maryland, and Nevada.

In those states, anyone who wishes to work as an interior designer has to complete six years of training and internships before they can even apply for a license. Those six years plus the cost of all that training limits the supply of interior designers and thereby raises the wages of the few who do obtain a license. Those few naturally lobby to maintain the licensing requirement.

Source: NSBAIDRD

The six years of training that are required to obtain an interior-design license in those three states stand in stark contrast to the average of just 33 days that are required across all 50 states to obtain an EMT license. The EMT licensing requirements are much less onerous because EMTs have not organized themselves politically the way interior designers have. So the EMT licensing requirements reflect only what is actually required for competence. There has been no attempt to artificially increase the EMT requirements in order to reduce the supply of EMTs and thereby artificially increase EMT wages.

There are dozens of examples of industries where occupational licensing is not obviously needed to protect the public or in which licensing requirements have been made artificially excessive to drive up wages. Thirty-six states "protect" the public by requiring make-up artists to spend an average of seven months earning a license. Forty-six states "safeguard" gym-goers by requiring personal trainers to take an average of four years of classes and internships. And three states "defend" the public by requiring eight months of classes and training to obtain a license to install home entertainment systems.

These examples of unnecessary licensing might be funny except for the burden they place on consumers and workers. Not only do consumers have to pay higher prices because of reduced supply, they also enjoy fewer choices because they cannot legally hire an unlicensed provider even if that person is perfectly capable of doing the job well. Even worse, unnecessary licensing requirements substantially limit job opportunities for poorer workers. Instead of being able to start working as soon as any honestly needed training is completed, they are forced to go through months or even years of costly artificial requirements whose only purpose is to limit competition for those who already have licenses.

These barriers to employment have grown more burdensome and pervasive in recent decades. Whereas only about 1 in 20 jobs required an occupational license in the 1950s, nearly 1 in 3 do today. And of the 1,100 or so occupations that require a license at either the federal or state level, over 100 are for lower-wage jobs in fields such as cosmetology, child care, floristry, barbering, bus driving, bartending, tree trimming, hair braiding, massage therapy, and travel agency. Thus, unnecessary occupational licensing presents a major impediment to millions of poorer people hoping to set up their own businesses or switch careers. If they live in a state that requires licensing, they will have to pay fees, take classes, endure internships, and pass tests to obtain jobs that many consumers would be happy to pay them to do without a license. Unfortunately, that state of affairs is likely to continue indefinitely due to the power of the *special-interest effect* under which a small group of insiders can impose large costs on outsiders.

Source: **http://www.nsbaidrd.org/?page=16**

SUMMARY

LO17.1 Explain why labor productivity and real hourly compensation track so closely over time.

The term "labor" encompasses all people who work for pay. The wage rate is the price paid per unit of time for labor. Labor earnings comprise total pay and are found by multiplying the number of hours worked by the hourly wage rate. The nominal wage rate is the amount of money received per unit of time; the real wage rate is the purchasing power of the nominal wage.

The long-run growth of real hourly compensation—the average real wage—roughly matches that of productivity, with both increasing over the long run.

Global comparisons suggest that real wages in the United States are relatively high, but not the highest, internationally. High real wages in the advanced industrial countries stem largely from high labor productivity.

LO17.2 Show how wage rates and employment levels are determined in competitive labor markets.

Specific wage rates depend on the structure of the particular labor market. In a competitive labor market the equilibrium wage rate and level of employment are determined at the intersection of the labor supply curve and labor demand curve. For the individual firm, the market wage rate establishes a horizontal labor supply curve, meaning that the wage rate equals the firm's constant marginal resource cost. The firm hires workers to the point where its MRP equals its MRC.

LO17.3 Demonstrate how monopsony (a market with a single employer) can reduce wages below competitive levels.

Under monopsony the marginal resource cost curve lies above the resource supply curve because the monopsonist must bid up the wage rate to hire extra workers and must pay that higher wage rate to all workers. The monopsonist hires fewer workers than are hired under competitive conditions, pays less-than-competitive wage rates (has lower labor costs), and thus obtains greater profit.

LO17.4 Discuss how unions increase wage rates by pursuing the demand-enhancement model, the craft union model, or the industrial union model.

A union may raise competitive wage rates by (a) increasing the derived demand for labor, (b) restricting the supply of labor through exclusive unionism, or (c) directly enforcing an above-equilibrium wage rate through inclusive unionism. On average, unionized workers realize wage rates 15 percent higher than those of comparable nonunion workers.

LO17.5 Explain why wages and employment are determined by collective bargaining in a situation of bilateral monopoly.

In many industries the labor market takes the form of bilateral monopoly, in which a strong union "sells" labor to a monopsonistic employer. The wage-rate outcome of this labor market model depends on union and employer bargaining power.

LO17.6 Discuss how minimum wage laws affect labor markets.

Economists disagree about the desirability of the minimum wage as an antipoverty mechanism. While it causes unemployment for some low-income workers, it raises the incomes of those who retain their jobs.

LO17.7 List the major causes of wage differentials.

Wage differentials are largely explainable in terms of (a) marginal revenue productivity of various groups of workers; (b) noncompeting groups arising from differences in the capacities and education of different groups of workers; (c) compensating wage differences, that is, wage differences that must be paid to offset nonmonetary differences in jobs; and (d) market imperfections in the form of lack of job information, geographic immobility, union and government restraints, and discrimination.

LO17.8 Identify the types, benefits, and costs of "pay-for-performance" plans.

As it a applies to labor, the principal-agent problem arises when workers provide less-than-expected effort. Firms may combat this by monitoring workers or by creating incentive pay schemes that link worker compensation to performance.

TERMS AND CONCEPTS

wage rate	occupational licensing	noncompeting groups
nominal wage	inclusive unionism	human capital
real wage	bilateral monopoly	compensating differences
purely competitive labor market	minimum wage	principal-agent problem
monopsony	wage differentials	incentive pay plan
exclusive unionism	marginal revenue productivity	

The following and additional problems can be found in ▄ᴄonnect

DISCUSSION QUESTIONS

1. Explain why the general level of wages is high in the United States and other industrially advanced countries. What is the single most important factor underlying the long-run increase in average real-wage rates in the United States? **LO17.1**
2. Why is a firm in a purely competitive labor market a wage taker? What would happen if it decided to pay less than the going market wage rate? **LO17.2**
3. Describe wage determination in a labor market in which workers are unorganized and many firms actively compete for the services of labor. Show this situation graphically, using W_1 to indicate the equilibrium wage rate and Q_1 to show the number of workers hired by the firms as a group. Show the labor supply curve of the individual firm, and compare it with that of the total market. Why the differences? In the diagram representing the firm, identify total revenue, total wage cost, and revenue available for the payment of non-labor resources. **LO17.2**
4. Suppose the formerly competing firms in the previous question form an employers' association that hires labor as a monopsonist would. Describe verbally the effect on wage rates and employment. Adjust the graph you drew for review question 1, showing the monopsonistic wage rate and employment level as W_2 and Q_2, respectively. Using this monopsony model, explain why hospital administrators sometimes complain about a "shortage" of nurses. How might such a shortage be corrected? **LO17.3**

5. Assume a monopsonistic employer is paying a wage rate of W_m and hiring Q_m workers, as indicated in Figure 17.8. Now suppose an industrial union is formed that forces the employer to accept a wage rate of W_c. Explain verbally and graphically why in this instance the higher wage rate will be accompanied by an increase in the number of workers hired. **LO17.5**
6. Have you ever worked for the minimum wage? If so, for how long? Would you favor increasing the minimum wage by a dollar? By two dollars? By five dollars? Explain your reasoning. **LO17.6**
7. "Many of the lowest-paid people in society—for example, short-order cooks—also have relatively poor working conditions. Hence, the notion of compensating wage differentials is disproved." Do you agree? Explain. **LO17.7**
8. What is meant by investment in human capital? Use this concept to explain (a) wage differentials and (b) the long-run rise of real-wage rates in the United States. **LO17.7**
9. What is the principal-agent problem? Have you ever worked in a setting where this problem has arisen? If so, do you think increased monitoring would have eliminated the problem? Why don't firms simply hire more supervisors to eliminate shirking? **LO17.8**
10. **LAST WORD** Speculate as to why we see unnecessary occupational licensing only in some industries but not others. Consider both costs and benefits, who gets them, and how hard it would be to organize opposition to unnecessary licensing in various industries.

REVIEW QUESTIONS

1. Brenda owns a construction company that employs bricklayers and other skilled tradesmen. Her firm's MRP for bricklayers is $22.25 per hour for each of the first seven bricklayers, $18.50 for an eighth bricklayer, and $17.75 for a ninth bricklayer. Given that she is a price taker when hiring bricklayers, how many bricklayers will she hire if the market equilibrium wage for bricklayers is $18.00 per hour? **LO17.2**
   a. Zero.
   b. Seven.
   c. Eight.
   d. Nine.
   e. More information is required to answer this question.
2. Because a perfectly competitive employer's MRC curve is _____, it will hire _____ workers than would a monopsony employer with the same MRP curve. **LO17.3**
   a. Upsloping; more.
   b. Upsloping; fewer.
   c. Flat; more.
   d. Flat; fewer.
   e. Downsloping; more.
   f. Downsloping; fewer.

3. True or false. When a labor market consists of a single monopsony buyer of labor interacting with a single monopoly seller of labor (such as a trade union), the resulting quantity of labor that is hired will always be inefficiently low. **LO17.5**
4. The market equilibrium wage is currently $12 per hour among hairdressers. At that wage, 17,323 hairdressers are currently employed in the state. The state legislature then sets a minimum wage of $11.50 per hour for hairdressers. If there are no changes to either the demand or supply for hairdressers when that minimum wage is imposed, the number of hairdressers employed in the state will be: **LO17.6**
   a. Fewer than 17,323.
   b. Still 17,323.
   c. More than 17,323.
   d. This is a bilateral monopsony so you can't tell.
5. On average, 50-year-old workers are paid several times more than workers in their teens and twenties. Which of the following options is the most likely explanation for that huge difference in average earnings? **LO17.7**
   a. Older workers have more human capital and higher MRPs.
   b. Employers engage in widespread discrimination against younger workers.

c. Young people lack information about the existence of the high-paying jobs occupied by older workers.

d. Older workers receive compensating differences because they do jobs that are more risky than the jobs done by younger workers.

6. Manny owns a local fast-food franchise. Angel runs it for him. So in this situation, Manny is the _____ and Angel is the _____. LO17.8
    a. Free rider; entrepreneur.
    b. Agent; principal.

c. Principal; agent.

d. Producer; consumer.

7. A principal is worried that her agent may not do what she wants. As a solution, she should consider: LO17.8
    a. Commissions.
    b. Bonuses.
    c. Profit sharing.
    d. All of the above.

PROBLEMS

1. Workers are compensated by firms with "benefits" in addition to wages and salaries. The most prominent benefit offered by many firms is health insurance. Suppose that in 2000, workers at one steel plant were paid $20 per hour and in addition received health benefits at the rate of $4 per hour. Also suppose that by 2010 workers at that plant were paid $21 per hour but received $9 in health insurance benefits. LO17.1

    a. By what percentage did total compensation (wages plus benefits) change at this plant from 2000 to 2010? What was the approximate average annual percentage change in total compensation?

    b. By what percentage did wages change at this plant from 2000 to 2010? What was the approximate average annual percentage change in wages?

    c. If workers value a dollar of health benefits as much as they value a dollar of wages, by what total percentage will they feel that their incomes have risen over this time period? What if they only consider wages when calculating their incomes?

    d. Is it possible for workers to feel as though their wages are stagnating even if total compensation is rising?

2. Complete the following labor supply table for a firm hiring labor competitively: LO17.2

Units of Labor	Wage Rate	Total Labor Cost	Marginal Resource (Labor) Cost
0	$14	$ _____	$ _____
1	14	_____	
2	14	_____	_____
3	14	_____	_____
4	14	_____	_____
5	14	_____	_____
6	14	_____	_____

    a. Show graphically the labor supply and marginal resource (labor) cost curves for this firm. Are the curves the same or different? If they are different, which one is higher?

    b. Plot the labor demand data of review question 2 in Chapter 16 on the graph used in part a above. What are the equilibrium wage rate and level of employment?

3. Assume a firm is a monopsonist that can hire its first worker for $6 but must increase the wage rate by $3 to attract each successive worker (so that the second worker must be paid $9, the third $12, and so on). LO17.3

    a. Draw the firm's labor supply and marginal resource cost curves. Are the curves the same or different? If they are different, which one is higher?

    b. On the same graph, plot the labor demand data of review question 2 in Chapter 16. What are the equilibrium wage rate and level of employment?

    c. Compare these answers with those you found in problem 2. By how much does the monopsonist reduce wages below the competitive wage? By how much does the monopsonist reduce employment below the competitive level?

4. Suppose that low-skilled workers employed in clearing woodland can each clear one acre per month if each is equipped with a shovel, a machete, and a chainsaw. Clearing one acre brings in $1,000 in revenue. Each worker's equipment costs the worker's employer $150 per month to rent and each worker toils 40 hours per week for four weeks each month. LO17.6

    a. What is the marginal revenue product of hiring one low-skilled worker to clear woodland for one month?

    b. How much revenue per hour does each worker bring in?

    c. If the minimum wage were $6.20, would the revenue per hour in part b exceed the minimum wage? If so, by how much per hour?

    d. Now consider the employer's total costs. These include the equipment costs as well as a normal profit of $50 per acre. If the firm pays workers the minimum wage of $6.20 per hour, what will the firm's economic profit or loss be per acre?

    e. At what value would the minimum wage have to be set so that the firm would make zero economic profit from employing an additional low-skilled worker to clear woodland?

5. Suppose that a car dealership wishes to see if efficiency wages will help improve its salespeople's productivity. Currently, each

salesperson sells an average of one car per day while being paid $20 per hour for an eight-hour day. **LO17.8**

a. What is the current labor cost per car sold?

b. Suppose that when the dealer raises the price of labor to $30 per hour the average number of cars sold by a salesperson increases to two per day. What is now the labor cost per car sold? By how much is it higher or lower than it was before? Has the efficiency of labor expenditures by the firm (cars sold per dollar of wages paid to salespeople) increased or decreased?

c. Suppose that if the wage is raised a second time to $40 per hour the number of cars sold rises to an average of 2.5 per day. What is now the labor cost per car sold?

d. If the firm's goal is to maximize the efficiency of its labor expenditures, which of the three hourly salary rates should it use: $20 per hour, $30 per hour, or $40 per hour?

e. By contrast, which salary maximizes the productivity of the car dealer's workers (cars sold per worker per day)?

Labor Unions and Their Impacts

LO17.9 Relate who belongs to U.S. unions, the basics of collective bargaining, and the economic effects of unions.

We have noted that unions can increase wage rates by augmenting the demand for labor (Figure 17.5) or by restricting or controlling the supply of labor (Figures 17.6 and 17.7). The purpose of this appendix is to provide some additional information about American unions, collective bargaining, and union impacts.

Union Membership

In 2015, about 16.4 million U.S. workers—11.1 percent of employed wage and salary workers—belonged to unions. Some 11.6 million of these U.S. union members belonged to one of many unions that are loosely and voluntarily affiliated with the **American Federation of Labor and the Congress of Industrial Organizations (AFL-CIO).** Examples of AFL-CIO unions are the United Autoworkers, Communications Workers, and United Steelworkers. Another 5.5 million union members belonged to one of the seven unions, including the Service Workers and Teamsters, loosely federated as **Change to Win.** The remaining union members belonged to other **independent unions** that were not affiliated with either federation.

The likelihood that any particular worker will be a union member depends mainly on the industry in which the worker is employed and his or her occupation. As shown in Figure 1a, the **unionization rate**—the percentage of workers unionized—is high in government, transportation, telecommunications, construction, and manufacturing. The unionization rate is very low in finance, agriculture, and retail trade. Figure 1b shows that unionism also varies greatly by occupation. Protective service workers (fire and police), teachers, production workers, transportation services employees, and social workers have high unionization rates; sales workers, food workers, and managers have very low rates.

Because disproportionately more men than women work in the industries and occupations with high unionization rates, men are more likely to be union members than women. Specifically, 12 percent of male wage and salary workers belong to unions compared with 11 percent of women. For the same reason, African Americans have higher unionization rates than whites: 14 percent compared with 11 percent. The unionization rate for Asians is 10 percent; Hispanics, 9 percent. Unionism in the United States is largely an urban phenomenon. Seven heavily urbanized, heavily industrialized states (New York, California, Pennsylvania, Illinois, Ohio, New Jersey, and Michigan) account for approximately half of all union members.

The Decline of Unionism

Since the mid-1950s, union membership has not kept pace with the growth of the labor force. While 25 percent of employed wage and salary workers belonged to unions in the

FIGURE 1 Union membership as a percentage of employed wage and salary workers, selected industries and occupations, 2015. In percentage terms, union membership varies greatly by (a) industry and (b) occupation.

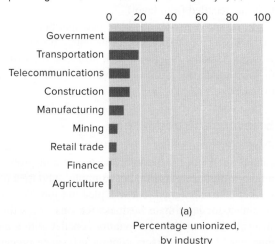

(a)
Percentage unionized,
by industry

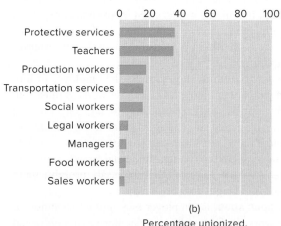

(b)
Percentage unionized,
by occupation

Source: Bureau of Labor Statistics, **www.bls.gov**.

mid-1950s, today only 11.1 percent are union members. Over recent years, even the absolute number of union members has declined significantly. More than 22 million workers were unionized in 1980 but only 16.4 million in 2015.

Some of the major reasons for the decline of U.S. unionism involve structural changes in the economy. Employment has shifted away from manufactured goods (where unions have been stronger) and toward services (where unions have been weaker). Consumer demand has shifted toward foreign manufactured goods and away from goods produced by union labor in the United States. Industry has shifted from the northeast and midwest, where unionism is "a way of life," to "hard-to-organize" areas of the south and southwest. These and other factors have reduced the growth of union membership.

Also, management has greatly intensified its opposition to unions and has increasingly engaged in aggressive collective bargaining, including the use of strikebreakers. Within unionized firms, employers have substituted machinery for workers, subcontracted work to nonunion suppliers, and shifted the production of components to low-wage nations. Nonunion firms have greatly improved their wage, fringe benefits, and working conditions. That has reduced the demand for unionism.

Collective Bargaining

Despite the overall decline of unionism, **collective bargaining** (the negotiation of labor contracts) remains an important feature of labor-management relations in several U.S. industries. The goal of collective bargaining is to establish a "work agreement" between the firm and the union.

Collective bargaining agreements (contracts) assume many forms, but typically cover several topics.

Union Status

Union status is the degree of security afforded a union by the work agreement. The strongest form of union security is a **closed shop,** in which a worker must be (or must become) a member of the union before being hired. Under federal labor law, such shops are illegal in industries other than transportation and construction.

In contrast, a **union shop** permits the employer to hire nonunion workers but provides that these workers must join the union within a specified period, say 30 days, or relinquish their jobs. An **agency shop** allows nonunion workers but requires nonunion workers to either pay union dues or donate an equivalent amount to charity. Union and agency shops are legal, except in the 25 states that expressly prohibit them through so-called **right-to-work laws.**

In an **open shop,** an employer may hire either union or nonunion workers. Those who are nonunion are not obligated to join the union or to pay union dues; they may continue on their jobs indefinitely as nonunion workers. Nevertheless, the wages, hours, and working conditions set forth in the work agreement apply to the nonunion workers as well as to the union workers.

Managerial Prerogatives

Most work agreements contain clauses outlining certain decisions that are reserved solely for management. These managerial prerogatives usually cover such matters as the size and location of plants, the products to be manufactured, and the types of equipment and materials to be used in production and in production scheduling.

Wages and Hours

The focal point of almost all bargaining agreements is wages (including fringe benefits) and hours. Both labor and management press for the advantage in wage bargaining. The arguments that unions use most frequently in demanding wage boosts are (1) "what others are getting"; (2) the employer's ability to pay, based on its profitability; (3) increases in the cost of living; and (4) increases in labor productivity.

Hours of work, voluntary versus mandatory overtime, holiday and vacation provisions, profit sharing, health plans, and pension benefits are other contract issues that must be addressed in the bargaining process.

Seniority and Job Protection

The uncertainty of employment in a market economy, along with the fear of antiunion discrimination on the part of employers, has made workers and their unions "job-conscious." The explicit and detailed provisions covering job opportunities that most agreements contain reflect this concern. Unions stress length of service, or *seniority,* as the basis for worker promotion and for layoff and recall. They want the worker with the longest continuous service to have the first chance at relevant promotions, to be the last one laid off, and to be the first one recalled from layoff.

In recent years, unions have become increasingly sensitive to losing jobs to nonunion subcontractors and to overseas workers. Unions sometimes seek limits on the firm's ability to subcontract out work or to relocate production facilities overseas.

Grievance Procedures

Even the most detailed and comprehensive work agreement cannot spell out all the specific issues and problems that might occur during its life. For example, suppose a particular worker gets reassigned to a less pleasant job. Was this reassignment for legitimate business reasons or, as the person suspects, because of a personality conflict with a particular manager? Labor contracts contain grievance procedures to resolve such matters.

The Bargaining Process

The date for the beginning of collective bargaining on a new contract is usually specified in the existing contract and is typically 60 days before the current one expires.

The union normally takes the initiative, presenting its demands in the form of specific wage, fringe-benefit, and other adjustments to the present union-management contract. The firm counters with an offer relating to these and other contract provisions. It is not unusual for the original union demand and the first offer by the firm to be far apart, not only because of the parties' conflicting goals but also because starting far apart leaves plenty of room for compromise and counteroffers during negotiations.

Hanging over the negotiations is the contract deadline, which occurs the moment the present contract expires. At that time there is a possibility of a **strike**—a work stoppage by the union—if it thinks its demands are not being satisfactorily met. But there is also the possibility that at the deadline the firm may engage in a **lockout,** in which it forbids the workers to return to work until a new contract is signed. In this setting of uncertainty prior to the deadline, both parties feel pressure to find mutually acceptable terms.

Although bluster and bickering often occur in collective bargaining, labor and management display a remarkable capacity for compromise and agreement. Typically they reach a compromise that is written into a new contract. Nevertheless, strikes and lockouts occasionally do occur. When they happen, workers lose income and firms lose profit. To stem their losses, both parties usually look for and eventually find ways to settle the labor dispute and get the workers back to work.

Bargaining, strikes, and lockouts occur within a framework of federal labor law, specifically the **National Labor Relations Act (NLRA).** This act was first passed as the Wagner Act of 1935 and later amended by the Taft-Hartley Act of 1947 and the Landrum-Griffin Act of 1959. The act sets forth the *dos and don'ts* of union and management labor practices. For example, while union members can picket in front of a firm's business, they cannot block access to the business by customers, coworkers, or strikebreakers hired by the firm. Another example: Firms cannot refuse to meet and talk with the union's designated representatives.

Either unions or management can file charges of unfair labor practices under the labor law. The **National Labor Relations Board (NLRB)** has the authority to investigate such charges and to issue cease-and-desist orders in the event of a violation. The board also conducts worker elections to decide which specific union, if any, a group of workers might want to have represent them in collective bargaining.

Economic Effects of Unions

The most straightforward effect of unions is an increase in the wage rates for their members. The consensus estimate is that the overall union wage premium (wage advantage) averages about 15 percent. The effects of unions on output and efficiency, however, are slightly more complicated.

Featherbedding and Work Rules

Some unions diminish output and efficiency by engaging in "make-work" or "featherbedding" practices and resisting the introduction of output-increasing machinery and equipment. These productivity-reducing practices often arise in periods of technological change. For example, in 2002 the ILWU (dockworkers' union) obtained a contract provision guaranteeing 40-hour-per-week jobs for all current ILWU clerical personnel for as long as they wish to continue working at their current jobs at West Coast ports. However, many of those workers will not be needed because the ports are rapidly moving toward labor-saving computerized systems for tracking cargo. Thus, many of the current clerical personnel will be paid for doing little or nothing. This will be very inefficient.

More generally, unions may reduce efficiency by establishing work rules and practices that impede putting the most productive workers in particular jobs. Under seniority rules, for example, workers may be promoted for their employment tenure rather than for their ability to perform the available job with the greatest efficiency. Also, unions might restrict the kinds of tasks workers may perform. Contract provisions may prohibit sheet-metal workers or bricklayers from doing the simple carpentry work often associated with their jobs. Observance of such rules means, in this instance, that firms must hire unneeded and under-used carpenters.

Finally, critics of unions contend that union contracts often chip away at managerial prerogatives to establish work schedules, determine production targets, introduce new technology, and make other decisions contributing to productive efficiency.

Output Losses from Strikes

A second way unions can impair efficiency and output is through strikes. If union and management reach an impasse during their contract negotiations, a strike may result and the firm's production may cease for the strike's duration. If so, the firm will forgo sales and profit; workers will sacrifice income; and the economy might lose output. U.S. strike activity, however, has dwindled in the past few decades. In 2015, there were 12 major work stoppages—strikes or lockouts involving 1,000 or more employees.

About 47,000 workers were idled by the 12 work stoppages in 2015, with the average length of stoppages being 26 days. It is estimated that the amount of work time lost to the stoppages was less than 0.005 percent of the total work time provided by employees that year.

But the amount of work time lost is an imprecise indicator of the potential economic costs of strikes. These costs may be greater than indicated if strikes disrupt production in nonstruck firms that either supply inputs to struck firms or buy products from them. Example: An extended strike in the auto industry might reduce output and cause layoffs in firms producing, say, glass, tires, paints, and fabrics used in producing cars. It also may reduce sales and cause layoffs in auto dealerships.

On the other hand, the costs of strikes may be less than is implied by the work time lost by strikers if nonstruck firms increase their output to offset the loss of production by struck firms. While the output of General Motors declines when its workers strike, auto buyers may shift their demand to Ford, Toyota, or Honda, which will respond by increasing their employment and output. Therefore, although GM and its employees are hurt by a strike, society as a whole may experience little or no decline in employment, real output, and income.

Efficiency Losses from Labor Misallocation

A third and more subtle way that unions might reduce efficiency and output is through the union wage advantage itself. Figure 2 splits the economy into two sectors, showing identical labor demand curves for the unionized sector and the non-unionized sector. If all markets are competitive and no union is initially present in either sector, the wage rate in both parts of the economy will be W_n and N_1 workers will be employed in each sector.

Now suppose workers form a union in one sector and succeed in increasing the wage rate from W_n to W_u. As a consequence, $N_1 - N_2$ workers lose their jobs in the union sector. Assume that they all move to the nonunion sector, where they are employed. This increase in labor supply (not shown) in the nonunion sector increases the quantity of labor supplied there from N_1 to N_3, reducing the wage rate from W_n to W_s.

Recall that the labor demand curves reflect the marginal revenue products (MRPs) of workers or, in other words, the contribution that each additional worker makes to domestic output. This means that area A + B + C in the union sector represents the sum of the MRPs—the total contributions to domestic output—of the workers displaced by the wage increase achieved by the union. The reemployment of these workers in the nonunion sector produces an increase in domestic output shown by area D + E. Because area A + B + C exceeds area D + E, a net loss of domestic output is the result.

More precisely, because A = D and C = E, the efficiency loss attributable to the union wage advantage is represented by area B. Because the same amount of employed labor is now producing a smaller output, labor is being misallocated and used inefficiently. After the shift of N_1N_2 workers to the nonunion sector has occurred, workers in both sectors will be paid wage rates according to their MRPs. But the workers who shifted sectors will be working at a lower MRP than before. An economy always obtains a larger domestic output when labor is reallocated from a low-MRP use to a high-MRP

FIGURE 2 The effects of the union wage advantage on the allocation of labor. (a) The higher wage rate W_u obtained by unions in the union sector displaces $N_1 - N_2$ workers and reduces output by area A + B + C. (b) The displaced workers from the union sector are reemployed in the nonunion sector, where employment increases from N_1 to N_3 and the wage rate declines from W_n to W_s. Output increases by area D + E in the nonunion sector, but that increase is less than the loss of output A + B + C in the union sector. The net loss of output, shown by area B in blue, means that the union wage advantage has caused a misallocation of resources and a decline in economic efficiency.

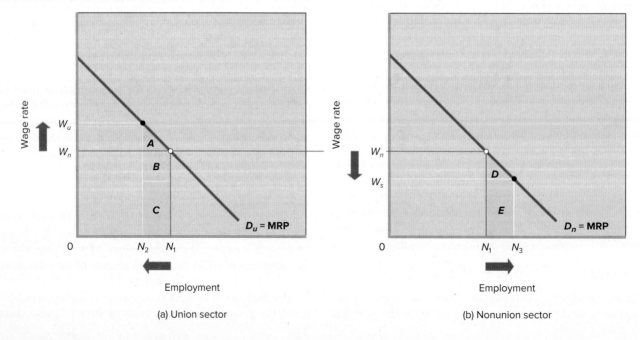

(a) Union sector

(b) Nonunion sector

use. But here the opposite has occurred. And assuming the union can maintain the W_u wage rate in its sector, a reallocation of labor from the nonunion sector to the union sector will never occur.

Attempts to estimate the efficiency loss associated with union wage gains, however, suggest that it is very small: perhaps 0.2 to 0.4 percent (or one-fifth of 1 percent to two-fifths of 1 percent) of U.S. GDP. In 2011 this cost would have amounted to about $32 billion to $63 billion.

Offsetting Factors

Some long-run consequences of unionization may enhance productivity and reduce the efficiency loss from unions. One such impact is lower worker turnover within unionized firms. Compared with the rates at nonunion firms, the quit rates (resignation rates) for union workers are 31 to 65 percent lower, depending on the industry.

The union wage premium may reduce worker turnover by increasing the desirability of the union job relative to alternative employment. In economic terms, the higher opportunity cost of quitting reduces the frequency of quitting. Unions also may reduce turnover by using collective communication—the

voice mechanism—to correct job dissatisfactions that otherwise would be "resolved" by workers quitting and taking other jobs—the **exit mechanism.** It might be risky for individual workers to express their dissatisfaction to employers because employers might retaliate by firing them as "troublemakers." But a union can provide workers with a collective voice to communicate problems and grievances to management and to press for satisfactory resolutions.

A lower quit rate may give a firm a more experienced, more productive workforce. Over time, that might offset a part of the higher costs and reduced profitability associated with the union premium. Also, having fewer resignations might reduce the firm's recruitment, screening, and hiring costs. Additionally, reduced turnover may encourage employers to invest more in the training (and therefore the productivity) of their workers. If a worker quits or "exits" at the end of, say, a year's training, the employer will get no return from providing that training. Lower turnover increases the likelihood that the employer will receive a return on the training it provides, thereby increasing its willingness to upgrade the skills of its workforce. All these factors may increase the long-run productivity of the unionized labor force and therefore reduce the efficiency loss caused by the union wage premium.

APPENDIX SUMMARY

LO17.9 Relate who belongs to U.S. unions, the basics of collective bargaining, and the economic effects of unions.

About 11.6 million of the 16.4 million union members in 2015 belonged to unions affiliated with the AFL-CIO; another 5.5 million belonged to 7 unions loosely federated under the name Change to Win. The rest were members of other independent unions. About 11.1 percent of U.S. wage and salary workers in 2015 were union members, with government employees having the highest unionization rates. As an occupation, protective service workers (fire and police) have the highest rate of unionization—36 percent.

Union membership has declined as a percentage of the labor force and in absolute numbers in recent decades. Some of the key causes are structural changes such as the shift from manufacturing employment to service employment. Other causes include improved

wages and working conditions in nonunion firms and increased managerial opposition to unions.

Collective bargaining determines the terms of union work agreements, which typically cover (*a*) union status and managerial prerogatives; (*b*) wages, hours, and working conditions; (*c*) control over job opportunities; and (*d*) grievance procedures. The bargaining process is governed by the National Labor Relations Act.

Union wages are on average about 15 percent higher than nonunion wages in comparable jobs. Restrictive union work rules, output losses from strikes, and labor misallocation from the union wage advantage are ways that unions may reduce efficiency, output, and productivity. The efficiency losses from unions may be partially offset in the long run by union productivity advances deriving from reduced labor turnover.

APPENDIX TERMS AND CONCEPTS

American Federation of Labor and the Congress of Industrial Organizations (AFL-CIO)

Change to Win

independent unions

unionization rate

collective bargaining

closed shop

union shop

agency shop

right-to-work laws

open shop

strike

lockout

National Labor Relations Act (NLRA)

National Labor Relations Board (NLRB)

voice mechanism

exit mechanism

The following and additional problems can be found in ▉ connect

APPENDIX DISCUSSION QUESTIONS

1. Which industries and occupations have the highest rates of unionization? Which the lowest? Speculate on the reasons for such large differences. **LO17.9**
2. What percentage of wage and salary workers are union members? Is this percentage higher, or is it lower, than in previous decades? Which of the factors explaining the trend do you think is most dominant? **LO17.9**
3. Explain how featherbedding and other restrictive work practices can reduce labor productivity. Why might strikes reduce the economy's output less than the loss of production by the struck firms? **LO17.9**

4. What is the estimated size of the union wage advantage? How might this advantage diminish the efficiency with which labor resources are allocated in the economy? Normally, labor resources of equal potential productivity flow from low-wage employment to high-wage employment. Why does that not happen to close the union wage advantage? **LO17.9**
5. Contrast the voice mechanism and the exit mechanism for communicating dissatisfaction. In what two ways do labor unions reduce labor turnover? How might such reductions increase productivity? **LO17.9**

APPENDIX REVIEW QUESTIONS

1. True or false. In the United States, unions have been gaining in membership and power for several decades. **LO17.9**
2. Suppose that you are president of a newly established local union about to bargain with an employer for the first time. List the basic areas you want covered in the work agreement. Why might you begin with a larger wage demand than you actually are willing to accept? What is the logic of a union threatening an employer with a strike during the collective bargaining process? Of an employer threatening the union with a lockout? What is the role of the deadline in encouraging agreement in collective bargaining? **LO17.9**
3. Look back at Figure 2. In the union sector, the union's ability to raise wages from W_n to W_u decreases total employment from N_1 to N_2. Thus $N_1 - N_2$ workers are displaced from the union sector and will seek employment in the nonunion sector. But

suppose that wages in the nonunion sector cannot fall (perhaps because of a minimum wage law). Suppose, more specifically, that they are fixed at W_n in the nonunion sector. If the union and nonunion sectors are the only two sectors in the economy, how many workers will become unemployed because of the union's ability to raise wages in the union sector? (Hint: $N_1 - N_2$ in the union sector is the same number of workers as $N_3 - N_1$ in the nonunion sector.) **LO17.9**
   a. N_1.
   b. N_2.
   c. N_3.
   d. $N_1 - N_2$.
   e. $N_1 + N_2$.
4. True or false. "To the extent that they succeed in their goals, unions only ever reduce productivity and efficiency." **LO17.9**

APPENDIX PROBLEMS

1. Suppose that a delivery company currently uses one employee per vehicle to deliver packages. Each driver delivers 50 packages per day, and the firm charges $20 per package for delivery. **LO17.9**
   a. What is the MRP per driver per day?
   b. Now suppose that a union forces the company to place a supervisor in each vehicle at a cost of $300 per supervisor per day. The presence of the supervisor causes the number of packages delivered per vehicle per day to rise to 60 packages per day. What is the MRP per supervisor per day? By how much per vehicle per day do firm profits fall after supervisors are introduced?
   c. How many packages per day would each vehicle have to deliver in order to maintain the firm's profit per vehicle after supervisors are introduced?
   d. Suppose that the number of packages delivered per day cannot be increased but that the price per delivery might potentially be raised. What price would the firm have to charge for each delivery in order to maintain the firm's profit per vehicle after supervisors are introduced?
2. Suppose that a car factory initially hires 1,500 workers at $30 per hour and that each worker works 40 hours per week. Then

the factory unionizes, and the new union demands that wages be raised by 10 percent. The firm accedes to that request in collective bargaining negotiations but then decides to cut the factory's labor force by 20 percent due to the higher labor costs. **LO17.9**
   a. What is the new union wage? How many workers does the factory employ after the agreement goes into effect?
   b. How much in total did the factory's workers receive in wage payments each week before the agreement? How much do the factory's remaining workers receive in wage payments each week after the agreement?
   c. Suppose that the workers who lose their jobs as a result of the agreement end up unemployed. By how much do the total wages received each week by the initial 1,500 workers (both those who continue to be employed at the factory and those who lose their jobs) change from before the agreement to after the agreement?
   d. If the workers who lose their jobs as a result of the agreement end up making $15 per hour at jobs where they work 40 hours per week, by how much do the total wages received each week by the initial 1,500 workers change from before the agreement to after the agreement?

Rent, Interest, and Profit

Learning Objectives

LO18.1 Explain the nature of economic rent and how it is determined.

LO18.2 Define interest and explain how interest rates vary based on risk, maturity, loan size, and taxability.

LO18.3 Explain the loanable funds theory of interest rates.

LO18.4 Demonstrate how interest rates relate to the time-value of money.

LO18.5 Explain the role of interest rates in allocating capital, modulating **R&D** spending, and helping to determine the economy's total output of goods and services.

LO18.6 Relate why economic profits occur and how profits, along with losses, allocate resources among alternative uses.

LO18.7 List the share of U.S. earnings received by each of the factors of production.

In Chapter 17, we focused on the wages and salaries paid by firms to obtain labor. Here our attention is focused on the rent, interest, and profit paid by firms to obtain, respectively, land, capital, and entrepreneurship. Our analysis will provide answers to numerous practical questions, including:

How do *land prices* and *land rents* get established, and why do they differ from property to property? For example, why do 20 acres of land in the middle of the Nevada desert sell for $5,000 while 20 acres along The Strip in Las Vegas command $500 million?

What determines *interest rates* and causes them to change? For instance, why were interest rates on 3-month bank certificates of deposit 1.3 percent in January 2003, 5.4 percent in June 2006, and 0.2 percent in November 2009? How does interest compound over time, and how does that compounding relate to the so-called present value and future value of a particular sum of money?

What are the sources of *profits* and *losses*, and why do they vary? For example, why did Walmart earn profits of nearly $17 billion in 2015 while financial firm RCS Capital went bankrupt after losing over $1.4 billion of its clients' money?

Economic Rent

LO18.1 Explain the nature of economic rent and how it is determined.

To most people, "rent" means the money paid for the use of an apartment or a room in a residence hall. To the business executive, "rent" is a payment made for the use of a factory building, machine, or warehouse facility owned by others. Such definitions of rent can be confusing and ambiguous, however. Residence hall room rent, for example, may include other payments as well: interest on money the university borrowed to finance the dormitory, wages for custodial services, utility payments, and so on.

Economists use "rent" in a much narrower sense. **Economic rent** is the price paid for the use of land and other natural resources that are completely fixed in total supply. As you will see, this fixed overall supply distinguishes rental payments from wage, interest, and profit payments.

Let's examine this idea and some of its implications through supply and demand analysis. We first assume that all land has a single use, for example, growing wheat. We assume, too, that all land is of the same grade or quality, meaning that each arable (tillable) acre of land is as productive as every other acre. And we suppose that land is rented or leased in a competitive market in which many producers are demanding land and many landowners are offering land in the market.

In Figure 18.1, curve S represents the supply of arable land available in the economy as a whole, and curve D_2 represents the demand of producers for use of that land. As with all economic resources, the demand for land is a derived demand, meaning that the demand for land is derived from the demand for the products that land helps to produce. Demand curves such as D_2 reflect the marginal revenue product ($MRP = MP \times P$) of land. The curve slopes downward because of diminishing returns (MP declines) and because, for producers as a group, additional units of land result in greater output and thus lower output prices (P is less).

Perfectly Inelastic Supply

The unique feature of our analysis is on the supply side. For all practical purposes the supply of land is perfectly inelastic (in both the short run and the long run), as reflected in supply curve S. Land has no production cost; it is a "free and nonreproducible gift of nature." The economy has only so much land, and that's that. Of course, within limits any parcel of land can be made more usable by clearing, drainage, and irrigation. But these are capital improvements and not changes in the amount of land itself. Moreover, increases in the usability of land affect only a small fraction of the total amount of land and do not change the basic fact that land and other nonrenewable natural resources are fixed in supply.

Equilibrium Rent and Changes in Demand

Because the supply of land is fixed, demand is the only active determinant of land rent. In this case, supply is passive. And what determines the demand for land? The factors we discussed in Chapter 16: the price of the products produced on the land, the productivity of land (which depends in part on the quantity and quality of the resources with which land is combined), and the prices of the other resources that are combined with land.

If demand is D_2, as we have suggested, the equilibrium rent will be R_2. The quantity of land L_0 that producers wish to rent will equal the quantity of land available (also L_0). But if the demand for land in Figure 18.1 increased from D_2 to D_1, land rent would rise from R_2 to R_1. On the other hand, if the demand for land declined from D_2 to D_3, land rent would fall from R_2 to R_3. Finally, if the demand for land were only D_4, land rent would be zero. In this situation, land would be a *free good*—a good for which demand is so weak relative to supply that an excess supply of it occurs even if the market price is zero. In Figure 18.1, we show this excess supply as distance $b - a$ at rent of zero. This essentially was the situation in the free-land era of U.S. history.

The ideas underlying Figure 18.1 help answer one of our chapter-opening questions. Land prices and rents are so high along the Las Vegas strip because the demand for that land is tremendous. It is capable of producing exceptionally high revenue from gambling, lodging, and entertainment. In contrast, the demand for isolated land in the middle of the desert is highly limited because very little revenue can be generated from its use. (It is an entirely different matter, of course, if gold can be mined from the land, as is true of some isolated parcels in Nevada!)

FIGURE 18.1 The determination of land rent. Because the supply S of land (and other natural resources) is perfectly inelastic, demand is the sole active determinant of land rent. An increase in demand from D_2 to D_1 or a decrease in demand from D_2 to D_3 will cause a considerable change in rent: from R_2 to R_1 in the first instance and from R_2 to R_3 in the second. But the amount of land supplied will remain at L_0. If demand is very weak (D_4) relative to supply, land will be a "free good," commanding no rent.

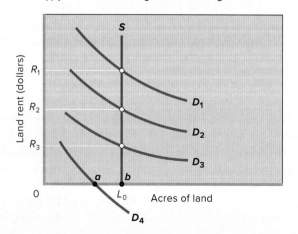

Productivity Differences and Rent Differences

So far we have assumed that all land is equally productive. That assumption is unrealistic because land varies widely in terms of productivity. As an example, differences in rainfall, soil quality, and other factors imply that while land in Kansas is excellently suited to wheat production, the sagebrush plains of Wyoming are much less well suited and the desert of Arizona is practically useless. Such productivity differences are reflected in resource demands and economic rents. Competitive bidding by producers will establish a high rent for highly productive Kansas land, less productive Wyoming land will command a much lower rent, and Arizona desert land may command no rent at all.

This process whereby differences in productivity lead to differences in rents can be understood graphically if we look at Figure 18.1 from a slightly different perspective. As before, assume that land can only be used for wheat production. But this time assume that there are four different plots of land. Each plot is of the same size L_0 but differs in productivity so that different marginal revenue products emerge when each plot of land is combined with identical amounts of labor, capital, and entrepreneurial talent.

These differences in marginal revenue products lead to four different demand curves: D_1, D_2, D_3, and D_4. D_1 is the highest demand curve because plot 1 has the highest productivity. D_4 is the lowest demand curve because plot 4 has the lowest productivity. When combined with supply curve S, the different demand curves yield different equilibrium rents: R_1, R_2, R_3, and R_4. The differences in rents mirror the differences in productivity so that plot 1 commands the highest rent, while plot 4 is so poor in quality that, given supply S, farmers won't pay anything to use it. It will be a free good because it is not sufficiently scarce in relation to its demand for it to command a price above zero.

As a final point, be aware that location itself can affect productivity and rent. Other things equal, renters will pay more for a unit of land that is strategically located with respect to materials, transportation, labor, and customers than they will for a unit of land whose location is remote from these things. Examples include the enormously high land prices near major ski resorts and the high price of land that contains oil beneath it.

Land Rent: A Surplus Payment

The supply of land is perfectly inelastic both in total and with respect to individual parcels of land. Whether land prices rise or fall, a nation will have the same total area to work with and individual plots of land will stay the same size.

The perfectly inelastic supply of land must be contrasted with the relatively elastic supply of nonland resources. Consider capital, which includes apartment buildings,

fiber optic networks, and machinery. When the prices of these and other capital goods rise, entrepreneurs respond by increasing the production of capital goods. Conversely, a decline in capital goods prices results in reduced production of capital goods. As a result, the supply curves of nonland resources are normally upsloping, so that the prices paid to such resources provide an **incentive function.** A high price provides an incentive to offer more of the resource, whereas a low price prompts resource suppliers to offer less.

Not so with unimproved land. Rent serves no incentive function because both the total area of land in a nation as well as the sizes of individual plots of land will always stay exactly the same no matter what land prices are. As a result, economists consider land rents to be *surplus payments* that are not necessary to ensure that land is made available for economic use. From this perspective, the sum of all the land rents paid across a nation constitutes a giant surplus payment because it has no effect on the total supply of land in the nation. And in the same way, the individual land rents paid on particular plots of land are also surplus payments because they likewise have no effect on the sizes of those individual plots.

Land Ownership: Fairness versus Allocative Efficiency

If land is a gift of nature, costs nothing to produce, and would be available even without rental payments, why should rent be paid to those who just happen to be landowners? Socialists have long argued that all land rents are unearned incomes because the act of owning land and renting it out to others produces nothing of value in and of itself. They urge that land should be nationalized (owned by the state) so that any payments for its use can be put to work by the government to further the well-being of the entire population.

Opponents of land nationalization argue that private land ownership allows Adam Smith's "invisible hand" to work its magic in terms of allocating scarce land resources to their best possible uses. In a nation where land is privately owned and rents are charged for the use of land, individuals and firms are forced to consider opportunity costs when deciding whether to secure the use of a particular piece of land. This gives them an incentive to allocate each piece of land to its highest-value use. In particular, renters will only allocate land to uses that generate enough revenue to both pay the rent and cover all other costs, including a normal profit.

Private land ownership and having to pay market-determined land rents also aid economic growth and development because as consumer tastes change and as new technologies are developed, the best uses to which particular pieces of land can be put also change. These changing opportunity costs are reflected in land rents, whose changing values thereby help to reallocate land from lower-value uses to higher-value uses as the economy evolves—thus, the often-heard remark, "The land was just too valuable for its previous use."

By contrast, if land were nationalized, government planners would have a difficult time assigning each piece of land to its best possible use and adjusting its use with changing circumstances without the guidance about opportunity costs provided by market-determined rents.

Along those lines, it is important to be clear that while economic rents are surplus payments when viewed from the perspective of society as a whole, they are most definitely costs to individual people and individual firms. To see why this is true, recall that because land is a free gift of nature, there is no cost to society as a whole for obtaining the current supply of land. Thus, economic rents are, from the perspective of society, surplus payments because they have no effect on land supply. But individuals must pay economic rents because such rents determine how society's fixed supply of land is allocated among competing potential uses. Those who are willing and able to pay the market rent get to use the land, while those who are unwilling or unable to pay the market rent do not. Put slightly differently: Economic rents do not cause land to be supplied—they cause land to be directed.

Application: A Single Tax on Land

In the United States, criticism of rental payments produced the **single-tax movement,** which gained significant support in the late nineteenth century. Spearheaded by Henry George's provocative book *Progress and Poverty* (1879), supporters of this reform movement held that economic rent could be heavily taxed without diminishing the available supply of land or reducing the efficiency with which it is allocated.

Henry George's Proposal George observed that, as population grew and the Western frontier closed, landowners enjoyed larger and larger rents (or lease incomes) from their landholdings. That increase in rents was the result of a growing demand for a resource whose supply was perfectly inelastic. Some landlords were receiving fabulously high incomes, not through any productive effort but solely through their ownership of highly prized land. George insisted that these increases in land rent belonged to society at large. Consequently, he argued that land rents should be heavily taxed and that the revenue generated by land taxes be spent for public uses. In seeking popular support for his ideas on land taxation, George proposed that a tax on rental income be the *only* tax levied by government.

George's case for taxing rental income was based not only on equity or fairness but also on efficiency. First, he wished

for land to remain in private hands so that the "invisible hand" would guide private landowners to allocate their land to its best possible use. Allocative efficiency would still be achieved because the most profitable use for a particular piece of land before it is taxed remains the most profitable use for that land after it is taxed. Thus, landowners would not have any incentive to shift the use of their land from one activity to another just because it was taxed. In addition, landlords would not withdraw land from production when the tax was imposed because doing so would mean no rental income at all. Because some rental income, no matter how small, is better than no rental income, landlords would continue to supply land.

George further argued that, in addition to maintaining allocative efficiency for land, his single tax would also be much better for society in terms of productive efficiency. His argument was based on the fact that because land is in fixed supply, it does not have an incentive function. Thus, when taxed, the quantity of land supplied does not change. By contrast, because other resources have incentive functions, taxing them would likely reduce their supply—something that would cause an underproduction of output and, consequently, productive inefficiency. For instance, if workers responded to a tax on labor by supplying less labor, output would decline. Similarly, if a property tax on buildings caused builders to supply fewer buildings, there would be less capital available to produce output and, hence, less output. But because land is in fixed supply, no such reductions in output need be feared when taxing land. Thus, if only land were taxed, society would never have to worry about taxes causing productive inefficiency by reducing output.

Criticisms The single tax on land has few remaining advocates. Critics of the idea have pointed out that:

- Current levels of government spending are such that a land tax alone would not bring in enough revenue.

- Most income payments consist of a mixture of interest, rent, wages, and profits. So in practice it would be difficult to isolate how much of any specific income payment is actually derived from rent.

- So-called unearned income accrues to many people other than landowners. For example, consider the capital-gains income received by someone who many years ago purchased or inherited stock that now delivers hefty dividend payments. Is such income more "earned" than the rental income of the landowner?

- Historically, a piece of land is likely to have changed ownership many times. It would therefore be highly unfair to impose a heavy tax on recent buyers who paid a high price for their land and thus did not gain in any way from previous price increases.

Interest

LO18.2 Define interest and explain how interest rates vary based on risk, maturity, loan size, and taxability.

Interest is the price paid for the use of money. It can be thought of as the amount of money that a borrower must pay a lender for the use of the lender's money over some period of time. As an example, a borrower might be required to pay $100 of interest for the use of $1,000 for one year.

Because borrowers pay for loans of money with money, interest can be stated as a percentage of the amount of money borrowed rather than as a dollar amount. This is useful because it is far less clumsy to say that interest is "12 percent annually" than to say that interest is "$120 per year per $1,000."

Stating interest as a percentage also makes it much easier to compare the interest paid on loans involving different amounts of money. By expressing interest as a percentage, we can immediately compare an interest payment of, say, $432 per year per $2,880 with one of $1,800 per year per $12,000. Both interest payments are 15 percent per year, which is not obvious from the actual dollar figures.

And to make things even simpler, an interest payment of 15 percent per year can also be referred to as a 15 percent interest rate.

Money Is Not a Resource

When considering why borrowers are willing to pay interest for the right to use borrowed money, it is important to remember that money is not itself an economic resource. Whether money comes in the form of coins, paper currency, or checking accounts, you cannot directly produce any goods and services with it.

Thus, borrowers do not value money for its own sake. Rather, they value money because of what it can purchase. Individuals and households are willing to pay interest to borrow for consumption spending because they would rather consume certain goods and services sooner rather than later. And businesses are willing to pay interest because the money that they borrow can be used to expand their businesses and increase their profits. In particular, borrowed money can be used to fund the acquisition of capital goods such as computers, machinery, and warehouses.

Interest Rates and Interest Income

The interest rate on money loans determines the *interest income* earned by households for providing capital to firms. This is true because firms have the choice of either leasing capital from households or purchasing their own capital. Because businesses have this option, households wishing to lease their capital to businesses cannot charge more for the use of their capital than what businesses would have to pay in terms of interest payments to borrow the money needed to purchase their own capital.

As an example, consider a custom T-shirt shop that needs a $10,000 embroidering machine to expand production. If the owners of the shop can borrow the money to buy such a machine at an interest rate of 8 percent per year, then anyone wishing to lease them an identical machine could charge them no more than $800 per year for it (since $800 is how much per year the shop would have to pay in interest to borrow $10,000 at an 8 percent interest rate.)

Range of Interest Rates

For convenience, economists often speak in terms of a single interest rate. However, there are actually a number of interest rates in the economy. Table 18.1 lists several interest rates often referred to in the media. On March 9, 2016, these rates ranged from 0.32 to 15.92 percent. Why the differences?

- *Risk* Loans to different borrowers for different purposes carry varying degrees of risk. The greater the chance that a borrower will not repay his loan, the higher the interest rate the lender will charge to compensate for that risk.

- *Maturity* The time length of a loan, or its *maturity* (when it needs to be paid back), also affects the interest rate. Other things equal, longer-term loans usually command higher interest rates than shorter-term loans. This is true because one function of interest rates is to compensate lenders for the inconvenience and potential financial sacrifices involved with forgoing alternative uses of their money until their loans are repaid. Longer-term loans must offer higher interest rates to compensate lenders for having to forgo alternative opportunities for longer periods of time.

- *Loan size* If there are two loans of equal maturity and risk, the interest rate on the smaller of the two loans usually will be higher. The administrative costs of

TABLE 18.1 Selected Interest Rates, March 9, 2016

Type of Interest Rate	Annual Percentage
20-year Treasury bond rate (interest rate on federal government securities used to finance the public debt)	2.28%
90-day Treasury Bill rate (interest rate on federal government securities used to finance the public debt)	0.32
Prime interest rate (interest rate used as a reference point for a wide range of bank loans)	3.50
30-year mortgage rate (fixed-interest rate on loans for houses)	3.78
4-year automobile loan rate (interest rate for new autos by automobile finance companies)	4.24
Tax-exempt state and municipal bond rate (interest rate paid on low-risk bonds issued by a state or local government)	3.42
Federal funds target rate (interest rate on overnight loans between banks)	0.50
Consumer credit card rate (interest rate charged for credit card purchases)	15.92

Sources: Federal Reserve, **www.federalreserve.gov**, and Bankrate.com, **www.bankrate.com**.

issuing a large loan and a small loan are about the same in dollars, but the cost is greater *as a percentage* of the smaller loan.

- *Taxability* Interest on certain state and municipal bonds is exempt from the federal income tax. Because lenders are interested in their after-tax rate of interest, the bonds issued by state and local governments can attract lenders even though they pay lower before-tax interest rates than other bonds of similar maturity and risk. Consider a lender who expects to pay a 35 percent federal income tax on any taxable interest payments. She may prefer a 5 percent interest rate on a tax-exempt municipal bond to a 6 percent interest rate on a taxable corporate bond because, after paying taxes on that taxable corporate bond, she will be left with an after-tax return of only 3.9 percent.

Pure Rate of Interest

When economists and financial specialists talk of "the" interest rate, they typically have in mind the **pure rate of interest.** This is the hypothetical interest rate that would serve purely and solely to compensate lenders for their willingness to patiently forgo alternative consumption and investment opportunities until their money is repaid.

The pure rate of interest is best approximated by the interest rates of long-term, virtually riskless securities, such as the 20-year Treasury bonds issued by the U.S. federal government.

Because such bonds involve minimal risk and negligible administrative costs, the interest that they pay can be thought of as compensating purely and solely for the use of money over an extended period of time. In March 2016, the pure rate of interest in the United States was 2.28 percent.

Loanable Funds Theory of Interest Rates

LO18.3 Explain the loanable funds theory of interest rates.

Because macroeconomics deals with the entire economy, it typically focuses on the pure rate of interest and assumes that it is determined by the total supply and demand for money in the economy. But because our present focus is on microeconomics, we will focus on a more micro-based theory of interest rates. By doing so, we will be able to explain why the interest rates on different types of loans vary so greatly, as in Table 18.1.

The **loanable funds theory of interest** explains the interest rate on any particular type of loan in terms of the supply of and demand for *funds available for lending* in the loanable funds market that exists for that particular type of loan. As Figure 18.2 shows, the equilibrium interest rate (here, 8 percent) on a particular type of loan is the rate at which the quantities of loanable funds supplied and demanded are equal for that type of loan.

To gain a deeper understanding of the loanable funds theory of interest, let's focus on a simplified lending market.

FIGURE 18.2 A loanable funds market. The upsloping supply curve S for loanable funds in a specific lending market reflects the idea that at higher interest rates, households will defer more of their present consumption (save more), making more funds available for lending. The downsloping demand curve D for loanable funds in such a market indicates that businesses will borrow more at lower interest rates than at higher interest rates. At the equilibrium interest rate (here, 8 percent), the quantities of loanable funds lent and borrowed are equal (here, F_0 each).

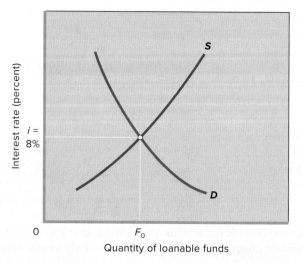

Quantity of loanable funds

First, assume that, for a particular type of loan, households or consumers are the sole suppliers of loanable funds, while businesses are the sole demanders of loanable funds. Also assume that lending occurs directly between households and businesses so that there are no financial institutions acting as intermediaries.

Supply of Loanable Funds

The supply of loanable funds in our simplified lending market is represented by curve S in Figure 18.2. Its upward slope indicates that households will make available a larger quantity of funds at high interest rates than at low interest rates. Most people prefer to use their incomes to purchase goods and services *today,* rather than delay purchases to sometime in the *future*. For people to delay consumption and increase their saving, they must be "bribed" or compensated by an interest payment. The larger the amount of that payment, the greater the deferral of household consumption and thus the greater the amount of money made available for loans.

Demand for Loanable Funds

Businesses borrow loanable funds primarily to add to their stocks of capital goods, such as new plants or warehouses, machinery, and equipment. Assume that a firm wants to buy a machine that will increase output and sales such that the firm's total revenue will rise by $110 for the year. Also assume that the machine costs $100 and has a useful life of just 1 year. Comparing the $10 earned with the $100 cost of the machine, we find that the expected rate of return on this investment is 10 percent (= $10/$100) for the 1 year.

To determine whether the investment would be profitable and whether it should be made, the firm must compare the interest rate—the price of loanable funds—with the 10 percent expected rate of return. If funds can be borrowed at some rate less than the rate of return, say, at 8 percent, as in Figure 18.2, then the investment is profitable and should be made. But if funds can be borrowed only at an interest rate above the 10 percent rate of return, say, at 14 percent, the investment is unprofitable and should not be made.

Why is the demand for loanable funds downsloping, as in Figure 18.2? At higher interest rates fewer investment projects will be profitable and therefore a smaller quantity of loanable funds will be demanded. At lower interest rates, more investment projects will be profitable and therefore more loanable funds will be demanded. Indeed, as we have just seen, purchasing the $100 machine is profitable if funds can be borrowed at 8 percent but not if the firm must borrow at 14 percent.

Extending the Model

There is a loanable funds market for nearly every type of loan in the economy. The best known are the markets for corporate and government bonds. But there are also loanable funds markets for student loans, home mortgages, and car loans. Each type of loan ends up with its own equilibrium interest rate determined by the demand and supply for loanable funds in its particular market.

We now extend the simple loanable funds model to make it more realistic and better able to capture the diversity of these many lending markets.

Financial Institutions Households rarely directly lend their savings to the businesses that are borrowing funds for investment. Instead, they place their savings in banks (and other financial institutions). The banks pay interest to savers in order to attract loanable funds and in turn lend those funds to businesses. Businesses borrow the funds from the banks, paying them interest for the use of the money. Financial institutions profit by charging borrowers higher interest rates than the interest rates they pay savers. Both interest rates, however, are based on the supply of and demand for loanable funds in their respective markets.

Changes in Supply Anything that causes households to be thriftier will prompt them to save more at each interest rate, shifting the supply curve rightward. For example, if interest earned on savings were to be suddenly exempted from taxation, we would expect the supply of loanable funds to increase and the equilibrium interest rate to decrease.

Conversely, a decline in thriftiness would shift the supply-of-loanable-funds curve leftward and increase the equilibrium interest rate. Illustration: If the government expanded social insurance to cover the costs of hospitalization, prescription drugs, and retirement living more fully, the incentive of households to save might diminish.

Changes in Demand On the demand side, anything that increases the rate of return on potential investments will increase the demand for loanable funds. Let's return to our earlier example, where a firm would receive additional revenue of $110 by purchasing a $100 machine and, therefore, would realize a 10 percent return on investment. What factors might increase or decrease the rate of return? Suppose a technological advance raised the productivity of the machine such that the firm's total revenue increased by $120 rather than $110. The rate of return would then be 20 percent, not 10 percent. Before the technological advance, the firm would have demanded zero loanable funds at, say, an interest rate of 14 percent. But now it will demand $100 of loanable funds at that interest rate, meaning that the demand curve for loanable funds has been shifted to the right.

Similarly, an increase in consumer demand for the firm's product will increase the price of its product. So even though the productivity of the machine is unchanged, its potential revenue will rise from $110 to perhaps $120, increasing the firm's rate of return from 10 to 20 percent. Again the firm will be willing to borrow more than previously at our presumed 8 or 14 percent interest rate, implying that the demand curve for loanable funds has shifted rightward. This shift in demand increases the equilibrium interest rate.

Conversely, a decline in productivity or in the price of the firm's product would shift the demand curve for loanable funds leftward, reducing the equilibrium interest rate.

Other Participants We must recognize that participation in many loanable funds markets may go well beyond our simplification of households as suppliers of funds and businesses as demanders of funds. For example, while households are suppliers of loanable funds, many are also demanders of such funds. Households borrow to finance expensive purchases such as housing, automobiles, furniture, and household appliances. Governments also are on the demand side of a loanable funds market when they borrow to finance budgetary deficits. And businesses that have revenues in excess of their current expenditures may offer some of those revenues in various loanable funds markets. Thus, like households, businesses operate on both the supply and the demand sides of various loanable funds markets.

Finally, in addition to gathering and making available the savings of households, banks and other financial institutions also increase funds through the lending process and decrease funds when the money that is used to pay off loans is retained by the banks rather than being lent out again to other borrowers. The Federal Reserve (the nation's central bank) controls the amount of this bank activity and thus influences a wide variety of interest rates.

This fact helps answer one of our chapter-opening questions: Why did the interest rate on 3-month certificates of deposit in the United States fall from 5.4 percent in June 2006 to only 0.2 percent in November 2009? There are two reasons: (1) The demand for loanable funds sharply declined because businesses reduced their desire to purchase more capital goods and (2) the Federal Reserve, fighting recession and sluggish recovery, took monetary actions that greatly increased the supply of loanable funds. In contrast, between 2003 and 2006 the Federal Reserve restricted the growth of loanable funds. Because the demand for loanable funds increased more rapidly than the supply of loanable funds, interest rates such as those on 3-month certificates of deposit rose. As indicated in the chapter opening, that rate increased from 1.3 percent in January 2003 to 5.4 percent in June 2006.

Time-Value of Money

LO18.4 Demonstrate how interest rates relate to the time-value of money.

Interest is central to understanding the **time-value of money**—the idea that a specific amount of money is more valuable to a person the sooner it is obtained. To see where money's time value comes from, suppose that you could choose between being paid $1,000 today or $1,000 in a year. The fact that $1,000 received today can be invested at interest and grow into more than $1,000 in a year implies that it is better to receive $1,000 today than $1,000 in a year. By how much is it better? By the amount of interest that can be gained over the course of the year. The higher the interest rate, the greater the time-value of money.

In addition to giving money its time value, the fact that money can be invested to earn interest also implies a way in which a given amount of money today can be thought of as being equivalent to a larger amount of money in the future and how a future amount of money can be thought of as being equivalent to a smaller amount of money today. We explore this idea next.

Compound Interest

Compound interest is the total interest that cumulates over time on money that is placed into an interest-bearing account. Table 18.2 helps us explain compound interest, as well as the related ideas of future value and present value. Suppose that Max places $1,000 into an interest-bearing account at 10 percent interest with the intent to let the *principal* (the initial deposit) and interest compound for 3 years. The first row of each column shows the beginning period sum; the second column shows the yearly computation as to how that sum grows, given a particular interest rate. That growth is found by multiplying the dollar amount at the beginning of each year by $1 + i$, where i is the interest rate expressed as a decimal.

In year 1 the 10 percent interest rate increases the money in the account from $1,000 to $1,100 (= $1,000 × 1.10). So,

TABLE 18.2 Compound Interest, Future Value, and Present Value, 10 Percent Interest Rate

(1) Beginning Period Value	(2) Computation	(3) Total Interest	(4) End Period Value
$1,000 (Year 1)	$1,000 × 1.10 = $1,100	$100	$1,100 (= $1,000 + $100)
$1,100 (Year 2)	$1,100 × 1.10 = $1,210	$210 (= $100 + $110)	$1,210 (= $1,000 + $210)
$1,210 (Year 3)	$1,210 × 1.10 = $1,331	$331 (= $100 + $110 + $121)	$1,331 (= $1,000 + $331)

as shown in Column 3, total interest is $100. Column 4 simply lists the $1,100 again but reinforces that this amount consists of the original principal plus the total interest. Similarly, in year 2, the $1,100 now in the account grows to $1,210 (= $1,100 × 1.10) because $110 of new interest accrues on the $1,100. At the end of year 2, the principal remains $1,000, but the total interest is $210 and the total amount in the account is $1,210. Interest in year 3 is $121 and total interest rises to $331. After this $331 of total interest is added to the $1,000 principal, the accumulation is $1,331. As shown in Column 3, compound interest builds and builds over time.

Future Value and Present Value

Now note from Table 18.2 that we can look at the time-value of money in two distinct ways. **Future value** is the amount to which some current amount of money will grow as interest compounds over time. In our table, the future value (FV) of $1,000 today at 10 percent interest is $1,331 three years from now. Future value is always forward-looking.

But we can just as easily look backward from the end value of $1,331 and ask how much that amount is worth today, given the 10 percent interest rate. **Present value** is today's value of some amount of money to be received in the future. In terms of the table, the present value (PV) of $1,331 is $1,000. Here, FV is "discounted" by three years at 10 percent to remove the $331 of compounded interest and therefore to obtain PV. (We will defer explaining the discounting procedure to our chapter on financial economics in the macro portion of *Economics*. But if you are interested in the mathematics, see the text within the footnote.)[1]

With any positive interest rate (and assuming no inflation), a person would prefer to receive $1,000 today rather than $1,000 at some time in the future. The higher the interest rate, the greater is the *future value* of a specific amount of money today. To confirm, substitute a 20 percent interest rate for the 10 percent rate in Table 18.2 and rework the analysis. Finally, you should know that the analysis presented in the table is extendable to any number of years.

The time-value of money is an important concept. For example, it helps explain the optimal timing of natural resource extraction (Chapter 19). It also is critical to the entire field of financial economics (Chapter 37). In our present chapter, our goal is simply to stress that *money has time value because of the potential for compound interest.*

---

[1]The mathematics is as follows:

$$FV = PV(1 + i)^t \quad \text{and} \quad PV = \frac{FV}{(1 + i)^t}$$

where i is the interest rate and t is time, here the number of years of compounding.

CONSIDER THIS . . .

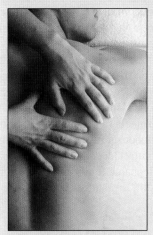

© Matthew Borkoski Photography/ Getty Images

That Is Interest

The following story told by economist Irving Fisher (1867–1947) helps illustrate the time-value of money.

In the process of a massage, a masseur informed Fisher that he was a socialist who believed that "interest is the basis of capitalism and is robbery." Following the massage, Fisher asked, "How much do I owe you?"

The masseur replied, "Thirty dollars."

"Very well," said Fisher, "I will give you a note payable a hundred years hence. I suppose you have no objections to taking this note without any interest. At the end of that time, you, or perhaps your grandchildren, can redeem it."

"But I cannot afford to wait that long," said the masseur.

"I thought you said that interest was robbery. If interest is robbery, you ought to be willing to wait indefinitely for the money. If you are willing to wait ten years, how much would you require?"

"Well, I would have to get more than thirty dollars."

His point now made, Fisher replied, "That is interest."*

---

*Irving Fisher, as quoted in Irving Norton Fisher, *My Father Irving Fisher* (New York: Comet Press Books, 1956), p. 77.

Role of Interest Rates

LO18.5 Explain the role of interest rates in allocating capital, modulating R&D spending, and helping to determine the economy's total output of goods and services.

We have already explained that interest rates on money loans determine the interest incomes earned by the owners of capital goods. This fact implies that interest rates are the critical prices determining both the *level* and *composition* of new investments in capital goods as well as the amount of research and development (R&D) spending in the economy.

Interest and Total Output

Lower equilibrium interest rates encourage businesses to borrow more for investment, other things equal. As a result, total spending in the economy rises, and if the economy has unused resources, so does total output. Conversely, higher equilibrium interest rates discourage businesses from borrowing for investment, thereby reducing investment and total spending. Such a decrease in spending may be desirable if an economy is experiencing inflation.

The Federal Reserve often manages interest rates to try to expand investment and output, on the one hand, or to reduce investment and inflation, on the other. It affects interest rates by changing the supply of money. Increases in the money supply increase the supply of loanable funds, causing equilibrium interest rates to fall. This boosts investment spending and expands the economy. In contrast, decreases in the money supply decrease the supply of loanable funds, boosting equilibrium interest rates. As a result, investment is constrained and so is the economy.

Interest and the Allocation of Capital

Prices are rationing devices. And interest rates are prices. Thus, when it comes to allocating capital in the economy, the interest rates charged on investment loans ration the available supply of loanable investment funds to investment projects that have expected rates of return at or above the interest rate cost of the borrowed funds.

If, say, the computer industry expects to earn a return of 12 percent on the money it invests in physical capital and it can secure the required funds at an interest rate of 8 percent, it can borrow and expand its physical capital. If the expected rate of return on additional capital in the steel industry is only 6 percent, that industry will find it unprofitable to expand its capital at 8 percent interest. The interest rate allocates money, and ultimately physical capital, to the industries in which it will be most productive and therefore most profitable. Such an allocation of capital goods benefits society.

But the interest rate on investment loans does not perfectly ration capital to its most productive uses. Large oligopolistic borrowers may be better able than competitive borrowers to pass interest costs on to consumers because they can change prices by controlling output. Also, the size, prestige, and monopsony power of large corporations may help them obtain funds on more favorable terms than can smaller firms, even when the smaller firms have similar rates of profitability.

Interest and R&D Spending

In Chapter 15, we pointed out that, similar to an investment decision, a decision on how much to spend on R&D depends on the cost of borrowing funds in relationship to the expected rate of return. Other things equal, the lower the interest rate and thus the lower the cost of borrowing funds for R&D, the greater is the amount of R&D spending that is potentially profitable. Low interest rates encourage R&D spending; high interest rates discourage it.

Also, the interest rate allocates R&D funds to firms and industries for which the expected rate of return on R&D is the greatest. Ace Microcircuits may have an expected rate of return of 16 percent on an R&D project, while Glow Paints has only a 2 percent expected rate of return on an R&D project. With the interest rate at 8 percent, loanable funds will flow to Ace, not to Glow. Society will benefit by having R&D spending allocated to projects that have high enough expected rates of return to justify using scarce resources for R&D rather than for other purposes.

Nominal and Real Interest Rates

This discussion of the role of interest in investment decisions and in R&D decisions assumes that there is no inflation. If inflation exists, we must distinguish between nominal and real interest rates, just like we needed to distinguish between nominal and real wages in Chapter 17. The **nominal interest rate** is the rate of interest expressed in dollars of current value. The **real interest rate** is the rate of interest expressed in purchasing power—dollars of inflation-adjusted value.

Example: Suppose the nominal interest rate and the rate of inflation are both 10 percent. If you borrow $100, you must pay back $110 a year from now. However, because of 10 percent inflation, each of these 110 dollars will be worth 10 percent less. Thus, the real value or purchasing power of your $110 at the end of the year is only $100. In inflation-adjusted dollars you are borrowing $100 and at year's end you are paying back $100. While the nominal interest rate is 10 percent, the real interest rate is zero. We determine the real interest rate by subtracting the 10 percent inflation rate from the 10 percent nominal interest rate. It is the real interest rate, not the nominal rate, that affects investment and R&D decisions.

For a comparison of nominal interest rates on bank loans in selected countries, see Global Perspective 18.1. Note that some countries now have negative nominal interest rates, meaning that a saver will get back less than the amount she invested. Negative nominal interest rates are the result of deliberate central bank monetary policies intended to get people to consume more. The central banks are hoping that consumers will save less and consume more when savings earns a negative return due to negative rates.

Application: Usury Laws

A number of states have passed **usury laws,** which specify a maximum interest rate at which loans can be made. Such rates are a special case of *price ceilings,* discussed in Chapter 3. The purpose of usury laws is to hold down the interest cost of borrowing, particularly for low-income borrowers. ("Usury" simply means exorbitant interest.)

Figure 18.2 helps us assess the impact of such legislation. The equilibrium interest rate there is 8 percent, but suppose a

GLOBAL PERSPECTIVE 18.1

Short-Term Nominal Interest Rates, Selected Nations

These data show the short-term nominal interest rates (percentage rates on 3-month loans) in various countries in 2015. Because these are nominal rates, much of the variation reflects differences in rates of inflation. But differences in central bank monetary policies and default risk also influence the variation.

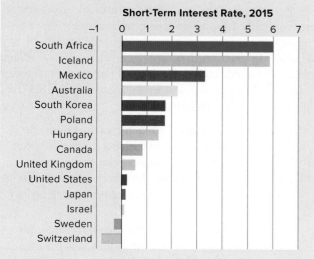

Short-Term Interest Rate, 2015

Source: OECD Economic Outlook, Organization for Economic Cooperation and Development, **www.oecd.org**.

usury law specifies that lenders cannot charge more than 6 percent. The effects are as follows:

- *Nonmarket rationing* At 6 percent, the quantity of loanable funds demanded exceeds the quantity supplied: There is a shortage of loanable funds. Because the market interest rate no longer can ration the available loanable funds to borrowers, lenders (banks) have to do the rationing. We can expect them to make loans only to the most creditworthy borrowers (mainly wealthy, high-income people), thus defeating the goal of the usury law. Low-income, riskier borrowers are excluded from the market and may be forced to turn to loan sharks who charge illegally high interest rates.

- *Gainers and losers* Creditworthy borrowers gain from usury laws because they pay below-market interest rates. Lenders (ultimately bank shareholders) are losers because they receive 6 percent rather than 8 percent on each dollar lent.

- *Inefficiency* We have just seen how the equilibrium interest rate allocates money to the investments and the R&D projects whose expected rates of return are

greatest. Under usury laws, funds are much less likely to be allocated by banks to the most productive projects. Suppose Mendez has a project so promising she would pay 10 percent for funds to finance it. Chen has a less-promising investment, and he would be willing to pay only 7 percent for financing. If the market were rationing funds, Mendez's highly productive project would be funded and Chen's would not. That allocation of funds would be in the interest of both Mendez and society. But with a 6 percent usury rate, Chen may get to the bank before Mendez and receive the loanable funds at 6 percent. So Mendez may not get funded. Legally controlled interest rates may thus inefficiently ration funds to less-productive investments or R&D projects.

QUICK REVIEW 18.2

✓ Interest is the price paid for the use of money and determines the interest income earned by households for providing capital to firms.

✓ The range of interest rates is influenced by risk, maturity, loan size, and taxability.

✓ In the loanable funds model, the equilibrium interest rate is determined by the demand for and supply of loanable funds.

✓ The time-value of money is the idea that $1 can be converted into more than $1 of future value through compound interest and therefore that $1 to be received sometime in the future has less than $1 of present value.

✓ Interest rates on investment loans affect the total level of investment and therefore the levels of total spending and total output; they also allocate money and real capital to specific industries and firms. Similarly, interest rates also affect the level and composition of R&D spending.

✓ Usury laws that establish an interest-rate ceiling below the market interest rate may (a) deny credit to low-income people, (b) subsidize high-income borrowers and penalize lenders, and (c) diminish the efficiency with which loanable funds are allocated to investment and R&D projects.

Economic Profit

LO18.6 Relate why economic profits occur and how profits, along with losses, allocate resources among alternative uses.

Recall from previous chapters that economists define profit narrowly. To accountants, "profit" is what remains of a firm's total revenue after it has paid individuals and other firms for the materials, capital, and labor they have supplied to the firm. To the economist, these "accounting profits" overstate profit.

The reason is that the accountant's view of profit considers only **explicit costs:** payments made by the firm to outsiders. It ignores **implicit costs:** the monetary income the firm sacrifices when it uses resources that it owns, rather than supplying those resources to the market. The economist considers implicit costs to be opportunity costs that must be accounted for in determining profit. **Economic**, or **pure, profit** is what remains after all costs—both explicit and implicit costs, the latter including a normal profit—have been subtracted from a firm's total revenue. Economic profit may be either positive or negative (a loss).

Entrepreneurship and Profit

Economic profit flows to individuals to motivate them to provide the economic resource known as entrepreneurship. For illustration, let's suppose that two entrepreneurs establish a start-up company called Upside and that they are the only owners. They do not incorporate or borrow and instead use their own funds to finance the firm.

As discussed in previous chapters, the resource that these entrepreneurs provide is clearly not labor. Typical workers simply complete assigned tasks and engage in routine activities. For their labor inputs, they are compensated with wages and salaries.

Entrepreneurs, by contrast, make nonroutine decisions that involve substantial financial risk. Among other things, they (1) decide their firm's strategy for combining land, labor, and capital to produce a good or service; (2) decide whether and how to develop new products and new production processes; and (3) personally bear the financial risks associated with the success or failure of their respective firms.

With regard to bearing those financial risks, it is crucial to understand that a firm's entrepreneurs are its *residual claimants,* meaning that they only receive whatever residual revenue—if any—remains after all the other factors of production have been paid. As residual claimants, the entrepreneurs at Upside receive whatever accounting profit or accounting loss the firm generates. Thus, the financial risks of running the firm are borne by its two entrepreneurs. If Upside loses money, it loses *their* money.

Insurable and Uninsurable Risks

As residual claimants, entrepreneurs face financial risks. These fall into two categories. **Insurable risks** are those risks for which it is possible to buy insurance from an insurance company, while **uninsurable risks** are those risks for which it is not possible to buy insurance from an insurance company.

Individuals and firms who purchase insurance policies (contracts) from an insurance company are referred to as policyholders. In exchange for an annual premium (fee), the policyholders obtain the insurance company's guarantee to reimburse them for any financial losses caused by any of the risks covered under the insurance contract. In order to be able

to keep that promise, the insurance company must be able to collect enough in premiums from its policyholders in the present to be able to fully reimburse the ones who eventually suffer losses in the future. This is only possible with risks like fire, flood, theft, accident, and death whose frequencies of occurrence can be predicted with relative accuracy. Risks whose frequencies of occurrence cannot be predicted with accuracy are uninsurable.

Sources of Uninsurable Risks

Because insurance is available for insurable risks, entrepreneurs only have to deal with uninsurable risks whose frequency of occurrence cannot be predicted with any accuracy. In practice, these are the result of uncontrollable and unpredictable changes in demand and supply that either reduce revenues or increase costs. These uninsurable risks fall into four main categories:

- *Changes in the general economic environment* An economy-wide downturn in business (a recession) can lead to greatly reduced demand, sales, and revenues, and thus to business losses. An otherwise prosperous firm may experience substantial losses through no fault of its own.
- *Changes in the structure of the economy* Consumer tastes, technology, resource availability, and prices change unpredictably in the real world, bringing changes in production costs and revenues. For example, an airline earning an economic profit one year may sustain substantial losses the next year as the result of a significant increase in the price of jet fuel.
- *Changes in government policy* A newly instituted regulation, the removal of a tariff, or a change in national defense policy may significantly alter the costs and revenues of the affected industry and firms.
- *New products or production methods pioneered by rivals* Any firm can suddenly find itself losing sales and revenue to popular new products brought out by rivals. Similarly, a firm may suddenly find itself having to sell its product at a loss if rival firms cut their prices after figuring out a lower-cost way to make the same product.

Profit as Compensation for Bearing Uninsurable Risks

Economists list entrepreneurship as its own economic resource—separate from land, labor, and capital—because it is not possible to run a business without somebody being willing to undertake and live with uninsurable risks. Entrepreneurs are rewarded with profit precisely to compensate them for personally taking on the uninsurable risks of running a business. Indeed, their willingness to bear those uninsurable risks means that the providers of the firm's other resource inputs (of land, labor, and capital) can almost completely ignore those risks.

To see why this is true, again consider our start-up company, Upside, and suppose that its two entrepreneurs used $100,000 of their own money to fund the firm. If revenues ever run below costs, the entrepreneurs will use that pile of money to cover the losses and make sure that the firm's workers and other resource suppliers get paid on time and in full. The resource suppliers are shielded from the losses because the entrepreneurs have taken it upon themselves to bear the firm's uninsurable financial risks. In such situations, no bill is sent to the workers or other resource suppliers asking them to help make up the firm's losses. The entrepreneurs, who took on the firm's uninsurable risks, are "on the hook."

The entrepreneurs' compensation for providing entrepreneurship and shielding the other resource suppliers from uninsurable risk is the opportunity to run the business and keep the firm's profits if things go well. Thus, entrepreneurship boils down to a simple bargain: In exchange for making sure that everyone else gets paid if things go wrong, the entrepreneur gets to receive the firm's profits if things go right.

Sources of Economic Profit

For bearing a firm's uninsurable risks, its entrepreneurs receive control of the firm. This allows them to try to make as much profit as possible in exchange for taking on those risks.

Along those lines, there are three main ways in which entrepreneurs can generate economic profits (that is, accounting profits that exceed normal profits):

- *Create popular new products* If an entrepreneur can develop a popular new product at a sufficiently low cost, his firm will be able to generate economic profits until competitors bring out competing products.

- *Reduce production costs below rivals' costs* Entrepreneurs who implement more efficient production methods for existing products can generate economic profits until their efficiency gains are matched or exceeded by competitors.

- *Create and maintain a profitable monopoly* Entrepreneurs who possess a monopoly for their product may be able to generate economic rent by restricting their outputs and raising their prices. And such economic profits may persist if entry to the industry is blocked. But remember from Chapter 12 that having a monopoly does not guarantee that a monopoly will be profitable. If demand is weak relative to production costs, monopolies can and will go bankrupt.

By reallocating resources toward the production of popular new products that consumers prefer to old products, entrepreneurs improve allocative efficiency. By reducing production costs, they improve productive efficiency. Thus,

CONSIDER THIS . . .

Profits and Efficiency

© E. Audras/PhotoAlto RF

Entrepreneurs focus on a single number: profit. That might make you think that entrepreneurs will end up neglecting the other aspects of their business. But a wonderful thing about the market system is that the only way for a firm to maximize profit is by paying close attention to *every* aspect of its operations.

This is true because entrepreneurs have to make many simultaneous decisions about how to spend their firm's limited budget. Should they allocate a little more money to research and development? Should they reduce spending on advertising? How about allocating more money for bonuses?

The only way to give one activity more resources is to give another activity fewer resources. If an entrepreneur wishes to maximize her firm's overall profit, she will have to get all of these marginal decisions right, and simultaneously. She will also have to find the correct allocation of the firm's limited resources across all possible tasks so that MB = MC for each budget item. So while profit is just a single number, focusing on profit forces entrepreneurs to be efficient in every aspect of her firm's operations.

with the important exception of monopoly, the entrepreneur's pursuit of profit clearly benefits society.

With monopolies, though, things are very different, because a monopoly's profit cannot be justified as rewarding its entrepreneurs for personally taking on a firm's financial risks or for making perceptive business decisions that enhance productive or allocative efficiency. As a result, governments use antitrust laws to impede monopolies from forming or, if they arise, break them up or restrict their business behaviors. In some instances, governments also regulate away their excessive profits.

Profit Rations Entrepreneurship

Even if a firm is making an accounting profit, its entrepreneurs may decide to quit and go into another line of business. This is because they will want their accounting profit to be at least as large as the typical accounting profit that their risk taking and decision making could on average be expected to earn in other business ventures. This typical accounting profit is known as their **normal profit.**

Because entrepreneurs will be comparing their current accounting profit with the normal profit that they could be making elsewhere, profit can be thought of as the "price" that allocates the scarce resource of entrepreneurship toward different possible economic activities. Just as wages must be

Determining the Price of Credit

A Variety of Lending Practices May Cause the Effective Interest Rate to Be Quite Different from What It Appears to Be.

Borrowing and lending—receiving and granting credit—are a way of life. Individuals receive credit when they negotiate a mortgage loan and when they use their credit cards. Individuals make loans when they open a savings account in a commercial bank or buy a government bond.

It is sometimes difficult to determine exactly how much interest we pay and receive when we borrow and lend. Let's suppose that you borrow $10,000 that you agree to repay plus $1,000 of interest at the end of 1 year. In this instance, the interest rate is 10 percent per year. To determine the interest rate i, we compare the interest paid with the amount borrowed:

$$i = \frac{\$1,000}{\$10,000} = 10\%$$

But in some cases a lender—say, a bank—will discount the interest payment from the loan amount at the time the loan is made. Thus, instead of giving the borrower $10,000, the bank discounts the $1,000 interest payment in advance, giving the borrower only $9,000. This increases the interest rate:

$$i = \frac{\$1,000}{\$9,000} = 11\%$$

Source: © JoeFox/Radharc Images/Alamy Stock Photo

While the absolute amount of interest paid is the same, in the second case the borrower has only $9,000 available for the year.

An even more subtle point is that, to simplify their calculations, many financial institutions assume a 360-day year (twelve 30-day months). This means the borrower has the use of the lender's funds

paid to attract and retain labor, profits must be paid to attract and retain entrepreneurial talent. And just as higher wages attract workers, higher profits attract entrepreneurs.

Entrepreneurs, Profits, and Corporate Stockholders

In the actual economy, economic profits are distributed widely beyond the entrepreneurs who first start new businesses. The corporate structure of business enterprise has allowed millions of individuals to purchase ownership shares in corporations and therefore to share in the risks and rewards of ownership.

Some of these people participate in the for-profit economy by purchasing the stock of individual firms or by investing in mutual funds, which in turn buy corporate stock. Millions of additional people share in the profits of corporations through the financial investments of their pension funds. But at their core, all of the profits that are shared with these

direct and indirect corporate shareholders are made possible in the first place by the activities of entrepreneurs. For instance, without Bill Gates and Paul Allen, there would have been no Microsoft Corporation—and, consequently, no Microsoft profits (dividends) to distribute to the millions of owners of Microsoft stock.

The desire on the part of so many millions of people to own corporate stock and thereby share in the risks and rewards of business reflects the fact that economic profit is the main energizer of the capitalistic economy. It influences both the level of economic output and the allocation of resources among alternative uses. The expectation of economic profit motivates firms to innovate. Innovation stimulates new investment, thereby increasing total output and employment. Thus, the pursuit of profit enhances economic growth by promoting innovation.

Profit also helps allocate resources among alternative lines of production, distribution, and sales. Entrepreneurs seek profit and shun losses. The occurrence of continuing profits in for 5 days less than the normal year. This use of a "short year" also increases the actual interest rate paid by the borrower.

The interest rate paid may change dramatically if a loan is repaid in installments. Suppose a bank lends you $10,000 and charges interest in the amount of $1,000 to be paid at the end of the year. But the loan contract requires that you repay the $10,000 loan in 12 equal monthly installments. As a result, the average amount of the loan outstanding during the year is only $5,000. Therefore:

$$i = \frac{\$1,000}{\$5,000} = 20\%$$

Here interest is paid on the total amount of the loan ($10,000) rather than on the outstanding balance (which averages $5,000 for the year), making for a much higher interest rate.

Another factor that influences the effective interest rate is whether or not interest is compounded. Suppose you deposit $10,000 in a savings account that pays a 10 percent interest rate compounded semiannually. In other words, interest is paid twice a year. At the end of the first 6 months, $500 of interest (10 percent of $10,000 for half a year) is added to your account. At the end of the year, interest is calculated on $10,500 so that the second interest payment is $525 (10 percent of $10,500 for half a year). Thus:

$$i = \frac{\$1,025}{\$10,000} = 10.25\%$$

This 10.25 percent return means that a bank offering a 10 percent interest rate compounded semiannually would pay more interest to its customers than a competitor offering a simple (noncompounded) rate of, say, 10.2 percent.

Two pieces of legislation have attempted to clarify interest charges and payments. The Truth in Lending Act of 1968 requires that lenders state the costs and terms of consumer credit in concise and uniform language, in particular, as an annual percentage rate (APR). More recently, the Truth in Savings Act of 1991 requires that all advertisements of deposit accounts by banks and other financial institutions disclose all fees connected with such accounts and the interest rates and APRs on each account. Nevertheless, some "payday" check-cashing firms that lend money to people in return for postdated personal checks have been found to receive interest payments on one- and two-week loans that are equivalent to APRs of hundreds of percent per year. These interest rates prompted calls for state legislators to protect consumers from "predatory lenders."

More recently, many banks have established fee-based "bounce (overdraft) protection" for checking accounts. The bank agrees to pay each overdraft for a flat fee of around $35. These fees are essentially interest on a loan for the amount of the overdraft. When the overdraft amount is small, the annual interest on the loan can easily exceed 1,000 percent.

Similarly, late-payment fees on credit card accounts can boost the actual interest rate paid on credit card balances to extremely high levels. Furthermore, low "teaser" rates designed to attract new customers often contain "fin e print" that raises the interest rate to 16 percent, or even 28 percent, if a payment on the account is late. Also, low initial rates on some variable rate mortgages eventually "reset" to higher rates, greatly increasing the monthly payments that are due. "Let the borrower (or depositor) beware" remains a fitting motto in the world of credit.

a firm or industry is a signal that society wants that particular firm or industry to expand. It attracts resources from firms and industries that are not profitable. But the rewards of profits are more than an inducement for a firm to expand; they also attract the financing needed for expansion. In contrast, continuing losses penalize firms or industries that fail to adjust their productive efforts to match consumer wants. Such losses signal society's desire for the afflicted entities to contract.

So, in terms of our chapter-opening question, Walmart garnered large profits because it was locating its stores close to customers and delivering the mix of products many consumers wanted at exceptionally low prices. These profits signaled that society wanted more of its scarce resources allocated to Walmart stores. RCS Capital, in contrast, was not delivering products equivalent in value to the costs of the resources used to provide them—so the firm suffered losses. The losses and RCS Capital's bankruptcy signaled that society would benefit from a reallocation of all or a part of those resources to some other use.

Income Shares

LO18.7 List the share of U.S. earnings received by each of the factors of production.

Our discussion in this and in the preceding chapter would not be complete without a brief examination of how U.S. income is distributed among wages, rent, interest, and profit.

Figure 18.3 shows how the income generated in the United States in 2015 was distributed among the five "functional" income categories tracked by the U.S. government. These five categories do not match up perfectly with the economic definitions of wages, rent, interest, and profit. The biggest difference is "proprietors' income," which is the income received by doctors, lawyers, small-business owners, farmers, and the owners of other unincorporated enterprises. In terms of our four economic categories, proprietors' income is a combination of wages and profit. The wages compensate for labor, while the profits compensate for entrepreneurship. The economists who have looked into this combination believe that the large majority of proprietors' income is implicitly composed of wages and salaries rather than profit. That is, the large majority of proprietors' income is compensation for labor rather than compensation for entrepreneurship.

Taking that into account, note the dominant role of labor income in the U.S. economy. Even with labor income narrowly defined as wages and salaries, labor receives 70 percent of all income earned by Americans in a typical year. But if we add in proprietors' income because most of it is believed to be a payment for labor, then labor's share of national income rises to almost 80 percent, a percentage that has been remarkably

FIGURE 18.3 The functional distribution of U.S. income, 2015. Seventy percent of U.S. income is received as wages and salaries. Income to property owners—corporate profit, interest, and rents—accounts for about 20 percent of total income. The dollar amounts are in billions of dollars.

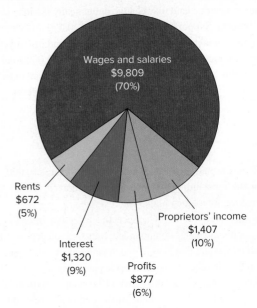

Source: Bureau of Economic Analysis, **www.bea.gov.**

stable since at least 1900. That leaves about 20 percent for "capitalists" in the form of rent, income, and profit. Ironically, income from capital is a relatively small share of the U.S. economy, though we call it a capitalist system.

SUMMARY

LO18.1 Explain the nature of economic rent and how it is determined.

Economic rent is the price paid for the use of land and other natural resources whose total supplies are fixed.

Differences in land rent result from differences in demand, often stemming from differences in the fertility and climate features of the land or differences in location.

Because the supply of land is fixed by nature, rent is a surplus payment that is socially unnecessary from the viewpoint of causing land to be supplied. The idea of land rent as a surplus payment gave rise to the single-tax movement of the late 1800s.

Although land rent is a surplus payment rather than a cost to the economy as a whole, to individuals and firms, land rents are correctly regarded as costs. The payment of land rents by individuals and firms is socially useful because it puts an opportunity cost on the use of land so that people are incentivized to put each piece of land to its best possible use.

LO18.2 Define interest and explain how interest rates vary based on risk, maturity, loan size, and taxability.

Interest is the price paid for the use of money. Because money is not itself an economic resource, people do not value money for its own sake; they value it for its purchasing power.

The interest rate on money loans determines the interest income earned by households for providing capital to firms.

Interest rates vary in size because loans differ as to risk, maturity, amount, and taxability.

The pure rate of interest is the hypothetical interest rate that would serve purely and solely to compensate lenders for their willingness to patiently forgo alternative consumption and investment opportunities until their money is repaid. The pure rate is best approximated by the interest rate on long-term, virtually riskless, 20-year U.S. Treasury bonds.

LO18.3 Explain the loanable funds theory of interest rates.

In the loanable funds theory of interest, the equilibrium interest rate in a loan market is determined by the demand for and supply of loanable funds in that market. Other things equal, an increase in the supply of loanable funds reduces the equilibrium interest rate, whereas a decrease in supply increases it. And increases in the demand for loanable funds raise the equilibrium interest rate, whereas decreases in demand reduce it.

LO18.4 Demonstrate how interest rates relate to the time-value of money.

The time-value of money is the idea that $1 today has more value than $1 sometime in the future because the $1 today can be placed in an interest-bearing account and earn compound interest over time. Future value is the amount to which a current amount of money will grow through interest compounding. Present value is the current value of some money payment to be received in the future.

LO18.5 Explain the role of interest rates in allocating capital, modulating R&D spending, and helping to determine the economy's total output of goods and services.

The equilibrium interest rate influences the level of investment and helps ration financial and physical capital to specific firms and industries. Similarly, this rate influences the size and composition of R&D spending. The real interest rate, not the nominal rate, is critical to investment and R&D decisions.

Although designed to make funds available to low-income borrowers, usury laws tend to allocate credit to high-income persons, subsidize high-income borrowers at the expense of lenders, and lessen the efficiency with which loanable funds are allocated.

LO18.6 Relate why economic profits occur and how profits, along with losses, allocate resources among alternative uses.

As residual claimants, entrepreneurs receive a firm's accounting profits (total revenue minus explicit costs) in exchange for assuming the uninsurable risks associated with running a business. An entrepreneur can earn an economic profit (total revenue minus both explicit and implicit costs, including a normal profit) if her firm's accounting profit exceeds the normal profit that her entrepreneurship could on average earn in other business ventures.

The corporate form of business organization has allowed the millions who own corporate stock to share in the financial risks and economic profits engendered by entrepreneurship. Profits are the key energizer of business firms within the capitalist system. Profit expectations influence innovating and investment activities and therefore the economy's levels of employment and economic growth. The basic function of profits and losses, however, is to allocate resources in accord with consumers' preferences.

LO18.7 List the share of U.S. earnings received by each of the factors of production.

The largest share of all income earned by Americans—about 70 percent—goes to labor, a share narrowly defined as "wages and salaries." When labor's share is more broadly defined to include "proprietors' income," it rises to about 80 percent of national income, leaving about 20 percent for rent, interest, and profit payments to the providers of land, capital, and entrepreneurship.

TERMS AND CONCEPTS

economic rent	compound interest	explicit costs
incentive function	future value	implicit costs
single-tax movement	present value	economic or pure profit
pure rate of interest	nominal interest rate	insurable risks
loanable funds theory of interest	real interest rate	uninsurable risks
time-value of money	usury laws	normal profit

The following and additional problems can be found in **connect**

DISCUSSION QUESTIONS

1. How does the economist's use of the term "rent" differ from everyday usage? Explain: "Though rent need not be paid by society to make land available, rental payments are useful in guiding land into the most productive uses." **LO18.1**

2. Explain why economic rent is a surplus payment when viewed by the economy as a whole but a cost of production from the standpoint of individual firms and industries.

Explain: "Land rent performs no 'incentive function' for the overall economy." **LO18.1**

3. How does Henry George's proposal for a single tax on land relate to the elasticity of the supply of land? Why are there so few remaining advocates of George's proposal? **LO18.1**

4. If money is not an economic resource, why is interest paid and received for its use? What considerations account for the fact

that interest rates differ greatly on various types of loans? Use those considerations to explain the relative sizes of the interest rates on the following: **LO18.2**

a. A 10-year $1,000 government bond.

b. A $20 pawnshop loan.

c. A 30-year mortgage loan on a $175,000 house.

d. A 24-month $12,000 commercial bank loan to finance the purchase of an automobile.

e. A 60-day $100 loan from a personal finance company.

5. Why is the supply of loanable funds upsloping? Why is the demand for loanable funds downsloping? Explain the equilibrium interest rate. List some factors that might cause it to change. **LO18.3**

6. Here is the deal: You can pay your college tuition at the beginning of the academic year or the same amount at the end of the academic year. You either already have the money in an interest-bearing account or will have to borrow it. Deal, or no deal? Explain your financial reasoning. Relate your answer to the time-value of money, present value, and future value. **LO18.4**

7. What are the major economic functions of the interest rate? How might the fact that many businesses finance their investment activities internally affect the efficiency with which the interest rate performs its functions? **LO18.5**

8. Distinguish between nominal and real interest rates. Which is more relevant in making investment and R&D decisions? If the nominal interest rate is 12 percent and the inflation rate is 8 percent, what is the real rate of interest? **LO18.5**

9. Historically, usury laws that put below-equilibrium ceilings on interest rates have been used by some states to make credit available to poor people who could not otherwise afford to borrow. Critics contend that poor people are those most likely to be hurt by such laws. Which view is correct? **LO18.5**

10. How do the concepts of accounting profit and economic profit differ? Why is economic profit smaller than accounting profit? What are the three basic sources of economic profit? Classify each of the following according to those sources: **LO18.6**

a. A firm's profit from developing and patenting a new medication that greatly reduces cholesterol and thus diminishes the likelihood of heart disease and stroke.

b. A restaurant's profit that results from the completion of a new highway past its door.

c. The profit received by a firm due to an unanticipated change in consumer tastes.

11. Why is the distinction between insurable and uninsurable risks significant for the theory of profit? Carefully evaluate: "All economic profit can be traced to either uncertainty or the desire to avoid it." What are the major functions of economic profit? **LO18.6**

12. What is the combined rent, interest, and profit share of the income earned by Americans in a typical year if proprietors' income is included within the labor (wage) share? **LO18.7**

13. **LAST WORD** Assume that you borrow $5,000, and you pay back the $5,000 plus $250 in interest at the end of the year. Assuming no inflation, what is the real interest rate? What would the interest rate be if the $250 of interest had been discounted at the time the loan was made? What would the interest rate be if you were required to repay the loan in 12 equal monthly installments?

REVIEW QUESTIONS

1. When using a supply-and-demand model to illustrate how land rents are set, economists typically draw the supply curve as a vertical line because: **LO18.1**

a. The supply of land is fixed.

b. The supply of land is perfectly inelastic.

c. The quantity supplied of land does not increase when rents go up.

d. All of the above.

2. In the 1980s land prices in Japan surged upward in a "speculative bubble." Land prices then fell for 11 straight years between 1990 and 2001. What can we safely assume happened to *land rent* in Japan over those 11 years? Use graphical analysis to illustrate your answer. **LO18.1**

3. The main argument put forth by advocates of the *single-tax movement* was that: **LO18.1**

a. Taxing only income would make for a more equal society.

b. Taxing only land would be very efficient because taxing land does not decrease its supply.

c. Taxing only imports would help to protect local jobs and stimulate local entrepreneurs.

d. Having only one tax would be much easier for people to understand and much less costly to administer than our current system with its wide variety of taxes.

4. Angela puts $1,000 in a savings account that pays 3 percent per year. What is the future value of her money one year from now? **LO18.4**

a. $970.

b. $1,000.

c. $1,003.

d. $1,030.

5. As shown in Table 18.2, $1,000 invested at 10 percent compound interest will grow into $1,331 after three years. What is the present value of $2,662 in three years if it is discounted back to the present at a 10 percent compound interest rate? (Hint: $2,662 is twice as much as $1,331.) **LO18.4**

6. Entrepreneurs are the residual claimants at their respective firms. This means that they: **LO18.6**

a. Only get paid if there is any money left over after all the other factors of production have been paid.

b. Must bear the financial risks of running their firms.

c. Receive whatever accounting profits or losses their firms generate.

d. All of the above.

7. True or false. As a capitalist economy, the vast majority of U.S. national income flows to the owners of capital. **LO18.7**

PROBLEMS

1. Suppose that you own a 10-acre plot of land that you would like to rent out to wheat farmers. For them, bringing in a harvest involves $30 per acre for seed, $80 per acre for fertilizer, and $70 per acre for equipment rentals and labor. With these inputs, the land will yield 40 bushels of wheat per acre. If the price at which wheat can be sold is $5 per bushel and if farmers want to earn a normal profit of $10 per acre, what is the most that any farmer would pay to rent your 10 acres? What if the price of wheat rose to $6 per bushel? LO18.1

2. Suppose that the demand for loanable funds for car loans in the Milwaukee area is $10 million per month at an interest rate of 10 percent per year, $11 million at an interest rate of 9 percent per year, $12 million at an interest rate of 8 percent per year, and so on. If the supply of loanable funds is fixed at $15 million, what will be the equilibrium interest rate? If the government imposes a usury law and says that car loans cannot exceed 3 percent per year, how big will the monthly shortage (or excess demand) for car loans be? What if the usury limit is raised to 7 percent per year? LO18.3

3. To fund its wars against Napoleon, the British government sold consol bonds. They were referred to as "perpetuities" because they would pay £3 every year in perpetuity (forever). If a citizen could purchase a consol for £25, what would its annual interest rate be? What if the price were £50? £100? Bonds are known as "fixed income" securities because the future payments that they will make to investors are fixed by the bond agreement in advance. Do the interest rates of bonds and other investments that offer fixed future payments vary positively or inversely with their current prices? LO18.4

4. Suppose that the interest rate is 4 percent. What is the future value of $100 four years from now? How much of the future value is total interest? By how much would total interest be greater at a 6 percent interest rate than at a 4 percent interest rate? LO18.4

5. You are currently a worker earning $60,000 per year but are considering becoming an entrepreneur. You will not switch unless you earn an accounting profit that is on average at least as great as your current salary. You look into opening a small grocery store. Suppose that the store has annual costs of $150,000 for labor, $40,000 for rent, and $30,000 for equipment. There is a one-half probability that revenues will be $200,000 and a one-half probability that revenues will be $400,000. LO18.6

   a. In the low-revenue situation, what will your accounting profit or loss be? In the high-revenue situation?

   b. *On average,* how much do you expect your revenue to be? Your accounting profit? Your economic profit? Will you quit your job and try your hand at being an entrepreneur?

   c. Suppose the government imposes a 25 percent tax on accounting profits. This tax is only levied if a firm is earning positive accounting profits. What will your after-tax accounting profit be in the low-revenue case? In the high-revenue case? What will your *average* after-tax accounting profit be? What about your *average* after-tax economic profit? Will you now want to quit your job and try your hand at being an entrepreneur?

   d. Other things equal, does the imposition of the 25 percent profit tax increase or decrease the supply of entrepreneurship in the economy?

Natural Resource and Energy Economics

Learning Objectives

LO19.1 Explain why falling birthrates mean that we are not likely to run out of natural resources.

LO19.2 Describe why using a mix of energy sources is efficient, even if some of them are quite costly.

LO19.3 Discuss why running out of oil would not mean running out of energy.

LO19.4 Show how the profit motive can encourage resource conservation.

LO19.5 Relate how to use property rights to prevent deforestation and species extinction.

People like to consume goods and services. But to produce those goods and services, natural resources must be used up. Some natural resources, such as solar energy, forests, and fish, are renewable and can potentially be exploited indefinitely. Other resources, such as oil and coal, are in fixed supply and can be used only once. This chapter explores two issues in relation to our supplies of resources and energy. The first is whether we are likely to run out of resources in the near or even distant future and thereby face the possibility of either a drastic reduction in living standards or even, perhaps, the collapse of civilization as we know it. The second is how to best utilize and manage our resources so that we can maximize the benefits that we receive from them both now and in the future.

We begin the chapter by addressing the issue of whether we are about to run out of resources. We then turn to energy economics and natural resource economics, focusing on the incentive structures that help to promote conservation and sustainability.

Resource Supplies: Doom or Boom?

LO19.1 Explain why falling birthrates mean that we are not likely to run out of natural resources.

Since the beginning of the Industrial Revolution in the late eighteenth century, a historically unprecedented increase in both population and living standards has taken place. The world's population has increased from 1 billion people in 1800 to about 7.4 billion today, and the average person living in the United States enjoys a standard of living at least 12 times higher than that of the average American living in 1800. Stated slightly differently, many more people are alive today and levels of consumption per person are much higher. These two factors mean that human beings are now consuming vastly more resources than before the Industrial Revolution both in absolute terms and in per capita terms. This fact has led many observers to wonder if our current economic system and its high living standards are sustainable. In particular, will the availability of natural resources be sufficient to meet the growing demand for them?

A sensible response clearly involves looking at *both* resource demand and resource supply. We begin by examining human population growth because larger populations mean greater demand for resources.

Population Growth

We can trace the debate over the sustainability of resources back to 1798, when an Anglican minister in England named Thomas Malthus published *An Essay on the Principle of Population*. In that essay, Malthus argued that human living standards could only temporarily rise above subsistence levels. Any temporary increase in living standards would cause people to have more children and thereby increase the population. With so many more people to feed, per capita living standards would be driven back down to subsistence levels.

Falling Birthrates Unfortunately for Malthus's theory—but fortunately for society—higher living standards have *not* produced higher birthrates. In fact, just the opposite has happened. Higher standards of living are associated with *lower* birthrates. Birthrates are falling rapidly throughout the world and the majority of the world's population is now living in countries that have birthrates that are lower than the **replacement rate** necessary to keep their respective populations stable over time.

Table 19.1 lists the total fertility rates for 12 selected nations including the United States. The **total fertility rate** is the average number of children that a woman is expected to have during her lifetime. Taking into account infant and child mortality, a total fertility rate of about 2.1 births per woman per lifetime is necessary to keep the population constant, since 2.1 children equals 1 child to replace the mother, 1 child to replace the father, and 0.1 extra child who can be expected to die before becoming old enough to reproduce.

As you can see from Table 19.1, total fertility rates in many nations are well below the 2.1 rate necessary to keep the population stable over time. As a result, populations are expected to fall rapidly in many countries over the next few decades, with, for instance, the population of Russia expected to fall by about 7 percent from its current level of 144 million people to fewer than 134 million in 2050. Russia is not alone. Over 30 countries are expected to see their populations decline by 2050, including Japan by 30 million (a 24 percent decrease) and Latvia by 600,000 (a 30 percent decrease).

Worldwide, the precipitous fall of birthrates means that many **demographers** (scientists who study human populations)

TABLE 19.1   Total Fertility Rates for Selected Countries, 2015

Country	Total Fertility Rate
Australia	1.77
Canada	1.59
China	1.60
France	2.08
Germany	1.44
Hong Kong	1.18
Italy	1.43
Japan	1.40
Russia	1.61
South Korea	1.25
Sweden	1.88
United States	1.87

Source: The World Factbook, **www.cia.gov**. Data are 2015 estimates.

now expect the world's population to reach a peak of 9 billion people or fewer sometime around the middle of this century before beginning to fall, perhaps quite rapidly. For instance, if the worldwide total fertility rate declines to 1 birth per woman per lifetime, then each generation will be only half as large as the previous one because there will be only one child on average for every two parents. Even a rate of 1.3 births per woman per lifetime will reduce a country's population by half in just under 45 years.

The Demographic Transition The world's population increased so rapidly from 1800 to the present day because the higher living standards that arrive when a country begins to modernize bring with them much lower death rates. Before modernization happens, death rates are typically so high that women have to give birth to more than six children per lifetime just to ensure that, on average, two will survive to adulthood. But once living standards begin to rise and modern medical care becomes available, death rates plummet so that nearly all children survive to adulthood. This causes a temporary population explosion because parents—initially unaware that such a revolutionary change in death rates has taken place—for a while keep having six or more children. The impression persists that they must have many children to ensure that at least two will survive to adulthood. The result is one or two generations of very rapid population growth until parents adjust to the new situation and reduce the number of children that they choose to have. Demographers refer to this three-step shift from (1) the traditional situation of simultaneously high birth and death rates through (2) a transition period of high birth rates and low death rates and then finally on to (3) the current situation of simultaneously low birth and death rates as the **demographic transition.**

The overall world population is still increasing because many countries such as India and Indonesia began modernizing only relatively recently and are still in the transition phase where death rates have fallen but birthrates are still relatively high. Nevertheless, birthrates are falling rapidly nearly everywhere. This means that the end of rapid population growth is at hand. Furthermore, because fertility rates tend to fall below the replacement rate as countries modernize, we can also expect total world population to begin to decline during the twenty-first century. This is a critical fact to keep in mind when considering whether we are likely to ever face a resource crisis: Fewer people means fewer demands placed on society's scarce resources.

Possible Explanations for Low Fertility Demographers have been surprised at just how low fertility rates have fallen and why they have fallen so far below the replacement rate in so many countries. The decline of fertility rates to such low levels is especially surprising given the fact that couples typically tell demographers that they would like to have *at least* two children. Because this implies that most couples would prefer higher total fertility rates than we actually observe, it seems probable that social or economic factors are constraining couples to have fewer children than they desire, thereby causing total fertility rates to fall so low. Demographers have not yet reached agreement on which factors are most important, but possible candidates include changing attitudes toward religion, the much wider career opportunities available to women in modern economies, and the expense of raising children in modern societies. Indeed, children have been transformed from economic assets that could be put to work at an early age in agricultural societies into economic liabilities that are very costly to raise in modern societies where child labor is illegal and where children must attend school until adulthood. The Consider This vignette discusses current government efforts to raise birthrates by offering financial incentives to parents.

Resource Consumption per Person

Thomas Malthus's tradition of predicting a collapse in living standards has been carried on to this day by various individuals and groups. One well-reported prediction was made by Stanford University butterfly expert Paul Ehrlich. In his 1968 book *The Population Bomb,* he made the Malthusian prediction that the population would soon outstrip resources so that "in the 1970s and 1980s hundreds of millions of people will starve to death in spite of any crash programs embarked upon now." Contrary to this prediction, no famines approaching these magnitudes materialized then and none appear likely today.

Falling Resource Prices One reason that Ehrlich's pessimism was not borne out was because the population growth rate slowed dramatically as living standards around the world

CONSIDER THIS . . .

Source: © Digital Vision/Getty Images RF

Can Governments Raise Birthrates?
Low birthrates pose major problems for countries encountering very slow population growth or actual population declines. The primary problem is that with very few children being born today, very few workers will be alive in a few decades to pay the large amounts of taxes that will be needed if governments are to keep their current promises regarding Social Security and other old-age pension programs. Too few young workers will be supporting too many elderly retirees. Another potential problem is a lack of soldiers. Consider Russia. With its population expected to fall by 12 percent by mid-century, defending its borders will be much harder.

As a response, Russian President Vladimir Putin announced a new policy in 2006 that would pay any Russian woman who chooses to have a second child a bounty worth 250,000 rubles ($9,280). In addition, the Russian government promised to double monthly child benefits in an effort to make having children less financially burdensome for parents. Many other countries have experimented with similar policies. In 2004, France began offering its mothers a payment of €800 ($1,040) for each child born and Italy began offering a €1,000 ($1,300) payment for second children.

As far as demographers can tell, however, these and other policies aimed at raising birthrates by offering maternity leave, free day care, or other subsidies to mothers or their children have not been able to generate any substantial increases in fertility levels in any country in which they have been attempted. For example, Australia's policy of paying mothers A$5,000 ($4,500) for each child increased the number of births by less than 4 percent. It therefore appears that the incentives to have more babies provided by these government plans are being swamped by the broader social and economic forces that are leading to declining overall fertility rates.

rose. Another reason is that the long-run evidence indicates that the supply of productive resources available to be made into goods and services has been increasing faster than the demand for those resources for at least 150 years. This is best seen by looking at Figure 19.1, which tracks *The Economist* magazine's commodity price index for the years 1850 to 2015. The index currently contains 25 important commodities including aluminum, copper, corn, rice, wheat, coffee, rubber, sugar, and soybeans. In earlier days, it included

FIGURE 19.1 *The Economist's* **commodity price index, 1850–2015.** *The Economist* magazine's commodity price index attempts to keep track of the prices of the commodities most common in international trade. It is adjusted for inflation and scaled so that commodity prices in the years 1845–1850 are set to an index value of 100. The figure shows that real commodity prices are volatile (vary considerably from year to year) but are now 60 percent lower than they were in the mid-nineteenth century. This implies that commodity supplies have increased faster than commodity demands.

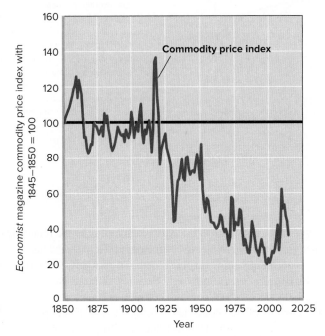

Source: The Economist, **www.economist.com,** from 1845 to 2015.

commodities such as candle wax, silk, and indigo, which were important at the time. The index also adjusts for inflation so that one can see how the real cost of commodities has evolved over time and it is standardized so that the real price of commodities during the years 1845 to 1850 is given a value of 100.

As Figure 19.1 demonstrates, a dramatic long-run decline in real commodity prices has occurred. With the current value of the index at about 50, the real cost of buying commodities today is roughly 50 percent lower than it was in the initial 1845–1850 period. This means that commodity supplies have increased faster than commodity demands, since the only way that commodity prices could have fallen so much in the face of increasing demand is if the supply curve for commodities shifted to the right faster than the demand curve for commodities shifted to the right.

A key point is that the long-run fall of commodity prices implies that commodity supplies have grown faster than the sum total of the two pressures that have acted over this time to increase commodity demands. The first is the huge rise in the total number of people alive and therefore consuming resources (since 1850, the world's population has risen from

1.25 billion to 7.4 billion). The second is the huge rise in the amount of consumption *per person*. That is, more people are alive today than in 1850, and each person alive today is on average consuming several times more than was consumed by the average person alive in 1850. Still, the long-run fall in commodity prices confirms that supplies have managed to grow fast enough to overcome both these demand-increasing pressures.

But will supplies be able to overcome these two pressures in the future? Prospects are hopeful. First, the rapid and continuing decline in birthrates means that the huge population increases that occurred during the nineteenth and twentieth centuries are not likely to continue in the future. Indeed, we have seen that population decline has begun in several countries and it now seems likely that overall world population will begin to decline within this century. This trend will moderate future increases in the total demand for goods and services. Second, resource consumption *per person* (as distinct from goods and services consumption per person) also has either leveled off or declined in the past decade or so in the richest countries, which currently consume the largest fraction of the world's resources.

Consumption Trends for Water, Energy, and Materials

The leveling off or decline of per capita resource consumption can be observed in Figures 19.2, 19.3, and 19.4, which show, respectively, how much water, energy, and other resources have been consumed on a daily or annual basis in both total and per capita terms over the last few decades in the United States. The red lines in each figure show total use while the blue lines trace per capita use. To accommodate both sets of data, the units measuring total use are on the vertical scales on the left side of each figure while the units measuring per capita use are shown on the vertical scales on the right side of each figure.

The blue line in Figure 19.2 shows that per capita water use in the United States peaked in 1975 at 1,941 gallons per person per day. It then fell by 42 percent to just 1,134 gallons per person per day in 2010.

The blue line in Figure 19.3 shows that annual per capita energy use peaked at 360 million British thermal units per person in 1979 before falling sharply during the early 1980s recession, gradually rising through the late 1990s and then falling again through 2014, when it ran at a rate of 309 BTUs per person per year. (A **British thermal unit,** or **BTU,** is the amount of energy required to raise the temperature of 1 pound of water by 1 degree Fahrenheit.)

Finally, Figure 19.4 takes advantage of a fundamental principle of physics to show that the per capita use of other resources has also leveled off since 1990. This principle states that matter is neither created nor destroyed—only transformed—by the sorts of chemical reactions that take place as raw materials are turned into finished products and

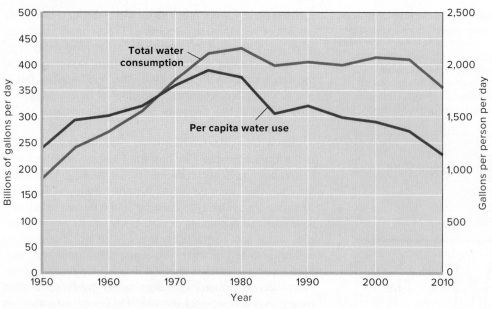

FIGURE 19.2 **Total and per capita water use in the United States, 1950–2010.** Average total water use in the United States peaked at 430 billion gallons per day in 1980 before declining to about 355 billion gallons per day in 2010, the last year for which data were available. Average per capita water consumption fell 42 percent from a peak of 1,941 gallons per person per day in 1975 to only 1,134 gallons per person per day in 2010. These data are reported every 5 years. The 2015 data were not available at the time of publication, but they may be available when you read this. If interested, check the U.S. Geological Survey website.

Source: *Estimated Use of Water in the United States in 2010*, United States Geological Survey, **www.usgs.gov**.

then consumed. As a result, we can measure how much use of solid objects like plastics, metals, and paper takes place by measuring how much solid waste (commonly called trash or garbage) is generated when they are thrown away. Consequently, because Figure 19.4 shows that per capita trash generation has leveled off at about 4.5 pounds per person per day since 1990, we can conclude that per capita consumption of solids has also leveled off since that time.

The Likely Long-Run Decline in Resource Demands

These three figures give further cause for optimism on the availability of future resource supplies. We have already provided evidence that the number of people in the world is not likely to increase substantially. Figures 19.2, 19.3, and 19.4 show that per capita consumption levels are also likely to either level off or decline. Together, these two facts suggest that the total

demand for resources is likely to reach a peak in the relatively near future before falling over time as populations decline.

That being said, resource demand is likely to increase substantially for the next few decades as large parts of the world modernize and begin to consume as much per capita as the citizens of rich countries do today. For instance, per capita energy use in the United States in 2014 was 309 million BTUs per person. If every person in the world were to use that much energy, total annual energy demand would be 2,287 quadrillion BTUs, or about 4.4 times the 2012 world production of 524 quadrillion BTUs. One of the world's great economic challenges over the coming decades will be to supply the resources that will be demanded as living standards in poorer countries rise to rich-country levels. But because population growth rates are slowing and because per capita resource uses in rich countries have leveled off, we can now

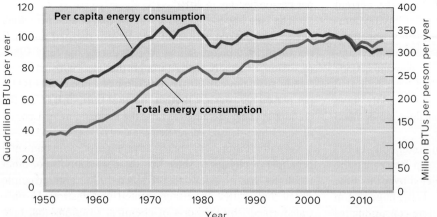

FIGURE 19.3 **Total and per capita energy consumption in the United States, 1950–2014.** Per capita energy consumption in the United States peaked at 360 million British thermal units (BTUs) per person per day in 1979. It fell dramatically during the early 1980s recession and then rose again until 1999, after which it has been mostly falling, down to a value of 312 million BTUs per person per day in 2011. Total energy consumption between 1950 and 2000 nearly tripled, increasing from 34.6 quadrillion BTUs in 1950 to 98.1 quadrillion BTUs in 2000. Since 2000, total energy usage has been approximately steady, with 98.5 quadrillion BTUs consumed in 2014.

Source: *February 2016 Monthly Energy Overview*, United States Energy Information Administration, **www.eia.doe.gov**.

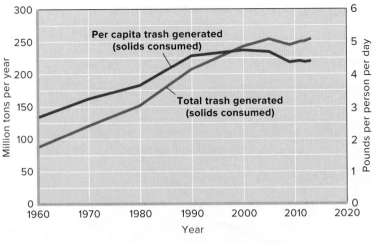

FIGURE 19.4 Total and per capita trash generation in the United States, 1960–2013. Although the total level of trash generated in the United States increased from 88.1 million tons in 1960 to 254.1 million tons in 2013, the amount of trash generated per person has held steady at approximately 4.5 pounds per person per day since 1990. Because *trash generated equals solids consumed,* we know that per capita consumption of solids has stayed relatively constant over the past 20 years.

Source: United States Environmental Protection Agency, **www.epa.gov.**

foresee a maximum total demand for resources even if living standards all over the world rise to rich-country levels. Given the ongoing improvements in technology and productivity that characterize modern economies and that allow us to produce increasingly more from any given set of inputs, it consequently seems unlikely that we will run into a situation where the total demand for resources exhausts their overall supply.

Regional Resource Challenges Significant challenges are likely to appear in those places where local supplies of certain resources are extremely limited. Water, for instance, is a rare and precious commodity in many places, including the Middle East and the American Southwest. Governments will have to work hard to ensure that the limited supplies of water

in such areas are used efficiently and that disputes over water rights are settled peacefully. Along the same lines, resources are often produced in certain areas but consumed in others with, for instance, one-quarter of the world's oil being produced in the Middle East but most of the demand for oil coming from Europe, North America, and East Asia. In such cases, institutions must be developed that can move such resources from the areas in which they originate to the areas in which they are used. If not, local shortages may develop in the areas that cannot produce these resources despite the fact that the resources in question may at the same time be in very plentiful supply in the areas in which they are produced.

Energy Economics

LO19.2 Describe why using a mix of energy sources is efficient, even if some of them are quite costly.

Energy economics studies how people deal with energy scarcity. This involves both demand and supply. In terms of energy supply, people are interested in attempting to find and exploit low-cost energy sources. But since energy is only one input into a production process, often the best energy source to use in a given situation is, paradoxically, actually rather expensive—yet still the best choice when other costs are taken into account. The economy therefore develops and exploits many different energy sources, from fossil fuels to nuclear power.

Energy Efficiency Is Increasing

In terms of energy demand, the most interesting fact is that per capita energy use has leveled off in recent years in developed countries, as we previously illustrated for the United States in Figure 19.3. This fact implies that our economy has become increasingly efficient at using energy to produce goods and services. This is best seen by noting that while per capita energy inputs fell from 338 BTUs per person per year in 1990 down to only 309 BTUs per person per year in 2014,

QUICK REVIEW 19.1

✓ Thomas Malthus and others have worried that increases in our demand for resources will outrun the supply of resources, but commodity prices have been falling for more than a century, indicating that supply has increased by more than demand.

✓ Because total fertility rates are very low and falling, population growth for the world will soon turn negative and thereby reduce the demand for natural resources.

✓ Per capita consumption of resources such as water, energy, and solids has either fallen or remained constant in the United States. If per capita consumption continues to stay the same or decrease while populations fall, total resource demand will fall—meaning that the demand for resources is unlikely to threaten to use up the available supply of resources.

✓ Significant increases in resource demands are likely over the next few decades, however, as living standards in poorer countries rise toward those in richer countries.

FIGURE 19.5 **Inflation-adjusted GDP per million BTUs of energy consumption in the United States, 1950–2014.** This figure shows the number of dollars' worth of real GDP the U.S. economy produced per million BTUs of energy consumed in each year from 1950 through 2014, when annual GDP figures are converted to year 2009 dollars to account for inflation. Energy efficiency has more than doubled during this period, with real output per energy input rising from $63.09 worth of GDP per million BTUs in 1950 to $162.07 worth of GDP per million BTUs in 2014.

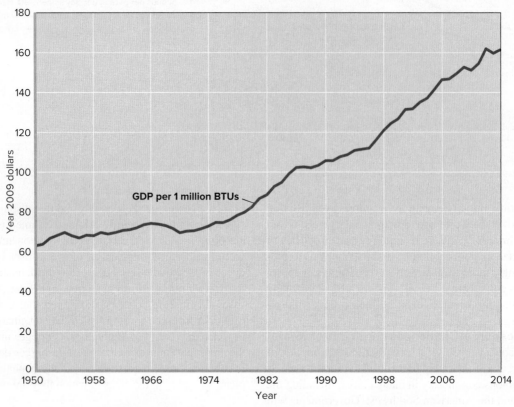

Source: United States Energy Information Administration, **www.eia.doe.gov**.

real GDP per person rose during that time period by 78 percent. As a result, people were able to make and consume nearly four-fifths more goods and services per person despite using about 8 percent less energy per person.

This increase in energy efficiency has been part of a long historical trend, as Figure 19.5 makes quite clear. For the years 1950 through 2014, it shows the number of inflation-adjusted dollars of GDP that the U.S. economy has produced each year for every 1 million BTUs of energy consumed in the United States. The figure demonstrates that technological improvements greatly increased energy efficiency, so much so that although 1 million BTUs of energy yielded only $63.09 worth of goods and services in 1950, 1 million BTUs of energy yielded $162.07 worth of goods and services in 2014 (when the comparison is made using year 2009 dollars to account for inflation).

Keep this huge increase in energy efficiency in mind when considering the magnitude of future energy demands. Because better technology means that more output can be produced with the same amount of energy input, rising living standards in the future will not necessarily depend on using more energy. The behavior of the U.S. economy since 1990 bears this out because, as we just pointed out, real GDP per person increased by nearly 80 percent between 1990 and 2014, while per capita energy inputs declined. Living standards can be raised without having to increase energy inputs.

Efficient Electricity Use

We just saw that the United States has grown increasingly efficient at using energy. The same is true for other developed countries. An interesting fact about energy efficiency, however, is that it often involves using a mix of energy inputs, some of which are much more expensive than others. The best way to see why this is true is to examine electric power generation.

The Challenge: Highly Variable Demand A typical electric plant has to serve tens of thousands of homes and businesses and is expected to deliver an uninterrupted supply of electricity 24 hours a day, 7 days a week. This task is not easy. The problem is that massive changes in energy demand occur over the course of a day. Demand is extremely low at night when people are sleeping, begins to rise rapidly in the morning as people wake up and turn on their lights, rises even more when they are at work, falls a bit as they commute home, rises back up a bit in the evening when they turn on their house lights to deal with the darkness and their televisions to deal with their boredom, and finally collapses as they turn out their lights and go to sleep.

The problem for electric companies as they try to minimize the cost of providing for such large variations in the demand for electricity is that the power plants that have the lowest operating costs also have the highest fixed costs in terms of construction. For instance, large coal-fired plants can produce energy at a cost of about 4 cents per kilowatt hour. But they can do this only if they are built large enough to exploit economies of scale and if they are then operated at full capacity. To see why this can be a problem, imagine that such a plant has a maximum generating capacity of 20 megawatts per hour but that its customers' peak afternoon demand for electricity is 25 megawatts per hour. One solution would be to build two 20-megawatt coal-fired plants. But that would be very wasteful because one would be operating at full capacity (and hence minimum cost), while the other would be producing only 5 megawatts of its 20-megawatt capacity. Given that such plants cost hundreds of millions of dollars to build, this would be highly inefficient.

The Solution: Mixing Generation Technologies

The solution that electric companies employ is to use a mix of different types of generation technology. This turns out to be optimal because even though some electricity generation plants have very high operating costs, they have low fixed costs (that is, they are very inexpensive to build). Thus, the power company in our example might build one large coal-fired plant to generate 20 of the required 25 megawatts of energy at 4 cents per kilowatt hour, but it would then build a small 5-megawatt natural gas generator to supply the rest. Such plants produce electricity at the much higher cost of 15 cents per kilowatt hour, but they are relatively inexpensive to build. As a result, this solution would save the electric company from having to build a second very expensive coal-fired plant that would wastefully operate well below its full capacity.

The result of this process of mixing generator technologies is that the United States currently generates electricity from a variety of energy sources, as we show in Figure 19.6. Seventy five percent of the total is generated at coal, petroleum, and natural gas plants. The rest comes from nuclear power and a variety of renewable energy sources including hydropower, geothermal, wind, and solar.

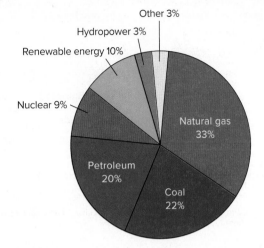

FIGURE 19.6 **Percentages of U.S. electricity generated using various energy sources, 2014.** About 22 percent of U.S. electricity was generated by coal-fired plants in 2014, with natural gas and petroleum accounting together for a further 53 percent of the total.

Source: United States Energy Information Administration, **www.eia.doe.gov**.

Running Out of Energy?

LO19.3 Discuss why running out of oil would not mean running out of energy.

Some observers worry that we may soon run out of the energy needed to power our economy. Their fears are based largely on the possibility that the world may run out of oil sometime in the next century. It is the case, however, that there is no likelihood of running out of energy. If anything, running out of oil would not mean running out of energy— just running out of *cheap* energy.

This is best seen by looking at Table 19.2, which compares oil prices with the prices at which other energy sources become economically viable. For instance, biodiesel, a type of diesel fuel made from decomposed plant wastes, is so expensive to produce that it becomes economically viable (that is, less costly to produce than oil) only if oil costs $80 or more per barrel. On the other hand, ethanol made from corn in the United States costs less to produce and would be an economically viable alternative to oil even if the price of oil were only $60 per barrel.

Multiple Sources of Supply The key point to gather from Table 19.2, however, is that even if we were to run out of oil, alternatives would quickly become available. At a price of $40 per barrel, vast reserves of energy derived from tar sands, the conversion of natural gas and coal to liquid petroleum, and even ethanol derived from cheap Brazilian sugar cane become economically viable alternatives. At $50 per barrel, shale oil becomes a viable alternative. At $60 per barrel, corn-based ethanol becomes viable. And at $80 per barrel, so does biodiesel.

TABLE 19.2 Oil Prices at which Alternative Energy Sources Become Economically Viable

Oil Price per Barrel at which Alternative Is Economically Viable	Alternative Fuel
$80	Biodiesel
60	U.S. corn-based ethanol*
50	Shale oil
40	Tar sands; Brazilian sugar-cane-based ethanol; gas to liquids;† coal-to-liquids‡
20	Conventional oil

*Excludes tax credits.
†Gas to liquid is economically viable at $40 if natural gas price is $2.50 or less per million BTUs.
‡Coal to liquid is economically viable at $40 if coal price is $15 per ton or less.

Sources: Cambridge Energy Research Associates, **www.cera.com**; *The Economist*, April 22, 2006, **www.economist.com**.

In fact, these prices can be thought of as a giant supply curve for energy, with rising energy prices leading to increased energy production. The result is that even if the supply of oil begins to dry up and oil prices consequently rise, other energy supplies will quickly be brought online to fill the energy gap created by the decline in the amount of oil available. Also, the alternative prices listed in Table 19.2 are *current* alternative prices. As technologies improve, the costs of producing these alternatives are likely to fall and, as a result, the potential costs of replacing oil if it runs out will be even lower than suggested by the prices in the table. As a result, economists do not worry about running out of oil or, more generally, running out of energy. There is plenty of energy—but the major concern is price and the impact that potentially increasing energy prices might have on the standard of living.

Environmental Impacts Finally, we need to acknowledge that energy sources differ not only in their prices but also with regard to the extent of negative externalities they may generate. Recall from Chapter 4 that negative externalities are costs—such as those associated with air pollution—that are transferred to society during the production process and therefore not reflected in product price. Such externalities need to be accounted for. Some energy sources are relatively "clean," creating little pollution or other externalities. Other sources currently are more problematic. For example, burning coal generates substantial particulate and carbon dioxide emissions that can contribute to health problems and global warming. But a caution is needed here: At sufficiently high electricity prices, burning coal can be both economical and clean. This is true because at sufficiently high electricity prices, the companies that burn coal to generate electricity are able to afford extensive expenditures on pollution reduction. Scrubbers can reduce soot from emissions and new

CONSIDER THIS . . .

Source: © Henglein and Steets/Getty Images RF

Storage Wars

Many governments have subsidized wind turbines and solar energy projects to generate zero-emissions electricity. The amount of electricity that can be generated by these alternative methods can be massive relative to demand. On a gusty day, domestic wind turbines can provide over 100 percent of Denmark's electricity.

Unfortunately, wind turbines supply nothing on windless days and solar works only when the sun is up.

Coal and gas plants can modulate their output to fill in for the fluctuations in wind and solar, but another strategy for maximizing the potential of wind and solar generation is to develop low-cost storage technologies so that electricity can be stored up on windy days for use on windless days and during the daytime for nighttime use.

Potential storage technologies include super-efficient lithium-ion batteries like those used in cell phones, supercapacitors that can discharge huge volumes of electricity very rapidly, and using flywheels to store energy. Wind and solar will reach their full potential when the marginal cost of energy storage falls below the marginal cost of using coal and gas to fill in for the fluctuations in wind and solar electricity generation. When that point is reached, unsubsidized market pressures can be expected to displace coal and gas in favor of wind and solar.

technologies can capture and sequester carbon dioxide in underground storage. At sufficiently high energy prices, clean methods of producing energy are not confined to wind, solar, and other so-called alternative energy sources.

QUICK REVIEW 19.2

✓ Energy efficiency has consistently improved so that more output can be produced for every unit of energy used by the economy.

✓ After taking the different fixed costs of different electricity-generating plants into account, utility companies find it efficient to use a variety of energy sources (coal, natural gas, nuclear) to deal with the large daily variations in energy demand with which they must cope.

✓ Even if we run out of oil, we will not run out of energy because many alternative sources of energy are available. These alternatives are, however, more costly than oil so that if we were to run out of oil, energy costs in the economy would most likely increase.

Natural Resource Economics

LO19.4 Show how the profit motive can encourage resource conservation.

The major focus of natural resource economics is to design policies for extracting or harvesting a natural resource that will maximize the **net benefits** from doing so. The net benefits are simply the total dollar value of all benefits minus the total dollar value of all costs, so that a project's net benefit is equal to the dollar value of the gains or losses to be made. A key feature of such policies is that they take into account the fact that present and future decisions about how fast to extract or harvest a resource typically cannot be made independently. Other things equal, taking more today means having less in the future, and having more in the future is possible only by taking less today.

Renewables vs. Nonrenewables

In applying this general rule, however, large differences between renewable natural resources and nonrenewable natural resources become apparent. **Renewable natural resources** include things like forests and wildlife, which are capable of growing back, or renewing themselves, if they are harvested at moderate rates. This leaves open the possibility of enjoying their benefits in perpetuity. Solar energy, the atmosphere, the oceans, and aquifers are also considered renewable natural resources either because they will continue providing us with their benefits no matter what we do (as is the case with solar energy) or because if we manage them well, we can continue to enjoy their benefits in perpetuity (as is the case with the atmosphere, the oceans, and aquifers). **Nonrenewable natural resources** include things like oil, coal, and metals, which either are in actual fixed supply (like the metals found in the earth's crust) or are renewed so slowly as to be in virtual fixed supply when viewed from a human time perspective (as is the case with fossil fuels like oil and coal, which take millions of years to form out of decaying plants and animals).

Optimal Resource Management

The key to optimally managing both renewable and nonrenewable resources is designing incentive structures that prompt decision makers to consider not only the net benefits to be made by using the resources under their control in the present but also the net benefits to be made by conserving the resources under their control in the present to be able to use more of them in the future. Once these incentive structures are in place, decision makers can weigh the costs and benefits of present use against the costs and benefits of future use to determine the optimal allocation of the resource between present and future uses. The key concept used in weighing these alternatives is present value, which allows decision makers to sensibly compare the net benefits of potential present uses with the net benefits of potential future uses.

Using Present Values to Evaluate Future Possibilities

Natural resource economics studies the optimal use of our limited supplies of resources. Decisions about optimal resource use typically involve choosing how resources will be exploited intertemporally, or over time. For instance, suppose that a poor country has just discovered that it possesses a small oil field. Should the country pump this oil today when it can make a profit of $50 per barrel, or should it wait 5 years to pump the oil given that it believes that in 5 years it will be able to make a profit of $60 per barrel due to lower production costs?

Answering this question requires consideration of the time-value of money, discussed in the previous chapter. We need a way to compare $60 worth of money in 5 years with $50 worth of money today. Economists make this comparison by converting the future quantity of money (in this case $60) into a present-day equivalent measured in present-day money. By making this conversion, the two quantities of money can be compared using the same unit of measurement, present-day dollars.

Understanding Present Values The formula for calculating the present-day equivalent, or **present value,** of any future sum of money (in this case, $60 in 5 years) is described in our macroeconomics chapter on financial economics, but the intuition is simple. Suppose that the current market rate of interest is 5 percent per year. How much money would a person have to save and invest today at 5 percent interest to end up with exactly $60 in 5 years? The correct answer turns out to be $47.01 because if $47.01 is invested at an interest rate of 5 percent per year, it will grow into precisely $60 in 5 years. Stated slightly differently, $47.01 today can be thought of as being equivalent to $60 in 5 years because it is possible to transform $47.01 today into $60 in 5 years by simply investing it at the market rate of interest.

This fact is very important because it allows for a direct comparison of the benefits from the country's two possible courses of action. If it pumps its oil today, it will get $50 per barrel worth of present-day dollars. But if it pumps its oil in 5 years and gets $60 per barrel at that time, it will only get $47.01 per barrel worth of present-day dollars since the present value of $60 in 5 years is precisely $47.01 today. By measuring both possibilities in present-day dollars, the better choice of action becomes obvious: The country should pump its oil today, since $50 worth of present-day money is obviously greater than $47.01 worth of present-day money.

The ability to calculate present values also allows decision makers to use cost-benefit analysis in situations where the costs and benefits happen at different points in time. For instance, suppose that a forestry company is considering spending $1,000 per acre to plant seedlings that it hopes will grow into trees that it will be able to harvest in 100 years. It expects that the wood from the trees will be worth $125,000 per acre in 100 years. Should it undertake this investment?

The answer is *no* because at the current market interest rate of 5 percent per year, the present value of $125,000 in 100 years is only $950.56 today, which is less than the $1,000 per acre that the firm would have to invest today to plant the seedlings. When both the benefits and costs of the project are measured in the same units (present-day dollars), it is clear that the project is a money loser and should be avoided.

Allocating Resources over Time   More generally, the ability of policymakers to calculate present values and put present-day dollar values on future possibilities is vitally important because it helps to ensure that resources are allocated to their best possible uses over time. By enabling a decision maker to compare the costs and benefits of present use with the costs and benefits of future use, present value calculations help to ensure that a resource will be used at whatever point in time it will be most valuable.

This is especially important when it comes to conservation because there is always a temptation to use up a resource as fast as possible in the present rather than conserving some or all of it for future use. By putting a present-day dollar value on the net benefits to be gained by conservation and future use, present value calculations provide a financial incentive to make sure that resources will be conserved for future use whenever doing so will generate higher net benefits than using them in the present. Indeed, a large part of natural resource economics focuses on nothing more than ensuring that the net benefits that can be gained from conservation and future use are accounted for by the governments, companies, and individuals that are in charge of deciding when and how to use our limited supply of resources. When these future net benefits are properly accounted for, resource use tends to be conservative and sustainable, whereas when they are not properly accounted for, environmental devastation tends to take place, including, as we will discuss in detail below, deforestation and fisheries collapse.

Nonrenewable Resources

Nonrenewable resources like oil, coal, and metals must be mined or pumped from the ground before they can be used. Oil companies and mining companies specialize in the extraction of nonrenewable resources and attempt to make a profit from extracting and then selling the resources that they mine or pump out of the ground. But because extraction is costly and because the price that they will get on the market for their products is uncertain, profits are not guaranteed and such companies must plan their operations carefully if they hope to realize a profit.

User Costs of Current Use   We must note, however, that because an oil field or a mineral deposit is typically very large and will take many years to fully extract, an extraction company's goal of "maximizing profits" actually involves attempting to choose an extraction strategy that will maximize a *stream* of profits—potential profits today as well as potential profits in the future. There is, of course, a trade-off. If the company extracts more today, its revenues will be larger today since it will have more product to sell today. On the other hand, more extraction today means that less of the resource will be left in the ground for future extraction and, consequently, future revenues will be smaller since future extraction will necessarily be reduced. Indeed, every bit of resource that is extracted and sold today comes at the cost of not being able to extract it and sell it in the future. Natural resource economists refer to this cost as the **user cost** of extraction because the user of a resource always faces the opportunity cost of reduced future extraction when choosing to extract a resource now rather than in the future.

Present Use versus Future Use   The concept of user cost is very helpful in showing how a resource extraction firm that is interested in maximizing its flow of profits over time will choose to behave in terms of how much it will extract in the present as opposed to the future. To give a simple example, consider the case of a coal mining company called Black Rock whose mine will have to shut down in two years, when the company's lease expires. Because the mine will close in two years, the mine's production can be thought of as taking place either during the current year or next year. Black Rock's problem is to figure out how much to mine this year so that it can maximize its stream of profits.

Extraction when Considering Only Current Costs   To see how Black Rock's managers might think about the problem, look at Figure 19.7, which shows the situation facing the company during the first year. Begin by noticing *P*, the market price at which Black Rock can sell each and every ton of coal that it extracts. The firm's managers will obviously want to take this price into consideration when deciding how much output to produce.

Next, consider the company's production costs, which we will refer to as **extraction costs,** or *EC*, since this is an extraction company. The extraction costs include all costs associated with running the mine, digging out the coal, and preparing the coal for sale. Notice that the *EC* curve that represents extraction costs in Figure 19.7 is upward sloping to reflect the fact that the company's marginal extraction costs increase the more the company extracts because faster extraction involves having to rent or buy more equipment and having to either hire more workers or pay overtime to existing workers. Rapid extraction is costly, and the *EC* curve slopes upward to reflect this fact.

Next, consider how much output the firm's managers will choose to produce if they fail to take user cost into account. If the firm's managers ignore user cost, then they will choose to

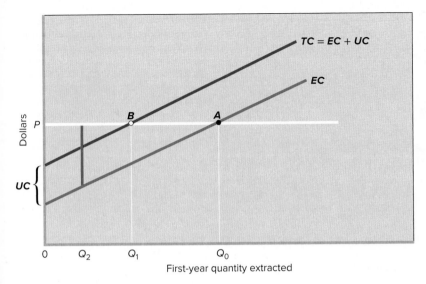

FIGURE 19.7 Choosing the optimal extraction level.
A firm that takes account only of current extraction costs, *EC*, will produce Q_0 units of output in the current period—that is, all units for which the market price *P* exceeds extraction costs, *EC*. If it also takes account of user cost, *UC*, and the fact that current output reduces future output and profits, it will produce only Q_1 units of output—that is, only those units for which price exceeds the sum of extraction costs and user cost.

extract and sell Q_0 tons of coal (shown by where the horizontal *P* line crosses the upward-sloping *EC* line at point *A*). They will do this because for each and every ton of coal that is extracted up to Q_0, the market price at which it can be sold exceeds its extraction cost—making each of those tons of coal profitable to produce.

Extraction when Also Considering User Costs The previous analysis considers only potential first-year profits. None of those tons of coal *has* to be mined this year. Each of them could be left in the ground and mined during the second year. The question that Black Rock's managers have to ask is whether the company's total stream of profits would be increased by leaving some or all of those tons of coal in the ground this year and instead mining and selling them next year.

This question can be answered by taking account of user cost. Specifically, the company's managers can put a dollar amount on how much future profits are reduced by current extraction and then take that dollar amount into account when determining the optimal amount to extract this year. This process is best understood by looking once again at Figure 19.7. There, each ton of coal that is extracted this year is assumed to have a user cost of *UC* dollars per ton that is set equal to the present value of the profits that the firm would earn if the extraction and sale of each ton of coal were delayed until the second year. Taking this user cost into account results in a total cost curve, or *TC*, that is exactly *UC* dollars higher than the extraction cost curve at every extraction level. This parallel upward shift reflects the fact that once the company takes user cost into account, its total costs must be equal to the sum of extraction costs and user cost. That is, $TC = EC + UC$.

If the firm's managers take user cost into account in this fashion, then they will choose to produce less output. In fact, they will choose to extract only Q_1 units of coal (shown by

where the horizontal *P* line crosses the upward-sloping *TC* line at point *B*). They will produce exactly this much coal because for each and every ton of coal that is extracted up to Q_1, the market price at which it can be sold exceeds its total cost—including not only the current extraction cost but also the cost of forgone future profits, *UC*.

Why Delay Is More Profitable for Some Units Another way to understand why Black Rock will limit its production to only Q_1 tons of coal is to realize that for every ton of coal up to Q_1, it is more profitable to extract during the current year than during the second year. This is best seen by looking at a particular ton of coal like Q_2. The profit that the firm can get by extracting Q_2 this year is equal to the difference between Q_2's extraction cost and the market price that it can fetch when it is sold. In terms of the figure, this first-year profit is equal to the length of the vertical red line that runs between the point on the *EC* curve above output level Q_2 and the horizontal *P* line.

Notice that the red line is longer than the vertical distance between the *EC* curve and the *TC* curve. This means that the first-year profit is greater than the present value of the second-year profit because the vertical distance between the *EC* curve and the *TC* curve is equal to *UC*, which is by definition the present value of the amount of profit that the company would get if it delayed producing Q_2 until the second year. It is therefore clear that if the firm wants to maximize its profit, it should produce Q_2 during the first year rather than during the second year since the profit to be made by current production exceeds the present value of the profit to be made by second-year production.

This is not true for the tons of coal between output levels Q_1 and Q_0. For these tons of coal, the first-year profit—which is, as before, equal to the vertical distance between the *EC*

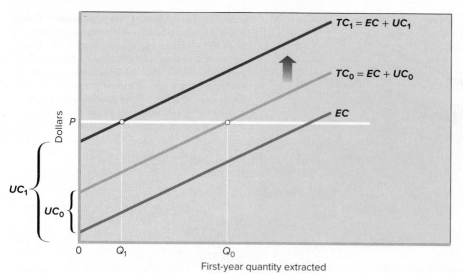

FIGURE 19.8 An increase in expected future profits leads to less current extraction. An increase in future profitability increases user cost from UC_0 to UC_1, thereby raising the total cost curve from TC_0 to TC_1. The firm responds by reducing current production from Q_0 to Q_1 so that it can extract more of the resource in the future and take advantage of the increase in future profitability.

curve and the horizontal P line—is less than UC, the present value of the second-year profit that can be obtained by delaying production until the second year. Consequently, the extraction of these units should be delayed until the second year.

Benefits of Efficient Delay The model presented in Figure 19.7 demonstrates that the goal of profit-maximizing extraction firms is not to simply mine coal or pump oil as fast as possible. Instead, they are interested in extracting resources at whatever rate will maximize their streams of profit over time. This incentive structure is very useful to society because it means that our limited supplies of nonrenewable resources will be conserved for future extraction and use if extraction firms expect that demand (and hence profits) in the future will be higher than they are today. This can be seen in Figure 19.8, where user cost has increased in the current period from UC_0 to UC_1 to reflect an increase in expected future profits. This increase in user cost causes Black Rock's total cost curve to shift up from $TC_0 = EC + UC_0$ to $TC_1 = EC + UC_1$. This shift, in turn, reduces the optimal amount of current extraction from Q_0 tons of coal to only Q_1 tons of coal.

This reduction in the amount of coal currently extracted conserves coal for extraction and use in the future when it will be in higher demand. Indeed, Black Rock's profit motive has caused it to reallocate extraction in a way that serves the interests of its customers and their desire to consume more in the future. Since the supply of this nonrenewable resource is limited, more consumption in the future implies less consumption today and Black Rock has accommodated this constraint by reducing extraction this year in order to increase it next year.

More generally speaking, Black Rock's behavior in this case demonstrates that under the right institutional structure, profit-maximizing firms will extract resources efficiently over time, meaning that each unit will tend to be extracted when the net benefits from extraction are the greatest.

Incomplete Property Rights Lead to Excessive Present Use

We just demonstrated that profit-maximizing extraction companies are very happy to decrease current extraction if they can benefit financially from doing so. In particular, they are willing to reduce current extraction if they have the ability to profit from the future extraction and sale of their product. Indeed, this type of a financial situation gives them the incentive to conserve any and all resources that would be more profitably extracted in the future.

This pleasant result breaks down completely if weak or uncertain property rights do not allow extraction companies to profit from conserving resources for future use. For instance, look back at Figure 19.7 and consider how much Black Rock would produce if it were suddenly told that its lease would expire at the end of this year rather than at the end of next year. This would be the equivalent of having a user cost equal to zero because there would be no way for the company to profit in the future by reducing current extraction. As a result, the firm will take into account only current extraction costs, EC. The result will be that it will extract and sell Q_0 tons of coal, more than the Q_1 tons that it would extract if it could profit from conservation.

Application: Conflict Diamonds

Resources tend to be extracted much too quickly if there is no way to profit from conservation. That certainly is the case with so-called **conflict diamonds,** which are diamonds mined by combatants in war zones in Africa to provide the hard currency that they need to finance their military activities. Most of these civil wars, however, are very unpredictable, so that control of the mines is tenuous, slipping from one army to another depending on the tide of war.

This fluidity has destroyed any incentive to conserve the resource since the only reason a person would reduce current extraction would be if he or she could benefit from that act of conservation by being able to extract more in the future. But because nobody can be sure of controlling a mine for more than a few months, extraction rates are always extremely high, with the only limit being extraction costs.

This behavior is very wasteful of the resource because once the war finally ends and money is needed to rebuild the country, whichever side wins will find precious few diamonds left to help pay for the reconstruction. Unfortunately, the incentive structures created by the uncertainty of war see to it that extraction takes place at far too rapid a pace, making no allowance for the possibility that future use would be better than present use.

QUICK REVIEW 19.3

✓ Because nonrenewable resources are finite, it is very important to allocate their limited supply efficiently between present and future uses.

✓ If resource extraction companies can benefit from both present and future extraction, they will limit current extraction to only those units that are more profitable to extract in the present rather than in the future. This conserves resources for future use.

✓ If resource users have no way of benefiting from the conservation of a resource, they will use too much of it in the present and not save enough of it for future use—even if future use would be more beneficial than present use.

Renewable Resources

LO19.5 Relate how to use property rights to prevent deforestation and species extinction.

We just saw that under the right circumstances, extraction companies have a strong profit incentive to moderate their current extraction rates and conserve nonrenewable resources for future use. A similar incentive can also hold true for companies and individuals dealing with renewable resources like forests and wildlife. If property rights are structured properly, then decision makers will have an incentive to preserve resources and manage them on a sustainable basis, meaning that they will harvest the resources slowly enough that the resources can always replenish themselves.

On the other hand, if proper incentives are not in place, then high and nonsustainable harvest rates can quickly wipe out a renewable resource. Indeed, ecologists and natural resource economists can cite numerous examples of fish and animal populations collapsing because of overfishing and overhunting, as well as rainforests being wiped out because of overlogging. This section discusses the economics of renewable resources as well as policies that promote the sustainable use of renewable resources. To keep things concrete, we provide a quick example of overhunting and then turn our main attention to forests and fisheries.

Elephant Preservation

If a renewable wildlife resource is used too fast, it can become extinct. This was the situation facing elephants in Africa during the 1970s and 1980s when elephant populations in most parts of Africa declined drastically due to the illegal poaching of elephants for their ivory tusks. It was the case, however, that elephant populations in a few countries expanded considerably. The difference resulted from the fact that in certain countries like Botswana and Zimbabwe, property rights over elephants were given to local villagers, thereby giving them a strong financial incentive to preserve their local elephant populations. In particular, local villagers were allowed to keep the money that could be earned by taking foreign tourists on safari to see the elephants in their area as well as the money that could be made by selling hunting rights to foreign sports hunters. This gave them a strong incentive to prevent poaching, and villagers quickly organized very effective patrols to protect and conserve their valuable resource.

By contrast, elephants belonged to the state in other countries, meaning that locals had no personal stake in the long-term survival of their local elephant populations since any elephant tourism money flowed to the state and other outsiders. This created the perverse incentive that the only way for a local to benefit financially from an elephant was by killing it to get its ivory. Indeed, most of the poaching in these countries was done by locals who had been given no way to benefit from the long-term survival of their local elephant populations. As with nonrenewable resources, the inability to benefit from conservation and future use causes people to increase their present use of renewable resources.

Forest Management

Forests provide many benefits including wildlife habitat, erosion prevention, oxygen production, recreation, and, of course, wood. In 2015, just under 10 billion acres, or about 30 percent of the world's land area, was forested and about 766 million acres, or about 34 percent of the United States' land area, was forested. The amount of land covered by forests is, however, growing in some places but declining in others. This fact is apparent in Global Perspective 19.1, which gives the total percentage change over the years 2010 to 2015 in the amount of forest-covered land in 12 selected countries as well as in the entire world.

The Importance of Property Rights Economists believe that the large variation in growth rates seen in Global Perspective 19.1 is largely the result of differences in property

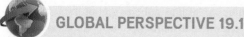

GLOBAL PERSPECTIVE 19.1

Percentage Change in the Amount of Land Covered by Forests, 2010–2015

The percentage change in the amount of land covered by forests varies greatly by nation.

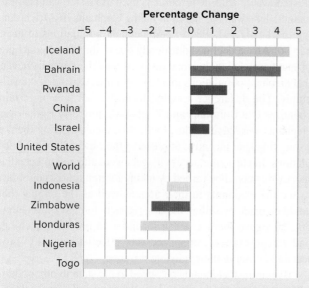

Source: Global Forests Resource Assessment 2015, Food and Agriculture Organization of the United Nations, **www.fao.org**.

rights. In certain areas, including the United States and western Europe, forests are either private property or strictly regulated government property. In either case, individuals or institutions have an incentive to harvest their forests on a sustainable basis because they can benefit not just from cutting down the trees currently alive but also from keeping their forests going to reap the benefits that they will give off in the future if they are managed on a sustainable basis.

By contrast, deforestation is proceeding rapidly in countries where property rights over forests are poorly enforced or nonexistent. To see why this is true, consider the situation facing competing loggers if nobody owns the property rights to a given forest. In such a situation, whoever chops down the forest first will be able to reap economic benefits because, while nobody can have ownership or control over a living tree, anybody can establish a property right to it by chopping it down and bringing it to market. In such a situation, everybody has an incentive to chop down as many trees as fast as they can to secure them before anyone else can. Sadly, nobody has an incentive to preserve trees for future use because—without enforceable property rights—person A has no way to prevent person B from chopping down the trees that person A would like to preserve.

To reduce and hopefully eliminate nonsustainable logging, governments and international agencies have been

taking increasingly strong steps to define and enforce property rights over forests. One major result is that in areas such as the United States and Europe where strong property rights over forests have been established, virtually all wood production is generated by commercially run forestry companies. These companies buy up large tracts of land on which they plant and harvest trees. Whenever a harvest takes place and the trees in a given area are chopped down, seedlings are planted to replace the felled trees, thereby replenishing the stock of trees. These companies are deeply concerned about the long-term sustainability of their operations and many often plant trees in the expectation that more than a century may pass before they are harvested.

Optimal Forest Harvesting In cases where the property rights to a forest are clear and enforceable (as they are in the United States), forest owners have a strong incentive to manage their forests on a sustainable basis because they can reap the long-term benefits that derive from current acts of conservation. A key part of their long-term planning is deciding how often to harvest and then replant their trees.

This is an interesting problem because a commercial forestry company that grows trees for lumber or paper production must take into consideration the fact that trees grow at different rates over the course of their lifetimes. Indeed, Figure 19.9 shows that if the company plants an acre of land with seedlings and lets those seedlings grow into mature trees, the amount of wood contained in the trees at first grows rather slowly as the seedlings slowly grow into saplings, then grows quite quickly as the saplings mature into adult trees, and then tapers off as the adult trees reach their maximum size.

FIGURE 19.9 A forest's growth rate depends on its age. Because trees do not reach their most rapid growth rates until middle age, forestry companies have an incentive not to harvest them too early. But because growth then tapers off as the trees reach their maximum adult sizes, there is an incentive to cut them down before they are fully mature to enable the replanting of the forest with faster-growing young trees.

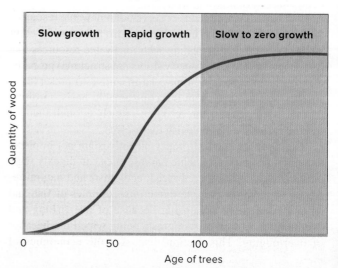

This growth pattern leads forestry companies to think very carefully about when to harvest their trees. If they harvest and replant the acre of land when the trees are only 50 years old, they will miss out on the most rapid years of growth. On the other hand, there is not much point in letting the trees get much more than 100 years old before harvesting and replanting since at that age very little growth is left in them. The result is that the forestry company will choose to harvest the trees and replant the land when the trees reach an age of somewhere between 50 and 100 years old. The precise age will be chosen to maximize firm profits and will be affected not only by the growth rate of trees but also by other factors including the cost of harvesting the trees and, of course, the market price of wood and how it is expected to vary over time.

The key point to keep in mind, however, is that forestry companies that have secure property rights over their trees do not harvest them as soon as possible. Instead, they shepherd their resource and harvest their trees only when replacing older, slow-growing trees with younger, fast-growing trees finally becomes more profitable. And, of course, it must also be emphasized that forestry companies *replant*. They do this because they know that they can benefit from the seedlings' eventual harvest, even if that is 50 or 100 years in the future. In countries where property rights are not secure, nobody replants after cutting down a forest because there is no way to prevent someone else from cutting down the new trees and stealing the harvest.

Optimal Fisheries Management

A **fishery** is a stock of fish or other marine animals that can be thought of as a logically distinct group. A fishery is typically identified by location and species—for example, Newfoundland cod, Pacific tuna, or Alaskan crab. Table 19.3 lists the top 10 U.S. fisheries in terms of how much their respective catches were worth in 2014.

TABLE 19.3 Top 10 U.S. Fisheries in Dollar Terms, 2014

Fishery	Market Value of Catch
Lobster	$566,563,000
Gulf shrimp	565,132,000
Sea scallop	424,448,000
Walleye pollock	399,884,000
Sockeye salmon	349,457,000
Oysters	240,301,000
Dungeness crab	209,508,000
Blue crab	205,705,000
Pacific cod	153,724,000
Opilio snow crab	115,366,000

Source: Fisheries of the United States, 2014, National Marine Fisheries Service Office of Science and Technology, **http://www.st.nmfs.noaa.gov/Assets/ commercial/fus/fus14/documents/FUS2014.pdf**.

The key difficulty with fishery management is that the only way to establish property rights over a fish swimming in the open ocean is to catch it and kill it. As long as the fish is alive and swimming in the open ocean, it belongs to nobody. But as soon as it is caught, it belongs to the person who catches it. This property rights system means that the only way to benefit economically from a fish is to catch it and thereby turn it into a private good.

This creates an incentive for fishers to be very aggressive and try to outfish each other, since the only way for them to benefit from a particular fish is to catch it before someone else does. The calamitous result of this perverse incentive has been tremendous overfishing, which has caused many fisheries to collapse and which threatens many others with collapse as well.

Two examples of fishery collapse are presented in Figure 19.10, which shows the number of metric tons per year

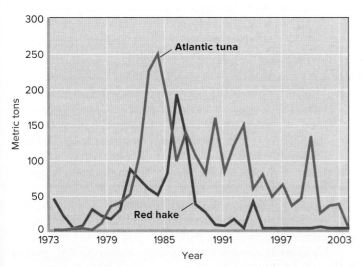

FIGURE 19.10 The collapse of two fisheries, 1973–2004. This figure shows how many metric tons of Atlantic tuna and Maine red hake were caught by U.S. fishing boats each year from 1973 to 2004. Overfishing has caused the population of both species to collapse, Maine red hake very abruptly and Atlantic tuna more slowly.

Source: National Marine Fisheries Service, National Oceanic and Atmospheric Administration, **www.nmfs.noaa.gov**.

of Maine red hake and Atlantic tuna that were caught between 1973 and 2004 by U.S. fishers. A **fishery collapse** happens when a fishery's population is sent into a rapid decline because fish are being harvested faster than they can reproduce. The speed of the decline depends on how much faster harvesting is than reproduction. In the case of Maine red hake, the decline was very abrupt, with the annual catch falling from 190.3 million metric tons in 1986 down to only 4.1 million tons 5 years later. After making a minor resurgence in 1994, the fishery then totally collapsed, so that the catch was less than 1 ton per year for most of the following decade despite the best efforts of fishers to catch more. The collapse of the Atlantic tuna fishery was more gradual, presumably because the ratio of harvest to reproduction was not as extreme as it was for Maine red hake. But even when harvesting exceeds reproduction by only a small amount in a given year, the population declines. And if that pattern holds for many years, the population will be forced into collapse. This was the case for Atlantic tuna. Its annual catch collapsed more gradually, from a peak of 248.9 million metric tons in 1984 down to only 4.1 million metric tons in 2004.

Overfishing and fishery collapse are now extremely common, so much so that worldwide stocks of large predatory fish like tuna, halibut, swordfish, and cod are believed to be 90 percent smaller than they were just 50 years ago. In addition, Table 19.4 shows that just 10 percent of world fisheries in 2014 were estimated to be underexploited, whereas just over 60 percent were categorized as fully exploited, and roughly 30 percent were categorized as overexploited, meaning they were either depleted or (hopefully) recovering from depletion.

Policies to Limit Catch Sizes

Governments have tried several different polices to limit the number of fish that are caught each year to prevent fisheries from collapsing. They also hope to lower annual catch sizes down to sustainable levels, where the size of the catch does not exceed the fishery's ability to regenerate. Unfortunately, many of these policies not only fail to reduce catch sizes but also create perverse incentives that raise fishing costs because they do not stop the fishing free-for-all in which each fisher tries to catch as many fish as possible as fast as possible before anyone else can get to them.

Shortening the Length of Fishing Seasons For example, some policies attempt to reduce catch sizes by limiting the number of days per year that a certain species can be caught. For instance, the duration of the legal crabbing season in Alaska was once cut down from several months to just 4 days. Unfortunately, this policy failed to reduce catch sizes because crabbers compensated for the short legal crabbing season by buying massive boats that could harvest in 4 days the same amount of crab that they had previously needed months to gather.

Fishers bought the new, massive boats because while the new policy limited the number of days over which crabbers were allowed to compete, it did not lessen their incentive to try to catch as many crabs as possible before anyone else could get to them. Indeed, the massive new boats were a sort of arms race, with each fisher trying to buy a bigger, faster, more powerful boat than his competitors to be able to capture more of the available crabs during the limited 4-day season. The result, however, was a stalemate because if everybody is buying bigger, faster, more powerful boats, then nobody gains an advantage. Consequently, the policy actually made the situation worse. Not only did it fail to reduce catch size; it also drove up fishing costs. This was an especially pernicious result because the policy had been designed to help fishers by preserving the resource upon which their livelihoods depended.

Limiting the Number of Boats Another failed policy attempted to limit catch size by limiting the number of fishing boats allowed to fish in a specific area. This policy failed because fishers compensated for the limit on the number of boats by operating bigger boats. That is, many small boats that could each catch only a few tons of fish were replaced by a few large boats that could each catch many tons of fish. Once again, catch sizes did not fall.

Limiting the Total Catch A policy that does work to reduce catch size goes by the acronym **TAC,** which stands for **total allowable catch.** Under this system, biologists determine the TAC for a given fishery, for instance, 100,000 tons per year. Fishers can then fish until a total of 100,000 tons have been brought to shore. At that point, fishing is halted for the year.

This policy has the benefit of actually limiting the size of the catch to sustainable levels. But it still encourages an arms race between the fishers because each fisher wants to try to catch as many fish as possible before the TAC limit is reached. The result is that even under a TAC, fishing costs

TABLE 19.4 Status of World's Fisheries in 2014

Status	Percentage
Nonfully exploited	10%
Fully exploited	61
Overexploited	29

Source: Seafish Summary, State of World Fisheries and Aquaculture (SOFIA) 2014, Seafish, www.seafish.org.

CONSIDER THIS . . .

© Digital Vision/PunchStock

The Tragedy of the Commons

In an article titled "The Tragedy of the Commons," ecologist Garret Hardin explained the crucial role that individual property rights play in resource preservation.

Hardin discussed the public plots of grazing land that were set aside in many villages in medieval Europe. These plots were called commons, after the fact that they were held in common and could be used by anyone. They were a form of welfare designed to help poor people graze and feed animals even if they couldn't afford any land of their own.

Hardin pointed out that this welfare system often failed due to a lack of individual property rights. In particular, the commons were overrun, overgrazed, and turned into barren patches of dirt because they were "first come, first served." The fact that anybody could use the commons meant that nobody had an individual incentive to try to preserve an existing patch of grass. That was because any grass that one person chose to preserve would just end up being eaten by somebody else's animals. So if a person saw any uneaten grass, his best strategy was to let his animals devour it before somebody else's animals did.

As soon as Hardin published his article, people realized that similar **tragedy of the commons** situations were prone to occur wherever individual property rights were lacking. Consider overfishing and deforestation. They both occur because a lack of individual property rights means that each user is incentivized to use as much as possible, as quickly as possible, before anyone else can get to the resource.

rise because fishers buy bigger, faster boats as each one tries to fulfill as much of the overall TAC catch limit as possible.

Assigning Individual Transferable Quotas The catch-limiting system that economists prefer not only limits the total catch size but also eliminates the arms race between fishers that drives up costs. The system is based on the issuance of **individual transferable quotas,** or **ITQs,** which are individual catch size limits that specify that the holder of an ITQ has the right to harvest a given quantity of a particular species during a given time period, for instance, 1,000 tons of Alaskan king crab during the year 2017.

The individual catch sizes of all the ITQs that are issued for a given fishery during a specific year add up to the fishery's overall TAC for the year so that they put a sustainable limit on the overall catch size. This preserves the fishery from overexploitation. But the fact that the ITQ quotas are *individual* also eliminates the need for an arms race. Because each fisherman knows that he can take as long as he wants to catch his individual quota, he does not need a superexpensive, technologically sophisticated boat that is capable of hauling in massive amounts of fish in only a few days in order to beat his competitors to the punch. Instead, he can use smaller, less expensive, and simpler boats since he knows that he can fish slowly—perhaps year round if it suits him.

Efficiency Gains This move toward smaller boats and more leisurely fishing greatly reduces fishing costs. But ITQs offer one more cost-saving benefit. They encourage all of the fishing to be done by the lowest-cost, most-efficient fishing vessels. This is true because ITQs are *tradable* fishing quotas, meaning that they can be sold and thereby traded to other fishers. As we will explain, market pressures will cause them to be sold to the fishers who can catch fish most efficiently, at the lowest possible cost.

To see how this works, imagine a situation in which the market price of tuna is $10 per ton but in which a fisherman named Sven can barely make a profit because his old, slow boat is so expensive that it costs him $9 per ton to catch tuna. At that cost, if he does his own fishing and uses his ITQ quota of 1,000 tons himself, he will make a profit of only $1,000 (= $1 per ton × 1,000 tons). At the same time, one of his neighbors, Tammy, has just bought a new, superefficient ship that can harvest fish at the very low cost of $6 per ton. This difference in costs means that Sven and Tammy will both find it advantageous to negotiate the sale of Sven's ITQ to Tammy. Sven, for his part, would be happy to accept any price higher than $1,000 since $1,000 is the most that he can make if he does his own fishing. Suppose that they agree on a price of $2 per ton, or $2,000 total. In such a case, both are better off. Sven is happy because he gets $2,000 rather than the $1,000 that he would have earned if he had done his own fishing. And Tammy is happy because she is about to make a tidy profit. The 1,000 tons of tuna that she can catch with Sven's ITQ will bring $10,000 in revenues when they are sold at $10 per ton, while her costs of bringing in that catch will be only $8,000 since it costs $6,000 in fishing costs at $6 per ton to bring in the catch plus the $2,000 that she pays to Sven for the right to use his 1,000-ton ITQ.

Social Benefits Notice, though, that society also benefits. If Sven had used his ITQ himself, he would have run up fishing costs of $9,000 harvesting the 1,000 tons of tuna that his quota allows. But because the permit was sold to

Is Economic Growth Bad for the Environment?

Measures of Environmental Quality Are Higher in Richer Countries.

Many people are deeply concerned that environmental degradation is an inevitable consequence of economic growth. Their concern is lent credence by sensational media events like oil and chemical spills and by the indisputable fact that modern chemistry and industry have created and released into the environment many toxic chemicals and substances that human beings did not even know how to make a couple of centuries ago.

Economists, however, tend to be rather positive about economic growth and its consequences for the environment. They feel this way because significant evidence indicates that richer societies spend much more money on keeping their respective environments healthy than do poorer societies. Viewed from this perspective, economic growth and rising living standards are good for the environment because as societies get richer, they tend to spend more on things like reducing emissions from smokestacks, preventing the dumping of toxic chemicals, and insisting that sewage be purified before its water is returned to the environment. They also tend to institute better protections for sensitive ecosystems and engage in greater amounts of habitat preservation for endangered species.

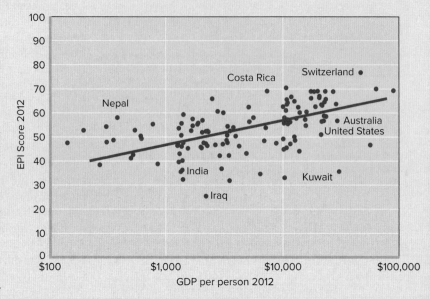

But are these increasing expenditures on environmentally beneficial goods and services enough to overcome the massive increases in environmental harm that seem likely to accompany the enormous amounts of production and consumption in which rich societies engage? The empirical record suggests that the answer is yes. The best evidence for this is given by the accompanying

Tammy, only $6,000 in fishing costs are actually incurred. The tradable nature of ITQs promotes overall economic efficiency by creating an incentive structure that tends to move production toward the producers who have the lowest production costs.

It remains to be seen, however, if ITQs and other catch-reduction policies will be enough to save the world's fisheries. Since current international law allows countries to enforce ITQs and other conservation measures only within 200 miles of their shores, most of the world's oceans are a fishing free-for-all. Unless this changes and incentive structures are put in place to limit catch sizes in international waters, economic theory suggests that the fisheries there will continue to decline as fishers compete to catch as many fish as possible as fast as possible before anyone else can get to them.

> ### QUICK REVIEW 19.4
>
> ✓ When property rights are absent, renewable resources tend to be depleted quickly because users have no way of benefiting from conservation.
>
> ✓ Governments that establish and enforce property rights over renewable resources encourage conservation by allowing users to benefit financially from future harvesting as well as present harvesting.
>
> ✓ Total allowable catch limits (TAQs) combined with individual transferrable quotas (ITQs) promote the preservation and efficient harvesting of fisheries. The TAQs preserve fisheries by capping total harvest sizes. The ITQs promote efficiency by providing financial incentives that encourage all the fishing to be done by the most efficient fishers.

figure, in which each of 125 countries is represented by a point that indicates both its GDP per capita (measured on the horizontal axis using a logarithmic scale) and its year 2012 score on the Environmental Performance Index, or EPI.

This index, produced by researchers at Yale University, compares countries based on how well they are doing in terms of 25 environmental indicators, including atmospheric carbon emissions, measures of air and water quality, the degree of wilderness protection, energy efficiency, and measures of whether a country's fisheries and forests are being overexploited. Out of a maximum possible EPI score of 100, Switzerland and Latvia received the highest scores of, respectively, 76.69 and 70.37. The United States was ranked 49th with a score of 56.59 while the lowest-ranked country, Iraq, received a score of 25.32.

When EPI scores are combined with measures of GDP per person in the figure, an extremely strong pattern emerges: Richer countries have higher EPI scores. In fact, the relationship between the two variables is so strong that 70 percent of the differences between countries in terms of EPI scores are explained by their differences in GDP per person. In addition, the logarithmic scale used on the horizontal axis allows us to look at the best-fit line drawn through the data and conclude that a 10-fold increase in

Source: © PhotoLink/Getty Images RF

GDP per capita (from, for instance, $1,000 to $10,000) is associated with a 10-point increase in EPI. The figure is therefore clear confirmation not only that economic growth can go together with a healthy environment, but that economic growth actually promotes a healthy environment by making people rich enough to pay for pollution-reduction technologies that people living in poorer countries cannot afford.

Looking to the future, many economists are hopeful that economic growth and rising living standards will pay for the invention and implementation of new technologies that could make for an even cleaner environment. If the current pattern continues to hold, increased standards of living will lead to better environmental outcomes.

Note: The horizontal axis within the graph is measured using a logarithmic scale, so that each successive horizontal unit represents a 10-fold increase in GDP per person. This is useful because it happens to be the case that the relationship between EPI and GDP per person is such that a 10-fold increase in GDP per person is associated with a 20-point increase in EPI. Graphing the data using a logarithmic scale makes this relationship obvious.

Sources: The EPI data as well as the purchasing-power-parity-adjusted per-person GDP data are from the Yale Center for Environmental Law and Policy (YCELP) and Center for International Earth Science Information Network (CIESIN), **epi.yale.edu.**

SUMMARY

LO19.1 Explain why falling birthrates mean that we are not likely to run out of natural resources.

Per capita living standards in the United States are at least 12 times higher than they were in 1800. This increase in living standards has entailed using much larger amounts of resources to produce the much larger amounts of goods and services that are currently consumed. The increase in resource use can be attributed to two factors. First, there has been a large increase in resource use per person. Second, there are now many more people alive and consuming resources than at any previous time.

The large increase in total resource use has led to a spirited debate about whether our high and rising living standards are sustainable. In particular, will our demand for resources soon outstrip the supply of resources? A proper answer to this question involves examining the demand for resources as well as the supply of resources.

A good way to examine the demand for resources is to think of total resource demand as being the product of the amount of resources used per person times the number of people alive. Thomas Malthus famously predicted that higher living standards would tend to lead to higher birthrates. The opposite, however, has held true. Higher living standards have led to lower birthrates and the majority of the world's population now lives in countries where the total fertility rate is less than the replacement rate of 2.1 births per woman per lifetime necessary to keep a country's population stable over time.

The result is that world population growth is not only slowing but is actually turning negative in many countries. What is more, the effect of low birthrates is so strong that many demographers believe that the world's population will reach a maximum of fewer than 9 billion people in the next 50 years before beginning to decline quite rapidly. That implies substantially reduced resource demand.

The evidence from the United States and other rich countries is that resource use per person has either fallen or leveled off during the past several decades. For instance, per capita water use in the United States fell 42 percent between 1975 and 2010. Per capita energy use has declined since the late 1980s. And because the per capita generation of trash has been stable since 1990, we can infer that the per capita use of solid objects like metals, paper, and plastics has been stable since that time as well.

Combined with the expected decline in population levels, the fact that per capita resource use has either fallen or leveled off implies that the total demand for resources is likely to reach a peak in the next 50 years before falling over time as populations decline.

Natural resource economists predict that resource supplies are likely to grow faster than resource demands in the future. This confidence is based on the fact that since 1850 the real (inflation-adjusted) prices of resources have fallen by about 50 percent. Because this decline in prices happened at the same time that total resource use was increasing dramatically, it seems likely that resource supplies will continue to grow faster than resource demands since, going forward, resource use should grow less quickly than it has in the past because population growth has slowed (and is expected to turn negative) and because per capita resource use in recent decades has leveled off or turned negative.

LO19.2 Describe why using a mix of energy sources is efficient, even if some of them are quite costly.

Living standards can continue to rise without consuming more energy thanks to more efficient productive technologies, which can produce more output using the same amount of energy input. Indeed, real GDP per person in the United States increased by nearly 80 percent between 1990 and 2014 despite the fact that annual per capita energy consumption fell 9 percent during those years.

Differences in fixed costs mean that a wide variety of energy sources are used in the economy despite the fact that some of these energy sources are much more costly than others. For instance, coal-fired electric generating plants use low-cost coal, but are extremely expensive to build so that they are used only in situations where very large generating capacities are required. By contrast, when smaller amounts of electricity are required, it often makes more sense to employ other generating technologies such as natural gas even though they use more expensive fuel.

LO19.3 Discuss why running out of oil would not mean running out of energy.

We are not running out of energy. Even if we run out of oil, there are plenty of other energy sources including biodiesel, ethanol made from corn or sugar cane, and oil made from organic waste products. The only question is cost.

LO19.4 Show how the profit motive can encourage resource conservation.

Renewable natural resources like forests and fisheries as well as nonrenewable natural resources like oil and coal tend to be overused in the present unless there are institutions created that provide resource users with a way to benefit from conservation. Governments can ensure this benefit by strictly defining and enforcing property rights so that users know that if they conserve a resource today, they will be able to use it or sell it in the future.

LO19.5 Relate how to use property rights to prevent deforestation and species extinction.

Encouraging conservation is especially difficult in the open ocean where it is impossible to either define or enforce property rights over fish because, by international law, nobody owns the open ocean and so anyone can fish there as much as he or she wants. This lack of property rights leads to severe overfishing and an eventual collapse of the fishery.

Closer to shore, however, governments can define property rights within their sovereign waters and impose limits on fishing. The best system involves combining total allowable catch (TAC) limits for a given fishery with individual transferable quotas (ITQs) for individual fishers.

TERMS AND CONCEPTS

replacement rate	renewable natural resources	fishery
total fertility rate	nonrenewable natural resources	fishery collapse
demographers	present value	total allowable catch (TAC)
demographic transition	user cost	tragedy of the commons
British thermal unit (BTU)	extraction cost	individual transferable quotas (ITQs)
net benefits	conflict diamonds	

The following and additional problems can be found in ▤ connect

DISCUSSION QUESTIONS

1. Describe Thomas Malthus's theory of human reproduction. Does it make sense for some species—say, bacteria or rabbits? What do you think makes humans different? **LO19.1**

2. Demographers have been surprised that total fertility rates have fallen below 2.0, especially because most people in most countries tell pollsters that they would like to have at least two

children. Can you think of any possible economic factors that may be causing women in so many countries to average fewer than two children per lifetime? What about other social or political changes? LO19.1

3. Resource consumption per person in the United States is either flat or falling, depending on the resource. Yet living standards are rising because of technological improvements that allow more output to be produced for every unit of input used in production. What does this say about the likelihood of our running out of resources? Could we possibly maintain or improve our living standards even if the population were expected to rise in the future rather than fall? LO19.1

4. A community has a nighttime energy demand of 50 megawatts but a peak daytime demand of 75 megawatts. It has the chance to build a 90-megawatt coal-fired plant that could easily supply all of its energy needs even at peak daytime demand. Should it necessarily proceed? Could there be lower-cost options? Explain. LO19.2

5. Suppose that you hear two people arguing about energy. One says that we are running out of energy. The other counters that we are running out of cheap energy. Explain which person is correct and why. LO19.3

6. Recall the model of nonrenewable resource extraction presented in Figure 19.7. Suppose that a technological breakthrough means that extraction costs will fall in the future (but not in the present). What will this do to future profits and, therefore, to current user cost? Will current extraction increase or decrease? Compare this to a situation where future extraction costs remain unchanged but current extraction costs fall. In this situation, does current extraction increase or decrease? Does the firm's behavior make sense in both situations? That is, does its response to the changes in production costs in each case maximize the firm's stream of profits over time? LO19.4

7. If the current market price rises, does current extraction increase or decrease? What if the future market price rises? Do these changes in current extraction help to ensure that the resource is extracted and used when it is most valuable? LO19.4

8. ADVANCED ANALYSIS Suppose that a government wants to reduce its economy's dependence on coal and decides as a result to tax coal mining companies $1 per ton for every ton of coal that they mine. Assuming that coal mining companies treat this tax as an increase in extraction costs this year, what effect will the tax have on current extraction in the model used in Figure 19.7? Now, think one step ahead. Suppose that the tax will be in place forever, so that it will also affect extraction costs in the future. Will the tax increase or decrease user cost? Does this effect increase or decrease the change in current extraction caused by the shift of the EC curve? Given your finding, should environmental taxes be temporary? LO19.4

9. ADVANCED ANALYSIS User cost is equal to the present value of future profits in the model presented in Figure 19.7. Will the optimal quantity to mine in the present year increase or decrease if the market rate of interest rises? Does your result make any intuitive sense? (Hint: If interest rates are up, would you want to have more or less money right now to invest at the market rate of interest?) LO19.4

10. Various cultures have come up with their own methods to limit catch size and prevent fishery collapse. In old Hawaii, certain fishing grounds near shore could be used only by certain individuals. And among lobstermen in Maine, strict territorial rights are handed out so that only certain people can harvest lobsters in certain waters. Discuss specifically how these systems provide incentives for conservation. Then think about the enforcement of these property rights. Do you think similar systems could be successfully enforced for deep-sea fishing, far off shore? LO19.5

11. Aquaculture is the growing of fish, shrimp, and other seafood in enclosed cages or ponds. The cages and ponds not only keep the seafood from swimming away but also provide aquaculturists with strong property rights over their animals. Does this provide a good incentive for low-cost production as compared with fishing in the open seas where there are few if any property rights? LO19.5

12. LAST WORD The figure in the Last Word section shows that a 10-fold increase in a country's GDP per person is associated with about a 20-point increase in EPI. On the other hand, GDP per person was $48,112 in the United States in 2011 but $36,254 in New Zealand; yet New Zealand had an EPI score of 66.05, while the United States had an EPI score of only 56.59. So does getting rich guarantee doing well environmentally? Discuss.

REVIEW QUESTIONS

1. The long-run downward trend in commodity prices is consistent with the idea that: LO19.1
   a. We are quickly running out of resources.
   b. Resource demands have been increasing faster than resource supplies.
   c. Birthrates will soon increase due to the falling cost of living.
   d. Resource supplies have increased faster than resource demands.

2. It would cost the town of Irondale $50 million to build a gas-powered generator that could produce a maximum of 5 megawatts of electricity at 15 cents per hour. Another alternative would be for Irondale to build a $100 million coal-fired generator that could produce a maximum of 15 megawatts of electricity at 5 cents per hour. Irondale should: LO19.2
   a. Build the coal-fired generator because its hourly operating costs are so much lower.
   b. Build the gas-powered generator since it is less expensive to build.
   c. Build the coal-fired generator because, while it would cost twice as much to build, it would produce three times as much electricity.
   d. Obtain more information before deciding what to do.

3. After mining 9,273 tons of coal, Blue Sky Mining's managers note that the marginal cost of mining the next ton of coal would be $40 per ton. They also calculate that the user cost of mining

that next ton of coal would be $35. If the market price of coal is $72, should Blue Sky mine an additional ton of coal? **LO19.4**
   a. Yes.
   b. No.
   c. More information is needed.

4. Good methods for helping to protect natural resources include: **LO19.5**
   a. Establishing property rights and giving them to local users.
   b. Encouraging first-come, first-served property rights.
   c. Teaching people to consider user cost.
   d. Having the government set up and enforce ITQs.

5. Ingvar and Olaf are the only two fishermen in their area. Each has been assigned an ITQ that allows him to catch 20 tons of salmon. Ingvar's MC of catching salmon is $6 per ton while Olaf's MC of catching salmon is $7 per ton. If the price of salmon is $10 per ton, then to maximize efficiency, the two guys should trade ITQs until Ingvar is in charge of catching _____ tons while Olaf catches _____ tons. **LO19.5**
   a. 20; 20.
   b. 30; 10.
   c. 40; 0.
   d. 0; 40.

PROBLEMS

1. Suppose that the current (first) generation consists of 1 million people, half of whom are women. If the total fertility rate is 1.3 and the only way people die is of old age, how big will the fourth generation (the great-grandchildren) be? How much smaller (in percentage terms) is each generation than the previous generation? How much smaller (in percentage terms) is the fourth generation than the first generation? Are you surprised by how quickly the population declines? **LO19.1**

2. A coal-fired power plant can produce electricity at a variable cost of 4 cents per kilowatt hour when running at its full capacity of 30 megawatts per hour, 16 cents per kilowatt hour when running at 20 megawatts per hour, and 24 cents per kilowatt hour when running at 10 megawatts per hour. A gas-fired power plant can produce electricity at a variable cost of 12 cents per kilowatt-hour at any capacity from 1 megawatt per hour to its full capacity of 5 megawatts per hour. The cost of constructing a coal-fired plant is $50 million, but it costs only $10 million to build a gas-fired plant. **LO19.2**
   a. Consider a city that has a peak afternoon demand of 80 megawatts of electricity. If it wants all plants to operate at full capacity, what combination of coal-fired plants and gas-fired plants would minimize construction costs?
   b. How much will the city spend on building that combination of plants?
   c. What will the average cost per kilowatt-hour be if you average over all 80 megawatts that are produced by that combination of plants? (Hint: A kilowatt is one thousand watts, while a megawatt is one million watts.)
   d. What would the average cost per kilowatt-hour be if the city had instead built three coal-fired plants?

3. Suppose that Sea Shell oil company (SS) is pumping oil at a field off the coast of Nigeria. At this site, it has an extraction cost of $30 per barrel for the first 10 million barrels it pumps each year and then $60 per barrel for all subsequent barrels that it pumps each year, up to the site's maximum capacity of 90 million barrels per year. **LO19.4**
   a. Suppose the user cost is $50 per barrel for all barrels and that the current market price for oil is $90 per barrel. How many barrels will SS pump this year? What is the total accounting profit on the total amount of oil it pumps? What is the total economic profit on those barrels of oil?

   b. What if the current market price for oil rises to $120 per barrel, while the user cost remains at $50 per barrel? How many barrels will SS pump and what will be its accounting profit and its economic profit?
   c. If the current market price remains at $120 per barrel but the user cost rises to $95 per barrel, how many barrels will SS pump this year and what will be its accounting profit and its economic profit?

4. Eric and Kyle are fishermen with different equipment and, as a result, different costs for catching fish. Eric's costs for catching fish are $1,000 per ton for the first five tons and then $2,500 per ton for any additional tons. Kyle can harvest fish at a cost of $3,000 for the first 15 tons and then $1,400 for any additional tons. **LO19.5**
   a. If society wants 30 tons of fish and for some reason will only allow one of the two guys to do all the fishing, which one should society choose if it wants to minimize the cost of catching those 30 tons of fish? How much will the total cost of catching the fish be? What will the average cost per ton be for the 30 tons?
   b. If society wants 30 tons of fish and wants them for the least cost regardless of who catches them, how much should Eric and Kyle each catch? How much will the total cost of catching 30 tons be? What will the average cost per ton be for the 30 tons?
   c. Suppose that Eric and Kyle can both sell whatever amount of fish they catch for $3,000 per ton. Also suppose that Eric is initially given ITQs for 30 tons of fish, while Kyle is given ITQs for zero tons of fish. Suppose that Kyle is willing to pay Eric $550 per ton for as many tons of ITQs as Eric is willing to sell to Kyle. How much profit would Eric make if he used all the ITQs himself? What if Eric sold 25 tons' worth of his ITQs to Kyle while using the other 5 tons of ITQs to fish for himself?
   d. What price per ton can Kyle offer to pay Eric for his 25 tons of ITQs such that Eric would make exactly as much money from that deal (in which he sells 25 tons' worth of ITQs to Kyle while using the rest to fish for himself) as he would by using all 30 tons of ITQs for himself?

Public Finance: Expenditures and Taxes

Learning Objectives

LO20.1 Use a circular flow diagram to illustrate how the allocation of resources is affected by government's revenue and expenditure decisions.

LO20.2 Identify the main categories of government spending and the main sources of government revenue.

LO20.3 List the main categories of federal revenue and spending and describe the difference between marginal and average tax rates.

LO20.4 List the main categories of state and local revenue and spending.

LO20.5 Discuss the magnitude and distribution across job categories of government employment at the local, state, and federal levels.

LO20.6 Summarize the different philosophies regarding the distribution of a nation's tax burden.

LO20.7 Explain the principles relating to tax shifting, tax incidence, and the efficiency losses caused by taxes.

LO20.8 Discuss the probable incidence of U.S. taxes and how the distribution of income between rich and poor is affected by government taxes, transfers, and spending.

As discussed in Chapter 2, the U.S. economy relies heavily on the private sector (households and businesses) and the market system to decide what gets produced, how it gets produced, and who gets the output. But the private sector is not the only entity in the decision process. The public sector (federal, state, and local government) also affects these economic decisions.

Government influences what gets produced and how it gets produced through laws that regulate the activities of private firms and also by directly producing certain goods and services, such as national defense and education. As discussed in Chapter 4, many of these government-produced goods and services are *public goods* that the private sector has trouble producing because of free-rider problems. Also, government influences who receives society's output of goods and services through various taxes and through welfare and income-transfer payments that redistribute income from the rich to the poor.

Government-provided goods, services, and transfer payments are funded by taxes, borrowing, and *proprietary income*—the income that governments receive from running government-owned enterprises such as hospitals, utilities, toll roads, and lotteries.

Public finance is the subdiscipline of economics that studies the various ways in which governments raise and expend money. In this chapter we view the economy through the lens of public finance. Our main goal is to understand how taxes and income transfers not only pay for government-produced goods and services but also affect the distribution of income between rich and poor.

Government and the Circular Flow

LO20.1 Use a circular flow diagram to illustrate how the allocation of resources is affected by government's revenue and expenditure decisions.

In Figure 20.1, we integrate government into the circular flow model first shown in Figure 2.2. Here flows (1) through (4) are the same as the corresponding flows in that figure. Flows (1) and (2) show business expenditures for the resources provided by households. These expenditures are costs to businesses but represent wage, rent, interest, and profit income to households. Flows (3) and (4) show household expenditures for the goods and services produced by businesses.

Now consider what happens when we add government. Flows (5) through (8) illustrate that government makes purchases in both product and resource markets. Flows (5) and (6) represent government purchases of such products as paper, computers, and military hardware from private businesses. Flows (7) and (8) represent government purchases of resources. The federal government employs and pays salaries to members of Congress, the armed forces, Justice Department lawyers, meat inspectors, and so on. State and local governments hire and pay teachers, bus drivers, police, and firefighters. The federal government might also lease or purchase land to expand a military base and a city might buy land on which to build a new elementary school.

Government then provides goods and services to both households and businesses, as shown by flows (9) and (10). Governments rely on three revenue sources to finance those

FIGURE 20.1 Government within the circular flow diagram. Government buys products from the product market and employs resources from the resource market to provide goods and services to households and businesses. Government finances its expenditures through the net taxes (taxes minus transfer payments) it receives from households and businesses.

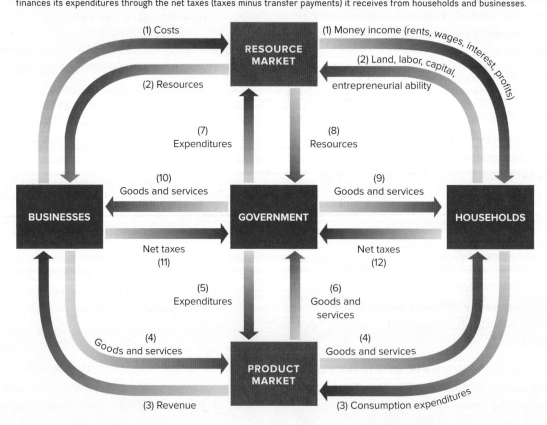

goods and services: taxes, borrowing, and the proprietary income generated by government-run or government-sponsored businesses like public utilities and state lotteries. These revenues flowing from households and businesses to government are included in flows (11) and (12), which are labeled as "net taxes" for two reasons. First, the vast majority of the money raised by these three revenue sources comes from taxes; thus, it is sensible to have these labels refer to taxes. Second, the labels refer to *net* taxes to indicate that they also include "taxes in reverse" in the form of transfer payments to households and subsidies to businesses. Thus, flow (11) entails various subsidies to farmers, shipbuilders, and airlines as well as income, sales, and excise taxes paid by businesses to government. Most subsidies to business are "concealed" in the form of low-interest loans, loan guarantees, tax concessions, or public facilities provided at prices below their cost. Similarly, flow (12) includes not only taxes (personal income taxes, payroll taxes) collected by government from households but also transfer payments made by government to households. These include welfare payments and Social Security benefits.

Government Finance

LO20.2 Identify the main categories of government spending and the main sources of government revenue.

How large is the U.S. public sector? What are the main expenditure categories of federal, state, and local governments? How are these expenditures financed?

Government Purchases and Transfers

We can get an idea of the size of government's economic role by examining government purchases of goods and services and government transfer payments. There is a significant difference between these two kinds of outlays:

- **Government purchases** are *exhaustive;* the products purchased directly absorb (require the use of) resources and are part of the domestic output. For example, the purchase of a missile absorbs the labor of physicists and engineers along with steel, explosives, and a host of other inputs.

- **Transfer payments** are *nonexhaustive;* they do not directly absorb resources or create output. Social Security benefits, welfare payments, veterans' benefits, and unemployment compensation are examples of transfer payments. Their key characteristic is that recipients make no current contribution to domestic output in return for them.

Federal, state, and local governments spent $5,879 billion (roughly $5.9 trillion) in 2015. Of that total, government purchases were $3,204 billion and government transfers were

FIGURE 20.2 Government purchases, transfers, and total spending as percentages of U.S. output, 1960 and 2015. Government purchases have declined as a percentage of U.S. output since 1960. Transfer payments, however, have increased by more than this drop, raising total government spending (purchases plus transfers) from 27 percent of U.S. GDP in 1960 to about 33 percent today.

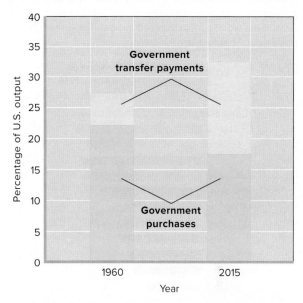

Source: Compiled from Bureau of Economic Analysis data, **www.bea.gov**.

$2,675 billion. Figure 20.2 shows these amounts as percentages of U.S. domestic output for 2015 and compares them to percentages for 1960. Government purchases have declined from about 22 to 18 percent of output since 1960. But transfer payments have tripled as a percentage of output—from 5 percent in 1960 to about 15 percent in 2015. Relative to U.S. output, total government spending is thus higher today than it was 55 years earlier. This means that the tax revenues required to finance government expenditures are also higher. Today, government spending and the tax revenues needed to finance it are about 33 percent of U.S. output.

In 2015, the so-called Tax Freedom Day in the United States was April 24. On that day the average worker had earned enough (from the start of the year) to pay his or her share of the taxes required to finance government spending for the year. Tax Freedom Day arrives even later in several other countries, as indicated in Global Perspective 20.1.

Government Revenues

The funds used to pay for government purchases and transfers come from three sources: taxes, proprietary income, and funds that are borrowed by selling bonds to the public.

Government Borrowing and Deficit Spending The ability to borrow allows a government to spend more in a given time period than it collects in tax revenues and proprietary

GLOBAL PERSPECTIVE 20.1

Total Tax Revenue as a Percentage of Total Output, Selected Nations, 2014*

A nation's "tax burden" is its tax revenue from all levels of government as a percentage of its total output (GDP). Among the world's industrialized nations, the United States has a very moderate tax burden.

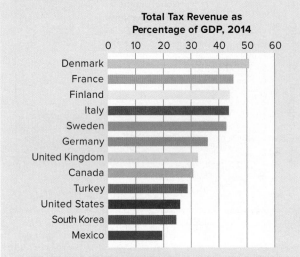

Total Tax Revenue as Percentage of GDP, 2014

(Nations listed top to bottom: Denmark, France, Finland, Italy, Sweden, Germany, United Kingdom, Canada, Turkey, United States, South Korea, Mexico. Horizontal scale 0 to 60.)

*Includes government nontax revenue from fees, charges, fines and sales of government property.

Source: OECD iLibrary, *Taxation: Key Tables from OECD*, **www.oecd-ilibrary.org**, accessed April 26, 2016. Numbers are 2014 estimates.

income during that period. This flexibility is useful during an economic downturn because a government can use borrowed funds to maintain high levels of spending on goods, services, and transfer payments even if tax revenues and proprietary income are falling due to the slowing economy.

Any money borrowed by a government, however, is money that cannot be put to other uses. During an economic downturn, this opportunity cost is likely to be small because any funds that the government does not borrow are likely to sit idle and unused by other parties due to the lack of economic activity during the downturn. But if the government borrows when the economy is doing well, many economists worry that the opportunity cost may be high. In particular, the government's borrowing may "crowd out" private-sector investment. As an example, a billion dollars borrowed and spent by the federal government on roads is a billion dollars that was not lent to private companies to fund the expansion of factories or the development of new technologies.

Government spending that is financed by borrowing is often referred to as *deficit spending* because a government's budget is said to be "in deficit" if the government's spending in a given time period exceeds the money that it collects from taxes and proprietary income during that period.

Federal Finance

LO20.3 List the main categories of federal revenue and spending and describe the difference between marginal and average tax rates.

Now let's look separately at each of the federal, state, and local units of government in the United States and compare their expenditures and taxes. Figure 20.3 tells the story for the federal government.

Federal Expenditures

Four areas of federal spending stand out: (1) pensions and income security, (2) national defense, (3) health, and (4) interest on the public debt. The *pensions and income security* category includes the many income-maintenance programs for the aged, persons with disabilities or handicaps, the unemployed, the retired, and families with no breadwinner. This category—dominated by the $888 billion pension portion of the Social Security program—accounts for 38 percent of total federal expenditures. *National defense* accounts for about 16 percent of the federal budget, underscoring the high cost of military preparedness. *Health* reflects the cost of government health programs for the retired (Medicare) and poor (Medicaid). *Interest on the public debt* accounts for 6 percent of federal spending.

Federal Tax Revenues

The revenue side of Figure 20.3 shows that the personal income tax, payroll taxes, and the corporate income tax are the largest revenue sources, accounting respectively for 47, 33, and 11 cents of each dollar collected.

Personal Income Tax The **personal income tax** is the kingpin of the federal tax system and merits special comment. This tax is levied on *taxable income,* that is, on the

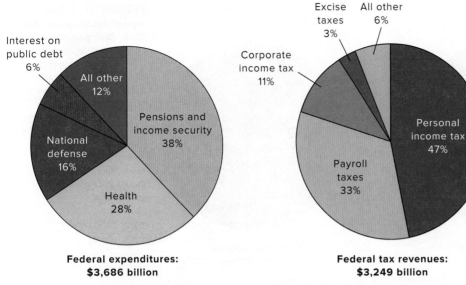

FIGURE 20.3 **Federal expenditures and tax revenues, 2015.** Federal expenditures are dominated by spending for pensions and income security, health, and national defense. A full 80 percent of federal tax revenue is derived from just two sources: the personal income tax and payroll taxes. The $437 billion difference between expenditures and revenues reflects a budget deficit.

Federal expenditures:
$3,686 billion

Federal tax revenues:
$3,249 billion

Source: U.S. Treasury, *Combined Statement of Receipts, Outlays, and Balances, 2015,* **fms.treas.gov**.

incomes of households and unincorporated businesses after certain exemptions ($4,050 for each household member) and deductions (business expenses, charitable contributions, home mortgage interest payments, certain state and local taxes) are taken into account.

The federal personal income tax is a *progressive tax,* meaning that people with higher incomes pay a larger percentage of their incomes as taxes than do people with lower incomes. The progressivity is achieved by applying higher tax rates to successive layers or brackets of income.

Columns 1 and 2 in Table 20.1 show the mechanics of the income tax for a married couple filing a joint return in 2016. Note that a 10 percent tax rate applies to all taxable income up to $18,550 and a 15 percent rate applies to additional income up to $75,300. The rates on additional layers of income then go up to 25, 28, 33, 35, and 39.6 percent.

The tax rates shown in column 2 in Table 20.1 are marginal tax rates. A **marginal tax rate** is the rate at which the tax is paid on each *additional* unit of taxable income. Thus, if a couple's taxable income is $80,000, they will pay the marginal rate of 10 percent on each dollar from $1 to $18,550, 15 percent on each dollar from $18,551 to $75,300, and 25 percent on each dollar from $75,301 to $80,000. You should confirm that their total income tax is $13,398.

The marginal tax rates in column 2 overstate the personal income tax bite because the rising rates in that column apply only to the income within each successive tax bracket. To get a better idea of the tax burden, we must consider average tax rates. The **average tax rate** is the total tax paid divided by total taxable income. The couple in our previous example is in the 25 percent tax bracket because they pay a top marginal tax rate of 25 percent on the highest dollar of their income. But their *average* tax rate is 17 percent (= $13,398/$80,000).

As we will discuss in more detail shortly, a tax whose average rate rises as income increases is said to be a *progressive tax* because it claims both a progressively larger absolute amount of income as well as a progressively larger proportion of income as income rises. Thus we can say that the federal personal income tax is progressive.

Payroll Taxes Social Security contributions are **payroll taxes**—taxes based on wages and salaries—used to finance two compulsory federal programs for retired workers: Social Security (an income-enhancement program) and Medicare (which pays for medical services). Employers and employees pay these taxes equally. In 2016, employees and employers each paid 7.65 percent on the first $118,500

TABLE 20.1 **Federal Personal Income Tax Rates, 2016***

(1) Total Taxable Income	(2) Marginal Tax Rate,%	(3) Total Tax on Highest Income In Bracket	(4) Average Tax Rate on Highest Income in Bracket,% (3) ÷ (1)
$0–$18,550	10	$1,855	10
$18,551–$75,300	15	10,368	14
$75,301–$151,900	25	29,518	19
$151,901–$231,450	28	51,792	22
$231,451–$413,350	33	111,819	27
$413,351–$466,950	35	130,579	28
$466,951 and above	39.6		

*For a married couple filing a joint return.

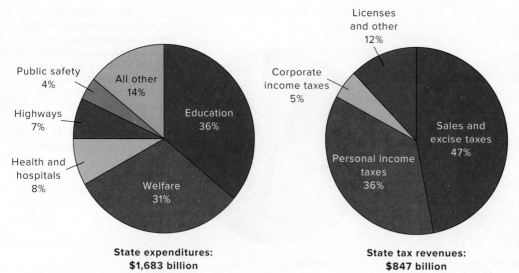

FIGURE 20.4 State expenditures and tax revenues, 2013. State governments spend largely on education and welfare. Their primary source of tax revenue is sales and excise taxes. The deficit between state expenditures and state tax revenues is filled by proprietary income and intergovernmental grants from the federal government. The state expenditures numbers here include state grants to local governments.

State expenditures: $1,683 billion

State tax revenues: $847 billion

Source: U.S. Census Bureau, *2013 Annual Survey of State Government Finances,* **www.census.gov**.

of an employee's annual earnings and 1.45 percent on all additional earnings.

Corporate Income Tax The federal government also taxes corporate income. The **corporate income tax** is levied on a corporation's profit—the difference between its total revenue and its total expenses. For almost all corporations, the tax rate is 35 percent.

Excise Taxes Taxes on commodities or on purchases take the form of **sales** and **excise taxes.** The two differ primarily in terms of coverage. Sales taxes fall on a wide range of products, whereas excises are levied individually on a small, select list of commodities. An additional difference is that sales taxes are calculated as a percentage of the price paid for a product, whereas excise taxes are levied on a per-unit basis—for example, $2 per pack of cigarettes or $0.50 per gallon of gasoline.

As Figure 20.3 suggests, the federal government collects excise taxes of various rates (on the sale of such commodities as alcoholic beverages, tobacco, and gasoline) but does not levy a general sales tax; sales taxes are, however, the primary revenue source of most state governments.

State and Local Finance

LO20.4 List the main categories of state and local revenue and spending.

State and local governments have different mixes of revenues and expenditures than the federal government has.

State Finances

Figure 20.4 shows that the primary source of tax revenue for state governments is sales and excise taxes, which account for about 47 percent of all their tax revenue. State personal income taxes, which have much lower rates than the federal income tax, are the second most important source of state tax revenue. They bring in about 36 percent of total state tax revenue. Corporate income taxes and license fees account for most of the remainder of state tax revenue.

Education expenditures account for about 36 percent of all state spending. State expenditures on public welfare are next in relative weight, at about 31 percent of the total. States also spend heavily on health and hospitals (8 percent), highway maintenance and construction (7 percent), and public safety (4 percent). That leaves about 14 percent of all state spending for a variety of other purposes.

These tax and expenditure percentages combine data from all the states, so they reveal little about the finances of individual states. States vary significantly in the taxes levied. Thus, although personal income taxes are a major source of revenue for all state governments combined, seven states do not levy a personal income tax. Also, there are great variations in the sizes of tax revenues and disbursements among the states, both in the aggregate and as percentages of personal income.

Forty-three states augment their tax revenues with state-run lotteries to help close the gap between their tax receipts and expenditures. Individual states also receive large intergovernmental grants from the federal government. In fact, about 25 percent of their total revenue is in that form. States also take in revenue from miscellaneous sources such as state-owned utilities and liquor stores.

Local Finances

The local levels of government include counties, municipalities, townships, and school districts as well as cities and towns. Figure 20.5 shows that local governments obtain about 73 percent

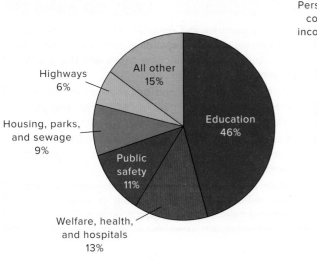

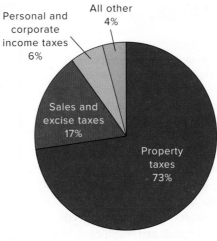

FIGURE 20.5 Local expenditures and tax revenues, 2013. The expenditures of local governments go largely to education, while a large majority of local tax collections are obtained via property taxes. The large deficit between local expenditures and local tax revenues is filled by proprietary income and federal and state intergovernmental grants.

Local expenditures:
$1,445 billion

Local tax revenues:
$608 billion

Source: U.S. Census Bureau, *2013 Annual Surveys of State and Local Government Finances,* **www.census.gov**.

of their tax revenue from **property taxes.** Sales and excise taxes contribute about 17 percent of all local government tax revenue.

About 46 percent of local government expenditures go to education. Welfare, health, and hospitals (13 percent); public safety (11 percent); housing, parks, and sewerage (9 percent); and streets and highways (6 percent) are also major spending categories.

The tax revenues of local government cover less than one-half of their expenditures. The bulk of the remaining revenue comes from intergovernmental grants from the federal and state governments. Also, local governments receive considerable amounts of proprietary income, for example, revenue from government-owned utilities providing water, electricity, natural gas, and transportation.

CONSIDER THIS . . .

Source: © Mark Steinmetz

State Lotteries: A Good Bet?

State lotteries generated about $64.6 billion in revenue in 2014. Of that amount, $40.3 billion went to prizes and $3.1 billion went to administrative costs. That left $21.2 billion that could be spent by the states as they saw fit.

Though nowadays common, state lotteries are still controversial. Critics argue that (1) it is morally wrong for states to sponsor gambling; (2) lotteries generate compulsive gamblers who impoverish themselves and their families; (3) low-income families spend a larger portion of their incomes on lotteries than do high-income families; (4) as a cash business, lotteries attract criminals and other undesirables; and (5) lotteries send the message that luck and fate—rather than education, hard work, and saving—are the route to wealth.

Defenders contend that (1) lotteries are preferable to taxes because they are voluntary rather than compulsory; (2) they are a relatively painless way to finance government services such as education, medical care, and welfare; and (3) lotteries compete with illegal gambling and are thus socially beneficial in curtailing organized crime.

As a further point for debate, also note that state lotteries are monopolies, with states banning competing private lotteries. The resulting lack of competition allows many states to restrict prizes to only about half the money wagered. These payout rates are substantially lower than the 80–95 percent payout rates typically found in private betting operations such as casinos.

Thus, while lotteries are indeed voluntary, they are overpriced and underprovided relative to what would happen if there were a free market in lotteries. But, then again, a free market in lotteries would eliminate monopoly profits for state lotteries and possibly add government costs for regulation and oversight. Consequently, the alternative of allowing a free market in lottery tickets and then taxing the firms selling lottery tickets would probably net very little additional revenue to support state spending programs.

Local, State, and Federal Employment

LO20.5 Discuss the magnitude and distribution across job categories of government employment at the local, state, and federal levels.

In 2014, U.S. governments (local, state, and federal) employed about 21.9 million workers, or about 14 percent of the U.S. labor force. Figure 20.6 shows the percentages of these government employees assigned to different tasks at both the federal level and the state and local level.

As Figure 20.6 makes clear, the types of jobs done by government workers depend on the level of government. Over half of state and local government employment is focused on education. The next largest sector is hospitals and health care, which accounts for about 8 percent of state and local government employment. Police and corrections make up another 9 percent. Smaller categories like highways, public welfare, and judicial together combine for less than 8 percent of state and local employment. The "other" category includes workers in areas such as parks and recreation, fire fighting, transit, and libraries.

Almost half of federal government jobs are in national defense or the postal service. A further 15 percent of federal government jobs are in hospitals or health care. The natural resources, police, and financial administration categories each account for between 4 and 7 percent of federal employment. The "other" category at the federal level is composed of workers in areas such as justice and law, corrections, air transportation, and social insurance administration.

QUICK REVIEW 20.2

✓ Income security and national defense are the main categories of federal spending; personal income, payroll, and corporate income taxes are the primary sources of federal revenue.

✓ States rely on sales and excise taxes for revenue; their spending is largely for education and public welfare.

✓ Education is the main expenditure for local governments, most of whose revenue comes from property taxes.

✓ State and local employment is dominated by education, while federal employment is dominated by national defense and the postal service.

Apportioning the Tax Burden

LO20.6 Summarize the different philosophies regarding the distribution of a nation's tax burden.

Taxes are the major source of funding for the goods and services provided by government and the wages and salaries paid to government workers. Without taxes, there would be no public schools, no national defense, no public highways, no courts, no police, and no other government-provided public and quasi-public goods. As stated by Supreme Court Justice Oliver Wendell Holmes, "Taxes are the price we pay for civilization."

FIGURE 20.6 Job functions of state and local employees and federal employees, 2014. A majority of state and local workers are employed in education. Federal employment is dominated by the postal service and national defense, which together employ just over half of federal employees.

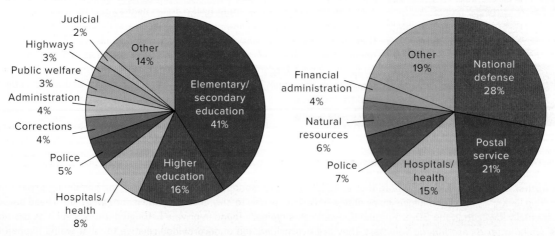

Local and state employees: 19.3 million

Federal employees: 2.7 million

Source: U.S. Census Bureau, *State and Local Government Employment and Payroll Data, by State and Function,* and *Federal Government Employment by Function,* **www.census.gov**.

But taxes are controversial. To begin with, many people would prefer to obtain government goods and services without paying for them. Many others argue that certain taxes cause more harm than good, either by discouraging beneficial economic activity or by unfairly reducing the income flowing to workers and investors. And millions more chafe at the huge variety of taxes that governments levy, including income taxes, Social Security taxes, Medicare taxes, property taxes, sales taxes, liquor taxes, cigarette taxes, cell phone taxes, hotel taxes, gasoline taxes, profit taxes, and estate taxes.

For these and other reasons, people are intently focused on the overall level of taxes, the amount they must personally pay, and the idea of tax fairness (which is often defined in terms of their own circumstances).

The public's attention to taxes has spurred public finance economists to undertake considerable research into the size, distribution, and impact of the total costs that taxes impose on society—the so-called tax burden. Their investigations reveal with reasonable clarity both the size of the tax burden as well as how it is apportioned across the income distribution.

Whether you consider their findings to be good news or bad news, however, depends significantly on your opinion about the fairest way to allocate taxes and the tax burden. So before turning to their findings, let's first discuss some of the major philosophical viewpoints regarding taxation.

Benefits Received versus Ability to Pay

Two basic philosophies coexist on how the economy's tax burden should be apportioned.

Benefits-Received Principle The **benefits-received principle** of taxation asserts that households should purchase the goods and services of government in the same way they buy other commodities. Those who benefit most from government-supplied goods or services should pay the taxes necessary to finance them. A few public goods are now financed on this basis. For example, money collected as gasoline taxes is typically used to finance highway construction and repairs. Thus people who benefit from good roads pay the cost of those roads. Difficulties immediately arise, however, when we consider widespread application of the benefits-received principle:

- How will the government determine the benefits that individual households and businesses receive from national defense, education, the court system, and police and fire protection? Recall from Chapter 4 that public goods are characterized by nonrivalry and nonexcludability. So benefits from public goods are especially widespread and diffuse. Even in the seemingly straightforward case of highway financing it is difficult to measure benefits. Good roads benefit owners of cars in different degrees. But others also

benefit. For example, businesses benefit because good roads bring them workers and customers.

- The benefits-received principle cannot logically be applied to income redistribution programs. It would be absurd and self-defeating to ask poor families to pay the taxes needed to finance their welfare payments. It would also be self-defeating to tax only unemployed workers to finance the unemployment benefits they receive.

Ability-to-Pay Principle The **ability-to-pay principle** of taxation asserts that the tax burden should be apportioned according to taxpayers' income and wealth. In practice, this means that individuals and businesses with larger incomes should pay more taxes in both absolute and relative terms than those with smaller incomes.

In justifying the ability-to-pay principle, proponents contend that each additional dollar of income received by a household yields a smaller amount of satisfaction or marginal utility when it is spent. Because consumers act rationally, the first dollars of income received in any time period will be spent on high-urgency goods that yield the greatest marginal utility. Successive dollars of income will go for less urgently needed goods and finally for trivial goods and services. This means that a dollar taken through taxes from a poor person who has few dollars represents a greater utility sacrifice than a dollar taken through taxes from a rich person who has many dollars. To balance the sacrifices that taxes impose on income receivers, taxes should be apportioned according to the amount of income a taxpayer receives.

This argument is appealing, but application problems arise here too. Although we might agree that the household earning $100,000 per year has a greater ability to pay taxes than a household receiving $10,000, we don't know exactly how much more ability to pay the first family has. Should the wealthier family pay the *same* percentage of its larger income, and hence a larger absolute amount, as taxes? Or should it be made to pay a *larger* percentage of its income as taxes? And how much larger should that percentage be? Who is to decide?

There is no scientific way of making utility comparisons among individuals and thus of measuring someone's relative ability to pay taxes. That is the main problem. In practice, the solution hinges on guesswork, the tax views of the political party in power, expediency, and how urgently the government needs revenue.

Progressive, Proportional, and Regressive Taxes

Any discussion of taxation leads ultimately to the question of tax rates. Taxes are classified as progressive, proportional, or regressive, depending on the relationship between average tax rates and taxpayer incomes. We focus on incomes because all taxes—whether on income, a product, a building, or a parcel of land—are ultimately paid out of someone's income.

- A tax is **progressive** if its average rate increases as income increases. Such a tax claims not only a larger absolute (dollar) amount but also a larger percentage of income as income increases.

- A tax is **regressive** if its average rate declines as income increases. Such a tax takes a smaller proportion of income as income increases. A regressive tax may or may not take a larger absolute amount of income as income increases. (You may want to develop an example to substantiate this fact.)

- A tax is **proportional** if its average rate *remains the same* regardless of the size of income. Proportional income taxes are often referred to as *flat taxes* or *flat-rate taxes* because their average rates do not vary with (are flat with respect to) income levels.

We can illustrate these ideas with the personal income tax. Suppose tax rates are such that a household pays 10 percent of its income in taxes regardless of the size of its income. This is a *proportional* income tax. Now suppose the rate structure is such that a household with an annual taxable income of less than $10,000 pays 5 percent in income taxes; a household with an income of $10,000 to $20,000 pays 10 percent; one with a $20,000 to $30,000 income pays 15 percent; and so forth. This is a *progressive* income tax. Finally, suppose the rate declines as taxable income rises: You pay 15 percent if you earn less than $10,000; 10 percent if you earn $10,000 to $20,000; 5 percent if you earn $20,000 to $30,000; and so forth. This is a *regressive* income tax.

In general, progressive taxes are those that fall relatively more heavily on people with high incomes; regressive taxes are those that fall relatively more heavily on the poor.

Let's examine the progressivity, or regressivity, of several taxes.

Personal Income Tax

As noted earlier, the federal personal income tax is progressive, with marginal tax rates (those assessed on additional income) ranging from 10 to 39.6 percent in 2016. Rules that allow individuals to deduct from income interest on home mortgages and property taxes and that exempt interest on state and local bonds from taxation tend to make the tax less progressive than these marginal rates suggest. Nevertheless, average tax rates rise with income.

Sales Taxes

At first thought, a general sales tax with, for example, a 5 percent rate would seem to be proportional. But in fact it is regressive with respect to income. A larger portion of a low-income person's income is exposed to the tax than is the case for a high-income person; the rich pay no tax on the part of income that is saved, whereas the poor are unable to save. Example: "Low-income" Smith has an income of $15,000 and spends it all. "High-income" Jones has an income of $300,000 but spends only $200,000 and saves the rest. Assuming a 5 percent sales tax applies to all expenditures of each individual, we find that Smith pays $750 (5 percent of $15,000) in sales taxes and Jones pays $10,000 (5 percent of $200,000). But Smith pays $750/$15,000, or 5 percent of income as sales taxes while Jones pays $10,000/$300,000, or 3.3 percent of income. The general sales tax therefore is regressive.

Corporate Income Tax

The federal corporate income tax is essentially a proportional tax with a flat 35 percent tax rate. In the short run, the corporate owners (shareholders) bear the tax through lower dividends and share values. In the long run, workers may bear some of the tax since it reduces the return on investment and therefore slows capital accumulation. It also causes corporations to relocate to other countries that have lower tax rates. With less capital per worker, U.S. labor productivity may decline and wages may fall. To the extent this happens, the corporate income tax may be somewhat regressive.

Payroll Taxes

Payroll taxes are taxes levied upon wages and salaries by certain states as well as by the federal government. The federal payroll tax is known as the FICA tax after the Federal Insurance Contributions Act, which mandated one payroll tax to fund the Social Security program and another to fund the Medicare program.

Both taxes are split equally between employer and employee. Thus, the 12.4 percent Social Security tax is split in half, with 6.2 percent paid by employees and an additional 6.2 percent paid by employers. In the same way, the 2.9 percent Medicare tax is also split in half, with 1.45 percent paid by employees and 1.45 percent paid by employers.

Crucially, however, only the Medicare tax applies to all wage and salary income without limit. The Social Security tax, by contrast, is "capped," meaning that it applies only up to a certain limit, or cap. In 2016, the cap was $118,500.

The fact that the Social Security tax applies only on income below the cap implies that the FICA tax is regressive. To see this, consider a person with $118,500 in wage income. He would pay $9,065.25, or 7.65 percent (= 6.2 percent + 1.45 percent) of his wages in FICA taxes. By contrast, someone with twice that income, or $237,000, would pay $10,783.50 (= $9,065.25 on the first $118,500 + 1,718.25 on the second $118,500), which is only 4.6 percent of his wage income. Thus the average FICA tax falls as income rises, thereby confirming that the FICA tax is regressive.

But payroll taxes are even more regressive than suggested by this example because they only apply to wage and salary income. People earning high incomes tend to derive a higher percentage of their total incomes from nonwage sources like rents and dividends than do people who have incomes below the $118,500 cap on which Social Security taxes are paid. Thus, if

The VAT: A Very Alluring Tax?

Source: © Steve Cole/Getty Images RF

A value-added tax (VAT) is like a retail sales tax except that it applies only to the *difference* between the value of a firm's sales and the value of its purchases from other firms. For instance, Intel would pay the VAT—say, 7 percent—only on the difference between the value of the microchips it sells and the value of the materials used to make them. Dell, Lenovo, and other firms that buy chips and other components to make computers would subtract the value of their materials from the value of their sales of personal computers. They would pay the 7 percent tax on that difference—on the value that *they* added.

Economists reason that because the VAT would apply to all firms, sellers could shift their VATs to buyers in the form of higher prices without having to worry that their higher prices might cause them to lose sales to competitors. Final consumers, who cannot shift the tax, would be the ones who ultimately end up paying the full VAT as 7 percent higher prices. So the VAT would amount to a national sales tax on consumer goods.

Most other nations besides the United States have a VAT in addition to other taxes. Why the attraction? Proponents argue that it encourages savings and investment because it penalizes consumption. Unlike income taxes and profits taxes, which reduce the returns to working and investing, the VAT only taxes consumption. Thus, people might be expected to save and invest more if the government switched from taxing income and profits to taxing consumption via a VAT.

Opponents counter, however, that the VAT discourages savings and investment just as much as do income and profit taxes because the whole point of working hard, saving, and investing is the ability to reward yourself in the future with increased consumption. By making consumption more expensive, the VAT reduces this future reward. Also, because VATs are regressive, opponents argue that VATs lead to higher and more progressive income taxes as governments try to use the progressivity of income taxes to counter the regressivity of the VAT. Finally, critics note that the VAT is deeply buried within product prices and therefore is a *hidden tax.* Such taxes are usually easier to increase than other taxes and therefore may result in excessively large government.

our individual with the $237,000 of wage income also received $237,000 of nonwage income, his $10,783.50 of FICA tax would be only 2.3 percent of his total income of $474,000.

Property Taxes Most economists conclude that property taxes on buildings are regressive for the same reasons as are sales taxes. First, property owners add the tax to the rents that tenants are charged. Second, property taxes, as a percentage of income, are higher for low-income families than for high-income families because the poor must spend a larger proportion of their incomes for housing.

Tax Incidence and Efficiency Loss

LO20.7 Explain the principles relating to tax shifting, tax incidence, and the efficiency losses caused by taxes.

Determining whether a particular tax is progressive, proportional, or regressive is complicated because those on whom taxes are levied do not always pay the taxes. This is true because some or all of the value of the tax may be passed on to others. We therefore need an understanding of **tax incidence,** the degree to which a tax falls on a particular person or group. The tools of elasticity of supply and demand will help. Let's focus on a hypothetical excise tax levied on wine producers. Do the producers really pay this tax, or is some fraction of the tax shifted to wine consumers?

Elasticity and Tax Incidence

In Figure 20.7, S and D represent the pretax market for a certain domestic wine; the no-tax equilibrium price and quantity are $8 per bottle and 15 million bottles. Suppose that government levies an excise tax of $2 per bottle at the winery. Who will actually pay this tax?

Division of Burden Since the government imposes the tax on the sellers (suppliers), we can view the tax as an addition to the marginal cost of the product. Now sellers must get $2 more for each bottle to receive the same per-unit profit they were getting before the tax. While sellers are willing to offer, for example, 5 million bottles of untaxed wine at $4 per bottle, they must now receive $6 per bottle (= $4 + $2 tax) to offer the same 5 million bottles. The tax shifts the supply curve upward (leftward) as shown in Figure 20.7, where S_t is the "after-tax" supply curve.

The after-tax equilibrium price is $9 per bottle, whereas the before-tax equilibrium price was $8. So, in this case, consumers pay half the $2 tax as a higher price; producers pay the other half in the form of a lower after-tax per-unit revenue. That is, after remitting the $2 tax per unit to government, producers receive $7 per bottle, or $1 less than the $8 before-tax price. So, in this case, consumers and producers share the burden of the tax equally: Half of the $2 per bottle tax is shifted to consumers in the form of a higher price and half is paid by producers.

Note also that the equilibrium quantity declines because of the tax levy and the higher price that it imposes on

FIGURE 20.7 The incidence of an excise tax. An excise tax of a specified amount (here, $2 per unit) shifts the supply curve upward by the amount of the tax per unit: the vertical distance between S and S_t. This results in a higher price (here, $9) to consumers and a lower after-tax price (here, $7) to producers. Thus consumers and producers share the burden of the tax in some proportion (here, equally at $1 per unit).

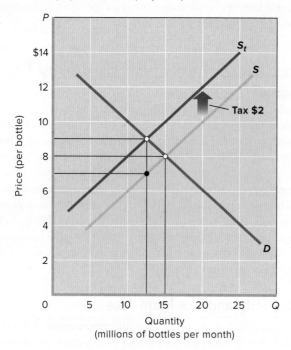

cases in which demand is perfectly elastic and perfectly inelastic. In the first case, the incidence of the tax is entirely on sellers; in the second, the tax is shifted entirely to consumers.

Figure 20.8 contrasts the more usual cases where demand is either relatively elastic or relatively inelastic in the relevant price range. With elastic demand (Figure 20.8a), a small portion of the tax ($P_2 - P_1$) is shifted to consumers and most of the tax ($P_1 - P_3$) is borne by the producers. With inelastic demand (Figure 20.8b), most of the tax ($P_5 - P_4$) is shifted to consumers and only a small amount ($P_4 - P_6$) is paid by producers. In both graphs the per-unit tax is represented by the vertical distance between S_t and S.

Note also that the decline in equilibrium quantity (from Q_1 to Q_2 in Figure 20.8a and from Q_4 to Q_5 in Figure 20.8b) is smaller when demand is more inelastic. This is the basis of our previous applications of the elasticity concept to taxation in earlier chapters: Revenue-seeking legislatures place heavy excise taxes on liquor, cigarettes, automobile tires, telephone service, and other products whose demand is thought to be inelastic. Since demand for these products is relatively inelastic, the tax does not reduce sales by much, so the tax revenue stays high.

The second generalization is that, with a specific demand, the more inelastic the supply, the larger is the portion of the tax borne by producers. When supply is elastic (Figure 20.9a), consumers bear most of the tax ($P_2 - P_1$) while producers bear only a small portion ($P_1 - P_3$) themselves. But where supply is inelastic (Figure 20.9b), the reverse is true: The major portion of the tax ($P_4 - P_6$) falls on sellers, and a relatively small amount ($P_5 - P_4$) is shifted to buyers. The equilibrium quantity also declines less with an inelastic supply than it does with an elastic supply.

Gold is an example of a product with an inelastic supply and therefore one where the burden of an excise tax (such as an extraction tax) would mainly fall on producers. On the other hand, because the supply of baseballs is relatively elastic, producers would pass on to consumers much of an excise tax on baseballs.

consumers. In Figure 20.7 that decline in quantity is from 15 million bottles to 12.5 million bottles per month.

Elasticities If the elasticities of demand and supply were different from those shown in Figure 20.7, the incidence of tax would also be different. Two generalizations are relevant.

With a specific supply, the more inelastic the demand for the product, the larger is the portion of the tax shifted to consumers. To verify this, sketch graphically the extreme

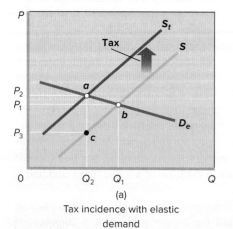

(a)
Tax incidence with elastic demand

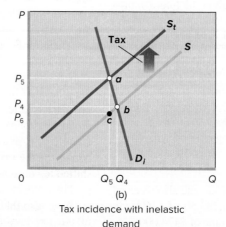

(b)
Tax incidence with inelastic demand

FIGURE 20.8 Demand elasticity and the incidence of an excise tax. (a) If demand is elastic in the relevant price range, price rises modestly (P_1 to P_2) when an excise tax is levied. Hence, the producers bear most of the tax burden. (b) If demand is inelastic, the price increases substantially (P_4 to P_5) and most of the tax is borne by consumers.

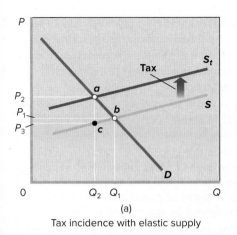

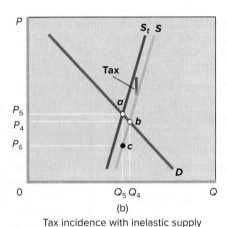

FIGURE 20.9 Supply elasticity and the incidence of an excise tax. (a) With elastic supply, an excise tax results in a large price increase (P_1 to P_2) and the tax is therefore paid mainly by consumers. (b) If supply is inelastic, the price rise is small (P_4 to P_5) and sellers bear most of the tax.

(a)
Tax incidence with elastic supply

(b)
Tax incidence with inelastic supply

Efficiency Loss of a Tax

We just observed that producers and consumers typically each bear part of an excise tax levied on producers. Let's now look more closely at the overall economic effect of the excise tax. Consider Figure 20.10, which is identical to Figure 20.7 but contains the additional detail we need for our discussion.

Tax Revenues In our example, a $2 excise tax on wine increases its market price from $8 to $9 per bottle and reduces the

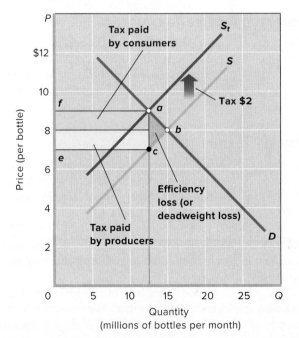

FIGURE 20.10 Efficiency loss (or deadweight loss) of a tax. The levy of a $2 tax per bottle of wine increases the price per bottle from $8 to $9 and reduces the equilibrium quantity from 15 million to 12.5 million. Tax revenue to the government is $25 million (area *efac*). The efficiency loss of the tax arises from the 2.5 million decline in output; the amount of that loss is shown as triangle *abc*.

equilibrium quantity from 15 million bottles to 12.5 million. Government tax revenue is $25 million (= $2 × 12.5 million bottles), an amount shown as the rectangle *efac* in Figure 20.10. The elasticities of supply and demand in this case are such that consumers and producers each pay half this total amount, or $12.5 million apiece (= $1 × 12.5 million bottles). The government uses this $25 million of tax revenue to provide public goods and services. So this transfer of dollars from consumers and producers to government involves no loss of well-being to society.

Efficiency Loss The $2 tax on wine does more than require consumers and producers to pay $25 million of taxes; it also reduces the equilibrium amount of wine produced and consumed by 2.5 million bottles. The fact that consumers and producers demanded and supplied 2.5 million more bottles of wine before the tax means that those 2.5 million bottles provided benefits in excess of their production costs. This is clear from the following analysis.

Segment *ab* of demand curve *D* in Figure 20.10 indicates the willingness to pay—the marginal benefit—associated with each of the 2.5 million bottles consumed before (but not after) the tax. Segment *cb* of supply curve *S* reflects the marginal cost of each of the bottles of wine. For all but the very last one of these 2.5 million bottles, the marginal benefit (shown by a point on *ab*) exceeds the marginal cost (shown by a point on *cb*). Not producing these 2.5 million bottles of wine reduces well-being by an amount represented by the triangle *abc*. The area of this triangle identifies the **efficiency loss of the tax** (also called the *deadweight loss of the tax*). This loss is society's sacrifice of net benefit because the tax reduces production and consumption of the product below their levels of economic efficiency, where marginal benefit and marginal cost are equal.

Role of Elasticities Most taxes create some degree of efficiency loss, but just how much depends on the supply and demand elasticities. Glancing back at Figure 20.8, we see that the efficiency loss area *abc* is greater in Figure 20.8a, where demand is relatively elastic, than in Figure 20.8b, where demand is relatively inelastic. Similarly, area *abc* is greater in Figure 20.9a than in Figure 20.9b, indicating a larger efficiency loss where supply is more elastic. Other things equal, the greater the elasticities of supply and demand, the greater the efficiency loss of a particular tax.

Two taxes yielding equal revenues do not necessarily impose equal costs on society. The government must keep this fact in mind in designing a tax system to finance beneficial public goods and services. In general, it should minimize the efficiency loss of the tax system in raising any specific dollar amount of tax revenue.

Qualifications We must acknowledge, however, that other tax goals may be as important as, or even more important than, minimizing efficiency losses from taxes. Here are two examples:

- **Redistributive goals** Government may wish to impose progressive taxes as a way to redistribute income. The 10 percent excise tax the federal government placed on selected luxuries in 1990 was an example. Because the demand for luxuries is elastic, substantial efficiency losses from this tax were to be expected. However, Congress apparently concluded that the benefits from the redistribution effects of the tax would exceed the efficiency losses.

  Ironically, in 1993 Congress repealed the luxury taxes on personal airplanes and yachts, mainly because the taxes had reduced quantity demanded so much that widespread layoffs of workers were occurring in those industries. But the 10 percent tax on luxury automobiles remained in place until it expired in 2003.

- **Reducing negative externalities** Our analysis of the efficiency loss of a tax assumes no negative externalities arising from either the production or consumption of the product in question. Where such spillover costs occur, an excise tax on producers might actually improve allocative efficiency by reducing output and thus lessening the negative externality. For example, the $2 excise tax on wine in our example might be part of a broader set of excise taxes on alcoholic beverages. The government may have concluded that the consumption of these beverages produces certain negative externalities. Therefore, it might have purposely levied this $2 tax to shift the market supply curve in Figure 20.10 to increase the price of wine, decrease alcohol consumption, and reduce the amount of resources devoted to wine.

  Excise taxes that are intended to reduce the production and consumption of products with negative externalities are sometimes referred to as *sin taxes*. This

name captures the idea that governments are motivated to impose these taxes to discourage activities that are perceived to be harmful or sinful. Excise taxes on cigarettes and alcohol in particular are commonly referred to as sin taxes.

> ### QUICK REVIEW 20.3
>
> ✓ The benefits-received principle of taxation asserts that those who benefit from government services should pay the taxes needed to finance them; by contrast, the ability-to-pay principle asserts that taxes should be apportioned by income and wealth.
>
> ✓ A tax is (*a*) progressive if the average amount taxed away increases with income, (*b*) regressive if the average amount taxed away decreases with income, and (*c*) proportional if the average amount taxed away remains constant as income increases.
>
> ✓ Given fixed demand, more elastic supply shifts tax burdens to consumers; given fixed supply, more elastic demand shifts tax burdens to producers.
>
> ✓ Taxes imposed in markets raise the market equilibrium price, reduce the market equilibrium output, and normally generate efficiency losses.

Probable Incidence of U.S. Taxes

LO20.8 Discuss the probable incidence of U.S. taxes and how the distribution of income between rich and poor is affected by government taxes, transfers, and spending.

Let's look now at the probable incidence of each of the major sources of tax revenue in the United States.

Personal Income Tax

The incidence of the personal income tax generally is on the individual because there is little chance for shifting it. For every dollar paid to the tax, individuals have one less dollar in their pocketbooks. The same ordinarily holds true for inheritance taxes.

Payroll Taxes

As discussed earlier, employees and employers in 2016 *each* paid 7.65 percent in FICA taxes on a worker's annual earnings up to the 2016 Social Security cap of $118,500 and then 1.45 percent on any additional earnings.

Workers bear the full burden of their half of the Social Security and Medicare payroll taxes. As is true for the income tax, they cannot shift the payroll taxes that they pay to anyone else.

But what about the other half of the FICA tax that is levied on employers? Who pays that? The consensus view is that part of the employers' half of the FICA tax gets shifted to workers in the form of lower before-tax wages. By making it more costly to hire workers, the payroll tax reduces the demand for labor relative to supply. That reduces the market wages that employers pay workers. In a sense, employers "collect" some of the payroll tax they owe from their workers.

Corporate Income Tax

In the short run, the incidence of the corporate income tax falls on the company's stockholders (owners), who bear the burden of the tax through lower dividends or smaller amounts of retained corporate earnings. Here is why. A firm currently charging the profit-maximizing price and producing the profit-maximizing output will have no reason to change product price, output, or wages when a tax on corporate income (profit) is imposed. The price and output combination yielding the greatest profit before the tax will still yield the greatest profit after a fixed percentage of the firm's profit is removed by a corporate income tax. So, the company's stockholders will not be able to shift the tax to consumers or workers.

As previously indicated, the situation may be different in the long run. Workers, in general, may bear a significant part of the corporate income tax in the form of lower wage growth. Because it reduces the return on investment, the corporate income tax may slow the accumulation of capital (plant and equipment). It also may prompt some U.S. firms to relocate abroad in countries that have lower corporate tax rates. In either case, the tax may slow the growth of U.S. labor productivity, which depends on American workers having access to more and better equipment. We know from Figure 17.1 that the growth of labor productivity is the main reason labor demand grows over time. If the corporate income tax reduces the growth of labor productivity, then labor demand and wages may rise less rapidly. In this indirect way—and over long periods of time—workers may bear part of the corporate income tax.

Sales and Excise Taxes

A *sales tax* is a general excise tax levied on a full range of consumer goods and services, whereas a *specific excise tax* is one levied only on a particular product. Sales taxes are usually transparent to the buyer, whereas excise taxes are often "hidden" in the price of the product. But whether they are hidden or clearly visible, both are often partly or largely shifted to consumers through higher equilibrium product prices (as in Figures 20.7 through 20.9). Sales taxes and excise taxes may get shifted to different extents, however. Because a sales tax covers a much wider range of products than an excise tax, there is little chance for consumers to avoid the price boosts that sales taxes entail. They cannot reallocate their expenditures to untaxed, lower-priced products. Therefore, sales taxes tend to be shifted in their entirety from producers to consumers.

Excise taxes, however, fall on a select list of goods. Therefore, the possibility of consumers turning to substitute goods and services is greater. An excise tax on theater tickets that does not apply to other types of entertainment might be difficult to pass on to consumers via price increases. Why? The answer is provided in Figure 20.8a, where demand is elastic. A price boost to cover the excise tax on theater tickets might cause consumers to substitute alternative types of entertainment. The higher price would reduce sales so much that a seller would be better off to bear all, or a large portion of, the excise tax.

With other products, modest price increases to cover taxes may have smaller effects on sales. The excise taxes on gasoline, cigarettes, and alcoholic beverages provide examples. Here consumers have few good substitute products to which they can turn as prices rise. For these goods, the seller is better able to shift nearly all the excise tax to consumers. Example: Prices of cigarettes have gone up nearly in lockstep with the recent, substantial increases in excise taxes on cigarettes.

As indicated in Global Perspective 20.2, the United States depends less on sales and excise taxes for tax revenue than do several other nations.

GLOBAL PERSPECTIVE 20.2

Taxes on General Consumption as a Percentage of GDP, Selected Nations

A number of advanced industrial nations rely much more heavily on consumption taxes—sales taxes, specific excise taxes, and value-added taxes—than does the United States. A value-added tax, which the United States does not have, applies only to the difference between the value of a firm's sales and the value of its purchases from other firms. As a percentage of GDP, the highest tax rates on consumption are in countries that have value-added taxes.

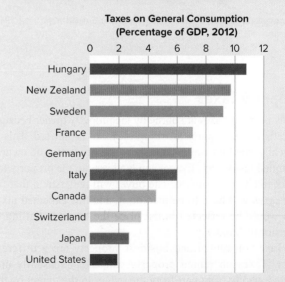

Taxes on General Consumption (Percentage of GDP, 2012)

Hungary	
New Zealand	
Sweden	
France	
Germany	
Italy	
Canada	
Switzerland	
Japan	
United States	

Source: Organization for Economic Cooperation and Development, OECD Stat Extracts, stats.oecd.org.

Taxation and Spending: Redistribution versus Recycling

Many Think of Taxes as the Best Way to Level the Income Distribution, but the Real Action Is in Expenditures.

Modern governments face substantial political pressure to ensure a fair distribution of society's economic benefits. In most people's minds, this boils down to taxing the rich more than the poor, which is why there is such a focus on whether particular taxes are progressive or regressive.

But taxing the rich cannot by itself alter the income distribution. One other thing is needed: The taxes taken from the rich have to flow to the poor. In particular, they have to be spent on goods, services, and programs that are used mostly by the poor rather than on goods, services, and programs that are used mostly by the rich. If government doesn't do this, the tax revenues of the rich will simply be recycled back to the rich rather than being redistributed to the poor.

Until recently, however, economists had only patchy evidence about whether our system of taxation and spending actually redistributes income from the rich to the poor. The problem was that the U.S. government only publishes statistics on whether the rich are being taxed more than the poor. It does not publish statistics on who receives most of its spending.

Fortunately, two economists from the nonpartisan Tax Foundation took it upon themselves to calculate those statistics. By combining data on government spending with household questionnaire responses in which people report what goods and services they consume, economists Gerald Prante and Scott A. Hodge generated reliable estimates of whether the government transfers significant amounts of income from the rich to the poor.*

---

*Gerald Prante and Scott A. Hodge, "The Distribution of Tax and Spending Policies in the United States," Tax Foundation *Special Report* No. 211, November 2013.

© PhotoDisc/Getty Images RF

As it turns out, the government *does* transfer an enormous amount of income from those with high incomes to those with low incomes. Not only do people with high incomes pay a much larger fraction of their incomes in taxes, it is also the case that the majority of that money gets transferred to the poor because government spending is indeed concentrated on programs that are used more by

Property Taxes

Many property taxes are borne by the property owner because there is no other party to whom they can be shifted. This is typically true for taxes on land, personal property, and owner-occupied residences. Even when land is sold, the property tax is not likely to be shifted. The buyer will understand that future taxes will have to be paid on it, and this expected taxation would be reflected in the price the buyer is willing to offer for the land.

Taxes on rented and business property are a different story. Taxes on rented property can be, and usually are, shifted wholly or in part from the owner to the tenant by the process of boosting the rent. Business property taxes are

treated as a business cost and are taken into account in establishing product price; hence such taxes are ordinarily shifted to the firm's customers.

Table 20.2 summarizes this discussion of the shifting and incidence of taxes.

The U.S. Tax Structure

Is the overall U.S. tax structure—federal, state, and local taxes combined—progressive, proportional, or regressive? The question is difficult to answer. Estimates of the distribution of the total tax burden depend on the extent to which the various taxes are shifted to others, and who bears the burden the poor than by the rich. These include welfare, subsidized health care, public education, and jobs programs. The poor also benefit from government-provided public goods that are available to everyone on an equal basis—things like public roads, clean drinking water, national defense, and so on.

The size and impact of the income transfers from rich to poor are most clearly understood by looking at the nearby figure, which groups the 133 million households living in the United States in 2012 into one of five equally sized groups (or quintiles) on the basis of household income. The quintiles are labeled Bottom 20%, Second 20%, Third 20%, Fourth 20%, and Top 20%. The yellow and blue bars above each quintile show, respectively, how much in taxes its members paid on average and how much in government spending they received on average during 2012.

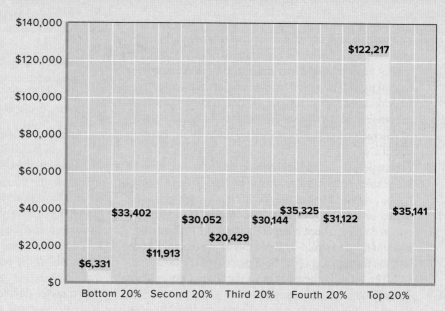

The first thing to notice is how much more money the poor received in government spending than they paid in taxes that year. A comparison of the yellow and blue bars for the bottom quintile reveals that the poorest households received $27,071 (= $33,402 in government spending − $6,331 in taxes) more in government spending than they paid in taxes in 2012. By contrast, households in the top 20 percent of the income distribution paid $87,076 more in taxes than they received in government spending that year.

This $87,076 per-household excess paid by households in the top quintile plus the $4,203 per-household excess paid by the households in the second-highest quintile provided the money that allowed the members of the lower three quintiles to receive more in government spending than they paid in taxes. In total, the transfers from the top two quintiles to the bottom three quintiles amounted to more than $1 trillion in 2012, or about 10 percent of all income earned by households that year.

The authors also found that the average tax rates paid by the five quintiles (on their total incomes, including government spending received) were, respectively, 14.7 percent for the bottom quintile, 19.5 percent for the second quintile, 23.5 percent for the third quintile, 26.9 percent for the fourth quintile, and 35.2 percent for the top quintile. Thus, the overall tax system is highly progressive (due to the federal income tax) despite many individual taxes being quite regressive.

But, more significantly, the spending made possible by taxing the rich more than the poor disproportionately flows back to the poor rather than being recycled to the rich. In fact, households in the top quintile receive back only 29 cents in government spending for each dollar they pay in taxes—which means that the remaining 71 cents are channeled to poorer households.

TABLE 20.2 The Probable Incidence of Taxes

Type of Tax	Probable Incidence
Personal income tax	The household or individual on which it is levied.
Payroll taxes	Workers pay the full tax levied on their earnings and part of the tax levied on their employers.
Corporate income tax	In the short run, the full tax falls on owners of the businesses. In the long run, some of the tax may be borne by workers through lower wages.
Sales tax	Consumers who buy the taxed products.
Specific excise taxes	Consumers, producers, or both, depending on elasticities of demand and supply.
Property taxes	Owners in the case of land and owner-occupied residences; tenants in the case of rented property; consumers in the case of business property.

is subject to dispute. But the majority view of economists who study taxes is as follows:

- **The federal tax system is progressive.** Overall, higher-income groups pay larger percentages of their income as federal taxes than do lower-income groups. Although federal payroll taxes and excise taxes are regressive, the federal income tax is sufficiently progressive to make the overall federal tax system progressive. About one-third of federal income tax filers owe no tax at all. In fact, because of fully refundable tax credits designed to reduce poverty and promote work, millions of households receive tax rebates even though their income tax bill is zero. Most of the federal income tax is paid by higher-income taxpayers. In 2013 (the latest year for which data have been compiled), the top 1 percent of income-tax filers paid 37.8 percent of the federal income tax; the top 5 percent paid 58.5 percent of the tax.

    The overall progressivity of the federal tax system is confirmed by comparing effective (average) tax rates, which are found by dividing the total of federal income, payroll, and excise taxes paid at various income levels by the total incomes earned by the people at those various income levels. In 2011, the 20 percent of the households with the lowest income paid an effective tax rate of 1.9 percent. The 20 percent of households with the highest income paid a 23.4 percent rate. The top 1 percent paid a 29.0 percent rate.[1]

- **The state and local tax structures are largely regressive.** As a percentage of income, property taxes and sales taxes fall as income rises. Also, state income taxes are generally less progressive than the federal income tax.

- **The overall U.S. tax system is progressive.** Higher-income people carry a substantially larger tax burden, as a percentage of their income, than do lower-income people, as discussed in this chapter's Last Word.

- **The overall U.S. tax system is more progressive than that of other rich countries.** A study by the Organization

for Economic Cooperation and Development (OECD) concluded that the U.S. tax system is the most progressive among OECD nations and therefore more progressive than those of countries such as Canada, Japan, France, Sweden, Germany, Korea, Australia, and the United Kingdom.[2] This is because those other nations rely much more heavily on national sales taxes and value-added taxes, both of which are regressive.

This chapter's Last Word also points out that the income tax system cannot be relied upon by itself to substantially alter the distribution of income because the government might choose to spend the taxes collected from the rich to pay for things that are used more by the rich than the poor. In actual fact, however, this does not happen in the United States because the government uses a large portion of the tax revenues collected from the rich to make income transfer payments to the poor and to pay for the provision of goods and services that are utilized more by the poor than the rich. The transfer payments by themselves are so large that they almost quadruple the incomes of the poorest fifth of U.S. households. Thus, the combined tax-transfer system levels the income distribution by much more than the tax system does on its own.

> ## QUICK REVIEW 20.4
>
> ✓ Some taxes are borne by those taxed while other taxes are shifted to someone else.
>
> ✓ The personal income tax and the corporate income tax (in the short run) are borne by those taxed.
>
> ✓ Sales taxes are shifted to consumers; the employer share of the payroll tax is shifted to workers; excise taxes may be shifted to consumers; and property taxes on rental properties are shifted to tenants.
>
> ✓ The federal tax structure is progressive. The state and local tax structures are regressive. The overall U.S. tax structure is progressive.

---

[1]*The Distribution of Household Income and Federal Taxes*, 2011, Congressional Budget Office, November 2014.

[2]*Growing Unequal? Income Distribution and Poverty in OECD Countries*, Organization for Economic Cooperation and Development, 2008.

SUMMARY

LO20.1 Use a circular flow diagram to illustrate how the allocation of resources is affected by government's revenue and expenditure decisions.

The funds used to pay for government purchases and transfers come from taxes, proprietary income, and borrowing. The ability to borrow allows governments to maintain high spending during economic

downturns, but government borrowing when the economy is doing well may "crowd out" private-sector investment.

LO20.2 Identify the main categories of government spending and the main sources of government revenue.

Government purchases exhaust (use up or absorb) resources; transfer payments do not. Government purchases have declined from about 22 percent of domestic output in 1960 to about 18 percent today. Transfer payments, however, have grown rapidly. As a percentage of GDP, total government spending (purchases plus transfers) now stands at about 33 percent, up from 27 percent in 1960.

LO20.3 List the main categories of federal revenue and spending and describe the difference between marginal and average tax rates.

The main categories of federal spending are pensions and income security, national defense, health, and interest on the public debt; federal revenues come primarily from personal income taxes, payroll taxes, and corporate income taxes.

It is important to distinguish between marginal and average tax rates. An income tax system may have different rates for different ranges of income. The tax rate that applies to any particular range is that range's marginal tax rate. The average tax rate is found by dividing the total amount of taxes paid on the full value of a taxpayer's taxable income and then dividing by the amount of the taxable income.

LO20.4 List the main categories of state and local revenue and spending.

States derive their revenue primarily from sales and excise taxes and personal income taxes; major state expenditures go to education, public welfare, health and hospitals, and highways. Local communities derive most of their revenue from property taxes; education is their most important expenditure. State and local tax revenues are supplemented by sizable revenue grants from the federal government.

LO20.5 Discuss the magnitude and distribution across job categories of government employment at the local, state, and federal levels.

Slightly over half of state and local government employees work in education. Just over half of federal government employees work for either the postal service or in national defense.

LO20.6 Summarize the different philosophies regarding the distribution of a nation's tax burden.

The benefits-received principle of taxation states that those who receive the benefits of goods and services provided by government should pay the taxes required to finance them. The ability-to-pay principle states that those who have greater income should be taxed more, absolutely and relatively, than those who have less income.

LO20.7 Explain the principles relating to tax shifting, tax incidence, and the efficiency losses causes by taxes.

Excise taxes affect supply and therefore equilibrium price and quantity. The more inelastic the demand for a product, the greater is the portion of an excise tax that is borne by consumers. The greater the inelasticity of supply, the larger is the portion of the tax that is borne by the seller.

Taxation involves the loss of some output whose marginal benefit exceeds its marginal cost. The more elastic the supply and demand curves, the greater is the efficiency loss (or deadweight loss) resulting from a particular tax.

LO20.8 Discuss the probable incidence of U.S. taxes and how the distribution of income between rich and poor is affected by government taxes, transfers, and spending.

The federal personal income tax is progressive. The corporate income tax is roughly proportional. General sales, excise, payroll, and property taxes are regressive.

Some taxes are borne by those taxed; other taxes are shifted to someone else. The income tax, the payroll tax levied on workers, and the corporate income tax (in the short run) are borne by those taxed. In contrast, sales taxes are shifted to consumers, part of the payroll tax levied on employers is shifted to workers, and, in the long run, part of the corporate income tax is shifted to workers. Specific excise taxes may or may not be shifted to consumers, depending on the elasticities of demand and supply. Property taxes on owner-occupied property are borne by the owner; those on rental property are borne by tenants.

The federal tax structure is progressive; the state and local tax structures are regressive; and the overall tax structure is progressive.

As discussed in the Last Word, the overall tax-spending system in the United States redistributes significant amounts of income from high-income individuals to low-income individuals. Because of the highly progressive federal income tax, the overall tax system is progressive. In addition, spending flows disproportionately to those with lower incomes, so that the tax collections from the rich are redistributed to the poor rather than being recycled back to the rich.

TERMS AND CONCEPTS

government purchases	corporate income tax	progressive tax
transfer payments	excise tax	regressive tax
personal income tax	sales tax	proportional tax
marginal tax rate	property taxes	tax incidence
average tax rate	benefits-received principle	efficiency loss of a tax
payroll taxes	ability-to-pay principle	

The following and additional problems can be found in ▇connect

DISCUSSION QUESTIONS

1. Use a circular flow diagram to show how the allocation of re-sources and the distribution of income are affected by each of the following government actions. **LO20.1**
   a. The construction of a new high school.
   b. A 2-percentage-point reduction of the corporate income tax.
   c. An expansion of preschool programs for disadvantaged children.
   d. The levying of an excise tax on polluters.

2. What do economists mean when they say government pur-chases are "exhaustive" expenditures whereas government transfer payments are "nonexhaustive" expenditures? Cite an example of a government purchase and a government transfer payment. **LO20.1**

3. What are the main categories of government spending? What are the main categories of government revenue? **LO20.2**

4. What is the most important source of revenue and the major type of expenditure at the federal level? **LO20.3**

5. For state and local governments, what are the three most impor-tant sources of revenue and types of expenditure? **LO20.4**

6. How do the top two categories of federal employment differ from the top two categories of local and state employment? **LO20.5**

7. Distinguish between the benefits-received and the ability-to-pay principles of taxation. Which philosophy is more evident in our present tax structure? Justify your answer. To which prin-ciple of taxation do you subscribe? Why? **LO20.6**

8. What is meant by a progressive tax? A regressive tax? A pro-portional tax? Comment on the progressivity or regressivity of each of the following taxes, indicating in each case where you think the tax incidence lies: (*a*) the federal personal income tax, (*b*) a 4 percent state general sales tax, (*c*) a federal excise tax on

automobile tires, (*d*) a municipal property tax on real estate, (*e*) the federal corporate income tax, (*f*) the portion of the payroll tax levied on employers. **LO20.6**

9. What is the tax incidence of an excise tax when demand is highly inelastic? Highly elastic? What effect does the elasticity of supply have on the incidence of an excise tax? What is the efficiency loss of a tax, and how does it relate to elasticity of demand and supply? **LO20.7**

10. Given the inelasticity of cigarette demand, discuss an excise tax on cigarettes in terms of efficiency loss and tax inci-dence. **LO20.7**

11. **ADVANCED ANALYSIS** Suppose the equation for the demand curve for some product X is $P = 8 - 0.6Q$ and the supply curve is $P = 2 + 0.4Q$. What are the equilibrium price and quantity? Now suppose an excise tax is imposed on X such that the new supply equation is $P = 4 + 0.4Q$. How much tax revenue will this excise tax yield the government? Graph the curves, and label the area of the graph that represents the tax collection "TC" and the area that represents the efficiency loss of the tax "EL." Briefly explain why area EL is the efficiency loss of the tax but TC is not. **LO20.7**

12. Is it possible for a country with a regressive tax system to have a tax-spending system that transfers resources from the rich to the poor? **LO20.8**

13. **LAST WORD** Does a progressive tax system by itself guaran-tee that resources will be redistributed from the rich to the poor? Explain. Is the *tax* system in the United States progres-sive, regressive, or proportional? Does the *tax-spending* system in the United States redistribute resources from higher-income earners to lower-income earners?

REVIEW QUESTIONS

1. The city of Joslyn has three sources of revenue: borrowing, proprietary income from running the local electric power util-ity, and taxes. If it received $10 million from running the elec-tric power utility and borrowed $40 million, how much did it collect in taxes? **LO20.2**
   a. $140 million.
   b. $110 million.
   c. $100 million.
   d. Nothing.

2. Suppose George made $20,000 last year and that he lives in the country of Harmony. The way Harmony levies income taxes, each citizen must pay 10 percent in taxes on their first $10,000 in earnings and then 50 percent in taxes on anything else they might earn. So given that George earned $20,000 last year, his marginal tax rate on the last dollar he earns will be _____ and his average tax rate for his entire income will be _____. **LO20.3**
   a. 50 percent; 50 percent.
   b. 50 percent; less than 50 percent.

   c. 10 percent; 50 percent.
   d. 10 percent; less than 50 percent.

3. The nation of Upstandia uses kroner for money and its tax code is such that a person making 100,000 kroner per year pays 40,000 kroner per year in income taxes; a person making 200,000 kroner per year pays 70,000 kroner per year in income taxes; and a person making 300,000 kroner per year pays 90,000 kroner per year in income taxes. Upstandia's income tax system is: **LO20.6**
   a. Progressive.
   b. Regressive.
   c. Proportional.

4. Identify each of the following taxes as being either progressive or regressive. **LO20.6**
   a. Personal income tax.
   b. Sales taxes.
   c. Payroll taxes.
   d. Property taxes.

5. The efficiency loss of imposing an excise tax is due to: **LO20.7**
   a. Paying a higher price per unit.
   b. Producing and consuming fewer units.

6. True or false. The incidence of property taxes that are levied on rented houses and apartments is high—meaning that they are paid almost entirely by the landlords, who are billed by the government for those taxes. **LO20.8**

PROBLEMS

1. Suppose a tax is such that an individual with an income of $10,000 pays $2,000 of tax, a person with an income of $20,000 pays $3,000 of tax, a person with an income of $30,000 pays $4,000 of tax, and so forth. What is each person's average tax rate? Is this tax regressive, proportional, or progressive? **LO20.7**

2. Suppose in Fiscalville there is no tax on the first $10,000 of income, but a 20 percent tax on earnings between $10,000 and $20,000 and a 30 percent tax on income between $20,000 and $30,000. Any income above $30,000 is taxed at 40 percent. If your income is $50,000, how much will you pay in taxes? Determine your marginal and average tax rates. Is this a progressive tax? **LO20.7**

3. For tax purposes, "gross income" is all the money a person receives in a given year from any source. But income taxes are levied on "taxable income" rather than gross income. The difference between the two is the result of many exemptions and deductions. To see how they work, suppose you made $50,000 last year in wages, earned $10,000 from investments, and were given $5,000 as a gift by your grandmother. Also assume that you are a single parent with one small child living with you. **LO20.7**
   a. What is your gross income?
   b. Gifts of up to $14,000 per year from any person are not counted as taxable income. Also, the "personal exemption" allows you to reduce your taxable income by $4,050 for each member of your household. Given these exemptions, what is your taxable income?

   c. Next, assume you paid $700 in interest on your student loans last year, put $2,000 into a health savings account (HSA), and deposited $4,000 into an individual retirement account (IRA). These expenditures are all *tax exempt*, meaning that any money spent on them reduces taxable income dollar-for-dollar. Knowing that fact, now what is your taxable income?
   d. Next, you can either take the so-called standard deduction or apply for itemized deductions (which involve a lot of tedious paperwork). You opt for the standard deduction that allows you as head of your household to exempt another $8,500 from your taxable income. Taking that into account, what is your taxable income?
   e. Apply the tax rates shown in Table 18.1 to your taxable income. How much federal income tax will you owe? What is the marginal tax rate that applies to your last dollar of taxable income?
   f. As the parent of a dependent child, you qualify for the government's $1,000 per-child "tax credit." Like all tax credits, this $1,000 credit "pays" for $1,000 of whatever amount of tax you owe. Given this credit, how much money will you actually have to pay in taxes? Using that actual amount, what is your average tax rate relative to your taxable income? What about your average tax rate relative to your gross income?

6

Microeconomic Issues and Policies

Antitrust Policy and Regulation

Learning Objectives

LO21.1 List and explain the core elements of the major antitrust (antimonopoly) laws in the United States.

LO21.2 Describe some of the key issues relating to the interpretation and application of antitrust laws.

LO21.3 Identify and explain the economic principles and difficulties relating to the setting of prices (rates) charged by so-called natural monopolies.

LO21.4 Discuss the nature of "social regulation," its benefits and costs, and its optimal level.

We now can apply the economics of product markets (Part 4) and the economics of resource markets and governments (Part 5) to selected microeconomic issues and policies.

In this chapter we look at three sets of government policies toward business: antitrust policy, industrial regulation, and social regulation. **Antitrust policy** consists of laws and government actions designed to prevent monopoly and promote competition. **Industrial regulation** pertains to government regulation of firms' prices (or "rates") within selected industries. **Social regulation** is government regulation of the conditions under which goods are produced, the physical characteristics of goods, and the impact of the production and consumption of goods on society.

Then, in the remaining four chapters of Part 6, we discuss issues and policies relating to agriculture, income inequality, health care, and immigration.

The Antitrust Laws

LO21.1 List and explain the core elements of the major antitrust (antimonopoly) laws in the United States.

The underlying purpose of antitrust policy (antimonopoly policy) is to prevent monopolization, promote competition, and achieve allocative efficiency. Although all economists would agree that these are meritorious goals, there is sharp conflict of opinion about the appropriateness and effectiveness of U.S. antitrust policy. As we will see, antitrust policy over the years has been neither clear-cut nor consistent.

Historical Background

Just after the U.S. Civil War (1861–1865), local markets widened into national markets because of improved transportation facilities, mechanized production methods, and sophisticated corporate structures. In the 1870s and 1880s, dominant firms formed in several industries, including petroleum, meatpacking, railroads, sugar, lead, coal, whiskey, and tobacco. Some of these oligopolists, near-monopolists, or monopolists were known as *trusts*—business combinations that assign control to a single decision group ("trustees"). Because these trusts "monopolized" industries, the word "trust" became synonymous with "monopoly" in common usage. The public, government, and historians began to define a business monopoly as a large-scale dominant seller, even though that seller was not always "a sole seller" as specified in the model of pure monopoly.

These dominant firms often used questionable tactics in consolidating their industries and then charged high prices to customers and extracted price concessions from resource suppliers. Farmers and owners of small businesses were particularly vulnerable to the power of large corporate monopolies and were among the first to oppose them. Consumers, labor unions, and economists were not far behind in their opposition.

The main economic case against monopoly is familiar to you from Chapter 12. Monopolists tend to produce less output and charge higher prices than would be the case if their industries were competitive. With pure competition, each competitive firm maximizes profit by producing the output level at which $P = MC$. That output level generates allocative efficiency because price P measures the marginal benefit to society of an extra unit of output while marginal cost MC reflects the cost of an extra unit. When $P = MC$, society cannot gain by producing 1 more or 1 less unit of the product. In contrast, a monopolist maximizes profit by producing the lower output level at which marginal revenue (rather than price) equals marginal cost. At this $MR = MC$ point, price exceeds marginal cost, meaning that society would obtain more benefit than it would incur cost by producing extra units. An underallocation of resources to the monopolized product occurs, and the economy suffers an efficiency loss. So society's economic well-being is less than it would be with greater competition.

But an efficiency loss isn't the only consequence of the monopolist's higher-than-competitive price. The higher price also transfers income from consumers to the monopolist. This transfer causes significant resentment because it results purely from the monopolist's ability to restrict output and cannot be justified on the basis of increased production costs. Consumers consequently express their ire to elected officials to "do something about the situation."

Responding to that pressure, government officials concluded in the late 1800s and early 1900s that monopolized industries lacked enough of the beneficial market forces that in competitive industries help to protect consumers, achieve fair competition, and achieve allocative efficiency. So the government instituted two alternative means of control as substitutes for, or supplements to, market forces:

- ***Regulatory agencies*** In the few markets where the nature of the product or technology creates a *natural monopoly,* the government established public regulatory agencies to control economic behavior.
- ***Antitrust laws*** In most other markets, government control took the form of antitrust (antimonopoly) legislation designed to inhibit or prevent the growth of monopoly.

Four particular pieces of federal legislation, as refined and extended by various amendments, constitute the basic law relating to monopoly structure and conduct.

Sherman Act of 1890

The public resentment of trusts that emerged in the 1870s and 1880s culminated in the **Sherman Act** of 1890. This cornerstone of antitrust legislation is surprisingly brief and, at first glance, directly to the point. The core of the act resides in two provisions:

- ***Section 1*** "Every contract, combination in the form of a trust or otherwise, or conspiracy, in restraint of trade or commerce among the several States, or with foreign nations is declared to be illegal."
- ***Section 2*** "Every person who shall monopolize, or attempt to monopolize, or combine or conspire with any person or persons, to monopolize any part of the trade or commerce among the several states, or with foreign nations, shall be deemed guilty of a felony" (as later amended from "misdemeanor").

The Sherman Act thus outlawed *restraints of trade* (for example, collusive price-fixing and dividing up markets) as well as *monopolization.* Today, the U.S. Department of Justice, the Federal Trade Commission, injured private parties, or state attorney generals can file antitrust suits against alleged violators of the act. The courts can issue injunctions to prohibit anticompetitive practices or, if necessary, break up monopolists into competing firms. Courts can also fine and imprison violators. Further, parties injured by illegal combinations and conspiracies can sue the perpetrators for *treble damages*—awards of three times the amount of the monetary injury done to them.

The Sherman Act seemed to provide a sound foundation for positive government action against business monopolies. However, early court interpretations limited the scope of the act and created ambiguities of law. It became clear that a more explicit statement of the government's antitrust sentiments was needed. The business community itself sought a clearer statement of what was legal and what was illegal.

Clayton Act of 1914

The **Clayton Act** of 1914 contained the desired elaboration of the Sherman Act. Four sections of the act, in particular, were designed to strengthen and make explicit the intent of the Sherman Act:

- Section 2 outlaws *price discrimination* when such discrimination is not justified on the basis of cost differences and when it reduces competition.

- Section 3 prohibits **tying contracts**, in which a producer requires that a buyer purchase another (or other) of its products as a condition for obtaining a desired product.

- Section 7 prohibits the acquisition of stocks of competing corporations when the outcome would be less competition.

- Section 8 prohibits the formation of **interlocking directorates**—situations where a director of one firm is also a board member of a competing firm—in large corporations where the effect would be reduced competition.

The Clayton Act simply sharpened and clarified the general provisions of the Sherman Act. It also sought to outlaw the techniques that firms might use to develop monopoly power and, in that sense, was a preventive measure. Section 2 of the Sherman Act, by contrast, was aimed more at breaking up existing monopolies.

Federal Trade Commission Act of 1914

The **Federal Trade Commission Act** created the five-member Federal Trade Commission (FTC), which has joint federal responsibility with the U.S. Justice Department for enforcing the antitrust laws. The act gave the FTC the power to investigate unfair competitive practices on its own initiative or at the request of injured firms. It can hold public hearings on such complaints and, if necessary, issue **cease-and-desist orders** in cases where it discovers "unfair methods of competition in commerce."

The **Wheeler-Lea Act** of 1938 amended the Federal Trade Commission Act to give the FTC the additional responsibility of policing "deceptive acts or practices in commerce." In so doing, the FTC tries to protect the public against false or misleading advertising and the misrepresentation of products. So the Federal Trade Commission Act, as modified by the Wheeler-Lea Act, (1) established the FTC as an independent antitrust agency and (2) made unfair and deceptive sales practices illegal.

The FTC is highly active in enforcing the deceptive advertising statutes. As one recent example, in 2007 the FTC fined four makers of over-the-counter diet pills a collective $25 million for claiming their products produced fast and permanent weight loss.

Celler-Kefauver Act of 1950

The **Celler-Kefauver Act** amended the Clayton Act, Section 7, which prohibits a firm from merging with a competing firm (and thereby lessening competition) by acquiring its stock. However, firms could evade Section 7 by acquiring the physical assets (plant and equipment) of competing firms without formally merging. The Celler-Kefauver Act closed that loophole by prohibiting one firm from obtaining the physical assets of another firm when the effect would be reduced competition. Section 7 of the Clayton Act now prohibits anticompetitive mergers no matter how they are undertaken.

Antitrust Policy: Issues and Impacts

LO21.2 Describe some of the key issues relating to the interpretation and application of antitrust laws.

The effectiveness of any law depends on how the courts interpret it and on the vigor of government enforcement. The courts have been inconsistent in interpreting the antitrust laws. At times, they have applied them vigorously, adhering closely to their spirit and objectives. At other times, their interpretations have rendered certain laws nearly powerless. The federal government itself has varied considerably in its aggressiveness in enforcing the antitrust laws. Some administrations have made tough antitrust enforcement a high priority. Other administrations have taken a more laissez-faire approach, initiating few antitrust actions or even scaling back the budgets of the enforcement agencies.

Issues of Interpretation

Differences in judicial interpretations have led to vastly different applications of the antitrust laws. Two questions, in particular, have arisen: (1) Should the focus of antitrust policy be on monopoly behavior or on monopoly structure? (2) How broadly should markets be defined in antitrust cases?

Monopoly Behavior versus Monopoly Structure A comparison of three landmark Supreme Court decisions reveals two distinct interpretations of Section 2 of the Sherman Act as it relates to monopoly behavior and structure.

In the 1911 **Standard Oil case**, the Supreme Court found Standard Oil guilty of monopolizing the petroleum industry through a series of abusive and anticompetitive actions. The Court's remedy was to divide Standard Oil into several competing firms. But the Standard Oil case left open an important question: Is every monopoly in violation of Section 2 of the Sherman Act or just those created or maintained by anticompetitive actions?

In the 1920 **U.S. Steel case,** the courts established the so-called **rule of reason,** under which not every monopoly is illegal. Only monopolies that "unreasonably" restrain trade violate Section 2 of the Sherman Act and are subject to antitrust action. Size alone is not an offense. Under the rule of reason, U.S. Steel was innocent of "monopolizing" because it had not resorted to illegal acts against competitors in obtaining and then maintaining its monopoly power. Unlike Standard Oil, which was a so-called bad trust, U.S. Steel was a "good trust" and therefore not in violation of the law.

In the **Alcoa case** of 1945 the courts touched off a 20-year turnabout. The Supreme Court sent the case to the U.S. court of appeals in New York because four of the Supreme Court justices had been involved with litigation of the case before their appointments. Led by Judge Learned Hand, the court of appeals held that, even though a firm's behavior might be legal, the mere possession of monopoly power (Alcoa held 90 percent of the aluminum ingot market) violated the antitrust laws. So Alcoa was found guilty of violating the Sherman Act.

These two cases point to a controversy in antitrust policy. Should a firm be judged by its behavior (as in the U.S. Steel case) or by its structure or market share (as in the Alcoa case)?

- "Structuralists" assume that any firm with a very high market share will behave like a monopoly. As a result, they assert that any firm with a very high market share is a legitimate target for antitrust action. Structuralists argue that changes in the structure of an industry, say, by splitting the monopolist into several smaller firms, will improve behavior and performance.

- "Behavioralists" assert that the relationships among structure, behavior, and performance are tenuous and unclear. They feel a monopolized or highly concentrated industry may be technologically progressive and have a good record of providing products of increasing quality at reasonable prices. If a firm has served society well and has engaged in no anticompetitive practices, it should not be accused of antitrust violation just because it has an extraordinarily large market share. That share may be the product of superior technology, superior products, and economies of scale. "Why use antitrust laws to penalize efficient, technologically progressive, well-managed firms?" they ask.

Over the past several decades, the courts have returned to the rule of reason first established in the 1920 U.S. Steel case, and most contemporary economists and antitrust enforcers reject strict structuralism. For instance, in 1982 the government dropped its 13-year-long monopolization case against IBM on the grounds that IBM had not unreasonably restrained trade, despite having possessed extremely high market share in the market for mainframe computers. More recently, the government has made no attempt to break up Intel's near monopoly in the sale of microprocessors for personal computers. And in prosecuting the Microsoft case, the federal government made it clear that the behavior used by Microsoft to maintain and extend its monopoly, not the presence of its large market share, violated the Sherman Act. In essence, the government declared Microsoft to be "a bad monopoly" that could become a good monopoly if it stopped doing bad things.

Defining the Relevant Market Courts often decide whether or not market power exists by considering the share of the market held by the dominant firm. They have roughly adhered to a "90-60-30 rule" in defining monopoly: If a firm has a 90 percent market share, it is definitely a monopolist; if it has a 60 percent market share, it probably is a monopolist; if it has a 30 percent market share, it clearly is not a monopolist. The market share will depend on how the market is defined. If the market is defined broadly to include a wide range of somewhat similar products, the firm's market share will appear small. If the market is defined narrowly to exclude such products, the market share will seem large. The Supreme Court has the final say on how broadly to define relevant markets, but the Supreme Court has not always been consistent.

In the Alcoa case, the Court used a narrow definition of the relevant market: the aluminum ingot market. But in the **DuPont cellophane case** of 1956 the Court defined the market very broadly. The government contended that DuPont, along with a licensee, controlled 100 percent of the cellophane market. But the Court accepted DuPont's contention that the relevant market included all "flexible packaging materials"—waxed paper, aluminum foil, and so forth, in addition to cellophane. Despite DuPont's monopoly in the "cellophane market," it controlled only 20 percent of the market for "flexible wrapping materials." The Court ruled that this did not constitute a monopoly.

Issues of Enforcement

Some U.S. presidential administrations have enforced the antitrust laws more strictly than others. The degree of federal antitrust enforcement makes a difference in the overall degree of antitrust action in the economy. It is true that individual firms can sue other firms under the antitrust laws. For example, in 2005 AMD—a maker of microprocessors—filed an antitrust suit against Intel, claiming that Intel was a monopolist that used anticompetitive business practices to thwart the growth of AMD's market share. But major antitrust suits often last years and are highly expensive. Injured parties therefore often look to the federal government to initiate and litigate such cases. Once the federal government gains a conviction, the injured parties no longer need to prove guilt and can simply sue the violator to obtain treble damages. In many cases, lack of federal antitrust action therefore means diminished legal action by firms.

Why might one administration enforce the antitrust laws more or less strictly than another? The main reason is differences in political philosophies about the market economy and the wisdom of intervention by government. There are two contrasting general perspectives on antitrust policy.

The *active antitrust perspective* is that competition is insufficient in some circumstances to achieve allocative efficiency and ensure fairness to consumers and competing firms. Firms occasionally use illegal tactics against competitors to dominate markets. In other instances, competitors collude to fix prices or merge to enhance their monopoly power. Active, strict enforcement of the antitrust laws is needed to stop illegal business practices, prevent anticompetitive mergers, and remedy monopoly. This type of government intervention maintains the viability and vibrancy of the market system and thus allows society to reap its full benefits. In this view, the antitrust authorities need to act much like the officials in a football game. They must observe the players, spot infractions, and enforce the rules.

In contrast, the *laissez-faire perspective* holds that antitrust intervention is largely unnecessary, particularly as it relates to monopoly. Economists holding this position view competition as a long-run dynamic process in which firms battle against each other for dominance of markets. In some markets, a firm successfully monopolizes the market, usually because of its superior innovativeness or business skill. But in exploiting its monopoly power to raise prices, these firms inadvertently create profit incentives and profit opportunities for other entrepreneurs and firms to develop alternative technologies and new products to better serve consumers. As discussed in Chapter 2 and expanded upon in Chapter 11, a process of *creative destruction* occurs in which today's monopolies are eroded and eventually destroyed by tomorrow's technologies and products. The government therefore should not try to break up a monopoly. It should stand aside and allow the long-run competitive process to work.

The extent to which a particular administration adheres to—or leans toward—one of these contrasting antitrust perspectives usually gets reflected in the appointments to the agencies overseeing antitrust policy. Those appointees help determine how strictly the laws are enforced.

Effectiveness of Antitrust Laws

Have the antitrust laws been effective? Although this question is difficult to answer, we can at least observe how the laws have been applied to monopoly, mergers, price-fixing, price discrimination, and tying contracts.

Monopoly On the basis of the rule of reason, the government has generally been lenient in applying antitrust laws to monopolies that have developed naturally. Generally, a firm will be sued by the federal government only if it has a very high market share and there is evidence of abusive conduct in achieving, maintaining, or extending its market dominance.

But even if the federal government wins the antitrust lawsuit, there is still the matter of *remedy:* What actions should the court order to correct for the anticompetitive practices of the monopoly that lost the lawsuit?

The issue of remedy arose in two particularly noteworthy monopoly cases. The first was the AT&T (American Telephone and Telegraph) case in which the government charged AT&T with violating the Sherman Act by engaging in anticompetitive practices designed to maintain its domestic telephone monopoly. As part of an out-of-court settlement between the government and AT&T, in 1982 AT&T agreed to divest itself of its 22 regional telephone-operating companies.

A second significant monopoly case was the **Microsoft case.** In 2000 Microsoft was found guilty of violating the Sherman Act by taking several unlawful actions designed to maintain its monopoly of operating systems for personal computers. A lower court ordered that Microsoft be split into two competing firms. A court of appeals upheld the lower-court finding of abusive monopoly but rescinded the breakup of Microsoft. Instead of the structural remedy, the eventual outcome was a behavioral remedy in which Microsoft was prohibited from engaging in a set of specific anticompetitive business practices.

The antitrust agency for the European Union (EU) has generally been more aggressive than the United States in prosecuting monopolists. For example, in 2015 the EU began to prosecute Google for showing a bias in search results in favor of products being sold on the Google online marketplace rather than on other online stores. Google faced €6.6 billion in fines in the EU despite having been investigated and cleared by U.S. antitrust authorities for the same behavior. (See this chapter's Last Word for details.)

Mergers The treatment of mergers, or combinations of existing firms, varies with the type of merger and its effect on competition.

Merger Types There are three basic types of mergers, as represented in Figure 21.1. This figure shows two stages of production (the input stage and the output, or final-product, stage) for two distinct final-goods industries (autos and blue jeans). Each rectangle (A, B, C, . . . X, Y, Z) represents a particular firm.

A **horizontal merger** is a merger between two competitors that sell similar products in the same geographic market. In Figure 21.1 this type of merger is shown as a combination

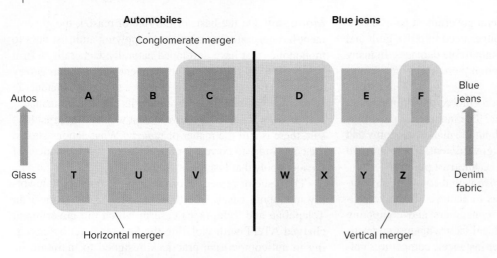

FIGURE 21.1 Types of mergers.
Horizontal mergers (T + U) bring together firms selling the same product in the same geographic market; vertical mergers (F + Z) connect firms having a buyer-seller relationship; and conglomerate mergers (C + D) join firms in different industries or firms operating in different geographic areas.

of glass producers T and U. Actual examples of such mergers include Chase Manhattan's merger with Chemical Bank, Boeing's merger with McDonnell Douglas, and Exxon's merger with Mobil.

A **vertical merger** is a merger between firms at different stages of the production process. In Figure 21.1, the merger between firm Z, a producer of denim fabric, and firm F, a producer of blue jeans, is a vertical merger. Vertical mergers are mergers between firms that have buyer-seller relationships. Actual examples of such mergers are PepsiCo's mergers with Pizza Hut, Taco Bell, and Kentucky Fried Chicken. PepsiCo supplies soft drinks to each of these fast-food outlets. (In 1997, PepsiCo spun off these entities into a separate company now called Yum! Brands.)

A **conglomerate merger** is officially defined as any merger that is not horizontal or vertical; in general, it is the combination of firms in different industries or firms operating in different geographic areas. Conglomerate mergers can extend the line of products sold, extend the territory in which products are sold, or combine totally unrelated companies. In Figure 21.1, the merger between firm C, an auto manufacturer, and firm D, a blue jeans producer, is a conglomerate merger. Real-world examples of conglomerate mergers include the merger between Walt Disney Company (movies) and the American Broadcasting Company (radio and television) and the merger between America Online (Internet service provider) and Time Warner (communications).

Merger Guidelines: The Herfindahl Index The federal government has established very loose merger guidelines based on the Herfindahl index. Recall from Chapter 14 that this measure of concentration is the sum of the squared percentage market shares of the firms within an industry. An industry of only four firms, each with a 25 percent market share, has a

Herfindahl index of 2,500 (= $25^2 + 25^2 + 25^2 + 25^2$). In pure competition, where each firm's market share is minuscule, the index approaches 0 (= $0^2 + 0^2 + \ldots + 0^2$). In pure monopoly, the index for that single firm is 10,000 (= 100^2).

The U.S. government uses Section 7 of the Clayton Act to block horizontal mergers that will substantially lessen competition. It is likely to challenge a horizontal merger if the post-merger Herfindahl index would be high (above 1,800) and if the merger has substantially increased the index (added 100 or more points). However, other factors, such as economies of scale, the degree of foreign competition, and the ease of entry of new firms, are also considered. Furthermore, horizontal mergers are usually allowed if one of the merging firms is suffering major and continuing losses. (This is one reason Boeing was allowed to acquire McDonnell Douglas in 1996: MD was losing money in producing its commercial airplanes.)

During the past several decades, the federal government has blocked several proposed horizontal mergers. For example, it blocked mergers between Staples and Office Depot, two major office-supply retailers; WorldCom and Sprint, two competing telecommunications firms; and Hughes (DirecTV) and Echostar (DISH Network), providers of direct-broadcast satellite television.

More recently, the federal government successfully challenged mergers between Snyder's of Hanover and Utz Quality Foods, makers of pretzels; Polypore and Microporous, battery-parts makers; and Blue Cross Blue Shield of Michigan and Physician's Health Plan of Michigan, health insurance providers.

Most *vertical mergers* escape antitrust prosecution because they do not substantially lessen competition in either of the two markets. (In Figure 21.1 neither the Herfindahl index in the industry producing denim fabric nor the index in the blue jeans industry changes when firms Z and F merge vertically.) However, a vertical merger between large firms in highly concentrated industries may be challenged. For example, in 1999 the threat of FTC action spurred Barnes & Noble to abandon its merger with Ingram Book Company, the nation's largest book wholesaler. The merger would have enabled Barnes & Noble to set the wholesale price of books charged to its direct retail competitors such as Borders and Amazon.com.

Conglomerate mergers are generally permitted. If an auto manufacturer acquires a blue jeans producer, no antitrust action is likely since neither firm has increased its own market share as a result. That means the Herfindahl index remains unchanged in each industry.

Price-Fixing Price-fixing among competitors is treated strictly. Evidence of price-fixing, even by small firms, will bring antitrust action, as will other collusive activities such as scheming to rig bids on government contracts or dividing up sales in a market. In antitrust law, these activities are known as **per se violations;** they are "in and of themselves" illegal, and therefore are *not* subject to the rule of reason. To gain a conviction, the government or other party making the charge need show only that there was a conspiracy to fix prices, rig bids, or divide up markets, not that the conspiracy succeeded or caused serious damage to other parties.

Price-fixing investigations and court actions are common. (See the Consider This box.)

Price Discrimination Price discrimination is a common business practice that rarely reduces competition and therefore is rarely challenged by government. The exception occurs when a firm engages in price discrimination as part of a strategy to block entry or drive out competitors.

Tying Contracts The federal government strictly enforces the prohibition of tying contracts, particularly when practiced by dominant firms. For example, it stopped movie distributors from forcing theaters to buy the projection rights to a full package of films as a condition of showing a blockbuster movie. Also, it prevented Kodak—the dominant maker of photographic film—from requiring that consumers process their film only through Kodak.

Conclusions So what can we conclude about the overall effectiveness of antitrust laws? Antitrust policy has not been very effective in restricting the rise of or in breaking up monopolies or oligopolies resulting from legally undertaken internal expansions of firms. But most economists do not deem that to be a flaw. The antitrust laws have been used more effectively against predatory or abusive monopoly, but that effectiveness has been diminished by the slow legal process and consequently long time between the filing of

CONSIDER THIS . . .

Of Airfare and eBooks (and Other Things in Common)

Examples of price-fixing are numerous. Here are just a few:

© APCortizasJr/Getty Images RF

- In 2007, British Airlines and Korean Air agreed to pay fines of $300 million each for conspiring to fix fuel surcharges on passenger tickets and cargo.

- Between 2008 and 2010, five manufacturers of liquid crystal displays (LCDs)—LG, Sharp, Hitachi, Chi Mei Optoelectronics, and Chunghwa Picture Tubes—were fined a total of over $860 million by the U.S. Justice Department for fixing the prices of the displays they sold to computer maker Dell Inc.

- In 2009, three international cargo airlines—Cargolux of Luxembourg, Nippon Cargo of Japan, and Asiana Airlines of South Korea—were fined $214 million by the U.S. Justice Department for conspiring to fix international airline cargo rates.

- In 2012, nine Japanese, German, and Swedish auto parts makers were fined a total of $790 million for conspiring to fix the prices of automobile heater control panels. Eleven corporate officers received jail sentences ranging from one to two years.

- In 2013, Apple was convicted along with five publishers—Harper Collins, Penguin, Simon & Schuster, Hachette, and Macmillan—of horizontal price-fixing in the market for e-books to be sold on Apple's iBook store. Apple was ordered to pay $450 million in reparations to those harmed by the scheme, which raised prices 20 percent in Apple's online bookstore.

charges and the implementation of remedies. In contrast, antitrust policy *has* been effective in prosecuting price-fixing and tying contracts.

Most economists conclude that, overall, U.S. antitrust policy has been moderately effective in achieving its goal of promoting competition and efficiency. Much of the success of antitrust policy arises from its deterrent effect on price-fixing and anticompetitive mergers. Some economists, however, think that enforcement of antitrust laws has been too weak. Others believe that parts of U.S. antitrust policy are anachronistic in an era of rapidly changing technology that continuously undermines existing monopoly power.

Industrial Regulation

LO21.3 Identify and explain the economic principles and difficulties relating to the setting of prices (rates) charged by so-called natural monopolies.

Antitrust policy assumes that society will benefit if a monopoly is prevented from evolving or if it is dissolved where it already exists. We now return to a special situation in which there is an economic reason for an industry to be organized monopolistically.

Natural Monopoly

A natural monopoly exists when economies of scale are so extensive that a single firm can supply the entire market at a lower average total cost than could a number of competing firms. Clear-cut circumstances of natural monopoly are relatively rare, but such conditions exist for many *public utilities*, such as local electricity, water, and natural gas providers. As discussed in Chapter 12, large-scale operations in some cases are necessary to obtain low unit costs and a low product price. Where natural monopoly occurs, competition is uneconomical.

If the market were divided among many producers, economies of scale would not be achieved and unit costs and prices would be higher than necessary.

There are two possible alternatives for promoting better economic outcomes where natural monopoly exists. One is public ownership, and the other is public regulation.

Public ownership or some approximation of it has been established in a few instances. Examples: the Postal Service, the Tennessee Valley Authority, and Amtrak at the national level and mass transit, water supply systems, and garbage collection at the local level.

But *public regulation,* or what economists call *industrial regulation,* has been the preferred option in the United States. In this type of regulation, government commissions regulate the prices (or "rates") charged by natural monopolists. Table 21.1 lists the two major federal regulatory commissions and their jurisdictions. It also notes that all 50 states have commissions that regulate the intrastate activities and "utility rates" of local natural monopolies.

The economic objective of industrial regulation is embodied in the **public interest theory of regulation.** In that theory, industrial regulation is necessary to keep a natural monopoly from charging monopoly prices and thus harming consumers and society. The goal of such regulation is to garner for society at least part of the cost reductions associated with natural monopoly while avoiding the restrictions of output and high prices associated with unregulated monopoly. If competition is inappropriate or impractical, society should allow or even encourage a monopoly but regulate its prices. Regulation should then be structured so that ratepayers benefit from the economies of scale—the lower per-unit costs—that natural monopolists are able to achieve.

In practice, regulators seek to establish rates that will cover production costs and yield a "fair" return to the enterprise. The goal is to set price equal to average total cost so that the regulated firm receives a normal profit, as described in the "Regulated Monopoly" section of Chapter 12. In particular, you should carefully review Figure 12.9.

TABLE 21.1 The Main Regulatory Commissions Providing Industrial Regulation

Commission (Year Established)	Jurisdiction
Federal Energy Regulatory Commission (1930)*	Electricity, gas, gas pipelines, oil pipelines, water-power sites
Federal Communications Commission (1934)	Telephones, television, cable television, radio, telegraph, CB radios, ham operators
State public utility commissions (various years)	Electricity, gas, telephones

*Originally called the Federal Power Commission; renamed in 1977.

Problems with Industrial Regulation

There is considerable disagreement on the effectiveness of industrial regulation. Let's examine two criticisms.

Costs and Inefficiency

An unregulated firm has a strong incentive to reduce its costs at each level of output because that will increase its profit. The regulatory commission, however, confines the regulated firm to a normal profit or a "fair return" on the value of its assets. If a regulated firm lowers its operating costs, the rising profit eventually will lead the regulatory commission to require that the firm lower its rates in order to return its profits to normal. The regulated firm therefore has little or no incentive to reduce its operating costs.

Worse yet, higher costs do not result in lower profit. Because the regulatory commission must allow the public utility a fair return, the regulated monopolist can simply pass through higher production costs to consumers by charging higher rates. A regulated firm may reason that it might as well have high salaries for its workers, opulent working conditions for management, and the like, since the "return" is the same in percentage terms whether costs are minimized or not. So, although a natural monopoly reduces costs through economies of scale, industrial regulation fosters considerable X-inefficiency (Figure 12.7). Due to the absence of competition, the potential cost savings from natural monopoly may never actually materialize.

Perpetuating Monopoly

A second general problem with industrial regulation is that it sometimes perpetuates monopoly long after the conditions of natural monopoly have ended.

Technological change often creates the potential for competition in some or even all portions of the regulated industry. Examples: Trucks began competing with railroads; transmission of voice and data by microwave and satellites began competing with transmission over telephone wires; satellite television began competing with cable television; and cell phones began competing with landline phones.

But spurred by the firms they regulate, commissions often protect the regulated firms from new competition by either blocking entry or extending regulation to competitors. Industrial regulation therefore may perpetuate a monopoly that is no longer a natural monopoly and would otherwise erode. Ordinary monopoly, protected by government, may supplant natural monopoly. If so, the regulated prices may exceed those that would occur with competition. The beneficiaries of outdated regulation are the regulated firms and their employees. The losers are consumers and the potential entrants.

Example: Regulation of the railroads by the Interstate Commerce Commission (ICC) was justified in the late 1800s and early 1900s. But by the 1930s, with the emergence of a network of highways, the trucking industry had seriously undermined the monopoly power of the railroads. That is, for the transport of many goods over many routes, railroad service was no longer a natural monopoly. At that time it would have been desirable to dismantle the ICC and let railroads and truckers, along with barges and airlines, compete with one another. Instead, in the 1930s the ICC extended regulation of rates to interstate truckers. The ICC remained in place until its elimination in 1996. It was eliminated because the deregulation of railroads and trucking in the late 1970s and early 1980s had made its work irrelevant.

Second example: Until the mid-1990s, both long-distance telephone companies such as AT&T as well as cable-television providers such as Time Warner were prohibited from offering local telephone services in competition with regulated local and regional telephone companies. But the very fact that AT&T, Time Warner, and other firms wanted to compete with regulated monopolies calls into question whether those local providers are in fact natural monopolies or government-protected monopolies.

Legal Cartel Theory

In Chapter 14, we noted that a *cartel* is formed when a group of previously competing firms makes a formal agreement to cease competing. They either control the price of a product by establishing the amounts of output that each cartel member will produce or they divide up the overall market for the product geographically so that each firm becomes a monopolist within its assigned region.

Privately organized cartels are illegal in the United States. But, in some cases, government regulations can have effects on prices and competition very similar to cartels. Thus, firms may seek to be regulated if they believe that regulation will reduce competition and raise prices in the same way a private cartel would. In essence, they see regulation as a way of creating a legal, publicly sanctioned cartel.

This possibility is known as the **legal cartel theory of regulation.** In place of having socially minded officials forcing regulation on natural monopolies to protect consumers, holders of this view see practical politicians "supplying" regulation to local, regional, and national firms that fear the impact of competition on their profits or even on their long-term survival. These firms desire regulation because it yields a legal monopoly that can virtually guarantee a profit. Specifically, the regulatory commission performs such functions as blocking entry (for example, in local telephone service). Or, where there are several firms, the commission divides up the market much like an illegal cartel (for example, prior to airline deregulation, the Civil Aeronautics Board assigned routes to specific airlines). The commission may also restrict potential competition by enlarging the "cartel" (for example, the ICC's addition of trucking to its regulatory domain).

While private cartels are illegal and unstable and often break down, the special attraction of a government-sponsored cartel under the guise of regulation is that it endures. The legal cartel theory of regulation suggests that regulation is a form of regulatory capture that results from the rent-seeking activities of private firms and the desire of politicians to be responsive in order to win reelection (Chapter 5).

Proponents of the legal cartel theory of regulation note that the Interstate Commerce Commission was welcomed by the railroads and that the trucking and airline industries both supported the extension of ICC regulation to their industries, arguing that unregulated competition was severe and destructive.

Occupational licensing is a labor market application of the legal cartel theory. Certain occupational groups—barbers, dentists, hairstylists, interior designers, dietitians, lawyers—demand stringent licensing on the grounds that it protects the public from charlatans and quacks. But skeptics say the real reason may be to limit entry into the occupational group so that practitioners can receive monopoly incomes.

Deregulation

Beginning in the 1970s, evidence of inefficiency in regulated industries and the contention that the government was regulating potentially competitive industries contributed to a wave of deregulation. Since then, Congress and many state legislatures have passed legislation that has deregulated in varying degrees the airline, trucking, banking, railroad, natural gas, television, and electricity industries. Deregulation has also occurred in the telecommunications industry, where antitrust authorities dismantled the regulated monopoly known as the Bell System (AT&T). Deregulation in the 1970s and 1980s was one of the most extensive experiments in economic policy to take place during the last 50 years.

The overwhelming consensus among economists is that deregulation has produced large net benefits for consumers and society. Most of the gains from deregulation have occurred in three industries: airlines, railroads, and trucking. Airfares (adjusted for inflation) declined by about one-third, and airline safety has continued to improve. Trucking and railroad freight rates (again, adjusted for inflation) dropped by about one-half.

Significant efficiency gains were also realized in long-distance telecommunications, and there have been slight efficiency gains in cable television, stock brokerage services, and the natural gas industry. Moreover, deregulation has unleashed a wave of technological advances that have resulted in such new and improved products and services as fax machines, cellular phones, fiber-optic cable, microwave communication systems, and the Internet.

The most recent and perhaps controversial industry to be deregulated is electricity. Deregulation is relatively advanced at the wholesale level, where firms can buy and sell electricity at market prices. They are also free to build generating facilities and sell electricity to local electricity providers at unregulated prices. In addition, several states have deregulated retail prices and encouraged households and businesses to choose among available electricity suppliers. This competition has generally lowered electricity rates for consumers and enhanced allocative efficiency.

But deregulation suffered a severe setback in California, where wholesale electricity prices, but not retail rates, were deregulated. Wholesale electricity prices surged in 2001 when California experienced electricity shortages. Because they could not pass on wholesale price increases to consumers, California electric utilities suffered large financial losses. California then filed lawsuits against several energy-trading companies that allegedly manipulated electricity supplies to boost the wholesale price of electricity during the California energy crisis. One multibillion-dollar energy trader—Enron—collapsed in 2002 when federal investigators uncovered a pattern of questionable and fraudulent business and accounting practices.

The California deregulation debacle and the Enron collapse have muddied the overall assessment of electricity deregulation in the United States. California's policy of deregulating only wholesale prices clearly did not work. So, even enthusiastic supporters of deregulation are now careful to reflect on the details of how, exactly, an industry should be dergulated.

> ## QUICK REVIEW 21.2
>
> ✓ Natural monopoly occurs where economies of scale are so extensive that only a single firm can produce the product at minimum average total cost.
>
> ✓ The public interest theory of regulation says that government must regulate natural monopolies to prevent abuses arising from monopoly power. Regulated firms, however, have less incentive than competitive firms to reduce costs. That is, regulated firms tend to be X-inefficient.
>
> ✓ The legal cartel theory of regulation suggests that some firms seek government regulation to reduce price competition and ensure stable profits.
>
> ✓ Deregulation initiated by government in the past several decades has yielded large annual efficiency gains for society.

Social Regulation

LO21.4 Discuss the nature of "social regulation," its benefits and costs, and its optimal level.

The industrial regulation discussed in the preceding section has focused on the regulation of prices (or rates) in natural monopolies. But in the early 1960s a new type of regulation began to emerge. This *social regulation* is concerned with the conditions under which goods and services are produced, the

TABLE 21.2 The Main Federal Regulatory Commissions Providing Social Regulation

Commission (Year Established)	Jurisdiction
Food and Drug Administration (1906)	Safety and effectiveness of food, drugs, and cosmetics
Equal Employment Opportunity Commission (1964)	Hiring, promotion, and discharge of workers
Occupational Safety and Health Administration (1971)	Industrial health and safety
Environmental Protection Agency (1972)	Air, water, and noise pollution
Consumer Product Safety Commission (1972)	Safety of consumer products
Consumer Financial Protection Bureau (2011)	Fairness and transparency in lending and other financial services

impact of production on society, and the physical qualities of the goods themselves.

The federal government carries out most of the social regulation, although states also play a role. In Table 21.2 we list the main federal regulatory commissions engaged in social regulation.

Distinguishing Features

Social regulation differs from industrial regulation in several ways.

First, social regulation applies to far more firms than does industrial regulation. Social regulation is often applied "across the board" to all industries and directly affects more producers than does industrial regulation. For instance, while the industrial regulation of the Federal Energy Regulatory Commission (FERC) applies to a relatively small number of firms, the rules and regulations issued by the Occupational Safety and Health Administration (OSHA) apply to firms in all industries.

Second, social regulation intrudes into the day-to-day production process to a greater extent than industrial regulation. While industrial regulation focuses on rates, costs, and profits, social regulation often dictates the design of products, the conditions of employment, and the nature of the production process. As examples, the Consumer Product Safety Commission (CPSC) regulates the design of potentially unsafe products, and the Environmental Protection Agency (EPA) regulates the amount of pollution allowed during production.

Finally, social regulation has expanded rapidly during the same period in which industrial regulation has waned. Between 1970 and 1980, the U.S. government created 20 new social regulatory agencies. More recently, Congress has established new social regulations to be enforced by existing regulatory agencies. For example, the Equal Employment Opportunity Commission, which is responsible for enforcing laws against workplace discrimination on the basis of race, gender, age, or religion, has been given the added duty of enforcing the Americans with Disabilities Act of 1990. Under this social regulation, firms must provide reasonable accommodations for qualified workers and job applicants with disabilities. Also, sellers must provide reasonable access for customers with disabilities.

The names of the regulatory agencies in Table 21.2 suggest the reasons for their creation and growth: As much of our society had achieved a fairly affluent standard of living by the 1960s, attention shifted to improvement in the nonmaterial quality of life. The new focus called for safer products, less pollution, improved working conditions, and greater equality of economic opportunity.

The Optimal Level of Social Regulation

While economists agree on the need for social regulation, they disagree on whether or not the current level of such regulation is optimal. Recall that an activity should be expanded as long as its marginal benefit (MB) exceeds its marginal cost (MC). If the MB of social regulation exceeds its MC, then there is too little social regulation. But if MC exceeds MB, there is too much (review Figure 4.9). Unfortunately, the marginal costs and benefits of social regulation are not always easy to measure. So ideology about the proper size and role of government often drives the debate over social regulation as much as, or perhaps more than, economic cost-benefit analysis.

In Support of Social Regulation Defenders of social regulation say that it has achieved notable successes and, overall, has greatly enhanced society's well-being. They point out that the problems that social regulation confronts are serious and substantial. According to the National Safety Council, about 5,000 workers die annually in job-related accidents and 3.7 million workers suffer injuries that force them to miss a day or more of work. Air pollution continues to cloud major U.S. cities, imposing large costs in terms of reduced property values and increased health care expense. Numerous children and adults die each year because of poorly designed or manufactured products (for example, car tires) or tainted food (for example, *E. coli* in beef). Discrimination against some ethnic and racial minorities, persons with disabilities, and older workers reduces their earnings and imposes heavy costs on society.

Proponents of social regulation acknowledge that social regulation is costly. But they correctly point out that a high "price" for something does not necessarily mean that it should not be purchased. They say that the appropriate economic test should be not whether the costs of social regulation are high or low but, rather, whether the benefits of social regulation exceed the costs. After decades of neglect, they further assert, society cannot expect to cleanse the environment, enhance the safety of the workplace, and promote economic opportunity for all without incurring substantial costs. So statements about the huge costs of social regulation are irrelevant, say defenders, since the benefits are even greater. The public often underestimates those benefits since they are more difficult to measure than costs and often become apparent only after some time has passed (for example, the benefits of reducing global warming).

Proponents of social regulation point to its many specific benefits. Here are just a few examples: It is estimated that highway fatalities would be 40 percent greater annually in the absence of auto safety features mandated through regulation. Compliance with child safety-seat and seat-belt laws has significantly reduced the auto fatality rate for small children. The national air quality standards set by law have been reached in nearly all parts of the nation for sulfur dioxide, nitrogen dioxide, and lead. Moreover, recent studies clearly link cleaner air, other things equal, with increases in the values of homes. Affirmative action regulations have increased the labor demand for racial and ethnic minorities and females. The use of childproof lids has resulted in a 90 percent decline in child deaths caused by accidental swallowing of poisonous substances.

Some defenders of social regulation say there are many remaining areas in which greater regulation would generate net benefits to society. For instance, some call for greater regulation of the meat, poultry, and seafood industries to improve food safety. Others favor greater regulation of health care organizations and insurance companies to ensure "patients' rights" for consumers of health care services. Still others say that more regulation is needed to ensure that violent movies, CDs, and video games are not marketed to children.

Advocates of social regulation say that the benefits of such regulation are well worth the considerable costs. The costs are simply the price we must pay to create a hospitable, sustainable, and just society.

Criticisms of Social Regulation Critics of social regulation contend that, in many instances, it has been expanded to the point where the marginal costs exceed the marginal benefits. In this view, society would achieve net benefits by cutting back on irritating social regulation. Critics say that many social regulation laws are poorly written, making regulatory objectives and standards difficult to understand. As a result, regulators pursue goals well beyond the original intent of the legislation. Businesses complain that regulators often press for additional increments of improvement, unmindful of costs.

Also, decisions must often be made and rules formed on the basis of inadequate information. Examples: CPSC officials may make decisions about certain ingredients in products on the basis of limited laboratory experiments that suggest that those ingredients might cause cancer. Or government agencies may establish costly pollution standards to attack the global-warming problem without knowing for certain whether pollution is the main cause of the problem. These efforts, say critics, lead to excessive regulation of business.

Moreover, critics argue that social regulations produce many unintended and costly side effects. For instance, the federal gas mileage standard for automobiles has been blamed for an estimated 2,000 to 3,900 traffic deaths a year because auto manufacturers have reduce d the weight of vehicles to meet the higher miles-per-gallon standards. Other things equal, drivers of lighter cars have a higher fatality rate than drivers of heavier vehicles.

Finally, opponents of social regulation say that the regulatory agencies may attract overzealous workers who are hostile toward the market system and "believe" too fervently in regulation. For example, some staff members of government agencies may see large corporations as "bad guys" who regularly cause pollution, provide inadequate safety for workers, deceive their customers, and generally abuse their power in the community. Such biases can lead to seemingly never-ending calls for still more regulation, rather than objective assessments of the costs and benefits of added regulation.

Two Reminders

The debate over the proper amount of social regulation will surely continue. By helping determine costs and benefits, economic analysis can lead to more informed discussions and to better decisions. In this regard, economic analysis provides pertinent reminders for both ardent supporters and ardent opponents of social regulation.

There Is No Free Lunch Fervent supporters of social regulation need to remember that "there is no free lunch." Social regulation can produce higher prices, stifle innovation, and reduce competition.

Social regulation raises product prices in two ways. It does so directly because compliance costs normally get passed on to consumers, and it does so indirectly by reducing labor productivity. Resources invested in making workplaces accessible to disabled workers, for example, are not available for investment in new machinery designed to increase output per worker. Where the wage rate is fixed, a drop in labor productivity increases the marginal and average total costs of production. In effect, the supply curve for the product shifts leftward, causing the price of the product to rise.

Social regulation may have a negative impact on the rate of innovation. Technological advance may be stifled by, say, the fear that a new plant will not meet EPA guidelines or that a new medicine will require years of testing before being approved by the Food and Drug Administration (FDA).

Social regulation may weaken competition since it usually places a relatively greater burden on small firms than on

LAST WORD

Antitrust Online

The Internet Has Presented Antitrust Authorities with Both Old and New Causes for Concern.

The Airline Tariff Publishing case was the first important example of how digital communication platforms could be used by businesses to engage in price-fixing. In the late 1980s, U.S. airlines began to post both current and future prices for airline tickets on a centralized computer system known as the Airline Tariff Publishing Company. The system was set up so that travel agents could comparison shop for their clients. But the airlines used the system's ability to list start dates and end dates for ticket purchases as a way of colluding.

As an example, suppose that American Airlines and Delta Airlines had both been charging $200 for a one-way ticket between New York and Chicago. American could then post a higher price of $250 for the route with the stipulation that nobody could start buying tickets at that price until the next month. Delta could then respond by also saying that it would start selling tickets at the higher price next month. In that way, the two airlines could tacitly coordinate their price setting ahead of time so as to collude on a major price increase.

The antitrust authorities at the U.S. Department of Justice stopped this practice in 1994 by getting the airlines to agree to the behavioral remedy that any fare changes would have to become immediately available to consumers. Airlines could no longer use suggested future prices as a way of signaling each other about how to collude.

The monopoly power gained during the 1990s and early 2000s by online giants such as Microsoft and Google has also led to business practices that have raised the ire of antitrust authorities. Microsoft, for example, was fined $2.7 billion after being convicted in 2000 of using the near-monopoly (95 percent market share) dominance of its Windows operating system software to coerce computer makers into favoring Microsoft's Internet Explorer web browser over rival browsers such as Netscape Navigator.

More recently, Google was indicted in 2015 by European Union antitrust officials for allegedly using its 90 percent share of the market for Internet searches in Europe to favor its Google Shopping price-comparison service over price-comparison services run by rival firms. For example, if a person in Germany types "prices for used iPhones" into Google's search bar, the top of the search results page will feature images of several used iPhones for sale on Google Shopping. By contrast, anyone wanting comparison prices for used iPhones that are listed on other price-comparison sites will have to click on links further down on the search-results page to get to those other sites and their respective lists of used iPhone prices. Google faces up to €6.6 billion in fines if convicted.

© grzegorz knec/Alamy Stock Photo

The most recent threat to competition spawned by the Internet is the rise of collusion via pieces of software that use pricing algorithms (automatically applied rules for setting prices) to constantly adjust a company's the online prices in response to seeing what rival firms are charging for similar products. The problem for regulators is that the pricing algorithms of different firms could end up interacting in ways that collusively raise prices for consumers. This is especially true for pieces of software that use artificial intelligence to learn how to achieve preset goals. Two such pieces of software could each be programmed to try to maximize profits and, as they interacted with each other, "realize" that the best way to do so is by coordinating rather than competing.

That possibility is especially challenging because, given the way antitrust laws are currently written, firms can be prosecuted for collusion only if they make an anticompetitive "agreement" with each other. If the algorithms come to collude on their own, there is no such agreement to prosecute. In fact, the behavior of the two pieces of software could just as easily be interpreted as independent parallel conduct rather than coordination since they don't even directly communicate with each other. And, in addition, should asking a piece of software to try to figure out how to maximize profits be illegal just by itself?

These issues are still very much up in the air but being faced squarely by U.S. regulators, who made their first prosecution against the collusive use of algorithmic pricing software in 2015 and who established the Office of Technology Research and Investigation as part of the Federal Trade Commission's Bureau of Consumer Protection that same year.

large ones. The costs of complying with social regulation are, in effect, fixed costs. Because smaller firms produce less output over which to distribute those costs, their compliance costs per unit of output put them at a competitive disadvantage with their larger rivals. Social regulation is more likely to force smaller firms out of business, thus contributing to the increased concentration of industry.

Finally, social regulation may prompt some U.S. firms to move their operations to countries in which the rules are not as burdensome and therefore production costs are lower.

Less Government Is Not Always Better Than More

On the opposite side of the issue, opponents of social regulation need to remember that less government is not always better than more government. While the market system is a powerful engine for producing goods and services and generating income, it has certain flaws and can camouflage certain abuses. Through appropriate amounts of social regulation, government can clearly increase economic efficiency and thus society's well-being. Ironically, by "taking the rough edges off of capitalism," social regulation may be a strong pro-capitalism force. Properly conceived and executed, social regulation helps maintain political support for the market system. Such support could quickly wane should there be a

steady drumbeat of reports of unsafe workplaces, unsafe products, discriminatory hiring, choking pollution, deceived loan customers, and the like. Social regulation helps the market system deliver not only goods and services but also a "good society."

QUICK REVIEW 21.3

✓ Social regulation is concerned with the conditions under which goods and services are produced, the effects of production on society, and the physical characteristics of the goods themselves.

✓ Defenders of social regulation point to the benefits arising from policies that keep dangerous products from the marketplace, reduce workplace injuries and deaths, contribute to clean air and water, and reduce employment discrimination.

✓ Critics of social regulation say uneconomical policy goals, inadequate information, unintended side effects, and overzealous personnel create excessive regulation, for which regulatory costs exceed regulatory benefits.

SUMMARY

LO21.1 List and explain the core elements of the major antitrust (antimonopoly) laws in the United States.

The cornerstones of antitrust policy are the Sherman Act of 1890 and the Clayton Act of 1914. The Sherman Act specifies that "every contract, combination . . . or conspiracy in the restraint of interstate trade . . . is . . . illegal" and that any person who monopolizes or attempts to monopolize interstate trade is guilty of a felony.

If a company is found guilty of violating the antimonopoly provisions of the Sherman Act, the government can either break up the monopoly into competing firms (a structural remedy) or prohibit it from engaging in specific anticompetitive business practices (a behavioral remedy).

The Clayton Act was designed to bolster and make more explicit the provisions of the Sherman Act. It declares that price discrimination, tying contracts, intercorporate stock acquisitions, and interlocking directorates are illegal when their effect is to reduce competition.

The Federal Trade Commission Act of 1914 created the Federal Trade Commission to investigate antitrust violations and to prevent the use of "unfair methods of competition." The FTC Act was amended by the Wheeler-Lea Act of 1938 to outlaw false and deceptive representation of products to consumers. Empowered by

cease-and-desist orders, the FTC serves as a watchdog agency over unfair, deceptive, or false claims made by firms about their own products or the products of their competitors.

The Celler-Kefauver Act of 1950 amended the Clayton Act of 1914 to prohibit one firm from acquiring the assets of another firm when doing so would substantially reduce competition.

LO21.2 Describe some of the key issues relating to the interpretation and application of antitrust laws.

Some of the key issues in applying antitrust laws include (a) determining whether an industry should be judged by its structure or by its behavior, (b) defining the scope and size of the dominant firm's market, and (c) deciding how strictly to enforce the antitrust laws.

The courts treat price-fixing among competitors as a *per se violation*, meaning that the conduct is illegal independently of whether the conspiracy causes harm. In contrast, a *rule of reason* is used to assess monopoly. Only monopolies that unreasonably (abusively) achieve or maintain their status violate the law. Antitrust officials are more likely to challenge price-fixing, tying contracts, and horizontal mergers than to try to break up existing monopolies. Nevertheless, antitrust suits by the federal government led to the breakup of the AT&T monopoly in the early 1980s.

LO21.3 Identify and explain the economic principles and difficulties relating to the setting of prices (rates) charged by so-called natural monopolies.

The objective of industrial regulation is to protect the public from the market power of natural monopolies by regulating prices and quality of service.

Critics of industrial regulation contend that it can lead to inefficiency and rising costs and that in many instances it constitutes a legal cartel for the regulated firms. Legislation passed in the late 1970s and the 1980s has brought about varying degrees of deregulation in the airline, trucking, banking, railroad, and television broadcasting industries.

Studies indicate that deregulation of airlines, railroads, trucking, and telecommunications is producing sizable annual gains to society through lower prices, lower costs, and increased output.

Less certain is the effect of the more recent deregulation of the electricity industry.

LO21.4 Discuss the nature of "social regulation," its benefits and costs, and its optimal level.

Social regulation is concerned with product safety, working conditions, and the effects of production on society. Whereas industrial regulation is on the wane, social regulation continues to expand. The optimal amount of social regulation occurs where MB = MC.

People who support social regulation point to its numerous specific successes and assert that it has greatly enhanced society's well-being. Critics of social regulation contend that businesses are excessively regulated to the point where marginal costs exceed marginal benefits. They also say that social regulation often produces unintended and costly side effects.

TERMS AND CONCEPTS

antitrust policy	cease-and-desist order	Microsoft case
industrial regulation	Wheeler-Lea Act	horizontal merger
social regulation	Celler-Kefauver Act	vertical merger
Sherman Act	Standard Oil case	conglomerate merger
Clayton Act	U.S. Steel case	per se violations
tying contracts	rule of reason	natural monopoly
interlocking directorates	Alcoa case	public interest theory of regulation
Federal Trade Commission Act	DuPont cellophane case	legal cartel theory of regulation

The following and additional problems can be found in ▇connect

DISCUSSION QUESTIONS

1. Both antitrust policy and industrial regulation deal with monopoly. What distinguishes the two approaches? How does government decide to use one form of remedy rather than the other? **LO21.1, LO21.3**

2. Describe the major provisions of the Sherman and Clayton acts. What government entities are responsible for enforcing those laws? Are firms permitted to initiate antitrust suits on their own against other firms? **LO21.1**

3. Contrast the outcomes of the Standard Oil and U.S. Steel cases. What was the main antitrust issue in the DuPont cellophane case? In what major way do the Microsoft and Standard Oil cases differ? **LO21.2**

4. Why might one administration interpret and enforce the antitrust laws more strictly than another? How might a change of administrations affect a major monopoly case in progress? **LO21.2**

5. Suppose a proposed merger of firms would simultaneously lessen competition and reduce unit costs through economies of scale. Do you think such a merger should be allowed? **LO21.2**

6. In the 1980s, PepsiCo Inc., which then had 28 percent of the soft-drink market, proposed to acquire the Seven-Up Company. Shortly thereafter, the Coca-Cola Company, with 39 percent of the market, indicated it wanted to acquire the Dr Pepper Company. Seven-Up and Dr Pepper each controlled about 7 percent of the market. In your judgment, was the government's decision to block these mergers appropriate? **LO21.2**

7. Why might a firm charged with violating the Clayton Act, Section 7, try arguing that the products sold by the merged firms are in separate markets? Why might a firm charged with violating Section 2 of the Sherman Act try convincing the court that none of its behavior in achieving and maintaining its monopoly was illegal? **LO21.2**

8. "The social desirability of any particular firm should be judged not on the basis of its market share but on the basis of its conduct and performance." Make a counterargument, referring to the monopoly model in your statement. **LO21.2**

9. What types of industries, if any, should be subjected to industrial regulation? What specific problems does industrial regulation entail? **LO21.3**

10. In view of the problems involved in regulating natural monopolies, compare socially optimal (marginal-cost) pricing and fair-return pricing by referring again to Figure 12.9. Assuming that a government subsidy might be used to cover any loss resulting from marginal-cost pricing, which pricing policy would you favor? Why? What problems might such a subsidy entail? **LO21.3**

11. How does social regulation differ from industrial regulation? What types of benefits and costs are associated with social regulation? **LO21.4**

12. Use economic analysis to explain why the optimal amount of product safety may be less than the amount that would totally eliminate the risk of accidents and deaths. Use automobiles as an example. **LO21.4**

13. **LAST WORD** On what basis were the airlines found guilty of violating antitrust laws in the Airline Tariff Publishing case? What was the remedy? By contrast, why might it be hard to prosecute algorithmic collusion, which also uses prices posted electronically?

REVIEW QUESTIONS

1. True or false: Under the "rule of reason" that was established by the Supreme Court in the U.S. Steel case, a monopoly seller should be found guilty of violating antitrust laws even if it is charging low prices to consumers and acting the same way a competitive firm would act. **LO21.2**

2. How would you expect antitrust authorities to react to: **LO21.2**
   a. A proposed merger of Ford and General Motors.
   b. Evidence of secret meetings by contractors to rig bids for highway construction projects.
   c. A proposed merger of a large shoe manufacturer and a chain of retail shoe stores.
   d. A proposed merger of a small life-insurance company and a regional candy manufacturer.
   e. An automobile rental firm that charges higher rates for last-minute rentals than for rentals reserved weeks in advance.

3. When confronted with a natural monopoly that restricts output and charges monopoly prices, the two methods that

governments have for promoting better outcomes are: **LO21.3**
   a. Public ownership and public regulation.
   b. Sole proprietorships and public goods.
   c. Antitrust law and horizontal mergers.
   d. Creative destruction and laissez-faire.

4. Which of the following is the correct name for the idea that certain firms prefer government regulation because regulation shields them from the pressures of competition and, in effect, guarantees them a regulated profit. **LO21.3**
   a. The public interest theory of regulation.
   b. The structuralists' theory of monopoly.
   c. The legal cartel theory of regulation.
   d. The public regulation theory of natural monopoly.

5. True or false: Economists believe that social regulation is an exception to the MB = MC rule because social regulation should in every case extend as far as possible in order to ensure safe products, less pollution, and improved working conditions. **LO21.4**

PROBLEMS

1. Suppose that there are only three types of fruit sold in the United States. Annual sales are 1 million tons of blueberries, 5 million tons of strawberries, and 10 million tons of bananas. Suppose that of those total amounts, the Sunny Valley Fruit Company sells 900,000 tons of blueberries, 900,000 tons of strawberries, and 7.9 million tons of bananas. **LO21.2**
   a. What is Sunny Valley's market share if the relevant market is blueberries? If a court applies the "90-60-30 rule" when considering just the blueberry market, would it rule that Sunny Valley is a monopoly?
   b. What is Sunny Valley's market share if the relevant market is all types of berries? Would the court rule Sunny Valley to be a monopolist in that market?
   c. What if the relevant market is all types of fruit? What is Sunny Valley's market share, and would the court consider Sunny Valley to be a monopolist?

2. Carrot Computers and its competitors purchase touch screens for their tablet computers from several suppliers. The six makers of touch screens have market shares of, respectively, 19 percent, 18 percent, 14 percent, 16 percent, 20 percent, and 13 percent. **LO21.2**
   a. What is the Herfindahl index for the touch screen manufacturing industry?
   b. By how much would a proposed merger between the two smallest touch screen makers increase the Herfindahl index? Would the government be likely to challenge that proposed merger?
   c. If Carrot Computers horizontally merges with its competitor Blueberry Handhelds, by how much would the Herfindahl index change for the touch screen industry?

Agriculture: Economics and Policy

Learning Objectives

LO22.1 Explain why agricultural prices and farm income are unstable.

LO22.2 Discuss why there has been a huge employment exodus from agriculture to other U.S. industries over the past several decades.

LO22.3 Relate the rationale for farm subsidies and the economics and politics of price supports (price floors).

LO22.4 Describe major criticisms of the price-support system in agriculture.

LO22.5 List the main elements of existing federal farm policy.

If you eat, you are part of agriculture! In the United States, agriculture is important for a number of reasons. It is one of the nation's largest industries and major segments of it provide real-world examples of the pure-competition model developed in Chapters 10 and 11. Also, agriculture clearly shows the effects of government policies that interfere with supply and demand. Further, the industry provides excellent illustrations of Chapter 5's special-interest effect and rent-seeking behavior. Finally, it demonstrates the globalization of markets for farm commodities.

This chapter examines the circumstances in agriculture that have resulted in government intervention, the types and outcomes of government intervention, and recent major changes in farm policy.

Economics of Agriculture

LO22.1 Explain why agricultural prices and farm income are unstable.

Although economists refer to *the* agriculture industry, this segment of the economy is extremely diverse. Agriculture encompasses cattle ranches, fruit orchards, dairies, poultry plants, pig farms, grain farms, feed lots, vegetable plots, sugar-cane plantations, and much more. Some farm commodities (for example, soybeans and corn) are produced by thousands of individual farmers. Other farm commodities (such as poultry) are produced by just a handful of large firms. Some farm products (for example, wheat, milk, and sugar) are heavily subsidized through federal government programs; other farm products (such as fruits, nuts, and potatoes) have much less government support.

Moreover, agriculture includes both farm products, or **farm commodities** (for example, wheat, soybeans, cattle, and rice), and also **food products** (items sold through restaurants or grocery stores). Generally, the number of competing firms in the market diminishes as farm products are refined into commercial food products. Although thousands of ranches and farms raise cattle, only four firms (Tyson, Cargill, JBS, and National) account for about 80 percent of red meat produced at cattle slaughtering/meat packing plants. And thousands of farms grow tomatoes, but only three companies (Heinz, Del-Monte, and Hunt) make the bulk of the ketchup sold in the United States.

Our focus in this chapter will be on farm commodities (or farm products) and the farms and ranches that produce them. Farm commodities usually are sold in highly competitive markets, whereas food products tend to be sold in markets characterized by monopolistic competition or oligopoly.

Partly because of large government subsidies, farming remains a generally profitable industry. U.S. consumers allocate 10 percent of their spending to food, and farmers and ranchers receive about $380 billion of revenue annually from sales of crops and livestock. Over the years, however, American farmers have experienced severely fluctuating prices and periodically low incomes. Further, they have had to adjust to the reality that agriculture is a declining industry. The farm share of GDP has declined from about 7 percent in 1950 to 1 percent today.

Let's take a close look at both the short-run and long-run economics of U.S. agriculture.

The Short Run: Price and Income Instability

Price and income instability in agriculture results from (1) an inelastic demand for agricultural products, combined with (2) fluctuations in farm output and (3) shifts of the demand curve for farm products.

Inelastic Demand for Agricultural Products
In industrially advanced economies, the price elasticity of demand for agricultural products is low. For agricultural products in the aggregate, the elasticity coefficient is between 0.20 and 0.25. These figures suggest that the prices of farm products would have to fall by 40 to 50 percent for consumers to increase their purchases by a mere 10 percent. Consumers apparently put a low value on additional farm output compared with the value they put on additional units of alternative goods.

Why is this so? Recall that the basic determinant of elasticity of demand is substitutability. When the price of one product falls, the consumer tends to substitute that product for other products whose prices have not fallen. But in relatively wealthy societies this "substitution effect" is very modest for food. Although people may eat more, they do not switch from three meals a day to, say, five or six meals a day in response to a decline in the relative prices of farm products. Real biological factors constrain an individual's capacity to substitute food for other products.

The inelasticity of agricultural demand is also related to diminishing marginal utility. In a high-income economy, the population is generally well fed and well clothed; it is relatively saturated with the food and fiber of agriculture. Additional farm products therefore are subject to rapidly diminishing marginal utility. So very large price cuts are needed to induce small increases in food and fiber consumption.

Fluctuations in Output
Farm output tends to fluctuate from year to year, mainly because farmers have limited control over their output. Floods, droughts, unexpected frost, insect damage, and similar disasters can mean poor crops, while an excellent growing season means bumper crops (unusually large outputs). Such natural occurrences are beyond the control of farmers, yet they exert an important influence on output.

In addition to natural phenomena, the highly competitive nature of many parts of farming and ranching makes it difficult for those producers to form huge combinations to control production. If the thousands of widely scattered and independent producers happened to plant an unusually large or abnormally small portion of their land one year, an extra-large or a very small farm output would result even if the growing season were normal.

Curve D in Figure 22.1 illustrates the inelastic demand for agricultural products. Combining that inelastic demand with the instability of farm production, we can see why agricultural prices and incomes are unstable. Even if the market demand for farm products remains fixed at D, its price inelasticity will magnify small changes in output into relatively large changes in agricultural prices and income. For example, suppose that a "normal" crop of Q_n results in a "normal" price of P_n and a "normal" farm income represented by the yellow rectangle. A bumper crop or a poor crop will cause large deviations from these normal prices and incomes because of the inelasticity of demand.

If a good growing season occurs, the resulting large crop of Q_b will reduce farm income to that of area $0P_b bQ_b$. When demand is inelastic, an increase in the quantity sold will be accompanied by a more-than-proportionate decline in price. The net result is that total revenue, that is, total farm income, will decline disproportionately.

Similarly, a small crop caused by, say, drought will boost total farm income to that represented by area $0P_p pQ_p$. A decline in output will cause more-than-proportionate increases in price and income when demand is inelastic. Ironically, for farmers as a group, a poor crop may be a blessing and a bumper crop a hardship.

Conclusion: With a stable market demand for farm products, the inelasticity of that demand will turn relatively small changes in output into relatively larger changes in agricultural prices and income.

FIGURE 22.1 The effects of changes in farm output on agricultural prices and income. Because of the inelasticity of demand for farm products, a relatively small change in farm output (from Q_n to Q_p or Q_b) will cause a relatively large change in agricultural prices (from P_n to P_p or P_b). Farm income will change from the yellow area to the larger $0P_ppQ_p$ area or to the smaller $0P_bbQ_b$ area.

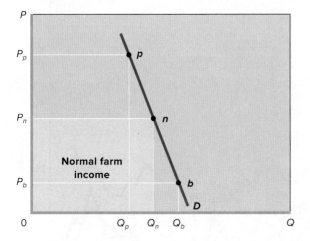

FIGURE 22.2 The effect of a demand shift on agricultural prices and income. Because of the highly inelastic demand for farm products, a small shift in demand (from D_1 to D_2) for farm products can drastically alter agricultural prices (P_1 to P_2) and farm income (area $0P_1aQ_n$ to area $0P_2bQ_n$), given a fixed level of production Q_n.

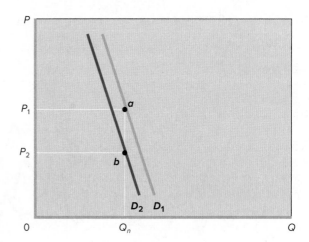

Fluctuations in Demand The third factor in the short-run instability of farm income results from shifts in the demand curve for agricultural products. Suppose that somehow farm output is stabilized at the "normal" level of Q_n in Figure 22.2. Now, because of the inelasticity of the demand for farm products, short-run changes in the demand for those products will cause markedly different prices and incomes to be associated with this fixed level of output.

A slight decline in demand from D_1 to D_2 will reduce farm income from area $0P_1aQ_n$ to $0P_2bQ_n$. So a relatively small decline in demand gives farmers significantly less income for the same amount of farm output. Conversely, a slight increase in

FIGURE 22.3 U.S. farm exports as a percentage of farm output, 1950–2014. Exports of farm output have increased as a percentage of total farm output (the value of agricultural-sector production) in the United States. But this percentage has been quite variable, contributing to the instability of the demand for U.S. farm output.

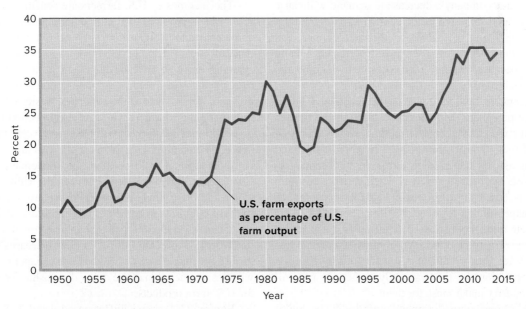

Source: Derived by the authors from *Foreign Agricultural Trade of the United States,* **www.ers.usda.gov/Data/FATUS**; and Bureau of Economic Analysis, **www.bea.gov**.

FIGURE 22.4 Inflation-adjusted U.S. agricultural prices, selected commodities, 1950–2015. Inflation-adjusted U.S. prices (in 2005 dollars) for cattle, hogs, corn, and wheat since 1950 indicate both volatility and general decline.

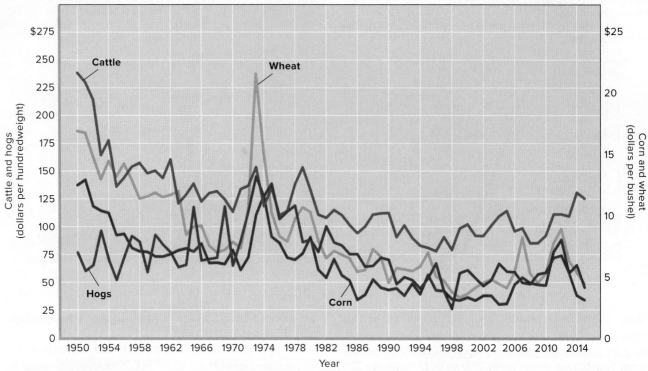

Source: Author calculations using nominal values from Global Financial Data, **globalfinancialdata.com**, adjusted for inflation with the GDP deflator published by the Bureau of Economic Analysis, **bea.gov**.

demand—as from D_2 to D_1—provides a sizable increase in farm income for the same volume of output. Again, large price and income changes occur because demand is inelastic.

It is tempting to argue that the sharp declines in agricultural prices that accompany a decrease in demand will cause many farmers to close down in the short run, reducing total output and alleviating the price and income declines. But farm production is relatively insensitive to price changes in the short run because farmers' fixed costs are high compared with their variable costs.

Interest, rent, tax, and mortgage payments on land, buildings, and equipment are the major costs faced by the farmer. These are all fixed charges. Furthermore, the labor supply of farmers and their families can also be regarded as a fixed cost. As long as they stay on their farms, farmers cannot reduce their costs by firing themselves. Their variable costs are the costs of the small amounts of extra help they may employ, as well as expenditures for seed, fertilizer, and fuel. As a result of their high proportion of fixed costs, farmers are usually better off working their land even when they are losing money since they would lose much more by shutting down their operations for the year. Only in the long run will exiting the industry make sense for them.

But why is agricultural demand unstable? The major source of demand volatility in U.S. agriculture springs from

its dependence on world markets. As we show in Figure 22.3, that dependency has increased since 1950. The yearly ups and downs of the line in the figure also reveal that, as a percentage of total U.S. farm output, farm exports are highly unstable.

The incomes of U.S. farmers are sensitive to changes in weather and crop production in other countries: Better crops abroad mean less foreign demand for U.S. farm products. Similarly, cyclical fluctuations in incomes in Europe or Southeast Asia, for example, may shift the demand for U.S. farm products. Changes in foreign economic policies may also change demand. For instance, if the nations of western Europe decide to provide their farmers with greater protection from foreign competition, U.S. farmers will have less access to those markets and demand for U.S. farm exports will fall.

International politics also add to demand instability. Changing political relations between the United States and China and the United States and Russia have boosted exports to those countries in some periods and reduced them in others. Changes in the international value of the dollar may also be critical. Depreciation of the dollar increases the demand for U.S. farm products (which become cheaper to foreigners), whereas appreciation of the dollar diminishes foreign demand for U.S. farm products.

Figure 22.4 shows inflation-adjusted U.S. prices for cattle, hogs, corn, and wheat from 1950 through 2012. The short-run economics of price volatility is evident. So, too, is the general decline of real (inflation-adjusted) agricultural prices from 1950 through the late 1990s.

Since the late 1990s, however, the prices of these four commodities have not continued the overall downward trend that they had previously followed. Prices continued to be volatile but remained in 2009 about where they had been in the late 1990s. Then, major price spikes took place between 2009 and 2012. For example, the inflation-adjusted price of wheat more than doubled, increasing from $3.75 per bushel in 2009 to $8.31 per bushel in 2012.

The lack of a downward trend in commodity prices starting in the late 1990s coupled with the major price spikes that occurred between 2009 and 2012 led some economists to wonder whether the era of inflation-adjusted price decreases in agriculture had come to an end. They speculated that the rising demand for food in emerging economies such as China together with the growing demand for farm products to produce ethanol might reverse the long-run downward trend. But, as Figure 22.4 reveals, several previous price spikes as well as flat periods in agricultural prices have occurred. Each of these events eventually yielded to the general historical downward trend in agricultural prices. That patterned reoccurred between 2012 and 2015 as the prices of hogs, corn, and wheat fell back down toward their all-time lows.

The Long Run: A Declining Industry

LO22.2 Discuss why there has been a huge employment exodus from agriculture to other U.S. industries over the past several decades.

Two dynamic characteristics of agricultural markets explain why agriculture has been a declining industry:

- Over time, the supply of farm products has increased rapidly because of technological progress.

- The demand for farm products has increased slowly because it is inelastic with respect to income and because it is largely limited by population growth, which has not been rapid in the United States.

Let's examine each of these supply and demand forces.

Technology and Supply Increases

A rapid rate of technological advance has significantly increased the supply of agricultural products. This technological progress has many roots: the mechanization of farms, improved techniques of land management, soil conservation, irrigation, development of hybrid crops, availability of improved fertilizers and insecticides, polymer-coated seeds, and improvements in the breeding and care of livestock. The amount of capital used per farmworker increased 15 times between 1930 and 1980,

permitting a fivefold increase in the amount of land cultivated per farmer. The simplest measure of these advances is the U.S. Agriculture Department's index of farm output per unit of farm labor. In 1950 a single unit of farm labor could produce 10 units of farm output. This amount increased to 30 in 1970, 42 in 1980, 64 in 1990, 90 in 2000, and 119 in 2009. Over the last half-century, productivity in agriculture has advanced twice as fast as productivity in the nonfarm economy.

Most of the technological advances in agriculture were not initiated by farmers. Rather, they are the result of government-sponsored programs of research and education and the initiative of the suppliers of farm inputs. Land-grant colleges, experiment stations, county agents of the Agricultural Extension Service, educational pamphlets issued by the U.S. Department of Agriculture (USDA), and the research departments of farm machinery, pesticide, and fertilizer producers have been the primary sources of technological advance in U.S. agriculture.

More recently, technological advance has been fueled by the incorporation of advanced information technologies into farming. Computers and the Internet give farmers instant access to information about soil conditions, estimated crop yields, farm-product prices, available land for purchase or lease, and much more. They also provide farmers with sophisticated business software to help track and manage their operations.

Lagging Demand

Increases in the demand for agricultural products have failed to keep pace with these technologically created increases in the supply of the products. The reason lies in the two major determinants of agricultural demand: income and population.

In developing countries, consumers must devote most of their meager incomes to agricultural products—food and clothing—to sustain themselves. But as income expands beyond subsistence and the problem of hunger diminishes, consumers increase their outlays on food at ever-declining rates. Once consumers' stomachs are filled, they turn to the amenities of life that manufacturing and services, not agriculture, provide. Economic growth in the United States has boosted average per capita income far beyond the level of subsistence. As a result, increases in the incomes of U.S. consumers now produce less-than-proportionate increases in spending on farm products.

The demand for farm products in the United States is income-inelastic; it is quite insensitive to increases in income. Estimates indicate that a 10 percent increase in real per capita after-tax income produces about a 1 percent increase in consumption of farm products. That means a coefficient of income elasticity of 0.1 ($= 0.01/0.10$). So as the incomes of Americans rise, the demand for farm products increases far less rapidly than the demand for goods and services in general.

The second reason for lagging demand relates to population growth. Once a certain income level has been reached, each consumer's intake of food and fiber becomes relatively

CONSIDER THIS . . .

© Digital Vision/PunchStock RF

Risky Business

The short-run instability of agricultural prices and farm income creates considerable risk in agriculture. Later in this chapter we will find that farm programs (direct payments, countercyclical payments, and "repay-or-default" loans) reduce the risk of farming for many farmers. But these programs are limited to certain crops, such as grains and oilseeds.

Fortunately, several private techniques for managing risk have become commonplace in agriculture. The purpose of these measures is to "smooth" income over time, "hedging" against short-run output and price fluctuations. Hedging is an action by a buyer or seller to protect against a change in future prices prior to an anticipated purchase or sale.

Farm risk-management techniques include:

- **Futures markets.** In the futures market, farmers can buy or sell farm products at prices fixed now, for delivery at a specified date in the future. If the price falls, farmers will still obtain revenue based on the higher price fixed in the futures market. If the price rises, the buyer will benefit by getting the farm commodity at the lower price fixed in the futures market.

- **Contracting with processors.** In advance of planting, farmers can directly contract with food processors (firms such as sugar beet refiners, ethanol plants, and feed lots) to assure themselves of a fixed price per unit of their farm or ranch output.

- **Crop revenue insurance.** Farmers can buy crop revenue insurance, which insures them against gross revenue losses resulting from storm damage and other natural occurrences.

- **Leasing land.** Farm operators can reduce their risk by leasing some of their land to other operators who pay them cash rent. The rent payment is stable, regardless of the quality of the crop and crop prices.

- **Nonfarm income.** Many farm households derive substantial parts of their total income from off-farm income, such as spousal work and agricultural investments. These more-stable elements of income cushion the instability of farm income.

Although farming remains a risky business, farm operators have found creative ways to manage the inherent risks of price and income instability.

FIGURE 22.5 The long-run decline of agricultural prices and farm income. In the long run, increases in the demand for U.S. farm products (from D_1 to D_2) have not kept pace with the increases in supply (from S_1 to S_2) resulting from technological advances. Because agricultural demand is inelastic, these shifts have tended to depress agricultural prices (from P_1 to P_2) and reduce farm income (from $0P_1aQ_1$ to $0P_2bQ_2$) while increasing output only modestly (from Q_1 to Q_2).

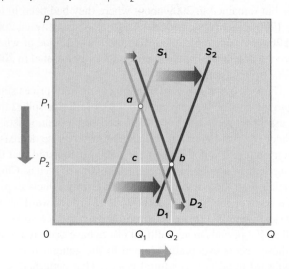

fixed. Thus subsequent increases in demand depend directly on growth in the number of consumers. In most advanced nations, including the United States, the demand for farm products increases at a rate roughly equal to the rate of population growth. Because U.S. population growth has not been rapid, the increase in U.S. demand for farm products has not kept pace with the rapid growth of farm output.

Graphical Portrayal

The combination of an inelastic and slowly increasing demand for agricultural products with a rapidly increasing supply puts strong downward pressure on agricultural prices and income. Figure 22.5 shows a large increase in agricultural supply accompanied by a very modest increase in demand. Because of the inelasticity of demand, those shifts result in a sharp decline in agricultural prices, accompanied by a relatively small increase in output. So farm income declines. On the graph, we see that farm income before the increases in demand and supply (measured by rectangle $0P_1aQ_1$) exceeds farm income after those increases ($0P_2bQ_2$). Because farm products have inelastic demand, an increase in supply relative to demand creates persistent downward pressure on farm income.

Consequences

The actual consequences of the demand and supply changes over time have been those predicted by the pure-competition model. The supply and demand conditions just outlined have increased the minimum efficient scale (MES) in agriculture and reduced crop prices. Farms that are too small to realize productivity gains and take advantage of economies of scale have discovered that their average total costs exceed the (declining) prices for their crops. So they can no longer operate

TABLE 22.1 U.S. Farm Employment and Number of Farms, 1950–2015

| | Farm Employment* | | |
| | | | |
Year	In Millions of People	As Percentage of Total Employment	Number of Farms, Thousands
1950	9.3	15.8	5,388
1960	6.2	9.4	3,962
1970	4.0	5.0	2,954
1980	3.5	3.5	2,440
1990	2.5	2.1	2,146
2000	2.2	1.6	2,172
2010	2.2	1.2	2,200
2015	2.4	1.5	2,110

*Includes self-employed farmers, unpaid farmworkers, and hired farmworkers.

Sources: Derived by the authors from *Economic Report of the President, 2012,* Table B-100 and *Economic Report of the President, 2015,* Table B-12; U.S. Bureau of Labor Statistics, **www.bls.gov**; and Department of Agriculture, Economic Research Service, **www.ers.usda.gov**.

profitably. In the long run, financial losses in agriculture have triggered a massive exit of workers to other sectors of the economy, as shown by Table 22.1. They have also caused a major consolidation of smaller farms into larger ones. A person farming, say, 240 acres of corn three decades ago is today likely to be farming two or three times that number of acres. Large corporate firms, collectively called **agribusiness**, have emerged in some areas of farming such as potatoes, beef, fruits, vegetables, and poultry. Today, there are 2.1 million farms compared to about 4 million in 1960, and farm labor constitutes about 1.5 percent of the U.S. labor force compared to 9.4 percent in 1960. (Global Perspective 22.1 compares the most recent labor-force percentages for several nations.)

Farm-Household Income

Traditionally, the income of farm households was well below that of nonfarm households. But even with the lower real crop prices, that imbalance has reversed. In 2014—a particularly good year for agriculture—the average income of farm households was about $134,000, compared to $75,738 for all U.S. households. Outmigration, consolidation, rising farm productivity, and significant government subsidies have boosted farm income *per farm household* (of which there are fewer than before).

Also, members of farm households operating smaller farms have increasingly taken jobs in nearby towns and cities. On average, only about 16 percent of the income of farm households derives from farming activities. This average, however, is pulled downward by the many households living in rural areas and operating small "residential farms." For households operating "commercial farms"—farms with

GLOBAL PERSPECTIVE 22.1

Average Percentage of Labor Force in Agriculture, Selected Nations, 2011–2014 Data

High-income nations devote a much smaller percentage of their labor forces to agriculture than do low-income nations. Because their workforces are so heavily committed to producing the food and fiber needed for their populations, low-income nations have relatively less labor available to produce housing, schools, autos, and the other goods and services that contribute to a high standard of living.

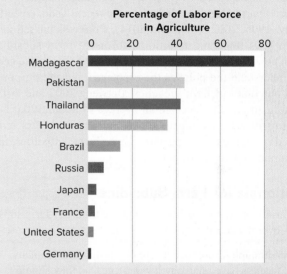

Percentage of Labor Force in Agriculture

Source: *World Development Indicators 2014,* World Bank, **databank.worldbank.org**.

annual sales of $350,000 or more—about 73 percent of the average income of $225,463 in 2014 derived from farming. Although agriculture is a declining industry, the 10 percent of farm households operating commercial farms in the United States are doing remarkably well, at least as a group.

QUICK REVIEW 22.1

✓ Agricultural prices and incomes are volatile in the short run because an inelastic demand converts small changes in farm output and demand into relatively larger changes in prices and income.

✓ Technological progress has generated large increases in the supply of farm products over time.

✓ Increases in demand for farm products have been modest in the United States because demand is inelastic with respect to income and because population growth has been modest.

✓ The combination of large increases in supply and small increases in demand has made U.S. agriculture a declining industry (as measured by the value of agricultural output as a percentage of GDP).

Economics of Farm Policy

LO22.3 Relate the rationale for farm subsidies and the economics and politics of price supports (price floors).

The U.S. government has subsidized agriculture since the 1930s with a "farm program" that includes (1) support for agricultural prices, income, and output; (2) soil and water conservation; (3) agricultural research; (4) farm credit; (5) crop insurance; and (6) subsidized sale of farm products in world markets.

We will focus on the main element of farm policy: the programs designed to prop up prices and income. This topic is particularly timely because in recent years (specifically, 1996, 2002, 2008, and 2014), Congress passed new farm laws replacing traditional forms of farm subsidies with new forms. To understand these new policies, we need to understand the policies they replaced and the purposes and outcomes of farm subsidies. Between 2002 and 2011, American farmers received an average of about $20.0 billion of direct government subsidies each year. (As indicated in Global Perspective 22.2, farm subsidies are common in many nations.)

Rationale for Farm Subsidies

A variety of arguments have been made to justify farm subsidies over the decades:

- Although farm products are necessities of life, many farmers have relatively low incomes, so they should receive higher prices and incomes through public help.

- The "family farm" is a fundamental U.S. institution and should be nurtured as a way of life.

- Farmers are subject to extraordinary hazards—floods, droughts, and insects—that most other industries do not face. Without government help, farmers cannot fully insure themselves against these disasters.

- While many farmers face purely competitive markets for their outputs, they buy inputs of fertilizer, farm machinery, and gasoline from industries that have considerable market power. Whereas those resource-supplying industries are able to control their prices, farmers are at the "mercy of the market" in selling their output. The supporters of subsidies argue that agriculture warrants public aid to offset the disadvantageous market-power imbalances faced by farmers.

Background: The Parity Concept

The Agricultural Adjustment Act of 1933 established the **parity concept** as a cornerstone of agricultural policy. The rationale of the parity concept can be stated in both real and nominal terms. In real terms, parity says that year after year for a fixed output of farm products, a farmer should be able to

GLOBAL PERSPECTIVE 22.2

Agricultural Subsidies, Selected Nations

Farmers in various countries receive large percentages of their incomes as government subsidies.

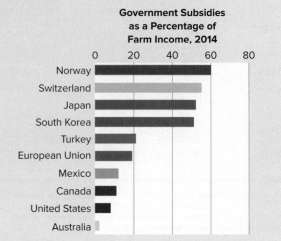

Government Subsidies as a Percentage of Farm Income, 2014

Source: *Producer and Consumer Support Estimates, 2015,* Organization for Economic Cooperation and Development, **www.oecd.org/agriculture/pse**.

acquire a specific total amount of other goods and services. A particular real output should always result in the same real income: "If a farmer could take a bushel of corn to town in 1912 and sell it for enough money to buy a shirt, he should be able to sell a bushel of corn today and buy a shirt." In nominal terms, the parity concept suggests that the relationship between the prices received by farmers for their output and the prices they must pay for goods and services should remain constant. The parity concept implies that if the price of shirts tripled over some time period, then the price of corn should have tripled too. Such a situation is said to represent 100 percent of parity.

The **parity ratio** is the ratio of prices received to prices paid, expressed as a percentage. That is:

$$\text{Parity ratio} = \frac{\text{Prices received by farmers}}{\text{Prices paid by farmers}}$$

Why farmers would benefit from having the prices of their products based on 100 percent of parity is obvious. By 2015 nominal prices paid by farmers had increased 29-fold since 1900–1914, whereas nominal prices received by farmers had increased only about 9-fold. In 2015 the parity ratio stood at 0.36 (or 36 percent), indicating that prices received in 2015 could buy 36 percent as much as prices received in the 1910–1914 period. So a farm policy that enforced 100 percent of parity would generate substantially higher prices for farmers.

FIGURE 22.6 Price supports, agricultural surpluses, and transfers to farmers. The market demand D and supply S of a farm product yield equilibrium price P_e and quantity Q_e. An above-equilibrium price support P_s results in consumption of quantity Q_c, production of quantity Q_s, and a surplus of quantity $Q_s - Q_c$. The yellow rectangle represents a transfer of money from taxpayers to farmers. Triangle bac within the yellow rectangle shows the efficiency loss (or a deadweight loss) to society.

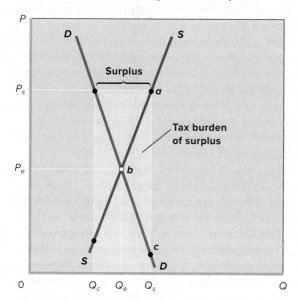

Economics of Price Supports

The concept of parity provides the rationale for government price floors on farm products. In agriculture those minimum prices are called **price supports**. We have shown that, in the long run, the market prices received by farmers have not kept up with the prices paid by them. One way to achieve parity, or some percentage thereof, is to have the government establish above-equilibrium price supports for farm products.

Many different price-support programs have been tried, but they all tend to have similar effects, some of which are subtle and negative. Suppose in Figure 22.6 that the equilibrium price is P_e and the price support is P_s. Then the major effects would be as follows.

Surplus Output The most obvious result is a product surplus. Consumers are willing to purchase only Q_c units at the supported price, while farmers supply Q_s units. What about the $Q_s - Q_c$ surplus that results? The government must buy it to make the above-equilibrium price support effective. As you will see, this surplus farm output means that agriculture receives an overallocation of resources.

Gain to Farmers Farmers benefit from price supports. In Figure 22.6, gross farm revenue rises from the free-market level represented by area $0P_ebQ_e$ to the larger, supported level shown by area $0P_saQ_s$.

Loss to Consumers Consumers lose; they pay a higher price (P_s rather than P_e) and consume less (Q_c rather than Q_e) of the product. In some instances differences between the market price and the supported price are substantial. For example, the U.S.-supported price of a pound of sugar is about 32 percent higher than the world market price, and a quart of fluid milk is estimated to cost consumers twice as much as it would without government programs. Moreover, the burden of higher food prices falls disproportionately on the poor because they spend a larger part of their incomes on food.

Efficiency Losses Society loses because price supports create allocative inefficiency by encouraging an overallocation of resources to agriculture. A price floor (P_s) attracts more resources to the agricultural sector than would the free-market price (P_e). Viewed through the pure-competition model, the market supply curve in Figure 22.6 represents the marginal costs of all farmers producing this product at the various output levels. An efficient allocation of resources occurs at point b, where the market price P_e is equal to marginal cost. So the output Q_e reflects that efficient allocation of resources.

In contrast, the output Q_s associated with the price support P_s represents an overallocation of resources; for all units of output between Q_e and Q_s, marginal costs (measured on curve S) exceed the prices people are willing to pay for those units (measured on curve D). Simply stated, the marginal cost of the extra production exceeds its marginal benefit to society. Society incurs an efficiency loss (or a deadweight loss) of area bac because of the price-support system.

Other Social Losses Society at large loses in other ways. Taxpayers pay higher taxes to finance the government's purchase of the surplus. This added tax burden is equal to the surplus output $Q_s - Q_c$ multiplied by its price P_s, as shown by the yellow area in Figure 22.6. Recall, too, that the mere collection of taxes imposes an efficiency loss (as was demonstrated in Chapter 20 in Figure 20.10). Also, the cost of storing surplus farm output adds to this tax burden.

Government's intervention in agriculture also entails administrative costs. Thousands of government workers are needed to administer U.S. price supports and other farm programs.

Finally, the rent-seeking activity involved—the pursuit of political support to maintain price supports—is costly and socially wasteful. Farm groups spend considerable sums to sustain political support for price floors and other programs that enhance farm incomes.

Environmental Costs We know from Figure 22.6 that price supports encourage additional production. Although some of that extra output may come from the use of additional land, much of it comes from heavier use of fertilizer and pesticides. Those pesticides and fertilizers may pollute the environment (for example, groundwater) and create residues in food that pose health risks to farmworkers and consumers. Research shows a positive relationship between the level of price-support subsidies and the use of agrochemicals.

Farm policy also may cause environmental problems in less obvious ways. Farmers benefit from price supports only when they use their land consistently for a specific crop such as corn or wheat. That creates a disincentive to practice crop rotation, which is a nonchemical technique for controlling pests. Farm policy thus encourages the substitution of chemicals for other forms of pest control.

Also, we know from the concept of derived demand that an increase in the price of a product will increase the demand for relevant inputs. In particular, price supports for farm products increase the demand for land. And the land that farmers bring into farm production is often environmentally sensitive "marginal" land, such as steeply sloped, erosion-prone land, or wetlands that provide wildlife habitat. Similarly, price supports result in the use of more water for irrigation, and the resulting runoff may contribute to soil erosion.

International Costs Actually, the costs of farm price supports go beyond those indicated by Figure 22.6. Price supports generate economic distortions that cross national boundaries. For example, the high prices caused by price supports make the U.S. agricultural market attractive to foreign producers. But inflows of foreign agricultural products would serve to increase supplies in the United States, aggravating the problem of U.S. surpluses. To prevent that from happening, the United States is likely to impose import barriers in the form of tariffs or quotas. Those barriers tend to restrict the output of more-efficient foreign producers while encouraging more output from less-efficient U.S. producers. The result is a less-efficient use of world agricultural resources. This chapter's Last Word suggests that this is indeed the case for sugar.

Similarly, as the United States and other industrially advanced countries with similar agricultural programs dump surplus farm products on world markets, the prices of such products are depressed. Developing countries are often heavily dependent on world commodity markets for their incomes. So they are particularly hurt because their export earnings are reduced. Thus, U.S. subsidies for rice production have imposed significant costs on Thailand, a major rice exporter. Similarly, U.S. cotton programs have adversely affected Egypt, Mexico, and other cotton-exporting nations.

Reduction of Surpluses

Figure 22.6 suggests that programs designed to reduce market supply (shift S leftward) or increase market demand (shift D rightward) would help boost the market price toward

the supported price P_s. Further, such programs would reduce or eliminate farm surpluses. The U.S. government has tried both supply and demand approaches to reduce or eliminate surpluses.

Restricting Supply Until recently, public policy focused mainly on restricting farm output. In particular, **acreage allotments** accompanied price supports. In return for guaranteed prices for their crops, farmers had to agree to limit the number of acres they planted in that crop. The U.S. Department of Agriculture first set the price support and then estimated the amount of the product consumers would buy at the supported price. It then translated that amount into the total number of planted acres necessary to provide it. The total acreage was apportioned among states, counties, and ultimately individual farmers.

These supply-restricting programs were only partially successful. They did not eliminate surpluses, mainly because acreage reduction did not result in a proportionate decline in production. Some farmers retired their worst land and kept their best land in production. They also cultivated their tilled acres more intensively. Superior seed, more and better fertilizer and insecticides, and improved farm equipment were used to enhance output per acre. And nonparticipating farmers expanded their planted acreage in anticipation of overall higher prices. Nevertheless, the net effect of acreage allotment undoubtedly was a reduction of farm surpluses and their associated costs to taxpayers.

Bolstering Demand Government has tried several ways to increase demand for U.S. agricultural products. For example, both government and private industry have spent large sums on research to create new uses for agricultural goods. The production of "gasohol," which is a blend of gasoline and alcohol (ethanol) made mainly from corn, is one such successful attempt to increase the demand for farm output. (See the nearby Consider This box for a fuller discussion of ethanol.) Recent attempts to promote "biodiesel," a fuel made from soybean oil and other natural vegetable oils, also fit the demand-enhancement approach.

The government has also created a variety of programs to stimulate consumption of farm products. For example, the objective of the food-stamp program is not only to reduce hunger but also to bolster the demand for food. Similarly, the Food for Peace program has enabled developing countries to buy U.S. surplus farm products with their own currencies, rather than having to use dollars. The federal government spends millions of dollars each year to advertise and promote global sales of U.S. farm products. Furthermore, U.S. negotiators have pressed hard in international trade negotiations to persuade foreign nations to reduce trade barriers to the importing of farm products.

CONSIDER THIS . . .

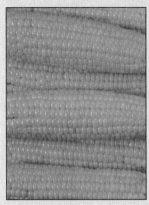

© Burke/Triolo Productions/Getty Images RF

Putting Corn in Your Gas Tank

Government's promotion of greater production and use of corn-based ethanol serves both as a good example of an attempt by government to bolster the demand for U.S. farm products and as an example of how price changes can ripple through markets and produce myriad secondary effects. Gasoline producers blend ethanol (an alcohol-like substance) with conventional gasoline refined from oil. The government's rationale for promoting ethanol is to reduce U.S. dependency on foreign oil, but the strongest proponents are from states in the Corn Belt.

The ethanol program has several facets, including tariffs on imported ethanol, subsidies to oil refineries that buy ethanol, and mandates to industry to increase their use of alternative fuels. The rising demand for ethanol that resulted contributed to tripling of the inflation-adjusted price of a bushel of corn between 2005 and 2012.

But numerous secondary effects from the increased price of corn also occurred. Farmers shifted production toward corn and away from soybeans, sorghum, and other crops. The decreases in the supply of these other crops raised their prices, too. Also, because corn is used as a major feedstock, the price of beef, pork, and chicken rose.

The ethanol subsidies had other secondary effects. The prices of seed, fertilizer, and farmland all increased. Because corn is a water-intensive crop, its expanded production resulted in faster withdrawals of irrigation water from underground aquifers. The refining of ethanol also depleted ground water or removed it from rivers. Moreover, the increased use of fertilizer in corn production increased the runoff of nitrogen from fertilizer into streams and rivers, causing environmental damage.

The price effects of ethanol subsidies, however, may moderate as farmers shift additional land to corn, increasing its supply and reducing its price. Nevertheless, the multiple impacts of public policy illustrate an important economic maxim: In the economy, it is difficult to do just *one* thing.

During the era of price supports, the government's supply-restricting and demand-increasing efforts boosted agricultural prices and reduced surplus production, but they did not succeed in eliminating the sizable surpluses.

Criticisms and Politics

LO22.4 Describe major criticisms of the price-support system in agriculture.

After decades of experience with government price-support programs, it became apparent in the 1990s that farm policy was not working well. Major criticisms of farm subsidies emerged, as did a more skeptical analysis of the politics of those subsidies.

Criticisms of the Parity Concept

Economists uniformly rejected the rationale of the parity concept. They found no economic logic in the proposition that if a bushel of wheat could buy a shirt in 1900, it should still be able to buy a shirt several decades later. The relative values of goods and services are established by supply and demand, and those relative values change over time as technology changes, resource prices change, tastes change, and substitute resources and new products emerge. A fully equipped personal computer, monitor, and printer cost as much as a cheap new automobile in 1985. That was not true just a decade later because the price of computer equipment had dropped so dramatically. Based on the parity concept, one could argue that price supports and subsidies were justified for computer manufacturers!

Criticisms of the Price-Support System

Criticisms of the price-support system were equally severe.

Symptoms, Not Causes The price-support strategy in agriculture was designed to treat the symptoms, not the causes of the farm problem. The root cause of the long-run farm problem was misallocation of resources between agriculture and the rest of the economy. Historically, the problem had been one of too many farmers. The effect of that misallocation was relatively low agricultural prices and low farm income. But the price and income supports encouraged people to stay in farming rather than move to nonfarm occupations. That is, the price and income orientation of the farm program slowed the reallocation of resources necessary to resolve the long-run farm problem.

Misguided Subsidies Because price supports were on a per-bushel basis, the subsidy system benefited those farmers who needed subsidies the least. If the goal of farm policy was to raise low farm incomes, it followed that any program of federal aid should have been aimed at farmers with the lowest incomes. But the poor, low-output farmer did not produce and sell enough in the market to get much aid from price supports. Instead, the large, prosperous farmer reaped the benefits because of sizable output. On equity grounds, direct income payments to struggling farmers are highly preferable to indirect price-support subsidies that go primarily to large-scale, prosperous farmers. Better yet, say many economists, would be transition and retraining support for farmers willing to move out of farming and into other occupations and businesses in greater demand.

A related point concerns land values. The price and income benefits that the price-support system provided increased the value of farmland. By making crops more valuable, price supports made the land itself more valuable. That was helpful to farmers who owned the land they farmed but not to farmers who rented land. Farmers rented about 40 percent of their farmland, mostly from well-to-do nonfarm landlords. So, price supports became a subsidy to people who were not actively engaged in farming.

Policy Contradictions Because farm policy had many objectives, it often led to contradictions. Whereas most subsidized research was aimed at increasing farm productivity and the supply of farm products, acreage-allotment programs required that farmers take land out of production in order to reduce supply. Price supports for crops meant increased feed costs for ranchers and farmers and high consumer prices for animal products. Tobacco farmers were subsidized even though tobacco consumption was causing serious health problems. The U.S. sugar program raised prices for domestic producers by imposing import quotas that conflicted with free-trade policies. Conservation programs called for setting aside land for wildlife habitat, while price supports provided incentives to bring such acreage into production.

All these criticisms helped spawn policy reform. Nevertheless, as we will see, those reforms turned out to be less substantive than originally conceived. Nearly all these criticisms are as valid for current farm policy as they were for the price-support program.

The Politics of Farm Policy

In view of these criticisms, why did the United States continue its price-support program for 60 years and why does it still continue that program for sugar, milk, and tobacco? Why do farm subsidies in the billions of dollars still occur?

Public Choice Theory Revisited Public choice theory (Chapter 5) helps answer these questions. Recall that rent-seeking behavior occurs when a group (a labor union, firms in a specific industry, or farmers producing a particular crop) uses political means to transfer income or wealth to itself at the expense of another group or of society as a whole. And recall that the special-interest effect involves a program or policy from which a small group receives large benefits at the expense of a much larger group whose members individually suffer small losses. Both rent-seeking behavior and the special-interest effect help explain the politics of farm subsidies.

Suppose a certain group of farmers, say, peanut or sugar producers, organize and establish a well-financed political action committee (PAC). The PAC's job is to promote government programs that will transfer income to the group (this is rent-seeking behavior). The PAC vigorously lobbies U.S. senators and representatives to enact or to continue price supports, production quotas, or import quotas for peanuts or sugar. The PAC does this in part by making political contributions to sympathetic legislators. Although peanut production is heavily concentrated in a few states such as Georgia, Alabama, and Texas, the peanut PAC will also make contributions to legislators from other states in order to gain support.

But how can a small interest group like peanut or sugar growers successfully lobby to increase its own income at the expense of society as a whole? Because even though the total cost of the group's programs might be considerable, the cost imposed on each individual taxpayer is small (this is the special-interest effect). Taxpayers are likely to be uninformed about and indifferent to such programs since they have little at stake. Unless you grow sugar beets or peanuts, you probably have no idea how much these programs cost you as an individual taxpayer and consumer and therefore do not object when your legislator votes for, say, a sugar-support program. Thus, the PAC encounters little or no lobbying against its efforts.

Political logrolling—the trading of votes on policies and programs—also works to perpetuate certain programs: Senator Foghorn agrees to vote for a program that benefits Senator Moribund's constituents, and Moribund returns the favor. Example: Many members of Congress who represent low-income urban areas vote in favor of farm subsidies. In return, representatives of agricultural areas support such programs as food stamps, which subsidize food for the poor. The result is a rural-urban coalition through which representatives from both areas provide benefits for their constituents and enhance their reelection chances. Such coalitions help explain why farm subsidies persist and why the food-stamp program has been expanded over the years.

Large agribusinesses that supply inputs to agriculture also lend political support to farm subsidies because subsidies increase the amounts of agrochemicals and farm machinery that farmers are able to buy. And most of the thousands of government employees whose jobs depend on farm programs are highly supportive. So, too, are owners of farmland.

Public choice theory also tells us that politicians are likely to favor programs that have hidden costs. As we have seen, that is often true of farm programs. Our discussion of Figure 22.6 indicated that price supports involve not simply a transfer of money from taxpayer to farmer but costs that are hidden as higher food prices, storage costs for surplus output, costs of administering farm programs, and costs associated with both domestic and international misallocations of resources. Because those costs are largely indirect and hidden, farm programs are much more acceptable to politicians and the public than they would be if all costs were explicit.

Changing Politics In spite of rent seeking, special interests, and logrolling, a combination of factors has somewhat altered the politics of farm subsidies in recent decades.

Declining Political Support As the farm population declines, agriculture's political power weakens. The farm population was about 25 percent of the general population in the 1930s, when many U.S. farm programs were established; now it is less than 2 percent. Urban congressional representatives now constitute a 10-to-1 majority over their rural colleagues. An increasing number of legislators are critically examining farm programs for their effects on consumers' grocery bills as well as on farm incomes. Also, more farmers themselves are coming to resent the intrusion of the federal government into their farming decisions. A few rural-state congressional members now support free-market agriculture.

World Trade Considerations The United States has taken the lead to reduce barriers to world trade in agricultural products. This has also contributed to the more critical attitude toward farm subsidies, particularly price supports. The nations of the European Union (EU) and many other nations support agricultural prices. And, to maintain their high domestic prices, they restrict imports of foreign farm products by imposing tariffs and quotas. They then try to rid themselves of their domestic surpluses by subsidizing exports into world markets. The effects on the United States are that (1) trade barriers hinder U.S. farmers from selling to EU nations and (2) subsidized exports from those nations depress world prices for agricultural products, making world markets less attractive to U.S. farmers.

Perhaps most important, farm programs such as those maintained by the EU and the United States distort both world agricultural trade and the international allocation of agricultural resources. Encouraged by artificially high prices, farmers in industrially advanced nations produce more food and fiber than they would otherwise. The resulting surpluses flow into world markets, where they depress prices. This means that farmers in countries with no farm programs—many of them developing countries—face artificially low prices for their exports, which signals them to produce less. Overall, the result is a shift in production away from what would occur on the basis of comparative advantage. As an example, price supports cause U.S. agricultural resources to be used for sugar production, even though sugar can be produced at perhaps half the cost in the Caribbean countries and Australia.

Recognizing these distortions, in 1994 the 128 nations then belonging to the World Trade Organization (WTO) agreed to reduce farm price-support programs by 20 percent by the year 2000 and to reduce tariffs and quotas on imported farm products by 15 percent. Larger, more significant, reductions of farm subsidies and agricultural tariffs are part of the agenda of the most recent round of trade negotiations (the Doha Development Agenda). But reaching agreement on those reductions has proved difficult. As of late 2016, negotiations over these issues were completely stalled.

Recent Farm Policies

LO22.5 List the main elements of existing federal farm policy.
In the mid-1990s there was a common feeling among economists and political leaders that the goals and techniques of farm policy needed to be reexamined and revised. Moreover, crop prices were relatively high at the time and Congress wanted to reduce large federal budget deficits.

Freedom to Farm Act of 1996

In 1996 Congress radically revamped 60 years of U.S. farm policy by passing the **Freedom to Farm Act.** The law ended price supports and acreage allotments for wheat, corn, barley, oats, sorghum, rye, cotton, and rice. Farmers were allowed to respond to changing crop prices by planting as much or as little of these crops as they chose. Also, they were free to plant crops of their choice. If the price of, say, oats increased, farmers could plant more oats and less barley. Markets, not government programs, were to determine the kinds and amounts of crops grown.

To ease the transition away from price supports, the Freedom to Farm Act granted declining annual "transition payments" through 2002. $37 billion of transition payments were scheduled through 2002 based on the production levels that had previously been imposed on farmers under the price-support

The Sugar Program: A Sweet Deal

The Sugar Program Is a Sweet Deal for Domestic Sugar Producers, but It Imposes Heavy Costs on Domestic Consumers, Domestic Candy Manufacturers, Foreign Producers, and the American Economy.

The continuing U.S. sugar program uses price supports and import quotas to guarantee a minimum price of sugar for domestic sugar producers. The program has significant effects, both domestically and internationally.

Domestic Costs Price supports and import quotas have boosted the domestic price of sugar to approximately 32 percent above the world price (for 2015, $0.25 per pound compared to the international price of $0.17 per pound). The aggregate cost to domestic consumers has been estimated at between $1.5 billion and $1.9 billion per year. In contrast, each sugar producer receives from subsidies alone an amount estimated to be twice the nation's average family income. In one particular year, a single producer received an estimated $30 million in benefits. Many sugar

© Envision/Corbis

producers obtain more than $1 million each year in benefits.

Import Quotas As a consequence of high U.S. domestic price supports, foreign sugar producers have a strong incentive to sell their output in the United States. But an influx of lower-priced foreign sugar into the U.S. domestic market would undermine U.S. price supports. The government therefore has imposed import quotas on foreign sugar. It decides how much sugar can be imported at a zero or very low tariff rate, and then it charges a prohibitively high tariff for any quantities above that amount. As the gap between U.S.-supported prices and world prices has widened, imports have declined as a percentage of sugar consumed in the United States. In 1975, about 30 percent of the sugar consumed in the United States was imported; currently about 20 percent

system. A previous wheat farmer, for example, was scheduled to receive transition payments for 7 years regardless of the current price of wheat or the amount of wheat the farmer chose to grow over those 7 years.

This ambitious plan to wean American agriculture from subsidies unraveled in 1998 and 1999, when sharply reduced export demand and strong crop production in the United States depressed the prices of many farm products. Congress responded by supplementing the previously scheduled transition payments with large "emergency aid" payments to farmers. Agricultural subsidies for 1999–2002 averaged $20 billion annually—even more than they were before passage of the Freedom to Farm Act.

The Food, Conservation, and Energy Act of 2008

Since 2002, agricultural policy in the United States has substantially retreated from the free-market intent of the Freedom to Farm Act of 1996. The three subsidy programs

introduced by the Food, Conservation, and Energy Act of 2008 continued the "freedom to plant" approach and provided revenue guarantees for farmers. But one of them transformed what were supposed to be temporary "transition payments" into "direct payments" that could be obtained year after year, without any time limit. These revenue guarantees kicked in automatically whenever crop prices (or total revenues) fell below target levels.

Direct Payments The **direct payments** under the 2008 law were similar to the transition payments paid under the Freedom to Farm Act. These cash payments were fixed for each crop based on a farmer's historical pattern of production and were unaffected by current crop prices or current production. Farmers could plant as much or as little of any particular crop as they wanted and still receive these payments. These direct payments did not decline from year to year. They were a permanent transfer payment from the federal government (general taxpayers) to farmers. The payments ranged from 2.4 cents per bushel for oats up to 54 cents per bushel for wheat.

comes from abroad. Domestic policy regarding the U.S. sugar industry largely dictates the nation's international trade policy with respect to sugar.

Developing Countries The loss of the U.S. market has had several harmful effects on sugar-exporting developing countries such as the Philippines, Brazil, and several Central American countries.

First, exclusion from the U.S. market has significantly reduced their export revenues—by an amount estimated to be many billions of dollars per year. That decline in export revenues is important because many of the sugar-producing countries depend on such revenues to pay interest and principal on large debts owed to the United States and other industrially advanced nations.

Second, barred by quotas from sale in the U.S. market, the sugar produced by the developing countries has been added to world markets, where the increased supply has depressed the world price of sugar.

Third, domestic price supports have caused U.S. sugar production to expand to the extent that the United States may soon change from a sugar-importing to a sugar-exporting nation. That is, the U.S. sugar program may soon be a source of new competition for the sugar producers of the developing countries. Sugar price supports in the European Union have already turned that group of nations into sugar exporters.

U.S. Efficiency Loss The sugar program benefits sugar producers by about $1 billion annually but costs U.S. consumers about $1.5 billion to $1.9 billion each year. The excess of losses over gains is therefore $500 million to $900 million annually. This efficiency loss (or deadweight loss) results from the overallocation of U.S. resources to growing and processing sugar beets and sugar cane.

As a secondary effect, the higher domestic sugar prices have encouraged several U.S. confectionery firms (candy manufacturers) to relocate their operations to Canada or Mexico. According to the U.S. Commerce Department, for every American job that has been added by the price supports in the cane sugar and sugar beet industries, three American jobs have been lost in the industries buying sugar. Government economists estimate that the confectionery industry has lost a total of about 24,000 jobs since 2003.

Global Resource Misallocation Both domestically and globally, the sugar price-support programs of the United States and other industrially advanced economies have distorted the worldwide allocation of agricultural resources. Price supports have caused a shift of resources to sugar production by less efficient U.S. producers, and U.S. import quotas and consequent low world sugar prices have caused more-efficient foreign producers to restrict their production. Thus high-cost producers are producing more sugar and low-cost producers are producing less, resulting in the inefficient use of the world's agricultural resources.

Adding to the inefficient use of world resources, the relocation of candy manufacturers—to avoid artificially sweetened U.S. sugar prices—is moving capital and labor resources away from their place of comparative advantage.

Countercyclical Payments This component of 2008 farm policy tied a separate set of subsidies to the difference between market prices of specified farm products and a target price set for each crop. Like direct payments, these **countercyclical payments (CCPs)** were based on previous crops grown and were received regardless of the current crop planted. For example, the target price for corn in the years 2008–2012 was $2.63 per bushel. If the price of corn stayed at or above $2.63, the farmer who qualified would have received no CCP. But if the price fell below $2.63, the farmer would have received a CCP payment geared to the size of the price gap. The CCP system returned a form of price supports to a prominent role in farm policy, but it based those supports on past crops grown, not current crops planted.

Marketing Loans The 2008 law contained a **marketing loan program** under which farmers could receive a loan (on a per-unit-of-output basis) from a government lender. If the crop price at harvest was higher than the price specified in the loan (the loan price), farmers had to repay their loans, with interest. If the crop price was lower than the loan price, farmers could forfeit their harvested crops to the lender and be free of their loans. In this second case, farmers received what amounted to a subsidy because the proceeds from the loan exceeded the revenues from the sale of the crop in the market.

The Agricultural Act of 2014

The **Agricultural Act of 2014** ended both direct payments and countercyclical payments because it was politically difficult to justify paying farmers for crops they didn't grow. The marketing loan program was continued as a way for farmers to reduce the risk of price and revenue variability.

To help farmers further reduce risk, the Act created two new **crop insurance** programs:

- Under **price loss coverage,** farmers who elect to participate and pay the insurance premium are guaranteed an insurance payment if the price of their crop falls below a specified value, such as $3.50 per bushel of wheat.

- By contrast, **agricultural risk coverage** depends on the total revenue generated by all of the farmers in a given county who plant the same crop in a given year. The program makes insurance payments to participating farmers if the total revenue collectively received by all the farmers planting the crop in the county falls below a specific value, such as $150 million for corn producers in Kossuth County, Iowa.

The 2014 Act also established the dairy margin protection program that makes payments if the price of milk falls too low or the cost of feed rises too high. The idea is to shield dairy producers' per-unit margin (= revenue per unit minus cost per unit).

The 2014 farm law reduced the risk of price and revenue variability for farmers and increased farm income. But the law failed to address the problem of subsidies. However structured, subsidies slow the exodus of resources from agriculture and maintain high production levels. This means lower crop prices and less market income for farmers. These lower prices and reduced market incomes, in turn, provide the rationale for continued government subsidies!

QUICK REVIEW 22.3

✓ Farm policy in the United States has been heavily criticized for delaying the shift of resources away from farming, directing most subsidies to wealthier farmers, and being fraught with policy contradictions.

✓ The persistence of farm subsidies can largely be explained in terms of rent-seeking behavior, the special-interest effect, political logrolling, and other aspects of public choice theory.

✓ The Freedom to Farm Act of 1996 eliminated price supports and acreage allotments for many of the nation's crops, while continuing direct subsidies to farmers.

✓ The Food, Conservation, and Energy Act of 2008 provided three major kinds of farm subsidies: direct payments, countercyclical payments, and marketing loans.

✓ The Agricultural Act of 2014 eliminated direct payments and countercyclical payments while introducing two types of crop insurance: price loss coverage and agricultural risk coverage.

SUMMARY

LO22.1 Explain why agricultural prices and farm income are unstable.

In the short run, the highly inelastic demand for farm products transforms small changes in output and small shifts in demand into large changes in prices and income.

LO22.2 Discuss why there has been a huge employment exodus from agriculture to other U.S. industries over the past several decades.

Over the long run, rapid technological advance, together with a highly inelastic and relatively slow-growing demand for agricultural output, has made agriculture a declining industry in the United States and dictated that resources exit the industry.

LO22.3 Relate the rationale for farm subsidies and the economics and politics of price supports (price floors).

Historically, farm policy has been centered on price and based on the parity concept, which suggests that the relationship between prices received and paid by farmers should be constant over time.

The use of price floors or price supports has a number of economic effects: It (a) causes surplus production, (b) increases the incomes of farmers, (c) causes higher consumer prices for farm products, (d) creates an overallocation of resources to agriculture, (e) obliges society to pay higher taxes to finance the purchase and storage of surplus output, (f) increases pollution because of the greater use of agrochemicals and vulnerable land, and (g) forces other nations to bear the costs associated with import barriers and depressed world agricultural prices.

With only limited success, the federal government has pursued programs to reduce agricultural supply and increase agricultural demand as a way to reduce the surpluses associated with price supports.

LO22.4 Describe major criticisms of the price-support system in agriculture.

Economists have criticized U.S. farm policy for (a) confusing symptoms (low farm incomes) with causes (excess capacity), (b) providing the largest subsidies to high-income farmers, and (c) creating contradictions among specific farm programs.

The persistence of agricultural subsidies can be explained by public choice theory and, in particular, as rent-seeking behavior, the special-interest effect, and political logrolling.

Political backing for price supports and acreage allotments has eroded for several reasons: (a) The number of U.S. farmers, and thus their political clout, has declined relative to the number of urban consumers of farm products, and (b) successful efforts by the United States to get other nations to reduce their farm subsidies have altered the domestic debate on the desirability of U.S. subsidies.

LO22.5 List the main elements of existing federal farm policy.

The Freedom to Farm Act of 1996 ended price supports and acreage allotments for wheat, corn, barley, oats, sorghum, rye, cotton, and rice. The law established declining annual transition payments through the year 2002, but those payments were no longer tied to crop prices or the current crop produced.

When crop prices plummeted in 1998 and 1999, Congress supplemented the transition payments of the Freedom to Farm Act with large amounts of emergency aid. Total subsidies to agriculture averaged $20 billion annually in the years 1999–2002.

Beginning in 2002, the federal government retreated from the free-market principles of the Freedom to Farm Act, setting up a system of permanent direct payments to farmers along with countercyclical farm-revenue guarantees.

The Food, Conservation, and Energy Act of 2008 provided farmers with direct payments (based on previous crops planted), countercyclical payments (based on the differences between market prices and targeted prices), and marketing loans (based on a specified crop price and an option to either pay back the loan or forfeit the crop to the government lender).

The Agricultural Act of 2014 preserved marketing loans but ended direct payments and countercyclical payments in favor of two types of crop insurance. Price loss coverage pays participating farmers if the market price of their crop falls below a predetermined value. Agricultural risk coverage pays out if the total revenue generated by a given crop in a given county falls below a preselected value.

TERMS AND CONCEPTS

farm commodities	price supports	marketing loan program
food products	acreage allotments	Agricultural Act of 2014
agribusiness	Freedom to Farm Act	crop insurance
parity concept	direct payments	price loss coverage
parity ratio	countercyclical payments (CCPs)	agricultural risk coverage

The following and additional problems can be found in ▪ connect

DISCUSSION QUESTIONS

1. Carefully evaluate: "The supply and demand for agricultural products are such that small changes in agricultural supply result in drastic changes in prices. However, large changes in agricultural prices have modest effects on agricultural output." (Hint: A brief review of the distinction between *supply* and *quantity supplied* may be helpful.) Do exports increase or reduce the instability of demand for farm products? Explain. **LO22.1**

2. What relationship, if any, can you detect between the facts that farmers' fixed costs of production are large and the supply of most agricultural products is generally inelastic? Be specific in your answer. **LO22.1**

3. Explain how each of the following contributes to the farm problem: **LO22.1, LO22.2**
   a. The inelasticity of demand for farm products.
   b. The rapid technological progress in farming.
   c. The modest long-run growth in demand for farm commodities.
   d. The volatility of export demand.

4. The key to efficient resource allocation is shifting resources from low-productivity to high-productivity uses. In view of the high and expanding physical productivity of agricultural resources, explain why many economists want to divert additional resources away from farming in order to achieve allocative efficiency. **LO22.2**

5. Explain and evaluate: "Industry complains of the higher taxes it must pay to finance subsidies to agriculture. Yet the trend of agricultural prices has been downward, while industrial prices have been moving upward, suggesting that on balance agriculture is actually subsidizing industry." **LO22.3**

6. "Because consumers as a group must ultimately pay the total income received by farmers, it makes no real difference whether the income is paid through free farm markets or through price supports supplemented by subsidies financed out of tax revenue." Do you agree? **LO22.3**

7. If in a given year the indexes of prices received and paid by farmers were 120 and 165, respectively, what would the parity ratio be? Explain the meaning of that ratio. **LO22.3**

8. Explain the economic effects of price supports. Explicitly include environmental and global impacts in your answer. On what grounds do economists contend that price supports cause a misallocation of resources? **LO22.3**

9. Do you agree with each of the following statements? Explain why or why not. **LO22.3, LO22.4**
   a. The problem with U.S. agriculture is that there are too many farmers. That is not the fault of farmers but the fault of government programs.
   b. The federal government ought to buy up all U.S. farm surpluses and give them away to developing nations.
   c. All industries would like government price supports if they could get them; agriculture has obtained price supports only because of its strong political clout.

10. What are the effects of farm subsidies such as those of the United States and the European Union on (a) domestic agricultural prices, (b) world agricultural prices, and (c) the international allocation of agricultural resources? **LO22.3**

11. Use public choice theory to explain the persistence of farm subsidies in the face of major criticisms of those subsidies. If the special-interest effect is so strong, what factors made it possible in 1996 for the government to end price supports and acreage allotments for several crops? **LO22.4**

12. What was the major intent of the Freedom to Farm Act of 1996? Do you agree with the intent? Why or why not? Did the law succeed in reducing overall farm subsidies? Why or why not? **LO22.5**

13. Distinguish between price loss coverage and agricultural risk coverage. How do they help reduce the volatility of farm income? In what way do farm subsidies perpetuate the long-standing problem of too many resources in agriculture? **LO22.5**

14. **LAST WORD** What groups benefit and what groups lose from the U.S. sugar subsidy program?

REVIEW QUESTIONS

1. Suppose that the demand for olive oil is highly inelastic. Also suppose that the supply of olive oil is fixed for the year. If the demand for olive oil suddenly increases because of a shortage of corn oil, you would expect a _____ in the price of olive oil. LO22.2
   a. Large increase.
   b. Small increase.
   c. Large decrease.
   d. Small decrease.
   e. No change.

2. Use supply and demand curves to depict equilibrium price and output in a competitive market for some farm product. Then show how an above-equilibrium price floor (price support) would cause a surplus in this market. Demonstrate in your graph how government could reduce the surplus through a policy that (a) changes supply or (b) changes demand. Identify each of the following actual government policies as primarily affecting the supply of or the demand for a particular farm product: acreage allotments, the food-stamp program, the Food for Peace program, a government buyout of dairy herds, and export promotion. LO22.3

3. Suppose that the government has been supporting the price of corn. Its free market price is $2.50 per bushel, but the government

has been setting a support price of $3.50 per bushel. Which of the following are ways that the government might try to reduce the size of the corn surplus? (Select one or more answers from the choices shown.) LO22.3
   a. Decrease the support price.
   b. Institute an acreage allotment program.
   c. Decrease demand by taxing purchases of corn.
   d. Raise the support price.

4. The majority of farm subsidies flow toward _____. LO22.4
   a. Poor, small-scale farmers.
   b. Rich, large-scale farmers.
   c. Government employees.
   d. Grain wholesalers.

5. Which of the following are elements of current U.S. farm policy? LO22.5
   a. Farmers are free to choose how much to plant of any particular crop.
   b. Direct payments.
   c. Price supports.
   d. Countercyclical payments.

PROBLEMS

1. Suppose that corn currently costs $4 per bushel and that wheat currently costs $3 per bushel. Also assume that the price elasticity of corn is 0.10, while the price elasticity of wheat is 0.15. For the following questions about elasticities, simply use the percentage changes that are provided rather than attempting to calculate those percentage changes yourself using the midpoint formula given in Chapter 6. LO22.1
   a. If the price of corn fell by 25 percent to $3 per bushel, by what percentage would the quantity demanded of corn increase? What if the price of corn fell by 50 percent to $2 per bushel?
   b. To what value would the price of wheat have to fall to induce consumers to increase their purchases of wheat by 5 percent?
   c. If the government imposes a $0.40 per bushel tax on corn so that the price of corn rises by 10 percent to $4.40 per bushel, by what percentage would the quantity demanded of corn decrease? If the initial quantity demanded is 10 billion bushels per year, by how many bushels would the quantity demanded decrease in response to this tax?

2. Suppose that both wheat and corn have an income elasticity of 0.1. LO22.1
   a. If the average income in the economy increases by 2 percent each year, by what percentage does the quantity demanded of wheat increase each year, holding all other factors constant? Holding all other factors constant, if 10 billion bushels are demanded this year, by how many bushels will the quantity demanded increase next year if incomes rise by 2 percent?
   b. Given that average personal income doubles in the United States about every 30 years, by about what percentage does

the quantity demanded of corn increase every 30 years, holding all other factors constant?

3. Suppose that 10 workers were required in 2010 to produce 40,000 bushels of wheat on a 1,000-acre farm. LO22.2
   a. What is the average output per acre? Per worker?
   b. If in 2020 only 8 workers produce 44,000 bushels of wheat on that same 1,000-acre farm, what will be the average output per acre? Per worker?
   c. By what percentage does productivity (output per worker) increase over those 10 years? Over those 10 years, what is the average annual percentage increase in productivity?

4. In 2013, it was estimated that the total value of all corn-production subsidies in the United States totaled about $4.8 billion. The population of the United States was approximately 315 million people that year. LO22.3
   a. On average, how much did corn subsidies cost per person in the United States in 2013? (Hint: A billion is a 1 followed by nine zeros. A million is a 1 followed by six zeros.)
   b. If each person in the United States is only willing to spend $0.50 to support efforts to overturn the corn subsidy, and if antisubsidy advocates can only raise funds from 10 percent of the population, how much money will they be able to raise for their lobbying efforts?
   c. If the recipients of corn subsidies donate just 1 percent of the total amount that they receive in subsidies, how much could they raise to support lobbying efforts to continue the corn subsidy?
   d. By how many dollars does the amount raised by the recipients of the corn subsidy exceed the amount raised by the opponents of the corn subsidy?

Income Inequality, Poverty, and Discrimination

Learning Objectives

LO23.1 Explain how income inequality in the United States is measured and described.

LO23.2 Discuss the extent and sources of income inequality.

LO23.3 Demonstrate how income inequality has changed since 1975.

LO23.4 Debate the economic arguments for and against income inequality.

LO23.5 Relate how poverty is measured and its incidence by age, gender, ethnicity, and other characteristics.

LO23.6 Identify the major components of the income-maintenance program in the United States.

LO23.7 Discuss labor market discrimination and how it might affect hiring decisions and wages.

Evidence that suggests wide income disparity in the United States is easy to find. In 2015 boxer Floyd Mayweather earned $300 million, singer Katy Perry earned $135 million, and celebrity chef Gordon Ramsay earned $60 million. In contrast, the salary of the president of the United States is $400,000, and the typical schoolteacher earns $56,000. A full-time minimum-wage worker at a fast-food restaurant makes about $15,000. Cash welfare payments to a mother with two children average $5,150 per year.

In 2014 about 46.7 million Americans—or 15.0 percent of the population—lived in poverty. An estimated 576,400 people were homeless that year. The richest fifth of American households received about 51.2 percent of total income, while the poorest fifth received about 3.1 percent.

What are the sources of income inequality? Is income inequality rising or falling? Is the United States making progress against poverty? What are the major income-maintenance programs in the United States? What role does discrimination play in reducing wages for some and increasing wages for others? These are some of the questions we will answer in this chapter.

Facts about Income Inequality

LO23.1 Explain how income inequality in the United States is measured and described.

Average household income in the United States is among the highest in the world; in 2014, it was $68,426 per household (one or more persons occupying a housing unit). But that average tells us nothing about income inequality. To learn about that, we must examine how income is distributed around the average.

Distribution by Income Category

One way to measure **income inequality** is to look at the percentages of households in a series of income categories. Table 23.1 shows that 23.6 percent of all households had annual before-tax incomes of less than $25,000 in 2014, while 24.7 percent had annual incomes of $100,000 or more. The data in the table suggest a wide dispersion of household income and considerable inequality of income in the United States.

Distribution by Quintiles (Fifths)

A second way to measure income inequality is to divide the total number of individuals, households, or families (two or more persons related by birth, marriage, or adoption) into five numerically equal groups, or *quintiles,* and examine the percentage of total personal (before-tax) income received by each quintile. We do this for households in the table in Figure 23.1, where we also provide the upper income limit for each quintile. Any amount of income greater than that listed in each row of column 3 would place a household into the next-higher quintile.

TABLE 23.1 The Distribution of U.S. Income by Households, 2014

(1) Personal Income Category	(2) Percentage of All Households in This Category
Under $15,000	12.6
$15,000–$24,999	11.0
$25,000–$34,999	10.1
$35,000–$49,999	13.1
$50,000–$74,999	17.0
$75,000–$99,999	11.5
$100,000 and above	24.7
Total	100.0

Source: Bureau of the Census, **www.census.gov**.

The Lorenz Curve and Gini Ratio

We can display the quintile distribution of personal income through a **Lorenz curve.** In Figure 23.1, we plot the cumulative percentage of households on the horizontal axis and the percentage of income they obtain on the vertical axis. The diagonal line 0e represents a *perfectly equal distribution of income* because each point along that line indicates that a particular percentage of households receive the same percentage of income. In other words, points representing 20 percent of all households receiving 20 percent of total income, 40 percent receiving 40 percent, 60 percent receiving 60 percent, and so on, all lie on the diagonal line.

By plotting the quintile data from the table in Figure 23.1, we obtain the Lorenz curve for 2014. The bottom 20 percent of all households received 3.1 percent of the income, as shown by point *a*; the bottom 40 percent received 11.3 percent (= 3.1 + 8.2), as shown by point *b*; and so forth. The blue area between the diagonal line and the Lorenz curve is determined by the extent that the Lorenz curve sags away from the diagonal and indicates the degree of income inequality. If the actual income distribution were perfectly equal, the Lorenz curve and the diagonal would coincide and the blue area would disappear.

At the opposite extreme is complete inequality, where all households but one have zero income. In that case the Lorenz curve would coincide with the horizontal axis from 0 to point *f* (at 0 percent of income) and then would move immediately up from *f* to point *e* along the vertical axis (indicating that a single household has 100 percent of the total income). The entire area below the diagonal line (triangle 0ef) would indicate this extreme degree of inequality. So the farther the Lorenz curve sags away from the diagonal, the greater is the degree of income inequality.

The income inequality described by the Lorenz curve can be transformed into a **Gini ratio**—a numerical measure of the overall dispersion of income:

$$\text{Gini ratio} = \frac{\text{Area between Lorenz curve and diagonal}}{\text{Total area below the diagonal}}$$
$$= \frac{A \text{ (blue are)}}{A + B \text{ (blue + green area)}}$$

The Gini ratio is 0.480 for the distribution of household income shown in Figure 23.1. As the area between the Lorenz curve and the diagonal gets larger, the Gini ratio rises to reflect greater inequality. Lower Gini ratios denote less inequality; higher ratios indicate more inequality. The Gini coefficient for complete income equality is zero and for complete inequality is 1.

Because Gini ratios are numerical, they are easier to use than Lorenz curves for comparing the income distributions of

FIGURE 23.1 **The Lorenz curve and Gini ratio.** The Lorenz curve is a convenient way to show the degree of income inequality (here, household income by quintile in 2014). The area between the diagonal (the line of perfect equality) and the Lorenz curve represents the degree of inequality in the distribution of total income. This inequality is measured numerically by the Gini ratio—area *A* (shown in blue) divided by area *A* + *B* (the blue + green area). The Gini ratio for the distribution shown is 0.480.

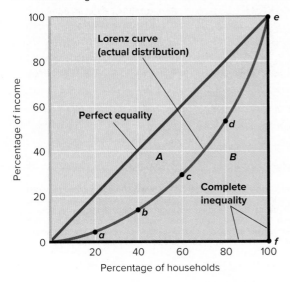

(1) Quintile (2011)	(2) Percentage of Total Income	(3) Upper Income Limit
Lowest 20 percent	3.1	$ 21,432
Second 20 percent	8.2	41,186
Third 20 percent	14.3	68,212
Fourth 20 percent	23.2	112,262
Highest 20 percent	51.2	No limit
Total	100.0	

Source: Bureau of the Census, **www.census.gov**.

different ethnic groups and countries. For example, in 2014 the Gini ratio of U.S. household income for Hispanics was 0.455; for whites, 0.472; for Asians, 0.463; and for African-Americans, 0.499.[1] In 2014, national Gini ratios ranged from a low of 0.247 in Ukraine to a high of 0.608 in Haiti. Examples within this range include Denmark, 0.291; Italy, 0.352; Mexico, 0.481; and Honduras, 0.574.[2]

Income Mobility: The Time Dimension

The income data used so far have a major limitation: The income accounting period of 1 year is too short to be very meaningful. Because the Census Bureau data portray the distribution of income in only a single year, they may conceal a more equal distribution over a few years, a decade, or even a lifetime. If Brad earns $1,000 in year 1 and $100,000 in year 2, while Jenny earns $100,000 in year 1 and only $1,000 in year 2, do we have income inequality? The answer depends on the period of measurement. Annual data would reveal great income inequality, but there would be complete equality over the 2-year period.

This point is important because evidence suggests considerable "churning around" in the distribution of income over time. Such movement of individuals or households from one income quintile to another over time is called **income mobility**. For most income receivers, income starts at a relatively low level during youth, reaches a peak during middle age, and then declines. It follows that if all people receive exactly the same stream of income over their lifetimes, considerable income inequality would still exist in any specific year because of age differences. In any single year, the young and the old would receive low incomes while the middle-aged receive high incomes.

If we change from a "snapshot" view of income distribution in a single year to a "time exposure" portraying incomes over much longer periods, we find considerable movement of income receivers among income classes. For instance, one study showed that between 1996 and 2005, half the individuals in the lowest quintile of the U.S. income distribution in 1996 were in a higher income quintile in 2005. Almost 25 percent made it to the middle fifth and 5 percent achieved the top quintile. There was income mobility in both directions. About 57 percent of the top 1 percent of income receivers in 1996 had dropped out of that category by 2005. Overall, income mobility between 1996 and 2005 was the same as it was the previous 10 years. All this correctly suggests that income is more equally distributed over a 5-, 10-, or 20-year period than in any single year.[3]

[1]U.S. Census Bureau, *Historical Income Tables,* **www.census.gov**.

[2]*CIA World Factbook,* 2014, **www.cia.gov**.

[3]U.S. Department of the Treasury, *Income Mobility in the U.S. from 1996–2005,* November 13, 2007, pp. 1–22.

FIGURE 23.2 The impact of taxes and transfers on U.S. income inequality. The distribution of household income is significantly more equal after taxes and transfers are taken into account than before. Transfers account for most of the lessening of inequality and provide most of the income received by the lowest quintile of households.

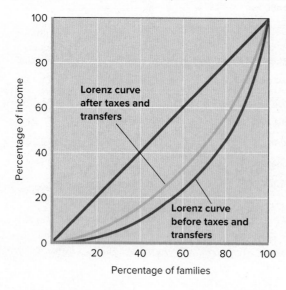

Quintile	Percentage of Total Income Received, 2013	
	(1) Before Taxes and Transfers	(2) After Taxes and Transfers
Lowest 20 percent	2.2	9.3
Second 20 percent	7.2	10.7
Third 20 percent	12.8	14.1
Fourth 20 percent	20.8	19.9
Highest 20 percent	57.0	46.0

Source: Congressional Budget Office, **www.cbo.gov**. Income received "before taxes and transfers" excludes government cash transfers, realized capital gains, and employer-provided health insurance. Income received "after taxes and transfers" includes both cash and noncash transfers as well as realized capital gains and employer-provided health insurance. Numbers may not add to 100 percent due to rounding.

In short, individual and family income mobility over time is significant; for many people, "low income" and "high income" are not permanent conditions. Also, the longer the time period considered, the more equal the distribution of income becomes.

Effect of Government Redistribution

The income data in Table 23.1 and Figure 23.1 include wages, salaries, dividends, and interest. They also include all cash transfer payments such as Social Security, unemployment compensation benefits, and welfare assistance to needy families. The data are before-tax data and therefore do not take into account the effects of personal income and payroll (Social Security) taxes that are levied directly on income receivers. Nor do they include in-kind or **noncash transfers,** which provide specific goods or services rather than cash. Noncash transfers include such things as Medicare, Medicaid, housing subsidies, subsidized school lunches, and food stamps. Such transfers are "incomelike," since they enable recipients to "purchase" goods and services.

One economic function of government is to redistribute income, if society so desires. Figure 23.2 and its table[4] reveal that government significantly redistributes income from higher- to lower-income households through taxes and transfers. Note that the U.S. distribution of household income before taxes and transfers are taken into account (dark red Lorenz curve) is

substantially less equal than the distribution after taxes and transfers (light red Lorenz curve). Without government redistribution, the lowest 20 percent of households in 2013 would have received only 2.2 percent of total income. *With* redistribution, they received 9.3 percent, or 4.2 times as much.

Which contributes more to redistribution, government taxes or government transfers? The answer is transfers. As discussed in Chapter 20's Last Word, the combined federal, state, and local tax system in the United States is only modestly progressive. As a result, nearly all the reduction in income inequality in the United States is attributable to transfer payments. Together with job opportunities, transfer payments have been the most important means of alleviating poverty in the United States.

Causes of Income Inequality

LO23.2 Discuss the extent and sources of income inequality.
There are several causes of income inequality in the United States. In general, the market system is permissive of a high degree of income inequality because it rewards individuals based on the contributions that they make, or the resources that they own, in producing society's output.

More specifically, the factors that contribute to income inequality are the following.

Ability

People have different mental, physical, and aesthetic talents. Some have inherited the exceptional mental qualities that are essential to such high-paying occupations as medicine, corporate leadership, and law. Others are blessed with the physical capacity and coordination to become highly paid

---

[4]The "before" data in this table differ from the data in the table in Figure 23.1 because the latter include cash transfers. Also, the data in Figure 23.2 are based on a broader concept of income than are the data in Figure 23.1.

professional athletes. A few have the talent to become great artists or musicians or have the beauty to become top fashion models. Others have very weak mental endowments and may work in low-paying occupations or may be incapable of earning any income at all. The intelligence and skills of most people fall somewhere in between.

Education and Training

Native ability alone rarely produces high income; people must develop and refine their capabilities through education and training. Individuals differ significantly in the amount of education and training they obtain and thus in their capacity to earn income. Such differences may be a matter of choice: Nguyen enters the labor force after graduating from high school, while Nyberg takes a job only after earning a college degree. Other differences may be involuntary: Nguyen and her parents may simply be unable to finance a college education.

People also receive varying degrees of on-the-job training, which contributes to income inequality. Some workers learn valuable new skills each year on the job and therefore experience significant income growth over time; others receive little or no on-the-job training and earn no more at age 50 than they did at age 30. Moreover, firms tend to select for advanced on-the-job training the workers who have the most formal education. That added training magnifies the education-based income differences between less-educated and better-educated individuals.

Discrimination

Discrimination in education, hiring, training, and promotion undoubtedly causes some income inequality. If discrimination confines certain racial, ethnic, or gender groups to lower-pay occupations, the supply of labor in those occupations will increase relative to demand, and hourly wages and income in those lower-pay jobs will decline. Conversely, labor supply will be artificially reduced in the higher-pay occupations populated by "preferred" workers, raising their wage rates and income. In this way, discrimination can add to income inequality. In fact, economists cannot account for all racial, ethnic, and gender differences in work earnings on the basis of differences in years of education, quality of education, occupations, and annual hours of work. Many economists attribute the unexplained residual to discrimination.

Economists, however, do not see discrimination by race, gender, and ethnicity as a dominant factor explaining income inequality. The income distributions *within* racial or ethnic groups that historically have been targets of discrimination— for example, African Americans—are similar to the income distribution for whites. Other factors besides discrimination are obviously at work.

Nevertheless, discrimination is an important concern since it harms individuals and reduces society's overall output and income. We will discuss it in more detail later in this chapter.

Preferences and Risks

Incomes also differ because of differences in preferences for market work relative to leisure, market work relative to work in the household, and types of occupations. People who choose to stay home with children, work part-time, or retire early usually have less income than those who make the opposite choices. Those who are willing to take arduous, unpleasant jobs (for example, underground mining or heavy construction), to work long hours with great intensity, or to "moonlight" will tend to earn more.

Individuals also differ in their willingness to assume risk. We refer here not only to the race-car driver or the professional boxer but also to the entrepreneur. Although many entrepreneurs fail, many of those who develop successful new products or services realize very substantial incomes. That contributes to income inequality.

Unequal Distribution of Wealth

Income is a *flow;* it represents a stream of wage and salary earnings, along with rent, interest, and profits, as depicted in Chapter 2's circular flow diagram. In contrast, wealth is a *stock,* reflecting at a particular moment the financial and real assets an individual has accumulated over time. A retired person may have very little income and yet own a home, mutual fund shares, and a pension plan that add up to considerable wealth. A new college graduate may be earning a substantial income as an accountant, middle manager, or engineer but has yet to accumulate significant wealth.

As you will discover in this chapter's Last Word, the ownership of wealth in the United States is more unequal than the distribution of income. This inequality of wealth leads to inequality in rent, interest, and dividends, which in turn contributes to income inequality. Those who own more machinery, real estate, farmland, stocks, and bonds and who have more money in savings accounts obviously receive greater income from that ownership than people with less or no such wealth.

Market Power

The ability to "rig the market" on one's own behalf also contributes to income inequality. For example, in *resource* markets certain unions and professional groups have adopted policies that limit the supply of their services, thereby boosting the incomes of those "on the inside." Also, legislation that requires occupational licensing for, say, doctors, dentists, and lawyers can bestow market power that favors the licensed groups. In *product* markets, "rigging the market" means gaining or enhancing monopoly power, which results in greater profit and thus greater income to the firms' owners.

Luck, Connections, and Misfortune

Other forces also play a role in producing income inequality. Luck and "being in the right place at the right time" have helped individuals stumble into fortunes. Discovering oil on a ranch, owning land along a proposed freeway interchange, and hiring the right press agent have accounted for some high incomes. Personal contacts and political connections are other potential routes to attaining high income.

In contrast, economic misfortunes such as prolonged illness, serious accident, the death of the family breadwinner, or unemployment may plunge a family into the low range of income. The burden of such misfortune is borne very unevenly by the population and thus contributes to income inequality.

Income inequality of the magnitude we have described is not exclusively an American phenomenon. Global Perspective 23.1 compares income inequality (here by individuals, not by households) in the United States with that in several other nations. Income inequality tends to be greatest in South American nations, where land and capital resources are highly concentrated in the hands of a relatively small number of wealthy families.

GLOBAL PERSPECTIVE 23.1

Percentage of Total Income Received by the Top One-Tenth of Income Receivers, Selected Nations

The share of income going to the highest 10 percent of income receivers varies among nations.

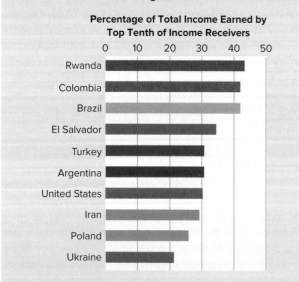

Source: Human Development Report, 2009, **hdr.undp.org**. United Nations Development Programme.

Income Inequality over Time

LO23.3 Demonstrate how income inequality has changed since 1975.

Over a period of years economic growth has raised incomes in the United States: In *absolute* dollar amounts, the entire distribution of income has been moving upward. But incomes may move up in *absolute* terms while leaving the *relative* distribution of income less equal, more equal, or unchanged. Table 23.2 shows how the distribution of household income has changed since 1975. This income is "before tax" and includes cash transfers but not noncash transfers.

Rising Income Inequality since 1975

It is clear from Table 23.2 that the distribution of income by quintiles has become more unequal since 1975. In 2014 the lowest 20 percent of households received 3.1 percent of total before-tax income, compared with 4.4 percent in 1975. Meanwhile, the income share received by the highest 20 percent rose from 43.2 in 1975 to 51.2 percent in 2014. The percentage of income received by the top 5 percent of households also rose significantly over the 1975–2014 period.

TABLE 23.2 Percentage of Total Before-Tax Income Received by Each One-Fifth, and by the Top 5 Percent, of Households, Selected Years

Quintile	1975	1980	1985	1990	1995	2000	2005	2014
Lowest 20 percent	4.4	4.3	4.0	3.7	3.6	3.4	3.4	3.1
Second 20 percent	10.5	10.3	9.7	9.1	8.9	8.6	8.6	8.2
Third 20 percent	17.1	16.9	16.3	15.2	14.8	14.6	14.6	14.3
Fourth 20 percent	24.8	24.9	24.0	23.3	23.0	23.0	23.0	23.2
Highest 20 percent	43.2	43.7	46.6	48.7	50.4	49.8	50.4	51.2
Total	100.0	100.0	100.0	100.0	100.0	100.0	100.0	100.0
Top 5 percent	15.9	15.8	17.0	18.6	21.0	22.1	22.2	21.9

Source: Bureau of the Census, **www.census.gov**. Numbers may not add to 100 percent due to rounding.

Causes of Growing Inequality

Economists suggest several major explanations for the increase in U.S. income inequality since 1975.

Greater Demand for Highly Skilled Workers

Perhaps the most significant contributor to the growing income inequality has been an increasing demand by many firms for workers who are highly skilled and well-educated. Moreover, several industries requiring highly skilled workers have either recently emerged or expanded greatly, such as the computer software, business consulting, biotechnology, health care, and Internet industries. Because highly skilled workers remain relatively scarce, their wages have been bid up. Consequently, the wage differences between them and less-skilled workers have increased.

Between 1980 and 2007 the wage difference between college graduates and high school graduates rose from 28 percent to 49 percent for women and from 22 percent to 44 percent for men. And the so-called *90-10 ratio*—how many times larger the hourly wage at the 90th percentile is compared to the hourly wage at the 10th percentile—rose from 3.6 in 1980 to 4.5 in 2007.[5]

The rising demand for skill has also shown up in rapidly rising pay for chief executive officers (CEOs), sizable increases in income from stock options, substantial increases in income for professional athletes and entertainers, and huge fortunes for successful entrepreneurs. This growth of "super-star" pay has also contributed to rising income inequality.

Demographic Changes

The entrance of large numbers of less-experienced and less-skilled "baby boomers" into the labor force during the 1970s and 1980s may have contributed to greater income inequality in those two decades.

Because younger workers tend to earn less income than older workers, their growing numbers contributed to income inequality. There has also been a growing tendency for men and women with high earnings potential to marry each other, thus increasing household income among the highest income quintiles. Finally, the number of households headed by single or divorced women has increased greatly. That trend has increased income inequality because such households lack a second major wage earner and also because the poverty rate for female-headed households is very high.

International Trade, Immigration, and Decline in Unionism

Other factors are probably at work as well. Stronger international competition from imports has reduced the demand for and employment of less-skilled (but highly paid) workers in such industries as the automobile and steel industries. The decline in such jobs has reduced the average wage for less-skilled workers. It also has swelled the ranks of workers in already low-paying industries, placing further downward pressure on wages there.

Similarly, the transfer of jobs to lower-wage workers in developing countries has exerted downward wage pressure on less-skilled workers in the United States. Also, an upsurge in the immigration of unskilled workers has increased the number of low-income households in the United States. Finally, the decline in unionism in the United States has undoubtedly contributed to wage inequality, since unions tend to equalize pay within firms and industries.

Two cautions: First, when we note growing income inequality, we are not saying that the "rich are getting richer and the poor are getting poorer" in terms of absolute income. Both the rich and the poor are experiencing rises in real income. Rather, what has happened is that, while incomes have risen in all quintiles, income growth has been fastest in the top quintile. Second, increased income inequality is not solely a U.S. phenomenon. The recent rise of inequality has also occurred in several other industrially advanced nations.

---

[5]Economic Policy Institute, **www.epinet.org**. The college wage premiums are adjusted for differences in earnings based on race, ethnicity, marital status, and region.

CONSIDER THIS . . .

Laughing at *The Lego Movie*

Source: © Moviestore collection Ltd/Alamy Stock Photo

Some economists say that the distribution of annual *consumption* is more meaningful for examining inequality of well-being than is the distribution of annual *income*. In a given year, people's consumption of goods and services may be above or below their income because they can save, draw down past savings, use credit cards, take out home mortgages, spend from inheritances, give money to charities, and so on.

A recent study of the distribution of consumption finds that annual consumption inequality is less than income inequality. Moreover, consumption inequality has remained relatively constant over several decades, even though income inequality has increased.[*]

The Economist magazine extends the argument even further, pointing out that despite the recent increase in income inequality, the products consumed by the rich and the poor are far closer in functionality today than at any other time in history.

More than 70 percent of Americans under the official poverty line own at least one car. The difference between driving a beat-up sedan and a high-end sports car is nigh undetectable when compared to the difference between driving and hiking through the mud. A flat panel television is lovely, but you do not need one to laugh at *The Lego Movie*.

The successful entrepreneurs who make fortunes by improving quality while dropping prices widen the income gap while reducing meaningful differences.[†]

Economists generally agree that products and experiences once reserved exclusively for the rich in the United States have, in fact, become more commonplace for nearly all income classes. But skeptics contend that *The Economist's* argument is too simplistic. Even though both are water outings, there is a fundamental difference between sailing among the Greek isles on your private yacht and paddling on a local pond in a rented kayak.

---

[*]Dirk Krueger and Fabrizio Perri, "Does Income Inequality Lead to Consumption Inequality?" *Review of Economic Studies*, 2006, pp. 163–193.

[†]*The Economist*, "Economic Focus: The New (Improved) Gilded Age," December 22, 2007, p. 122.

The Lorenz curve can be used to contrast the distribution of income at different points in time. If we plotted Table 23.2's data as Lorenz curves, we would find that the curves shifted farther away from the diagonal between 1975 and 2014. The Gini ratio rose from 0.397 in 1975 to 0.480 in 2014.

Equality versus Efficiency

LO23.4 Debate the economic arguments for and against income inequality.

The main policy issue concerning income inequality is how much is necessary and justified. While there is no general agreement on the justifiable amount, we can gain insight by exploring the cases for and against greater equality.

The Case for Equality: Maximizing Total Utility

The basic argument for an equal distribution of income is that income equality maximizes total consumer satisfaction (utility) from any particular level of output and income. The rationale for this argument is shown in Figure 23.3, in which we assume that the money incomes of two individuals, Anderson and Brooks, are subject to diminishing marginal utility. In any time period, income receivers spend the first dollars received on the products they value most—products whose marginal utility is high. As their most pressing wants become satisfied, consumers then spend additional dollars of income on less-important, lower-marginal-utility goods. The identical diminishing-marginal-utility-from-income curves (MU_A and MU_B in the figure) reflect the assumption that Anderson and Brooks have the same capacity to derive utility from income.

Now suppose that there is $10,000 worth of income (output) to be distributed between Anderson and Brooks. According to proponents of income equality, the optimal distribution is an equal distribution, which causes the marginal utility of the last dollar spent to be the same for both persons. We can prove this by demonstrating that if the income distribution is initially unequal, then distributing income more equally can increase the combined utility of the two individuals.

Suppose that the $10,000 of income initially is distributed unequally, with Anderson getting $2,500 and Brooks $7,500. The marginal utility, *a*, from the last dollar received by Anderson is high, and the marginal utility, *b*, from Brooks's last dollar of income is low. If a single dollar of income is shifted from Brooks to Anderson—that is, toward greater equality—then Anderson's utility increases by *a* and Brooks's utility decreases by *b*. The combined utility then increases by *a* minus *b* (Anderson's large gain minus Brooks's small loss). The transfer of another dollar from Brooks to Anderson again increases their combined utility, this time by a slightly smaller amount. Continued transfer of dollars from Brooks to Anderson increases their combined utility until the income is evenly distributed and both receive $5,000. At that time their marginal utilities from the last dollar of income are equal (at *a′* and *b′*), and any further income redistribution beyond the $2,500 already transferred would begin to create inequality and decrease their combined utility.

FIGURE 23.3 The utility-maximizing distribution of income. With identical marginal-utility-of-income curves MU_A and MU_B, Anderson and Brooks will maximize their combined utility when any amount of income (say, $10,000) is equally distributed. If income is unequally distributed (say, $2,500 to Anderson and $7,500 to Brooks), the marginal utility derived from the last dollar will be greater for Anderson than for Brooks, and a redistribution of income toward equality will result in a net increase in total utility. The utility gained by equalizing income at $5,000 each, shown by the blue area below curve MU_A in panel (a), exceeds the utility lost, indicated by the red area below curve MU_B in (b).

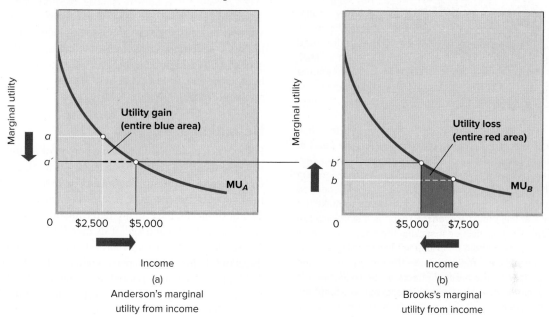

(a)
Anderson's marginal
utility from income

(b)
Brooks's marginal
utility from income

The area under the MU curve and to the left of the individual's particular level of income represents the total utility of that income. Therefore, as a result of the transfer of the $2,500, Anderson has gained utility represented by the blue area below curve MU_A, and Brooks has lost utility represented by the red area below curve MU_B. The blue area is obviously greater than the red area, so income equality yields greater combined total utility than income inequality does.

The Case for Inequality: Incentives and Efficiency

Although the logic of the argument for equality might seem solid, critics of income equality say that the transfer of income required to create income equality is both unfair and unwise. They say that income inequality largely reflects rewards to individuals for supplying their talents and resources to the economy. They conclude that it is not fair to take some of Brooks's income and give it to Anderson. Further, critics of income equality point out that proponents of income equality falsely assume that there is some fixed amount of output produced and therefore income to be distributed. These critics argue that the way in which income is distributed is an important determinant of the amount of output or income that is produced and is available for distribution.

Suppose once again in Figure 23.3 that Anderson earns $2,500 and Brooks earns $7,500. In moving toward equality, society (the government) must tax away some of Brooks's income and transfer it to Anderson. This tax and transfer process diminishes the income rewards of high-income Brooks and raises the income rewards of low-income Anderson; in so doing, it reduces the incentives of both to earn high incomes. Why should high-income Brooks work hard, save and invest, or undertake entrepreneurial risks when the rewards from such activities will be reduced by taxation? And why should low-income Anderson be motivated to increase his income through market activities when the government stands ready to transfer income to him? Taxes are a reduction in the rewards from increased productive effort; redistribution through transfers is a reward for diminished effort.

In the extreme, imagine a situation in which the government levies a 100 percent tax on income and distributes the tax revenue equally to its citizenry. Why would anyone work hard? Why would anyone work at all? Why would anyone assume business risk? Or why would anyone save (forgo current consumption) in order to invest? The economic incentives to "get ahead" will have been removed, greatly reducing society's total production and income. That is, the way income is distributed affects the size of that income. The basic argument for income inequality therefore is twofold: (1) income inequality is justified because it results from differences in

Source: © Fuse/Getty Images RF

Slicing the Pizza

The equality-efficiency trade-off might better be understood through an analogy. Assume that society's income is a huge pizza, baked year after year, *with the sizes of the pieces going to people on the basis of their contribution to making it.* Now suppose that for fairness reasons, society decides some people are getting pieces that are too large and others are getting pieces too small. But when society redistributes the pizza to make the sizes more equal, they discover the result is a smaller pizza than before. Why participate in making the pizza if you get a decent-size piece without contributing? The shrinkage of the pizza represents the efficiency loss—the loss of output and income—caused by the harmful effects of the redistribution on incentives to work, to save and invest, and to accept entrepreneurial risk. The shrinkage also reflects the resources that society must divert to the bureaucracies that administer the redistribution system.

How much pizza shrinkage will society accept while continuing to agree to the redistribution? If redistributing pizza to make it less unequal reduces the size of the pizza, what amount of pizza loss will society tolerate? Is a loss of 10 percent acceptable? 25 percent? 75 percent? This is the basic question in any debate over the ideal size of a nation's income redistribution program.

the quantity and quality of labor and other resources supplied by individuals to the economy, and (2) it is an unavoidable consequence of maintaining the incentives needed to motivate people to produce output and income year after year.

The Equality-Efficiency Trade-off

At the essence of the income equality-inequality debate is a fundamental trade-off between equality and efficiency. In this **equality-efficiency trade-off,** greater income equality (achieved through redistribution of income) comes at the opportunity cost of reduced production and income. And greater production and income (through reduced redistribution) comes at the expense of less equality of income. The trade-off obligates society to choose how much redistribution it wants, in view of the costs. If society decides it wants to redistribute income, it needs to determine methods that

minimize the adverse effects on fairness, incentives, productivity, and economic efficiency.

The Economics of Poverty

LO23.5 Relate how poverty is measured and its incidence by age, gender, ethnicity, and other characteristics.

We now turn from the broader issue of income distribution to the more specific issue of very low income, or "poverty." A society with a high degree of income inequality can have a high, moderate, or low amount of poverty. We therefore need a separate examination of poverty.

Definition of Poverty

Poverty is a condition in which a person or a family does not have the means to satisfy basic needs for food, clothing, shelter, and transportation. The means include currently earned income, transfer payments, past savings, and property owned. The basic needs have many determinants, including family size and the health and age of its members.

The federal government has established minimum income thresholds below which a person or a family is "in poverty." In 2014 an unattached individual receiving less than $12,071 per year was said to be living in poverty. For a family of four, the poverty line was $24,230; for a family of six, it was $32,473. Based on these thresholds, in 2014 about 46.7 million Americans lived in poverty. In 2014 the **poverty rate**—the percentage of the population living in poverty—was 14.8 percent.

Incidence of Poverty

The poor are heterogeneous: They can be found in all parts of the nation; they are of all races and ethnicities, rural and urban, young and old. But as Figure 23.4 indicates, poverty is far from randomly distributed. For example, the poverty rate for African Americans is above the national average, as is the rate for Hispanics, while the rates for whites and Asians are below the average. In 2014, the poverty rates for African Americans and Hispanics were 25.2 and 23.6, respectively; for whites and Asians, 12.9 and 13.1 percent, respectively.[6]

Figure 23.4 shows that female-headed households (no husband present), foreign-born noncitizens, and children under 18 years of age have very high incidences of poverty. Marriage and full-time, year-round work are associated with low poverty rates, and, because of the Social Security system, the incidence of poverty among the elderly is less than that for the population as a whole.

The high poverty rate for children is especially disturbing because poverty tends to breed poverty. Poor children are at greater risk for a range of long-term problems, including poor health and inadequate education, crime, drug use, and teenage pregnancy. Many of today's impoverished children will

[6]Bureau of the Census, **www.census.gov**.

Population group

Percentage in poverty, 2014

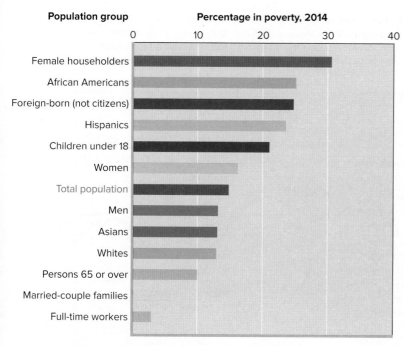

Source: Bureau of the Census, **www.census.gov**.

FIGURE 23.4 **Poverty rates among selected population groups, 2014.** Poverty is disproportionately borne by African Americans, Hispanics, children, foreign-born residents who are not citizens, and families headed by women. People who are employed full-time, have a college degree, or are married tend to have low poverty rates.

reach adulthood unhealthy and illiterate and unable to earn above-poverty incomes.

As many as half of people in poverty are poor for only one or two years before climbing out of poverty. But poverty is much more long-lasting among some groups than among others. In particular, African American and Hispanic families, families headed by women, persons with little education and few labor market skills, and people who are dysfunctional because of drug use, alcoholism, or mental illness are more likely than others to remain in poverty. Also, long-lasting poverty is heavily present in depressed areas of cities, parts of the Deep South, and some Indian reservations.

Poverty Trends

As Figure 23.5 shows, the total poverty rate fell significantly between 1959 and 1969, stabilized at 11 to 13 percent over the next decade, and then rose in the early 1980s. In 1993 the rate was 15.1 percent, the highest since 1983. Between 1993 and 2000 the rate turned downward, falling to 11.3 percent in 2000. Because of recession, slow employment growth, and relatively slow wage growth, the poverty rate rose from 11.7 percent in 2001 to 12.7 percent in 2004. During the second half of the 1990s, poverty rates plunged for African Americans, Hispanics, and Asians, and they have remained historically low. Nevertheless, in 2008 African Americans and Hispanics still had poverty rates that were roughly double the rate for whites.

The recession that began in December 2007 increased poverty rates for all groups with, for instance, the Asian poverty rate rising from 10.2 percent in 2007 to 11.8 percent in

2008. As data became available for the years 2009 to 2011, many economists were surprised that poverty rates appeared to level off or fall despite the widespread and lingering unemployment caused by the so-called Great Recession.

Measurement Issues

The poverty rates and trends in Figures 23.4 and 23.5 should be interpreted cautiously. The official income thresholds for defining poverty are necessarily arbitrary and therefore may inadequately measure the true extent of poverty in the United States.

Some observers say that the high cost of living in major metropolitan areas means that the official poverty thresholds exclude millions of families whose income is slightly above the poverty level but clearly inadequate to meet basic needs for food, housing, and medical care. These observers use city-by-city studies on "minimal income needs" to argue that poverty in the United States is much more widespread than officially measured and reported.

In contrast, some economists point out that using income to measure poverty understates the standard of living of many of the people who are officially poor. When individual, household, or family *consumption* is considered rather than family *income,* some of the poverty in the United States disappears. Some low-income families maintain their consumption by drawing down past savings, borrowing against future income, or selling homes. Moreover, many poor families receive substantial noncash benefits such as food stamps and rent subsidies that boost their living standards. Such "in-kind" benefits are not included in determining a family's official poverty status.

FIGURE 23.5 Poverty-rate trends, 1959–2014. Although the national poverty rate declined sharply between 1959 and 1969, it stabilized in the 1970s only to increase significantly in the early 1980s. Between 1993 and 2000 it substantially declined, before rising slightly again in the immediate years following the 2001 recession. Although poverty rates for African Americans and Hispanics are much higher than the average, they significantly declined during the 1990s. Poverty rates rose in 2008 in response to the recession that began in December 2007.

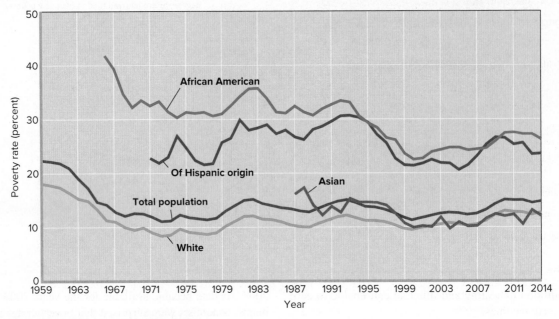

Source: Bureau of the Census, **www.census.gov**.

The U.S. Income-Maintenance System

LO23.6 Identify the major components of the income-maintenance program in the United States.

Regardless of how poverty is measured, economists agree that considerable poverty exists in the United States. Helping those who have very low income is a widely accepted goal of public policy. A wide array of antipoverty programs, including education and training programs, subsidized employment, minimum-wage laws, and antidiscrimination policies, are designed to increase the earnings of the poor. In addition, a number of income-maintenance programs were devised to reduce poverty; the most important are listed in Table 23.3. These programs involve large expenditures and have numerous beneficiaries.

The U.S. income-maintenance system consists of two kinds of programs: (1) social insurance and (2) public assistance, or "welfare." Both are known as **entitlement programs** because all eligible persons are legally entitled to receive the benefits set forth in the programs.

Social Insurance Programs

Social insurance programs partially replace earnings that have been lost due to retirement, disability, or temporary unemployment; they also provide health insurance for the elderly. The main social insurance programs are Social Security, unemployment compensation, and Medicare. Benefits are viewed as earned rights and do not carry the stigma of public charity. These programs are financed primarily out of federal payroll taxes. In these programs the entire population shares the risk of an individual's losing income because of retirement, unemployment, disability, or illness. Workers (and employers) pay a part of wages into a government fund while they are working. The workers are then entitled to benefits when they retire or when a specified misfortune occurs.

Social Security and Medicare The major social insurance program is known as **Social Security.** It is a federal pension program that replaces part of the earnings lost when workers retire, become disabled, or die. This gigantic program ($882 billion in 2014) is financed by compulsory payroll taxes levied on both employers and employees. Workers currently may retire at age 65 and receive full retirement benefits or retire early at age 62 with reduced benefits. When a worker dies, benefits accrue to his or her family survivors. Special provisions provide benefits for disabled workers.

Social Security covers over 90 percent of the workforce; some 59 million people receive Social Security benefits, with benefits for retirees averaging about $1,230 per month. In 2014, those benefits were financed with a combined Social Security and Medicare payroll tax of 15.3 percent, with both

TABLE 23.3 Characteristics of Major Income-Maintenance Programs

Program	Basis of Eligibility	Source of Funds	Form of Aid	Expenditures,* Billions	Beneficiaries, Millions
Social Insurance Programs					
Social Security	Age, disability, or death of parent or spouse; life-time work earnings	Federal payroll tax on employers and employees	Cash	$882	59
Medicare	Age or disability	Federal payroll tax on employers and employees	Subsidized health insurance	$634	54
Unemployment compensation	Unemployment	State and federal payroll taxes on employers	Cash	$32	7.4
Public Assistance Programs					
Supplemental Security Income (SSI)	Age or disability; income	Federal revenues	Cash	$55	8.3
Temporary Assistance for Needy Families (TANF)	Certain families with children; income	Federal-state-local revenues	Cash and services	$10	4
Supplemental Nutrition Assistance Program (SNAP)	Income	Federal revenues	Cash via EBT cards	$76	46
Medicaid	Persons eligible for TANF or SSI and medically indigent	Federal-state-local revenues	Subsidized medical services	$495	67
Earned-income tax credit (EITC)	Low-wage working families	Federal revenues	Refundable tax credit, cash	$61	28

*Expenditures by federal, state, and local governments; excludes administrative expenses.

Source: Social Security Administration, *Annual Statistical Supplement, 2014,* **www.socialsecurity.gov**; U.S. Department of Agriculture, **www.fns.usda.gov**; Internal Revenue Service, **www.irs.gov/taxstats**; and other government sources. Latest data.

the worker and the employer paying 7.65 percent on their first $118,500 of earnings. The 7.65 percent tax comprises 6.2 percent for Social Security and 1.45 percent for Medicare. Self-employed workers pay a tax of 15.3 percent.

Medicare is a federal insurance program that provides health insurance benefits to those 65 or older and people who are disabled. It is financed by payroll taxes on employers and employees. This overall 2.9 percent tax is paid on all work income, not just on the first $118,500. Medicare also makes available supplementary low-cost insurance programs that help pay for doctor visits and prescription drug expenses. In 2014, some 54 million people received Medicare benefits. The benefits paid to recipients totaled $634 billion.

The number of retirees drawing Social Security and Medicare benefits is rapidly rising relative to the number of workers paying payroll taxes. As a result, Social Security and Medicare face serious long-term funding problems. These fiscal imbalances have spawned calls to reform the programs.

Unemployment Compensation All 50 states sponsor unemployment insurance programs called **unemployment compensation,** a federal–state social insurance program that makes income available to workers who are unemployed.

This insurance is financed by a relatively small payroll tax, paid by employers, which varies by state and by the size of the firm's payroll. Any insured worker who becomes unemployed can, after a short waiting period, become eligible for benefit payments. The program covers almost all wage and salary workers. The size of payments and the number of weeks they are made available vary considerably from state to state. Generally, benefits approximate 33 percent of a worker's wages up to a certain maximum payment. In 2014 benefits averaged about $333 weekly. The number of beneficiaries and the level of total disbursements varies with economic conditions.

Typically, unemployment compensation payments last a maximum of 26 weeks. But during recessions—when unemployment rates soar—Congress extends the benefits for additional weeks.

Public Assistance Programs

Public assistance programs (welfare) provide benefits to people who are unable to earn income because of permanent disabling conditions or who have no or very low income and also have dependent children. These programs are financed out of

CONSIDER THIS . . .

Source: © Christopher Kimmel/Getty Images RF

Welfare Cliffs

A **welfare cliff** occurs when an employed welfare recipient's overall income (= wages they earn from work + government benefits) will fall if they earn more money at work. This happens because many types of welfare benefits are withdrawn abruptly if the recipient's income rises above a particular level.

As an example, a single mother named Linda earning wages of $30,000 per year in the state of Pennsylvania would qualify for about $7,000 in housing credits, which would raise her overall income to $37,000. But the housing credits are withdrawn for anyone earning more than $30,000 per year. Thus, if Linda went out and earned an extra $1,000 per year, her overall income would actually fall by $6,000 (= $1,000 more earned income minus $7,000 of lost housing credits).

Welfare cliffs discourage welfare recipients from working more, transitioning into higher-paying jobs, or undertaking the education and training that could lead to higher income levels. One solution would be to have welfare benefits taper off gently as earned income rises. In our example, suppose that Linda's housing credit fell by only $500 (rather than $7,000) when she earned that extra $1,000. In that case, she would come out $500 ahead and thus have an incentive to work more.

general tax revenues and are regarded as public charity. They include "means tests" that require that individuals and families demonstrate low incomes in order to qualify for aid. The federal government finances about two-thirds of the welfare program expenditures, and the rest is paid for by the states.

Many needy persons who do not qualify for social insurance programs are assisted through the federal government's **Supplemental Security Income (SSI)** program. This is a federal program (financed by general tax revenues) that provides a uniform nationwide minimum income for the aged, blind, and disabled who are unable to work and who do not qualify for Social Security aid. In 2014 the average monthly payment was $733 for individuals and $1,100 for couples with both people eligible. More than half the states provide additional income supplements to the aged, blind, and disabled.

Temporary Assistance for Needy Families (TANF) is the basic welfare program for low-income families in the United States. The program is financed through general

federal tax revenues and consists of lump-sum payments of federal money to states to operate their own welfare and work programs. These lump-sum payments are called TANF funds, and in 2014 about 3.5 million people (including children) received TANF assistance. TANF expenditures in 2014 were about $10 billion.

In 1996 TANF replaced the six-decade-old Aid for Families with Dependent Children (AFDC) program. Unlike that welfare program, TANF established work requirements and placed limits on the length of time a family can receive welfare payments. Specifically, the TANF program:

- Set a lifetime limit of 5 years on receiving TANF benefits and requires able-bodied adults to work after receiving assistance for 2 years.

- Ended food-stamp eligibility for able-bodied persons age 18 to 50 (with no dependent children) who are not working or engaged in job-training programs.

- Tightened the definition of "disabled children" as it applies for eligibility of low-income families for Supplemental Security Income (SSI) assistance.

- Established a 5-year waiting period on public assistance for new legal immigrants who have not become citizens.

In 1996, about 12.6 million people, or about 4.8 percent of the U.S. population, were welfare recipients. By the middle of 2007 those totals had declined to 3.9 million and 1.3 percent of the population. The recession that began in December 2007 pushed the number of welfare recipients up to about 4.4 million by December 2009. These recipients accounted for about 1.4 percent of the population in December 2009.

The welfare program has greatly increased the employment rate (= employment/population) for single mothers with children under age 6—a group particularly prone to welfare dependency. Today, that rate is about 13 percentage points higher than it was in 1996.

The **Supplemental Nutrition Assistance Program (SNAP)** was formerly known as the food-stamp program. SNAP is a federal program (financed through general tax revenues) that permits eligible low-income persons to obtain vouchers that can be used to buy food. It is designed to provide all low-income Americans with a nutritionally adequate diet. Under the program, eligible households receive monthly deposits of spendable electronic money on specialized debit cards known as Electronic Benefit Transfer (EBT) cards. The EBT cards are designed so that the deposits can be spent only on food. The amount deposited onto a family's EBT card varies inversely with the family's earned income.

Medicaid is a federal program (financed by general tax revenues) that provides medical benefits to people covered by the SSI and TANF (basic welfare) programs. It helps finance the medical expenses of individuals participating in those programs.

The **earned-income tax credit (EITC)** is a refundable federal tax credit provided to low-income wage earners to supplement their families' incomes and encourage work. It is available for low-income working families, with or without children. The credit reduces the federal income taxes that such families owe or provides them with cash payments if the credit exceeds their tax liabilities. The purpose of the credit is to offset Social Security taxes paid by low-wage earners and thus keep the federal government from "taxing families into poverty." In essence, EITC is a wage subsidy from the federal government that works out to be as much as $2 per hour for the lowest-paid workers with families. Under the program many people owe no income tax and receive direct checks from the federal government once a year. According to the Internal Revenue Service, 28 million taxpayers received $61 billion in payments from the EITC in 2014.

Several other welfare programs are not listed in Table 23.3. Some provide help in the form of noncash transfers. Head Start provides education, nutrition, and social services to economically disadvantaged 3- and 4-year-olds. Housing assistance in the form of rent subsidies and funds for construction is available to low-income families. Pell grants provide assistance to undergraduate students from low-income families. Low-income home energy assistance provides help with home heating bills. Other programs—such as veteran's assistance and black lung benefits—provide cash assistance to those eligible.

QUICK REVIEW 23.2

✓ The basic argument for income equality is that it maximizes total utility by equalizing the marginal utility of the last dollar of income received by all people.

✓ The basic argument for income inequality is that it is an unavoidable consequence of maintaining the economic incentives for production.

✓ By government standards, 46.7 million people in the United States, or 15 percent of the population, lived in poverty in 2014.

✓ The U.S. income-maintenance system includes both social insurance programs and public assistance (welfare) programs.

Economic Analysis of Discrimination

LO23.7 Discuss labor market discrimination and how it might affect hiring decisions and wages.

Although the majority of Americans who are in the lowest income quintile or in poverty are white, African Americans and Hispanics are in those two categories disproportionally to

their total populations. For that reason, the percentages of all African Americans and Hispanics receiving public assistance from the TANF, SSI, and food stamp programs are also well above the average for the entire population. This fact raises the question of what role, if any, discrimination plays in reducing wages for some and increasing wages for others.

Discrimination is the practice of according people inferior treatment (for example, in hiring, occupational access, education and training, promotion, wage rate, or working conditions) on the basis of some factor such as race, gender, or ethnicity. People who practice discrimination are said to exhibit a prejudice or a bias against the groups they discriminate against.

Prejudice reflects complex, multifaceted, and deeply ingrained beliefs and attitudes. Thus, economics can contribute some insights into discrimination but no detailed explanations. With this caution in mind, let's look more deeply into the economics of discrimination.

Taste-for-Discrimination Model

The **taste-for-discrimination model** examines prejudice by using the emotion-free language of demand theory. It views discrimination as resulting from a preference or taste for which the discriminator is willing to pay. The model assumes that, for whatever reason, prejudiced people experience a subjective or psychic cost—a disutility—whenever they must interact with those they are biased against. Consequently, they are willing to pay a certain "price" to avoid interactions with the nonpreferred group. The size of this price depends directly on the degree of prejudice.

The taste-for-discrimination model is general, since it can be applied to race, gender, age, and religion. But our discussion focuses on employer discrimination, in which employers discriminate against nonpreferred workers. For concreteness, we will look at a white employer discriminating against African-American workers.

Discrimination Coefficient A prejudiced white employer behaves as if employing African-American workers would add a cost. The amount of this cost—this disutility—is reflected in a **discrimination coefficient**, d, measured in monetary units. Because the employer is not prejudiced against whites, the cost of employing a white worker is the white wage rate, W_w. However, the employer's perceived "cost" of employing an African-American worker is the African-American worker's wage rate, W_{aa}, *plus* the cost d involved in the employer's prejudice, or $W_{aa} + d$.

The prejudiced white employer will have no preference between African-American and white workers when the total cost per worker is the same, that is, when $W_w = W_{aa} + d$. Suppose the market wage rate for whites is $10 and the monetary value of the disutility the employer attaches to hiring African

Americans is $2 (that is, $d = \$2$). This employer will be indifferent between hiring African Americans and whites only when the African-American wage rate is $8, since at this wage the perceived cost of hiring either a white or an African-American worker is $10:

$$\$10 \text{ white wage} = \$8 \text{ African-American wage} + \$2 \text{ discrimination coefficient}$$

It follows that our prejudiced white employer will hire African Americans only if their wage rate is sufficiently below that of whites. By "sufficiently" we mean at least the amount of the discrimination coefficient.

The greater a white employer's taste for discrimination as reflected in the value of d, the larger the difference between white wages and the lower wages at which African Americans will be hired. A "color-blind" employer whose d is $0 will hire equally productive African Americans and whites impartially if their wages are the same. A blatantly prejudiced white employer whose d is infinity would refuse to hire African Americans even if the African-American wage were zero.

Most prejudiced white employers will not refuse to hire African Americans under all conditions. They will, in fact, *prefer* to hire African Americans if the actual white-black wage difference in the market exceeds the value of d. In our example, if whites can be hired at $10 and equally productive African Americans at only $7.50, the biased white employer will hire African Americans. That employer is willing to pay a wage difference of up to $2 per hour for whites to satisfy his or her bias, but no more. At the $2.50 actual difference, the employer will hire African Americans.

Conversely, if whites can be hired at $10 and African Americans at $8.50, whites will be hired. Again, the biased employer is willing to pay a wage difference of up to $2 for whites; a $1.50 actual difference means that hiring whites is a "bargain" for this employer.

Prejudice and the Market African-American–White Wage Ratio

For a particular supply of African-American workers, the actual African-American–white wage ratio—the ratio determined in the labor market—will depend on the collective prejudice of white employers. To see why, consider Figure 23.6, which shows a labor market for African-American workers. Initially, suppose the relevant labor demand curve is D_1, so the equilibrium African-American wage is $8 and the equilibrium level of African-American employment is 16 million. If we assume that the white wage (not shown) is $10, then the initial African-American–white wage ratio is 0.8 (= $8/$10).

Now assume that prejudice against African-American workers increases—that is, the collective d of white employers rises. An increase in d means an increase in the perceived cost of African-American labor at each African-American wage rate, and that reduces the demand for African-American

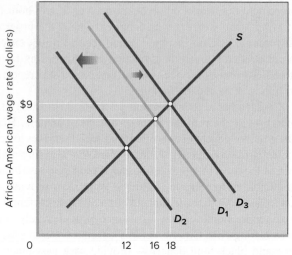

FIGURE 23.6   The African-American wage and employment level in the taste-for-discrimination model. An increase in prejudice by white employers as reflected in higher discrimination coefficients would decrease the demand for African-American workers, here from D_1 to D_2, and reduce the African-American wage rate and level of African-American employment. Not shown, this drop in the African-American wage rate would lower the African-American–white wage ratio. In contrast, if prejudice were reduced such that discrimination coefficients of employers declined, the demand for African-American labor would increase, as from D_1 to D_3, boosting the African-American wage rate and level of employment. The higher African-American wage rate would increase the African-American–white wage ratio.

labor, say, from D_1 to D_2. The African-American wage rate falls from $8 to $6 in the market, and the level of African-American employment declines from 16 million to 12 million. The increase in white employer prejudice reduces the African-American wage rate and thus the actual African-American–white wage ratio. If the white wage rate remains at $10, the new African-American–white ratio is 0.6 (= $6/$10).

Conversely, suppose social attitudes change such that white employers become less biased and their discrimination coefficient as a group declines. This decreases the perceived cost of African-American labor at each African-American wage rate, so the demand for African-American labor increases, as from D_1 to D_3. In this case, the African-American wage rate rises to $9, and employment of African-American workers increases to 18 million. The decrease in white employer prejudice increases the African-American wage rate and thus the actual African-American–white wage ratio. If the white wage remains at $10, the new African-American–white wage ratio is 0.9 (= $9/$10).

Competition and Discrimination

The taste-for-discrimination model suggests that competition will reduce discrimination in the very long run, as follows: The actual African-American–white wage difference for equally productive workers—say, $2—allows nondiscriminators to hire African Americans for less than whites. Firms that hire African-American workers will therefore have lower actual wage costs per unit of output and lower average total costs than will the firms that discriminate. These lower costs will allow non-discriminators to underprice discriminating competitors, eventually driving them out of the market.

But critics of this implication of the taste-for-discrimination model say that it overlooks entry barriers to new firms and point out that progress in eliminating racial discrimination has been slow. Discrimination based on race has persisted in the United States and other market economies decade after decade. To explain why, economists have proposed alternative models.

Statistical Discrimination

A second theory of discrimination centers on the concept of **statistical discrimination,** in which people are judged on the basis of the average characteristics of the group to which they belong, rather than on their own personal characteristics or productivity. For example, insurance rates for teenage males are higher than those for teenage females. The difference is based on factual evidence indicating that, on average, young males are more likely than young females to be in accidents. But many young men are actually less accident-prone than the average young woman, and those men are discriminated against by having to pay higher insurance rates. The uniqueness of the theory of statistical discrimination is its suggestion that discriminatory outcomes are possible even where there is no prejudice.

Labor Market Example How does statistical discrimination show itself in labor markets? Employers with job openings want to hire the most productive workers available. They have their personnel department collect information concerning each job applicant, including age, education, and prior work experience. They may supplement that information with preemployment tests, which they feel are helpful indicators of potential job performance. But collecting detailed information about job applicants is very expensive, and predicting job performance on the basis of limited data is difficult. Consequently, some employers looking for inexpensive information may consider the *average* characteristics of women and minorities in determining whom to hire. They are in fact practicing statistical discrimination when they do so. They are using gender, race, or ethnic background as a crude indicator of production-related attributes.

Example: Suppose an employer who plans to invest heavily in training a worker knows that on average women are less likely to be career-oriented than men, more likely to quit work in order to care for young children, and more likely to refuse geographic transfers. Thus, on average, the return on the employer's investment in training is likely to be less when choosing a woman than when choosing a man. All else equal, when choosing between two job applicants, one a woman and the other a man, this employer is likely to hire the man.

Note what is happening here. Average characteristics for a *group* are being applied to *individual* members of that group. The employer is falsely assuming that *each and every* woman worker has the same employment tendencies as the *average* woman. Such stereotyping means that numerous women who are career-oriented, who do not plan on quitting work in order to care for young children, and who are flexible as to geographic transfers will be discriminated against.

Profitable, Undesirable, but Not Malicious The firm that practices statistical discrimination is not being malicious in its hiring behavior (although it may be violating antidiscrimination laws). The decisions it makes will be rational and profitable because *on average* its hiring decisions are likely to be correct. Nevertheless, many people suffer because of statistical discrimination, since it blocks the economic betterment of capable people. And since it is profitable, statistical discrimination tends to persist.

Occupational Segregation: The Crowding Model

The practice of **occupational segregation**—the crowding of women, African Americans, and certain ethnic groups into less desirable, lower-paying occupations—is still apparent in the U.S. economy. Statistics indicate that women are disproportionately concentrated in a limited number of occupations such as teaching, nursing, and secretarial and clerical jobs. African Americans and Hispanics are crowded into low-paying jobs such as those of laundry workers, cleaners and household aides, hospital orderlies, agricultural workers, and other manual laborers.

Let's look at a model of occupational segregation, using women and men as an example.

The Model The character and income consequences of occupational discrimination are revealed through a labor supply and demand model. We make the following assumptions:

- The labor force is equally divided between men and women workers. Let's say there are 6 million male and 6 million female workers.

- The economy comprises three occupations, X, Y, and Z, with identical labor demand curves, as shown in Figure 23.7.

- Men and women have the same labor-force characteristics; each of the three occupations could be filled equally well by men or by women.

FIGURE 23.7 The economics of occupational segregation. (a) Because 1 million women are excluded from occupation X, the wage rate for men in that occupation is *M* rather than *B*. (b) Because another 1 million women are excluded from occupation Y, the wage for men in occupation Y is also *M* rather than *B*. (c) Because the 2 million women excluded from occupations X and Y are crowded into occupation Z, the wage rate for women there is *W* rather *B*. The elimination of discrimination will create flows of 1 million women to occupation X and 1 million women to occupation Y. The wage rate will equalize at *B* in all three occupations and the nation's output will rise by the sum of the two blue areas minus the single green area.

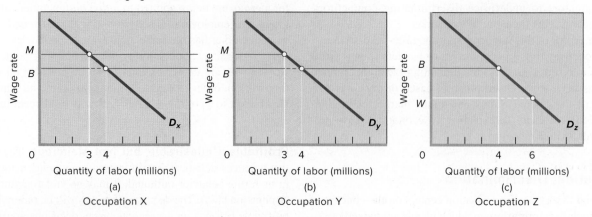

Effects of Crowding Suppose that, as a consequence of discrimination, the 6 million women are excluded from occupations X and Y and crowded into occupation Z, where they earn wage *W*. The men distribute themselves equally among occupations X and Y, meaning that 3 million male workers are in each occupation and have a common wage of *M*. (If we assume that there are no barriers to mobility between X and Y, any initially different distribution of males between X and Y would result in a wage differential between the two occupations. That would prompt labor shifts from the low- to the high-wage occupation until an equal distribution occurred.)

Because women are crowded into occupation Z, labor supply (not shown) is larger and their wage rate *W* is much lower than *M*. Because of the discrimination, this is an equilibrium situation that will persist as long as the crowding occurs. The occupational barrier means women cannot move into occupations X and Y in pursuit of a higher wage.

The result is a loss of output for society. To see why, recall again that labor demand reflects labor's marginal revenue product, which is labor's contribution to domestic output. Thus, the blue areas for occupations X and Y in Figure 23.7 show the decrease in domestic output—the market value of the marginal output—caused by subtracting 1 million women from each of these occupations. Similarly, the green area for occupation Z shows the increase in domestic output caused by moving 2 million women into occupation Z. Although society would gain the added output represented by the green area in occupation Z, it would lose the output represented by the sum of the two blue areas in occupations X and Y. That output loss exceeds the output gain, producing a net output loss for society.

Eliminating Occupational Segregation Now assume that through legislation or sweeping changes in social attitudes,

discrimination disappears. Women, attracted by higher wage rates, shift from occupation Z to X and Y; 1 million women move into X and another 1 million move into Y. Now there are 4 million workers in Z, and occupational segregation is eliminated. At that point there are 4 million workers in each occupation, and wage rates in all three occupations are equal, here at *B*. That wage equality eliminates the incentive for further reallocations of labor.

The new, nondiscriminatory equilibrium clearly benefits women, who now receive higher wages; it hurts men, who now receive lower wages. But women were initially harmed and men benefited through discrimination; removing discrimination corrects that situation.

Society also gains. The elimination of occupational segregation reverses the net output loss just discussed. Adding 1 million women to each of occupations X and Y in Figure 23.7 increases domestic output by the sum of the two blue areas. The decrease in domestic output caused by losing 2 million women from occupation Z is shown by the green area. The sum of the two increases in domestic output in X and Y exceeds the decrease in domestic output in Z. With the end of the discrimination, 2 million women workers have moved from occupation Z, where their contribution to domestic output (their MRP) is low, to higher-paying occupations X and Y, where their contribution to domestic output is high. Thus society gains a more efficient allocation of resources from the removal of occupational discrimination.

Example: The easing of occupational barriers has led to a surge of women gaining advanced degrees in some high-paying professions. In recent years, for instance, the percentage of law degrees and medical degrees awarded to women has exceeded 50 percent, compared with less than 10 percent in 1970.

U.S. Family Wealth and Its Distribution

Between 1995 and 2010, Family Wealth Rose Rapidly for Both the Typical Family as Well as Very Well-Off Families. But Then the Collapse of the Housing Bubble and the Recession of 2007–2009 Greatly Reduced the Typical Family's Level of Wealth.

The latest findings on U.S. family wealth (= net worth = assets *minus* liabilities) were reported in 2014. The data were obtained from the Survey of Consumer Finances and *The State of Working America*. The information includes data on median family wealth, average family wealth, and the distribution of wealth in the United States. *Median family wealth* is the wealth received by the family at the midpoint of the wealth distribution; *average family wealth* is simply total wealth divided by the number of families.

As shown in Table 1, median and average family wealth, adjusted for inflation, both grew rapidly between 1995 and 2007. But then the 2007–2009 recession caused both to drop precipitously. Median wealth, in particular, fell so far that its 2010 value of $77,300 was nearly 8 percent lower than the $84,000 value observed 15 years earlier, in 1995. Even worse, the decline continued over the next few years, with the 2013 value falling to $76,000, or about 10 percent less than the 1995 value.

Most of the decline was due to the 30 percent fall in average housing prices that took place during and after the recession. Millions of people who had taken out loans to buy houses found themselves "underwater" on their home mortgages because the market values of their homes had fallen below what they owed on their loans. That meant that they had *negative* wealth in terms of their housing purchases. As a result, overall wealth levels dropped sharply.

Table 2 looks at the distribution of family wealth for various percentile groups and reveals that the distribution of wealth is highly unequal. In 2010 the wealthiest 10 percent of families owned almost 77 percent of the total wealth and the top 1 percent owned about 35 percent. By contrast, the bottom 90 percent held only about 23 percent of the total wealth. Moreover, the general trend is toward greater inequality. The

Source: © Kelly Ryerson/Getty Images

lowest 90 percent of families saw their share fall from about 32 percent of total U.S. wealth in 1995 to only about 23 percent in 2010.

Tables 1 and 2 raise many interesting questions: Will the inequality of wealth continue to grow in the future? If so, what are the implications for the future character of American society? Should government do more, or less, in the future to try to redistribute wealth? Would new government policies to redistribute wealth endanger or slow the creation of wealth and the growth of income for average Americans? As of 2016, the federal estate (inheritance) tax had a zero percent rate up to $5.43 million and then a 40 percent rate on anything above $5.43 million. There is a vigorous debate about whether this represents too much or too little in the way of estate taxation.

Sources: "Changes in U.S. Family Finances from 2004 to 2007: Evidence from the Survey of Consumer Finances," *Federal Reserve Bulletin,* vol. 95 (February 2009); "Ponds and Streams: Wealth and Income in the U.S., 1989 to 2007," Survey of Consumer Finances working paper, January 2009, p. 35; Lawrence Mishel, Josh Bivens, Elise Gould, and Heidi Shierholz, *The State of Working America,* 12th ed., Economic Policy Institute (2012).

TABLE 1 Median and Average Family Wealth, Survey Years 1995–2010 (in 2010 Dollars)

Year	Median	Average*
1995	$ 84,000	$307,900
1998	98,100	386,700
2001	106,100	487,000
2004	107,200	517,100
2007	126,400	584,600
2010	77,300	498,800
2013	76,000	500,400

*The averages greatly exceed the medians because the averages are boosted by the multibillion-dollar wealth of a relatively few families.

TABLE 2 Percentage of Total Family Wealth Held by Different Groups, Survey Years 1995–2010

Year	Percentage of Total Wealth by Group		
	Bottom 90%	Top 10%	Top 1%
1995	32.2%	67.8%	34.6%
1998	31.4	68.6	33.9
2001	30.2	69.8	32.7
2004	30.4	69.5	33.4
2007	28.5	71.5	33.8
2010	23.3	76.7	35.4

Cost to Society as Well as to Individuals

It is obvious from all three models of discrimination that discrimination by characteristics such as race, ethnicity, gender, or age imposes costs on those who are discriminated against. They have lower wages, less access to jobs, or both. Preferred workers in turn benefit from discrimination through less job competition, greater job access, and higher wages. But discrimination does more than simply transfer earnings from some people to others, thus contributing to income inequality and increasing poverty. Where it exists, discrimination also diminishes the economy's total output and income. In that regard, discrimination acts much like any other artificial barrier to free competition. By arbitrarily blocking qualified individuals from high-productivity (and thus high-wage) jobs, discrimination keeps those discriminated against from providing their maximum contribution to society's total output and total income. In terms of production possibilities analysis, discrimination locates society inside the production possibilities curve that would be available to it if there were no discrimination.

Discrimination redistributes a diminished amount of total income.

QUICK REVIEW 23.3

✓ Discrimination occurs when workers who have the same abilities, education, training, and experience as other workers receive inferior treatment with respect to hiring, occupational access, promotion, or wages.

✓ The taste-for-discrimination model sees discrimination as representing a preference or "taste" for which the discriminator is willing to pay.

✓ The theory of statistical discrimination says that employers often wrongly judge individuals on the basis of average group characteristics rather than on personal characteristics, thus harming those discriminated against.

✓ The crowding model of discrimination suggests that when women and minorities are systematically excluded from high-paying occupations and crowded into low-paying ones, their wages and society's domestic output are reduced.

SUMMARY

LO23.1 Explain how income inequality in the United States is measured and described.

The distribution of income in the United States reflects considerable inequality. The richest 20 percent of households receive 51.2 percent of total income, while the poorest 20 percent receive 3.1 percent.

The Lorenz curve shows the percentage of total income received by each percentage of households. The extent of the gap between the Lorenz curve and a line of total equality illustrates the degree of income inequality.

The Gini ratio measures the overall dispersion of the income distribution and is found by dividing the area between the diagonal and the Lorenz curve by the entire area below the diagonal. The Gini ratio ranges from zero to 1, with higher ratios signifying greater degrees of income inequality.

LO23.2 Discuss the extent and sources of income inequality.

Recognizing that the positions of individual families in the distribution of income change over time and incorporating the effects of noncash transfers and taxes would reveal less income inequality than do standard census data. Government transfers (cash and noncash) greatly lessen the degree of income inequality; taxes also reduce inequality, but not nearly as much as transfers.

Causes of income inequality include differences in abilities, in education and training, and in job tastes, along with discrimination, inequality in the distribution of wealth, and an unequal distribution of market power.

LO23.3 Demonstrate how income inequality has changed since 1975.

Census data show that income inequality has increased since 1975. The major cause of the recent increases in income inequality is a rising demand for highly skilled workers, which has boosted their earnings significantly.

LO23.4 Debate the economic arguments for and against income inequality.

The basic argument for income equality is that it maximizes consumer satisfaction (total utility) from a particular level of total income. The main argument for income inequality is that it provides the incentives to work, invest, and assume risk and is necessary for the production of output, which, in turn, creates income that is then available for distribution.

LO23.5 Relate how poverty is measured and its incidence by age, gender, ethnicity, and other characteristics.

Current statistics reveal that 15 percent of the U.S. population lives in poverty. Poverty rates are particularly high for female-headed families, young children, African Americans, and Hispanics.

LO23.6 Identify the major components of the income-maintenance program in the United States.

The present income-maintenance program in the United States consists of social insurance programs (Social Security, Medicare, and unemployment compensation) and public assistance programs (SSI, TANF, food stamps, Medicaid, and the earned-income tax credit).

LO23.7 Discuss labor market discrimination and how it might affect hiring decisions and wages.

Discrimination relating to the labor market occurs when women or minorities having the same abilities, education, training, and experience as men or white workers are given inferior treatment with respect to hiring, occupational choice, education and training, promotion, and wage rates. Discrimination redistributes national income and, by creating inefficiencies, diminishes its size.

In the taste-for-discrimination model, some white employers have a preference for discrimination, measured by a discrimination coefficient d. Prejudiced white employers will hire African-American workers only if their wages are at least d dollars below those of whites. The model indicates that declines in the discrimination coefficients of white employers will increase the demand for African-American workers, raising the African-American wage rate and the ratio of African-American wages to white wages. It also suggests that competition may eliminate discrimination in the long run.

Statistical discrimination occurs when employers base employment decisions about *individuals* on the average characteristics of *groups* of workers. That can lead to discrimination against individuals even in the absence of prejudice.

The crowding model of occupational segregation indicates how white males gain higher earnings at the expense of women and certain minorities who are confined to a limited number of occupations. The model shows that discrimination also causes a net loss of domestic output.

TERMS AND CONCEPTS

income inequality	Social Security	earned-income tax credit (EITC)
Lorenz curve	Medicare	discrimination
Gini ratio	unemployment compensation	taste-for-discrimination model
income mobility	public assistance programs	discrimination coefficient
noncash transfers	welfare cliff	statistical discrimination
equality-efficiency trade-off	Supplemental Security Income (SSI)	occupational segregation
poverty rate	Temporary Assistance for Needy Families (TANF)	
entitlement programs	Supplemental Nutrition Assistance Program (SNAP)	
social insurance programs	Medicaid	

The following and additional problems can be found in **connect**

DISCUSSION QUESTIONS

1. Use quintiles to briefly summarize the degree of income inequality in the United States. How and to what extent does government reduce income inequality? **LO23.1**

2. Assume that Al, Beth, Carol, David, and Ed receive incomes of $500, $250, $125, $75, and $50, respectively. Construct and interpret a Lorenz curve for this five-person economy. What percentage of total income is received by the richest quintile and by the poorest quintile? **LO23.1**

3. How does the Gini ratio relate to the Lorenz curve? Why can't the Gini ratio exceed 1? What is implied about the direction of income inequality if the Gini ratio declines from 0.42 to 0.35? How would one show that change of inequality in the Lorenz diagram? **LO23.1**

4. Why is the lifetime distribution of income more equal than the distribution in any specific year? **LO23.1**

5. Briefly discuss the major causes of income inequality. With respect to income inequality, is there any difference between inheriting property and inheriting a high IQ? Explain. **LO23.2**

6. What factors have contributed to increased income inequality since 1975? **LO23.3**

7. Should a nation's income be distributed to its members according to their contributions to the production of that total income or according to the members' needs? Should society attempt to equalize income or economic opportunities? Are the issues of equity and equality in the distribution of income synonymous? To what degree, if any, is income inequality equitable? **LO23.4**

8. Do you agree or disagree? Explain your reasoning. "There need be no trade-off between equality and efficiency. An 'efficient' economy that yields an income distribution that many regard as unfair may cause those with meager incomes to become discouraged and stop trying. So efficiency may be undermined. A fairer distribution of rewards may generate a higher average productive effort on the part of the population, thereby enhancing efficiency. If people think they are playing a fair economic game and this belief causes them to try harder, an economy with an equitable income distribution may be efficient as well."[7] **LO23.4**

---

[7]Paraphrased from Andrew Schotter, *Free Market Economics* (New York: St. Martin's Press, 1985), pp. 30–31.

9. Comment on or explain: **LO23.4**
   a. Endowing everyone with equal income will make for very unequal enjoyment and satisfaction.
   b. Equality is a "superior good"; the richer we become, the more of it we can afford.
   c. The mob goes in search of bread, and the means it employs is generally to wreck the bakeries.
   d. Some freedoms may be more important in the long run than freedom from want on the part of every individual.
   e. Capitalism and democracy are really a most improbable mixture. Maybe that is why they need each other—to put some rationality into equality and some humanity into efficiency.
   f. The incentives created by the attempt to bring about a more equal distribution of income are in conflict with the incentives needed to generate increased income.

10. How do government statisticians determine the poverty rate? How could the poverty rate fall while the number of people in poverty rises? Which group in each of the following pairs has the higher poverty rate: (*a*) children or people age 65 or over? (*b*) African Americans or foreign-born noncitizens? (*c*) Asians or Hispanics? **LO23.5**

11. What are the essential differences between social insurance and public assistance programs? Why is Medicare a social insurance program, whereas Medicaid is a public assistance program? Why is the earned-income tax credit considered to be a public assistance program? **LO23.6**

12. The labor demand and supply data in the following table relate to a single occupation. Use them to answer the questions that follow. Base your answers on the taste-for-discrimination model. **LO23.7**

Quantity of Hispanic Labor Demanded, Thousands	Hispanic Wage Rate	Quantity of Hispanic Labor Supplied, Thousands
24	$16	52
30	14	44
35	12	35
42	10	28
48	8	20

   a. Plot the labor demand and supply curves for Hispanic workers in this occupation.
   b. What are the equilibrium Hispanic wage rate and quantity of Hispanic employment?
   c. Suppose the white wage rate in this occupation is $16. What is the Hispanic-to-white wage ratio?
   d. Suppose a particular employer has a discrimination coefficient *d* of $5 per hour. Will that employer hire Hispanic or white workers at the Hispanic-white wage ratio indicated in part *c*? Explain.
   e. Suppose employers as a group become less prejudiced against Hispanics and demand 14 more units of Hispanic labor at each Hispanic wage rate in the table. What are the new equilibrium Hispanic wage rate and level of Hispanic employment? Does the Hispanic-white wage ratio rise or fall? Explain.
   f. Suppose Hispanics as a group increase their labor services in that occupation, collectively offering 14 more units of labor at each Hispanic wage rate. Disregarding the changes indicated in part *e*, what are the new equilibrium Hispanic wage rate and level of Hispanic employment? Does the Hispanic-white wage ratio rise, or does it fall?

13. Males under the age of 25 must pay far higher auto insurance premiums than females in this age group. How does this fact relate to statistical discrimination? Statistical discrimination implies that discrimination can persist indefinitely, while the taste-for-discrimination model suggests that competition might reduce discrimination in the long run. Explain the difference. **LO23.7**

14. Use a demand-and-supply model to explain the impact of occupational segregation or "crowding" on the relative wage rates and earnings of men and women. Who gains and who loses from the elimination of occupational segregation? Is there a net gain or a net loss to society? Explain. **LO23.7**

15. **LAST WORD** Go to Table 1 in the Last Word and compute the ratio of average wealth to median wealth for each of the 7 years. What trend do you find? What is your explanation for the trend? The federal estate tax redistributes wealth in two ways: by encouraging charitable giving, which reduces the taxable estate, and by heavily taxing extraordinarily large estates and using the proceeds to fund government programs. Do you favor repealing the estate tax? Explain.

REVIEW QUESTIONS

1. Suppose that the United States has a Gini ratio of 0.41 while Sweden has a Gini ratio of 0.31. Which country has a more equal distribution of income? **LO23.1**
   a. The United States.
   b. Sweden.
   c. They are actually equal.

2. Some part of income inequality is likely to be the result of discrimination. But other factors responsible for inequality include (select as many as apply): **LO23.2**
   a. Differences in abilities and talents.
   b. Differences in education and training.
   c. Different preferences for work versus leisure.
   d. Different preferences for low-paying but safe jobs relative to high-paying but dangerous jobs.

3. Suppose that a society contains only two members, a lawyer named Monique and a handyman named James. Five years ago, Monique made $100,000 while James made $50,000. This year, Monique will make $300,000 while James will make $100,000. Which of the following statements about this society's income distribution are true? **LO23.2**

*Select **one or more** answers from the choices shown.*

a. In absolute dollar amounts, the entire distribution of income has been moving upward.

b. In absolute dollar amounts, the entire distribution of income has been stagnant.

c. The relative distribution of income has become more equal.

d. The relative distribution of income has become less equal.

e. The relative distribution of income has remained constant.

f. The rich are getting richer while the poor are getting poorer.

g. The rich are getting richer faster than the poor are getting richer.

4. Suppose that the last dollar that Victoria receives as income brings her a marginal utility of 10 utils while the last dollar that Fredrick receives as income brings him a marginal utility of 15 utils. If our goal is to maximize the combined total utility of Victoria and Fredrick, we should: **LO23.4**

a. Redistribute income from Victoria to Fredrick.

b. Redistribute income from Fredrick to Victoria.

c. Not engage in any redistribution because the current situation already maximizes total utility.

d. None of the above.

5. If women are crowded into elementary education and away from fire fighting, wages in fire fighting will tend to be _____ than if women weren't crowded into elementary education. **LO23.7**

a. Higher.

b. Lower.

6. In the taste-for-discrimination model, an increase in employer prejudice against African-American workers would cause the discrimination coefficient to _____ and the demand curve for African-American labor to shift _____. **LO23.7**

a. Decrease; right.

b. Decrease; left.

c. Increase; right.

d. Increase; left.

PROBLEMS

1. In 2015, *Forbes* magazine listed Bill Gates, the founder of Microsoft, as the richest person in the United States. His personal wealth was estimated to be $76 billion. Given that there were about 322 million people living in the United States that year, how much could each person have received if Gates's wealth had been divided equally among the population of the United States? (Hint: A billion is a 1 followed by 9 zeros while a million is a 1 followed by six zeros.) **LO23.1**

2. Imagine an economy with only two people. Larry earns $20,000 per year, while Roger earns $80,000 per year. As shown in the following figure, the Lorenz curve for this two-person economy consists of two line segments. The first runs from the origin to point *a*, while the second runs from point *a* to point *b*. **LO23.1**

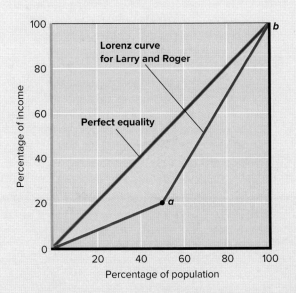

a. Calculate the Gini ratio for this two-person economy using the geometric formulas for the area of a triangle ($= \frac{1}{2} \times$ base $\times$ height) and the area of a rectangle ($=$ base $\times$ height). (Hint: The area under the line segment from point *a* to point *b* can be thought of as the sum of the area of a particular triangle and the area of a particular rectangle.)

b. What would the Gini ratio be if the government taxed $20,000 away from Roger and gave it to Larry? (Hint: The figure will change.)

c. Start again with Larry earning $20,000 per year and Roger earning $80,000 per year. What would the Gini ratio be if both their incomes doubled? How much has the Gini ratio changed from before the doubling in incomes to after the doubling in incomes?

3. In 2015, many unskilled workers in the United States earned the federal minimum wage of $7.25 per hour. By contrast, average earnings in 2015 were about $23 per hour, and certain highly skilled professionals, such as doctors and lawyers, earned $100 or more per hour. **LO23.6**

a. If we assume that wage differences are caused solely by differences in productivity, how many times more productive was the average worker than a worker being paid the federal minimum wage? How many times more productive was a $100-per-hour lawyer compared to a worker earning minimum wage?

b. Assume that there are 20 minimum-wage workers in the economy for each $100-per-hour lawyer. Also assume that both lawyers and minimum-wage workers work the same number of hours per week. If everyone works 40 hours per week, how much does a $100-per-hour lawyer earn a week? How much does a minimum-wage worker earn a week?

c. Suppose that the government pairs each $100-per-hour lawyer with 20 nearby minimum-wage workers. If the government taxes 25 percent of each lawyer's income each week and distributes it equally among the 20 minimum-wage workers with whom each lawyer is paired, how much will each of those minimum-wage workers receive each week? If we divide by the number of hours worked each week, how much does each minimum-wage worker's weekly transfer amount to on an hourly basis?

d. What if instead the government taxed each lawyer 100 percent before dividing the money equally among the 20 minimum-wage workers with whom each lawyer is paired—how much per week will each minimum-wage worker receive? And how much is that on an hourly basis?

4. The desire to maximize profits can work against racial and other types of discrimination. To see this, consider two equally productive accountants named Ted and Jared. Ted is black, and Jared is white. Both can complete 10 audits per month. **LO23.7**

a. Suppose that for any accounting firm that hires either Ted or Jared, all the other costs of performing an audit (besides paying either Ted or Jared) come to $1,000 per audit. If the going rate that must be paid to hire an accountant is $7,000 per month, how much will it cost an accounting firm to produce one audit if it hires either Ted or Jared to do the work?

b. If the market price that accounting firms charge their clients for an audit is $1,800, what would the accounting profit per audit be for a firm that hired either Ted or Jared? What is the profit rate as a percentage?

c. Suppose that firm *A* dislikes hiring black accountants, while firm *B* is happy to hire them. So Ted ends up working at firm *B* rather than firm *A*. If Ted works 11 months per year, how many audits will he complete for firm *B* each year? How much in accounting profits will firm *B* earn each year from those audits?

d. Because firm *A* passed on hiring Ted because he was black, firm *A* is forgoing the profits it could have earned if it had hired Ted. If the firm is willing to forgo up to $5,000 per year in profit to avoid hiring blacks, by how many dollars will firm *A* regret its decision not to hire Ted?

24

Health Care

Learning Objectives

LO24.1 Convey important facts about rising health care costs in the United States.

LO24.2 Relate the economic implications of rising health care costs.

LO24.3 Discuss the problem of limited access to health care for those without insurance.

LO24.4 List the demand and supply factors explaining rising health care costs.

LO24.5 Describe the cost-containment strategies that rely on altering the financial incentives facing either patients or health service providers.

LO24.6 Summarize the goals of the Patient Protection and Affordable Care Act and the major changes that it institutes.

On March 23, 2010, President Barack Obama signed into law the **Patient Protection and Affordable Care Act (PPACA),** a wide-ranging law that proponents claimed would lower health care costs while increasing access to quality health care for millions of poorer Americans.

At over 2,400 pages, the legislation was designed to address a wide set of concerns relating to the provision, delivery, and cost of health care. These included the high and rapidly rising cost of health insurance for those who did have health insurance, the fact that tens of millions of Americans at any given moment were without health insurance, and the inability of many people with preexisting conditions to obtain health insurance.

The controversial law gave the federal government sweeping new powers to promote universal insurance coverage and to regulate the details of insurance policies. Because health care spending was 17.9 percent of GDP in 2010, the law effectively put the federal government in control of nearly one-fifth of the U.S. economy. This chapter applies microeconomic analysis to help explain the origin of the problems that the law was designed to address as well as the heated debate over whether the policies prescribed by the law are likely to achieve their goals.

The Health Care Industry

LO24.1 Convey important facts about rising health care costs in the United States.

Because the boundaries of the health care industry are not precise, defining the industry is difficult. In general, it includes services provided in hospitals, nursing homes, laboratories, and physicians' and dentists' offices. It also includes prescription and nonprescription drugs, artificial limbs, and eyeglasses. Note, however, that many goods and services that may affect health are not included, for example, low-fat foods, vitamins, and health club services.

Health care is one of the largest U.S. industries, employing about 19 million people, including about 708,300 practicing physicians, or 245 doctors per 100,000 of population. There are about 5,600 hospitals containing 902,200 beds. Americans make more than 1 billion visits to office-based physicians each year.

The U.S. Emphasis on Private Health Insurance

Many of the provisions of the Patient Protection and Affordable Care Act are focused on health insurance. This is because a high proportion of health care spending in the United States is provided through private health insurance policies paid for by employers. By contrast, many countries such as Canada have systems of **national health insurance** in which the government uses tax revenues to provide a basic package of health care to every resident at either no charge or at low cost-sharing levels. In such countries only a relatively few people bother to buy private health insurance—and then only to cover services that are not paid for by the national health insurance system.

The uniquely American emphasis on private health insurance paid for by employers is a relatively recent phenomenon. It began during the Second World War in response to price and wage controls that the federal government imposed to prevent inflation. The wage controls were problematic for the private companies charged with building the tanks, planes, and boats needed to win the war. These firms needed to expand output rapidly and knew that doing so would be possible only if they could attract workers away from other industries. Several manufacturers stumbled on the strategy of offering free health insurance as a way of attracting workers. Unable to raise wages, the companies recruited the workers they needed by offering health insurance as a fringe benefit paid for by the employer.

After the war, price and wage controls were lifted. Nevertheless, more and more companies began to offer "free" health insurance to their employees. They did so because of a provision in the federal tax law that makes it cheaper for companies to purchase insurance for their employees than it would be for employees to purchase insurance on their own behalf. By 2007, this incentive structure led to a situation in which nearly 88 percent of people with private health insurance received it as a benefit provided by their employer rather than by purchasing it themselves directly from an insurance company.

The prominence of employer-provided health insurance in the United States has had several important consequences. Perhaps the most important is that health care paid for via insurance can create perverse incentives for overuse that, in turn, lead to higher prices.

Another consequence of employer-provided health care is that health care reform efforts have focused on regulating the health insurance system with which most people are familiar rather than attempting alternatives that most people have never experienced. Later, we will explore how this tendency to regulate—rather than replace—the current insurance system has affected recent reform efforts including the Patient Protection and Affordable Care Act.

Twin Problems: Costs and Access

In recent decades, the U.S. health care system has suffered from two highly publicized problems:

- The cost of health care has risen rapidly in response to higher prices and an increase in the quantity of services provided. (Spending on health care involves both "prices" and "quantities" and is often loosely referred to as "health care costs.") The price of medical care has traditionally increased faster than the overall price level in nearly all periods. The December-to-December index of medical care prices rose by 3.3 percent in 2010, 3.5 percent in 2011, 3.2 percent in 2012, 2.0 percent in 2013, and 3.0 percent in 2014, for a five-year average of 3.0 percent. At the same time, the overall price index for all consumer goods increased by an annual average of 2.0 percent for those five years. However, health care spending (price × quantity) grew by 3.9 percent in 2010, 3.9 percent in 2011, 3.8 percent is 2012, 2.9 percent in 2013, and 5.3 percent in 2014. It is projected to grow at an annual rate of 5.8 percent over the next 10 years, far faster than inflation.

- Some 30 million Americans in 2015 did not have health insurance coverage and, as a result, had significantly reduced access to quality health care.

Efforts to reform health care have focused on controlling costs and making it accessible to everyone. Those two goals are related, since high and rising prices make health care services unaffordable to a significant portion of the U.S. population. In fact, a dual system of health care may be evolving in the United States. Those with insurance or other financial means receive world-class medical treatment, but many people, because of their inability to pay, often fail to seek out even the most basic treatment. When they do seek treatment, they may receive poorer care than those who have insurance. Free county hospitals and private charity hospitals do provide services to those without insurance, but the quality of care can be considerably lower than that available to people who have insurance.

High and Rising Health Care Costs

We need to examine several aspects of health care costs, or, alternatively, health care spending.

FIGURE 24.1 **Health care expenditures and finance.** Total U.S. health care expenditures are extremely large ($3.0 trillion in 2014). (a) Most health care expenditures are for hospitals and the services of physicians and other skilled professionals. (b) Public and private insurance pay for four-fifths of health care.

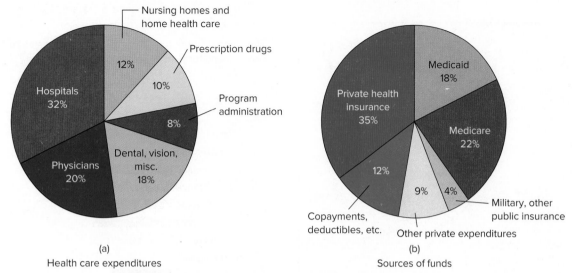

(a)
Health care expenditures

(b)
Sources of funds

Source: Centers for Medicare and Medicaid Services, **cms.hhs.gov.** Data are for 2014 and are compiled by the authors.

Health Care Spending

Health care spending in the United States is high and rising in both absolute terms and as a percentage of domestic output.

Total Spending on Health Care Figure 24.1a gives an overview of the major types of U.S. health care spending ($3.0 trillion in 2014). It shows that 32 cents of each health care dollar goes to hospitals, while 20 cents goes to physicians, and 18 cents is spent on dental, vision, and other miscellaneous health care services.

Figure 24.1b shows the sources of funds for health care spending. It reveals that four-fifths of health care spending is financed by insurance. Public insurance (Medicaid, Medicare, and insurance for veterans, current military personnel, and government employees) is the source of 44 cents of each dollar spent. Private insurance accounts for 35 cents. So public and private insurance combined provide 79 cents of each dollar spent. The remaining 21 cents comes directly out of the health care consumer's pocket. It is paid mainly as insurance **deductibles** (that is, the insured pays the first $250 or $500 of each year's health care costs before the insurer begins paying) or **copayments** (that is, the insured pays, say, 20 percent of all health care costs and the insurance company pays 80 percent).

As discussed in Chapter 23, Medicare is a nationwide federal health care program available to Social Security beneficiaries and persons with disabilities. One part of Medicare is a hospital insurance program that, after a deductible of $1,100 in 2010, covers all reasonable costs for the first 60 days of inpatient care per "benefit period" and lesser amounts (on a cost-sharing basis) for additional days. Coverage is also provided for posthospital nursing services, home health care, and hospice care for the terminally ill. Other parts of Medicare

(including insurance programs for physicians' services, laboratory and other diagnostic tests, outpatient hospital services, and prescription drugs) are voluntary but heavily subsidized by government. The monthly premiums that most participants pay cover about one-fourth of the cost of the benefits provided.

Medicaid provides payment for medical benefits to certain low-income people, including the elderly, the blind, persons with disabilities, children, and adults with dependent children. Those who qualify for Temporary Aid for Needy Families (TANF) and the Supplemental Security Income (SSI) program are automatically eligible for Medicaid. Nevertheless, Medicaid covers less than half of those living in poverty. The federal government and the states share the cost of Medicaid. On average, the states fund 40 percent and the federal government 60 percent of each Medicaid dollar spent.

Overall, about 21 percent of each dollar spent on health care is financed by direct out-of-pocket payments by individuals. The fact that most U.S. health care is paid for by private insurance companies or the government is an important contributor to rising health care costs.

Percentage of GDP Figure 24.2 shows how U.S. health care spending has been increasing as a percentage of GDP. Health care spending absorbed 5.2 percent of GDP in 1960 but rose to 17.5 percent in 2014.

International Comparisons Global Perspective 24.1 reveals that among the industrialized nations, health care spending as a percentage of GDP is highest in the United States. It is reasonable to assume that health care spending varies positively with output and incomes, but that doesn't account for the higher U.S. health expenditures as a percentage of GDP. Later

FIGURE 24.2 **U.S. health care expenditures as a percentage of GDP.** U.S. health care spending as a percentage of GDP has greatly increased since 1960.

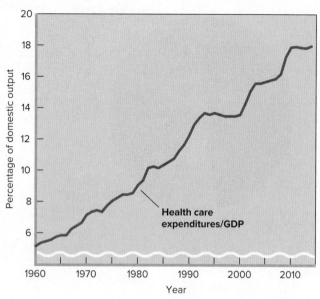

Source: Centers for Medicare and Medicaid Services, **cms.hhs.gov**.

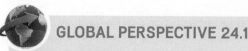

GLOBAL PERSPECTIVE 24.1

Health Care Spending as a Percentage of GDP, Selected Nations

The United States tops the chart when it comes to health care expenditures as a percentage of GDP.

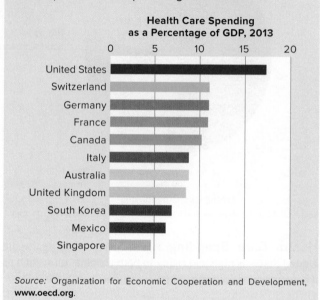

Source: Organization for Economic Cooperation and Development, **www.oecd.org**.

in the chapter we discuss various explanations for why the United States is "in a league of its own" as to its proportion of output devoted to health care.

Quality of Care: Are We Healthier?

To compare the quality of health care from country to country is difficult. Yet there is general agreement that medical care (although not health and not "preventive treatment") in the United States is among the best in the world. Average life expectancy in the United States has increased by about 7 years since 1970, and U.S. physicians and hospitals employ the most advanced medical equipment and technologies. Also, more than half the world's medical research funding is done in the United States. As a result, the incidence of disease has been declining and the quality of treatment has been improving. Polio has been virtually eliminated, ulcers are successfully treated without surgery, angioplasty and coronary bypass surgery greatly benefit those with heart disease, sophisticated body scanners are increasingly available diagnostic tools, and organ transplants and prosthetic joint replacements are more and more common.

That is the good news. But there is other news as well. Despite new screening and treatment technologies, the breast cancer mortality rate has shown only modest improvement. Tuberculosis, a virtually forgotten disease, has reappeared. The AIDS epidemic has claimed more than 658,000 American lives. More generally, some experts say that high levels of health care spending have not produced significantly better health and well-being. U.S. health care expenditures are the highest in the world absolutely, as a proportion of GDP, and on a per capita basis. Yet many nations have lower rates of maternal and infant mortality and longer life expectancies.

Economic Implications of Rising Costs

LO24.2 Relate the economic implications of rising health care costs.

The most visible economic effects of rising health care costs are higher health insurance premiums to employers and higher out-of-pocket costs to workers. But rising health care costs have other economic effects as well.

Reduced Access to Care

Higher health care costs and insurance premiums reduce access to health care. Some employers reduce or eliminate health insurance as part of their pay packages and some uninsured workers go without private health insurance. Consequently, the number of uninsured grows. We will consider this issue in detail momentarily.

Labor Market Effects

Surging health care costs have three main effects on labor markets:

- *Slower wage growth* First, gains in workers' total compensation (wages plus fringe benefits, including health insurance paid for by employers) generally match gains in productivity. When health care costs (and thus insurance prices) rise more rapidly than productivity, firms wanting to maintain the existing level of health care benefits for their workers must reduce the growth of the wage portion of the total compensation package. Thus, in the long run, workers bear the burden of rising health care costs in the form of slower-growing wages.

- *Use of part-time and temporary workers* The high cost of employer-provided health insurance has led some employers to restructure their workforces: Full-time workers with health insurance benefits are employed in smaller numbers, and uninsured part-time or temporary workers are employed in greater numbers. Similarly, an employer with a generous but expensive health care plan might reduce its health insurance expense by discharging its insured lower-wage workers—janitors, gardeners, and cafeteria staff—and replacing them with workers employed by outside independent contractors that provide little or no health insurance for their employees.

- *Outsourcing (and offshoring)* Burdened by rising insurance costs, some firms may find it profitable to shift part of their production to outside suppliers that may be either domestic or international. This outsourcing may lower labor costs in situations where the outside suppliers provide fewer medical benefits to their workers. Offshoring (international outsourcing) has shifted jobs to developing economies such as Mexico, India, and China. Although labor productivity in these countries is considerably lower than that in the United States, lower wages and employer-provided medical benefits may be sufficient to make offshoring profitable. Rising domestic medical expenses therefore may join a host of other factors, including shifts in comparative advantage, in encouraging this practice.

Personal Bankruptcies

Large, uninsured medical bills are one of the major causes of personal bankruptcy. Health care experts point out that medical bills are often the last to be paid because unlike other bills there is nothing to repossess, shut off, or foreclose. So medical bills sometimes build up beyond the point of a realistic means for full repayment. Even individuals who pay all bills in a timely fashion can find themselves in tremendous financial difficulty when they face large, uninsured medical bills for major operations (such as open-heart surgery) and expensive medical procedures (such as cancer treatment).

Impact on Government Budgets

The budgets of federal, state, and local governments are negatively affected by spiraling and sometimes unpredictable health care expenditures. In the past two decades, spending for health care through Medicare and Medicaid has been by far the fastest-growing segment of the federal budget. To cover those rising expenditures, the government must either raise taxes or reduce the portion of the budget used for national defense, education, environmental programs, scientific research, and other spending categories.

The states are also finding it difficult to cover their share of the Medicaid bill. Most of them have been forced to raise their tax rates and search for new sources of revenue, and many of them have had to reduce spending on nonhealth programs such as infrastructure maintenance, welfare, and education. Local governments face similar budget strains in trying to finance public health services, hospitals, and clinics.

Too Much Spending?

Increased spending on computers or houses would be a sign of prosperity, not a cause for alarm, because society is obtaining more of each. What is different about increased spending on health care? Maybe nothing, say some economists. William Nordhaus of Yale, for example, estimated that the economic value of increases in longevity over the last 100 years nearly equals the total value of the additional GDP produced during that period. According to Kevin Murphy and Robert Topel, economists at the University of Chicago, reduced mortality from heart disease alone contributes $1.5 trillion of benefits a year in the United States. That nearly equals the entire annual GDP of Canada.

While all economists agree that improved health care has greatly contributed to society's GDP and well-being, many economists think that health care expenditures in the United States are inefficiently large. The production of health care requires scarce resources such as capital in the form of hospitals and diagnostic equipment and the highly skilled labor of physicians, technicians, and nurses. The total output of health care in the United States may be so large that health care, at the margin, is worth less than the alternative goods and services these resources could otherwise have produced. The United States therefore may be consuming health care beyond the MB = MC point that defines efficiency.

If resources are overallocated to health care, society incurs an efficiency loss. Resources used excessively in health care could be used more productively to build new factories, support research and development, construct new bridges and roads, support education, improve the environment, or provide more consumer goods.

The suggested "too much of a good thing" results from peculiarities in the market for health care. We will see that the possibility of overspending arises from the way health care is financed, the asymmetry of information between consumers and providers, and the interaction of health insurance with technological progress in the industry.

Limited Access

LO24.3 Discuss the problem of limited access to health care for those without insurance.

The other health care problem is limited access. Even though there may be an overallocation of resources to health care, not all Americans can obtain the health care they need. Extrapolations from government surveys indicate that in 2015 about 30 million Americans, or roughly 9 percent of the population, had no health insurance for the entire year. As health care costs (and therefore health care insurance premiums) continue to rise, the number of uninsured could grow.

Who are the medically uninsured? As incomes rise, so does the probability of being insured. So it is no surprise that the uninsured are concentrated among the poor. Medicaid is designed to provide health care for the poor who are on welfare. But many poor people work at low or minimum-wage jobs without health care benefits, earning "too much" to qualify for Medicaid yet not enough to afford private health insurance. About half of the uninsured have a family head who works full time. Many single-parent families, African Americans, and Hispanics are uninsured simply because they are more likely to be poor.

Curiously, those with excellent health and those with the poorest health also tend to be uninsured. Many young people with excellent health simply choose not to buy health insurance. The chronically ill find it very difficult and too costly to obtain insurance because of the likelihood that they will incur substantial health care costs in the future. Because private health insurance is most frequently obtained through an employer, the unemployed are also likely to lack insurance.

Workers for smaller firms are also less likely to have health insurance. The main reason is that administrative expenses for a small firm may be 30 to 40 percent of insurance premiums, as opposed to only 10 percent for a large firm. Also, corporations can deduct health insurance premiums from income to obtain substantial tax savings. Small unincorporated businesses can deduct only part of their health insurance expenses.

Low-wage workers are also less likely to be insured. Earlier we noted that in the long run employers pass on the increasing expense of health care insurance to workers as lower wages. This option is not available to employers who are paying the minimum wage. Thus as health care insurance premiums rise, employers cut or eliminate this benefit from the compensation package for their minimum- and low-wage workers. As a result, these workers are typically uninsured.

Although many of the uninsured forgo health care, some do not. A few are able to pay for it out of pocket. Others may wait until their illness reaches a critical stage and then go to a hospital for admittance or to be treated in the emergency room. This form of treatment is more costly than if the patient had insurance and therefore had been treated earlier by a physician. It is estimated that hospitals provide about $40 billion of uncompensated ("free") health care per year. The hospitals then try to shift these costs to those who have insurance or who can pay out of pocket.

> ### QUICK REVIEW 24.1
> ✓ Private, employer-funded health insurance plays a much larger role in the delivery of health care in the United States than it does in other countries.
> ✓ Health care spending in the United States has been increasing absolutely and as a percentage of gross domestic output.
> ✓ Rising health care costs have caused (a) more people to find health insurance unaffordable; (b) adverse labor market effects, including slower real-wage growth and increased use of part-time and temporary workers; and (c) restriction of nonhealth spending by governments.
> ✓ Rising health care spending may reflect an overallocation of resources to the health care industry.
> ✓ Approximately 9 percent of all Americans have no health insurance and, hence, inferior access to quality health care.

Why the Rapid Rise in Costs?

LO24.4 List the demand and supply factors explaining rising health care costs.

The rising prices, quantities, and costs of health care services are the result of the demand for health care increasing much more rapidly than supply. We will examine the reasons for this in some detail. But first it will be helpful to understand certain characteristics of the health care market.

Peculiarities of the Health Care Market

We know that purely competitive markets achieve both allocative and productive efficiency: The most desired products are produced in the least costly way. We also have found that many imperfectly competitive markets, perhaps aided by regulation or the threat of antitrust action, provide outcomes generally accepted as efficient. What, then, are the special features of the health care market that have contributed to rising prices and thus escalating costs to buyers?

- *Ethical and equity considerations* Ethical questions inevitably intervene in markets when decisions involve the quality of life, or literally life or death. Although we might not consider it immoral or unfair if a person cannot buy a Mercedes or a personal computer, society regards it as unjust for people to be denied access to basic health care or even to the best available health care. In general, society regards health care as an "entitlement" or a "right" and is reluctant to ration it solely by price and income.

- *Asymmetric information* Health care buyers typically have little or no understanding of complex diagnostic and treatment procedures, while the physicians, who are the health care sellers of those procedures, possess detailed information. This creates the unusual situation in which the doctor (supplier) as the agent of the patient (consumer) tells the patient what health care services he or she should consume. We will say more about this shortly.

- *Positive externalities* The medical care market often generates positive externalities (spillover benefits). For example, an immunization against polio, smallpox, or measles benefits the immediate purchaser, but it also benefits society because it reduces the risk that other members of society will be infected with a highly contagious disease. Similarly, a healthy labor force is more productive, contributing to the general prosperity and well-being of society.

- *Third-party payments: insurance* Because four-fifths of all health care expenses are paid through public or private insurance, health care consumers pay much lower out-of-pocket "prices" than they would otherwise. Those lower prices are a distortion that results in "excess" consumption of health care services.

The Increasing Demand for Health Care

With these four features in mind, let's consider some factors that have increased the demand for health care over time.

Rising Incomes: The Role of Elasticities Because health care is a normal good, increases in domestic income have caused increases in the demand for health care. While there is some disagreement as to the exact income elasticity of demand for health care, several studies for industrially advanced countries suggest that the income elasticity coefficient is about 1. This means that per capita health care spending rises approximately in proportion to increases in per capita income. For example, a 3 percent increase in income will generate a 3 percent increase in health care expenditures. Some evidence suggests that income elasticity may be higher in the United States, perhaps as high as 1.5.

Estimates of the price elasticity of demand for health care imply that it is quite inelastic, with this coefficient being as low as 0.2. This means that the quantity of health care consumed declines relatively little as price increases. For example, a 10 percent increase in price would reduce quantity demanded by only 2 percent. An important consequence is that total health care spending will increase as the price of health care rises.

The relative insensitivity of health care spending to price changes results from four factors. First, people consider health care a necessity, not a luxury. Few, if any, good substitutes exist for medical care in treating injuries and infections and alleviating various ailments. Second, medical treatment is often provided in an emergency situation in which price considerations are secondary or irrelevant. Third, most consumers prefer a long-term relationship with their doctors and therefore do not "shop around" when health care prices rise. Fourth, most patients have insurance and are therefore not directly affected by the price of health care. If insured patients pay, for example, only 20 percent of their health care expenses, they are less concerned with price increases or price differences between hospitals and between doctors than they would be if they paid 100 percent themselves.

An Aging Population The U.S. population is aging. People 65 years of age and older constituted approximately 9 percent of the population in 1960 but 14 percent in 2014. Projections for the year 2030 indicate 19 percent of the population will be 65 or over by that year.

This aging of the population affects the demand for health care because older people encounter more frequent and more prolonged spells of illness. Specifically, those 65 and older consume about three and one-half times as much health care as those between 19 and 64. In turn, people over 84 consume almost two and one-half times as much health care as those in the 65 to 69 age group. Health care expenditures are often extraordinarily high in the last year of one's life.

In 2011 the oldest of the 76 million members of the baby boom generation born between 1946 and 1964 began turning 65. We can expect that fact to create a substantial surge in the demand for health care.

Unhealthy Lifestyles Substance abuse helps drive up health care costs. The abuse of alcohol, tobacco, and illicit drugs damages health and is therefore an important component of the demand for health care services. Alcohol is a major cause of injury-producing traffic accidents and liver disease. Tobacco use markedly increases the probability of cancer, heart disease, bronchitis, and emphysema. Illicit drugs are a major contributor to violent crime, health problems in infants, and the spread of AIDS. In addition, illicit-drug users make hundreds of thousands of costly visits to hospital emergency rooms each year. And overeating and lack of exercise contribute to heart disease, diabetes, and many other ailments. One study estimated that obesity-related medical conditions may account for 21 percent of all U.S. medical spending.

The Role of Doctors Physicians may increase the demand for health care in several ways.

Supplier-Induced Demand As we mentioned before, doctors, the suppliers of medical services, have much more information about those services than consumers, who are the demanders. While a patient might be well informed about food products or more complex products such as cameras, he or she is not likely to be well informed about diagnostic tests such as magnetic resonance imaging or medical procedures such as joint replacements. Because of this asymmetric information (informational imbalance), a principal-agent problem emerges: The supplier, not the demander, decides what types and amounts of health care are to be consumed. This situation creates a possibility of "supplier-induced demand."

This possibility becomes especially relevant when doctors are paid on a **fee-for-service** basis, that is, paid separately for each service they perform. In light of the asymmetric information and fee-for-service arrangement, doctors have an opportunity and an incentive to suggest more health care services than are absolutely necessary (just as an auto repair shop has an opportunity and an incentive to recommend replacement of parts that are worn but still working).

More surgery is performed in the United States, where many doctors are paid a fee for each operation, than in foreign countries, where doctors are often paid fixed salaries unrelated to the number of operations they perform. Furthermore, doctors who own X-ray or ultrasound machines do four times as many tests as doctors who refer their patients to radiologists. More generally, studies suggest that up to one-third of common medical tests and procedures are either inappropriate or of questionable value.

The seller's control over consumption decisions has another result: It eliminates much of the power buyers might have in controlling the growth of health care prices and spending.

Defensive Medicine "Become a doctor and support a lawyer," says a bumper sticker. The number of medical malpractice lawsuits admittedly is high. To a medical doctor, each patient represents not only a person in need but also a possible malpractice suit. As a result, physicians tend to practice **defensive medicine.** They recommend more tests and procedures than are warranted medically or economically to protect themselves against malpractice suits.

Medical Ethics Medical ethics may drive up the demand for health care in two ways. First, doctors are legally and ethically committed to using "best-practice" techniques in serving their patients. This often means the use of costly medical procedures that may be of only slight benefit to patients.

Second, public values seem to support the medical ethic that human life should be sustained as long as possible. This makes it difficult to confront the notion that health care is

---

CONSIDER THIS . . .

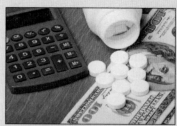

Source: © Oleg (RF)/Alamy Stock Photo RF

Why Do Hospitals Sometimes Charge $25 for an Aspirin?

To save taxpayers money, Medicare and Medicaid set their payment rates for medical services above marginal cost but below average total cost. Doing so gives health care providers an incentive to provide services to Medicare and Medicaid patients because MR > MC. But it also means that government health insurance programs are not reimbursing the full cost of treating Medicare and Medicaid patients. In particular, the programs are not picking up their share of the fixed costs associated with providing health care.

As an example, consider an elderly person who uses Medicare. If he gets into a car accident and is taken to the local emergency room, the hospital will run up a wide variety of marginal costs, including ambulance charges, X-rays, medications, and the time of the nurses and doctors who help him. But the hospital also has a wide variety of fixed costs including rent, utility bills, computer networks, and lots of hideously expensive medical equipment.

These costs have to be borne by somebody. So when Medicare and Medicaid fail to pay their full share of the fixed costs, other patients must pick up the slack. The result has been for hospitals to transfer as much as possible of the fixed costs onto patients with private health insurance. The hospitals overbill private insurance companies so as to make up for the fixed costs that the government refuses to pay.

That is why you will hear stories about hospitals charging patients with private insurance $25 for a single aspirin or $100 for a newborn baby's first pair of diapers. They are making up for the fact that hospitals around the country lost over $51 billion in 2014 because Medicare and Medicaid on average only reimbursed hospitals about 90 percent of the total cost of providing medical services to Medicare and Medicaid patients.

---

provided with scarce resources and therefore must be rationed like any other good. Can society afford to provide $5,000-per-day intensive care to a comatose patient unlikely to be restored to reasonable health? Public priorities seem to indicate that such care should be provided, and those values again increase the demand for health care.

Role of Health Insurance

As we noted in Figure 24.1, 79 percent of health care spending is done not by health care consumers through direct out-of-pocket payments but by private health insurance companies or by the government through Medicare and Medicaid.

Individuals and families face potentially devastating monetary losses from a variety of hazards. Your house may burn down, you may be in an auto accident, or you may suffer a serious illness. An insurance program is a means of protection against the huge monetary losses that can result from such hazards. A number of people agree to pay certain amounts (premiums) periodically in return for the guarantee that they will be compensated if they should incur a particular misfortune. Insurance is a means of paying a relatively small known cost in exchange for obtaining protection against an uncertain but potentially much larger cost.

This financial arrangement can be highly advantageous to those purchasing insurance, but it also alters incentives in ways that can contribute to rising costs and the overconsumption of health care.

The Moral Hazard Problem

The moral hazard problem is the tendency of one party to an agreement to alter her or his behavior in a way that is costly to the other party. Health care insurance can change behavior in two ways. First, some insured people may be less careful about their health, taking fewer steps to prevent accident or illness. Second, insured individuals have greater incentives to use health care more intensively than they would if they did not have insurance. Let's consider both aspects of moral hazard.

Less Prevention Health insurance may increase the demand for health care by encouraging behaviors that require more health care. Although most people with health care insurance are probably as careful about their health as are those without insurance, some may be more inclined to smoke, avoid exercise, and eat unhealthful foods, knowing they have insurance. Similarly, some individuals may take up ski jumping or rodeo bull riding if they have insurance covering the costs of orthopedic surgeons. And if their insurance covers rehabilitation programs, some people may be more inclined to experiment with alcohol or drugs.

Overconsumption Insured people go to doctors more often and request more diagnostic tests and more complex treatments than they would if they were uninsured because, with health insurance, the price or opportunity cost of consuming health care is minimal. For example, many individuals with private insurance pay a fixed premium for coverage, and beyond that, aside from a modest deductible, their health care is "free." This situation differs from most markets, in which the price to the consumer reflects the full opportunity cost of each unit of the good or service. In all markets, price provides a direct economic incentive to restrict use of the product. The minimal direct price to the insured consumer of health care, in contrast, creates an incentive to overuse the health care system. Of course, the penalty for overuse will ultimately show up in higher insurance premiums, but all policyholders will share those premiums. The cost increase for the individual health consumer will be relatively small.

Also, the availability of insurance removes the consumer's budget constraint (spending limitation) when he or she decides to consume health care. Recall from Chapter 7 that budget constraints limit the purchases of most products. But insured patients face minimal or no out-of-pocket expenditures at the time they purchase health care. Because affordability is not the issue, health care may be overconsumed.

Government Tax Subsidy

Federal tax policy toward employer-financed health insurance works as a **tax subsidy** that strengthens the demand for health care services. Specifically, employees do not pay federal income or payroll tax (Social Security) on the value of the health insurance they receive as an employee benefit. Employees thus request and receive more of their total compensation as nontaxed health care benefits and less in taxed wages and salaries.

The government rationale for this tax treatment is that positive spillover benefits are associated with having a healthy, productive workforce. So it is appropriate to encourage health insurance for workers. The tax break does enable more of the population to have health insurance, but it also contributes to greater consumption of health care. Combined with other factors, the tax break may result in an overconsumption of health care.

To illustrate: If the marginal tax rate is, say, 28 percent, $1 worth of health insurance is equivalent to 72 cents in after-tax pay. Because the worker can get more insurance for $1 than for 72 cents, the exclusion of health insurance from taxation increases purchases of health insurance, thus increasing the demand for health care. In essence, the 28-cent difference acts as a government subsidy to health care. One estimate suggests that this subsidy costs the federal government $120 billion per year in forgone tax revenue and boosts private health insurance spending by about one-third. Actual health care spending may be 10 to 20 percent higher than otherwise because of the subsidy.

Graphical Portrayal

A simple demand and supply model illustrates the effect of health insurance on the health care market. Figure 24.3a depicts a competitive market for health care services; curve D shows the demand for health care services if all consumers are uninsured, and S represents the supply of health care. At market price P_a the equilibrium quantity of health care is Q_a.

Recall from our discussion of competitive markets that output Q_a results in allocative efficiency, which means there is no better alternative use for the resources allocated to producing that level of health care. To see what we mean by "no better use," recall that:

- As we move down along demand curve D, each succeeding point indicates, via the price it represents, the marginal benefit that consumers receive from that unit.

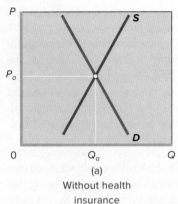

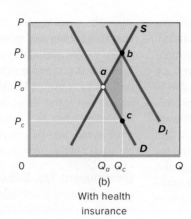

FIGURE 24.3 Insurance and the overallocation of resources to health care. (a) Without health insurance, the optimal amount of health care consumed is Q_a, where the marginal benefit and marginal cost of health care are equal. (b) The availability of private and public insurance increases the demand for health care, as from D to D_i, and reduces the price to the consumer from P_a to P_c (here, equal to one-third of the full price P_b). This lower after-insurance price results in overconsumption (Q_c rather than Q_a). Area abc represents the efficiency loss (or deadweight loss) from the overallocation of resources to health care.

- The supply curve is the producers' marginal-cost curve. As we move up along supply curve S, each succeeding point indicates the marginal cost of each successive unit of health care.

- For each unit produced up to the equilibrium quantity Q_a, marginal benefit exceeds marginal cost (because points on D are above those on S). At Q_a marginal benefit equals marginal cost, designating allocative efficiency. No matter what else those resources could have produced, the greatest net benefit to society is obtained by using those resources to produce Q_a units of health care.

But allocative efficiency occurs only when consumers pay the full market price for a product, as is assumed in Figure 24.3a. What happens when we introduce health insurance that covers, say, two-thirds of all health care costs? In Figure 24.3b, with private or public health insurance in place, consumers increase their demand for health care, as from D to D_i. At each possible price they desire more health care than before because insurance will pick up a large part of the bill. Given the supply curve of health care S, this increase in demand raises the price of health care to P_b. But with the insurance, consumers pay only one-third of the new higher price. This is less than without the insurance because the new price is only $P_c\,(=\frac{1}{3}P_b)$—rather than the previous price P_a. So they increase their consumption of health care from Q_a to Q_c.

The added consumption (and production) of health care is inefficient. Between Q_a and Q_c each unit's marginal cost to society (measured on curve S) exceeds its marginal benefit (measured on before-insurance demand curve D). Each unit of health care between Q_a and Q_c is an overallocation of resources to health care. Area abc shows the efficiency loss (or deadweight loss) that results.

Figure 24.3b implies that a trade-off exists between efficiency and equity. Standards of fairness or equity in the United States lead people to believe that all citizens should have access to basic health care, which is why government created social insurance in the form of Medicare and

Medicaid. Also, it helps explain the federal tax subsidy to private health insurance, which again makes health care more accessible. The problem, as Figure 24.3b shows, is that the greater the availability of insurance (and thus the more equitable society makes access to health care), the greater the overallocation of resources to the health care industry. This overallocation would be even greater if health care were provided completely "free" under a program of national health insurance. Consumers would purchase health care as long as the marginal benefit to themselves as individuals was positive, regardless of the true cost to society.

Rationing to Control Costs We have just seen that by reducing the marginal costs facing patients, both private health insurance and government health insurance drive up prices. But then why is it that the United States, with its emphasis on private health insurance, spends so much more on health care than countries like the United Kingdom and Canada that provide national health insurance? If both types of insurance promote higher prices, why do we see higher health care spending in the United States than in those other countries?

One contributing factor is that the countries with national health insurance use various nonprice mechanisms to ration care. These mechanisms restrict the quantity of health care services supplied and, consequently, the amount of money spent providing health care.

Some nonprice rationing is done by committees of medical and budgetary experts. In the United Kingdom, for instance, the National Committee for Health and Clinical Excellence has set a general limit of £30,000 (approximately $44,000) on the cost of extending life for a year. Applying this rule to a specific situation, if an anticancer treatment would cost more than £30,000 to extend a cancer patient's life for a year, the United Kingdom's national health service would not pay for it. This cost rule keeps a lid on expenditures.

Waiting is another nonprice mechanism that rations care in countries with national health insurance. In the Canadian system, patients often have waits of weeks, months, or even years for certain diagnostic procedures and surgeries. This is the result of the Canadian government's effort to control expenditures by restricting hospitals' capital spending. To illustrate, there are only one-fifth as many magnetic resonance imaging (MRI) machines per million people in Canada as in the United States. This results in a substantial waiting list for MRI scans in Canada.

By contrast, private health insurers in the United States have not had to obey national committees that set spending limits. Nor have they had to answer to government budget officials attempting to control expenditures by restricting capital spending. Instead, private health insurers have faced a very different regulatory system that has tended to increase rather than decrease spending.

To see why this is true, note that until the Patient Protection and Affordable Care Act, private health insurers were regulated almost entirely at the state level. In addition, each state insurance regulator had very different incentives compared to the national health insurance regulators found in other countries.

In a country with national health insurance, regulators are confronted by their government's budget constraint and the fact that the government has a limited supply of tax dollars to spend on health care. As a result, they have a strong incentive to deny care and limit spending. By contrast, state insurance regulators in the United States did not have to worry about exhausting government budgets because private health insurance is paid for with private money rather than government money. This led to a tendency for state insurance regulators to focus on benefits more than costs.

To see why this happened, note that requiring insurance companies to cover more people or treat more conditions is politically popular, while requiring them to cut coverage to save money is politically unpopular. With many states having popularly elected state insurance commissioners and the rest having insurance commissioners appointed by either the governor or the legislature, there was constant political pressure for state insurance regulators to pass new regulations requiring insurance companies to spend more rather than less. States incrementally imposed various rules expanding the number of conditions that had to be covered by insurers as well as the amounts that insurers had to spend on patient care.

Because these requirements involved the costly provision of additional care, insurance companies responded by raising insurance premiums. Thus, America's state-based system of government insurance regulation tended to increase rather than decrease the amount spent on health care.

Many economists view this regulatory system as one of the factors that has contributed to the United States spending more of its GDP on health care than any other nation on earth. While regulators in other countries have sought out ways to deny care and reduce costs, state regulators in America have tended to mandate that insurance companies expand treatment and incur additional costs.

As we will discuss later, the Patient Protection and Affordable Care Act creates a new set of federal insurance regulators that will largely supersede state insurance regulators. Part of the controversy related to the bill is whether the new federal regulators might eventually be tasked with denying care in the way that European regulators have.

Supply Factors in Rising Health Care Prices

Supply factors have also played a role in rising health care prices. Specifically, the supply of health care services has increased, but more slowly than demand. A combination of factors has produced this relatively slow growth of supply.

Supply of Physicians The supply of physicians in the United States has increased over the years; in 1975 there were 169 physicians per 100,000 people; by 2011 there were 245. But this increase in supply has not kept up with the increase in the demand for physicians' services. As a result, physicians' fees and incomes have increased more rapidly than average prices and incomes for the economy as a whole.

Conventional wisdom has been that physician groups, for example, the American Medical Association, have purposely kept admissions to medical schools, and therefore the supply of doctors, artificially low. But that is too simplistic. A rapidly rising cost of medical education seems to be the main cause of the relatively slow growth of doctor supply. Medical training requires 4 years of college, 4 years of medical school, an internship, and perhaps 3 or 4 years of training in a medical specialty. The opportunity cost of this education has increased because the salaries of similarly capable people have soared in other professions. The direct expenses have also increased, largely due to the increasingly sophisticated levels of medical care and therefore of medical training.

High and rising education and training costs have necessitated high and rising doctors' fees to ensure an adequate return on this sort of investment in human capital. Physicians' incomes are indeed high, averaging in 2015 from about $195,000 for family care physicians up to $541,000 for neurosurgeons. But the costs of obtaining the skills necessary to become a physician are also very high. Data show that while doctors have high rates of return on their educational expenses, those returns are below the returns for the holders of masters of business administration degrees.

Slow Productivity Growth Productivity growth in an industry tends to reduce costs and increase supply. In the health care industry, such productivity growth has been modest. One reason is that health care is a service, and it is generally more difficult to increase productivity for services than for goods. It is relatively easy to increase productivity in manufacturing by mechanizing the production process. With more and better machinery, the same number of workers can produce greater output. But services often are a different matter. It is not easy, for example, to mechanize haircuts, child care, and pizza delivery. How do you significantly increase the productivity of physicians, nurses, and home care providers?

Also, competition for patients among many providers of health care has not been sufficiently brisk to force them to look for ways to reduce costs by increasing productivity. When buying most goods, customers typically shop around for the lowest price. This shopping requires that sellers keep their prices low and look to productivity increases to maintain or expand their profits. But patients rarely shop for the lowest prices when seeking medical care. In fact, a patient may feel uncomfortable about being operated on by a physician who charges the lowest price. Moreover, if insurance pays for the surgery, there is no reason to consider price at all. The point is that unusual features of the market for health care limit competitive pricing and thus reduce incentives to achieve cost saving via advances in productivity.

Changes in Medical Technology
Some technological advances in medicine have lowered costs. For example, the development of vaccines for polio, smallpox, and measles has greatly reduced health care expenditures for the treatment of those diseases. And reduced lengths of stays in hospitals have lowered the costs of medical care.

But many medical technologies developed since the Second World War have significantly increased the cost of medical care either by increasing prices or by extending procedures to a greater number of people. For example, because they give more accurate information, advanced body scanners costing up to $1,000 per scan are often used in place of X-rays that cost less than $100 for each scan. Desiring to offer the highest quality of service, hospitals want to use the very latest equipment and procedures. These newer, more expensive treatments are believed to be more effective than older ones. But doctors and hospital administrators both realize that the high fixed cost of such equipment means it must be used extensively to reduce the average cost per patient and recoup the investment at "fair return" charges per procedure.

As another example, organ transplants are extremely costly. Before the development of this technology, a person with a serious liver malfunction died. Now a liver transplant can cost $200,000 or more, with subsequent medical attention costing $10,000 to $20,000 per year for the rest of the patient's life.

Finally, consider new prescription medications. Pharmaceutical companies have developed very expensive drugs that often replace less expensive ones and are prescribed for a much wider range of physical and mental illnesses. Although these remarkable new medications greatly improve health care, they also contribute to rising health care costs.

The historical willingness of private and public insurance to pay for new treatments without regard to price and

---

CONSIDER THIS . . .

Source: © Blend Images/Alamy Stock Photo

Electronic Medical Records

The Health Information Technology for Economic and Clinical Health (HITECH) Act of 2009 provides $20 billion of subsidies to encourage hospitals and physicians to adopt electronic medical records.

The subsidies are designed to get doctors and nurses to switch from traditional paper records to electronic databases. That way, hospital administrators should be able to easily search for instances where costs might be cut. They could, for instance, notice whether doctors are overprescribing certain medications or scheduling expensive MRI scans when less-expensive X-rays would suffice.

Unfortunately, these systems seem to raise costs and lower the quality of care. When records are done with pen and paper, doctors only write down the information they think is relevant. By contrast, electronic systems demand that during every appointment, the doctor fill out every single item from a comprehensive list of questions and drop-down menus. That is wasteful because the vast majority of those items are going to be totally irrelevant for any particular patient. The systems are so time-intensive that many doctors report that they are now seeing fewer patients because it takes so long to fill out the forms.

At the same time, insurance billings have gone up because hospitals using electronic systems now have a comprehensive record of *everything* that was discussed at each appointment. Armed with that information, they are billing insurance companies and Medicare and Medicaid for many more procedures than was the case when records were kept by hand and doctors only wrote down the most important information about each patient.

The projected efficiency gains from being able to search for patterns of overuse have not materialized because the financial incentive for each hospital is not to look for patterns of overuse but, instead, to bill for every little thing that it can. As a result, care is down while costs are up.

---

number of patients has contributed to the incentive to develop and use new technologies. Insurers, in effect, have encouraged research into and development of health care technologies, regardless of their cost. Recently, when insurance companies resisted paying for new expensive treatments such as bone marrow transplants, public outcries led them to change their minds. So expanding insurance coverage leads to new, often more expensive medical technologies, which in turn lead to a demand for a wider definition of what should be covered by insurance.

Relative Importance

According to most analysts, the demand and supply factors we have discussed vary in their impact on escalating health care costs. As we noted, the income elasticity of demand for health care is estimated to be upward of 1.5 in the United States, meaning that increased income brings with it more-than-proportionate increases in health care spending. But rising income does not alone explain the rocketing increase in health care spending as a percentage of total domestic output (income). Furthermore, government studies estimate that the aging population accounts for less than 10 percent of the current increase in per capita health care spending.

Most experts attribute the relative rise in health care spending to (1) advances in medical technology, combined with (2) the medical ethic of providing the best treatment available, (3) private and public health insurance, and (4) fee-for-service physicians' payments by health insurance firms. Through technological progress, great strides have been made in the diagnosis, treatment, and prevention of illness. But the third-party (insurance) payment system provides little incentive to limit the development or use of such technologies because it has no mechanism to force an equating of marginal costs and marginal benefits. And the "best treatment available" ethic, together with the fee-for-service payment system, ensures that any new technology with a positive marginal benefit will get used and be billed for, regardless of the marginal cost to society.

QUICK REVIEW 24.2

✓ Characteristics of the health care market are (a) the widespread view of health care as a "right," (b) asymmetric information between consumers and suppliers, (c) the presence of positive externalities, and (d) payment mostly by insurance.

✓ The demand for health care has increased for many reasons, including rising incomes, an aging population, unhealthy lifestyles, the role of doctors as advisers to patients, the practice of defensive medicine, and a fee-for-service payment system via health insurance.

✓ Countries with national health insurance systems contain costs by denying care for certain procedures and by limiting capital expenditures.

✓ The supply of health care has grown slowly, primarily because of (a) relatively slow productivity growth in the health care industry, (b) rising costs of medical education and training, and (c) greater use of very-high-cost health care technologies.

Cost Containment: Altering Incentives

LO24.5 Describe the cost-containment strategies that rely on altering the financial incentives facing either patients or health service providers.

The Patient Protection and Affordable Care Act is the latest in a long series of attempts to control the growth of health care costs, prices, and spending. Many of these efforts have been focused on reducing the incentives to overconsume health care.

Deductibles and Copayments

Insurance companies have reacted to rising health care costs by imposing sizable deductibles and copayments on those they insure. Instead of covering all of an insured's medical costs, a policy might now specify that the insured pay the first $250 or $500 of each year's health care costs (the deductible) and 15 or 20 percent of all additional costs (the copayment). The deductible and copayment are intended to alleviate the overuse problem by creating a direct payment and therefore an opportunity cost to the health care consumer. The deductible has the added advantage of reducing the administrative costs of insurance companies in processing many small claims.

Health Savings Accounts

A federal law enacted in 2003 established **health savings accounts (HSAs).** These accounts are available to all workers who are covered by health insurance plans with annual deductibles of $1,000 or more and do not have other first-dollar insurance coverage. Individuals can make tax-deductible contributions into their HSAs, even if they do not itemize deductions on their tax forms. Employers can also make tax-free contributions to workers' accounts if they choose. Earnings on the funds in HSAs are not taxable, and the owners of these accounts can use them to pay for approved medical expenses. Unused funds in HSAs accumulate and remain available for later out-of-pocket medical expenses. Account holders can place additional money into their accounts each year between age 55 and the year they become eligible for Medicare.

HSAs are designed to promote personal saving out of which workers can pay routine health care expenses while working and Medicare copayments and deductibles later, during retirement. HSAs are also designed to reduce escalating medical expenses by injecting an element of competition into health care delivery. Because individuals are using some of their own HSA money to pay for health care, they presumably will assess their personal marginal costs and marginal benefits in choosing how much and what type of health care to obtain. They will also have a strong incentive to inquire about and compare prices charged by various qualified medical providers. Holders of HSAs never lose their accumulated funds. They can remove money for nonmedical purchases but must pay income taxes and a 10 percent penalty on such withdrawals.

Managed Care

Managed-care organizations (or systems) are those in which medical services are controlled or coordinated by insurance companies or health care organizations to reduce health care expenditures. In 2009 nearly 90 percent of all U.S. workers received health care through such "managed care." These organizations are of two main types.

Some insurance companies have set up **preferred provider organizations (PPOs)**, which require that hospitals and physicians accept discounted prices for their services as a condition for being included in the insurance plan. The policyholder receives a list of participating hospitals and doctors and is given, say, 80 to 100 percent reimbursement of health care costs when treated by PPO physicians and hospitals. If a patient chooses a doctor or hospital outside the PPO, the insurance company reimburses only 60 to 70 percent. In return for being included as a PPO provider, doctors and hospitals agree to rates set by the insurance company for each service. Because these fees are less than those usually charged, PPOs reduce health insurance premiums and health care expenditures.

Many Americans now receive their medical care from **health maintenance organizations (HMOs),** which provide health care services to a specific group of enrollees in exchange for a set annual fee per enrollee. HMOs employ their own physicians and contract for specialized services with outside providers and hospitals. They then contract with firms or government units to provide medical care for their workers, who thereby become HMO members. Because HMOs have fixed annual revenue, they may lose money if they provide "too much" care. So they have an incentive to hold down costs. They also have an incentive to provide preventive care in order to reduce the potentially far larger expense of corrective care.

Both PPOs and HMOs are managed-care organizations because medical use and spending are "managed" by closely monitoring physicians' and hospitals' behavior. The purpose of close monitoring is to eliminate unnecessary tests and treatments. Doctors in managed-care organizations might not order an MRI scan or an ultrasound test or suggest surgery because their work is monitored and because they may have a fixed budget. In contrast, an independent fee-for-service physician facing little or no oversight may have a financial incentive to order the test or do the surgery. Doctors and hospitals in a managed-care organization often share in an "incentive pool" of funds when they meet their cost-control goals.

The advantages of managed-care plans are that they provide health care at lower prices than traditional insurance and emphasize preventive medicine. The disadvantages are that the patient usually is restricted to physicians employed by or under contract with the managed-care plan. Also, some say that the focus on reducing costs has gone too far, resulting in

denial of highly expensive, but effective, treatment. This "too far" criticism was mainly leveled at HMOs, where incentives to reduce costs were the greatest. Perhaps because of a backlash against HMOs, firms have increasingly shifted workers from managed care toward PPOs.

Medicare and DRG

In 1983 the federal government altered the way it makes payments for hospital services received by Medicare patients. Rather than automatically paying all costs related to a patient's treatment and length of hospital stay, Medicare authorized payments based on a **diagnosis-related group (DRG) system**. Under DRG, a hospital receives a fixed payment for treating each patient; that payment is an amount associated with the diagnosis—one of several hundred carefully detailed diagnostic categories—that best characterizes the patient's condition and needs.

DRG payments obviously give hospitals the incentive to restrict the amount of resources used in treating patients. It is no surprise that under DRG the length of hospital stays has fallen sharply and more patients are treated on an outpatient basis. Critics, however, argue that this is evidence of diminished health care quality.

Limits on Malpractice Awards

Congress has, for many years, debated whether to cap (at, say, $250,000 or $500,000) the "pain and suffering" awards on medical malpractice lawsuits against physicians. Those who support malpractice caps say that patients should receive full compensation for economic losses but not be made wealthy through huge jury awards. They contend that capping the awards will reduce medical malpractice premiums and therefore lower health care costs. Opponents of caps counter that large "pain and suffering" awards deter medical malpractice. If so, such awards improve the overall quality of the health care system. Opponents also point out that malpractice awards are a negligible percentage of total health care costs. Thirty-three states have placed caps on the "pain and suffering" portion of malpractice awards.

QUICK REVIEW 24.3

✓ Policymakers have pursued several strategies when attempting to contain health care spending and prices.

✓ Insurance deductibles and copayments confront consumers with opportunity costs; managed-care organizations attempt to restrict their members' use of health services; the diagnosis-related group (DRG) system caps the amount Medicare will spend on any procedure; and health savings accounts (HSAs) confront individuals with the marginal cost of routine health care expenses.

The Patient Protection and Affordable Care Act

LO24.6 Summarize the goals of the Patient Protection and Affordable Care Act and the major changes that it institutes.

The primary goal of the Patient Protection and Affordable Care Act (PPACA) passed in 2010 was not cost containment but rather the extension of health insurance coverage to all Americans. In truth, covering every single citizen would have been possible only if America had moved to a national health insurance system similar to that used in Canada. Such a move would have been impossible politically, however, because opinion polls indicated that 75 percent of Americans with employer-provided health insurance rated their coverage as good or very good.

Thus, President Obama and like-minded members of Congress did not pursue the creation of a national health insurance system. Rather, they moved to extend and expand the existing system in which nearly all Americans receive their health care through either employer-provided health insurance or government-provided health insurance (Medicaid and Medicare). In promoting the PPACA, the president reassured audiences by telling them, "If you like your health care plan, you can keep it."

Major Provisions

The authors of the PPACA understood that extending insurance coverage to millions of previously uninsured people would be costly. As with any group of people enrolled in a health insurance program, many would eventually become sick and need costly treatments. This problem was exacerbated by the fact that many of those without insurance were known to suffer from extremely costly medical conditions. These individuals were without insurance coverage precisely because private insurance companies (which have to either break even or go bankrupt) considered them to be too expensive to insure. Thus, if those with costly medical conditions were to be covered, significant new revenue sources would have had to be found.

The PPACA aimed to obtain the needed revenue from two main sources: a personal mandate to buy insurance and an assortment of other new taxes. We will discuss each as we go over the PPACA's major provisions.

Preexisting Conditions, Caps, and Drops The PPACA made it illegal for insurance companies to deny coverage to anyone on the basis of a preexisting medical condition. As just discussed, this ban lead to the enrollment of millions of individuals with costly health conditions.

The PPACA also increased the amount of money that insurance companies had to pay out by prohibiting them from imposing annual or lifetime expenditure caps.

To prevent insurance companies from dropping policyholders just because they developed a costly illness, the PPACA also made fraud the only legal reason that an insurance company could drop a policyholder. Because this provision forced insurance companies to keep very sick people enrolled, it also entailed significant cost increases for insurance companies.

Employer Mandate The PPACA has an **employer mandate** (requirement) that every firm with 50 or more full-time employees must either purchase health insurance for each of their full-time employees or pay a fine of $2,000 per employee. This provision of the law is intended to extend employer-paid health insurance to as many workers as possible so that private employers, rather than the government, will bear as much of the cost of extending insurance coverage to the uninsured as possible.

Firms with fewer than 50 full-time employees are exempt from the employer mandate because the high cost of health insurance might bankrupt many smaller firms.

Personal Mandate The PPACA contains a **personal mandate** (requirement) that individuals must purchase health insurance for themselves and their dependents unless they are already covered by either government insurance or employer-provided insurance. Anyone refusing will be fined. The fine is the larger of either $695 per uninsured family member or 2.5 percent of family income.

As we will explain next, the PPACA contains extensive subsidies to ensure that poorer people will not be financially devastated by the personal mandate's requirement to buy health insurance. However, it must be understood that the point of the personal mandate is to force higher-income healthy people (especially healthy young workers) to buy health insurance so that their insurance premiums can help pay for the high health care bills of those with costly medical conditions as well as the subsidies needed to make health insurance affordable for those with lower incomes.

Covering the Poor In the years before the PPACA was passed, millions of poorer Americans lacked private health insurance either (*a*) because they were unemployed and thus not receiving employer-provided health insurance or (*b*) because their employers did not provide health insurance. Some of these poorer Americans could obtain government health insurance through either Medicaid or Medicare, but those who did not found themselves without any sort of health insurance, either private or public.

The PPACA attempts to cover those with lower incomes in three ways. First, the employer mandate will induce many larger employers to provide insurance for all of their full-time employees, including the poorer ones. Second, the law expands the Medicaid system to cover anyone whose income is less than 133 percent of the poverty level. Third, the PPACA subsidizes the purchase price of health insurance for those who must buy their own health insurance to comply with the individual mandate.

The subsidies actually extend well into the middle class because they extend upward along the income scale even to persons making up to four times the federal poverty level. Taking into account the fact that individuals and households have different federal poverty levels, the subsidies would extend to individuals making up to about $44,000 per year and families of four making up to about $88,000 per year. By comparison, full-time workers had median annual earnings of about $41,560 in 2011, while the median family income in 2011 was about $50,054. The subsidies extend into the upper half of the income distribution because health insurance is so expensive that the personal mandate would have been financially ruinous for even middle-income workers if it had not been accompanied by subsidies.

A complicated formula adjusts the size of the subsidies by income level. The formula kicks in at 133 percent of the federal poverty level because anyone earning less will receive free government health insurance through Medicaid. For those earning slightly more than 133 percent of the poverty level (about $15,000 for an individual and about $30,700 for a family of four), the subsidies would be large enough so that they would not have to spend more than about 4 percent of their incomes purchasing health insurance. The subsidies get progressively less generous as incomes rise, so that those earning three to four times the poverty level would be subsidized such that they would have to pay about 10 percent of their incomes to buy health insurance.

Insurance Exchanges Individuals shopping for their own insurance will do so in government-regulated markets called **insurance exchanges**. There will be one exchange for each state, and federal regulators will only allow policies meeting certain standards to be offered. The regulators cannot set prices directly but will have the authority to withdraw approval from any insurer that requests a price increase that regulators deem to be unjustified on the basis of higher costs. It is hoped that the exchanges will reduce the growth of health care spending by fostering competition among insurance companies.

Other Provisions The 2,400-page PPACA contains hundreds of additional provisions. Some of the more publicized include:

- Mandating that the adult children of parents with employer-provided health insurance remain covered by their parents' insurance through age 26.
- Making it illegal for insurance companies to charge copayments or apply deductibles to annual checkups or preventive care.

- Requiring insurers to spend at least 80 percent of the money they receive in premiums on either health care or improving health care.

Taxes To help pay for the extension of health insurance to millions of previously uninsured people, the PPACA imposes several new taxes. The more prominent are:

- A 0.9 percentage point increase in the Medicare payroll tax for individuals earning more than $200,000 per year and for married couples earning more than $250,000 per year.

Singapore's Efficient and Effective Health Care System

How Does Singapore Deliver Some of the Best Health Care in the World while Spending 72 Percent Less per Person than the United States?

In every health quality category monitored by the World Health Organization, the small island nation of Singapore is either number one in the world or near the top of the list. Among other achievements, Singapore has the world's lowest rate of infant mortality and the world's fourth-highest life expectancy.

One might expect that achieving these exceptional outcomes would be extremely expensive. But Singapore is also number one in another category. It spends less per person on health care than any other developed nation. In 2015 the United States spent 17.5 percent of its GDP on health care. Singapore spent just 4.9 percent.

How does Singapore deliver world-class health care while spending less than any other developed nation? The answer is a unique combination of government mandates to encourage competition, high out-of-pocket costs for consumers, and laws requiring people to save for future health expenditures.

Competition is encouraged by forcing hospitals to post prices for each of their services. Armed with this information, patients can shop around for the best deal. The government also publishes the track record of each hospital on each service so that consumers can make informed decisions about quality as well as price. With consumers choosing on the basis of cost and quality, local hospitals compete to reduce costs and improve quality.

Singapore also insists upon high out-of-pocket costs to avoid the overconsumption and high prices that result when insurance policies pick up most of the price for medical procedures. Indeed, out-of-pocket spending represents about 92 percent of all nongovernment health care spending in Singapore, compared to just 11 percent in the United States.

Having to pay for most medical spending out of pocket, however, means that Singapore's citizens are faced with having to pay for most of their health care themselves. How can this be done without bankrupting the average citizen? The answer is mandatory health savings accounts.

Singapore's citizens are required to save about 6 percent of their incomes into "MediSave" accounts. MediSave deposits are private property, so people have an incentive to spend the money in their accounts wisely. In addition, the citizens of Singapore also know that they won't be left helpless if the money in their MediSave accounts runs out. The government subsidizes the health care of those who have

Source: © Comstock Images/PictureQuest RF

exhausted their MediSave accounts as well as the health care of the poor and others who have not been able to accumulate much money in their MediSave accounts.

Could elements of Singapore's system help to hold down medical costs in the United States? Two cases suggest that the answer is yes.

First, consider the health care plan offered by Whole Foods Markets to its employees. The company deposits $1,800 per year into a "personal wellness account" for each of its full-time employees. It simultaneously pays for a high-deductible health insurance plan that will pick up 100 percent of all medical expenses exceeding $2,500 in a given year. This combination implies that employees are *at most* on the hook for $700 a year—that is, for the difference between the $1,800 in their personal wellness accounts and the $2,500 deductible on their health insurance policy (above which, all medical expenses are covered).

Because both the money in the personal wellness account as well as the $700 that employees might have to spend before reaching the $2,500 deductible are personal property, Whole Foods Markets has effectively created a system in which all medical spending up to $2,500 is an out-of-pocket expense. This forces employees to examine the opportunity cost of any potential medical expenditure. The result is less spending.

A similar plan offered to employees of the State of Indiana puts $2,750 per year into a health savings account and then provides an insurance policy that covers 80 percent of any medical expenses between $2,750 and $8,000 and 100 percent of any expenses above $8,000. The Indiana plan's design means that any state employee volunteering for the plan must pay 100 percent of all spending up to $2,750 from their health savings accounts. As with Singapore's system and Whole Foods' system, this encourages prudence. The result has been a 35 percent decline in total health care spending for those who volunteered for the plan versus state employees who opted to stick with the state's traditional PPO option. In addition, an independent audit showed that participants in the new plan were not cutting corners by skimping on preventive care like annual mammogram screenings for cancer. Thus, the savings appear to be permanent and sustainable.

The program is also popular, with positive personal recommendations causing voluntary participation to rise from 2 percent of state employees in the program's first year to 70 percent of state employees in the program's second year.

- A 3.8 percentage point increase in the capital gains tax for individuals earning more than $200,000 per year and for married couples earning more than $250,000 per year.

- A 40 percent tax payable by employers on any employer-provided insurance policy whose premium exceeds $10,200 per year for individual coverage or $27,500 per year for family coverage.

- A 2.9 percent excise tax applied to everything sold by medical device manufacturers.

- A 10 percent tax levied on indoor tanning.

Objections and Alternatives

The PPACA was strongly opposed and passed Congress without a single approving vote in either chamber of Congress from members of the minority (Republican) party. The legislation also failed to achieve majority support in public opinion polls conducted on the eve of the legislation's passage.

Some of those voicing objections worried that federal control over the pricing and content of insurance policies would lead to greater inefficiencies in health care by adding additional layers of bureaucracy. Others objected because they felt that the PPACA might be the first step toward the creation of a national health insurance system in which non-price rationing might become necessary to hold down expenditures. Yet others pointed to financial projections indicating that the revenue sources legislated by the PPACA would not be nearly sufficient to cover future health care expenses, especially over the longer run.

An additional concern was whether the PPACA would reduce the growth rate of health care expenditures and thereby fulfill the president's promise that the law would "bend the cost curve down." Many economists worried that the large subsidies provided by the law would raise prices and increase consumption (as in Figure 24.3 and the nearby discussion). With even middle-class individuals and families eligible for significant government subsidies, inefficient health care spending might increase significantly.

As an alternative, some opponents of the PPACA pointed to the health care system in Singapore and recent experiments with the health insurance offered to employees of the State of Indiana. Both systems reduce wasteful expenditures by increasing the percentage of health care spending that comes directly out of consumers' pockets, thereby forcing them to consider opportunity costs and weigh marginal benefits against marginal costs. (See this chapter's Last Word for more.)

In evaluating the pros and cons of the PPACA, one thing seems clear. It will not be the last word on health care reform in America. Indeed, the economic challenges related to health care will only get stronger. The combination of an aging population and advances in medical technology seem to be on a collision course with the reality of economic scarcity such that individuals and society will face increasingly difficult choices about how much health care to consume and how to pay for it.

QUICK REVIEW 24.4

✓ The Patient Protection and Affordable Care Act (PPACA) is an attempt to extend either private or public insurance coverage to all U.S. citizens and legal residents.

✓ The PPACA includes (1) a *personal mandate* that requires all citizens and legal residents to purchase insurance coverage for themselves and their dependents if they are not already provided with insurance by their employer or by the government as well as (2) an *employer mandate* that requires all firms with more than 50 full-time employees to either offer health insurance coverage to their full-time employees or pay large fines.

✓ The PPACA also bans insurance companies from denying coverage on the basis of preexisting conditions; includes various subsidies so that the personal mandate will not bankrupt the poor and middle class; provides for the creation of state insurance exchanges, where individuals can comparison shop for government-approved health insurance policies; and imposes various taxes to help pay for the increased expenditures that will be required to extend insurance coverage to the previously uninsured.

SUMMARY

LO24.1 Convey important facts about rising health care costs in the United States.

The U.S. health care industry comprises 19 million workers (including about 708,300 practicing physicians) and 5,600 hospitals.

Unlike nations with publicly funded systems of national health insurance, the United States delivers a large fraction of its health care through private, employer-provided health insurance.

U.S. health care spending has increased both absolutely and as a percentage of GDP.

LO24.2 Relate the economic implications of rising health care costs.

Rising health care costs and prices have (*a*) reduced access to the health care system, (*b*) contributed to slower real wage growth and expanded the employment of part-time and temporary workers, and (*c*) caused governments to restrict spending on nonhealth programs and to raise taxes.

The core of the health care problem is an alleged overallocation of resources to the health care industry.

LO24.3 Discuss the problem of limited access to health care for those without insurance.

About 30 million Americans, or 9 percent of the population, did not have health insurance in 2015. The uninsured were concentrated among the poor, the chronically ill, the unemployed, the young, those employed by small firms, and low-wage workers.

LO24.4 List the demand and supply factors explaining rising health care costs.

Special characteristics of the health care market include (*a*) the belief that health care is a "right," (*b*) an imbalance of information between consumers and suppliers, (*c*) the presence of positive externalities, and (*d*) the payment of most health care expenses by private or public insurance.

While rising incomes, an aging population, and substance abuse have all contributed to an increasing demand for health care, the role of doctors is also significant. Because of asymmetric information, physicians influence the demand for their own services. The fee-for-service payment system, combined with defensive medicine to protect against malpractice suits, also increases the demand for health care.

The moral hazard problem arising from health insurance takes two forms: (*a*) people may be less careful of their health and (*b*) there is an incentive to overconsume health care.

The exemption of employer-paid health insurance from the federal income tax subsidizes health care. The subsidy increases demand, leading to higher prices and a likely overallocation of resources to health care.

Countries with systems of national health insurance also increase demand by subsidizing health care. Facing limited budgets, those countries engage in nonprice rationing to restrict health care expenditures. Rationing mechanisms include waiting lists, committees that set standards for denial of service, and restrictions on capital spending.

Because private insurance does not involve government expenditures, the state regulators charged with regulating private insurance companies in the United States focus more on expanding politically popular benefits than on restricting costs.

Slow productivity growth in the health care industry and, more important, cost-increasing advances in health care technology have restricted the expansion of the supply of medical care and have boosted prices.

LO24.5 Describe the cost-containment strategies that rely on altering the financial incentives facing either patients or health service providers.

Strategies that have attempted to contain health care prices and spending include (*a*) insurance deductibles and copayments to confront consumers with opportunity costs, (*b*) managed-care organizations—preferred provider organizations (PPOs) and health maintenance organizations (HMOs)—that attempt to restrict their members' use of health services, (*c*) the diagnosis-related-group (DRG) system that caps the amount Medicare will spend on any procedure, and (*d*) health savings accounts (HSAs) that also confront individuals with opportunity costs when they spend out of their tax-free HSA accounts.

LO24.6 Summarize the goals of the Patient Protection and Affordable Care Act and the major changes that it institutes.

The Patient Protection and Affordable Care Act (PPACA) of 2010 is an attempt to extend either private or public (Medicare and Medicaid) insurance coverage to all U.S. citizens and legal residents.

Enrolling millions of previously uninsured people (including the chronically ill) into health insurance will be costly, so the PPACA includes a personal mandate that requires all citizens and legal residents to purchase insurance coverage for themselves and their dependents if they are not already provided with insurance by their employer or by the government. The goal is to compel healthy people to purchase insurance so that their premiums can help to pay for the health care costs of the previously uninsured (many of whom are likely to be chronically ill.)

The PPACA also (*a*) bans insurance companies from denying coverage on the basis of preexisting conditions, (*b*) includes various subsidies so that the personal mandate will not bankrupt the poor and middle class, (*c*) provides for the creation of state insurance exchanges where individuals can comparison shop for government-approved health insurance policies, and (*d*) imposes various taxes to help pay for the increased expenditures that will be required to extend insurance coverage to the previously uninsured.

TERMS AND CONCEPTS

Patient Protection and Affordable
   Care Act (PPACA)

national health insurance

deductibles

copayments

fee for service

defensive medicine

tax subsidy

health savings accounts (HSAs)

preferred provider organizations (PPOs)

health maintenance organizations (HMOs)

diagnosis-related group
   (DRG) system

employer mandate

personal mandate

insurance exchanges

The following and additional problems can be found in ▦connect

DISCUSSION QUESTIONS

1. Why would increased spending as a percentage of GDP on, say, household appliances or education in a particular economy be regarded as economically desirable? Why, then, is there so much concern about rising expenditures as a percentage of GDP on health care? **LO24.1**

2. What are the "twin problems" of the health care industry as viewed by society? How are they related? **LO24.1**

3. Briefly describe the main features of Medicare and Medicaid, indicating how each is financed **LO24.1**

4. What are the implications of rapidly rising health care prices and spending for (a) the growth of real wage rates, (b) government budgets, and (c) offshoring of U.S. jobs? Explain **LO24.2**

5. What are the main groups without health insurance? **LO24.3**

6. List the special characteristics of the U.S. health care market and specify how each affects health care problems **LO24.3**

7. What are the estimated income and price elasticities of demand for health care? How does each relate to rising health care costs? **LO24.4**

8. Briefly discuss the demand and supply factors that contribute to rising health costs. Specify how (a) asymmetric information, (b) fee-for-service payments, (c) defensive medicine, and (d) medical ethics might cause health care costs to rise **LO24.4**

9. How do advances in medical technology and health insurance interact to drive up the cost of medical care? **LO24.4**

10. Using the concepts in Chapter 7's discussion of consumer behavior, explain how health care insurance results in an overallocation of resources to the health care industry. Use a demand and supply diagram to specify the resulting efficiency loss **LO24.4**

11. How is the moral hazard problem relevant to the health care market? **LO24.4**

12. What is the rationale for exempting a firm's contribution to its workers' health insurance from taxation as worker income? What is the impact of this exemption on allocative efficiency in the health care industry? **LO24.5**

13. What are (a) preferred provider organizations and (b) health maintenance organizations? In your answer, explain how each is designed to alleviate the overconsumption of health care **LO24.5**

14. What are health savings accounts (HSAs)? How might they reduce the overconsumption of health care resulting from traditional insurance? How might they introduce an element of price competition into the health care system? **LO24.5**

15. Why is the PPACA's attempt to extend insurance coverage to all Americans so costly? How does the PPACA attempt to obtain the funds needed to extend insurance coverage to all Americans? **LO24.6**

16. How does the PPACA attempt to ensure affordable health insurance for the poor? **LO24.6**

17. What were the objections made by opponents of the PPACA? **LO24.6**

18. **LAST WORD** What are the three major cost-reducing features of the Singapore health care system? Which one do you think has the largest effect on holding down the price of medical care in Singapore? What element of the Singapore system is shared by the Whole Foods and State of Indiana systems? What elements are missing? How difficult do you think it would be to implement those missing elements in the United States? Explain.

REVIEW QUESTIONS

1. Which of the following best describes the United States' level of health care spending as compared to that of other nations? **LO24.1**
   a. The lowest of all nations.
   b. A bit lower than average.
   c. Average.
   d. A bit higher than average.
   e. The highest of all nations.

2. Which of the following make a person *less* likely to have health insurance? (Select one or more answers from the choices shown.) **LO24.3**
   a. Working for a larger firm.
   b. Being a low-wage worker.
   c. Being employed.
   d. Having excellent health.
   e. Being chronically ill.

3. A patient named Jen visits Dr. Jan. Dr. Jan is nearly certain that Jen only has a cold. But because Dr. Jan is afraid of malpractice lawsuits, she orders an extensive battery of tests just to make sure that Jen can never claim—if she turns out to have something more severe—that Dr. Jan shirked her duties as a medical professional. Dr. Jan's behavior is an example of: **LO24.4**
   a. Asymmetric information.
   b. Fee-for-service.
   c. Defensive medicine.
   d. Positive externalities.

4. All MegaCorp employees who stay on the job for more than three years are rewarded with a 10 percent pay increase and coverage under a private health insurance plan that MegaCorp pays for. Tina just passed three years as a MegaCorp employee and reacts to having health insurance by taking up several dangerous sports because now she knows that the insurance plan will pay for any injuries that she may sustain. This change in Tina's behavior is known as: **LO24.4**
   a. Defensive medicine.
   b. Asymmetric information.
   c. The moral hazard problem.
   d. The personal mandate.

5. By increasing demand, health insurance creates: **LO24.4**
   a. A deadweight loss related to overconsumption.
   b. A deadweight loss related to underconsumption.
   c. Neither of the above.
6. Ralph will consume any health care service just as long as its MB exceeds the money he must pay out of pocket. His insurance policy has a zero deductible and a 10 percent copay, so Ralph only has to pay 10 percent of the price charged for any medical procedure. Which of the following procedures will Ralph choose to consume? **LO24.5**

a. An $800 eye exam that has an MB of $100 to Ralph.
b. A $90 hearing test that has an MB of $5 to Ralph.
c. A $35,000 knee surgery that has an MB of $3,000 to Ralph.
d. A $10,000 baldness treatment that has an MB of $16,000 to Ralph.

7. True or False. Under the PPACA, Americans are free to decide for themselves whether or not they should have health insurance coverage. **LO24.6**

PROBLEMS

1. Suppose that the price elasticity for hip replacement surgeries is 0.2. Further suppose that hip replacement surgeries are originally not covered by health insurance and that at a price of $50,000 each, 10,000 such surgeries are demanded each year. **LO24.2**
   a. Suppose that health insurance begins to cover hip replacement surgeries and that everyone interested in getting a hip replacement has health insurance. If insurance covers 50 percent of the cost of the surgery, by what percentage would you expect the quantity demanded of hip replacements to increase? What if insurance covered 90 percent of the price? (Hint: Do not bother to calculate the percentage changes using the midpoint formula given in Chapter 6. If insurance covers 50 percent of the bill, just assume that the price paid by consumers falls 50 percent.)
   b. Suppose that with insurance companies covering 90 percent of the price, the increase in demand leads to a jump in the price per hip surgery from $50,000 to $100,000. How much will each insured patient now pay for a hip replacement surgery? Compared to the original situation, where hip replacements cost $50,000 each but people had no insurance to help subsidize the cost, will the quantity demanded increase or decrease? By how much?

2. The federal tax code allows businesses but not individuals to deduct the cost of health insurance premiums from their taxable income. Consider a company named HeadBook that could either spend $5,000 on an insurance policy for an employee named Vanessa or increase her annual salary by $5,000 instead. **LO24.4**
   a. As far as the tax code is concerned, HeadBook will increase its expenses by $5,000 in either case. If it pays for the policy, it incurs a $5,000 health care expense. If it raises Vanessa's salary by $5,000, it incurs $5,000 of salary expense. If HeadBook is profitable and pays corporate profit taxes at a marginal 35 percent rate, by how much will HeadBook's tax liability be reduced in either case?

   b. Suppose that Vanessa pays personal income tax at a marginal 20 percent rate. If HeadBook increases her salary by $5,000, how much of that increase will she have after paying taxes on that raise? If Vanessa can only devote what remains after paying taxes on the $5,000 to purchasing health insurance, how much will she be able to spend on health insurance for herself?
   c. If HeadBook spends the $5,000 on a health insurance policy for Vanessa instead of giving it to her as a raise, how many more dollars will HeadBook be able to spend on Vanessa's health insurance than if she had to purchase it herself after being given a $5,000 raise and paying taxes on that raise?
   d. Would Vanessa prefer to have the raise or to have HeadBook purchase insurance for her? Would HeadBook have any profit motive for denying Vanessa her preference?
   e. Suppose the government changes the tax law so that individuals can now deduct the cost of health insurance from their personal incomes. If Vanessa gets the $5,000 raise and then spends all of it on health insurance, how much will her tax liability change? How much will she be able to spend on health insurance? Will she now have a preference for HeadBook to buy insurance on her behalf?

3. Preventive care is not always cost-effective. Suppose that it costs $100 per person to administer a screening exam for a particular disease. Also suppose that if the screening exam finds the disease, the early detection given by the exam will avert $1,000 of costly future treatment. **LO24.4**
   a. Imagine giving the screening test to 100 people. How much will it cost to give those 100 tests? Imagine a case in which 15 percent of those receiving the screening exam test positive. How much in future costly treatments will be averted? How much is saved by setting up a screening system?
   b. Imagine that everything is the same as in part *a* except that now only 5 percent of those receiving the screening exam test positive. In this case, how much in future costly treatments will be averted? How much is lost by setting up a screening system?

25 Chapter

Immigration

Learning Objectives

LO25.1 Describe the extent of legal and illegal immigration into the United States.

LO25.2 Discuss why economists view economic immigration as a personal human capital investment.

LO25.3 Explain how immigration affects average wages, resource allocation, domestic output, and group income shares.

LO25.4 Relate how illegal immigration affects employment and wages in low-wage labor markets and impacts state and local budgets.

LO25.5 Demonstrate how economics can inform current immigration discussions and attempts to reform immigration laws.

The population of the United States is composed largely of immigrants and their descendants, yet immigration has long been a matter of heated controversy. Some immigration issues are political, social, and legal; others are economic. Our focus will be on economic issues and **economic immigrants**—international migrants motivated by economic gain. How many such immigrants come to the United States each year? What is their motivation and what economic impact do they make? Should more or fewer people be allowed to enter legally? What criteria, if any, should be used in allowing legal entry? How should the United States handle illegal immigration?[1]

Number of Immigrants

LO25.1 Describe the extent of legal and illegal immigration into the United States.

U.S. immigration consists of **legal immigrants**—immigrants who have permission to reside and work in the United States—and **illegal immigrants**—immigrants who arrive illegally or who enter legally on temporary visas but then fail to leave as stipulated. Legal immigrants include *permanent legal residents* ("green card" recipients) who have the right to stay in the country indefinitely and *temporary legal immigrants,* who have visas that allow them to stay until a specific date. Illegal immigrants are alternatively called unauthorized immigrants, illegal aliens, or, if working, undocumented workers.

---

[1] Some of our discussion is drawn from our more advanced treatment of mobility and migration in our textbook on labor economics: Campbell R. McConnell, Stanley L. Brue, and David A. Macpherson, *Contemporary Labor Economics,* 10th ed. (New York: McGraw-Hill, 2013), pp. 263–290.

FIGURE 25.1 **Legal immigration to the United States, 1980–2013.** Legal immigration grew slowly between 1980 and 1988 and then spiked from 1989 to 1991 when previous illegal immigrants gained legal status as permanent residents under the terms of an amnesty program. Since that spike, legal immigration has remained relatively high, partly because the annual legal immigration quota was raised from 500,000 to 700,000. Within the totals are thousands of refugees, grantees of political asylum, and entrants under special provisions of the immigration law.

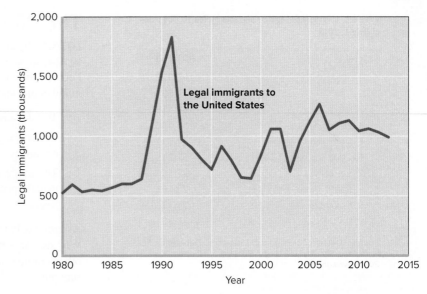

Source: Office of Immigration Statistics, Department of Homeland Security, **www.dhs.gov.**

Legal Immigrants

Figure 25.1 shows the annual levels of legal immigration into the United States since 1980. The spike in legal immigration from 1989 to 1991 resulted from an amnesty program through which many formerly illegal immigrants became legal residents. Between 2004 and 2013, legal immigration averaged 1 million persons per year. This number is higher than for earlier decades because beginning in 1990 the federal government increased the annual immigration quota from 500,000 to 700,000.

Augmenting quota immigrants in some years are thousands of legal immigrants who are refugees (people who flee their country for safety) or are entrants to the United States under special provisions of the immigration law. As an example of the latter, the current **H1-B provision** of the immigration law allows 65,000 high-skilled workers in "specialty occupations" to enter and work continuously in the United States for six years. Such high-skilled occupations include high-tech workers, scientists, and professors.

A total of 990,553 people became permanent legal residents of the United States in 2013. About 55 percent of them were women and 45 percent were men. Around 58 percent of all legal immigrants were married.

As shown in Figure 25.2, about 66 percent of the 990,553 legal immigrants in 2013 were family-sponsored. They were parents, children, siblings, or other qualified relatives of legal permanent U.S. residents. Another 16 percent were admitted based on employment-based preferences. Most of these immigrants were sponsored by employers. Refugees, "diversity immigrants," and others accounted for the remaining 18 percent. The 50,000 quota for diversity immigrants is filled with qualified immigrants who are from countries with low rates

of immigration to the United States. Because applications by diversity immigrants exceed the 50,000 quota, the slots are filled through an annual lottery.

Although the percentage varies somewhat each year, current U.S. immigration law is heavily weighted toward family reunification. This weighting is much heavier than that in Canada, which gives considerably stronger preference to immigrants with high levels of education and work skill. Of course, immigration by family ties and immigration by employment preferences are not necessarily mutually exclusive since a portion of the immigrants admitted through family ties are highly educated and skilled.

FIGURE 25.2 **Legal immigration by major category of admission, 2013.** The large bulk of legal U.S. immigrants obtain their legal status via family ties to American residents.

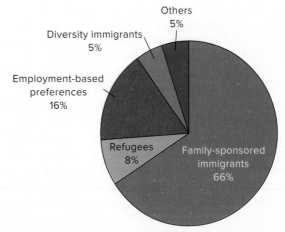

Source: Office of Immigration Statistics, Department of Homeland Security, **www.dhs.gov.**

TABLE 25.1 U.S. Legal Immigrants by Top 10 Countries of Origin, 2013

Total	990,553
1. Mexico	135,028
2. China	71,798
3. India	68,458
4. Philippines	54,446
5. Dominican Republic	41,311
6. Cuba	32,219
7. Vietnam	27,101
8. South Korea	23,166
9. Colombia	21,131
10. Haiti	20,351

Source: Office of Immigration Statistics, Department of Homeland Security, *U.S. Legal Permanent Resident Report, 2013,* **www.dhs.gov.**

Table 25.1 shows the 10 leading countries of origin of U.S. legal permanent immigrants in 2013. Mexico topped the list with 135,028 immigrants, accounting for 14 percent of the total. China, the Philippines, and India were also heavy contributors to U.S. immigration in 2013. In recent years immigration has composed about one-third of the total growth of the U.S. population and one-half the growth of the U.S. labor force.

Illegal Immigrants

Our figures and tables do not include illegal immigrants. The U.S. Census Bureau estimates the number of illegal immigrants living in the United States through a residual approach. It finds the current total number of *all* immigrants through census surveys and then subtracts the sum of the past annual inflows of *legal* immigrants. The residuals are large. In fact, the net annual inflow of illegal immigrants averaged about 250,000 per year from 2000 to 2009, with over 60 percent arriving from Mexico and Central America. As this chapter's Last Word describes, however, the net annual inflow reversed during the 2007–2008 recession and then remained near zero through 2014.

While some illegal immigrants do move back and forth across the U.S.–Mexican border, in 2014 about 11.3 million illegal immigrants were residing continuously in the United States. Increasingly, illegal immigrants are continuous residents, not temporary workers who follow the agricultural harvest (as was typical several decades ago). An estimated 49 percent of the 11.3 million illegal immigrants originally came from Mexico, with many others arriving from nations spanning the globe. Illegal Mexican immigrants who work continuously in the United States work mainly outside of agriculture and, on average, have higher educational levels than Mexicans who do not migrate to the United States.

The Decision to Migrate

LO25.2 Discuss why economists view economic immigration as a personal human capital investment.

People immigrate into the United States (emigrate from their home countries) legally or illegally:

- To take advantage of superior economic opportunities.
- To escape political or religious oppression in their home countries.
- To reunite with family members or other loved ones, usually prior immigrants, who are already in the United States.

As previously stated, our interest is in economic immigration. Why do some workers uproot their lives to move from some other country to the United States? Why do other workers stay put?

Earnings Opportunities

The main driver of economic immigration is the opportunity to improve the immigrant's earnings and therefore standard of living. The chief attractor for economic immigrants is the availability of higher pay in the United States. In particular, immigrants can earn much higher wages in the United States than doing identical or nearly identical jobs in their home countries. Stated in terms of economic theory, immigrants reap larger financial rewards from their respective stocks of human capital when working in the United States rather than in their home countries.

Recall that **human capital** is the stock of knowledge, know-how, and skills that enables a person to be productive, and thus to earn income. Other things equal, greater stocks of human capital (for example, more education or better training) result in greater personal productivity and earnings. But whatever someone's stock of education and skill, the value of that human capital depends critically on the capacity for it to earn income. That is where economic migration comes in. By securing higher earnings, migrants can increase—often quickly and dramatically—the value of their human capital. Economic migrants move from one country to another for the same reason many internal migrants move from one city or state to another within their home country: to increase their pay and therefore achieve a higher standard of living.

Other things equal, larger wage differences between nations strengthen the incentive to migrate and therefore increase the flow of immigrants toward the country providing the greater wage opportunities. Today, major "magnet countries" that attract a lot of immigrants include Australia, Switzerland, the United States, and several Western European nations. Global Perspective 25.1 shows the percentage of labor forces composed of foreign-born workers in selected nations in 2013, the latest year for which data are available. Along with earnings opportunities, significant differences in educational opportunities, health care availability, and public pensions and welfare benefits play a role in international migration decisions.

Moving Costs

Immigration can be viewed as an investment decision. As with other investments, current sacrifices are necessary to achieve future benefits. In moving from one nation to another, workers incur personal costs. Some of these costs are explicit, out-of-pocket costs such as paying application fees (for example, $1,010 for a green card) and a number of moving expenses. For illegal immigrants, a major explicit cost may be a payment to an expediter—a "coyote"—who charges as much as $2,000 to smuggle someone into the United States and transport him or her to a major city such as Chicago, New York, Houston, or Los Angeles. Other costs of migrating are implicit. They are opportunity costs such as the income given up while the worker is moving and looking for a job in the new country. Still more subtle costs are incurred in leaving family and friends and adapting to a new culture, language, and climate. For illegal immigrants, there is the additional potential cost of being caught, jailed, and deported.

The prospective immigrant estimates and weighs all such costs against the expected benefits of the higher earnings in the new country. A person who estimates that the stream of future earnings exceeds the explicit and implicit costs of moving will migrate; a person who sees those costs as exceeding the future stream of earnings will stay put.[2]

Factors Affecting Costs and Benefits

Earnings differences provide the major incentive to migrate, but many nonwage factors also affect the cost-benefit evaluation of moving to another nation. Let's look at two key factors.

Distance Other things equal, greater distance reduces the likelihood of migration. Most obvious, transportation costs rise with distance. In addition, migration to more distant countries is often seen as riskier because information about job market conditions in distant countries is usually less certain than about job market conditions in nearby countries (although the Internet has greatly reduced this difference in recent years). Finally, the farther the move, the greater the possible costs of maintaining contact with friends and family. In terms of expense, a short trip back across a border by automobile is one thing; an airline flight to a different continent, quite another.

The majority of international migrants move to countries relatively close to their home countries. Most Mexican

GLOBAL PERSPECTIVE 25.1

Immigrants as a Percent of the Labor Force, Selected Advanced Industrial Countries

Immigrants make up relatively large percentages of the labor forces in several advanced industrial countries, including Australia, Austria, and the United States, but not in other countries such as Finland.

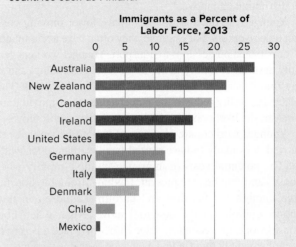

Immigrants as a Percent of Labor Force, 2013

Source: Organization for Economic Cooperation and Development, **www.oecd.org.**

migrants move to the United States. The majority of Eastern European migrants move to Western Europe. Close proximity reduces the cost of the move relative to anticipated benefits.

Some migrants, of course, *do* move to far-away lands. They often reduce their costs of these long moves by following **beaten paths**—routes taken previously by family, relatives, and friends. They also tend to cluster, at least for awhile, in cities and neighborhoods populated by former and current immigrants. For example, thousands of Russian immigrants have located in Brooklyn, New York. Numerous Asian immigrants have located in San Francisco.

The earlier immigrants ease the transition for those who follow by providing job information, employment contacts, temporary living quarters, language help, and cultural continuity. That reduces the costs and increases the benefits of migration to those who follow. Eventually, some new immigrants exploit even better economic opportunities by moving from the original place of migration to other cities within the country to which they have migrated. New clusters of immigrants emerge and new migration networks result. For instance, these new clusters and networks help explain the rapid northward expansion of Latino immigrants during the past decade.

Age Younger workers are much more likely to migrate than older workers. Age affects both benefits and costs in the calculation to move or stay put. Particularly relevant, younger

---

[2]As with other investment decisions, the decision to move internationally requires a comparison of the present value of the stream of additional earnings and the present value of the costs of moving. Present value considerations (discussed in Chapters 18 and 19) complicate the decision to migrate but do not alter the basic analytical framework.

migrants have more years to recoup their costs of moving. Spread over decades, the higher wage in the new country builds to a large accumulation of additional earnings relative to the earnings that would have accrued if the person had not moved. In contrast, older people are closer to retirement and therefore may conclude that moving abroad simply is not worth the effort. Their added earnings over their remaining work years simply will not be sufficient to cover the costs of the disruption and move.

Younger migrants also tend to have lower moving costs than older workers. For example, they often have accumulated fewer personal possessions to transport. Younger workers generally have fewer roots and ties to the local community and so may find it easier to adapt to new customs and cultures. This greater flexibility reduces the perceived costs of moving and increases the likelihood that the younger person will move.

Younger workers are also more likely to be single or, if married, less likely to have started families than older workers. The potential costs of migrating multiply rapidly when spouses and families are present. Finding affordable housing large enough for families and enrolling children in new schools complicate the potential move. Also, when both spouses work, the secondary wage earner may face a period of unemployment before finding a new job in the new country.

Other Factors Several other factors may affect the cost and benefit calculations of immigrants into the United States. Studies show that immigrants who lack English language skills do not, in general, fare as well in the U.S. workforce as immigrants who have those skills when they arrive. For some highly skilled immigrants, lower tax rates or opportunities to set up businesses in the United States may be the draw. Also, some immigrants to the United States may be willing to endure low or even negative personal returns on immigration simply so that their children have greater economic opportunities than at home.

QUICK REVIEW 25.1

✓ An average of 1 million legal immigrants entered the United States each year between 2004 and 2013.

✓ In 2013 Mexico was the greatest single contributor (14 percent) to U.S. legal immigration. Hundreds of thousands of additional legal immigrants arrived from China, the Philippines, India, and many other nations.

✓ Economists view economic migration as a personal investment; a worker will move internationally when the expected gain in earnings exceeds the explicit and implicit costs of moving.

✓ Other things equal, the greater the migration distance and the older the prospective migrant, the less likely the person will move.

Economic Effects of Immigration

LO25.3 Explain how immigration affects average wages, resource allocation, domestic output, and group income shares.
Immigration creates personal gains for movers, and also affects wage rates, efficiency, output, and the division of income. Like international trade, migration produces large economic benefits but also creates short-term winners and losers. In particular, we will see that the wage-rate and division-of-income aspects of immigration are two main sources of controversy.

Personal Gains

The fact that economic immigration to the United States is sizable and continuous affirms that in general the economic benefits of immigration to the immigrants exceed their costs. In economic terms, the inflows of legal and illegal immigration indicate that this investment has a positive return to movers. Studies confirm that the returns to immigrating to the United States are, on average, quite substantial. This should not be a surprise. For example, the real wages earned by recent Mexican male migrants to the United States are as much as six times higher than those earned by similarly educated men in Mexico.

Nevertheless, not all economic immigrants to the United States succeed. Migration decisions are based on expected benefits and are made under circumstances of uncertainty and imperfect information. High average rates of return do not guarantee that all migrants will benefit. In some cases the expected gain from immigration does not materialize—the anticipated job is not found in the new country, the living costs are higher than anticipated, the anticipated raises and promotions are not forthcoming, the costs of being away from family and friends are greater than expected. Major **backflows**—return migration to the home country—therefore occur in most international migration patterns, including those between the United States and other countries.

Although this return migration may be costly to those involved, it increases the availability of information about the United States to other potential migrants. These people are then able to better assess the benefits and costs of their own potential moves.

Also, although economic immigrants on average improve their standard of living, they may or may not achieve pay parity with similarly educated native-born workers. The skills that migrants possess are not always perfectly transferable between employers in different countries because of occupational licensing requirements, specific training, or differing languages. This lack of **skill transferability** may mean that migrants, although improving their own wage, may earn less than similarly employed native-born workers in the United States. Studies find that this is particularly true for immigrants who lack English-language skills.

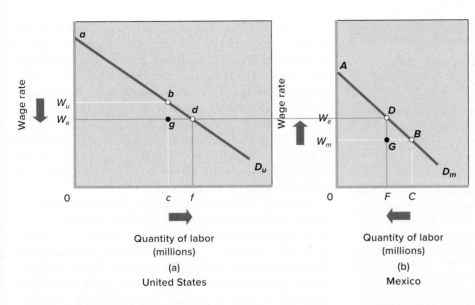

FIGURE 25.3 A simple immigration model. (a) The migration of low-wage Mexican labor by the amount *cf* to the United States increases U.S. domestic output by *cbdf*, reduces the U.S. wage rate from W_u to W_e, and increases U.S. business income by $W_e W_u bd$. (b) The out-migration of labor of *CF* from Mexico reduces Mexican domestic output by *FDBC*, raises the wage rate from W_m to W_e, and lowers Mexican business income by $W_m W_e DB$. Because the U.S. gain in domestic output of *cbdf* exceeds Mexico's loss of domestic output of *FDBC*, the migration depicted increases economic efficiency and produces a net gain of world output.

On the other hand, a great deal of economic migration is characterized by **self-selection.** Because migrants choose to move while others with similar skills do not, it is possible that those who move possess greater motivation for personal economic gain and greater willingness to sacrifice current consumption for higher levels of later consumption. If so, these migrants may overcome the problem of imperfect skill transferability and eventually outdo domestic-born workers in wage and salary advancement. This possibility is particularly true of highly skilled immigrants such as scientists, engineers, physicians, and entrepreneurs.

Many U.S. firms have been founded by immigrants or their children. Their impact has been large, with fully 40 percent of the businesses listed in the Fortune 500 ranking of the largest U.S. companies having been founded by immigrants or their offspring. These companies employed over 10 million people worldwide in 2010 and had combined annual revenues of $4.2 trillion dollars, a figure larger than the respective gross domestic products (GDPs) of all but three countries, the United States, China, and Japan. Famous American companies founded by immigrants or their children include Apple, AT&T, Budweiser, eBay, General Electric, Google, IBM, and McDonald's.

Impacts on Wage Rates, Efficiency, and Output

Although the personal outcomes of immigration are relatively straightforward and easy to understand, the broader economic outcomes are somewhat complicated and obscure. A simple economic model of migration will help us sort through key cause-effect relationships and identify broader economic outcomes. In Figure 25.3a, D_u is the demand for labor in the United States; in Figure 25.3b, D_m is the demand for labor in Mexico. The demand for labor presumably is greater in the

United States because it has more capital, advanced technology, and better infrastructure that enhance the productivity of labor. (Recall from Chapter 16 that the strength of labor demand is based on the marginal revenue productivity of labor.) Conversely, labor demand in Mexico is weaker since machinery and equipment are less abundant relative to labor, technology is less advanced, and infrastructure is less developed. We also assume that the before-migration labor forces of the United States and Mexico are *c* and *C*, respectively; that neither country is experiencing substantial long-term unemployment; and that labor quality in the two countries is the same.

If we further suppose that migration (1) has no cost, (2) occurs solely in response to wage differentials, and (3) is unimpeded by law in both countries, then workers will migrate from Mexico to the United States until wage rates in the two countries are equal at W_e. At that level, $C - F$ (equals $f - c$) workers will have migrated from Mexico to the United States. Although the U.S. wage level will fall from W_u to W_e, domestic output (the sum of the marginal revenue products of the entire workforce) will increase from 0*abc* to 0*adf*. This domestic output is the total output produced within the borders of the United States and equals U.S. domestic income.

In Mexico, the wage rate will rise from W_m to W_e, but domestic output will decline from 0*ABC* to 0*ADF*. Observe that the gain in domestic output *cbdf* in the United States exceeds the loss of domestic output *FDBC* in Mexico. The migration from Mexico to the United States has clearly increased the world's output and income.

The elimination of barriers to the international flow of labor tends to create worldwide **efficiency gains from migration.** The same number of workers—rearranged among countries—produces greater total output and income after migration than before migration. The world gains output (and income) because the freedom to migrate enables people to move to countries where they can contribute more to world

production. Economic migration not only provides a positive investment return to the mover, it produces an overall efficiency gain. Migration enables the world to produce a larger output with its currently available resources. So labor mobility joins capital mobility and international trade in enhancing the world's standard of living.

Income Shares

With personal gains and overall productivity gains, why would anyone oppose immigration? Our graphical model helps answer that question. There are specific groups of gainers and losers from immigration in both nations.

In Figure 25.3, as workers move from Mexico to the United States in search of higher wages, U.S. output will increase while Mexican output will decrease. These gains partly explain why the United States encourages a relatively high level of immigration through high annual quotas. It also explains why

some countries try to discourage outflows of labor from their countries. In particular, countries are rightfully concerned about the emigration of highly educated workers, particularly when those citizens received subsidized education at home. Such undesirable outflows are commonly called **brain drains.**

Figure 25.3 reveals a second consequence of immigration on income shares. The decline in the wage rate from W_u to W_e in the United States reduces the wage income of native-born U.S. workers from $0W_ubc$ to $0W_egc$. The opposite outcome occurs in Mexico, where the average wage for the native-born workers who do not migrate rises.

Although we can specify income gains and losses to domestic-born workers, we cannot say what will happen to the total wage income (= domestic-born wage income + immigrant wage income) in each country. That depends on the elasticities of labor demand. For example, if labor demand is elastic, the wage decrease in the United States will increase total wage income. In contrast, if labor demand is inelastic, the same wage decrease will cause total wage income to fall.

The immigration-caused decline in wage income for native-born U.S. workers is a major reason that many U.S. labor unions oppose increasing immigration quotas in the United States. Unions tend to resist policies that reduce the wages of their current membership or undercut their bargaining power by creating larger pools of potential workers for nonunion firms. In direct contrast, the increase in wages in the outflow country is a possible reason why labor groups in Mexico show little concern about the large-scale outflow of Mexican labor to the United States.

Finally, Figure 25.3 shows that the immigration enhances business income in the United States while reducing it in Mexico. The before-immigration domestic output and income in the United States is represented by area $0abc$. Total wage income is $0W_ubc$—the wage rate multiplied by the number of workers. The remaining triangular area W_uab shows business income before immigration. The same reasoning applies to Mexico, where the triangle W_mAB represents before-immigration business income.

Unimpeded immigration increases business income from W_uab to W_ead in the United States and reduces it from W_mAB to W_eAD in Mexico. Other things equal, owners of U.S. businesses benefit from immigration; owners of Mexican businesses are hurt by emigration. These outcomes are what we would expect intuitively; the United States is gaining "cheap" labor and Mexico is losing "cheap" labor. This conclusion is consistent with the historical fact that U.S. employers have often actively recruited immigrants and have generally supported higher immigration quotas, liberal guest-worker programs, and expanded specialized work visas such as H1-Bs.

Complications and Modifications

Our model is a purposeful simplification of the much more complex actual reality. Thus, it is not surprising that the model includes simplifying assumptions and overlooks some factors that may be important in certain situations. Relaxing some of the assumptions and introducing the omitted factors may affect our conclusions.

Costs of Migration Our model assumed that the movement of workers from Mexico to the United States is without personal cost, but we know that migrants incur explicit, out-of-pocket costs of physically moving and the implicit opportunity costs of forgone income during the move and transition.

In Figure 25.3, the presence of migration costs means that the flow of labor from Mexico to the United States will stop short of that required to close the wage differential entirely. Wage rates will remain somewhat higher in the United States than in Mexico, and that wage-rate difference will not encourage further migration to close up the wage gap. At some point, the remaining earnings gap between the two countries will not be sufficient to cover the marginal cost of migration. Migration will end, and the total output and income gain from migration will be less because wages have not equalized.

Remittances and Backflows Although most of the workers who acquire skills in the country of immigration do not return home, some migrants see their moves as temporary. They move to a more highly developed country; accumulate some wealth, training, or education through hard work and frugality; and return home to establish their own enterprises. During their time in the new country, these and other migrants frequently make sizable **remittances** to their families at home. These money transfers to the home country redistribute the net gain from migration between the countries involved.

In Figure 25.3, remittances by Mexican workers in the United States to their relatives in Mexico would cause the gain in U.S. income retained in the United States to be less than the domestic output and income gain shown. Similarly, the loss of income available in Mexico would be less than the domestic output and income loss shown. The World Bank estimates that $25 billion of remittances—an amount equal to 2 percent of Mexico's GDP—flowed to Mexico from other countries in 2015. Most of these remittances originate in the United States and are a major reason Mexico favors liberal U.S. immigration laws and generally opposes U.S. policies to stem the flow of illegal immigrants across the U.S. border. (Global Perspective 25.2 shows selected developing countries receiving remittances by emigrants in 2015. For many developing countries, remittances exceed foreign direct investment—purchases by foreigners of lasting ownership interests in domestic firms—as a source of foreign currencies available to buy imported goods and services.)

Along with remittances, backflows of migrants to their home countries might also alter gains and losses through time. For example, if some Mexican workers who migrated to

GLOBAL PERSPECTIVE 25.2

Emigrant Remittances, Selected Developing Countries, 2015

Although both developing nations and advanced industrial nations receive remittances from their emigrants, most remittances flow toward developing nations. For some of these nations, the amount of remittances each year exceeds their direct foreign investment (economic investment by foreign individuals and firms).

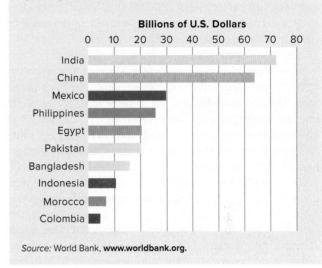

Source: World Bank, **www.worldbank.org.**

the United States acquired substantial labor market or managerial skills and then returned home, their enhanced human capital might contribute substantially to economic development in Mexico. Further, some of the more successful U.S. immigrants eventually may use their expertise and wealth to help build new businesses in Mexico. Both will eventually increase labor demand in Mexico and raise wage rates there.

Complementary versus Substitute Resources Although the average wage rate of domestic-born workers may decline because of immigration, not all such workers will see their wages fall. Many immigrant workers and domestic-born workers are **complementary resources** rather than **substitute resources** (Chapter 16). When that is the case, the lower wage rate resulting from large-scale immigration reduces production costs, creating an output effect that raises labor demand for certain domestic-born workers. For example, the large number of immigrants working in the home building industry lowers construction wages and reduces the cost of home building. That in turn increases the number of houses built and sold, which increases the demand for domestic-born residents who help manufacture sheet rock, plumbing products, air conditioners, major appliances, and other home products.

Expansion of Capital Long-run effects on capital are another reason native-born citizens may not be permanently harmed to the extent suggested by the simple immigration model. The stock of capital was implicitly constant in both countries in Figure 25.3, fixing the demand curves in place. But the rise in business income in the United States relative to the stock of capital produces a higher rate of return on capital. The higher rate of return stimulates overall investment, which in the long run adds to the size of the nation's stock of capital. Normally, the addition of new capital such as plant and equipment raises labor productivity, lowers production costs, and reduces product prices. As a result, wages and salaries rise because of increased demand for labor.

On the other hand, the inflow of illegal workers into certain low-wage occupations such as field harvesting may stifle R&D, technological advance, and investment in some industries. The easy availability of inexpensive legal or illegal immigrant labor provides little incentive to mechanize or otherwise economize on the use of labor. In this regard, economists note that the temporary slowing of the flow of illegal agricultural workers after the terrorist attacks of September 11, 2001, increased the purchase of mechanical harvesting equipment such as tree-trunk shakers used to harvest oranges.

Full Employment versus Unemployment Our model conveniently assumes full employment in both countries. Mexican workers presumably leave low-paying jobs to take higher-paying jobs in the United States (more or less immediately). However, in many circumstances, the factor that pushes immigrants from their homelands is not simply low wages but chronic unemployment or underemployment. Many developing countries have large populations and surplus labor. A sizable number of workers are either unemployed or so grossly underemployed that their contribution to domestic output is zero or near zero.

If we allow for this possibility, then Mexico would gain rather than lose by having such workers emigrate. Unemployed Mexicans are making no or little contribution to Mexico's domestic output and must be sustained by transfers from the rest of the labor force. The remaining Mexican labor force will be better off by the amount of the transfers after the unemployed workers have migrated to the United States.

The unemployed workers moving to the United States may reflect **negative self-selection,** in which movers are less capable and perhaps less motivated than similarly educated people who did not immigrate. This possibility could conceivably join higher domestic wages and large remittances as an explanation of why Mexico generally opposes stronger border enforcement by the United States.

Conversely, if the Mexican immigrant workers are unable to find jobs in the United States and are sustained through transfers from employed U.S. workers, then the after-tax income of working Americans will decline. This fear is one reason many Americans oppose immigration of low-education, low-skilled workers to the United States.

Fiscal Impacts

What effects do immigrants have on tax revenues and government spending in the United States? Do they contribute to U.S. GDP, as our model suggests, or do they go on welfare and use "free" public goods, draining the government treasury?

Before the 1970s, the immigrant population was less likely to receive public assistance than people born in the United States. Migrants were typically young, single men with significant education and job training. They were readily employable in average-paying jobs and therefore were net contributors to the tax-expenditure system.

But the situation reversed between the 1970s and 1998, when immigrants began to use the welfare system proportionately more than natives. The changing mix of immigrants from relatively skilled workers toward unskilled workers explained the turnabout. Critics claimed that U.S. welfare programs were drawing unskilled (and often illegal) workers to the United States from some of the world's poorest nations. Immigrants made up more than 10 percent of Supplemental Security Income (SSI) rolls in 1998 compared to only 3.3 percent a decade before.

As a result of this trend, the major overhaul of the U.S. welfare system that was passed into law in 1996 denied welfare benefits to new legal immigrants for their first five years in the United States. As a result, between 1996 and 2006 cash welfare payments to immigrants declined by 73 percent, food stamps by 39 percent, and SSI payments by 20 percent.

It remained the case, however, that rates of welfare utilization continued to be higher among immigrants than nonimmigrants. In 2009, for instance, a survey of all households with minor children revealed that 57 percent of immigrant households used at least one form of welfare as compared with only 39 percent of nonimmigrant households. Among households headed by an illegal immigrant, the percentage stood even higher, at 71 percent.

In addition to utilizing welfare at high rates, low-income immigrants impose costs on state and local governments by enrolling children in public schools, using emergency health care facilities, and straining the criminal justice system. For low-income immigrants, these fiscal burdens substantially exceed taxes paid. We will say more about this later.

Research Findings

All economists agree that U.S. immigration increases U.S. domestic output and income and that highly educated immigrants and successful entrepreneurs add to the vitality of American enterprise. But in light of the complications just discussed, no single generalization is possible as to the impact of immigration on the wages of native-born U.S. workers.

The best evidence indicates that immigration reduces the wages of native-born workers who have low levels of education, and also may reduce the salaries of some highly trained native-born workers. For example, studies show that immigration reduces the wages of native-born Americans who do not have high school diplomas, native-born African American men, and native-born holders of doctorate degrees.

The overall effect of immigration on the average American wage is much less clear. Scholarly estimates on that effect range from minus 3 percent to plus 2 percent.[3]

> **QUICK REVIEW 25.2**
>
> ✓ Other things equal, immigration reduces the average wage rate, increases domestic output, lowers the total wage income of native-born workers, and bolsters business income in the destination nation; it has the opposite effects in the origin nation.
>
> ✓ Assessing the impacts of immigration is complicated by such factors as remittances and backflows, complementary versus substitute labor, investment impacts, unemployment, and fiscal effects.

The Illegal Immigration Debate

LO25.4 Relate how illegal immigration affects employment and wages in low-wage labor markets and impacts state and local budgets.

Much of the recent concern about immigration has focused on illegal immigration, not immigration per se. Economists point out that a strong inflow of undocumented workers to some extent reflects the increasing scarcity of domestic unskilled labor in the United States. Only about 12 percent of the native-born U.S. workforce has less than a high-school diploma today, compared to about 50 percent in 1960. That scarcity has created significant employment opportunities for unskilled illegal immigrants. Illegal workers make up roughly 26 percent of all agricultural workers, 24 percent of all cleaning workers, 20 percent of all employees in clothing manufacturing, and 14 percent of all construction workers.

Many Americans fear that illegal immigrants and their families depress wage rates in these and other already low-wage U.S. occupations and also burden American citizens through their use of public services such as emergency medical care and public schools. Are these concerns justified?

Employment Effects

Two extreme views on illegal immigration are often expressed. Some observers suggest that the employment of illegal workers decreases the employment of legal workers on a one-for-one basis. They erroneously suggest that the economy has only a fixed number of jobs at any time. Supposedly, every job taken by an illegal worker deprives a legal resident of that job. At the other extreme is the claim that illegal workers accept only work that legal residents will not perform. Viewed this way, illegal workers displace *no* legal residents from their jobs.

Both views are misleading. Consider Figure 25.4, which illustrates a market for unskilled field workers in agriculture. The downsloping curve D is the labor demand curve for field workers. The upsloping supply curve S_d is the labor supply of domestic-born workers, while curve S_t reflects the combined total supply of domestic-born workers and illegal immigrants. The horizontal distances between S_t and S_d at the various wage rates measure the number of illegal immigrants offering their labor services at those wage rates.

With illegal workers present, as implied by curve S_t, the equilibrium wage and level of employment in this labor market are W_t and Q_t. At the low wage of W_t, only *ab* domestic-born workers are willing to work as field hands; the other workers—*bd*—are illegal immigrants. The low employment of domestic-born workers presumably is caused by their better wage opportunities and working conditions in alternative occupations or by the availability of government transfer payments. Recall that illegal workers are not eligible for most welfare benefits.

Can we therefore conclude from Figure 25.4 that illegal workers have filled field jobs that most U.S.-born workers do

FIGURE 25.4 The impacts of illegal workers in a low-wage labor market. Illegal workers in a low-wage labor market shift the labor supply curve, as from S_d to S_t, and reduce the market wage from W_d to W_t. At wage W_t, *ab* workers are domestic-born (or legal residents) and *bd* workers are illegal immigrants. If all the illegal workers were deported, however, Q_d American workers would be employed. To say that illegal workers do jobs that Americans are not willing to do (at any wage rate), therefore, is somewhat misleading. Similarly misleading is the conclusion that the deportation of illegal workers would boost the employment of American workers on a one-for-one basis.

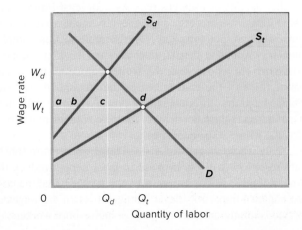

Quantity of labor

---

[3]The research conclusions summarized in this section are based on recent studies conducted individually or jointly by several prominent economists, including George Borjas, David Card, Richard Freeman, Jeffrey Grogger, Gordon Hanson, Lawrence Katz, Gianmarco Ottaviano, and Giovanni Peri.

not want? The answer is "yes," but only with the proviso: "at wage rate W_t." With fewer illegal immigrants in this labor market, labor supply would be less than that shown by curve S_t. The wage rate would be higher than W_t, and more legal residents would offer their services as field hands. For example, if the United States cut off the full inflow of illegal workers to this market, the relevant supply curve would be S_d and the wage rate would rise to W_d. Then Q_d domestic-born workers as opposed to ab workers would work as field hands. The critical point is that the willingness of Americans to work at any particular job depends significantly on the wage rate being paid. A sufficiently high **compensating wage differential** (wage premium to compensate for undesirable work) will attract U.S. workers even to otherwise undesirable work.

The opposite argument, that illegal workers reduce the employment of Americans by an amount equal to the employment of illegal workers, is also misleading. Figure 25.4 reveals that the illegal workers increase the total number of jobs in the labor market. With illegal workers, the number of jobs is Q_t. Without those workers, it is only Q_d. The deportation of the illegal workers would not increase domestic employment on a one-for-one basis. Native-born employment would increase by the amount bc in this specific labor market, not by bd.

Generally, illegal immigration causes some substitution of illegal workers for domestic workers, but the amount of displacement is less than the total employment of the illegal workers. Illegal immigration—as with legal immigration—increases total employment in the United States.

Wage Effects

Large flows of illegal workers into specific low-wage labor markets reduce wage rates in those markets. Note in Figure 25.4 that the greater supply of field workers reduces their wage rate from W_d to W_t. Some U.S. wages—including those of field laborers, food preparers, and house cleaners—are lower than otherwise because of illegal immigration.

As discussed previously, the overall effect of illegal immigration on the average wage rate in the economy is either a smaller decline or even positive. As with legal immigrants, some illegal workers are complementary inputs to domestic-born workers, not substitutes. An example of this complementarity would be illegal fruit pickers and the domestic-born truck drivers who deliver the fruit to grocery stores. The lower price of the fruit increases the amount of fruit demanded and thus the amount of it that needs to be delivered. That increases the labor demand for the complementary truck drivers, whose wage rates rise.

Only where illegal workers and legal workers are substitute resources will the increase in labor supply reduce the wages of other workers. Ironically, studies show that the largest negative impact of illegal immigrants is on the wages of previous immigrants, not on those of native-born workers.

Illegal immigration has very little effect on the average level of wages in the United States. That average wage level depends mainly on the nation's overall level of labor productivity, which illegal immigration does not appreciably affect.

Price Effects

Because illegal immigrants work at lower pay than would be necessary to attract native-born workers, the prices of goods and services that illegal workers produce are lower than they would be otherwise. The extent of such price reduction depends on several factors, including how much of the total cost of producing and delivering a product involves the services performed by illegal immigrants. In industries where illegal immigrants are heavily used—for example, construction, agriculture, landscaping, home cleaning, restaurant meals, and lodging—the presence of illegal workers may have a discernable downward price effect. Lower prices raise the standard of living of all Americans and their families.

Fiscal Impacts on Local and State Governments

One major and very legitimate concern about illegal immigration is the negative fiscal impact it has on local and state governments. Cities and states with high concentrations of illegal immigrants bear the main burden. The federal government receives the payroll taxes and income taxes withheld from the earnings of some illegal immigrants, but the state and local governments bear most of the costs of their presence. Immigrants place their children in local schools, use local emergency medical care, and add to the cost of the criminal justice system, most of which is provided by state and local governments. Immigrants do, however, pay state sales taxes and taxes on gasoline, and indirectly pay property taxes built into rent.

The average fiscal burden (government benefits minus taxes paid) on state and local government for each low-skilled immigrant household may be as high as $19,500 per household per year. In 2006 about 40 percent of the 4.5 million households falling into this low-skilled category were headed by illegal immigrants. One recent estimate of the fiscal burden for these households as a group is nearly $50 billion annually.

Other Concerns

Critics of illegal immigration point to other reasons to be concerned about illegal immigration. First, they say that allowing immigrants to enter the United States unlawfully undermines general respect for the law. If immigration laws can be broken, why can't other laws also be broken? The success of many immigrants in entering the United States and working for employers illegally rests on other criminal activity such as the creation of fake birth certificates, Social Security cards, and

The Startling Slowdown in Illegal Immigration

Illegal Immigration Fell Precipitously during the 2007–2009 Recession. Why Did It Happen? And Will It Continue?

The number of illegal immigrants living in the United States more than tripled between 1990 and 2007, increasing from 3.5 million in 1990 to 12.2 million in 2007. But during the 2007–2009 recession, the trend reversed and the number of illegal immigrants living in the United States fell by nearly 8 percent, down to 11.3 million in 2009.

The decline occurred because the backflow of illegal immigrants returning to their home countries exceeded the inflow of illegal immigrants entering the United States. The most important underlying cause for the backflow exceeding the inflow was quite simple: decreased job prospects for illegal immigrants.

There had been a major boom in housing prices and new home construction during the early 2000s, but it peaked in 2006 before crashing in 2007. When it did, the demand for unskilled labor fell dramatically. The ensuing recession cut the demand for unskilled labor even further.

As a result, most economists concluded that illegal immigration had declined due to low employment demand. Following the same logic, they also assumed that when the economy picked up again, so would illegal immigration.

Thus, it was a major surprise when the overall size of the illegal immigrant population stayed steady at around 11.3 million not only immediately after the Great Recession of 2007–2009 but all the way through 2014 (the most recent year for which data are available). Economic growth had returned, but the net flow of illegal immigrants remained at about zero.

Economists have come up with several explanations for this leveling-off in the overall number of illegal immigrants. Taken together, they offer a plausible explanation for why illegal immigration remained subdued after the Great Recession—and for why it may decrease in coming years.

The first major factor has been the rapid decline in birth rates in the countries that have historically sent the most illegal immigrants to the United States. Consider Mexico. In 1960, Mexican women were having, on average, 7.3 births per woman per lifetime. By 2009, that number had tumbled to an average of just 2.4 births per lifetime—and, indeed, that number is expected to fall even further in coming years. As a result, the number of young

Source: © Sandy Huffaker/Getty Images

Mexicans entering the job market each year in Mexico is now far lower than it was just a decade ago. One result has been far fewer young Mexicans deciding to seek their fortunes in the United States.

At the same time, economic growth has picked up substantially in most of the countries that have traditionally sent the most illegal immigrants to the United States. Consider Mexico once again. Mexico's economy grew rapidly between 2010 and 2014. That rapid growth drove up local wages—thereby making the wages available in the United States seem relatively less attractive than they had seemed just a few years earlier.

Government policies have also played a role. The North American Free Trade Agreement (NAFTA) that was signed by the governments of Canada, Mexico, and the United States in 1992 created a continent-wide free trade zone that spurred the creation of a larger manufacturing sector in Mexico. Mexico passed China and South Korea to become the world's largest producer of flat-screen TVs in 2009 and, in addition, Mexico has also become one of the world's top car and truck producers. Thus, many Mexicans now work in Mexican factories producing goods for export. Because they are employed in good-paying jobs in Mexico, they are less likely to want to immigrate illegally to the United States.

U.S. immigration-enforcement activities have also increased in recent years. A fence was built along several hundred miles of the U.S.-Mexican border and border patrols were strengthened after the 9/11 terrorist attack. As a result, the number of illegal immigrants deported by the U.S. Department of Homeland Security each year more than tripled between 2001 and 2014, rising from 189,026 removals in 2001 to 577,295 removals in 2014.

The factors just discussed—falling birth rates, better local job opportunities, and stronger border enforcement—lead many economists to conclude that illegal immigration is more likely to decrease than increase in coming years. If so, the debate over illegal immigration will likely take a less-prominent place in American political life. Whether one believes illegal immigration to be a serious problem or a net benefit, there will be less to argue over if the number of illegal immigrants declines in coming years.

driver's licenses. Also, some unauthorized immigrants engage in illegal activities such as drug smuggling, identity theft, and insurance fraud. Although legal U.S. immigrants have considerably lower incarceration rates than the native-born U.S. population, the crime rate for illegal immigrants is much higher than that of the native-born U.S. population.

Second, critics of the ineffective enforcement of border and employment laws point out that illegal immigration is highly unfair to the thousands of people enduring the expense and long waits associated with the process for legally gaining the right to live and work in the United States.

Finally, some observers see national defense as the greatest long-term risk from porous borders. The flow of illegal entrants into the United States is clearly at odds with the goal of homeland security. Ineffective border enforcement against illegal immigrants allows career criminals and even terrorists to enter the United States undetected.

> ### QUICK REVIEW 25.3
>
> ✓ Illegal immigrants reduce wage rates in low-wage labor markets, take jobs that some Americans do not want, and expand total employment in low-wage occupations.
>
> ✓ The deportation of illegal immigrants would increase the wage rate in low-skilled labor markets but not increase employment on a one-to-one basis with the number of illegal workers deported.
>
> ✓ Illegal immigration imposes a high net fiscal burden on state and local governments.

Optimal Immigration

LO25.5 Demonstrate how economics can inform current immigration discussions and attempts to reform immigration laws.

The immigration issues relating to quotas and illegal immigrants go well beyond economics. They are also political and cultural issues. Nevertheless, economics can help inform the debate. Economic analysis suggests that immigration can either benefit or harm a nation, depending on the number of immigrants; their education, skills, and work ethic; and the rate at which they can be absorbed into the economy without disruption.

From a strictly economic perspective, immigration should be expanded until its marginal benefit equals its marginal cost. The MB = MC conceptual framework explicitly recognizes that there can be too few immigrants, just as there can be too many. Moreover, it recognizes that from a strictly economic standpoint, not all immigrants are alike. Some immigrants generate more benefits to the U.S. economy than others; and some immigrants impose more costs on taxpayers than others. The immigration of, say, a highly educated scientist obviously has a different net economic impact than does the immigration of a long-term welfare recipient.

A nation sets the level of legal immigration through quotas and special provisions. In effect, it also sets the size of illegal immigration through how effectively it secures its borders and enforces its immigration laws. This chapter's Last Word examines the surprising recent decline in illegal immigration into the United States and the various causes of that decline, including increased enforcement activities.

SUMMARY

LO25.1 Describe the extent of legal and illegal immigration into the United States.

Legal immigrants may be either permanent immigrants (green card holders) or temporary immigrants who are legally in the country until a specific date. The United States admitted 990,553 legal permanent residents in 2013. About 55 percent of these immigrants were women; 45 percent were men. Roughly 58 percent of legal immigrants were married. The largest number of legal immigrants (135,028) was from Mexico, but Mexicans made up only 14 percent of the total number of legal immigrants in 2013. The vast majority of legal immigrants gain that status because of family ties with U.S. citizens and other legal residents.

Illegal immigrants (also called unauthorized immigrants, illegal aliens, or undocumented workers) are people who enter the country unlawfully or overstay their prescribed exit dates. An estimated 11.3 million illegal immigrants live in the United States. That number has held steady since 2009, with the net number of new arrivals and returns about equal. The vast majority of illegal immigrants come from Mexico.

LO25.2 Discuss why economists view economic immigration as a personal human capital investment.

An economic migrant's decision to move to another country can be viewed as an investment, in which present sacrifices (explicit and implicit costs) are incurred to obtain larger lifetime gains (higher earnings). Other things equal, the shorter the distance of the move and the younger the potential economic migrant, the more likely the person will move to the destination country.

LO25.3 Explain how immigration affects average wages, resource allocation, domestic output, and group income shares.

The simple immigration model suggests that, for a high-wage country, the movement of migrants from a low-wage country (a) increases domestic output (= domestic income), (b) reduces the average wage rate, (c) reduces the total wage income of native-born workers, and (d) increases business income. The opposite effects occur in the low-wage country. Because the domestic output gains in the high-wage country exceed the domestic output losses in the low-wage country, labor resources are more efficiently allocated globally and world output rises.

The outcomes of immigration predicted by the simple immigration model become more complicated when considering (*a*) the costs of moving, (*b*) the possibility of remittances and backflows, (*c*) complementary rather than substitute labor, (*d*) impacts on investment, (*e*) the levels of unemployment in each country, and (*f*) the fiscal impact on the taxpayers of each country.

LO25.4 Relate how illegal immigration affects employment and wages in low-wage labor markets and impacts state and local budgets.

Legal U.S. residents who have less than a high school education seem to bear the brunt of the wage impact of immigration, although some highly educated workers are also affected. Immigration has little discernable effect on the overall average wage rate in the U.S. economy, with estimates ranging from minus 3 percent to plus 2 percent.

Illegal workers in the United States reduce wage rates in narrowly defined low-wage labor markets, but they do not reduce native-born employment by the full extent of the employment of the illegal workers. American workers who are complementary to illegal immigrant labor may experience an increase in the demand for their services and wages because of the illegal immigrants.

LO25.5 Demonstrate how economics can inform current immigration discussions and attempts to reform immigration laws.

Illegal workers may increase the overall rate of return on capital, thus promoting greater national investment. However, large numbers of illegal workers in specific industries may reduce the incentive for those industries to mechanize. A legitimate concern is that illegal workers and their families impose greater fiscal costs on state and local governments than they contribute in tax revenues to those jurisdictions.

TERMS AND CONCEPTS

economic immigrants	backflows	complementary resources
legal immigrants	skill transferability	substitute resources
illegal immigrants	self-selection	negative self-selection
H1-B provision	efficiency gains from migration	compensating wage differential
human capital	brain drains	
beaten paths	remittances	

The following and additional problems can be found in ▦ connect

DISCUSSION QUESTIONS

1. Which of the following statements are true? Which are false? Explain why the false statements are untrue. **LO25.1**
   a. More immigrants arrive to the United States each year illegally than legally.
   b. The majority of legal immigrants are men.
   c. Over half the new legal immigrants to the United States each year are from Mexico.
   d. Most legal immigrants to the United States gain their legal status through employment-based preferences.
2. In what respect is the economic decision to move across international borders an investment decision? Why do economic migrants move to some countries but not to others? Cite an example of an explicit cost of moving; an implicit cost of moving. How do distance and age affect the migration decision? How does the presence of a large number of previous movers to a country affect the projected costs and benefits of subsequent movers? **LO25.2**
3. Suppose that the projected lifetime earnings gains from migration exceed the costs of moving. Explain how the decision to move might be reversed when a person considers present value. **LO25.2**
4. How might the output and income gains from immigration shown by the simple immigration model be affected by (*a*) unemployment in the originating nation, (*b*) remittances by

immigrants to the home country, and (*c*) backflows of migrants to the home country? **LO25.3**
5. Suppose initially that immigrant labor and native-born labor are complementary resources. Explain how substantial immigration might change the demand for native-born workers, altering their wages. (Review the relevant portion of Chapter 16 if necessary to help answer this question.) Next, suppose that new immigrant labor and previous immigrant labor (not native-born) are substitute resources. Explain how substantial immigration of new workers might affect the demand for previous immigrants, altering their wages. **LO25.3**
6. What is a "brain drain" as it relates to international migration? If emigrants are highly educated and received greatly subsidized education in the home country, is there any justification for that country to levy a "brain drain" tax on them? Do you see any problems with this idea? **LO25.3**
7. In July 2007 *The Wall Street Journal (WSJ)* reported that a growing shortage of skilled labor in Eastern European countries such as Slovakia was driving up wages in key industries and reducing business income. The reason for the shortages was a large migration of skilled Eastern European workers to Western European countries. Use the simple immigration model to demonstrate the key elements of the *WSJ* story as just described. **LO25.3**

8. Why is each of these statements somewhat misleading? (*a*) "Illegal immigrants take only jobs that no American wants." (*b*) "Deporting 100,000 illegal immigrants would create 100,000 job openings for Americans." LO25.4

9. Why are so many state and local governments greatly concerned about the federal government's allegedly lax enforcement of the immigration laws and congressional proposals to grant legal status (amnesty) to the 11.3 million illegal immigrants in the United States? How might an amnesty program affect the flow of future border crossings? LO25.5

10. If someone favors the free movement of labor within the United States, is it inconsistent for that person to also favor restrictions on the international movement of labor? Why or why not? LO25.5

11. **LAST WORD** What was the single most important reason for the decline in illegal immigration between 2007 and 2009? What other factors were at play? Going forward, why might people think it more likely that illegal immigration will fall rather than rise?

REVIEW QUESTIONS

1. Each year, the number of legal immigrants to the United States is _____ the number of illegal immigrants. LO25.1
   a. Less than.
   b. Equal to.
   c. Greater than.
   d. Less than, but only in *most* years, not every year.

2. The primary reason people immigrate to the United States is: LO25.2
   a. To escape political or religious oppression back home.
   b. To reunite with family members.
   c. To improve earnings and living standards.
   d. None of the above.

3. True or False. Because older adults have more human capital, they are more likely to migrate to another country than younger adults. LO25.2

4. Use the accompanying tables for Neon and Zeon to answer the questions that follow. Assume that the wage rate shown equals hourly output and income, and that the accumulated output and income are the sum of the marginal revenue products (MRPs) of each worker. LO25.3

Neon

Workers	Wage Rate = MRP	Domestic Output and Income
1	$21	$ 21
2	19	40 (= 21 + 19)
3	17	57 (= 21 + 19 + 17)
4	15	72
5	13	85
6	11	96
7	9	105

Zeon

Workers	Wage Rate = MRP	Domestic Output and Income
1	$15	$ 15
2	13	28 (= 15 + 13)
3	11	39 (= 15 + 13 + 11)
4	9	48
5	7	55
6	5	60
7	3	63

a. Which country has the greater stock of capital and technological prowess? How can you tell?

b. Suppose the equilibrium wage rate is $19 in Neon and $7 in Zeon. What is the domestic output (= domestic income) in the two countries?

c. Assuming zero migration costs and initial wage rates of $19 in Neon and $7 in Zeon, how many workers will move to Neon? Why will not more than that number of workers move to Neon?

d. After the move of workers, what will the equilibrium wage rate be in each country? What will the domestic output be after the migration? What is the amount of the combined gain in domestic output produced by the migration? Which country will gain output; which will lose output? How will the income of native-born workers be affected in each country?

5. Migration between North Korea and South Korea has been prohibited since the end of the Korean War in 1953. South Korea is now much richer than North Korea and has a much higher marginal product of labor and a much higher wage rate than North Korea. If workers could migrate from North Korea to South Korea, we would expect: LO25.3
   a. Output to fall in South Korea but rise in North Korea.
   b. Output to rise in each country.
   c. Total combined output in the two countries to fall.
   d. Total combined output in the two countries to rise.

6. True or False. Research indicates that immigration causes large decreases in the average American wage. LO25.3

7. True or False. The MB = MC level of immigration is likely to be achieved if we simply let in every person who wishes to immigrate to the United States. LO25.5

PROBLEMS

1. Mexico has daily (rather than hourly) minimum wage laws. In 2016, the daily minimum wage in Mexico was about 73 pesos per day, and the exchange rate between Mexican pesos and U.S. dollars was about 17 pesos per dollar. LO25.3

   a. In 2016, what was the Mexican minimum daily wage in terms of dollars?

   b. Given that Mexican employees typically work 8-hour days, about how much *per hour* is the Mexican minimum wage in terms of dollars?

   c. In 2016, the federal minimum wage in the United States was $7.25 per hour. How many times larger was the hourly U.S. federal minimum wage than the hourly Mexican minimum wage?

   d. If unskilled workers have a tendency to migrate to where they can obtain the highest compensation for their labor, which country is more likely to be receiving low-skilled immigrants?

2. Differences in productivity are usually the major force behind differences in wages and unit labor costs. Suppose that a single unskilled worker at a pottery factory in Mexico can produce 1 mug per hour. By comparison, suppose that a single unskilled worker at a pottery factory in the United States can produce 14 mugs per hour because more and better machinery generates higher labor productivity. The Mexican mugs and the American mugs are identical in quality and durability and sell for the same price. LO25.3

   a. If unskilled pottery workers are paid the local minimum wage in both countries, how much is the labor cost *per mug* for mugs produced in Mexico? For mugs produced in the United States? (Use the minimum wages from problem 1 and make all calculations in dollars.)

   b. With regard to mug production, how much higher are labor costs *per hour* in the United States?

   c. With regard to mug production, how much higher are labor costs *per unit* in Mexico?

   d. Do higher labor costs per hour always imply higher labor costs per unit?

   e. If firms with lower labor costs per unit expand, while those with higher labor costs per unit contract, in which country will mug-making firms be increasing in size and hiring more employees? If unskilled pottery workers relocate to where they can find jobs, to which country will they be moving?

3. There is evidence that, other things equal, a 10 percent increase in the number of workers having a particular skill level leads to about a 4 percent decline in wages for workers with that skill level. In addition, this 10-to-4 ratio appears to hold true whether the increase in labor supply is caused by domestic changes in labor supply or by an influx of foreign immigrants. LO25.3

   a. Suppose that 42,000 computer programmers work in Silicon Valley. If the number of computer programmers in Silicon Valley increases by 1,260 because of a change in U.S. immigration laws, by how many percentage points would you expect the wage of computer programmers to fall in Silicon Valley?

   b. Suppose that 8,000 full-time cooks work in restaurants in the Denver area. If Denver becomes popular both with U.S. citizens and with foreigners such that 400 full-time cooks move to Denver from other parts of the United States while 80 full-time cooks move to Denver from other countries, by how much would you expect the wages of full-time cooks to fall in Denver?

4. In 2012, an estimated 7.8 million Mexican-born immigrants were employed in the United States. LO25.3

   a. If 60 percent of the Mexican-born immigrants remitted money to family members in Mexico in 2012, and if they each sent $100 per month, how much money did they remit in total?

   b. If, instead, 100 percent of the Mexican-born immigrants remitted money to family members in Mexico in 2012, and if they each sent $250 per month, how much money did they remit in total?

   c. The actual amount remitted to Mexico in 2012 by Mexican-born immigrants living in the United States was about $23 billion. If we assume that 75 percent of the Mexican-born immigrants remitted money to Mexico that year and if we further assume that each of those immigrants remitted an equal amount each month, how much per month did each of those immigrants have to remit to total $23 billion for the year?

International Economics

7

26 Chapter

International Trade*

Learning Objective

LO26.1 List and discuss several key facts about international trade.

LO26.2 Define comparative advantage and demonstrate how specialization and trade add to a nation's output.

LO26.3 Describe how differences between world prices and domestic prices prompt exports and imports.

LO26.4 Analyze the economic effects of tariffs and quotas.

LO26.5 Analyze the validity of the most frequently presented arguments for protectionism.

LO26.6 Identify and explain the objectives of **GATT**, **WTO**, **EU**, eurozone, and **NAFTA** and discuss offshoring and trade adjustment assistance.

Backpackers in the wilderness like to think they are "leaving the world behind," but, like Atlas, they carry the world on

their shoulders. Much of their equipment is imported—knives from Switzerland, rain gear from South Korea, cameras from Japan, aluminum pots from England, sleeping bags from China, and compasses from Finland. Moreover, they may have driven to the trailheads in Japanese-made Toyotas or German-made BMWs, sipping coffee from Brazil or snacking on bananas from Honduras.

International trade and the global economy affect all of us daily, whether we are hiking in the wilderness, driving our cars, buying groceries, or working at our jobs. We cannot "leave the world behind." We are enmeshed in a global web of economic relationships, such as trading goods and services, multinational corporations, cooperative ventures among the world's firms, and ties among the world's financial markets.

The focus of this chapter is the trading of goods and services. Then in Chapter 27, we examine the U.S. balance of payments, exchange rates, and U.S. trade deficits.

---

*Note to Instructors: If you prefer to cover international trade early in your course, you can assign this chapter at the end of either Part 1 or Part 2. This chapter builds on the introductory ideas of opportunity costs, supply and demand analysis, and economic efficiency but does not require an understanding of either market failures or government failures.

Some Key Trade Facts

LO26.1 List and discuss several key facts about international trade.

The following are several important facts relating to international trade.

- U.S. exports and imports have more than doubled as percentages of GDP since 1980.

- A *trade deficit* occurs when imports exceed exports. The United States has a trade deficit in goods. In 2015, U.S. imports of goods exceeded U.S. exports of goods by $529 billion.

- A *trade surplus* occurs when exports exceed imports. The United States has a trade surplus in services (such as air transportation services and financial services). In 2015, U.S. exports of services exceeded U.S. imports of services by $220 billion.

- Principal U.S. exports include chemicals, agricultural products, consumer durables, semiconductors, and aircraft; principal imports include petroleum, automobiles, metals, household appliances, and computers.

- As with other advanced industrial nations, the United States imports many goods that are in some of the same categories as the goods that it exports. Examples: automobiles, computers, chemicals, semiconductors, and telecommunications equipment.

- Canada is the United States' most important trading partner quantitatively. In 2015, about 19 percent of U.S. exported goods were sold to Canadians, who in turn provided 13 percent of imported U.S. goods.

- The United States has a sizable trade deficit with China. In 2015 it was $366 billion.

- Starting in 2012, the shale oil boom in the Plains States greatly reduced U.S. dependence on foreign oil, as can be seen in the statistics that keep track of trade between the United States and the members of OPEC. In 2011, before the boom, the United States imported $191.5 billion of goods (mainly oil) from OPEC while exporting $64.8 billion of goods to those countries. By 2015, U.S. imports had fallen to just $66.2 billion while exports had risen to $72.8 billion. The United States' oil usage had fallen so much that the United States ran its first-ever trade surplus with OPEC in 2015.

- The United States leads the world in the combined volume of exports and imports, as measured in dollars. China, the United States, Germany, Japan, and the Netherlands were the top five exporters by dollar in 2015.

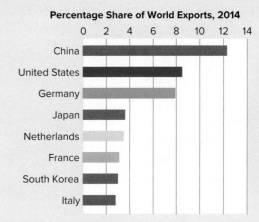

GLOBAL PERSPECTIVE 26.1

Shares of World Exports, Selected Nations

China has the largest share of world exports, followed by Germany and the United States. The eight largest export nations account for about 44.8 percent of world exports.

Percentage Share of World Exports, 2014

Source: International Trade Statistics, 2015, WTO Publications.

- Currently, the United States provides about 8.5 percent of the world's exports. (See Global Perspective 26.1.)

- Exports of goods and services (on a national income account basis) make up about 13 percent of total U.S. output. That percentage is much lower than the percentage in many other nations, including Belgium, the Netherlands, Germany, Canada, and the United Kingdom. (See Global Perspective 26.2.)

- China has become a major international trader, with an estimated $2.2 trillion of exports in 2015. Other Asian economies—including South Korea, Taiwan, and Singapore—are also active in international trade. Their combined exports exceed those of France, Britain, or Italy.

- International trade links world economies. Through trade, changes in economic conditions in one place on the globe can quickly affect other places.

- International trade is often at the center of debates over economic policy, both within the United States and internationally.

With this information in mind, let's turn to the economics of international trade.

GLOBAL PERSPECTIVE 26.2

Exports of Goods and Services as a Percentage of GDP, Selected Countries

Although the United States is one of the world's largest exporters, as a percentage of GDP, its exports are quite low relative to many other countries.

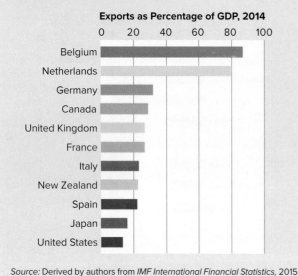

Exports as Percentage of GDP, 2014

Source: Derived by authors from *IMF International Financial Statistics*, 2015.

The Economic Basis for Trade

LO26.2 Define comparative advantage and demonstrate how specialization and trade add to a nation's output.

Sovereign nations, like individuals and the regions of a nation, can gain by specializing in the products they can produce with the greatest relative efficiency and by trading for the goods they cannot produce as efficiently. The simple answer to the question "Why do nations trade?" is "They trade because it is beneficial." The benefits that emerge relate to three underlying facts:

• The distribution of natural, human, and capital resources among nations is uneven; nations differ in their endowments of economic resources.

• Efficient production of various goods requires different technologies, and not all nations have the same level of technological expertise.

• Products are differentiated as to quality and other attributes, and some people may prefer certain goods imported from abroad rather than similar goods produced domestically.

To recognize the character and interaction of these three facts, think of China, which has abundant and inexpensive labor. As a result, China can produce efficiently (at low cost of other goods forgone) a variety of **labor-intensive goods,** such as textiles, electronics, apparel, toys, and sporting goods.

In contrast, Australia has vast amounts of land and can inexpensively produce such **land-intensive goods** as beef, wool, and meat. Mexico has the soil, tropical climate, rainfall, and ready supply of unskilled labor that allow for the efficient, low-cost production of vegetables. Industrially advanced economies such as the United States and Germany that have relatively large amounts of capital can inexpensively produce goods whose production requires much capital, including such **capital-intensive goods** as airplanes, automobiles, agricultural equipment, machinery, and chemicals.

Also, regardless of their resource intensities, nations can develop individual products that are in demand worldwide because of their special qualities. Examples: fashions from Italy, chocolates from Belgium, software from the United States, and watches from Switzerland.

The distribution of resources, technology, and product distinctiveness among nations is relatively stable in short time periods but certainly can change over time. When that distribution changes, the relative efficiency and success that nations have in producing and selling goods also change. For example, in the past several decades, South Korea has greatly expanded its stock of capital. Although South Korea was primarily an exporter of agricultural products and raw materials a half-century ago, it now exports large quantities of manufactured goods. Similarly, the new technologies that gave us synthetic fibers and synthetic rubber drastically altered the resource mix needed to produce fibers and rubber and changed the relative efficiency of nations in manufacturing them.

As national economies evolve, the size and quality of their labor forces may change, the volume and composition of their capital stocks may shift, new technologies may develop, and even the quality of land and the quantity of natural resources may be altered. As such changes take place, the relative efficiency with which a nation can produce specific goods will also change. As economists would say, comparative advantage can and does sometimes change.

Comparative Advantage

In an open economy (one with an international sector), a country produces more of certain goods (exports) and fewer of other goods (imports) than it would otherwise. Thus, the country shifts the use of labor and other productive resources toward export industries and away from import industries. For example, in the presence of international trade, the United States uses more resources to make commercial aircraft and to grow wheat and fewer resources to make television sets and sew clothes. So we ask: Do such shifts of resources make economic sense? Do they enhance U.S. total output and thus the U.S. standard of living?

CONSIDER THIS . . .

A CPA and a House Painter

Source: © Digital Vision/Getty Images RF

Suppose that Madison, a certified public accountant (CPA), is a swifter painter than Mason, the professional painter she is thinking of hiring. Also assume that Madison can earn $50 per hour as an accountant but would have to pay Mason $15 per hour. And suppose that Madison would need 30 hours to paint her house but Mason would need 40 hours.

Should Madison take time from her accounting to paint her own house, or should she hire the painter? Madison's opportunity cost of painting her house is $1,500 (= 30 hours of sacrificed CPA time × $50 per CPA hour). The cost of hiring Mason is only $600 (= 40 hours of painting × $15 per hour of painting). Although Madison is better at both accounting and painting, she will get her house painted at lower cost by specializing in accounting and using some of her earnings from accounting to hire a house painter.

Similarly, Mason can reduce his cost of obtaining accounting services by specializing in painting and using some of his income to hire Madison to prepare his income tax forms. Suppose Mason would need 10 hours to prepare his tax return, while Madison could handle the task in 2 hours. Mason would sacrifice $150 of income (= 10 hours of painting time × $15 per hour) to do something he could hire Madison to do for $100 (= 2 hours of CPA time × $50 per CPA hour). By specializing in painting and hiring Madison to prepare his tax return, Mason lowers the cost of getting his tax return prepared.

We will see that what is true for our CPA and house painter is also true for nations. Specializing on the basis of comparative advantage enables nations to reduce the cost of obtaining the goods and services they desire.

The answers are affirmative. Specialization and international trade increase the productivity of U.S. resources and allow the United States to obtain greater total output than otherwise would be possible. These benefits are the result of exploiting both *absolute advantages* and *comparative advantages*. A country is said to have an *absolute advantage* over other producers of a product if it is the most efficient producer of that product (by which we mean that it can produce more output of that product from any given amount of resource inputs than can any other producer). A country is said to have a *comparative advantage* over other producers of a product if it can produce the product at a lower opportunity cost (by which we mean that it must forgo less output of alternative products when allocating productive resources to producing the product in question).

In 1776, Adam Smith used the concept of absolute advantage to argue for international specialization and trade. His point was that nations would be better off if each specialized in the production of those products in which it had an absolute advantage and was therefore the most efficient producer:

> It is the maxim of every prudent master of a family, never to attempt to make at home what it will cost him more to make than to buy. The taylor does not attempt to make his own shoes, but buys them of the shoemaker. The shoemaker does not attempt to make his own clothes, but employs a taylor. The farmer attempts to make neither the one nor the other, but employs those different artificers. . . .
>
> What is prudence in the conduct of every private family, can scarce be folly in that of a great kingdom. If a foreign country can supply us with a commodity cheaper than we can make it, better buy it of them with some part of the produce of our own industry, employed in a way in which we have some advantage.[1]

In the early 1800s, David Ricardo extended Smith's idea by demonstrating that it is advantageous for a country to specialize and trade with another country even if it is more productive in all economic activities than that other country. Stated more formally, a nation does not need Smith's absolute advantage—total superiority in the efficiency with which it produces products—to benefit from specialization and trade. It needs only a comparative advantage.

The nearby Consider This box (A CPA and a House Painter) provides a simple, two-person illustration of Ricardo's principle of comparative advantage. Be sure to read it now because it will greatly help you understand the graphical analysis that follows.

QUICK REVIEW 26.1

- ✓ International trade enables nations to specialize, increase productivity, and increase the amount of output available for consumption.
- ✓ A country is said to have an *absolute advantage* over the other producers of a product if it can produce the product more efficiently, by which we mean that it can produce more of the product from any given amount of resource inputs than can any other producer.
- ✓ A country is said to have a *comparative advantage* over the other producers of a product if it can produce the product at a lower opportunity cost, by which we mean that it must forgo less of the output of alternative products when allocating resources to producing the product in question.

[1] Adam Smith, *The Wealth of Nations* (originally published, 1776; New York: Modern Library, 1937), p. 424.

Two Isolated Nations

Our goal is to place the idea of comparative advantage into the context of trading nations. Our method is to build a simple model that relies on the familiar concepts of production possibilities curves. Suppose the world consists of just two nations, the United States and Mexico. Also for simplicity, suppose that the labor forces in the United States and Mexico are of equal size. Each nation can produce both beef and raw (unprocessed) vegetables but at different levels of economic efficiency. Suppose the U.S. and Mexican domestic production possibilities curves for beef and vegetables are those shown in Figure 26.1a and Figure 26.1b. Note three realities relating to the production possibilities curves in the two graphs:

- **Constant costs** The curves derive from the data in Table 26.1 and are drawn as straight lines, in contrast to the bowed-outward production possibilities frontiers we examined in Chapter 1. This means that we have replaced the law of increasing opportunity costs with the assumption of constant costs. This substitution simplifies our discussion but does not impair the validity of our analysis and conclusions. Later we will consider the effects of increasing opportunity costs.

- **Different costs** The production possibilities curves of the United States and Mexico reflect different resource mixes and differing levels of technology. Specifically, the differing slopes of the two curves reflect the numbers in the figures and reveal that the opportunity costs of producing beef and vegetables differ between the two nations.

- **U.S. absolute advantage in both** A producer (an individual, firm, or country) has an *absolute advantage*

over another producer if it can produce more of a product than the other producer using the same amount of resources. Because of our convenient assumption that the U.S. and Mexican labor forces are the same size, the two production possibilities curves show that the United States has an absolute advantage in producing both products. If the United States and Mexico use their entire (equal-size) labor forces to produce either vegetables or beef, the United States can produce more of either than Mexico. The United States, using the same number of workers as Mexico, has greater production possibilities. So output per worker—labor productivity—in the United States exceeds that in Mexico in producing both products.

Opportunity-Cost Ratio in the United States In Figure 26.1a, with full employment, the United States will operate at some point on its production possibilities curve. On that curve, it can increase its output of beef from 0 tons to 30 tons by forgoing 30 tons of vegetables output. So the slope of the production possibilities curve is 1 (= 30 vegetables/ 30 beef), meaning that 1 ton of vegetables must be sacrificed for each extra ton of beef. In the United States the **opportunity-cost ratio** (domestic exchange ratio) for the two products is 1 ton of vegetables (V) for 1 ton of beef (B), or

$$\text{United States: } 1V \equiv 1B \text{ (The "}\equiv\text{" sign simply means "equivalent to.")}$$

Within its borders, the United States can "exchange" a ton of vegetables from itself for a ton of beef from itself. Our constant-cost assumption means that this exchange or opportunity-cost relationship prevails for all possible moves from one point to another along the U.S. production possibilities curve.

FIGURE 26.1 Production possibilities for the United States and Mexico. The two production possibilities curves show the combinations of vegetables and beef that the United States and Mexico can produce domestically. The curves for both countries are straight lines because we are assuming constant opportunity costs. (a) As reflected by the slope of *VB* in the left graph, the opportunity-cost ratio in the United States is 1 vegetable ≡ 1 beef. (b) The production possibilities curve *vb* in the right graph has a steeper slope, reflecting the different opportunity-cost ratio in Mexico of 2 vegetables ≡ 1 beef. The difference in the opportunity-cost ratios between the two countries defines their comparative advantages and is the basis for specialization and international trade.

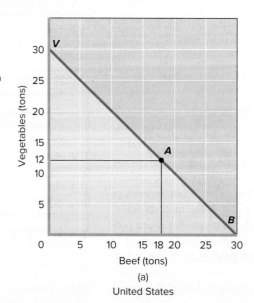

(a)
United States

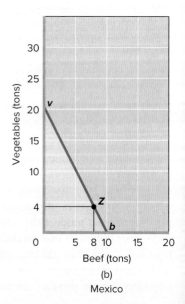

(b)
Mexico

TABLE 26.1 International Specialization According to Comparative Advantage and the Gains from Trade

Country	(1) Outputs before Specialization	(2) Outputs after Specialization	(3) Amounts Exported (−) and Imported (+)	(4) Outputs Available after Trade	(5) Gains from Specialization and Trade (4) − (1)
United States	18 beef	30 beef	−10 beef	20 beef	2 beef
	12 vegetables	0 vegetables	+15 vegetables	15 vegetables	3 vegetables
Mexico	8 beef	0 beef	+10 beef	10 beef	2 beef
	4 vegetables	20 vegetables	−15 vegetables	5 vegetables	1 vegetables

Opportunity-Cost Ratio in Mexico

Mexico's production possibilities curve in Figure 26.1b represents a different full-employment opportunity-cost ratio. In Mexico, 20 tons of vegetables must be given up to obtain 10 tons of beef. The slope of the production possibilities curve is 2 (= 20 vegetables/ 10 beef). This means that in Mexico the opportunity-cost ratio for the two goods is 2 tons of vegetables for 1 ton of beef, or

$$\text{Mexico: } 2V \equiv 1B$$

Self-Sufficiency Output Mix

If the United States and Mexico are isolated and self-sufficient, then each country must choose some output mix on its production possibilities curve. It will select the mix that provides the greatest total utility or satisfaction. Let's assume that combination point A in Figure 26.1a is the optimal mix in the United States. That is, society deems the combination of 18 tons of beef and 12 tons of vegetables preferable to any other combination of the goods available along the production possibilities curve. Suppose Mexico's optimal product mix is 8 tons of beef and 4 tons of vegetables, indicated by point Z in Figure 26.1b. These choices by the two countries are reflected in column 1 of Table 26.1.

Specializing Based on Comparative Advantage

A producer (an individual, firm, or nation) has a **comparative advantage** in producing a particular product if it can produce that product at a lower opportunity cost than other producers. Comparative advantage is the key determinant in whether or not nations can gain from specialization and trade. In fact, absolute advantage turns out to be irrelevant.

In our example, for instance, the United States has an absolute advantage over Mexico in producing both vegetables and beef. But it is still the case that the United States can gain from specialization and trade with Mexico. That is because what actually matters is whether the opportunity costs of producing the two products (beef and vegetables) differ in the two countries. If they do, then each nation will enjoy a comparative advantage in one of the products, meaning that it can produce that product at a lower opportunity cost than the other country. As a result, total output can increase if each country specializes in the production of the good in which it has the lower opportunity cost.

This idea is summarized in the **principle of comparative advantage,** which says that total output will be greatest when each good is produced by the nation that has the lowest domestic opportunity cost for producing that good. In our two-nation illustration, the United States has the lower domestic opportunity cost for beef; the United States must forgo only 1 ton of vegetables to produce 1 ton of beef, whereas Mexico must forgo 2 tons of vegetables for 1 ton of beef. The United States has a comparative (cost) advantage in beef and should specialize in beef production. The "world" (that is, the United States and Mexico) in our example would clearly not be economizing in the use of its resources if a high-cost producer (Mexico) produced a specific product (beef) when a low-cost producer (the United States) could have produced it. Having Mexico produce beef would mean that the world economy would have to give up more vegetables than is necessary to obtain a ton of beef.

Mexico has the lower domestic opportunity cost for vegetables. It must sacrifice only $\frac{1}{2}$ ton of beef to produce 1 ton of vegetables, while the United States must forgo 1 ton of beef to produce 1 ton of vegetables. Mexico has a comparative advantage in vegetables and should specialize in vegetable production. Again, the world would not be employing its resources economically if vegetables were produced by a high-cost producer (the United States) rather than by a low-cost producer (Mexico). If the United States produced vegetables, the world would be giving up more beef than necessary to obtain each ton of vegetables. Economizing requires that any particular good be produced by the nation having the lowest domestic opportunity cost or the nation having the comparative advantage for that good. The United States should produce beef, and Mexico should produce vegetables. The situation is summarized in Table 26.2.

A comparison of columns 1 and 2 in Table 26.1 verifies that specialized production enables the world to obtain more

TABLE 26.2 Comparative-Advantage Example: A Summary

Beef	Vegetables
Mexico: Must give up 2 tons of vegetables to get 1 ton of beef.	**Mexico:** Must give up $\frac{1}{2}$ ton of beef to get 1 ton of vegetables.
United States: Must give up 1 ton of vegetables to get 1 ton of beef.	**United States:** Must give up 1 ton of beef to get 1 ton of vegetables.
Comparative advantage: United States	**Comparative advantage:** Mexico

output from its fixed amount of resources. By specializing completely in beef, the United States can produce 30 tons of beef and no vegetables. Mexico, by specializing completely in vegetables, can produce 20 tons of vegetables and no beef. These figures exceed the yields generated without specialization: 26 tons of beef (= 18 in the United States + 8 in Mexico) and 16 tons of vegetables (= 12 in the United States + 4 in Mexico). As a result, the world ends up with 4 more tons of beef (= 30 tons − 26 tons) and 4 more tons of vegetables (= 20 tons − 16 tons) than it would if there were self-sufficiency and unspecialized production.

Terms of Trade

We have just seen that specialization in production will allow for the largest possible amounts of both beef and vegetables to be produced. But with each country specializing in the production of only one item, how will the vegetables that are all produced by Mexico and the beef that is all produced by the United States be divided between consumers in the two countries? The key turns out to be the **terms of trade,** the exchange ratio at which the United States and Mexico trade beef and vegetables.

Crucially, the terms of trade also establish whether each country will find it in its own better interest to bother specializing at all. This is because the terms of trade determine whether each country can "get a better deal" by specializing and trading than it could if it opted instead for self sufficiency. To see how this works, note that because $1B \equiv 1V$ ($= 1V \equiv 1B$) in the United States, it must get more than 1 ton of vegetables for each 1 ton of beef exported; otherwise, it will not benefit from exporting beef in exchange for Mexican vegetables. The United States must get a better "price" (more vegetables) for its beef through international trade than it can get domestically; otherwise, no gain from trade exists and such trade will not occur.

Similarly, because $1B \equiv 2V$ ($= 2V \equiv 1B$) in Mexico, Mexico must obtain 1 ton of beef by exporting less than 2 tons of vegetables to get it. Mexico must be able to pay a lower "price" for beef in the world market than it must pay domestically, or else it will not want to trade. The international

exchange ratio or terms of trade must therefore lie somewhere between

$$1B \equiv 1V \text{ (United States' cost conditions)}$$

and

$$1B \equiv 2V \text{ (Mexico's cost conditions)}$$

Where between these limits will the world exchange ratio fall? The United States will prefer a rate close to $1B \equiv 2V$, say, $1B \equiv 1\frac{3}{4}V$. The United States wants to obtain as many vegetables as possible for each 1 ton of beef it exports. By contrast, Mexico wants a rate near $1B \equiv 1V$, say, $1B \equiv 1\frac{1}{4}V$. This is true because Mexico wants to export as few vegetables as possible for each 1 ton of beef it receives in exchange.

The actual exchange ratio depends on world supply and demand for the two products. If overall world demand for vegetables is weak relative to its supply and if the demand for beef is strong relative to its supply, the price of vegetables will be lower and the price of beef will be higher. The exchange ratio will settle nearer the $1B \equiv 2V$ figure the United States prefers. If overall world demand for vegetables is great relative to its supply and if the demand for beef is weak relative to its supply, the ratio will settle nearer the $1B \equiv 1V$ level favorable to Mexico. In this manner, the actual exchange ratio that is set by world supply and demand determines how the gains from international specialization and trade are divided between the two nations and, consequently, how the beef that is all produced in the United States and the vegetables that are all produced in Mexico get divided among consumers in the two countries. (We discuss equilibrium world prices later in this chapter.)

Gains from Trade

Suppose the international terms of trade are $1B \equiv 1\frac{1}{2}V$. The possibility of trading on these terms permits each nation to supplant its domestic production possibilities curve with a trading possibilities line (or curve), as shown in **Figure 26.2 (Key Graph).** Just as a production possibilities curve shows the amounts of these products that a full-employment economy can obtain by shifting resources from one to the other, a **trading possibilities line** shows the amounts of the two products that a nation can obtain by specializing in one product and trading for the other. The trading possibilities lines in Figure 26.2 reflect the assumption that both nations specialize on the basis of comparative advantage: The United States specializes completely in beef (at point B in Figure 26.2a), and Mexico specializes completely in vegetables (at point v in Figure 26.2b).

Improved Alternatives With specialization and trade, the United States is no longer constrained by its domestic production possibilities line, which requires it to give up 1 ton of

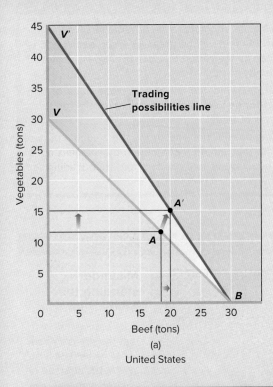

(a)
United States

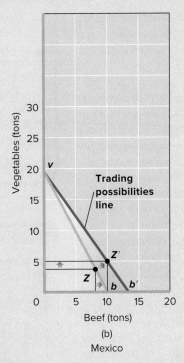

(b)
Mexico

FIGURE 26.2 Trading possibilities lines and the gains from trade. As a result of specialization and trade, both the United States and Mexico can have higher levels of output than the levels attainable on their domestic production possibilities curves. (a) The United States can move from point A on its domestic production possibilities curve to, say, A' on its trading possibilities line. (b) Mexico can move from Z to Z'.

QUICK QUIZ FOR FIGURE 26.2

1. The production possibilities curves in graphs (a) and (b) imply:
   a. increasing domestic opportunity costs.
   b. decreasing domestic opportunity costs.
   c. constant domestic opportunity costs.
   d. first decreasing, then increasing domestic opportunity costs.

2. Before specialization, the domestic opportunity cost of producing 1 unit of beef is:
   a. 1 unit of vegetables in both the United States and Mexico.
   b. 1 unit of vegetables in the United States and 2 units of vegetables in Mexico.
   c. 2 units of vegetables in the United States and 1 unit of vegetables in Mexico.
   d. 1 unit of vegetables in the United States and $\frac{1}{2}$ unit of vegetables in Mexico.

3. After specialization and international trade, the world output of beef and vegetables is:
   a. 20 tons of beef and 20 tons of vegetables.
   b. 45 tons of beef and 15 tons of vegetables.
   c. 30 tons of beef and 20 tons of vegetables.
   d. 10 tons of beef and 30 tons of vegetables.

4. After specialization and international trade:
   a. the United States can obtain units of vegetables at less cost than it could before trade.
   b. Mexico can obtain more than 20 tons of vegetables, if it so chooses.
   c. the United States no longer has a comparative advantage in producing beef.
   d. Mexico can benefit by prohibiting vegetables imports from the United States.

Answers: 1. c; 2. b; 3. c; 4. a

---

beef for every 1 ton of vegetables it wants as it moves up its domestic production possibilities line from, say, point B. Instead, the United States, through trade with Mexico, can get $1\frac{1}{2}$ tons of vegetables for every ton of beef that it exports to Mexico, as long as Mexico has vegetables to export. Trading possibilities line BV' thus represents the $1B \equiv 1\frac{1}{2}V$ trading ratio.

Similarly, Mexico, starting at, say, point v, no longer has to move down its domestic production possibilities curve,

giving up 2 tons of vegetables for each ton of beef it wants. It can now export just $1\frac{1}{2}$ tons of vegetables for each 1 ton of beef that it wants by moving down its trading possibilities line vb'.

Specialization and trade create a new exchange ratio between beef and vegetables, and that ratio is reflected in each nation's trading possibilities line. For both nations, this exchange ratio is superior to the unspecialized exchange ratio embodied in their respective production possibilities curves.

By specializing in beef and trading for Mexico's vegetables, the United States can obtain more than 1 ton of vegetables for 1 ton of beef. By specializing in vegetables and trading for U.S. beef, Mexico can obtain 1 ton of beef for less than 2 tons of vegetables. In both cases, self-sufficiency is inefficient and therefore undesirable.

Greater Output By specializing on the basis of comparative advantage and by trading for goods that are produced in the nation with greater domestic efficiency, the United States and Mexico can achieve combinations of beef and vegetables beyond their own individual production possibilities curves. Specialization according to comparative advantage results in a more efficient allocation of world resources, and larger outputs of both products are therefore available to both nations.

Suppose that at the $1B \equiv 1\frac{1}{2}V$ terms of trade, the United States exports 10 tons of beef to Mexico and, in return, Mexico exports 15 tons of vegetables to the United States. How do the new quantities of beef and vegetables available to the two nations compare with the optimal product mixes that existed before specialization and trade? Point A in Figure 26.2a reminds us that the United States chose 18 tons of beef and 12 tons of vegetables originally. But by producing 30 tons of beef and no vegetables and by trading 10 tons of beef for 15 tons of vegetables, the United States can obtain 20 tons of beef and 15 tons of vegetables. This new, superior combination of beef and vegetables is indicated by point A' in Figure 26.2a. Compared with the no-trade amounts of 18 tons of beef and 12 tons of vegetables, the United States' **gains from trade** are 2 tons of beef and 3 tons of vegetables.

Similarly, recall that Mexico's optimal product mix was 4 tons of vegetables and 8 tons of beef (point Z) before specialization and trade. Now, after specializing in vegetables and trading for beef, Mexico can have 5 tons of vegetables and 10 tons of beef. It accomplishes that by producing 20 tons of vegetables and no beef and exporting 15 tons of its vegetables in exchange for 10 tons of American beef. This new position is indicated by point Z' in Figure 26.2b. Mexico's gains from trade are 1 ton of vegetables and 2 tons of beef.

Points A' and Z' in Figure 26.2 are superior economic positions to points A and Z. This fact is enormously important! We know that a nation can expand its production possibilities boundary by (1) expanding the quantity and improving the quality of its resources or (2) realizing technological progress. We have now established that international trade can enable a nation to circumvent the output constraint illustrated by its production possibilities curve. An economy can grow by expanding international trade. The outcome of international specialization and trade is equivalent to having more and better resources or discovering and implementing improved production techniques.

Table 26.1 summarizes the transactions and outcomes in our analysis. Please give it one final careful review.

CONSIDER THIS . . .

Source: © Bloomberg/Getty Images

Misunderstanding the Gains from Trade

It is a common myth that the greatest benefit to be derived from international trade is greater domestic employment in the export sector. This suggests that exports are "good" because they increase domestic employment, whereas imports are "bad" because they deprive people of jobs at home. As we have demonstrated, the true benefit created by international trade is the overall increase in output available through specialization and exchange.

A nation does not need international trade to operate *on* its production possibilities curve. It can fully employ its resources, including labor, with or without international trade. International trade, however, enables a country to reach a point of consumption beyond its domestic production possibilities curve. The gain from trade to a nation is the extra output obtained from abroad—the imports obtained for less sacrifice of other goods than if they were produced at home.

Trade with Increasing Costs

To explain the basic principles underlying international trade, we simplified our analysis in several ways. For example, we limited discussion to two products and two nations. But multiproduct and multinational analysis yield the same conclusions. We also assumed constant opportunity costs (linear production possibilities curves), which is a more substantive simplification. Let's consider the effect of allowing increasing opportunity costs (concave-to-the-origin production possibilities curves) to enter the picture.

Suppose that the United States and Mexico initially are at positions on their concave production possibilities curves where their domestic cost ratios are $1B \equiv 1V$ and $1B \equiv 2V$, as they were in our constant-cost analysis. As before, comparative advantage indicates that the United States should specialize in beef and Mexico in vegetables. But now, as the United States begins to expand beef production, its cost of beef will rise; it will have to sacrifice more than 1 ton of vegetables to get 1 additional ton of beef. Resources are no longer perfectly substitutable between alternative uses, as the constant-cost assumption implied. Resources less and less suitable to beef production must be allocated to the U.S. beef industry in expanding beef output, and that means increasing costs—the sacrifice of larger and larger amounts of vegetables for each additional ton of beef.

Similarly, suppose that Mexico expands vegetable production starting from its $1B \equiv 2V$ cost ratio position. As production increases, it will find that its $1B \equiv 2V$ cost ratio begins to rise. Sacrificing 1 ton of beef will free resources that are capable of producing only something less than 2 tons of vegetables because those transferred resources are less suitable to vegetable production.

As the U.S. cost ratio falls from $1B \equiv 1V$ and the Mexican ratio rises from $1B \equiv 2V$, a point will be reached where the cost ratios are equal in the two nations, perhaps at $1B \equiv 1\frac{3}{4}V$. At this point, the underlying basis for further specialization and trade—differing cost ratios—has disappeared, and further specialization is therefore uneconomical. And, most important, this point of equal cost ratios may be reached while the United States is still producing some vegetables along with its beef and Mexico is producing some beef along with its vegetables. The primary effect of increasing opportunity costs is less-than-complete specialization. For this reason, we often find domestically produced products competing directly against identical or similar imported products within a particular economy.

The Case for Free Trade

The case for free trade reduces to one compelling argument: Through free trade based on the principle of comparative advantage, the world economy can achieve a more efficient allocation of resources and a higher level of material well-being than it can without free trade.

Since the resource mixes and technological knowledge of the world's nations are all somewhat different, each nation can produce particular commodities at different real costs. Each nation should produce goods for which its domestic opportunity costs are lower than the domestic opportunity costs of other nations and exchange those goods for products for which its domestic opportunity costs are high relative to those of other nations. If each nation does this, the world will realize the advantages of geographic and human specialization. The

world and each free-trading nation can obtain a larger real income from the fixed supplies of resources available to it.

Government trade barriers lessen or eliminate gains from specialization. If nations cannot trade freely, they must shift resources from efficient (low-cost) to inefficient (high-cost) uses to satisfy their diverse wants. A recent study suggests that the elimination of trade barriers since the Second World War has increased the income of the average U.S. household by at least $7,000 and perhaps by as much as $13,000. These income gains are recurring; they happen year after year.[2]

One side benefit of free trade is that it promotes competition and deters monopoly. The increased competition from foreign firms forces domestic firms to find and use the lowest-cost production techniques. It also compels them to be innovative with respect to both product quality and production methods, thereby contributing to economic growth. And free trade gives consumers a wider range of product choices. The reasons to favor free trade are the same as the reasons to endorse competition.

A second side benefit of free trade is that it links national interests and breaks down national animosities. Confronted with political disagreements, trading partners tend to negotiate rather than make war.

QUICK REVIEW 26.3

✓ International trade enables nations to specialize, increase productivity, and increase output available for consumption.

✓ Comparative advantage means total world output will be greatest when each good is produced by the nation that has the lowest domestic opportunity cost.

✓ Specialization is less than complete among nations because opportunity costs normally rise as any specific nation produces more of a particular good.

Supply and Demand Analysis of Exports and Imports

LO26.3 Describe how differences between world prices and domestic prices prompt exports and imports.

Supply and demand analysis reveals how equilibrium prices and quantities of exports and imports are determined. The amount of a good or a service a nation will export or import depends on differences between the equilibrium world price and the equilibrium domestic price. The interaction of *world* supply and demand determines the equilibrium **world price**—the price that equates the quantities supplied and

---

[2]Scott C. Bradford, Paul L. E. Grieco, and Gary C. Hufbauer, "The Payoff to America from Globalization," *The World Economy,* July 2006, pp. 893–916.

demanded globally. *Domestic* supply and demand determine the equilibrium **domestic price**—the price that would prevail in a closed economy that does not engage in international trade. The domestic price equates quantity supplied and quantity demanded domestically.

In the absence of trade, the domestic prices in a closed economy may or may not equal the world equilibrium prices. When economies are opened for international trade, differences between world and domestic prices encourage exports or imports. To see how, consider the international effects of such price differences in a simple two-nation world, consisting of the United States and Canada, that are both producing aluminum. We assume there are no trade barriers, such as tariffs and quotas, and no international transportation costs.

Supply and Demand in the United States

Figure 26.3a shows the domestic supply curve S_d and the domestic demand curve D_d for aluminum in the United States, which for now is a closed economy. The intersection of S_d and D_d determines the equilibrium domestic price of $1 per pound and the equilibrium domestic quantity of 100 million pounds. Domestic suppliers produce 100 million pounds and sell them all at $1 a pound. So there are no domestic surpluses or shortages of aluminum.

But what if the U.S. economy were opened to trade and the world price of aluminum were above or below this $1 domestic price?

U.S. Export Supply If the aluminum price in the rest of the world (that is, Canada) exceeds $1, U.S. firms will produce more than 100 million pounds and will export the excess domestic output. First, consider a world price of $1.25. We see from the supply curve S_d that U.S. aluminum firms will produce 125 million pounds of aluminum at that price. The demand curve D_d tells us that the United States will purchase only 75 million pounds at $1.25. The outcome is a domestic surplus of 50 million pounds of aluminum. U.S. producers will export those 50 million pounds at the $1.25 world price.

What if the world price were $1.50? The supply curve shows that U.S. firms will produce 150 million pounds of aluminum, while the demand curve tells us that U.S. consumers will buy only 50 million pounds. So U.S. producers will export the domestic surplus of 100 million pounds.

Toward the top of Figure 26.3b we plot the domestic surpluses—the U.S. exports—that occur at world prices above the $1 domestic equilibrium price. When the world and domestic prices are equal (= $1), the quantity of exports supplied is zero (point a). There is no surplus of domestic output

FIGURE 26.3 U.S. export supply and import demand. (a) Domestic supply S_d and demand D_d set the domestic equilibrium price of aluminum at $1 per pound. At world prices above $1, there are domestic surpluses of aluminum. At prices below $1, there are domestic shortages. (b) Surpluses are exported (top curve), and shortages are met by importing aluminum (lower curve). The export supply curve shows the direct relationship between world prices and U.S. exports; the import demand curve portrays the inverse relationship between world prices and U.S. imports.

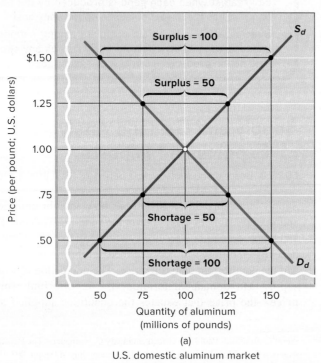

(a)

U.S. domestic aluminum market

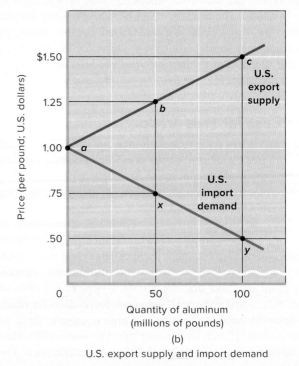

(b)

U.S. export supply and import demand

to export. But when the world price is $1.25, U.S. firms export 50 million pounds of surplus aluminum (point *b*). At a $1.50 world price, the domestic surplus of 100 million pounds is exported (point *c*).

The U.S. **export supply curve,** found by connecting points *a*, *b*, and *c*, shows the amount of aluminum U.S. producers will export at each world price above $1. This curve *slopes upward,* indicating a direct or positive relationship between the world price and the amount of U.S. exports. As world prices increase relative to domestic prices, U.S. exports rise.

U.S. Import Demand

If the world price is below the domestic $1 price, the United States will import aluminum. Consider a $0.75 world price. The supply curve in Figure 26.3a reveals that at that price U.S. firms produce only 75 million pounds of aluminum. But the demand curve shows that the United States wants to buy 125 million pounds at that price. The result is a domestic shortage of 50 million pounds. To satisfy that shortage, the United States will import 50 million pounds of aluminum.

At an even lower world price, $0.50, U.S. producers will supply only 50 million pounds. Because U.S. consumers want to buy 150 million pounds at that price, there is a domestic shortage of 100 million pounds. Imports will flow to the United States to make up the difference. That is, at a $0.50

world price U.S. firms will supply 50 million pounds and 100 million pounds will be imported.

In Figure 26.3b, we plot the U.S. **import demand curve** from these data. This *downsloping curve* shows the amounts of aluminum that will be imported at world prices below the $1 U.S. domestic price. The relationship between world prices and imported amounts is inverse or negative. At a world price of $1, domestic output will satisfy U.S. demand; imports will be zero (point *a*). But at $0.75 the United States will import 50 million pounds of aluminum (point *x*); at $0.50, the United States will import 100 million pounds (point *y*). Connecting points *a*, *x*, and *y* yields the *downsloping* U.S. import demand curve. It reveals that as world prices fall relative to U.S. domestic prices, U.S. imports increase.

Supply and Demand in Canada

We repeat our analysis in Figure 26.4, this time from the viewpoint of Canada. (We have converted Canadian dollar prices to U.S. dollar prices via the exchange rate.) Note that the domestic supply curve S_d and the domestic demand curve D_d for aluminum in Canada yield a domestic price of $0.75, which is $0.25 lower than the $1 U.S. domestic price.

The analysis proceeds exactly as above except that the domestic price is now the Canadian price. If the world price is $0.75, Canadians will neither export nor import aluminum

FIGURE 26.4 Canadian export supply and import demand. (a) At world prices above the $0.75 domestic price, production in Canada exceeds domestic consumption. At world prices below $0.75, domestic shortages occur. (b) Surpluses result in exports, and shortages result in imports. The Canadian export supply curve and import demand curve depict the relationships between world prices and exports or imports.

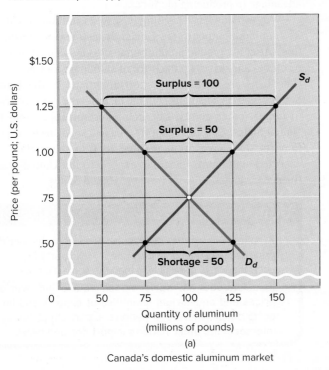

(a)
Canada's domestic aluminum market

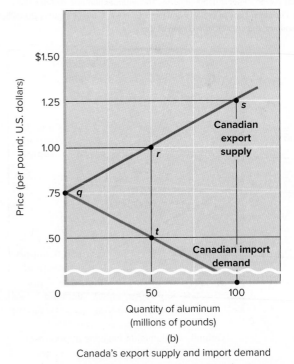

(b)
Canada's export supply and import demand

(giving us point *q* in Figure 26.4b). At world prices above $0.75, Canadian firms will produce more aluminum than Canadian consumers will buy. Canadian firms will export the surplus. At a $1 world price, Figure 26.4b tells us that Canada will have and export a domestic surplus of 50 million pounds (yielding point *r*). At $1.25, it will have and will export a domestic surplus of 100 million pounds (point *s*). Connecting these points yields the upsloping Canadian export supply curve, which reflects the domestic surpluses (and hence the exports) that occur when the world price exceeds the $0.75 Canadian domestic price.

At world prices below $0.75, domestic shortages occur in Canada. At a $0.50 world price, Figure 26.4a shows that Canadian consumers want to buy 125 million pounds of aluminum but Canadian firms will produce only 75 million pounds. The shortage will bring 50 million pounds of imports to Canada (point *t* in Figure 26.4b). The Canadian import demand curve in that figure shows the Canadian imports that will occur at all world aluminum prices below the $0.75 Canadian domestic price.

Equilibrium World Price, Exports, and Imports

We now have the tools for determining the **equilibrium world price** of aluminum and the equilibrium world levels of exports and imports when the world is opened to trade. Figure 26.5 combines the U.S. export supply curve and import demand curve in Figure 26.3b and the Canadian export supply curve and import demand curve in Figure 26.4b. The two U.S. curves proceed rightward from the $1 U.S. domestic price; the two Canadian curves proceed rightward from the $0.75 Canadian domestic price.

International equilibrium occurs in this two-nation model where one nation's import demand curve intersects another nation's export supply curve. In this case, the U.S. import demand curve intersects Canada's export supply curve at *e*. There, the world price of aluminum is $0.88. The Canadian export supply curve indicates that Canada will export 25 million pounds of aluminum at this price. Also at this price the United States will import 25 million pounds from Canada, indicated by the U.S. import demand curve. The $0.88 world price equates the quantity of imports demanded and the quantity of exports supplied (25 million pounds). Thus, there will be world trade of 25 million pounds of aluminum at $0.88 per pound.

Note that after trade, the single $0.88 world price will prevail in both Canada and the United States. Only one price for a standardized commodity can persist in a highly competitive world market. With trade, all consumers can buy a pound of aluminum for $0.88, and all producers can sell it for that price. This world price means that Canadians will pay more for aluminum with trade ($0.88) than without it ($0.75). The increased Canadian output caused by trade raises Canadian per-unit production costs and therefore raises the price of aluminum in Canada. The United States, however, pays less for aluminum with trade ($0.88) than without it ($1). The U.S. gain comes from Canada's comparative cost advantage in producing aluminum.

Why would Canada willingly send 25 million pounds of its aluminum output to the United States for U.S. consumption? After all, producing this output uses up scarce Canadian resources and drives up the price of aluminum for Canadians. Canadians are willing to export aluminum to the United States because Canadians gain the means—the U.S. dollars—to import other goods, say, computer software, from the United States. Canadian exports enable Canadians to acquire imports that have greater value to Canadians than the exported aluminum. Canadian exports to the United States finance Canadian imports from the United States.

FIGURE 26.5 Equilibrium world price and quantity of exports and imports. In a two-nation world, the equilibrium world price (= $0.88) is determined by the intersection of one nation's export supply curve and the other nation's import demand curve. This intersection also decides the equilibrium volume of exports and imports. Here, Canada exports 25 million pounds of aluminum to the United States.

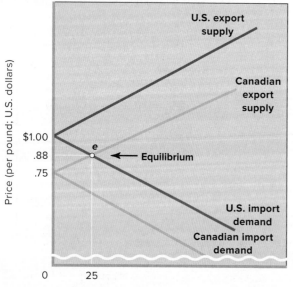

Quantity of aluminum (millions of pounds)

QUICK REVIEW 26.4

✓ A nation will export a particular product if the world price exceeds the domestic price; it will import the product if the world price is less than the domestic price.

✓ In a two-country world model, equilibrium world prices and equilibrium quantities of exports and imports occur where one nation's export supply curve intersects the other nation's import demand curve.

Trade Barriers and Export Subsidies

LO26.4 Analyze the economic effects of tariffs and quotas.

While a nation as a whole gains from trade, trade may harm particular domestic industries and their workers. Those industries might seek to preserve their economic positions by persuading their respective governments to protect them from imports—perhaps through tariffs, import quotas, or other trade barriers.

Indeed, the public may be won over by the apparent plausibility ("Cut imports and prevent domestic unemployment") and the patriotic ring ("Buy American!") of the arguments. The alleged benefits of tariffs are immediate and clear-cut to the public, but the adverse effects cited by economists are obscure and dispersed over the entire economy. When political deal-making is added in—"You back tariffs for the apparel industry in my state, and I'll back tariffs for the auto industry in your state"—the outcome can be a politically robust network of trade barriers. These impediments to free international trade can take several forms.

Tariffs are excise taxes or "duties" on the dollar values or physical quantities of imported goods. They may be imposed to obtain revenue or to protect domestic firms. A **revenue tariff** is usually applied to a product that is not being produced domestically, for example, tin, coffee, or bananas in the case of the United States. Rates on revenue tariffs tend to be modest and are designed to provide the federal government with revenue. A **protective tariff** is implemented to shield domestic producers from foreign competition. These tariffs impede free trade by increasing the prices of imported goods and therefore shifting sales toward domestic producers. Although protective tariffs are usually not high enough to stop the importation of foreign goods, they put foreign producers at a competitive disadvantage. A tariff on imported auto tires, for example, would make domestically produced tires more attractive to consumers.

An **import quota** is a limit on the quantities or total values of specific items that are imported in some period. Once a quota is filled, further imports of that product are choked off. Import quotas are more effective than tariffs in impeding international trade. With a tariff, a product can go on being imported in large quantities. But with an import quota, all imports are prohibited once the quota is filled.

A **nontariff barrier (NTB)** includes onerous licensing requirements, unreasonable standards pertaining to product quality, or simply bureaucratic hurdles and delays in customs procedures. Some nations require that importers of foreign goods obtain licenses and then restrict the number of licenses issued. Although many nations carefully inspect imported agricultural products to prevent the introduction of potentially

harmful insects, some countries use lengthy inspections to impede imports. Japan and the European countries frequently require that their domestic importers of foreign goods obtain licenses. By restricting the issuance of licenses, governments can limit imports.

A **voluntary export restriction (VER)** is a trade barrier by which foreign firms "voluntarily" limit the amount of their exports to a particular country. VERs have the same effect as import quotas and are agreed to by exporters to avoid more stringent tariffs or quotas. In the late 1990s, for example, Canadian producers of softwood lumber (fir, spruce, cedar, pine) agreed to a VER on exports to the United States under the threat of a permanently higher U.S. tariff.

An **export subsidy** consists of a government payment to a domestic producer of export goods and is designed to aid that producer. By reducing production costs, the subsidies enable the domestic firm to charge a lower price and thus to sell more exports in world markets. Two examples: Some European governments have heavily subsidized Airbus Industries, a European firm that produces commercial aircraft. The subsidies help Airbus compete against the American firm Boeing. The United States and other nations have subsidized domestic farmers to boost the domestic food supply. Such subsidies have artificially lowered export prices on agricultural produce.

Later in this chapter we will discuss some of the specific arguments and appeals that are made to justify protection.

Economic Impact of Tariffs

We will confine our in-depth analysis of the effects of trade barriers to the two most common forms: tariffs and quotas. Once again, we turn to supply and demand analysis for help. Curves D_d and S_d in Figure 26.6 show domestic demand and supply for a product in which a nation, say, the United States, does *not* have a comparative advantage—for example, smartphones. (Disregard curve $S_d + Q$ for now.) Without world trade, the domestic price and output would be P_d and q, respectively.

Assume now that the domestic economy is opened to world trade and that China, which *does* have a comparative advantage in smartphones, begins to sell its smartphones in the United States. We assume that with free trade the domestic price cannot differ from the world price, which here is P_w. At P_w, domestic consumption is d and domestic production is a. The horizontal distance between the domestic supply and demand curves at P_w represents imports of ad. Thus far, our analysis is similar to the analysis of world prices in Figure 26.3.

Direct Effects Suppose now that the United States imposes a tariff on each imported smartphone. The tariff, which raises the price of imported smartphones from P_w to P_t, has four effects:

- **Decline in consumption** Consumption of smartphones in the United States declines from d to c as the higher price moves buyers up and to the left along their

demand curve. The tariff prompts consumers to buy fewer smartphones and reallocate a portion of their expenditures to less desired substitute products. U.S. consumers are clearly injured by the tariff, since they pay $P_t - P_w$ more for each of the c units they buy at price P_t.

- **Increased domestic production** U.S. producers—who are not subject to the tariff—receive the higher price P_t per unit. Because this new price is higher than the pretariff world price P_w, the domestic smartphone industry moves up and to the right along its supply curve S_d, increasing domestic output from a to b. Domestic producers thus enjoy both a higher price and expanded sales; this explains why domestic producers lobby for protective tariffs. But from a social point of view, the increase in domestic production from a to b means that the tariff permits domestic producers of smartphones to bid resources away from other, more efficient, U.S. industries.

- **Decline in imports** Chinese producers are hurt. Although the sales price of each smartphone is higher by $P_t - P_w$, that amount accrues to the U.S. government, not to Chinese producers. The after-tariff world price, or the per-unit revenue to Chinese producers, remains at P_w, but the volume of U.S. imports (Chinese exports) falls from ad to bc.

- **Tariff revenue** The yellow rectangle represents the amount of revenue the tariff yields. Total revenue from the tariff is determined by multiplying the tariff, $P_t - P_w$ per unit, by the number of smartphones imported, bc. This tariff revenue is a transfer of income from consumers to government and does not represent any net change in the nation's economic well-being. The result is that government gains this portion of what consumers lose by paying more for smartphones.

Indirect Effect Tariffs have a subtle effect beyond what our supply and demand diagram can show. Because China sells fewer smartphones in the United States, it earns fewer dollars and so must buy fewer U.S. exports. U.S. export industries must then cut production and release resources. These are highly efficient industries, as we know from their comparative advantage and their ability to sell goods in world markets.

Tariffs directly promote the expansion of inefficient industries that do not have a comparative advantage; they also indirectly cause the contraction of relatively efficient industries that do have a comparative advantage. Put bluntly, tariffs cause resources to be shifted in the wrong direction—and that is not surprising. We know that specialization and world trade lead to more efficient use of world resources and greater world output. But protective

FIGURE 26.6 The economic effects of a protective tariff or an import quota. A tariff that increases the price of a good from P_w to P_t will reduce domestic consumption from d to c. Domestic producers will be able to sell more output (b rather than a) at a higher price (P_t rather than P_w). Foreign exporters are injured because they sell less output (bc rather than ad). The yellow area indicates the amount of tariff paid by domestic consumers. An import quota of bc units has the same effect as the tariff, with one exception: The amount represented by the yellow area will go to foreign producers rather than to the domestic government.

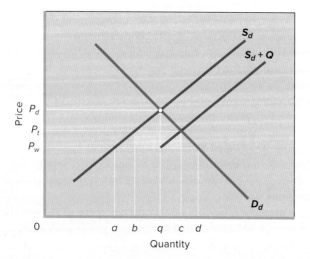

tariffs reduce world trade. Therefore, tariffs also reduce efficiency and the world's real output.

Economic Impact of Quotas

We noted earlier that an import quota is a legal limit placed on the amount of some product that can be imported in a given year. Quotas have the same economic impact as a tariff, with one big difference: While tariffs generate revenue for the domestic government, a quota transfers that revenue to foreign producers.

Suppose in Figure 26.6 that, instead of imposing a tariff, the United States prohibits any imports of Chinese smartphones players in excess of bc units. In other words, an import quota of bc smartphones is imposed on China. We deliberately chose the size of this quota to be the same amount as imports would be under a $P_t - P_w$ tariff so that we can compare "equivalent" situations. As a consequence of the quota, the supply of smartphones is $S_d + Q$ in the United States. This supply consists of the domestic supply plus the fixed amount bc $(= Q)$ that importers will provide at each domestic price. The supply curve $S_w + Q$ does not extend below price P_w because Chinese producers would not export smartphones to the United States at any price below P_w; instead, they would sell them to other countries at the world market price of P_w.

Most of the economic results are the same as those with a tariff. Prices of smartphones are higher (P_t instead of P_w) because imports have been reduced from ad to bc. Domestic consumption of smartphones is down from d to c. U.S. producers enjoy both a higher price (P_t rather than P_w) and increased sales (b rather than a).

The difference is that the price increase of $P_t - P_w$ paid by U.S. consumers on imports of bc—the yellow area—no longer goes to the U.S. Treasury as tariff (tax) revenue but flows to the Chinese firms that have acquired the quota rights to sell smartphones in the United States. For consumers in the United States, a tariff produces a better economic outcome than a quota, other things being the same. A tariff generates government revenue that can be used to cut other taxes or to finance public goods and services that benefit the United States. In contrast, the higher price created by quotas results in additional revenue for foreign producers.

QUICK REVIEW 26.5

✓ A tariff on a product increases its price, reduces its consumption, increases its domestic production, reduces its imports, and generates tariff revenue for the government.

✓ An import quota does the same, except a quota generates revenue for foreign producers rather than for the government imposing the quota.

Net Costs of Tariffs and Quotas

Figure 26.6 shows that tariffs and quotas impose costs on domestic consumers but provide gains to domestic producers and, in the case of tariffs, revenue to the federal government. The consumer costs of trade restrictions are calculated by determining the effect the restrictions have on consumer prices. Protection raises the price of a product in three ways: (1) The price of the imported product goes up; (2) the higher price of imports causes some consumers to shift their purchases to higher-priced domestically produced goods; and (3) the prices of domestically produced goods rise because import competition has declined.

Study after study finds that the costs to consumers substantially exceed the gains to producers and government. A sizable net cost or efficiency loss to society arises from trade protection. Furthermore, industries employ large amounts of economic resources to influence Congress to pass and retain protectionist laws. Because these rent-seeking efforts divert resources away from more socially desirable purposes, trade restrictions impose these additional costs on society as well.

Conclusion: The gains that U.S. trade barriers create for protected industries and their workers come at the expense of much greater losses for the entire economy. The result is economic inefficiency, reduced consumption, and lower standards of living.

The Case for Protection: A Critical Review

LO26.5 Analyze the validity of the most frequently presented arguments for protectionism.

Despite the logic of specialization and trade, there are still protectionists in some union halls, corporate boardrooms, and congressional conference rooms. What arguments do protectionists make to justify trade barriers? How valid are those arguments?

Military Self-Sufficiency Argument

The argument here is not economic but political-military: Protective tariffs are needed to preserve or strengthen industries that produce the materials essential for national defense. In an uncertain world, the political-military objectives (self-sufficiency) sometimes must take precedence over economic goals (efficiency in the use of world resources).

Unfortunately, it is difficult to measure and compare the benefit of increased national security against the cost of economic inefficiency when protective tariffs are imposed. The economist can only point out that when a nation levies tariffs to increase military self-sufficiency, it incurs economic costs.

All people in the United States would agree that relying on hostile nations for necessary military equipment is not a good idea, yet the self-sufficiency argument is open to serious abuse. Nearly every industry can claim that it makes direct or indirect contributions to national security and hence deserves protection from imports.

Diversification-for-Stability Argument

Highly specialized economies such as Saudi Arabia (based on oil) and Cuba (based on sugar) are dependent on international markets for their income. In these economies, wars, international political developments, recessions abroad, and random fluctuations in world supply and demand for one or two particular goods can cause deep declines in export revenues and therefore in domestic income. Tariff and quota protection are allegedly needed in such nations to enable greater industrial diversification. That way, these economies will not be so dependent on exporting one or two products to obtain the other goods they need. Such goods will be available domestically, thereby providing greater domestic stability.

There is some truth in this diversification-for-stability argument. But the argument has little or no relevance to the United States and other advanced economies. Also, the economic costs of diversification may be great; for example, one-crop economies may be highly inefficient at manufacturing.

Infant Industry Argument

The infant industry argument contends that protective tariffs are needed to allow new domestic industries to establish themselves. Temporarily shielding young domestic firms from the severe competition of more mature and more efficient foreign firms will give infant industries a chance to develop and become efficient producers.

This argument for protection rests on an alleged exception to the case for free trade. The exception is that young industries have not had, and if they face mature foreign competition will never have, the chance to make the long-run adjustments needed for larger scale and greater efficiency in production. In this view, tariff protection for such infant industries will correct a misallocation of world resources perpetuated by historically different levels of economic development between domestic and foreign industries.

There are some logical problems with the infant industry argument. In the developing nations, it is difficult to determine which industries are the infants that are capable of achieving economic maturity and therefore deserving protection. Also, protective tariffs may persist even after industrial maturity has been realized.

Most economists feel that if infant industries are to be subsidized, there are better means than tariffs for doing so. Direct subsidies, for example, have the advantage of making explicit which industries are being aided and to what degree.

Protection-against-Dumping Argument

The protection-against-dumping argument contends that tariffs are needed to protect domestic firms from "dumping" by foreign producers. **Dumping** is the sale of a product in a foreign country at prices either below cost or below the prices commonly charged at home.

Economists cite two plausible reasons for this behavior. First, with regard to below-cost dumping, firms in country A may dump goods at below cost into country B in an attempt to drive their competitors in country B out of business. If the firms in country A succeed in driving their competitors in country B out of business, they will enjoy monopoly power and monopoly prices and profits on the goods they subsequently sell in country B. Their hope is that the longer-term monopoly profits will more than offset the losses from below-cost sales that must take place while they are attempting to drive their competitors in country B out of business.

Second, dumping that involves selling abroad at a price that is below the price commonly charged in the home country (but that is still at or above production costs) may be a form of price discrimination, which is charging different prices to different customers. As an example, a foreign seller that has a monopoly in its home market may find that it can maximize its overall profit by charging a high price in its monopolized domestic market while charging a lower price in the United States, where it must compete with U.S. producers. Curiously, it may pursue this strategy even if it makes no profit at all from its sales in the United States, where it must charge the competitive price. So why bother selling in the United States? Because the increase in overall production that comes about by exporting to the United States may allow the firm to obtain the per-unit cost savings often associated with large-scale production. These cost savings imply even higher profits in the monopolized domestic market.

Because dumping is an "unfair trade practice," most nations prohibit it. For example, where dumping is shown to injure U.S. firms, the federal government imposes tariffs called *antidumping duties* on the goods in question. But relatively few documented cases of dumping occur each year, and specific instances of unfair trade do not justify widespread, permanent tariffs. Moreover, antidumping duties can be abused. Often, what appears to be dumping is simply comparative advantage at work.

Increased Domestic Employment Argument

Arguing for a tariff to "save U.S. jobs" becomes fashionable when the economy encounters a recession (such as the severe recession of 2007–2008 in the United States). In an economy that engages in international trade, exports involve spending on domestic output and imports reflect spending to obtain part of another nation's output. So, in this argument, reducing imports will divert spending on another nation's output to spending on domestic output. Thus, domestic output and employment will rise. But this argument has several shortcomings.

While imports may eliminate some U.S. jobs, they create others. Imports may have eliminated the jobs of some U.S. steel and textile workers in recent years, but other workers have gained jobs unloading ships, flying imported aircraft, and selling imported electronic equipment. Import restrictions alter the composition of employment, but they may have little or no effect on the volume of employment.

The *fallacy of composition*—the false idea that what is true for the part is necessarily true for the whole—is also present in this rationale for tariffs. All nations cannot simultaneously succeed in restricting imports while maintaining their exports; what is true for one nation is not true for all nations. The exports of one nation must be the imports of another nation. To the extent that one country is able to expand its economy through an excess of exports over imports, the resulting excess of imports over exports worsens another economy's unemployment problem. It is no wonder that tariffs and import quotas meant to achieve domestic full employment are called "beggar my neighbor" policies: They achieve short-run domestic goals by making trading partners poorer.

Moreover, nations adversely affected by tariffs and quotas are likely to retaliate, causing a "trade war" (more precisely, a *trade barrier war*) that will choke off trade and make all nations worse off. The **Smoot-Hawley Tariff Act** of 1930 is a classic example. Although that act was meant to reduce imports and stimulate U.S. production, the high tariffs it authorized prompted adversely affected nations to retaliate with tariffs equally high. International trade fell, lowering the output and income of all nations. Economic historians generally agree that the Smoot-Hawley Tariff Act was a contributing cause of the Great Depression.

Finally, forcing an excess of exports over imports cannot succeed in raising domestic employment over the long run. It is through U.S. imports that foreign nations earn dollars for buying U.S. exports. In the long run, a nation must import in order to export. The long-run impact of tariffs is not an increase in domestic employment but, at best, a reallocation of workers away from export industries and to protected domestic industries. This shift implies a less efficient allocation of resources.

Cheap Foreign Labor Argument

The cheap foreign labor argument says that domestic firms and workers must be shielded from the ruinous competition of countries where wages are low. If protection is not provided, cheap imports will flood U.S. markets and the prices of U.S. goods—along with the wages of U.S. workers—will be pulled down. That is, domestic living standards in the United States will be reduced.

This argument can be rebutted at several levels. The logic of the argument suggests that it is not mutually beneficial for rich and poor persons to trade with one another. However, that is not the case. A low-income farmworker may pick lettuce or tomatoes for a rich landowner, and both may benefit from the transaction. And both U.S. consumers and Chinese workers gain when they "trade" a pair of athletic shoes priced at $30 as opposed to U.S. consumers being restricted to buying a similar shoe made in the United States for $60.

Also, recall that gains from trade are based on comparative advantage, not on absolute advantage. Look back at Figure 26.1, where we supposed that the United States and Mexico had labor forces of exactly the same size. Noting the positions of the production possibilities curves, observe that U.S. labor can produce more of either good. Thus, it is more productive. Because of this greater productivity, we can expect wages and living standards to be higher for U.S. labor. Mexico's less productive labor will receive lower wages.

The cheap foreign labor argument suggests that, to maintain its standard of living, the United States should not trade with low-wage Mexico. What if it does not trade with Mexico? Will wages and living standards rise in the United States as a result? No. To obtain vegetables, the United States will have to reallocate a portion of its labor from its relatively more-efficient beef industry to its relatively less-efficient vegetables industry. As a result, the average productivity of U.S. labor will fall, as will real wages and living standards. The labor forces of both countries will have diminished standards of living because without specialization and trade they will have less output available to them. Compare column 4 with column 1 in Table 26.1 or points A' and Z' with A and Z in Figure 26.2 to confirm this point.

Another problem with the cheap foreign labor argument is that its proponents incorrectly focus on labor costs per hour when what really matters is labor costs per unit of output. As an example, suppose that a U.S. factory pays its workers $20 per hour while a factory in a developing country pays its workers $4 per hour. The proponents of the cheap foreign labor argument look at these numbers and conclude—incorrectly—that it is impossible for the U.S. factory to compete with the factory in the developing country. But this conclusion fails to take into account two crucial facts:

- What actually matters is labor costs *per unit of output*, not labor costs *per hour of work*.
- Differences in productivity typically mean that labor costs per unit of output are often nearly identical despite huge differences in hourly labor costs.

To see why these points matter so much, let's take into account how productive the two factories are. Because the U.S. factory uses much more sophisticated technology, better-trained workers, and a lot more capital per worker, one worker in one hour can produce 20 units of output. Since the U.S. workers get paid $20 per hour, this means the U.S. factory's labor cost *per unit of output* is $1. The factory in the developing country is much less productive since it uses less efficient technology and its relatively untrained workers have a lot less machinery and equipment to work with. A worker there produces only 4 units per hour. Given the foreign wage of $4 per hour, this means that the labor cost per unit of output at the factory in the developing country is also $1.

As you can see, the lower wage rate per hour at the factory in the developing country does not translate into lower labor costs per unit—meaning that it won't be able to undersell its U.S. competitor just because its workers get paid lower wages per hour.

Proponents of the cheap foreign labor argument tend to focus exclusively on the large international differences that exist in labor costs per hour. They typically fail to mention that these differences in labor costs per hour are mostly the result of tremendously large differences in productivity and that these large differences in productivity serve to equalize labor costs per unit of output. As a result, firms in developing countries only *sometimes* have an advantage in terms of labor costs per unit of output. Whether they do in any specific situation will vary by industry and firm and will depend on differences in productivity as well as differences in labor costs per hour. For many goods, labor productivity in high-wage countries like the United States is so much higher than labor productivity in low-wage countries that it is actually cheaper *per unit of output* to manufacture those goods in high-wage countries. That is why, for instance, Intel still makes microchips in the United States and why most automobiles are still produced in the United States, Japan, and Europe rather than in low-wage countries.

QUICK REVIEW 26.6

✓ Most rationales for trade protections are special-interest requests that, if followed, would create gains for protected industries and their workers at the expense of greater losses for the economy.

Multilateral Trade Agreements and Free-Trade Zones

LO26.6 Identify and explain the objectives of GATT, WTO, EU, eurozone, and NAFTA and discuss offshoring and trade adjustment assistance.

Aware of the detrimental effects of trade wars and the general weaknesses of arguments for trade protections, nations have worked to lower tariffs worldwide. Their pursuit of freer trade has been aided by recently emerged special-interest groups that have offset the more-established special-interest groups that have traditionally supported tariffs and quotas. Specifically, lower tariffs are now supported by exporters of goods and services, importers of foreign components used in "domestic" products, and domestic sellers of imported products.

General Agreement on Tariffs and Trade

In 1947, 23 nations, including the United States, signed the **General Agreement on Tariffs and Trade (GATT).** GATT was based on three principles: (1) equal, nondiscriminatory trade treatment for all member nations; (2) the reduction of tariffs by multilateral negotiation; and (3) the elimination of import quotas. Basically, GATT provided a forum for the multilateral negotiation of reduced trade barriers.

Since the Second World War, member nations have completed eight "rounds" of GATT negotiations to reduce trade barriers. The eighth round of negotiations began in Uruguay in 1986. After seven years of complex discussions, in 1993 a new agreement was reached by the 128 nations that were by that time members of GATT. The Uruguay Round agreement took effect on January 1, 1995, and its provisions were phased in through 2005.

Under this agreement, tariffs on thousands of products were eliminated or reduced, with overall tariffs dropping by 33 percent. The agreement also liberalized government rules that in the past impeded the global market for such services as advertising, legal services, tourist services, and financial services. Quotas on imported textiles and apparel were phased out and replaced with tariffs. Other provisions reduced agricultural subsidies paid to farmers and protected intellectual property (patents, trademarks, and copyrights) against piracy.

World Trade Organization

The Uruguay Round agreement established the **World Trade Organization (WTO)** as GATT's successor. Some 161 nations belonged to the WTO in 2015. The WTO oversees trade agreements reached by the member nations, and rules on trade disputes among them. It also provides forums for further rounds of trade negotiations. The ninth and latest round of negotiations—the **Doha Development Agenda**—was launched in Doha, Qatar, in late 2001. (The trade rounds occur over several years in several venues but are named after the city or country of origination.) The negotiations are aimed at further reducing tariffs and quotas, as well as agricultural subsidies that distort trade. You can get an update on the status of the complex negotiations at **www.wto.org.**

GATT and the WTO have been positive forces in the trend toward liberalized world trade. The trade rules agreed upon by the member nations provide a strong and necessary bulwark against the protectionism called for by the special-interest groups in the various nations.

For that reason and others, the WTO is quite controversial. Critics are concerned that rules crafted to expand international trade and investment enable firms to circumvent national laws that protect workers and the environment. Critics ask: What good are minimum-wage laws, worker-safety laws, collective-bargaining rights, and environmental laws if firms can easily shift their production to nations that have weaker laws or if consumers can buy goods produced in those countries?

Proponents of the WTO respond that labor and environmental protections should be pursued directly in nations that have low standards and via international organizations other than the WTO. These issues should not be linked to the process of trade liberalization, which confers widespread economic benefits across nations. Moreover, say proponents of the WTO, many environmental and labor concerns are greatly overblown. Most world trade is among advanced industrial countries, not between them and countries that have lower environmental and labor standards. Moreover, the free flow of goods and resources raises output and income in the developing nations. Historically, such increases in living standards have eventually resulted in stronger, not weaker, protections for the environment and for workers.

The European Union

Countries have also sought to reduce tariffs by creating regional free-trade zones. The most dramatic example is the **European Union (EU).** Initiated in 1958 as the Common Market, in 2003 the EU comprised 15 European nations—Austria, Belgium, Denmark, Finland, France, Germany, Greece, Ireland, Italy, Luxembourg, the Netherlands, Portugal, Spain, Sweden, and the United Kingdom. In 2004, the EU expanded by 10 additional European countries—Cyprus, the Czech Republic, Estonia, Hungary, Latvia, Lithuania, Malta, Poland, Slovakia, and Slovenia. The 2007 addition of Bulgaria and Romania plus the 2013 addition of Croatia expanded the EU to 28 nations.

The EU has abolished tariffs and import quotas on nearly all products traded among the participating nations and established a common system of tariffs applicable to all goods received from nations outside the EU. It has also liberalized the movement of capital and labor within the EU and has created common policies in other economic matters of joint concern, such as agriculture, transportation, and business practices.

EU integration has achieved for Europe what the U.S. constitutional prohibition on tariffs by individual states has achieved for the United States: increased regional specialization, greater productivity, greater output, and faster economic growth. The free flow of goods and services has created large markets for EU industries. The resulting economies of large-scale production have enabled these industries to achieve much lower costs than they could have achieved in their small, single-nation markets.

One of the most significant accomplishments of the EU was the establishment of the so-called **eurozone** or euro area in the early 2000s. As of 2015, 19 members of the EU (Austria, Belgium, Cyprus, Estonia, Finland, France, Germany, Greece, Ireland, Italy, Latvia, Lithuania, Luxembourg, Malta, the Netherlands, Portugal, Slovenia, Slovakia, and Spain) use the euro as a common currency. Notably, the United Kingdom, Denmark, and Sweden have opted not to use the common currency, at least for now. But gone are French francs, German marks, Italian liras, and other national currencies that were once used by eurozone countries.

Economists expect the adoption of the euro to raise the standard of living in the eurozone nations over time. By ending the inconvenience and expense of exchanging currencies, the euro has enhanced the free flow of goods, services, and resources among the eurozone members. Companies that previously sold products in only one or two European nations have found it easier to price and sell their products in all 19 eurozone countries. The euro has also allowed consumers and businesses to comparison shop for outputs and inputs, and this capability has increased competition, reduced prices, and lowered costs.

North American Free Trade Agreement

In 1993 Canada, Mexico, and the United States created a major free-trade zone. The **North American Free Trade Agreement (NAFTA)** established a free-trade area that has about the same combined output as the EU but encompasses a much larger geographic area. NAFTA has eliminated tariffs and other trade barriers among Canada, Mexico, and the United States for most goods and services.

Critics of NAFTA feared that it would cause a massive loss of U.S. jobs as firms moved to Mexico to take advantage of lower wages and weaker regulations on pollution and workplace safety. Also, they were concerned that Japan and South Korea would build plants in Mexico and transport goods tariff-free to the United States, further hurting U.S. firms and workers.

In retrospect, critics were much too pessimistic. Since the passage of NAFTA in 1993, employment in the United States has increased by more than 25 million workers. NAFTA has increased trade among Canada, Mexico, and the United States and has enhanced the standard of living in all three countries.

QUICK REVIEW 26.7

✓ The General Agreement on Tariffs and Trade (GATT) of 1947 reduced tariffs and quotas and established a process for numerous subsequent rounds of multinational trade negotiations that have liberalized international trade.

✓ The World Trade Organization (WTO)—GATT's successor—rules on trade disputes and provides forums for negotiations on further rounds of trade liberalization. The current round of negotiations is called the Doha Development Agenda.

✓ The European Union (EU) and the North American Free Trade Agreement (NAFTA) have reduced internal trade barriers among their member nations by establishing multination free-trade zones.

Recognizing Those Hurt by Free Trade

Shifts in patterns of comparative advantage and removal of long-standing trade protection can hurt specific groups of workers. For example, the erosion of the United States' once strong comparative advantage in steel has caused production plant shutdowns and layoffs in the U.S. steel industry. The textile and apparel industries in the United States face similar difficulties. Clearly, not everyone wins from free trade (or freer trade). Some workers lose.

Trade Adjustment Assistance

The **Trade Adjustment Assistance Act** of 2002 introduced some innovative policies to help those hurt by shifts in international trade patterns. The law provides cash assistance (beyond unemployment insurance) for up to 78 weeks for workers displaced by imports or plant relocations abroad. To obtain the assistance, workers must participate in job searches, training programs, or remedial education. Also provided are relocation allowances to help displaced workers move geographically to new jobs within the United States. Refundable tax credits for health insurance serve as payments to help workers maintain their insurance coverage during the retraining and job-search period. Workers who are 50 years of age or older are eligible for "wage insurance," which replaces some of the difference in pay (if any) between their old and new jobs. Many economists support trade adjustment assistance because it not only helps workers hurt by international trade but also helps create the political support necessary to reduce trade barriers and export subsidies.

But not all economists favor trade adjustment assistance. Loss of jobs from imports, sending some work abroad, and plant relocations to other countries are only a small fraction (about 4 percent in recent years) of total job losses in the economy each year. Many workers also lose their jobs because of changing patterns of demand, changing technology, bad management, and other dynamic aspects of a market economy. Some critics ask, "What makes losing one's job to international trade worthy of such special treatment, compared to losing one's job to, say, technological change or domestic competition?" Economists can find no totally satisfying answer.

Offshoring of Jobs

Not only are some U.S. jobs lost because of international trade, but some are lost because of globalization of resource markets. In recent years, U.S. firms have found the outsourcing of work abroad to be increasingly profitable. Economists call this business activity **offshoring**—shifting work previously done by American workers to workers located in other nations. Offshoring is not a new practice but traditionally has involved components for U.S. manufacturing goods. For example, Boeing has long offshored the production of major airplane parts for its "American" aircraft.

Recent advances in computer and communications technology have enabled U.S. firms to offshore service jobs such as data entry, book composition, software coding, call-center operations, medical transcription, and claims processing to countries such as India. Where offshoring occurs, some of the value added in the production process accrues to foreign countries rather than the United States. So part of the income generated from the production of U.S. goods is paid to foreigners, not to American workers.

Offshoring is a wrenching experience for many Americans who lose their jobs, but it is not necessarily bad for the overall economy. Offshoring simply reflects growing specialization and international trade in services, or, more descriptively, "tasks." That growth has been made possible by recent trade agreements and new information and communication technologies. As with trade in goods, trade in services reflects comparative advantage and is beneficial to both trading parties. Moreover, the United States has a sizable trade surplus with other nations in services. The United States gains by specializing in high-valued services such as transportation services, accounting services, legal services, and advertising services, where it still has a comparative advantage. It then "trades" to obtain lower-valued services such as call-center and data-entry work, for which comparative advantage has gone abroad.

Offshoring also increases the demand for complementary jobs in the United States. Jobs that are close substitutes for existing U.S. jobs are lost, but complementary jobs in the United States are expanded. For example, the lower price of writing software code in India may mean a lower cost of software sold in the United States and abroad. That, in turn, may create more jobs for U.S.-based workers such as software designers, marketers, and distributors. Moreover, offshoring may encourage domestic investment and the expansion of firms in the United States by reducing their production costs and keeping them competitive worldwide. In some instances, "offshoring jobs" may equate to "importing competitiveness." Entire firms that might otherwise disappear abroad may remain profitable in the United States only because they can offshore some of their work.

> ### QUICK REVIEW 26.8
> ✓ Increased international trade and offshoring of jobs have harmed some specific U.S. workers and have led to policies such as trade adjustment assistance to try to help them with their transitions to new lines of work.

Petition of the Candlemakers, 1845

French Economist Frédéric Bastiat (1801–1850) Devastated the Proponents of Protectionism by Satirically Extending Their Reasoning to Its Logical and Absurd Conclusions.

Petition of the Manufacturers of Candles, Waxlights, Lamps, Candlesticks, Street Lamps, Snuffers, Extinguishers, and of the Producers of Oil Tallow, Rosin, Alcohol, and, Generally, of Everything Connected with Lighting.

TO MESSIEURS THE MEMBERS OF THE CHAMBER OF DEPUTIES.

Gentlemen—You are on the right road. You reject abstract theories, and have little consideration for cheapness and plenty. Your chief care is the interest of the producer. You desire to emancipate him from external competition, and reserve the national market for national industry.

We are about to offer you an admirable opportunity of applying your—what shall we call it? your theory? No; nothing is more deceptive than theory; your doctrine? your system? your principle? but you dislike doctrines, you abhor systems, and as for principles, you deny that there are any in social economy: we shall say, then, your practice, your practice without theory and without principle.

We are suffering from the intolerable competition of a foreign rival, placed, it would seem, in a condition so far superior to ours for the production of light, that he absolutely inundates our national market with it at a price fabulously reduced. The moment he shows himself, our trade leaves us—all consumers apply to him; and a branch of native industry, having countless ramifications, is all at once rendered completely stagnant. This rival . . . is no other than the Sun.

What we pray for is, that it may please you to pass a law ordering the shutting up of all windows, skylights, dormer windows, outside and inside shutters, curtains, blinds, bull's-eyes; in a word, of all openings, holes, chinks, clefts, and fissures, by or through which the light of the sun has been in use to enter houses, to the prejudice of the meritorious manufacturers with which we flatter ourselves we have accommodated our country,—a country which, in gratitude, ought not to abandon us now to a strife so unequal.

Source: © J. Luke/PhotoLink/Getty Images RF

If you shut up as much as possible all access to natural light, and create a demand for artificial light, which of our French manufacturers will not be encouraged by it? If more tallow is consumed, then there must be more oxen and sheep; and, consequently, we shall behold the multiplication of artificial meadows, meat, wool, hides, and, above all, manure, which is the basis and foundation of all agricultural wealth.

The same remark applies to navigation. Thousands of vessels will proceed to the whale fishery; and, in a short time, we shall possess a navy capable of maintaining the honor of France, and gratifying the patriotic aspirations of your petitioners, the undersigned candle-makers and others.

Only have the goodness to reflect, Gentlemen, and you will be convinced that there is, perhaps, no Frenchman, from the wealthy coalmaster to the humblest vender of lucifer matches, whose lot will not be ameliorated by the success of this our petition.

Source: Frédéric Bastiat, *Economic Sophisms* (Irvington-on-Hudson, NY: The Foundation for Economic Education, Inc., 1996), abridged, **www.FEE.org**.

SUMMARY

LO26.1 List and discuss several key facts about international trade.

The United States leads the world in the combined volume of exports and imports. Other major trading nations are Germany, Japan, the western European nations, and the Asian economies of China, South Korea, Taiwan, and Singapore. The United States' principal exports include chemicals, agricultural products, consumer durables, semiconductors, and aircraft; principal imports include petroleum, automobiles, metals, household appliances, and computers.

LO26.2 Define comparative advantage and demonstrate how specialization and trade add to a nation's output.

World trade is based on three considerations: the uneven distribution of economic resources among nations, the fact that efficient production of various goods requires particular techniques or combinations of resources, and the differentiated products produced among nations.

Mutually advantageous specialization and trade are possible between any two nations if they have different domestic opportunity-cost ratios for any two products. By specializing on the basis of comparative advantage, nations can obtain larger real incomes with fixed amounts of resources. The terms of trade determine how this increase in world output is shared by the trading nations. Increasing (rather than constant) opportunity costs limit specialization and trade.

LO26.3 Describe how differences between world prices and domestic prices prompt exports and imports.

A nation's export supply curve shows the quantities of a product the nation will export at world prices that exceed the domestic price (the price in a closed, no-international-trade economy). A nation's import demand curve reveals the quantities of a product it will import at world prices below the domestic price.

In a two-nation model, the equilibrium world price and the equilibrium quantities of exports and imports occur where one nation's export supply curve intersects the other nation's import demand curve. A nation will export a particular product if the world price exceeds the domestic price; it will import the product if the world price is less than the domestic price. The country with the lower costs of production will be the exporter and the country with the higher costs of production will be the importer.

LO26.4 Analyze the economic effects of tariffs and quotas.

Trade barriers take the form of protective tariffs, quotas, nontariff barriers, and "voluntary" export restrictions. Export subsidies also distort international trade. Supply and demand analysis demonstrates that protective tariffs and quotas increase the prices and reduce the quantities demanded of the affected goods. Sales by foreign exporters diminish; domestic producers, however, gain higher prices and enlarged sales. Consumer losses from trade restrictions greatly exceed producer and government gains, creating an efficiency loss to society.

LO26.5 Analyze the validity of the most frequently presented arguments for protectionism.

The strongest arguments for protection are the infant industry and military self-sufficiency arguments. Most other arguments for protection are interest-group appeals or reasoning fallacies that emphasize producer interests over consumer interests or stress the immediate effects of trade barriers while ignoring long-run consequences.

The cheap foreign labor argument for protection fails because it focuses on labor costs per hour rather than on what really matters, labor costs per unit of output. Due to higher productivity, firms in high-wage countries like the United States can have lower wage costs per unit of output than competitors in low-wage countries. Whether they do will depend on how their particular wage and productivity levels compare with those of their competitors in low-wage countries.

LO26.6 Identify and explain the objectives of GATT, WTO, EU, eurozone, and NAFTA and discuss offshoring and trade adjustment assistance.

In 1947 the General Agreement on Tariffs and Trade (GATT) was formed to encourage nondiscriminatory treatment for all member nations, to reduce tariffs, and to eliminate import quotas. The Uruguay Round of GATT negotiations (1993) reduced tariffs and quotas, liberalized trade in services, reduced agricultural subsidies, reduced pirating of intellectual property, and phased out quotas on textiles.

GATT's successor, the World Trade Organization (WTO), had 161 member nations in 2015. It implements WTO agreements, rules on trade disputes between members, and provides forums for continued discussions on trade liberalization. The latest round of trade negotiations—the Doha Development Agenda—began in late 2001 and as of 2016 was still in progress.

Free-trade zones liberalize trade within regions. Two examples of free-trade arrangements are the 28-member European Union (EU) and the North American Free Trade Agreement (NAFTA), comprising Canada, Mexico, and the United States. Nineteen EU nations have abandoned their national currencies for a common currency called the euro.

The Trade Adjustment Assistance Act of 2002 recognizes that trade liberalization and increased international trade can create job loss for many workers. The Act therefore provides cash assistance, education and training benefits, health care subsidies, and wage subsidies (for persons aged 50 or older) to qualified workers displaced by imports or relocations of plants from the United States to abroad.

Offshoring is the practice of shifting work previously done by Americans in the United States to workers located in other nations. Although offshoring reduces some U.S. jobs, it lowers production costs, expands sales, and therefore may create other U.S. jobs. Less than 4 percent of all job losses in the United States each year are caused by imports, offshoring, and plant relocation abroad.

TERMS AND CONCEPTS

labor-intensive goods	export supply curve	Smoot-Hawley Tariff Act
land-intensive goods	import demand curve	General Agreement on Tariffs and Trade (GATT)
capital-intensive goods	equilibrium world price	World Trade Organization (WTO)
opportunity-cost ratio	tariffs	Doha Development Agenda
comparative advantage	revenue tariff	European Union (EU)
principle of comparative advantage	protective tariff	eurozone
terms of trade	import quota	North American Free Trade Agreement (NAFTA)
trading possibilities line	nontariff barrier (NTB)	Trade Adjustment Assistance Act
gains from trade	voluntary export restriction (VER)	offshoring
world price	export subsidy	
domestic price	dumping	

The following and additional problems can be found in ∎connect

DISCUSSION QUESTIONS

1. Quantitatively, how important is international trade to the United States relative to the importance of trade to other nations? What country is the United States' most important trading partner, quantitatively? With what country does the United States have the largest trade deficit? **LO26.1**

2. Distinguish among land-, labor-, and capital-intensive goods, citing an example of each without resorting to book examples. How do these distinctions relate to international trade? How do distinctive products, unrelated to resource intensity, relate to international trade? **LO26.1, LO26.2**

3. Explain: "The United States can make certain toys with greater productive efficiency than can China. Yet we import those toys from China." Relate your answer to the ideas of Adam Smith and David Ricardo. **LO26.2**

4. Suppose Big Country can produce 80 units of X by using all its resources to produce X or 60 units of Y by devoting all its resources to Y. Comparable figures for Small Nation are 60 units of X and 60 units of Y. Assuming constant costs, in which product should each nation specialize? Explain why. What are the limits of the terms of trade between these two countries? How would rising costs (rather than constant costs) affect the extent of specialization and trade between these two countries? **LO26.2**

5. What is an export supply curve? What is an import demand curve? How do such curves relate to the determination of the equilibrium world price of a tradable good? **LO26.3**

6. Why is a quota more detrimental to an economy than a tariff that results in the same level of imports as the quota? What is the net outcome of either tariffs or quotas for the world economy? **LO26.4**

7. "The potentially valid arguments for tariff protection—military self-sufficiency, infant industry protection, and diversification for stability—are also the most easily abused." Why are these arguments susceptible to abuse? **LO26.4**

8. Evaluate the effectiveness of artificial trade barriers, such as tariffs and import quotas, as a way to achieve and maintain full employment throughout the U.S. economy. How might such policies reduce unemployment in one U.S. industry but increase it in another U.S. industry? **LO26.4**

9. In 2013, manufacturing workers in the United States earned average compensation of $36.34 per hour. That same year, manufacturing workers in Mexico earned average compensation of $6.82 per hour. How can U.S. manufacturers possibly compete? Why isn't all manufacturing done in Mexico and other low-wage countries? **LO26.4**

10. How might protective tariffs reduce both the imports and the exports of the nation that levies tariffs? In what way do foreign firms that "dump" their products onto the U.S. market in effect provide bargains to American consumers? How might the import competition lead to quality improvements and cost reductions by American firms? **LO26.4**

11. Identify and state the significance of each of the following trade-related entities: (*a*) the WTO; (*b*) the EU; (*c*) the eurozone; and (*d*) NAFTA. **LO26.6**

12. What form does trade adjustment assistance take in the United States? How does such assistance promote political support for free-trade agreements? Do you think workers who lose their jobs because of changes in trade laws deserve special treatment relative to workers who lose their jobs because of other changes in the economy, say, changes in patterns of government spending? **LO26.6**

13. What is offshoring of white-collar service jobs and how does that practice relate to international trade? Why has offshoring increased over the past few decades? Give an example (other than that in the textbook) of how offshoring can eliminate some American jobs while creating other American jobs. **LO26.6**

14. **LAST WORD** What was the central point that Bastiat was trying to make in his imaginary petition of the candlemakers?

REVIEW QUESTIONS

1. In Country A, a worker can make 5 bicycles per hour. In Country B, a worker can make 7 bicycles per hour. Which country has an absolute advantage in making bicycles? **LO26.2**
   a. Country A.
   b. Country B.

2. In Country A, the production of 1 bicycle requires using resources that could otherwise be used to produce 11 lamps. In Country B, the production of 1 bicycle requires using resources that could otherwise be used to produce 15 lamps. Which country has a comparative advantage in making bicycles? **LO26.2**
   a. Country A.
   b. Country B.

3. True or False: If Country B has an absolute advantage over Country A in producing bicycles, it will also have a comparative advantage over Country A in producing bicycles. **LO26.2**

4. Suppose that the opportunity-cost ratio for sugar and almonds is $4S \equiv 1A$ in Hawaii but $1S \equiv 2A$ in California. Which state has the comparative advantage in producing almonds? **LO26.2**
   a. Hawaii.
   b. California.
   c. Neither.

5. Suppose that the opportunity-cost ratio for fish and lumber is $1F \equiv 1L$ in Canada but $2F \equiv 1L$ in Iceland. Then _____ should specialize in producing fish while _____ should specialize in producing lumber. **LO26.2**
   a. Canada; Iceland.
   b. Iceland; Canada.

6. Suppose that the opportunity-cost ratio for watches and cheese is $1C \equiv 1W$ in Switzerland but $1C \equiv 4W$ in Japan. At which of the following international exchange ratios (terms of trade) will Switzerland and Japan be willing to specialize and engage in trade with each other? **LO26.2**
   *Select **one or more** answers from the choices shown.*
   a. $1C \equiv 3W$.
   b. $1C \equiv \frac{1}{2}W$.
   c. $1C \equiv 5W$.
   d. $\frac{1}{2}C \equiv 1W$.
   e. $2C \equiv 1W$.

7. We see quite a bit of international trade in the real world. And trade is driven by specialization. So why don't we see full specialization—for instance, all cars in the world being made in South Korea, or all the mobile phones in the world being made in China? Choose the best answer from among the following choices. **LO26.2**
   a. High tariffs.
   b. Extensive import quotas.

c. Increasing opportunity costs.
d. Increasing returns.

8. Which of the following are benefits of international trade? **LO26.2**
   *Choose **one or more** answers from the choices shown.*
   a. A more efficient allocation of resources.
   b. A higher level of material well-being.
   c. Gains from specialization.
   d. Promoting competition.
   e. Deterring monopoly.
   f. Reducing the threat of war.

9. True or False: If a country is open to international trade, the domestic price can differ from the international price. **LO26.3**

10. Suppose that the current international price of wheat is $6 per bushel and that the United States is currently exporting 30 million bushels per year. If the United States suddenly became a closed economy with respect to wheat, would the domestic price of wheat in the United States end up higher or lower than $6? **LO26.3**
    a. Higher.
    b. Lower.
    c. The same.

11. Suppose that if Iceland and Japan were both closed economies, the domestic price of fish would be $100 per ton in Iceland and $90 per ton in Japan. If the two countries decided to open up to international trade with each other, which of the following could be the equilibrium international price of fish once they begin trading? **LO26.3**
    a. $75.
    b. $85.
    c. $95.
    d. $105.

12. Draw a domestic supply-and-demand diagram for a product in which the United States does not have a comparative advantage. What impact do foreign imports have on domestic price and quantity? On your diagram show a protective tariff that eliminates approximately one-half of the assumed imports. What are the price-quantity effects of this tariff on (*a*) domestic consumers, (*b*) domestic producers, and (*c*) foreign exporters? How would the effects of a quota that creates the same amount of imports differ? **LO26.4**

13. American apparel makers complain to Congress about competition from China. Congress decides to impose either a tariff or a quota on apparel imports from China. Which policy would Chinese apparel manufacturers prefer? **LO26.4**
    a. Tariff.
    b. Quota.

PROBLEMS

1. Assume that the comparative-cost ratios of two products—baby formula and tuna fish—are as follows in the nations of Canswicki and Tunata:

   Canswicki: 1 can baby formula $\equiv$ 2 cans tuna fish
   Tunata: 1 can baby formula $\equiv$ 4 cans tuna fish

   In what product should each nation specialize? Which of the following terms of trade would be acceptable to both nations: (a) 1 can baby formula $\equiv 2\frac{1}{2}$ cans tuna fish; (b) 1 can baby formula $\equiv$ 1 can tuna fish; (c) 1 can baby formula $\equiv$ 5 cans tuna fish? **LO26.2**

2. The accompanying hypothetical production possibilities tables are for New Zealand and Spain. Each country can produce apples and plums. Plot the production possibilities data for each of the two countries separately. Referring to your graphs, answer the following: **LO26.2**

New Zealand's Production Possibilities Table
(Millions of Bushels)

Product	Production Alternatives			
	A	**B**	**C**	**D**
Apples	0	20	40	60
Plums	15	10	5	0

Spain's Production Possibilities Table
(Millions of Bushels)

Product	Production Alternatives			
	R	**S**	**T**	**U**
Apples	0	20	40	60
Plums	60	40	20	0

a. What is each country's cost ratio of producing plums and apples?
b. Which nation should specialize in which product?
c. Show the trading possibilities lines for each nation if the actual terms of trade are 1 plum for 2 apples. (Plot these lines on your graph.)
d. Suppose the optimum product mixes before specialization and trade were alternative B in New Zealand and alternative S in Spain. What would be the gains from specialization and trade?

3. The following hypothetical production possibilities tables are for China and the United States. Assume that before specialization and trade, the optimal product mix for China is alternative B and for the United States is alternative U. **LO26.2**
   a. Are comparative-cost conditions such that the two areas should specialize? If so, what product should each produce?
   b. What is the total gain in apparel and chemical output that would result from such specialization?
   c. What are the limits of the terms of trade? Suppose that the actual terms of trade are 1 unit of apparel for 1 unit of chemicals and that 4 units of apparel are exchanged for 6 units of chemicals. What are the gains from specialization and trade for each nation?

	China Production Possibilities					
Product	**A**	**B**	**C**	**D**	**E**	**F**
Apparel (in thousands)	30	24	18	12	6	0
Chemicals (in tons)	0	6	12	18	24	30

	U.S. Production Possibilities					
Product	**R**	**S**	**T**	**U**	**V**	**W**
Apparel (in thousands)	10	8	6	4	2	0
Chemicals (in tons)	0	4	8	12	16	20

4. Refer to Figure 3.6. Assume that the graph depicts the U.S. domestic market for corn. How many bushels of corn, if any, will the United States export or import at a world price of $1, $2, $3, $4, and $5? Use this information to construct the U.S. export supply curve and import demand curve for corn. Suppose that the only other corn-producing nation is France, where the domestic price is $4. Which country will export corn; which country will import it? **LO26.3**

The Balance of Payments, Exchange Rates, and Trade Deficits

Learning Objectives

LO27.1 Explain how currencies of different nations are exchanged when international transactions take place.

LO27.2 Analyze the balance sheet the United States uses to account for the international payments it makes and receives.

LO27.3 Discuss how exchange rates are determined in currency markets that have flexible exchange rates.

LO27.4 Describe the differences between flexible and fixed exchange rates, including how changes in foreign exchange reserves bring about automatic changes in the domestic money supply under a fixed exchange rate.

LO27.5 Explain the current system of managed floating exchange rates.

LO27.6 Identify the causes and consequences of recent U.S. trade deficits.

LO27.7 (Appendix) Explain how exchange rates worked under the gold standard and Bretton Woods.

If you take a U.S. dollar to the bank and ask to exchange it for U.S. currency, you will get a puzzled look. If you persist, you may get a dollar's worth of change: One U.S. dollar can buy exactly one U.S. dollar. But on April 5, 2016, for example, 1 U.S. dollar could buy 3,087 Colombian pesos, 1.32 Australian dollars, 0.71 British pound, 1.31 Canadian dollars, 0.88 European euro, 110.48 Japanese yen, or 17.64 Mexican pesos. What explains this seemingly haphazard array of exchange rates?

In Chapter 26 we examined comparative advantage as the underlying economic basis of world trade and discussed the effects of barriers to free trade. Now we introduce the highly important monetary and financial aspects of international trade.

International Financial Transactions

LO27.1 Explain how currencies of different nations are exchanged when international transactions take place.

This chapter focuses on international financial transactions, the vast majority of which fall into two broad categories: international trade and international asset transactions. International trade involves either purchasing or selling currently produced goods or services across an international border.

Examples include an Egyptian firm exporting cotton to the United States and an American company hiring an Indian call center to answer its phones. International asset transactions involve the transfer of the property rights to either real or financial assets between the citizens of one country and the citizens of another country. International asset transactions include activities like buying foreign stocks or selling your house to a foreigner.

These two categories of international financial transactions reflect the fact that whether they live in different countries or the same country, individuals and firms can only exchange two things with each other: currently produced goods and services or assets. With regard to assets, however, money is by far the most commonly exchanged asset. Only rarely will you encounter a barter situation in which people directly exchange one nonmoney asset for another nonmoney asset—such as trading a car for 500 shares of Microsoft stock or a cow for 30 chickens and a tank of diesel fuel.

As a result, there are two basic types of transactions:

- People trading either goods or services for money.
- People trading assets for money.

In either case, money flows from the buyers of the goods, services, or assets to the sellers of the goods, services, or assets. In the context of international trade, importers are buyers and exporters are sellers. As a result, *imports cause outflows of money while exports cause inflows of money.*

When the buyers and sellers are both from places that use the same currency, there is no confusion about what type of money to use. Americans from California and Wisconsin will use their common currency, the dollar. People from France and Germany will use their common currency, the euro. However, when the buyers and sellers are from places that use different currencies, intermediate asset transactions have to take place: The buyers must convert their own currencies into the currencies that the sellers use and accept.

As an example, consider the case of an English software company that wants to buy a supercomputer made by an American company. The American company sells these high-powered machines for $300,000. To pay for the machine, the English company has to convert some of the money it has (British pounds) into the money that the American company will accept (U.S. dollars). This process is not difficult. As we will soon explain in detail, there are many easy-to-use foreign exchange markets in which those who wish to sell pounds and buy dollars can interact with others who wish to sell dollars and buy pounds. The demand and supply created by these two groups determine the equilibrium exchange rate, which, in turn, determines how many pounds our English company will have to convert to pay for the supercomputer. For instance, if the exchange rate is £1= $2, then the English company will have to convert £150,000 to obtain the $300,000 necessary to purchase the computer.

The Balance of Payments

LO27.2 Analyze the balance sheet the United States uses to account for the international payments it makes and receives.

A nation's **balance of payments** is the sum of all the financial transactions that take place between its residents and the residents of foreign nations. Most of these transactions fall into the two main categories that we have just discussed: international trade and international asset transactions. As a result, nearly all the items included in the balance of payments are things such as exports and imports of goods, exports and imports of services, and international purchases and sales of financial and real assets. But the balance of payments also includes international transactions that fall outside of these main categories—things such as tourist expenditures, interest and dividends received or paid abroad, debt forgiveness, and remittances made by immigrants to their relatives back home.

The Bureau of Economic Analysis at the U.S. Department of Commerce compiles a balance-of-payments statement each year. This statement summarizes all of the millions of payments that individuals and firms in the United States receive from foreigners as well as all of the millions of payments that individuals and firms in the United States make to foreigners. It shows "flows" of inpayments of money *to* the United States and outpayments of money *from* the United States. For convenience, all of these money payments are given in terms of dollars. This is true despite the fact that some of them actually may have been made using foreign currencies—as when, for instance, an American company converts dollars into euros to buy something from an Italian company. When including this outpayment of money from the United States, the accountants who compile the balance-of-payments statement use the number of dollars the American company converted—rather than the number of euros that were actually used to make the purchase.

Table 27.1 is a simplified balance-of-payments statement for the United States in 2015. Because most international financial transactions fall into only two categories—international trade and international asset transactions—the balance-of-payments statement is organized into two broad

TABLE 27.1 **The U.S. Balance of Payments, 2015 (in Billions)**

CURRENT ACCOUNT		
(1) U.S. goods exports	$+1,513	
(2) U.S. goods imports	−2,273	
(3) *Balance on goods*		$−760
(4) U.S. exports of services	+710	
(5) U.S. imports of services	−491	
(6) *Balance on services*		+219
(7) *Balance on goods and services*		−541
(8) Net investment income	+191*	
(9) Net transfers	−136	
(10) **Balance on current account**		**−486**
CAPITAL AND FINANCIAL ACCOUNT		
Capital account		
(11) *Balance on capital account*		0
Financial account		
(12) Foreign purchases of assets in the United States	+589†	
(13) U.S. purchases of assets abroad	−103†	
(14) *Balance on financial account*		+486
(15) **Balance on capital and financial account**		+486
		$ 0

*Includes other, less significant, categories of income.
†Includes one-half of a $275 billion statistical discrepancy that is listed in the capital account.

Source: U.S. Department of Commerce, Bureau of Economic Analysis, **www.bea.gov**. Preliminary 2015 data. The export and import data are on a "balance-of-payment basis" and usually vary from the data on exports and imports reported in the National Income and Product Accounts.

categories. *The current account* located at the top of the table primarily treats international trade. *The capital and financial account* at the bottom of the table primarily treats international asset transactions.

Current Account

The top portion of Table 27.1 that mainly summarizes U.S. trade in currently produced goods and services is called the **current account.** Items 1 and 2 show U.S. exports and imports of goods (merchandise) in 2015. U.S. exports have a *plus* (+) sign because they are a *credit*; they generate flows of money toward the United States. U.S. imports have a *minus* (−) sign because they are a *debit*; they cause flows of money out of the United States.

Balance on Goods Items 1 and 2 in Table 27.1 reveal that in 2015 U.S. goods exports of $1,513 billion were less than U.S. goods imports of $2,273 billion. A country's *balance of trade on goods* is the difference between its exports and its imports of goods. If exports exceed imports, the result is a surplus on the balance of goods. If imports exceed exports, there is a trade deficit on the balance of goods. We note in item 3 that, in 2015, the United States incurred a trade deficit on goods of $760 billion.

Balance on Services The United States exports not only goods, such as airplanes and computer software, but also services, such as insurance, consulting, travel, and investment advice, to residents of foreign nations. Item 4 in Table 27.1 shows that these service "exports" totaled $710 billion in 2015. Since they generate flows of money toward the United States, they are a credit (thus the + sign). Item 5 indicates that the United States "imports" similar services from foreigners. Those service imports were $491 billion in 2015, and since they generate flows of money out of the United States, they are a debit (thus the − sign). Summed together, items 4 and 5 indicate that the balance on services (item 6) in 2015 was $219 billion. The **balance on goods and services** shown as item 7 is the difference between U.S. exports of goods and services (items 1 and 4) and U.S. imports of goods and services (items 2 and 5). In 2015, U.S. imports of goods and services exceeded U.S. exports of goods and services by $541 billion. So a **trade deficit** of that amount occurred. In contrast, a **trade surplus** occurs when exports of goods and services exceed imports of goods and services. (Global Perspective 27.1 shows U.S. trade deficits and surpluses with selected nations.)

Balance on Current Account Items 8 and 9 are not items relating directly to international trade in goods and

GLOBAL PERSPECTIVE 27.1

U.S. Trade Balances in Goods and Services, Selected Nations, 2015

The United States has large trade deficits in goods and services with several nations, in particular, China, Germany, and Japan.

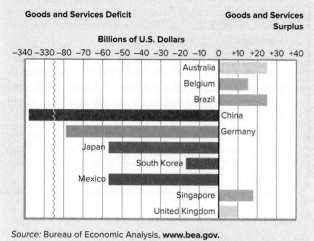

Source: Bureau of Economic Analysis, **www.bea.gov.**

services. But they are listed as part of the current account (which is mostly about international trade in goods and services) because they are international financial flows that in some sense compensate for things that can be conceptualized as being *like* international trade in either goods or services. For instance, item 8, *net investment income*, represents the difference between (1) the interest and dividend payments foreigners paid U.S. citizens and companies for the services provided by U.S. capital invested abroad ("exported" capital) and (2) the interest and dividends the U.S. citizens and companies paid for the services provided by foreign capital invested here ("imported" capital). Observe that in 2015 U.S. net investment income was a positive $191 billion.

Item 9 shows net transfers, both public and private, between the United States and the rest of the world. Included here is foreign aid, pensions paid to U.S. citizens living abroad, and remittances by immigrants to relatives abroad. These $136 billion of transfers are net U.S. outpayments (and therefore listed as a negative number in Table 27.1). They are listed as part of the current account because they can be thought of as the financial flows that accompany the exporting of goodwill and the importing of "thank you notes."

By adding all transactions in the current account, we obtain the **balance on current account** shown in item 10. In 2015 the United States had a current account deficit of

$486 billion. This means that the U.S. current account transactions created outpayments from the United States greater than inpayments to the United States.

Capital and Financial Account

The bottom portion of the current account statement summarizes U.S. international asset transactions. It is called the **capital and financial account** and consists of two separate accounts: the *capital account* and the *financial account*.

Capital Account The capital account mainly measures debt forgiveness—which is an asset transaction because the person forgiving a debt essentially hands the IOU back to the borrower. It is a "net" account (one that can be either + or −). The $0 billion listed in line 11 tells us that in 2015 foreigners forgave exactly as much debt owed to them by Americans as Americans forgave debt owed to them by foreigners. Any positive (+) entry in line 11 would indicate a credit; positive amounts are an "on-paper" inpayment (asset transfer) by the net amount of debt forgiven.

Financial Account The financial account summarizes international asset transactions having to do with international purchases and sales of real or financial assets. Line 12 lists the amount of foreign purchases of assets in the United States. It has a + sign because any purchase of an American-owned asset by a foreigner generates a flow of money toward the American who sells the asset. Line 13 lists U.S. purchases of assets abroad. These have a − sign because such purchases generate a flow of money from the Americans who buy foreign assets toward the foreigners who sell them those assets.

Items 12 and 13 added together yield a $486 billion balance on the financial account for 2015 (line 14). In 2015 the United States "exported" $589 billion of ownership of its real and financial assets and "imported" $103 billion. Thought of differently, this surplus in the financial account brought in income of $486 billion to the United States. The **balance on capital and financial account** (line 15) is also $486 billion. It is the sum of the $0 billion credit on the capital account and the $486 billion surplus on the financial account. Observe that this $486 billion surplus in the capital and financial account equals the $486 billion deficit in the current account. This is not an accident. The two numbers always equal—or "balance." That's why the statement is called the *balance* of payments. It has to balance. Let's see why.

Why the Balance?

The balance on the current account and the balance on the capital and financial account must always sum to zero because any deficit or surplus in the current account automatically creates an offsetting entry in the capital and financial account. People can only trade one of two things with each other: currently produced goods and services or preexisting assets. Therefore, if trading partners have an imbalance in their trade of currently produced goods and services, the only way to make up for that imbalance is with a net transfer of assets from one party to the other.

To see why this is true, suppose that John (an American) makes shoes and Henri (a Swiss citizen) makes watches and that the pair only trade with each other. Assume that their financial assets consist entirely of money, with each beginning the year with $1,000 in his bank account. Suppose that this year John exports $300 of shoes to Henri and imports $500 of watches from Henri. John therefore ends the year with a $200 goods deficit with Henri.

John and Henri's goods transactions, however, also result in asset exchanges that cause a net transfer of assets from John to Henri equal in size to John's $200 goods deficit with Henri. This is true because Henri pays John $300 for his shoes while John pays Henri $500 for his watches. The *net* result of these opposite-direction asset movements is that $200 of John's initial assets of $1,000 are transferred to Henri. This is unavoidable because the $300 John receives from his exports pays for only the first $300 of his $500 of imports. The only way for John to pay for the remaining $200 of imports is for him to transfer $200 of his initial asset holdings to Henri. Consequently, John's assets decline by $200 from $1,000 to $800, and Henri's assets rise from $1,000 to $1,200.

Consider how the transaction between John and Henri affects the U.S. balance-of-payments statement (Table 27.1), other things equal. John's $200 goods deficit with Henri shows up in the U.S. current account as a −$200 entry in the balance on goods account (line 3) and carries down to a −$200 entry in the balance on current account (line 10).

In the capital and financial account, this $200 is recorded as +$200 in the account labeled foreign purchases of assets in the United States (line 12). This +$200 then carries down to the balance on capital and financial account (line 15). Think of it this way: Henri has in essence used $200 worth of watches to purchase $200 of John's initial $1,000 holding of assets. The +$200 entry in line 12 (foreign purchases of assets in the United States) simply recognizes this fact. This +$200 exactly offsets the −$200 in the current account.

Thus, the balance of payments always balances. Any current account deficit or surplus in the top half of the statement automatically generates an offsetting international asset transfer that shows up in the capital and financial account in the bottom half of the statement. More specifically, current account deficits simultaneously generate transfers of assets to foreigners, while current account surpluses automatically generate transfers of assets from foreigners.

QUICK REVIEW 27.2

✓ A nation's balance-of-payments statement summarizes all of the international financial transactions that take place between its residents and the residents of all foreign nations. It includes the current account balance and the capital and financial account balance.

✓ The current account balance is a nation's exports of goods and services less its imports of goods and services plus its net investment income and net transfers.

✓ The capital and financial account balance includes the net amount of the nation's debt forgiveness as well as the nation's sale of real and financial assets to people living abroad less its purchases of real and financial assets from foreigners.

✓ The current account balance and the capital and financial account balance always sum to zero because any current account imbalance automatically generates an offsetting international asset transfer.

Flexible Exchange Rates

LO27.3 Discuss how exchange rates are determined in currency markets that have flexible exchange rates.

There are two pure types of exchange-rate systems:

- A **flexible- or floating-exchange-rate system** through which demand and supply determine exchange rates and in which no government intervention occurs.

- A **fixed-exchange-rate system** through which governments determine exchange rates and make necessary adjustments in their economies to maintain those rates.

We begin by looking at flexible exchange rates. Let's examine the rate, or price, at which U.S. dollars might be exchanged for British pounds in the market for foreign currency. In **Figure 27.1 (Key Graph)** we show demand D_1 and supply S_1 of pounds. Note that both the demand and supply of pounds are expressed in terms of U.S. dollars. They interact to determine the equilibrium price for pounds—which is expressed in terms of how many dollars are required to purchase one pound.

The *demand-for-pounds curve* D_1 is downsloping because all British goods and services will be cheaper to Americans if pounds become less expensive. That is, at lower dollar prices for pounds, Americans can obtain more pounds and therefore more British goods and services per dollar. To buy those cheaper British goods, U.S. consumers will increase the quantity of pounds they demand.

As a concrete example, suppose that you are a U.S. citizen on vacation in London. If it only takes 50 cents to buy 1 pound,

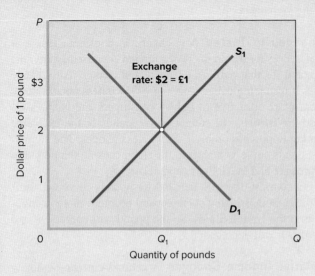

FIGURE 27.1 The market for foreign currency (pounds). The intersection of the demand-for-pounds curve D_1 and the supply-of-pounds curve S_1 determines the equilibrium dollar price of pounds, here, $2. That means that the exchange rate is $2 = £1. Not shown: An increase in demand for pounds or a decrease in supply of pounds will increase the dollar price of pounds and thus cause the pound to appreciate. Also not shown: A decrease in demand for pounds or an increase in the supply of pounds will reduce the dollar price of pounds, meaning that the pound has depreciated.

QUICK QUIZ FOR FIGURE 27.1

1. Which of the following statements is true?
   a. The quantity of pounds demanded falls when the dollar appreciates.
   b. The quantity of pounds supplied declines as the dollar price of the pound rises.
   c. At the equilibrium exchange rate, the pound price of $1 is $£\frac{1}{2}$.
   d. The dollar appreciates if the demand for pounds increases.

2. At the price of $2 for £1 in this figure:
   a. the dollar-pound exchange rate is unstable.
   b. the quantity of pounds supplied equals the quantity demanded.
   c. the dollar price of £1 equals the pound price of $1.
   d. U.S. goods exports to Britain must equal U.S. goods imports from Britain.

3. Other things equal, a leftward shift of the demand curve in this figure:
   a. would depreciate the dollar.
   b. would create a shortage of pounds at the previous price of $2 for £1.

   c. might be caused by a major recession in the United States.
   d. might be caused by a significant rise of real interest rates in Britain.

4. Other things equal, a rightward shift of the supply curve in this figure would:
   a. depreciate the dollar and might be caused by a significant rise of real interest rates in Britain.
   b. depreciate the dollar and might be caused by a significant fall of real interest rates in Britain.
   c. appreciate the dollar and might be caused by a significant rise of real interest rates in the United States.
   d. appreciate the dollar and might be caused by a significant fall of real interest rates in the United States.

you will end up wanting to buy a lot more souvenirs to take home than if it takes $1.50 to buy 1 pound. The lower the dollar price of purchasing a pound, the less expensive British goods and services will appear to you and the more dollars you will want to sell for pounds in order to get "cheap" British products. So the demand curve for pounds slopes downward.

The *supply-of-pounds curve* S_1 is upsloping because the British will purchase more U.S. goods when the dollar price of pounds rises (that is, as the pound price of dollars falls). When the British buy more U.S. goods, they supply a greater quantity of pounds to the foreign exchange market. In other words, they must exchange pounds for dollars to purchase U.S. goods. So, when the dollar price of pounds rises, the quantity of pounds supplied goes up.

As a concrete example, suppose that a Facebook friend from London wants to buy Google stock. Because Google is a U.S. company, he will need dollars to buy Google shares. If he can convert 1 pound into $3, he will want to buy a lot more shares of Google than if each pound only converts into $1.75. The more dollars he can get from selling a pound, the less expensive Google stock will appear to him and the more pounds he will want to sell in order to get "cheap" Google stock. So the supply curve for pounds slopes upward.

The intersection of the supply curve and the demand curve will determine the dollar price of pounds. Here, that price (exchange rate) is $2 for £1. At this exchange rate, the quantities of pounds supplied and demanded are equal; neither a shortage nor a surplus of pounds occurs.

Depreciation and Appreciation

An exchange rate determined by market forces can, and often does, change daily like stock and bond prices. When the dollar price of pounds *rises*, for example, from $2 = £1 to $3 = £1, the dollar has *depreciated* relative to the pound (and the pound has appreciated relative to the dollar). When a currency depreciates, more units of it (dollars) are needed to buy a single unit of some other currency (a pound).

When the dollar price of pounds *falls*, for example, from $2 = £1 to $1 = £1, the dollar has *appreciated* relative to the pound. When a currency appreciates, fewer units of it (dollars) are needed to buy a single unit of some other currency (pounds).

In our U.S.-Britain example, depreciation of the dollar means an appreciation of the pound, and vice versa. When the dollar price of a pound jumps from $2 = £1 to $3 = £1, the pound has appreciated relative to the dollar because it takes fewer pounds to buy $1. At $2 = £1, it took £$\frac{1}{2}$ to buy $1; at $3 = £1, it takes only £$\frac{1}{3}$ to buy $1. Conversely, when the dollar appreciated relative to the pound, the pound depreciated relative to the dollar. More pounds were needed to buy a dollar.

In general, the relevant terminology and relationships between the U.S. dollar and another currency are as follows (where the "≡" sign means "is equivalent to").

- Dollar price of foreign currency increases ≡ dollar depreciates relative to the foreign currency ≡ foreign currency price of dollar decreases ≡ foreign currency appreciates relative to the dollar.

- Dollar price of foreign currency decreases ≡ dollar appreciates relative to the foreign currency ≡ foreign currency price of dollar increases ≡ foreign currency depreciates relative to the dollar.

Determinants of Flexible Exchange Rates

What factors would cause a nation's currency to appreciate or depreciate in the market for foreign exchange? Here are three generalizations:

- If the demand for a nation's currency increases (other things equal), that currency will appreciate; if the demand declines, that currency will depreciate.

- If the supply of a nation's currency increases, that currency will depreciate; if the supply decreases, that currency will appreciate.

- If a nation's currency appreciates, some foreign currency depreciates relative to it.

With these generalizations in mind, let's examine the determinants of exchange rates—the factors that shift the demand or supply curve for a certain currency. As we do so, keep in mind that the other-things-equal assumption is always in force. Also note that we are discussing factors *that change the exchange rate*, not things that change *as a result of* a change in the exchange rate.

Changes in Tastes Any change in consumer tastes or preferences for the products of a foreign country may alter the demand for that nation's currency and change its exchange rate. If technological advances in U.S. wireless phones make them more attractive to British consumers and businesses, then the British will supply more pounds in the exchange market to purchase more U.S. wireless phones. The supply-of-pounds curve will shift to the right, causing the pound to depreciate and the dollar to appreciate.

In contrast, the U.S. demand-for-pounds curve will shift to the right if British woolen apparel becomes more fashionable in the United States. So the pound will appreciate and the dollar will depreciate.

Relative Income Changes A nation's currency is likely to depreciate if its growth of national income is more rapid than that of other countries. Here's why: A country's imports vary directly with its income level. As national income rises in the United States, Americans will buy both more domestic goods and more foreign goods. If the U.S. economy is expanding rapidly and the British economy is stagnant, U.S. imports of British goods, and therefore U.S. demands for pounds, will increase. The dollar price of pounds will rise, so the dollar will depreciate.

Relative Inflation Rate Changes Other things equal, changes in the relative rates of inflation of two nations change their relative price levels and alter the exchange rate between their currencies. The currency of the nation with the higher inflation rate—the more rapidly rising price level—tends to depreciate. Suppose, for example, that inflation is zero percent in Great Britain and 5 percent in the United States so that prices, on average, are rising by 5 percent per year in the United States while, on average, remaining unchanged in Great Britain. U.S. consumers will seek out more of the now relatively lower-priced British goods, increasing the demand for pounds. British consumers will purchase less of the now relatively higher-priced U.S. goods, reducing the supply of pounds. This combination of increased demand for pounds and reduced supply of pounds will cause the pound to appreciate and the dollar to depreciate.

According to the **purchasing-power-parity theory**, exchange rates should eventually adjust such that they equate the purchasing power of various currencies. If a certain market basket of identical products costs $10,000 in the United States and £5,000 in Great Britain, the exchange rate should move to $2 = £1. That way, a dollar spent in the United States will buy exactly as much output as it would if it were first converted to pounds (at the $2 = £1 exchange rate) and used to buy output in Great Britain.

In terms of our example, 5 percent inflation in the United States will increase the price of the market basket from $10,000 to $10,500, while the zero percent inflation in Great Britain will leave the market basket priced at £5,000. For purchasing power parity to hold, the exchange rate would have to move from $2 = £1 to $2.10 = £1. That means the dollar therefore would depreciate and the pound would appreciate. In practice, however, not all exchange rates move precisely to equate the purchasing power of various currencies and thereby achieve "purchasing power parity," even over long periods.

Relative Interest Rates Changes in relative interest rates between two countries may alter their exchange rate. Suppose that real interest rates rise in the United States but stay constant in Great Britain. British citizens will then find the United States a more attractive place in which to loan money directly or loan money indirectly by buying bonds. To make these loans, they will have to supply pounds in the foreign exchange market to obtain dollars. The increase in the supply of pounds results in depreciation of the pound and appreciation of the dollar.

Changes in Relative Expected Returns on Stocks, Real Estate, and Production Facilities International investing extends beyond buying foreign bonds. It includes international investments in stocks and real estate as well as foreign purchases of factories and production facilities. Other things equal, the extent of this foreign investment depends on relative expected returns. To make the investments, investors in one country must sell their currencies to purchase the foreign currencies needed for the foreign investments.

For instance, suppose that investing in England suddenly becomes more popular due to a more positive outlook regarding expected returns on stocks, real estate, and production facilities there. U.S. investors therefore will sell U.S. assets to buy more assets in England. The U.S. assets will be sold for dollars, which will then be brought to the foreign exchange market and exchanged for pounds, which will in turn be used to purchase British assets. The increased demand for pounds in the foreign exchange market will cause the pound to appreciate and therefore the dollar to depreciate relative to the pound.

Speculation Currency speculators are people who buy and sell currencies with an eye toward reselling or repurchasing them at a profit. Suppose speculators expect the U.S. economy to (1) grow more rapidly than the British economy and (2) experience more rapid inflation than Britain. These expectations translate into an anticipation that the pound will appreciate and the dollar will depreciate. Speculators who are holding dollars will therefore try to convert them into pounds. This effort will increase the demand for pounds and cause the dollar price of pounds to rise (that is, cause the dollar to depreciate). A self-fulfilling prophecy occurs: The pound appreciates and the dollar depreciates because speculators act on the belief that these changes will in fact take place. In this way, speculation can cause changes in exchange rates.

Table 27.2 has more illustrations of the determinants of exchange rates; the table is worth careful study.

Disadvantages of Flexible Exchange Rates

Flexible exchange rates may cause several significant problems. These are all related to the fact that flexible exchange rates are often volatile and can change by a large amount in

TABLE 27.2 **Determinants of Exchange Rates: Factors That Change the Demand for or the Supply of a Particular Currency and Thus Alter the Exchange Rate**

Determinant	Examples
Change in tastes	Japanese electronic equipment declines in popularity in the United States (Japanese yen depreciates; U.S. dollar appreciates).
	European tourists reduce visits to the United States (U.S. dollar depreciates; European euro appreciates).
Change in relative incomes	England encounters a recession, reducing its imports, while U.S. real output and real income surge, increasing U.S. imports (British pound appreciates; U.S. dollar depreciates).
Change in relative inflation rates	Switzerland experiences a 3% inflation rate compared to Canada's 10% rate (Swiss franc appreciates; Canadian dollar depreciates).
Change in relative real interest rates	The Federal Reserve drives up interest rates in the United States, while the Bank of England takes no such action (U.S. dollar appreciates; British pound depreciates).
Changes in relative expected returns on stocks, real estate, or production facilities	Corporate tax cuts in the United States raise expected after-tax investment returns in the United States relative to those in Europe (U.S. dollar appreciates; the euro depreciates).
Speculation	Currency traders believe South Korea will have much greater inflation than Taiwan (South Korean won depreciates; Taiwanese dollar appreciates).
	Currency traders think Norway's interest rates will plummet relative to Denmark's rates (Norway's krone depreciates; Denmark's krone appreciates).

FIGURE 27.2 The dollar-pound exchange rate, 1970–2015. Before January 1971, the dollar-pound exchange rate was fixed at $2.40 = £1. Since that time, its value has been determined almost entirely by market forces, with only occasional government interventions. Under these mostly flexible conditions, the dollar-pound exchange rate has varied considerably. For instance, in 1981 it took $2.02 to buy a pound, but by 1985 only $1.50 was needed to buy a pound. In contrast, between 2001 and 2007 the dollar price of a pound rose from $1.44 to $2.00, indicating that the dollar had depreciated relative to the pound. The dollar then sank back to $1.57 per British pound in 2009 and remained at about that level through 2015.

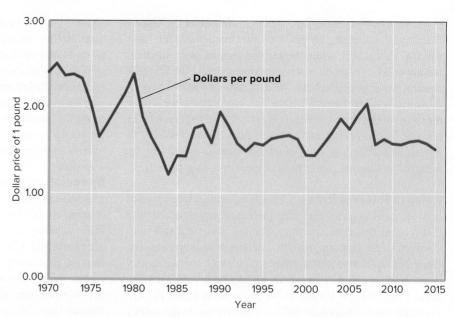

Source: Economic Report of the President, 2015, Table B-110. Earlier years from prior *Economic Reports*.

just a few weeks or months. In addition, they often take substantial swings that can last several years or more. This can be seen in Figure 27.2, which plots the dollar-pound exchange rate from 1970 through 2016. [You can track other exchange rates, for example, the dollar-euro or dollar-yen rate, by going to the Federal Reserve website, **www.federal-reserve.gov,** selecting Economic Research & Data, then Data Releases, and then clicking on "Foreign Exchange Rates (H.10/G.5)" under the heading that reads Exchange Rates and International Data.]

Uncertainty and Diminished Trade The risks and uncertainties associated with flexible exchange rates may discourage the flow of trade. Suppose a U.S. automobile dealer contracts to purchase 10 British cars for £150,000. At the current exchange rate of, say, $2 for £1, the U.S. importer expects to pay $300,000 for these automobiles. But if during the 3-month delivery period the rate of exchange shifts to $3 for £1, the £150,000 payment contracted by the U.S. importer will be $450,000.

That increase in the dollar price of pounds may thus turn the U.S. importer's anticipated profit into a substantial loss. Aware of the possibility of an adverse change in the exchange rate, the U.S. importer may not be willing to assume the risks involved. The U.S. firm may confine its operations to domestic automobiles, so international trade in this product will not occur.

The same thing can happen with investments. Assume that when the exchange rate is $3 to £1, a U.S. firm invests $30,000 (or £10,000) in a British enterprise. It estimates a return of 10 percent; that is, it anticipates annual earnings of

$3,000 or £1,000. Suppose these expectations prove correct in that the British firm earns £1,000 in the first year on the £10,000 investment. But suppose that during the year, the value of the dollar appreciates to $2 = £1. The absolute return is now only $2,000 (rather than $3,000), and the rate of return falls from the anticipated 10 percent to only $6\frac{2}{3}$ percent (= $2,000/$30,000). Investment is risky in any case. The added risk of changing exchange rates may persuade the U.S. investor not to venture overseas.

Terms-of-Trade Changes A decline in the international value of its currency will worsen a nation's terms of trade. For example, an increase in the dollar price of a pound will mean that the United States must export more goods and services to finance a specific level of imports from Britain.

Instability Flexible exchange rates may destabilize the domestic economy because wide fluctuations stimulate and then depress industries producing exported goods. If the U.S. economy is operating at full employment and its currency depreciates, the results will be inflationary, for two reasons. (1) Foreign demand for U.S. goods may rise, increasing total spending and pulling up U.S. prices. Also, the prices of all U.S. imports will increase. (2) Conversely, appreciation of the dollar will lower U.S. exports and increase imports, possibly causing unemployment.

Flexible or floating exchange rates also may complicate the use of domestic stabilization policies in seeking full employment and price stability. This is especially true for nations whose exports and imports are large relative to their total domestic output.

Fixed Exchange Rates

LO27.4 Describe the differences between flexible and fixed exchange rates, including how changes in foreign exchange reserves bring about automatic changes in the domestic money supply under a fixed exchange rate.

To circumvent the disadvantages of flexible exchange rates, governments have at times fixed or "pegged" their exchange rates. Under a fixed exchange rate, the government stands ready to buy and sell as much currency as is demanded or supplied at the constant (fixed) exchange rate that it announces.

To see how this works, suppose that the U.S. government decides to fix the dollar-pound exchange rate at $2 = £1. To enforce that peg, the U.S. government must stand ready to exchange both pounds for dollars as well as dollars for pounds at the fixed ratio of $2 = £1. If Americans want to exchange $20 billion for pounds, the U.S. government will need to come up with £10 billion pounds (= the required number of pounds at the $2 = £1 exchange rate). And if Britons wish to exchange £6 billion for dollars, the U.S. government will have to come up with $12 billion dollars (= required number of dollars at the $2 = £1 exchange rate).

Foreign Exchange Market Replaced by Government Peg

As long as the U.S. government is able to come up with the necessary amounts of both dollars (to satisfy exchange requests for pounds) and pounds (to satisfy exchange requests for dollars), the fixed exchange rate will preempt the foreign exchange market. All buying and selling of pounds for dollars or dollars for pounds will take place with the U.S. government. The U.S. government will *become* the dollar-pound foreign exchange market.

There will be no other dollar-pound market because, as long as the U.S. government can maintain the peg, there will be no other exchange rate that buyers and sellers would both simultaneously prefer, and thus no possibility of a given buyer and a given seller ever voluntarily agreeing to exchange dollars for pounds at any other exchange rate. To see why, consider an exchange rate like $3 = £1. U.K. citizens wishing to convert pounds to dollars would prefer $3 = £1 to the $2 = £1 exchange rate being offered by the U.S. government because each of their pounds would convert into $3 rather than $2. But would U.K. citizens be able to find anyone willing to take the opposite end of the deal and exchange dollars for pounds at a $3 = £1 exchange rate? The answer is no because anyone wishing to convert dollars to pounds would be able to go to the U.S. government and exchange money at the rate of $2 = £1, under which they would only have to give up $2 (rather than $3) to buy £1. So while U.K. citizens would prefer any exchange rate that gives them more dollars per pound than the $2 = £1 rate being offered by the U.S. government, they are not going to find anybody willing to exchange money at those rates. So anybody who wants to exchange pounds for dollars will end up dealing with the U.S. government and exchanging money at the $2 = £1 fixed rate.

You should take a moment to convince yourself that the reverse is also true: While Americans would prefer an exchange rate that requires them to give up less that $2 for each £1, no U.K. citizen would willingly accept a rate lower than $2 = £1 because doing so would mean receiving fewer dollars for their pounds than if they exchanged their pounds at the $2 = £1 exchange rate being offered by the U.S. government. So everyone wishing to exchange dollars for pounds will also end up dealing with the U.S. government and exchanging money at the $2 = £1 fixed exchange rate.

Please note, however, that if the U.S. government were ever to stop honoring its pledge to exchange dollars for pounds and pounds for dollars at the $2 = £1 exchange rate, a private market for foreign exchange would instantly pop back into existence to connect the buyers and sellers of dollars and pounds. Because the exchange rate would be determined by supply and demand, it could end up at an equilibrium value that is substantially different from the value of the fixed exchange rate that was just abandoned.

Official Reserves

A government that opts for a fixed exchange rate typically places its central bank in charge of day-to-day operations. It thus becomes the central bank's task to exchange as much local currency for foreign currency and as much foreign currency for local currency as is necessary each day to maintain the peg.

Satisfying requests to exchange foreign currency for local currency is easy, as the central bank has the legal right to print up as much local currency as it wants. But to satisfy requests to exchange local currency for foreign currency, the central bank must maintain a stock (inventory) of foreign currency since it can't legally create additional units of any other country's money.

The stock of the particular foreign currency that is used to maintain the fixed exchange rate will be just one component of the **official reserves** that the central bank will maintain for the government. The official reserves will consist not only of stockpiles of various foreign currencies but also stockpiles of bonds issued by foreign governments, gold reserves, and special reserves held at the International Monetary Fund. The stockpiles of foreign currencies are referred to as **foreign-exchange reserves,** or, less formally, FX reserves.

The Sizes of Currency Purchases and Sales

The amount of foreign and local currency that the central bank will have to buy and sell each day will depend on supply and demand. Consider Figure 27.3, in which we assume that the Fed is fixing the dollar-pound exchange rate at $2 = £1.

Begin by looking at the intersection of demand curve D_1 with supply curve S_1. If this were a free market, the equilibrium exchange rate (determined by where D_1 intersects S_1) would be equal to $2 = £1. But because the Fed is preempting the market by guaranteeing to exchange as many pounds for dollars and as many dollars for pounds as anyone might want to exchange at a price of $2 = £1, there will be no free market for foreign exchange. Instead, the Fed will act as a monopoly currency dealer (middleman) on all currency transactions. It will buy from those who wish to sell and sell to those who wish to buy.

In undertaking those sales, the Fed will find that its reserve of pounds will either remain constant, rise, or fall, depending upon the positions of the demand and supply curves.

FX Reserves Are Constant When Purchases Equal Sales

If the demand and supply curves for pounds happen to intersect at the $2 = £1 value of the fixed exchange rate, the Fed's reserve of pounds will remain unchanged in size. This situation is illustrated in Figure 27.3. Demand curve D_1 happens to intersect supply curve S_1 at the fixed exchange rate of $2 = £1. That implies that the quantity supplied of pounds and the quantity demanded of pounds will both equal b at the fixed exchange rate of $2 = £1. So the Fed will be buying and selling an equal number of pounds, which implies that its reserve of pounds will remain constant.

FX Reserves Increase When Sales Exceed Purchases

Next, imagine a situation in which the quantity demanded of pounds at the fixed exchange rate exceeds the quantity supplied of pounds at the fixed exchange rate. That happens in Figure 27.3 when the demand curve shifts left to

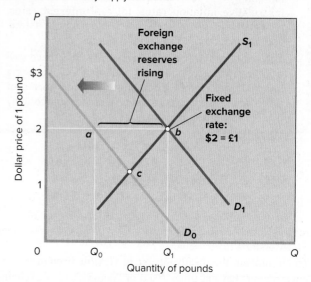

FIGURE 27.3 Fixed exchange rate with increasing foreign exchange reserves. To maintain a fixed exchange rate of $2 = £1, the central bank will have to buy whatever amount of pounds sellers supply at that price and sell whatever amount of pounds buyers demand at that price. If the demand curve for pounds shifts left to D_0, the quantity of pounds a that the central bank will have to sell to buyers at the fixed exchange rate will be less than the quantity of pounds b that the central bank will have to buy from sellers at that price. The central bank's reserve of pounds will consequently increase by amount ab. Not shown: As the reserve of pounds increases, so will the domestic money supply of dollars.

D_0 while the supply curve remains at S_1. In this situation, the Fed will *not* be exchanging equal quantities of pounds for dollars and dollars for pounds. At the fixed $2 = £1 exchange rate, the quantity demanded of pounds along demand curve D_0 will be a while the quantity supplied of pounds along supply curve S_1 will be b. There will be an excess supply of pounds ab that the Fed will end up owning.

That happens because Fed must satisfy both the buyers' desire to purchase a pounds for dollars and the sellers' desire to sell b pounds for dollars. After satisfying both of those desires, the Fed will find that its reserve of pounds has increased by the amount ab since it will have bought more pounds from suppliers than it sold to demanders. *The general rule is that if the quantity supplied of the foreign currency exceeds the quantity demanded at the fixed exchange rate, the central bank will accumulate foreign currency reserves as it accommodates the excess supply.*

Increasing Reserves = Increasing Domestic Money Supply
There is a flip side to accumulating foreign currency reserves: The net amount of local currency will also be increasing. This is because when the Fed buys ab more pounds than it sells, it will have to pay for those extra ab pounds by printing up dollars. Those new dollars initially go into the hands of the people who converted pounds into dollars. But as those people spend the newly created dollars for American goods, services,

and assets, the general level of prices will tend to rise. Other things equal, rising reserves are inflationary.

Locating Increasing Reserves in the Balance of Payments

Increases in foreign exchange reserves appear as a negative (−) item in the U.S. balance of payments statement, specifically as U.S. purchases of foreign assets (line 13 of Table 27.1). Increases in FX reserves are a debit because they represent an outflow of dollars.

Please note that in addition to the possibility of obtaining increased FX reserves as part of a fixed exchange rate regime (as in Figure 27.3), central banks and national governments may also increase FX reserves (whether or not they are pegging the exchange rate) by purchasing foreign currency with either domestic tax revenues or by printing up additional domestic currency. Those increases would also go into line 13 as a negative item.

FX Reserves Decrease When Purchases Exceed Sales

Consider Figure 27.4, which reproduces demand curve D_1 and supply curve S_1 from Figure 27.3, but in which we now have a rightward shift of the demand curve from D_1 to D_2. At the fixed exchange rate of $2 = £1, there will now be more pounds demanded d than there will be pounds supplied b. As a result of this shortage of pounds, the Fed will find that its reserve of pounds will decrease by bd as it sells

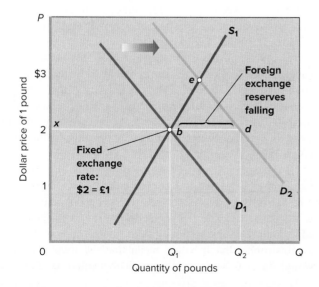

FIGURE 27.4 Fixed exchange rate with decreasing foreign exchange reserves. To maintain a fixed exchange rate of $2 = £1, the central bank will have to buy whatever amount of pounds sellers supply at that price and sell whatever amount of pounds buyers demand at that price. If the demand curve for pounds shifts right to D_2, the quantity of pounds d that the central bank will have to sell to buyers at the fixed exchange rate will be less than the quantity of pounds b that the central bank will have to buy from sellers. The central bank's reserve of pounds will consequently decrease by amount bd. Not shown: As the reserve of pounds decreases, so will the domestic money supply of dollars.

more pounds for dollars (point d along demand curve D_2) than it buys pounds for dollars (point b along supply curve S_1). *The general rule is that if the quantity demanded of the foreign currency exceeds the quantity supplied at the fixed exchange rate, the central bank will shed foreign currency reserves as it accommodates the excess demand.*

Decreasing Reserves = Decreasing Domestic Money Supply

The fall in pound reserves will automatically cause a decrease in the supply of dollars in the U.S. economy because as the Fed sells more pounds than it buys, it will receive more dollars in payment for the d pounds that it sells than the number of dollars it has to pay for the b pounds that it buys. Because those extra dollars go into the Fed's vaults, they no longer circulate. So in situations such as the one shown in Figure 27.4, there will be fewer dollars flowing around the U.S. economy and thus a tendency for a lower overall price level. Other things equal, decreasing reserves are deflationary.

Locating Decreasing Reserves in the Balance of Payments

Decreases in foreign exchange reserves appear as a plus (+) item in the U.S. balance of payments statement, specifically as foreign purchases of U.S. assets (line 12 of Table 27.1). The decreases are a credit because they represent an inflow of dollars.

Please note that in addition to FX reserves declining as part of a fixed exchange rate regime (as in Figure 27.4), central banks and national governments may also decrease FX reserves (whether or not they are fixing an exchange rate) by selling them in exchange for the local currency. Any such decreases would also go into line 12 as a positive item.

Small and Alternating Changes in FX Reserves and the Domestic Money Supply

If the periods of time when the Fed is buying more pounds than it sells (such as ab in Figure 27.3) alternate frequently enough with the periods of time when the Fed is selling more pounds than it buys (such as bd in Figure 27.4), then the Fed will not have to worry too much about inflation or deflation because any inflationary pressures caused by buying more pounds than it sells will be offset by deflationary pressures caused by selling more pounds than it buys. If the alternation is often enough and the number of dollars is small enough, then the changes in the domestic money supply caused by changes in FX reserves will have very little effect on the domestic price level.

It is also the case that if the periods of surplus and deficit in pound buying and selling alternate frequently enough or only involve modest quantities, the Fed will not have to worry about there being any long-term trend in the size of its pound reserves. The periods of buying more pounds will offset the periods of selling more pounds and the overall quantity of pound reserves will tend to stay about the same on average as time passes.

As a rule of thumb, the changes in both the domestic money supply and the size of the central bank's FX reserves will tend to be small and offsetting if the fixed exchange rate is close in value to the equilibrium exchange rate that would obtain if a free market determined the exchange rate. When the fixed rate is close to the equilibrium rate, any difference between the number of pounds sold and the number of pounds bought will tend to be small and, consequently, there will be little effect on either the domestic money supply or FX reserves.

Large and Continuous Changes in FX Reserves and the Domestic Money Supply

Major economic difficulties can arise if a nation's fixed exchange rate remains either substantially above or substantially below the equilibrium exchange rate for a long period of time.

Large and Continuous Increases in FX Reserves and the Domestic Money Supply

First imagine that the disequilibrium situation depicted in Figure 27.3 continued month after month and perhaps even year after year. With the fixed exchange rate substantially above the equilibrium exchange rate determined by where demand curve D_0 intersects supply curve S_1, both FX reserves and the local money supply will increase substantially. The continual increase in the local money supply will impel inflation.

If the anticipated increase in inflation is only modest, the central bank may choose to do nothing in response, and just allow the resulting inflation to occur. But if the injections of new dollars are likely to cause too large an increase in inflation, the central bank will have to either:

- Reset the peg lower (at, say, $1.9 = £1 in Figure 27.3) so that the peg moves closer to the equilibrium exchange rate and thereby reduces the volume of new-dollar creation.

- Abandon the peg altogether so that the equilibrium exchange rate (point *c* in Figure 27.3) would prevail and new-dollar creation would halt.

- Keep the peg the same, but offset the *ab* dollars created in Figure 27.3 with other policy interventions that reduce the domestic money supply. These **sterilization** operations can be accomplished by using either open market operations to sell bonds for dollars or by increasing the banking system's reserve requirements so as to limit the creation of checkable-deposit money. The amount of sterilization will depend upon the central bank's preferences. It can range from just a few dollars all the way up to a complete offset of *ab*. (See the nearby Consider This piece for an example of sterilization in action.)

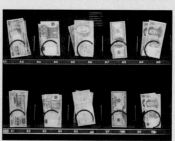
China's Inflationary Peg

China's economy boomed in the 1990s and 2000s after it abandoned communism for a market-based economy. China also fixed the value of its currency, the yuan, against the dollar and other foreign currencies to insulate local exporters and investors against exchange rate movements.

The peg that China chose was consistently below the free market equilibrium exchange rate throughout the 2000s so that China's foreign exchange reserves ballooned from just $165 billion in 2000 to a peak of just over $4 trillion in 2014.

China did attempt to gradually reset the peg lower, dropping the fixed exchange rate from about 8.3 yuan = $1 in the early 2000s to about 6.2 yuan = $1 by 2014. But because the yuan price of a dollar remained higher than equilibrium, China aroused accusations in other countries of unfairly subsidizing its export industries by making the yuan artificially cheap.

China also ensured substantial inflationary pressures at home as the number of yuan soared along with the increasing mountain of FX reserves. Inflation spiked as high as 8 percent despite aggressive sterilization efforts and an increase in the reserve ratio for bank lending from 6 percent to 21.5 percent, which left China with the highest reserve ratio by far of any major economy.

Large and Continuous Decreases in FX Reserves and the Domestic Money Supply

There is an important difference between having large and continuous increases in FX reserves and the domestic money supply on the one hand (Figure 27.3) and having large and continuous decreases in FX reserves and the domestic money supply on the other hand (Figure 27.4). The difference is caused by the fact that a country's central bank can only legally print the domestic currency. It has no right to print any other country's currency. So if its FX reserves are declining, it cannot simply print up more foreign money to make up for an ongoing decline in its FX reserves.

If the central bank finds itself continually in a situation like Figure 27.4, it has to face the reality that its FX reserves might soon be exhausted. If that were to happen, the country would have to abandon its peg and allow the exchange rate to adjust to its free-market equilibrium value. That might not be a catastrophe, but it would mean that the local economy would have to begin dealing with the volatility and risk associated with a flexible exchange rate. If the central bank wishes to avoid those problems, it will have to figure out a way to either halt, or at least slow, the decline in FX reserves.

One way for the central bank to reduce the rate at which its FX reserves are running out is to reset the peg higher (to, say, $2.25 = £1 in Figure 27.4). Resetting the peg higher moves the peg closer to the equilibrium exchange rate and thereby reduces the rate at which the central bank's foreign exchange reserves are falling.

Please note, however, that resetting the peg at a higher value will only *slow* the decline in FX reserves if the new value remains below the free-market equilibrium exchange rate. So it is important to consider the policy measures that could be taken to prevent the total exhaustion of the country's FX reserves if the peg cannot be reset all the way up to the free-market equilibrium value.

Trade Policies To maintain a fixed exchange rate, a nation can try to control the flow of trade and finance directly. The United States could try to maintain the $2 = £1 exchange rate in the face of a shortage of pounds by discouraging imports (thereby reducing the demand for pounds) and encouraging exports (thus increasing the supply of pounds). Imports could be reduced by means of new tariffs or import quotas; special taxes could be levied on the interest and dividends U.S. financial investors receive from foreign investments. Also, the U.S. government could subsidize certain U.S. exports to increase the supply of pounds.

The fundamental problem is that these policies reduce the volume of world trade and change its makeup from what is economically desirable. When nations impose tariffs, quotas, and the like, they lose some of the economic benefits of a free flow of world trade. That loss should not be underestimated: Trade barriers by one nation lead to retaliatory responses from other nations, multiplying the loss.

Exchange Controls and Rationing Another option is to adopt rationing via exchange controls (which are also sometimes referred to as capital controls). Under **exchange controls,** the U.S. government could handle the problem of a pound shortage by requiring that all pounds obtained by U.S. exporters be sold to the federal government. Then the government would allocate or ration this short supply of pounds (represented by *xb* in Figure 27.4) among various U.S. importers, who demand the quantity *xd*. This policy would restrict the value of U.S. imports to the amount of foreign exchange earned by U.S. exports. Assuming balance in the capital and financial account, there would then be no balance-of-payments deficit. U.S. demand for British imports with the value *bd* would simply not be fulfilled.

There are major objections to exchange controls:

- *Distorted trade* Like *trade controls* (tariffs, quotas, and export subsidies), exchange controls would distort the

pattern of international trade away from the pattern suggested by comparative advantage.

- *Favoritism* The process of rationing scarce foreign exchange might lead to government favoritism toward selected importers (big contributors to reelection campaigns, for example).

- *Restricted choice* Controls would limit freedom of consumer choice. The U.S. consumers who prefer Volkswagens might have to buy Chevrolets. The business opportunities for some U.S. importers might be impaired if the government were to limit imports.

- *Black markets* Enforcement problems are likely under exchange controls. U.S. importers might want foreign exchange badly enough to pay more than the $2 = £1 official rate, setting the stage for black-market dealings between importers and illegal sellers of foreign exchange.

Domestic Macroeconomic Adjustments A final way to maintain a fixed exchange rate would be to use domestic stabilization policies (monetary policy and fiscal policy) to eliminate the shortage of foreign currency. Tax hikes, reductions in government spending, and a high-interest-rate policy would reduce total spending in the U.S. economy and, consequently, domestic income. Because the volume of imports varies directly with domestic income, demand for British goods, and therefore for pounds, would be restrained.

If these "contractionary" policies served to reduce the domestic price level relative to Britain's, U.S. buyers of consumer and capital goods would divert their demands from British goods to U.S. goods, reducing the demand for pounds. Moreover, the high-interest-rate policy would lift U.S. interest rates relative to those in Britain.

Lower prices on U.S. goods and higher U.S. interest rates would increase British imports of U.S. goods and would increase British financial investment in the United States. Both developments would increase the supply of pounds. The combination of a decrease in the demand for and an increase in the supply of pounds would reduce or eliminate the original U.S. balance-of-payments deficit. In Figure 27.4, the new supply and demand curves would intersect at some new equilibrium point on line *bd*, where the exchange rate remains at $2 = £1.

Maintaining fixed exchange rates by such means is hardly appealing. The "price" of exchange-rate stability for the United States would be a decline in output, employment, and price levels—in other words, a recession. Eliminating a balance-of-payments deficit and achieving domestic stability are both important national economic goals, but to sacrifice macroeconomic stability simply to defend a currency peg would be to let the tail wag the dog. This chapter's Last Word discusses these concerns in the context of the European monetary union, which can be thought of as a system of permanently fixed exchange rates.

Confusing Payments Terminology

We know that a nation's balance of payments must always balance. It therefore is understandably confusing when economists or the press occasionally refer to a decrease of FX reserves in a country with a fixed exchange rate as a "balance of payments deficit" or an increase of FX reserves as a "balance of payments surplus." This unfortunate terminology often leads to inaccurate interpretations.

When a central bank fixes the exchange rate, all international payments (for trade, services, assets, remittances, etc.) will go through the central bank. If the quantities of foreign currency demanded and supplied aren't equal, the central bank's FX reserves will necessarily rise or fall, as you know from Figures 27.3 and 27.4.

Where FX reserves are rising, the "balance of payments surplus" terminology leads some people to falsely conclude that the United States is in some way "winning" a battle for international payments. After all, it is achieving a larger pile of wealth in the form of increased FX reserves.

What this mistaken interpretation misses is that the increase in FX reserves was not free. Anything gained by one country in terms of higher FX reserves had to be paid for by giving up assets, goods, or services *of an equal value* to another country. What looks like something achieved—a "balance of payments surplus"—results from a failure to account for the items that had to be given up to obtain the increase in FX reserves. This mistake in interpretation is equivalent to a coin dealer exchanging some rare Roman coins for euros but then only counting the increase in the number of euros in his cash box. That would be foolish because he will be failing to account for the fact that he now has fewer rare Roman coins in his possession. Euros were gained, but Roman coins were lost.

So don't be misled by this confusing terminology if you hear or read it. A **balance of payments deficit** is simply a decrease in FX reserves within the overall balance of payments that takes place when a country on a fixed exchange rate is forced to sell FX reserves in order to maintain its currency peg. A **balance of payments surplus** is simply an increase in FX reserves within the overall balance of payments that takes place when a country on a fixed exchange rate is forced to buy FX reserves in order to maintain its currency peg. The balance of payments will always balance. Any increase or decrease in FX reserves in lines 12 or 13 of the Capital and Financial Account in Table 27.1 will be exactly offset by one or more entries of the same total size, but of the opposite sign in lines 1 through 9 of the Current Account. Flows of goods, services, and transfer payments will perfectly offset any increase or decrease in the stock of FX reserves.

The Current Exchange Rate System: The Managed Float

LO27.5 Explain the current system of managed floating exchange rates.

Over the past 130 years, the world's nations have used three different exchange-rate systems. From 1879 to 1934, most nations used a gold standard, which implicitly created fixed exchange rates. From 1944 to 1971, most countries participated in the Bretton Woods system, which was a fixed-exchange-rate system indirectly tied to gold. And since 1971, most have used managed floating exchange rates, which mix mostly flexible exchange rates with occasional **currency interventions** during which a government buys or sells foreign exchange in the foreign exchange market in order to alter either supply or demand in a way that will push the exchange rate in the direction the government wants. Naturally, our focus here is on the current exchange-rate system. However, the history of the previous systems and why they broke down is highly fascinating.

The current international exchange-rate system (1971–present) is an "almost" flexible system called **managed floating exchange rates.** Exchange rates among major currencies are free to float to their equilibrium market levels, but nations occasionally use currency interventions in the foreign exchange market to stabilize or alter market exchange rates.

Normally, the major trading nations allow their exchange rates to float up or down to equilibrium levels based on supply and demand in the foreign exchange market. They recognize that changing economic conditions among nations require continuing changes in equilibrium exchange rates. They rely on freely operating foreign exchange markets to accomplish the necessary adjustments. The result has been considerably more volatile exchange rates than those during the Bretton Woods era.

But nations also recognize that certain trends in the movement of equilibrium exchange rates may be at odds with national or international objectives. On occasion, nations therefore intervene in the foreign exchange market by buying or selling large amounts of specific currencies. This way, they can "manage" or stabilize exchange rates by influencing currency demand and supply. In some cases, the interventions are sterilized via open market operations to prevent any change in the domestic money supply.

The current exchange-rate system is thus an "almost" flexible exchange-rate system. The "almost" refers mainly to the occasional currency interventions by governments; it also refers to the fact that the actual system is more complicated than described. While the major currencies such as dollars, euros, pounds, and yen fluctuate in response to changing supply and demand, some developing nations peg their currencies to the dollar and allow their currencies to fluctuate with it against other currencies. Also, some nations peg the value of their currencies to a "basket" or group of other currencies.

How well has the managed float worked? It has both proponents and critics.

In Support of the Managed Float
Proponents of the managed-float system argue that it has functioned far better than many experts anticipated. Skeptics had predicted that fluctuating exchange rates would reduce world trade and finance. But in real terms, world trade under the managed float has grown tremendously over the past several decades. Moreover, as supporters are quick to point out, currency crises such as those in Mexico and southeast Asia in the last half of the 1990s were not the result of the floating-exchange-rate system itself. Rather, the abrupt currency devaluations and depreciations resulted from internal problems in those nations, in conjunction with the nations' tendency to peg their currencies to the dollar or to a basket of currencies. In some cases, flexible exchange rates would have made these adjustments far more gradual.

Proponents also point out that the managed float has weathered severe economic turbulence that might have caused a fixed-rate system to break down. Such events as extraordinary oil price increases in 1973–1974 and again in 1981–1983, inflationary recessions in several nations in the mid-1970s, major national recessions in the early 1980s, and large U.S. budget deficits in the 1980s and the first half of the 1990s all caused substantial imbalances in international trade and finance, as did the large U.S. budget deficits and soaring world oil prices that occurred in the middle of the first decade of the 2000s. The U.S. financial crisis and the severe recession of 2007–2009 greatly disrupted world trade. Flexible rates enabled the system to adjust to all these events, whereas the same events would have put unbearable pressures on a fixed-rate system.

Concerns with the Managed Float There is still much sentiment in favor of greater exchange-rate stability. Those favoring more stable exchange rates see problems with the current system. They argue that the excessive volatility of exchange rates under the managed float threatens the prosperity of economies that rely heavily on exports. Several financial crises in individual nations (for example, Mexico, South Korea, Indonesia, Thailand, Russia, and Brazil) were exacerbated by abrupt changes in exchange rates. These crises have led to massive "bailouts" of those economies via loans from the International Monetary Fund (IMF). But the availability of IMF bailouts may spur moral hazard. Nations may undertake risky and inappropriate economic policies because they expect the IMF to bail them out if problems arise. Moreover, some exchange-rate volatility has occurred even when underlying economic and financial conditions were relatively stable, suggesting that speculation plays too large a role in determining exchange rates.

Skeptics say the managed float is basically a "nonsystem" because the guidelines as to what each nation may or may not do with its exchange rates are not specific enough to keep the system working in the long run. Nations inevitably will be tempted to intervene in the foreign exchange market, not merely to smooth out short-term fluctuations in exchange rates but to prop up their currency if it is chronically weak or to manipulate the exchange rate to achieve domestic stabilization goals.

So what are we to conclude? Flexible exchange rates have not worked perfectly, but they have not failed miserably. Thus far they have survived, and no doubt have eased, several major shocks to the international trading system. Meanwhile, the "managed" part of the float has given nations some sense of control over their collective economic destinies. On balance, most economists favor continuation of the present system of "almost" flexible exchange rates.

QUICK REVIEW 27.5

✓ The managed floating system of exchange rates (1971–present) relies on foreign exchange markets to establish equilibrium exchange rates.

✓ Under the system, nations can buy and sell official reserves of foreign currency to stabilize short-term changes in exchange rates or to correct exchange-rate imbalances that are negatively affecting the world economy.

✓ Proponents point out that international trade and investment have grown tremendously under the system. Critics say that it is a "nonsystem" and argue that the exchange rate volatility allowed under the managed float discourages international trade and investment. That is, trade and investment would be even larger if exchange rates were more stable.

Recent U.S. Trade Deficits

LO27.6 Identify the causes and consequences of recent U.S. trade deficits.

As shown in Figure 27.5a, the United States has experienced large and persistent trade deficits in recent years. These deficits rose rapidly between 2002 and 2006, with the trade deficit on goods and services peaking at $761 billion in 2006.

FIGURE 27.5 **U.S. trade deficits, 2002–2015.** (a) The United States experienced large deficits in *goods* and in *goods and services* between 2002 and 2012. (b) The U.S. current account, generally reflecting the goods and services deficit, was also in substantial deficit. Although reduced significantly by the recession of 2007–2009, large current account deficits are expected to continue for many years to come.

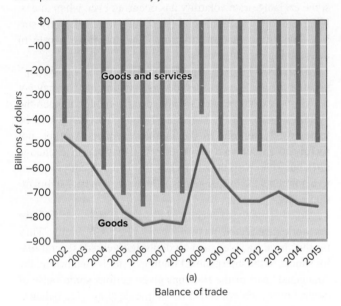

(a)
Balance of trade

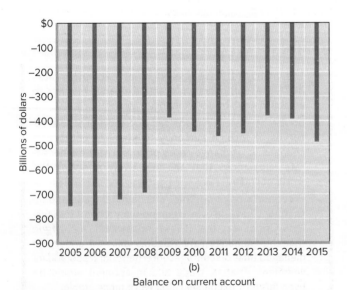

(b)
Balance on current account

Source: Bureau of Economic Analysis, **www.bea.gov.**

The trade deficit on goods and services then declined precipitously to just $383 billion in 2009 as consumers and businesses greatly curtailed their purchases of imports during the recession of 2007–2009. As the economy recovered from the recession, the trade deficit on goods and services began rising again and reached $500 billion in 2015. The current account deficit (Figure 27.5b) reached a record high of $800 billion in 2006, and that amount was 6.0 percent of GDP. The current account deficit declined to $382 billion—2.6 percent of GDP—in the recession year 2009. After the recession, the current account deficit expanded slowly, to $486 billion in 2015. But because GDP had also been growing, the 2015 current account deficit amounted to 2.7 percent of GDP, or about the same percentage as in 2009.

Causes of the Trade Deficits

The large U.S. trade deficits have several causes. First, the U.S. economy expanded more rapidly between 2002 and 2007 than the economies of several U.S. trading partners. The strong U.S. income growth that accompanied that economic growth enabled Americans to greatly increase their purchases of imported products. In contrast, Japan and some European nations suffered recession or experienced relatively slow income growth over that same period. So consumers in those countries increased their purchases of U.S. exports much less rapidly than Americans increased their purchases of foreign imports.

Another factor explaining the large trade deficits is the enormous U.S. trade imbalance with China. In 2015 the United States imported $366 billion more of goods and services from China than it exported to China. Even in the recession year 2009, the trade deficit with China was $220 billion. The 2015 deficit with China was 82 percent larger than the combined deficits with Mexico ($58 billion), Germany ($74 billion), and Japan ($69 billion). The United States is China's largest export market, and although China has greatly increased its imports from the United States, its standard of living has not yet risen sufficiently for its households to afford large quantities of U.S. products. Adding to the problem, China's government has fixed the exchange rate of its currency, the yuan, to a basket of currencies that includes the U.S. dollar. Therefore, China's large trade surpluses with the United States have not caused the yuan to appreciate much against the U.S. dollar. Greater appreciation of the yuan would have made Chinese goods more expensive in the United States and reduced U.S. imports from China. In China a stronger yuan would have reduced the dollar price of U.S. goods and increased Chinese purchases of U.S. exports. That combination—reduced U.S. imports from China and increased U.S. exports to China—would have reduced the large U.S. trade imbalance.

A declining U.S. saving rate (= saving/total income) also contributed to the large U.S. trade deficits. Up until the recession of 2007–2009, the U.S. saving rate declined substantially, while its investment rate (= investment/total income) increased. The gap between U.S. investment and U.S. saving was filled by foreign purchases of U.S. real and financial assets, which created a large surplus on the U.S. capital and financial account. Because foreign savers were willing to finance a large part of U.S. investment, Americans were able to save less and consume more. Part of that added consumption spending was on imported goods.

Finally, many foreigners simply view U.S. assets favorably because of the relatively high risk-adjusted rates of return they provide. The purchase of those assets provides foreign currency to Americans that enables them to finance their strong appetite for imported goods. The capital account surpluses, therefore, may partially cause the high U.S. trade deficits, not just result from those high deficits. The point is that the causes of the high U.S. trade deficits are numerous and not so easy to disentangle.

Implications of U.S. Trade Deficits

The prerecession U.S. trade deficits were the largest ever run by a major industrial nation. Whether the large trade deficits should be of significant concern to the United States and the rest of the world is debatable. Most economists see both benefits and costs to trade deficits.

Increased Current Consumption At the time a trade deficit or a current account deficit is occurring, American consumers benefit. A trade deficit means that the United States is receiving more goods and services as imports from abroad than it is sending out as exports. Taken alone, a trade deficit allows the United States to consume outside its production possibilities curve. It augments the domestic standard of living. But here is a catch: The gain in present consumption may come at the expense of reduced future consumption. When and if the current account deficit declines, Americans may have to consume less than before and perhaps even less than they produce.

Increased U.S. Indebtedness A trade deficit is considered unfavorable because it must be financed by borrowing from the rest of the world, selling off assets, or dipping into official reserves. Recall that current account deficits are financed by surpluses in the capital and financial accounts. Such surpluses require net inpayments of dollars to buy U.S. assets, including debt issued by Americans. Therefore, when U.S. exports are insufficient to finance U.S. imports, the United States increases both its debt to people abroad and the value of foreign claims against assets in the United States. Financing of the U.S. trade deficit has resulted in a larger foreign accumulation of claims against U.S. financial and real assets than the U.S. claim against foreign assets. In 2015, foreigners owned about $7.4 trillion more of U.S. assets (corporations, land, stocks, bonds, loan notes) than U.S. citizens and institutions owned of foreign assets.

If the United States wants to regain ownership of these domestic assets, at some future time it will have to export more than it imports. At that time, domestic consumption will be lower because the United States will need to send more of its output abroad than it receives as imports. Therefore, the current consumption gains delivered by U.S. current account deficits may mean permanent debt, permanent foreign ownership, or large sacrifices of future consumption.

We say "may mean" above because the foreign lending to U.S. firms and foreign investment in the United States increases the U.S. capital stock. U.S. production capacity therefore might increase more rapidly than otherwise because of a large surplus on the capital and financial account. Faster increases in production capacity and real GDP enhance the economy's ability to service foreign debt and buy back real capital, if that is desired.

Trade deficits therefore are a mixed blessing. The long-term impacts of the record-high U.S. trade deficits are largely unknown. That "unknown" worries some economists, who are concerned that foreigners will lose financial confidence in the United States. If that happens, they would restrict their lending to American households and businesses and also reduce their purchases of U.S. assets. Both actions would decrease the demand for U.S. dollars in the foreign exchange market and cause the U.S. dollar to depreciate. A sudden, large depreciation of the U.S. dollar might disrupt world trade and negatively affect economic growth worldwide. Other economists, however, downplay this scenario. Because any decline in the U.S. capital and financial account surplus is automatically met with a decline in the current account deficit, U.S. net exports would rise and the overall impact on the American economy would be slight.

QUICK REVIEW 27.6

✓ The United States has had large trade deficits in recent decades.

✓ Causes include (a) more rapid income growth in the United States than in Japan and some European nations, resulting in expanding U.S. imports relative to exports; (b) the emergence of a large trade deficit with China; (c) continuing large trade deficits with oil-exporting nations; and (d) a large surplus in the capital and financial account, which enabled Americans to reduce their saving and buy more imports.

✓ The severe recession of 2007–2009 in the United States substantially lowered the U.S. trade deficit by reducing American spending on imports.

✓ U.S. trade deficits have produced current increases in the living standards of U.S. consumers but the accompanying surpluses on the capital and financial account have increased U.S. debt to the rest of the world and increased foreign ownership of assets in the United States.

Are Common Currencies Common Sense?

A Shared Currency Precludes Independent Monetary Policies and External Adjustments

When countries use different currencies, international trade is hampered by the deadweight cost of currency-conversion fees, difficulties comparing costs when prices are given in multiple currencies, and exchange-rate risk.

Taken together, these problems suggest a simple solution: Why not use the same currency?

The 19 nations that are members of the eurozone did just that, eliminating their respective local currencies in favor of the euro. When they did, cross-border trade and investment surged, improving the economic prospects of all member nations. Unfortunately, life is full of costs as well as benefits. So while the eurozone countries did dramatically improve international trade and investment among their members, they incurred two major costs.

The Loss of Independent Monetary Policy When a country joins the European Monetary Union, it retains its own central bank, but cedes control over monetary policy to the central authority of the European Central Bank (ECB). To see why this can be problematic, consider a situation in which eurozone member Slovakia is in a recession while the rest of Europe is booming. The ECB has to set a single policy for all members. Because the large majority have booming economies, the ECB will choose to either keep interest rates constant or even raise them—just the opposite of what recessionary Slovakia needs.

The same problem confronts countries such as Zimbabwe, Panama, and El Salvador that have opted to use the U.S. dollar. By switching to U.S. dollars, they have ceded control over monetary policy to the Fed—which will put zero weight on their various local business cycles when setting monetary policy and interest rates for the United States.

The Loss of External Adjustments A country that joins a currency union also loses the ability to maintain competitiveness in international trade by making "external adjustments" to its current account balance. As an example, suppose that Greek goods and services are expensive relative to those produced by other eurozone countries because Greece has restrictive labor laws, low industrial productivity, unnecessarily high tax rates, and a bloated and corrupt public sector. These high costs will tend to cause both a trade deficit and a current account deficit in Greece because Greek consumers will favor less expensive foreign imports while at the same time Greek exporters will be hampered by high production costs.

This situation is not overly problematic if the Greek economy is growing. But if a recession starts, it would be helpful for Greece to figure out a way to boost its competitiveness in international trade and thereby increase the aggregate demand for its goods and services.

Source: © Maryna Pleshkun/Shutterstock.com

If Greece had retained its own currency, the Greek government could simply intervene in the foreign exchange market and devalue the Greek currency. The devaluation would be equivalent to putting all Greek goods and services on sale simultaneously, thereby making them more attractive to foreign consumers. At the same time, the price of foreign goods in Greece would rise, thereby causing local consumers to substitute domestic goods and services for imports. Aggregate demand within Greece would increase. The current account would move toward surplus. The "external adjustment" of devaluation would help Greece with its recession.

But Greece can't devalue; it no longer has its own currency. It can't use the external adjustment of devaluation to help resolve its high costs and lack of competitiveness. Its only way forward will be "internal adjustments" in which changes in the domestic economy lower the Greek cost structure so as to make its products internationally competitive again.

The Greek government could attempt to lower taxes, liberalize labor laws, and reform the bloated and corrupt public sector. But in most countries, those sorts of "structural changes" will be difficult to implement because of strong resistance by special interests or because of prior spending commitments. If they cannot be implemented, a country like Greece will be left with only the most painful type of internal adjustment: a recession-induced deflation in which falling aggregate demand slowly leads to a lower domestic price level. The recession will end, but only after downward price stickiness is overcome and the price level falls by enough to induce consumers both at home and abroad to buy more Greek products.

SUMMARY

LO27.1 Explain how currencies of different nations are exchanged when international transactions take place.

International financial transactions involve trade either in currently produced goods and services or in preexisting assets. Exports of goods, services, and assets create inflows of money, while imports cause outflows of money. If buyers and sellers use different currencies, then foreign exchange transactions take place so that the exporter can be paid in his or her own currency.

LO27.2 Analyze the balance sheet the United States uses to account for the international payments it makes and receives.

The balance of payments records all international trade and financial transactions taking place between a given nation and the rest of the world. The balance on goods and services (the trade balance) compares exports and imports of both goods and services. The current account balance includes not only goods and services transactions but also net investment income and net transfers.

The capital and financial account includes (*a*) the net amount of the nation's debt forgiveness and (*b*) the nation's sale of real and financial assets to people living abroad less its purchases of real and financial assets from foreigners.

The current account and the capital and financial account always sum to zero. A deficit in the current account is always offset by a surplus in the capital and financial account. Conversely, a surplus in the current account is always offset by a deficit in the capital and financial account.

LO27.3 Discuss how exchange rates are determined in currency markets that have flexible exchange rates.

Flexible or floating exchange rates between international currencies are determined by the demand for and supply of those currencies. Under flexible rates, a currency will depreciate or appreciate as a result of changes in tastes, relative income changes, relative changes in inflation rates, relative changes in real interest rates, and speculation. But the fluctuations in the exchange rate that occur under a flexible exchange rate system introduce uncertainty that can reduce the volume of international trade and destabilize the local economy.

LO27.4 Describe the differences between flexible and fixed exchange rates, including how changes in foreign exchange reserves bring about automatic changes in the domestic money supply under a fixed exchange rate.

Some countries have their central banks fix, or peg, their exchange rates to a particular value in order to eliminate the uncertainty about future exchange rates that arises under a floating exchange rate system. Because fixing requires buying and selling foreign currencies, the central bank will maintain reserves (stockpiles) of various foreign currencies. Those foreign exchange (FX) reserves

are a subset of a nation's overall collection of official reserves, which can include gold, foreign bonds, and special reserves held with the International Monetary Fund in addition to its holdings of FX reserves.

To maintain a fixed exchange rate, a central bank will simultaneously stand ready to sell as much foreign currency as buyers demand at the fixed exchange rate and buy as much foreign currency as sellers wish to supply at the fixed exchange rate. Those amounts will only be equal if the fixed exchange rate happens to equal the free-market exchange rate that would prevail if the country let the currency float. In other cases, the central bank's stockpile of foreign currency will either be rising or falling.

If FX reserves fall continuously, they may become exhausted. In such situations, the country will have to either abandon the peg, alter the peg, invoke protectionist trade policies, engage in exchange controls, or endure undesirable domestic macroeconomic adjustments.

Countries operating fixed exchange rates must also grapple with the fact that whenever the fixed exchange rate differs from the free-market exchange rate, the domestic money supply will be either rising or falling in tandem with its foreign currency (FX) reserves. That rise or fall in the domestic money supply will cause inflationary or deflationary pressures that policymakers will have to either accept or offset via open-market sterilization operations (bond purchases or sales) or changes in bank reserve ratios.

LO27.5 Explain the current system of managed floating exchange rates.

Since 1971 the world's major nations have used a system of managed floating exchange rates. Market forces generally set rates, although governments intervene with varying frequency to alter their exchange rates.

LO27.6 Identify the causes and consequences of recent U.S. trade deficits.

Between 1997 and 2007, the United States had large and rising trade deficits, which are projected to last well into the future. Causes of the trade deficits include (*a*) more rapid income growth in the United States than in Japan and some European nations, resulting in expanding U.S. imports relative to exports; (*b*) the emergence of a large trade deficit with China; (*c*) continuing large trade deficits with oil-exporting nations; and (*d*) a large surplus in the capital and financial account, which enabled Americans to reduce their saving and buy more imports. The severe recession of 2007–2009 in the United States substantially lowered the U.S. trade deficit by reducing American spending on imports.

U.S. trade deficits have produced current increases in the living standards of U.S. consumers. The accompanying surpluses on the capital and financial account have increased U.S. debt to the rest of the world and increased foreign ownership of assets in the United States. This greater foreign investment in the United States, however, has undoubtedly increased U.S. production possibilities.

TERMS AND CONCEPTS

balance of payments

current account

balance on goods and services

trade deficit

trade surplus

balance on current account

capital and financial account

balance on capital and financial account

flexible- or floating-exchange-rate system

fixed-exchange-rate system

purchasing-power-parity theory

official reserves

foreign exchange reserves

sterilization

exchange controls

balance of payments deficits

balance of payments surplus

currency interventions

managed floating exchange rates

The following and additional problems can be found in ▤ connect

DISCUSSION QUESTIONS

1. Do all international financial transactions necessarily involve exchanging one nation's distinct currency for another? Explain. Could a nation that neither imports goods and services nor exports goods and services still engage in international financial transactions? **LO27.1**

2. Explain: "U.S. exports earn supplies of foreign currencies that Americans can use to finance imports." Indicate whether each of the following creates a demand for or a supply of European euros in foreign exchange markets: **LO27.1**
   a. A U.S. airline firm purchases several Airbus planes assembled in France.
   b. A German automobile firm decides to build an assembly plant in South Carolina.
   c. A U.S. college student decides to spend a year studying at the Sorbonne in Paris.
   d. An Italian manufacturer ships machinery from one Italian port to another on a Liberian freighter.
   e. The U.S. economy grows faster than the French economy.
   f. A U.S. government bond held by a Spanish citizen matures, and the loan amount is paid back to that person.
   g. It is widely expected that the euro will depreciate in the near future.

3. What do the plus signs and negative signs signify in the U.S. balance-of-payments statement? Which of the following items appear in the current account and which appear in the capital and financial account? U.S. purchases of assets abroad; U.S. services imports; foreign purchases of assets in the United States; U.S. goods exports; U.S. net investment income. Why must the current account and the capital and financial account sum to zero? **LO27.2**

4. "Exports pay for imports. Yet in 2012 the nations of the world exported about $540 billion more of goods and services to the United States than they imported from the United States." Resolve the apparent inconsistency of these two statements. **LO27.2**

5. Generally speaking, how is the dollar price of euros determined? Cite a factor that might increase the dollar price of euros. Cite a different factor that might decrease the dollar price of euros. Explain: "A rise in the dollar price of euros necessarily means a fall in the euro price of dollars." Illustrate and elaborate: "The dollar-euro exchange rate provides a direct link between the prices of goods and services produced in the eurozone and in the United States." Explain the purchasing-power-parity theory of exchange rates, using the euro-dollar exchange rate as an illustration. **LO27.3**

6. Suppose that a Swiss watchmaker imports watch components from Sweden and exports watches to the United States. Also suppose the dollar depreciates, and the Swedish krona appreciates, relative to the Swiss franc. Speculate as to how each would hurt the Swiss watchmaker. **LO27.3**

7. Explain why the U.S. demand for Mexican pesos is downsloping and the supply of pesos to Americans is upsloping. Assuming a system of flexible exchange rates between Mexico and the United States, indicate whether each of the following would cause the Mexican peso to appreciate or depreciate, other things equal: **LO27.3**
   a. The United States unilaterally reduces tariffs on Mexican products.
   b. Mexico encounters severe inflation.
   c. Deteriorating political relations reduce American tourism in Mexico.
   d. The U.S. economy moves into a severe recession.
   e. The United States engages in a high-interest-rate monetary policy.
   f. Mexican products become more fashionable to U.S. consumers.
   g. The Mexican government encourages U.S. firms to invest in Mexican oil fields.
   h. The rate of productivity growth in the United States diminishes sharply.

8. Explain why you agree or disagree with the following statements. Assume other things equal. **LO27.3**
   a. A country that grows faster than its major trading partners can expect the international value of its currency to depreciate.

b. A nation whose interest rate is rising more rapidly than interest rates in other nations can expect the international value of its currency to appreciate.

c. A country's currency will appreciate if its inflation rate is less than that of the rest of the world.

9. Would it be accurate to think of a fixed exchange rate as a simultaneous price ceiling and price floor? **LO27.2**

10. What have been the major causes of the large U.S. trade deficits in recent years? What are the major benefits and costs associated with trade deficits? Explain: "A trade deficit means that a nation is receiving more goods and services from abroad than it is sending abroad." How can that be considered to be "unfavorable"? **LO27.6**

11. LAST WORD If a country like Greece that has joined the European Monetary Union can no longer use an independent monetary policy to offset a recession, what sorts of fiscal policy initiatives might it undertake? Give at least two examples.

REVIEW QUESTIONS

1. An American company wants to buy a television from a Chinese company. The Chinese company sells its TVs for 1,200 yuan each. The current exchange rate between the U.S. dollar and the Chinese yuan is $1 = 6$ yuan. How many dollars will the American company have to convert into yuan to pay for the television? **LO27.1**
   a. $7,200.
   b. $1,200.
   c. $200.
   d. $100.

2. Suppose that a country has a trade surplus of $50 billion, a balance on the capital account of $10 billion, and a balance on the current account of −$200 billion. The balance on the capital and financial account will be: **LO27.2**
   a. $10 billion.
   b. $50 billion.
   c. $200 billion.
   d. −$200 billion.

3. The exchange rate between the U.S. dollar and the British pound starts at $1 = £0.5$. It then changes to $1 = £0.75$. Given this change, we would say that the U.S. dollar has _____ while the British pound has _____. **LO27.3**
   a. Depreciated; appreciated.
   b. Depreciated; depreciated.
   c. Appreciated; depreciated.
   d. Appreciated; appreciated.

4. A meal at a McDonald's restaurant in New York costs $8. The identical meal at a McDonald's restaurant in London costs £4. According to the purchasing-power-parity theory of exchange rates, the exchange rate between U.S. dollars and British pounds should tend to move toward: **LO27.3**
   a. $2 = £1$.
   b. $1 = £2$.
   c. $4 = £1$.
   d. $1 = £4$.

5. Suppose that the Fed is fixing the dollar-pound exchange rate at $2.50 = £1$. If the Fed's reserve of pounds falls by £500 million, by how much would the supply of dollars increase, all other things equal? **LO27.3**

6. Diagram a market in which the equilibrium dollar price of 1 unit of fictitious currency zee (Z) is $5 (the exchange rate is $5 = Z1$). Then show on your diagram a decline in the demand for zee. **LO27.4**
   a. Referring to your diagram, discuss the adjustment options the United States would have in maintaining the exchange rate at $5 = Z1$ under a fixed-exchange-rate system.
   b. Suppose that the Fed's FX reserves increase by 40 million zees as a result of the decline in demand. How many millions of dollars worth of bonds will the Fed have to sell in order to sterilize the accompanying increase in the domestic money supply?

7. Suppose that the government of China is currently fixing the exchange rate between the U.S. dollar and the Chinese yuan at a rate of $1 = 6$ yuan. Also suppose that at this exchange rate, the people who want to convert dollars to yuan are asking to convert $10 billion per day of dollars into yuan, while the people who are wanting to convert yuan into dollars are asking to convert 36 billion yuan into dollars. What will happen to the size of China's official reserves of dollars? **LO27.4**
   a. Increase.
   b. Decrease.
   c. Stay the same.

8. Suppose that a country follows a managed-float policy but that its exchange rate is currently floating freely. In addition, suppose that it has a massive current account deficit. Other things equal, are its official reserves increasing, decreasing, or staying the same? If it decides to engage in a currency intervention to reduce the size of its current account deficit, will it buy or sell its own currency? As it does so, will its official reserves of foreign currencies get larger or smaller? **LO27.5**

9. If the economy booms in the United States while going into recession in other countries, the U.S. trade deficit will tend to _____. **LO27.6**
   a. Increase.
   b. Decrease.
   c. Remain the same.

10. Other things equal, if the United States continually runs trade deficits, foreigners will own _____ U.S. assets. **LO27.6**
   a. More and more.
   b. Less and less.
   c. The same amount of.

PROBLEMS

1. Alpha's balance-of-payments data for 2016 are shown below. All figures are in billions of dollars. What are the (*a*) balance on goods, (*b*) balance on goods and services, (*c*) balance on current account, and (*d*) balance on capital and financial account? **LO27.2**

Goods exports	$+40
Goods imports	−30
Service exports	+15
Service imports	−10
Net investment income	−5
Net transfers	+10
Balance on capital account	0
Foreign purchases of Alpha assets	+20
Alpha purchases of assets abroad	−40

2. China had a $214 billion overall current account surplus in 2012. Assuming that China's net debt forgiveness was zero in 2012 (its capital account balance was zero), by how much did Chinese purchases of financial and real assets abroad exceed foreign purchases of Chinese financial and real assets? **LO27.2**

3. Refer to the following table, in which Q_d is the quantity of loonies demanded, P is the dollar price of loonies, Q_s is the quantity of loonies supplied in year 1, and Q_s' is the quantity of loonies supplied in year 2. All quantities are in billions and the dollar-loonie exchange rate is fully flexible. **LO27.3**

Q_d	P	Q_s	Q_s'
10	125	30	20
15	120	25	15
20	115	20	10
25	110	15	5

a. What is the equilibrium dollar price of loonies in year 1?
b. What is the equilibrium dollar price of loonies in year 2?
c. Did the loonie appreciate or did it depreciate relative to the dollar between years 1 and 2?
d. Did the dollar appreciate or did it depreciate relative to the loonie between years 1 and 2?
e. Which one of the following could have caused the change in relative values of the dollar (used in the United States) and the loonie (used in Canadia) between years 1 and 2: (1) More rapid inflation in the United States than in Canadia, (2) an increase in the real interest rate in the United States but not in Canadia, or (3) faster income growth in the United States than in Canadia?

4. Suppose that the current Canadian dollar (CAD) to U.S. dollar exchange rate is $0.85 CAD = $1 US and that the U.S. dollar price of an Apple iPhone is $300. What is the Canadian dollar price of an iPhone? Next, suppose that the CAD to U.S. dollar exchange rate moves to $0.96 CAD = $1 US. What is the new Canadian dollar price of an iPhone? Other things equal, would you expect Canada to import more or fewer iPhones at the new exchange rate? **LO27.3**

5. Return to problem 3 and assume that the exchange rate is fixed at 110. In year 1, what would be the minimum initial size of the U.S. reserve of loonies such that the United States could maintain the peg throughout the year? What about the minimum initial size that would be necessary at the start of year 2? Next, consider only the data for year 1. What peg should the U.S. set if it wants the fixed exchange rate to increase the domestic money supply by $1.2 trillion? **LO27.6**

Previous International Exchange-Rate Systems

LO27.7 Explain how exchange rates worked under the gold standard and Bretton Woods.

This chapter discussed the current system of managed floating exchange rates in some detail. But before this system began in 1971, the world had previously used two other exchange rate systems: the gold standard, which implicitly created fixed exchange rates, and the Bretton Woods system, which was an explicit fixed-rate system indirectly tied to gold. Because the features and problems of these two systems help explain why we have the current system, they are well worth knowing more about.

The Gold Standard: Fixed Exchange Rates

Between 1879 and 1934 the major nations of the world adhered to a fixed-rate system called the **gold standard.** Under this system, each nation must:

- Define its currency in terms of a quantity of gold.
- Maintain a fixed relationship between its stock of gold and its money supply.
- Allow gold to be freely exported and imported.

If each nation defines its currency in terms of gold, the various national currencies will have fixed relationships to one another. For example, if the United States defines $1 as worth 25 grains of gold, and Britain defines £1 as worth 50 grains of gold, then a British pound is worth 2×25 grains, or $2. This exchange rate was fixed under the gold standard. The exchange rate did not change in response to changes in currency demand and supply.

Gold Flows If we ignore the costs of packing, insuring, and shipping gold between countries, under the gold standard the rate of exchange would not vary from this $2 = £1 rate. No one in the United States would pay more than $2 = £1 because 50 grains of gold could always be bought for $2 in the United States and sold for £1 in Britain. Nor would the British pay more than £1 for $2. Why should they when they could buy 50 grains of gold in Britain for £1 and sell it in the United States for $2?

Under the gold standard, the potential free flow of gold between nations resulted in fixed exchange rates.

Domestic Macroeconomic Adjustments When currency demand or supply changes, the gold standard requires domestic macroeconomic adjustments to maintain the fixed exchange rate. To see why, suppose that U.S. tastes change such that U.S. consumers want to buy more British goods. The resulting increase in the demand for pounds creates a shortage of pounds in the United States (recall Figure 27.4), implying a U.S. balance-of-payments deficit.

What will happen? Remember that the rules of the gold standard prohibit the exchange rate from moving from the fixed $2 = £1 rate. The rate cannot move to, say, a new equilibrium at $3 = £1 to correct the imbalance. Instead, gold will flow from the United States to Britain to correct the payments imbalance.

But recall that the gold standard requires that participants maintain a fixed relationship between their domestic money supplies and their quantities of gold. The flow of gold from the United States to Britain will require a reduction of the money supply in the United States. Other things equal, that will reduce total spending in the United States and lower U.S. real domestic output, employment, income, and, perhaps, prices. Also, the decline in the money supply will boost U.S. interest rates.

The opposite will occur in Britain. The inflow of gold will increase the money supply, and this will increase total spending in Britain. Domestic output, employment, income, and, perhaps, prices will rise. The British interest rate will fall.

Declining U.S. incomes and prices will reduce the U.S. demand for British goods and therefore reduce the U.S. demand for pounds. Lower interest rates in Britain will make it less attractive for U.S. investors to make financial investments there, also lessening the demand for pounds. For all these reasons, the demand for pounds in the United States will decline. In Britain, higher incomes, prices, and interest rates will make U.S. imports and U.S. financial investments more attractive. In buying these imports and making these financial investments, British citizens will supply more pounds in the exchange market.

In short, domestic macroeconomic adjustments in the United States and Britain, triggered by the international flow of gold, will produce new demand and supply conditions for pounds such that the $2 = £1 exchange rate is maintained. After all the adjustments are made, the United States will not have a payments deficit and Britain will not have a payments surplus.

So the gold standard has the advantage of maintaining stable exchange rates and correcting balance-of-payments deficits and surpluses automatically. However, its critical drawback is that nations must accept domestic adjustments in such distasteful forms as unemployment and falling incomes, on the one hand, or inflation, on the other hand. Under the gold standard, a nation's money supply is altered by changes in supply and demand in currency markets, and nations cannot establish their own monetary policy in their own national interest. If the United States, for example, were to experience declining output and income, the loss of gold under the gold standard would reduce the U.S. money supply. That would increase interest rates, retard borrowing and spending, and produce further declines in output and income.

Collapse of the Gold Standard

The gold standard collapsed under the weight of the worldwide Depression of the 1930s. As domestic output and employment fell worldwide, the restoration of prosperity became the primary goal of afflicted nations. They responded by enacting protectionist measures to reduce imports. The idea was to get their economies moving again by promoting consumption of domestically produced goods. To make their exports less expensive abroad, many nations redefined their currencies at lower levels in terms of gold. For example, a country that had previously defined the value of its currency at 1 unit = 25 grains of gold might redefine it as 1 unit = 10 grains of gold. Such redefining is an example of **devaluation**—a deliberate action by government to reduce the international value of its currency. A series of such devaluations in the 1930s meant that exchange rates were no longer fixed. That violated a major tenet of the gold standard, and the system broke down.

The Bretton Woods System

The Great Depression and the Second World War left world trade and the world monetary system in shambles. To lay the groundwork for a new international monetary system, in 1944, major nations held an international conference at Bretton Woods, New Hampshire. The conference produced a commitment to a modified fixed-exchange-rate system called an *adjustable-peg system,* or, simply, the **Bretton Woods system.** The new system sought to capture the advantages of the old gold standard (fixed exchange rate) while avoiding its disadvantages (painful domestic macroeconomic adjustments).

Furthermore, the conference created the **International Monetary Fund (IMF)** to make the new exchange-rate system feasible and workable. The new international monetary system managed through the IMF prevailed with modifications until 1971. (The IMF still plays a basic role in international finance; in recent years it has performed a major role in providing loans to developing countries, nations experiencing financial crises, and nations making the transition from communism to capitalism.)

IMF and Pegged Exchange Rates

How did the adjustable-peg system of exchange rates work? First, as with the gold standard, each IMF member had to define its currency in terms of gold (or dollars), thus establishing rates of exchange between its currency and the currencies of all other members. In addition, each nation was obligated to keep its exchange rate stable with respect to every other currency. To do so, nations would have to use their official currency reserves to intervene in foreign exchange markets.

Assume again that the U.S. dollar and the British pound were "pegged" to each other at $2 = £1. And suppose again that the demand for pounds temporarily increases so that a shortage of pounds occurs in the United States (the United States has a balance-of-payments deficit). How can the United States keep its pledge to maintain a $2 = £1 exchange rate when the new equilibrium rate is, say, $3 = £1? As we noted previously, the United States can supply additional pounds to the exchange market, increasing the supply of pounds such that the equilibrium exchange rate falls back to $2 = £1.

Under the Bretton Woods system, there were three main sources of the needed pounds:

- *Official reserves* The United States might currently possess pounds in its official reserves as the result of past actions against a payments surplus.

- *Gold sales* The U.S. government might sell some of its gold to Britain for pounds. The proceeds would then be offered in the exchange market to augment the supply of pounds.

- *IMF borrowing* The needed pounds might be borrowed from the IMF. Nations participating in the Bretton Woods system were required to make contributions to the IMF based on the size of their national income, population, and volume of trade. If necessary, the United States could borrow pounds on a short-term basis from the IMF by supplying its own currency as collateral.

Fundamental Imbalances: Adjusting the Peg

The Bretton Woods system recognized that from time to time a nation may be confronted with persistent and sizable balance-of-payments problems that cannot be corrected through the means listed above. In such cases, the nation would eventually run out of official reserves and be unable to maintain its current fixed exchange rate. The Bretton Woods remedy was correction by devaluation, that is, by an "orderly" reduction of the nation's pegged exchange rate. Also, the IMF allowed each member nation to alter the value of its currency by 10 percent, on its own, to correct a so-called fundamental (persistent and continuing) balance-of-payments deficit. Larger exchange-rate changes required the permission of the Fund's board of directors.

By requiring approval of significant rate changes, the Fund guarded against arbitrary and competitive currency devaluations by nations seeking only to boost output in their own countries at the expense of other countries. In our example, devaluation of the dollar would increase U.S. exports and lower U.S. imports, helping to correct the United States' persistent payments deficit.

Demise of the Bretton Woods System Under this adjustable-peg system, nations came to accept gold and the dollar as international reserves. The acceptability of gold as an international medium of exchange derived from its earlier use under the gold standard. Other nations accepted the dollar as international money because the United States had accumulated large quantities of gold, and between 1934 and 1971 it maintained a policy of buying gold from, and selling gold to, foreign governments at a fixed price of $35 per ounce. The dollar was convertible into gold on demand, so the dollar came to be regarded as a substitute for gold, or "as good as gold." The discovery of new gold was limited, but a growing volume of dollars helped facilitate the expanding volume of world trade during this period.

But a major problem arose. The United States had persistent payments deficits throughout the 1950s and 1960s. Those deficits were financed in part by U.S. gold reserves but mostly by payment of U.S. dollars. As the amount of dollars held by foreigners soared and the U.S. gold reserves dwindled, other nations began to question whether the dollar was really "as good as gold." The ability of the United States to continue to convert dollars into gold at $35 per ounce became increasingly doubtful, as did the role of dollars as international monetary reserves. Thus the dilemma was: To maintain the dollar as a reserve medium, the U.S. payments deficit had to be eliminated. But elimination of the payments deficit would remove the source of additional dollar reserves and thus limit the growth of international trade and finance.

The problem culminated in 1971 when the United States ended its 37-year-old policy of exchanging gold for dollars at $35 per ounce. It severed the link between gold and the international value of the dollar, thereby "floating" the dollar and letting market forces determine its value. The floating of the dollar withdrew U.S. support from the Bretton Woods system of fixed exchange rates and effectively ended the system. Nearly all major currencies began to float. This led to the current regime of "managed floating exchange rates" that is described at length in this chapter.

APPENDIX SUMMARY

LO27.7 Explain how exchange rates worked under the gold standard and Bretton Woods.

Before the current system of managed floating exchange rates started in 1971, several different international monetary systems were used.

Between 1879 and 1934, most major trading nations were on the gold standard, in which each nation fixed an exchange rate between its currency and gold. With each nation's currency fixed to gold, the system also implicitly set fixed exchange rates between different national currencies.

Any balance-of-payments imbalance would automatically lead to offsetting international flows of gold. This, in turn, led to automatically occurring domestic macroeconomic adjustments as the country exporting gold automatically encountered a decrease in its money supply while the country importing gold automatically felt an increase in its money supply. When the Great Depression hit, many countries found these automatic adjustments too hard to bear and they abandoned the gold standard.

The Bretton Woods system was implemented after the end of the Second World War and lasted until 1971. Under this system, the United States fixed the value of the U.S. dollar to gold at a rate of $35 per ounce. Other countries then set fixed exchange rates with the dollar so that their currencies were indirectly fixed to gold through the dollar.

The International Monetary Fund was created to administer the Bretton Woods system, which had some flexibility because exchange rates between countries could be adjusted to help offset balance-of-payments imbalances.

As the United States encountered increasingly large balance-of-payments imbalances in the 1960s and early 1970s, its ability to maintain its gold peg of $35 per ounce lost credibility. The United States abandoned the gold standard in 1971, thereby ending the Bretton Woods system. All major currencies then began the current regime of managed floating exchange rates.

APPENDIX TERMS AND CONCEPTS

gold standard

devaluation

Bretton Woods system

International Monetary Fund (IMF)

The following and additional problems can be found in ▤ **connect**

APPENDIX DISCUSSION QUESTIONS

1. Compare and contrast the Bretton Woods system of exchange rates with that of the gold standard. What caused the collapse of the gold standard? What caused the demise of the Bretton Woods system? **LO27.7**

APPENDIX REVIEW QUESTIONS

1. Think back to the gold standard period. If the United States suffered a recession, to what degree could it engage in expansionary monetary policy? **LO27.7**

APPENDIX PROBLEMS

1. Suppose Zeeland pegs its currency, the zee, at 1 zee = 36 grains of gold while Aeeland pegs its currency, the aeellar, at 1 aellar = 10 grains of gold. **LO27.7**

   a. What would the exchange rate be between the zee and the aellar?

   b. How many aellars could you get for 7 zees?

   c. In terms of gold, would you rather have 14.5 zees or 53 aellars?

The Economics of Developing Countries

Learning Objectives

LO28.1 Describe how the World Bank distinguishes between industrially advanced countries and developing countries.

LO28.2 List some of the obstacles to economic development.

LO28.3 Explain the vicious circle of poverty that afflicts low-income nations.

LO28.4 Discuss the role of government in promoting economic development within low-income nations.

LO28.5 Describe how industrial nations attempt to aid low-income countries.

It is difficult for those of us in the United States, where per capita GDP in 2015 was about $55,904, to grasp the fact that about 2.5 billion people, or nearly half the world's population, live on $2 or less a day. And about 1.3 billion live on less than $1.25 a day. Hunger, squalor, and disease are the norm in many nations of the world.

In this chapter we identify the developing countries, discuss their characteristics, and explore the obstacles that have impeded their growth. We also examine the appropriate roles of the private sector and government in economic development. Finally, we look at policies that might help developing countries increase their growth rates.

The Rich and the Poor

LO28.1 Describe how the World Bank distinguishes between industrially advanced countries and developing countries.

Just as there is considerable income inequality among families within a nation, so too is there great income inequality among the family of nations. According to the United Nations, the richest 20 percent of the world's population receive more than 75 percent of the world's income; the poorest 20 percent receive less than 2 percent. The poorest 60 percent receive less than 6 percent of the world's income.

Classifications

The World Bank classifies countries into high-income, upper-middle-income, lower-middle-income, and low-income countries on the basis of national income per capita, as shown in Figure 28.1. The *high-income nations*, shown in dark green, are known as the **industrially advanced countries (IACs);**

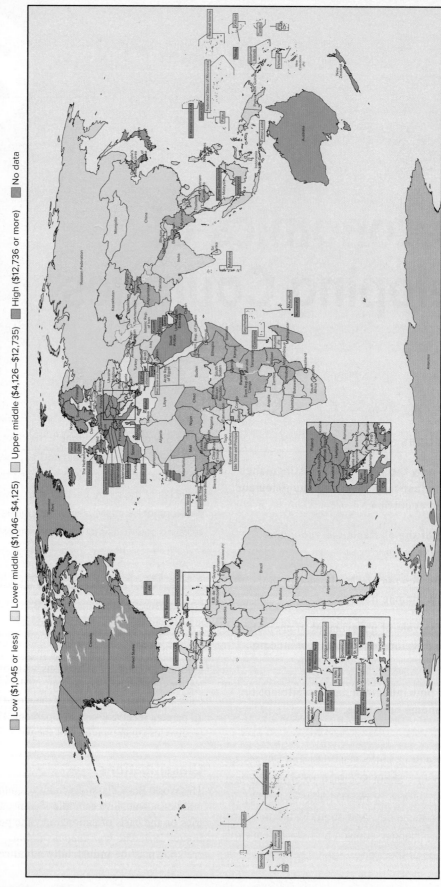

FIGURE 28.1 Groups of economies. The world's nations are grouped into industrially advanced countries (IACs) and developing countries (DVCs). The IACs (shown in dark green) are high-income countries. The DVCs are upper-middle-income, lower-middle-income, and low-income countries (shown respectively in light green, yellow, and orange).

Low ($1,045 or less) Lower middle ($1,046–$4,125) Upper middle ($4,126–$12,735) High ($12,736 or more) No data

Source: World Bank data, **www.worldbank.org.** National income per capita is converted to U.S. dollars using the World Bank's Atlas Method, which adjusts national amounts to U.S. dollars using 3-year exchange rate averages. See the World Bank's website for more details.

they include the United States, Japan, Canada, Australia, New Zealand, and most of the nations of western Europe. In general, these nations have well-developed market economies based on large stocks of capital goods, advanced production technologies, and well-educated workers. In 2014 this group of economies had a per capita income of $38,300.

The remaining nations of the world are called **developing countries (DVCs).** They have wide variations of income per capita and are mainly located in Africa, Asia, and Latin America. The DVCs are a highly diverse group that can be subdivided into three groups:

- The *upper-middle-income nations,* shown in light green in Figure 28.1, include countries such as Brazil, Iran, South Africa, Mexico, China, and Thailand. The per capita output of these nations ranged all the way from $4,126 to $12,735 in 2014 and averaged $7,926.

- The *lower-middle-income nations,* shown in yellow, had per capita incomes ranging from $1,046 to $4,125 in 2014 with an average per capita income of $2,018. This category includes Armenia, India, Indonesia, Pakistan, Vietnam, and Zambia.

- The *low-income nations,* shown in orange, had a per capita income of $1,045 or less in 2014 and averaged only $628 of income per person. The sub-Saharan nations of Africa dominate this group. Low-income DVCs have relatively low levels of industrialization. In general, literacy rates are low, unemployment is high, population growth is rapid, and exports consist largely of agricultural produce (such as cocoa, bananas, sugar, raw cotton) and raw materials (such as copper, iron ore, natural rubber). Capital equipment is minimal, production technologies are simple, and labor productivity is very low. About 9 percent of the world's population live in these low-income DVCs, all of which suffer widespread poverty.

Comparisons

Several comparisons will bring the differences in world income into sharper focus:

- In 2014, U.S. GDP was $17.3 trillion; the combined GDPs of the 135 DVCs in that year added up to $25 trillion.

- The United States, with only 4.4 percent of the world's population in 2014, produced 22.3 percent of the world's output.

- Per capita GDP of the United States in 2014 was 70 times greater than per capita GDP in the Democratic Republic of the Congo, one of the world's poorest nations.

- The annual sales of the world's largest corporations exceed the national incomes of many of the DVCs. Walmart's annual world revenues of $473 billion in 2014 were greater than the national incomes of all but 26 nations.

Growth, Decline, and Income Gaps

Two other points relating to the nations shown in Figure 28.1 should be noted. First, the various nations have demonstrated considerable differences in their ability to improve circumstances over time. On the one hand, DVCs such as Chile, China, India, Malaysia, and Thailand achieved high annual growth rates in their GDPs in recent decades. Consequently, their real output per capita increased severalfold. Several former DVCs, such as Singapore, Greece, and Hong Kong (now part of China), have achieved IAC status. In contrast, a number of DVCs in sub-Saharan Africa and the Middle East have recently been experiencing stagnant or even declining per capita GDPs.

Second, the absolute income gap between rich and poor nations has been widening. Suppose the per capita incomes of the advanced and developing countries were growing at about 2 percent per year. Because the income base in the advanced countries is initially much higher, the absolute income gap grows. If per capita income is $400 a year in a DVC, a 2 percent growth rate means an $8 increase in income. Where per capita income is $20,000 per year in an IAC, the same 2 percent growth rate translates into a $400 increase in income. Thus the absolute income gap will have increased from $19,600 (= $20,000 − $400) to $19,992 (= $20,400 − $408). The DVCs must grow faster than the IACs for the gap to be narrowed.

The Human Realities of Poverty

Development economist Michael Todaro points out that mere statistics conceal the human implications of the extreme poverty in the low-income DVCs:

> Let us examine a typical "extended" family in rural Asia. The Asian household is likely to comprise ten or more people, including parents, five to seven children, two grandparents, and some aunts and uncles. They have a combined annual income, both in money and in "kind" (i.e., they consume a share of the food they grow), of $250 to $300. Together they live in a poorly constructed one-room house as tenant farmers on a large agricultural estate ... The father, mother, uncle, and the older children must work all day on the land. None of the adults can read or write ... There is only one meal a day ... The house has no electricity, sanitation, or fresh water supply. There is much sickness, but qualified doctors and medical practitioners are far away in the cities attending to the needs of wealthier families. The work is hard, the sun is hot and aspirations for a better life are constantly being snuffed out. In this part of the world the only relief from the daily struggle for physical survival lies in the spiritual traditions of the people.[1]

---

[1]Todaro, Michael P., *Economic Development,* 7th edition, © 2000. Printed and Electronically reproduced by permission of Pearson Education, Inc., Upper Saddle River, New Jersey.

TABLE 28.1 **Selected Socioeconomic Indicators of Development**

Country	(1) Per Capita Income, 2014*	(2) Life Expectancy at Birth, 2014	(3) Under-5 Mortality Rate per 1,000, 2014	(4) Adult Illiteracy Rate, Percent, 2015	(5) Internet Users per 100, 2014	(6) Per Capita Energy Consumption, 2013**
United States	$55,230	79	7	1	87.4	6,914
Japan	42,000	84	3	1	90.6	3,570
Brazil	11,790	74	16	7	57.6	1,439
China	7,400	76	11	4	49.3	2,226
India	1,570	68	50	28	18.0	660
Mauritania	1,270	63	86	48	10.7	529
Bangladesh	1,080	72	40	39	9.6	216
Mozambique	600	55	81	41	5.9	407
Ethiopia	550	64	62	51	2.9	507

*Purchasing power parity basis (see World Bank website for definition and methodology).
**Kilograms of oil equivalent.

Source: World Bank, *World Development Indicators 2015* and *World Development Report 2015,* UNESCO Institute of Statistics, **dada.uis.unesco.org**.

Table 28.1 contrasts various socioeconomic indicators for selected DVCs with those for the United States and Japan. These data confirm the major points stressed in the quotation from Todaro.

Obstacles to Economic Development

LO28.2 List some of the obstacles to economic development.

The paths to economic development are essentially the same for developing countries and industrially advanced economies:

- The DVCs must use their existing supplies of resources more efficiently. This means that they must eliminate unemployment and underemployment and also combine labor and capital resources in a way that will achieve lowest-cost production. They must also direct their scarce resources so that they will achieve allocative efficiency.

- The DVCs must expand their available supplies of resources. By achieving greater supplies of raw materials, capital equipment, and productive labor, and by advancing its technological knowledge, a DVC can push its production possibilities curve outward.

All DVCs are aware of these two paths to economic development. Why, then, have some of them traveled those paths while others have lagged far behind? The difference lies in the physical, human, and socioeconomic environments of the various nations.

Natural Resources

No simple generalization is possible as to the role of natural resources in the economic development of DVCs because the distribution of natural resources among them is so uneven. Some DVCs have valuable deposits of bauxite, tin, copper, tungsten, nitrates, and petroleum and have been able to use their natural resource endowments to achieve rapid growth. This is true, for instance, of Kuwait and several other members of the Organization of Petroleum Exporting Countries (OPEC). In other instances, natural resources are owned or controlled by the multinational corporations of industrially advanced countries, with the economic benefits from these resources largely diverted abroad. Furthermore, world markets for many of the farm products and raw materials that the DVCs export are subject to large price fluctuations that contribute to instability in their economies.

Other DVCs lack mineral deposits, have little arable land, and have few sources of power. Moreover, most of the poor countries are situated in Central and South America, Africa, the Indian subcontinent, and southeast Asia, where tropical climates prevail. The heat and humidity hinder productive labor; human, crop, and livestock diseases are widespread; and weed and insect infestations plague agriculture.

A weak resource base can be a serious obstacle to growth. Real capital can be accumulated and the quality of the labor force improved through education and training. But it is not as easy to augment the natural resource base. It may be unrealistic for many of the DVCs to envision an economic destiny comparable with that of, say, the United States or Canada. But we must be careful in generalizing: Japan, for example, has achieved a high standard of living despite limited natural resources. It simply imports the large quantities of natural resources that it needs to produce goods for consumption at home and export abroad.

Human Resources

Three statements describe many of the poorest DVCs with respect to human resources:

- Populations are large.
- Unemployment and underemployment are widespread.
- Educational levels and labor productivity are low.

Large Populations As demonstrated by equation (1), a nation's standard of living or real income per capita depends on the size of its total output (or income) relative to its total population:

$$\text{Standard of living} = \frac{\text{Total output (or income)}}{\text{Population}} \quad (1)$$

Some of the DVCs with the most meager natural and capital resources not only have low total incomes but also large populations. These large populations often produce high population densities (population per square mile). In column 2 of Table 28.2, note the high population densities of the selected DVCs relative to the lower densities of the United States and the world.

The high population densities of many DVCs have resulted from decades of higher rates of population growth than most IACs. Column 3 of Table 28.2 shows the varying rates of population growth in selected countries over a recent period: 2013–2014. Although *total fertility rates*—the number of children per woman's lifetime—are dramatically declining in most DVCs, the population growth rates of the DVCs remain considerably higher than for the IACs. Between 2000 and 2010, the annual population growth rate was 2.1 percent for the low-income DVCs and 1.2 percent for the middle-income DVCs. Those numbers compare to only a 0.7 percent

rate of population growth for the IACs. Because a large percentage of the world's current population already lives in DVCs, their population growth remains significant. Over the next 15 years, 9 out of every 10 people added to the world population are projected to be born in developing nations. Figure 28.2 dramatically illustrates the effect of population growth in the DVCs on past, present, and projected world population numbers. Population growth in the DVCs will continue to increase the world's population through midcentury, at which time world population is expected to begin to level off.

In some of the poorest DVCs, rapid population growth actually strains the levels of income growth so severely that per capita income remains stagnant or even falls toward subsistence levels. In the worst instances, death rates rise sharply as war, drought, and natural disasters cause severe malnutrition and disease.

Boosting the standard of living in countries that have subsistence or near-subsistence levels of income is a daunting task. When a DVC is just starting to modernize its economy, initial increases in real income can for a time increase population and short-circuit the process. If population increases are sufficiently large, they simply spread the higher level of total income among more people such that the original gain in per capita income disappears.

Why might income gains in the poorest DVC increase population growth, at least for a while? First, such income growth often reduces the nation's death rate. The increase in income means better nutrition and that improves health and

TABLE 28.2 Population Statistics, Selected Countries

(1) Country	(2) Population per Square Kilometer, 2014*	(3) Annual Rate of Population Increase, 2013–2014
United States	35	0.7
Pakistan	240	2.1
Bangladesh	1,222	1.2
Venezuela	35	1.4
India	436	1.2
China	145	0.5
Kenya	79	2.6
Philippines	332	1.6
Yemen	50	2.5
World	**56**	**1.2**

*1 square kilometer (km) = 0.386 square mile.

Source: *World Development Indicators 2015*, **www.worldbank.org**

FIGURE 28.2 Population growth in developing countries and advanced industrial countries, 1950–2050. The majority of the world's population lives in the developing nations, and those nations will account for most of the increase in population through the middle of the twenty-first century.

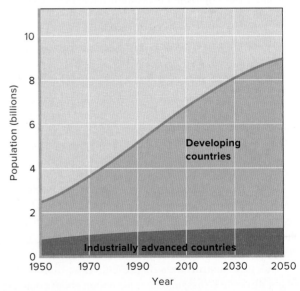

Source: Population Reference Bureau, **www.prb.org**. The underlying data are from the United Nations Population Division, *World Population Prospects: The 2012 Revision*.

increases life expectancy. Also, the death rate falls as a result of the basic medical and sanitation programs that accompany greater economic development. Second, the birthrate initially rises, particularly if medical and sanitation programs reduce infant mortality. For these reasons, the rapid population growth that results from income increases can convert an expanding standard of living into a stagnant or very-slow-growing standard of living.

Population expansion can also impede economic development in four additional ways:

- *Reduced saving and investment* The expenses associated with raising large families often reduce the capacity of households to save, thereby restricting the economy's ability to accumulate capital.

- *Lower productivity* As population increases, added investment is required to maintain the amount of real capital per person. If investment fails to keep pace, then on average each worker will have fewer tools and less equipment, and that will reduce worker productivity (output per worker). Declining productivity implies stagnating or declining per capita incomes.

- *Overuse of land resources* Because most developing countries are heavily dependent on agriculture, rapid population growth may cause an overuse of land resources. The much-publicized African famines of the 1980s and 1990s were partly the result of overgrazing and overplanting of land caused by the pressing need to feed a growing population. Population pressures also can encourage excessive cutting down of trees for use as fuel. This denuding of the landscape contributes to severe soil erosion from wind and water. Finally, in some cases population pressure leads to the use of crop waste and animal dung as needed fuel rather than as fertilizer to replenish the productivity of the soil.

- *Contribution to urban problems* Rapid population growth in the cities of the DVCs, accompanied by unprecedented inflows of rural migrants, generates massive urban problems. Rapid population growth aggravates problems such as substandard housing, poor public services, congestion, pollution, and crime. Resolving or reducing these difficulties necessitates diverting resources from growth-oriented uses.

Most authorities see birth control as a key strategy for breaking out of the population dilemma. And breakthroughs in contraceptive technology in recent decades have made this solution increasingly relevant. As we have indicated, fertility rates have dropped significantly in the DVCs. But obstacles to population control are still present. Low literacy rates make it difficult to disseminate information about contraceptive devices. In peasant agriculture, large families are a major source of labor. Adults may regard having many children as a kind of informal social security system; the more children, the greater the probability of the parents' having a relative to care for them in old age.

Chinese authorities took a harsh stance on fertility choices in 1980, when they instituted a "one child per family" law that imposed fines, removed social benefits, and in some cases forced abortions on any family that had, or attempted to have, more than one child. The law was widely credited with assisting in the dramatic increase in living standards that accompanied China's subsequent economic boom. But the policy may have been too effective over the long run because, by 2015, China's labor force was declining and the government faced a situation in which too few workers would be paying taxes to support too many retirees. The law was overturned in late 2015 in hopes of encouraging Chinese families to have more children.

Qualifications We need to qualify our focus on population growth as a major cause of low per-capita incomes, however. As with the relationship between natural resources and living standards, the relationship between population sizes and living standards is less clear than one might expect. High population density certainly does not consign a nation to poverty. China and India have immense populations and are poor, but Japan, Singapore, and Hong Kong are densely populated and are wealthy. Moreover, the standard of living in many parts of China and India has rapidly increased in recent years.

Also, the population growth rate for the DVCs as a group has declined significantly in recent decades. Between 2000 and 2010, their annual population growth rate was about 1.3 percent; for 2010 through 2020, it is projected to fall to 1.1 percent (compared to 0.4 percent in the IACs). The world's population actually is projected to decline in the last part of this century.

Finally, not everyone agrees that reducing population growth is the best way to increase per capita GDP in the developing countries. Economists point to a **demographic transition** that occurs as economic growth takes off. In this transition, rising income transforms the population dynamics of a nation by reducing birthrates. In this view, high fertility rates and large populations are a consequence of low income, not the underlying cause. The task of a nation is to increase output and income. With success, declining birthrates will automatically follow.

This view recognizes both marginal benefits and marginal costs of having another child. In DVCs, the marginal benefits are relatively large because the extra child becomes an extra worker who can help support the family. Extra children can provide financial support and security for parents in their old age, so people in poor countries have high birthrates. But in wealthy IACs, the marginal cost of having another child is relatively high. Care of children may require that one of the parents incur the opportunity cost of sacrificing high earnings or that the parents purchase expensive child care. Also, children require extended and expensive education for the highly skilled jobs characteristic of the IAC economies. At the same time, the marginal benefits of having a child may also be lower in a wealthy IAC. In particular, most IACs are wealthy enough to afford extensive "social safety nets" (such as retirement and disability benefits) that protect adults from the insecurity associated with old age and the inability to work. People in the IACs therefore recognize that high birthrates are not in the family's short-term or long-term interest. Thus, many of them choose to have fewer children.

Note the differences in causation between the traditional view and the demographic transition view of population. The traditional view is that reduced birthrates must first be achieved and then higher per capita income can follow. Lower birthrates enable per capita income to rise. The demographic transition view is that higher output and income should first be achieved and then lower rates of population growth eventually will follow. Higher incomes reduce population growth.

Development economists typically suggest a dual approach to development that combines both views. The surest way for the poorest DVCs to break out of their poverty is to implement policies that expand output and income while establishing independent policies that give families greater access to birth control information and methods. In terms of the standard of living equation (1) earlier in this section, a set of policies that raises the numerator (total income) and holds constant or lowers the denominator (population) will provide the biggest lift to a developing nation's standard of living.

Unemployment and Underemployment

A second human resource dimension of developing countries relates to employment. For many DVCs, employment-related data are either nonexistent or highly unreliable. But observation suggests that unemployment is high. There is also significant **underemployment,** which means that a large number of people are employed fewer hours per week than they want, work at jobs unrelated to their training, or spend much of the time on their jobs unproductively.

Many economists contend that unemployment may be as high as 15 to 20 percent in the rapidly growing urban areas of the DVCs. There has been substantial migration in most developing countries from rural to urban areas, motivated by the expectation of finding jobs with higher wage rates than are available in agricultural and other rural employment. But this huge migration to the cities reduces a migrant's chance of obtaining a job. In many cases, migration to the cities has greatly exceeded the growth of urban job opportunities, resulting in very high urban unemployment rates. Thus, rapid rural-urban migration has given rise to urban unemployment rates that are two or three times as great as rural rates.

Underemployment is widespread and characteristic of most DVCs. In many of the poorer DVCs, rural agricultural labor is so abundant relative to capital and natural resources that a significant percentage of the labor contributes little or nothing to agricultural output. Similarly, many DVC workers are self-employed as proprietors of small shops, in handicrafts, or as street vendors. Unfortunately, however, many of them must endure long stretches of idle time at work due to a lack of demand. While they are not unemployed, they are clearly underemployed.

Low Labor Productivity   The final human resource reality in developing nations is that labor productivity is low. As we will see, DVCs have found it difficult to invest in physical capital. As a result, their workers are poorly equipped with machinery and tools and therefore are relatively unproductive. Remember that rapid population growth tends to reduce the amount of physical capital available per worker, and that reduction erodes labor productivity and decreases real per capita incomes.

Moreover, most poor countries have not been able to invest adequately in their human capital (see Table 28.1, columns 3 and 4); consequently, expenditures on health and education have been meager. Low levels of literacy, malnutrition, lack of proper medical care, and insufficient educational facilities all contribute to populations that are ill equipped for industrialization and economic expansion. Attitudes may also play a role: In countries where hard work is associated with slavery and inferiority, many people try to avoid it. Also, by denying educational and work opportunities to women, many of the poorest DVCs forgo vast amounts of productive human capital.

Particularly vital is the absence of a vigorous entrepreneurial class willing to bear risks, accumulate capital, and provide the organizational requisites essential to economic growth. Closely related is the lack of labor trained to handle the routine supervisory functions basic to any program of development. Ironically, the higher-education systems of some DVCs emphasize the humanities and offer relatively few courses in business, engineering, and the sciences. Some DVCs are characterized by an authoritarian view of human relations, sometimes fostered by repressive governments, that creates an environment hostile to thinking independently, taking initiatives, and assuming economic risks. Authoritarianism discourages experimentation and change, which are the essence of entrepreneurship.

While migration from the DVCs has modestly offset rapid population growth, it has also deprived some DVCs of highly productive workers. Often the best-trained and most highly motivated workers, such as physicians, engineers, teachers, and nurses, leave the DVCs to better their circumstances in the IACs. This so-called **brain drain** contributes to the deterioration in the overall skill level and productivity of the labor force.

Capital Accumulation

The accumulation of capital goods is an important focal point of economic development. All DVCs have a relative dearth of capital goods such as factories, machinery and equipment, and public utilities. Better-equipped labor forces would greatly enhance productivity and would help boost per capita output. There is a close relationship between output per worker (labor productivity) and real income per worker. A nation must produce more goods and services per worker as output to enjoy more goods and services per worker as income. One way of increasing labor productivity is to provide each worker with more tools and equipment.

Increasing the stock of capital goods is crucial because the possibility of augmenting the supply of arable land is slight. An alternative is to supply the available agricultural workforce with more and better capital equipment. And, once initiated, the process of capital accumulation may be cumulative. If capital accumulation increases output faster than the growth in population, a margin of saving may arise that permits further capital formation. In a sense, capital accumulation feeds on itself.

Let's first consider the possibility that developing nations will manage to accumulate capital domestically. Then we will consider the possibility that foreign funds will flow into developing nations to support capital expansion.

Domestic Capital Formation

A developing nation, like any other nation, accumulates capital through saving and investing. A nation must save (refrain from consumption) to free some of its resources from the production of consumer goods. Investment spending must then absorb those released resources in the production of capital goods. But impediments to saving and investing are much greater in a low-income nation than they are in an advanced economy.

Savings Potential

Consider first the savings side of the picture. The situation here is mixed and varies greatly between countries. Some of the very poor countries, such as Burundi, Chad, Ghana, Guinea, Liberia, Madagascar, Mozambique, and Sierra Leone, have negative saving or save only 0 to 7 percent of their GDPs. The people are simply too poor to save a significant portion of their incomes. Interestingly, however, some middle-income countries save a larger percentage of their domestic outputs than do advanced industrial countries. In 2010 India and China saved 34 and 53 percent of their domestic outputs, respectively, compared to 24 percent for Japan, 23 percent for Germany, and 11 percent for the United States. The problem is that the domestic outputs of the DVCs are so low that even when saving rates are larger than those of advanced nations, the total volume of saving is not large.

Capital Flight

Some of the developing countries have suffered **capital flight,** the transfer of private DVC savings to accounts held in the IACs. (In this usage, "capital" is simply "money," "money capital," or "financial capital.") Many wealthy citizens of DVCs have used their savings to invest in the more economically advanced nations, enabling them to avoid the high investment risks at home, such as loss of savings or real capital from government expropriation, abrupt changes in taxation, potential hyperinflation, or high volatility of exchange rates. If a DVC's political climate is unsettled, savers may shift their funds overseas to a "safe haven" in fear that a new government might confiscate their wealth. Rapid or skyrocketing inflation in a DVC would have similar detrimental effects. The transfer of savings overseas may also be a means of evading high domestic taxes on interest income or capital gains. Finally, money capital may flow to the IACs to achieve higher interest rates or a greater variety of investment opportunities.

Whatever the motivation, the amount of capital flight from some DVCs is significant and offsets much of the IACs' lending and granting of other financial aid to developing nations.

Investment Obstacles

There are as many obstacles on the investment side of capital formation in DVCs as on the saving side. Those obstacles include a lack of investors and a lack of incentives to invest.

In some developing nations, the major obstacle to investment is the lack of entrepreneurs who are willing to assume the risks associated with investment. This is a special case of the human capital limitations of the labor force mentioned above.

But the incentive to invest may be weak even in the presence of substantial savings and a large number of willing entrepreneurs. Several factors may combine in a DVC to reduce investment incentives, including political instability, high rates of inflation, and lack of economies of scale. Similarly, very low incomes in a DVC result in a lack of buying power and thus weak demand for all but agricultural goods. This factor is crucial because the chances of competing successfully with mature industries in the international market are slim. Then, too, lack of trained administrative personnel may be a factor in retarding investment.

Finally, the **infrastructure** (stock of public capital goods) in many DVCs is insufficient to enable private firms to achieve adequate returns on their investments. Poor roads and bridges, inadequate railways, little gas and electricity production, poor communications, unsatisfactory housing, and inadequate educational and public health facilities create an inhospitable environment for private investment. A substantial portion of any new private investment would have to be used to create the infrastructure needed by all firms. Rarely can firms provide an investment in infrastructure themselves and still earn a positive return on their overall investment.

For all these reasons, investment incentives in many DVCs are lacking. It is significant that four-fifths of the overseas investments of multinational firms go to the IACs and only one-fifth to the DVCs. If the multinationals are reluctant to invest in the DVCs, we can hardly blame local entrepreneurs for being reluctant too.

How then can developing nations build up the infrastructure needed to attract investment? The higher-income DVCs may be able to accomplish this through taxation and public spending. But, in the poorest DVCs, there is little income to tax. Nevertheless, with leadership and a willingness to cooperate, a poor DVC can accumulate capital by transferring surplus agricultural labor to the improvement of the infrastructure. If each agricultural village allocated its surplus labor to the construction of irrigation canals, wells, schools, sanitary facilities, and roads, significant amounts of capital might be accumulated at no significant sacrifice of consumer goods production. Such investment bypasses the problems inherent in the financial aspects of the capital accumulation process. It does not require that consumers save portions of their money income, nor does it presume the presence of an entrepreneurial class eager to invest. When leadership and cooperative spirit are present, this "in-kind" investment is a promising avenue for accumulation of basic capital goods.

Technological Advance

Technological advance and capital formation are frequently part of the same process. Yet there are advantages in discussing technological advance separately.

Given the rudimentary state of technology in the DVCs, they are far from the frontiers of technological advance. But the IACs have accumulated an enormous body of technological knowledge that the developing countries might adopt and apply without expensive research. Crop rotation and contour plowing require no additional capital equipment and would contribute significantly to productivity. By raising grain storage bins a few inches above ground, a large amount of grain spoilage could be avoided. Although such changes may sound trivial to people of advanced nations, the resulting gains in productivity might mean the difference between subsistence and starvation in some poverty-ridden nations.

The application of either existing or new technological knowledge often requires the use of new and different capital goods. But, within limits, a nation can obtain at least part of that capital without an increase in the rate of capital formation. If a DVC channels the annual flow of replacement investment from technologically inferior to technologically superior capital equipment, it can increase productivity even with a constant level of investment spending. Actually, it can achieve some advances through **capital-saving technology** rather than **capital-using technology.** A new fertilizer, better adapted to a nation's topography and climate, might be cheaper than the fertilizer currently being used. A seemingly high-priced metal plow that will last 10 years may be cheaper in the long run than an inexpensive but technologically inferior wooden plow that has to be replaced every year.

To what extent have DVCs adopted and effectively used available IAC technological knowledge? The picture is mixed. There is no doubt that such technological borrowing has been instrumental in the rapid growth of such Pacific Rim countries as Japan, South Korea, Taiwan, and Singapore. Similarly, the OPEC nations have benefited significantly from IAC knowledge of oil exploration, production, and refining. Recently Russia, the nations of eastern Europe, and China have adopted Western technology to hasten their conversion to market-based economies.

Still, the transfer of advanced technologies to the poorest DVCs is not an easy matter. In IACs technological advances usually depend on the availability of highly skilled labor and abundant capital. Such advances tend to be capital-using or, to put it another way, labor-saving. Developing economies require technologies appropriate to quite different resource endowments: abundant unskilled labor and very limited quantities of capital goods. Although labor-using and capital-saving technologies are appropriate to DVCs, much of the highly advanced technology of advanced nations is inappropriate to them. They must develop their own appropriate technologies. Moreover, many DVCs have "traditional economies" and are not highly receptive to change. That is particularly true of peasant agriculture, which dominates the economies of most of the poorer DVCs. Since technological change that fails may well mean hunger and malnutrition, there is a strong tendency to retain traditional production techniques.

Sociocultural and Institutional Factors

Economic considerations alone do not explain why an economy does or does not grow. Substantial sociocultural and institutional readjustments are usually an integral part of the growth process. Economic development means not only changes in a nation's physical environment (new transportation and communications facilities, new schools, new housing, new plants and equipment) but also changes in the way people think, behave, and associate with one another. Emancipation from custom and tradition is frequently a prerequisite of economic development. A critical but intangible ingredient in that development is the **will to develop.** Economic growth may hinge on what individuals within DVCs want for themselves and their children. Do they want more material abundance? If so, are they willing to make the necessary changes in their institutions and old ways of doing things?

Sociocultural Obstacles Sociocultural impediments to growth are numerous and varied. Some of the very-low-income countries have failed to achieve the preconditions for a national economic entity. Tribal and ethnic allegiances take precedence over national allegiance. Each tribe confines its economic activity to the tribal unit, eliminating any possibility for production-increasing specialization and trade.

The desperate economic circumstances in Somalia, Sudan, Libya, Syria, and Afghanistan are due in no small measure to military and political conflicts among rival groups.

In countries with a formal or informal caste system, labor is allocated to occupations on the basis of status or tradition rather than on the basis of skill or merit. The result is a misallocation of human resources.

Religious beliefs and observances may seriously restrict the length of the workday and divert to ceremonial uses resources that might have been used for investment. Some religious and philosophical beliefs are dominated by the fatalistic view that the universe is capricious, the idea that there is little or no correlation between an individual's activities and endeavors and the outcomes or experiences that person encounters. The **capricious-universe view** leads to a fatalistic attitude. If "providence" rather than hard work, saving, and investing is the cause of one's lot in life, why save, work hard, and invest? Why engage in family planning? Why innovate?

Other attitudes and cultural factors may impede economic activity and growth: emphasis on the performance of duties rather than on individual initiative; focus on the group rather than on individual achievement; and the belief in reincarnation, which reduces the importance of one's current life.

Institutional Obstacles   Political corruption and bribery are common in many DVCs. School systems and public service agencies are often ineptly administered, and their functioning is frequently impaired by petty politics. Tax systems are frequently arbitrary, unjust, cumbersome, and detrimental to incentives to work and invest. Political decisions are often motivated by a desire to enhance the nation's international prestige rather than to foster development.

Because of the predominance of farming in DVCs, the problem of achieving an optimal institutional environment in agriculture is a vital consideration in any growth program. Specifically, the institutional problem of **land reform** demands attention in many DVCs. But the reform that is needed may vary tremendously from nation to nation. In some DVCs the problem is excessive concentration of land ownership in the hands of a few wealthy families. This situation is demoralizing for tenants, weakens their incentive to produce, and typically does not promote capital improvements. At the other extreme is the situation in which each family owns and farms a piece of land far too small for the use of modern agricultural technology. An important complication to the problem of land reform is that political considerations sometimes push reform in the direction of farms that are too small to achieve economies of scale. For many nations, land reform is the most acute institutional problem to be resolved in initiating economic development.

Examples: Land reform in South Korea weakened the political control of the landed aristocracy and opened the way for the emergence of strong commercial and industrial middle classes, all to the benefit of the country's economic development. In contrast, the prolonged dominance of the landed aristocracy in the Philippines may have stifled economic development in that nation.

QUICK REVIEW 28.1

✓ About 9 percent of the world's population lives in the low-income DVCs, which typically are characterized by scarce natural resources, inhospitable climates, large populations, high unemployment and underemployment, low education levels, and low labor productivity.

✓ For DVCs just beginning to modernize, high birthrates caused by improved medical care and sanitation can increase population faster than income growth, leading to lower living standards; but as development continues, the opportunity costs of having children rise and population growth typically slows.

✓ Low saving rates, capital flight, weak infrastructures, and lack of investors impair capital accumulation in many DVCs.

✓ Sociocultural and institutional factors are often serious impediments to economic growth in DVCs.

The Vicious Circle

LO28.3 Explain the vicious circle of poverty that afflicts low-income nations.

Many of the characteristics of the poorest of the DVCs just described are both causes and consequences of their poverty. These countries are caught in a **vicious circle of poverty.** They stay poor because they are poor! Consider Figure 28.3. Common to most DVCs is low per capita income. A family that is poor has little ability or incentive to save. Furthermore, low incomes mean low levels of product demand. Thus, there are few available resources, on the one hand, and no strong incentives, on the other hand, for investment in physical or human capital. Consequently, labor productivity is low. And since output per person is real income per person, it follows that per capita income is low.

Many economists think that the key to breaking out of this vicious circle is to increase the rate of capital accumulation, to achieve a level of investment of, say, 10 percent of the national income. But Figure 28.3 reminds us that rapid population growth may partially or entirely undo the potentially beneficial effects of a higher rate of capital accumulation. Suppose that initially a DVC is realizing no growth in its real GDP but somehow manages to increase saving and investment to 10 percent of its GDP. As a result, real GDP begins to grow at, say, 2.5 percent per year. With a stable population, real GDP per capita will also grow at 2.5 percent per year. If that growth persists, the standard of living will double in

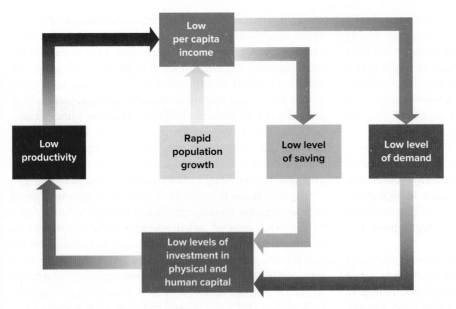

FIGURE 28.3 **The vicious circle of poverty.** Low per capita incomes make it difficult for poor nations to save and invest, a condition that perpetuates low productivity and low incomes. Furthermore, rapid population growth may quickly absorb increases in per capita real income and thereby destroy the possibility of breaking out of the poverty circle.

about 28 years. But what if population also grows at the rate of 2.5 percent per year, as it does in parts of the Middle East, northern Africa, and sub-Saharan Africa? Then real income per person will remain unchanged and the vicious circle will persist.

But if population can be kept constant or limited to some growth rate significantly below 2.5 percent, real income per person will rise. Then the possibility arises of further enlargement of the flows of saving and investment, continuing advances in productivity, and the continued growth of per capita real income. If a process of self-sustaining expansion of income, saving, investment, and productivity can be achieved, the self-perpetuating vicious circle of poverty can be transformed into a self-regenerating, beneficent circle of economic progress. The challenge is to make effective policies and strategies that will accomplish that transition.

The Role of Government

LO28.4 Discuss the role of government in promoting economic development within low-income nations.

Economists see a positive role for government in fostering DVC growth, but they generally agree that government efforts must support private efforts, not substitute for them. That is not always the case in practice.

A Positive Role

Economists suggest that developing nations have several avenues for fostering economic growth and improving their standards of living.

Establishing the Rule of Law Some of the poorest countries of the world are plagued by banditry and intertribal warfare

that divert attention and resources from the task of development. A strong, stable national government is needed to establish domestic law and order and to achieve peace and unity. Research demonstrates that political instability (as measured by the number of revolutions and coups per decade) and slow economic growth go hand in hand.

Clearly defined and strictly enforced property rights bolster economic growth by ensuring that individuals receive and retain the fruits of their labor. Because legal protections reduce investment risk, the rule of law encourages direct investments by firms in the IACs. Government itself must live by the law. The presence of corruption in the government sanctions criminality throughout the economic system. Such criminality discourages the growth of output because it lowers the returns available to honest workers and honest businesspeople.

Building Infrastructure Many obstacles to economic growth are related to an inadequate infrastructure. Sanitation and basic medical programs, education, irrigation and soil conservation projects, and construction of transportation links and communication facilities are all essentially nonmarketable goods and services that yield widespread spillover benefits. Government is the only institution that is in a position to provide public infrastructure. But it need not do all the work through government entities. It can contract out much of the work to private enterprises.

With respect to both private and public infrastructure, DVCs have an unexpected advantage over more developed countries because they can act as *follower countries* when it comes to technology. DVCs can simply adopt technologies that were developed at high cost in the more technologically advanced *leader countries* without having to pay any of the development costs of those technologies. DVCs can often jump directly to the most modern and highly productive infrastructure without going through the long process of development and replacement that was required in the IACs. As a good example, many DVCs have developed Internet-capable wireless phone networks instead of using their scarce resources to build and expand landline systems.

Embracing Globalization Other things equal, open economies that participate in international trade grow faster than closed economies. Also, DVCs that welcome foreign direct investment enjoy greater growth rates than DVCs that view such investment suspiciously or even as exploitation and therefore put severe obstacles in its way.

Realistic exchange-rate policies by government also help. Exchange rates that are fixed at unrealistic levels invite balance-of-payments problems and speculative trading in currencies. Often, such trading forces a nation into an abrupt devaluation of its currency, sending shock waves throughout its economy. More flexible exchange rates enable more gradual adjustments and thus less susceptibility to major currency shocks and the domestic disruption they cause.

Building Human Capital Government programs that encourage literacy, education, and labor market skills enhance economic growth by building human capital. In particular, policies that close the education gap between women and men spur economic growth in developing countries. Promoting the education of women pays off in terms of reduced fertility, greater productivity, and greater emphasis on educating children.

And government is in a position to nurture the will to develop, to change a philosophy of "Heaven and faith will determine the course of events" to one of "God helps those who help themselves." That change encourages personal educational attainment and enhanced human capital.

Promoting Entrepreneurship The lack of a sizable and vigorous entrepreneurial class, ready and willing to accumulate capital and initiate production, indicates that in some DVCs, private enterprise is not capable of spearheading the growth process. Government may have to take the lead, at least at first. But many DVCs would benefit by converting some of their state enterprises into private firms. State enterprises often are inefficient, more concerned with providing maximum employment than with introducing modern technology and delivering goods and services at minimum per-unit cost. Moreover, state enterprises are poor "incubators" for developing profit-focused, entrepreneurial persons who leave the firm to set up their own businesses.

Developing Credit Systems The banking systems in some of the poorest DVCs are nearly nonexistent and that

makes it difficult for domestic savers and international lenders to lend money to DVC borrowers, who in turn wish to create capital goods. An effective first step in developing credit systems is through **microcredit,** in which groups of people pool their money and make small loans to budding entrepreneurs and owners of small businesses. People from the IACs can do the same, helping nurture the spirit of enterprise and foster the benefits that it brings. The benefits of microlending accrue not only to the entrepreneurs in the DVCs but to the country as a whole because the lending creates jobs, expands output, and raises the standard of living.

At the national level, DVC governments must guard against excessive money creation and the high inflation that it brings. High rates of inflation simply are not conducive to economic investment and growth because inflation lowers the real returns generated by investments. DVCs can help keep inflation in check by establishing independent central banks to maintain proper control over their money supplies. Studies indicate that DVCs that control inflation enjoy higher growth rates than those that do not.

Controlling Population Growth Government can provide information about birth control options. We have seen that slower population growth can convert increases in real output and income to increases in real *per capita* output and income. Families with fewer children consume less and save more; they also free up time for women for education and participation in the labor market. As women participate in the labor market, they tend to reduce their fertility rate, which further helps to control population growth.

Making Peace with Neighbors Countries at war or in fear of war with neighboring nations divert scarce resources to armaments, rather than to private capital or public infrastructure. Sustained peace among neighboring nations eventually leads to economic cooperation and integration, broadened markets, and stronger economic growth.

Public-Sector Problems

Although the public sector can positively influence economic development, serious problems can and do arise with government-directed initiatives. If entrepreneurial talent is lacking in the private sector, are quality leaders likely to surface in the ranks of government? Is there not a real danger that government bureaucracy will impede, not stimulate, social and economic change? And what of the tendency of some political leaders to favor spectacular "showpiece" projects at the expense of less showy but more productive programs? Might not political objectives take precedence over the economic goals of a governmentally directed development program?

Development experts are less enthusiastic about the role of government in the growth process than they were 30 years

GLOBAL PERSPECTIVE 28.1

The Corruption Perceptions Index, Selected Nations, 2015*

The corruption perceptions index measures the degree of corruption existing among public officials and politicians as seen by business people, risk analysts, and the general public. An index value of 100 is highly clean and 0 is highly corrupt.

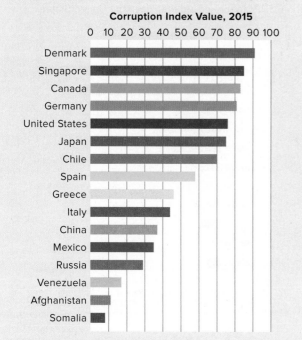

Corruption Index Value, 2015

0 10 20 30 40 50 60 70 80 90 100

Denmark
Singapore
Canada
Germany
United States
Japan
Chile
Spain
Greece
Italy
China
Mexico
Russia
Venezuela
Afghanistan
Somalia

*Index values are subject to change on the basis of election outcomes, military coups, and so on.

Source: Corruption Perceptions Index 2015, Transparency International. For more information, visit **http://www.transparency.org**.

ago. Unfortunately, government misadministration and **corruption** are common in many DVCs, and government officials sometimes line their own pockets with foreign-aid funds. Moreover, political leaders often confer monopoly privileges on relatives, friends, and political supporters and grant exclusive rights to relatives or friends to produce, import, or export certain products. Such monopoly privileges lead to higher domestic prices and diminish the DVC's ability to compete in world markets.

Similarly, managers of state-owned enterprises are often appointed on the basis of cronyism rather than competence. Many DVC governments, particularly in Africa, have created "marketing boards" as the sole purchaser of agricultural products from local farmers. The boards buy farm products at artificially low prices and sell them at higher world prices; the "profit" ends up in the pockets of government officials. In recent years the perception of government has shifted from that of catalyst and promoter of growth to that of a potential

impediment to development. According to a recent ranking of 176 nations based on perceived corruption, the 40 nations at the bottom of the list (most corrupt) were DVCs. Global Perspective 28.1 shows the corruption scores for 16 selected nations, including the two least corrupt (Denmark and Singapore) and the two most corrupt (Afghanistan and Somalia).

The Role of Advanced Nations

LO28.5 Describe how industrial nations attempt to aid low-income countries.

How can the IACs help developing countries in their pursuit of economic growth? To what degree have IACs provided assistance?

Expanding Trade

Some authorities maintain that the simplest and most effective way for the United States and other industrially advanced nations to aid developing nations is to lower international trade barriers. Such action would enable DVCs to elevate their national incomes through increased trade. Trade barriers instituted by the IACs are often highest for labor-intensive manufactured goods, such as textiles, clothing, footwear, and processed agricultural products. These are precisely the sorts of products for which the DVCs have a comparative advantage. Also, many IACs' tariffs rise as the degree of product processing increases; for example, tariffs on chocolates are higher than those on cocoa. This practice discourages the DVCs from developing processing industries of their own.

Additionally, large agricultural subsidies in the IACs encourage excessive production of food and fiber in the IACs. The overproduction flows into world markets, where it depresses agricultural prices. DVCs, which typically do not subsidize farmers, therefore face artificially low prices for their farm exports. The IACs could greatly help DVCs by reducing farm subsidies along with tariffs.

But lowering trade barriers is certainly not a panacea. Some poor nations need only large foreign markets for their raw materials to achieve growth. But the problem for many poor nations is not to obtain markets in which to sell existing products or relatively abundant raw materials but to get the capital and technical assistance they need to produce products for domestic consumption.

Also, close trade ties with advanced nations entail certain disadvantages. Dependence by the DVCs on exports to the IACs leaves the DVCs highly vulnerable to recessions in the IACs. As firms cut back production in the IACs, the demand for DVC resources declines; and as income in the IACs declines, the demand for DVC-produced goods declines. By reducing the demand for DVC exports, recessions in the IACs can severely reduce the prices of raw materials exported by the DVCs. For example, during the recession of 2007–2009, the world price of zinc fell from $2.02 per pound to $0.49 per pound, and the world price of copper fell from $4.05 per pound to $1.40 per pound. These declines in prices severely reduce the export earnings of the DVCs. Because mineral exports are a significant source of DVC income, stability and growth in IACs are important to improved standards of living in the developing nations.

Admitting Temporary Workers

Some economists recommend that the IACs help the DVCs by accepting more seasonal or other temporary workers from the DVCs. Temporary migration provides an outlet for surplus DVC labor. Moreover, migrant remittances to families in the home country serve as a sorely needed source of income. The problem, of course, is that some temporary workers illegally blend into the fabric of the IACs and do not leave when their visas or work permits expire. That may not be in the long-run best interest of the IACs.

Discouraging Arms Sales

Finally, the IACs can help the DVCs as a group by discouraging the sale of military equipment to the DVCs. Such purchases by the DVCs divert public expenditures from infrastructure and education and heighten tensions in DVCs that have long-standing disputes with neighbors.

Foreign Aid: Public Loans and Grants

Official development assistance (ODA), or simply "foreign aid," is another route through which IACs can help DVCs. This aid can play a crucial role in breaking an emerging country's circle of poverty by supplementing its saving and investment. As previously noted, many DVCs lack the infrastructure needed to attract either domestic or foreign private capital. The infusion of foreign aid that strengthens infrastructure could enhance the flow of private capital to the DVCs.

Direct Aid The United States and other IACs have assisted DVCs directly through a variety of programs designed to stimulate economic development. Over the past 10 years, U.S. loans and grants to the DVCs totaled $20 billion to $31 billion per year. The U.S. Agency for International Development (USAID) administers most of this aid. Some of it, however, consists of grants of surplus food under the Food for Peace program. Other advanced nations also have substantial foreign aid programs. In 2015 foreign aid from the IACs to the developing nations totaled $132 billion. This amounted to about one-fourth of 1 percent of the collective GDP of the IACs that year (see Global Perspective 28.2 for percentages for selected nations).

A large portion of foreign aid is distributed on the basis of political and military rather than strictly economic considerations. Afghanistan, Egypt, Iraq, Israel, Pakistan, and Turkey,

GLOBAL PERSPECTIVE 28.2

Development Assistance as a Percentage of GDP, Selected Nations

In terms of absolute amounts, the United States was the leading provider of development assistance in 2015. It provided $31.0 billion to developing nations. But many other industrialized nations contribute a larger percentage of their GDPs to foreign aid than does the United States.

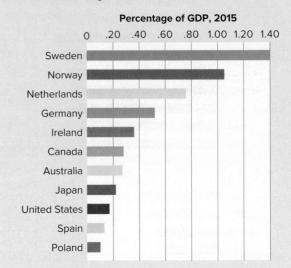

Percentage of GDP, 2015

Source: Development Co-operation Report, 2015, Organization for Economic Cooperation and Development (OECD), www.oecd.org/dac.

for example, are major recipients of U.S. aid. Asian, Latin American, and African nations with lower standards of living receive less.

Only one-fourth of foreign aid goes to the 10 countries in which 70 percent of the world's poorest people live. The most affluent 40 percent of the DVC population receives over twice as much aid as the poorest 40 percent. Many economists argue that the IACs should shift foreign aid away from the middle-income DVCs and toward the poorest DVCs.

Some of the world's poorest nations *do* receive large amounts of foreign aid relative to their meager GDPs. For example, in 2014 foreign aid relative to GDP was 63 percent in Tuvalu, 44 percent in Liberia, 23 percent in Afghanistan, 21 percent in Sierra Leone, and 13 percent in Mozambique.

Also, these and many other low-income developing nations receive large amounts of support from private donors in the IACs. In fact, in recent years the private giving to the DVCs by private U.S. universities, foundations (such as the Gates Foundation), voluntary organizations, and religious organizations has exceeded the foreign aid provided by the U.S. government.

The large accumulated debts of some of the poorest DVCs have become a severe roadblock to their growth. Therefore, some of the recent direct assistance by the IACs to the DVCs has taken the form of forgiving parts of the past IAC-government loans to low-income DVCs. In 2005 the G8 nations canceled $55 billion of debt owed by developing countries to the World Bank, the International Monetary Fund, and the African Development Bank. Of course, debt forgiveness creates a *moral hazard problem*. If current debt forgiveness creates an expectation of later debt forgiveness, a country has little incentive against running up a new debt. Therefore, future loans by the IACs must be extended cautiously to the low-income developing nations that receive current debt forgiveness.

The World Bank Group The United States and other IACs also support the DVCs by participating in the **World Bank,** whose major objective is helping DVCs achieve economic growth. The World Bank was established in 1945, along with the International Monetary Fund (IMF). Supported by about 188 member nations, the World Bank not only lends out of its capital funds but also sells bonds and lends the proceeds and guarantees and insures private loans:

- The World Bank is a "last-resort" lending agency; its loans are limited to economic projects for which private funds are not readily available.

- Many World Bank loans have been for basic development projects—dams, irrigation projects, health and sanitation programs, communications, and transportation facilities. Consequently, the Bank has helped finance the infrastructure needed to encourage the flow of private capital.

- The Bank has provided technical assistance to the DVCs by helping them determine what avenues of growth seem appropriate for their economic development.

Affiliates of the World Bank function in areas where the World Bank has proved weak. The *International Finance Corporation (IFC)*, for example, invests in private enterprises in the DVCs. The *International Development Association (IDA)* makes "soft loans" (which may not be self-liquidating) to the poorest DVCs on more liberal terms than does the World Bank.

Foreign Harm? Although official development assistance directly from the IACs and indirectly through the World Bank has generally helped the DVCs expand their economies, the foreign-aid approach to helping DVCs has met with several criticisms.

Dependency and Incentives A basic criticism is that foreign aid may promote dependency rather than self-sustaining growth. Critics argue that injections of funds from the IACs encourage the DVCs to ignore the painful economic decisions, the institutional and cultural reforms, and the changes in attitudes toward thrift, industry, hard work, and self-reliance that are needed for economic growth. They say that, after some five decades of foreign aid, the DVCs' demand for foreign aid has increased rather than decreased. These aid programs should have withered away if they had been successful in promoting sustainable growth.

Bureaucracy and Centralized Government IAC aid is given to the governments of the DVCs, not to their residents or businesses. The consequence is that the aid typically generates massive, ineffective government bureaucracies and centralizes government power over the economy. The stagnation and collapse of the Soviet Union and communist countries of eastern Europe is evidence that highly bureaucratized economies are not very conducive to economic growth and development. Furthermore, not only does the bureaucratization of the DVCs divert valuable human resources from the private to the public sector, but it often shifts the nation's focus from producing more output to bickering over how unearned "income" should be distributed.

Corruption and Misuse Critics also allege that foreign aid is being used ineffectively. As we noted previously, corruption is a major problem in many DVCs, and some estimates suggest that from 10 to 20 percent of the aid is diverted to government officials. Also, IAC-based aid consultants and multinational corporations are major beneficiaries of aid programs. Some economists contend that as much as one-fourth of each year's aid is spent on expert consultants. Furthermore, because IAC corporations manage many of the aid projects, they are major beneficiaries of, and lobbyists for, foreign aid.

Current Level of Foreign Aid After declining in the late 1990s, foreign aid increased between 2000 and 2008. This increase resulted from a renewed international emphasis on reducing global poverty and also from expanded efforts by the IACs to enlist the cooperation of DVCs in fighting terrorism. In 2015 foreign direct aid by IAC governments to developing countries was $132 billion.

Flows of Private Capital

The IACs also send substantial amounts of private capital to the DVCs. Among the private investors are corporations, commercial banks, and, more recently, financial investment companies. General Motors or Ford might finance the construction of plants in Mexico or Brazil to assemble autos or produce auto parts. JPMorgan Chase or Bank of America might make loans to private firms operating in Argentina or China or to the governments of Thailand and Malaysia. And individuals living in IACs might purchase shares in "emerging markets" mutual funds run by investment companies like Fidelity. Those funds make financial investments in the stock of promising firms in DVCs such as Hungary and Chile.

The total flow of private capital to DVCs was $172 billion in 2014, but the makeup of this flow differed from the

LAST WORD

Microfinance and Cash Transfers

Development Efforts Have Increasingly Focused on Lending, Granting, or Gifting Money to Individuals.

For the most of the twentieth century, international development efforts focused on infrastructure projects, such as building roads, bridges, and electrical grids. Efforts aimed directly at individuals were relatively rare and poorly funded. That has changed drastically in the last few decades as development efforts have become increasingly focused on delivering cash directly to poor individuals. The results, however, have been mixed.

Microcredit In the mid-1970s, a Bangladeshi economics professor named Muhammad Yunus discovered that making small loans to poor villagers in his native Bangladesh could sometimes facilitate economic growth and advancement at the individual level. A group of women could, for instance, start a modest but profitable textile company if they could borrow amounts of money as small as $10 or $20 to purchase looms and other equipment.

The even more startling part was that these small loans, or **microcredit,** were nearly always paid back. Whereas the poor had often been thought of by development experts as being too uneducated or inexperienced to help themselves out of poverty, Yunus showed that the poor often had good business sense and were in some cases constrained not by ignorance but by a lack of capital.

In 1983, Yunus established the Grameen Bank (literally the "Village Bank") to provide microcredit throughout Bangladesh. The

Source: © Tim Gerard Barker/Getty Images

Grameen Bank later expanded beyond microcredit into banking and insurance services for the poor, a set of activities that came to be referred to as **microfinance.** Its individual-focused approach to development spawned hundreds of imitators in scores of nations and earned Yunus the 2006 Nobel Peace Prize.

Unfortunately, development economists have found that microfinance does not offer a consistent way out of poverty by itself.

flow in earlier decades. The main private investors and lenders are now private IAC firms and individuals, not commercial banks. Also, more of the flow is in the form of **foreign direct investment** in DVCs, rather than loans to DVC governments. Such direct investment includes the building of new factories in DVCs by multinational firms and the purchase of DVC firms (or parts of them). Whereas DVCs once viewed foreign direct investment as "exploitation," many of them now seek out foreign direct investment as a way to expand their capital stock and improve their citizens' job opportunities and wages. Those wages are often very low by IAC standards but high by DVC standards. Another benefit of direct investment in DVCs is that management skills and technological knowledge often accompany the capital.

Unfortunately for the low-income DVCs, the strong flow of private capital to the DVCs has been very selective. The vast majority of IAC investment and lending has been directed toward China, India, Mexico, and other middle-income DVCs, with only small amounts flowing toward such extremely impoverished DVCs as those in Africa.

In fact, as we have indicated, many of the lowest-income countries face staggering debt burdens from previous government and private loans. Payment of interest and principal on this external debt is diverting expenditures away from maintenance of infrastructure, new infrastructure, education, and private investment.

Further, the flows of private capital to both the middle-income and low-income DVCs plummeted after the worldwide recession of 2007–2009. It may be several years before foreign direct investment regains its momentum.

QUICK REVIEW 28.2

- ✓ The IACs can assist the DVCs through expanded trade, foreign aid, and flows of private capital.
- ✓ Many of the poorest DVCs have large external debts that pose an additional obstacle to economic growth.
- ✓ The worldwide recession of 2007–2009 greatly reduced direct investment by the IACs in the DVC economies.

Randomized experiments show that, on average, the households and individuals receiving microcredit usually do no better than non-recipients on economic, health, and social outcomes such as family income, the total number of calories consumed, and rates of school attendance.

Conditional Cash Transfers Conditional cash transfer programs provide poor families with transfers (grants) of cash if they send their children to school and participate in preventative health programs. As just one example, the Mexican government's *Oportunidades* program gives bi-weekly cash grants to poor families who keep their kids in school and participate in health screenings and nutritional programs.

Conditional cash transfer programs have been in place since the early 1990s, which makes them old enough for us to be able to draw some conclusions about their effectiveness. Some very positive outcomes are apparent. The programs have been shown to increase school enrollment by up to 30 percent and to improve health and nutrition so much that rates of illness among young children fall by more than 10 percent. Children enrolled in conditional cash transfer programs also end up taller than children who are not enrolled.

Unfortunately, the effectiveness of conditional cash transfers in relieving poverty in developing countries is limited by other factors. As just one example, school enrollment goes up but test scores stay the same, probably because the schools themselves are poorly funded and often ineffective. Similarly, the wages earned by the students who stay in school longer don't seem to be much higher than those of the students who dropped out earlier, probably because of the low quality of many schools as well as high rates of unemployment in many local labor markets.

Unconditional Cash Transfers The newest antipoverty initiatives targeted at individuals are known as **unconditional cash transfers** because they simply hand cash to poor adults with no conditions attached. They operate under the theory that many poor people are held back by a lack of either physical or human capital, and that if you were to give them no-strings-attached cash, they would use the money to pay for tools and training.

That assumption has proven true in early testing. As an example, a randomized study in Uganda that started in 2008 offered the chance to receive unconditional cash transfers to young people who were willing to submit essays detailing what they planned to do with any money received. Half of the participants were then randomly selected to receive the money, with it being made explicitly clear that nobody would be following up to see if the recipients actually spent the money on what they had written in their essays (which, for the most part, indicated a desire to spend cash transfers on vocational training and business equipment).

The researchers running the study found that the half who were randomly selected to receive unconditional cash transfers ended up "65 percent more likely to practice a skilled trade such as carpentry, metalworking, tailoring, or hairstyling" than those who did not receive unconditional cash transfers. Even better, the results were long lasting, with recipients earning salaries that were 41 percent higher four years later.

Because unconditional cash transfer programs are quite new, however, it is not yet clear whether their early promise can be replicated in other places or even why granting cash unconditionally seems to work better than either conditional cash transfers or microfinance. Experiments are under way to find out.

SUMMARY

LO28.1 Describe how the World Bank distinguishes between industrially advanced countries and developing countries.

The majority of the world's nations are developing countries (low- and middle-income nations). While some DVCs have been realizing rapid growth rates in recent years, others have experienced little or no growth.

LO28.2 List some of the obstacles to economic development.

Scarcities of natural resources make it more challenging—but certainly not impossible—for a nation to develop.

The large and rapidly growing populations in many DVCs contribute to low per capita incomes. Increases in per capita incomes frequently induce greater population growth, often reducing per capita incomes to near-subsistence levels. The demographic transition view, however, suggests that rising living standards must precede declining birthrates.

Most DVCs suffer from unemployment and underemployment. Labor productivity is low because of insufficient investment in physical and human capital.

In many DVCs, formidable obstacles impede both saving and investment. In some of the poorest DVCs, the savings potential is very low, and many savers transfer their funds to the IACs rather than invest them domestically. The lack of a vigorous entrepreneurial class and the weakness of investment incentives also impede capital accumulation.

Appropriate social and institutional changes and, in particular, the presence of the will to develop are essential ingredients in economic development.

LO28.3 Explain the vicious circle of poverty that afflicts low-income nations.

The vicious circle of poverty brings together many of the obstacles to growth, supporting the view that poor countries stay poor because of their poverty. Low incomes inhibit saving and the accumulation of physical and human capital, making it difficult to increase productivity and incomes. Overly rapid population growth, however, may offset promising attempts to break the vicious circle.

LO28.4 Discuss the role of government in promoting economic development within low-income nations.

The nature of the obstacles to growth—the absence of an entrepreneurial class, the dearth of infrastructure, the saving-investment dilemma, and the presence of social-institutional obstacles to growth—suggests that government should play a major role in initiating growth. Economists suggest that DVCs could make further development progress through such policies as establishing the rule of law, building infrastructure, opening their economies to international trade, setting realistic exchange rates, encouraging foreign direct investment, building human capital, encouraging entrepreneurship, controlling population growth, and making peace with neighbors. However, the corruption and maladministration that are common to the public sectors of many DVCs suggest that government may not be very effective in instigating growth.

LO28.5 Describe how industrial nations attempt to aid low-income countries.

Advanced nations can encourage development in the DVCs by reducing IAC trade barriers and by directing foreign aid (official development assistance) to the neediest nations, providing debt forgiveness to the poorest DVCs, allowing temporary low-skilled immigration from the DVCs, and discouraging arms sales to the DVCs. Critics of foreign aid, however, say that it (a) creates DVC dependency, (b) contributes to the growth of bureaucracies and centralized economic control, and (c) is rendered ineffective by corruption and mismanagement.

In recent years the IACs have reduced foreign aid to the DVCs but have increased direct investment and other private capital flows to the DVCs. Little of the foreign direct investment, however, has gone to the poorest DVCs. Also, foreign direct investment plummeted during the worldwide recession of 2007–2009.

TERMS AND CONCEPTS

industrially advanced countries (IACs)

developing countries (DVCs)

demographic transition

underemployment

brain drain

capital flight

infrastructure

capital-saving technology

capital-using technology

will to develop

capricious universe view

land reform

vicious circle of poverty

microcredit

corruption

World Bank

foreign direct investment

microfinance

conditional cash transfers

unconditional cash transfers

The following and additional problems can be found in connect

DISCUSSION QUESTIONS

1. What are the four categories used by the World Bank to classify nations on the basis of national income per capita? Identify any two nations of your choice for each of the four categories. **LO28.1**

2. Explain how the absolute per capita income gap between rich and poor nations might increase, even though per capita income (or output) is growing faster in DVCs than in IACs. **LO28.1**

3. Explain how each of the following can be obstacles to the growth of income per capita in the DVCs: lack of natural resources, large populations, low labor productivity, poor infrastructure, and capital flight. **LO28.2**

4. What is the demographic transition? Contrast the demographic transition view of population growth with the traditional view that slower population growth is a prerequisite for rising living standards in the DVCs. **LO28.2**

5. As it relates to the vicious circle of poverty, what is meant by the saying "Some DVCs stay poor because they are poor"? Change the box labels as necessary in Figure 28.3 to explain rapid economic growth in countries such as South Korea and Chile. What factors other than those contained in the figure might contribute to that growth? **LO28.3**

6. Because real capital is supposed to earn a higher return where it is scarce, how do you explain the fact that most international investment flows to the IACs (where capital is relatively abundant) rather than to the DVCs (where capital is very scarce)? **LO28.3**

7. List and discuss five policies that DVC governments might undertake to promote economic development and expansion of income per capita in their countries? **LO28.4**

8. Do you think that the nature of the problems the DVCs face requires a government-directed or a private-sector-directed development process? Explain your reasoning. **LO28.4**

9. Why do you think there is so much government corruption in some developing countries? LO28.4
10. What types of products do the DVCs typically export? How do those exports relate to the law of comparative advantage? How do tariffs by IACs reduce the standard of living of DVCs? LO28.5
11. Do you favor debt forgiveness to all DVCs, just the poorest ones, or none at all? What incentive problem might debt relief create? Would you be willing to pay $20 a year more in personal income taxes for debt forgiveness? How about $200? How about $2,000? LO28.5
12. Do you think that IACs such as the United States should open their doors wider to the immigration of low-skilled DVC workers as a way to help DVCs develop? Do you think that it is appropriate for students from DVC nations to stay in IAC nations to work and build careers? LO28.5
13. **LAST WORD** Explain the differences among microcredit, conditional cash transfers, and unconditional cash transfers. Then explain how effective each policy has been.

REVIEW QUESTIONS

1. True or False: The term *developing country* (DVC) is applied to rich nations like the United States and Germany because their economies are always growing quickly by developing new technologies. LO28.1
2. True or False: A DVC that has little in the way of natural resources is destined to remain poor. LO28.2
3. Suppose a country's total output is growing 10 percent per year, but its population is growing 11 percent per year. What will happen to living standards? LO28.2
   a. Rise.
   b. Fall.
   c. Remain the same.
4. A DVC's population is growing 2 percent per year and output is growing 3 percent per year. If the government wants to improve living standards over coming decades, which of the following would probably be the best savings rate for the economy? LO28.2
   a. 0 percent.
   b. 2 percent.
   c. 5 percent.
   d. 10 percent.
5. Compare a hypothetical DVC with a hypothetical IAC. In the DVC, average per capita income is $500 per year. In the IAC, average per capita income is $40,000 per year. If both countries have a savings rate of 10 percent per year, the amount of savings per capita in the DVC will be _____ per person per year, while in the IAC it will be _____ per person per year. LO28.3
   a. $50; $4,000.
   b. $5; $400.
   c. $450; $36,000.
   d. None of the above.
6. Which of the following policies would economists consider to be actions that a DVC government might take that would *improve* growth prospects? LO28.4
   Choose one or more answers from the choices shown.
   a. Helping to extend the banking system to the rural poor.
   b. Passing high tariffs against foreign products.
   c. Constructing better ports, roads, and Internet networks.
   d. Charging high fees for public elementary schools.
7. True or False: Economists are unanimous that foreign aid greatly helps DVCs. LO28.5
8. True or False: Some economists argue that the single best thing that IACs could do for DVCs in terms of economic growth would be to eliminate trade barriers between IACs and DVCs. LO28.5

PROBLEMS

1. Assume a DVC and an IAC currently have real per capita outputs of $500 and $5,000, respectively. If both nations have a 3 percent increase in their real per capita outputs, by how much will the per capita output gap change? LO28.1
2. Assume that a very tiny and very poor DVC has income per capita of $300 and total national income of $3 million. How large is its population? If its population grows by 2 percent in some year while its total income grows by 3 percent, what will be its new income per capita rounded to full dollars? If the population had not grown during the year, what would have been its income per capita? LO28.2

Note: Terms set in *italic type* are defined separately in this glossary.

ability-to-pay principle   The idea that those who have greater *income* (or *wealth*) should pay a greater proportion of it as taxes than those who have less income (or wealth).

accounting profit   The *total revenue* of a *firm* less its *explicit costs;* the profit (or net income) that appears on accounting statements and that is reported to the government for tax purposes.

acreage allotments   A pre-1996 government program that limited the total number of acres to be used in producing (reduced amounts of) various food and fiber products and allocated these acres among individual farmers. These farmers had to limit their plantings to the allotted number of acres to obtain *price supports* for their crops.

adverse selection problem   A problem arising when information known to one party to a contract or agreement is not known to the other party, causing the latter to incur major costs. Example: Individuals who have the poorest health are most likely to buy health insurance.

AFL-CIO   An acronym for the American Federation of Labor–Congress of Industrial Organizations; the largest federation of *labor unions* in the United States.

agency shop   A place of employment where the employer may hire either *labor union* members or nonmembers but where those employees who do not join the union must either pay union dues or donate an equivalent amount of money to a charity.

aggregate   A collection of specific economic units treated as if they were one unit. Examples: the *prices* of all individual *goods* and *services* are combined into the *price level,* and all units of output are aggregated into *gross domestic product.*

agribusiness   The portion of the agricultural and food product industries that is dominated by large corporations.

agricultural risk coverage   A form of crop insurance that pays out if the total revenue generated by all the farmers planting a given crop in a given county falls below a predetermined value.

Alcoa case   A 1945 case in which the courts ruled that the possession of monopoly power, no matter how reasonably that power had been used, was a violation of the antitrust laws; temporarily overturned the *rule of reason* applied in the *U.S. Steel case.*

allocative efficiency   The apportionment of resources among *firms* and industries to obtain the production of the products most wanted by society (consumers); the output of each product at which its *marginal cost* and *price* or *marginal benefit* are equal, and at which the sum of *consumer surplus* and *producer surplus* is maximized.

anchoring   The tendency people have to unconsciously base, or "anchor," the valuation of an item they are currently thinking about on recently considered but logically irrelevant information.

antitrust laws   Legislation (including the *Sherman Act* and *Clayton Act*) that prohibits anticompetitive business activities such as *price fixing,* bid rigging, monopolization, and *tying contracts.*

antitrust policy   The use of the *antitrust laws* to promote *competition* and *economic efficiency.*

asymmetric information   A situation where one party to a market transaction has much more information about a product or service than the other. The result may be an under- or overallocation of resources.

average fixed cost (AFC)   A *firm*'s total *fixed cost* divided by output (the quantity of product produced).

average product (AP)   The total output produced per unit of a *resource* employed (*total product* divided by the quantity of that employed resource).

average revenue   Total revenue from the sale of a product divided by the quantity of the product sold (demanded); equal to the *price* at which the product is sold when all units of the product are sold at the same price.

average tax rate   Total tax paid divided by total *taxable income* or some other base (such as total income) against which to compare the amount of tax paid. Expressed as a percentage.

average total cost (ATC)   A firm's *total cost* divided by output (the quantity of product produced); equal to *average fixed cost* plus *average variable cost.*

average variable cost (AVC)   A firm's total *variable cost* divided by output (the quantity of product produced).

backflows   The return of workers to the countries from which they originally emigrated.

backward induction   A method for solving for the *subgame perfect Nash equilibrium* of a *sequential game* that is presented in *extensive form.*

balance of payments   A summary of all the financial transactions that take place between the individuals, *firms,* and governmental units of one nation and those of all other nations during a year.

balance on capital and financial account   The sum of the *capital account balance* and the *financial account balance.*

balance on current account   The exports of *goods* and *services* of a nation less its imports of goods and services plus its *net investment income* and *net transfers* in a year.

balance on goods and services   The exports of *goods* and *services* of a nation less its imports of goods and services in a year.

balance-of-payments deficit   Misleading term used in the financial press to describe a net decline in a country's *foreign exchange reserves* as it buys and sells foreign exchange in order to maintain a *fixed exchange rate.* The term is misleading because a nation's *balance of payments* statement must always balance (be zero) and can never be in deficit (less than zero).

balance-of-payments surplus   Misleading term used in the financial press to describe a net increase in a country's *foreign exchange reserves* as it buys and sells foreign exchange in order to maintain a *fixed exchange rate.* The term is misleading because a nation's *balance of payments* statement must always balance (be zero) and can never be in surplus (greater than zero).

barrier to entry Anything that artificially prevents the entry of *firms* into an *industry.*

barter The direct exchange of one *good* or *service* for another good or service.

beaten paths Migration routes taken previously by family, relatives, friends, and other migrants.

behavioral economics The branch of economic theory that combines insights from economics, psychology, and biology to make more accurate predictions about human behavior than conventional *neoclassical economics,* which is hampered by its core assumptions that people are fundamentally *rational* and almost entirely self-interested. Behavioral economics can explain *framing effects, anchoring, mental accounting,* the *endowment effect, status quo bias, time inconsistency,* and *loss aversion.*

benefits-received principle The idea that those who receive the benefits of *goods* and *services* provided by government should pay the taxes required to finance them.

bilateral monopoly A market in which there is a single seller (*monopoly*) and a single buyer (*monopsony*).

brain drains The exit or *emigration* of highly educated, highly skilled workers from a country.

break-even point An output at which a *firm* makes a *normal profit* (*total revenue = total cost*) but not an *economic profit.*

Bretton Woods system The international monetary system developed after the Second World War in which *adjustable pegs* were employed, the *International Monetary Fund* help stabilize foreign exchange rates, and gold and the dollar were used as *international monetary reserves.*

British thermal unit (BTU) The amount of energy required to raise the temperature of 1 pound of water by 1 degree Fahrenheit.

budget constraint The limit that the size of a consumer's income (and the *prices* that must be paid for *goods* and *services*) imposes on the ability of that consumer to obtain goods and services.

budget deficit The amount by which expenditures exceed revenues in any year.

budget line A line that shows the different combinations of two products a consumer can purchase with a specific money income, given the products' *prices.*

businesses Economic entities (*firms*) that purchase resources and provide *goods* and *services* to the economy.

capital Human-made resources (buildings, machinery, and equipment) used to produce *goods* and *services;* goods that do not directly satisfy human wants; also called capital goods. One of the four *economic resources.*

capital and financial account The section of a nation's *international balance of payments* that records (1) debt forgiveness by and to foreigners and (2) foreign purchases of assets in the United States and U.S. purchases of assets abroad.

capital goods (See *capital.*)

capital-intensive goods Products that require relatively large amounts of *capital* to produce.

cartel A formal agreement among *firms* (or countries) in an *industry* to set the *price* of a product and establish the outputs of the individual firms (or countries) or to divide the market for the product geographically.

cease-and-desist order An order from a court or government agency to a corporation or individual to stop engaging in a specified practice.

Celler-Kefauver Act The federal law of 1950 that amended the *Clayton Act* by prohibiting the acquisition of the assets of one *firm* by another firm when the effect would be less competition.

change in demand A movement of an entire *demand curve* or schedule such that the *quantity demanded* changes at every particular *price;* caused by a change in one or more of the *determinants of demand.*

change in quantity demanded A change in the *quantity demanded* along a fixed *demand curve* (or within a fixed demand schedule) as a result of a change in the *price* of the product.

change in quantity supplied A change in the *quantity supplied* along a fixed *supply curve* (or within a fixed supply schedule) as a result of a change in the product's *price.*

change in supply A movement of an entire *supply curve* or schedule such that the *quantity supplied* changes at every particular *price;* caused by a change in one or more of the *determinants of supply.*

Change to Win A loose federation of American unions that includes the Service Workers and Teamsters unions; the second largest union federation after the *AFL-CIO.*

circular flow diagram An illustration showing the flow of *resources* from *households* to *firms* and of products from firms to households. These flows are accompanied by reverse flows of money from firms to households and from households to firms.

Clayton Act The federal antitrust law of 1914 that strengthened the *Sherman Act* by making it illegal for *firms* to engage in certain specified practices including *tying contracts, interlocking directorates,* and certain forms of *price discrimination.*

closed shop A place of employment where only workers who are already members of a labor union may be hired.

Coase theorem The idea, first stated by economist Ronald Coase, that some *externalities* can be resolved through private negotiations among the affected parties.

cognitive biases Misperceptions or misunderstandings that cause *systematic errors.* Most result either (1) from *heuristics* that are prone to *systematic errors* or (2) because the brain is attempting to solve a type of problem (such as a calculus problem) for which it was not evolutionarily evolved and for which it has little innate capability.

collective bargaining The negotiation of labor contracts between *labor unions* and *firms* or government entities.

collective-action problem The idea that getting a group to pursue a common, collective goal gets harder the larger the group's size. Larger groups are more costly to organize and their members more difficult to motivate because the larger the group, the smaller each member's share of the benefits if the group succeeds.

collusion A situation in which *firms* act together and in agreement (collude) to fix *prices,* divide a market, or otherwise restrict competition.

command system A method of organizing an economy in which property resources are publicly owned and government uses *central* *economic planning* to direct and coordinate economic activities; *socialism; communism.* Compare with *market system.*

comparative advantage   A situation in which a person or country can produce a specific product at a lower opportunity cost than some other person or country; the basis for specialization and trade.

compensating differences   Differences in the *wages* received by workers in different jobs to compensate for the nonmonetary differences between the jobs.

compensating wage differential   (See *compensating differences.*)

competition   The effort and striving between two or more independent rivals to secure the business of one or more third parties by offering the best possible terms.

complementary goods   Products and *services* that are used together. When the *price* of one falls, the demand for the other increases (and conversely).

complementary resources   Productive inputs that are used jointly with other inputs in the production process; resources for which a decrease in the *price* of one leads to an increase in the demand for the other.

compound interest   The accumulation of money that builds over time in an investment or interest-bearing account as new interest is earned on previous interest that is not withdrawn.

conflict diamonds   Diamonds that are mined and sold by combatants in war zones in Africa as a way to provide the currency needed to finance their military activities.

conglomerate merger   The merger of two *firms* operating in separate industries or separate geographic areas so that neither firm is a supplier, customer, or competitor of the other; any merger that is neither a *horizontal merger* nor a *vertical merger.*

constant returns to scale   The situation when a firm's *average total cost* of producing a product remains unchanged in the *long run* as the firm varies the size of its *plant* (and, hence, its output).

constant-cost industry   An *industry* in which the entry and exit of *firms* have no effect on the *prices* firms in the industry must pay for resources and thus no effect on production costs.

consumer equilibrium   In marginal utility theory, the combination of goods purchased that maximizes *total utility* by applying the *utility-maximizing rule.* In indifference curve analysis, the combination of goods purchased that maximizes *total utility* by enabling the consumer to reach the highest *indifference curve,* given the consumer's *budget line* (or *budget constraint*).

consumer goods   Products and *services* that satisfy human wants directly.

consumer sovereignty   The determination by consumers of the types and quantities of *goods* and *services* that will be produced with the scarce resources of the economy; consumers' direction of production through their *dollar votes.*

consumer surplus   The difference between the maximum *price* a consumer is (or consumers are) willing to pay for an additional unit of a product and its market price; the triangular area below the demand curve and above the market price.

copayment   The percentage of (say, health care) costs that an insured individual pays while the insurer pays the remainder.

corporate income tax   A tax levied on the net income (accounting profit) of corporations.

corporation   A legal entity ("person") chartered by a state or the federal government that is distinct and separate from the individuals who own it.

cost-benefit analysis   A comparison of the *marginal costs* of a project or program with the *marginal benefits* to decide whether or not to employ resources in that project or program and to what extent.

countercyclical payments (CCPs)   Cash *subsidies* paid to farmers when market *prices* for certain crops drop below targeted prices. Payments are based on previous production and are received regardless of the current crop grown.

creative destruction   The hypothesis that the creation of new products and production methods destroys the market power of existing monopolies.

credible threat   In a *sequential game* with two players, a statement made by Player 1 that truthfully (credibly) threatens a penalizing action against Player 2 if Player 2 does something that Player 1 does not want Player 2 to do. Opposite of *empty threat.*

crop insurance   Insurance that farmers can purchase that will pay out if crop selling prices or crop revenues fall below predetermined values.

cross elasticity of demand   The ratio of the percentage change in *quantity demanded* of one good to the percentage change in the *price* of some other good. A positive coefficient indicates the two products are *substitute goods;* a negative coefficient indicates they are *complementary goods.*

currency intervention   A government's buying and selling of its own currency or foreign currencies to alter international exchange rates.

current account   The section in a nation's *international balance of payments* that records its exports and imports of *goods* and *services,* its net *investment income,* and its *net transfers.*

deadweight loss   (See *efficiency loss.*)

debt crisis   An economic crisis in which government debt has risen so high that the government is unable to borrow any more money due to people losing faith in the government's ability to repay. Leads to either massive spending cuts or large tax increases, either of which will likely plunge the economy into a *recession.*

decision node   In a *strategic game* that is presented in *extensive form,* a point (node) at which a player must make a decision. The decision leads to either another *decision node* or a *terminal node.*

decreasing-cost industry   An *industry* in which expansion through the entry of *firms* lowers the *prices* that firms in the industry must pay for resources and therefore decreases their production costs.

deductible   The dollar sum of (for example, health care) costs that an insured individual must pay before the insurer begins to pay.

defensive medicine   The recommendation by physicians of more tests and procedures than are warranted medically or economically as a way of protecting themselves against later malpractice suits.

demand A schedule or curve that shows the various amounts of a product that consumers are willing and able to purchase at each of a series of possible *prices* during a specified period of time.

demand curve A curve that illustrates the *demand* for a product by showing how each possible *price* (on the *vertical axis*) is associated with a specific *quantity demanded* (on the *horizontal axis*).

demand schedule A table of numbers showing the amounts of a *good* or *service* buyers are willing and able to purchase at various *prices* over a specified period of time.

demand-side market failures Underallocations of resources that occur when private demand curves understate consumers' full willingness to pay for a *good* or *service*.

demographers Scientists who study the characteristics of human populations.

demographic transition The massive decline in birth rates that occurs once a developing country achieves higher standards of living because the perceived marginal cost of additional children begins to exceed the perceived marginal benefit.

dependent variable A variable that changes as a consequence of a change in some other (independent) variable; the "effect" or outcome.

deregulation The removal of most or even all of the government regulation and laws designed to supervise an industry. Sometimes undertaken to combat *regulatory capture.*

derived demand The demand for a resource that depends on the demand for the products it helps to produce.

determinants of demand Factors other than *price* that determine the quantities demanded of a *good* or *service*. Also referred to as "demand shifters" because changes in the determinants of demand will cause the *demand curve* to shift either right or left.

determinants of supply Factors other than *price* that determine the quantities supplied of a *good* or *service*. Also referred to as "supply shifters" because changes in the determinants of supply will cause the *supply curve* to shift either right or left.

devaluation A decrease in the governmentally defined value of a currency.

diagnosis-related group (DRG) system Payments to doctors and hospitals under *Medicare* based on which of hundreds of carefully detailed diagnostic categories best characterize each patient's condition and needs.

dictator game A mutually anonymous behavioral economics game in which one person ("the dictator") unilaterally determines how to split an amount of money with the second player.

differentiated oligopoly An *oligopoly* in which *firms* produce a *differentiated product.*

diffusion The spread of an *innovation* through its widespread imitation.

diminishing marginal utility (See *law of diminishing marginal utility.*)

direct payments Cash subsidies paid to farmers based on past production levels; a permanent transfer payment unaffected by current crop *prices* and current production.

direct relationship The relationship between two variables that change in the same direction, for example, product *price* and quantity supplied; a positive relationship.

discrimination The practice of according individuals or groups inferior treatment in hiring, occupational access, education and training, promotion, wage rates, or working conditions even though they have the same abilities, education, skills, and work experience as other workers.

discrimination coefficient A measure of the cost or disutility of prejudice; the monetary amount an employer is willing to pay to hire a preferred worker rather than a nonpreferred worker of the same ability.

diseconomies of scale The situation when a firm's *average total cost* of producing a product increases in the *long run* as the firm increases the size of its *plant* (and, hence, its output).

division of labor The separation of the work required to produce a product into a number of different tasks that are performed by different workers; *specialization* of workers.

Doha Development Agenda The latest, uncompleted (as of late 2013) sequence of trade negotiations by members of the *World Trade Organization;* named after Doha, Qatar, where the set of negotiations began. Also called the Doha Round.

dollar votes The "votes" that consumers cast for the production of preferred products when they purchase those products rather than the alternatives that were also available.

domestic price The *price* of a *good* or *service* within a country, determined by domestic demand and supply.

dominant strategy In a strategic interaction (*game*) between two or more players, a course of action (strategy) that a player will wish to undertake no matter what the other players choose to do.

dumping The sale of a product in a foreign country at *prices* either below cost or below the prices commonly charged at home.

DuPont cellophane case The antitrust case brought against DuPont in which the U.S. Supreme Court ruled (in 1956) that while DuPont had a monopoly in the narrowly defined market for cellophane, it did not monopolize the more broadly defined market for flexible packaging materials. It was thus not guilty of violating the *Sherman Act.*

earmarks Narrow, specially designated spending authorizations placed in broad legislation by senators and representatives for the purpose of providing benefits to *firms* and organizations within their constituencies. Earmarked projects are exempt from competitive bidding and normal evaluation procedures.

earned-income tax credit (EITC) A refundable federal *tax credit* for low-income working people designed to reduce poverty and encourage labor-force participation.

economic cost A payment that must be made to obtain and retain the *services* of a *resource;* the income a *firm* must provide to a resource supplier to attract the resource away from an alternative use; equal to the quantity of other products that cannot be produced when resources are instead used to make a particular product.

economic growth (1) An outward shift in the *production possibilities curve* that results from an increase in resource supplies or quality or an improvement in *technology;* (2) an increase of real output (*gross domestic product*) or real output per capita.

economic immigrants International migrants who have moved from one country to another to obtain economic gains such as better employment opportunities.

economic perspective   A viewpoint that envisions individuals and institutions making rational decisions by comparing the marginal benefits and marginal costs associated with their actions.

economic principle   A widely accepted generalization about the economic behavior of individuals or institutions.

economic profit   The return flowing to those who provide the economy with the *economic resource* of *entrepreneurial ability;* the *total revenue* of a *firm* less its *economic costs* (which include both *explicit costs* and *implicit costs*); also called "pure profit" and "above-normal profit."

economic rent   The *price* paid for the use of land and other natural resources that are in fixed (*perfectly inelastic*) supply.

economic resources   The *land, labor, capital,* and *entrepreneurial ability* that are used to produce *goods* and *services;* the *factors of production.*

economic system   A particular set of institutional arrangements and a coordinating mechanism for solving the *economizing problem*; a method of organizing an economy, of which the *market system* and the *command system* are the two general types.

economics   The social science concerned with how individuals, institutions, and society make optimal (best) choices under conditions of scarcity.

economies of scale   The situation when a firm's *average total cost* of producing a product decreases in the *long run* as the firm increases the size of its *plant* (and, hence, its output).

economizing problem   The choices necessitated because society's economic wants for *goods* and *services* are unlimited but the resources available to satisfy these wants are limited (scarce).

efficiency gains from migration   The increases in total worldwide output that take place if the additions to output from *immigration* in the destination nation exceed the loss of output from *emigration* from the origin nation.

efficiency loss   Reductions in combined consumer and producer surplus caused by an underallocation or overallocation of resources to the production of a *good* or *service.* Also called *deadweight loss.*

efficiency loss of a tax   The loss of *net benefits* to society because a tax reduces the production and consumption of a taxed good below the level of *allocative efficiency.* Also called the *deadweight loss* of the tax.

elastic demand   Product or resource demand whose *price elasticity of demand* is greater than 1, so that any given percentage change in *price* leads to a larger percentage change in *quantity demanded.* As a result, quantity demanded is relatively sensitive to (elastic with respect to) price.

elasticity of resource demand   A measure of the responsiveness of *firms* to a change in the *price* of a particular *resource* they employ or use; the percentage change in the quantity demanded of the *resource* divided by the percentage change in its *price.*

employer mandate   The requirement under the *Patient Protection and Affordable Care Act (PPACA)* of 2010 that firms with 50 or more employees pay for insurance policies for their employees or face a fine of $2,000 per employee per year. Firms with fewer than 50 employees are exempt.

empty threat   In a *sequential game* with two players, a non-credible (bluffing) statement made by Player 1 that threatens a penalizing action against Player 2 if Player 2 does something that Player 1 does not want Player 2 to do. Opposite of *credible threat.*

endowment effect   The tendency people have to place higher valuations on items they possess (are endowed with) than on identical items that they do not possess; perhaps caused by *loss aversion.*

entitlement programs   Government programs such as *social insurance, Medicare,* and *Medicaid* that guarantee (entitle) particular levels of transfer payments or noncash benefits to all who fit the programs' criteria.

entrepreneurial ability   The human resource that combines the other *economic resources* of *land, labor,* and *capital* to produce new products or make innovations in the production of existing products; provided by *entrepreneurs.*

entrepreneurs   Individuals who provide *entrepreneurial ability* to *firms* by setting strategy, advancing innovations, and bearing the financial risk if their firms do poorly.

equality-efficiency trade-off   The decrease in *economic efficiency* that may accompany a decrease in *income inequality;* the presumption that some income inequality is required to achieve economic efficiency.

equilibrium position   In the indifference curve model, the combination of two goods at which a consumer maximizes his or her *utility* (reaches the highest attainable *indifference curve*), given a limited amount to spend (a *budget constraint*).

equilibrium price   The *price* in a competitive market at which the *quantity demanded* and the *quantity supplied* are equal, there is neither a shortage nor a surplus, and there is no tendency for price to rise or fall.

equilibrium quantity   (1) The quantity at which the intentions of buyers and sellers in a particular market match at a particular *price* such that the *quantity demanded* and the *quantity supplied* are equal; (2) the profit-maximizing output of a *firm.*

equilibrium world price   The *price* of an internationally traded product that equates the quantity of the product demanded by importers with the quantity of the product supplied by exporters; the price determined at the intersection of the export supply curve and the import demand curve.

European Union (EU)   An association of 28 European nations (as of mid-2013) that has eliminated tariffs and quotas among them, established common tariffs for imported goods from outside the member nations, eliminated barriers to the free movement of capital, and created other common economic policies.

eurozone   The 17 nations (as of 2013) of the 28-member (as of 2013) *European Union* that use the *euro* as their common *currency.* The eurozone countries are Austria, Belgium, Cyprus, Estonia, Finland, France, Germany, Greece, Ireland, Italy, Luxembourg, Malta, the Netherlands, Portugal, Slovakia, Slovenia, and Spain.

excess capacity   *Plant* resources that are underused when imperfectly competitive *firms* produce less output than that associated with achieving minimum *average total cost.*

exchange controls   Restrictions that a government may impose over the quantity of foreign currency demand by its citizens and *firms* and over the *rate of exchange* as a way to limit the nation's quantity of *outpayments* relative to its quantity of *inpayments* (in order to eliminate a *payments deficit*).

excise tax A tax levied on the production of a specific product or on the quantity of the product purchased.

excludability The characteristic of a *private good,* for which the seller can keep nonbuyers from obtaining the good.

exclusive unionism The policy, pursued by many *craft unions,* in which a *union* first gets employers to agree to hire only union workers and then excludes many workers from joining the union so as to restrict the supply of labor and drive up wages. Compare with *inclusive unionism.* The policies typically employed by a *craft union.*

exit mechanism The method of resolving workplace dissatisfaction by quitting one's job and searching for another.

expected-rate-of-return curve As it relates to research and development (*R&D*), a curve showing the anticipated gain in *profit,* as a percentage of R&D expenditure, from an additional dollar spent on R&D.

explicit cost The monetary payment made by a *firm* to an outsider to obtain a *resource.*

export subsidy A government payment to a domestic producer to enable the *firm* to reduce the *price* of a *good* or *service* to foreign buyers.

export supply curve An upward-sloping curve that shows the amount of a product that domestic *firms* will export at each *world price* that is above the *domestic price.*

externality A cost or benefit from production or consumption that accrues to to someone other than the immediate buyers and sellers of the product being produced or consumed (see *negative externality* and *positive externality*).

extraction cost All costs associated with extracting a natural resource and readying it for sale.

factors of production The four *economic resources: land, labor, capital,* and *entrepreneurial ability.*

fair-return price For *natural monopolies* subject to rate (*price*) regulation, the price that would allow the regulated monopoly to earn a *normal profit;* a price equal to *average total cost.*

fairness A person's opinion as to whether a price, wage, or allocation is considered morally or ethically acceptable.

farm commodities Agricultural products such as grains, milk, cattle, fruits, and vegetables that are usually sold to processors, who use the products as inputs in creating *food products.*

fast-second strategy An approach by a dominant *firm* in which it allows other firms in its *industry* to bear the risk of innovation and then quickly becomes the second firm to offer any successful new product or adopt any improved production process.

Federal Trade Commission Act The federal law of 1914 that established the *Federal Trade Commission.*

fee for service In the health care *industry*, payment to physicians for each visit made or procedure performed.

first-mover advantage In *game theory,* the benefit obtained by the party that moves first in a *sequential game.*

first-mover advantage A situation that occurs in a *sequential game* if the player who gets to move first has an advantage in terms of final outcomes over the player(s) who move subsequently.

fiscal policy Changes in government spending and tax collections designed to achieve full employment, price stability, and economic growth; also called *discretionary fiscal policy.*

fishery A stock of fish or other marine animal that is composed of a distinct group, for example New England cod, Pacific tuna, or Alaskan crab.

fishery collapse A rapid decline in a *fishery's* population because its fish are being harvested faster than they can reproduce.

fixed cost Any cost that in total does not change when the *firm* changes its output.

fixed exchange rate A *rate of exchange* that is set in some way and therefore prevented from rising or falling with changes in currency supply and demand.

flexible exchange rate A *rate of exchange* that is determined by the international demand for and supply of a nation's money and that is consequently free to rise or fall because it is not subject to *currency interventions.* Also referred to as a "floating exchange rate."

food products Processed *farm commodities* sold through grocery stores and restaurants. Examples: bread, meat, fish, chicken, pork, lettuce, peanut butter, and breakfast cereal.

foreign-exchange reserves Stockpiles of foreign currencies maintained by a nation's *central bank.* Obtained when the *central bank* sells local currency in exchange for foreign currency in the *foreign exchange market.*

four-firm concentration ratio The percentage of total *industry* sales accounted for by the top four *firms* in an industry.

framing effects In *prospect theory,* changes in people's decision making caused by new information that alters the context, or "frame of reference," that they use to judge whether options are viewed as gains or losses relative to the *status quo.*

free-rider problem The inability of potential providers of an economically desirable *good* or *service* to obtain payment from those who benefit, because of *nonexcludability.*

freedom of choice The freedom of owners of property resources to employ or dispose of them as they see fit, of workers to enter any line of work for which they are qualified, and of consumers to spend their incomes in a manner that they think is appropriate.

freedom of enterprise The freedom of *firms* to obtain economic resources, to use those resources to produce products of the firm's own choosing, and to sell their products in markets of their choice.

Freedom to Farm Act A law passed in 1996 that revamped 60 years of U.S. farm policy by ending *price supports* and *acreage allotments* for wheat, corn, barley, oats, sorghum, rye, cotton, and rice.

future value The amount to which some current amount of *money* will grow if *interest* earned on the amount is left to compound over time. (*See compound interest.*)

gains from trade The extra output that trading partners obtain through specialization of production and exchange of *goods* and *services.*

game An interaction between two or more participants (players) that is strategic so that the choices (strategies) of every participant affect the incentives facing—and thus the choices made by—all of the other participants

game theory The study of how people behave in strategic situations in which individuals must take into account not only their own possible actions but also the possible reactions of others. Originally developed to analyze the best ways to play games like poker and chess.

General Agreement on Tariffs and Trade (GATT)   The international agreement reached in 1947 in which 23 nations agreed to eliminate *import quotas*, negotiate reductions in *tariff* rates, and give each other equal and nondiscriminatory treatment. It now includes most nations and has become the *World Trade Organization*.

Gini ratio   A numerical measure of the overall dispersion of income among *households*, families, or individuals; found graphically by dividing the area between the diagonal line and the *Lorenz curve* by the entire area below the diagonal line.

gold standard   A historical system of fixed exchange rates in which nations defined their currencies in terms of gold, maintained fixed relationships between their stocks of gold and their money supplies, and allowed gold to be freely exported and imported.

government failure   Inefficiencies in resource allocation caused by problems in the operation of the *public sector* (government). Specific examples include the *principal-agent problem*, the *special-interest effect*, the *collective-action problem*, *rent seeking*, and *political corruption*.

government purchases (G)   Expenditures by government for *goods* and *services* that government consumes in providing public services as well as expenditures for publicly owned capital that has a long lifetime; the expenditures of all governments in the economy for those *final goods* and final *services*.

H1-B provision   A provision of the U.S. immigration law that allows the annual entry of 65,000 high-skilled workers in "specialty occupations" such as science, *R&D*, and computer programming to work legally and continuously in the United States for six years.

health maintenance organizations (HMOs)   Health care providers that contract with employers, insurance companies, labor unions, or government units to provide health care for their workers or others who are insured.

health savings accounts (HSAs)   Tax-free savings accounts into which people with high-deductible health insurance plans can place funds each year. Accumulated funds can be used to pay out-of-pocket medical expenses such as *deductibles* and *copayments*. Unused funds accumulate from year to year and can be used after retirement to supplement *Medicare*.

Herfindahl index   A measure of the concentration and competitiveness of an *industry;* calculated as the sum of the squared percentage market shares of the individual *firms* in the industry.

heuristics   The brain's low-energy mental shortcuts for making decisions. They are "fast and frugal" and work well in most situations but in other situations result in *systematic errors*.

homogeneous oligopoly   An *oligopoly* in which *firms* produce a *standardized product*.

horizontal axis   The "left-right" or "west-east" measurement line on a graph or grid.

horizontal merger   The merger into a single *firm* of two firms producing the same product and selling it in the same geographic market.

households   Economic entities (of one or more persons occupying a housing unit) that provide *resources* to the economy and use the

income received to purchase *goods* and *services* that satisfy economic wants.

human capital   The knowledge and skills that make a person productive.

illegal immigrants   People who have entered a country unlawfully to reside there; also called unauthorized immigrants.

imitation problem   The potential for a *firm's* rivals to produce a close variation of (imitate) a firm's new product or process, greatly reducing the originator's profit from *R&D* and *innovation*.

immediate market period   The length of time during which the producers of a product are unable to change the quantity supplied in response to a change in price and in which there is a *perfectly inelastic supply*.

imperfect competition   All *market structures* except *pure competition;* includes *monopoly, monopolistic competition,* and *oligopoly.*

implicit cost   The monetary income a *firm* sacrifices when it uses a *resource* it owns rather than supplying the resource in the market; equal to what the resource could have earned in the best-paying alternative employment; includes a *normal profit*.

import competition   The competition that domestic *firms* encounter from the products and *services* of foreign producers.

import demand curve   A downsloping curve showing the amount of a product that an economy will import at each *world price* below the *domestic price*.

import quota   A limit imposed by a nation on the quantity (or total value) of a good that may be imported during some period of time.

incentive function   The inducement that an increase in the price of a commodity gives to sellers to make more of it available (and conversely for a decrease in *price*), and the inducement that an increase in price offers to buyers to purchase smaller quantities (and conversely for a decrease in price).

incentive pay plan   A compensation structure that ties worker pay directly to performance. Such plans include piece rates, bonuses, *stock options*, commissions, and *profit-sharing plans*.

inclusive unionism   The policy, pursued by *industrial unions*, in which a *union* attempts to include every worker in a given *industry* so as to be able to restrict the entire industry's labor supply and thereby raise wages. Compare with *exclusive unionism*.

income effect   A change in the quantity demanded of a product that results from the change in *real income* (purchasing power) caused by a change in the product's *price*.

income elasticity of demand   The ratio of the percentage change in the *quantity demanded* of a good to a percentage change in consumer *income;* measures the responsiveness of consumer purchases to income changes.

income inequality   The unequal distribution of an economy's total *income* among *households* or families.

income mobility   The extent to which *income* receivers move from one part of the income distribution to another over some period of time.

increasing-cost industry   An *industry* in which expansion through the entry of new *firms* raises the *prices* firms in the industry must pay for *resources* and therefore increases their production costs.

independent unions   U.S. unions that are not affiliated with the *AFL-CIO* or *Change to Win.*

independent variable   The variable causing a change in some other (dependent) variable.

indifference curve   A curve showing the different combinations of two products that yield the same satisfaction or *utility* to a consumer.

indifference map   A set of *indifference curves,* each representing a different level of *utility,* that together show the preferences of a consumer.

individual transferable quotas (ITQs)   Limits (quotas) set by a government or a fisheries commission on the total number or total weight of a species that an individual fisher can harvest during some particular time period; fishers can sell (transfer) the right to use all or part of their respective individual quotas to other fishers.

industrial regulation   The older and more traditional type of regulation in which government is concerned with the *prices* charged and the *services* provided to the public in specific *industries.* Differs from *social regulation.*

inelastic demand   Product or resource demand for which the *price elasticity of demand* is less than 1, so that any given percentage change in *price* leads to a smaller percentage change in *quantity demanded.* As a result, quantity demanded is relatively insensitive to (inelastic with respect to) price.

inferior good   A *good* or *service* whose consumption declines as *income* rises, *prices* held constant.

innovation   The first commercially successful introduction of a new product, use of a new method of production, or creation of a new form of business organization.

insurable risk   An eventuality for which both the frequency and magnitude of potential losses can be estimated with considerable accuracy. Insurance companies are willing to sell insurance against such risks.

insurance exchanges   Government-regulated markets for health insurance in which individuals seeking to purchase health insurance to comply with the *personal mandate* of the *Patient Protection and Affordable Care Act* (*PPACA*) of 2010 will be able to comparison shop among insurance policies approved by regulators. Each state will have its own exchange.

interest-rate-cost-of-funds curve   As it relates to research and development (*R&D*), a curve showing the *interest rate* a *firm* must pay to obtain any particular amount of funds to finance R&D.

interindustry competition   The competition for sales between the products of one *industry* and the products of another industry.

interlocking directorate   A situation where one or more members of the board of directors of a *corporation* are also on the board of directors of a competing corporation; illegal under the *Clayton Act.*

International Monetary Fund (IMF)   The international association of nations that was formed after the Second World War to make loans of foreign monies to nations with temporary *balance of payments deficits* and, until the early 1970s, manage the international system of pegged exchange rates agreed upon at the Bretton Woods conference. It now mainly makes loans to nations facing possible defaults on private and government loans.

invention   The conception of a new product or process combined with the first proof that it will work.

inverse relationship   The relationship between two variables that change in opposite directions, for example, product *price* and quantity demanded; a negative relationship.

inverted-U theory (of R&D)   The idea that, other things equal, *R&D* expenditures as a percentage of sales rise with *industry* concentration, reach a peak at a *four-firm concentration ratio* of about 50 percent, and then fall as the ratio further increases.

investment   In economics, spending for the production and accumulation of *capital* and additions to *inventories.* (For contrast, see *financial investment.*)

invisible hand   The tendency of competition to cause individuals and firms to unintentionally but quite effectively promote the interests of society even when each individual or firm is only attempting to pursue its own interests.

kinked-demand curve   A *demand curve* that has a flatter slope above the current *price* than below the current price. Applies to a *noncollusive oligopoly* firm if its rivals will match any price decrease but ignore any price increase.

labor   Any mental or physical exertion on the part of a human being that is used in the production of a *good* or *service.* One of the four *economic resources.*

labor-intensive goods   Products requiring relatively large amounts of *labor* to produce.

laissez-faire capitalism   A hypothetical *economic system* in which the government's economic role is limited to protecting private property and establishing a legal environment appropriate to the operation of *markets* in which only mutually agreeable transactions would take place between buyers and sellers; sometimes referred to as "pure *capitalism.*"

land   In addition to the part of the earth's surface not covered by water, this term refers to any and all natural resources ("free gifts of nature") that are used to produce *goods* and *services.* Thus, it includes the oceans, sunshine, coal deposits, forests, the electromagnetic spectrum, and *fisheries.* Note that land is one of the four *economic resources.*

land-intensive goods   Products requiring relatively large amounts of land to produce.

law of demand   The principle that, other things equal, an increase in a product's *price* will reduce the quantity of it demanded, and conversely for a decrease in price.

law of diminishing marginal utility   The principle that as a consumer increases the consumption of a *good* or *service,* the *marginal utility* obtained from each additional unit of the good or service decreases.

law of diminishing returns   The principle that as successive increments of a variable *resource* are added to a fixed resource, the *marginal product* of the variable resource will eventually decrease.

law of increasing opportunity costs   The principle that as the production of a good increases, the *opportunity cost* of producing an additional unit rises.

law of supply   The principle that, other things equal, an increase in the *price* of a product will increase the quantity of it supplied, and conversely for a price decrease.

least-cost combination of resources   The quantity of each *resource* that a *firm* must employ in order to produce a particular output at the lowest total cost; the combination at which the ratio of the *marginal product* of a resource to its *marginal resource cost* (to its *price* if the resource is employed in a competitive market) is the same for the last dollar spent on each of the resources employed.

legal cartel theory of regulation   The hypothesis that some *industries* seek regulation or want to maintain regulation so that they may form or maintain a legal *cartel.*

legal immigrant   A person who lawfully enters a country for the purpose of residing there.

loan guarantees   A type of investment *subsidy* in which the government agrees to guarantee (pay off) the money borrowed by a private company to fund investment projects if the private company itself fails to repay the loan.

loanable funds theory of interest   The concept that the supply of and demand for *loanable funds* determine the equilibrium rate of *interest.*

lockout   A negotiating tactic in which a *firm* forbids its unionized workers to return to work until a new *collective bargaining* agreement is signed; a means of imposing costs (lost wages) on union workers.

logrolling   The trading of votes by legislators to secure favorable outcomes on decisions concerning the provision of *public goods* and *quasi-public goods.*

long run   (1) In *microeconomics,* a period of time long enough to enable producers of a product to change the quantities of all the resources they employ, so that all resources and costs are variable and no resources or costs are fixed. (2) In *macroeconomics,* a period sufficiently long for *nominal wages* and other input *prices* to change in response to a change in a nation's *price level.*

long-run supply curve   As it applies to *macroeconomics*, a *supply curve* for which *price*, but not real output, changes when the *demand curves* shifts; a vertical supply curve that implies fully flexible *prices.*

Lorenz curve   A curve showing the distribution of income in an economy. The cumulated percentage of families (income receivers) is measured along the horizontal axis and the cumulated percentage of income is measured along the vertical axis.

loss aversion   In *prospect theory*, the property of most people's preferences that the pain generated by losses feels substantially more intense than the pleasure generated by gains.

macroeconomics   The part of *economics* concerned with the performance and behavior of the economy as a whole. Focuses on *economic growth*, the *business cycle*, *interest rates*, *inflation*, and the behavior of major economic *aggregates* such as the household, business, and government sectors.

managed floating exchange rate   An *exchange rate* that is allowed to change (float) as a result of changes in *currency* supply and demand but at times is altered (managed) by governments via their buying and selling of particular currencies.

marginal analysis   The comparison of *marginal* ("extra" or "additional") *benefits* and *marginal costs*, usually for decision making.

marginal cost (MC)   The extra (additional) cost of producing 1 more unit of output; equal to the change in *total cost* divided by the change in output (and, in the short run, to the change in total *variable cost* divided by the change in output).

marginal cost-marginal benefit rule   As it applies to *cost-benefit analysis*, the tenet that a government project or program should be expanded to the point where the *marginal cost* and *marginal benefit* of additional expenditures are equal.

marginal product (MP)   The additional output produced when 1 additional unit of a resource is employed (the quantity of all other resources employed remaining constant); equal to the change in *total product* divided by the change in the quantity of a resource employed.

marginal productivity theory of income distribution   The contention that the distribution of *income* is equitable when each unit of each *resource* receives a *money* payment equal to its *marginal revenue product* (its marginal contribution to the revenue of the *firm* using the unit).

marginal rate of substitution (MRS)   The rate at which a consumer is willing to substitute one good for another (from a given combination of goods) and remain equally satisfied (have the same *total utility*)*;* equal to the slope of a consumer's *indifference curve* at each point on the curve.

marginal resource cost (MRC)   The amount by which the total cost of employing a *resource* increases when a *firm* employs 1 additional unit of the resource (the quantity of all other resources employed remaining constant); equal to the change in the *total cost* of the resource divided by the change in the quantity of the resource employed.

marginal revenue   The change in *total revenue* that results from the sale of 1 additional unit of a *firm*'s product; equal to the change in total revenue divided by the change in the quantity of the product sold.

marginal revenue product (MRP)   The change in a firm's *total revenue* when it employs 1 additional unit of a *resource* (the quantity of all other resources employed remaining constant); equal to the change in *total revenue* divided by the change in the quantity of the resource employed.

marginal revenue productivity   (See *marginal revenue product.*)

marginal tax rate   The *tax* rate paid on an additional dollar of *income.*

marginal utility   The extra *utility* a consumer obtains from the consumption of 1 additional unit of a *good* or *service;* equal to the change in *total utility* divided by the change in the quantity consumed.

market   Any institution or mechanism that brings together buyers (demanders) and sellers (suppliers) of a particular *good* or *service.*

market failure   The inability of a *market* to bring about the allocation of *resources* that best satisfies the wants of society; in particular, the overallocation or underallocation of resources to the production of a particular *good* or *service* because of *externalities* or informational problems or because markets do not provide desired *public goods.*

market structure The characteristics of an *industry* that define the likely behavior and performance of its *firms*. The primary characteristics are the number of firms in the industry, whether they are selling a *differentiated product*, the ease of entry, and how much control firms have over output prices. The most commonly discussed market structures are *pure competition*, *monopolistic competition*, *oligopoly*, pure *monopoly*, and *monopsony*.

market system (1) An *economic system* in which individuals own most *economic resources* and in which *markets* and *prices* serve as the dominant coordinating mechanism used to allocate those resources; *capitalism*. Compare with *command system*. (2) All the product and resource markets of a *market economy* and the relationships among them.

marketing loan program A federal farm subsidy under which certain farmers can receive a loan (on a per-unit-of-output basis) to plant a crop and then, depending on the harvest *price* of the crop, either pay back the loan with interest or keep the loan proceeds while forfeiting their harvested crop to the lender.

median-voter model The theory that under majority rule the median (middle) voter will be in the dominant position to determine the outcome of an election.

Medicaid A federal program that helps finance the medical expenses of individuals covered by the *Supplemental Security Income* (*SSI*) and *Temporary Assistance for Needy Families* (*TANF*) programs.

Medicare A federal program that provides for (1) compulsory hospital insurance for senior citizens, (2) low-cost voluntary insurance to help older Americans pay physicians' fees, and (3) subsidized insurance to buy prescription drugs. Financed by *payroll taxes*.

medium of exchange Any item sellers generally accept and buyers generally use to pay for a *good* or *service; money;* a convenient means of exchanging goods and *services* without engaging in *barter*.

mental accounting The tendency people have to create separate "mental boxes" (or "accounts") in which they deal with particular financial transactions in isolation rather than dealing with them as part of an overall decision-making process that would consider how to best allocate their limited budgets across all possible options by using the *utility-maximizing rule*.

microeconomics The part of economics concerned with (1) decision making by individual units such as a *household,* a *firm,* or an *industry* and (2) individual markets, specific *goods* and *services*, and product and resource *prices*.

Microsoft case A 2002 antitrust case in which Microsoft was found guilty of violating the *Sherman Act* by engaging in a series of unlawful activities designed to maintain its *monopoly* in operating systems for personal computers; as a remedy the company was prohibited from engaging in a set of specific anticompetitive business practices.

midpoint formula A method for calculating *price elasticity of demand* or *price elasticity of supply* that averages the starting and ending *prices* and quantities when computing percentages.

minimum efficient scale (MES) The lowest level of output at which a *firm* can minimize long-run *average total cost*.

minimum wage The lowest *wage* that employers may legally pay for an hour of work.

monetary policy A central bank's changing of the *money supply* to influence *interest* rates and assist the economy in achieving *price-level stability*, *full employment*, and *economic growth*.

money Any item that is generally acceptable to sellers in exchange for *goods* and *services*.

monopolistic competition A *market structure* in which many *firms* sell a *differentiated product,* entry is relatively easy, each firm has some control over its product *price*, and there is considerable *nonprice competition*.

monopsony A *market structure* in which there is only a single buyer of a good, *service*, or *resource*.

moral hazard problem The possibility that individuals or institutions will change their behavior as the result of a contract or agreement. Example: A bank whose deposits are insured against losses may make riskier loans and investments.

MR = MC rule The principle that a *firm* will maximize its profit (or minimize its losses) by producing the output at which *marginal revenue* and *marginal cost* are equal, provided product *price* is equal to or greater than *average variable cost*.

MRP = MRC rule The principle that to maximize profit (or minimize losses), a *firm* should employ the quantity of a resource at which its *marginal revenue product* (MRP) is equal to its *marginal resource cost* (MRC), the latter being the wage rate in a purely competitive labor market.

mutual interdependence A situation in which a change in *price* strategy (or in some other strategy) by one *firm* will affect the sales and profits of another firm (or other firms). Any firm that makes such a change can expect its rivals to react to the change.

myopia Refers to the difficulty human beings have with conceptualizing the more distant future. Leads to decisions that overly favor present and near-term options at the expense of more distant future possibilities.

Nash equilibrium The situation that occurs in some *simultaneous games* wherein every player is playing his or her *dominant strategy* at the same time and thus no player has any reason to change behavior.

national health insurance A program in which a nation's government provides a basic package of health care to all citizens at no direct charge or at a low cost-sharing level. Financing is out of general *tax* revenues.

National Labor Relations Act (NLRA) The basic labor-relations law in the United States. Defines the legal rights of unions and management and identifies unfair union and management labor practices; established the *National Labor Relations Board*. Often referred to as the Wagner Act, after the legislation's sponsor, New York Senator Robert F. Wagner.

National Labor Relations Board (NLRB) The board established by the *National Labor Relations Act* of 1935 to investigate unfair labor practices, issue *cease-and-desist orders,* and conduct elections among employees to determine if they wish to be represented by a *labor union*.

natural monopoly An *industry* in which *economies of scale* are so great that a single *firm* can produce the industry's product at a lower average total cost than would be possible if more than one firm produced the product.

negative self-selection   As it relates to international migration, the idea that those who choose to move to another country have poorer *wage* opportunities in the origin country than those with similar skills who choose not to *emigrate.*

negative-sum game   In *game theory,* a game in which the gains (+) and losses (−) add up to some amount less than zero; one party's losses exceed the other party's gains. A strategic interaction (*game*) between two or more parties (players) in which the winners' gains are less than the losers' losses so that the gains and losses sum to a negative number.

neoclassical economics   The dominant and conventional branch of economic theory that attempts to predict human behavior by building economic models based on simplifying assumptions about people's motives and capabilities. These include that people are fundamentally *rational;* motivated almost entirely by *self-interest;* good at math; and unaffected by *heuristics, time inconsistency,* and *self-control problems.*

net benefits   The total benefits of some activity or policy less the total costs of that activity or policy.

network effects   Increases in the value of a product to each user, including existing users, as the total number of users rises.

nominal interest rate   The *interest rate* expressed in terms of annual amounts currently charged for *interest* and not adjusted for *inflation.*

nominal wage   The amount of *money* received by a worker per unit of time (hour, day, etc.); money wage.

noncash transfer   A *government transfer payment* in the form of *goods* and *services* rather than *money,* for example, food stamps, housing assistance, and job training; also called *in-kind transfers.*

noncompeting groups   Collections of workers who do not compete with each other for employment because the skill and training of the workers in one group are substantially different from those of the workers in other groups.

nonexcludability   The inability to keep nonpayers (free riders) from obtaining benefits from a certain good; a characteristic of a *public good.*

nonprice competition   Competition based on distinguishing one's product by means of *product differentiation* and then *advertising* the distinguished product to consumers.

nonrenewable natural resource   Things such as oil, natural gas, and metals, that are either in actual fixed supply or that renew so slowly as to be in virtual fixed supply when viewed from a human time perspective.

nonrivalry   The idea that one person's benefit from a certain *good* does not reduce the benefit available to others; a characteristic of a *public good.*

nontariff barriers (NTBs)   All barriers other than *protective tariffs* that nations erect to impede international trade, including *import quotas,* licensing requirements, unreasonable product-quality standards, unnecessary bureaucratic detail in customs procedures, and so on.

normal good   A *good* or *service* whose consumption increases when *income* increases and falls when income decreases, *price* remaining constant.

normal profit   The payment made by a *firm* to obtain and retain *entrepreneurial ability;* the minimum *income* that entrepreneurial ability must receive to induce *entrepreneurs* to provide their entrepreneurial ability to a firm; the level of *accounting profit* at which a firm generates an *economic profit* of zero after paying for entrepreneurial ability.

normative economics   The part of economics involving value judgments about what the economy should be like; focused on which economic goals and policies should be implemented; policy economics.

North American Free Trade Agreement (NAFTA)   The 1993 treaty that established an international free-trade zone composed of Canada, Mexico, and the United States.

occupational licensing   The laws of state or local governments that require that a worker satisfy certain specified requirements and obtain a license from a licensing board before engaging in a particular occupation.

occupational segregation   The crowding of women or minorities into less desirable, lower-paying occupations.

official reserves   Foreign *currencies* owned by the central bank of a nation.

offshoring   The practice of shifting work previously done by domestic workers to workers located abroad.

oligopoly   A *market structure* in which a few *firms* sell either a *standardized* or *differentiated product,* into which entry is difficult, in which the firm has limited control over product *price* because of *mutual interdependence* (except when there is collusion among firms), and in which there is typically *nonprice competition.*

one-time game   A strategic interaction (*game*) between two or more parties (players) that all parties know will take place only once.

open shop   A place of employment in which the employer may hire nonunion workers and in which the workers need not become members of a *labor union.*

opportunity cost   The amount of other products that must be forgone or sacrificed to produce a unit of a product.

opportunity-cost ratio   An equivalency showing the number of units of two products that can be produced with the same *resources;* the equivalency 1 corn ≡ 3 olives shows that the resources required to produce 3 units of olives must be shifted to corn production to produce 1 unit of corn.

optimal amount of R&D   The level of *R&D* at which the *marginal benefit* and *marginal cost* of R&D expenditures are equal.

optimal reduction of an externality   The reduction of a *negative externality* such as pollution to the level at which the *marginal benefit* and *marginal cost* of reduction are equal.

other-things-equal assumption   The assumption that factors other than those being considered are held constant; *ceteris paribus* assumption.

output effect   The possibility that when the *price* of the first of a pair of *substitute resources* falls, the *quantity demanded* of both resources will rise because the reduction in the price of the first resource so greatly reduces production costs that the volume of output created with the two resources increases by so much that the quantity demanded of the second resource increases even after accounting for the *substitution effect*. (See the second definition listed in the entry for *substitution effect*.)

paradox of voting A situation where paired-choice voting by majority rule fails to provide a consistent ranking of society's preferences for *public goods* or *public services*.

parity concept The idea that year after year the sale of a specific output of a farm product should enable a farmer to purchase a constant amount of nonagricultural *goods* and *services*.

parity ratio The ratio of the *price* received by farmers from the sale of an agricultural commodity to the prices of other goods paid by them; usually expressed as a percentage; used as a rationale for *price supports*.

partnership An unincorporated *firm* owned and operated by two or more persons.

patent An exclusive right given to inventors to produce and sell a new product or machine for 20 years from the time of patent application.

Patient Protection and Affordable Care Act (PPACA) A major health care law passed by the federal government in 2010. Major provisions include an individual health insurance mandate, a ban on insurers refusing to accept patients with preexisting conditions, and federal (rather than state) regulation of health insurance policies.

payroll tax A *tax* levied on employers of labor equal to a percentage of all or part of the *wages* and salaries paid by them and on employees equal to a percentage of all or part of the wages and salaries received by them.

per se violations Collusive actions, such as attempts by *firms* to fix *prices* or divide a market, that are violations of the *antitrust laws*, even if the actions themselves are unsuccessful.

perfectly elastic demand Product or *resource* demand in which *quantity demanded* can be of any amount at a particular product or resource *price*; graphs as a horizontal *demand curve*.

perfectly inelastic demand Product or *resource* demand in which *price* can be of any amount at a particular quantity of the product or resource that is demanded; when the *quantity demanded* does not respond to a change in price; graphs as a vertical *demand curve*.

personal income tax A *tax* levied on the taxable income of individuals, *households*, and unincorporated *firms*.

personal mandate The requirement under the *Patient Protection and Affordable Care Act* (*PPACA*) of 2010 that all U.S. citizens and legal residents purchase health insurance unless they are already covered by employer-sponsored health insurance or government-sponsored health insurance (*Medicaid* or *Medicare*).

Pigovian tax A *tax* or charge levied on the production of a product that generates *negative externalities*. If set correctly, the tax will precisely offset the overallocation (overproduction) generated by the negative externality.

political corruption The unlawful misdirection of governmental resources or actions that occurs when government officials abuse their entrusted powers for personal gain. (Also see *corruption*.)

positive economics The analysis of facts or data to establish scientific generalizations about economic behavior.

positive-sum game In *game theory*, a game in which the gains (+) and losses (−) add up to more than zero; one party's gains exceed the other party's losses. A strategic interaction (*game*) between two or more parties (players) in which the winners' gains exceed the losers' losses so that the gains and losses sum to something positive.

poverty rate The percentage of the population with incomes below the official poverty income levels that are established by the federal government.

precommittments Actions taken ahead of time that make it difficult for the future self to avoid doing what the present self desires. See *time inconsistency* and *self-control problems*.

preferred provider organization (PPO) An arrangement in which doctors and hospitals agree to provide health care to insured individuals at rates negotiated with an insurer.

present value Today's value of some amount of *money* that is to be received sometime in the future.

price ceiling A legally established maximum *price* for a *good*, or *service*. Normally set at a price below the *equilibrium price*.

price discrimination The selling of a product to different buyers at different *prices* when the price differences are not justified by differences in cost.

price elasticity of demand The ratio of the percentage change in *quantity demanded* of a product or *resource* to the percentage change in its *price*; a measure of the responsiveness of buyers to a change in the price of a product or resource.

price elasticity of supply The ratio of the percentage change in *quantity supplied* of a product or *resource* to the percentage change in its *price*; a measure of the responsiveness of producers to a change in the price of a product or resource.

price floor A legally established minimum *price* for a *good*, or service. Normally set at a price above the *equilibrium price*.

price leadership An informal method that *firms* in an *oligopoly* may employ to set the *price* of their product: One firm (the leader) is the first to announce a change in price, and the other firms (the followers) soon announce identical or similar changes.

price loss coverage A form of *crop insurance* that pays participating farmers if the market price of their output falls below a predetermined value.

price support The term used to refer to *price floors* applied to *farm commodities*; the minimum *price* that the government allows farmers to receive for farm commodities like wheat or corn.

price taker A seller (or buyer) that is unable to affect the *price* at which a product or *resource* sells by changing the amount it sells (or buys).

price war Successive, competitive, and continued decreases in the *prices* charged by *firms* in an oligopolistic *industry*. At each stage of the price war, one *firm* lowers its price below its rivals' price, hoping to increase its sales and revenues at its rivals' expense. The war ends when the price decreases cease.

principal-agent problem (1) At a *firm*, a conflict of interest that occurs when agents (workers or managers) pursue their own objectives to the detriment of the principals' (stockholders') goals. (2) In *public choice theory*, a conflict of interest that arises when elected officials (who are the agents of the people) pursue policies that are in their own interests rather than policies that would be in the better interests of the public (the principals).

principle of comparative advantage The proposition that an individual, region, or nation will benefit if it specializes in producing goods for which its own *opportunity costs* are lower than the opportunity costs of a trading partner, and then exchanging some of the products in which it specializes for other desired products produced by others.

private good A *good,* or *service* that is individually consumed and that can be profitably provided by privately owned *firms* because they can exclude nonpayers from receiving the benefits.

private property The right of private persons and *firms* to obtain, own, control, employ, dispose of, and bequeath *land, capital,* and other property.

process innovation The development and use of new or improved production or distribution methods.

producer surplus The difference between the actual *price* a producer receives (or producers receive) and the minimum acceptable price; the triangular area above the *supply curve* and below the market price.

product differentiation A strategy in which one *firm*'s product is distinguished from competing products by means of its design, related *services*, quality, location, or other attributes (except *price*).

product innovation The development and sale of a new or improved product (or service).

product market A market in which products are sold by *firms* and bought by *households.*

production possibilities curve A curve showing the different combinations of two goods or *services* that can be produced in a *full-employment, full-production* economy where the available supplies of *resources* and technology are fixed.

productive efficiency The production of a *good* in the least costly way; occurs when production takes place at the output at which *average total cost* is a minimum and *marginal product* per dollar's worth of input is the same for all inputs.

profit-maximizing combination of resources The quantity of each *resource* a *firm* must employ to maximize its *profit* or minimize its loss; the combination of resource inputs at which the *marginal revenue product* of each resource is equal to its *marginal resource cost* (to its *price* if the resource is employed in a competitive market).

progressive tax At the individual level, a *tax* whose *average tax rate* increases as the taxpayer's *income* increases. At the national level, a *tax* for which the *average tax rate* (= tax revenue/GDP) rises with *GDP.*

property tax A *tax* on the value of property (*capital, land, stocks* and *bonds,* and other *assets*) owned by *firms* and *households.*

proportional tax At the individual level, a *tax* whose *average tax rate* remains constant as the taxpayer's *income* increases or decreases. At the national level, a *tax* for which the *average tax rate* (= tax revenue/GDP) remains constant as *GDP* rises or falls.

prospect theory A *behavioral economics* theory of preferences having three main features: (1) people evaluate options on the basis of whether they generate gains or losses relative to the *status quo;* (2) gains are subject to *diminishing marginal utility*, while losses are subject to diminishing marginal disutility; and (3) people are prone to *loss aversion.*

protective tariff A *tariff* designed to shield domestic producers of a *good* or *service* from the competition of foreign producers.

public assistance programs Government programs that pay benefits to those who are unable to earn *income* (because of permanent disabilities or because they have very low income and dependent children); financed by general *tax* revenues and viewed as public charity (rather than earned rights).

public choice theory The economic analysis of government decision making, politics, and elections.

public good A *good* or *service* that is characterized by *nonrivalry* and *nonexcludability*. These characteristics typically imply that no private *firm* can break even when attempting to provide such products. As a result, they are often provided by governments, who pay for them using general *tax* revenues.

public interest theory of regulation The presumption that the purpose of the regulation of an *industry* is to protect the public (consumers) from abuse of the power possessed by *natural monopolies.*

purchasing-power-parity theory The idea that if countries have *flexible exchange rates* (rather than *fixed exchange rates*), the exchange rates between national currencies will adjust to equate the purchasing power of various currencies. In particular, the exchange rate between any two national currencies will adjust to reflect the *price-level* differences between the two countries.

pure competition A *market structure* in which a very large number of *firms* sells a *standardized product,* into which entry is very easy, in which the individual seller has no control over the product *price*, and in which there is no nonprice competition; a market characterized by a very large number of buyers and sellers.

pure monopoly A *market structure* in which one *firm* sells a unique product, into which entry is blocked, in which the single firm has considerable control over product *price*, and in which *nonprice competition* may or may not be found.

pure profit (See *economic profit.*)

pure rate of interest The hypothetical *interest rate* that is completely *risk*-free and not subject to market imperfections; the hypothetical interest rate that would only compensate investors for *time preference.*

purely competitive labor market A *resource market* in which many *firms* compete with one another in hiring a specific kind of *labor*, numerous equally qualified workers supply that labor, and no one controls the market *wage rate.*

quasi-public good A *good* or *service* to which *excludability* could apply but that has such a large *positive externality* that government sponsors its production to prevent an underallocation of resources.

rational Behaviors and decisions that maximize a person's chances of achieving his or her goals. See *rational behavior.*

rational behavior Human behavior based on comparison of *marginal costs* and *marginal benefits;* behavior designed to maximize *total utility.* See *rational.*

real interest rate The *interest rate* expressed in dollars of constant value (adjusted for *inflation*) and equal to the *nominal interest rate* less the expected rate of inflation.

real wage The amount of *goods* and *services* a worker can purchase with his or her *nominal wage;* the *purchasing power* of the *nominal wage.*

regressive tax At the individual level, a *tax* whose *average tax rate* decreases as the taxpayer's *income* increases. At the national level, a *tax* for which the *average tax rate* (= tax revenue/*GDP*) falls as *GDP* rises.

regulatory agency An agency, commission, or board established by the federal government or a state government to control the *prices* charged and the *services* offered by a *natural monopoly* or *public utility.*

regulatory capture The situation that occurs when a governmental *regulatory agency* ends up being controlled by the industry that it is supposed to be regulating.

remittances Payments by *immigrants* to family members and others located in the immigrants' home countries.

renewable natural resources Things such as forests, water in reservoirs, and wildlife that are capable of growing back or building back up (renewing themselves) if they are harvested at moderate rates.

rent-seeking behavior The actions by persons, *firms*, or unions to gain special benefits from government at the taxpayers' or someone else's expense.

repeated game A strategic interaction (*game*) between two or more parties (players) that all parties know will take place repeatedly.

replacement rate The *total fertility rate* necessary to offset deaths in a country and thereby keep the size of its population constant (without relying on immigration). For most countries, a total fertility rate of about 2.1 births per woman per lifetime.

residual claimant In a market system, the economic agent who receives (is claimant to) whatever profit or loss remains (is residual) at a firm after all other *input* providers have been paid. The residual is compensation for providing the economic input of *entrepreneurial ability* and flows to the firm's owners.

resource market A market in which *households* sell and *firms* buy *resources* or the services of resources.

revenue tariff A *tariff* designed to produce *income* for the federal government.

right-to-work law A state law (in 23 states) that makes it illegal to require that a worker join a *labor union* in order to retain his or her job; laws that make *union shops* and *agency shops* illegal.

rivalry (1) The characteristic of a *private good,* the consumption of which by one party excludes other parties from obtaining the benefit; (2) the attempt by one *firm* to gain strategic advantage over another firm to enhance market share or *profit.*

rule of reason The rule stated and applied in the *U.S. Steel* case that only combinations and contracts unreasonably restraining trade are subject to actions under the antitrust laws and that size and possession of *monopoly* power are not by themselves illegal. Compare with *per se violation.*

sales tax A *tax* levied on the cost (at retail) of a broad group of products.

scarcity The limits placed on the amounts and types of *goods* and *services* available for consumption as the result of there being only limited *economic resources* from which to produce output; the fundamental economic constraint that creates *opportunity costs* and that necessitates the use of *marginal analysis* (*cost-benefit analysis*) to make optimal choices.

scientific method The procedure for the systematic pursuit of knowledge involving the observation of facts and the formulation and testing of hypotheses to obtain theories, principles, and laws.

self-control problems Refers to the difficulty people have in sticking with earlier plans and avoiding suboptimal decisions when finally confronted with a particular decision-making situation. A manifestation of *time inconsistency* and potentially avoidable by using *precommitments.*

self-interest That which each *firm*, property owner, worker, and consumer believes is best for itself and seeks to obtain.

self-selection As it relates to international migration, the idea that those who choose to move to a new country tend to have greater motivation for economic gain or greater willingness to sacrifice current consumption for future consumption than those with similar skills who choose to remain at home.

sequential game A strategic interaction (*game*) between two or more parties (players) in which each party moves (makes a decision) in a predetermined order (sequence).

Sherman Act The federal antitrust law of 1890 that makes *monopoly* and conspiracies to restrain trade criminal offenses.

short run (1) In *microeconomics*, a period of time in which producers are able to change the quantities of some but not all of the *resources* they employ; a period in which some resources (usually *plant*) are fixed and some are variable. (2) In *macroeconomics*, a period in which *nominal wages* and other input *prices* do not change in response to a change in the *price level.*

short-run supply curve A *supply curve* that shows the quantity of a product a *firm* in a purely competitive *industry* will offer to sell at various *prices* in the *short run;* the portion of the firm's short-run *marginal cost* curve that lies above its *average-variable-cost* curve.

shortage The amount by which the *quantity demanded* of a product exceeds the *quantity supplied* at a particular (below-equilibrium) *price.*

simultaneous consumption The same-time derivation of *utility* from some product by a large number of consumers.

simultaneous game A strategic interaction (*game*) between two or more parties (players) in which every player moves (makes a decision) at the same time.

single-tax movement The political efforts by followers of Henry George (1839–1897) to impose a single *tax* on the value of land and eliminate all other taxes.

skill transferability The ease with which people can shift their work talents from one job, region, or country to another job, region, or country.

slope of a straight line The ratio of the vertical change (the rise or fall) to the horizontal change (the run) between any two points on a straight line. The slope of an upward-sloping line is positive, reflecting a direct relationship between two variables; the slope of a downward-sloping line is negative, reflecting an inverse relationship between two variables.

Smoot-Hawley Tariff Act Legislation passed in 1930 that established very high *tariffs*. Its objective was to reduce *imports* and stimulate the domestic economy, but it resulted only in retaliatory tariffs by other nations.

social insurance programs Programs that replace the earnings lost when people retire or are temporarily unemployed, that are financed by payroll *taxes*, and that are viewed as earned rights (rather than charity).

social regulation Regulation in which government is concerned with the conditions under which *goods* and *services* are produced, their physical characteristics, and the impact of their production on society. Differs from *industrial regulation.*

Social Security The social insurance program in the United States financed by federal *payroll taxes* on employers and employees and designed to replace a portion of the earnings lost when workers become disabled, retire, or die.

socially optimal price The *price* of a product that results in the most efficient allocation of an economy's *resources* and that is equal to the *marginal cost* of the product.

sole proprietorship An unincorporated *firm* owned and operated by one person.

special-interest effect Any political outcome in which a small group ("special interest") gains substantially at the expense of a much larger number of persons who each individually suffers a small loss.

specialization The use of the *resources* of an individual, a *firm*, a region, or a nation to concentrate production on one or a small number of *goods* and *services.*

Standard Oil case A 1911 antitrust case in which Standard Oil was found guilty of violating the *Sherman Act* by illegally monopolizing the petroleum *industry*. As a remedy the company was divided into several competing *firms.*

start-ups Newly formed firms that are attempting to pioneer a new product or production method.

statistical discrimination The practice of judging an individual on the basis of the average characteristics of the group to which he or she belongs rather than on his or her own personal characteristics.

status quo The existing state of affairs; in *prospect theory,* the current situation from which gains and losses are calculated.

status quo bias The tendency most people have when making choices to select any option that is presented as the default (*status quo*) option. Explainable by *prospect theory* and *loss aversion.*

sterilization *Open market operations* or changes in bank *reserve ratios* undertaken by a *central bank* to offset changes in the domestic *money supply* caused either by the operation of a *fixed exchange rate* or by *currency interventions* made under a *managed floating exchange rate.*

strategic behavior Self-interested economic actions that take into account the expected reactions of others.

strategic form A matrix representation of a *game* that shows the payouts to every combination of player choices. Can be used for both *simultaneous games* and *sequential games.*

strike The withholding of *labor* services by an organized group of workers (a *labor union*).

subgame A subset of a larger *game* that begins with a single initial decision node. It includes all subsequent *decision nodes* and/or *terminal nodes.* Most easily seen in *sequential games* presented in *strategic form.*

subgame perfect Nash equilibrium In *sequential games,* a sequence of decisions made by the various players such that no player has an incentive to deviate.

substitute goods Products or *services* that can be used in place of each other. When the *price* of one falls, the *demand* for the other product falls; conversely, when the price of one product rises, the demand for the other product rises.

substitute resources Productive inputs that can be used instead of other inputs in the production process; resources for which an increase in the *price* of one leads to an increase in the demand for the other.

substitution effect (1) A change in the quantity demanded of a *consumer good* that results from a change in its relative expensiveness caused by a change in the good's own *price.* (2) The reduction in the *quantity demanded* of the second of a pair of *substitute resources* that occurs when the price of the first resource falls and causes *firms* that employ both resources to switch to using more of the first resource (whose price has fallen) and less of the second resource (whose price has remained the same).

Supplemental Nutrition Assistance Program (SNAP) A government program that provides food money to low-income recipients by depositing electronic money onto *Electronic Benefit Transfer* (*EBT*) *cards.* Formerly known as the food-stamp program.

Supplemental Security Income (SSI) A federally financed and administered program that provides a uniform nationwide minimum *income* for the aged, blind, and disabled who do not qualify for benefits under *Social Security* in the United States.

supply A schedule or curve that shows the various amounts of a product that producers are willing and able to make available for sale at each of a series of possible *prices* during a specified period of time.

supply curve A curve that illustrates the *supply* for a product by showing how each possible *price* (on the *vertical axis*) is associated with a specific *quantity supplied* (on the *horizontal axis*).

supply schedule A table of numbers showing the amounts of a *good* or *service* producers are willing and able to make available for sale at each of a series of possible *prices* during a specified period of time.

supply-side market failures Overallocations of *resources* that occur when private supply curves understate the full cost of producing a *good* or *service.*

surplus The amount by which the *quantity supplied* of a product exceeds the *quantity demanded* at a specific (above-equilibrium) *price.*

systematic errors Suboptimal choices that (1) are not *rational* because they do not maximize a person's chances of achieving his or her goals and (2) occur routinely, repeatedly, and predictably.

tariff A *tax* imposed by a nation on an imported good.

taste-for-discrimination model A theory that views discrimination as a preference for which an employer is willing to pay.

tax incidence   The degree to which a *tax* falls on a particular person or group.

tax subsidy   A grant in the form of reduced *taxes* through favorable *tax* treatment. For example, employer-paid health insurance is exempt from federal *income taxes* and *payroll taxes*.

technological advance   (1) An improvement in the quality of existing products, the invention of entirely new products, or the creation of new or better ways of producing or distributing products. (2) Any improvement in the methods by which resources are combined such that the same quantity of inputs can be made to yield a combination of outputs that is prefered to any combination of outputs that was previously possible.

Temporary Assistance for Needy Families (TANF)   A state-administered and partly federally funded program in the United States that provides financial aid to poor families; the basic welfare program for low-income families in the United States; contains time limits and work requirements.

terminal node   In a *sequential game* presented in *extensive form*, a final outcome point (node) showing the payouts to each player if the game ends at that point.

terms of trade   The rate at which units of one product can be exchanged for units of another product; the *price* of a *good* or *service;* the amount of one good or service that must be given up to obtain 1 unit of another good or service.

time inconsistency   The human tendency to systematically misjudge at the present time what will actually end up being desired at a future time.

time-value of money   The idea that a specific amount of *money* is more valuable to a person the sooner it is received because the money can be placed in a financial account or *investment* and earn *compound interest* over time; the *opportunity cost* of receiving a sum of money later rather than earlier.

total allowable catch (TAC)   The overall limit set by a government or a fisheries commission on the total number of fish or tonnage of fish that fishers collectively can harvest during some particular time period. Used to set the fishing limits for *individual transferable quotas* (*ITQs*).

total cost   The sum of *fixed cost* and *variable cost*.

total fertility rate   The average number of children per lifetime birthed by a nation's women.

total product (TP)   The total output of a particular *good* or *service* produced by a *firm* (or a group of firms or the entire economy).

total revenue (TR)   The total number of dollars received by a *firm* (or firms) from the sale of a product; equal to the total expenditures for the product produced by the firm (or firms); equal to the quantity sold (demanded) multiplied by the *price* at which it is sold.

total utility   The total amount of satisfaction derived from the consumption of a single product or a combination of products.

total-revenue test   A test to determine *elasticity of demand.* Demand is elastic if *total revenue* moves in the opposite direction from a *price* change; it is inelastic when it moves in the same direction as a price change; and it is of unitary elasticity when it does not change when price changes.

Trade Adjustment Assistance Act   A U.S. law passed in 2002 that provides cash assistance, education and training benefits, health care subsidies, and *wage* subsidies (for persons age 50 or older) to workers displaced by *imports* or relocations of U.S. *plants* to other countries.

trade deficit   The amount by which a nation's *imports* of *goods* (or goods and *services*) exceed its *exports* of goods (or goods and services).

trade surplus   The amount by which a nation's *exports* of *goods* (or goods and *services*) exceed its *imports* of goods (or goods and services).

trading possibilities line   A line that shows the different combinations of two products that an economy is able to obtain (consume) when it specializes in the production of one product and trades (exports) it to obtain the other product.

tragedy of the commons   The tendency for commonly owned *natural resources* to be overused, neglected, or degraded because their common ownership gives nobody an incentive to maintain or improve them.

transfer payment   A payment of *money* (or *goods* and *services*) by a government to a *household* or *firm* for which the payer receives no *good* or *service* directly in return.

tying contract   A requirement imposed by a seller that a buyer purchase another (or other) of its products as a condition for buying a desired product; a practice forbidden by the *Clayton Act*.

U.S. Steel case   The antitrust action brought by the federal government against the U.S. Steel Corporation in which the courts ruled (in 1920) that only unreasonable restraints of trade were illegal and that size and the possession of monopoly power were not by themselves violations of the *antitrust laws*.

ultimatum game   A *behavioral economics* game in which a mutually anonymous pair of players interact to determine how an amount of money is to be split. The first player suggests a division. The second player either accepts that proposal (in which case the split is made accordingly) or rejects it (in which case neither player gets anything).

unemployment compensation   (See *unemployment insurance*).

unfunded liability   A future government spending commitment (liability) for which the government has not legislated an offsetting revenue source.

uninsurable risk   An eventuality for which the frequency or magnitude of potential losses is unpredictable or unknowable. Insurance companies are not willing to sell insurance against such risks.

union shop   A place of employment where the employer may hire either *labor union* members or nonmembers but where nonmembers must become members within a specified period of time or lose their jobs.

unionization rate   The percentage of a particular population of workers that belongs to *labor unions;* alternatively, the percentage of a population of workers that is represented by one union or another in *collective bargaining*.

unit elasticity   *Demand* or *supply* for which the *elasticity coefficient* is equal to 1; means that the percentage change in the *quantity demanded* or *quantity supplied* is equal to the percentage change in *price*.

user cost The *opportunity cost* of extracting and selling a *nonrenewable natural resource* today rather than waiting to extract and sell the resource in the future; the *present value* of the decline in future revenue that will occur because a nonrenewable natural resource is extracted and sold today rather than being extracted and sold in the future.

usury laws State laws that specify the maximum legal *interest rate* at which loans can be made.

utility The want-satisfying power of a *good* or *service;* the satisfaction or pleasure a consumer obtains from the consumption of a good or service (or from the consumption of a collection of *goods* and *services*).

utility-maximizing rule The principle that to obtain the greatest *total utility,* a consumer should allocate *money income* so that the last dollar spent on each *good* or *service* yields the same *marginal utility* (MU). For two goods X and Y, with prices P_x and P_y, total utility will be maximized by purchasing the amounts of X and Y such that $MU_x/P_x = MU_y/P_y$ for the last dollar spent on each good.

variable cost A cost that increases when the *firm* increases its output and decreases when the firm reduces its output.

venture capital That part of household *savings* used to finance high-risk business enterprises in exchange for *stock* (and thus a share of any *profit* if the enterprises are successful).

vertical axis The "up-down" or "north-south" measurement line on a graph or grid.

vertical intercept The point at which a line meets the vertical axis of a graph.

vertical merger The merger of one or more *firms* engaged in different stages of the production of a particular *final good.*

very long run In microeconomics, a period of time long enough that *technology* can change and *firms* can introduce new products.

voice mechanism Communication by workers through their *union* to resolve grievances with an employer.

voluntary export restrictions (VER) Voluntary limitations by countries or *firms* of their exports to a particular foreign nation; undertaken to avoid the enactment of formal trade barriers by the foreign nation.

wage differential The difference between the *wage* received by one worker or group of workers and that received by another worker or group of workers.

wage rate (See *wage.*)

welfare cliff A situation in which a welfare recipient's overall income (= welfare benefits plus earned income) would decline if they got a raise or worked more hours. Caused by the abrupt withdrawal of certain welfare benefits at particular income thresholds.

Wheeler-Lea Act The federal law of 1938 that amended the *Federal Trade Commission Act* by prohibiting unfair and deceptive acts or practices of commerce (such as false and misleading advertising and the misrepresentation of products).

world price The international market *price* of a *good* or *service,* determined by world demand and supply.

World Trade Organization (WTO) An organization of 159 nations (as of mid-2013) that oversees the provisions of the current world trade agreement, resolves trade disputes stemming from it, and holds forums for further rounds of trade negotiations.

X-inefficiency The production of output, whatever its level, at a higher average (and total) cost than is necessary for producing that level of output.

zero-sum game In *game theory,* a game in which the gains (+) and losses (−) add up to zero; one party's gain equals the other party's loss. A strategic interaction (*game*) between two or more parties (players) in which the winners' gains exactly offset the losers' losses so that the gains and losses sum to zero.

INDEX